# OSW
## OFFICIAL SCRABBLE® WORDS

# OSW

## OFFICIAL SCRABBLE® WORDS

Second edition

Chambers

Published 1990 by W & R Chambers Ltd, 43–45 Annandale Street, Edinburgh EH7 4AZ.

Second edition © W & R Chambers Ltd 1990. First edition 1988.

**British Library Cataloguing in Publication Data**

Francis, Darryl
  OSW: Official Scrabble Words.
  2nd ed, by *Darryl Francis, Philip Nelkon, Allan Simmons*
  1. Scrabble
  I. Title II. Nelkon, Philip   III. Simmons, Allan
  793.7

ISBN 0 550 19022 8

The publishers wish to acknowledge the computing help of Peter Schwarz in the compilation and revision of *Official Scrabble® Words*.

The book was prepared and revised on a Sirius microcomputer using programs run under the UCSD-p system and the large-file editor ASE. The text was sorted on the Edinburgh University Multi-Access System (EMAS).

Typeset by Pillans & Wilson Specialist Litho Printers Ltd. Edinburgh.

Printed in England by Clay Ltd, St Ives plc

# Preface to first edition

At last we have the book which Scrabble® players have been wanting for many years. *Official Scrabble® Words (OSW)* is the definitive work which will save family arguments in social games and enable challenges to be dealt with quickly and efficiently in Scrabble Clubs and tournaments.

J W Spear & Sons and Chambers have had a close relationship going back to when the UK Scrabble Club movement adopted *Chambers 20th Century Dictionary* as its reference work. *Chambers* (now published as *Chambers English Dictionary*) is loved by Scrabble players throughout most of the English-speaking world because of the rich fund of useful Scrabble words it contains.

*Official Scrabble Words* uses this source so it almost certainly contains your pet Scrabble words and thousands of others. *OSW* is complementary to *Chambers English Dictionary,* which remains the reference work when you want to check a definition.

The task of adjudicating on well over 150,000 words was a mammoth one. I would like to thank the main adjudicating committee, the groups of volunteer Scrabble players who acted as the initial adjudicators (all named below) and, of course, Catherine Schwarz and her colleagues at Chambers for the dedicated way they handled the many problems. I also thank the members of the Australian Scrabble Players' Association who have made their contribution in helping Chambers' editorial team.

I am sure that the work they all have done will add to the enjoyment and satisfaction that you obtain from playing Scrabble.

Francis A Spear
*Chairman*
J W Spear & Sons PLC

### Main committee

Darryl Francis, *London Scrabble League*
Leonard Hodge, *Scrabble Club Co-ordinator and Chairman*
Angus Macdonald, *Mapperley Scrabble Club*
Philip Nelkon, *London Scrabble League*
Allan Simmons, *Postal Scrabble Club*

### Initial adjudicating committee

Steve Ablitt-Jones, *Croydon SC*          Josef Kollar, *Hythe SC*
Olive Behan, *Glenthorn SC*              Kevin Morris, *Bristol SC*
Jackie Fallows, *Isle of Wight SC*       Jane McLeman, *Frodsham SC*
Raye Green, *Leicester SC*               Norman Smith, *Edinburgh SC*
Mary Grylls, *Grantham SC*               Roy Upton, *Derby SC*
Ian Gucklhorn, *London Scrabble League*  Mike Willis, *Milton Keynes SC*
Dorothy Harrison, *Plymouth SC*

v

# Preface to second edition

Since its publication in 1988 *Official Scrabble® Words* has proved its worth as the Scrabble-players' authority from fireside to National championship finals.

In the course of using it, and its source and contemporary, *Chambers English Dictionary*, Scrabble players and dictionary users have brought to light a number of inconsistencies and infelicities. These have been scrutinised, extended, decided on and dealt with by original main committee members Darryl Francis, Philip Nelkon and Allan Simmons, in conjunction with Catherine Schwarz of Chambers. As before, we are grateful to members of the Australian Scrabble Players' Association for their constructive and courteous contribution. With *Chambers English Dictionary* complementing it for meanings and longer words, the revised *Official Scrabble Words* now takes its predecessor's place as the definitive Scrabble adjudication tool.

Francis A Spear
*Chairman*
J W Spear & Sons PLC

# Introduction

This revised edition of *Official Scrabble® Words* is the final authority on allowed Scrabble® words. It is based on the 1988 edition of *Chambers English Dictionary*. All words listed in that dictionary are permitted in Scrabble except:

> those only spelt with an initial capital letter;
>
> abbreviations;
>
> prefixes and suffixes;
>
> those requiring apostrophes and hyphens.

*Official Scrabble Words* fully takes account of the 1988 revision of the rules used for the National Scrabble Championship and other official Scrabble events. The differences between the revised rules and the earlier rules can be summarised here:

> foreign words are allowed;
>
> names of letters and letter sounds are allowed;
>
> obsolete words and words from the works of Shakespeare, Spenser and Milton are allowed;
>
> adverbs are only allowed if in *Chambers*.

Let us look at these differences in slightly more detail, as well as at the approaches that have been taken towards certain groups of words.

## Foreign words

Foreign words appearing in *Chambers English Dictionary* have been included in *Official Scrabble Words*. Where a specific plural form appears in *Chambers,* we have included only that form, but where no plural is shown in the dictionary, we have used our judgment, and the appropriate plural form has been included. In some instances, this will be a foreign plural; in others, it will be an English plural (usually the addition of an -S); occasionally both types of plural will be included. Do be aware that not all plural forms in *OSW* are explicitly shown in *Chambers*. For example, as no plural form is shown in the dictionary for DEUS, we have included the plural forms DEI and DI in preference to an unlisted -ES plural of DEUS.

## Letters and letter sounds

Names of letters and letter sounds appearing in *Chambers English Dictionary* are included in *Official Scrabble Words*. The reasons for barring these from the National Scrabble Championship and other official events were never clear, and these words are now welcomed back into the realm of valid Scrabble words. This allows the inclusion here of a flurry of words such as MU, NU and XI, as well as AITCH, VAU and YPSILON. Their plural forms are also included.

## Obsolete words

Obsolete words are included in *Official Scrabble Words*, along with many of their relevant inflected forms (such as plurals and verb inflections). We have included plurals of most obsolete nouns. We have included verb inflections of most, but not all, obsolete verbs. We have not included comparative and superlative forms of obsolete adjectives. We have not included derivatives of obsolete words, unless explicitly shown in *Chambers*. (For example, BROACH and BROACHER are both allowable words, and BROCH is in the dictionary as an obsolete spelling of BROACH – so BROACH, BROACHER and BROCH are all allowable, but we have not included the assumed BROCHER.)

Words marked in *Chambers* as being from the works of Shakespeare, Spenser and Milton have been treated in the same way as obsolete words.

## Adverbs

Adverbs have only been included in *Official Scrabble Words* if they are included in *Chambers*. No attempt has been made to include adverbial forms which are not explicitly shown in the dictionary.

Users of OSW may find it helpful if we outline our thinking on certain other groups of words, as well as on the word lengths included in the book.

## Plurals

With few exceptions, we have included in *Official Scrabble Words* the plurals of all nouns. Plural forms have been shown for all nouns ending in -ISM, -ITY and -NESS. While these plurals may be little used in regular English, all are available for use if needed in the English language. We have also included the plural forms of chemicals, chemical elements, minerals, man-made materials, natural materials, fibres, drugs, gases, rocks, oils, vitamins, enzymes, diseases, illnesses, and the like.

## Comparatives and superlatives

We have included a wide range of comparatives and superlatives in *Official Scrabble Words*. We have considered the possible comparative and superlative forms of all adjectives in *OSW*, and we have based our final selection on a range of criteria. These have included commonness or familiarity of the adjective, number of syllables, meaning, and whether the adjective is dialect, obsolete or foreign. We also took into account the euphony of the -ER and -EST forms, current usage, and listings in other dictionaries. We cannot say that we have applied a mechanical formula in deciding which comparatives and superlatives to include. We have allowed the -IER and -IEST forms of most one- and two-syllable adjectives ending in -Y, and some of three syllables, but not all. We have excluded comparative and superlative forms of obsolete and archaic adjectives ending in -Y. We have not excluded the comparatives and superlatives of all adjectives of three syllables or more – some have been included. We have not excluded the comparatives and superlatives of all adjectives ending with certain specific groups of letters, such as -ATE, -ENT, -ETE and -ID. We have certainly included some of these comparatives and superlatives. This revised edition of *Official Scrabble Words* contains many more comparative and superlative forms than the original edition, having taken into account comments from Scrabble players around the world.

## Interjections

Interjections are treated not as nouns, but as parts of speech which do not permit plurals. In *Official Scrabble Words*, an interjection has no inflected forms, unless explicitly indicated in *Chambers*. A plural is only allowed if an interjection is also shown to be a noun; and verb forms are only allowed if an interjection is shown to be a verb. Some examples:

> AH, QUOTHA and UM are interjections only, so no inflected forms are allowed;
>
> EH is an interjection and a verb, so the inflected verb forms EHS, EHED and EHING are allowed;
>
> OOH is an interjection, verb and noun, so the verb forms OOHS, OOHED and OOHING are allowed; OOHS is also the plural form of the noun.

If *Chambers* quite clearly lists a plural form of an interjection (for example, as at LO), then that is allowable.

## Accents

Accented letters have been retained in *Official Scrabble Words*, even though there are no accents in English-language Scrabble sets. Accents are to be ignored. Occasionally, two forms of an allowable Scrabble word are given in *OSW*, one accented, one not. An example is PATE and PÂTÉ. Retention of accents has been considered desirable because we have anticipated that *OSW* may well be used as the authority for other word-games which do *not* allow accented words. Inclusion of the accents will enable the players of those other games to discard accented words if they wish to.

## Word lengths

*Official Scrabble Words* users may well want to understand what criteria have been employed in considering word lengths. In compiling *OSW* we began by listing all the valid but uninflected words of length up to (and including) 9 letters. We then allowed the relevant inflections of these (namely plurals, verb forms, and comparatives and superlatives), resulting in words up to 13 letters long. (It is possible for a 9-letter verb to double a final consonant before adding -ING, giving 13 letters in all!) Here are some examples:

> the 9-letter noun CACODEMON gives rise to the 10-letter plural CACODEMONS;
>
> the 9-letter noun CACOPHONY gives rise to the 11-letter plural CACOPHONIES;
>
> the 9-letter noun CANTHARIS gives rise to the 11-letter plural CANTHARIDES;
>
> the 9-letter verb CALCULATE gives rise to these verb inflections: CALCULATED, CALCULATES and CALCULATING, having 10 or 11 letters;
>
> the 8-letter verb CARBURET gives rise to these verb inflections: CARBURETS, CARBURETTED and CARBURETTING, having 9, 11 or 12 letters.

If any inflected form of a 9-letter word is also a singular noun in its own right, then a plural form of that noun is also included. For example:

> the 9-letter verb CATERWAUL gives rise to these verb inflections: CATERWAULS, CATERWAULED and CATERWAULING; but since CATERWAULING is also shown in *Chambers* as a noun, the plural form CATERWAULINGS has been included here; the 8-letter verb CROSSCUT gives rise to these verb inflections: CROSSCUTS and CROSSCUTTING; but since CROSSCUTTING is also shown in *Chambers* as a noun, the plural form CROSSCUTTINGS has been included here.

There are a few instances of 9-letter adjectives which add an -S to become 10-letter nouns. For example, CANONICAL is an adjective only, yet CANONICALS is a noun. In such cases, we have included the -S form. After all, if CANONICAL was a noun rather than an adjective, we would have included its plural form CANONICALS. There are instances of singular nouns having more than 9 letters, but with plurals of 9 letters or less. The singulars have not been included here, but the plurals have. For example, the singular CYNOMOLGUS has 10 letters, so hasn't been included, but its plural CYNOMOLGI has 9 letters, so is included.

## Order of words

All the words in *Official Scrabble Words* are listed in strict alphabetical sequence regardless of length. It is important to bear this in mind, particularly when checking the validity of plurals. For example:

> the plural of FAD is not listed immediately after FAD but is shown at its correct alphabetical place beween FADOS and FADY;
>
> to determine whether FAB has a plural or not, it is necessary to check between the entries FABRICS and FABULAR. It is not listed there, so FABS is not allowed.

*Official Scrabble Words* does not list the definitions of any words. If you wish to discover the meaning of a word included, then it is necessary to consult *Chambers English Dictionary*.

## Apparent misspellings

There are some instances where it may appear that a word has been misspelt. This can occur when the normal spelling is greater than 9 letters and therefore excluded, but an older or obsolete spelling of the same word qualifies for inclusion. For example:

> SENSUALTY and its plural form SENSUALTIES both appear in *Official Scrabble Words* because SENSUALTY is a 9-letter noun. The regular spelling SENSUALITY and its plural form SENSUALITIES are not listed because SENSUALITY is longer than 9 letters.

*Official Scrabble Words* will not answer every possible enquiry regarding the validity of words. For uninflected words longer than 9 letters, you will have to turn to

*Chambers* itself. For example, CYNOMOLGUS, mentioned above, is perfectly valid for use in Scrabble; it's just that it isn't included here. There are plenty of other 10-15 letter words which could be played on a Scrabble board and are in *Chambers*. However, we felt that such words fell outside the scope of *OSW*.

## Why a revised edition?

This revised edition of *Official Scrabble Words* contains about 1300 words *not* listed in the original edition. Some were accidentally omitted from the original edition, but many are added as the result of reconsidering derivative forms. This is especially the case with comparatives and superlatives of adjectives ending in -Y, and the verbal derivatives of obsolete words. While these 1300 new words represent less than 1% of the total stock of words in *Official Scrabble Words*, it is felt that Scrabble players will welcome their introduction here in an attempt to make this revised edition as accurate and consistent as possible.

The revised *Official Scrabble Words* omits about 500 words which appeared in the original edition. Some were too long, some were misprints, and some were inappropriate plurals and other derivative forms. Again, although these deletions represent about one-third of 1% of the stock of words in *Official Scrabble Words*, it is felt that Scrabble players everywhere will welcome this improved level of accuracy and consistency.

The 1300 additions and the 500 deletions have all been individually and carefully considered. Many other words have been considered for inclusion and exclusion, but have remained excluded or included. In several cases it has been particularly difficult to decide over a word's validity for inclusion (or otherwise) here. However, if after considering the guidelines here you believe you have found an error, either of inclusion or omission, then please write to Catherine Schwarz at W and R Chambers, Edinburgh.

Darryl Francis, Leonard Hodge,
Philip Nelkon, Allan Simmons
UK *Official Scrabble® Words Committee*

# A

AA
AARDVARK
AARDVARKS
AARDWOLF
AARDWOLVES
AAS
AASVOGEL
AASVOGELS
ABA
ABAC
ABACA
ABACAS
ABACI
ABACK
ABACS
ABACTINAL
ABACTOR
ABACTORS
ABACUS
ABACUSES
ABAFT
ABALONE
ABALONES
ABAMPERE
ABAMPERES
ABAND
ABANDED
ABANDING
ABANDON
ABANDONED
ABANDONEE
ABANDONEES
ABANDONING
ABANDONS
ABANDS
ABAS
ABASE
ABASED
ABASEMENT
ABASEMENTS
ABASES
ABASH
ABASHED
ABASHES
ABASHING
ABASHLESS
ABASHMENT
ABASHMENTS
ABASING
ABASK
ABATABLE
ABATE
ABATED
ABATEMENT
ABATEMENTS
ABATES
ABATING
ABATIS
ABATOR
ABATORS
ABATTIS
ABATTOIR
ABATTOIRS

ABATTU
ABATURE
ABATURES
ABAXIAL
ABAYA
ABAYAS
ABB
ABBA
ABBACIES
ABBACY
ABBAS
ABBATIAL
ABBÉ
ABBÉS
ABBESS
ABBESSES
ABBEY
ABBEYS
ABBOT
ABBOTS
ABBOTSHIP
ABBOTSHIPS
ABBS
ABCEE
ABCEES
ABDABS
ABDICABLE
ABDICANT
ABDICATE
ABDICATED
ABDICATES
ABDICATING
ABDOMEN
ABDOMENS
ABDOMINAL
ABDUCE
ABDUCED
ABDUCENT
ABDUCES
ABDUCING
ABDUCT
ABDUCTED
ABDUCTEE
ABDUCTEES
ABDUCTING
ABDUCTION
ABDUCTIONS
ABDUCTOR
ABDUCTORS
ABDUCTS
ABEAM
ABEAR
ABEARING
ABEARS
ABED
ABEIGH
ABELE
ABELES
ABELIA
ABELIAS
ABERRANCE
ABERRANCES
ABERRANCIES

ABERRANCY
ABERRANT
ABERRATE
ABERRATED
ABERRATES
ABERRATING
ABESSIVE
ABESSIVES
ABET
ABETMENT
ABETMENTS
ABETS
ABETTED
ABETTER
ABETTERS
ABETTING
ABETTOR
ABETTORS
ABEYANCE
ABEYANCES
ABEYANCIES
ABEYANCY
ABEYANT
ABHOR
ABHORRED
ABHORRENT
ABHORRER
ABHORRERS
ABHORRING
ABHORRINGS
ABHORS
ABID
ABIDANCE
ABIDANCES
ABIDDEN
ABIDE
ABIDED
ABIDES
ABIDING
ABIDINGLY
ABIDINGS
ABIES
ABIGAIL
ABIGAILS
ABILITIES
ABILITY
ABIOSES
ABIOSIS
ABIOTIC
ABJECT
ABJECTED
ABJECTING
ABJECTION
ABJECTIONS
ABJECTLY
ABJECTS
ABJOINT
ABJOINTED
ABJOINTING
ABJOINTS
ABJURE
ABJURED
ABJURER

ABJURERS
ABJURES
ABJURING
ABLATE
ABLATED
ABLATES
ABLATING
ABLATION
ABLATIONS
ABLATIVAL
ABLATIVE
ABLATIVES
ABLATOR
ABLATORS
ABLAUT
ABLAUTS
ABLAZE
ABLE
ABLED
ABLER
ABLES
ABLEST
ABLET
ABLETS
ABLING
ABLINS
ABLOOM
ABLOW
ABLUSH
ABLUTION
ABLUTIONS
ABLY
ABNEGATE
ABNEGATED
ABNEGATES
ABNEGATING
ABNEGATOR
ABNEGATORS
ABNORMAL
ABNORMITIES
ABNORMITY
ABNORMOUS
ABOARD
ABODE
ABODED
ABODEMENT
ABODEMENTS
ABODES
ABODING
ABOIDEAU
ABOIDEAUS
ABOIL
ABOITEAU
ABOITEAUS
ABOLISH
ABOLISHED
ABOLISHES
ABOLISHING
ABOLITION
ABOLITIONS
ABOLLA
ABOLLAE
ABOLLAS

ABOMASA
ABOMASUM
ABOMASUS
ABOMASUSES
ABOMINATE
ABOMINATED
ABOMINATES
ABOMINATING
ABONDANCE
ABONDANCES
ABORAL
ABORD
ABORDED
ABORDING
ABORDS
ABORE
ABORIGEN
ABORIGENS
ABORIGIN
ABORIGINE
ABORIGINES
ABORIGINS
ABORNE
ABORT
ABORTED
ABORTING
ABORTION
ABORTIONS
ABORTIVE
ABORTS
ABOUGHT
ABOULIA
ABOULIAS
ABOUND
ABOUNDED
ABOUNDING
ABOUNDS
ABOUT
ABOUTS
ABOVE
ABRADANT
ABRADANTS
ABRADE
ABRADED
ABRADES
ABRADING
ABRAID
ABRAIDED
ABRAIDING
ABRAIDS
ABRAM
ABRASION
ABRASIONS
ABRASIVE
ABRASIVES
ABRAXAS
ABRAXASES
ABRAY
ABRAYED
ABRAYING
ABRAYS
ABRAZO
ABRAZOS

ABREACT
ABREACTED
ABREACTING
ABREACTS
ABREAST
ABRÉGÉ
ABRÉGÉS
ABRICOCK
ABRICOCKS
ABRIDGE
ABRIDGED
ABRIDGER
ABRIDGERS
ABRIDGES
ABRIDGING
ABRIM
ABRIN
ABRINS
ABROACH
ABROAD
ABROADS
ABROGATE
ABROGATED
ABROGATES
ABROGATING
ABROGATOR
ABROGATORS
ABROOKE
ABROOKED
ABROOKES
ABROOKING
ABRUPT
ABRUPTER
ABRUPTEST
ABRUPTION
ABRUPTIONS
ABRUPTLY
ABRUPTS
ABSCESS
ABSCESSES
ABSCIND
ABSCINDED
ABSCINDING
ABSCINDS
ABSCISE
ABSCISED
ABSCISES
ABSCISIN
ABSCISING
ABSCISINS
ABSCISS
ABSCISSA
ABSCISSAE
ABSCISSAS
ABSCISSE
ABSCISSES
ABSCISSIN
ABSCISSINS
ABSCOND
ABSCONDED
ABSCONDER
ABSCONDERS
ABSCONDING
ABSCONDS
ABSEIL
ABSEILED
ABSEILING
ABSEILINGS
ABSEILS
ABSENCE

ABSENCES
ABSENT
ABSENTED
ABSENTEE
ABSENTEES
ABSENTING
ABSENTLY
ABSENTS
ABSEY
ABSEYS
ABSINTH
ABSINTHE
ABSINTHES
ABSINTHS
ABSIT
ABSITS
ABSOLUTE
ABSOLUTES
ABSOLVE
ABSOLVED
ABSOLVER
ABSOLVERS
ABSOLVES
ABSOLVING
ABSONANT
ABSORB
ABSORBATE
ABSORBATES
ABSORBED
ABSORBENT
ABSORBENTS
ABSORBER
ABSORBERS
ABSORBING
ABSORBS
ABSTAIN
ABSTAINED
ABSTAINER
ABSTAINERS
ABSTAINING
ABSTAINS
ABSTERGE
ABSTERGED
ABSTERGES
ABSTERGING
ABSTINENT
ABSTRACT
ABSTRACTED
ABSTRACTER
ABSTRACTEST
ABSTRACTING
ABSTRACTS
ABSTRICT
ABSTRICTED
ABSTRICTING
ABSTRICTS
ABSTRUSE
ABSTRUSER
ABSTRUSEST
ABSURD
ABSURDER
ABSURDEST
ABSURDITIES
ABSURDITY
ABSURDLY
ABTHANE
ABTHANES
ABULIA
ABULIAS
ABUNA

ABUNAS
ABUNDANCE
ABUNDANCES
ABUNDANCIES
ABUNDANCY
ABUNDANT
ABUNE
ABURST
ABUSAGE
ABUSAGES
ABUSE
ABUSED
ABUSER
ABUSERS
ABUSES
ABUSING
ABUSION
ABUSIONS
ABUSIVE
ABUSIVELY
ABUT
ABUTILON
ABUTILONS
ABUTMENT
ABUTMENTS
ABUTS
ABUTTAL
ABUTTALS
ABUTTED
ABUTTER
ABUTTERS
ABUTTING
ABUZZ
ABVOLT
ABVOLTS
ABY
ABYE
ABYEING
ABYES
ABYING
ABYSM
ABYSMAL
ABYSMALLY
ABYSMS
ABYSS
ABYSSAL
ABYSSES
ACACIA
ACACIAS
ACADEME
ACADEMES
ACADEMIA
ACADEMIAS
ACADEMIC
ACADEMICS
ACADEMIES
ACADEMIST
ACADEMISTS
ACADEMY
ACAJOU
ACAJOUS
ACALEPH
ACALEPHA
ACALEPHAN
ACALEPHANS
ACALEPHAS
ACALEPHE
ACALEPHES
ACALEPHS
ACANTH

ACANTHA
ACANTHAS
ACANTHIN
ACANTHINE
ACANTHINS
ACANTHOID
ACANTHOUS
ACANTHS
ACANTHUS
ACANTHUSES
ACAPNIA
ACAPNIAS
ACARI
ACARIAN
ACARIASES
ACARIASIS
ACARICIDE
ACARICIDES
ACARID
ACARIDAN
ACARIDANS
ACARIDEAN
ACARIDEANS
ACARIDIAN
ACARIDIANS
ACARIDS
ACARINE
ACAROID
ACAROLOGIES
ACAROLOGY
ACARPOUS
ACARUS
ACATER
ACATERS
ACATES
ACATOUR
ACATOURS
ACAUDAL
ACAUDATE
ACAULINE
ACAULOSE
ACCABLÉ
ACCEDE
ACCEDED
ACCEDENCE
ACCEDENCES
ACCEDER
ACCEDERS
ACCEDES
ACCEDING
ACCEND
ACCENDED
ACCENDING
ACCENDS
ACCENSION
ACCENSIONS
ACCENT
ACCENTED
ACCENTING
ACCENTOR
ACCENTORS
ACCENTS
ACCENTUAL
ACCEPT
ACCEPTANT
ACCEPTANTS
ACCEPTED
ACCEPTER
ACCEPTERS
ACCEPTING

ACCEPTIVE
ACCEPTOR
ACCEPTORS
ACCEPTS
ACCESS
ACCESSARIES
ACCESSARY
ACCESSED
ACCESSES
ACCESSING
ACCESSION
ACCESSIONED
ACCESSIONING
ACCESSIONS
ACCESSORIES
ACCESSORY
ACCIDENCE
ACCIDENCES
ACCIDENT
ACCIDENTS
ACCIDIE
ACCIDIES
ACCINGE
ACCINGED
ACCINGES
ACCINGING
ACCITE
ACCITED
ACCITES
ACCITING
ACCLAIM
ACCLAIMED
ACCLAIMING
ACCLAIMS
ACCLIMATE
ACCLIMATED
ACCLIMATES
ACCLIMATING
ACCLIVITIES
ACCLIVITY
ACCLIVOUS
ACCLOY
ACCLOYED
ACCLOYING
ACCLOYS
ACCOAST
ACCOASTED
ACCOASTING
ACCOASTS
ACCOIED
ACCOIL
ACCOILS
ACCOLADE
ACCOLADES
ACCOMPANIED
ACCOMPANIES
ACCOMPANY
ACCOMPANYING
ACCOMPT
ACCOMPTED
ACCOMPTING
ACCOMPTS
ACCORAGE
ACCORAGED
ACCORAGES
ACCORAGING
ACCORD
ACCORDANT
ACCORDED
ACCORDER

ACCORDERS
ACCORDING
ACCORDION
ACCORDIONS
ACCORDS
ACCOST
ACCOSTED
ACCOSTING
ACCOSTS
ACCOUNT
ACCOUNTED
ACCOUNTING
ACCOUNTINGS
ACCOUNTS
ACCOURAGE
ACCOURAGED
ACCOURAGES
ACCOURAGING
ACCOURT
ACCOURTED
ACCOURTING
ACCOURTS
ACCOUTRE
ACCOUTRED
ACCOUTRES
ACCOUTRING
ACCOY
ACCOYED
ACCOYING
ACCOYLD
ACCOYS
ACCREDIT
ACCREDITED
ACCREDITING
ACCREDITS
ACCRETE
ACCRETED
ACCRETES
ACCRETING
ACCRETION
ACCRETIONS
ACCRETIVE
ACCREW
ACCREWED
ACCREWING
ACCREWS
ACCRUAL
ACCRUALS
ACCRUE
ACCRUED
ACCRUES
ACCRUING
ACCUMBENT
ACCURACIES
ACCURACY
ACCURATE
ACCURSE
ACCURSED
ACCURSES
ACCURSING
ACCURST
ACCUSABLE
ACCUSAL
ACCUSALS
ACCUSE
ACCUSED
ACCUSER
ACCUSERS
ACCUSES
ACCUSING

ACCUSTOM
ACCUSTOMED
ACCUSTOMING
ACCUSTOMS
ACE
ACED
ACEDIA
ACEDIAS
ACELLULAR
ACERB
ACERBATE
ACERBATED
ACERBATES
ACERBATING
ACERBER
ACERBEST
ACERBIC
ACERBITIES
ACERBITY
ACEROSE
ACEROUS
ACERVATE
ACES
ACESCENCE
ACESCENCES
ACESCENCIES
ACESCENCY
ACESCENT
ACETABULA
ACETAL
ACETALS
ACETAMIDE
ACETAMIDES
ACETATE
ACETATES
ACETIC
ACETIFIED
ACETIFIES
ACETIFY
ACETIFYING
ACETONE
ACETONES
ACETOSE
ACETOUS
ACETYL
ACETYLENE
ACETYLENES
ACETYLS
ACHAENIUM
ACHAENIUMS
ACHAGE
ACHAGES
ACHARNÉ
ACHARYA
ACHARYAS
ACHATES
ACHE
ACHED
ACHENE
ACHENES
ACHENIAL
ACHENIUM
ACHENIUMS
ACHES
ACHIER
ACHIEST
ACHIEVE
ACHIEVED
ACHIEVER
ACHIEVERS

ACHIEVES
ACHIEVING
ACHIMENES
ACHING
ACHINGS
ACHKAN
ACHKANS
ACHROMAT
ACHROMATS
ACHY
ACICULAR
ACICULATE
ACID
ACIDER
ACIDEST
ACIDFREAK
ACIDFREAKS
ACIDIC
ACIDIFIED
ACIDIFIES
ACIDIFY
ACIDIFYING
ACIDITIES
ACIDITY
ACIDOSES
ACIDOSIS
ACIDS
ACIDULATE
ACIDULATED
ACIDULATES
ACIDULATING
ACIDULOUS
ACIERAGE
ACIERAGES
ACIERATE
ACIERATED
ACIERATES
ACIERATING
ACIFORM
ACING
ACINI
ACINIFORM
ACINOSE
ACINOUS
ACINUS
ACKEE
ACKEES
ACKERS
ACKNEW
ACKNOW
ACKNOWING
ACKNOWN
ACKNOWNE
ACKNOWS
ACLINIC
ACME
ACMES
ACMITE
ACMITES
ACNE
ACNES
ACOCK
ACOEMETI
ACOLD
ACOLUTHIC
ACOLYTE
ACOLYTES
ACOLYTH
ACOLYTHS
ACONITE

ACONITES
ACONITIC
ACONITINE
ACONITINES
ACONITUM
ACONITUMS
ACORN
ACORNED
ACORNS
ACOSMISM
ACOSMISMS
ACOSMIST
ACOSMISTS
ACOUCHIES
ACOUCHY
ACOUSTIC
ACOUSTICS
ACQUAINT
ACQUAINTED
ACQUAINTING
ACQUAINTS
ACQUEST
ACQUESTS
ACQUIESCE
ACQUIESCED
ACQUIESCES
ACQUIESCING
ACQUIGHT
ACQUIGHTING
ACQUIGHTS
ACQUIRAL
ACQUIRALS
ACQUIRE
ACQUIRED
ACQUIRES
ACQUIRING
ACQUIST
ACQUISTS
ACQUIT
ACQUITE
ACQUITES
ACQUITING
ACQUITS
ACQUITTAL
ACQUITTALS
ACQUITTED
ACQUITTING
ACRAWL
ACRE
ACREAGE
ACREAGES
ACRED
ACRES
ACRID
ACRIDER
ACRIDEST
ACRIDIN
ACRIDINE
ACRIDINES
ACRIDINS
ACRIDITIES
ACRIDITY
ACRIMONIES
ACRIMONY
ACROBAT
ACROBATIC
ACROBATICS
ACROBATS
ACROGEN
ACROGENS

ACROLEIN
ACROLEINS
ACROLITH
ACROLITHS
ACROMIAL
ACROMION
ACROMIONS
ACRONYM
ACRONYMIC
ACRONYMS
ACROPETAL
ACROPHONIES
ACROPHONY
ACROPOLIS
ACROPOLISES
ACROSPIRE
ACROSPIRES
ACROSS
ACROSTIC
ACROSTICS
ACROTER
ACROTERIA
ACROTERS
ACROTISM
ACROTISMS
ACRYLIC
ACRYLICS
ACT
ACTA
ACTED
ACTIN
ACTINAL
ACTING
ACTINGS
ACTINIA
ACTINIAE
ACTINIAN
ACTINIANS
ACTINIAS
ACTINIC
ACTINIDE
ACTINIDES
ACTINISM
ACTINISMS
ACTINIUM
ACTINIUMS
ACTINOID
ACTINOIDS
ACTINON
ACTINONS
ACTINS
ACTION
ACTIONIST
ACTIONISTS
ACTIONS
ACTIVATE
ACTIVATED
ACTIVATES
ACTIVATING
ACTIVATOR
ACTIVATORS
ACTIVE
ACTIVELY
ACTIVISM
ACTIVISMS
ACTIVIST
ACTIVISTS
ACTIVITIES
ACTIVITY
ACTON

ACTONS
ACTOR
ACTORS
ACTRESS
ACTRESSES
ACTS
ACTUAL
ACTUALISE
ACTUALISED
ACTUALISES
ACTUALISING
ACTUALIST
ACTUALISTS
ACTUALITIES
ACTUALITY
ACTUALIZE
ACTUALIZED
ACTUALIZES
ACTUALIZING
ACTUALLY
ACTUARIAL
ACTUARIES
ACTUARY
ACTUATE
ACTUATED
ACTUATES
ACTUATING
ACTUATION
ACTUATIONS
ACTUATOR
ACTUATORS
ACTURE
ACTURES
ACUITIES
ACUITY
ACULEATE
ACULEATED
ACUMEN
ACUMENS
ACUMINATE
ACUMINATED
ACUMINATES
ACUMINATING
ACUPOINTS
ACUSHLA
ACUSHLAS
ACUTE
ACUTELY
ACUTENESS
ACUTENESSES
ACUTER
ACUTES
ACUTEST
ACYCLIC
ACYCLOVIR
ACYCLOVIRS
ACYL
ACYLS
AD
ADAGE
ADAGES
ADAGIO
ADAGIOS
ADAMANT
ADAMANTS
ADAPT
ADAPTABLE
ADAPTED
ADAPTER
ADAPTERS

ADAPTING
ADAPTION
ADAPTIONS
ADAPTIVE
ADAPTOR
ADAPTORS
ADAPTS
ADAW
ADAWED
ADAWING
ADAWS
ADAXIAL
ADAYS
ADD
ADDAX
ADDAXES
ADDED
ADDEEM
ADDEEMED
ADDEEMING
ADDEEMS
ADDEND
ADDENDA
ADDENDS
ADDENDUM
ADDER
ADDERS
ADDERWORT
ADDERWORTS
ADDICT
ADDICTED
ADDICTING
ADDICTION
ADDICTIONS
ADDICTIVE
ADDICTS
ADDING
ADDIO
ADDIOS
ADDITION
ADDITIONS
ADDITIVE
ADDITIVES
ADDLE
ADDLED
ADDLEMENT
ADDLEMENTS
ADDLES
ADDLING
ADDOOM
ADDOOMED
ADDOOMING
ADDOOMS
ADDORSED
ADDRESS
ADDRESSED
ADDRESSEE
ADDRESSEES
ADDRESSER
ADDRESSERS
ADDRESSES
ADDRESSING
ADDRESSOR
ADDRESSORS
ADDREST
ADDS
ADDUCE
ADDUCED
ADDUCENT
ADDUCER

ADDUCERS
ADDUCES
ADDUCIBLE
ADDUCING
ADDUCT
ADDUCTED
ADDUCTING
ADDUCTION
ADDUCTIONS
ADDUCTIVE
ADDUCTOR
ADDUCTORS
ADDUCTS
ADEEM
ADEEMED
ADEEMING
ADEEMS
ADEMPTION
ADEMPTIONS
ADENINE
ADENINES
ADENITIS
ADENITISES
ADENOID
ADENOIDAL
ADENOIDS
ADENOMA
ADENOMAS
ADENOMATA
ADENOSINE
ADENOSINES
ADEPT
ADEPTER
ADEPTEST
ADEPTNESS
ADEPTNESSES
ADEPTS
ADEQUACIES
ADEQUACY
ADEQUATE
ADERMIN
ADERMINS
ADESPOTA
ADESSIVE
ADESSIVES
ADHARMA
ADHARMAS
ADHERE
ADHERED
ADHERENCE
ADHERENCES
ADHERENT
ADHERENTS
ADHERER
ADHERERS
ADHERES
ADHERING
ADHESION
ADHESIONS
ADHESIVE
ADHESIVES
ADHIBIT
ADHIBITED
ADHIBITING
ADHIBITS
ADIABATIC
ADIAPHORA
ADIEU
ADIEUS
ADIEUX

ADIOS
ADIPIC
ADIPOCERE
ADIPOCERES
ADIPOSE
ADIPOSITIES
ADIPOSITY
ADIT
ADITS
ADJACENCIES
ADJACENCY
ADJACENT
ADJECTIVE
ADJECTIVES
ADJOIN
ADJOINED
ADJOINING
ADJOINS
ADJOINT
ADJOINTS
ADJOURN
ADJOURNED
ADJOURNING
ADJOURNS
ADJUDGE
ADJUDGED
ADJUDGES
ADJUDGING
ADJUNCT
ADJUNCTLY
ADJUNCTS
ADJURE
ADJURED
ADJURES
ADJURING
ADJUST
ADJUSTED
ADJUSTER
ADJUSTERS
ADJUSTING
ADJUSTOR
ADJUSTORS
ADJUSTS
ADJUTAGE
ADJUTAGES
ADJUTANCIES
ADJUTANCY
ADJUTANT
ADJUTANTS
ADJUVANCIES
ADJUVANCY
ADJUVANT
ADJUVANTS
ADMASS
ADMASSES
ADMEASURE
ADMEASURED
ADMEASURES
ADMEASURING
ADMIN
ADMINICLE
ADMINICLES
ADMINS
ADMIRABLE
ADMIRABLY
ADMIRAL
ADMIRALS
ADMIRANCE
ADMIRANCES
ADMIRE

ADMIRED
ADMIRER
ADMIRERS
ADMIRES
ADMIRING
ADMISSION
ADMISSIONS
ADMISSIVE
ADMIT
ADMITS
ADMITTED
ADMITTING
ADMIX
ADMIXED
ADMIXES
ADMIXING
ADMIXTURE
ADMIXTURES
ADMONISH
ADMONISHED
ADMONISHES
ADMONISHING
ADMONITOR
ADMONITORS
ADNASCENT
ADNATE
ADNATION
ADNATIONS
ADO
ADOBE
ADOBES
ADONISE
ADONISED
ADONISES
ADONISING
ADONIZE
ADONIZED
ADONIZES
ADONIZING
ADOORS
ADOPT
ADOPTED
ADOPTER
ADOPTERS
ADOPTING
ADOPTION
ADOPTIONS
ADOPTIOUS
ADOPTIVE
ADOPTS
ADORABLE
ADORABLY
ADORATION
ADORATIONS
ADORE
ADORED
ADORER
ADORERS
ADORES
ADORING
ADORINGLY
ADORN
ADORNED
ADORNING
ADORNMENT
ADORNMENTS
ADORNS
ADOS
ADOWN
ADPRESS

# A

AA
AARDVARK
AARDVARKS
AARDWOLF
AARDWOLVES
AAS
AASVOGEL
AASVOGELS
ABA
ABAC
ABACA
ABACAS
ABACI
ABACK
ABACS
ABACTINAL
ABACTOR
ABACTORS
ABACUS
ABACUSES
ABAFT
ABALONE
ABALONES
ABAMPERE
ABAMPERES
ABAND
ABANDED
ABANDING
ABANDON
ABANDONED
ABANDONEE
ABANDONEES
ABANDONING
ABANDONS
ABANDS
ABAS
ABASE
ABASED
ABASEMENT
ABASEMENTS
ABASES
ABASH
ABASHED
ABASHES
ABASHING
ABASHLESS
ABASHMENT
ABASHMENTS
ABASING
ABASK
ABATABLE
ABATE
ABATED
ABATEMENT
ABATEMENTS
ABATES
ABATING
ABATIS
ABATOR
ABATORS
ABATTIS
ABATTOIR
ABATTOIRS

ABATTU
ABATURE
ABATURES
ABAXIAL
ABAYA
ABAYAS
ABB
ABBA
ABBACIES
ABBACY
ABBAS
ABBATIAL
ABBÉ
ABBÉS
ABBESS
ABBESSES
ABBEY
ABBEYS
ABBOT
ABBOTS
ABBOTSHIP
ABBOTSHIPS
ABBS
ABCEE
ABCEES
ABDABS
ABDICABLE
ABDICANT
ABDICATE
ABDICATED
ABDICATES
ABDICATING
ABDOMEN
ABDOMENS
ABDOMINAL
ABDUCE
ABDUCED
ABDUCENT
ABDUCES
ABDUCING
ABDUCT
ABDUCTED
ABDUCTEE
ABDUCTEES
ABDUCTING
ABDUCTION
ABDUCTIONS
ABDUCTOR
ABDUCTORS
ABDUCTS
ABEAM
ABEAR
ABEARING
ABEARS
ABED
ABEIGH
ABELE
ABELES
ABELIA
ABELIAS
ABERRANCE
ABERRANCES
ABERRANCIES

ABERRANCY
ABERRANT
ABERRATE
ABERRATED
ABERRATES
ABERRATING
ABESSIVE
ABESSIVES
ABET
ABETMENT
ABETMENTS
ABETS
ABETTED
ABETTER
ABETTERS
ABETTING
ABETTOR
ABETTORS
ABEYANCE
ABEYANCES
ABEYANCIES
ABEYANCY
ABEYANT
ABHOR
ABHORRED
ABHORRENT
ABHORRER
ABHORRERS
ABHORRING
ABHORRINGS
ABHORS
ABID
ABIDANCE
ABIDANCES
ABIDDEN
ABIDE
ABIDED
ABIDES
ABIDING
ABIDINGLY
ABIDINGS
ABIES
ABIGAIL
ABIGAILS
ABILITIES
ABILITY
ABIOSES
ABIOSIS
ABIOTIC
ABJECT
ABJECTED
ABJECTING
ABJECTION
ABJECTIONS
ABJECTLY
ABJECTS
ABJOINT
ABJOINTED
ABJOINTING
ABJOINTS
ABJURE
ABJURED
ABJURER

ABJURERS
ABJURES
ABJURING
ABLATE
ABLATED
ABLATES
ABLATING
ABLATION
ABLATIONS
ABLATIVAL
ABLATIVE
ABLATIVES
ABLATOR
ABLATORS
ABLAUT
ABLAUTS
ABLAZE
ABLE
ABLED
ABLER
ABLES
ABLEST
ABLET
ABLETS
ABLING
ABLINS
ABLOOM
ABLOW
ABLUSH
ABLUTION
ABLUTIONS
ABLY
ABNEGATE
ABNEGATED
ABNEGATES
ABNEGATING
ABNEGATOR
ABNEGATORS
ABNORMAL
ABNORMITIES
ABNORMITY
ABNORMOUS
ABOARD
ABODE
ABODED
ABODEMENT
ABODEMENTS
ABODES
ABODING
ABOIDEAU
ABOIDEAUS
ABOIL
ABOITEAU
ABOITEAUS
ABOLISH
ABOLISHED
ABOLISHES
ABOLISHING
ABOLITION
ABOLITIONS
ABOLLA
ABOLLAE
ABOLLAS

ABOMASA
ABOMASUM
ABOMASUS
ABOMASUSES
ABOMINATE
ABOMINATED
ABOMINATES
ABOMINATING
ABONDANCE
ABONDANCES
ABORAL
ABORD
ABORDED
ABORDING
ABORDS
ABORE
ABORIGEN
ABORIGENS
ABORIGIN
ABORIGINE
ABORIGINES
ABORIGINS
ABORNE
ABORT
ABORTED
ABORTING
ABORTION
ABORTIONS
ABORTIVE
ABORTS
ABOUGHT
ABOULIA
ABOULIAS
ABOUND
ABOUNDED
ABOUNDING
ABOUNDS
ABOUT
ABOUTS
ABOVE
ABRADANT
ABRADANTS
ABRADE
ABRADED
ABRADES
ABRADING
ABRAID
ABRAIDED
ABRAIDING
ABRAIDS
ABRAM
ABRASION
ABRASIONS
ABRASIVE
ABRASIVES
ABRAXAS
ABRAXASES
ABRAY
ABRAYED
ABRAYING
ABRAYS
ABRAZO
ABRAZOS

ABREACT
ABREACTED
ABREACTING
ABREACTS
ABREAST
ABRÉGÉ
ABRÉGÉS
ABRICOCK
ABRICOCKS
ABRIDGE
ABRIDGED
ABRIDGER
ABRIDGERS
ABRIDGES
ABRIDGING
ABRIM
ABRIN
ABRINS
ABROACH
ABROAD
ABROADS
ABROGATE
ABROGATED
ABROGATES
ABROGATING
ABROGATOR
ABROGATORS
ABROOKE
ABROOKED
ABROOKES
ABROOKING
ABRUPT
ABRUPTER
ABRUPTEST
ABRUPTION
ABRUPTIONS
ABRUPTLY
ABRUPTS
ABSCESS
ABSCESSES
ABSCIND
ABSCINDED
ABSCINDING
ABSCINDS
ABSCISE
ABSCISED
ABSCISES
ABSCISIN
ABSCISING
ABSCISINS
ABSCISS
ABSCISSA
ABSCISSAE
ABSCISSAS
ABSCISSE
ABSCISSES
ABSCISSIN
ABSCISSINS
ABSCOND
ABSCONDED
ABSCONDER
ABSCONDERS
ABSCONDING
ABSCONDS
ABSEIL
ABSEILED
ABSEILING
ABSEILINGS
ABSEILS
ABSENCE

ABSENCES
ABSENT
ABSENTED
ABSENTEE
ABSENTEES
ABSENTING
ABSENTLY
ABSENTS
ABSEY
ABSEYS
ABSINTH
ABSINTHE
ABSINTHES
ABSINTHS
ABSIT
ABSITS
ABSOLUTE
ABSOLUTES
ABSOLVE
ABSOLVED
ABSOLVER
ABSOLVERS
ABSOLVES
ABSOLVING
ABSONANT
ABSORB
ABSORBATE
ABSORBATES
ABSORBED
ABSORBENT
ABSORBENTS
ABSORBER
ABSORBERS
ABSORBING
ABSORBS
ABSTAIN
ABSTAINED
ABSTAINER
ABSTAINERS
ABSTAINING
ABSTAINS
ABSTERGE
ABSTERGED
ABSTERGES
ABSTERGING
ABSTINENT
ABSTRACT
ABSTRACTED
ABSTRACTER
ABSTRACTEST
ABSTRACTING
ABSTRACTS
ABSTRICT
ABSTRICTED
ABSTRICTING
ABSTRICTS
ABSTRUSE
ABSTRUSER
ABSTRUSEST
ABSURD
ABSURDER
ABSURDEST
ABSURDITIES
ABSURDITY
ABSURDLY
ABTHANE
ABTHANES
ABULIA
ABULIAS
ABUNA

ABUNAS
ABUNDANCE
ABUNDANCES
ABUNDANCIES
ABUNDANCY
ABUNDANT
ABUNE
ABURST
ABUSAGE
ABUSAGES
ABUSE
ABUSED
ABUSER
ABUSERS
ABUSES
ABUSING
ABUSION
ABUSIONS
ABUSIVE
ABUSIVELY
ABUT
ABUTILON
ABUTILONS
ABUTMENT
ABUTMENTS
ABUTS
ABUTTAL
ABUTTALS
ABUTTED
ABUTTER
ABUTTERS
ABUTTING
ABUZZ
ABVOLT
ABVOLTS
ABY
ABYE
ABYEING
ABYES
ABYING
ABYSM
ABYSMAL
ABYSMALLY
ABYSMS
ABYSS
ABYSSAL
ABYSSES
ACACIA
ACACIAS
ACADEME
ACADEMES
ACADEMIA
ACADEMIAS
ACADEMIC
ACADEMICS
ACADEMIES
ACADEMIST
ACADEMISTS
ACADEMY
ACAJOU
ACAJOUS
ACALEPH
ACALEPHA
ACALEPHAN
ACALEPHANS
ACALEPHAS
ACALEPHE
ACALEPHES
ACALEPHS
ACANTH

ACANTHA
ACANTHAS
ACANTHIN
ACANTHINE
ACANTHINS
ACANTHOID
ACANTHOUS
ACANTHS
ACANTHUS
ACANTHUSES
ACAPNIA
ACAPNIAS
ACARI
ACARIAN
ACARIASES
ACARIASIS
ACARICIDE
ACARICIDES
ACARID
ACARIDAN
ACARIDANS
ACARIDEAN
ACARIDEANS
ACARIDIAN
ACARIDIANS
ACARIDS
ACARINE
ACAROID
ACAROLOGIES
ACAROLOGY
ACARPOUS
ACARUS
ACATER
ACATERS
ACATES
ACATOUR
ACATOURS
ACAUDAL
ACAUDATE
ACAULINE
ACAULOSE
ACCABLÉ
ACCEDE
ACCEDED
ACCEDENCE
ACCEDENCES
ACCEDER
ACCEDERS
ACCEDES
ACCEDING
ACCEND
ACCENDED
ACCENDING
ACCENDS
ACCENSION
ACCENSIONS
ACCENT
ACCENTED
ACCENTING
ACCENTOR
ACCENTORS
ACCENTS
ACCENTUAL
ACCEPT
ACCEPTANT
ACCEPTANTS
ACCEPTED
ACCEPTER
ACCEPTERS
ACCEPTING

ACCEPTIVE
ACCEPTOR
ACCEPTORS
ACCEPTS
ACCESS
ACCESSARIES
ACCESSARY
ACCESSED
ACCESSES
ACCESSING
ACCESSION
ACCESSIONED
ACCESSIONING
ACCESSIONS
ACCESSORIES
ACCESSORY
ACCIDENCE
ACCIDENCES
ACCIDENT
ACCIDENTS
ACCIDIE
ACCIDIES
ACCINGE
ACCINGED
ACCINGES
ACCINGING
ACCITE
ACCITED
ACCITES
ACCITING
ACCLAIM
ACCLAIMED
ACCLAIMING
ACCLAIMS
ACCLIMATE
ACCLIMATED
ACCLIMATES
ACCLIMATING
ACCLIVITIES
ACCLIVITY
ACCLIVOUS
ACCLOY
ACCLOYED
ACCLOYING
ACCLOYS
ACCOAST
ACCOASTED
ACCOASTING
ACCOASTS
ACCOIED
ACCOIL
ACCOILS
ACCOLADE
ACCOLADES
ACCOMPANIED
ACCOMPANIES
ACCOMPANY
ACCOMPANYING
ACCOMPT
ACCOMPTED
ACCOMPTING
ACCOMPTS
ACCORAGE
ACCORAGED
ACCORAGES
ACCORAGING
ACCORD
ACCORDANT
ACCORDED
ACCORDER

| | | | | |
|---|---|---|---|---|
| ACCORDERS | ACCUSTOM | ACHIEVES | ACONITES | ACROLEIN |
| ACCORDING | ACCUSTOMED | ACHIEVING | ACONITIC | ACROLEINS |
| ACCORDION | ACCUSTOMING | ACHIMENES | ACONITINE | ACROLITH |
| ACCORDIONS | ACCUSTOMS | ACHING | ACONITINES | ACROLITHS |
| ACCORDS | ACE | ACHINGS | ACONITUM | ACROMIAL |
| ACCOST | ACED | ACHKAN | ACONITUMS | ACROMION |
| ACCOSTED | ACEDIA | ACHKANS | ACORN | ACROMIONS |
| ACCOSTING | ACEDIAS | ACHROMAT | ACORNED | ACRONYM |
| ACCOSTS | ACELLULAR | ACHROMATS | ACORNS | ACRONYMIC |
| ACCOUNT | ACERB | ACHY | ACOSMISM | ACRONYMS |
| ACCOUNTED | ACERBATE | ACICULAR | ACOSMISMS | ACROPETAL |
| ACCOUNTING | ACERBATED | ACICULATE | ACOSMIST | ACROPHONIES |
| ACCOUNTINGS | ACERBATES | ACID | ACOSMISTS | ACROPHONY |
| ACCOUNTS | ACERBATING | ACIDER | ACOUCHIES | ACROPOLIS |
| ACCOURAGE | ACERBER | ACIDEST | ACOUCHY | ACROPOLISES |
| ACCOURAGED | ACERBEST | ACIDFREAK | ACOUSTIC | ACROSPIRE |
| ACCOURAGES | ACERBIC | ACIDFREAKS | ACOUSTICS | ACROSPIRES |
| ACCOURAGING | ACERBITIES | ACIDIC | ACQUAINT | ACROSS |
| ACCOURT | ACERBITY | ACIDIFIED | ACQUAINTED | ACROSTIC |
| ACCOURTED | ACEROSE | ACIDIFIES | ACQUAINTING | ACROSTICS |
| ACCOURTING | ACEROUS | ACIDIFY | ACQUAINTS | ACROTER |
| ACCOURTS | ACERVATE | ACIDIFYING | ACQUEST | ACROTERIA |
| ACCOUTRE | ACES | ACIDITIES | ACQUESTS | ACROTERS |
| ACCOUTRED | ACESCENCE | ACIDITY | ACQUIESCE | ACROTISM |
| ACCOUTRES | ACESCENCES | ACIDOSES | ACQUIESCED | ACROTISMS |
| ACCOUTRING | ACESCENCIES | ACIDOSIS | ACQUIESCES | ACRYLIC |
| ACCOY | ACESCENCY | ACIDS | ACQUIESCING | ACRYLICS |
| ACCOYED | ACESCENT | ACIDULATE | ACQUIGHT | ACT |
| ACCOYING | ACETABULA | ACIDULATED | ACQUIGHTING | ACTA |
| ACCOYLD | ACETAL | ACIDULATES | ACQUIGHTS | ACTED |
| ACCOYS | ACETALS | ACIDULATING | ACQUIRAL | ACTIN |
| ACCREDIT | ACETAMIDE | ACIDULOUS | ACQUIRALS | ACTINAL |
| ACCREDITED | ACETAMIDES | ACIERAGE | ACQUIRE | ACTING |
| ACCREDITING | ACETATE | ACIERAGES | ACQUIRED | ACTINGS |
| ACCREDITS | ACETATES | ACIERATE | ACQUIRES | ACTINIA |
| ACCRETE | ACETIC | ACIERATED | ACQUIRING | ACTINIAE |
| ACCRETED | ACETIFIED | ACIERATES | ACQUIST | ACTINIAN |
| ACCRETES | ACETIFIES | ACIERATING | ACQUISTS | ACTINIANS |
| ACCRETING | ACETIFY | ACIFORM | ACQUIT | ACTINIAS |
| ACCRETION | ACETIFYING | ACING | ACQUITE | ACTINIC |
| ACCRETIONS | ACETONE | ACINI | ACQUITES | ACTINIDE |
| ACCRETIVE | ACETONES | ACINIFORM | ACQUITING | ACTINIDES |
| ACCREW | ACETOSE | ACINOSE | ACQUITS | ACTINISM |
| ACCREWED | ACETOUS | ACINOUS | ACQUITTAL | ACTINISMS |
| ACCREWING | ACETYL | ACINUS | ACQUITTALS | ACTINIUM |
| ACCREWS | ACETYLENE | ACKEE | ACQUITTED | ACTINIUMS |
| ACCRUAL | ACETYLENES | ACKEES | ACQUITTING | ACTINOID |
| ACCRUALS | ACETYLS | ACKERS | ACRAWL | ACTINOIDS |
| ACCRUE | ACHAENIUM | ACKNEW | ACRE | ACTINON |
| ACCRUED | ACHAENIUMS | ACKNOW | ACREAGE | ACTINONS |
| ACCRUES | ACHAGE | ACKNOWING | ACREAGES | ACTINS |
| ACCRUING | ACHAGES | ACKNOWN | ACRED | ACTION |
| ACCUMBENT | ACHARNÉ | ACKNOWNE | ACRES | ACTIONIST |
| ACCURACIES | ACHARYA | ACKNOWS | ACRID | ACTIONISTS |
| ACCURACY | ACHARYAS | ACLINIC | ACRIDER | ACTIONS |
| ACCURATE | ACHATES | ACME | ACRIDEST | ACTIVATE |
| ACCURSE | ACHE | ACMES | ACRIDIN | ACTIVATED |
| ACCURSED | ACHED | ACMITE | ACRIDINE | ACTIVATES |
| ACCURSES | ACHENE | ACMITES | ACRIDINES | ACTIVATING |
| ACCURSING | ACHENES | ACNE | ACRIDINS | ACTIVATOR |
| ACCURST | ACHENIAL | ACNES | ACRIDITIES | ACTIVATORS |
| ACCUSABLE | ACHENIUM | ACOCK | ACRIDITY | ACTIVE |
| ACCUSAL | ACHENIUMS | ACOEMETI | ACRIMONIES | ACTIVELY |
| ACCUSALS | ACHES | ACOLD | ACRIMONY | ACTIVISM |
| ACCUSE | ACHIER | ACOLUTHIC | ACROBAT | ACTIVISMS |
| ACCUSED | ACHIEST | ACOLYTE | ACROBATIC | ACTIVIST |
| ACCUSER | ACHIEVE | ACOLYTES | ACROBATICS | ACTIVISTS |
| ACCUSERS | ACHIEVED | ACOLYTH | ACROBATS | ACTIVITIES |
| ACCUSES | ACHIEVER | ACOLYTHS | ACROGEN | ACTIVITY |
| ACCUSING | ACHIEVERS | ACONITE | ACROGENS | ACTON |

ACTONS
ACTOR
ACTORS
ACTRESS
ACTRESSES
ACTS
ACTUAL
ACTUALISE
ACTUALISED
ACTUALISES
ACTUALISING
ACTUALIST
ACTUALISTS
ACTUALITIES
ACTUALITY
ACTUALIZE
ACTUALIZED
ACTUALIZES
ACTUALIZING
ACTUALLY
ACTUARIAL
ACTUARIES
ACTUARY
ACTUATE
ACTUATED
ACTUATES
ACTUATING
ACTUATION
ACTUATIONS
ACTUATOR
ACTUATORS
ACTURE
ACTURES
ACUITIES
ACUITY
ACULEATE
ACULEATED
ACUMEN
ACUMENS
ACUMINATE
ACUMINATED
ACUMINATES
ACUMINATING
ACUPOINTS
ACUSHLA
ACUSHLAS
ACUTE
ACUTELY
ACUTENESS
ACUTENESSES
ACUTER
ACUTES
ACUTEST
ACYCLIC
ACYCLOVIR
ACYCLOVIRS
ACYL
ACYLS
AD
ADAGE
ADAGES
ADAGIO
ADAGIOS
ADAMANT
ADAMANTS
ADAPT
ADAPTABLE
ADAPTED
ADAPTER
ADAPTERS

ADAPTING
ADAPTION
ADAPTIONS
ADAPTIVE
ADAPTOR
ADAPTORS
ADAPTS
ADAW
ADAWED
ADAWING
ADAWS
ADAXIAL
ADAYS
ADD
ADDAX
ADDAXES
ADDED
ADDEEM
ADDEEMED
ADDEEMING
ADDEEMS
ADDEND
ADDENDA
ADDENDS
ADDENDUM
ADDER
ADDERS
ADDERWORT
ADDERWORTS
ADDICT
ADDICTED
ADDICTING
ADDICTION
ADDICTIONS
ADDICTIVE
ADDICTS
ADDING
ADDIO
ADDIOS
ADDITION
ADDITIONS
ADDITIVE
ADDITIVES
ADDLE
ADDLED
ADDLEMENT
ADDLEMENTS
ADDLES
ADDLING
ADDOOM
ADDOOMED
ADDOOMING
ADDOOMS
ADDORSED
ADDRESS
ADDRESSED
ADDRESSEE
ADDRESSEES
ADDRESSER
ADDRESSERS
ADDRESSES
ADDRESSING
ADDRESSOR
ADDRESSORS
ADDREST
ADDS
ADDUCE
ADDUCED
ADDUCENT
ADDUCER

ADDUCERS
ADDUCES
ADDUCIBLE
ADDUCING
ADDUCT
ADDUCTED
ADDUCTING
ADDUCTION
ADDUCTIONS
ADDUCTIVE
ADDUCTOR
ADDUCTORS
ADDUCTS
ADEEM
ADEEMED
ADEEMING
ADEEMS
ADEMPTION
ADEMPTIONS
ADENINE
ADENINES
ADENITIS
ADENITISES
ADENOID
ADENOIDAL
ADENOIDS
ADENOMA
ADENOMAS
ADENOMATA
ADENOSINE
ADENOSINES
ADEPT
ADEPTER
ADEPTEST
ADEPTNESS
ADEPTNESSES
ADEPTS
ADEQUACIES
ADEQUACY
ADEQUATE
ADERMIN
ADERMINS
ADESPOTA
ADESSIVE
ADESSIVES
ADHARMA
ADHARMAS
ADHERE
ADHERED
ADHERENCE
ADHERENCES
ADHERENT
ADHERENTS
ADHERER
ADHERERS
ADHERES
ADHERING
ADHESION
ADHESIONS
ADHESIVE
ADHESIVES
ADHIBIT
ADHIBITED
ADHIBITING
ADHIBITS
ADIABATIC
ADIAPHORA
ADIEU
ADIEUS
ADIEUX

ADIOS
ADIPIC
ADIPOCERE
ADIPOCERES
ADIPOSE
ADIPOSITIES
ADIPOSITY
ADIT
ADITS
ADJACENCIES
ADJACENCY
ADJACENT
ADJECTIVE
ADJECTIVES
ADJOIN
ADJOINED
ADJOINING
ADJOINS
ADJOINT
ADJOINTS
ADJOURN
ADJOURNED
ADJOURNING
ADJOURNS
ADJUDGE
ADJUDGED
ADJUDGES
ADJUDGING
ADJUNCT
ADJUNCTLY
ADJUNCTS
ADJURE
ADJURED
ADJURES
ADJURING
ADJUST
ADJUSTED
ADJUSTER
ADJUSTERS
ADJUSTING
ADJUSTOR
ADJUSTORS
ADJUSTS
ADJUTAGE
ADJUTAGES
ADJUTANCIES
ADJUTANCY
ADJUTANT
ADJUTANTS
ADJUVANCIES
ADJUVANCY
ADJUVANT
ADJUVANTS
ADMASS
ADMASSES
ADMEASURE
ADMEASURED
ADMEASURES
ADMEASURING
ADMIN
ADMINICLE
ADMINICLES
ADMINS
ADMIRABLE
ADMIRABLY
ADMIRAL
ADMIRALS
ADMIRANCE
ADMIRANCES
ADMIRE

ADMIRED
ADMIRER
ADMIRERS
ADMIRES
ADMIRING
ADMISSION
ADMISSIONS
ADMISSIVE
ADMIT
ADMITS
ADMITTED
ADMITTING
ADMIX
ADMIXED
ADMIXES
ADMIXING
ADMIXTURE
ADMIXTURES
ADMONISH
ADMONISHED
ADMONISHES
ADMONISHING
ADMONITOR
ADMONITORS
ADNASCENT
ADNATE
ADNATION
ADNATIONS
ADO
ADOBE
ADOBES
ADONISE
ADONISED
ADONISES
ADONISING
ADONIZE
ADONIZED
ADONIZES
ADONIZING
ADOORS
ADOPT
ADOPTED
ADOPTER
ADOPTERS
ADOPTING
ADOPTION
ADOPTIONS
ADOPTIOUS
ADOPTIVE
ADOPTS
ADORABLE
ADORABLY
ADORATION
ADORATIONS
ADORE
ADORED
ADORER
ADORERS
ADORES
ADORING
ADORINGLY
ADORN
ADORNED
ADORNING
ADORNMENT
ADORNMENTS
ADORNS
ADOS
ADOWN
ADPRESS

| | | | | |
|---|---|---|---|---|
| ADPRESSED | ADVECTION | ADVOWSONS | AEROBOMB | AESTIVATES |
| ADPRESSES | ADVECTIONS | ADWARD | AEROBOMBS | AESTIVATING |
| ADPRESSING | ADVENE | ADWARDED | AEROBUS | AETHER |
| ADRAD | ADVENED | ADWARDING | AEROBUSES | AETHERS |
| ADREAD | ADVENES | ADWARDS | AERODART | AETIOLOGIES |
| ADREADED | ADVENING | ADYNAMIA | AERODARTS | AETIOLOGY |
| ADREADING | ADVENT | ADYNAMIAS | AERODROME | AFALD |
| ADREADS | ADVENTIVE | ADYNAMIC | AERODROMES | AFAR |
| ADRED | ADVENTIVES | ADYTA | AERODYNE | AFARA |
| ADRENAL | ADVENTS | ADYTUM | AERODYNES | AFARAS |
| ADRENALS | ADVENTURE | ADZE | AEROFOIL | AFAWLD |
| ADRIFT | ADVENTURED | ADZES | AEROFOILS | AFEAR |
| ADROIT | ADVENTURES | AE | AEROGRAM | AFEARD |
| ADROITER | ADVENTURING | AECIA | AEROGRAMS | AFEARED |
| ADROITEST | ADVERB | AECIDIA | AEROGRAPH | AFEARING |
| ADROITLY | ADVERBIAL | AECIDIUM | AEROGRAPHS | AFEARS |
| ADRY | ADVERBS | AECIUM | AEROLITE | AFFABLE |
| ADS | ADVERSARIES | AEDILE | AEROLITES | AFFABLY |
| ADSCRIPT | ADVERSARY | AEDILES | AEROLITH | AFFAIR |
| ADSCRIPTS | ADVERSE | AEFALD | AEROLITHS | AFFAIRE |
| ADSORB | ADVERSELY | AEFAULD | AEROLITIC | AFFAIRES |
| ADSORBATE | ADVERSER | AEFAWLD | AEROLOGIES | AFFAIRS |
| ADSORBATES | ADVERSEST | AEGIRINE | AEROLOGY | AFFEAR |
| ADSORBED | ADVERSITIES | AEGIRINES | AEROMANCIES | AFFEARD |
| ADSORBENT | ADVERSITY | AEGIRITE | AEROMANCY | AFFEARE |
| ADSORBENTS | ADVERT | AEGIRITES | AEROMETER | AFFEARED |
| ADSORBING | ADVERTED | AEGIS | AEROMETERS | AFFEARES |
| ADSORBS | ADVERTENT | AEGISES | AEROMETRIES | AFFEARING |
| ADSUM | ADVERTING | AEGLOGUE | AEROMETRY | AFFEARS |
| ADULARIA | ADVERTISE | AEGLOGUES | AEROMOTOR | AFFECT |
| ADULARIAS | ADVERTISED | AEGROTAT | AEROMOTORS | AFFECTED |
| ADULATE | ADVERTISES | AEGROTATS | AERONAUT | AFFECTER |
| ADULATED | ADVERTISING | AEMULE | AERONAUTS | AFFECTERS |
| ADULATES | ADVERTISINGS | AEMULED | AERONOMIES | AFFECTING |
| ADULATING | ADVERTS | AEMULES | AERONOMY | AFFECTION |
| ADULATION | ADVEW | AEMULING | AEROPHONE | AFFECTIONED |
| ADULATIONS | ADVEWED | AEOLIAN | AEROPHONES | AFFECTIONING |
| ADULATOR | ADVEWING | AEOLIPILE | AEROPHYTE | AFFECTIONS |
| ADULATORS | ADVEWS | AEOLIPILES | AEROPHYTES | AFFECTIVE |
| ADULATORY | ADVICE | AEOLIPYLE | AEROPLANE | AFFECTS |
| ADULT | ADVICEFUL | AEOLIPYLES | AEROPLANES | AFFEER |
| ADULTERER | ADVICES | AEON | AEROSHELL | AFFEERED |
| ADULTERERS | ADVISABLE | AEONIAN | AEROSHELLS | AFFEERING |
| ADULTERIES | ADVISABLY | AEONS | AEROSOL | AFFEERS |
| ADULTERY | ADVISE | AERATE | AEROSOLS | AFFERENT |
| ADULTHOOD | ADVISED | AERATED | AEROSPACE | AFFIANCE |
| ADULTHOODS | ADVISEDLY | AERATES | AEROSPACES | AFFIANCED |
| ADULTS | ADVISER | AERATING | AEROSTAT | AFFIANCES |
| ADUMBRATE | ADVISERS | AERATION | AEROSTATS | AFFIANCING |
| ADUMBRATED | ADVISES | AERATIONS | AEROTAXES | AFFICHE |
| ADUMBRATES | ADVISING | AERATOR | AEROTAXIS | AFFICHES |
| ADUMBRATING | ADVISINGS | AERATORS | AEROTRAIN | AFFIDAVIT |
| ADUNC | ADVISOR | AERIAL | AEROTRAINS | AFFIDAVITS |
| ADUNCATE | ADVISORS | AERIALIST | AERY | AFFIED |
| ADUNCATED | ADVISORY | AERIALISTS | AESC | AFFIES |
| ADUNCITIES | ADVOCAAT | AERIALITIES | AESCES | AFFILIATE |
| ADUNCITY | ADVOCAATS | AERIALITY | AESCULIN | AFFILIATED |
| ADUNCOUS | ADVOCACIES | AERIALLY | AESCULINS | AFFILIATES |
| ADUST | ADVOCACY | AERIALS | AESIR | AFFILIATING |
| ADUSTED | ADVOCATE | AERIE | AESTHESES | AFFINE |
| ADUSTING | ADVOCATED | AERIER | AESTHESIA | AFFINED |
| ADUSTS | ADVOCATES | AERIES | AESTHESIAS | AFFINES |
| ADVANCE | ADVOCATING | AERIEST | AESTHESIS | AFFINITIES |
| ADVANCED | ADVOCATOR | AERIFORM | AESTHETE | AFFINITY |
| ADVANCES | ADVOCATORS | AEROBE | AESTHETES | AFFIRM |
| ADVANCING | ADVOUTRER | AEROBES | AESTHETIC | AFFIRMANT |
| ADVANTAGE | ADVOUTRERS | AEROBIC | AESTHETICS | AFFIRMANTS |
| ADVANTAGED | ADVOUTRIES | AEROBICS | AESTIVAL | AFFIRMED |
| ADVANTAGES | ADVOUTRY | AEROBIONT | AESTIVATE | AFFIRMER |
| ADVANTAGING | ADVOWSON | AEROBIONTS | AESTIVATED | AFFIRMERS |

AFFIRMING
AFFIRMS
AFFIX
AFFIXED
AFFIXES
AFFIXING
AFFLATED
AFFLATION
AFFLATIONS
AFFLATUS
AFFLATUSES
AFFLICT
AFFLICTED
AFFLICTING
AFFLICTINGS
AFFLICTS
AFFLUENCE
AFFLUENCES
AFFLUENT
AFFLUENTS
AFFLUX
AFFLUXES
AFFLUXION
AFFLUXIONS
AFFOORD
AFFOORDED
AFFOORDING
AFFOORDS
AFFORCE
AFFORCED
AFFORCES
AFFORCING
AFFORD
AFFORDED
AFFORDING
AFFORDS
AFFOREST
AFFORESTED
AFFORESTING
AFFORESTS
AFFRAP
AFFRAPPED
AFFRAPPING
AFFRAPS
AFFRAY
AFFRAYED
AFFRAYING
AFFRAYS
AFFRENDED
AFFRET
AFFRETS
AFFRICATE
AFFRICATES
AFFRIGHT
AFFRIGHTED
AFFRIGHTING
AFFRIGHTS
AFFRONT
AFFRONTÉ
AFFRONTED
AFFRONTÉE
AFFRONTEE
AFFRONTING
AFFRONTINGS
AFFRONTS
AFFUSION
AFFUSIONS
AFFY
AFFYDE
AFFYING

AFGHAN
AFGHANS
AFIELD
AFIRE
AFLAJ
AFLAME
AFLATOXIN
AFLATOXINS
AFLOAT
AFOOT
AFORE
AFOREHAND
AFORESAID
AFORETIME
AFOUL
AFRAID
AFREET
AFREETS
AFRESH
AFRIT
AFRITS
AFRO
AFRONT
AFROS
AFT
AFTER
AFTERCARE
AFTERCARES
AFTEREYE
AFTEREYED
AFTEREYEING
AFTEREYES
AFTEREYING
AFTERGAME
AFTERGAMES
AFTERGLOW
AFTERGLOWS
AFTERINGS
AFTERMATH
AFTERMATHS
AFTERMOST
AFTERNOON
AFTERNOONS
AFTERS
AFTERTIME
AFTERTIMES
AFTERWARD
AFTERWARDS
AFTERWORD
AFTERWORDS
AFTMOST
AGA
AGAÇANT
AGAÇANTE
AGACERIE
AGACERIES
AGAIN
AGAINST
AGALACTIA
AGALACTIAS
AGALLOCH
AGALLOCHS
AGAMI
AGAMIC
AGAMID
AGAMIDS
AGAMIS
AGAMOID
AGAMOIDS
AGAMOUS

AGAPAE
AGAPE
AGAR
AGARIC
AGARICS
AGARS
AGAS
AGAST
AGATE
AGATES
AGAVE
AGAVES
AGAZE
AGAZED
AGE
AGED
AGEDNESS
AGEDNESSES
AGEE
AGEING
AGEINGS
AGEISM
AGEISMS
AGEIST
AGEISTS
AGELAST
AGELASTIC
AGELASTS
AGELESS
AGELONG
AGEN
AGENCIES
AGENCY
AGENDA
AGENDAS
AGENE
AGENES
AGENT
AGENTED
AGENTIAL
AGENTING
AGENTS
AGES
AGGER
AGGERS
AGGRACE
AGGRACED
AGGRACES
AGGRACING
AGGRADE
AGGRADED
AGGRADES
AGGRADING
AGGRATE
AGGRATED
AGGRATES
AGGRATING
AGGRAVATE
AGGRAVATED
AGGRAVATES
AGGRAVATING
AGGREGATE
AGGREGATED
AGGREGATES
AGGREGATING
AGGRESS
AGGRESSED
AGGRESSES
AGGRESSING
AGGRESSOR

AGGRESSORS
AGGRI
AGGRIEVE
AGGRIEVED
AGGRIEVES
AGGRIEVING
AGGRO
AGGROS
AGGRY
AGHA
AGHAS
AGHAST
AGILA
AGILAS
AGILE
AGILELY
AGILER
AGILEST
AGILITIES
AGILITY
AGIN
AGING
AGINGS
AGINNER
AGINNERS
AGIO
AGIOS
AGIOTAGE
AGIOTAGES
AGIST
AGISTED
AGISTER
AGISTERS
AGISTING
AGISTMENT
AGISTMENTS
AGISTOR
AGISTORS
AGISTS
AGITATE
AGITATED
AGITATES
AGITATING
AGITATION
AGITATIONS
AGITATIVE
AGITATO
AGITATOR
AGITATORS
AGITPROP
AGITPROPS
AGLEE
AGLET
AGLETS
AGLEY
AGLIMMER
AGLITTER
AGLOW
AGMA
AGMAS
AGNAIL
AGNAILS
AGNAME
AGNAMED
AGNAMES
AGNATE
AGNATES
AGNATIC
AGNATICAL
AGNATION

AGNATIONS
AGNISE
AGNISED
AGNISES
AGNISING
AGNIZE
AGNIZED
AGNIZES
AGNIZING
AGNOMEN
AGNOMENS
AGNOMINA
AGNOSTIC
AGNOSTICS
AGO
AGOG
AGOGE
AGOGES
AGOGIC
AGOGICS
AGOING
AGON
AGONE
AGONIC
AGONIES
AGONISE
AGONISED
AGONISES
AGONISING
AGONIST
AGONISTES
AGONISTIC
AGONISTICS
AGONISTS
AGONIZE
AGONIZED
AGONIZES
AGONIZING
AGONS
AGONY
AGOOD
AGORA
AGORAS
AGOROT
AGOUTA
AGOUTAS
AGOUTI
AGOUTIES
AGOUTIS
AGOUTY
AGRAFFE
AGRAFFES
AGRAPHA
AGRAPHIA
AGRAPHIAS
AGRAPHIC
AGRAPHON
AGRARIAN
AGRASTE
AGRAVIC
AGREE
AGREEABLE
AGREEABLY
AGREED
AGREEING
AGREEMENT
AGREEMENTS
AGREES
AGRÉGÉ
AGRÉGÉS

AGRÉMENS
AGRÉMENT
AGRÉMENTS
AGRESTAL
AGRESTIAL
AGRESTIC
AGRIMONIES
AGRIMONY
AGRIN
AGRIOLOGIES
AGRIOLOGY
AGRISE
AGRISED
AGRISES
AGRISING
AGRIZE
AGRIZED
AGRIZES
AGRIZING
AGROLOGIES
AGROLOGY
AGRONOMIC
AGRONOMICS
AGRONOMIES
AGRONOMY
AGROUND
AGRYZE
AGRYZED
AGRYZES
AGRYZING
AGUACATE
AGUACATES
AGUE
AGUED
AGUES
AGUISE
AGUISED
AGUISES
AGUISH
AGUISHLY
AGUISING
AGUIZE
AGUIZED
AGUIZES
AGUIZING
AGUTI
AGUTIS
AH
AHA
AHEAD
AHEAP
AHEIGHT
AHEM
AHIGH
AHIMSA
AHIMSAS
AHIND
AHINT
AHOLD
AHORSE
AHOY
AHULL
AHUNGERED
AHUNGRY
AI
AIA
AIAS
AIBLINS
AID
AIDANCE

AIDANCES
AIDANT
AIDE
AIDED
AIDER
AIDERS
AIDES
AIDFUL
AIDING
AIDLESS
AIDOI
AIDOS
AIDS
AIERIES
AIERY
AIGLET
AIGLETS
AIGRETTE
AIGRETTES
AIGUILLE
AIGUILLES
AIKIDO
AIKIDOS
AIKONA
AIL
AILANTHUS
AILANTHUSES
AILANTO
AILANTOS
AILED
AILERON
AILERONS
AILETTE
AILETTES
AILING
AILMENT
AILMENTS
AILS
AIM
AIMED
AIMING
AIMLESS
AIMLESSLY
AIMS
AIN
AÎNÉ
AÎNÉE
AIOLI
AIOLIS
AIR
AIRBORNE
AIRBURST
AIRBURSTS
AIRCRAFT
AIRDRAWN
AIRDROME
AIRDROMES
AIRED
AIRER
AIRERS
AIRFIELD
AIRFIELDS
AIRFRAME
AIRFRAMES
AIRGAP
AIRGAPS
AIRGRAPH
AIRGRAPHS
AIRHOLE
AIRHOLES

AIRIER
AIRIEST
AIRILY
AIRINESS
AIRINESSES
AIRING
AIRINGS
AIRLESS
AIRLIFT
AIRLIFTED
AIRLIFTING
AIRLIFTS
AIRLINE
AIRLINER
AIRLINERS
AIRLINES
AIRMAIL
AIRMAILED
AIRMAILING
AIRMAILS
AIRMAN
AIRMEN
AIRN
AIRNED
AIRNING
AIRNS
AIRPLANE
AIRPLANES
AIRPORT
AIRPORTS
AIRS
AIRSCREW
AIRSCREWS
AIRSHAFT
AIRSHAFTS
AIRSHIP
AIRSHIPS
AIRSICK
AIRSPACE
AIRSPACES
AIRSTOP
AIRSTOPS
AIRSTREAM
AIRSTREAMS
AIRSTRIP
AIRSTRIPS
AIRT
AIRTED
AIRTIGHT
AIRTIME
AIRTIMES
AIRTING
AIRTS
AIRWARD
AIRWARDS
AIRWAVE
AIRWAVES
AIRWAY
AIRWAYS
AIRWOMAN
AIRWOMEN
AIRWORTHY
AIRY
AIS
AISLE
AISLED
AISLES
AISLING
AISLINGS
AIT

AITCH
AITCHBONE
AITCHBONES
AITCHES
AITS
AITU
AITUS
AIZLE
AIZLES
AJAR
AJEE
AJOWAN
AJOWANS
AJUTAGE
AJUTAGES
AJWAN
AJWANS
AKE
AKED
AKEDAH
AKEDAHS
AKEE
AKEES
AKENE
AKENES
AKES
AKIMBO
AKIN
AKINESES
AKINESIA
AKINESIAS
AKINESIS
AKING
AKKAS
AKOLUTHOS
AKOLUTHOSES
AKVAVIT
AKVAVITS
ALA
ALAAP
ALAAPS
ALABAMINE
ALABAMINES
ALABASTER
ALABASTERS
ALACK
ALACRITIES
ALACRITY
ALAE
ALAIMENT
ALAIMENTS
ALALAGMOI
ALALAGMOS
ALALIA
ALALIAS
ALAMEDA
ALAMEDAS
ALAMODE
ALAMODES
ALAMORT
ALAND
ALANG
ALANGS
ALANNAH
ALANNAHS
ALAP
ALAPA
ALAPAS
ALAPS
ALAR

ALARM
ALARMED
ALARMEDLY
ALARMING
ALARMISM
ALARMISMS
ALARMIST
ALARMISTS
ALARMS
ALARUM
ALARUMED
ALARUMING
ALARUMS
ALARY
ALAS
ALASTRIM
ALASTRIMS
ALATE
ALATED
ALAY
ALAYED
ALAYING
ALAYS
ALB
ALBACORE
ALBACORES
ALBARELLI
ALBARELLO
ALBARELLOS
ALBATA
ALBATAS
ALBATROSS
ALBATROSSES
ALBE
ALBEDO
ALBEDOS
ALBEE
ALBEIT
ALBERGHI
ALBERGO
ALBERT
ALBERTITE
ALBERTITES
ALBERTS
ALBESCENT
ALBESPINE
ALBESPINES
ALBESPYNE
ALBESPYNES
ALBICORE
ALBICORES
ALBINESS
ALBINESSES
ALBINISM
ALBINISMS
ALBINO
ALBINOISM
ALBINOISMS
ALBINOS
ALBINOTIC
ALBITE
ALBITES
ALBITISE
ALBITISED
ALBITISES
ALBITISING
ALBITIZE
ALBITIZED
ALBITIZES
ALBITIZING

ALBRICIAS
ALBS
ALBUGO
ALBUGOS
ALBUM
ALBUMEN
ALBUMENS
ALBUMIN
ALBUMINS
ALBUMS
ALBURNOUS
ALBURNUM
ALBURNUMS
ALCAHEST
ALCAHESTS
ALCAIDE
ALCAIDES
ALCALDE
ALCALDES
ALCARRAZA
ALCARRAZAS
ALCATRAS
ALCATRASES
ALCAYDE
ALCAYDES
ALCÁZAR
ALCÁZARS
ALCHEMIC
ALCHEMIES
ALCHEMIST
ALCHEMISTS
ALCHEMY
ALCHERA
ALCHERAS
ALCHYMIES
ALCHYMY
ALCOHOL
ALCOHOLIC
ALCOHOLICS
ALCOHOLS
ALCORZA
ALCORZAS
ALCOVE
ALCOVES
ALDEA
ALDEAS
ALDEHYDE
ALDEHYDES
ALDER
ALDERMAN
ALDERMEN
ALDERN
ALDERS
ALDOSE
ALDOSES
ALDRIN
ALDRINS
ALE
ALEATORIC
ALEATORIES
ALEATORY
ALEBENCH
ALEBENCHES
ALECOST
ALECOSTS
ALECTRYON
ALECTRYONS
ALEE
ALEFT
ALEGAR

ALEGARS
ALEGGE
ALEGGED
ALEGGES
ALEGGING
ALEMBIC
ALEMBICS
ALEMBROTH
ALEMBROTHS
ALENGTH
ALEPH
ALEPHS
ALEPINE
ALEPINES
ALERCE
ALERCES
ALERION
ALERIONS
ALERT
ALERTED
ALERTER
ALERTEST
ALERTING
ALERTLY
ALERTNESS
ALERTNESSES
ALERTS
ALES
ALEURON
ALEURONE
ALEURONES
ALEURONS
ALEVIN
ALEVINS
ALEW
ALEWASHED
ALEWIFE
ALEWIVES
ALEWS
ALEXIA
ALEXIAS
ALEXIC
ALEXIN
ALEXINS
ALEYE
ALEYED
ALEYES
ALEYING
ALFA
ALFALFA
ALFALFAS
ALFAQUÍ
ALFAQUÍS
ALFAS
ALFÉRECES
ALFÉREZ
ALFORJA
ALFORJAS
ALFRESCO
ALGA
ALGAE
ALGAL
ALGAROBA
ALGAROBAS
ALGARROBA
ALGARROBAS
ALGARROBO
ALGARROBOS
ALGATE
ALGATES

ALGEBRA
ALGEBRAIC
ALGEBRAS
ALGERINE
ALGERINES
ALGESES
ALGESIA
ALGESIAS
ALGESIS
ALGICIDE
ALGICIDES
ALGID
ALGIDITIES
ALGIDITY
ALGIN
ALGINATE
ALGINATES
ALGINIC
ALGINS
ALGOID
ALGOLOGIES
ALGOLOGY
ALGORISM
ALGORISMS
ALGORITHM
ALGORITHMS
ALGUACIL
ALGUACILS
ALGUAZIL
ALGUAZILS
ALGUM
ALGUMS
ALIAS
ALIASES
ALIBI
ALIBIS
ALICANT
ALICANTS
ALICYCLIC
ALIDAD
ALIDADE
ALIDADES
ALIDADS
ALIEN
ALIENABLE
ALIENAGE
ALIENAGES
ALIENATE
ALIENATED
ALIENATES
ALIENATING
ALIENATOR
ALIENATORS
ALIENED
ALIENEE
ALIENEES
ALIENING
ALIENISM
ALIENISMS
ALIENIST
ALIENISTS
ALIENOR
ALIENORS
ALIENS
ALIFORM
ALIGARTA
ALIGARTAS
ALIGHT
ALIGHTED
ALIGHTING

ALIGHTS
ALIGN
ALIGNED
ALIGNING
ALIGNMENT
ALIGNMENTS
ALIGNS
ALIKE
ALIMENT
ALIMENTAL
ALIMENTED
ALIMENTING
ALIMENTS
ALIMONIES
ALIMONY
ALINE
ALINED
ALINEMENT
ALINEMENTS
ALINES
ALINING
ALIPED
ALIPEDS
ALIPHATIC
ALIQUANT
ALIQUOT
ALISMA
ALISMAS
ALIT
ALIUNDE
ALIVE
ALIZARI
ALIZARIN
ALIZARINE
ALIZARINES
ALIZARINS
ALIZARIS
ALKAHEST
ALKAHESTS
ALKALI
ALKALIES
ALKALIFIED
ALKALIFIES
ALKALIFY
ALKALIFYING
ALKALINE
ALKALIS
ALKALISE
ALKALISED
ALKALISES
ALKALISING
ALKALIZE
ALKALIZED
ALKALIZES
ALKALIZING
ALKALOID
ALKALOIDS
ALKALOSES
ALKALOSIS
ALKANE
ALKANES
ALKANET
ALKANETS
ALKENE
ALKENES
ALKYD
ALKYDS
ALKYL
ALKYLS
ALKYNE

ALKYNES
ALL
ALLANTOIC
ALLANTOID
ALLANTOIDS
ALLANTOIS
ALLANTOISES
ALLATIVE
ALLATIVES
ALLAY
ALLAYED
ALLAYER
ALLAYERS
ALLAYING
ALLAYINGS
ALLAYMENT
ALLAYMENTS
ALLAYS
ALLEDGE
ALLEDGED
ALLEDGES
ALLEDGING
ALLÉE
ALLÉES
ALLEGE
ALLEGED
ALLEGEDLY
ALLEGER
ALLEGERS
ALLEGES
ALLEGGE
ALLEGGED
ALLEGGES
ALLEGGING
ALLEGIANT
ALLEGING
ALLEGORIC
ALLEGORIES
ALLEGORY
ALLEGRO
ALLEGROS
ALLEL
ALLELE
ALLELES
ALLELS
ALLELUIA
ALLELUIAH
ALLELUIAHS
ALLELUIAS
ALLEMANDE
ALLEMANDES
ALLENARLY
ALLERGEN
ALLERGENS
ALLERGIC
ALLERGICS
ALLERGIES
ALLERGY
ALLERION
ALLERIONS
ALLEVIATE
ALLEVIATED
ALLEVIATES
ALLEVIATING
ALLEY
ALLEYED
ALLEYS
ALLEYWAY
ALLEYWAYS
ALLHEAL

ALLHEALS
ALLIANCE
ALLIANCES
ALLICE
ALLICES
ALLICHOLIES
ALLICHOLY
ALLIED
ALLIES
ALLIGARTA
ALLIGARTAS
ALLIGATE
ALLIGATED
ALLIGATES
ALLIGATING
ALLIGATOR
ALLIGATORS
ALLIS
ALLISES
ALLNESS
ALLNESSES
ALLNIGHT
ALLOCABLE
ALLOCARPIES
ALLOCARPY
ALLOCATE
ALLOCATED
ALLOCATES
ALLOCATING
ALLOD
ALLODIAL
ALLODIUM
ALLODIUMS
ALLODS
ALLOGAMIES
ALLOGAMY
ALLOGRAPH
ALLOGRAPHS
ALLOMETRIES
ALLOMETRY
ALLOMORPH
ALLOMORPHS
ALLONGE
ALLONGES
ALLONS
ALLONYM
ALLONYMS
ALLOPATH
ALLOPATHIES
ALLOPATHS
ALLOPATHY
ALLOPHONE
ALLOPHONES
ALLOPLASM
ALLOPLASMS
ALLOSAUR
ALLOSAURS
ALLOSTERIES
ALLOSTERY
ALLOT
ALLOTMENT
ALLOTMENTS
ALLOTROPE
ALLOTROPES
ALLOTROPIES
ALLOTROPY
ALLOTS
ALLOTTED
ALLOTTEE
ALLOTTEES

ALLOTTERIES
ALLOTTERY
ALLOTTING
ALLOW
ALLOWABLE
ALLOWABLY
ALLOWANCE
ALLOWANCED
ALLOWANCES
ALLOWANCING
ALLOWED
ALLOWEDLY
ALLOWING
ALLOWS
ALLOY
ALLOYED
ALLOYING
ALLOYS
ALLS
ALLSEED
ALLSEEDS
ALLSPICE
ALLSPICES
ALLUDE
ALLUDED
ALLUDES
ALLUDING
ALLURE
ALLURED
ALLURER
ALLURERS
ALLURES
ALLURING
ALLUSION
ALLUSIONS
ALLUSIVE
ALLUVIA
ALLUVIAL
ALLUVION
ALLUVIONS
ALLUVIUM
ALLY
ALLYCHOLIES
ALLYCHOLY
ALLYING
ALLYL
ALLYLS
ALMA
ALMAH
ALMAHS
ALMAIN
ALMAINS
ALMANAC
ALMANACS
ALMANDINE
ALMANDINES
ALMAS
ALME
ALMEH
ALMEHS
ALMERIES
ALMERY
ALMES
ALMIGHTY
ALMIRAH
ALMIRAHS
ALMOND
ALMONDS
ALMONER
ALMONERS

ALMONRIES
ALMONRY
ALMOST
ALMOUS
ALMS
ALMUG
ALMUGS
ALNAGE
ALNAGER
ALNAGERS
ALNAGES
ALOD
ALODIAL
ALODIUM
ALODIUMS
ALODS
ALOE
ALOED
ALOES
ALOETIC
ALOETICS
ALOFT
ALOGIA
ALOGIAS
ALOGICAL
ALOHA
ALOHAS
ALONE
ALONELY
ALONENESS
ALONENESSES
ALONG
ALONGSIDE
ALONGST
ALOOF
ALOOFLY
ALOOFNESS
ALOOFNESSES
ALOPECIA
ALOPECIAS
ALOPECOID
ALOUD
ALOW
ALOWE
ALP
ALPACA
ALPACAS
ALPARGATA
ALPARGATAS
ALPEEN
ALPEENS
ALPENHORN
ALPENHORNS
ALPHA
ALPHABET
ALPHABETED
ALPHABETING
ALPHABETS
ALPHAS
ALPHASORT
ALPHASORTED
ALPHASORTING
ALPHASORTS
ALPHORN
ALPHORNS
ALPINE
ALPINES
ALPINISM
ALPINISMS
ALPINIST

ALPINISTS
ALPS
ALREADY
ALRIGHT
ALS
ALSIKE
ALSIKES
ALSO
ALSOON
ALSOONE
ALT
ALTAR
ALTARAGE
ALTARAGES
ALTARS
ALTARWISE
ALTER
ALTERABLE
ALTERANT
ALTERANTS
ALTERCATE
ALTERCATED
ALTERCATES
ALTERCATING
ALTERED
ALTERING
ALTERITIES
ALTERITY
ALTERN
ALTERNANT
ALTERNANTS
ALTERNAT
ALTERNATE
ALTERNATED
ALTERNATES
ALTERNATING
ALTERNATS
ALTERNE
ALTERNES
ALTERS
ALTESSE
ALTESSES
ALTEZA
ALTEZAS
ALTEZZA
ALTEZZAS
ALTHAEA
ALTHAEAS
ALTHORN
ALTHORNS
ALTHOUGH
ALTIMETER
ALTIMETERS
ALTISSIMO
ALTITUDE
ALTITUDES
ALTO
ALTOS
ALTRICES
ALTRICIAL
ALTRUISM
ALTRUISMS
ALTRUIST
ALTRUISTS
ALTS
ALUDEL
ALUDELS
ALULA
ALULAS
ALUM

ALUMINA
ALUMINAS
ALUMINATE
ALUMINATES
ALUMINISE
ALUMINISED
ALUMINISES
ALUMINISING
ALUMINIUM
ALUMINIUMS
ALUMINIZE
ALUMINIZED
ALUMINIZES
ALUMINIZING
ALUMINOUS
ALUMINUM
ALUMINUMS
ALUMISH
ALUMIUM
ALUMIUMS
ALUMNA
ALUMNAE
ALUMNI
ALUMNUS
ALUMS
ALUNITE
ALUNITES
ALURE
ALURES
ALVEARIES
ALVEARY
ALVEATED
ALVEOLAR
ALVEOLATE
ALVEOLE
ALVEOLES
ALVEOLI
ALVEOLUS
ALVINE
ALWAY
ALWAYS
ALYSSUM
ALYSSUMS
AM
AMABILE
AMADAVAT
AMADAVATS
AMADOU
AMADOUS
AMAH
AMAHS
AMAIN
AMALGAM
AMALGAMS
AMANDINE
AMANDINES
AMANITA
AMANITAS
AMARACUS
AMARACUSES
AMARANT
AMARANTH
AMARANTHS
AMARANTIN
AMARANTS
AMARYLLID
AMARYLLIDS
AMARYLLIS
AMARYLLISES
AMASS

AMASSABLE
AMASSED
AMASSES
AMASSING
AMASSMENT
AMASSMENTS
AMATE
AMATED
AMATES
AMATEUR
AMATEURS
AMATING
AMATION
AMATIONS
AMATIVE
AMATOL
AMATOLS
AMATORIAL
AMATORIAN
AMATORY
AMAUROSES
AMAUROSIS
AMAUROTIC
AMAZE
AMAZED
AMAZEDLY
AMAZEMENT
AMAZEMENTS
AMAZES
AMAZING
AMAZINGLY
AMAZON
AMAZONIAN
AMAZONITE
AMAZONITES
AMAZONS
AMBAGE
AMBAGES
AMBAGIOUS
AMBAN
AMBANS
AMBASSAGE
AMBASSAGES
AMBASSIES
AMBASSY
AMBATCH
AMBATCHES
AMBER
AMBERED
AMBERGRIS
AMBERGRISES
AMBERITE
AMBERITES
AMBERJACK
AMBERJACKS
AMBEROID
AMBEROIDS
AMBEROUS
AMBERS
AMBERY
AMBIANCE
AMBIANCES
AMBIENCE
AMBIENCES
AMBIENT
AMBIENTS
AMBIGUITIES
AMBIGUITY
AMBIGUOUS
AMBIT

AMBITION
AMBITIONS
AMBITIOUS
AMBITS
AMBITTY
AMBIVERT
AMBIVERTS
AMBLE
AMBLED
AMBLER
AMBLERS
AMBLES
AMBLING
AMBLINGS
AMBLYOPIA
AMBLYOPIAS
AMBO
AMBONES
AMBOS
AMBRIES
AMBROID
AMBROIDS
AMBROSIA
AMBROSIAL
AMBROSIAN
AMBROSIAS
AMBROTYPE
AMBROTYPES
AMBRY
AMBULACRA
AMBULANCE
AMBULANCES
AMBULANT
AMBULANTS
AMBULATE
AMBULATED
AMBULATES
AMBULATING
AMBULATOR
AMBULATORS
AMBUSCADE
AMBUSCADED
AMBUSCADES
AMBUSCADING
AMBUSCADO
AMBUSCADOES
AMBUSCADOS
AMBUSH
AMBUSHED
AMBUSHES
AMBUSHING
AMEARST
AMEBA
AMEBAE
AMEBAS
AMEBIC
AMEER
AMEERS
AMELCORN
AMELCORNS
AMELIA
AMELIAS
AMEN
AMENABLE
AMENABLY
AMENAGE
AMENAGED
AMENAGES
AMENAGING
AMENAUNCE

AMENAUNCES
AMEND
AMENDABLE
AMENDE
AMENDED
AMENDER
AMENDERS
AMENDES
AMENDING
AMENDMENT
AMENDMENTS
AMENDS
AMENE
AMENED
AMENING
AMENITIES
AMENITY
AMENS
AMENT
AMENTA
AMENTAL
AMENTIA
AMENTIAS
AMENTS
AMENTUM
AMERCE
AMERCED
AMERCES
AMERCING
AMERICIUM
AMERICIUMS
AMETHYST
AMETHYSTS
AMI
AMIABLE
AMIABLY
AMIANTHUS
AMIANTHUSES
AMIANTUS
AMIANTUSES
AMICABLE
AMICABLY
AMICE
AMICES
AMID
AMIDE
AMIDES
AMIDMOST
AMIDSHIPS
AMIDST
AMIE
AMIES
AMIGO
AMIGOS
AMILDAR
AMILDARS
AMINE
AMINES
AMIR
AMIRS
AMIS
AMISES
AMISS
AMISSES
AMISSIBLE
AMISSING
AMITIES
AMITOSES
AMITOSIS
AMITOTIC

AMITY
AMLA
AMLAS
AMMAN
AMMANS
AMMETER
AMMETERS
AMMIRAL
AMMIRALS
AMMO
AMMON
AMMONAL
AMMONALS
AMMONIA
AMMONIAC
AMMONIAS
AMMONITE
AMMONITES
AMMONIUM
AMMONIUMS
AMMONOID
AMMONOIDS
AMMONS
AMMOS
AMNESIA
AMNESIAC
AMNESIACS
AMNESIAS
AMNESIC
AMNESICS
AMNESTIED
AMNESTIES
AMNESTY
AMNESTYING
AMNIA
AMNION
AMNIOTIC
AMOEBA
AMOEBAE
AMOEBAEAN
AMOEBAS
AMOEBIC
AMOEBOID
AMOK
AMOMUM
AMOMUMS
AMONG
AMONGST
AMOOVE
AMOOVED
AMOOVES
AMOOVING
AMORAL
AMORALISM
AMORALISMS
AMORALIST
AMORALISTS
AMORCE
AMORCES
AMORET
AMORETS
AMORETTI
AMORETTO
AMORINI
AMORINO
AMORISM
AMORISMS
AMORIST
AMORISTS
AMORNINGS

AMOROSA
AMOROSAS
AMOROSITIES
AMOROSITY
AMOROSO
AMOROSOS
AMOROUS
AMOROUSLY
AMORPHISM
AMORPHISMS
AMORPHOUS
AMORT
AMORTISE
AMORTISED
AMORTISES
AMORTISING
AMORTIZE
AMORTIZED
AMORTIZES
AMORTIZING
AMOSITE
AMOSITES
AMOUNT
AMOUNTED
AMOUNTING
AMOUNTS
AMOUR
AMOURETTE
AMOURETTES
AMOURS
AMOVE
AMOVED
AMOVES
AMOVING
AMP
AMPASSIES
AMPASSY
AMPERAGE
AMPERAGES
AMPERE
AMPERES
AMPERSAND
AMPERSANDS
AMPERZAND
AMPERZANDS
AMPHIBIAN
AMPHIBIANS
AMPHIBOLE
AMPHIBOLES
AMPHIBOLIES
AMPHIBOLY
AMPHIGORIES
AMPHIGORY
AMPHIOXUS
AMPHIOXUSES
AMPHIPOD
AMPHIPODS
AMPHOLYTE
AMPHOLYTES
AMPHORA
AMPHORAE
AMPHORIC
AMPLE
AMPLENESS
AMPLENESSES
AMPLER
AMPLEST
AMPLIFIED
AMPLIFIER
AMPLIFIERS

| | | | | |
|---|---|---|---|---|
| AMPLIFIES | AMYLOPSINS | ANALOGIZES | ANARCHS | ANCLE |
| AMPLIFY | AMYLS | ANALOGIZING | ANARCHY | ANCLES |
| AMPLIFYING | AMYLUM | ANALOGON | ANAS | ANCOME |
| AMPLITUDE | AMYLUMS | ANALOGONS | ANASARCA | ANCOMES |
| AMPLITUDES | AN | ANALOGOUS | ANASARCAS | ANCON |
| AMPLOSOME | ANA | ANALOGS | ANASTASES | ANCONES |
| AMPLOSOMES | ANABAS | ANALOGUE | ANASTASIS | ANCORA |
| AMPLY | ANABASES | ANALOGUES | ANASTATIC | ANCRESS |
| AMPOULE | ANABASIS | ANALOGY | ANATASE | ANCRESSES |
| AMPOULES | ANABATIC | ANALYSAND | ANATASES | AND |
| AMPS | ANABIOSES | ANALYSANDS | ANATHEMA | ANDANTE |
| AMPUL | ANABIOSIS | ANALYSE | ANATHEMAS | ANDANTES |
| AMPULE | ANABIOTIC | ANALYSED | ANATOMIC | ANDANTINO |
| AMPULES | ANABLEPS | ANALYSER | ANATOMIES | ANDANTINOS |
| AMPULLA | ANABLEPSES | ANALYSERS | ANATOMISE | ANDESINE |
| AMPULLAE | ANABOLIC | ANALYSES | ANATOMISED | ANDESINES |
| AMPULS | ANABOLISM | ANALYSING | ANATOMISES | ANDESITE |
| AMPUTATE | ANABOLISMS | ANALYSIS | ANATOMISING | ANDESITES |
| AMPUTATED | ANABRANCH | ANALYST | ANATOMIST | ANDESITIC |
| AMPUTATES | ANABRANCHES | ANALYSTS | ANATOMISTS | ANDIRON |
| AMPUTATING | ANACHARIS | ANALYTIC | ANATOMIZE | ANDIRONS |
| AMPUTATOR | ANACHARISES | ANALYTICS | ANATOMIZED | ANDROECIA |
| AMPUTATORS | ANACONDA | ANALYZE | ANATOMIZES | ANDROGEN |
| AMPUTEE | ANACONDAS | ANALYZED | ANATOMIZING | ANDROGENS |
| AMPUTEES | ANACRUSES | ANALYZER | ANATOMY | ANDROGYNE |
| AMRIT | ANACRUSIS | ANALYZERS | ANATROPIES | ANDROGYNES |
| AMRITA | ANADEM | ANALYZES | ANATROPY | ANDROGYNIES |
| AMRITAS | ANADEMS | ANALYZING | ANATTA | ANDROGYNY |
| AMRITS | ANAEMIA | ANAMNESES | ANATTAS | ANDROID |
| AMTMAN | ANAEMIAS | ANAMNESIS | ANATTO | ANDROIDS |
| AMTMANS | ANAEMIC | ANAN | ANATTOS | ANDROLOGIES |
| AMTRACK | ANAEROBE | ANANA | ANBURIES | ANDROLOGY |
| AMTRACKS | ANAEROBES | ANANAS | ANBURY | ANDROMEDA |
| AMUCK | ANAEROBIC | ANANASES | ANCE | ANDROMEDAS |
| AMULET | ANAGLYPH | ANANDROUS | ANCESTOR | ANDS |
| AMULETIC | ANAGLYPHS | ANANKE | ANCESTORS | ANDVILE |
| AMULETS | ANAGOGE | ANANKES | ANCESTRAL | ANDVILES |
| AMUSABLE | ANAGOGES | ANANTHOUS | ANCESTRIES | ANE |
| AMUSE | ANAGOGIC | ANAPAEST | ANCESTRY | ANEAR |
| AMUSED | ANAGOGIES | ANAPAESTS | ANCHOR | ANEARED |
| AMUSEDLY | ANAGOGY | ANAPEST | ANCHORAGE | ANEARING |
| AMUSEMENT | ANAGRAM | ANAPESTS | ANCHORAGES | ANEARS |
| AMUSEMENTS | ANAGRAMMED | ANAPHASE | ANCHORED | ANEATH |
| AMUSER | ANAGRAMMING | ANAPHASES | ANCHORESS | ANECDOTAL |
| AMUSERS | ANAGRAMS | ANAPHORA | ANCHORESSES | ANECDOTE |
| AMUSES | ANAL | ANAPHORAS | ANCHORET | ANECDOTES |
| AMUSETTE | ANALCIME | ANAPHORIC | ANCHORETS | ANECHOIC |
| AMUSETTES | ANALCIMES | ANAPLASTIES | ANCHORING | ANELACE |
| AMUSING | ANALCITE | ANAPLASTY | ANCHORITE | ANELACES |
| AMUSINGLY | ANALCITES | ANAPTYXES | ANCHORITES | ANELE |
| AMUSIVE | ANALECTA | ANAPTYXIS | ANCHORS | ANELED |
| AMYGDAL | ANALECTIC | ANARAK | ANCHOVETA | ANELES |
| AMYGDALA | ANALECTS | ANARAKS | ANCHOVETAS | ANELING |
| AMYGDALAS | ANALEPTIC | ANARCH | ANCHOVIES | ANEMIA |
| AMYGDALE | ANALGESIA | ANARCHAL | ANCHOVY | ANEMIAS |
| AMYGDALES | ANALGESIAS | ANARCHIAL | ANCHYLOSE | ANEMIC |
| AMYGDALIN | ANALGESIC | ANARCHIC | ANCHYLOSED | ANEMOGRAM |
| AMYGDALINS | ANALGESICS | ANARCHIES | ANCHYLOSES | ANEMOGRAMS |
| AMYGDALS | ANALLY | ANARCHISE | ANCHYLOSING | ANEMOLOGIES |
| AMYGDULE | ANALOG | ANARCHISED | ANCHYLOSIS | ANEMOLOGY |
| AMYGDULES | ANALOGIC | ANARCHISES | ANCIENT | ANEMONE |
| AMYL | ANALOGIES | ANARCHISING | ANCIENTLY | ANEMONES |
| AMYLASE | ANALOGISE | ANARCHISM | ANCIENTRIES | ANENT |
| AMYLASES | ANALOGISED | ANARCHISMS | ANCIENTRY | ANERLY |
| AMYLENE | ANALOGISES | ANARCHIST | ANCIENTS | ANEROID |
| AMYLENES | ANALOGISING | ANARCHISTS | ANCILE | ANEROIDS |
| AMYLOID | ANALOGIST | ANARCHIZE | ANCILES | ANES |
| AMYLOIDAL | ANALOGISTS | ANARCHIZED | ANCILLARIES | ANESTRA |
| AMYLOIDS | ANALOGIZE | ANARCHIZES | ANCILLARY | ANESTRI |
| AMYLOPSIN | ANALOGIZED | ANARCHIZING | ANCIPITAL | ANESTROUS |

ANESTRUM
ANESTRUS
ANETIC
ANEURIN
ANEURINS
ANEURISM
ANEURISMS
ANEURYSM
ANEURYSMS
ANEW
ANGARIES
ANGARY
ANGEKKOK
ANGEKKOKS
ANGEKOK
ANGEKOKS
ANGEL
ANGELHOOD
ANGELHOODS
ANGELIC
ANGELICA
ANGELICAL
ANGELICAS
ANGELS
ANGELUS
ANGELUSES
ANGER
ANGERED
ANGERING
ANGERLESS
ANGERLY
ANGERS
ANGICO
ANGICOS
ANGINA
ANGINAL
ANGINAS
ANGIOGRAM
ANGIOGRAMS
ANGIOMA
ANGIOMAS
ANGIOMATA
ANGLE
ANGLED
ANGLER
ANGLERS
ANGLES
ANGLESITE
ANGLESITES
ANGLEWISE
ANGLICE
ANGLICISE
ANGLICISED
ANGLICISES
ANGLICISING
ANGLICISM
ANGLICISMS
ANGLICIST
ANGLICISTS
ANGLICIZE
ANGLICIZED
ANGLICIZES
ANGLICIZING
ANGLIFIED
ANGLIFIES
ANGLIFY
ANGLIFYING
ANGLING
ANGLINGS
ANGLIST

ANGLISTS
ANGLOPHIL
ANGLOPHILS
ANGORA
ANGORAS
ANGRIER
ANGRIES
ANGRIEST
ANGRILY
ANGRINESS
ANGRINESSES
ANGRY
ANGST
ANGSTROM
ANGSTROMS
ANGSTS
ANGUIFORM
ANGUINE
ANGUIPED
ANGUIPEDE
ANGUISH
ANGUISHED
ANGUISHES
ANGUISHING
ANGULAR
ANGULATE
ANGULATED
ANHEDONIA
ANHEDONIAS
ANHEDRAL
ANHUNGRED
ANHYDRIDE
ANHYDRIDES
ANHYDRITE
ANHYDRITES
ANHYDROUS
ANICONIC
ANICONISM
ANICONISMS
ANICONIST
ANICONISTS
ANICUT
ANICUTS
ANIGH
ANIGHT
ANIL
ANILE
ANILINE
ANILINES
ANILITIES
ANILITY
ANILS
ANIMA
ANIMAL
ANIMALIC
ANIMALISE
ANIMALISED
ANIMALISES
ANIMALISING
ANIMALISM
ANIMALISMS
ANIMALIST
ANIMALISTS
ANIMALITIES
ANIMALITY
ANIMALIZE
ANIMALIZED
ANIMALIZES
ANIMALIZING
ANIMALLY

ANIMALS
ANIMAS
ANIMATE
ANIMATED
ANIMATES
ANIMATING
ANIMATION
ANIMATIONS
ANIMATISM
ANIMATISMS
ANIMATOR
ANIMATORS
ANIMÉ
ANIME
ANIMÉS
ANIMES
ANIMISM
ANIMISMS
ANIMIST
ANIMISTIC
ANIMISTS
ANIMOSITIES
ANIMOSITY
ANIMUS
ANIMUSES
ANION
ANIONIC
ANIONS
ANISE
ANISEED
ANISEEDS
ANISES
ANISETTE
ANISETTES
ANKER
ANKERITE
ANKERITES
ANKERS
ANKH
ANKHS
ANKLE
ANKLED
ANKLES
ANKLET
ANKLETS
ANKUS
ANKUSES
ANKYLOSE
ANKYLOSED
ANKYLOSES
ANKYLOSING
ANKYLOSIS
ANLACE
ANLACES
ANLAGE
ANLAGES
ANN
ANNA
ANNAL
ANNALISE
ANNALISED
ANNALISES
ANNALISING
ANNALIST
ANNALISTS
ANNALIZE
ANNALIZED
ANNALIZES
ANNALIZING
ANNALS

ANNAS
ANNAT
ANNATES
ANNATS
ANNATTA
ANNATTAS
ANNATTO
ANNATTOS
ANNEAL
ANNEALED
ANNEALER
ANNEALERS
ANNEALING
ANNEALINGS
ANNEALS
ANNECTENT
ANNELID
ANNELIDS
ANNEX
ANNEXE
ANNEXED
ANNEXES
ANNEXING
ANNEXION
ANNEXIONS
ANNEXMENT
ANNEXMENTS
ANNEXURE
ANNEXURES
ANNICUT
ANNICUTS
ANNO
ANNOTATE
ANNOTATED
ANNOTATES
ANNOTATING
ANNOTATOR
ANNOTATORS
ANNOUNCE
ANNOUNCED
ANNOUNCER
ANNOUNCERS
ANNOUNCES
ANNOUNCING
ANNOY
ANNOYANCE
ANNOYANCES
ANNOYED
ANNOYING
ANNOYS
ANNS
ANNUAL
ANNUALISE
ANNUALISED
ANNUALISES
ANNUALISING
ANNUALIZE
ANNUALIZED
ANNUALIZES
ANNUALIZING
ANNUALLY
ANNUALS
ANNUITANT
ANNUITANTS
ANNUITIES
ANNUITY
ANNUL
ANNULAR
ANNULARS
ANNULATE

ANNULATED
ANNULATES
ANNULET
ANNULETS
ANNULI
ANNULLED
ANNULLING
ANNULMENT
ANNULMENTS
ANNULOSE
ANNULS
ANNULUS
ANOA
ANOAS
ANODAL
ANODE
ANODES
ANODIC
ANODISE
ANODISED
ANODISES
ANODISING
ANODIZE
ANODIZED
ANODIZES
ANODIZING
ANODYNE
ANODYNES
ANOESES
ANOESIS
ANOESTRA
ANOESTRI
ANOESTRUM
ANOESTRUS
ANOETIC
ANOINT
ANOINTED
ANOINTING
ANOINTS
ANOMALIES
ANOMALOUS
ANOMALY
ANOMIC
ANOMIE
ANOMIES
ANOMY
ANON
ANONYM
ANONYMA
ANONYMAS
ANONYMITIES
ANONYMITY
ANONYMOUS
ANONYMS
ANOPHELES
ANORAK
ANORAKS
ANORECTIC
ANORECTICS
ANORETIC
ANORETICS
ANOREXIA
ANOREXIAS
ANOREXIC
ANOREXICS
ANOREXIES
ANOREXY
ANORTHIC
ANORTHITE
ANORTHITES

| | | | | |
|---|---|---|---|---|
| ANOSMIA | ANTHEM | ANTINOMIC | ANTRORSE | APAYD |
| ANOSMIAS | ANTHEMED | ANTINOMIES | ANTRUM | APAYING |
| ANOTHER | ANTHEMIA | ANTINOMY | ANTRUMS | APAYS |
| ANOUGH | ANTHEMING | ANTIPAPAL | ANTS | APE |
| ANOUROUS | ANTHEMION | ANTIPASTO | ANUCLEATE | APEAK |
| ANOW | ANTHEMS | ANTIPASTOS | ANURIA | APED |
| ANOXIA | ANTHER | ANTIPATHIES | ANURIAS | APEDOM |
| ANOXIAS | ANTHERS | ANTIPATHY | ANUROUS | APEDOMS |
| ANOXIC | ANTHESES | ANTIPHON | ANUS | APEEK |
| ANSATE | ANTHESIS | ANTIPHONIES | ANUSES | APEHOOD |
| ANSATED | ANTHOCARP | ANTIPHONS | ANVIL | APEHOODS |
| ANSERINE | ANTHOCARPS | ANTIPHONY | ANVILS | APEMAN |
| ANSWER | ANTHOCYAN | ANTIPODAL | ANXIETIES | APEMEN |
| ANSWERED | ANTHOCYANS | ANTIPODE | ANXIETY | APEPSIA |
| ANSWERER | ANTHOID | ANTIPODES | ANXIOUS | APEPSIAS |
| ANSWERERS | ANTHOLOGIES | ANTIPOLE | ANXIOUSLY | APEPSIES |
| ANSWERING | ANTHOLOGY | ANTIPOLES | ANY | APEPSY |
| ANSWERS | ANTHRACIC | ANTIPOPE | ANYBODIES | APERÇU |
| ANT | ANTHRAX | ANTIPOPES | ANYBODY | APERÇUS |
| ANTA | ANTHRAXES | ANTIQUARIES | ANYHOW | APERIENT |
| ANTACID | ANTHROPIC | ANTIQUARK | ANYONE | APERIENTS |
| ANTACIDS | ANTHURIUM | ANTIQUARKS | ANYONES | APERIES |
| ANTAE | ANTHURIUMS | ANTIQUARY | ANYROAD | APERIODIC |
| ANTAR | ANTI | ANTIQUATE | ANYTHING | APÉRITIF |
| ANTARS | ANTIAR | ANTIQUATED | ANYTHINGS | APÉRITIFS |
| ANTBEAR | ANTIARS | ANTIQUATES | ANYTIME | APERITIVE |
| ANTBEARS | ANTIBODIES | ANTIQUATING | ANYWAY | APERITIVES |
| ANTE | ANTIBODY | ANTIQUE | ANYWAYS | APERT |
| ANTECEDE | ANTIC | ANTIQUED | ANYWHEN | APERTNESS |
| ANTECEDED | ANTICHLOR | ANTIQUELY | ANYWHERE | APERTNESSES |
| ANTECEDES | ANTICHLORS | ANTIQUES | ANYWISE | APERTURE |
| ANTECEDING | ANTICIVIC | ANTIQUING | ANZIANI | APERTURES |
| ANTECHOIR | ANTICIZE | ANTIQUITIES | AORIST | APERY |
| ANTECHOIRS | ANTICIZED | ANTIQUITY | AORISTIC | APES |
| ANTED | ANTICIZES | ANTIS | AORISTS | APETALIES |
| ANTEDATE | ANTICIZING | ANTISCIAN | AORTA | APETALOUS |
| ANTEDATED | ANTICK | ANTISCIANS | AORTAL | APETALY |
| ANTEDATES | ANTICKE | ANTISERA | AORTAS | APEX |
| ANTEDATING | ANTICKED | ANTISERUM | AORTIC | APEXES |
| ANTEFIX | ANTICKING | ANTISERUMS | AORTITIS | APHAGIA |
| ANTEFIXA | ANTICLINE | ANTISHIP | AORTITISES | APHAGIAS |
| ANTEFIXAL | ANTICLINES | ANTISPAST | AOUDAD | APHANITE |
| ANTEFIXES | ANTICOUS | ANTISPASTS | AOUDADS | APHANITES |
| ANTEING | ANTICS | ANTISTAT | APACE | APHASIA |
| ANTELOPE | ANTIDOTAL | ANTISTATS | APACHE | APHASIAC |
| ANTELOPES | ANTIDOTE | ANTITHET | APACHES | APHASIACS |
| ANTELUCAN | ANTIDOTES | ANTITHETS | APAGE | APHASIAS |
| ANTENATAL | ANTIENT | ANTITOXIC | APAGOGE | APHASIC |
| ANTENATI | ANTIENTS | ANTITOXIN | APAGOGES | APHELIA |
| ANTENNA | ANTIGEN | ANTITOXINS | APAGOGIC | APHELIAN |
| ANTENNAE | ANTIGENIC | ANTITRADE | APAID | APHELIC |
| ANTENNAL | ANTIGENS | ANTITRADES | APANAGE | APHELION |
| ANTENNARY | ANTIHELICES | ANTITRAGI | APANAGED | APHERESES |
| ANTENNAS | ANTIHELIX | ANTITRAGUS | APANAGES | APHERESIS |
| ANTENNULE | ANTIKNOCK | ANTITYPAL | APART | APHESES |
| ANTENNULES | ANTIKNOCKS | ANTITYPE | APARTHEID | APHESIS |
| ANTEPAST | ANTILOG | ANTITYPES | APARTHEIDS | APHETIC |
| ANTEPASTS | ANTILOGIES | ANTITYPIC | APARTMENT | APHETISE |
| ANTERIOR | ANTILOGS | ANTIVENIN | APARTMENTS | APHETISED |
| ANTEROOM | ANTILOGY | ANTIVENINS | APARTNESS | APHETISES |
| ANTEROOMS | ANTIMASK | ANTIVIRAL | APARTNESSES | APHETISING |
| ANTES | ANTIMASKS | ANTLER | APATETIC | APHETIZE |
| ANTEVERT | ANTIMONIC | ANTLERED | APATHATON | APHETIZED |
| ANTEVERTED | ANTIMONIES | ANTLERS | APATHATONS | APHETIZES |
| ANTEVERTING | ANTIMONY | ANTLIA | APATHETIC | APHETIZING |
| ANTEVERTS | ANTING | ANTLIAE | APATHIES | APHICIDE |
| ANTHELIA | ANTINGS | ANTLIATE | APATHY | APHICIDES |
| ANTHELICES | ANTINODAL | ANTONYM | APATITE | APHID |
| ANTHELION | ANTINODE | ANTONYMS | APATITES | APHIDES |
| ANTHELIX | ANTINODES | ANTRE | APAY | APHIDIAN |
| | | ANTRES | | |

APHIDIANS
APHIDICAL
APHIDS
APHIS
APHONIA
APHONIAS
APHONIC
APHONIES
APHONOUS
APHONY
APHORISE
APHORISED
APHORISER
APHORISERS
APHORISES
APHORISING
APHORISM
APHORISMS
APHORIST
APHORISTS
APHORIZE
APHORIZED
APHORIZER
APHORIZERS
APHORIZES
APHORIZING
APHOTIC
APHTHA
APHTHAE
APHTHOUS
APHYLLIES
APHYLLOUS
APHYLLY
APIAN
APIARIAN
APIARIES
APIARIST
APIARISTS
APIARY
APICAL
APICALLY
APICES
APICULATE
APIECE
APING
APIOL
APIOLS
APISH
APISHLY
APISHNESS
APISHNESSES
APISM
APISMS
APIVOROUS
APLANAT
APLANATIC
APLANATS
APLASIA
APLASIAS
APLASTIC
APLENTY
APLITE
APLITES
APLOMB
APLOMBS
APLUSTRE
APLUSTRES
APNEA
APNEAS
APNOEA

APNOEAS
APOCOPATE
APOCOPATED
APOCOPATES
APOCOPATING
APOCOPE
APOCOPES
APOCRINE
APOCRYPHA
APOD
APODAL
APODE
APODES
APODICTIC
APODOSES
APODOSIS
APODOUS
APODS
APOENZYME
APOENZYMES
APOGAEIC
APOGAMIES
APOGAMOUS
APOGAMY
APOGEAL
APOGEAN
APOGEE
APOGEES
APOGRAPH
APOGRAPHS
APOLLINE
APOLLO
APOLLOS
APOLOGIA
APOLOGIAS
APOLOGIES
APOLOGISE
APOLOGISED
APOLOGISES
APOLOGISING
APOLOGIST
APOLOGISTS
APOLOGIZE
APOLOGIZED
APOLOGIZES
APOLOGIZING
APOLOGUE
APOLOGUES
APOLOGY
APOMICTIC
APOMIXES
APOMIXIS
APOOP
APOPHATIC
APOPHYGE
APOPHYGES
APOPHYSES
APOPHYSIS
APOPLEX
APOPLEXED
APOPLEXES
APOPLEXIES
APOPLEXING
APOPLEXY
APORIA
APORIAS
APORT
APOSITIA
APOSITIAS
APOSPORIES

APOSPORY
APOSTASIES
APOSTASY
APOSTATE
APOSTATES
APOSTATIC
APOSTIL
APOSTILLE
APOSTILLES
APOSTILS
APOSTLE
APOSTLES
APOSTOLIC
APOTHECIA
APOTHEGM
APOTHEGMS
APOTHEM
APOTHEMS
APOZEM
APOZEMS
APPAID
APPAIR
APPAIRED
APPAIRING
APPAIRS
APPAL
APPALLED
APPALLING
APPALS
APPALTI
APPALTO
APPANAGE
APPANAGED
APPANAGES
APPARAT
APPARATS
APPARATUS
APPARATUSES
APPAREL
APPARELLED
APPARELLING
APPARELS
APPARENCIES
APPARENCY
APPARENT
APPARENTS
APPARITOR
APPARITORS
APPAY
APPAYD
APPAYING
APPAYS
APPEACH
APPEACHED
APPEACHES
APPEACHING
APPEAL
APPEALED
APPEALING
APPEALS
APPEAR
APPEARED
APPEARER
APPEARERS
APPEARING
APPEARS
APPEASE
APPEASED
APPEASES
APPEASING

APPELLANT
APPELLANTS
APPELLATE
APPEND
APPENDAGE
APPENDAGES
APPENDANT
APPENDANTS
APPENDED
APPENDICES
APPENDING
APPENDIX
APPENDIXES
APPENDS
APPERIL
APPERILL
APPERILLS
APPERILS
APPERTAIN
APPERTAINED
APPERTAINING
APPERTAINS
APPESTAT
APPESTATS
APPETENCE
APPETENCES
APPETENCIES
APPETENCY
APPETENT
APPETIBLE
APPETISE
APPETISED
APPETISER
APPETISERS
APPETISES
APPETISING
APPETITE
APPETITES
APPETIZE
APPETIZED
APPETIZER
APPETIZERS
APPETIZES
APPETIZING
APPLAUD
APPLAUDED
APPLAUDER
APPLAUDERS
APPLAUDING
APPLAUDS
APPLAUSE
APPLAUSES
APPLE
APPLES
APPLIABLE
APPLIANCE
APPLIANCES
APPLICANT
APPLICANTS
APPLICATE
APPLIED
APPLIES
APPLIQUÉ
APPLIQUÉS
APPLY
APPLYING
APPOINT
APPOINTED
APPOINTEE
APPOINTEES

APPOINTING
APPOINTOR
APPOINTORS
APPOINTS
APPORT
APPORTION
APPORTIONED
APPORTIONING
APPORTIONS
APPORTS
APPOSE
APPOSED
APPOSER
APPOSERS
APPOSES
APPOSING
APPOSITE
APPRAISAL
APPRAISALS
APPRAISE
APPRAISED
APPRAISER
APPRAISERS
APPRAISES
APPRAISING
APPREHEND
APPREHENDED
APPREHENDING
APPREHENDS
APPRESS
APPRESSED
APPRESSES
APPRESSING
APPRISE
APPRISED
APPRISES
APPRISING
APPRIZE
APPRIZED
APPRIZER
APPRIZERS
APPRIZES
APPRIZING
APPRIZINGS
APPROACH
APPROACHED
APPROACHES
APPROACHING
APPROBATE
APPROBATED
APPROBATES
APPROBATING
APPROOF
APPROOFS
APPROVAL
APPROVALS
APPROVE
APPROVED
APPROVER
APPROVERS
APPROVES
APPROVING
APPUI
APPUIED
APPUIS
APPULSE
APPULSES
APPUY
APPUYED
APPUYING

| | | | | |
|---|---|---|---|---|
| APPUYS | AQUANAUTS | ARAK | ARCADE | ARCHIVOLT |
| APRAXIA | AQUAPLANE | ARAKS | ARCADED | ARCHIVOLTS |
| APRAXIAS | AQUAPLANED | ARALIA | ARCADES | ARCHLET |
| APRÈS | AQUAPLANES | ARALIAS | ARCADING | ARCHLETS |
| APRICATE | AQUAPLANING | ARAME | ARCADINGS | ARCHLUTE |
| APRICATED | AQUAPLANINGS | ARAMES | ARCANA | ARCHLUTES |
| APRICATES | AQUARELLE | ARANEID | ARCANE | ARCHLY |
| APRICATING | AQUARELLES | ARANEIDS | ARCANELY | ARCHNESS |
| APRICOCK | AQUARIA | ARANEOUS | ARCANIST | ARCHNESSES |
| APRICOCKS | AQUARIAN | ARAPAIMA | ARCANISTS | ARCHOLOGIES |
| APRICOT | AQUARIANS | ARAPAIMAS | ARCANUM | ARCHOLOGY |
| APRICOTS | AQUARIIST | ARAPONGA | ARCCOS | ARCHON |
| APRIORISM | AQUARIISTS | ARAPONGAS | ARCCOSES | ARCHONS |
| APRIORISMS | AQUARIST | ARAPUNGA | ARCED | ARCHONTIC |
| APRIORIST | AQUARISTS | ARAPUNGAS | ARCH | ARCHWAY |
| APRIORISTS | AQUARIUM | ARAR | ARCHAEI | ARCHWAYS |
| APRIORITIES | AQUARIUMS | ARAROBA | ARCHAEUS | ARCHWISE |
| APRIORITY | AQUAS | ARAROBAS | ARCHAIC | ARCING |
| APRON | AQUATIC | ARARS | ARCHAISE | ARCINGS |
| APRONED | AQUATICS | ARAUCARIA | ARCHAISED | ARCKED |
| APRONFUL | AQUATINT | ARAUCARIAS | ARCHAISER | ARCKING |
| APRONFULS | AQUATINTA | ARAYSE | ARCHAISERS | ARCKINGS |
| APRONING | AQUATINTAS | ARAYSED | ARCHAISES | ARCO |
| APRONS | AQUATINTED | ARAYSES | ARCHAISING | ARCS |
| APROPOS | AQUATINTING | ARAYSING | ARCHAISM | ARCSECOND |
| APSE | AQUATINTS | ARBA | ARCHAISMS | ARCSECONDS |
| APSES | AQUAVIT | ARBALEST | ARCHAIST | ARCSIN |
| APSIDAL | AQUAVITS | ARBALESTS | ARCHAISTS | ARCSINS |
| APSIDES | AQUEDUCT | ARBALIST | ARCHAIZE | ARCTAN |
| APSIDIOLE | AQUEDUCTS | ARBALISTS | ARCHAIZED | ARCTANS |
| APSIDIOLES | AQUEOUS | ARBAS | ARCHAIZER | ARCTIC |
| APSIS | AQUIFER | ARBITER | ARCHAIZERS | ARCTICS |
| APT | AQUIFERS | ARBITERS | ARCHAIZES | ARCTOID |
| APTED | AQUILEGIA | ARBITRAGE | ARCHAIZING | ARCTOPHIL |
| APTER | AQUILEGIAS | ARBITRAGED | ARCHANGEL | ARCTOPHILS |
| APTERAL | AQUILINE | ARBITRAGES | ARCHANGELS | ARCUATE |
| APTERIA | AQUIVER | ARBITRAGING | ARCHDUCAL | ARCUATED |
| APTERIUM | AR | ARBITRAL | ARCHDUCHIES | ARCUATION |
| APTEROUS | ARABA | ARBITRARY | ARCHDUCHY | ARCUATIONS |
| APTERYX | ARABAS | ARBITRATE | ARCHDUKE | ARCUS |
| APTERYXES | ARABESQUE | ARBITRATED | ARCHDUKES | ARCUSES |
| APTEST | ARABESQUES | ARBITRATES | ARCHED | ARDEB |
| APTING | ARABICA | ARBITRATING | ARCHEI | ARDEBS |
| APTITUDE | ARABICAS | ARBITRESS | ARCHER | ARDENCIES |
| APTITUDES | ARABIN | ARBITRESSES | ARCHERESS | ARDENCY |
| APTLY | ARABINOSE | ARBITRIUM | ARCHERESSES | ARDENT |
| APTNESS | ARABINOSES | ARBITRIUMS | ARCHERIES | ARDENTLY |
| APTNESSES | ARABINS | ARBLAST | ARCHERS | ARDOUR |
| APTOTE | ARABISE | ARBLASTER | ARCHERY | ARDOURS |
| APTOTES | ARABISED | ARBLASTERS | ARCHES | ARDRI |
| APTOTIC | ARABISES | ARBLASTS | ARCHEST | ARDRIGH |
| APTS | ARABISING | ARBOR | ARCHETYPE | ARDRIGHS |
| APYRETIC | ARABIZE | ARBOREAL | ARCHETYPES | ARDRIS |
| APYREXIA | ARABIZED | ARBOREOUS | ARCHEUS | ARDUOUS |
| APYREXIAS | ARABIZES | ARBORET | ARCHIL | ARDUOUSLY |
| AQUA | ARABIZING | ARBORETA | ARCHILOWE | ARE |
| AQUABATIC | ARABLE | ARBORETS | ARCHILOWES | AREA |
| AQUABATICS | ARACEOUS | ARBORETUM | ARCHILS | AREACH |
| AQUABOARD | ARACHIS | ARBORIST | ARCHIMAGE | AREACHED |
| AQUABOARDS | ARACHISES | ARBORISTS | ARCHIMAGES | AREACHES |
| AQUACADE | ARACHNID | ARBOROUS | ARCHING | AREACHING |
| AQUACADES | ARACHNIDS | ARBORS | ARCHITECT | AREAD |
| AQUADROME | ARACHNOID | ARBOUR | ARCHITECTED | AREADING |
| AQUADROMES | ARACHNOIDS | ARBOURED | ARCHITECTING | AREADS |
| AQUAE | ARAGONITE | ARBOURS | ARCHITECTS | AREAL |
| AQUAFER | ARAGONITES | ARBUTE | ARCHIVAL | AREAR |
| AQUAFERS | ARAISE | ARBUTES | ARCHIVE | AREAS |
| AQUALUNG | ARAISED | ARBUTUS | ARCHIVES | ARECA |
| AQUALUNGS | ARAISES | ARBUTUSES | ARCHIVIST | ARECAS |
| AQUANAUT | ARAISING | ARC | ARCHIVISTS | ARED |

AREDD
AREDE
AREDES
AREDING
AREFIED
AREFIES
AREFY
AREFYING
ARENA
ARENAS
ARENATION
ARENATIONS
AREOLA
AREOLAE
AREOLAR
AREOLATE
AREOLATED
AREOLE
AREOLES
AREOMETER
AREOMETERS
AREOSTYLE
AREOSTYLES
ARERE
ARES
ARET
ARÊTE
ARÊTES
ARETS
ARETT
ARETTED
ARETTING
ARETTS
AREW
ARGAL
ARGALA
ARGALAS
ARGALI
ARGALIS
ARGAN
ARGAND
ARGANDS
ARGANS
ARGEMONE
ARGEMONES
ARGENT
ARGENTINE
ARGENTINES
ARGENTITE
ARGENTITES
ARGENTS
ARGHAN
ARGHANS
ARGIL
ARGILLITE
ARGILLITES
ARGILS
ARGININE
ARGININES
ARGOL
ARGOLS
ARGON
ARGONAUT
ARGONAUTS
ARGONS
ARGOSIES
ARGOSY
ARGOT
ARGOTS
ARGUABLE

ARGUABLY
ARGUE
ARGUED
ARGUER
ARGUERS
ARGUES
ARGUFIED
ARGUFIES
ARGUFY
ARGUFYING
ARGUING
ARGULI
ARGULUS
ARGUMENT
ARGUMENTS
ARGUS
ARGUSES
ARGUTE
ARGUTELY
ARGYLE
ARGYLES
ARGYRIA
ARGYRIAS
ARGYRITE
ARGYRITES
ARHYTHMIA
ARHYTHMIAS
ARHYTHMIC
ARIA
ARIAS
ARID
ARIDER
ARIDEST
ARIDITIES
ARIDITY
ARIDLY
ARIDNESS
ARIDNESSES
ARIEL
ARIELS
ARIETTA
ARIETTAS
ARIETTE
ARIETTES
ARIGHT
ARIL
ARILLARY
ARILLATE
ARILLATED
ARILLI
ARILLODE
ARILLODES
ARILLUS
ARILS
ARIOSI
ARIOSO
ARIOSOS
ARIOT
ARIPPLE
ARIS
ARISE
ARISEN
ARISES
ARISH
ARISHES
ARISING
ARISTA
ARISTAE
ARISTAS
ARISTATE

ARISTO
ARISTOS
ARK
ARKED
ARKING
ARKITE
ARKITES
ARKOSE
ARKOSES
ARKS
ARLES
ARLESED
ARLESES
ARLESING
ARM
ARMADA
ARMADAS
ARMADILLO
ARMADILLOS
ARMAMENT
ARMAMENTS
ARMATURE
ARMATURES
ARMBAND
ARMBANDS
ARMCHAIR
ARMCHAIRS
ARMED
ARMET
ARMETS
ARMFUL
ARMFULS
ARMGAUNT
ARMHOLE
ARMHOLES
ARMIES
ARMIGER
ARMIGERAL
ARMIGERO
ARMIGEROS
ARMIGERS
ARMIL
ARMILLA
ARMILLAE
ARMILLARY
ARMILLAS
ARMILS
ARMING
ARMISTICE
ARMISTICES
ARMLESS
ARMLET
ARMLETS
ARMLOCK
ARMLOCKS
ARMOIRE
ARMOIRES
ARMOR
ARMORIAL
ARMORIALS
ARMORIES
ARMORIST
ARMORISTS
ARMORS
ARMORY
ARMOUR
ARMOURED
ARMOURER
ARMOURERS
ARMOURIES

ARMOURS
ARMOURY
ARMOZEEN
ARMOZEENS
ARMOZINE
ARMOZINES
ARMPIT
ARMPITS
ARMS
ARMURE
ARMURES
ARMY
ARNA
ARNAS
ARNICA
ARNICAS
ARNOTTO
ARNOTTOS
ARNUT
ARNUTS
AROBA
AROBAS
AROID
AROIDS
AROINT
AROINTED
AROINTING
AROINTS
AROLLA
AROLLAS
AROMA
AROMAS
AROMATIC
AROMATICS
AROMATISE
AROMATISED
AROMATISES
AROMATISING
AROMATIZE
AROMATIZED
AROMATIZES
AROMATIZING
AROSE
AROUND
AROUSAL
AROUSALS
AROUSE
AROUSED
AROUSER
AROUSERS
AROUSES
AROUSING
AROW
AROYNT
AROYNTED
AROYNTING
AROYNTS
ARPEGGIO
ARPEGGIOS
ARPENT
ARPENTS
ARQUEBUS
ARQUEBUSE
ARQUEBUSES
ARRACACHA
ARRACACHAS
ARRACK
ARRACKS
ARRAH
ARRAIGN

ARRAIGNED
ARRAIGNER
ARRAIGNERS
ARRAIGNING
ARRAIGNINGS
ARRAIGNS
ARRANGE
ARRANGED
ARRANGER
ARRANGERS
ARRANGES
ARRANGING
ARRANT
ARRANTLY
ARRAS
ARRASED
ARRASENE
ARRASENES
ARRASES
ARRAUGHT
ARRAY
ARRAYED
ARRAYING
ARRAYMENT
ARRAYMENTS
ARRAYS
ARREAR
ARREARAGE
ARREARAGES
ARREARS
ARRECT
ARREEDE
ARREEDES
ARREEDING
ARREST
ARRESTED
ARRESTEE
ARRESTEES
ARRESTER
ARRESTERS
ARRESTING
ARRESTIVE
ARRESTOR
ARRESTORS
ARRESTS
ARRÊT
ARRÊTS
ARRIAGE
ARRIAGES
ARRIDE
ARRIDED
ARRIDES
ARRIDING
ARRIÉRÉ
ARRIERO
ARRIEROS
ARRIS
ARRISES
ARRISH
ARRISHES
ARRIVAL
ARRIVALS
ARRIVANCE
ARRIVANCES
ARRIVANCIES
ARRIVANCY
ARRIVE
ARRIVED
ARRIVES
ARRIVING

ARRIVISME
ARRIVISMES
ARRIVISTE
ARRIVISTES
ARROBA
ARROBAS
ARROGANCE
ARROGANCES
ARROGANCIES
ARROGANCY
ARROGANT
ARROGATE
ARROGATED
ARROGATES
ARROGATING
ARROW
ARROWED
ARROWING
ARROWROOT
ARROWROOTS
ARROWS
ARROWWOOD
ARROWWOODS
ARROWY
ARROYO
ARROYOS
ARS
ARSE
ARSEHOLE
ARSEHOLES
ARSENAL
ARSENALS
ARSENATE
ARSENATES
ARSENIATE
ARSENIATES
ARSENIC
ARSENICAL
ARSENICS
ARSENIDE
ARSENIDES
ARSENIOUS
ARSENITE
ARSENITES
ARSES
ARSHEEN
ARSHEENS
ARSHIN
ARSHINE
ARSHINES
ARSHINS
ARSINE
ARSINES
ARSIS
ARSON
ARSONIST
ARSONISTS
ARSONITE
ARSONITES
ARSONS
ART
ARTAL
ARTEFACT
ARTEFACTS
ARTEL
ARTELS
ARTEMISIA
ARTEMISIAS
ARTERIAL
ARTERIES

ARTERIOLE
ARTERIOLES
ARTERITIS
ARTERITISES
ARTERY
ARTESIAN
ARTFUL
ARTFULLY
ARTHRITIC
ARTHRITICS
ARTHRITIS
ARTHRITISES
ARTHROPOD
ARTHROPODS
ARTHROSES
ARTHROSIS
ARTIC
ARTICHOKE
ARTICHOKES
ARTICLE
ARTICLED
ARTICLES
ARTICLING
ARTICS
ARTICULAR
ARTIER
ARTIEST
ARTIFACT
ARTIFACTS
ARTIFICE
ARTIFICER
ARTIFICERS
ARTIFICES
ARTILLERIES
ARTILLERY
ARTISAN
ARTISANAL
ARTISANS
ARTIST
ARTISTE
ARTISTES
ARTISTIC
ARTISTRIES
ARTISTRY
ARTISTS
ARTLESS
ARTLESSLY
ARTS
ARTSIER
ARTSIEST
ARTSMAN
ARTSMEN
ARTSY
ARTWORK
ARTWORKS
ARTY
ARUM
ARUMS
ARVAL
ARVO
ARVOS
ARY
ARYBALLOS
ARYBALLOSES
ARYL
ARYLS
ARYTENOID
ARYTENOIDS
AS
ASAFETIDA

ASAFETIDAS
ASANA
ASANAS
ASAR
ASARUM
ASARUMS
ASBESTIC
ASBESTINE
ASBESTOS
ASBESTOSES
ASBESTOUS
ASCARID
ASCARIDES
ASCARIDS
ASCARIS
ASCAUNT
ASCEND
ASCENDANT
ASCENDANTS
ASCENDED
ASCENDENT
ASCENDENTS
ASCENDER
ASCENDERS
ASCENDING
ASCENDS
ASCENSION
ASCENSIONS
ASCENSIVE
ASCENT
ASCENTS
ASCERTAIN
ASCERTAINED
ASCERTAINING
ASCERTAINS
ASCESES
ASCESIS
ASCETIC
ASCETICAL
ASCETICS
ASCI
ASCIAN
ASCIANS
ASCIDIA
ASCIDIAN
ASCIDIANS
ASCIDIUM
ASCITES
ASCITIC
ASCITICAL
ASCLEPIAD
ASCLEPIADS
ASCLEPIAS
ASCLEPIASES
ASCONCE
ASCORBATE
ASCORBATES
ASCORBIC
ASCOSPORE
ASCOSPORES
ASCOT
ASCOTS
ASCRIBE
ASCRIBED
ASCRIBES
ASCRIBING
ASCUS
ASEISMIC
ASEITIES
ASEITY

ASEPALOUS
ASEPSES
ASEPSIS
ASEPTATE
ASEPTIC
ASEPTICS
ASEXUAL
ASEXUALLY
ASH
ASHAKE
ASHAME
ASHAMED
ASHAMEDLY
ASHAMES
ASHAMING
ASHEN
ASHERIES
ASHERY
ASHES
ASHET
ASHETS
ASHIER
ASHIEST
ASHINE
ASHIVER
ASHLAR
ASHLARED
ASHLARING
ASHLARINGS
ASHLARS
ASHLER
ASHLERED
ASHLERING
ASHLERINGS
ASHLERS
ASHORE
ASHRAM
ASHRAMA
ASHRAMAS
ASHRAMS
ASHY
ASIDE
ASIDES
ASINICO
ASINICOS
ASININE
ASININITIES
ASININITY
ASK
ASKANCE
ASKANCED
ASKANCES
ASKANCING
ASKANT
ASKANTED
ASKANTING
ASKANTS
ASKARI
ASKARIS
ASKED
ASKER
ASKERS
ASKESES
ASKESIS
ASKEW
ASKING
ASKLENT
ASKS
ASLAKE
ASLAKED

ASLAKES
ASLAKING
ASLANT
ASLEEP
ASLOPE
ASMEAR
ASMOULDER
ASOCIAL
ASP
ASPARAGUS
ASPARAGUSES
ASPARTAME
ASPARTAMES
ASPECT
ASPECTED
ASPECTING
ASPECTS
ASPECTUAL
ASPEN
ASPENS
ASPER
ASPERATE
ASPERATED
ASPERATES
ASPERATING
ASPERGE
ASPERGED
ASPERGER
ASPERGERS
ASPERGES
ASPERGILL
ASPERGILLS
ASPERGING
ASPERITIES
ASPERITY
ASPEROUS
ASPERS
ASPERSE
ASPERSED
ASPERSES
ASPERSING
ASPERSION
ASPERSIONS
ASPERSIVE
ASPERSOIR
ASPERSOIRS
ASPERSORIES
ASPERSORY
ASPHALT
ASPHALTED
ASPHALTIC
ASPHALTING
ASPHALTS
ASPHALTUM
ASPHALTUMS
ASPHODEL
ASPHODELS
ASPHYXIA
ASPHYXIAS
ASPHYXIES
ASPHYXY
ASPIC
ASPICK
ASPICKS
ASPICS
ASPIDIA
ASPIDIOID
ASPIDIUM
ASPINE
ASPINES

ASPIRANT
ASPIRANTS
ASPIRATE
ASPIRATED
ASPIRATES
ASPIRATING
ASPIRATOR
ASPIRATORS
ASPIRE
ASPIRED
ASPIRES
ASPIRIN
ASPIRING
ASPIRINS
ASPORT
ASPORTED
ASPORTING
ASPORTS
ASPOUT
ASPRAWL
ASPREAD
ASPROUT
ASPS
ASQUAT
ASQUINT
ASS
ASSAGAI
ASSAGAIED
ASSAGAIING
ASSAGAIS
ASSAI
ASSAIL
ASSAILANT
ASSAILANTS
ASSAILED
ASSAILING
ASSAILS
ASSAIS
ASSART
ASSARTED
ASSARTING
ASSARTS
ASSASSIN
ASSASSINS
ASSAULT
ASSAULTED
ASSAULTER
ASSAULTERS
ASSAULTING
ASSAULTS
ASSAY
ASSAYABLE
ASSAYED
ASSAYER
ASSAYERS
ASSAYING
ASSAYINGS
ASSAYS
ASSEGAAI
ASSEGAAIED
ASSEGAAIING
ASSEGAAIS
ASSEGAI
ASSEGAIED
ASSEGAIING
ASSEGAIS
ASSEMBLE
ASSEMBLÉ
ASSEMBLED
ASSEMBLER

ASSEMBLERS
ASSEMBLES
ASSEMBLÉS
ASSEMBLIES
ASSEMBLING
ASSEMBLY
ASSENT
ASSENTED
ASSENTER
ASSENTERS
ASSENTING
ASSENTIVE
ASSENTOR
ASSENTORS
ASSENTS
ASSERT
ASSERTED
ASSERTER
ASSERTERS
ASSERTING
ASSERTION
ASSERTIONS
ASSERTIVE
ASSERTOR
ASSERTORS
ASSERTORY
ASSERTS
ASSES
ASSESS
ASSESSED
ASSESSES
ASSESSING
ASSESSOR
ASSESSORS
ASSET
ASSETS
ASSEVER
ASSEVERED
ASSEVERING
ASSEVERS
ASSHOLE
ASSHOLES
ASSIDUITIES
ASSIDUITY
ASSIDUOUS
ASSIEGE
ASSIEGED
ASSIEGES
ASSIEGING
ASSIENTO
ASSIENTOS
ASSIGN
ASSIGNAT
ASSIGNATS
ASSIGNED
ASSIGNEE
ASSIGNEES
ASSIGNING
ASSIGNOR
ASSIGNORS
ASSIGNS
ASSIST
ASSISTANT
ASSISTANTS
ASSISTED
ASSISTING
ASSISTS
ASSIZE
ASSIZED
ASSIZER

ASSIZERS
ASSIZES
ASSIZING
ASSOCIATE
ASSOCIATED
ASSOCIATES
ASSOCIATING
ASSOIL
ASSOILED
ASSOILING
ASSOILS
ASSOILZIE
ASSOILZIED
ASSOILZIEING
ASSOILZIES
ASSONANCE
ASSONANCES
ASSONANT
ASSONATE
ASSONATED
ASSONATES
ASSONATING
ASSORT
ASSORTED
ASSORTER
ASSORTERS
ASSORTING
ASSORTS
ASSOT
ASSOTS
ASSOTT
ASSOTTED
ASSOTTING
ASSUAGE
ASSUAGED
ASSUAGES
ASSUAGING
ASSUAGINGS
ASSUASIVE
ASSUETUDE
ASSUETUDES
ASSUMABLE
ASSUMABLY
ASSUME
ASSUMED
ASSUMEDLY
ASSUMES
ASSUMING
ASSUMINGS
ASSUMPSIT
ASSUMPSITS
ASSURABLE
ASSURANCE
ASSURANCES
ASSURE
ASSURED
ASSUREDLY
ASSUREDS
ASSURER
ASSURERS
ASSURES
ASSURGENT
ASSURING
ASSWAGE
ASSWAGED
ASSWAGES
ASSWAGING
ASTABLE
ASTARE
ASTART

ASTARTED
ASTARTING
ASTARTS
ASTATIC
ASTATINE
ASTATINES
ASTATKI
ASTATKIS
ASTEISM
ASTEISMS
ASTELIC
ASTELIES
ASTELY
ASTER
ASTERIA
ASTERIAS
ASTERID
ASTERIDS
ASTERISK
ASTERISKED
ASTERISKING
ASTERISKS
ASTERISM
ASTERISMS
ASTERN
ASTEROID
ASTEROIDS
ASTERS
ASTERT
ASTERTED
ASTERTING
ASTERTS
ASTHENIA
ASTHENIAS
ASTHENIC
ASTHENICS
ASTHMA
ASTHMAS
ASTHMATIC
ASTHORE
ASTHORES
ASTICHOUS
ASTIGMIA
ASTIGMIAS
ASTILBE
ASTILBES
ASTIR
ASTOMOUS
ASTONE
ASTONED
ASTONES
ASTONIED
ASTONIES
ASTONING
ASTONISH
ASTONISHED
ASTONISHES
ASTONISHING
ASTONY
ASTONYING
ASTOOP
ASTOUND
ASTOUNDED
ASTOUNDING
ASTOUNDS
ASTRADDLE
ASTRAGAL
ASTRAGALS
ASTRAKHAN
ASTRAKHANS

ASTRAL
ASTRAND
ASTRAY
ASTRICT
ASTRICTED
ASTRICTING
ASTRICTS
ASTRIDE
ASTRINGE
ASTRINGED
ASTRINGER
ASTRINGERS
ASTRINGES
ASTRINGING
ASTRODOME
ASTRODOMES
ASTROFELL
ASTROFELLS
ASTROID
ASTROIDS
ASTROLABE
ASTROLABES
ASTROLOGIES
ASTROLOGY
ASTRONAUT
ASTRONAUTS
ASTRONOMIES
ASTRONOMY
ASTROPHEL
ASTROPHELS
ASTRUT
ASTUCIOUS
ASTUCITIES
ASTUCITY
ASTUN
ASTUNNED
ASTUNNING
ASTUNS
ASTUTE
ASTUTELY
ASTUTER
ASTUTEST
ASTYLAR
ASUDDEN
ASUNDER
ASWARM
ASWAY
ASWIM
ASWING
ASWIRL
ASWOON
ASYLUM
ASYLUMS
ASYMMETRIES
ASYMMETRY
ASYMPTOTE
ASYMPTOTES
ASYNDETIC
ASYNDETON
ASYNDETONS
ASYNERGIA
ASYNERGIAS
ASYSTOLE
ASYSTOLES
AT
ATABAL
ATABALS
ATABEG
ATABEGS
ATABEK

| | | | | |
|---|---|---|---|---|
| ATABEKS | ATHETISES | ATOMISTIC | ATTACKS | ATTITUDE |
| ATABRIN | ATHETISING | ATOMISTS | ATTAIN | ATTITUDES |
| ATABRINS | ATHETIZE | ATOMIZE | ATTAINDER | ATTOLLENT |
| ATACAMITE | ATHETIZED | ATOMIZED | ATTAINDERS | ATTOLLENTS |
| ATACAMITES | ATHETIZES | ATOMIZER | ATTAINED | ATTONCE |
| ATACTIC | ATHETIZING | ATOMIZERS | ATTAINING | ATTONE |
| ATAGHAN | ATHETOID | ATOMIZES | ATTAINS | ATTONES |
| ATAGHANS | ATHETOIDS | ATOMIZING | ATTAINT | ATTORN |
| ATALAYA | ATHETOSES | ATOMS | ATTAINTED | ATTORNED |
| ATALAYAS | ATHETOSIS | ATOMY | ATTAINTING | ATTORNEY |
| ATAMAN | ATHIRST | ATONAL | ATTAINTS | ATTORNEYED |
| ATAMANS | ATHLETA | ATONALISM | ATTAP | ATTORNEYING |
| ATAP | ATHLETAS | ATONALISMS | ATTAPS | ATTORNEYS |
| ATAPS | ATHLETE | ATONALITIES | ATTAR | ATTORNING |
| ATARACTIC | ATHLETES | ATONALITY | ATTARS | ATTORNS |
| ATARACTICS | ATHLETIC | ATONE | ATTASK | ATTRACT |
| ATARAXIA | ATHLETICS | ATONED | ATTASKED | ATTRACTED |
| ATARAXIAS | ATHRILL | ATONEMENT | ATTASKING | ATTRACTING |
| ATARAXIC | ATHROB | ATONEMENTS | ATTASKS | ATTRACTOR |
| ATARAXICS | ATHROCYTE | ATONER | ATTASKT | ATTRACTORS |
| ATARAXIES | ATHROCYTES | ATONERS | ATTEMPER | ATTRACTS |
| ATARAXY | ATHWART | ATONES | ATTEMPERED | ATTRAHENT |
| ATAVISM | ATILT | ATONIC | ATTEMPERING | ATTRAHENTS |
| ATAVISMS | ATIMIES | ATONICITIES | ATTEMPERS | ATTRAP |
| ATAVISTIC | ATIMY | ATONICITY | ATTEMPT | ATTRAPPED |
| ATAXIA | ATINGLE | ATONIES | ATTEMPTED | ATTRAPPING |
| ATAXIAS | ATLAS | ATONING | ATTEMPTER | ATTRAPS |
| ATAXIC | ATLASES | ATONINGLY | ATTEMPTERS | ATTRIBUTE |
| ATAXIES | ATMAN | ATONY | ATTEMPTING | ATTRIBUTED |
| ATAXY | ATMANS | ATOP | ATTEMPTS | ATTRIBUTES |
| ATCHIEVE | ATMOLOGIES | ATOPIC | ATTEND | ATTRIBUTING |
| ATCHIEVED | ATMOLOGY | ATOPIES | ATTENDANT | ATTRIST |
| ATCHIEVES | ATMOLYSE | ATOPY | ATTENDANTS | ATTRISTED |
| ATCHIEVING | ATMOLYSED | ATRAMENT | ATTENDED | ATTRISTING |
| ATE | ATMOLYSES | ATRAMENTS | ATTENDEE | ATTRISTS |
| ATEBRIN | ATMOLYSING | ATREMBLE | ATTENDEES | ATTRITE |
| ATEBRINS | ATMOLYSIS | ATRESIA | ATTENDER | ATTRITION |
| ATELIER | ATMOLYZE | ATRESIAS | ATTENDERS | ATTRITIONS |
| ATELIERS | ATMOLYZED | ATRIA | ATTENDING | ATTUENT |
| ATHANASIES | ATMOLYZES | ATRIAL | ATTENDS | ATTUITE |
| ATHANASY | ATMOLYZING | ATRIP | ATTENT | ATTUITED |
| ATHANOR | ATMOMETER | ATRIUM | ATTENTAT | ATTUITES |
| ATHANORS | ATMOMETERS | ATROCIOUS | ATTENTATS | ATTUITING |
| ATHEISE | ATOC | ATROCITIES | ATTENTION | ATTUITION |
| ATHEISED | ATOCIA | ATROCITY | ATTENTIONS | ATTUITIONS |
| ATHEISES | ATOCIAS | ATROPHIED | ATTENTIVE | ATTUITIVE |
| ATHEISING | ATOCS | ATROPHIES | ATTENTS | ATTUNE |
| ATHEISM | ATOK | ATROPHY | ATTENUANT | ATTUNED |
| ATHEISMS | ATOKAL | ATROPHYING | ATTENUANTS | ATTUNES |
| ATHEIST | ATOKE | ATROPIA | ATTENUATE | ATTUNING |
| ATHEISTIC | ATOKES | ATROPIAS | ATTENUATED | ATWAIN |
| ATHEISTS | ATOKOUS | ATROPIN | ATTENUATES | ATWEEL |
| ATHEIZE | ATOKS | ATROPINE | ATTENUATING | ATWEEN |
| ATHEIZED | ATOLL | ATROPINES | ATTERCOP | ATWIXT |
| ATHEIZES | ATOLLS | ATROPINS | ATTERCOPS | ATYPICAL |
| ATHEIZING | ATOM | ATROPISM | ATTEST | AUBADE |
| ATHELING | ATOMIC | ATROPISMS | ATTESTED | AUBADES |
| ATHELINGS | ATOMICAL | ATROPOUS | ATTESTER | AUBERGE |
| ATHEMATIC | ATOMICITIES | ATTABOY | ATTESTERS | AUBERGES |
| ATHEOLOGIES | ATOMICITY | ATTACH | ATTESTING | AUBERGINE |
| ATHEOLOGY | ATOMIES | ATTACHÉ | ATTESTOR | AUBERGINES |
| ATHEOUS | ATOMISE | ATTACHED | ATTESTORS | AUBRIETIA |
| ATHERINE | ATOMISED | ATTACHES | ATTESTS | · AUBRIETIAS |
| ATHERINES | ATOMISER | ATTACHÉS | ATTIC | AUBURN |
| ATHEROMA | ATOMISERS | ATTACHING | ATTICS | AUCEPS |
| ATHEROMAS | ATOMISES | ATTACK | ATTIRE | AUCEPSES |
| ATHETESES | ATOMISING | ATTACKED | ATTIRED | AUCTION |
| ATHETESIS | ATOMISM | ATTACKER | ATTIRES | AUCTIONED |
| ATHETISE | ATOMISMS | ATTACKERS | ATTIRING | AUCTIONING |
| ATHETISED | ATOMIST | ATTACKING | ATTIRINGS | AUCTIONS |

AUCTORIAL
AUCUBA
AUCUBAS
AUDACIOUS
AUDACITIES
AUDACITY
AUDIBLE
AUDIBLY
AUDIENCE
AUDIENCES
AUDIENT
AUDIENTS
AUDILE
AUDILES
AUDIO
AUDIOGRAM
AUDIOGRAMS
AUDIOLOGIES
AUDIOLOGY
AUDIOPHIL
AUDIOPHILS
AUDIOS
AUDIPHONE
AUDIPHONES
AUDIT
AUDITED
AUDITING
AUDITION
AUDITIONED
AUDITIONING
AUDITIONS
AUDITIVE
AUDITOR
AUDITORIA
AUDITORIES
AUDITORS
AUDITORY
AUDITRESS
AUDITRESSES
AUDITS
AUF
AUFGABE
AUFGABES
AUFS
AUGER
AUGERS
AUGHT
AUGHTS
AUGITE
AUGITES
AUGITIC
AUGMENT
AUGMENTED
AUGMENTER
AUGMENTERS
AUGMENTING
AUGMENTOR
AUGMENTORS
AUGMENTS
AUGUR
AUGURAL
AUGURED
AUGURER
AUGURERS
AUGURIES
AUGURING
AUGURS
AUGURSHIP
AUGURSHIPS
AUGURY

AUGUST
AUGUSTE
AUGUSTER
AUGUSTES
AUGUSTEST
AUGUSTLY
AUGUSTS
AUK
AUKLET
AUKLETS
AUKS
AULA
AULARIAN
AULARIANS
AULAS
AULD
AULDER
AULDEST
AULIC
AULNAGE
AULNAGER
AULNAGERS
AULNAGES
AULOI
AULOS
AUMAIL
AUMAILED
AUMAILING
AUMAILS
AUMBRIES
AUMBRY
AUMIL
AUMILS
AUNT
AUNTER
AUNTERS
AUNTIE
AUNTIES
AUNTS
AUNTY
AURA
AURAE
AURAL
AURALLY
AURAS
AURATE
AURATED
AURATES
AUREATE
AUREI
AUREITIES
AUREITY
AURELIA
AURELIAN
AURELIANS
AURELIAS
AUREOLA
AUREOLAS
AUREOLE
AUREOLED
AUREOLES
AUREUS
AURIC
AURICLE
AURICLED
AURICLES
AURICULA
AURICULAR
AURICULAS
AURIFIED

AURIFIES
AURIFORM
AURIFY
AURIFYING
AURISCOPE
AURISCOPES
AURIST
AURISTS
AUROCHS
AUROCHSES
AURORA
AURORAE
AURORAL
AURORALLY
AURORAS
AUROREAN
AUROUS
AUSPICATE
AUSPICATED
AUSPICATES
AUSPICATING
AUSPICE
AUSPICES
AUSTENITE
AUSTENITES
AUSTERE
AUSTERELY
AUSTERER
AUSTEREST
AUSTERITIES
AUSTERITY
AUSTRAL
AUTACOID
AUTACOIDS
AUTARCHIC
AUTARCHIES
AUTARCHY
AUTARKIC
AUTARKIES
AUTARKIST
AUTARKISTS
AUTARKY
AUTEUR
AUTEURS
AUTHENTIC
AUTHOR
AUTHORED
AUTHORESS
AUTHORESSES
AUTHORIAL
AUTHORING
AUTHORINGS
AUTHORISE
AUTHORISED
AUTHORISES
AUTHORISH
AUTHORISING
AUTHORISM
AUTHORISMS
AUTHORITIES
AUTHORITY
AUTHORIZE
AUTHORIZED
AUTHORIZES
AUTHORIZING
AUTHORS
AUTISM
AUTISMS
AUTISTIC
AUTO

AUTOBAHN
AUTOBAHNS
AUTOBUS
AUTOBUSES
AUTOCADE
AUTOCADES
AUTOCAR
AUTOCARP
AUTOCARPS
AUTOCARS
AUTOCLAVE
AUTOCLAVES
AUTOCRACIES
AUTOCRACY
AUTOCRAT
AUTOCRATS
AUTOCROSS
AUTOCROSSES
AUTOCUE
AUTOCUES
AUTOCYCLE
AUTOCYCLES
AUTODYNE
AUTOFLARE
AUTOFLARES
AUTOGAMIC
AUTOGAMIES
AUTOGAMY
AUTOGENIC
AUTOGENICS
AUTOGENIES
AUTOGENY
AUTOGIRO
AUTOGIROS
AUTOGRAFT
AUTOGRAFTED
AUTOGRAFTING
AUTOGRAFTS
AUTOGRAPH
AUTOGRAPHED
AUTOGRAPHING
AUTOGRAPHS
AUTOGYRO
AUTOGYROS
AUTOHARP
AUTOHARPS
AUTOLATRIES
AUTOLATRY
AUTOLOGIES
AUTOLOGY
AUTOLYSE
AUTOLYSED
AUTOLYSES
AUTOLYSING
AUTOLYSIS
AUTOLYTIC
AUTOLYZE
AUTOLYZED
AUTOLYZES
AUTOLYZING
AUTOMAT
AUTOMATA
AUTOMATE
AUTOMATED
AUTOMATES
AUTOMATIC
AUTOMATICS
AUTOMATING
AUTOMATON
AUTOMATONS

AUTOMATS
AUTONOMIC
AUTONOMICS
AUTONOMIES
AUTONOMY
AUTONYM
AUTONYMS
AUTOPHAGIES
AUTOPHAGY
AUTOPHOBIES
AUTOPHOBY
AUTOPHONIES
AUTOPHONY
AUTOPILOT
AUTOPILOTS
AUTOPISTA
AUTOPISTAS
AUTOPOINT
AUTOPOINTS
AUTOPSIA
AUTOPSIAS
AUTOPSIED
AUTOPSIES
AUTOPSY
AUTOPSYING
AUTOPTIC
AUTOROUTE
AUTOROUTES
AUTOS
AUTOSCOPIES
AUTOSCOPY
AUTOSOMAL
AUTOSOME
AUTOSOMES
AUTOTELIC
AUTOTIMER
AUTOTIMERS
AUTOTOMIES
AUTOTOMY
AUTOTOXIN
AUTOTOXINS
AUTOTROPH
AUTOTROPHS
AUTOTYPE
AUTOTYPED
AUTOTYPES
AUTOTYPING
AUTOVAC
AUTOVACS
AUTUMN
AUTUMNAL
AUTUMNS
AUTUMNY
AUTUNITE
AUTUNITES
AUXESES
AUXESIS
AUXETIC
AUXETICS
AUXILIAR
AUXILIARIES
AUXILIARS
AUXILIARY
AUXIN
AUXINS
AUXOMETER
AUXOMETERS
AVA
AVADAVAT
AVADAVATS

AVAIL
AVAILABLE
AVAILABLY
AVAILE
AVAILED
AVAILES
AVAILFUL
AVAILING
AVAILS
AVAL
AVALANCHE
AVALANCHED
AVALANCHES
AVALANCHING
AVALE
AVALED
AVALES
AVALING
AVANT
AVANTI
AVARICE
AVARICES
AVAS
AVAST
AVATAR
AVATARS
AVAUNT
AVAUNTED
AVAUNTING
AVAUNTS
AVE
AVENGE
AVENGED
AVENGEFUL
AVENGER
AVENGERS
AVENGES
AVENGING
AVENIR
AVENIRS
AVENS
AVENSES
AVENTAIL
AVENTAILE
AVENTAILES
AVENTAILS
AVENTRE
AVENTRED
AVENTRES
AVENTRING
AVENTURE
AVENTURES
AVENUE
AVENUES
AVER
AVERAGE
AVERAGED
AVERAGES
AVERAGING
AVERMENT
AVERMENTS
AVERRED
AVERRING
AVERS
AVERSE
AVERSELY
AVERSION
AVERSIONS
AVERSIVE
AVERT

AVERTABLE
AVERTED
AVERTEDLY
AVERTIBLE
AVERTING
AVERTS
AVES
AVGAS
AVGASES
AVIAN
AVIARIES
AVIARIST
AVIARISTS
AVIARY
AVIATE
AVIATED
AVIATES
AVIATING
AVIATION
AVIATIONS
AVIATOR
AVIATORS
AVIATRIX
AVIATRIXES
AVID
AVIDER
AVIDEST
AVIDITIES
AVIDITY
AVIDLY
AVIETTE
AVIETTES
AVIFAUNA
AVIFAUNAE
AVIFAUNAS
AVIFORM
AVINE
AVION
AVIONIC
AVIONICS
AVIONS
AVISANDUM
AVISANDUMS
AVISE
AVISED
AVISEMENT
AVISEMENTS
AVISES
AVISING
AVISO
AVISOS
AVITAL
AVIZANDUM
AVIZANDUMS
AVIZE
AVIZED
AVIZEFULL
AVIZES
AVIZING
AVOCADO
AVOCADOS
AVOCATION
AVOCATIONS
AVOCET
AVOCETS
AVOID
AVOIDABLE
AVOIDANCE
AVOIDANCES
AVOIDED

AVOIDING
AVOIDS
AVOISION
AVOISIONS
AVOSET
AVOSETS
AVOUCH
AVOUCHED
AVOUCHES
AVOUCHING
AVOUÉ
AVOUÉS
AVOURE
AVOURES
AVOUTERER
AVOUTERERS
AVOUTRER
AVOUTRERS
AVOUTRIES
AVOUTRY
AVOW
AVOWABLE
AVOWAL
AVOWALS
AVOWED
AVOWEDLY
AVOWING
AVOWRIES
AVOWRY
AVOWS
AVOYER
AVOYERS
AVULSE
AVULSED
AVULSES
AVULSING
AVULSION
AVULSIONS
AVUNCULAR
AVYZE
AVYZED
AVYZES
AVYZING
AW
AWA
AWAIT
AWAITED
AWAITING
AWAITS
AWAKE
AWAKED
AWAKEN
AWAKENED
AWAKENING
AWAKENINGS
AWAKENS
AWAKES
AWAKING
AWAKINGS
AWANTING
AWARD
AWARDED
AWARDING
AWARDS
AWARE
AWARENESS
AWARENESSES
AWARER
AWAREST
AWARN

AWARNED
AWARNING
AWARNS
AWASH
AWATCH
AWAVE
AWAY
AWAYES
AWAYS
AWDL
AWDLS
AWE
AWEARIED
AWEARY
AWED
AWEEL
AWELESS
AWES
AWESOME
AWESOMELY
AWESTRIKE
AWESTRIKES
AWESTRIKING
AWESTRUCK
AWETO
AWETOS
AWFUL
AWFULLER
AWFULLEST
AWFULLY
AWFULNESS
AWFULNESSES
AWHAPE
AWHAPED
AWHAPES
AWHAPING
AWHEEL
AWHEELS
AWHILE
AWING
AWKWARD
AWKWARDER
AWKWARDEST
AWKWARDLY
AWL
AWLBIRD
AWLBIRDS
AWLS
AWMOUS
AWMRIE
AWMRIES
AWMRY
AWN
AWNED
AWNER
AWNERS
AWNIER
AWNIEST
AWNING
AWNINGS
AWNLESS
AWNS
AWNY
AWOKE
AWOKEN
AWORK
AWRACK
AWRONG
AWRY
AWSOME

AX
AXE
AXED
AXEL
AXELS
AXES
AXIAL
AXIALLY
AXIL
AXILE
AXILLA
AXILLAE
AXILLAR
AXILLARY
AXILS
AXING
AXINITE
AXINITES
AXIOLOGIES
AXIOLOGY
AXIOM
AXIOMATIC
AXIOMATICS
AXIOMS
AXIS
AXISES
AXLE
AXLES
AXOID
AXOIDS
AXOLOTL
AXOLOTLS
AXON
AXONS
AXOPLASM
AXOPLASMS
AY
AYAH
AYAHS
AYAHUASCO
AYAHUASCOS
AYATOLLAH
AYATOLLAHS
AYE
AYELP
AYENBITE
AYENBITES
AYES
AYGRE
AYONT
AYRE
AYRES
AYRIE
AYRIES
AYU
AYURVEDIC
AYUS
AYWORD
AYWORDS
AZALEA
AZALEAS
AZAN
AZANS
AZEOTROPE
AZEOTROPES
AZIDE
AZIDES
AZIMUTH
AZIMUTHAL
AZIMUTHS

| AZIONE | AZOTH | AZOTIZES | AZURINES | AZYME |
| AZIONES | AZOTHS | AZOTIZING | AZURITE | AZYMES |
| AZOIC | AZOTIC | AZOTOUS | AZURITES | AZYMITE |
| AZOLLA | AZOTISE | AZULEJO | AZURN | AZYMITES |
| AZOLLAS | AZOTISED | AZULEJOS | AZURY | AZYMOUS |
| AZONAL | AZOTISES | AZURE | AZYGIES | AZYMS |
| AZONIC | AZOTISING | AZUREAN | AZYGOUS | |
| AZOTE | AZOTIZE | AZURES | AZYGY | |
| AZOTES | AZOTIZED | AZURINE | AZYM | |

# B

| | | | | |
|---|---|---|---|---|
| BA | BABUDOMS | BACKBITINGS | BACKSEYS | BACTERIC |
| BAA | BABUISM | BACKBITTEN | BACKSHISH | BACTERISE |
| BAAED | BABUISMS | BACKBOND | BACKSHISHES | BACTERISED |
| BAAING | BABUL | BACKBONDS | BACKSIDE | BACTERISES |
| BAAINGS | BABULS | BACKBONE | BACKSIDES | BACTERISING |
| BAAS | BABUS | BACKBONED | BACKSIGHT | BACTERIUM |
| BAASES | BABUSHKA | BACKBONES | BACKSIGHTS | BACTERIZE |
| BAASSKAP | BABUSHKAS | BACKCHAT | BACKSLID | BACTERIZED |
| BAASSKAPS | BABY | BACKCHATS | BACKSLIDE | BACTERIZES |
| BABA | BABYFOOD | BACKCHATTED | BACKSLIDES | BACTERIZING |
| BABACOOTE | BABYFOODS | BACKCHATTING | BACKSLIDING | BACTEROID |
| BABACOOTES | BABYHOOD | BACKCOURT | BACKSLIDINGS | BACTEROIDS |
| BABAS | BABYHOODS | BACKCOURTS | BACKSPACE | BACULINE |
| BABASSU | BABYING | BACKDOWN | BACKSPACED | BACULITE |
| BABASSUS | BABYISH | BACKDOWNS | BACKSPACES | BACULITES |
| BABBITT | BACCA | BACKDROP | BACKSPACING | BAD |
| BABBITTED | BACCAE | BACKDROPS | BACKSPEER | BADDIE |
| BABBITTING | BACCARA | BACKED | BACKSPEERED | BADDIES |
| BABBITTS | BACCARAS | BACKER | BACKSPEERING | BADDISH |
| BABBLE | BACCARAT | BACKERS | BACKSPEERS | BADDY |
| BABBLED | BACCARATS | BACKET | BACKSPEIR | BADE |
| BABBLER | BACCARE | BACKETS | BACKSPEIRED | BADGE |
| BABBLERS | BACCAS | BACKFALL | BACKSPEIRING | BADGER |
| BABBLES | BACCATE | BACKFALLS | BACKSPEIRS | BADGERED |
| BABBLIER | BACCHANAL | BACKFILL | BACKSPIN | BADGERING |
| BABBLIEST | BACCHANALS | BACKFILLED | BACKSPINS | BADGERLY |
| BABBLING | BACCHANT | BACKFILLING | BACKSTAGE | BADGERS |
| BABBLINGS | BACCHANTE | BACKFILLS | BACKSTALL | BADGES |
| BABBLY | BACCHANTES | BACKFIRE | BACKSTALLS | BADINAGE |
| BABE | BACCHANTS | BACKFIRED | BACKSTAYS | BADINAGES |
| BABEL | BACCHIAC | BACKFIRES | BACKSTOP | BADIOUS |
| BABELDOM | BACCHII | BACKFIRING | BACKSTOPS | BADLANDS |
| BABELDOMS | BACCHIUS | BACKFISCH | BACKSWORD | BADLY |
| BABELISH | BACCIES | BACKFISCHES | BACKSWORDS | BADMAN |
| BABELISM | BACCIFORM | BACKHAND | BACKTRACK | BADMASH |
| BABELISMS | BACCO | BACKHANDS | BACKTRACKED | BADMASHES |
| BABELS | BACCOES | BACKHOE | BACKTRACKING | BADMEN |
| BABES | BACCOS | BACKHOES | BACKTRACKINGS | BADMINTON |
| BABICHE | BACCY | BACKING | BACKTRACKS | BADMINTONS |
| BABICHES | BACH | BACKINGS | BACKVELD | BADMOUTH |
| BABIED | BACHARACH | BACKLASH | BACKVELDS | BADMOUTHED |
| BABIER | BACHARACHS | BACKLASHES | BACKWARD | BADMOUTHING |
| BABIES | BACHED | BACKLIST | BACKWARDS | BADMOUTHS |
| BABIEST | BACHELOR | BACKLISTS | BACKWASH | BADNESS |
| BABIRUSSA | BACHELORS | BACKLOG | BACKWASHED | BADNESSES |
| BABIRUSSAS | BACHES | BACKLOGS | BACKWASHES | BAEL |
| BABLAH | BACHING | BACKMOST | BACKWASHING | BAELS |
| BABLAHS | BACILLAR | BACKPACK | BACKWATER | BAETYL |
| BABOO | BACILLARY | BACKPACKED | BACKWATERS | BAETYLS |
| BABOON | BACILLI | BACKPACKING | BACKWOODS | BAFF |
| BABOONERIES | BACILLUS | BACKPACKINGS | BACKWORD | BAFFED |
| BABOONERY | BACK | BACKPACKS | BACKWORDS | BAFFIES |
| BABOONISH | BACKACHE | BACKPAY | BACKWORK | BAFFING |
| BABOONS | BACKACHES | BACKPAYS | BACKWORKS | BAFFLE |
| BABOOS | BACKARE | BACKPIECE | BACKYARD | BAFFLED |
| BABOOSH | BACKBAND | BACKPIECES | BACKYARDS | BAFFLEGAB |
| BABOOSHES | BACKBANDS | BACKROOM | BACLAVA | BAFFLEGABS |
| BABOUCHE | BACKBIT | BACKS | BACLAVAS | BAFFLER |
| BABOUCHES | BACKBITE | BACKSAW | BACON | BAFFLERS |
| BABU | BACKBITER | BACKSAWS | BACONS | BAFFLES |
| BABUCHE | BACKBITERS | BACKSET | BACTERIA | BAFFLING |
| BABUCHES | BACKBITES | BACKSETS | BACTERIAL | BAFFS |
| BABUDOM | BACKBITING | BACKSEY | BACTERIAN | BAFFY |

BAFT
BAFTS
BAG
BAGARRE
BAGARRES
BAGASSE
BAGASSES
BAGATELLE
BAGATELLES
BAGEL
BAGELS
BAGFUL
BAGFULS
BAGGAGE
BAGGAGES
BAGGED
BAGGIER
BAGGIEST
BAGGILY
BAGGING
BAGGINGS
BAGGIT
BAGGITS
BAGGY
BAGMAN
BAGMEN
BAGNIO
BAGNIOS
BAGPIPE
BAGPIPER
BAGPIPERS
BAGPIPES
BAGPIPING
BAGPIPINGS
BAGS
BAGUETTE
BAGUETTES
BAGUIO
BAGUIOS
BAGWASH
BAGWASHES
BAGWIG
BAGWIGS
BAH
BAHADA
BAHADAS
BAHT
BAHTS
BAHUVRIHI
BAHUVRIHIS
BAIGNOIRE
BAIGNOIRES
BAIL
BAILABLE
BAILBOND
BAILBONDS
BAILED
BAILEE
BAILEES
BAILER
BAILERS
BAILEY
BAILEYS
BAILIE
BAILIES
BAILIFF
BAILIFFS
BAILING
BAILIWICK
BAILIWICKS

BAILLI
BAILLIAGE
BAILLIAGES
BAILLIE
BAILLIES
BAILLIS
BAILMENT
BAILMENTS
BAILOR
BAILORS
BAILS
BAILSMAN
BAILSMEN
BAININ
BAININS
BAIRN
BAIRNLIKE
BAIRNLY
BAIRNS
BAISEMAIN
BAISEMAINS
BAIT
BAITED
BAITER
BAITERS
BAITFISH
BAITFISHES
BAITING
BAITINGS
BAITS
BAIZE
BAIZED
BAIZES
BAIZING
BAJADA
BAJADAS
BAJAN
BAJANS
BAJRA
BAJRAS
BAJREE
BAJREES
BAJRI
BAJRIS
BAKE
BAKEAPPLE
BAKEAPPLES
BAKEBOARD
BAKEBOARDS
BAKED
BAKEHOUSE
BAKEHOUSES
BAKEMEAT
BAKEMEATS
BAKEN
BAKER
BAKERIES
BAKERS
BAKERY
BAKES
BAKESTONE
BAKESTONES
BAKEWARE
BAKEWARES
BAKHSHISH
BAKHSHISHES
BAKING
BAKINGS
BAKLAVA
BAKLAVAS

BAKSHEESH
BAKSHEESHES
BALADIN
BALADINE
BALADINES
BALADINS
BALALAIKA
BALALAIKAS
BALANCE
BALANCED
BALANCER
BALANCERS
BALANCES
BALANCING
BALANITIS
BALANITISES
BALAS
BALASES
BALATA
BALATAS
BALBOA
BALBOAS
BALCONET
BALCONETS
BALCONIED
BALCONIES
BALCONY
BALD
BALDACHIN
BALDACHINS
BALDAQUIN
BALDAQUINS
BALDER
BALDEST
BALDING
BALDISH
BALDLY
BALDMONEY
BALDMONEYS
BALDNESS
BALDNESSES
BALDPATE
BALDPATED
BALDPATES
BALDRIC
BALDRICK
BALDRICKS
BALDRICS
BALE
BALECTION
BALECTIONS
BALED
BALEEN
BALEENS
BALEFUL
BALEFULLY
BALER
BALERS
BALES
BALING
BALISTA
BALISTAE
BALISTAS
BALK
BALKANISE
BALKANISED
BALKANISES
BALKANISING
BALKANIZE
BALKANIZED

BALKANIZES
BALKANIZING
BALKED
BALKER
BALKERS
BALKIER
BALKIEST
BALKINESS
BALKINESSES
BALKING
BALKINGLY
BALKINGS
BALKLINE
BALKLINES
BALKS
BALKY
BALL
·BALLABILE
BALLABILES
BALLABILI
BALLAD
BALLADE
BALLADED
BALLADEER
BALLADEERED
BALLADEERING
BALLADEERS
BALLADES
BALLADIN
BALLADINE
BALLADINES
BALLADINS
BALLADING
BALLADIST
BALLADISTS
BALLADRIES
BALLADRY
BALLADS
BALLAN
BALLANS
BALLANT
BALLANTS
BALLAST
BALLASTED
BALLASTING
BALLASTS
BALLAT
BALLATS
BALLCOCK
BALLCOCKS
BALLED
BALLERINA
BALLERINAS
BALLERINE
BALLET
BALLETIC
BALLETS
BALLING
BALLINGS
BALLISTA
BALLISTAE
BALLISTAS
BALLISTIC
BALLISTICS
BALLIUM
BALLIUMS
BALLOCKS
BALLOCKSED
BALLOCKSES
BALLOCKSING

BALLON
BALLONET
BALLONETS
BALLONS
BALLOON
BALLOONED
BALLOONING
BALLOONINGS
BALLOONS
BALLOT
BALLOTED
BALLOTEE
BALLOTEES
BALLOTING
BALLOTS
BALLOW
BALLOWS
BALLPARK
BALLS
BALLY
BALLYHOO
BALLYHOOS
BALLYRAG
BALLYRAGGED
BALLYRAGGING
BALLYRAGS
BALM
BALMED
BALMIER
BALMIEST
BALMILY
BALMINESS
BALMINESSES
BALMING
BALMORAL
BALMORALS
BALMS
BALMY
BALNEAL
BALNEARIES
BALNEARY
BALONEY
BALONEYS
BALOO
BALOOS
BALSA
BALSAM
BALSAMED
BALSAMIC
BALSAMING
BALSAMS
BALSAMY
BALSAS
BALTHASAR
BALTHASARS
BALTHAZAR
BALTHAZARS
BALU
BALUS
BALUSTER
BALUSTERS
BALZARINE
BALZARINES
BAM
BAMBINI
BAMBINO
BAMBINOS
BAMBOO
BAMBOOS
BAMBOOZLE

| | | | | |
|---|---|---|---|---|
| BAMBOOZLED | BANDITTIS | BANISTERS | BANTERER | BARBECUED |
| BAMBOOZLES | BANDOBAST | BANJAX | BANTERERS | BARBECUES |
| BAMBOOZLING | BANDOBASTS | BANJAXED | BANTERING | BARBECUING |
| BAMMED | BANDOG | BANJAXES | BANTERINGS | BARBED |
| BAMMER | BANDOGS | BANJAXING | BANTERS | BARBEL |
| BAMMERS | BANDOLEER | BANJO | BANTING | BARBELS |
| BAMMING | BANDOLEERS | BANJOES | BANTINGS | BARBER |
| BAMPOT | BANDOLERO | BANJOIST | BANTLING | BARBERED |
| BAMPOTS | BANDOLEROS | BANJOISTS | BANTLINGS | BARBERING |
| BAMS | BANDOLIER | BANJOS | BANTS | BARBERRIES |
| BAN | BANDOLIERS | BANJULELE | BANXRING | BARBERRY |
| BANAL | BANDOLINE | BANJULELES | BANXRINGS | BARBERS |
| BANALER | BANDOLINES | BANK | BANYAN | BARBES |
| BANALEST | BANDOOK | BANKABLE | BANYANS | BARBET |
| BANALITIES | BANDOOKS | BANKED | BANZAI | BARBETS |
| BANALITY | BANDORA | BANKER | BAOBAB | BARBETTE |
| BANALLY | BANDORAS | BANKERS | BAOBABS | BARBETTES |
| BANANA | BANDORE | BANKET | BAP | BARBICAN |
| BANANAS | BANDORES | BANKETS | BAPS | BARBICANS |
| BANAUSIAN | BANDROL | BANKING | BAPTISE | BARBICEL |
| BANAUSIC | BANDROLS | BANKINGS | BAPTISED | BARBICELS |
| BANC | BANDS | BANKROLL | BAPTISES | BARBIE |
| BANCO | BANDSMAN | BANKROLLED | BAPTISING | BARBIES |
| BANCOS | BANDSMEN | BANKROLLING | BAPTISM | BARBING |
| BANCS | BANDSTAND | BANKROLLS | BAPTISMAL | BARBITAL |
| BAND | BANDSTANDS | BANKRUPT | BAPTISMS | BARBITALS |
| BANDAGE | BANDSTER | BANKRUPTED | BAPTIST | BARBITONE |
| BANDAGED | BANDSTERS | BANKRUPTING | BAPTISTRIES | BARBITONES |
| BANDAGES | BANDURA | BANKRUPTS | BAPTISTRY | BARBOLA |
| BANDAGING | BANDURAS | BANKS | BAPTISTS | BARBOLAS |
| BANDALORE | BANDWAGON | BANKSIA | BAPTIZE | BARBOTINE |
| BANDALORES | BANDWAGONS | BANKSIAS | BAPTIZED | BARBOTINES |
| BANDANA | BANDWIDTH | BANKSMAN | BAPTIZES | BARBS |
| BANDANAS | BANDWIDTHS | BANKSMEN | BAPTIZING | BARBULE |
| BANDANNA | BANDY | BANLIEUE | BAPU | BARBULES |
| BANDANNAS | BANDYING | BANLIEUES | BAPUS | BARCA |
| BANDAR | BANDYINGS | BANNED | BAR | BARCAROLE |
| BANDARS | BANDYMAN | BANNER | BARACAN | BARCAROLES |
| BANDBRAKE | BANDYMEN | BANNERALL | BARACANS | BARCAS |
| BANDBRAKES | BANE | BANNERALLS | BARAGOUIN | BARCHAN |
| BANDEAU | BANEBERRIES | BANNERED | BARAGOUINS | BARCHANE |
| BANDEAUX | BANEBERRY | BANNERET | BARATHEA | BARCHANES |
| BANDED | BANED | BANNERETS | BARATHEAS | BARCHANS |
| BANDELET | BANEFUL | BANNEROL | BARATHRUM | BARD |
| BANDELETS | BANEFULLY | BANNEROLS | BARATHRUMS | BARDASH |
| BANDELIER | BANES | BANNERS | BARB | BARDASHES |
| BANDELIERS | BANG | BANNING | BARBARIAN | BARDED |
| BANDEROL | BANGED | BANNOCK | BARBARIANS | BARDIC |
| BANDEROLE | BANGER | BANNOCKS | BARBARIC | BARDIER |
| BANDEROLES | BANGERS | BANNS | BARBARISE | BARDIEST |
| BANDEROLS | BANGING | BANQUET | BARBARISED | BARDING |
| BANDH | BANGLE | BANQUETED | BARBARISES | BARDLING |
| BANDHED | BANGLED | BANQUETER | BARBARISING | BARDLINGS |
| BANDHING | BANGLES | BANQUETERS | BARBARISM | BARDS |
| BANDHS | BANGS | BANQUETING | BARBARISMS | BARDSHIP |
| BANDICOOT | BANGSRING | BANQUETINGS | BARBARITIES | BARDSHIPS |
| BANDICOOTED | BANGSRINGS | BANQUETS | BARBARITY | BARDY |
| BANDICOOTING | BANGSTER | BANQUETTE | BARBARIZE | BARE |
| BANDICOOTS | BANGSTERS | BANQUETTES | BARBARIZED | BAREBACK |
| BANDIED | BANI | BANS | BARBARIZES | BAREBOAT |
| BANDIER | BANIA | BANSHEE | BARBARIZING | BAREBONE |
| BANDIES | BANIAN | BANSHEES | BARBAROUS | BAREBONES |
| BANDIEST | BANIANS | BANT | BARBASCO | BARED |
| BANDING | BANIAS | BANTAM | BARBASCOS | BAREFACED |
| BANDINGS | BANING | BANTAMS | BARBASTEL | BAREFOOT |
| BANDIT | BANISH | BANTED | BARBASTELS | BAREGE |
| BANDITRIES | BANISHED | BANTENG | BARBATE | BAREGES |
| BANDITRY | BANISHES | BANTENGS | BARBATED | BAREGINE |
| BANDITS | BANISHING | BANTER | BARBE | BAREGINES |
| BANDITTI | BANISTER | BANTERED | BARBECUE | BARELY |

| | | | | |
|---|---|---|---|---|
| BARENESS | BARKLESS | BAROSTAT | BARRIERED | BASEMENT |
| BARENESSES | BARKS | BAROSTATS | BARRIERING | BASEMENTS |
| BARER | BARKY | BAROUCHE | BARRIERS | BASENESS |
| BARES | BARLEY | BAROUCHES | BARRING | BASENESSES |
| BARESARK | BARLEYS | BARP | BARRINGS | BASENJI |
| BARESARKS | BARM | BARPERSON | BARRIO | BASENJIS |
| BAREST | BARMAID | BARPERSONS | BARRIOS | BASEPLATE |
| BARF | BARMAIDS | BARPS | BARRISTER | BASEPLATES |
| BARFED | BARMAN | BARQUE | BARRISTERS | BASER |
| BARFING | BARMBRACK | BARQUES | BARROW | BASES |
| BARFLIES | BARMBRACKS | BARRACAN | BARROWS | BASEST |
| BARFLY | BARMEN | BARRACANS | BARRULET | BASH |
| BARFS | BARMIER | BARRACE | BARRULETS | BASHAW |
| BARFUL | BARMIEST | BARRACES | BARS | BASHAWISM |
| BARGAIN | BARMINESS | BARRACK | BARTENDER | BASHAWISMS |
| BARGAINED | BARMINESSES | BARRACKED | BARTENDERS | BASHAWS |
| BARGAINER | BARMIZVAH | BARRACKER | BARTER | BASHED |
| BARGAINERS | BARMIZVAHS | BARRACKERS | BARTERED | BASHER |
| BARGAINING | BARMKIN | BARRACKING | BARTERER | BASHERS |
| BARGAINS | BARMKINS | BARRACKINGS | BARTERERS | BASHES |
| BARGAIST | BARMS | BARRACKS | BARTERING | BASHFUL |
| BARGAISTS | BARMY | BARRACOON | BARTERS | BASHFULLY |
| BARGANDER | BARN | BARRACOONS | BARTISAN | BASHING |
| BARGANDERS | BARNACLE | BARRACUDA | BARTISANED | BASHINGS |
| BARGE | BARNACLED | BARRACUDAS | BARTISANS | BASHLESS |
| BARGED | BARNACLES | BARRAGE | BARTIZAN | BASHLYK |
| BARGEE | BARNED | BARRAGES | BARTIZANS | BASHLYKS |
| BARGEES | BARNEY | BARRANCA | BARTON | BASIC |
| BARGEESE | BARNEYS | BARRANCAS | BARTONS | BASICALLY |
| BARGELLO | BARNING | BARRANCO | BARWOOD | BASICITIES |
| BARGELLOS | BARNS | BARRANCOS | BARWOODS | BASICITY |
| BARGEMAN | BARNSTORM | BARRAT | BARYE | BASICS |
| BARGEMEN | BARNSTORMED | BARRATOR | BARYES | BASIDIA |
| BARGEPOLE | BARNSTORMING | BARRATORS | BARYON | BASIDIAL |
| BARGEPOLES | BARNSTORMS | BARRATRIES | BARYONS | BASIDIUM |
| BARGES | BARNYARD | BARRATRY | BARYTA | BASIFIXED |
| BARGEST | BARNYARDS | BARRATS | BARYTAS | BASIFUGAL |
| BARGESTS | BAROCCO | BARRÉ | BARYTES | BASIL |
| BARGHEST | BAROCCOS | BARRE | BARYTIC | BASILAR |
| BARGHESTS | BAROCK | BARRED | BARYTON | BASILICA |
| BARGING | BAROCKS | BARREFULL | BARYTONE | BASILICAL |
| BARGOOSE | BAROGRAM | BARREL | BARYTONES | BASILICAN |
| BARIC | BAROGRAMS | BARRELAGE | BARYTONS | BASILICAS |
| BARILLA | BAROGRAPH | BARRELAGES | BAS | BASILICON |
| BARILLAS | BAROGRAPHS | BARRELFUL | BASAL | BASILICONS |
| BARING | BAROMETER | BARRELFULS | BASALT | BASILISK |
| BARISH | BAROMETERS | BARRELLED | BASALTIC | BASILISKS |
| BARITE | BAROMETRIES | BARRELLING | BASALTS | BASILS |
| BARITES | BAROMETRY | BARRELS | BASAN | BASIN |
| BARITONE | BAROMETZ | BARREN | BASANITE | BASINET |
| BARITONES | BAROMETZES | BARRENER | BASANITES | BASINETS |
| BARIUM | BARON | BARRENEST | BASANS | BASINFUL |
| BARIUMS | BARONAGE | BARRES | BASBLEU | BASINFULS |
| BARK | BARONAGES | BARRET | BASBLEUS | BASING |
| BARKAN | BARONESS | BARRETS | BASCULE | BASINS |
| BARKANS | BARONESSES | BARRETTE | BASCULES | BASIPETAL |
| BARKED | BARONET | BARRETTES | BASE | BASIS |
| BARKEEPER | BARONETCIES | BARRICADE | BASEBALL | BASK |
| BARKEEPERS | BARONETCY | BARRICADED | BASEBALLS | BASKED |
| BARKEN | BARONETS | BARRICADES | BASEBOARD | BASKET |
| BARKENED | BARONIAL | BARRICADING | BASEBOARDS | BASKETFUL |
| BARKENING | BARONIES | BARRICADO | BASECOURT | BASKETFULS |
| BARKENS | BARONNE | BARRICADOED | BASECOURTS | BASKETRIES |
| BARKER | BARONNES | BARRICADOES | BASED | BASKETRY |
| BARKERS | BARONS | BARRICADOING | BASELARD | BASKETS |
| BARKHAN | BARONY | BARRICADOS | BASELARDS | BASKING |
| BARKHANS | BAROQUE | BARRICO | BASELESS | BASKS |
| BARKIER | BAROQUES | BARRICOES | BASELY | BASMIZVAH |
| BARKIEST | BAROSCOPE | BARRICOS | BASEMAN | BASMIZVAHS |
| BARKING | BAROSCOPES | BARRIER | BASEMEN | BASNET |

BASNETS
BASOCHE
BASOCHES
BASON
BASONS
BASQUE
BASQUED
BASQUES
BASQUINE
BASQUINES
BASS
BASSE
BASSED
BASSER
BASSES
BASSEST
BASSET
BASSETED
BASSETING
BASSETS
BASSI
BASSIER
BASSIEST
BASSINET
BASSINETS
BASSING
BASSIST
BASSISTS
BASSO
BASSOON
BASSOONS
BASSOS
BASSWOOD
BASSWOODS
BASSY
BAST
BASTA
BASTARD
BASTARDIES
BASTARDLY
BASTARDS
BASTARDY
BASTE
BASTED
BASTER
BASTERS
BASTES
BASTIDE
BASTIDES
BASTILLE
BASTILLES
BASTINADE
BASTINADED
BASTINADES
BASTINADING
BASTINADO
BASTINADOED
BASTINADOES
BASTINADOING
BASTING
BASTINGS
BASTION
BASTIONED
BASTIONS
BASTLE
BASTLES
BASTO
BASTOS
BASTS
BAT

BATABLE
BATATA
BATATAS
BATCH
BATCHED
BATCHES
BATCHING
BATE
BATEAU
BATEAUX
BATED
BATELESS
BATELEUR
BATELEURS
BATEMENT
BATEMENTS
BATES
BATH
BATHCUBE
BATHCUBES
BATHE
BATHED
BATHER
BATHERS
BATHES
BATHETIC
BATHHOUSE
BATHHOUSES
BATHING
BATHMIC
BATHMISM
BATHMISMS
BATHOLITE
BATHOLITES
BATHOLITH
BATHOLITHS
BATHORSE
BATHORSES
BATHOS
BATHOSES
BATHROBE
BATHROBES
BATHROOM
BATHROOMS
BATHS
BATHTUB
BATHTUBS
BATHYAL
BATHYBIUS
BATHYBIUSES
BATHYLITE
BATHYLITES
BATHYLITH
BATHYLITHS
BATIK
BATIKS
BATING
BATISTE
BATISTES
BATLER
BATLERS
BATLET
BATLETS
BATMAN
BATMEN
BATMIZVAH
BATMIZVAHS
BATOLOGIES
BATOLOGY
BATON

BATONED
BATONING
BATONS
BATOON
BATOONED
BATOONING
BATOONS
BATRACHIA
BATS
BATSMAN
BATSMEN
BATSWING
BATSWINGS
BATT
BATTA
BATTALIA
BATTALIAS
BATTALION
BATTALIONS
BATTAS
BATTED
BATTEL
BATTELED
BATTELER
BATTELERS
BATTELING
BATTELS
BATTEMENT
BATTEMENTS
BATTEN
BATTENED
BATTENING
BATTENINGS
BATTENS
BATTER
BATTERED
BATTERIE
BATTERIES
BATTERING
BATTERO
BATTEROS
BATTERS
BATTERY
BATTIER
BATTIEST
BATTILL
BATTING
BATTINGS
BATTLE
BATTLED
BATTLER
BATTLERS
BATTLES
BATTLING
BATTOLOGIES
BATTOLOGY
BATTS
BATTUE
BATTUES
BATTUTA
BATTUTAS
BATTY
BATWOMAN
BATWOMEN
BAUBLE
BAUBLES
BAUBLING
BAUCHLE
BAUCHLED
BAUCHLES

BAUCHLING
BAUD
BAUDEKIN
BAUDEKINS
BAUDRIC
BAUDRICK
BAUDRICKE
BAUDRICKES
BAUDRICKS
BAUDRICS
BAUDS
BAUERA
BAUERAS
BAUHINIA
BAUHINIAS
BAUK
BAUKED
BAUKING
BAUKS
BAULK
BAULKED
BAULKING
BAULKS
BAUR
BAURS
BAUSOND
BAUXITE
BAUXITES
BAUXITIC
BAVARDAGE
BAVARDAGES
BAVIN
BAVINS
BAWBEE
BAWBEES
BAWBLE
BAWBLES
BAWCOCK
BAWCOCKS
BAWD
BAWDIER
BAWDIES
BAWDIEST
BAWDILY
BAWDINESS
BAWDINESSES
BAWDKIN
BAWDKINS
BAWDRIES
BAWDRY
BAWDS
BAWDY
BAWL
BAWLED
BAWLER
BAWLERS
BAWLEY
BAWLEYS
BAWLING
BAWLINGS
BAWLS
BAWN
BAWNS
BAWR
BAWRS
BAXTER
BAXTERS
BAY
BAYADÈRE
BAYADÈRES

BAYARD
BAYARDS
BAYBERRIES
BAYBERRY
BAYE
BAYED
BAYES
BAYING
BAYLE
BAYLES
BAYONET
BAYONETED
BAYONETING
BAYONETS
BAYOU
BAYOUS
BAYS
BAYT
BAYTED
BAYTING
BAYTS
BAZAAR
BAZAARS
BAZAR
BAZARS
BAZAZZ
BAZAZZES
BAZOOKA
BAZOOKAS
BDELLIUM
BDELLIUMS
BE
BEACH
BEACHED
BEACHES
BEACHHEAD
BEACHHEADS
BEACHIER
BEACHIEST
BEACHING
BEACHY
BEACON
BEACONED
BEACONING
BEACONS
BEAD
BEADED
BEADIER
BEADIEST
BEADING
BEADINGS
BEADLE
BEADLEDOM
BEADLEDOMS
BEADLES
BEADMAN
BEADMEN
BEADS
BEADSMAN
BEADSMEN
BEADY
BEAGLE
BEAGLED
BEAGLER
BEAGLERS
BEAGLES
BEAGLING
BEAGLINGS
BEAK
BEAKED

BEAKER
BEAKERS
BEAKS
BEAM
BEAMED
BEAMER
BEAMERS
BEAMIER
BEAMIEST
BEAMILY
BEAMINESS
BEAMINESSES
BEAMING
BEAMINGLY
BEAMINGS
BEAMISH
BEAMLESS
BEAMS
BEAMY
BEAN
BEANED
BEANFEAST
BEANFEASTS
BEANIE
BEANIES
BEANING
BEANO
BEANOS
BEANPOLE
BEANPOLES
BEANS
BEANSTALK
BEANSTALKS
BEAR
BEARABLE
BEARABLY
BEARBINE
BEARBINES
BEARD
BEARDED
BEARDIE
BEARDIES
BEARDING
BEARDLESS
BEARDS
BEARE
BEARED
BEARER
BEARERS
BEARES
BEARING
BEARINGS
BEARISH
BÉARNAISE
BÉARNAISES
BEARS
BEARSKIN
BEARSKINS
BEARWARD
BEARWARDS
BEAST
BEASTHOOD
BEASTHOODS
BEASTIE
BEASTIES
BEASTILY
BEASTINGS
BEASTLIER
BEASTLIEST
BEASTLIKE

BEASTLY
BEASTS
BEAT
BEATABLE
BEATEN
BEATER
BEATERS
BEATH
BEATHED
BEATHING
BEATHS
BEATIFIC
BEATIFIED
BEATIFIES
BEATIFY
BEATIFYING
BEATING
BEATINGS
BEATITUDE
BEATITUDES
BEATNIK
BEATNIKS
BEATS
BEAU
BEAUFET
BEAUFETS
BEAUFFET
BEAUFFETS
BEAUFIN
BEAUFINS
BEAUISH
BEAUT
BEAUTEOUS
BEAUTIED
BEAUTIES
BEAUTIFIED
BEAUTIFIES
BEAUTIFUL
BEAUTIFY
BEAUTIFYING
BEAUTS
BEAUTY
BEAUTYING
BEAUX
BEAUXITE
BEAUXITES
BEAVER
BEAVERED
BEAVERIES
BEAVERS
BEAVERY
BEBEERINE
BEBEERINES
BEBEERU
BEBEERUS
BEBOP
BEBOPPED
BEBOPPING
BEBOPS
BEBUNG
BEBUNGS
BECALL
BECALLED
BECALLING
BECALLS
BECALM
BECALMED
BECALMING
BECALMS
BECAME

BÉCASSE
BÉCASSES
BECAUSE
BECCACCIA
BECCACCIAS
BECCAFICO
BECCAFICOS
BÉCHAMEL
BÉCHAMELS
BECHANCE
BECHANCED
BECHANCES
BECHANCING
BECHARM
BECHARMED
BECHARMING
BECHARMS
BECK
BECKE
BECKED
BECKES
BECKET
BECKETS
BECKING
BECKON
BECKONED
BECKONING
BECKONS
BECKS
BECLOUD
BECLOUDED
BECLOUDING
BECLOUDS
BECOME
BECOMES
BECOMING
BECQUEREL
BECQUERELS
BECURL
BECURLED
BECURLING
BECURLS
BED
BEDABBLE
BEDABBLED
BEDABBLES
BEDABBLING
BEDAD
BEDAGGLE
BEDAGGLED
BEDAGGLES
BEDAGGLING
BEDARKEN
BEDARKENED
BEDARKENING
BEDARKENS
BEDASH
BEDASHED
BEDASHES
BEDASHING
BEDAUB
BEDAUBED
BEDAUBING
BEDAUBS
BEDAWIN
BEDAWINS
BEDAZE
BEDAZED
BEDAZES
BEDAZING

BEDAZZLE
BEDAZZLED
BEDAZZLES
BEDAZZLING
BEDBUG
BEDBUGS
BEDCOVER
BEDCOVERS
BEDDABLE
BEDDED
BEDDER
BEDDERS
BEDDING
BEDDINGS
BEDE
BEDEAFEN
BEDEAFENED
BEDEAFENING
BEDEAFENS
BEDECK
BEDECKED
BEDECKING
BEDECKS
BEDEGUAR
BEDEGUARS
BEDEL
BEDELL
BEDELLS
BEDELS
BEDELSHIP
BEDELSHIPS
BEDEMAN
BEDEMEN
BEDERAL
BEDERALS
BEDES
BEDESMAN
BEDESMEN
BEDEVIL
BEDEVILLED
BEDEVILLING
BEDEVILS
BEDEW
BEDEWED
BEDEWING
BEDEWS
BEDFAST
BEDFELLOW
BEDFELLOWS
BEDIDE
BEDIGHT
BEDIGHTING
BEDIGHTS
BEDIM
BEDIMMED
BEDIMMING
BEDIMMINGS
BEDIMS
BEDIZEN
BEDIZENED
BEDIZENING
BEDIZENS
BEDLAM
BEDLAMISM
BEDLAMISMS
BEDLAMITE
BEDLAMITES
BEDLAMS
BEDMAKER
BEDMAKERS

BEDOUIN
BEDOUINS
BEDPAN
BEDPANS
BEDPOST
BEDPOSTS
BEDRAGGLE
BEDRAGGLED
BEDRAGGLES
BEDRAGGLING
BEDRAL
BEDRALS
BEDRENCH
BEDRENCHED
BEDRENCHES
BEDRENCHING
BEDRID
BEDRIDDEN
BEDRIGHT
BEDRIGHTS
BEDRITE
BEDRITES
BEDROCK
BEDROCKS
BEDROOM
BEDROOMS
BEDROP
BEDROPPED
BEDROPPING
BEDROPS
BEDROPT
BEDS
BEDSIDE
BEDSIDES
BEDSOCKS
BEDSORE
BEDSORES
BEDSPREAD
BEDSPREADS
BEDSTEAD
BEDSTEADS
BEDSTRAW
BEDSTRAWS
BEDTICK
BEDTICKS
BEDTIME
BEDTIMES
BEDUCK
BEDUCKED
BEDUCKING
BEDUCKS
BEDUIN
BEDUINS
BEDUNG
BEDUNGED
BEDUNGING
BEDUNGS
BEDUST
BEDUSTED
BEDUSTING
BEDUSTS
BEDWARD
BEDWARDS
BEDWARF
BEDWARFED
BEDWARFING
BEDWARFS
BEDYDE
BEDYE
BEDYED

| | | | | |
|---|---|---|---|---|
| BEDYEING | BEFALLS | BEGGARED | BEGUILER | BEHOVING |
| BEDYES | BEFANA | BEGGARIES | BEGUILERS | BEHOWL |
| BEE | BEFANAS | BEGGARING | BEGUILES | BEHOWLED |
| BEECH | BEFELD | BEGGARLY | BEGUILING | BEHOWLING |
| BEECHEN | BEFELL | BEGGARS | BEGUIN | BEHOWLS |
| BEECHES | BEFFANA | BEGGARY | BEGUINAGE | BEIGE |
| BEEF | BEFFANAS | BEGGED | BEGUINAGES | BEIGEL |
| BEEFALO | BEFIT | BEGGING | BEGUINE | BEIGELS |
| BEEFALOES | BEFITS | BEGGINGLY | BEGUINES | BEIGES |
| BEEFALOS | BEFITTED | BEGGINGS | BEGUINS | BEIGNET |
| BEEFCAKE | BEFITTING | BEGHARD | BEGUM | BEIGNETS |
| BEEFCAKES | BEFLOWER | BEGHARDS | BEGUMS | BEIN |
| BEEFEATER | BEFLOWERED | BEGIFT | BEGUN | BEING |
| BEEFEATERS | BEFLOWERING | BEGIFTED | BEGUNK | BEINGLESS |
| BEEFED | BEFLOWERS | BEGIFTING | BEGUNKED | BEINGNESS |
| BEEFIER | BEFLUM | BEGIFTS | BEGUNKING | BEINGNESSES |
| BEEFIEST | BEFLUMMED | BEGILD | BEGUNKS | BEINGS |
| BEEFING | BEFLUMMING | BEGILDED | BEHALF | BEINKED |
| BEEFS | BEFLUMS | BEGILDING | BEHALVES | BEINNESS |
| BEEFSTEAK | BEFOAM | BEGILDS | BEHAPPEN | BEINNESSES |
| BEEFSTEAKS | BEFOAMED | BEGILT | BEHAPPENED | BEJABERS |
| BEEFY | BEFOAMING | BEGIN | BEHAPPENING | BEJADE |
| BEEGAH | BEFOAMS | BEGINNE | BEHAPPENS | BEJADED |
| BEEGAHS | BEFOG | BEGINNER | BEHATTED | BEJADES |
| BEEHIVE | BEFOGGED | BEGINNERS | BEHAVE | BEJADING |
| BEEHIVES | BEFOGGING | BEGINNES | BEHAVED | BEJANT |
| BEEKEEPER | BEFOGS | BEGINNING | BEHAVES | BEJANTS |
| BEEKEEPERS | BEFOOL | BEGINNINGS | BEHAVING | BEJESUIT |
| BEEN | BEFOOLED | BEGINS | BEHAVIOR | BEJESUITED |
| BEENAH | BEFOOLING | BEGIRD | BEHAVIORS | BEJESUITING |
| BEENAHS | BEFOOLS | BEGIRDED | BEHAVIOUR | BEJESUITS |
| BEEP | BEFORE | BEGIRDING | BEHAVIOURS | BEJEWEL |
| BEEPED | BEFORTUNE | BEGIRDS | BEHEAD | BEJEWELLED |
| BEEPER | BEFORTUNED | BEGIRT | BEHEADAL | BEJEWELLING |
| BEEPERS | BEFORTUNES | BEGLAMOUR | BEHEADALS | BEJEWELS |
| BEEPING | BEFORTUNING | BEGLAMOURED | BEHEADED | BEKAH |
| BEEPS | BEFOUL | BEGLAMOURING | BEHEADING | BEKAHS |
| BEER | BEFOULED | BEGLAMOURS | BEHEADINGS | BEKISS |
| BEERHALL | BEFOULING | BEGLERBEG | BEHEADS | BEKISSED |
| BEERHALLS | BEFOULS | BEGLERBEGS | BEHELD | BEKISSES |
| BEERIER | BEFRIEND | BEGLOOM | BEHEMOTH | BEKISSING |
| BEERIEST | BEFRIENDED | BEGLOOMED | BEHEMOTHS | BEKNAVE |
| BEERINESS | BEFRIENDING | BEGLOOMING | BEHEST | BEKNAVED |
| BEERINESSES | BEFRIENDS | BEGLOOMS | BEHESTS | BEKNAVES |
| BEERS | BEFRINGE | BEGNAW | BEHIGHT | BEKNAVING |
| BEERY | BEFRINGED | BEGNAWED | BEHIGHTING | BEKNOWN |
| BEES | BEFRINGES | BEGNAWING | BEHIGHTS | BEL |
| BEESOME | BEFRINGING | BEGNAWS | BEHIND | BELABOUR |
| BEESTINGS | BEFUDDLE | BEGO | BEHINDS | BELABOURED |
| BEESWAX | BEFUDDLED | BEGOES | BEHOLD | BELABOURING |
| BEESWAXED | BEFUDDLES | BEGOING | BEHOLDEN | BELABOURS |
| BEESWAXES | BEFUDDLING | BEGONE | BEHOLDER | BELACE |
| BEESWAXING | BEG | BEGONIA | BEHOLDERS | BELACED |
| BEESWING | BEGAD | BEGONIAS | BEHOLDING | BELACES |
| BEESWINGED | BEGAN | BEGORED | BEHOLDINGS | BELACING |
| BEESWINGS | BEGAR | BEGORRA | BEHOLDS | BELAH |
| BEET | BEGARS | BEGORRAH | BEHOOF | BELAHS |
| BEETED | BEGAT | BEGOT | BEHOOFS | BELAID |
| BEETING | BEGEM | BEGOTTEN | BEHOOVE | BELAMIES |
| BEETLE | BEGEMMED | BEGRIME | BEHOOVED | BELAMOURE |
| BEETLED | BEGEMMING | BEGRIMED | BEHOOVES | BELAMOURES |
| BEETLES | BEGEMS | BEGRIMES | BEHOOVING | BELAMY |
| BEETLING | BEGET | BEGRIMING | BEHOTE | BELATE |
| BEETROOT | BEGETS | BEGRUDGE | BEHOTES | BELATED |
| BEETROOTS | BEGETTER | BEGRUDGED | BEHOTING | BELATES |
| BEETS | BEGETTERS | BEGRUDGES | BEHOVE | BELATING |
| BEEVES | BEGETTING | BEGRUDGING | BEHOVED | BELAUD |
| BEFALL | BEGGAR | BEGS | BEHOVEFUL | BELAUDED |
| BEFALLEN | BEGGARDOM | BEGUILE | BEHOVELY | BELAUDING |
| BEFALLING | BEGGARDOMS | BEGUILED | BEHOVES | BELAUDS |

BELAY
BELAYING
BELAYS
BELCH
BELCHED
BELCHER
BELCHERS
BELCHES
BELCHING
BELDAM
BELDAME
BELDAMES
BELDAMS
BELEAGUER
BELEAGUERED
BELEAGUERING
BELEAGUERS
BELEE
BELEED
BELEEING
BELEES
BELEMNITE
BELEMNITES
BELFRIED
BELFRIES
BELFRY
BELGA
BELGARD
BELGARDS
BELGAS
BELIE
BELIED
BELIEF
BELIEFS
BELIER
BELIERS
BELIES
BELIEVE
BELIEVED
BELIEVER
BELIEVERS
BELIEVES
BELIEVING
BELIKE
BELITTLE
BELITTLED
BELITTLES
BELITTLING
BELIVE
BELL
BELLBIND
BELLBINDS
BELLCOTE
BELLCOTES
BELLE
BELLED
BELLES
BELLETER
BELLETERS
BELLHOP
BELLHOPS
BELLIBONE
BELLIBONES
BELLICOSE
BELLIED
BELLIES
BELLING
BELLMAN
BELLMEN
BELLOW

BELLOWED
BELLOWER
BELLOWERS
BELLOWING
BELLOWS
BELLPUSH
BELLPUSHES
BELLS
BELLWORT
BELLWORTS
BELLY
BELLYFUL
BELLYFULS
BELLYING
BELLYINGS
BELOMANCIES
BELOMANCY
BELONG
BELONGED
BELONGER
BELONGERS
BELONGING
BELONGINGS
BELONGS
BELOVE
BELOVED
BELOVEDS
BELOVES
BELOVING
BELOW
BELS
BELT
BELTED
BELTER
BELTERS
BELTING
BELTINGS
BELTS
BELTWAY
BELTWAYS
BELUGA
BELUGAS
BELVEDERE
BELVEDERES
BELYING
BEMA
BEMAD
BEMADDED
BEMADDING
BEMADS
BEMAS
BEMATA
BEMAUL
BEMAULED
BEMAULING
BEMAULS
BEMAZED
BEMEAN
BEMEANED
BEMEANING
BEMEANS
BEMEANT
BEMEDAL
BEMEDALLED
BEMEDALLING
BEMEDALS
BEMETE
BEMETED
BEMETES
BEMETING

BEMIRE
BEMIRED
BEMIRES
BEMIRING
BEMOAN
BEMOANED
BEMOANER
BEMOANERS
BEMOANING
BEMOANINGS
BEMOANS
BEMOCK
BEMOCKED
BEMOCKING
BEMOCKS
BEMOIL
BEMOILED
BEMOILING
BEMOILS
BEMONSTER
BEMONSTERED
BEMONSTERING
BEMONSTERS
BEMOUTH
BEMOUTHED
BEMOUTHING
BEMOUTHS
BEMUD
BEMUDDED
BEMUDDING
BEMUDDLE
BEMUDDLED
BEMUDDLES
BEMUDDLING
BEMUDS
BEMUFFLE
BEMUFFLED
BEMUFFLES
BEMUFFLING
BEMUSE
BEMUSED
BEMUSES
BEMUSING
BEN
BENAME
BENAMED
BENAMES
BENAMING
BENCH
BENCHED
BENCHER
BENCHERS
BENCHES
BENCHING
BEND
BENDED
BENDER
BENDERS
BENDIER
BENDIEST
BENDING
BENDINGLY
BENDINGS
BENDLET
BENDLETS
BENDS
BENDWISE
BENDY
BENE
BENEATH

BENEDICT
BENEDIGHT
BENEFACT
BENEFACTED
BENEFACTING
BENEFACTS
BENEFIC
BENEFICE
BENEFICED
BENEFICES
BENEFIT
BENEFITED
BENEFITING
BENEFITS
BENEMPT
BENES
BENET
BENETS
BENETTED
BENETTING
BENGALINE
BENGALINES
BENI
BENIGHT
BENIGHTED
BENIGHTEN
BENIGHTENED
BENIGHTENING
BENIGHTENINGS
BENIGHTENS
BENIGHTER
BENIGHTERS
BENIGHTING
BENIGHTINGS
BENIGHTS
BENIGN
BENIGNANT
BENIGNER
BENIGNEST
BENIGNITIES
BENIGNITY
BENIGNLY
BENIS
BENISEED
BENISEEDS
BENISON
BENISONS
BÉNITIER
BÉNITIERS
BENJ
BENJAMIN
BENJAMINS
BENJES
BENNE
BENNES
BENNET
BENNETS
BENNI
BENNIES
BENNIS
BENNY
BENS
BENT
BENTHIC
BENTHOAL
BENTHONIC
BENTHOS
BENTHOSES
BENTIER
BENTIEST

BENTONITE
BENTONITES
BENTS
BENTWOOD
BENTWOODS
BENTY
BENUMB
BENUMBED
BENUMBING
BENUMBS
BENZAL
BENZALS
BENZENE
BENZENES
BENZIDINE
BENZIDINES
BENZIL
BENZILS
BENZINE
BENZINES
BENZOATE
BENZOATES
BENZOIC
BENZOIN
BENZOINS
BENZOL
BENZOLE
BENZOLES
BENZOLINE
BENZOLINES
BENZOLS
BENZOYL
BENZOYLS
BENZYL
BENZYLS
BEPAINT
BEPAINTED
BEPAINTING
BEPAINTS
BEPAT
BEPATCHED
BEPATS
BEPATTED
BEPATTING
BEPEARL
BEPEARLED
BEPEARLING
BEPEARLS
BEPELT
BEPELTED
BEPELTING
BEPELTS
BEPEPPER
BEPEPPERED
BEPEPPERING
BEPEPPERS
BEPESTER
BEPESTERED
BEPESTERING
BEPESTERS
BEPITIED
BEPITIES
BEPITY
BEPITYING
BEPLASTER
BEPLASTERED
BEPLASTERING
BEPLASTERS
BEPLUMED
BEPOMMEL

| | | | | |
|---|---|---|---|---|
| BEPOMMELLED | BERGHAANS | BESCREENED | BESLAVED | BESPICED |
| BEPOMMELLING | BERGMEHL | BESCREENING | BESLAVER | BESPICES |
| BEPOMMELS | BERGMEHLS | BESCREENS | BESLAVERED | BESPICING |
| BEPOWDER | BERGOMASK | BESCRIBBLE | BESLAVERING | BESPIT |
| BEPOWDERED | BERGOMASKS | BESCRIBBLED | BESLAVERS | BESPITS |
| BEPOWDERING | BERGS | BESCRIBBLES | BESLAVES | BESPITTING |
| BEPOWDERS | BERGYLT | BESCRIBBLING | BESLAVING | BESPOKE |
| BEPRAISE | BERGYLTS | BESEE | BESLOBBER | BESPOKEN |
| BEPRAISED | BERIBERI | BESEECH | BESLOBBERED | BESPORT |
| BEPRAISES | BERIBERIS | BESEECHED | BESLOBBERING | BESPORTED |
| BEPRAISING | BERK | BESEECHER | BESLOBBERS | BESPORTING |
| BEPROSE | BERKELIUM | BESEECHERS | BESLUBBER | BESPORTS |
| BEPROSED | BERKELIUMS | BESEECHES | BESLUBBERED | BESPOT |
| BEPROSES | BERKS | BESEECHING | BESLUBBERING | BESPOTS |
| BEPROSING | BERLEY | BESEECHINGS | BESLUBBERS | BESPOTTED |
| BEPUFF | BERLEYS | BESEEING | BESMEAR | BESPOTTING |
| BEPUFFED | BERLIN | BESEEKE | BESMEARED | BESPOUT |
| BEPUFFING | BERLINE | BESEEKES | BESMEARING | BESPOUTED |
| BEPUFFS | BERLINES | BESEEKING | BESMEARS | BESPOUTING |
| BEQUEATH | BERLINS | BESEEM | BESMIRCH | BESPOUTS |
| BEQUEATHED | BERM | BESEEMED | BESMIRCHED | BESPREAD |
| BEQUEATHING | BERMS | BESEEMING | BESMIRCHES | BESPREADING |
| BEQUEATHS | BEROB | BESEEMINGS | BESMIRCHING | BESPREADS |
| BEQUEST | BEROBBED | BESEEMLY | BESMUT | BESPRENT |
| BEQUESTS | BEROBBING | BESEEMS | BESMUTCH | BEST |
| BERATE | BEROBS | BESEEN | BESMUTCHED | BESTAD |
| BERATED | BERRET | BESEES | BESMUTCHES | BESTADDE |
| BERATES | BERRETS | BESET | BESMUTCHING | BESTAIN |
| BERATING | BERRIED | BESETMENT | BESMUTS | BESTAINED |
| BERAY | BERRIES | BESETMENTS | BESMUTTED | BESTAINING |
| BERAYED | BERRY | BESETS | BESMUTTING | BESTAINS |
| BERAYING | BERRYING | BESETTER | BESOGNIO | BESTAR |
| BERAYS | BERRYINGS | BESETTERS | BESOGNIOS | BESTARRED |
| BERBERINE | BERSERK | BESETTING | BESOIN | BESTARRING |
| BERBERINES | BERSERKER | BESHADOW | BESOINS | BESTARS |
| BERBERIS | BERSERKERS | BESHADOWED | BESOM | BESTEAD |
| BERBERISES | BERSERKLY | BESHADOWING | BESOMS | BESTEADED |
| BERCEAU | BERSERKS | BESHADOWS | BESORT | BESTEADING |
| BERCEAUX | BERTH | BESHAME | BESORTED | BESTEADS |
| BERCEUSE | BERTHA | BESHAMED | BESORTING | BESTED |
| BERCEUSES | BERTHAGE | BESHAMES | BESORTS | BESTIAL |
| BERDACHE | BERTHAGES | BESHAMING | BESOT | BESTIALS |
| BERDACHES | BERTHAS | BESHINE | BESOTS | BESTIARIES |
| BERDASH | BERTHE | BESHINES | BESOTTED | BESTIARY |
| BERDASHES | BERTHED | BESHINING | BESOTTING | BESTICK |
| BERE | BERTHES | BESHONE | BESOUGHT | BESTICKING |
| BEREAVE | BERTHING | BESHREW | BESOULED | BESTICKS |
| BEREAVED | BERTHS | BESHREWED | BESPAKE | BESTILL |
| BEREAVEN | BERYL | BESHREWING | BESPANGLE | BESTILLED |
| BEREAVES | BERYLLIA | BESHREWS | BESPANGLED | BESTILLING |
| BEREAVING | BERYLLIAS | BESIDE | BESPANGLES | BESTILLS |
| BEREFT | BERYLLIUM | BESIDES | BESPANGLING | BESTING |
| BERES | BERYLLIUMS | BESIEGE | BESPAT | BESTIR |
| BERET | BERYLS | BESIEGED | BESPATE | BESTIRRED |
| BERETS | BESAINT | BESIEGER | BESPATTER | BESTIRRING |
| BERG | BESAINTED | BESIEGERS | BESPATTERED | BESTIRS |
| BERGAMA | BESAINTING | BESIEGES | BESPATTERING | BESTORM |
| BERGAMAS | BESAINTS | BESIEGING | BESPATTERS | BESTORMED |
| BERGAMASK | BESANG | BESIEGINGS | BESPEAK | BESTORMING |
| BERGAMASKS | BESAT | BESIGH | BESPEAKING | BESTORMS |
| BERGAMOT | BESAW | BESIGHED | BESPEAKS | BESTOW |
| BERGAMOTS | BESCATTER | BESIGHING | BESPECKLE | BESTOWAL |
| BERGANDER | BESCATTERED | BESIGHS | BESPECKLED | BESTOWALS |
| BERGANDERS | BESCATTERING | BESING | BESPECKLES | BESTOWED |
| BERGENIA | BESCATTERS | BESINGING | BESPECKLING | BESTOWER |
| BERGENIAS | BESCRAWL | BESINGS | BESPED | BESTOWERS |
| BERGÈRE | BESCRAWLED | BESIT | BESPEED | BESTOWING |
| BERGFALL | BESCRAWLING | BESITS | BESPEEDING | BESTOWS |
| BERGFALLS | BESCRAWLS | BESITTING | BESPEEDS | BESTREAK |
| BERGHAAN | BESCREEN | BESLAVE | BESPICE | BESTREAKED |

| | | | | |
|---|---|---|---|---|
| BESTREAKING | BETHUMBS | BETTERED | BEWITCH | BIBBING |
| BESTREAKS | BETHUMP | BETTERING | BEWITCHED | BIBCOCK |
| BESTREW | BETHUMPED | BETTERINGS | BEWITCHES | BIBCOCKS |
| BESTREWED | BETHUMPING | BETTERS | BEWITCHING | BIBELOT |
| BESTREWING | BETHUMPS | BETTIES | BEWRAY | BIBELOTS |
| BESTREWN | BETHWACK | BETTING | BEWRAYED | BIBLE |
| BESTREWS | BETHWACKED | BETTINGS | BEWRAYING | BIBLES |
| BESTRID | BETHWACKING | BETTOR | BEWRAYS | BIBLICAL |
| BESTRIDDEN | BETHWACKS | BETTORS | BEY | BIBLICISM |
| BESTRIDE | BETID | BETTY | BEYOND | BIBLICISMS |
| BESTRIDES | BETIDE | BETUMBLED | BEYONDS | BIBLICIST |
| BESTRIDING | BETIDED | BETWEEN | BEYS | BIBLICISTS |
| BESTRODE | BETIDES | BETWEENS | BEZ | BIBLIST |
| BESTROWN | BETIDING | BETWIXT | BEZANT | BIBLISTS |
| BESTS | BETIGHT | BEURRÉ | BEZANTS | BIBS |
| BESTSELL | BETIME | BEURRE | BEZAZZ | BIBULOUS |
| BESTSELLING | BETIMED | BEURRÉS | BEZAZZES | BICAMERAL |
| BESTSELLS | BETIMES | BEURRES | BEZEL | BICARB |
| BESTSOLD | BETIMING | BEVATRON | BEZELS | BICARBS |
| BESTUCK | BETING | BEVATRONS | BEZES | BICE |
| BESTUD | BÊTISE | BEVEL | BEZIQUE | BICEPS |
| BESTUDDED | BÊTISES | BEVELLED | BEZIQUES | BICEPSES |
| BESTUDDING | BETITLE | BEVELLER | BEZOAR | BICES |
| BESTUDS | BETITLED | BEVELLERS | BEZOARDIC | BICHORD |
| BESUNG | BETITLES | BEVELLING | BEZOARS | BICIPITAL |
| BET | BETITLING | BEVELLINGS | BEZONIAN | BICKER |
| BETA | BETOIL | BEVELMENT | BEZONIANS | BICKERED |
| BETACISM | BETOILED | BEVELMENTS | BEZZLE | BICKERING |
| BETACISMS | BETOILING | BEVELS | BEZZLED | BICKERS |
| BETAINE | BETOILS | BEVER | BEZZLES | BICONCAVE |
| BETAINES | BETOKEN | BEVERAGE | BEZZLING | BICONVEX |
| BETAKE | BETOKENED | BEVERAGES | BHAJAN | BICUSPID |
| BETAKEN | BETOKENING | BEVERS | BHAJANS | BICUSPIDS |
| BETAKES | BETOKENS | BEVIES | BHAKTI | BICYCLE |
| BETAKING | BÉTON | BEVUE | BHAKTIS | BICYCLED |
| BETAS | BETONIES | BEVUES | BHANG | BICYCLES |
| BETATRON | BÉTONS | BEVVIED | BHANGS | BICYCLING |
| BETATRONS | BETONY | BEVVIES | BHARAL | BICYCLIST |
| BÊTE | BETOOK | BEVVY | BHARALS | BICYCLISTS |
| BETE | BETOSS | BEVY | BHEESTIE | BID |
| BETED | BETOSSED | BEWAIL | BHEESTIES | BIDDABLE |
| BETEEM | BETOSSES | BEWAILED | BHEESTY | BIDDEN |
| BETEEME | BETOSSING | BEWAILING | BHEL | BIDDER |
| BETEEMED | BETRAY | BEWAILINGS | BHELS | BIDDERS |
| BETEEMES | BETRAYAL | BEWAILS | BHINDI | BIDDIES |
| BETEEMING | BETRAYALS | BEWARE | BHINDIS | BIDDING |
| BETEEMS | BETRAYED | BEWARED | BHISTEE | BIDDINGS |
| BETEL | BETRAYER | BEWARES | BHISTEES | BIDDY |
| BETELS | BETRAYERS | BEWARING | BHISTI | BIDE |
| BÊTES | BETRAYING | BEWEEP | BHISTIS | BIDED |
| BETES | BETRAYS | BEWEEPING | BIANNUAL | BIDENT |
| BETH | BETREAD | BEWEEPS | BIAS | BIDENTAL |
| BETHANKIT | BETREADING | BEWENT | BIASED | BIDENTALS |
| BETHANKITS | BETREADS | BEWEPT | BIASES | BIDENTATE |
| BETHEL | BETRIM | BEWET | BIASING | BIDENTS |
| BETHELS | BETRIMMED | BEWETS | BIASINGS | BIDES |
| BETHESDA | BETRIMMING | BEWETTED | BIASSED | BIDET |
| BETHESDAS | BETRIMS | BEWETTING | BIASSES | BIDETS |
| BETHINK | BETROD | BEWHORE | BIASSING | BIDING |
| BETHINKING | BETRODDEN | BEWHORED | BIATHLON | BIDINGS |
| BETHINKS | BETROTH | BEWHORES | BIATHLONS | BIDON |
| BETHOUGHT | BETROTHAL | BEWHORING | BIAXAL | BIDONS |
| BETHRALL | BETROTHALS | BEWIG | BIAXIAL | BIDS |
| BETHRALLED | BETROTHED | BEWIGGED | BIB | BIELD |
| BETHRALLING | BETROTHEDS | BEWIGGING | BIBACIOUS | BIELDIER |
| BETHRALLS | BETROTHING | BEWIGS | BIBATION | BIELDIEST |
| BETHS | BETROTHS | BEWILDER | BIBATIONS | BIELDS |
| BETHUMB | BETS | BEWILDERED | BIBBED | BIELDY |
| BETHUMBED | BETTED | BEWILDERING | BIBBER | BIEN |
| BETHUMBING | BETTER | BEWILDERS | BIBBERS | BIENNIAL |

| | | | | |
|---|---|---|---|---|
| BIENNIALS | BIKED | BILLIARD | BINGLING | BIOPARENTS |
| BIER | BIKER | BILLIARDS | BINGO | BIOPHOR |
| BIERS | BIKERS | BILLIE | BINGOS | BIOPHORE |
| BIESTINGS | BIKES | BILLIES | BINGS | BIOPHORES |
| BIFACIAL | BIKIE | BILLING | BINK | BIOPHORS |
| BIFARIOUS | BIKIES | BILLINGS | BINKS | BIOPIC |
| BIFF | BIKING | BILLION | BINNACLE | BIOPICS |
| BIFFED | BIKINGS | BILLIONS | BINNACLES | BIOPLASM |
| BIFFIN | BIKINI | BILLIONTH | BINNED | BIOPLASMS |
| BIFFING | BIKINIS | BILLIONTHS | BINNING | BIOPLAST |
| BIFFINS | BILABIAL | BILLMAN | BINOCLE | BIOPLASTS |
| BIFFS | BILABIALS | BILLMEN | BINOCLES | BIOPSIES |
| BIFID | BILABIATE | BILLON | BINOCULAR | BIOPSY |
| BIFILAR | BILANDER | BILLONS | BINOCULARS | BIOS |
| BIFOCAL | BILANDERS | BILLOW | BINOMIAL | BIOSCOPE |
| BIFOCALS | BILATERAL | BILLOWED | BINOMIALS | BIOSCOPES |
| BIFOLD | BILBERRIES | BILLOWIER | BINOMINAL | BIOSPHERE |
| BIFOLIATE | BILBERRY | BILLOWIEST | BINS | BIOSPHERES |
| BIFORM | BILBO | BILLOWING | BINT | BIOSTABLE |
| BIFURCATE | BILBOES | BILLOWS | BINTS | BIOTA |
| BIFURCATED | BILBOS | BILLOWY | BINTURONG | BIOTAS |
| BIFURCATES | BILE | BILLS | BINTURONGS | BIOTIC |
| BIFURCATING | BILES | BILLY | BIO | BIOTIN |
| BIG | BILGE | BILLYBOY | BIOASSAY | BIOTINS |
| BIGA | BILGED | BILLYBOYS | BIOASSAYS | BIOTITE |
| BIGAE | BILGES | BILLYCOCK | BIOBLAST | BIOTITES |
| BIGAMIES | BILGIER | BILLYCOCKS | BIOBLASTS | BIOTYPE |
| BIGAMIST | BILGIEST | BILOBAR | BIOCIDAL | BIOTYPES |
| BIGAMISTS | BILGING | BILOBATE | BIOCIDE | BIPAROUS |
| BIGAMOUS | BILGY | BILOBED | BIOCIDES | BIPARTITE |
| BIGAMY | BILHARZIA | BILOBULAR | BIODATA | BIPED |
| BIGENER | BILHARZIAS | BILOCULAR | BIOETHICS | BIPEDAL |
| BIGENERIC | BILIAN | BILTONG | BIOG | BIPEDS |
| BIGENERS | BILIANS | BILTONGS | BIOGAS | BIPHENYL |
| BIGG | BILIARIES | BIMANAL | BIOGASES | BIPHENYLS |
| BIGGED | BILIARY | BIMANOUS | BIOGEN | BIPINNATE |
| BIGGER | BILIMBI | BIMBASHI | BIOGENIC | BIPLANE |
| BIGGEST | BILIMBING | BIMBASHIS | BIOGENIES | BIPLANES |
| BIGGIE | BILIMBINGS | BIMBO | BIOGENOUS | BIPOD |
| BIGGIES | BILIMBIS | BIMBOS | BIOGENS | BIPODS |
| BIGGIN | BILINGUAL | BIMONTHLY | BIOGENY | BIPOLAR |
| BIGGING | BILIOUS | BIN | BIOGRAPH | BIPYRAMID |
| BIGGINS | BILIOUSLY | BINARIES | BIOGRAPHIES | BIPYRAMIDS |
| BIGGISH | BILIRUBIN | BINARY | BIOGRAPHS | BIRCH |
| BIGGS | BILIRUBINS | BINATE | BIOGRAPHY | BIRCHED |
| BIGGY | BILITERAL | BINAURAL | BIOGS | BIRCHEN |
| BIGHA | BILK | BIND | BIOHAZARD | BIRCHES |
| BIGHAS | BILKED | BINDER | BIOHAZARDS | BIRCHING |
| BIGHEADED | BILKER | BINDERIES | BIOLOGIES | BIRD |
| BIGHORN | BILKERS | BINDERS | BIOLOGIST | BIRDBATH |
| BIGHORNS | BILKING | BINDERY | BIOLOGISTS | BIRDBATHS |
| BIGHT | BILKS | BINDING | BIOLOGY | BIRDCAGE |
| BIGHTS | BILL | BINDINGS | BIOMASS | BIRDCAGES |
| BIGNESS | BILLABONG | BINDS | BIOMASSES | BIRDCALL |
| BIGNESSES | BILLABONGS | BINDWEED | BIOME | BIRDCALLS |
| BIGOT | BILLBOARD | BINDWEEDS | BIOMES | BIRDED |
| BIGOTED | BILLBOARDS | BINE | BIOMETRIC | BIRDER |
| BIGOTRIES | BILLBOOK | BINERVATE | BIOMETRICS | BIRDERS |
| BIGOTRY | BILLBOOKS | BINES | BIOMETRIES | BIRDIE |
| BIGOTS | BILLED | BING | BIOMETRY | BIRDIED |
| BIGS | BILLET | BINGE | BIOMORPH | BIRDIEING |
| BIGWIG | BILLETED | BINGED | BIOMORPHS | BIRDIES |
| BIGWIGS | BILLETING | BINGEING | BIONIC | BIRDING |
| BIJECTION | BILLETS | BINGER | BIONICS | BIRDINGS |
| BIJECTIONS | BILLFOLD | BINGERS | BIONOMIC | BIRDMAN |
| BIJOU | BILLFOLDS | BINGES | BIONOMICS | BIRDMEN |
| BIJOUX | BILLHEAD | BINGING | BIONT | BIRDS |
| BIJWONER | BILLHEADS | BINGLE | BIONTIC | BIRDSEED |
| BIJWONERS | BILLHOOK | BINGLED | BIONTS | BIRDSEEDS |
| BIKE | BILLHOOKS | BINGLES | BIOPARENT | BIRDSHOT |

| | | | | |
|---|---|---|---|---|
| BIRDSHOTS | BISHES | BITTERLY | BLACKBIRD | BLAEST |
| BIRDWING | BISHOP | BITTERN | BLACKBIRDS | BLAG |
| BIRDWINGS | BISHOPDOM | BITTERNS | BLACKBOY | BLAGGED |
| BIREME | BISHOPDOMS | BITTERS | BLACKBOYS | BLAGGING |
| BIREMES | BISHOPED | BITTIE | BLACKBUCK | BLAGS |
| BIRETTA | BISHOPESS | BITTIER | BLACKBUCKS | BLAGUE |
| BIRETTAS | BISHOPESSES | BITTIES | BLACKCAP | BLAGUES |
| BIRIYANI | BISHOPING | BITTIEST | BLACKCAPS | BLAGUEUR |
| BIRIYANIS | BISHOPRIC | BITTING | BLACKCOCK | BLAGUEURS |
| BIRK | BISHOPRICS | BITTOCK | BLACKCOCKS | BLAH |
| BIRKEN | BISHOPS | BITTOCKS | BLACKED | BLAHED |
| BIRKIE | BISK | BITTOR | BLACKEN | BLAHING |
| BIRKIES | BISKS | BITTORS | BLACKENED | BLAHS |
| BIRKS | BISMAR | BITTOUR | BLACKENING | BLAIN |
| BIRL | BISMARS | BITTOURS | BLACKENS | BLAINS |
| BIRLE | BISMILLAH | BITTS | BLACKER | BLAISE |
| BIRLED | BISMUTH | BITTUR | BLACKEST | BLAIZE |
| BIRLER | BISMUTHS | BITTURS | BLACKFISH | BLAMABLE |
| BIRLERS | BISON | BITTY | BLACKFISHES | BLAMABLY |
| BIRLES | BISONS | BITUMED | BLACKGAME | BLAME |
| BIRLIEMAN | BISQUE | BITUMEN | BLACKGAMES | BLAMEABLE |
| BIRLIEMEN | BISQUES | BITUMENS | BLACKHEAD | BLAMEABLY |
| BIRLING | BISSON | BIVALENCE | BLACKHEADS | BLAMED |
| BIRLINGS | BISTABLE | BIVALENCES | BLACKING | BLAMEFUL |
| BIRLINN | BISTER | BIVALENCIES | BLACKINGS | BLAMELESS |
| BIRLINNS | BISTERS | BIVALENCY | BLACKISH | BLAMES |
| BIRLS | BISTORT | BIVALENT | BLACKJACK | BLAMING |
| BIRR | BISTORTS | BIVALENTS | BLACKJACKS | BLANCH |
| BIRRS | BISTOURIES | BIVALVE | BLACKLEAD | BLANCHED |
| BIRSE | BISTOURY | BIVALVES | BLACKLEADS | BLANCHES |
| BIRSES | BISTRE | BIVARIANT | BLACKLEG | BLANCHING |
| BIRSIER | BISTRED | BIVARIANTS | BLACKLEGGED | BLANCO |
| BIRSIEST | BISTRES | BIVARIATE | BLACKLEGGING | BLANCOED |
| BIRSLE | BISTRO | BIVARIATES | BLACKLEGS | BLANCOING |
| BIRSLED | BISTROS | BIVIOUS | BLACKLIST | BLANCOS |
| BIRSLES | BISULCATE | BIVIUM | BLACKLISTED | BLAND |
| BIRSLING | BIT | BIVIUMS | BLACKLISTING | BLANDER |
| BIRSY | BITCH | BIVOUAC | BLACKLISTINGS | BLANDEST |
| BIRTH | BITCHED | BIVOUACKED | BLACKLISTS | BLANDISH |
| BIRTHDAY | BITCHERIES | BIVOUACKING | BLACKMAIL | BLANDISHED |
| BIRTHDAYS | BITCHERY | BIVOUACS | BLACKMAILED | BLANDISHES |
| BIRTHDOM | BITCHES | BIVVIED | BLACKMAILING | BLANDISHING |
| BIRTHDOMS | BITCHIER | BIVVIES | BLACKMAILS | BLANDLY |
| BIRTHMARK | BITCHIEST | BIVVY | BLACKNESS | BLANDNESS |
| BIRTHMARKS | BITCHILY | BIVVYING | BLACKNESSES | BLANDNESSES |
| BIRTHS | BITCHING | BIZ | BLACKOUT | BLANDS |
| BIRTHWORT | BITCHY | BIZARRE | BLACKOUTS | BLANK |
| BIRTHWORTS | BITE | BIZAZZ | BLACKS | BLANKED |
| BIRYANI | BITER | BIZAZZES | BLACKTOP | BLANKER |
| BIRYANIS | BITERS | BIZCACHA | BLACKTOPS | BLANKEST |
| BIS | BITES | BIZCACHAS | BLACKWASH | BLANKET |
| BISCACHA | BITING | BIZONAL | BLACKWASHES | BLANKETED |
| BISCACHAS | BITINGS | BIZONE | BLACKWOOD | BLANKETIES |
| BISCUIT | BITO | BIZONES | BLACKWOODS | BLANKETING |
| BISCUITS | BITONAL | BIZZES | BLAD | BLANKETINGS |
| BISCUITY | BITOS | BLAB | BLADDED | BLANKETS |
| BISE | BITS | BLABBED | BLADDER | BLANKETY |
| BISECT | BITSIER | BLABBER | BLADDERED | BLANKIES |
| BISECTED | BITSIEST | BLABBERS | BLADDERS | BLANKING |
| BISECTING | BITSY | BLABBING | BLADDERY | BLANKINGS |
| BISECTION | BITT | BLABBINGS | BLADDING | BLANKLY |
| BISECTIONS | BITTACLE | BLABS | BLADE | BLANKNESS |
| BISECTOR | BITTACLES | BLACK | BLADED | BLANKNESSES |
| BISECTORS | BITTE | BLACKBALL | BLADES | BLANKS |
| BISECTS | BITTED | BLACKBALLED | BLADS | BLANKY |
| BISERIAL | BITTEN | BLACKBALLING | BLAE | BLANQUET |
| BISERRATE | BITTER | BLACKBALLINGS | BLAEBERRIES | BLANQUETS |
| BISES | BITTERER | BLACKBALLS | BLAEBERRY | BLARE |
| BISEXUAL | BITTEREST | BLACKBAND | BLAER | BLARED |
| BISH | BITTERISH | BLACKBANDS | BLAES | BLARES |

BLARING
BLARNEY
BLARNEYED
BLARNEYING
BLARNEYS
BLASÉ
BLASH
BLASHES
BLASHIER
BLASHIEST
BLASHY
BLASPHEME
BLASPHEMED
BLASPHEMES
BLASPHEMIES
BLASPHEMING
BLASPHEMY
BLAST
BLASTED
BLASTEMA
BLASTEMAS
BLASTER
BLASTERS
BLASTING
BLASTINGS
BLASTMENT
BLASTMENTS
BLASTOID
BLASTOIDS
BLASTS
BLASTULA
BLASTULAE
BLASTULAR
BLASTULAS
BLAT
BLATANT
BLATANTLY
BLATE
BLATER
BLATEST
BLATHER
BLATHERED
BLATHERING
BLATHERS
BLATS
BLATT
BLATTANT
BLATTED
BLATTER
BLATTERED
BLATTERING
BLATTERS
BLATTING
BLATTS
BLAUBOK
BLAUBOKS
BLAUD
BLAUDED
BLAUDING
BLAUDS
BLAWORT
BLAWORTS
BLAY
BLAYS
BLAZE
BLAZED
BLAZER
BLAZERS
BLAZES
BLAZING

BLAZON
BLAZONED
BLAZONER
BLAZONERS
BLAZONING
BLAZONRIES
BLAZONRY
BLAZONS
BLEACH
BLEACHED
BLEACHER
BLEACHERIES
BLEACHERS
BLEACHERY
BLEACHES
BLEACHING
BLEACHINGS
BLEAK
BLEAKER
BLEAKEST
BLEAKIER
BLEAKIEST
BLEAKLY
BLEAKNESS
BLEAKNESSES
BLEAKS
BLEAKY
BLEAR
BLEARED
BLEARER
BLEAREST
BLEAREYED
BLEARIER
BLEARIEST
BLEARING
BLEARS
BLEARY
BLEAT
BLEATED
BLEATER
BLEATERS
BLEATING
BLEATINGS
BLEATS
BLEB
BLEBS
BLED
BLEE
BLEED
BLEEDER
BLEEDERS
BLEEDING
BLEEDINGS
BLEEDS
BLEEP
BLEEPED
BLEEPER
BLEEPERS
BLEEPING
BLEEPS
BLEES
BLEMISH
BLEMISHED
BLEMISHES
BLEMISHING
BLENCH
BLENCHED
BLENCHES
BLENCHING
BLEND

BLENDE
BLENDED
BLENDER
BLENDERS
BLENDES
BLENDING
BLENDINGS
BLENDS
BLENNIES
BLENNY
BLENT
BLESBOK
BLESBOKS
BLESS
BLESSED
BLESSEDER
BLESSEDEST
BLESSEDLY
BLESSES
BLESSING
BLESSINGS
BLEST
BLET
BLETHER
BLETHERED
BLETHERING
BLETHERINGS
BLETHERS
BLETS
BLETTED
BLETTING
BLEUÂTRE
BLEW
BLEWART
BLEWARTS
BLEWITS
BLEWITSES
BLEY
BLEYS
BLIGHT
BLIGHTED
BLIGHTER
BLIGHTERS
BLIGHTIES
BLIGHTING
BLIGHTINGS
BLIGHTS
BLIGHTY
BLIMBING
BLIMBINGS
BLIMEY
BLIMP
BLIMPISH
BLIMPS
BLIMY
BLIN
BLIND
BLINDAGE
BLINDAGES
BLINDED
BLINDER
BLINDERS
BLINDEST
BLINDFISH
BLINDFISHES
BLINDFOLD
BLINDFOLDED
BLINDFOLDING
BLINDFOLDS
BLINDING

BLINDINGS
BLINDLESS
BLINDLY
BLINDNESS
BLINDNESSES
BLINDS
BLINDWORM
BLINDWORMS
BLINI
BLINIS
BLINK
BLINKARD
BLINKARDS
BLINKED
BLINKER
BLINKERED
BLINKERING
BLINKERS
BLINKING
BLINKS
BLINNED
BLINNING
BLINS
BLINTZ
BLINTZE
BLINTZES
BLIP
BLIPPED
BLIPPING
BLIPS
BLISS
BLISSES
BLISSFUL
BLISSLESS
BLIST
BLISTER
BLISTERED
BLISTERING
BLISTERS
BLISTERY
BLITE
BLITES
BLITHE
BLITHELY
BLITHER
BLITHERED
BLITHERING
BLITHERS
BLITHEST
BLITZ
BLITZED
BLITZES
BLITZING
BLIVE
BLIZZARD
BLIZZARDS
BLOAT
BLOATED
BLOATER
BLOATERS
BLOATING
BLOATINGS
BLOATS
BLOB
BLOBBED
BLOBBING
BLOBS
BLOC
BLOCK
BLOCKADE

BLOCKADED
BLOCKADES
BLOCKADING
BLOCKAGE
BLOCKAGES
BLOCKED
BLOCKER
BLOCKERS
BLOCKHEAD
BLOCKHEADS
BLOCKHOLE
BLOCKHOLES
BLOCKIER
BLOCKIEST
BLOCKING
BLOCKINGS
BLOCKISH
BLOCKS
BLOCKWORK
BLOCKWORKS
BLOCKY
BLOCS
BLOKE
BLOKES
BLONCKET
BLOND
BLONDE
BLONDER
BLONDES
BLONDEST
BLONDS
BLOOD
BLOODED
BLOODHEAT
BLOODHEATS
BLOODIED
BLOODIER
BLOODIES
BLOODIEST
BLOODILY
BLOODING
BLOODLESS
BLOODLUST
BLOODLUSTS
BLOODROOT
BLOODROOTS
BLOODS
BLOODSHED
BLOODSHEDS
BLOODSHOT
BLOODWOOD
BLOODWOODS
BLOODY
BLOODYING
BLOOM
BLOOMED
BLOOMER
BLOOMERIES
BLOOMERS
BLOOMERY
BLOOMIER
BLOOMIEST
BLOOMING
BLOOMLESS
BLOOMS
BLOOMY
BLOOP
BLOOPED
BLOOPER
BLOOPERS

| | | | | |
|---|---|---|---|---|
| BLOOPING | BLOWSES | BLUEPRINTED | BLURB | BOATBILLS |
| BLOOPS | BLOWSIER | BLUEPRINTING | BLURBS | BOATED |
| BLOOSME | BLOWSIEST | BLUEPRINTS | BLURRED | BOATEL |
| BLOOSMED | BLOWSY | BLUER | BLURRING | BOATELS |
| BLOOSMES | BLOWTORCH | BLUES | BLURS | BOATER |
| BLOOSMING | BLOWTORCHES | BLUESIER | BLURT | BOATERS |
| BLORE | BLOWY | BLUESIEST | BLURTED | BOATHOUSE |
| BLORES | BLOWZE | BLUEST | BLURTING | BOATHOUSES |
| BLOSSOM | BLOWZED | BLUESTONE | BLURTINGS | BOATING |
| BLOSSOMED | BLOWZES | BLUESTONES | BLURTS | BOATINGS |
| BLOSSOMING | BLOWZIER | BLUESY | BLUSH | BOATMAN |
| BLOSSOMINGS | BLOWZIEST | BLUETTE | BLUSHED | BOATMEN |
| BLOSSOMS | BLOWZY | BLUETTES | BLUSHER | BOATRACE |
| BLOSSOMY | BLUB | BLUEWEED | BLUSHERS | BOATRACES |
| BLOT | BLUBBED | BLUEWEEDS | BLUSHES | BOATS |
| BLOTCH | BLUBBER | BLUEWING | BLUSHET | BOATSWAIN |
| BLOTCHED | BLUBBERED | BLUEWINGS | BLUSHETS | BOATSWAINS |
| BLOTCHES | BLUBBERING | BLUEY | BLUSHFUL | BOATTAIL |
| BLOTCHIER | BLUBBERS | BLUEYS | BLUSHING | BOATTAILS |
| BLOTCHIEST | BLUBBING | BLUFF | BLUSHINGS | BOB |
| BLOTCHING | BLUBS | BLUFFED | BLUSHLESS | BOBA |
| BLOTCHINGS | BLUCHER | BLUFFER | BLUSTER | BOBAC |
| BLOTCHY | BLUCHERS | BLUFFERS | BLUSTERED | BOBACS |
| BLOTS | BLUDE | BLUFFEST | BLUSTERER | BOBAK |
| BLOTTED | BLUDES | BLUFFING | BLUSTERERS | BOBAKS |
| BLOTTER | BLUDGE | BLUFFLY | BLUSTERIER | BOBAS |
| BLOTTERS | BLUDGED | BLUFFNESS | BLUSTERIEST | BOBBED |
| BLOTTIER | BLUDGEON | BLUFFNESSES | BLUSTERING | BOBBERIES |
| BLOTTIEST | BLUDGEONED | BLUFFS | BLUSTERINGS | BOBBERY |
| BLOTTING | BLUDGEONING | BLUGGY | BLUSTERS | BOBBIES |
| BLOTTINGS | BLUDGEONS | BLUID | BLUSTERY | BOBBIN |
| BLOTTO | BLUDGER | BLUIDIER | BLUSTROUS | BOBBINET |
| BLOTTY | BLUDGERS | BLUIDIEST | BLUTWURST | BOBBINETS |
| BLOUBOK | BLUDGES | BLUIDS | BLUTWURSTS | BOBBING |
| BLOUBOKS | BLUDGING | BLUIDY | BO | BOBBINS |
| BLOUSE | BLUDIE | BLUIER | BOA | BOBBISH |
| BLOUSED | BLUDIER | BLUIEST | BOAK | BOBBLE |
| BLOUSES | BLUDIEST | BLUING | BOAKED | BOBBLED |
| BLOUSING | BLUDY | BLUINGS | BOAKING | BOBBLES |
| BLOUSON | BLUE | BLUISH | BOAKS | BOBBLING |
| BLOUSONS | BLUEBACK | BLUNDER | BOAR | BOBBY |
| BLOW | BLUEBACKS | BLUNDERED | BOARD | BOBBYSOCK |
| BLOWBALL | BLUEBEARD | BLUNDERER | BOARDED | BOBBYSOCKS |
| BLOWBALLS | BLUEBEARDS | BLUNDERERS | BOARDER | BOBCAT |
| BLOWDOWN | BLUEBELL | BLUNDERING | BOARDERS | BOBCATS |
| BLOWDOWNS | BLUEBELLS | BLUNDERINGS | BOARDING | BOBOLINK |
| BLOWED | BLUEBERRIES | BLUNDERS | BOARDINGS | BOBOLINKS |
| BLOWER | BLUEBERRY | BLUNGE | BOARDROOM | BOBS |
| BLOWERS | BLUEBIRD | BLUNGED | BOARDROOMS | BOBSLED |
| BLOWFLIES | BLUEBIRDS | BLUNGER | BOARDS | BOBSLEDS |
| BLOWFLY | BLUEBUCK | BLUNGERS | BOARDWALK | BOBSLEIGH |
| BLOWGUN | BLUEBUCKS | BLUNGES | BOARDWALKS | BOBSLEIGHS |
| BLOWGUNS | BLUECAP | BLUNGING | BOARFISH | BOBSTAYS |
| BLOWHARD | BLUECAPS | BLUNK | BOARFISHES | BOBTAIL |
| BLOWHARDS | BLUECOAT | BLUNKED | BOARISH | BOBTAILED |
| BLOWHOLE | BLUECOATS | BLUNKER | BOARS | BOBTAILING |
| BLOWHOLES | BLUED | BLUNKERS | BOART | BOBTAILS |
| BLOWIE | BLUEFISH | BLUNKING | BOARTS | BOBWHEEL |
| BLOWIER | BLUEFISHES | BLUNKS | BOAS | BOBWHEELS |
| BLOWIES | BLUEGOWN | BLUNT | BOAST | BOBWIG |
| BLOWIEST | BLUEGOWNS | BLUNTED | BOASTED | BOBWIGS |
| BLOWING | BLUEGRASS | BLUNTER | BOASTER | BOCAGE |
| BLOWLAMP | BLUEGRASSES | BLUNTEST | BOASTERS | BOCAGES |
| BLOWLAMPS | BLUEING | BLUNTING | BOASTFUL | BOCCA |
| BLOWN | BLUEINGS | BLUNTISH | BOASTING | BOCCAS |
| BLOWPIPE | BLUENESS | BLUNTLY | BOASTINGS | BOCHE |
| BLOWPIPES | BLUENESSES | BLUNTNESS | BOASTLESS | BOCHES |
| BLOWS | BLUENOSE | BLUNTNESSES | BOASTS | BOCK |
| BLOWSE | BLUENOSES | BLUNTS | BOAT | BOCKED |
| BLOWSED | BLUEPRINT | BLUR | BOATBILL | BOCKING |

BOCKS
BOD
BODACH
BODACHS
BODDLE
BODDLES
BODE
BODED
BODEFUL
BODEGA
BODEGAS
BODEGUERO
BODEGUEROS
BODEMENT
BODEMENTS
BODES
BODGE
BODGED
BODGER
BODGERS
BODGES
BODGIE
BODGIES
BODGING
BODICE
BODICES
BODIED
BODIES
BODIKIN
BODIKINS
BODILESS
BODILY
BODING
BODINGS
BODKIN
BODKINS
BODLE
BODLES
BODRAG
BODRAGS
BODS
BODY
BODYGUARD
BODYGUARDS
BODYING
BODYLINE
BODYLINES
BODYSHELL
BODYSHELLS
BODYWORK
BODYWORKS
BOEREWORS
BOEREWORSES
BOFF
BOFFED
BOFFIN
BOFFING
BOFFINS
BOFFS
BOG
BOGAN
BOGANS
BOGBEAN
BOGBEANS
BOGEY
BOGEYISM
BOGEYISMS
BOGEYS
BOGGARD
BOGGARDS

BOGGART
BOGGARTS
BOGGED
BOGGIER
BOGGIEST
BOGGINESS
BOGGINESSES
BOGGING
BOGGLE
BOGGLED
BOGGLER
BOGGLERS
BOGGLES
BOGGLING
BOGGY
BOGIE
BOGIES
BOGLAND
BOGLANDS
BOGLE
BOGLES
BOGOAK
BOGOAKS
BOGONG
BOGONGS
BOGS
BOGUS
BOGY
BOGYISM
BOGYISMS
BOH
BOHEA
BOHEAS
BOHUNK
BOHUNKS
BOIL
BOILED
BOILER
BOILERIES
BOILERS
BOILERY
BOILING
BOILINGS
BOILS
BOING
BOINGED
BOINGING
BOINGS
BOINK
BOINKED
BOINKING
BOINKS
BOK
BOKE
BOKED
BOKES
BOKING
BOKO
BOKOS
BOKS
BOLAS
BOLASES
BOLD
BOLDEN
BOLDENED
BOLDENING
BOLDENS
BOLDER
BOLDEST
BOLDLY

BOLDNESS
BOLDNESSES
BOLE
BOLECTION
BOLECTIONS
BOLERO
BOLEROS
BOLES
BOLETI
BOLETUS
BOLETUSES
BOLIDE
BOLIDES
BOLIVAR
BOLIVARES
BOLIVARS
BOLIVIANO
BOLIVIANOS
BOLIX
BOLIXES
BOLL
BOLLARD
BOLLARDS
BOLLED
BOLLEN
BOLLETRIE
BOLLETRIES
BOLLING
BOLLIX
BOLLIXES
BOLLOCK
BOLLOCKED
BOLLOCKING
BOLLOCKINGS
BOLLOCKS
BOLLOCKSED
BOLLOCKSES
BOLLOCKSING
BOLLS
BOLO
BOLOMETER
BOLOMETERS
BOLOMETRIES
BOLOMETRY
BOLONEY
BOLONEYS
BOLOS
BOLSHEVIK
BOLSHEVIKS
BOLSHIE
BOLSHIER
BOLSHIES
BOLSHIEST
BOLSHY
BOLSTER
BOLSTERED
BOLSTERING
BOLSTERINGS
BOLSTERS
BOLT
BOLTED
BOLTER
BOLTERS
BOLTHEAD
BOLTHEADS
BOLTHOLE
BOLTHOLES
BOLTING
BOLTINGS
BOLTS

BOLUS
BOLUSES
BOMA
BOMAS
BOMB
BOMBARD
BOMBARDED
BOMBARDING
BOMBARDON
BOMBARDONS
BOMBARDS
BOMBASINE
BOMBASINES
BOMBAST
BOMBASTED
BOMBASTIC
BOMBASTING
BOMBASTS
BOMBAX
BOMBAXES
BOMBAZINE
BOMBAZINES
BOMBE
BOMBÉ
BOMBED
BOMBER
BOMBERS
BOMBES
BOMBILATE
BOMBILATED
BOMBILATES
BOMBILATING
BOMBINATE
BOMBINATED
BOMBINATES
BOMBINATING
BOMBING
BOMBO
BOMBORA
BOMBORAS
BOMBOS
BOMBS
BOMBSHELL
BOMBSHELLS
BOMBSITE
BOMBSITES
BOMBYCID
BOMBYCIDS
BON
BONA
BONAMANI
BONAMANO
BONANZA
BONANZAS
BONASSUS
BONASSUSES
BONASUS
BONASUSES
BONBON
BONBONS
BONCE
BONCES
BOND
BONDAGE
BONDAGER
BONDAGERS
BONDAGES
BONDED
BONDER
BONDERS

BONDING
BONDINGS
BONDMAID
BONDMAIDS
BONDMAN
BONDMEN
BONDS
BONDSMAN
BONDSMEN
BONDSTONE
BONDSTONES
BONDUC
BONDUCS
BONE
BONED
BONEHEAD
BONEHEADS
BONELESS
BONER
BONERS
BONES
BONESET
BONESETS
BONEYARD
BONEYARDS
BONFIRE
BONFIRES
BONG
BONGED
BONGING
BONGO
BONGOS
BONGRACE
BONGRACES
BONGS
BONHOMIE
BONHOMIES
BONHOMMIE
BONHOMMIES
BONHOMOUS
BONIBELL
BONIBELLS
BONIE
BONIER
BONIEST
BONIFACE
BONIFACES
BONILASSE
BONILASSES
BONINESS
BONINESSES
BONING
BONINGS
BONISM
BONISMS
BONIST
BONISTS
BONITO
BONITOS
BONJOUR
BONK
BONKED
BONKERS
BONKING
BONKS
BONNE
BONNES
BONNET
BONNETED
BONNETING

BONNETS
BONNIBELL
BONNIBELLS
BONNIE
BONNIER
BONNIES
BONNIEST
BONNILY
BONNINESS
BONNINESSES
BONNY
BONSAI
BONSAIS
BONSOIR
BONSPIEL
BONSPIELS
BONTEBOK
BONTEBOKS
BONUS
BONUSES
BONXIE
BONXIES
BONY
BONZE
BONZER
BONZES
BOO
BOOB
BOOBED
BOOBIES
BOOBING
BOOBOO
BOOBOOK
BOOBOOKS
BOOBOOS
BOOBS
BOOBY
BOOBYISH
BOOBYISM
BOOBYISMS
BOODIE
BOODIED
BOODIES
BOODLE
BOODLES
BOODY
BOODYING
BOOED
BOOGIE
BOOGIED
BOOGIEING
BOOGIES
BOOH
BOOHED
BOOHING
BOOHS
BOOING
BOOK
BOOKABLE
BOOKCASE
BOOKCASES
BOOKED
BOOKFUL
BOOKIE
BOOKIER
BOOKIES
BOOKIEST
BOOKING
BOOKINGS
BOOKISH

BOOKLAND
BOOKLANDS
BOOKLESS
BOOKLET
BOOKLETS
BOOKLICE
BOOKLORE
BOOKLORES
BOOKLOUSE
BOOKMAKER
BOOKMAKERS
BOOKMAN
BOOKMARK
BOOKMARKS
BOOKMEN
BOOKPLATE
BOOKPLATES
BOOKREST
BOOKRESTS
BOOKS
BOOKSHELF
BOOKSHELVES
BOOKSHOP
BOOKSHOPS
BOOKSIE
BOOKSIER
BOOKSIEST
BOOKSTALL
BOOKSTALLS
BOOKSTAND
BOOKSTANDS
BOOKSTORE
BOOKSTORES
BOOKSY
BOOKWORK
BOOKWORKS
BOOKWORM
BOOKWORMS
BOOKY
BOOM
BOOMED
BOOMER
BOOMERANG
BOOMERANGED
BOOMERANGING
BOOMERANGS
BOOMERS
BOOMING
BOOMINGS
BOOMS
BOOMSLANG
BOOMSLANGS
BOON
BOONDOCKS
BOONG
BOONGS
BOONIES
BOONS
BOOR
BOORD
BOORDE
BOORDES
BOORDS
BOORISH
BOORISHLY
BOORS
BOORTREE
BOORTREES
BOOS
BOOSE

BOOSED
BOOSES
BOOSING
BOOST
BOOSTED
BOOSTER
BOOSTERS
BOOSTING
BOOSTS
BOOT
BOOTBLACK
BOOTBLACKS
BOOTED
BOOTEE
BOOTEES
BOOTH
BOOTHOSE
BOOTHS
BOOTIES
BOOTIKIN
BOOTIKINS
BOOTING
BOOTLACE
BOOTLACES
BOOTLAST
BOOTLASTS
BOOTLEG
BOOTLEGGED
BOOTLEGGING
BOOTLEGGINGS
BOOTLEGS
BOOTLESS
BOOTLICK
BOOTLICKED
BOOTLICKING
BOOTLICKINGS
BOOTLICKS
BOOTMAKER
BOOTMAKERS
BOOTS
BOOTTREE
BOOTTREES
BOOTY
BOOZE
BOOZED
BOOZER
BOOZERS
BOOZES
BOOZEY
BOOZIER
BOOZIEST
BOOZILY
BOOZING
BOOZY
BOP
BOPPED
BOPPER
BOPPERS
BOPPING
BOPS
BOR
BORA
BORACHIO
BORACHIOS
BORACIC
BORACITE
BORACITES
BORAGE
BORAGES
BORANE

BORANES
BORAS
BORATE
BORATES
BORAX
BORAXES
BORAZON
BORAZONS
BORD
BORDAR
BORDARS
BORDE
BORDEL
BORDELLO
BORDELLOS
BORDELS
BORDER
BORDEREAU
BORDEREAUX
BORDERED
BORDERER
BORDERERS
BORDERING
BORDERS
BORDES
BORDS
BORDURE
BORDURES
BORE
BOREAL
BORECOLE
BORECOLES
BORED
BOREDOM
BOREDOMS
BOREE
BOREEN
BOREENS
BOREES
BOREHOLE
BOREHOLES
BOREL
BORER
BORERS
BORES
BORGHETTO
BORGHETTOS
BORGO
BORGOS
BORIC
BORIDE
BORIDES
BORING
BORINGS
BORN
BORNE
BORNÉ
BORNITE
BORNITES
BORON
BORONIA
BORONIAS
BORONS
BOROUGH
BOROUGHS
BORREL
BORRELL
BORROW
BORROWED
BORROWER

BORROWERS
BORROWING
BORROWINGS
BORROWS
BORS
BORSCH
BORSCHES
BORSCHT
BORSCHTS
BORSTAL
BORSTALL
BORSTALLS
BORSTALS
BORT
BORTS
BORTSCH
BORTSCHES
BORTSCHT
BORTSCHTS
BORZOI
BORZOIS
BOS
BOSBOK
BOSBOKS
BOSCAGE
BOSCAGES
BOSCHBOK
BOSCHBOKS
BOSCHE
BOSCHES
BOSCHVELD
BOSCHVELDS
BOSH
BOSHES
BOSHTA
BOSHTER
BOSK
BOSKER
BOSKET
BOSKETS
BOSKIER
BOSKIEST
BOSKINESS
BOSKINESSES
BOSKS
BOSKY
BOSOM
BOSOMED
BOSOMING
BOSOMS
BOSOMY
BOSON
BOSONS
BOSS
BOSSED
BOSSER
BOSSES
BOSSEST
BOSSIER
BOSSIEST
BOSSILY
BOSSINESS
BOSSINESSES
BOSSING
BOSSY
BOSTANGI
BOSTANGIS
BOSTON
BOSTONS
BOSTRYX

BOSTRYXES
BOSUN
BOSUNS
BOT
BOTANIC
BOTANICAL
BOTANICALS
BOTANIES
BOTANISE
BOTANISED
BOTANISES
BOTANISING
BOTANIST
BOTANISTS
BOTANIZE
BOTANIZED
BOTANIZES
BOTANIZING
BOTANY
BOTARGO
BOTARGOES
BOTARGOS
BOTCH
BOTCHED
BOTCHER
BOTCHERIES
BOTCHERS
BOTCHERY
BOTCHES
BOTCHIER
BOTCHIEST
BOTCHING
BOTCHINGS
BOTCHY
BOTEL
BOTELS
BOTFLIES
BOTFLY
BOTH
BOTHAN
BOTHANS
BOTHER
BOTHERED
BOTHERING
BOTHERS
BOTHIE
BOTHIES
BOTHOLE
BOTHOLES
BOTHY
BOTHYMAN
BOTHYMEN
BOTONÉ
BOTRYOID
BOTRYOSE
BOTS
BOTT
BOTTE
BOTTED
BOTTEGA
BOTTEGAS
BOTTES
BOTTIES
BOTTINE
BOTTINES
BOTTING
BOTTLE
BOTTLED
BOTTLEFUL
BOTTLEFULS

BOTTLER
BOTTLERS
BOTTLES
BOTTLING
BOTTOM
BOTTOMED
BOTTOMING
BOTTOMS
BOTTONY
BOTTS
BOTTY
BOTULISM
BOTULISMS
BOUCHE
BOUCHÉ
BOUCHÉE
BOUCHÉES
BOUCHES
BOUCHÉS
BOUCLÉ
BOUCLÉS
BOUDERIE
BOUDERIES
BOUDOIR
BOUDOIRS
BOUFFANT
BOUGE
BOUGED
BOUGES
BOUGET
BOUGETS
BOUGH
BOUGHPOT
BOUGHPOTS
BOUGHS
BOUGHT
BOUGHTEN
BOUGHTS
BOUGIE
BOUGIES
BOUGING
BOUILLI
BOUILLIS
BOUILLON
BOUILLONS
BOUK
BOUKS
BOULDER
BOULDERS
BOULE
BOULES
BOULEVARD
BOULEVARDS
BOULLE
BOULLES
BOULT
BOULTED
BOULTER
BOULTERS
BOULTING
BOULTINGS
BOULTS
BOUN
BOUNCE
BOUNCED
BOUNCER
BOUNCERS
BOUNCES
BOUNCIER
BOUNCIEST

BOUNCILY
BOUNCING
BOUNCY
BOUND
BOUNDARIES
BOUNDARY
BOUNDED
BOUNDEN
BOUNDER
BOUNDERS
BOUNDING
BOUNDLESS
BOUNDS
BOUNED
BOUNING
BOUNS
BOUNTEOUS
BOUNTIES
BOUNTIFUL
BOUNTREE
BOUNTREES
BOUNTY
BOUNTYHED
BOUNTYHEDS
BOUQUET
BOUQUETS
BOURASQUE
BOURASQUES
BOURBON
BOURBONS
BOURD
BOURDER
BOURDERS
BOURDON
BOURDONS
BOURDS
BOURG
BOURGEOIS
BOURGEOISES
BOURGEON
BOURGEONED
BOURGEONING
BOURGEONS
BOURGS
BOURKHA
BOURKHAS
BOURLAW
BOURLAWS
BOURN
BOURNE
BOURNES
BOURNS
BOURREE
BOURREES
BOURSE
BOURSES
BOURSIER
BOURSIERS
BOURTREE
BOURTREES
BOUSE
BOUSED
BOUSES
BOUSIER
BOUSIEST
BOUSING
BOUSY
BOUT
BOUTADE
BOUTADES

BOUTIQUE
BOUTIQUES
BOUTON
BOUTONNÉ
BOUTONNÉE
BOUTONS
BOUTS
BOUZOUKI
BOUZOUKIS
BOVATE
BOVATES
BOVINE
BOVVER
BOVVERS
BOW
BOWAT
BOWATS
BOWBENT
BOWED
BOWEL
BOWELLED
BOWELLING
BOWELS
BOWER
BOWERED
BOWERIES
BOWERING
BOWERS
BOWERY
BOWES
BOWET
BOWETS
BOWFIN
BOWFINS
BOWGET
BOWGETS
BOWHEAD
BOWHEADS
BOWING
BOWL
BOWLDER
BOWLDERS
BOWLED
BOWLER
BOWLERED
BOWLERING
BOWLERS
BOWLINE
BOWLINES
BOWLING
BOWLINGS
BOWLS
BOWMAN
BOWMEN
BOWNE
BOWNED
BOWNES
BOWNING
BOWPOT
BOWPOTS
BOWR
BOWRS
BOWS
BOWSE
BOWSED
BOWSER
BOWSERS
BOWSES
BOWSHOT
BOWSHOTS

BOWSING
BOWSPRIT
BOWSPRITS
BOWSTRING
BOWSTRINGED
BOWSTRINGING
BOWSTRINGS
BOWSTRUNG
BOWWOW
BOWWOWS
BOWYER
BOWYERS
BOX
BOXCAR
BOXCARS
BOXED
BOXEN
BOXER
BOXERS
BOXES
BOXFUL
BOXFULS
BOXIER
BOXIEST
BOXINESS
BOXINESSES
BOXING
BOXINGS
BOXKEEPER
BOXKEEPERS
BOXROOM
BOXROOMS
BOXWALLAH
BOXWALLAHS
BOXWOOD
BOXWOODS
BOXY
BOY
BOYAR
BOYARS
BOYAU
BOYAUX
BOYCOTT
BOYCOTTED
BOYCOTTING
BOYCOTTS
BOYED
BOYFRIEND
BOYFRIENDS
BOYG
BOYGS
BOYHOOD
BOYHOODS
BOYING
BOYISH
BOYISHLY
BOYO
BOYOS
BOYS
BOZZETTI
BOZZETTO
BRA
BRABBLE
BRABBLED
BRABBLES
BRABBLING
BRACCATE
BRACCIA
BRACCIO
BRACE

BRACED
BRACELET
BRACELETS
BRACER
BRACERS
BRACES
BRACH
BRACHES
BRACHET
BRACHETS
BRACHIAL
BRACING
BRACK
BRACKEN
BRACKENS
BRACKET
BRACKETED
BRACKETING
BRACKETS
BRACKISH
BRACKS
BRACT
BRACTEAL
BRACTEATE
BRACTEATES
BRACTEOLE
BRACTEOLES
BRACTLESS
BRACTLET
BRACTLETS
BRACTS
BRAD
BRADAWL
BRADAWLS
BRADS
BRAE
BRAES
BRAG
BRAGGART
BRAGGARTS
BRAGGED
BRAGGING
BRAGLY
BRAGS
BRAID
BRAIDE
BRAIDED
BRAIDER
BRAIDEST
BRAIDING
BRAIDINGS
BRAIDS
BRAIL
BRAILED
BRAILING
BRAILS
BRAIN
BRAINCASE
BRAINCASES
BRAINED
BRAINIER
BRAINIEST
BRAINING
BRAINISH
BRAINLESS
BRAINPAN
BRAINPANS
BRAINS
BRAINSICK
BRAINWASH

BRAINWASHED
BRAINWASHES
BRAINWASHING
BRAINWASHINGS
BRAINY
BRAIRD
BRAIRDED
BRAIRDING
BRAIRDS
BRAISE
BRAISED
BRAISES
BRAISING
BRAIZE
BRAIZES
BRAKE
BRAKED
BRAKELESS
BRAKEMAN
BRAKEMEN
BRAKES
BRAKIER
BRAKIEST
BRAKING
BRAKY
BRALESS
BRAMBLE
BRAMBLES
BRAMBLIER
BRAMBLIEST
BRAMBLING
BRAMBLINGS
BRAMBLY
BRAME
BRAMES
BRAN
BRANCARD
BRANCARDS
BRANCH
BRANCHED
BRANCHER
BRANCHERIES
BRANCHERS
BRANCHERY
BRANCHES
BRANCHIA
BRANCHIAE
BRANCHIAL
BRANCHIER
BRANCHIEST
BRANCHING
BRANCHINGS
BRANCHLET
BRANCHLETS
BRANCHY
BRAND
BRANDADE
BRANDADES
BRANDED
BRANDER
BRANDERED
BRANDERING
BRANDERS
BRANDIED
BRANDIES
BRANDING
BRANDISE
BRANDISES
BRANDISH
BRANDISHED

BRANDISHES
BRANDISHING
BRANDLING
BRANDLINGS
BRANDRETH
BRANDRETHS
BRANDS
BRANDY
BRANGLE
BRANGLED
BRANGLES
BRANGLING
BRANGLINGS
BRANK
BRANKED
BRANKIER
BRANKIEST
BRANKING
BRANKS
BRANKY
BRANLE
BRANLES
BRANNIER
BRANNIEST
BRANNY
BRANS
BRANSLE
BRANSLES
BRANTLE
BRANTLES
BRAS
BRASERO
BRASEROS
BRASES
BRASH
BRASHED
BRASHER
BRASHES
BRASHEST
BRASHIER
BRASHIEST
BRASHING
BRASHY
BRASIER
BRASIERS
BRASS
BRASSARD
BRASSARDS
BRASSART
BRASSARTS
BRASSERIE
BRASSERIES
BRASSES
BRASSET
BRASSETS
BRASSICA
BRASSICAS
BRASSIE
BRASSIER
BRASSIÈRE
BRASSIÈRES
BRASSIES
BRASSIEST
BRASSILY
BRASSY
BRAST
BRASTING
BRASTS
BRAT
BRATCHET

BRATCHETS
BRATLING
BRATLINGS
BRATS
BRATTICE
BRATTICED
BRATTICES
BRATTICING
BRATTICINGS
BRATTIER
BRATTIEST
BRATTISH
BRATTISHED
BRATTISHES
BRATTISHING
BRATTISHINGS
BRATTLE
BRATTLED
BRATTLES
BRATTLING
BRATTLINGS
BRATTY
BRATWURST
BRATWURSTS
BRAUNCH
BRAUNCHED
BRAUNCHES
BRAUNCHING
BRAVA
BRAVADO
BRAVADOED
BRAVADOES
BRAVADOING
BRAVADOS
BRAVE
BRAVED
BRAVELY
BRAVER
BRAVERIES
BRAVERY
BRAVES
BRAVEST
BRAVI
BRAVING
BRAVO
BRAVOES
BRAVOS
BRAVURA
BRAVURAS
BRAW
BRAWER
BRAWEST
BRAWL
BRAWLED
BRAWLER
BRAWLERS
BRAWLIER
BRAWLIEST
BRAWLING
BRAWLINGS
BRAWLS
BRAWLY
BRAWN
BRAWNED
BRAWNIER
BRAWNIEST
BRAWNS
BRAWNY
BRAWS
BRAXIES

BRAXY
BRAY
BRAYED
BRAYER
BRAYERS
BRAYING
BRAYS
BRAZE
BRAZED
BRAZELESS
BRAZEN
BRAZENED
BRAZENING
BRAZENLY
BRAZENRIES
BRAZENRY
BRAZENS
BRAZES
BRAZIER
BRAZIERS
BRAZIL
BRAZILS
BRAZING
BREACH
BREACHED
BREACHES
BREACHING
BREAD
BREADED
BREADHEAD
BREADHEADS
BREADING
BREADLINE
BREADLINES
BREADNUT
BREADNUTS
BREADROOM
BREADROOMS
BREADROOT
BREADROOTS
BREADS
BREADTH
BREADTHS
BREAK
BREAKABLE
BREAKABLES
BREAKAGE
BREAKAGES
BREAKAWAY
BREAKAWAYS
BREAKBACK
BREAKDOWN
BREAKDOWNS
BREAKER
BREAKERS
BREAKFAST
BREAKFASTED
BREAKFASTING
BREAKFASTS
BREAKING
BREAKINGS
BREAKNECK
BREAKS
BREAM
BREAMED
BREAMING
BREAMS
BREARE
BREARES
BREASKIT

| | | | | |
|---|---|---|---|---|
| BREASKITS | BRENNING | BRICKED | BRIGADES | BRIOCHE |
| BREAST | BRENS | BRICKEN | BRIGADIER | BRIOCHES |
| BREASTED | BRENT | BRICKIE | BRIGADIERS | BRIONIES |
| BREASTING | BRENTER | BRICKIER | BRIGADING | BRIONY |
| BREASTPIN | BRENTEST | BRICKIES | BRIGAND | BRIOS |
| BREASTPINS | BRER | BRICKIEST | BRIGANDRIES | BRIQUET |
| BREASTS | BRERE | BRICKING | BRIGANDRY | BRIQUETS |
| BREATH | BRERES | BRICKINGS | BRIGANDS | BRIQUETTE |
| BREATHE | BRERS | BRICKLE | BRIGHT | BRIQUETTES |
| BREATHED | BRETASCHE | BRICKS | BRIGHTEN | BRISÉ |
| BREATHER | BRETASCHES | BRICKWALL | BRIGHTENED | BRISÉS |
| BREATHERS | BRETESSE | BRICKWALLS | BRIGHTENING | BRISK |
| BREATHES | BRETESSES | BRICKWORK | BRIGHTENS | BRISKED |
| BREATHFUL | BRETHREN | BRICKWORKS | BRIGHTER | BRISKEN |
| BREATHIER | BRETON | BRICKY | BRIGHTEST | BRISKENED |
| BREATHIEST | BRETONS | BRICKYARD | BRIGHTLY | BRISKENING |
| BREATHILY | BRETTICE | BRICKYARDS | BRIGS | BRISKENS |
| BREATHING | BRETTICED | BRICOLE | BRIGUE | BRISKER |
| BREATHINGS | BRETTICES | BRICOLES | BRIGUED | BRISKEST |
| BREATHS | BRETTICING | BRIDAL | BRIGUES | BRISKET |
| BREATHY | BREVE | BRIDALS | BRIGUING | BRISKETS |
| BRECCIA | BREVES | BRIDE | BRIGUINGS | BRISKING |
| BRECCIAS | BREVET | BRIDECAKE | BRILL | BRISKISH |
| BRECHAM | BREVETÉ | BRIDECAKES | BRILLIANT | BRISKLY |
| BRECHAMS | BREVETED | BRIDED | BRILLIANTED | BRISKNESS |
| BRED | BREVETING | BRIDEMAID | BRILLIANTING | BRISKNESSES |
| BREDE | BREVETS | BRIDEMAIDS | BRILLIANTS | BRISKS |
| BREDED | BREVETTED | BRIDEMAN | BRILLS | BRISKY |
| BREDES | BREVETTING | BRIDEMEN | BRIM | BRISLING |
| BREDING | BREVIARIES | BRIDES | BRIMFUL | BRISLINGS |
| BREE | BREVIARY | BRIDESMAN | BRIMING | BRISTLE |
| BREECH | BREVIATE | BRIDESMEN | BRIMINGS | BRISTLED |
| BREECHED | BREVIATES | BRIDEWELL | BRIMLESS | BRISTLES |
| BREECHES | BREVIER | BRIDEWELLS | BRIMMED | BRISTLIER |
| BREECHING | BREVIERS | BRIDGE | BRIMMER | BRISTLIEST |
| BREECHINGS | BREVITIES | BRIDGED | BRIMMERS | BRISTLING |
| BREED | BREVITY | BRIDGES | BRIMMING | BRISTLY |
| BREEDER | BREW | BRIDGING | BRIMS | BRISTOLS |
| BREEDERS | BREWAGE | BRIDGINGS | BRIMSTONE | BRISURE |
| BREEDING | BREWAGES | BRIDIE | BRIMSTONES | BRISURES |
| BREEDINGS | BREWED | BRIDIES | BRIMSTONY | BRIT |
| BREEDS | BREWER | BRIDING | BRINDED | BRITCHES |
| BREEKS | BREWERIES | BRIDLE | BRINDISI | BRITS |
| BREEM | BREWERS | BRIDLED | BRINDISIS | BRITSCHKA |
| BREER | BREWERY | BRIDLER | BRINDLE | BRITSCHKAS |
| BREERED | BREWING | BRIDLERS | BRINDLED | BRITSKA |
| BREERING | BREWINGS | BRIDLES | BRINDLES | BRITSKAS |
| BREERS | BREWIS | BRIDLING | BRINE | BRITTLE |
| BREES | BREWISES | BRIDOON | BRINED | BRITTLER |
| BREESE | BREWS | BRIDOONS | BRINES | BRITTLES |
| BREESES | BREWSTER | BRIEF | BRING | BRITTLEST |
| BREEZE | BREWSTERS | BRIEFED | BRINGER | BRITZKA |
| BREEZED | BRIAR | BRIEFER | BRINGERS | BRITZKAS |
| BREEZES | BRIARED | BRIEFEST | BRINGING | BRITZSKA |
| BREEZIER | BRIARS | BRIEFING | BRINGINGS | BRITZSKAS |
| BREEZIEST | BRIBE | BRIEFINGS | BRINGS | BRIZE |
| BREEZILY | BRIBED | BRIEFLESS | BRINIER | BRIZES |
| BREEZING | BRIBER | BRIEFLY | BRINIEST | BRO |
| BREEZY | BRIBERIES | BRIEFNESS | BRINING | BROACH |
| BREGMA | BRIBERS | BRIEFNESSES | BRINISH | BROACHED |
| BREGMATA | BRIBERY | BRIEFS | BRINJAL | BROACHER |
| BREGMATIC | BRIBES | BRIER | BRINJALS | BROACHERS |
| BREHON | BRIBING | BRIERED | BRINJARRIES | BROACHES |
| BREHONS | BRICABRAC | BRIERIER | BRINJARRY | BROACHING |
| BRELOQUE | BRICABRACS | BRIERIEST | BRINK | BROAD |
| BRELOQUES | BRICK | BRIERS | BRINKMAN | BROADBAND |
| BREME | BRICKBAT | BRIERY | BRINKMEN | BROADCAST |
| BREN | BRICKBATS | BRIG | BRINKS | BROADCASTED |
| BRENNE | BRICKCLAY | BRIGADE | BRINY | BROADCASTING |
| BRENNES | BRICKCLAYS | BRIGADED | BRIO | BROADCASTINGS |

BROADCASTS
BROADEN
BROADENED
BROADENING
BROADENS
BROADER
BROADEST
BROADISH
BROADLOOM
BROADLY
BROADNESS
BROADNESSES
BROADS
BROADSIDE
BROADSIDES
BROADTAIL
BROADTAILS
BROADWAY
BROADWAYS
BROADWISE
BROCADE
BROCADED
BROCADES
BROCAGE
BROCAGES
BROCARD
BROCARDS
BROCATEL
BROCATELS
BROCCOLI
BROCCOLIS
BROCH
BROCHAN
BROCHANS
BROCHÉ
BROCHÉS
BROCHS
BROCHURE
BROCHURES
BROCK
BROCKAGE
BROCKAGES
BROCKED
BROCKET
BROCKETS
BROCKIT
BROCKRAM
BROCKRAMS
BROCKS
BROD
BRODDED
BRODDING
BRODEKIN
BRODEKINS
BRODKIN
BRODKINS
BRODS
BROG
BROGAN
BROGANS
BROGGED
BROGGING
BROGH
BROGHS
BROGS
BROGUE
BROGUES
BROIDER
BROIDERED
BROIDERER

BROIDERERS
BROIDERIES
BROIDERING
BROIDERINGS
BROIDERS
BROIDERY
BROIL
BROILED
BROILER
BROILERS
BROILING
BROILS
BROKAGE
BROKAGES
BROKE
BROKED
BROKEN
BROKENLY
BROKER
BROKERAGE
BROKERAGES
BROKERIES
BROKERS
BROKERY
BROKES
BROKING
BROKINGS
BROLGA
BROLGAS
BROLLIES
BROLLY
BROMATE
BROMATES
BROMELIA
BROMELIAD
BROMELIADS
BROMELIAS
BROMIC
BROMIDE
BROMIDES
BROMIDIC
BROMINE
BROMINES
BROMMER
BROMMERS
BROMOFORM
BROMOFORMS
BRONCHI
BRONCHIA
BRONCHIAL
BRONCHO
BRONCHOS
BRONCHUS
BRONCO
BRONCOS
BROND
BRONDS
BRONDYRON
BRONDYRONS
BRONZE
BRONZED
BRONZEN
BRONZES
BRONZIER
BRONZIEST
BRONZIFIED
BRONZIFIES
BRONZIFY
BRONZIFYING
BRONZING

BRONZINGS
BRONZITE
BRONZITES
BRONZY
BROO
BROOCH
BROOCHED
BROOCHES
BROOCHING
BROOD
BROODED
BROODER
BROODERS
BROODIER
BROODIEST
BROODING
BROODMARE
BROODMARES
BROODS
BROODY
BROOK
BROOKED
BROOKING
BROOKITE
BROOKITES
BROOKLET
BROOKLETS
BROOKLIME
BROOKLIMES
BROOKS
BROOKWEED
BROOKWEEDS
BROOL
BROOLS
BROOM
BROOMBALL
BROOMBALLS
BROOMED
BROOMIER
BROOMIEST
BROOMING
BROOMRAPE
BROOMRAPES
BROOMS
BROOMY
BROOS
BROOSE
BROOSES
BROS
BROSE
BROSES
BROTH
BROTHEL
BROTHELS
BROTHER
BROTHERLY
BROTHERS
BROTHS
BROUGH
BROUGHAM
BROUGHAMS
BROUGHS
BROUGHT
BROUHAHA
BROUHAHAS
BROUZE
BROUZES
BROW
BROWBEAT
BROWBEATEN

BROWBEATING
BROWBEATS
BROWLESS
BROWN
BROWNED
BROWNER
BROWNEST
BROWNIE
BROWNIER
BROWNIES
BROWNIEST
BROWNING
BROWNINGS
BROWNISH
BROWNNESS
BROWNNESSES
BROWNOUT
BROWNOUTS
BROWNS
BROWNY
BROWS
BROWSE
BROWSED
BROWSES
BROWSING
BROWSINGS
BROWST
BROWSTS
BRUCHID
BRUCHIDS
BRUCINE
BRUCINES
BRUCITE
BRUCITES
BRUCKLE
BRUHAHA
BRUHAHAS
BRUILZIE
BRUILZIES
BRUISE
BRUISED
BRUISER
BRUISERS
BRUISES
BRUISING
BRUISINGS
BRUIT
BRUITED
BRUITING
BRUITS
BRÛLÉ
BRULYIE
BRULYIES
BRULZIE
BRULZIES
BRUMAL
BRUMBIES
BRUMBY
BRUME
BRUMES
BRUMMER
BRUMMERS
BRUMOUS
BRUNCH
BRUNCHES
BRUNET
BRUNETS
BRUNETTE
BRUNETTES
BRUNT

BRUNTED
BRUNTING
BRUNTS
BRUSH
BRUSHED
BRUSHER
BRUSHERS
BRUSHES
BRUSHIER
BRUSHIEST
BRUSHING
BRUSHINGS
BRUSHWOOD
BRUSHWOODS
BRUSHWORK
BRUSHWORKS
BRUSHY
BRUSQUE
BRUSQUELY
BRUSQUER
BRUSQUEST
BRUST
BRUSTING
BRUSTS
BRUT
BRUTAL
BRUTALISE
BRUTALISED
BRUTALISES
BRUTALISING
BRUTALISM
BRUTALISMS
BRUTALIST
BRUTALISTS
BRUTALITIES
BRUTALITY
BRUTALIZE
BRUTALIZED
BRUTALIZES
BRUTALIZING
BRUTALLY
BRUTE
BRUTED
BRUTENESS
BRUTENESSES
BRUTES
BRUTIFIED
BRUTIFIES
BRUTIFY
BRUTIFYING
BRUTING
BRUTISH
BRUTISHLY
BRUXISM
BRUXISMS
BRYOLOGIES
BRYOLOGY
BRYONIES
BRYONY
BRYOPHYTE
BRYOPHYTES
BUAT
BUATS
BUAZE
BUAZES
BUB
BUBA
BUBAL
BUBALINE
BUBALIS

BUBALISES
BUBALS
BUBAS
BUBBIES
BUBBLE
BUBBLED
BUBBLES
BUBBLIER
BUBBLIES
BUBBLIEST
BUBBLING
BUBBLY
BUBBY
BUBINGA
BUBINGAS
BUBO
BUBOES
BUBONIC
BUBS
BUBUKLE
BUBUKLES
BUCCAL
BUCCANEER
BUCCANEERED
BUCCANEERING
BUCCANEERINGS
BUCCANEERS
BUCCANIER
BUCCANIERED
BUCCANIERING
BUCCANIERS
BUCCINA
BUCCINAS
BUCELLAS
BUCELLASES
BUCHU
BUCHUS
BUCK
BUCKAROO
BUCKAROOS
BUCKAYRO
BUCKAYROS
BUCKBEAN
BUCKBEANS
BUCKBOARD
BUCKBOARDS
BUCKCART
BUCKCARTS
BUCKED
BUCKEEN
BUCKEENS
BUCKER
BUCKEROO
BUCKEROOS
BUCKERS
BUCKET
BUCKETED
BUCKETFUL
BUCKETFULS
BUCKETING
BUCKETINGS
BUCKETS
BUCKHORN
BUCKHORNS
BUCKHOUND
BUCKHOUNDS
BUCKIE
BUCKIES
BUCKING
BUCKINGS

BUCKISH
BUCKLE
BUCKLED
BUCKLER
BUCKLERS
BUCKLES
BUCKLING
BUCKLINGS
BUCKO
BUCKOES
BUCKRA
BUCKRAM
BUCKRAMED
BUCKRAMING
BUCKRAMS
BUCKRAS
BUCKS
BUCKSAW
BUCKSAWS
BUCKSHEE
BUCKSHEES
BUCKSHISH
BUCKSHISHES
BUCKSHOT
BUCKSHOTS
BUCKSKIN
BUCKSKINS
BUCKSOM
BUCKTEETH
BUCKTHORN
BUCKTHORNS
BUCKTOOTH
BUCKU
BUCKUS
BUCKWHEAT
BUCKWHEATS
BUCOLIC
BUCOLICAL
BUCOLICS
BUD
BUDDED
BUDDIER
BUDDIES
BUDDIEST
BUDDING
BUDDINGS
BUDDLE
BUDDLED
BUDDLEIA
BUDDLEIAS
BUDDLES
BUDDLING
BUDDY
BUDGE
BUDGED
BUDGER
BUDGEREE
BUDGERO
BUDGEROS
BUDGEROW
BUDGEROWS
BUDGERS
BUDGES
BUDGET
BUDGETARY
BUDGETED
BUDGETING
BUDGETS
BUDGIE
BUDGIES

BUDGING
BUDLESS
BUDMASH
BUDMASHES
BUDO
BUDOS
BUDS
BUFF
BUFFA
BUFFALO
BUFFALOED
BUFFALOES
BUFFALOING
BUFFE
BUFFED
BUFFER
BUFFERED
BUFFERING
BUFFERS
BUFFET
BUFFETED
BUFFETING
BUFFETINGS
BUFFETS
BUFFI
BUFFING
BUFFO
BUFFOON
BUFFOONS
BUFFS
BUFO
BUFOS
BUG
BUGABOO
BUGABOOS
BUGBANE
BUGBANES
BUGBEAR
BUGBEARS
BUGGAN
BUGGANE
BUGGANES
BUGGANS
BUGGED
BUGGER
BUGGERED
BUGGERIES
BUGGERING
BUGGERS
BUGGERY
BUGGIES
BUGGIN
BUGGING
BUGGINGS
BUGGINS
BUGGY
BUGHOUSE
BUGHOUSES
BUGLE
BUGLED
BUGLER
BUGLERS
BUGLES
BUGLET
BUGLETS
BUGLING
BUGLOSS
BUGLOSSES
BUGONG
BUGONGS

BUGS
BUGWORT
BUGWORTS
BUHL
BUHLS
BUHRSTONE
BUHRSTONES
BUIK
BUIKS
BUILD
BUILDED
BUILDER
BUILDERS
BUILDING
BUILDINGS
BUILDS
BUILT
BUIRDLIER
BUIRDLIEST
BUIRDLY
BUIST
BUISTED
BUISTING
BUISTS
BUKE
BUKES
BUKSHEE
BUKSHEES
BUKSHI
BUKSHIS
BULB
BULBAR
BULBED
BULBIL
BULBILS
BULBING
BULBOUS
BULBS
BULBUL
BULBULS
BULGE
BULGED
BULGER
BULGERS
BULGES
BULGIER
BULGIEST
BULGINE
BULGINES
BULGINESS
BULGINESSES
BULGING
BULGY
BULIMIA
BULIMIAS
BULIMIC
BULIMICS
BULIMIES
BULIMUS
BULIMUSES
BULIMY
BULK
BULKED
BULKER
BULKERS
BULKHEAD
BULKHEADS
BULKIER
BULKIEST
BULKILY

BULKINESS
BULKINESSES
BULKING
BULKS
BULKY
BULL
BULLA
BULLACE
BULLACES
BULLAE
BULLARIES
BULLARY
BULLAS
BULLATE
BULLBAT
BULLBATS
BULLDOG
BULLDOGGED
BULLDOGGING
BULLDOGS
BULLDOZE
BULLDOZED
BULLDOZER
BULLDOZERS
BULLDOZES
BULLDOZING
BULLDUST
BULLDUSTS
BULLED
BULLER
BULLERED
BULLERING
BULLERS
BULLET
BULLETIN
BULLETINS
BULLETRIE
BULLETRIES
BULLETS
BULLFIGHT
BULLFIGHTS
BULLFINCH
BULLFINCHES
BULLFROG
BULLFROGS
BULLGINE
BULLGINES
BULLHEAD
BULLHEADS
BULLIED
BULLIER
BULLIES
BULLIEST
BULLING
BULLION
BULLIONS
BULLISH
BULLISHLY
BULLOCK
BULLOCKS
BULLS
BULLSHIT
BULLSHITS
BULLSHITTED
BULLSHITTING
BULLWHACK
BULLWHACKED
BULLWHACKING
BULLWHACKS
BULLY

BULLYING
BULLYISM
BULLYISMS
BULLYRAG
BULLYRAGGED
BULLYRAGGING
BULLYRAGS
BULRUSH
BULRUSHES
BULRUSHY
BULSE
BULSES
BULWARK
BULWARKED
BULWARKING
BULWARKS
BUM
BUMALO
BUMBAZE
BUMBAZED
BUMBAZES
BUMBAZING
BUMBLE
BUMBLED
BUMBLES
BUMBLING
BUMBO
BUMBOS
BUMF
BUMFS
BUMKIN
BUMKINS
BUMMALO
BUMMALOTI
BUMMALOTIS
BUMMAREE
BUMMAREES
BUMMED
BUMMEL
BUMMELS
BUMMER
BUMMERS
BUMMING
BUMMLE
BUMMLED
BUMMLES
BUMMLING
BUMMOCK
BUMMOCKS
BUMP
BUMPED
BUMPER
BUMPERED
BUMPERING
BUMPERS
BUMPH
BUMPHS
BUMPIER
BUMPIEST
BUMPINESS
BUMPINESSES
BUMPING
BUMPKIN
BUMPKINS
BUMPOLOGIES
BUMPOLOGY
BUMPS
BUMPTIOUS
BUMPY
BUMS

BUMSUCKER
BUMSUCKERS
BUN
BUNA
BUNAS
BUNCE
BUNCED
BUNCES
BUNCH
BUNCHED
BUNCHES
BUNCHIER
BUNCHIEST
BUNCHING
BUNCHINGS
BUNCHY
BUNCING
BUNCO
BUNCOED
BUNCOING
BUNCOMBE
BUNCOMBES
BUNCOS
BUND
BUNDED
BUNDING
BUNDLE
BUNDLED
BUNDLES
BUNDLING
BUNDLINGS
BUNDOBUST
BUNDOBUSTS
BUNDOOK
BUNDOOKS
BUNDS
BUNDU
BUNDUS
BUNG
BUNGALOID
BUNGALOIDS
BUNGALOW
BUNGALOWS
BUNGED
BUNGEE
BUNGEES
BUNGEY
BUNGEYS
BUNGIE
BUNGIES
BUNGING
BUNGLE
BUNGLED
BUNGLER
BUNGLERS
BUNGLES
BUNGLING
BUNGLINGS
BUNGS
BUNGY
BUNIA
BUNIAS
BUNION
BUNIONS
BUNJE
BUNJEE
BUNJEES
BUNJES
BUNJIE
BUNJIES

BUNJY
BUNK
BUNKED
BUNKER
BUNKERED
BUNKERING
BUNKERS
BUNKHOUSE
BUNKHOUSES
BUNKING
BUNKO
BUNKOED
BUNKOING
BUNKOS
BUNKS
BUNKUM
BUNKUMS
BUNNIA
BUNNIAS
BUNNIES
BUNNY
BUNODONT
BUNRAKU
BUNRAKUS
BUNS
BUNT
BUNTED
BUNTER
BUNTERS
BUNTIER
BUNTIEST
BUNTING
BUNTINGS
BUNTLINE
BUNTLINES
BUNTS
BUNTY
BUNYA
BUNYAS
BUNYIP
BUNYIPS
BUONAMANI
BUONAMANO
BUOY
BUOYAGE
BUOYAGES
BUOYANCE
BUOYANCES
BUOYANCIES
BUOYANCY
BUOYANT
BUOYED
BUOYING
BUOYS
BUPLEVER
BUPLEVERS
BUR
BURAN
BURANS
BURBLE
BURBLED
BURBLES
BURBLING
BURBLINGS
BURBOT
BURBOTS
BURD
BURDASH
BURDASHES
BURDEN

BURDENED
BURDENING
BURDENOUS
BURDENS
BURDIE
BURDIES
BURDOCK
BURDOCKS
BURDS
BUREAU
BUREAUS
BUREAUX
BURETTE
BURETTES
BURG
BURGAGE
BURGAGES
BURGANET
BURGANETS
BURGEE
BURGEES
BURGEON
BURGEONED
BURGEONING
BURGEONS
BURGER
BURGERS
BURGESS
BURGESSES
BURGH
BURGHAL
BURGHER
BURGHERS
BURGHS
BURGLAR
BURGLARED
BURGLARIES
BURGLARING
BURGLARS
BURGLARY
BURGLE
BURGLED
BURGLES
BURGLING
BURGONET
BURGONETS
BURGOO
BURGOOS
BURGRAVE
BURGRAVES
BURGS
BURGUNDIES
BURGUNDY
BURHEL
BURHELS
BURIAL
BURIALS
BURIED
BURIES
BURIN
BURINIST
BURINISTS
BURINS
BURITI
BURITIS
BURK
BURKA
BURKAS
BURKE
BURKED

BURKES
BURKHA
BURKHAS
BURKING
BURKS
BURL
BURLAP
BURLAPS
BURLED
BURLER
BURLERS
BURLESQUE
BURLESQUED
BURLESQUES
BURLESQUING
BURLETTA
BURLETTAS
BURLEY
BURLEYS
BURLIER
BURLIEST
BURLINESS
BURLINESSES
BURLING
BURLS
BURLY
BURN
BURNED
BURNER
BURNERS
BURNET
BURNETS
BURNING
BURNINGS
BURNISH
BURNISHED
BURNISHER
BURNISHERS
BURNISHES
BURNISHING
BURNISHINGS
BURNOUS
BURNOUSE
BURNOUSES
BURNS
BURNSIDE
BURNSIDES
BURNT
BUROO
BUROOS
BURP
BURPED
BURPING
BURPS
BURQA
BURQAS
BURR
BURRED
BURREL
BURRELL
BURRELLS
BURRELS
BURRHEL
BURRHELS
BURRIER
BURRIEST
BURRING
BURRO
BURROS
BURROW

BURROWED
BURROWING
BURROWS
BURRS
BURRSTONE
BURRSTONES
BURRY
BURS
BURSA
BURSAE
BURSAL
BURSAR
BURSARIAL
BURSARIES
BURSARS
BURSARY
BURSE
BURSES
BURSIFORM
BURSITIS
BURSITISES
BURST
BURSTED
BURSTEN
BURSTER
BURSTERS
BURSTING
BURSTS
BURTHEN
BURTHENED
BURTHENING
BURTHENS
BURTON
BURTONS
BURWEED
BURWEEDS
BURY
BURYING
BUS
BUSBIES
BUSBOY
BUSBOYS
BUSBY
BUSED
BUSES
BUSGIRL
BUSGIRLS
BUSH
BUSHCRAFT
BUSHCRAFTS
BUSHED
BUSHEL
BUSHELLED
BUSHELLER
BUSHELLERS
BUSHELLING
BUSHELLINGS
BUSHELS
BUSHES
BUSHFIRE
BUSHFIRES
BUSHIDO
BUSHIDOS
BUSHIER
BUSHIES
BUSHIEST

BUSHINESS
BUSHINESSES
BUSHING
BUSHMAN
BUSHMEN
BUSHVELD
BUSHVELDS
BUSHWALK
BUSHWALKED
BUSHWALKING
BUSHWALKINGS
BUSHWALKS
BUSHWHACK
BUSHWHACKED
BUSHWHACKING
BUSHWHACKINGS
BUSHWHACKS
BUSHY
BUSIED
BUSIER
BUSIES
BUSIEST
BUSILY
BUSINESS
BUSINESSES
BUSING
BUSINGS
BUSK
BUSKED
BUSKER
BUSKERS
BUSKET
BUSKETS
BUSKIN
BUSKINED
BUSKING
BUSKINGS
BUSKINS
BUSKS
BUSKY
BUSMAN
BUSMEN
BUSS
BUSSED
BUSSES
BUSSING
BUSSINGS
BUSSU
BUSSUS
BUST
BUSTARD
BUSTARDS
BUSTED
BUSTEE
BUSTEES
BUSTER
BUSTERS
BUSTIER
BUSTIERS
BUSTIEST
BUSTING
BUSTINGS
BUSTLE
BUSTLED
BUSTLER
BUSTLERS

BUSTLES
BUSTLING
BUSTS
BUSTY
BUSY
BUSYBODIES
BUSYBODY
BUSYING
BUSYNESS
BUSYNESSES
BUT
BUTADIENE
BUTADIENES
BUTANE
BUTANES
BUTANOL
BUTANOLS
BUTCH
BUTCHER
BUTCHERED
BUTCHERIES
BUTCHERING
BUTCHERINGS
BUTCHERLY
BUTCHERS
BUTCHERY
BUTCHES
BUTCHEST
BUTCHING
BUTCHINGS
BUTE
BUTENE
BUTENES
BUTES
BUTLER
BUTLERAGE
BUTLERAGES
BUTLERED
BUTLERIES
BUTLERING
BUTLERS
BUTLERY
BUTMENT
BUTMENTS
BUTS
BUTT
BUTTE
BUTTED
BUTTER
BUTTERBUR
BUTTERBURS
BUTTERCUP
BUTTERCUPS
BUTTERED
BUTTERFLIES
BUTTERFLY
BUTTERIER
BUTTERIES
BUTTERIEST
BUTTERINE
BUTTERINES
BUTTERING
BUTTERNUT
BUTTERNUTS
BUTTERS
BUTTERY

BUTTES
BUTTIES
BUTTING
BUTTLE
BUTTLED
BUTTLES
BUTTLING
BUTTOCK
BUTTOCKED
BUTTOCKING
BUTTOCKS
BUTTON
BUTTONED
BUTTONING
BUTTONS
BUTTONY
BUTTRESS
BUTTRESSED
BUTTRESSES
BUTTRESSING
BUTTS
BUTTY
BUTTYMAN
BUTTYMEN
BUTYL
BUTYLENE
BUTYLENES
BUTYLS
BUTYRATE
BUTYRATES
BUTYRIC
BUVETTE
BUVETTES
BUXOM
BUXOMER
BUXOMEST
BUXOMNESS
BUXOMNESSES
BUY
BUYABLE
BUYABLES
BUYER
BUYERS
BUYING
BUYS
BUZZ
BUZZARD
BUZZARDS
BUZZED
BUZZER
BUZZERS
BUZZES
BUZZIER
BUZZIEST
BUZZING
BUZZINGLY
BUZZINGS
BUZZY
BWANA
BWANAS
BWAZI
BWAZIS
BY
BYCATCH
BYCATCHES
BYCOKET

BYCOKETS
BYE
BYES
BYGOING
BYGOINGS
BYGONE
BYGONES
BYKE
BYKED
BYKES
BYKING
BYLANDER
BYLANDERS
BYLAW
BYLAWS
BYLINE
BYLINES
BYLIVE
BYNEMPT
BYPASS
BYPASSED
BYPASSES
BYPASSING
BYPATH
BYPATHS
BYPLACE
BYPLACES
BYRE
BYREMAN
BYREMEN
BYRES
BYREWOMAN
BYREWOMEN
BYRLADY
BYRLAKIN
BYRLAW
BYRLAWS
BYRNIE
BYRNIES
BYROAD
BYROADS
BYROOM
BYROOMS
BYS
BYSSAL
BYSSINE
BYSSOID
BYSSUS
BYSSUSES
BYSTANDER
BYSTANDERS
BYTE
BYTES
BYTOWNITE
BYTOWNITES
BYWAY
BYWAYS
BYWONER
BYWONERS
BYWORD
BYWORDS
BYWORK
BYWORKS
BYZANT
BYZANTS

# C

CAATINGA
CAATINGAS
CAB
CABA
CABAL
CABALA
CABALAS
CABALETTA
CABALETTAS
CABALETTE
CABALISM
CABALISMS
CABALIST
CABALISTS
CABALLED
CABALLER
CABALLERO
CABALLEROS
CABALLERS
CABALLINE
CABALLING
CABALS
CABANA
CABANAS
CABARET
CABARETS
CABAS
CABBAGE
CABBAGED
CABBAGES
CABBAGING
CABBAGY
CABBALA
CABBALAS
CABBALISM
CABBALISMS
CABBALIST
CABBALISTS
CABBIE
CABBIES
CABBY
CABER
CABERS
CABIN
CABINED
CABINET
CABINETS
CABINING
CABINS
CABLE
CABLED
CABLEGRAM
CABLEGRAMS
CABLES
CABLEWAY
CABLEWAYS
CABLING
CABLINGS
CABMAN
CABMEN
CABOB
CABOBS
CABOC

CABOCEER
CABOCEERS
CABOCHED
CABOCHON
CABOCHONS
CABOCS
CABOODLE
CABOODLES
CABOOSE
CABOOSES
CABOSHED
CABOTAGE
CABOTAGES
CABRÉ
CABRIE
CABRIES
CABRIOLE
CABRIOLES
CABRIOLET
CABRIOLETS
CABRIT
CABRITS
CABS
CACAFOGO
CACAFOGOS
CACAFUEGO
CACAFUEGOS
CACAO
CACAOS
CACHAEMIA
CACHAEMIAS
CACHAEMIC
CACHALOT
CACHALOTS
CACHE
CACHECTIC
CACHED
CACHES
CACHET
CACHETS
CACHEXIA
CACHEXIAS
CACHEXIES
CACHEXY
CACHING
CACHOLONG
CACHOLONGS
CACHOLOT
CACHOLOTS
CACHOU
CACHOUS
CACHUCHA
CACHUCHAS
CACIQUE
CACIQUES
CACIQUISM
CACIQUISMS
CACKLE
CACKLED
CACKLER
CACKLERS
CACKLES
CACKLING

CACODEMON
CACODEMONS
CACODOXIES
CACODOXY
CACODYL
CACODYLIC
CACODYLS
CACOEPIES
CACOEPY
CACOETHES
CACOLET
CACOLETS
CACOLOGIES
CACOLOGY
CACOMIXL
CACOMIXLS
CACOON
CACOONS
CACOPHONIES
CACOPHONY
CACOTOPIA
CACOTOPIAS
CACTI
CACTIFORM
CACTUS
CACTUSES
CACUMEN
CACUMENS
CACUMINAL
CAD
CADASTRAL
CADASTRE
CADASTRES
CADAVER
CADAVERIC
CADAVERS
CADDICE
CADDICES
CADDIE
CADDIED
CADDIES
CADDIS
CADDISES
CADDISH
CADDY
CADDYING
CADDYSS
CADDYSSES
CADE
CADEAU
CADEAUX
CADENCE
CADENCED
CADENCES
CADENCIES
CADENCY
CADENT
CADENTIAL
CADENZA
CADENZAS
CADES
CADET
CADETS

CADETSHIP
CADETSHIPS
CADGE
CADGED
CADGER
CADGERS
CADGES
CADGIER
CADGIEST
CADGING
CADGY
CADI
CADIE
CADIES
CADIS
CADMIUM
CADMIUMS
CADRANS
CADRANSES
CADRE
CADRES
CADS
CADUAC
CADUACS
CADUCEAN
CADUCEI
CADUCEUS
CADUCITIES
CADUCITY
CADUCOUS
CAECA
CAECAL
CAECILIAN
CAECILIANS
CAECUM
CAERULE
CAERULEAN
CAESAR
CAESARS
CAESE
CAESIOUS
CAESIUM
CAESIUMS
CAESTUS
CAESTUSES
CAESURA
CAESURAL
CAESURAS
CAFARD
CAFARDS
CAFÉ
CAFÉS
CAFETERIA
CAFETERIAS
CAFF
CAFFEINE
CAFFEINES
CAFFEISM
CAFFEISMS
CAFFILA
CAFFILAS
CAFFS
CAFILA

CAFILAS
CAFTAN
CAFTANS
CAGE
CAGEBIRD
CAGEBIRDS
CAGED
CAGELING
CAGELINGS
CAGES
CAGEWORK
CAGEWORKS
CAGEY
CAGEYNESS
CAGEYNESSES
CAGIER
CAGIEST
CAGILY
CAGINESS
CAGINESSES
CAGING
CAGOT
CAGOTS
CAGOUL
CAGOULE
CAGOULES
CAGOULS
CAGY
CAGYNESS
CAGYNESSES
CAHIER
CAHIERS
CAHOOT
CAHOOTS
CAILLACH
CAILLACHS
CAILLEACH
CAILLEACHS
CAILLIACH
CAILLIACHS
CAIMAC
CAIMACAM
CAIMACAMS
CAIMACS
CAIMAN
CAIMANS
CAIN
CAINS
CAÏQUE
CAIQUE
CAÏQUES
CAIQUES
CAIRD
CAIRDS
CAIRN
CAIRNED
CAIRNGORM
CAIRNGORMS
CAIRNS
CAISSON
CAISSONS
CAITIFF
CAITIFFS

CAITIVE
CAITIVES
CAJEPUT
CAJEPUTS
CAJOLE
CAJOLED
CAJOLER
CAJOLERIES
CAJOLERS
CAJOLERY
CAJOLES
CAJOLING
CAJUN
CAJUPUT
CAJUPUTS
CAKE
CAKED
CAKES
CAKEWALK
CAKEWALKED
CAKEWALKING
CAKEWALKS
CAKIER
CAKIEST
CAKING
CAKINGS
CAKY
CALABASH
CALABASHES
CALABOOSE
CALABOOSES
CALABRESE
CALABRESES
CALAMANCO
CALAMANCOS
CALAMARIES
CALAMARY
CALAMI
CALAMINE
CALAMINES
CALAMINT
CALAMINTS
CALAMITE
CALAMITES
CALAMITIES
CALAMITY
CALAMUS
CALANDO
CALANDRIA
CALANDRIAS
CALANTHE
CALANTHES
CALASH
CALASHES
CALAVANCE
CALAVANCES
CALCANEAL
CALCANEAN
CALCANEUM
CALCANEUMS
CALCAR
CALCARATE
CALCARINE
CALCARS
CALCEATE
CALCEATED
CALCEATES
CALCEATING
CALCED
CALCEDONIES

CALCEDONY
CALCES
CALCIC
CALCICOLE
CALCIFIC
CALCIFIED
CALCIFIES
CALCIFUGE
CALCIFY
CALCIFYING
CALCINE
CALCINED
CALCINES
CALCINING
CALCITE
CALCITES
CALCIUM
CALCIUMS
CALCSPAR
CALCSPARS
CALCULAR
CALCULARY
CALCULATE
CALCULATED
CALCULATES
CALCULATING
CALCULI
CALCULOSE
CALCULOUS
CALCULUS
CALCULUSES
CALDARIA
CALDARIUM
CALDARIUMS
CALDERA
CALDERAS
CALDRON
CALDRONS
CALEFIED
CALEFIES
CALEFY
CALEFYING
CALEMBOUR
CALEMBOURS
CALENDAR
CALENDARED
CALENDARING
CALENDARS
CALENDER
CALENDERED
CALENDERING
CALENDERINGS
CALENDERS
CALENDRER
CALENDRERS
CALENDRIES
CALENDRY
CALENDS
CALENDULA
CALENDULAS
CALENTURE
CALENTURES
CALF
CALFDOZER
CALFDOZERS
CALFLESS
CALFS
CALFSKIN
CALFSKINS
CALIATOUR

CALIATOURS
CALIBER
CALIBERED
CALIBERS
CALIBRATE
CALIBRATED
CALIBRATES
CALIBRATING
CALIBRE
CALIBRED
CALIBRES
CALICES
CALICHE
CALICHES
CALICO
CALICOES
CALICOS
CALID
CALIDITIES
CALIDITY
CALIF
CALIFS
CALIGO
CALIGOES
CALIGOS
CALIOLOGIES
CALIOLOGY
CALIPASH
CALIPASHES
CALIPEE
CALIPEES
CALIPER
CALIPERS
CALIPH
CALIPHAL
CALIPHATE
CALIPHATES
CALIPHS
CALISAYA
CALISAYAS
CALIVER
CALIVERS
CALIX
CALIXES
CALK
CALKED
CALKER
CALKERS
CALKIN
CALKING
CALKINS
CALKS
CALL
CALLA
CALLANT
CALLANTS
CALLAS
CALLED
CALLER
CALLERS
CALLET
CALLETS
CALLID
CALLIDITIES
CALLIDITY
CALLIGRAM
CALLIGRAMS
CALLING
CALLINGS
CALLIOPE

CALLIOPES
CALLIPER
CALLIPERED
CALLIPERING
CALLIPERS
CALLOSITIES
CALLOSITY
CALLOUS
CALLOUSLY
CALLOW
CALLOWER
CALLOWEST
CALLOWS
CALLS
CALLUS
CALLUSES
CALM
CALMANT
CALMANTS
CALMATIVE
CALMATIVES
CALMED
CALMER
CALMEST
CALMIER
CALMIEST
CALMING
CALMLY
CALMNESS
CALMNESSES
CALMS
CALMSTANE
CALMSTANES
CALMSTONE
CALMSTONES
CALMY
CALOMEL
CALOMELS
CALORIC
CALORICS
CALORIE
CALORIES
CALORIFIC
CALORIST
CALORISTS
CALOTTE
CALOTTES
CALOTYPE
CALOTYPES
CALOYER
CALOYERS
CALP
CALPA
CALPAC
CALPACK
CALPACKS
CALPACS
CALPAS
CALPS
CALQUE
CALQUED
CALQUES
CALQUING
CALTHA
CALTHAS
CALTHROP
CALTHROPS
CALTRAP
CALTRAPS
CALTROP

CALTROPS
CALUMBA
CALUMBAS
CALUMET
CALUMETS
CALUMNIES
CALUMNY
CALVE
CALVED
CALVER
CALVERED
CALVERING
CALVERS
CALVES
CALVING
CALVITIES
CALX
CALXES
CALYCES
CALYCINAL
CALYCINE
CALYCLE
CALYCLED
CALYCLES
CALYCOID
CALYCULE
CALYCULES
CALYPSO
CALYPSOS
CALYPTRA
CALYPTRAS
CALYX
CALYXES
CALZONE
CALZONES
CALZONI
CAM
CAMAIEU
CAMAIEUX
CAMAN
CAMANACHD
CAMANACHDS
CAMANS
CAMARILLA
CAMARILLAS
CAMARON
CAMARONS
CAMAS
CAMASES
CAMASH
CAMASHES
CAMASS
CAMASSES
CAMBER
CAMBERED
CAMBERING
CAMBERS
CAMBIAL
CAMBIFORM
CAMBISM
CAMBISMS
CAMBIST
CAMBISTRIES
CAMBISTRY
CAMBISTS
CAMBIUM
CAMBIUMS
CAMBOGE
CAMBOGES
CAMBREL

CAMBRELS
CAMBRIC
CAMBRICS
CAMCORDER
CAMCORDERS
CAME
CAMEL
CAMELBACK
CAMELBACKS
CAMELEER
CAMELEERS
CAMELEON
CAMELEONS
CAMELID
CAMELIDS
CAMELINE
CAMELINES
CAMELISH
CAMELLIA
CAMELLIAS
CAMELOID
CAMELOIDS
CAMELOT
CAMELOTS
CAMELRIES
CAMELRY
CAMELS
CAMEO
CAMEOS
CAMERA
CAMERAL
CAMERAMAN
CAMERAMEN
CAMERAS
CAMERATED
CAMES
CAMESE
CAMESES
CAMION
CAMIONS
CAMIS
CAMISADE
CAMISADES
CAMISADO
CAMISADOS
CAMISARD
CAMISARDS
CAMISE
CAMISES
CAMISOLE
CAMISOLES
CAMLET
CAMLETS
CAMMED
CAMMING
CAMOMILE
CAMOMILES
CAMOUFLET
CAMOUFLETS
CAMP
CAMPAGNA
CAMPAGNAS
CAMPAIGN
CAMPAIGNED
CAMPAIGNING
CAMPAIGNS
CAMPANA
CAMPANAS
CAMPANERO
CAMPANEROS

CAMPANILE
CAMPANILES
CAMPANILI
CAMPANIST
CAMPANISTS
CAMPEADOR
CAMPEADORS
CAMPED
CAMPER
CAMPERS
CAMPESINO
CAMPESINOS
CAMPEST
CAMPHANE
CAMPHANES
CAMPHENE
CAMPHENES
CAMPHINE
CAMPHINES
CAMPHIRE
CAMPHIRES
CAMPHOR
CAMPHORIC
CAMPHORS
CAMPIER
CAMPIEST
CAMPING
CAMPION
CAMPIONS
CAMPLE
CAMPLED
CAMPLES
CAMPLING
CAMPS
CAMPSITE
CAMPSITES
CAMPUS
CAMPUSES
CAMPY
CAMS
CAMSHAFT
CAMSHAFTS
CAMSHEUGH
CAMSHO
CAMSHOCH
CAMSTAIRY
CAMSTANE
CAMSTANES
CAMSTEARY
CAMSTONE
CAMSTONES
CAMUS
CAMUSES
CAN
CAÑADA
CAÑADAS
CANAIGRE
CANAIGRES
CANAILLE
CANAILLES
CANAKIN
CANAKINS
CANAL
CANALISE
CANALISED
CANALISES
CANALISING
CANALIZE
CANALIZED
CANALIZES

CANALIZING
CANALS
CANAPÉ
CANAPÉS
CANARD
CANARDS
CANARIED
CANARIES
CANARY
CANARYING
CANASTA
CANASTAS
CANASTER
CANASTERS
CANCAN
CANCANS
CANCEL
CANCELEER
CANCELEERED
CANCELEERING
CANCELEERS
CANCELIER
CANCELIERED
CANCELIERING
CANCELIERS
CANCELLED
CANCELLI
CANCELLING
CANCELS
CANCER
CANCERATE
CANCERATED
CANCERATES
CANCERATING
CANCEROUS
CANCERS
CANCRINE
CANCROID
CANCROIDS
CANDELA
CANDELAS
CANDENT
CANDID
CANDIDA
CANDIDACIES
CANDIDACY
CANDIDAS
CANDIDATE
CANDIDATES
CANDIDER
CANDIDEST
CANDIDLY
CANDIE
CANDIED
CANDIES
CANDLE
CANDLED
CANDLES
CANDLING
CANDOCK
CANDOCKS
CANDOR
CANDORS
CANDOUR
CANDOURS
CANDY
CANDYING
CANDYTUFT
CANDYTUFTS
CANE

CANED
CANEFRUIT
CANEFRUITS
CANEH
CANEHS
CANELLA
CANELLAS
CANEPHOR
CANEPHORA
CANEPHORAS
CANEPHORE
CANEPHORES
CANEPHORS
CANES
CANESCENT
CANFUL
CANFULS
CANG
CANGLE
CANGLED
CANGLES
CANGLING
CANGS
CANGUE
CANGUES
CANICULAR
CANID
CANIDS
CANIER
CANIEST
CANIKIN
CANIKINS
CANINE
CANINES
CANING
CANINGS
CANINITIES
CANINITY
CANISTER
CANISTERED
CANISTERING
CANISTERS
CANITIES
CANKER
CANKERED
CANKERING
CANKEROUS
CANKERS
CANKERY
CANN
CANNA
CANNABIC
CANNABIN
CANNABINS
CANNABIS
CANNABISES
CANNACH
CANNACHS
CANNAE
CANNAS
CANNED
CANNEL
CANNELS
CANNELURE
CANNELURES
CANNER
CANNERIES
CANNERS
CANNERY
CANNIBAL

CANNIBALS
CANNIER
CANNIEST
CANNIKIN
CANNIKINS
CANNILY
CANNINESS
CANNINESSES
CANNING
CANNON
CANNONADE
CANNONADED
CANNONADES
CANNONADING
CANNONED
CANNONEER
CANNONEERS
CANNONIER
CANNONIERS
CANNONING
CANNONRIES
CANNONRY
CANNONS
CANNOT
CANNS
CANNULA
CANNULAE
CANNULAS
CANNULATE
CANNY
CANOE
CANOED
CANOEING
CANOEINGS
CANOEIST
CANOEISTS
CANOES
CANON
CAÑON
CANONESS
CANONESSES
CANONIC
CANONICAL
CANONICALS
CANONISE
CANONISED
CANONISES
CANONISING
CANONIST
CANONISTS
CANONIZE
CANONIZED
CANONIZES
CANONIZING
CANONRIES
CANONRY
CANONS
CAÑONS
CANOODLE
CANOODLED
CANOODLES
CANOODLING
CANOPIED
CANOPY
CANOPYING
CANOROUS
CANS
CANST
CANSTICK

| | | | | |
|---|---|---|---|---|
| CANSTICKS | CANTOR | CAPILLARY | CAPRIFOIL | CAPTIVING |
| CANT | CANTORIAL | CAPING | CAPRIFOILS | CAPTIVITIES |
| CANTABANK | CANTORIS | CAPITA | CAPRIFOLE | CAPTIVITY |
| CANTABANKS | CANTORS | CAPITAL | CAPRIFOLES | CAPTOR |
| CANTABILE | CANTOS | CAPITALLY | CAPRIFORM | CAPTORS |
| CANTABILES | CANTRED | CAPITALS | CAPRIFY | CAPTURE |
| CANTALOUP | CANTREDS | CAPITAN | CAPRIFYING | CAPTURED |
| CANTALOUPS | CANTREF | CAPITANI | CAPRINE | CAPTURES |
| CANTAR | CANTREFS | CAPITANO | CAPRIOLE | CAPTURING |
| CANTARS | CANTRIP | CAPITANOS | CAPRIOLED | CAPUCCIO |
| CANTATA | CANTRIPS | CAPITANS | CAPRIOLES | CAPUCCIOS |
| CANTATAS | CANTS | CAPITATE | CAPRIOLING | CAPUCHE |
| CANTATE | CANTUS | CAPITAYN | CAPROATE | CAPUCHES |
| CANTATES | CANTY | CAPITAYNS | CAPROATES | CAPUCHIN |
| CANTDOG | CANVAS | CAPITELLA | CAPROIC | CAPUCHINS |
| CANTDOGS | CANVASED | CAPITULA | CAPRYLATE | CAPUL |
| CANTED | CANVASES | CAPITULAR | CAPRYLATES | CAPULS |
| CANTEEN | CANVASING | CAPITULARS | CAPRYLIC | CAPUT |
| CANTEENS | CANVASS | CAPITULUM | CAPS | CAPYBARA |
| CANTER | CANVASSED | CAPLE | CAPSAICIN | CAPYBARAS |
| CANTERED | CANVASSER | CAPLES | CAPSAICINS | CAR |
| CANTERING | CANVASSERS | CAPLIN | CAPSICUM | CARABIN |
| CANTERS | CANVASSES | CAPLINS | CAPSICUMS | CARABINE |
| CANTEST | CANVASSING | CAPO | CAPSID | CARABINES |
| CANTHARI | CANY | CAPOCCHIA | CAPSIDS | CARABINS |
| CANTHARID | CANYON | CAPOCCHIAS | CAPSIZAL | CARACAL |
| CANTHARIDES | CANYONS | CAPON | CAPSIZALS | CARACALS |
| CANTHARIDS | CANZONA | CAPONIER | CAPSIZE | CARACARA |
| CANTHARIS | CANZONAS | CAPONIERE | CAPSIZED | CARACARAS |
| CANTHARUS | CANZONE | CAPONIERES | CAPSIZES | CARACK |
| CANTHI | CANZONET | CAPONIERS | CAPSIZING | CARACKS |
| CANTHOOK | CANZONETS | CAPONISE | CAPSTAN | CARACOL |
| CANTHOOKS | CANZONI | CAPONISED | CAPSTANS | CARACOLE |
| CANTHUS | CAP | CAPONISES | CAPSTONE | CARACOLED |
| CANTICLE | CAPA | CAPONISING | CAPSTONES | CARACOLES |
| CANTICLES | CAPABLE | CAPONIZE | CAPSULAR | CARACOLING |
| CANTICO | CAPABLER | CAPONIZED | CAPSULARY | CARACOLLED |
| CANTICOED | CAPABLEST | CAPONIZES | CAPSULATE | CARACOLLING |
| CANTICOING | CAPACIOUS | CAPONIZING | CAPSULE | CARACOLS |
| CANTICOS | CAPACITIES | CAPONS | CAPSULES | CARACT |
| CANTICOY | CAPACITOR | CAPORAL | CAPSULISE | CARACTS |
| CANTICOYED | CAPACITORS | CAPORALS | CAPSULISED | CARACUL |
| CANTICOYING | CAPACITY | CAPOS | CAPSULISES | CARACULS |
| CANTICOYS | CAPARISON | CAPOT | CAPSULISING | CARAFE |
| CANTICUM | CAPARISONED | CAPOTASTO | CAPSULIZE | CARAFES |
| CANTICUMS | CAPARISONING | CAPOTASTOS | CAPSULIZED | CARAMBA |
| CANTIER | CAPARISONS | CAPOTE | CAPSULIZES | CARAMBOLA |
| CANTIEST | CAPAS | CAPOTES | CAPSULIZING | CARAMBOLAS |
| CANTILENA | CAPE | CAPOTS | CAPTAIN | CARAMBOLE |
| CANTILENAS | CAPED | CAPOTTED | CAPTAINCIES | CARAMBOLED |
| CANTINA | CAPELET | CAPOTTING | CAPTAINCY | CARAMBOLES |
| CANTINAS | CAPELETS | CAPPED | CAPTAINED | CARAMBOLING |
| CANTINESS | CAPELIN | CAPPER | CAPTAINING | CARAMEL |
| CANTINESSES | CAPELINE | CAPPERS | CAPTAINRIES | CARAMELLED |
| CANTING | CAPELINES | CAPPING | CAPTAINRY | CARAMELLING |
| CANTINGS | CAPELINS | CAPPINGS | CAPTAINS | CARAMELS |
| CANTION | CAPELLET | CAPRATE | CAPTAN | CARANGID |
| CANTIONS | CAPELLETS | CAPRATES | CAPTANS | CARANGIDS |
| CANTLE | CAPELLINE | CAPRIC | CAPTION | CARANGOID |
| CANTLED | CAPELLINES | CAPRICCI | CAPTIONED | CARANGOIDS |
| CANTLES | CAPER | CAPRICCIO | CAPTIONING | CARANNA |
| CANTLET | CAPERED | CAPRICCIOS | CAPTIONS | CARANNAS |
| CANTLETS | CAPERER | CAPRICE | CAPTIOUS | CARANX |
| CANTLING | CAPERERS | CAPRICES | CAPTIVATE | CARAP |
| CANTO | CAPERING | CAPRID | CAPTIVATED | CARAPACE |
| CANTON | CAPERS | CAPRIDS | CAPTIVATES | CARAPACES |
| CANTONAL | CAPES | CAPRIFIED | CAPTIVATING | CARAPS |
| CANTONED | CAPIAS | CAPRIFIES | CAPTIVE | CARAT |
| CANTONING | CAPIASES | CAPRIFIG | CAPTIVED | CARATS |
| CANTONS | CAPILLARIES | CAPRIFIGS | CAPTIVES | CARAUNA |

| | | | | |
|---|---|---|---|---|
| CARAUNAS | CARBURETTING | CARED | CARINA | CARNIED |
| CARAVAN | CARBURISE | CAREEN | CARINAS | CARNIER |
| CARAVANCE | CARBURISED | CAREENAGE | CARINATE | CARNIES |
| CARAVANCES | CARBURISES | CAREENAGES | CARING | CARNIEST |
| CARAVANED | CARBURISING | CAREENED | CARIOCA | CARNIFEX |
| CARAVANER | CARBURIZE | CAREENING | CARIOCAS | CARNIFEXES |
| CARAVANERS | CARBURIZED | CAREENS | CARIOLE | CARNIVAL |
| CARAVANING | CARBURIZES | CAREER | CARIOLES | CARNIVALS |
| CARAVANNED | CARBURIZING | CAREERED | CARIOUS | CARNIVORE |
| CARAVANNING | CARCAJOU | CAREERING | CARITAS | CARNIVORES |
| CARAVANS | CARCAJOUS | CAREERISM | CARITATES | CARNOSE |
| CARAVEL | CARCAKE | CAREERISMS | CARJACOU | CARNOSITIES |
| CARAVELS | CARCAKES | CAREERIST | CARJACOUS | CARNOSITY |
| CARAWAY | CARCANET | CAREERISTS | CARK | CARNOTITE |
| CARAWAYS | CARCANETS | CAREERS | CARKED | CARNOTITES |
| CARB | CARCASE | CAREFREE | CARKING | CARNY |
| CARBAMATE | CARCASED | CAREFUL | CARKS | CARNYING |
| CARBAMATES | CARCASES | CAREFULLY | CARL | CAROB |
| CARBAMIDE | CARCASING | CARELESS | CARLINE | CAROBS |
| CARBAMIDES | CARCASS | CARÈME | CARLINES | CAROCHE |
| CARBARYL | CARCASSED | CARÈMES | CARLISH | CAROCHES |
| CARBARYLS | CARCASSES | CARER | CARLOAD | CAROL |
| CARBIDE | CARCASSING | CARERS | CARLOADS | CAROLLED |
| CARBIDES | CARCINOMA | CARES | CARLOCK | CAROLLER |
| CARBINE | CARCINOMAS | CARESS | CARLOCKS | CAROLLERS |
| CARBINEER | CARCINOMATA | CARESSED | CARLOT | CAROLLING |
| CARBINEERS | CARD | CARESSES | CARLOTS | CAROLS |
| CARBINES | CARDAMINE | CARESSING | CARLS | CAROM |
| CARBINIER | CARDAMINES | CARESSINGS | CARMAN | CAROMED |
| CARBINIERS | CARDAMOM | CARET | CARMELITE | CAROMEL |
| CARBOLIC | CARDAMOMS | CARETAKE | CARMELITES | CAROMELLED |
| CARBOLICS | CARDAMON | CARETAKEN | CARMEN | CAROMELLING |
| CARBON | CARDAMONS | CARETAKER | CARMINE | CAROMELS |
| CARBONADE | CARDAMUM | CARETAKERS | CARMINES | CAROMING |
| CARBONADES | CARDAMUMS | CARETAKES | CARNAGE | CAROMS |
| CARBONADO | CARDBOARD | CARETAKING | CARNAGES | CAROTENE |
| CARBONADOED | CARDBOARDS | CARETOOK | CARNAHUBA | CAROTENES |
| CARBONADOES | CARDECU | CARETS | CARNAHUBAS | CAROTID |
| CARBONADOING | CARDECUE | CAREWORN | CARNAL | CAROTIN |
| CARBONADOS | CARDECUES | CAREX | CARNALISE | CAROTINS |
| CARBONATE | CARDECUS | CARFAX | CARNALISED | CAROUSAL |
| CARBONATED | CARDED | CARFAXES | CARNALISES | CAROUSALS |
| CARBONATES | CARDER | CARFOX | CARNALISING | CAROUSE |
| CARBONATING | CARDERS | CARFOXES | CARNALISM | CAROUSED |
| CARBONIC | CARDI | CARFUFFLE | CARNALISMS | CAROUSEL |
| CARBONISE | CARDIAC | CARFUFFLED | CARNALIST | CAROUSELS |
| CARBONISED | CARDIACAL | CARFUFFLES | CARNALISTS | CAROUSER |
| CARBONISES | CARDIACS | CARFUFFLING | CARNALITIES | CAROUSERS |
| CARBONISING | CARDIALGIES | CARGEESE | CARNALITY | CAROUSES |
| CARBONIZE | CARDIALGY | CARGO | CARNALIZE | CAROUSING |
| CARBONIZED | CARDIES | CARGOED | CARNALIZED | CARP |
| CARBONIZES | CARDIGAN | CARGOES | CARNALIZES | CARPAL |
| CARBONIZING | CARDIGANS | CARGOING | CARNALIZING | CARPALS |
| CARBONS | CARDINAL | CARGOOSE | CARNALLED | CARPARK |
| CARBONYL | CARDINALS | CARIACOU | CARNALLING | CARPARKS |
| CARBONYLS | CARDING | CARIACOUS | CARNALLY | CARPED |
| CARBOXYL | CARDIOID | CARIAMA | CARNALS | CARPEL |
| CARBOXYLS | CARDIOIDS | CARIAMAS | CARNATION | CARPELS |
| CARBOY | CARDIS | CARIBE | CARNATIONS | CARPENTER |
| CARBOYS | CARDITIS | CARIBES | CARNAUBA | CARPENTERED |
| CARBS | CARDITISES | CARIBOU | CARNAUBAS | CARPENTERING |
| CARBUNCLE | CARDOON | CARIBOUS | CARNELIAN | CARPENTERS |
| CARBUNCLES | CARDOONS | CARICES | CARNELIANS | CARPENTRIES |
| CARBURATE | CARDPUNCH | CARIERE | CARNEOUS | CARPENTRY |
| CARBURATED | CARDPUNCHES | CARIERES | CARNET | CARPER |
| CARBURATES | CARDS | CARIES | CARNETS | CARPERS |
| CARBURATING | CARDUUS | CARILLON | CARNEY | CARPET |
| CARBURET | CARDUUSES | CARILLONED | CARNEYED | CARPETED |
| CARBURETS | CARDY | CARILLONING | CARNEYING | CARPETING |
| CARBURETTED | CARE | CARILLONS | CARNEYS | CARPETINGS |

CARPETS
CARPING
CARPINGLY
CARPINGS
CARPORT
CARPORTS
CARPS
CARPUS
CARPUSES
CARR
CARRACK
CARRACKS
CARRACT
CARRACTS
CARRAGEEN
CARRAGEENS
CARRAT
CARRATS
CARRAWAY
CARRAWAYS
CARRECT
CARRECTS
CARREL
CARRELL
CARRELLS
CARRELS
CARRIAGE
CARRIAGES
CARRIED
CARRIER
CARRIERS
CARRIES
CARRIOLE
CARRIOLES
CARRION
CARRIONS
CARRITCH
CARRITCHES
CARRONADE
CARRONADES
CARROT
CARROTS
CARROTY
CARROUSEL
CARROUSELS
CARRS
CARRY
CARRYCOT
CARRYCOTS
CARRYING
CARRYTALE
CARRYTALES
CARS
CARSE
CARSES
CART
CARTA
CARTAGE
CARTAGES
CARTAS
CARTE
CARTED
CARTEL
CARTELISE
CARTELISED
CARTELISES
CARTELISING
CARTELIZE
CARTELIZED
CARTELIZES

CARTELIZING
CARTELS
CARTER
CARTERS
CARTES
CARTILAGE
CARTILAGES
CARTING
CARTLOAD
CARTLOADS
CARTOGRAM
CARTOGRAMS
CARTOLOGIES
CARTOLOGY
CARTON
CARTONAGE
CARTONAGES
CARTONED
CARTONING
CARTONS
CARTOON
CARTOONED
CARTOONING
CARTOONS
CARTOUCH
CARTOUCHE
CARTOUCHES
CARTRIDGE
CARTRIDGES
CARTROAD
CARTROADS
CARTS
CARTULARIES
CARTULARY
CARTWAY
CARTWAYS
CARTWHEEL
CARTWHEELED
CARTWHEELING
CARTWHEELS
CARUCAGE
CARUCAGES
CARUCATE
CARUCATES
CARUNCLE
CARUNCLES
CARVACROL
CARVACROLS
CARVE
CARVED
CARVEL
CARVELS
CARVEN
CARVER
CARVERS
CARVES
CARVIES
CARVING
CARVINGS
CARVY
CARYATIC
CARYATID
CARYATIDES
CARYATIDS
CARYOPSES
CARYOPSIDES
CARYOPSIS
CASA
CASAS
CASBAH

CASBAHS
CASCABEL
CASCABELS
CASCADE
CASCADED
CASCADES
CASCADING
CASCARA
CASCARAS
CASCHROM
CASCHROMS
CASCO
CASCOS
CASE
CASEATION
CASEATIONS
CASEBOOK
CASEBOOKS
CASED
CASEIN
CASEINS
CASEMAKER
CASEMAKERS
CASEMAN
CASEMATE
CASEMATED
CASEMATES
CASEMEN
CASEMENT
CASEMENTS
CASEOUS
CASERN
CASERNE
CASERNES
CASERNS
CASES
CASH
CASHAW
CASHAWS
CASHED
CASHES
CASHEW
CASHEWS
CASHIER
CASHIERED
CASHIERER
CASHIERERS
CASHIERING
CASHIERINGS
CASHIERS
CASHING
CASHLESS
CASHMERE
CASHMERES
CASING
CASINGS
CASINO
CASINOS
CASK
CASKED
CASKET
CASKETS
CASKING
CASKS
CASQUE
CASQUES
CASSAREEP
CASSAREEPS
CASSARIPE
CASSARIPES

CASSATA
CASSATAS
CASSATION
CASSATIONS
CASSAVA
CASSAVAS
CASSEROLE
CASSEROLED
CASSEROLES
CASSEROLING
CASSETTE
CASSETTES
CASSIA
CASSIAS
CASSIMERE
CASSIMERES
CASSINO
CASSINOS
CASSIS
CASSISES
CASSOCK
CASSOCKED
CASSOCKS
CASSONADE
CASSONADES
CASSONE
CASSONES
CASSOULET
CASSOULETS
CASSOWARIES
CASSOWARY
CAST
CASTANETS
CASTAWAY
CASTAWAYS
CASTE
CASTED
CASTELESS
CASTELLA
CASTELLAN
CASTELLANS
CASTELLUM
CASTELLUMS
CASTER
CASTERS
CASTES
CASTIGATE
CASTIGATED
CASTIGATES
CASTIGATING
CASTING
CASTINGS
CASTLE
CASTLED
CASTLES
CASTLING
CASTOCK
CASTOCKS
CASTOR
CASTOREUM
CASTOREUMS
CASTORIES
CASTORS
CASTORY
CASTRAL
CASTRATE
CASTRATED
CASTRATES
CASTRATI
CASTRATING

CASTRATO
CASTS
CASUAL
CASUALISE
CASUALISED
CASUALISES
CASUALISING
CASUALISM
CASUALISMS
CASUALIZE
CASUALIZED
CASUALIZES
CASUALIZING
CASUALLY
CASUALS
CASUALTIES
CASUALTY
CASUARINA
CASUARINAS
CASUIST
CASUISTIC
CASUISTRIES
CASUISTRY
CASUISTS
CAT
CATACLASM
CATACLASMS
CATACLYSM
CATACLYSMS
CATACOMB
CATACOMBS
CATAFALCO
CATAFALCOES
CATALASE
CATALASES
CATALEPSIES
CATALEPSY
CATALEXES
CATALEXIS
CATALO
CATALOES
CATALOG
CATALOGED
CATALOGER
CATALOGERS
CATALOGING
CATALOGS
CATALOGUE
CATALOGUED
CATALOGUES
CATALOGUING
CATALOS
CATALPA
CATALPAS
CATALYSE
CATALYSED
CATALYSER
CATALYSERS
CATALYSES
CATALYSING
CATALYSIS
CATALYST
CATALYSTS
CATALYTIC
CATALYZE
CATALYZED
CATALYZER
CATALYZERS
CATALYZES
CATALYZING

CATAMARAN
CATAMARANS
CATAMENIA
CATAMITE
CATAMITES
CATAMOUNT
CATAMOUNTS
CATAPAN
CATAPANS
CATAPHYLL
CATAPHYLLS
CATAPLASM
CATAPLASMS
CATAPLEXIES
CATAPLEXY
CATAPULT
CATAPULTED
CATAPULTING
CATAPULTS
CATARACT
CATARACTS
CATARHINE
CATARRH
CATARRHAL
CATARRHS
CATASTA
CATASTAS
CATATONIA
CATATONIAS
CATATONIC
CATATONICS
CATATONIES
CATATONY
CATAWBA
CATAWBAS
CATBIRD
CATBIRDS
CATBOAT
CATBOATS
CATCALL
CATCALLED
CATCALLING
CATCALLS
CATCH
CATCHABLE
CATCHED
CATCHEN
CATCHER
CATCHERS
CATCHES
CATCHFLIES
CATCHFLY
CATCHIER
CATCHIEST
CATCHING
CATCHINGS
CATCHMENT
CATCHMENTS
CATCHPOLE
CATCHPOLES
CATCHPOLL
CATCHPOLLS
CATCHT
CATCHUP
CATCHUPS
CATCHWEED
CATCHWEEDS
CATCHWORD
CATCHWORDS
CATCHY

CATE
CATECHISE
CATECHISED
CATECHISES
CATECHISING
CATECHISINGS
CATECHISM
CATECHISMS
CATECHIST
CATECHISTS
CATECHIZE
CATECHIZED
CATECHIZES
CATECHIZING
CATECHIZINGS
CATECHOL
CATECHOLS
CATECHU
CATECHUS
CATEGORIES
CATEGORY
CATELOG
CATELOGS
CATENA
CATENAE
CATENARIES
CATENARY
CATENAS
CATENATE
CATENATED
CATENATES
CATENATING
CATER
CATERAN
CATERANS
CATERED
CATERER
CATERERS
CATERESS
CATERESSES
CATERING
CATERINGS
CATERS
CATERWAUL
CATERWAULED
CATERWAULING
CATERWAULINGS
CATERWAULS
CATES
CATFISH
CATFISHES
CATGUT
CATGUTS
CATHARISE
CATHARISED
CATHARISES
CATHARISING
CATHARIZE
CATHARIZED
CATHARIZES
CATHARIZING
CATHARSES
CATHARSIS
CATHARTIC
CATHARTICS
CATHEAD
CATHEADS
CATHECTIC
CATHEDRA
CATHEDRAL

CATHEDRALS
CATHEDRAS
CATHETER
CATHETERS
CATHETUS
CATHETUSES
CATHEXES
CATHEXIS
CATHISMA
CATHISMAS
CATHODAL
CATHODE
CATHODES
CATHODIC
CATHOLIC
CATHOOD
CATHOODS
CATHOUSE
CATHOUSES
CATION
CATIONS
CATKIN
CATKINS
CATLING
CATLINGS
CATMINT
CATMINTS
CATNAP
CATNAPS
CATNEP
CATNEPS
CATNIP
CATNIPS
CATOPTRIC
CATOPTRICS
CATS
CATSKIN
CATSKINS
CATSUIT
CATSUITS
CATSUP
CATSUPS
CATTABU
CATTABUS
CATTALO
CATTALOES
CATTALOS
CATTED
CATTERIES
CATTERY
CATTIER
CATTIES
CATTIEST
CATTILY
CATTINESS
CATTINESSES
CATTING
CATTISH
CATTISHLY
CATTLE
CATTLEMAN
CATTLEMEN
CATTY
CAUCHEMAR
CAUCHEMARS
CAUCUS
CAUCUSED
CAUCUSES
CAUCUSING
CAUDAD

CAUDAL
CAUDATE
CAUDATED
CAUDEX
CAUDEXES
CAUDICES
CAUDICLE
CAUDICLES
CAUDILLO
CAUDILLOS
CAUDLE
CAUDLED
CAUDLES
CAUDLING
CAUDRON
CAUDRONS
CAUF
CAUGHT
CAUK
CAUKER
CAUKERS
CAUKS
CAUL
CAULD
CAULDER
CAULDEST
CAULDRIFE
CAULDRON
CAULDRONS
CAULDS
CAULES
CAULICLE
CAULICLES
CAULIFORM
CAULINARY
CAULINE
CAULIS
CAULK
CAULKED
CAULKER
CAULKERS
CAULKING
CAULKINGS
CAULKS
CAULOME
CAULOMES
CAULS
CAUM
CAUMED
CAUMING
CAUMS
CAUMSTANE
CAUMSTANES
CAUMSTONE
CAUMSTONES
CAUP
CAUPS
CAUSAL
CAUSALITIES
CAUSALITY
CAUSALLY
CAUSATION
CAUSATIONS
CAUSATIVE
CAUSATIVES
CAUSE
CAUSED
CAUSELESS
CAUSEN
CAUSER

CAUSERIE
CAUSERIES
CAUSERS
CAUSES
CAUSEWAY
CAUSEWAYED
CAUSEWAYING
CAUSEWAYS
CAUSEY
CAUSEYED
CAUSEYING
CAUSEYS
CAUSING
CAUSTIC
CAUSTICS
CAUTEL
CAUTELOUS
CAUTELS
CAUTER
CAUTERANT
CAUTERANTS
CAUTERIES
CAUTERISE
CAUTERISED
CAUTERISES
CAUTERISING
CAUTERISM
CAUTERISMS
CAUTERIZE
CAUTERIZED
CAUTERIZES
CAUTERIZING
CAUTERS
CAUTERY
CAUTION
CAUTIONED
CAUTIONER
CAUTIONERS
CAUTIONING
CAUTIONRIES
CAUTIONRY
CAUTIONS
CAUTIOUS
CAUVES
CAVALCADE
CAVALCADED
CAVALCADES
CAVALCADING
CAVALIER
CAVALIERED
CAVALIERING
CAVALIERO
CAVALIEROS
CAVALIERS
CAVALLA
CAVALLAS
CAVALLIES
CAVALLY
CAVALRIES
CAVALRY
CAVASS
CAVASSES
CAVATINA
CAVATINAS
CAVE
CAVEAT
CAVEATS
CAVED
CAVEL
CAVELS

CAVEMAN
CAVEMEN
CAVENDISH
CAVENDISHES
CAVER
CAVERN
CAVERNED
CAVERNING
CAVERNOUS
CAVERNS
CAVERS
CAVES
CAVESSON
CAVESSONS
CAVETTI
CAVETTO
CAVIAR
CAVIARE
CAVIARES
CAVIARIE
CAVIARIES
CAVIARS
CAVICORN
CAVICORNS
CAVIE
CAVIER
CAVIERS
CAVIES
CAVIL
CAVILLED
CAVILLER
CAVILLERS
CAVILLING
CAVILLINGS
CAVILS
CAVING
CAVINGS
CAVITATE
CAVITATED
CAVITATES
CAVITATING
CAVITIED
CAVITIES
CAVITY
CAVORT
CAVORTED
CAVORTING
CAVORTS
CAVY
CAW
CAWED
CAWING
CAWINGS
CAWK
CAWKER
CAWKERS
CAWKS
CAWS
CAXON
CAXONS
CAY
CAYENNE
CAYENNED
CAYENNES
CAYMAN
CAYMANS
CAYS
CAYUSE
CAYUSES
CAZIQUE

CAZIQUES
CEAS
CEASE
CEASED
CEASELESS
CEASES
CEASING
CEASINGS
CEAZE
CEAZED
CEAZES
CEAZING
CEBADILLA
CEBADILLAS
CECA
CECILS
CECITIES
CECITY
CECUM
CEDAR
CEDARED
CEDARN
CEDARS
CEDARWOOD
CEDARWOODS
CEDE
CEDED
CEDES
CEDI
CEDILLA
CEDILLAS
CEDING
CEDIS
CEDRATE
CEDRATES
CEDRINE
CEDULA
CEDULAS
CEE
CEES
CEIL
CEILED
CEILI
CEILIDH
CEILIDHS
CEILING
CEILINGED
CEILINGS
CEILIS
CEILS
CEINTURE
CEINTURES
CEL
CELADON
CELADONS
CELANDINE
CELANDINES
CELEBRANT
CELEBRANTS
CELEBRATE
CELEBRATED
CELEBRATES
CELEBRATING
CELEBRITIES
CELEBRITY
CELERIAC
CELERIACS
CELERIES
CELERITIES
CELERITY

CELERY
CELESTA
CELESTAS
CELESTE
CELESTES
CELESTIAL
CELESTIALS
CELESTINE
CELESTINES
CELIAC
CELIACS
CELIBACIES
CELIBACY
CELIBATE
CELIBATES
CELL
CELLA
CELLAE
CELLAR
CELLARAGE
CELLARAGES
CELLARED
CELLARER
CELLARERS
CELLARET
CELLARETS
CELLARING
CELLARIST
CELLARISTS
CELLARMAN
CELLARMEN
CELLAROUS
CELLARS
CELLED
CELLIST
CELLISTS
CELLO
CELLOS
CELLPHONE
CELLPHONES
CELLS
CELLULAR
CELLULE
CELLULES
CELLULITE
CELLULITES
CELLULOID
CELLULOIDS
CELLULOSE
CELLULOSES
CELOM
CELOMS
CELS
CELSITUDE
CELSITUDES
CELT
CELTS
CEMBALIST
CEMBALISTS
CEMBALO
CEMBALOS
CEMBRA
CEMBRAS
CEMENT
CEMENTA
CEMENTED
CEMENTING
CEMENTITE
CEMENTITES
CEMENTS

CEMENTUM
CEMETERIES
CEMETERY
CEMITARE
CEMITARES
CENACLE
CENACLES
CENDRÉ
CENOBITE
CENOBITES
CENOTAPH
CENOTAPHS
CENOTE
CENOTES
CENSE
CENSED
CENSER
CENSERS
CENSES
CENSING
CENSOR
CENSORED
CENSORIAL
CENSORIAN
CENSORING
CENSORS
CENSUAL
CENSURE
CENSURED
CENSURES
CENSURING
CENSUS
CENSUSED
CENSUSES
CENSUSING
CENT
CENTAGE
CENTAGES
CENTAL
CENTALS
CENTAUR
CENTAURIES
CENTAURS
CENTAURY
CENTAVO
CENTAVOS
CENTENARIES
CENTENARY
CENTENIER
CENTENIERS
CENTER
CENTERED
CENTERING
CENTERINGS
CENTERS
CENTESES
CENTESIS
CENTIARE
CENTIARES
CENTIGRAM
CENTIGRAMS
CENTIME
CENTIMES
CENTINEL
CENTINELL
CENTINELLS
CENTINELS
CENTIPEDE
CENTIPEDES
CENTNER

CENTNERS
CENTO
CENTOIST
CENTOISTS
CENTONATE
CENTONEL
CENTONELL
CENTONELLS
CENTONELS
CENTONIST
CENTONISTS
CENTOS
CENTRAL
CENTRALLY
CENTRE
CENTRED
CENTREING
CENTREINGS
CENTRES
CENTRIC
CENTRICAL
CENTRIES
CENTRING
CENTRINGS
CENTRISM
CENTRISMS
CENTRIST
CENTRISTS
CENTRODE
CENTRODES
CENTROID
CENTROIDS
CENTRUM
CENTRUMS
CENTRY
CENTS
CENTUM
CENTUMS
CENTUMVIR
CENTUMVIRI
CENTUPLE
CENTUPLED
CENTUPLES
CENTUPLING
CENTURIAL
CENTURIES
CENTURION
CENTURIONS
CENTURY
CEORL
CEORLS
CEP
CEPHALAD
CEPHALATE
CEPHALIC
CEPHALICS
CEPHALOUS
CEPHEID
CEPHEIDS
CEPS
CERACEOUS
CERAMET
CERAMETS
CERAMIC
CERAMICS
CERAMIST
CERAMISTS
CERASIN
CERASINS
CERASTES

CERATE
CERATED
CERATES
CERATITIS
CERATITISES
CERATODUS
CERATODUSES
CERATOID
CERBERIAN
CERCAL
CERCARIA
CERCARIAE
CERCARIAN
CERCARIAS
CERCI
CERCUS
CERCUSES
CERE
CEREAL
CEREALIST
CEREALISTS
CEREALS
CEREBELLA
CEREBRAL
CEREBRATE
CEREBRATED
CEREBRATES
CEREBRATING
CEREBRIC
CEREBRUM
CEREBRUMS
CERED
CEREMENT
CEREMENTS
CEREMONIES
CEREMONY
CEREOUS
CERES
CERESIN
CERESINE
CERESINES
CERESINS
CERGE
CERGES
CERIA
CERIAS
CERING
CERIPH
CERIPHS
CERISE
CERISES
CERITE
CERITES
CERIUM
CERIUMS
CERMET
CERMETS
CERNE
CERNED
CERNES
CERNING
CERNUOUS
CEROGRAPH
CEROGRAPHS
CEROMANCIES
CEROMANCY
CEROON
CEROONS
CERRIAL
CERRIS

CERRISES
CERT
CERTAIN
CERTAINLY
CERTAINTIES
CERTAINTY
CERTES
CERTIFIED
CERTIFIER
CERTIFIERS
CERTIFIES
CERTIFY
CERTIFYING
CERTITUDE
CERTITUDES
CERTS
CERULEAN
CERULEIN
CERULEINS
CERULEOUS
CERUMEN
CERUMENS
CERUSE
CERUSES
CERUSITE
CERUSITES
CERUSSITE
CERUSSITES
CERVELAT
CERVELATS
CERVICAL
CERVINE
CERVIX
CERVIXES
CESAREVNA
CESAREVNAS
CESIUM
CESIUMS
CESPITOSE
CESS
CESSATION
CESSATIONS
CESSE
CESSED
CESSER
CESSERS
CESSES
CESSING
CESSION
CESSIONS
CESSPIT
CESSPITS
CESSPOOL
CESSPOOLS
CESTODE
CESTODES
CESTOID
CESTOIDS
CESTUI
CESTUIS
CESTUS
CESTUSES
CESURA
CESURAS
CESURE
CESURES
CETACEAN
CETACEANS
CETACEOUS
CETANE

CETANES
CETE
CETERACH
CETERACHS
CETES
CETOLOGIES
CETOLOGY
CETYL
CETYLS
CETYWALL
CETYWALLS
CEVADILLA
CEVADILLAS
CEYLANITE
CEYLANITES
CEYLONITE
CEYLONITES
CH
CHA
CHABAZITE
CHABAZITES
CHABOUK
CHABOUKS
CHACE
CHACED
CHACES
CHACING
CHACK
CHACKED
CHACKING
CHACKS
CHACMA
CHACMAS
CHACO
CHACOES
CHACONNE
CHACONNES
CHACOS
CHAD
CHADAR
CHADARS
CHADDAR
CHADDARS
CHADOR
CHADORS
CHADS
CHAETA
CHAETAE
CHAETODON
CHAETODONS
CHAETOPOD
CHAETOPODS
CHAFE
CHAFED
CHAFER
CHAFERS
CHAFES
CHAFF
CHAFFED
CHAFFER
CHAFFERED
CHAFFERER
CHAFFERERS
CHAFFERIES
CHAFFERING
CHAFFERS
CHAFFERY
CHAFFIER
CHAFFIEST
CHAFFINCH

CHAFFINCHES
CHAFFING
CHAFFINGS
CHAFFLESS
CHAFFRON
CHAFFRONS
CHAFFS
CHAFFY
CHAFING
CHAFT
CHAFTS
CHAGAN
CHAGANS
CHAGRIN
CHAGRINED
CHAGRINING
CHAGRINS
CHAI
CHAIN
CHAINED
CHAINING
CHAINLESS
CHAINLET
CHAINLETS
CHAINS
CHAINSAW
CHAINSAWS
CHAINWORK
CHAINWORKS
CHAIR
CHAIRDAYS
CHAIRED
CHAIRING
CHAIRLIFT
CHAIRLIFTS
CHAIRMAN
CHAIRMEN
CHAIRS
CHAIS
CHAISE
CHAISES
CHAKRA
CHAKRAS
CHAL
CHALAN
CHALANED
CHALANING
CHALANS
CHALAZA
CHALAZAE
CHALAZAS
CHALDAISM
CHALDAISMS
CHALDER
CHALDERS
CHALDRON
CHALDRONS
CHALET
CHALETS
CHALICE
CHALICED
CHALICES
CHALK
CHALKED
CHALKFACE
CHALKFACES
CHALKIER
CHALKIEST
CHALKING
CHALKPIT

CHALKPITS
CHALKS
CHALKY
CHALLAN
CHALLANED
CHALLANING
CHALLANS
CHALLENGE
CHALLENGED
CHALLENGES
CHALLENGING
CHALLIS
CHALLISES
CHALONE
CHALONES
CHALONIC
CHALS
CHALUMEAU
CHALUMEAUX
CHALYBITE
CHALYBITES
CHAM
CHAMADE
CHAMADES
CHAMBER
CHAMBERED
CHAMBERER
CHAMBERERS
CHAMBERING
CHAMBERINGS
CHAMBERS
CHAMBRÉ
CHAMELEON
CHAMELEONS
CHAMELOT
CHAMELOTS
CHAMFER
CHAMFERED
CHAMFERING
CHAMFERS
CHAMFRAIN
CHAMFRAINS
CHAMFRON
CHAMFRONS
CHAMISAL
CHAMISALS
CHAMISE
CHAMISES
CHAMISO
CHAMISOS
CHAMLET
CHAMLETS
CHAMOIS
CHAMOMILE
CHAMOMILES
CHAMP
CHAMPAC
CHAMPACS
CHAMPAGNE
CHAMPAGNES
CHAMPAIGN
CHAMPAIGNS
CHAMPAK
CHAMPAKS
CHAMPART
CHAMPARTS
CHAMPED
CHAMPERS
CHAMPERTIES
CHAMPERTY

CHAMPING
CHAMPION
CHAMPIONED
CHAMPIONING
CHAMPIONS
CHAMPLEVÉ
CHAMPLEVÉS
CHAMPS
CHAMS
CHANCE
CHANCED
CHANCEFUL
CHANCEL
CHANCELS
CHANCER
CHANCERS
CHANCES
CHANCIER
CHANCIEST
CHANCING
CHANCRE
CHANCRES
CHANCROID
CHANCROIDS
CHANCROUS
CHANCY
CHANDLER
CHANDLERIES
CHANDLERS
CHANDLERY
CHANGE
CHANGED
CHANGEFUL
CHANGER
CHANGERS
CHANGES
CHANGING
CHANK
CHANKS
CHANNEL
CHANNELLED
CHANNELLING
CHANNELS
CHANOYU
CHANOYUS
CHANSON
CHANSONS
CHANT
CHANTAGE
CHANTAGES
CHANTED
CHANTER
CHANTERS
CHANTEUSE
CHANTEUSES
CHANTEY
CHANTEYS
CHANTIE
CHANTIES
CHANTING
CHANTOR
CHANTORS
CHANTRESS
CHANTRESSES
CHANTRIES
CHANTRY
CHANTS
CHANTY
CHAOS
CHAOSES

CHAOTIC
CHAP
CHAPARRAL
CHAPARRALS
CHAPATI
CHAPATIS
CHAPATTI
CHAPATTIS
CHAPBOOK
CHAPBOOKS
CHAPE
CHAPEAU
CHAPEAUS
CHAPEL
CHAPELESS
CHAPELRIES
CHAPELRY
CHAPELS
CHAPERON
CHAPERONE
CHAPERONED
CHAPERONES
CHAPERONING
CHAPERONS
CHAPES
CHAPESS
CHAPESSES
CHAPITER
CHAPITERS
CHAPKA
CHAPKAS
CHAPLAIN
CHAPLAINS
CHAPLESS
CHAPLET
CHAPLETED
CHAPLETS
CHAPMAN
CHAPMEN
CHAPPED
CHAPPESS
CHAPPESSES
CHAPPIE
CHAPPIER
CHAPPIES
CHAPPIEST
CHAPPING
CHAPPY
CHAPRASSI
CHAPRASSIS
CHAPS
CHAPTER
CHAPTERED
CHAPTERING
CHAPTERS
CHAPTREL
CHAPTRELS
CHAR
CHARA
CHARABANC
CHARABANCS
CHARACIN
CHARACINS
CHARACT
CHARACTER
CHARACTERED
CHARACTERING
CHARACTERS
CHARACTS
CHARADE

CHARADES
CHARAS
CHARASES
CHARCOAL
CHARCOALS
CHARD
CHARDS
CHARE
CHARED
CHARES
CHARET
CHARETS
CHARGE
CHARGED
CHARGEFUL
CHARGER
CHARGERS
CHARGES
CHARGING
CHARIER
CHARIEST
CHARILY
CHARINESS
CHARINESSES
CHARING
CHARIOT
CHARIOTED
CHARIOTING
CHARIOTS
CHARISM
CHARISMA
CHARISMAS
CHARISMS
CHARITIES
CHARITY
CHARIVARI
CHARIVARIS
CHARK
CHARKED
CHARKING
CHARKS
CHARLADIES
CHARLADY
CHARLATAN
CHARLATANS
CHARLEY
CHARLEYS
CHARLIE
CHARLIES
CHARLOCK
CHARLOCKS
CHARLOTTE
CHARLOTTES
CHARM
CHARMED
CHARMER
CHARMERS
CHARMEUSE
CHARMEUSES
CHARMFUL
CHARMING
CHARMLESS
CHARMS
CHARNECO
CHARNECOS
CHARNEL
CHARNELS
CHAROSET
CHAROSETH
CHAROSETHS

CHAROSETS
CHARPIE
CHARPIES
CHARPOY
CHARPOYS
CHARQUI
CHARQUIS
CHARR
CHARRED
CHARRING
CHARRS
CHARRY
CHARS
CHART
CHARTA
CHARTAS
CHARTED
CHARTER
CHARTERED
CHARTERER
CHARTERERS
CHARTERING
CHARTERS
CHARTING
CHARTISM
CHARTISMS
CHARTIST
CHARTISTS
CHARTLESS
CHARTS
CHARWOMAN
CHARWOMEN
CHARY
CHAS
CHASE
CHASED
CHASER
CHASERS
CHASES
CHASING
CHASINGS
CHASM
CHASMED
CHASMIC
CHASMIER
CHASMIEST
CHASMS
CHASMY
CHASSÉ
CHASSE
CHASSÉED
CHASSÉING
CHASSÉS
CHASSES
CHASSEUR
CHASSEURS
CHASSIS
CHASTE
CHASTELY
CHASTEN
CHASTENED
CHASTENER
CHASTENERS
CHASTENING
CHASTENS
CHASTER
CHASTEST
CHASTISE
CHASTISED
CHASTISES

CHASTISING
CHASTITIES
CHASTITY
CHASUBLE
CHASUBLES
CHAT
CHÂTEAU
CHÂTEAUX
CHÂTELAIN
CHÂTELAINS
CHATON
CHATONS
CHATOYANT
CHATS
CHATTA
CHATTAS
CHATTED
CHATTEL
CHATTELS
CHATTER
CHATTERED
CHATTERER
CHATTERERS
CHATTERING
CHATTERINGS
CHATTERS
CHATTIER
CHATTIES
CHATTIEST
CHATTING
CHATTY
CHAUFE
CHAUFED
CHAUFES
CHAUFF
CHAUFFED
CHAUFFER
CHAUFFERS
CHAUFFEUR
CHAUFFEURED
CHAUFFEURING
CHAUFFEURS
CHAUFFING
CHAUFFS
CHAUFING
CHAUMER
CHAUMERS
CHAUNCE
CHAUNCED
CHAUNCES
CHAUNCING
CHAUNGE
CHAUNGED
CHAUNGES
CHAUNGING
CHAUNT
CHAUNTED
CHAUNTER
CHAUNTERS
CHAUNTING
CHAUNTRIES
CHAUNTRY
CHAUNTS
CHAUSSES
CHAUSSURE
CHAUSSURES
CHAUVIN
CHAUVINS
CHAVE
CHAVENDER

CHAVENDERS
CHAW
CHAWDRON
CHAWDRONS
CHAWED
CHAWING
CHAWS
CHAY
CHAYA
CHAYAS
CHAYOTE
CHAYOTES
CHAYS
CHE
CHEAP
CHEAPEN
CHEAPENED
CHEAPENER
CHEAPENERS
CHEAPENING
CHEAPENS
CHEAPER
CHEAPEST
CHEAPIE
CHEAPIES
CHEAPLY
CHEAPNESS
CHEAPNESSES
CHEAPO
CHEAPS
CHEAPY
CHEAT
CHEATED
CHEATER
CHEATERIES
CHEATERS
CHEATERY
CHEATING
CHEATS
CHECHAKO
CHECHAKOES
CHECHAKOS
CHECHAQUA
CHECHAQUAS
CHECHAQUO
CHECHAQUOS
CHÉCHIA
CHÉCHIAS
CHECK
CHECKED
CHECKER
CHECKERED
CHECKERS
CHECKIER
CHECKIEST
CHECKING
CHECKLIST
CHECKLISTS
CHECKMATE
CHECKMATED
CHECKMATES
CHECKMATING
CHECKROOM
CHECKROOMS
CHECKS
CHECKY
CHEECHAKO
CHEECHAKOES
CHEECHAKOS
CHEEK

CHEEKED
CHEEKIER
CHEEKIEST
CHEEKILY
CHEEKING
CHEEKS
CHEEKY
CHEEP
CHEEPED
CHEEPER
CHEEPERS
CHEEPING
CHEEPS
CHEER
CHEERED
CHEERER
CHEERERS
CHEERFUL
CHEERFULLER
CHEERFULLEST
CHEERIER
CHEERIEST
CHEERILY
CHEERING
CHEERIO
CHEERIOS
CHEERLESS
CHEERLY
CHEERO
CHEEROS
CHEERS
CHEERY
CHEESE
CHEESED
CHEESES
CHEESIER
CHEESIEST
CHEESING
CHEESY
CHEETAH
CHEETAHS
CHEEWINK
CHEEWINKS
CHEF
CHEFS
CHEKA
CHEKAS
CHEKIST
CHEKISTS
CHELA
CHELAE
CHELAS
CHELASHIP
CHELASHIPS
CHELATE
CHELATED
CHELATES
CHELATING
CHELATION
CHELATIONS
CHELATOR
CHELATORS
CHELICERA
CHELICERAE
CHELIPED
CHELIPEDS
CHELOID
CHELOIDAL
CHELOIDS
CHELONIAN

CHELONIANS
CHEMIC
CHEMICAL
CHEMICALS
CHEMICKED
CHEMICKING
CHEMICS
CHEMISE
CHEMISES
CHEMISM
CHEMISMS
CHEMIST
CHEMISTRIES
CHEMISTRY
CHEMISTS
CHEMITYPE
CHEMITYPES
CHEMITYPIES
CHEMITYPY
CHEMMIES
CHEMMY
CHEMOSTAT
CHEMOSTATS
CHEMURGIC
CHEMURGIES
CHEMURGY
CHENAR
CHENARS
CHENET
CHENETS
CHENILLE
CHENILLES
CHENIX
CHENIXES
CHEQUE
CHEQUER
CHEQUERED
CHEQUERING
CHEQUERS
CHEQUES
CHEQUIER
CHEQUIEST
CHEQUY
CHER
CHERALITE
CHERALITES
CHÈRE
CHERIMOYA
CHERIMOYAS
CHERISH
CHERISHED
CHERISHES
CHERISHING
CHERNOZEM
CHERNOZEMS
CHEROOT
CHEROOTS
CHERRIED
CHERRIER
CHERRIES
CHERRIEST
CHERRY
CHERRYING
CHERT
CHERTIER
CHERTIEST
CHERTS
CHERTY
CHERUB
CHERUBIC

CHERUBIM
CHERUBIMS
CHERUBIN
CHERUBINS
CHERUBS
CHERUP
CHERUPED
CHERUPING
CHERUPS
CHERVIL
CHERVILS
CHESIL
CHESILS
CHESNUT
CHESNUTS
CHESS
CHESSEL
CHESSELS
CHESSES
CHESSMAN
CHESSMEN
CHEST
CHESTED
CHESTFUL
CHESTFULS
CHESTIER
CHESTIEST
CHESTNUT
CHESTNUTS
CHESTS
CHESTY
CHEVALET
CHEVALETS
CHEVALIER
CHEVALIERS
CHEVELURE
CHEVELURES
CHEVEN
CHEVENS
CHEVEREL
CHEVERELS
CHEVERIL
CHEVERILS
CHEVERON
CHEVERONS
CHEVERYE
CHEVERYES
CHEVIED
CHEVIES
CHEVILLE
CHEVILLES
CHEVIN
CHEVINS
CHEVRETTE
CHEVRETTES
CHEVRON
CHEVRONED
CHEVRONS
CHEVRONY
CHEVY
CHEVYING
CHEW
CHEWED
CHEWET
CHEWETS
CHEWIER
CHEWIEST
CHEWING
CHEWINK
CHEWINKS

CHEWS
CHEWY
CHEZ
CHI
CHIACK
CHIACKED
CHIACKING
CHIACKINGS
CHIACKS
CHIAO
CHIASM
CHIASMA
CHIASMAS
CHIASMS
CHIASMUS
CHIASMUSES
CHIASTIC
CHIAUS
CHIAUSED
CHIAUSES
CHIAUSING
CHIBOL
CHIBOLS
CHIBOUK
CHIBOUKS
CHIBOUQUE
CHIBOUQUES
CHIC
CHICA
CHICANE
CHICANED
CHICANER
CHICANERIES
CHICANERS
CHICANERY
CHICANES
CHICANING
CHICANINGS
CHICANO
CHICANOS
CHICAS
CHICCORIES
CHICCORY
CHICER
CHICEST
CHICH
CHICHA
CHICHAS
CHICHES
CHICHI
CHICHIS
CHICK
CHICKADEE
CHICKADEES
CHICKAREE
CHICKAREES
CHICKEN
CHICKENED
CHICKENING
CHICKENS
CHICKLING
CHICKLINGS
CHICKS
CHICKWEED
CHICKWEEDS
CHICLE
CHICLES
CHICLY
CHICON
CHICONS

CHICORIES
CHICORY
CHICS
CHID
CHIDDEN
CHIDE
CHIDED
CHIDER
CHIDERS
CHIDES
CHIDING
CHIDINGS
CHIDLINGS
CHIEF
CHIEFDOM
CHIEFDOMS
CHIEFER
CHIEFERIES
CHIEFERY
CHIEFESS
CHIEFESSES
CHIEFEST
CHIEFLESS
CHIEFLING
CHIEFLINGS
CHIEFLY
CHIEFRIES
CHIEFRY
CHIEFS
CHIEFSHIP
CHIEFSHIPS
CHIEFTAIN
CHIEFTAINS
CHIEL
CHIELD
CHIELDS
CHIELS
CHIFFON
CHIFFONS
CHIGGER
CHIGGERS
CHIGNON
CHIGNONS
CHIGOE
CHIGOES
CHIGRE
CHIGRES
CHIHUAHUA
CHIHUAHUAS
CHIK
CHIKARA
CHIKARAS
CHIKHOR
CHIKHORS
CHIKOR
CHIKORS
CHIKS
CHILBLAIN
CHILBLAINS
CHILD
CHILDBED
CHILDBEDS
CHILDE
CHILDED
CHILDER
CHILDHOOD
CHILDHOODS
CHILDING
CHILDISH
CHILDLESS

CHILDLIKE
CHILDLY
CHILDNESS
CHILDNESSES
CHILDREN
CHILDS
CHILE
CHILES
CHILI
CHILIAD
CHILIADS
CHILIAGON
CHILIAGONS
CHILIARCH
CHILIARCHS
CHILIASM
CHILIASMS
CHILIAST
CHILIASTS
CHILIS
CHILL
CHILLED
CHILLER
CHILLERS
CHILLEST
CHILLI
CHILLIER
CHILLIES
CHILLIEST
CHILLILY
CHILLING
CHILLINGS
CHILLIS
CHILLNESS
CHILLNESSES
CHILLS
CHILLUM
CHILLUMS
CHILLY
CHIMAERA
CHIMAERAS
CHIMAERID
CHIMAERIDS
CHIMB
CHIMBS
CHIME
CHIMED
CHIMER
CHIMERA
CHIMERAS
CHIMERE
CHIMERES
CHIMERIC
CHIMERS
CHIMES
CHIMING
CHIMLEY
CHIMLEYED
CHIMLEYING
CHIMLEYS
CHIMNEY
CHIMNEYED
CHIMNEYING
CHIMNEYS
CHIMP
CHIMPS
CHIN
CHINA
CHINAMPA
CHINAMPAS

CHINAR
CHINAROOT
CHINAROOTS
CHINARS
CHINAS
CHINCAPIN
CHINCAPINS
CHINCH
CHINCHES
CHINCOUGH
CHINCOUGHS
CHINDIT
CHINDITS
CHINÉ
CHINE
CHINED
CHINES
CHINESE
CHINING
CHINK
CHINKAPIN
CHINKAPINS
CHINKARA
CHINKARAS
CHINKED
CHINKIE
CHINKIER
CHINKIES
CHINKIEST
CHINKING
CHINKS
CHINKY
CHINLESS
CHINO
CHINOOK
CHINOOKS
CHINOS
CHINOVNIK
CHINOVNIKS
CHINS
CHINSTRAP
CHINSTRAPS
CHINTZ
CHINTZES
CHINTZIER
CHINTZIEST
CHINTZY
CHINWAG
CHINWAGGED
CHINWAGGING
CHINWAGS
CHIP
CHIPBOARD
CHIPBOARDS
CHIPMUCK
CHIPMUCKS
CHIPMUNK
CHIPMUNKS
CHIPOCHIA
CHIPOCHIAS
CHIPOLATA
CHIPOLATAS
CHIPPED
CHIPPER
CHIPPIE
CHIPPIER
CHIPPIES
CHIPPIEST
CHIPPING
CHIPPINGS

CHIPPY
CHIPS
CHIRAGRA
CHIRAGRAS
CHIRAGRIC
CHIRAL
CHIRALITIES
CHIRALITY
CHIRIMOYA
CHIRIMOYAS
CHIRK
CHIRKED
CHIRKING
CHIRKS
CHIRL
CHIRLED
CHIRLING
CHIRLS
CHIRM
CHIRMED
CHIRMING
CHIRMS
CHIROLOGIES
CHIROLOGY
CHIRONOMIES
CHIRONOMY
CHIROPODIES
CHIROPODY
CHIRP
CHIRPED
CHIRPER
CHIRPERS
CHIRPIER
CHIRPIEST
CHIRPILY
CHIRPING
CHIRPS
CHIRPY
CHIRR
CHIRRED
CHIRRING
CHIRRS
CHIRRUP
CHIRRUPED
CHIRRUPING
CHIRRUPS
CHIRRUPY
CHIRT
CHIRTED
CHIRTING
CHIRTS
CHIS
CHISEL
CHISELLED
CHISELLING
CHISELLINGS
CHISELS
CHIT
CHITAL
CHITALS
CHITCHAT
CHITCHATS
CHITCHATTED
CHITCHATTING
CHITIN
CHITINOUS
CHITINS
CHITLINGS
CHITON
CHITONS

CHITS
CHITTED
CHITTER
CHITTERED
CHITTERING
CHITTERINGS
CHITTERS
CHITTIER
CHITTIES
CHITTIEST
CHITTING
CHITTY
CHIV
CHIVALRIC
CHIVALRIES
CHIVALRY
CHIVE
CHIVED
CHIVES
CHIVIED
CHIVIES
CHIVING
CHIVS
CHIVVED
CHIVVIED
CHIVVIES
CHIVVING
CHIVVY
CHIVVYING
CHIVY
CHIVYING
CHLAMYDES
CHLAMYDIA
CHLAMYDIAS
CHLAMYS
CHLOASMA
CHLOASMAS
CHLORACNE
CHLORACNES
CHLORAL
CHLORALS
CHLORATE
CHLORATES
CHLORDAN
CHLORDANE
CHLORDANES
CHLORDANS
CHLORIC
CHLORIDE
CHLORIDES
CHLORINE
CHLORINES
CHLORITE
CHLORITES
CHLORITIC
CHLOROSES
CHLOROSIS
CHLOROTIC
CHLOROUS
CHOBDAR
CHOBDARS
CHOC
CHOCHO
CHOCHOS
CHOCK
CHOCKED
CHOCKER
CHOCKING
CHOCKS
CHOCOLATE

CHOCOLATES
CHOCS
CHOCTAW
CHOCTAWS
CHODE
CHOENIX
CHOENIXES
CHOICE
CHOICEFUL
CHOICELY
CHOICER
CHOICES
CHOICEST
CHOIR
CHOIRBOY
CHOIRBOYS
CHOIRED
CHOIRING
CHOIRMAN
CHOIRMEN
CHOIRS
CHOKE
CHOKEBORE
CHOKEBORES
CHOKED
CHOKEDAMP
CHOKEDAMPS
CHOKER
CHOKERS
CHOKES
CHOKEY
CHOKEYS
CHOKIDAR
CHOKIDARS
CHOKIER
CHOKIES
CHOKIEST
CHOKING
CHOKY
CHOLAEMIA
CHOLAEMIAS
CHOLAEMIC
CHOLECYST
CHOLECYSTS
CHOLELITH
CHOLELITHS
CHOLER
CHOLERA
CHOLERAIC
CHOLERAS
CHOLERIC
CHOLERS
CHOLI
CHOLIAMB
CHOLIAMBS
CHOLIC
CHOLINE
CHOLINES
CHOLIS
CHOLTRIES
CHOLTRY
CHOMP
CHOMPED
CHOMPING
CHOMPS
CHONDRAL
CHONDRE
CHONDRES
CHONDRI
CHONDRIFIED

CHONDRIFIES
CHONDRIFY
CHONDRIFYING
CHONDRIN
CHONDRINS
CHONDRITE
CHONDRITES
CHONDROID
CHONDRULE
CHONDRULES
CHONDRUS
CHOOK
CHOOKIE
CHOOKIES
CHOOKS
CHOOM
CHOOMS
CHOOSE
CHOOSER
CHOOSERS
CHOOSES
CHOOSEY
CHOOSIER
CHOOSIEST
CHOOSING
CHOOSY
CHOP
CHOPIN
CHOPINE
CHOPINES
CHOPINS
CHOPPED
CHOPPER
CHOPPERS
CHOPPIER
CHOPPIEST
CHOPPING
CHOPPINGS
CHOPPY
CHOPS
CHORAGI
CHORAGIC
CHORAGUS
CHORAGUSES
CHORAL
CHORALE
CHORALES
CHORALLY
CHORALS
CHORD
CHORDAL
CHORDATE
CHORDATES
CHORDS
CHORE
CHOREA
CHOREAS
CHOREE
CHOREES
CHOREGI
CHOREGIC
CHOREGUS
CHOREGUSES
CHORES
CHOREUS
CHOREUSES
CHORIA
CHORIAMB
CHORIAMBS
CHORIC

CHORINE
CHORINES
CHORIOID
CHORIOIDS
CHORION
CHORIONIC
CHORISES
CHORISIS
CHORIST
CHORISTER
CHORISTERS
CHORISTS
CHORIZO
CHORIZONT
CHORIZONTS
CHORIZOS
CHOROID
CHOROIDS
CHOROLOGIES
CHOROLOGY
CHORTLE
CHORTLED
CHORTLES
CHORTLING
CHORUS
CHORUSED
CHORUSES
CHORUSING
CHOSE
CHOSEN
CHOSES
CHOU
CHOUGH
CHOUGHS
CHOULTRIES
CHOULTRY
CHOUNTER
CHOUNTERED
CHOUNTERING
CHOUNTERS
CHOUSE
CHOUSED
CHOUSES
CHOUSING
CHOUT
CHOUTS
CHOUX
CHOW
CHOWDER
CHOWDERS
CHOWKIDAR
CHOWKIDARS
CHOWRI
CHOWRIES
CHOWRIS
CHOWRY
CHOWS
CHRISM
CHRISMAL
CHRISMALS
CHRISMS
CHRISOM
CHRISOMS
CHRISTEN
CHRISTENED
CHRISTENING
CHRISTENINGS
CHRISTENS
CHRISTIE
CHRISTIES

CHRISTOM
CHRISTOMS
CHRISTY
CHROMA
CHROMAKEY
CHROMAKEYS
CHROMAS
CHROMATE
CHROMATES
CHROMATIC
CHROMATICS
CHROMATIN
CHROMATINS
CHROME
CHROMED
CHROMES
CHROMIC
CHROMIDIA
CHROMING
CHROMITE
CHROMITES
CHROMIUM
CHROMIUMS
CHROMO
CHROMOS
CHRONIC
CHRONICAL
CHRONICLE
CHRONICLED
CHRONICLES
CHRONICLING
CHRONICS
CHRONON
CHRONONS
CHRYSALID
CHRYSALIDES
CHRYSALIDS
CHRYSALIS
CHRYSALISES
CHRYSANTH
CHRYSANTHS
CHTHONIAN
CHTHONIC
CHUB
CHUBBED
CHUBBIER
CHUBBIEST
CHUBBY
CHUBS
CHUCK
CHUCKED
CHUCKIE
CHUCKIES
CHUCKING
CHUCKLE
CHUCKLED
CHUCKLES
CHUCKLING
CHUCKLINGS
CHUCKS
CHUDDAH
CHUDDAHS
CHUDDAR
CHUDDARS
CHUFA
CHUFAS
CHUFF
CHUFFED
CHUFFIER
CHUFFIEST

CHUFFS
CHUFFY
CHUG
CHUGGED
CHUGGING
CHUGS
CHUKAR
CHUKARS
CHUKKA
CHUKKAS
CHUKKER
CHUKKERS
CHUKOR
CHUKORS
CHUM
CHUMLEY
CHUMLEYED
CHUMLEYING
CHUMLEYS
CHUMMAGE
CHUMMAGES
CHUMMED
CHUMMIER
CHUMMIES
CHUMMIEST
CHUMMING
CHUMMY
CHUMP
CHUMPS
CHUMS
CHUNDER
CHUNDERED
CHUNDERING
CHUNDERS
CHUNK
CHUNKIER
CHUNKIEST
CHUNKS
CHUNKY
CHUNNEL
CHUNNELS
CHUNNER
CHUNNERED
CHUNNERING
CHUNNERS
CHUNTER
CHUNTERED
CHUNTERING
CHUNTERS
CHUPATI
CHUPATIS
CHUPATTI
CHUPATTIS
CHUPRASSIES
CHUPRASSY
CHURCH
CHURCHED
CHURCHES
CHURCHIER
CHURCHIEST
CHURCHING
CHURCHINGS
CHURCHISM
CHURCHISMS
CHURCHLY
CHURCHMAN
CHURCHMEN
CHURCHWAY
CHURCHWAYS
CHURCHY

CHURINGA
CHURINGAS
CHURL
CHURLISH
CHURLS
CHURN
CHURNED
CHURNING
CHURNINGS
CHURNS
CHURR
CHURRED
CHURRING
CHURRS
CHURRUS
CHURRUSES
CHUSE
CHUSES
CHUSING
CHUT
CHUTE
CHUTES
CHUTIST
CHUTISTS
CHUTNEY
CHUTNEYS
CHUTZPAH
CHUTZPAHS
CHYACK
CHYACKED
CHYACKING
CHYACKS
CHYLDE
CHYLE
CHYLES
CHYLURIA
CHYLURIAS
CHYME
CHYMES
CHYMIFIED
CHYMIFIES
CHYMIFY
CHYMIFYING
CHYMISTRIES
CHYMISTRY
CHYMOUS
CHYND
CHYPRE
CHYPRES
CIAO
CIAOS
CIBATION
CIBATIONS
CIBOL
CIBOLS
CIBORIA
CIBORIUM
CICADA
CICADAS
CICALA
CICALAS
CICATRICE
CICATRICES
CICATRISE
CICATRISED
CICATRISES
CICATRISING
CICATRIX
CICATRIXES
CICATRIZE

CICATRIZED
CICATRIZES
CICATRIZING
CICELIES
CICELY
CICERO
CICERONE
CICERONED
CICERONEING
CICERONES
CICERONI
CICEROS
CICHLID
CICHLIDS
CICHLOID
CICINNUS
CICINNUSES
CICISBEI
CICISBEO
CICLATON
CICLATONS
CICLATOUN
CICLATOUNS
CICUTA
CICUTAS
CIDARIS
CIDARISES
CIDE
CIDED
CIDER
CIDERKIN
CIDERKINS
CIDERS
CIDERY
CIDES
CIDING
CIEL
CIELED
CIELING
CIELINGS
CIELS
CIERGE
CIERGES
CIG
CIGAR
CIGARETTE
CIGARETTES
CIGARILLO
CIGARILLOS
CIGARS
CIGGIE
CIGGIES
CIGGY
CIGS
CILIA
CILIARY
CILIATE
CILIATED
CILICE
CILICES
CILICIOUS
CILIOLATE
CILIUM
CILL
CILLS
CIMAR
CIMARS
CIMELIA
CIMEX
CIMICES

CIMIER
CIMIERS
CIMINITE
CIMINITES
CIMOLITE
CIMOLITES
CINCH
CINCHED
CINCHES
CINCHING
CINCHONA
CINCHONAS
CINCHONIC
CINCINNUS
CINCINNUSES
CINCT
CINCTURE
CINCTURED
CINCTURES
CINCTURING
CINDER
CINDERS
CINDERY
CINEAST
CINEASTE
CINÉASTE
CINEASTES
CINÉASTES
CINEASTS
CINEMA
CINEMAS
CINEMATIC
CINEOL
CINEOLE
CINEOLES
CINEOLS
CINERAMIC
CINERARIA
CINERARIAS
CINERARY
CINERATOR
CINERATORS
CINEREA
CINEREAL
CINEREAS
CINEREOUS
CINGULUM
CINGULUMS
CINNABAR
CINNABARS
CINNAMIC
CINNAMON
CINNAMONS
CINQUAIN
CINQUAINS
CINQUE
CINQUES
CION
CIONS
CIPHER
CIPHERED
CIPHERING
CIPHERINGS
CIPHERS
CIPOLIN
CIPOLINS
CIPOLLINO
CIPOLLINOS
CIPPI
CIPPUS

CIRCA
CIRCADIAN
CIRCAR
CIRCARS
CIRCINATE
CIRCITER
CIRCLE
CIRCLED
CIRCLER
CIRCLERS
CIRCLES
CIRCLET
CIRCLETS
CIRCLING
CIRCLINGS
CIRCS
CIRCUIT
CIRCUITED
CIRCUITIES
CIRCUITING
CIRCUITRIES
CIRCUITRY
CIRCUITS
CIRCUITY
CIRCULAR
CIRCULARS
CIRCULATE
CIRCULATED
CIRCULATES
CIRCULATING
CIRCULATINGS
CIRCUS
CIRCUSES
CIRCUSSY
CIRCUSY
CIRÉ
CIRÉS
CIRL
CIRLS
CIRQUE
CIRQUES
CIRRATE
CIRRHOPOD
CIRRHOPODS
CIRRHOSES
CIRRHOSIS
CIRRHOTIC
CIRRI
CIRRIFORM
CIRRIPED
CIRRIPEDE
CIRRIPEDES
CIRRIPEDS
CIRROSE
CIRROUS
CIRRUS
CISCO
CISCOES
CISCOS
CISELEUR
CISELEURS
CISELURE
CISELURES
CISLUNAR
CISSIER
CISSIES
CISSIEST
CISSOID
CISSOIDS
CISSY

CIST
CISTED
CISTERN
CISTERNS
CISTIC
CISTRON
CISTRONS
CISTS
CISTUS
CISTUSES
CISTVAEN
CISTVAENS
CIT
CITABLE
CITADEL
CITADELS
CITAL
CITALS
CITATION
CITATIONS
CITATORY
CITE
CITED
CITER
CITERS
CITES
CITESS
CITESSES
CITHARA
CITHARAS
CITHARIST
CITHARISTS
CITHER
CITHERN
CITHERNS
CITHERS
CITIES
CITIFIED
CITIFIES
CITIFY
CITIFYING
CITIGRADE
CITING
CITIZEN
CITIZENRIES
CITIZENRY
CITIZENS
CITO
CITOLE
CITOLES
CITRANGE
CITRANGES
CITRATE
CITRATES
CITREOUS
CITRIC
CITRIN
CITRINE
CITRINES
CITRINS
CITRON
CITRONS
CITROUS
CITRUS
CITRUSES
CITS
CITTERN
CITTERNS
CITY
CITYSCAPE

CITYSCAPES
CIVE
CIVES
CIVET
CIVETS
CIVIC
CIVICALLY
CIVICS
CIVIL
CIVILIAN
CIVILIANS
CIVILISE
CIVILISED
CIVILISER
CIVILISERS
CIVILISES
CIVILISING
CIVILIST
CIVILISTS
CIVILITIES
CIVILITY
CIVILIZE
CIVILIZED
CIVILIZER
CIVILIZERS
CIVILIZES
CIVILIZING
CIVILLY
CIVISM
CIVISMS
CIVVIES
CIVVY
CIZERS
CLABBER
CLABBERS
CLACHAN
CLACHANS
CLACK
CLACKBOX
CLACKBOXES
CLACKDISH
CLACKDISHES
CLACKED
CLACKER
CLACKERS
CLACKING
CLACKS
CLAD
CLADDED
CLADDER
CLADDERS
CLADDING
CLADDINGS
CLADE
CLADES
CLADISM
CLADISMS
CLADIST
CLADISTIC
CLADISTICS
CLADISTS
CLADODE
CLADODES
CLADOGRAM
CLADOGRAMS
CLADS
CLAES
CLAG
CLAGGED
CLAGGIER

CLAGGIEST
CLAGGING
CLAGGY
CLAGS
CLAIM
CLAIMABLE
CLAIMANT
CLAIMANTS
CLAIMED
CLAIMER
CLAIMERS
CLAIMING
CLAIMS
CLAM
CLAMANCIES
CLAMANCY
CLAMANT
CLAMANTLY
CLAMBAKE
CLAMBAKES
CLAMBE
CLAMBER
CLAMBERED
CLAMBERING
CLAMBERS
CLAME
CLAMES
CLAMMED
CLAMMIER
CLAMMIEST
CLAMMILY
CLAMMING
CLAMMY
CLAMOR
CLAMORED
CLAMORING
CLAMOROUS
CLAMORS
CLAMOUR
CLAMOURED
CLAMOURER
CLAMOURERS
CLAMOURING
CLAMOURS
CLAMP
CLAMPDOWN
CLAMPDOWNS
CLAMPED
CLAMPER
CLAMPERED
CLAMPERING
CLAMPERS
CLAMPING
CLAMPS
CLAMS
CLAN
CLANG
CLANGED
CLANGER
CLANGERS
CLANGING
CLANGINGS
CLANGOR
CLANGORED
CLANGORING
CLANGORS
CLANGOUR
CLANGOURED
CLANGOURING
CLANGOURS

CLANGS
CLANK
CLANKED
CLANKING
CLANKINGS
CLANKLESS
CLANKS
CLANNISH
CLANS
CLANSHIP
CLANSHIPS
CLANSMAN
CLANSMEN
CLAP
CLAPBOARD
CLAPBOARDS
CLAPBREAD
CLAPBREADS
CLAPDISH
CLAPDISHES
CLAPNET
CLAPNETS
CLAPPED
CLAPPER
CLAPPERED
CLAPPERING
CLAPPERINGS
CLAPPERS
CLAPPING
CLAPPINGS
CLAPS
CLAPTRAP
CLAPTRAPS
CLAQUE
CLAQUES
CLAQUEUR
CLAQUEURS
CLARENCE
CLARENCES
CLARENDON
CLARENDONS
CLARET
CLARETED
CLARETING
CLARETS
CLARIES
CLARIFIED
CLARIFIER
CLARIFIERS
CLARIFIES
CLARIFY
CLARIFYING
CLARINET
CLARINETS
CLARINI
CLARINO
CLARINOS
CLARION
CLARIONET
CLARIONETS
CLARIONS
CLARITIES
CLARITY
CLARKIA
CLARKIAS
CLARSACH
CLARSACHS
CLART
CLARTED
CLARTIER

CLARTIEST
CLARTING
CLARTS
CLARTY
CLARY
CLASH
CLASHED
CLASHES
CLASHING
CLASHINGS
CLASP
CLASPED
CLASPER
CLASPERS
CLASPING
CLASPINGS
CLASPS
CLASS
CLASSABLE
CLASSED
CLASSES
CLASSIBLE
CLASSIC
CLASSICAL
CLASSICS
CLASSIER
CLASSIEST
CLASSIFIC
CLASSIFIED
CLASSIFIES
CLASSIFY
CLASSIFYING
CLASSING
CLASSIS
CLASSLESS
CLASSMAN
CLASSMATE
CLASSMATES
CLASSMEN
CLASSROOM
CLASSROOMS
CLASSY
CLASTIC
CLAT
CLATCH
CLATCHED
CLATCHES
CLATCHING
CLATHRATE
CLATS
CLATTED
CLATTER
CLATTERED
CLATTERER
CLATTERERS
CLATTERING
CLATTERS
CLATTING
CLAUCHT
CLAUCHTED
CLAUCHTING
CLAUCHTS
CLAUGHT
CLAUGHTED
CLAUGHTING
CLAUGHTS
CLAUSAL
CLAUSE
CLAUSES
CLAUSTRA

CLAUSTRAL
CLAUSTRUM
CLAUSULA
CLAUSULAE
CLAUSULAR
CLAUT
CLAUTED
CLAUTING
CLAUTS
CLAVATE
CLAVATED
CLAVATION
CLAVATIONS
CLAVE
CLAVECIN
CLAVECINS
CLAVER
CLAVERED
CLAVERING
CLAVERS
CLAVES
CLAVICLE
CLAVICLES
CLAVICORN
CLAVICORNS
CLAVICULA
CLAVICULAS
CLAVIE
CLAVIER
CLAVIERS
CLAVIES
CLAVIFORM
CLAVIGER
CLAVIGERS
CLAVIS
CLAVULATE
CLAW
CLAWBACK
CLAWBACKS
CLAWED
CLAWING
CLAWLESS
CLAWS
CLAY
CLAYED
CLAYEY
CLAYIER
CLAYIEST
CLAYING
CLAYISH
CLAYMORE
CLAYMORES
CLAYPAN
CLAYPANS
CLAYS
CLEAN
CLEANED
CLEANER
CLEANERS
CLEANEST
CLEANING
CLEANINGS
CLEANLIER
CLEANLIEST
CLEANLY
CLEANNESS
CLEANNESSES
CLEANS
CLEANSE
CLEANSED

CLEANSER
CLEANSERS
CLEANSES
CLEANSING
CLEANSINGS
CLEANSKIN
CLEANSKINS
CLEAR
CLEARAGE
CLEARAGES
CLEARANCE
CLEARANCES
CLEARCOLE
CLEARCOLES
CLEARED
CLEARER
CLEARERS
CLEAREST
CLEARING
CLEARINGS
CLEARLY
CLEARNESS
CLEARNESSES
CLEARS
CLEARSKIN
CLEARSKINS
CLEARWAY
CLEARWAYS
CLEARWING
CLEARWINGS
CLEAT
CLEATED
CLEATING
CLEATS
CLEAVABLE
CLEAVAGE
CLEAVAGES
CLEAVE
CLEAVED
CLEAVER
CLEAVERS
CLEAVES
CLEAVING
CLEAVINGS
CLECHÉ
CLECK
CLECKED
CLECKING
CLECKINGS
CLECKS
CLEEK
CLEEKED
CLEEKING
CLEEKIT
CLEEKS
CLEEP
CLEEPED
CLEEPING
CLEEPS
CLEEVE
CLEEVES
CLEF
CLEFS
CLEFT
CLEFTS
CLEG
CLEGS
CLEITHRAL
CLEM
CLEMATIS

CLEMATISES
CLEMENCE
CLEMENCES
CLEMENCIES
CLEMENCY
CLEMENT
CLEMENTLY
CLEMMED
CLEMMING
CLEMS
CLENCH
CLENCHED
CLENCHES
CLENCHING
CLEPE
CLEPED
CLEPES
CLEPING
CLEPSYDRA
CLEPSYDRAS
CLERECOLE
CLERECOLES
CLERGIES
CLERGY
CLERGYMAN
CLERGYMEN
CLERIC
CLERICAL
CLERICALS
CLERICATE
CLERICATES
CLERICITIES
CLERICITY
CLERICS
CLERIHEW
CLERIHEWS
CLERISIES
CLERISY
CLERK
CLERKDOM
CLERKDOMS
CLERKED
CLERKESS
CLERKESSES
CLERKING
CLERKISH
CLERKLESS
CLERKLIER
CLERKLIEST
CLERKLING
CLERKLINGS
CLERKLY
CLERKS
CLERKSHIP
CLERKSHIPS
CLERUCH
CLERUCHIA
CLERUCHIAS
CLERUCHIES
CLERUCHS
CLERUCHY
CLEUCH
CLEUCHS
CLEUGH
CLEUGHS
CLEVE
CLEVEITE
CLEVEITES
CLEVER
CLEVERER

CLEVEREST
CLEVERISH
CLEVERLY
CLEVES
CLEVIS
CLEVISES
CLEW
CLEWED
CLEWING
CLEWS
CLIANTHUS
CLIANTHUSES
CLICHÉ
CLICHÉD
CLICHÉS
CLICK
CLICKED
CLICKER
CLICKERS
CLICKET
CLICKETED
CLICKETING
CLICKETS
CLICKING
CLICKINGS
CLICKS
CLIED
CLIENT
CLIENTAGE
CLIENTAGES
CLIENTAL
CLIENTÈLE
CLIENTÈLES
CLIENTS
CLIES
CLIFF
CLIFFED
CLIFFHANG
CLIFFHANGING
CLIFFHANGINGS
CLIFFHANGS
CLIFFHUNG
CLIFFIER
CLIFFIEST
CLIFFS
CLIFFY
CLIFT
CLIFTED
CLIFTIER
CLIFTIEST
CLIFTS
CLIFTY
CLIMACTIC
CLIMATAL
CLIMATE
CLIMATED
CLIMATES
CLIMATIC
CLIMATING
CLIMATISE
CLIMATISED
CLIMATISES
CLIMATISING
CLIMATIZE
CLIMATIZED
CLIMATIZES
CLIMATIZING
CLIMATURE
CLIMATURES
CLIMAX

CLIMAXED
CLIMAXES
CLIMAXING
CLIMB
CLIMBABLE
CLIMBED
CLIMBER
CLIMBERS
CLIMBING
CLIMBINGS
CLIMBS
CLIME
CLIMES
CLINAMEN
CLINAMENS
CLINCH
CLINCHED
CLINCHER
CLINCHERS
CLINCHES
CLINCHING
CLINE
CLINES
CLING
CLINGER
CLINGERS
CLINGIER
CLINGIEST
CLINGING
CLINGS
CLINGY
CLINIC
CLINICAL
CLINICIAN
CLINICIANS
CLINICS
CLINIQUE
CLINIQUES
CLINK
CLINKED
CLINKER
CLINKERS
CLINKING
CLINKS
CLINOAXES
CLINOAXIS
CLINQUANT
CLINQUANTS
CLINT
CLINTS
CLIP
CLIPBOARD
CLIPBOARDS
CLIPE
CLIPED
CLIPES
CLIPING
CLIPPED
CLIPPER
CLIPPERS
CLIPPIE
CLIPPIES
CLIPPING
CLIPPINGS
CLIPS
CLIPT
CLIQUE
CLIQUES
CLIQUEY
CLIQUIER

CLIQUIEST
CLIQUISH
CLIQUISM
CLIQUISMS
CLIQUY
CLITELLA
CLITELLAR
CLITELLUM
CLITHRAL
CLITIC
CLITICS
CLITORAL
CLITORIS
CLITORISES
CLITTER
CLITTERED
CLITTERING
CLITTERS
CLIVERS
CLOACA
CLOACAE
CLOACAL
CLOACALIN
CLOACINAL
CLOAK
CLOAKED
CLOAKING
CLOAKROOM
CLOAKROOMS
CLOAKS
CLOAM
CLOAMS
CLOBBER
CLOBBERED
CLOBBERING
CLOBBERS
CLOCHARD
CLOCHARDS
CLOCHE
CLOCHES
CLOCK
CLOCKED
CLOCKER
CLOCKERS
CLOCKING
CLOCKS
CLOCKWISE
CLOCKWORK
CLOCKWORKS
CLOD
CLODDED
CLODDIER
CLODDIEST
CLODDING
CLODDISH
CLODDY
CLODLY
CLODPATE
CLODPATED
CLODPATES
CLODPOLE
CLODPOLL
CLODPOLLS
CLODS
CLOFF
CLOFFS
CLOG
CLOGDANCE
CLOGDANCES

CLOGGED
CLOGGER
CLOGGERS
CLOGGIER
CLOGGIEST
CLOGGING
CLOGGY
CLOGS
CLOISON
CLOISONNÉ
CLOISONNÉS
CLOISONS
CLOISTER
CLOISTERED
CLOISTERING
CLOISTERS
CLOISTRAL
CLOKE
CLOKED
CLOKES
CLOKING
CLOMB
CLONAL
CLONE
CLONED
CLONES
CLONIC
CLONING
CLONK
CLONKED
CLONKING
CLONKS
CLONUS
CLONUSES
CLOOP
CLOOPS
CLOOT
CLOOTS
CLOP
CLOPPED
CLOPPING
CLOPS
CLOQUÉ
CLOQUÉS
CLOSE
CLOSED
CLOSELY
CLOSENESS
CLOSENESSES
CLOSER
CLOSERS
CLOSES
CLOSEST
CLOSET
CLOSETED
CLOSETING
CLOSETS
CLOSING
CLOSINGS
CLOSURE
CLOSURED
CLOSURES
CLOSURING
CLOT
CLOTBUR
CLOTBURS
CLOTE
CLOTEBUR
CLOTEBURS
CLOTES

CLOTH
CLOTHE
CLOTHED
CLOTHES
CLOTHIER
CLOTHIERS
CLOTHING
CLOTHINGS
CLOTHS
CLOTPOLL
CLOTPOLLS
CLOTS
CLOTTED
CLOTTER
CLOTTERED
CLOTTERING
CLOTTERS
CLOTTIER
CLOTTIEST
CLOTTING
CLOTTINGS
CLOTTY
CLOTURE
CLOTURED
CLOTURES
CLOTURING
CLOU
CLOUD
CLOUDAGE
CLOUDAGES
CLOUDED
CLOUDIER
CLOUDIEST
CLOUDILY
CLOUDING
CLOUDINGS
CLOUDLAND
CLOUDLANDS
CLOUDLESS
CLOUDLET
CLOUDLETS
CLOUDS
CLOUDY
CLOUGH
CLOUGHS
CLOUR
CLOURED
CLOURING
CLOURS
CLOUS
CLOUT
CLOUTED
CLOUTER
CLOUTERLY
CLOUTERS
CLOUTING
CLOUTS
CLOVE
CLOVEN
CLOVER
CLOVERED
CLOVERS
CLOVERY
CLOVES
CLOW
CLOWDER
CLOWDERS
CLOWN
CLOWNED
CLOWNERIES

CLOWNERY
CLOWNING
CLOWNINGS
CLOWNISH
CLOWNS
CLOWNSHIP
CLOWNSHIPS
CLOWS
CLOY
CLOYE
CLOYED
CLOYES
CLOYING
CLOYLESS
CLOYMENT
CLOYMENTS
CLOYS
CLOYSOME
CLOZE
CLUB
CLUBABLE
CLUBBABLE
CLUBBED
CLUBBING
CLUBBINGS
CLUBBISH
CLUBBISM
CLUBBISMS
CLUBBIST
CLUBBISTS
CLUBHOUSE
CLUBHOUSES
CLUBLAND
CLUBLANDS
CLUBMAN
CLUBMEN
CLUBROOM
CLUBROOMS
CLUBROOT
CLUBROOTS
CLUBS
CLUBWOMAN
CLUBWOMEN
CLUCK
CLUCKED
CLUCKIER
CLUCKIEST
CLUCKING
CLUCKS
CLUCKY
CLUDGIE
CLUDGIES
CLUE
CLUED
CLUEING
CLUELESS
CLUES
CLUING
CLUMBER
CLUMBERS
CLUMP
CLUMPED
CLUMPIER
CLUMPIEST
CLUMPING
CLUMPS
CLUMPY
CLUMSIER
CLUMSIEST
CLUMSILY

CLUMSY
CLUNCH
CLUNCHES
CLUNG
CLUNK
CLUNKED
CLUNKING
CLUNKS
CLUPEID
CLUPEIDS
CLUPEOID
CLUPEOIDS
CLUSIA
CLUSIAS
CLUSTER
CLUSTERED
CLUSTERING
CLUSTERS
CLUSTERY
CLUTCH
CLUTCHED
CLUTCHES
CLUTCHING
CLUTTER
CLUTTERED
CLUTTERING
CLUTTERS
CLY
CLYING
CLYPE
CLYPEAL
CLYPEATE
CLYPED
CLYPEI
CLYPES
CLYPEUS
CLYPING
CLYSTER
CLYSTERS
CNIDA
CNIDAE
CNIDARIA
COACH
COACHDOG
COACHDOGS
COACHED
COACHEE
COACHEES
COACHER
COACHERS
COACHES
COACHIES
COACHING
COACHINGS
COACHMAN
COACHMEN
COACHWHIP
COACHWHIPS
COACHWORK
COACHWORKS
COACHY
COACT
COACTED
COACTING
COACTION
COACTIONS
COACTIVE
COACTS
COADJUTOR
COADJUTORS

COADUNATE
COADUNATED
COADUNATES
COADUNATING
COAGULANT
COAGULANTS
COAGULATE
COAGULATED
COAGULATES
COAGULATING
COAGULUM
COAGULUMS
COAITA
COAITAS
COAL
COALBALL
COALBALLS
COALED
COALER
COALERS
COALESCE
COALESCED
COALESCES
COALESCING
COALFIELD
COALFIELDS
COALFISH
COALFISHES
COALIER
COALIEST
COALING
COALISE
COALISED
COALISES
COALISING
COALITION
COALITIONS
COALIZE
COALIZED
COALIZES
COALIZING
COALMAN
COALMEN
COALS
COALY
COAMING
COAMINGS
COAPT
COAPTED
COAPTING
COAPTS
COARB
COARBS
COARCTATE
COARSE
COARSELY
COARSEN
COARSENED
COARSENING
COARSENS
COARSER
COARSEST
COARSISH
COAST
COASTAL
COASTED
COASTER
COASTERS
COASTING
COASTINGS

COASTLINE
COASTLINES
COASTS
COASTWARD
COASTWARDS
COASTWISE
COAT
COATE
COATED
COATEE
COATEES
COATER
COATERS
COATES
COATI
COATING
COATINGS
COATIS
COATLESS
COATRACK
COATRACKS
COATS
COATSTAND
COATSTANDS
COAX
COAXED
COAXER
COAXERS
COAXES
COAXIAL
COAXIALLY
COAXING
COAXINGLY
COB
COBALT
COBALTIC
COBALTITE
COBALTITES
COBALTS
COBB
COBBED
COBBER
COBBERS
COBBIER
COBBIEST
COBBING
COBBLE
COBBLED
COBBLER
COBBLERIES
COBBLERS
COBBLERY
COBBLES
COBBLING
COBBLINGS
COBBS
COBBY
COBIA
COBIAS
COBLE
COBLES
COBLOAF
COBLOAVES
COBNUT
COBNUTS
COBRA
COBRAS
COBRIC
COBRIFORM
COBS

COBURG
COBURGS
COBWEB
COBWEBBED
COBWEBBIER
COBWEBBIEST
COBWEBBING
COBWEBBY
COBWEBS
COCA
COCAINE
COCAINES
COCAINISE
COCAINISED
COCAINISES
COCAINISING
COCAINISM
COCAINISMS
COCAINIST
COCAINISTS
COCAINIZE
COCAINIZED
COCAINIZES
COCAINIZING
COCAS
COCCAL
COCCI
COCCID
COCCIDIA
COCCIDIUM
COCCIDS
COCCO
COCCOID
COCCOLITE
COCCOLITES
COCCOLITH
COCCOLITHS
COCCOS
COCCUS
COCCYGEAL
COCCYGES
COCCYGIAN
COCCYX
COCH
COCHES
COCHINEAL
COCHINEALS
COCHLEA
COCHLEAE
COCHLEAR
COCHLEARE
COCHLEARES
COCHLEARS
COCHLEAS
COCHLEATE
COCK
COCKADE
COCKADES
COCKATEEL
COCKATEELS
COCKATIEL
COCKATIELS
COCKATOO
COCKATOOS
COCKBIRD
COCKBIRDS
COCKBOAT
COCKBOATS
COCKED
COCKER

COCKERED
COCKEREL
COCKERELS
COCKERING
COCKERS
COCKET
COCKETS
COCKEYE
COCKEYED
COCKEYES
COCKFIGHT
COCKFIGHTS
COCKHORSE
COCKHORSES
COCKIER
COCKIES
COCKIEST
COCKILY
COCKINESS
COCKINESSES
COCKING
COCKLAIRD
COCKLAIRDS
COCKLE
COCKLED
COCKLES
COCKLING
COCKLOFT
COCKLOFTS
COCKMATCH
COCKMATCHES
COCKNEY
COCKNEYFIED
COCKNEYFIES
COCKNEYFY
COCKNEYFYING
COCKNEYS
COCKPIT
COCKPITS
COCKROACH
COCKROACHES
COCKS
COCKSCOMB
COCKSCOMBS
COCKSFOOT
COCKSFOOTS
COCKSHIES
COCKSHOOT
COCKSHOOTS
COCKSHOT
COCKSHOTS
COCKSHUT
COCKSHUTS
COCKSHY
COCKSIER
COCKSIEST
COCKSPUR
COCKSPURS
COCKSURE
COCKSWAIN
COCKSWAINED
COCKSWAINING
COCKSWAINS
COCKSY
COCKTAIL
COCKTAILS
COCKY
COCKYOLLIES
COCKYOLLY
COCO

COCOA
COCOANUT
COCOANUTS
COCOAS
COCONUT
COCONUTS
COCOON
COCOONED
COCOONERIES
COCOONERY
COCOONING
COCOONS
COCOPLUM
COCOPLUMS
COCOS
COCOTTE
COCOTTES
COCTILE
COCTION
COCTIONS
COD
CODA
CODAS
CODDED
CODDING
CODDLE
CODDLED
CODDLES
CODDLING
CODE
CODED
CODEINE
CODEINES
CODES
CODEX
CODFISH
CODFISHES
CODGER
CODGERS
CODICES
CODICIL
CODICILS
CODIFIED
CODIFIER
CODIFIERS
CODIFIES
CODIFY
CODIFYING
CODILLA
CODILLAS
CODILLE
CODILLES
CODING
CODINGS
CODIST
CODISTS
CODLIN
CODLING
CODLINGS
CODLINS
CODON
CODONS
CODS
COED
COEDS
COEHORN
COEHORNS
COELIAC
COELIACS
COELOM

COELOMATE
COELOMATES
COELOME
COELOMES
COELOMIC
COELOMS
COELOSTAT
COELOSTATS
COEMPTION
COEMPTIONS
COENOBIA
COENOBITE
COENOBITES
COENOBIUM
COENOSARC
COENOSARCS
COENZYME
COENZYMES
COEQUAL
COEQUALLY
COEQUALS
COERCE
COERCED
COERCES
COERCIBLE
COERCIBLY
COERCING
COERCION
COERCIONS
COERCIVE
COEVAL
COEVALS
COFF
COFFEE
COFFEES
COFFER
COFFERED
COFFERING
COFFERS
COFFIN
COFFINED
COFFING
COFFINING
COFFINITE
COFFINITES
COFFINS
COFFLE
COFFLES
COFFRET
COFFRETS
COFFS
COFT
COG
COGENCE
COGENCES
COGENCIES
COGENCY
COGENER
COGENERS
COGENT
COGENTLY
COGGED
COGGER
COGGERS
COGGIE
COGGIES
COGGING
COGGLE
COGGLED
COGGLES

COGGLIER
COGGLIEST
COGGLING
COGGLY
COGIE
COGIES
COGITABLE
COGITATE
COGITATED
COGITATES
COGITATING
COGNATE
COGNATES
COGNATION
COGNATIONS
COGNISANT
COGNISE
COGNISED
COGNISES
COGNISING
COGNITION
COGNITIONS
COGNITIVE
COGNIZANT
COGNIZE
COGNIZED
COGNIZES
COGNIZING
COGNOMEN
COGNOMENS
COGNOMINA
COGNOSCE
COGNOSCED
COGNOSCES
COGNOSCING
COGNOVIT
COGNOVITS
COGS
COGUE
COGUES
COHABIT
COHABITED
COHABITEE
COHABITEES
COHABITING
COHABITS
COHERE
COHERED
COHERENCE
COHERENCES
COHERENCIES
COHERENCY
COHERENT
COHERER
COHERERS
COHERES
COHERING
COHERITOR
COHERITORS
COHESIBLE
COHESION
COHESIONS
COHESIVE
COHIBIT
COHIBITED
COHIBITING
COHIBITS
COHO
COHOE
COHOES

COHOG
COHOGS
COHORN
COHORNS
COHORT
COHORTS
COHOS
COHUNE
COHUNES
COIF
COIFED
COIFFEUR
COIFFEURS
COIFFEUSE
COIFFEUSES
COIFFURE
COIFFURED
COIFFURES
COIFFURING
COIFING
COIFS
COIGN
COIGNE
COIGNED
COIGNES
COIGNING
COIGNS
COIL
COILED
COILING
COILS
COIN
COINAGE
COINAGES
COINCIDE
COINCIDED
COINCIDES
COINCIDING
COINED
COINER
COINERS
COINING
COININGS
COINS
COIR
COIRS
COISTREL
COISTRELS
COISTRIL
COISTRILS
COITAL
COITION
COITIONS
COITUS
COITUSES
COJOIN
COJOINED
COJOINING
COJOINS
COKE
COKED
COKERNUT
COKERNUTS
COKES
COKESES
COKIER
COKIEST
COKING
COKY
COL

COLA
COLANDER
COLANDERS
COLAS
COLATION
COLATIONS
COLATURE
COLATURES
COLCANNON
COLCANNONS
COLCHICA
COLCHICUM
COLCHICUMS
COLCOTHAR
COLCOTHARS
COLD
COLDBLOOD
COLDBLOODS
COLDER
COLDEST
COLDHOUSE
COLDHOUSES
COLDISH
COLDLY
COLDNESS
COLDNESSES
COLDS
COLE
COLES
COLEUS
COLEUSES
COLEY
COLEYS
COLIBRI
COLIBRIS
COLIC
COLICKY
COLICS
COLIFORM
COLIFORMS
COLIN
COLINS
COLISEUM
COLISEUMS
COLITIS
COLITISES
COLL
COLLAGE
COLLAGEN
COLLAGENS
COLLAGES
COLLAGIST
COLLAGISTS
COLLAPSE
COLLAPSED
COLLAPSES
COLLAPSING
COLLAR
COLLARD
COLLARDS
COLLARED
COLLARING
COLLARS
COLLATE
COLLATED
COLLATES
COLLATING
COLLATION
COLLATIONS
COLLATIVE

COLLATOR
COLLATORS
COLLEAGUE
COLLEAGUED
COLLEAGUES
COLLEAGUING
COLLECT
COLLECTED
COLLECTING
COLLECTINGS
COLLECTOR
COLLECTORS
COLLECTS
COLLED
COLLEEN
COLLEENS
COLLEGE
COLLEGER
COLLEGERS
COLLEGES
COLLEGIA
COLLEGIAL
COLLEGIAN
COLLEGIANS
COLLEGIUM
COLLEGIUMS
COLLET
COLLETS
COLLIDE
COLLIDED
COLLIDES
COLLIDING
COLLIE
COLLIED
COLLIER
COLLIERIES
COLLIERS
COLLIERY
COLLIES
COLLIGATE
COLLIGATED
COLLIGATES
COLLIGATING
COLLIMATE
COLLIMATED
COLLIMATES
COLLIMATING
COLLINEAR
COLLING
COLLINGS
COLLISION
COLLISIONS
COLLOCATE
COLLOCATED
COLLOCATES
COLLOCATING
COLLODION
COLLODIONS
COLLOGUE
COLLOGUED
COLLOGUES
COLLOGUING
COLLOID
COLLOIDAL
COLLOIDS
COLLOP
COLLOPS
COLLOQUE
COLLOQUED
COLLOQUES

COLLOQUIA
COLLOQUIED
COLLOQUIES
COLLOQUING
COLLOQUY
COLLOQUYING
COLLOTYPE
COLLOTYPES
COLLS
COLLUDE
COLLUDED
COLLUDER
COLLUDERS
COLLUDES
COLLUDING
COLLUSION
COLLUSIONS
COLLUSIVE
COLLUVIES
COLLY
COLLYING
COLLYRIA
COLLYRIUM
COLLYRIUMS
COLOBI
COLOBUS
COLOBUSES
COLOCYNTH
COLOCYNTHS
COLON
COLONEL
COLONELCIES
COLONELCY
COLONELS
COLONES
COLONIAL
COLONIALS
COLONIC
COLONICS
COLONIES
COLONISE
COLONISED
COLONISES
COLONISING
COLONIST
COLONISTS
COLONIZE
COLONIZED
COLONIZES
COLONIZING
COLONNADE
COLONNADES
COLONS
COLONY
COLOPHON
COLOPHONIES
COLOPHONS
COLOPHONY
COLOR
COLORANT
COLORANTS
COLORED
COLORIFIC
COLORING
COLORS
COLOSSAL
COLOSSEUM
COLOSSEUMS
COLOSSI
COLOSSUS

COLOSSUSES
COLOSTOMIES
COLOSTOMY
COLOSTRIC
COLOSTRUM
COLOSTRUMS
COLOTOMIES
COLOTOMY
COLOUR
COLOURANT
COLOURANTS
COLOURED
COLOUREDS
COLOURER
COLOURERS
COLOURFUL
COLOURING
COLOURINGS
COLOURIST
COLOURISTS
COLOURMAN
COLOURMEN
COLOURS
COLOURY
COLS
COLT
COLTED
COLTER
COLTERS
COLTING
COLTISH
COLTS
COLTSFOOT
COLTSFOOTS
COLTWOOD
COLTWOODS
COLUBER
COLUBERS
COLUBRIAD
COLUBRIADS
COLUBRINE
COLUGO
COLUGOS
COLUMBARIES
COLUMBARY
COLUMBATE
COLUMBATES
COLUMBIC
COLUMBINE
COLUMBINES
COLUMBITE
COLUMBITES
COLUMBIUM
COLUMBIUMS
COLUMEL
COLUMELLA
COLUMELLAE
COLUMELS
COLUMN
COLUMNAL
COLUMNAR
COLUMNED
COLUMNIST
COLUMNISTS
COLUMNS
COLURE
COLURES
COLZA
COLZAS
COMA

COMAE
COMAL
COMARB
COMARBS
COMART
COMARTS
COMAS
COMATE
COMATES
COMATOSE
COMB
COMBAT
COMBATANT
COMBATANTS
COMBATED
COMBATING
COMBATIVE
COMBATS
COMBE
COMBED
COMBER
COMBERS
COMBES
COMBIER
COMBIEST
COMBINATE
COMBINE
COMBINED
COMBINES
COMBING
COMBINGS
COMBINING
COMBLE
COMBLES
COMBLESS
COMBO
COMBOS
COMBRETUM
COMBRETUMS
COMBS
COMBUST
COMBUSTED
COMBUSTING
COMBUSTS
COMBWISE
COMBY
COME
COMEDIAN
COMEDIANS
COMEDIC
COMEDIES
COMEDO
COMEDOS
COMEDOWN
COMEDOWNS
COMEDY
COMELIER
COMELIEST
COMELY
COMER
COMERS
COMES
COMET
COMETARY
COMETHER
COMETHERS
COMETIC
COMETS
COMFIER
COMFIEST

COMFIT
COMFITS
COMFITURE
COMFITURES
COMFORT
COMFORTED
COMFORTER
COMFORTERS
COMFORTING
COMFORTS
COMFREY
COMFREYS
COMFY
COMIC
COMICAL
COMICALLY
COMICS
COMING
COMINGS
COMIQUE
COMIQUES
COMITADJI
COMITADJIS
COMITAL
COMITATUS
COMITATUSES
COMITIA
COMITIES
COMITY
COMMA
COMMAND
COMMANDED
COMMANDER
COMMANDERS
COMMANDING
COMMANDO
COMMANDOS
COMMANDS
COMMAS
COMMENCE
COMMENCED
COMMENCES
COMMENCING
COMMEND
COMMENDAM
COMMENDAMS
COMMENDED
COMMENDING
COMMENDS
COMMENSAL
COMMENSALS
COMMENT
COMMENTED
COMMENTER
COMMENTERS
COMMENTING
COMMENTOR
COMMENTORS
COMMENTS
COMMER
COMMERCE
COMMERCED
COMMERCES
COMMERCING
COMMÈRE
COMMÈRES
COMMERGE
COMMERGED
COMMERGES
COMMERGING

COMMERS
COMMIE
COMMIES
COMMINATE
COMMINATED
COMMINATES
COMMINATING
COMMINGLE
COMMINGLED
COMMINGLES
COMMINGLING
COMMINUTE
COMMINUTED
COMMINUTES
COMMINUTING
COMMIS
COMMISSAR
COMMISSARS
COMMIT
COMMITS
COMMITTAL
COMMITTALS
COMMITTED
COMMITTEE
COMMITTEES
COMMITTING
COMMIX
COMMIXED
COMMIXES
COMMIXING
COMMO
COMMODE
COMMODES
COMMODITIES
COMMODITY
COMMODORE
COMMODORES
COMMON
COMMONAGE
COMMONAGES
COMMONED
COMMONER
COMMONERS
COMMONEST
COMMONEY
COMMONEYS
COMMONING
COMMONLY
COMMONS
COMMORANT
COMMORANTS
COMMOS
COMMOT
COMMOTE
COMMOTES
COMMOTION
COMMOTIONS
COMMOTS
COMMOVE
COMMOVED
COMMOVES
COMMOVING
COMMUNAL
COMMUNARD
COMMUNARDS
COMMUNE
COMMUNED
COMMUNES
COMMUNING
COMMUNINGS

COMMUNION
COMMUNIONS
COMMUNISE
COMMUNISED
COMMUNISES
COMMUNISING
COMMUNISM
COMMUNISMS
COMMUNIST
COMMUNISTS
COMMUNITIES
COMMUNITY
COMMUNIZE
COMMUNIZED
COMMUNIZES
COMMUNIZING
COMMUTATE
COMMUTATED
COMMUTATES
COMMUTATING
COMMUTE
COMMUTED
COMMUTER
COMMUTERS
COMMUTES
COMMUTING
COMMUTUAL
COMOSE
COMOUS
COMP
COMPACT
COMPACTED
COMPACTER
COMPACTEST
COMPACTING
COMPACTLY
COMPACTOR
COMPACTORS
COMPACTS
COMPAGE
COMPAGES
COMPANDER
COMPANDERS
COMPANDOR
COMPANDORS
COMPANIED
COMPANIES
COMPANING
COMPANION
COMPANIONED
COMPANIONING
COMPANIONS
COMPANY
COMPANYING
COMPARE
COMPARED
COMPARES
COMPARING
COMPART
COMPARTED
COMPARTING
COMPARTS
COMPASS
COMPASSED
COMPASSES
COMPASSING
COMPASSINGS
COMPAST
COMPEAR
COMPEARED

COMPEARING
COMPEARS
COMPEER
COMPEERED
COMPEERING
COMPEERS
COMPEL
COMPELLED
COMPELLING
COMPELS
COMPEND
COMPENDIA
COMPENDS
COMPERE
COMPERED
COMPERES
COMPERING
COMPESCE
COMPESCED
COMPESCES
COMPESCING
COMPETE
COMPETED
COMPETENT
COMPETES
COMPETING
COMPILE
COMPILED
COMPILER
COMPILERS
COMPILES
COMPILING
COMPITAL
COMPLAIN
COMPLAINED
COMPLAINING
COMPLAININGS
COMPLAINS
COMPLAINT
COMPLAINTS
COMPLEAT
COMPLECT
COMPLECTED
COMPLECTING
COMPLECTS
COMPLETE
COMPLETED
COMPLETER
COMPLETES
COMPLETEST
COMPLETING
COMPLEX
COMPLEXED
COMPLEXER
COMPLEXES
COMPLEXEST
COMPLEXING
COMPLEXLY
COMPLEXUS
COMPLEXUSES
COMPLIANT
COMPLICE
COMPLICES
COMPLIED
COMPLIER
COMPLIERS
COMPLIES
COMPLIN
COMPLINE
COMPLINES

COMPLINS
COMPLISH
COMPLISHED
COMPLISHES
COMPLISHING
COMPLOT
COMPLOTS
COMPLOTTED
COMPLOTTING
COMPLUVIA
COMPLY
COMPLYING
COMPO
COMPONÉ
COMPONENT
COMPONENTS
COMPONY
COMPORT
COMPORTED
COMPORTING
COMPORTS
COMPOS
COMPOSE
COMPOSED
COMPOSER
COMPOSERS
COMPOSES
COMPOSING
COMPOSITE
COMPOSITED
COMPOSITES
COMPOSITING
COMPOST
COMPOSTED
COMPOSTER
COMPOSTERS
COMPOSTING
COMPOSTS
COMPOSURE
COMPOSURES
COMPOT
COMPOTE
COMPOTES
COMPOTIER
COMPOTIERS
COMPOTS
COMPOUND
COMPOUNDED
COMPOUNDING
COMPOUNDS
COMPRADOR
COMPRADORS
COMPRESS
COMPRESSED
COMPRESSES
COMPRESSING
COMPRINT
COMPRINTED
COMPRINTING
COMPRINTS
COMPRISAL
COMPRISALS
COMPRISE
COMPRISED
COMPRISES
COMPRISING
COMPS
COMPT
COMPTABLE
COMPTED

COMPTER
COMPTERS
COMPTIBLE
COMPTING
COMPTROLL
COMPTROLLED
COMPTROLLING
COMPTROLLS
COMPTS
COMPULSE
COMPULSED
COMPULSES
COMPULSING
COMPUTANT
COMPUTANTS
COMPUTE
COMPUTED
COMPUTER
COMPUTERS
COMPUTES
COMPUTING
COMPUTIST
COMPUTISTS
COMRADE
COMRADELY
COMRADES
COMS
COMUS
COMUSES
CON
CONACRE
CONACRED
CONACRES
CONACRING
CONARIA
CONARIAL
CONARIUM
CONATION
CONATIONS
CONATIVE
CONATUS
CONCAUSE
CONCAUSES
CONCAVE
CONCAVED
CONCAVELY
CONCAVES
CONCAVING
CONCAVITIES
CONCAVITY
CONCEAL
CONCEALED
CONCEALING
CONCEALS
CONCEDE
CONCEDED
CONCEDER
CONCEDERS
CONCEDES
CONCEDING
CONCEIT
CONCEITED
CONCEITING
CONCEITS
CONCEITY
CONCEIVE
CONCEIVED
CONCEIVES
CONCEIVING
CONCENT

CONCENTED
CONCENTER
CONCENTERED
CONCENTERING
CONCENTERS
CONCENTING
CONCENTRE
CONCENTRED
CONCENTRES
CONCENTRING
CONCENTS
CONCEPT
CONCEPTI
CONCEPTS
CONCEPTUS
CONCEPTUSES
CONCERN
CONCERNED
CONCERNING
CONCERNS
CONCERT
CONCERTED
CONCERTING
CONCERTO
CONCERTOS
CONCERTS
CONCETTI
CONCETTO
CONCH
CONCHA
CONCHAE
CONCHATE
CONCHE
CONCHED
CONCHES
CONCHIE
CONCHIES
CONCHING
CONCHITIS
CONCHITISES
CONCHOID
CONCHOIDS
CONCHS
CONCHY
CONCIERGE
CONCIERGES
CONCILIAR
CONCISE
CONCISED
CONCISELY
CONCISER
CONCISES
CONCISEST
CONCISING
CONCISION
CONCISIONS
CONCLAVE
CONCLAVES
CONCLUDE
CONCLUDED
CONCLUDES
CONCLUDING
CONCOCT
CONCOCTED
CONCOCTER
CONCOCTERS
CONCOCTING
CONCOCTOR
CONCOCTORS
CONCOCTS

CONCOLOR
CONCORD
CONCORDAT
CONCORDATS
CONCORDED
CONCORDING
CONCORDS
CONCOURS
CONCOURSE
CONCOURSES
CONCREATE
CONCREATED
CONCREATES
CONCREATING
CONCRETE
CONCRETED
CONCRETES
CONCRETING
CONCREW
CONCREWED
CONCREWING
CONCREWS
CONCUBINE
CONCUBINES
CONCUPIES
CONCUPY
CONCUR
CONCURRED
CONCURRING
CONCURS
CONCUSS
CONCUSSED
CONCUSSES
CONCUSSING
CONCYCLIC
COND
CONDEMN
CONDEMNED
CONDEMNING
CONDEMNS
CONDENSE
CONDENSED
CONDENSER
CONDENSERS
CONDENSES
CONDENSING
CONDER
CONDERS
CONDIDDLE
CONDIDDLED
CONDIDDLES
CONDIDDLING
CONDIGN
CONDIGNLY
CONDIMENT
CONDIMENTED
CONDIMENTING
CONDIMENTS
CONDITION
CONDITIONED
CONDITIONING
CONDITIONINGS
CONDITIONS
CONDOLE
CONDOLED
CONDOLENT
CONDOLES
CONDOLING
CONDOM
CONDOMS

CONDONE
CONDONED
CONDONES
CONDONING
CONDOR
CONDORS
CONDUCE
CONDUCED
CONDUCES
CONDUCING
CONDUCIVE
CONDUCT
CONDUCTED
CONDUCTI
CONDUCTING
CONDUCTOR
CONDUCTORS
CONDUCTS
CONDUCTUS
CONDUIT
CONDUITS
CONDYLAR
CONDYLE
CONDYLES
CONDYLOID
CONDYLOMA
CONDYLOMATA
CONE
CONED
CONES
CONEY
CONEYS
CONFAB
CONFABBED
CONFABBING
CONFABS
CONFECT
CONFECTED
CONFECTING
CONFECTS
CONFER
CONFEREE
CONFEREES
CONFERRED
CONFERRER
CONFERRERS
CONFERRING
CONFERS
CONFERVA
CONFERVAE
CONFESS
CONFESSED
CONFESSES
CONFESSING
CONFESSOR
CONFESSORS
CONFEST
CONFESTLY
CONFETTI
CONFIDANT
CONFIDANTS
CONFIDE
CONFIDED
CONFIDENT
CONFIDENTS
CONFIDER
CONFIDERS
CONFIDES
CONFIDING
CONFIGURE

CONFIGURED
CONFIGURES
CONFIGURING
CONFINE
CONFINED
CONFINER
CONFINERS
CONFINES
CONFINING
CONFIRM
CONFIRMED
CONFIRMEE
CONFIRMEES
CONFIRMER
CONFIRMERS
CONFIRMING
CONFIRMINGS
CONFIRMOR
CONFIRMORS
CONFIRMS
CONFISEUR
CONFISEURS
CONFIT
CONFITEOR
CONFITEORS
CONFITS
CONFITURE
CONFITURES
CONFIX
CONFIXED
CONFIXES
CONFIXING
CONFLATE
CONFLATED
CONFLATES
CONFLATING
CONFLICT
CONFLICTED
CONFLICTING
CONFLICTS
CONFLUENT
CONFLUENTS
CONFLUX
CONFLUXES
CONFORM
CONFORMAL
CONFORMED
CONFORMER
CONFORMERS
CONFORMING
CONFORMS
CONFOUND
CONFOUNDED
CONFOUNDING
CONFOUNDS
CONFRÈRE
CONFRÈRES
CONFRÉRIE
CONFRÉRIES
CONFRONT
CONFRONTÉ
CONFRONTED
CONFRONTING
CONFRONTS
CONFUSE
CONFUSED
CONFUSES
CONFUSING
CONFUSION
CONFUSIONS

CONFUTE
CONFUTED
CONFUTES
CONFUTING
CONGA
CONGAED
CONGAING
CONGAS
CONGÉ
CONGEAL
CONGEALED
CONGEALING
CONGEALS
CONGÉD
CONGEE
CONGEED
CONGEEING
CONGEES
CONGÉING
CONGENER
CONGENERS
CONGENIAL
CONGER
CONGERIES
CONGERS
CONGERY
CONGÉS
CONGEST
CONGESTED
CONGESTING
CONGESTS
CONGIARIES
CONGIARY
CONGLOBE
CONGLOBED
CONGLOBES
CONGLOBING
CONGO
CONGOS
CONGOU
CONGOUS
CONGREE
CONGREED
CONGREEING
CONGREES
CONGREET
CONGREETED
CONGREETING
CONGREETS
CONGRESS
CONGRESSED
CONGRESSES
CONGRESSING
CONGRUE
CONGRUED
CONGRUENT
CONGRUES
CONGRUING
CONGRUITIES
CONGRUITY
CONGRUOUS
CONIA
CONIAS
CONIC
CONICAL
CONICALLY
CONICS
CONIDIA
CONIDIAL
CONIDIUM

CONIES
CONIFER
CONIFERS
CONIFORM
CONIINE
CONIINES
CONIMA
CONIMAS
CONINE
CONINES
CONING
CONJECT
CONJECTED
CONJECTING
CONJECTS
CONJEE
CONJEED
CONJEEING
CONJEES
CONJOIN
CONJOINED
CONJOINING
CONJOINS
CONJOINT
CONJUGAL
CONJUGANT
CONJUGANTS
CONJUGATE
CONJUGATED
CONJUGATES
CONJUGATING
CONJUGATINGS
CONJUNCT
CONJURE
CONJURED
CONJURER
CONJURERS
CONJURES
CONJURIES
CONJURING
CONJURINGS
CONJUROR
CONJURORS
CONJURY
CONK
CONKED
CONKER
CONKERS
CONKIES
CONKING
CONKS
CONKY
CONN
CONNATE
CONNATION
CONNATIONS
CONNATURE
CONNATURES
CONNE
CONNECT
CONNECTED
CONNECTER
CONNECTERS
CONNECTING
CONNECTOR
CONNECTORS
CONNECTS
CONNED
CONNER
CONNERS

CONNES
CONNEXION
CONNEXIONS
CONNEXIVE
CONNING
CONNINGS
CONNIVE
CONNIVED
CONNIVENT
CONNIVER
CONNIVERS
CONNIVES
CONNIVING
CONNOTATE
CONNOTATED
CONNOTATES
CONNOTATING
CONNOTE
CONNOTED
CONNOTES
CONNOTING
CONNOTIVE
CONNS
CONNUBIAL
CONODONT
CONODONTS
CONOID
CONOIDAL
CONOIDIC
CONOIDS
CONQUER
CONQUERED
CONQUERING
CONQUEROR
CONQUERORS
CONQUERS
CONQUEST
CONQUESTS
CONS
CONSCIENT
CONSCIOUS
CONSCIOUSES
CONSCRIBE
CONSCRIBED
CONSCRIBES
CONSCRIBING
CONSCRIPT
CONSCRIPTED
CONSCRIPTING
CONSCRIPTS
CONSEIL
CONSEILS
CONSENSUS
CONSENSUSES
CONSENT
CONSENTED
CONSENTING
CONSENTS
CONSERVE
CONSERVED
CONSERVER
CONSERVERS
CONSERVES
CONSERVING
CONSIDER
CONSIDERED
CONSIDERING
CONSIDERINGS
CONSIDERS
CONSIGN

CONSIGNED
CONSIGNEE
CONSIGNEES
CONSIGNER
CONSIGNERS
CONSIGNING
CONSIGNOR
CONSIGNORS
CONSIGNS
CONSIST
CONSISTED
CONSISTING
CONSISTS
CONSOLATE
CONSOLATED
CONSOLATES
CONSOLATING
CONSOLE
CONSOLED
CONSOLER
CONSOLERS
CONSOLES
CONSOLING
CONSOLS
CONSOMMÉ
CONSOMMÉS
CONSONANT
CONSONANTS
CONSONOUS
CONSORT
CONSORTED
CONSORTER
CONSORTERS
CONSORTIA
CONSORTING
CONSORTS
CONSPIRE
CONSPIRED
CONSPIRER
CONSPIRERS
CONSPIRES
CONSPIRING
CONSTABLE
CONSTABLES
CONSTANCIES
CONSTANCY
CONSTANT
CONSTANTS
CONSTATE
CONSTATED
CONSTATES
CONSTATING
CONSTER
CONSTERED
CONSTERING
CONSTERS
CONSTRAIN
CONSTRAINED
CONSTRAINING
CONSTRAINS
CONSTRICT
CONSTRICTED
CONSTRICTING
CONSTRICTS
CONSTRUCT
CONSTRUCTED
CONSTRUCTING
CONSTRUCTS
CONSTRUE
CONSTRUED

CONSTRUER
CONSTRUERS
CONSTRUES
CONSTRUING
CONSUL
CONSULAGE
CONSULAGES
CONSULAR
CONSULARS
CONSULATE
CONSULATES
CONSULS
CONSULT
CONSULTA
CONSULTAS
CONSULTED
CONSULTEE
CONSULTEES
CONSULTER
CONSULTERS
CONSULTING
CONSULTOR
CONSULTORS
CONSULTS
CONSUME
CONSUMED
CONSUMER
CONSUMERS
CONSUMES
CONSUMING
CONSUMINGS
CONSUMPT
CONSUMPTS
CONTACT
CONTACTED
CONTACTING
CONTACTOR
CONTACTORS
CONTACTS
CONTADINA
CONTADINAS
CONTADINE
CONTADINI
CONTADINO
CONTAGION
CONTAGIONS
CONTAGIUM
CONTAGIUMS
CONTAIN
CONTAINED
CONTAINER
CONTAINERS
CONTAINING
CONTAINS
CONTANGO
CONTANGOED
CONTANGOING
CONTANGOS
CONTE
CONTECK
CONTECKS
CONTEMN
CONTEMNED
CONTEMNER
CONTEMNERS
CONTEMNING
CONTEMNOR
CONTEMNORS
CONTEMNS
CONTEMPER

CONTEMPERED
CONTEMPERING
CONTEMPERS
CONTEMPT
CONTEMPTS
CONTEND
CONTENDED
CONTENDER
CONTENDERS
CONTENDING
CONTENDINGS
CONTENDS
CONTENT
CONTENTED
CONTENTING
CONTENTS
CONTES
CONTEST
CONTESTED
CONTESTER
CONTESTERS
CONTESTING
CONTESTS
CONTEXT
CONTEXTS
CONTICENT
CONTINENT
CONTINENTS
CONTINUA
CONTINUAL
CONTINUE
CONTINUED
CONTINUER
CONTINUERS
CONTINUES
CONTINUING
CONTINUO
CONTINUOS
CONTINUUM
CONTLINE
CONTLINES
CONTO
CONTORNO
CONTORNOS
CONTORT
CONTORTED
CONTORTING
CONTORTS
CONTOS
CONTOUR
CONTOURED
CONTOURING
CONTOURS
CONTRA
CONTRACT
CONTRACTED
CONTRACTING
CONTRACTS
CONTRAIL
CONTRAILS
CONTRAIR
CONTRALTI
CONTRALTO
CONTRALTOS
CONTRARIED
CONTRARIES
CONTRARY
CONTRARYING
CONTRAS
CONTRAST

CONTRASTED
CONTRASTING
CONTRASTS
CONTRASTY
CONTRATE
CONTRIST
CONTRISTED
CONTRISTING
CONTRISTS
CONTRITE
CONTRIVE
CONTRIVED
CONTRIVER
CONTRIVERS
CONTRIVES
CONTRIVING
CONTROL
CONTROLLED
CONTROLLING
CONTROLS
CONTROUL
CONTROULED
CONTROULING
CONTROULS
CONTUMACIES
CONTUMACY
CONTUMELIES
CONTUMELY
CONTUND
CONTUNDED
CONTUNDING
CONTUNDS
CONTUSE
CONTUSED
CONTUSES
CONTUSING
CONTUSION
CONTUSIONS
CONTUSIVE
CONUNDRUM
CONUNDRUMS
CONURBAN
CONURBIA
CONURBIAS
CONVECTOR
CONVECTORS
CONVENE
CONVENED
CONVENER
CONVENERS
CONVENES
CONVENING
CONVENOR
CONVENORS
CONVENT
CONVENTED
CONVENTING
CONVENTS
CONVERGE
CONVERGED
CONVERGES
CONVERGING
CONVERSE
CONVERSED
CONVERSES
CONVERSING
CONVERT
CONVERTED
CONVERTER
CONVERTERS

CONVERTING
CONVERTOR
CONVERTORS
CONVERTS
CONVEX
CONVEXED
CONVEXES
CONVEXITIES
CONVEXITY
CONVEXLY
CONVEY
CONVEYAL
CONVEYALS
CONVEYED
CONVEYER
CONVEYERS
CONVEYING
CONVEYOR
CONVEYORS
CONVEYS
CONVICT
CONVICTED
CONVICTING
CONVICTS
CONVINCE
CONVINCED
CONVINCES
CONVINCING
CONVIVE
CONVIVED
CONVIVES
CONVIVIAL
CONVIVING
CONVOCATE
CONVOCATED
CONVOCATES
CONVOCATING
CONVOKE
CONVOKED
CONVOKES
CONVOKING
CONVOLUTE
CONVOLVE
CONVOLVED
CONVOLVES
CONVOLVING
CONVOY
CONVOYED
CONVOYING
CONVOYS
CONVULSE
CONVULSED
CONVULSES
CONVULSING
CONY
COO
COOED
COOEE
COOEED
COOEEING
COOEES
COOEY
COOEYED
COOEYING
COOEYS
COOF
COOFS
COOING
COOINGLY
COOINGS

COOK
COOKABLE
COOKED
COOKER
COOKERIES
COOKERS
COOKERY
COOKHOUSE
COOKHOUSES
COOKIE
COOKIES
COOKING
COOKMAID
COOKMAIDS
COOKOUT
COOKOUTS
COOKROOM
COOKROOMS
COOKS
COOKSHOP
COOKSHOPS
COOKWARE
COOKWARES
COOKY
COOL
COOLABAH
COOLABAHS
COOLABAR
COOLABARS
COOLAMON
COOLAMONS
COOLANT
COOLANTS
COOLED
COOLER
COOLERS
COOLEST
COOLIBAH
COOLIBAHS
COOLIBAR
COOLIBARS
COOLIE
COOLIES
COOLING
COOLISH
COOLLY
COOLNESS
COOLNESSES
COOLS
COOLTH
COOLTHS
COOLY
COOM
COOMB
COOMBS
COOMED
COOMIER
COOMIEST
COOMING
COOMS
COOMY
COON
COONS
COONTIE
COONTIES
COONTY
COOP
COOPED
COOPER
COOPERAGE

COOPERAGES
COOPERANT
COOPERATE
COOPERATED
COOPERATES
COOPERATING
COOPERED
COOPERIES
COOPERING
COOPERINGS
COOPERS
COOPERY
COOPING
COOPS
COOS
COOSEN
COOSENED
COOSENING
COOSENS
COOSER
COOSERS
COOSIN
COOSINED
COOSINING
COOSINS
COOST
COOT
COOTIKIN
COOTIKINS
COOTS
COP
COPACETIC
COPAIBA
COPAIBAS
COPAIVA
COPAIVAS
COPAL
COPALS
COPARTNER
COPARTNERS
COPATAINE
COPATRIOT
COPATRIOTS
COPE
COPECK
COPECKS
COPED
COPEPOD
COPEPODS
COPER
COPERED
COPERING
COPERS
COPES
COPIED
COPIER
COPIERS
COPIES
COPILOT
COPILOTS
COPING
COPINGS
COPIOUS
COPIOUSLY
COPITA
COPITAS
COPPED
COPPER
COPPERAS
COPPERASES

COPPERED
COPPERING
COPPERINGS
COPPERISH
COPPERS
COPPERY
COPPICE
COPPICED
COPPICES
COPPICING
COPPICINGS
COPPIES
COPPIN
COPPING
COPPINS
COPPLE
COPPLES
COPPY
COPRA
COPRAS
COPRESENT
COPROLITE
COPROLITES
COPROLOGIES
COPROLOGY
COPS
COPSE
COPSED
COPSES
COPSEWOOD
COPSEWOODS
COPSIER
COPSIEST
COPSING
COPSY
COPULA
COPULAR
COPULAS
COPULATE
COPULATED
COPULATES
COPULATING
COPY
COPYBOOK
COPYBOOKS
COPYHOLD
COPYHOLDS
COPYING
COPYISM
COPYISMS
COPYIST
COPYISTS
COPYRIGHT
COPYRIGHTED
COPYRIGHTING
COPYRIGHTS
COQUET
COQUETRIES
COQUETRY
COQUETS
COQUETTE
COQUETTED
COQUETTES
COQUETTING
COQUILLA
COQUILLAS
COQUILLE
COQUILLES
COQUITO
COQUITOS

COR
CORACLE
CORACLES
CORACOID
CORACOIDS
CORAGGIO
CORAGGIOS
CORAL
CORALLA
CORALLINE
CORALLINES
CORALLITE
CORALLITES
CORALLOID
CORALLUM
CORALS
CORAMINE
CORAMINES
CORANACH
CORANACHS
CORANTO
CORANTOES
CORANTOS
CORBAN
CORBANS
CORBE
CORBEAU
CORBEAUS
CORBEIL
CORBEILLE
CORBEILLES
CORBEILS
CORBEL
CORBELLED
CORBELS
CORBES
CORBICULA
CORBICULAE
CORBIE
CORBIES
CORCASS
CORCASSES
CORD
CORDAGE
CORDAGES
CORDATE
CORDED
CORDIAL
CORDIALLY
CORDIALS
CORDIFORM
CORDINER
CORDINERS
CORDING
CORDINGS
CORDITE
CORDITES
CORDLESS
CÓRDOBA
CÓRDOBAS
CORDON
CORDONED
CORDONING
CORDONS
CORDOTOMIES
CORDOTOMY
CORDOVAN
CORDOVANS
CORDS
CORDUROY

CORDUROYS
CORDWAIN
CORDWAINS
CORDYLINE
CORDYLINES
CORE
CORED
CORELESS
CORELLA
CORELLAS
COREOPSIS
COREOPSISES
CORER
CORERS
CORES
CORF
CORGI
CORGIS
CORIA
CORIANDER
CORIANDERS
CORING
CORIOUS
CORIUM
CORIUMS
CORK
CORKAGE
CORKAGES
CORKED
CORKER
CORKERS
CORKIER
CORKIEST
CORKINESS
CORKINESSES
CORKING
CORKIR
CORKIRS
CORKS
CORKWING
CORKWINGS
CORKWOOD
CORKWOODS
CORKY
CORM
CORMORANT
CORMORANTS
CORMOUS
CORMS
CORMUS
CORMUSES
CORN
CORNACRE
CORNACRES
CORNAGE
CORNAGES
CORNBRASH
CORNBRASHES
CORNCRAKE
CORNCRAKES
CORNEA
CORNEAL
CORNEAS
CORNED
CORNEL
CORNELIAN
CORNELIANS
CORNELS
CORNEMUSE
CORNEMUSES

CORNEOUS
CORNER
CORNERED
CORNERING
CORNERS
CORNET
CORNETCIES
CORNETCY
CORNETIST
CORNETISTS
CORNETS
CORNETT
CORNETTI
CORNETTO
CORNETTS
CORNFIELD
CORNFIELDS
CORNFLIES
CORNFLOUR
CORNFLOURS
CORNFLY
CORNHUSK
CORNHUSKS
CORNI
CORNICE
CORNICED
CORNICES
CORNICHE
CORNICHES
CORNICING
CORNICLE
CORNICLES
CORNIER
CORNIEST
CORNIFIC
CORNIFORM
CORNING
CORNIST
CORNISTS
CORNLAND
CORNLANDS
CORNLOFT
CORNLOFTS
CORNO
CORNOPEAN
CORNOPEANS
CORNPIPE
CORNPIPES
CORNS
CORNSTALK
CORNSTALKS
CORNSTONE
CORNSTONES
CORNU
CORNUA
CORNUAL
CORNUTE
CORNUTED
CORNUTES
CORNUTING
CORNUTO
CORNUTOS
CORNWORM
CORNWORMS
CORNY
COROCORE
COROCORES
COROCORO
COROCOROS
CORODIES

CORODY
COROLLA
COROLLARIES
COROLLARY
COROLLAS
COROLLINE
CORONA
CORONACH
CORONACHS
CORONAE
CORONAL
CORONALS
CORONARIES
CORONARY
CORONAS
CORONATE
CORONATED
CORONER
CORONERS
CORONET
CORONETED
CORONETS
CORONIS
CORONISES
CORONIUM
CORONIUMS
CORONOID
COROZO
COROZOS
CORPORA
CORPORAL
CORPORALS
CORPORAS
CORPORASES
CORPORATE
CORPOREAL
CORPORIFIED
CORPORIFIES
CORPORIFY
CORPORIFYING
CORPOSANT
CORPOSANTS
CORPS
CORPSE
CORPSED
CORPSES
CORPSING
CORPULENT
CORPUS
CORPUSCLE
CORPUSCLES
CORRADE
CORRADED
CORRADES
CORRADING
CORRAL
CORRALLED
CORRALLING
CORRALS
CORRASION
CORRASIONS
CORRECT
CORRECTED
CORRECTER
CORRECTEST
CORRECTING
CORRECTLY
CORRECTOR
CORRECTORS
CORRECTS

CORRELATE
CORRELATED
CORRELATES
CORRELATING
CORRIDA
CORRIDAS
CORRIDOR
CORRIDORS
CORRIE
CORRIES
CORRIGENT
CORRIGENTS
CORRIVAL
CORRIVALLED
CORRIVALLING
CORRIVALS
CORRODE
CORRODED
CORRODENT
CORRODENTS
CORRODES
CORRODIES
CORRODING
CORRODY
CORROSION
CORROSIONS
CORROSIVE
CORROSIVES
CORRUGATE
CORRUGATED
CORRUGATES
CORRUGATING
CORRUPT
CORRUPTED
CORRUPTER
CORRUPTERS
CORRUPTEST
CORRUPTING
CORRUPTLY
CORRUPTS
CORS
CORSAGE
CORSAGES
CORSAIR
CORSAIRS
CORSE
CORSELET
CORSELETS
CORSES
CORSET
CORSETED
CORSETIER
CORSETIERS
CORSETING
CORSETRIES
CORSETRY
CORSETS
CORSIVE
CORSIVES
CORSLET
CORSLETED
CORSLETS
CORSNED
CORSNEDS
CORSO
CORSOS
CORTÈGE
CORTÈGES
CORTEX
CORTEXES

CORTICAL
CORTICATE
CORTICES
CORTICOID
CORTICOIDS
CORTILE
CORTILES
CORTISOL
CORTISOLS
CORTISONE
CORTISONES
CORUNDUM
CORUNDUMS
CORUSCANT
CORUSCATE
CORUSCATED
CORUSCATES
CORUSCATING
CORVÉE
CORVÉES
CORVES
CORVET
CORVETED
CORVETING
CORVETS
CORVETTE
CORVETTED
CORVETTES
CORVETTING
CORVID
CORVIDS
CORVINE
CORVUS
CORVUSES
CORYBANT
CORYBANTES
CORYBANTS
CORYMB
CORYMBOSE
CORYMBS
CORYPHAEI
CORYPHE
CORYPHEE
CORYPHEES
CORYPHENE
CORYPHENES
CORYPHES
CORYZA
CORYZAS
COS
COSE
COSECANT
COSECANTS
COSECH
COSECHS
COSED
COSEISMAL
COSEISMIC
COSES
COSH
COSHED
COSHER
COSHERED
COSHERER
COSHERERS
COSHERIES
COSHERING
COSHERINGS
COSHERS
COSHERY

COSHES
COSHING
COSIER
COSIERS
COSIES
COSIEST
COSILY
COSINE
COSINES
COSINESS
COSINESSES
COSING
COSMEA
COSMEAS
COSMESES
COSMESIS
COSMETIC
COSMETICS
COSMIC
COSMICAL
COSMISM
COSMISMS
COSMIST
COSMISTS
COSMOCRAT
COSMOCRATS
COSMOGENIES
COSMOGENY
COSMOGONIES
COSMOGONY
COSMOLOGIES
COSMOLOGY
COSMONAUT
COSMONAUTS
COSMORAMA
COSMORAMAS
COSMOS
COSMOSES
COSMOTRON
COSMOTRONS
COSPONSOR
COSPONSORED
COSPONSORING
COSPONSORS
COSS
COSSES
COSSET
COSSETED
COSSETING
COSSETS
COSSIE
COSSIES
COST
COSTA
COSTAE
COSTAL
COSTALS
COSTARD
COSTARDS
COSTATE
COSTATED
COSTE
COSTEAN
COSTEANED
COSTEANING
COSTEANINGS
COSTEANS
COSTED
COSTER
COSTERS

COSTES
COSTING
COSTIVE
COSTIVELY
COSTLIER
COSTLIEST
COSTLY
COSTMARIES
COSTMARY
COSTREL
COSTRELS
COSTS
COSTUME
COSTUMED
COSTUMER
COSTUMERS
COSTUMES
COSTUMIER
COSTUMIERS
COSTUMING
COSTUS
COSTUSES
COSY
COT
COTANGENT
COTANGENTS
COTE
COTEAU
COTEAUX
COTED
CÔTELETTE
CÔTELETTES
COTELINE
COTELINES
COTERIE
COTERIES
COTES
COTH
COTHS
COTHURN
COTHURNI
COTHURNS
COTHURNUS
COTICULAR
COTILLION
COTILLIONS
COTILLON
COTILLONS
COTING
COTINGA
COTINGAS
COTISE
COTISED
COTISES
COTISING
COTLAND
COTLANDS
COTQUEAN
COTQUEANS
COTS
COTT
COTTA
COTTABUS
COTTABUSES
COTTAGE
COTTAGED
COTTAGER
COTTAGERS
COTTAGES
COTTAGEY

COTTAR
COTTARS
COTTAS
COTTED
COTTER
COTTERS
COTTIER
COTTIERS
COTTISE
COTTISED
COTTISES
COTTISING
COTTOID
COTTOIDS
COTTON
COTTONADE
COTTONADES
COTTONED
COTTONING
COTTONS
COTTONY
COTTOWN
COTTOWNS
COTTS
COTWAL
COTWALS
COTYLAE
COTYLE
COTYLEDON
COTYLEDONS
COTYLES
COTYLOID
COUCAL
COUCALS
COUCH
COUCHANT
COUCHÉ
COUCHED
COUCHEE
COUCHÉE
COUCHEES
COUCHÉES
COUCHÉS
COUCHES
COUCHETTE
COUCHETTES
COUCHING
COUCHINGS
COUDÉ
COUGAR
COUGARS
COUGH
COUGHED
COUGHER
COUGHERS
COUGHING
COUGHINGS
COUGHS
COUGUAR
COUGUARS
COULD
COULÉE
COULÉES
COULIS
COULISSE
COULISSES
COULOIR
COULOIRS
COULOMB
COULOMBS

COULTER
COULTERS
COUMARIC
COUMARIN
COUMARINS
COUNCIL
COUNCILOR
COUNCILORS
COUNCILS
COUNSEL
COUNSELLED
COUNSELLING
COUNSELLINGS
COUNSELS
COUNT
COUNTABLE
COUNTED
COUNTER
COUNTERED
COUNTERING
COUNTERS
COUNTESS
COUNTESSES
COUNTIES
COUNTING
COUNTLESS
COUNTRIES
COUNTROL
COUNTROLLED
COUNTROLLING
COUNTROLS
COUNTRY
COUNTS
COUNTSHIP
COUNTSHIPS
COUNTY
COUP
COUPE
COUPÉ
COUPED
COUPEE
COUPEES
COUPER
COUPERS
COUPES
COUPÉS
COUPING
COUPLE
COUPLED
COUPLER
COUPLERS
COUPLES
COUPLET
COUPLETS
COUPLING
COUPLINGS
COUPON
COUPONS
COUPS
COUPURE
COUPURES
COUR
COURAGE
COURAGES
COURANT
COURANTE
COURANTES
COURANTS
COURB
COURBARIL

COURBARILS
COURBED
COURBETTE
COURBETTES
COURBING
COURBS
COURD
COURE
COURED
COURES
COURGETTE
COURGETTES
COURIER
COURIERS
COURING
COURLAN
COURLANS
COURS
COURSE
COURSED
COURSER
COURSERS
COURSES
COURSING
COURSINGS
COURT
COURTED
COURTEOUS
COURTESAN
COURTESANS
COURTESIED
COURTESIES
COURTESY
COURTESYING
COURTEZAN
COURTEZANS
COURTIER
COURTIERS
COURTING
COURTINGS
COURTLET
COURTLETS
COURTLIER
COURTLIEST
COURTLIKE
COURTLING
COURTLINGS
COURTLY
COURTROOM
COURTROOMS
COURTS
COURTSHIP
COURTSHIPS
COURTYARD
COURTYARDS
COUSCOUS
COUSCOUSES
COUSIN
COUSINAGE
COUSINAGES
COUSINLY
COUSINRIES
COUSINRY
COUSINS
COUTER
COUTERS
COUTH
COUTHER
COUTHEST
COUTHIE

COUTHIER
COUTHIEST
COUTHY
COUTIL
COUTILLE
COUTILLES
COUTILS
COUTURE
COUTURES
COUTURIER
COUTURIERS
COUVADE
COUVADES
COUVERT
COUVERTS
COVALENCIES
COVALENCY
COVALENT
COVARIANT
COVARIANTS
COVARIED
COVARIES
COVARY
COVARYING
COVE
COVED
COVELET
COVELETS
COVELLITE
COVELLITES
COVEN
COVENANT
COVENANTED
COVENANTING
COVENANTS
COVENS
COVENT
COVENTS
COVER
COVERAGE
COVERAGES
COVERALL
COVERALLS
COVERED
COVERING
COVERINGS
COVERLET
COVERLETS
COVERLID
COVERLIDS
COVERS
COVERSLIP
COVERSLIPS
COVERT
COVERTLY
COVERTS
COVERTURE
COVERTURES
COVES
COVET
COVETABLE
COVETED
COVETING
COVETISE
COVETISES
COVETOUS
COVETS
COVEY
COVEYS
COVIN

COVING
COVINGS
COVINOUS
COVINS
COVYNE
COVYNES
COW
COWAGE
COWAGES
COWAN
COWANS
COWARD
COWARDED
COWARDICE
COWARDICES
COWARDING
COWARDLY
COWARDREE
COWARDREES
COWARDRIES
COWARDRY
COWARDS
COWBANE
COWBANES
COWBELL
COWBELLS
COWBERRIES
COWBERRY
COWBIRD
COWBIRDS
COWBOY
COWBOYS
COWED
COWER
COWERED
COWERING
COWERS
COWFEEDER
COWFEEDERS
COWFISH
COWFISHES
COWGIRL
COWGIRLS
COWGRASS
COWGRASSES
COWHAGE
COWHAGES
COWHAND
COWHANDS
COWHEARD
COWHEARDS
COWHEEL
COWHEELS
COWHERD
COWHERDS
COWHIDE
COWHIDED
COWHIDES
COWHIDING
COWHOUSE
COWHOUSES
COWING
COWISH
COWITCH
COWITCHES
COWL
COWLED
COWLICK
COWLICKS
COWLING

COWLINGS
COWLS
COWMAN
COWMEN
COWP
COWPAT
COWPATS
COWPED
COWPING
COWPOKE
COWPOKES
COWPOX
COWPOXES
COWPS
COWRIE
COWRIES
COWRY
COWS
COWSHED
COWSHEDS
COWSLIP
COWSLIPS
COX
COXA
COXAE
COXAL
COXALGIA
COXALGIAS
COXCOMB
COXCOMBIC
COXCOMBRIES
COXCOMBRY
COXCOMBS
COXED
COXES
COXIER
COXIEST
COXINESS
COXINESSES
COXING
COXSWAIN
COXSWAINED
COXSWAINING
COXSWAINS
COXY
COY
COYED
COYER
COYEST
COYING
COYISH
COYISHLY
COYLY
COYNESS
COYNESSES
COYOTE
COYOTES
COYPU
COYPUS
COYS
COYSTREL
COYSTRELS
COYSTRIL
COYSTRILS
COZ
COZE
COZED
COZEN
COZENAGE
COZENAGES

COZENED
COZENER
COZENERS
COZENING
COZENS
COZES
COZIER
COZIERS
COZIES
COZIEST
COZING
COZY
COZZES
CRAB
CRABBED
CRABBEDLY
CRABBIER
CRABBIEST
CRABBILY
CRABBING
CRABBY
CRABLIKE
CRABS
CRABSTICK
CRABSTICKS
CRABWISE
CRACK
CRACKDOWN
CRACKDOWNS
CRACKED
CRACKER
CRACKERS
CRACKING
CRACKJAW
CRACKLE
CRACKLED
CRACKLES
CRACKLIER
CRACKLIEST
CRACKLING
CRACKLINGS
CRACKLY
CRACKNEL
CRACKNELS
CRACKPOT
CRACKPOTS
CRACKS
CRACKSMAN
CRACKSMEN
CRACOWE
CRACOWES
CRADLE
CRADLED
CRADLES
CRADLING
CRADLINGS
CRAFT
CRAFTED
CRAFTIER
CRAFTIEST
CRAFTILY
CRAFTING
CRAFTLESS
CRAFTS
CRAFTSMAN
CRAFTSMEN
CRAFTWORK
CRAFTWORKS
CRAFTY
CRAG

CRAGFAST
CRAGGED
CRAGGIER
CRAGGIEST
CRAGGY
CRAGS
CRAGSMAN
CRAGSMEN
CRAIG
CRAIGS
CRAKE
CRAKED
CRAKES
CRAKING
CRAM
CRAMBO
CRAMBOES
CRAME
CRAMES
CRAMESIES
CRAMESY
CRAMMABLE
CRAMMED
CRAMMER
CRAMMERS
CRAMMING
CRAMOISIES
CRAMOISY
CRAMP
CRAMPED
CRAMPET
CRAMPETS
CRAMPIER
CRAMPIEST
CRAMPING
CRAMPIT
CRAMPITS
CRAMPON
CRAMPONS
CRAMPS
CRAMPY
CRAMS
CRAN
CRANAGE
CRANAGES
CRANBERRIES
CRANBERRY
CRANCH
CRANCHED
CRANCHES
CRANCHING
CRANE
CRANED
CRANES
CRANIA
CRANIAL
CRANING
CRANIUM
CRANIUMS
CRANK
CRANKCASE
CRANKCASES
CRANKED
CRANKER
CRANKEST
CRANKIER
CRANKIEST
CRANKILY
CRANKING
CRANKLE

CRANKLED
CRANKLES
CRANKLING
CRANKNESS
CRANKNESSES
CRANKS
CRANKY
CRANNIED
CRANNIES
CRANNOG
CRANNOGS
CRANNY
CRANNYING
CRANREUCH
CRANREUCHS
CRANS
CRANTS
CRANTSES
CRAP
CRAPE
CRAPED
CRAPES
CRAPIER
CRAPIEST
CRAPING
CRAPLE
CRAPLES
CRAPPED
CRAPPING
CRAPS
CRAPULENT
CRAPULOUS
CRAPY
CRARE
CRARES
CRASES
CRASH
CRASHED
CRASHES
CRASHING
CRASHPAD
CRASHPADS
CRASIS
CRASS
CRASSER
CRASSEST
CRASSLY
CRASSNESS
CRASSNESSES
CRATCH
CRATCHES
CRATE
CRATED
CRATER
CRATEROUS
CRATERS
CRATES
CRATING
CRATON
CRATONS
CRATUR
CRATURS
CRAUNCH
CRAUNCHED
CRAUNCHES
CRAUNCHING
CRAVAT
CRAVATS
CRAVATTED
CRAVATTING

CRAVE
CRAVED
CRAVEN
CRAVENED
CRAVENING
CRAVENLY
CRAVENS
CRAVER
CRAVERS
CRAVES
CRAVING
CRAVINGS
CRAW
CRAWFISH
CRAWFISHES
CRAWL
CRAWLED
CRAWLER
CRAWLERS
CRAWLIER
CRAWLIEST
CRAWLING
CRAWLINGS
CRAWLS
CRAWLY
CRAWS
CRAYER
CRAYERS
CRAYFISH
CRAYFISHES
CRAYON
CRAYONED
CRAYONING
CRAYONS
CRAZE
CRAZED
CRAZES
CRAZIER
CRAZIES
CRAZIEST
CRAZILY
CRAZINESS
CRAZINESSES
CRAZING
CRAZY
CREACH
CREACHS
CREAGH
CREAGHS
CREAK
CREAKED
CREAKIER
CREAKIEST
CREAKILY
CREAKING
CREAKS
CREAKY
CREAM
CREAMED
CREAMER
CREAMERIES
CREAMERS
CREAMERY
CREAMIER
CREAMIEST
CREAMING
CREAMS
CREAMY
CREANCE
CREANCES

CREANT
CREASE
CREASED
CREASES
CREASIER
CREASIEST
CREASING
CREASOTE
CREASOTED
CREASOTES
CREASOTING
CREASY
CREATABLE
CREATE
CREATED
CREATES
CREATIC
CREATINE
CREATINES
CREATING
CREATION
CREATIONS
CREATIVE
CREATOR
CREATORS
CREATRESS
CREATRESSES
CREATRIX
CREATRIXES
CREATURAL
CREATURE
CREATURES
CRÈCHE
CRÈCHES
CREDAL
CREDENCE
CREDENCES
CREDENDA
CREDENDUM
CREDENT
CREDENZA
CREDENZAS
CREDIBLE
CREDIBLY
CREDIT
CREDITED
CREDITING
CREDITOR
CREDITORS
CREDITS
CREDO
CREDOS
CREDULITIES
CREDULITY
CREDULOUS
CREE
CREED
CREEDAL
CREEDS
CREEING
CREEK
CREEKIER
CREEKIEST
CREEKS
CREEKY
CREEL
CREELS
CREEP
CREEPER
CREEPERED

CREEPERS
CREASE
CREEPIE
CREEPIER
CREEPIES
CREEPIEST
CREEPING
CREEPS
CREEPY
CREES
CREESE
CREESED
CREESES
CREESH
CREESHED
CREESHES
CREESHING
CREESHY
CREESING
CREMASTER
CREMASTERS
CREMATE
CREMATED
CREMATES
CREMATING
CREMATION
CREMATIONS
CREMATOR
CREMATORIES
CREMATORS
CREMATORY
CRÈME
CRÊME
CRÈMES
CRÊMES
CREMOCARP
CREMOCARPS
CREMONA
CREMONAS
CREMOR
CREMORNE
CREMORNES
CREMORS
CREMOSIN
CREMSIN
CRENA
CRENAS
CRENATE
CRENATED
CRENATION
CRENATIONS
CRENATURE
CRENATURES
CRENEL
CRENELATE
CRENELATED
CRENELATES
CRENELATING
CRENELLED
CRENELLING
CRENELS
CRENULATE
CREODONT
CREODONTS
CREOLE
CREOLES
CREOLIAN
CREOLIANS
CREOLIST
CREOLISTS
CREOSOTE

CREOSOTED
CREOSOTES
CREOSOTING
CREPANCE
CREPANCES
CRÊPE
CRÊPED
CRÊPES
CRÊPIER
CRÊPIEST
CRÊPING
CREPITANT
CREPITATE
CREPITATED
CREPITATES
CREPITATING
CREPITUS
CREPITUSES
CREPOLINE
CREPOLINES
CREPON
CREPONS
CREPT
CREPUSCLE
CREPUSCLES
CRÊPY
CRESCENDO
CRESCENDOED
CRESCENDOING
CRESCENDOS
CRESCENT
CRESCENTS
CRESCIVE
CRESOL
CRESOLS
CRESS
CRESSES
CRESSET
CRESSETS
CRESSIER
CRESSIEST
CRESSY
CREST
CRESTED
CRESTING
CRESTLESS
CRESTS
CRETIC
CRETICS
CRETIN
CRETINISM
CRETINISMS
CRETINOID
CRETINOUS
CRETINS
CRETISM
CRETISMS
CRETONNE
CRETONNES
CREUTZER
CREUTZERS
CREVASSE
CREVASSED
CREVASSES
CREVASSING
CREVICE
CREVICES
CREW
CREWE
CREWED

CREWEL
CREWELIST
CREWELISTS
CREWELLED
CREWELLING
CREWELS
CREWES
CREWING
CREWS
CRIANT
CRIB
CRIBBAGE
CRIBBAGES
CRIBBED
CRIBBING
CRIBBLE
CRIBBLED
CRIBBLES
CRIBBLING
CRIBELLA
CRIBELLAR
CRIBELLUM
CRIBLÉ
CRIBRATE
CRIBROSE
CRIBS
CRIBWORK
CRIBWORKS
CRICK
CRICKED
CRICKET
CRICKETED
CRICKETER
CRICKETERS
CRICKETING
CRICKETINGS
CRICKETS
CRICKEY
CRICKING
CRICKS
CRICKY
CRICOID
CRICOIDS
CRIED
CRIER
CRIERS
CRIES
CRIKEY
CRIME
CRIMED
CRIMEFUL
CRIMELESS
CRIMES
CRIMINAL
CRIMINALS
CRIMINATE
CRIMINATED
CRIMINATES
CRIMINATING
CRIMINE
CRIMING
CRIMINI
CRIMINOUS
CRIMMER
CRIMMERS
CRIMP
CRIMPED
CRIMPER
CRIMPERS
CRIMPIER

CRIMPIEST
CRIMPING
CRIMPLE
CRIMPLED
CRIMPLES
CRIMPLING
CRIMPS
CRIMPY
CRIMSON
CRIMSONED
CRIMSONING
CRIMSONS
CRINAL
CRINATE
CRINATED
CRINE
CRINED
CRINES
CRINGE
CRINGED
CRINGER
CRINGERS
CRINGES
CRINGING
CRINGINGS
CRINGLE
CRINGLES
CRINING
CRINITE
CRINITES
CRINKLE
CRINKLED
CRINKLES
CRINKLIER
CRINKLIES
CRINKLIEST
CRINKLING
CRINKLY
CRINOID
CRINOIDAL
CRINOIDS
CRINOLINE
CRINOLINES
CRINOSE
CRINUM
CRINUMS
CRIOLLO
CRIOLLOS
CRIPES
CRIPPLE
CRIPPLED
CRIPPLES
CRIPPLING
CRIPPLINGS
CRISE
CRISES
CRISIS
CRISP
CRISPATE
CRISPATED
CRISPED
CRISPER
CRISPERS
CRISPEST
CRISPIER
CRISPIEST
CRISPIN
CRISPING
CRISPINS
CRISPLY

CRISPNESS
CRISPNESSES
CRISPS
CRISPY
CRISSA
CRISSUM
CRISTA
CRISTAE
CRISTATE
CRIT
CRITERIA
CRITERION
CRITH
CRITHS
CRITIC
CRITICAL
CRITICISE
CRITICISED
CRITICISES
CRITICISING
CRITICISM
CRITICISMS
CRITICIZE
CRITICIZED
CRITICIZES
CRITICIZING
CRITICS
CRITIQUE
CRITIQUES
CRITS
CRITTER
CRITTERS
CRITTUR
CRITTURS
CRIVENS
CRIVVENS
CROAK
CROAKED
CROAKER
CROAKERS
CROAKIER
CROAKIEST
CROAKILY
CROAKING
CROAKINGS
CROAKS
CROAKY
CROC
CROCEATE
CROCEOUS
CROCHE
CROCHES
CROCHET
CROCHETED
CROCHETING
CROCHETINGS
CROCHETS
CROCK
CROCKED
CROCKERIES
CROCKERY
CROCKET
CROCKETS
CROCKING
CROCKS
CROCODILE
CROCODILES
CROCOITE
CROCOITES
CROCS

CROCUS
CROCUSES
CROFT
CROFTER
CROFTERS
CROFTING
CROFTINGS
CROFTS
CROISSANT
CROISSANTS
CROMACK
CROMACKS
CROMB
CROMBED
CROMBIE
CROMBIES
CROMBING
CROMBS
CROME
CROMED
CROMES
CROMING
CROMLECH
CROMLECHS
CROMORNA
CROMORNAS
CROMORNE
CROMORNES
CRONE
CRONES
CRONET
CRONETS
CRONIES
CRONK
CRONKER
CRONKEST
CRONY
CRONYISM
CRONYISMS
CROODLE
CROODLED
CROODLES
CROODLING
CROOK
CROOKBACK
CROOKBACKS
CROOKED
CROOKEDER
CROOKEDEST
CROOKEDLY
CROOKER
CROOKEST
CROOKING
CROOKS
CROON
CROONED
CROONER
CROONERS
CROONING
CROONINGS
CROONS
CROP
CROPBOUND
CROPFUL
CROPFULL
CROPFULS
CROPLAND
CROPLANDS
CROPPED
CROPPER

CROPPERS
CROPPIES
CROPPING
CROPPINGS
CROPPY
CROPS
CROPSICK
CROQUET
CROQUETED
CROQUETING
CROQUETS
CROQUETTE
CROQUETTES
CROQUIS
CRORE
CRORES
CROSIER
CROSIERED
CROSIERS
CROSS
CROSSBAND
CROSSBANDS
CROSSBAR
CROSSBARS
CROSSBEAM
CROSSBEAMS
CROSSBILL
CROSSBILLS
CROSSBIT
CROSSBITE
CROSSBITES
CROSSBITING
CROSSBITTEN
CROSSBOW
CROSSBOWS
CROSSBRED
CROSSCUT
CROSSCUTS
CROSSCUTTING
CROSSCUTTINGS
CROSSE
CROSSED
CROSSER
CROSSES
CROSSEST
CROSSETTE
CROSSETTES
CROSSFALL
CROSSFALLS
CROSSFIRE
CROSSFIRES
CROSSFISH
CROSSFISHES
CROSSING
CROSSINGS
CROSSISH
CROSSJACK
CROSSJACKS
CROSSLET
CROSSLETS
CROSSLY
CROSSNESS
CROSSNESSES
CROSSOVER
CROSSOVERS
CROSSROAD
CROSSROADS
CROSSTREE
CROSSTREES
CROSSWALK

CROSSWALKS
CROSSWAY
CROSSWAYS
CROSSWIND
CROSSWINDS
CROSSWISE
CROSSWORD
CROSSWORDS
CROSSWORT
CROSSWORTS
CROST
CROTAL
CROTALA
CROTALINE
CROTALISM
CROTALISMS
CROTALS
CROTALUM
CROTCH
CROTCHED
CROTCHES
CROTCHET
CROTCHETS
CROTCHETY
CROTON
CROTONS
CROTTLE
CROTTLES
CROUCH
CROUCHED
CROUCHES
CROUCHING
CROUP
CROUPADE
CROUPADES
CROUPE
CROUPED
CROUPER
CROUPERS
CROUPES
CROUPIER
CROUPIERS
CROUPIEST
CROUPING
CROUPON
CROUPONS
CROUPOUS
CROUPS
CROUPY
CROUSE
CROUSELY
CROUSTADE
CROUSTADES
CROUT
CROÛTE
CROÛTES
CROÛTON
CROÛTONS
CROUTS
CROW
CROWD
CROWDED
CROWDER
CROWDERS
CROWDIE
CROWDIES
CROWDING
CROWDS
CROWED
CROWFEET

CROWFOOT
CROWFOOTS
CROWING
CROWN
CROWNED
CROWNER
CROWNERS
CROWNET
CROWNETS
CROWNING
CROWNINGS
CROWNLESS
CROWNLET
CROWNLETS
CROWNS
CROWNWORK
CROWNWORKS
CROWS
CROZE
CROZES
CROZIER
CROZIERS
CRU
CRUBEEN
CRUBEENS
CRUCES
CRUCIAL
CRUCIAN
CRUCIANS
CRUCIATE
CRUCIATED
CRUCIATES
CRUCIATING
CRUCIBLE
CRUCIBLES
CRUCIFER
CRUCIFERS
CRUCIFIED
CRUCIFIER
CRUCIFIERS
CRUCIFIES
CRUCIFIX
CRUCIFIXES
CRUCIFORM
CRUCIFY
CRUCIFYING
CRUCK
CRUCKS
CRUD
CRUDDIER
CRUDDIEST
CRUDDLE
CRUDDLED
CRUDDLES
CRUDDLING
CRUDDY
CRUDE
CRUDELY
CRUDENESS
CRUDENESSES
CRUDER
CRUDES
CRUDEST
CRUDITÉS
CRUDITIES
CRUDITY
CRUDS
CRUDY
CRUE
CRUEL

CRUELLER
CRUELLEST
CRUELLS
CRUELLY
CRUELNESS
CRUELNESSES
CRUELS
CRUELTIES
CRUELTY
CRUES
CRUET
CRUETS
CRUISE
CRUISED
CRUISER
CRUISERS
CRUISES
CRUISEWAY
CRUISEWAYS
CRUISIE
CRUISIES
CRUISING
CRUIVE
CRUIVES
CRULLER
CRULLERS
CRUMB
CRUMBED
CRUMBIER
CRUMBIEST
CRUMBING
CRUMBLE
CRUMBLED
CRUMBLES
CRUMBLIER
CRUMBLIES
CRUMBLIEST
CRUMBLING
CRUMBLY
CRUMBS
CRUMBY
CRUMEN
CRUMENAL
CRUMENALS
CRUMENS
CRUMHORN
CRUMHORNS
CRUMMACK
CRUMMACKS
CRUMMIER
CRUMMIES
CRUMMIEST
CRUMMOCK
CRUMMOCKS
CRUMMY
CRUMP
CRUMPED
CRUMPER
CRUMPEST
CRUMPET
CRUMPETS
CRUMPIER
CRUMPIEST
CRUMPING
CRUMPLE
CRUMPLED
CRUMPLES
CRUMPLING
CRUMPLINGS
CRUMPS

CRUMPY
CRUNCH
CRUNCHED
CRUNCHES
CRUNCHIER
CRUNCHIEST
CRUNCHING
CRUNCHY
CRUNKLE
CRUNKLED
CRUNKLES
CRUNKLING
CRUOR
CRUORS
CRUPPER
CRUPPERS
CRURAL
CRUS
CRUSADE
CRUSADED
CRUSADER
CRUSADERS
CRUSADES
CRUSADING
CRUSADO
CRUSADOS
CRUSE
CRUSES
CRUSET
CRUSETS
CRUSH
CRUSHABLE
CRUSHED
CRUSHER
CRUSHERS
CRUSHES
CRUSHING
CRUSIAN
CRUSIANS
CRUSIE
CRUSIES
CRUST
CRUSTA
CRUSTAE
CRUSTAL
CRUSTATE
CRUSTATED
CRUSTED
CRUSTIER
CRUSTIEST
CRUSTILY
CRUSTING
CRUSTLESS
CRUSTS
CRUSTY
CRUSY
CRUTCH
CRUTCHED
CRUTCHES
CRUTCHING
CRUVE
CRUVES
CRUX
CRUXES
CRUZEIRO
CRUZEIROS
CRWTH
CRWTHS
CRY
CRYING

CRYINGS
CRYOGEN
CRYOGENIC
CRYOGENICS
CRYOGENIES
CRYOGENS
CRYOGENY
CRYOLITE
CRYOLITES
CRYOMETER
CRYOMETERS
CRYONIC
CRYONICS
CRYOPROBE
CRYOPROBES
CRYOSCOPE
CRYOSCOPES
CRYOSCOPIES
CRYOSCOPY
CRYOSTAT
CRYOSTATS
CRYOTRON
CRYOTRONS
CRYPT
CRYPTADIA
CRYPTAL
CRYPTIC
CRYPTICAL
CRYPTO
CRYPTOGAM
CRYPTOGAMS
CRYPTON
CRYPTONS
CRYPTONYM
CRYPTONYMS
CRYPTOS
CRYPTS
CRYSTAL
CRYSTALS
CSÁRDÁS
CSÁRDÁSES
CTENE
CTENES
CTENIFORM
CTENOID
CUB
CUBAGE
CUBAGES
CUBATURE
CUBATURES
CUBBED
CUBBIES
CUBBING
CUBBINGS
CUBBISH
CUBBY
CUBE
CUBEB
CUBEBS
CUBED
CUBES
CUBHOOD
CUBHOODS
CUBIC
CUBICA
CUBICAL
CUBICALLY
CUBICAS
CUBICLE
CUBICLES

CUBIFORM
CUBING
CUBISM
CUBISMS
CUBIST
CUBISTS
CUBIT
CUBITAL
CUBITS
CUBITUS
CUBITUSES
CUBLESS
CUBOID
CUBOIDAL
CUBOIDS
CUBS
CUCKOLD
CUCKOLDED
CUCKOLDING
CUCKOLDLY
CUCKOLDOM
CUCKOLDOMS
CUCKOLDRIES
CUCKOLDRY
CUCKOLDS
CUCKOLDY
CUCKOO
CUCKOOS
CUCULLATE
CUCUMBER
CUCUMBERS
CUCURBIT
CUCURBITS
CUD
CUDBEAR
CUDBEARS
CUDDEEHIH
CUDDEEHIHS
CUDDEN
CUDDENS
CUDDIE
CUDDIES
CUDDIN
CUDDINS
CUDDLE
CUDDLED
CUDDLES
CUDDLIER
CUDDLIEST
CUDDLING
CUDDLY
CUDDY
CUDGEL
CUDGELLED
CUDGELLER
CUDGELLERS
CUDGELLING
CUDGELLINGS
CUDGELS
CUDS
CUDWEED
CUDWEEDS
CUE
CUED
CUEING
CUEIST
CUEISTS
CUES
CUESTA
CUESTAS

| | | | | |
|---|---|---|---|---|
| CUFF | CULLYISM | CUMBRANCES | CUPPAS | CURDINESS |
| CUFFED | CULLYISMS | CUMBROUS | CUPPED | CURDINESSES |
| CUFFIN | CULM | CUMEC | CUPPER | CURDING |
| CUFFING | CULMED | CUMECS | CUPPERS | CURDLE |
| CUFFINS | CULMEN | CUMIN | CUPPING | CURDLED |
| CUFFLE | CULMENS | CUMINS | CUPPINGS | CURDLES |
| CUFFLED | CULMINANT | CUMMER | CUPREOUS | CURDLING |
| CUFFLES | CULMINATE | CUMMERS | CUPRIC | CURDS |
| CUFFLING | CULMINATED | CUMMIN | CUPRITE | CURDY |
| CUFFO | CULMINATES | CUMMINS | CUPRITES | CURE |
| CUFFS | CULMINATING | CUMQUAT | CUPROUS | CURÉ |
| CUIF | CULMING | CUMQUATS | CUPS | CURED |
| CUIFS | CULMS | CUMSHAW | CUPULAR | CURELESS |
| CUING | CULOTTE | CUMSHAWS | CUPULATE | CURER |
| CUIRASS | CULOTTES | CUMULATE | CUPULE | CURERS |
| CUIRASSED | CULPABLE | CUMULATED | CUPULES | CURES |
| CUIRASSES | CULPABLY | CUMULATES | CUR | CURÉS |
| CUIRASSING | CULPATORY | CUMULATING | CURABLE | CURETTAGE |
| CUISH | CULPRIT | CUMULI | CURAÇAO | CURETTAGES |
| CUISHES | CULPRITS | CUMULOSE | CURAÇAOS | CURETTE |
| CUISINE | CULT | CUMULUS | CURAÇIES | CURETTED |
| CUISINES | CULTCH | CUNABULA | CURAÇOA | CURETTES |
| CUISINIER | CULTCHES | CUNCTATOR | CURAÇOAS | CURETTING |
| CUISINIERS | CULTER | CUNCTATORS | CURACY | CURFEW |
| CUISSE | CULTERS | CUNEAL | CURARA | CURFEWS |
| CUISSER | CULTIC | CUNEATE | CURARAS | CURFUFFLE |
| CUISSERS | CULTIGEN | CUNEATIC | CURARE | CURFUFFLED |
| CUISSES | CULTIGENS | CUNEIFORM | CURARES | CURFUFFLES |
| CUIT | CULTISH | CUNEIFORMS | CURARI | CURFUFFLING |
| CUITER | CULTISM | CUNETTE | CURARINE | CURIA |
| CUITERED | CULTISMS | CUNETTES | CURARINES | CURIAE |
| CUITERING | CULTIST | CUNJEVOI | CURARIS | CURIALISM |
| CUITERS | CULTISTS | CUNJEVOIS | CURARISE | CURIALISMS |
| CUITIKIN | CULTIVAR | CUNNER | CURARISED | CURIALIST |
| CUITIKINS | CULTIVARS | CUNNERS | CURARISES | CURIALISTS |
| CUITS | CULTIVATE | CUNNING | CURARISING | CURIAS |
| CUITTLE | CULTIVATED | CUNNINGLY | CURARIZE | CURIE |
| CUITTLED | CULTIVATES | CUNNINGS | CURARIZED | CURIES |
| CUITTLES | CULTIVATING | CUNT | CURARIZES | CURIET |
| CUITTLING | CULTORIST | CUNTS | CURARIZING | CURIETS |
| CULCH | CULTORISTS | CUP | CURASSOW | CURING |
| CULCHES | CULTRATE | CUPBEARER | CURASSOWS | CURIO |
| CULET | CULTRATED | CUPBEARERS | CURAT | CURIOS |
| CULETS | CULTS | CUPBOARD | CURATE | CURIOSA |
| CULEX | CULTURAL | CUPBOARDED | CURATES | CURIOSITIES |
| CULICES | CULTURE | CUPBOARDING | CURATIVE | CURIOSITY |
| CULICID | CULTURED | CUPBOARDS | CURATOR | CURIOUS |
| CULICIDS | CULTURES | CUPEL | CURATORS | CURIOUSER |
| CULICINE | CULTURING | CUPELLED | CURATORY | CURIOUSLY |
| CULINARY | CULTURIST | CUPELLING | CURATRIX | CURIUM |
| CULL | CULTURISTS | CUPELS | CURATRIXES | CURIUMS |
| CULLED | CULTUS | CUPFUL | CURATS | CURL |
| CULLENDER | CULTUSES | CUPFULS | CURB | CURLED |
| CULLENDERS | CULVER | CUPGALL | CURBABLE | CURLER |
| CULLER | CULVERIN | CUPGALLS | CURBED | CURLERS |
| CULLERS | CULVERINS | CUPHEAD | CURBING | CURLEW |
| CULLET | CULVERS | CUPHEADS | CURBLESS | CURLEWS |
| CULLETS | CULVERT | CUPID | CURBS | CURLICUE |
| CULLIED | CULVERTS | CUPIDITIES | CURCH | CURLICUES |
| CULLIES | CUM | CUPIDITY | CURCHES | CURLIER |
| CULLING | CUMARIN | CUPIDS | CURCULIO | CURLIEST |
| CULLINGS | CUMARINS | CUPMAN | CURCULIOS | CURLINESS |
| CULLION | CUMBENT | CUPMEN | CURCUMA | CURLINESSES |
| CULLIONLY | CUMBER | CUPOLA | CURCUMAS | CURLING |
| CULLIONS | CUMBERED | CUPOLAED | CURCUMINE | CURLINGS |
| CULLIS | CUMBERER | CUPOLAING | CURCUMINES | CURLS |
| CULLISES | CUMBERERS | CUPOLAR | CURD | CURLY |
| CULLS | CUMBERING | CUPOLAS | CURDED | CURN |
| CULLY | CUMBERS | CUPOLATED | CURDIER | CURNEY |
| CULLYING | CUMBRANCE | CUPPA | CURDIEST | CURNIER |

CURNIEST
CURNS
CURNY
CURPEL
CURPELS
CURR
CURRACH
CURRACHS
CURRAGH
CURRAGHS
CURRAJONG
CURRAJONGS
CURRANT
CURRANTS
CURRANTY
CURRAWONG
CURRAWONGS
CURRED
CURRENCIES
CURRENCY
CURRENT
CURRENTLY
CURRENTS
CURRICLE
CURRICLES
CURRICULA
CURRIE
CURRIED
CURRIER
CURRIERS
CURRIES
CURRING
CURRISH
CURRISHLY
CURRS
CURRY
CURRYING
CURRYINGS
CURS
CURSAL
CURSE
CURSED
CURSEDLY
CURSENARY
CURSER
CURSERS
CURSES
CURSING
CURSINGS
CURSITOR
CURSITORS
CURSITORY
CURSIVE
CURSIVELY
CURSOR
CURSORARY
CURSORES
CURSORIAL
CURSORILY
CURSORS
CURSORY
CURST
CURSTNESS
CURSTNESSES
CURSUS
CURSUSES
CURT
CURTAIL
CURTAILED
CURTAILING

CURTAILS
CURTAIN
CURTAINED
CURTAINING
CURTAINS
CURTAL
CURTALS
CURTANA
CURTANAS
CURTATE
CURTATION
CURTATIONS
CURTAXE
CURTAXES
CURTER
CURTEST
CURTILAGE
CURTILAGES
CURTLY
CURTNESS
CURTNESSES
CURTSEY
CURTSEYED
CURTSEYING
CURTSEYS
CURTSIED
CURTSIES
CURTSY
CURTSYING
CURULE
CURVATE
CURVATED
CURVATION
CURVATIONS
CURVATIVE
CURVATURE
CURVATURES
CURVE
CURVED
CURVES
CURVESOME
CURVET
CURVETED
CURVETING
CURVETS
CURVETTED
CURVETTING
CURVIER
CURVIEST
CURVIFORM
CURVING
CURVITAL
CURVITIES
CURVITY
CURVY
CUSCUS
CUSCUSES
CUSEC
CUSECS
CUSH
CUSHAT
CUSHATS
CUSHAW
CUSHAWS
CUSHES
CUSHIER
CUSHIEST
CUSHION
CUSHIONED
CUSHIONET

CUSHIONETS
CUSHIONING
CUSHIONS
CUSHIONY
CUSHY
CUSK
CUSKS
CUSP
CUSPATE
CUSPED
CUSPID
CUSPIDAL
CUSPIDATE
CUSPIDOR
CUSPIDORE
CUSPIDORES
CUSPIDORS
CUSPS
CUSS
CUSSED
CUSSER
CUSSERS
CUSSES
CUSSING
CUSTARD
CUSTARDS
CUSTOCK
CUSTOCKS
CUSTODE
CUSTODES
CUSTODIAL
CUSTODIAN
CUSTODIANS
CUSTODIER
CUSTODIERS
CUSTODIES
CUSTODY
CUSTOM
CUSTOMARIES
CUSTOMARY
CUSTOMED
CUSTOMER
CUSTOMERS
CUSTOMISE
CUSTOMISED
CUSTOMISES
CUSTOMISING
CUSTOMIZE
CUSTOMIZED
CUSTOMIZES
CUSTOMIZING
CUSTOMS
CUSTOS
CUSTREL
CUSTRELS
CUSTUMARIES
CUSTUMARY
CUT
CUTANEOUS
CUTAWAY
CUTAWAYS
CUTBACK
CUTBACKS
CUTCH
CUTCHA
CUTCHERIES
CUTCHERRIES
CUTCHERRY
CUTCHERY
CUTCHES

CUTE
CUTER
CUTES
CUTESIER
CUTESIEST
CUTEST
CUTESY
CUTEY
CUTEYS
CUTICLE
CUTICLES
CUTICULAR
CUTIE
CUTIES
CUTIKIN
CUTIKINS
CUTIN
CUTINISE
CUTINISED
CUTINISES
CUTINISING
CUTINIZE
CUTINIZED
CUTINIZES
CUTINIZING
CUTINS
CUTIS
CUTISES
CUTLASS
CUTLASSES
CUTLER
CUTLERIES
CUTLERS
CUTLERY
CUTLET
CUTLETS
CUTLINE
CUTLINES
CUTPURSE
CUTPURSES
CUTS
CUTTER
CUTTERS
CUTTIER
CUTTIES
CUTTIEST
CUTTING
CUTTINGS
CUTTLE
CUTTLES
CUTTO
CUTTOE
CUTTOES
CUTTY
CUTWORM
CUTWORMS
CUVÉE
CUVÉES
CUVETTE
CUVETTES
CUZ
CUZZES
CWM
CWMS
CYAN
CYANAMIDE
CYANAMIDES
CYANATE
CYANATES
CYANIC

CYANIDE
CYANIDED
CYANIDES
CYANIDING
CYANIDINGS
CYANIN
CYANINE
CYANINES
CYANINS
CYANISE
CYANISED
CYANISES
CYANISING
CYANITE
CYANITES
CYANIZE
CYANIZED
CYANIZES
CYANIZING
CYANOGEN
CYANOGENS
CYANOSED
CYANOSES
CYANOSIS
CYANOTIC
CYANOTYPE
CYANOTYPES
CYANS
CYANURET
CYANURETS
CYATHI
CYATHIA
CYATHIUM
CYATHUS
CYATHUSES
CYCAD
CYCADS
CYCLAMATE
CYCLAMATES
CYCLAMEN
CYCLAMENS
CYCLE
CYCLED
CYCLER
CYCLERS
CYCLES
CYCLEWAY
CYCLEWAYS
CYCLIC
CYCLICAL
CYCLICISM
CYCLICISMS
CYCLICITIES
CYCLICITY
CYCLING
CYCLINGS
CYCLIST
CYCLISTS
CYCLO
CYCLOID
CYCLOIDAL
CYCLOIDS
CYCLOLITH
CYCLOLITHS
CYCLONE
CYCLONES
CYCLONIC
CYCLOPEAN
CYCLOPES
CYCLOPIAN

CYCLOPIC
CYCLOPS
CYCLORAMA
CYCLORAMAS
CYCLOS
CYCLOSES
CYCLOSIS
CYCLOTRON
CYCLOTRONS
CYCLUS
CYCLUSES
CYDER
CYDERS
CYESES
CYESIS
CYGNET
CYGNETS
CYLICES
CYLINDER
CYLINDERS
CYLINDRIC
CYLIX
CYMA
CYMAGRAPH
CYMAGRAPHS
CYMAR
CYMARS
CYMAS
CYMATIUM

CYMATIUMS
CYMBAL
CYMBALIST
CYMBALISTS
CYMBALO
CYMBALOES
CYMBALOS
CYMBALS
CYMBIDIA
CYMBIDIUM
CYMBIDIUMS
CYMBIFORM
CYME
CYMES
CYMOGRAPH
CYMOGRAPHS
CYMOID
CYMOPHANE
CYMOPHANES
CYMOSE
CYMOUS
CYNANCHE
CYNANCHES
CYNEGETIC
CYNIC
CYNICAL
CYNICALLY
CYNICISM
CYNICISMS

CYNICS
CYNOMOLGI
CYNOSURE
CYNOSURES
CYPHER
CYPHERED
CYPHERING
CYPHERS
CYPRESS
CYPRESSES
CYPRIAN
CYPRIANS
CYPRID
CYPRIDES
CYPRIDS
CYPRINE
CYPRINOID
CYPRIS
CYPRUS
CYPRUSES
CYST
CYSTIC
CYSTID
CYSTIDEAN
CYSTIDEANS
CYSTIDS
CYSTIFORM
CYSTITIS
CYSTITISES

CYSTOCARP
CYSTOCARPS
CYSTOCELE
CYSTOCELES
CYSTOID
CYSTOIDS
CYSTOLITH
CYSTOLITHS
CYSTOTOMIES
CYSTOTOMY
CYSTS
CYTASE
CYTASES
CYTE
CYTES
CYTISI
CYTISINE
CYTISINES
CYTISUS
CYTODE
CYTODES
CYTOID
CYTOKININ
CYTOKININS
CYTOLOGIES
CYTOLOGY
CYTOLYSES
CYTOLYSIS
CYTON

CYTONS
CYTOPLASM
CYTOPLASMS
CYTOSINE
CYTOSINES
CYTOTOXIC
CYTOTOXIN
CYTOTOXINS
CZAPKA
CZAPKAS
CZAR
CZARDAS
CZARDASES
CZARDOM
CZARDOMS
CZAREVICH
CZAREVICHES
CZAREVNA
CZAREVNAS
CZARINA
CZARINAS
CZARISM
CZARISMS
CZARIST
CZARISTS
CZARITZA
CZARITZAS
CZARS

# D

DA
DAB
DABBED
DABBER
DABBERS
DABBING
DABBITIES
DABBITY
DABBLE
DABBLED
DABBLER
DABBLERS
DABBLES
DABBLING
DABBLINGS
DABCHICK
DABCHICKS
DABS
DABSTER
DABSTERS
DACE
DACES
DACHA
DACHAS
DACHSHUND
DACHSHUNDS
DACITE
DACITES
DACKER
DACKERED
DACKERING
DACKERS
DACOIT
DACOITAGE
DACOITAGES
DACOITIES
DACOITS
DACOITY
DACTYL
DACTYLAR
DACTYLIC
DACTYLIST
DACTYLISTS
DACTYLS
DAD
DADDED
DADDIES
DADDING
DADDLE
DADDLED
DADDLES
DADDLING
DADDOCK
DADDOCKS
DADDY
DADO
DADOED
DADOES
DADOING
DADOS
DADS
DAEDAL
DAEDALE

DAEDALIC
DAEMON
DAEMONIC
DAEMONS
DAFF
DAFFED
DAFFIER
DAFFIES
DAFFIEST
DAFFING
DAFFINGS
DAFFODIL
DAFFODILS
DAFFS
DAFFY
DAFT
DAFTAR
DAFTARS
DAFTER
DAFTEST
DAFTIE
DAFTIES
DAFTLY
DAFTNESS
DAFTNESSES
DAG
DAGABA
DAGABAS
DAGGA
DAGGAS
DAGGED
DAGGER
DAGGERS
DAGGING
DAGGLE
DAGGLED
DAGGLES
DAGGLING
DAGLOCK
DAGLOCKS
DAGO
DAGOBA
DAGOBAS
DAGOES
DAGS
DAGWOOD
DAGWOODS
DAH
DAHABEEAH
DAHABEEAHS
DAHABIEH
DAHABIEHS
DAHABIYAH
DAHABIYAHS
DAHABIYEH
DAHABIYEHS
DAHL
DAHLIA
DAHLIAS
DAHLS
DAHS
DAIDLE
DAIDLED

DAIDLES
DAIDLING
DAIKER
DAIKERED
DAIKERING
DAIKERS
DAIKON
DAIKONS
DAILIES
DAILY
DAIMEN
DAIMIO
DAIMIOS
DAIMON
DAIMONIC
DAIMONS
DAINE
DAINED
DAINES
DAINING
DAINT
DAINTIER
DAINTIES
DAINTIEST
DAINTILY
DAINTY
DAIQUIRI
DAIQUIRIS
DAIRIES
DAIRY
DAIRYING
DAIRYINGS
DAIRYMAID
DAIRYMAIDS
DAIRYMAN
DAIRYMEN
DAIS
DAISES
DAISIED
DAISIES
DAISY
DAK
DAKER
DAKERED
DAKERING
DAKERS
DAKOIT
DAKOITI
DAKOITIS
DAKOITS
DAKS
DAL
DALE
DALES
DALESMAN
DALESMEN
DALI
DALIS
DALLE
DALLES
DALLIANCE
DALLIANCES
DALLIED

DALLIER
DALLIERS
DALLIES
DALLOP
DALLOPS
DALLY
DALLYING
DALMAHOY
DALMAHOYS
DALMATIC
DALMATICS
DALS
DALT
DALTON
DALTONS
DALTS
DAM
DAMAGE
DAMAGED
DAMAGES
DAMAGING
DAMAN
DAMANS
DAMAR
DAMARS
DAMASCENE
DAMASCENED
DAMASCENES
DAMASCENING
DAMASCENINGS
DAMASK
DAMASKED
DAMASKEEN
DAMASKEENED
DAMASKEENING
DAMASKEENS
DAMASKIN
DAMASKINED
DAMASKING
DAMASKINING
DAMASKINS
DAMASKS
DAMASQUIN
DAMASQUINED
DAMASQUINING
DAMASQUINS
DAMASSIN
DAMASSINS
DAMBOARD
DAMBOARDS
DAMBROD
DAMBRODS
DAME
DAMES
DAMFOOL
DAMMAR
DAMMARS
DAMME
DAMMED
DAMMER
DAMMERS
DAMMING
DAMMIT

DAMN
DAMNABLE
DAMNABLY
DAMNATION
DAMNATIONS
DAMNATORY
DAMNED
DAMNEDER
DAMNEDEST
DAMNIFIED
DAMNIFIES
DAMNIFY
DAMNIFYING
DAMNING
DAMNS
DAMOISEL
DAMOISELS
DAMOSEL
DAMOSELS
DAMOZEL
DAMOZELS
DAMP
DAMPED
DAMPEN
DAMPENED
DAMPENING
DAMPENS
DAMPER
DAMPERS
DAMPEST
DAMPIER
DAMPIEST
DAMPING
DAMPINGS
DAMPISH
DAMPLY
DAMPNESS
DAMPNESSES
DAMPS
DAMPY
DAMS
DAMSEL
DAMSELFLIES
DAMSELFLY
DAMSELS
DAMSON
DAMSONS
DAN
DANCE
DANCEABLE
DANCED
DANCER
DANCERS
DANCES
DANCETTE
DANCETTÉ
DANCETTEE
DANCETTEES
DANCETTY
DANCING
DANCINGS
DANDELION
DANDELIONS

| | | | | |
|---|---|---|---|---|
| DANDER | DANSEURS | DARKMANS | DASHES | DAUGHTERS |
| DANDERED | DANSEUSE | DARKNESS | DASHIKI | DAULT |
| DANDERING | DANSEUSES | DARKNESSES | DASHIKIS | DAULTS |
| DANDERS | DANT | DARKROOM | DASHING | DAUNDER |
| DANDIACAL | DANTED | DARKROOMS | DASHINGLY | DAUNDERED |
| DANDIER | DANTING | DARKS | DASSIE | DAUNDERING |
| DANDIES | DANTON | DARKSOME | DASSIES | DAUNDERS |
| DANDIEST | DANTONED | DARKY | DASTARD | DAUNER |
| DANDIFIED | DANTONING | DARLING | DASTARDIES | DAUNERED |
| DANDIFIES | DANTONS | DARLINGS | DASTARDLY | DAUNERING |
| DANDIFY | DANTS | DARN | DASTARDS | DAUNERS |
| DANDIFYING | DAP | DARNED | DASTARDY | DAUNT |
| DANDILY | DAPHNE | DARNEDER | DASYPOD | DAUNTED |
| DANDIPRAT | DAPHNES | DARNEDEST | DASYPODS | DAUNTER |
| DANDIPRATS | DAPHNID | DARNEL | DASYURE | DAUNTERS |
| DANDLE | DAPHNIDS | DARNELS | DASYURES | DAUNTING |
| DANDLED | DAPPED | DARNER | DATA | DAUNTLESS |
| DANDLER | DAPPER | DARNERS | DATABANK | DAUNTON |
| DANDLERS | DAPPERER | DARNING | DATABANKS | DAUNTONED |
| DANDLES | DAPPEREST | DARNINGS | DATABASE | DAUNTONING |
| DANDLING | DAPPERLY | DARNS | DATABASES | DAUNTONS |
| DANDRIFF | DAPPERS | DARRAIGN | DATABLE | DAUNTS |
| DANDRIFFS | DAPPING | DARRAIGNE | DATABUS | DAUPHIN |
| DANDRUFF | DAPPLE | DARRAIGNED | DATABUSES | DAUPHINE |
| DANDRUFFS | DAPPLED | DARRAIGNES | DATAL | DAUPHINES |
| DANDY | DAPPLES | DARRAIGNING | DATALLER | DAUPHINS |
| DANDYFUNK | DAPPLING | DARRAIGNS | DATALLERS | DAUR |
| DANDYFUNKS | DAPS | DARRAIN | DATALS | DAURED |
| DANDYISH | DAPSONE | DARRAINE | DATARIA | DAURING |
| DANDYISM | DAPSONES | DARRAINED | DATARIAS | DAURS |
| DANDYISMS | DARAF | DARRAINES | DATARIES | DAUT |
| DANDYPRAT | DARAFS | DARRAINING | DATARY | DAUTED |
| DANDYPRATS | DARBIES | DARRAINS | DATE | DAUTIE |
| DANEGELD | DARE | DARRAYN | DATEABLE | DAUTIES |
| DANEGELDS | DARED | DARRAYNED | DATED | DAUTING |
| DANEGELT | DAREFUL | DARRAYNING | DATELESS | DAUTS |
| DANEGELTS | DARES | DARRAYNS | DATER | DAVENPORT |
| DANELAGH | DARG | DARRE | DATERS | DAVENPORTS |
| DANELAGHS | DARGA | DARRED | DATES | DAVIT |
| DANELAW | DARGAS | DARRES | DATING | DAVITS |
| DANELAWS | DARGLE | DARRING | DATINGS | DAW |
| DANG | DARGLES | DARSHAN | DATIVAL | DAWBRIES |
| DANGED | DARGS | ⁓ DARSHANS | DATIVE | DAWBRY |
| DANGER | DARI | DART | DATIVES | DAWCOCK |
| DANGERED | DARIC | DARTED | DATOLITE | DAWCOCKS |
| DANGERING | DARICS | DARTER | DATOLITES | DAWD |
| DANGEROUS | DARING | DARTERS | DATUM | DAWDED |
| DANGERS | DARINGLY | DARTING | DATURA | DAWDING |
| DANGING | DARINGS | DARTINGLY | DATURAS | DAWDLE |
| DANGLE | DARIOLE | DARTLE | DATURINE | DAWDLED |
| DANGLED | DARIOLES | DARTLED | DATURINES | DAWDLER |
| DANGLER | DARIS | DARTLES | DAUB | DAWDLERS |
| DANGLERS | DARK | DARTLING | DAUBE | DAWDLES |
| DANGLES | DARKEN | DARTRE | DAUBED | DAWDLING |
| DANGLING | DARKENED | DARTRES | DAUBER | DAWDS |
| DANGLINGS | DARKENING | DARTROUS | DAUBERIES | DAWED |
| DANGS | DARKENS | DARTS | DAUBERS | DAWING |
| DANIO | DARKER | DARZI | DAUBERY | DAWISH |
| DANIOS | DARKEST | DARZIS | DAUBES | DAWK |
| DANK | DARKEY | DAS | DAUBIER | DAWKS |
| DANKER | DARKEYS | DASH | DAUBIEST | DAWN |
| DANKEST | DARKIE | DASHBOARD | DAUBING | DAWNED |
| DANKISH | DARKIES | DASHBOARDS | DAUBINGS | DAWNER |
| DANKNESS | DARKISH | DASHED | DAUBS | DAWNERED |
| DANKNESSES | DARKLE | DASHEEN | DAUBY | DAWNERING |
| DANKS | DARKLED | DASHEENS | DAUD | DAWNERS |
| DANNEBROG | DARKLES | DASHEKI | DAUDED | DAWNING |
| DANNEBROGS | DARKLING | DASHEKIS | DAUDING | DAWNINGS |
| DANS | DARKLINGS | DASHER | DAUDS | DAWNS |
| DANSEUR | DARKLY | DASHERS | DAUGHTER | DAWS |

| | | | | |
|---|---|---|---|---|
| DAWT | DEADLINES | DEATHIER | DEBBY | DECADENCES |
| DAWTED | DEADLOCK | DEATHIEST | DEBEL | DECADENCIES |
| DAWTIE | DEADLOCKED | DEATHLESS | DEBELLED | DECADENCY |
| DAWTIES | DEADLOCKING | DEATHLIER | DEBELLING | DECADENT |
| DAWTING | DEADLOCKS | DEATHLIEST | DEBELS | DECADENTS |
| DAWTS | DEADLY | DEATHLIKE | DEBENTURE | DECADES |
| DAY | DEADNESS | DEATHLY | DEBENTURES | DECADS |
| DAYBREAK | DEADNESSES | DEATHS | DEBILE | DECAGON |
| DAYBREAKS | DEADPAN | DEATHSMAN | DEBILITIES | DECAGONAL |
| DAYDREAM | DEADPANS | DEATHSMEN | DEBILITY | DECAGONS |
| DAYDREAMED | DEADS | DEATHWARD | DEBIT | DECAGRAM |
| DAYDREAMING | DEAF | DEATHWARDS | DEBITED | DECAGRAMS |
| DAYDREAMS | DEAFEN | DEATHY | DEBITING | DECAL |
| DAYDREAMT | DEAFENED | DEAVE | DEBITOR | DECALCIFIED |
| DAYGLO | DEAFENING | DEAVED | DEBITORS | DECALCIFIES |
| DAYLIGHT | DEAFENINGS | DEAVES | DEBITS | DECALCIFY |
| DAYLIGHTS | DEAFENS | DEAVING | DEBONAIR | DECALCIFYING |
| DAYLONG | DEAFER | DEAW | DEBOSH | DECALITRE |
| DAYMARK | DEAFEST | DEAWIE | DEBOSHED | DECALITRES |
| DAYMARKS | DEAFLY | DEAWS | DEBOSHES | DECALOGUE |
| DAYNT | DEAFNESS | DEAWY | DEBOSHING | DECALOGUES |
| DAYS | DEAFNESSES | DEB | DEBOUCH | DECALS |
| DAYSMAN | DEAL | DEBACLE | DÉBOUCHÉ | DECAMETRE |
| DAYSMEN | DEALBATE | DÉBÂCLE | DEBOUCHED | DECAMETRES |
| DAYSPRING | DEALER | DEBACLES | DÉBOUCHÉS | DECAMP |
| DAYSPRINGS | DEALERS | DÉBÂCLES | DEBOUCHES | DECAMPED |
| DAYSTAR | DEALFISH | DEBAG | DEBOUCHING | DECAMPING |
| DAYSTARS | DEALFISHES | DEBAGGED | DEBRIDE | DECAMPS |
| DAYTALE | DEALING | DEBAGGING | DEBRIDED | DECANAL |
| DAYTALER | DEALINGS | DEBAGGINGS | DEBRIDES | DECANE |
| DAYTALERS | DEALS | DEBAGS | DEBRIDING | DECANES |
| DAYTALES | DEALT | DEBAR | DEBRIEF | DECANI |
| DAYTIME | DEAN | DEBARK | DEBRIEFED | DECANT |
| DAYTIMES | DEANER | DEBARKED | DEBRIEFING | DECANTATE |
| DAZE | DEANERIES | DEBARKING | DEBRIEFINGS | DECANTATED |
| DAZED | DEANERS | DEBARKS | DEBRIEFS | DECANTATES |
| DAZEDLY | DEANERY | DEBARMENT | DEBRIS | DECANTATING |
| DAZES | DEANS | DEBARMENTS | DEBRUISED | DECANTED |
| DAZING | DEANSHIP | DEBARRASS | DEBS | DECANTER |
| DAZZLE | DEANSHIPS | DEBARRASSED | DEBT | DECANTERS |
| DAZZLED | DEAR | DEBARRASSES | DEBTED | DECANTING |
| DAZZLER | DEARE | DEBARRASSING | DEBTEE | DECANTS |
| DAZZLERS | DEARED | DEBARRED | DEBTEES | DECAPOD |
| DAZZLES | DEARER | DEBARRING | DEBTOR | DECAPODAL |
| DAZZLING | DEARES | DEBARS | DEBTORS | DECAPODAN |
| DAZZLINGS | DEAREST | DEBASE | DEBTS | DECAPODS |
| DEACON | DEARIE | DEBASED | DEBUG | DECARB |
| DEACONESS | DEARIES | DEBASER | DEBUGGED | DECARBED |
| DEACONESSES | DEARING | DEBASERS | DEBUGGING | DECARBING |
| DEACONRIES | DEARLING | DEBASES | DEBUGS | DECARBS |
| DEACONRY | DEARLINGS | DEBASING | DEBUNK | DECARE |
| DEACONS | DEARLY | DEBATABLE | DEBUNKED | DECARES |
| DEAD | DEARN | DEBATE | DEBUNKING | DECASTERE |
| DEADED | DEARNESS | DEBATED | DEBUNKS | DECASTERES |
| DEADEN | DEARNESSES | DEBATEFUL | DEBUS | DECASTICH |
| DEADENED | DEARNFUL | DEBATER | DEBUSSED | DECASTICHS |
| DEADENER | DEARNLY | DEBATERS | DEBUSSES | DECASTYLE |
| DEADENERS | DEARNS | DEBATES | DEBUSSING | DECASTYLES |
| DEADENING | DEARS | DEBATING | DÉBUT | DECATHLON |
| DEADENINGS | DEARTH | DEBAUCH | DÉBUTANT | DECATHLONS |
| DEADENS | DEARTHS | DEBAUCHED | DÉBUTANTE | DECAUDATE |
| DEADER | DEARY | DEBAUCHEE | DÉBUTANTES | DECAUDATED |
| DEADERS | DEASIL | DEBAUCHEES | DÉBUTANTS | DECAUDATES |
| DEADEST | DEASILS | DEBAUCHER | DÉBUTS | DECAUDATING |
| DEADHOUSE | DEASIUL | DEBAUCHERS | DECACHORD | DECAY |
| DEADHOUSES | DEASIULS | DEBAUCHES | DECACHORDS | DECAYED |
| DEADING | DEASOIL | DEBAUCHING | DECAD | DECAYING |
| DEADLIER | DEASOILS | DEBBIER | DECADAL | DECAYS |
| DEADLIEST | DEATH | DEBBIES | DECADE | DECCIE |
| DEADLINE | DEATHFUL | DEBBIEST | DECADENCE | DECCIES |

DECEASE
DECEASED
DECEASES
DECEASING
DECEDENT
DECEDENTS
DECEIT
DECEITFUL
DECEITS
DECEIVE
DECEIVED
DECEIVER
DECEIVERS
DECEIVES
DECEIVING
DECEMVIR
DECEMVIRI
DECEMVIRS
DECENCIES
DECENCY
DECENNARIES
DECENNARY
DECENNIA
DECENNIAL
DECENNIUM
DECENNIUMS
DECENT
DECENTER
DECENTEST
DECENTLY
DECEPTION
DECEPTIONS
DECEPTIVE
DECEPTORY
DECERN
DECERNED
DECERNING
DECERNS
DECESSION
DECESSIONS
DÉCHÉANCE
DÉCHÉANCES
DECIARE
DECIARES
DECIBEL
DECIBELS
DECIDABLE
DECIDE
DECIDED
DECIDEDLY
DECIDER
DECIDERS
DECIDES
DECIDING
DECIDUA
DECIDUAL
DECIDUAS
DECIDUATE
DECIDUOUS
DECIGRAM
DECIGRAMS
DECILITRE
DECILITRES
DECILLION
DECILLIONS
DECIMAL
DECIMALLY
DECIMALS
DECIMATE
DECIMATED

DECIMATES
DECIMATING
DECIMATOR
DECIMATORS
DÉCIME
DÉCIMES
DECIMETRE
DECIMETRES
DECIPHER
DECIPHERED
DECIPHERING
DECIPHERS
DECISION
DECISIONS
DECISIVE
DECISORY
DECISTERE
DECISTERES
DECK
DECKCHAIR
DECKCHAIRS
DECKED
DECKER
DECKERS
DECKING
DECKINGS
DECKLE
DECKLED
DECKLES
DECKO
DECKOED
DECKOING
DECKOS
DECKS
DECLAIM
DECLAIMED
DECLAIMER
DECLAIMERS
DECLAIMING
DECLAIMINGS
DECLAIMS
DECLARANT
DECLARANTS
DECLARE
DECLARED
DECLARER
DECLARERS
DECLARES
DECLARING
DECLASS
DÉCLASSÉ
DECLASSED
DÉCLASSÉE
DECLASSES
DECLASSING
DECLINAL
DECLINANT
DECLINATE
DECLINE
DECLINED
DECLINES
DECLINING
DECLIVITIES
DECLIVITY
DECLIVOUS
DECLUTCH
DECLUTCHED
DECLUTCHES
DECLUTCHING
DECO

DECOCT
DECOCTED
DECOCTING
DECOCTION
DECOCTIONS
DECOCTIVE
DECOCTS
DECOCTURE
DECOCTURES
DECODE
DECODED
DECODER
DECODERS
DECODES
DECODING
DECOHERER
DECOHERERS
DECOKE
DECOKED
DECOKES
DECOKING
DECOLLATE
DECOLLATED
DECOLLATES
DECOLLATING
DÉCOLLETÉ
DECOLOR
DECOLORED
DECOLORING
DECOLORS
DECOLOUR
DECOLOURED
DECOLOURING
DECOLOURS
DECOMPLEX
DECOMPOSE
DECOMPOSED
DECOMPOSES
DECOMPOSING
DECONGEST
DECONGESTED
DECONGESTING
DECONGESTS
DECONTROL
DECONTROLLED
DECONTROLLING
DECONTROLS
DÉCOR
DECORATE
DECORATED
DECORATES
DECORATING
DECORATOR
DECORATORS
DECOROUS
DÉCORS
DECORUM
DECORUMS
DECOUPAGE
DECOUPAGES
DECOUPLE
DECOUPLED
DECOUPLES
DECOUPLING
DECOUPLINGS
DECOY
DECOYED
DECOYING
DECOYS
DECREASE

DECREASED
DECREASES
DECREASING
DECREE
DECREED
DECREEING
DECREES
DECREET
DECREETS
DECREMENT
DECREMENTED
DECREMENTING
DECREMENTS
DECREPIT
DECRETAL
DECRETALS
DECRETIST
DECRETISTS
DECRETIVE
DECRETORY
DECREW
DECREWED
DECREWING
DECREWS
DECRIAL
DECRIALS
DECRIED
DECRIER
DECRIERS
DECRIES
DECROWN
DECROWNED
DECROWNING
DECROWNS
DECRY
DECRYING
DECRYPT
DECRYPTED
DECRYPTING
DECRYPTS
DECTET
DECTETS
DECUBITI
DECUBITUS
DECUMAN
DECUMANS
DECUMBENT
DECUPLE
DECUPLED
DECUPLES
DECUPLING
DECURIA
DECURIAS
DECURIES
DECURION
DECURIONS
DECURRENT
DECURSION
DECURSIONS
DECURSIVE
DECURVE
DECURVED
DECURVES
DECURVING
DECURY
DECUSSATE
DECUSSATED
DECUSSATES
DECUSSATING
DEDAL

DEDALIAN
DEDANS
DEDICANT
DEDICANTS
DEDICATE
DEDICATED
DEDICATEE
DEDICATEES
DEDICATES
DEDICATING
DEDICATOR
DEDICATORS
DEDIMUS
DEDIMUSES
DEDUCE
DEDUCED
DEDUCES
DEDUCIBLE
DEDUCING
DEDUCT
DEDUCTED
DEDUCTING
DEDUCTION
DEDUCTIONS
DEDUCTIVE
DEDUCTS
DEE
DEED
DEEDED
DEEDER
DEEDEST
DEEDFUL
DEEDIER
DEEDIEST
DEEDILY
DEEDING
DEEDLESS
DEEDS
DEEDY
DEEING
DEEJAY
DEEJAYED
DEEJAYING
DEEJAYS
DEEM
DEEMED
DEEMING
DEEMS
DEEMSTER
DEEMSTERS
DEEN
DEENS
DEEP
DEEPEN
DEEPENED
DEEPENING
DEEPENS
DEEPER
DEEPEST
DEEPFELT
DEEPIE
DEEPIES
DEEPLY
DEEPMOST
DEEPNESS
DEEPNESSES
DEEPS
DEER
DEERBERRIES
DEERBERRY

DEERE
DEERHORN
DEERHORNS
DEERLET
DEERLETS
DEERSKIN
DEERSKINS
DEES
DEEV
DEEVE
DEEVED
DEEVES
DEEVING
DEEVS
DEFACE
DEFACED
DEFACER
DEFACERS
DEFACES
DEFACING
DEFAECATE
DEFAECATED
DEFAECATES
DEFAECATING
DEFALCATE
DEFALCATED
DEFALCATES
DEFALCATING
DEFAME
DEFAMED
DEFAMES
DEFAMING
DEFAMINGS
DEFAST
DEFASTE
DEFAT
DEFATS
DEFATTED
DEFATTING
DEFAULT
DEFAULTED
DEFAULTER
DEFAULTERS
DEFAULTING
DEFAULTS
DEFEAT
DEFEATED
DEFEATING
DEFEATISM
DEFEATISMS
DEFEATIST
DEFEATISTS
DEFEATS
DEFEATURE
DEFEATURED
DEFEATURES
DEFEATURING
DEFECATE
DEFECATED
DEFECATES
DEFECATING
DEFECATOR
DEFECATORS
DEFECT
DEFECTED
DEFECTING
DEFECTION
DEFECTIONS
DEFECTIVE
DEFECTIVES

DEFECTOR
DEFECTORS
DEFECTS
DEFENCE
DEFENCED
DEFENCES
DEFEND
DEFENDANT
DEFENDANTS
DEFENDED
DEFENDER
DEFENDERS
DEFENDING
DEFENDS
DEFENSE
DEFENSES
DEFENSIVE
DEFENSIVES
DEFER
DEFERABLE
DEFERENCE
DEFERENCES
DEFERENT
DEFERENTS
DEFERMENT
DEFERMENTS
DEFERRAL
DEFERRALS
DEFERRED
DEFERRER
DEFERRERS
DEFERRING
DEFERS
DEFFLY
DEFIANCE
DEFIANCES
DEFIANT
DEFIANTLY
DEFICIENT
DEFICIENTS
DEFICIT
DEFICITS
DEFIED
DEFIER
DEFIERS
DEFIES
DEFILADE
DEFILADED
DEFILADES
DEFILADING
DEFILE
DEFILED
DEFILER
DEFILERS
DEFILES
DEFILING
DEFINABLE
DEFINABLY
DEFINE
DEFINED
DEFINER
DEFINERS
DEFINES
DEFINING
DEFINITE
DEFLATE
DEFLATED
DEFLATER
DEFLATERS
DEFLATES

DEFLATING
DEFLATION
DEFLATIONS
DEFLATOR
DEFLATORS
DEFLECT
DEFLECTED
DEFLECTING
DEFLECTOR
DEFLECTORS
DEFLECTS
DEFLEX
DEFLEXED
DEFLEXES
DEFLEXING
DEFLEXION
DEFLEXIONS
DEFLEXURE
DEFLEXURES
DEFLORATE
DEFLORATED
DEFLORATES
DEFLORATING
DEFLOWER
DEFLOWERED
DEFLOWERING
DEFLOWERS
DEFLUENT
DEFLUXION
DEFLUXIONS
DEFOLIANT
DEFOLIANTS
DEFOLIATE
DEFOLIATED
DEFOLIATES
DEFOLIATING
DEFORCE
DEFORCED
DEFORCES
DEFORCING
DEFOREST
DEFORESTED
DEFORESTING
DEFORESTS
DEFORM
DEFORMED
DEFORMER
DEFORMERS
DEFORMING
DEFORMITIES
DEFORMITY
DEFORMS
DEFOUL
DEFOULED
DEFOULING
DEFOULS
DEFRAUD
DEFRAUDED
DEFRAUDER
DEFRAUDERS
DEFRAUDING
DEFRAUDS
DEFRAY
DEFRAYAL
DEFRAYALS
DEFRAYED
DEFRAYER
DEFRAYERS
DEFRAYING
DEFRAYS

DEFREEZE
DEFREEZES
DEFREEZING
DEFROCK
DEFROCKED
DEFROCKING
DEFROCKS
DEFROST
DEFROSTED
DEFROSTER
DEFROSTERS
DEFROSTING
DEFROSTS
DEFROZE
DEFROZEN
DEFT
DEFTER
DEFTEST
DEFTLY
DEFTNESS
DEFTNESSES
DEFUNCT
DEFUNCTS
DEFUSE
DEFUSED
DEFUSES
DEFUSING
DEFUZE
DEFUZED
DEFUZES
DEFUZING
DEFY
DEFYING
DÉGAGÉ
DEGARNISH
DEGARNISHED
DEGARNISHES
DEGARNISHING
DEGAS
DEGASSED
DEGASSES
DEGASSING
DEGAUSS
DEGAUSSED
DEGAUSSES
DEGAUSSING
DEGENDER
DEGENDERED
DEGENDERING
DEGENDERS
DÉGOÛT
DÉGOÛTS
DEGRADE
DEGRADED
DEGRADES
DEGRADING
DEGRAS
DEGREASE
DEGREASED
DEGREASES
DEGREASING
DEGREE
DEGREES
DEGUM
DEGUMMED
DEGUMMING
DEGUMS
DEGUST
DEGUSTATE
DEGUSTATED

DEGUSTATES
DEGUSTATING
DEGUSTED
DEGUSTING
DEGUSTS
DEHISCE
DEHISCED
DEHISCENT
DEHISCES
DEHISCING
DEHORN
DEHORNED
DEHORNER
DEHORNERS
DEHORNING
DEHORNS
DEHORT
DEHORTED
DEHORTER
DEHORTERS
DEHORTING
DEHORTS
DEHYDRATE
DEHYDRATED
DEHYDRATES
DEHYDRATING
DEI
DEICIDAL
DEICIDE
DEICIDES
DEICTIC
DEICTICS
DEID
DEIDER
DEIDEST
DEIDS
DEIFIC
DEIFICAL
DEIFIED
DEIFIER
DEIFIERS
DEIFIES
DEIFORM
DEIFY
DEIFYING
DEIGN
DEIGNED
DEIGNING
DEIGNS
DEIL
DEILS
DEINOSAUR
DEINOSAURS
DEIPAROUS
DEISEAL
DEISEALS
DEISHEAL
DEISHEALS
DEISM
DEISMS
DEIST
DEISTIC
DEISTICAL
DEISTS
DEITIES
DEITY
DEIXES
DEIXIS
DEJECT
DEJECTA

| | | | | |
|---|---|---|---|---|
| DEJECTED | DELICACIES | DELUSION | DEMERGED | DEMOLISHING |
| DEJECTING | DELICACY | DELUSIONS | DEMERGER | DEMOLOGIES |
| DEJECTION | DELICATE | DELUSIVE | DEMERGERS | DEMOLOGY |
| DEJECTIONS | DELICATES | DELUSORY | DEMERGES | DEMON |
| DEJECTORY | DELICE | DELVE | DEMERGING | DEMONESS |
| DEJECTS | DELICES | DELVED | DEMERIT | DEMONESSES |
| DEJEUNE | DELICIOUS | DELVER | DEMERITS | DEMONIAC |
| DÉJEUNER | DELICT | DELVERS | DEMERSAL | DEMONIACS |
| DÉJEUNERS | DELICTS | DELVES | DEMERSE | DEMONIAN |
| DEJEUNES | DELIGHT | DELVING | DEMERSED | DEMONIC |
| DEKALOGIES | DELIGHTED | DEMAGOGIC | DEMERSES | DEMONISE |
| DEKALOGY | DELIGHTING | DEMAGOGIES | DEMERSING | DEMONISED |
| DEKKO | DELIGHTS | DEMAGOGUE | DEMERSION | DEMONISES |
| DEKKOED | DELIMIT | DEMAGOGUES | DEMERSIONS | DEMONISING |
| DEKKOING | DELIMITED | DEMAGOGY | DEMES | DEMONISM |
| DEKKOS | DELIMITING | DEMAIN | DEMESNE | DEMONISMS |
| DEL | DELIMITS | DEMAINE | DEMESNES | DEMONIST |
| DELAINE | DELINEATE | DEMAINES | DEMIC | DEMONISTS |
| DELAINES | DELINEATED | DEMAINS | DEMIES | DEMONIZE |
| DELAPSE | DELINEATES | DEMAN | DEMIGOD | DEMONIZED |
| DELAPSED | DELINEATING | DEMAND | DEMIGODS | DEMONIZES |
| DELAPSES | DELIQUIUM | DEMANDANT | DEMIJOHN | DEMONIZING |
| DELAPSING | DELIQUIUMS | DEMANDANTS | DEMIJOHNS | DEMONRIES |
| DELAPSION | DELIRIA | DEMANDED | DEMIPIQUE | DEMONRY |
| DELAPSIONS | DELIRIANT | DEMANDER | DEMIPIQUES | DEMONS |
| DELATE | DELIRIANTS | DEMANDERS | DEMIREP | DEMOS |
| DELATED | DELIRIOUS | DEMANDING | DEMIREPS | DEMOSES |
| DELATES | DELIRIUM | DEMANDS | DEMISABLE | DEMOTE |
| DELATING | DELIRIUMS | DEMANNED | DEMISE | DEMOTED |
| DELATION | DELIS | DEMANNING | DEMISED | DEMOTES |
| DELATIONS | DELIVER | DEMANNINGS | DEMISES | DEMOTIC |
| DELATOR | DELIVERED | DEMANS | DEMISING | DEMOTING |
| DELATORS | DELIVERER | DEMARCATE | DEMISS | DEMOTION |
| DELAY | DELIVERERS | DEMARCATED | DEMISSION | DEMOTIONS |
| DELAYED | DELIVERIES | DEMARCATES | DEMISSIONS | DEMOTIST |
| DELAYER | DELIVERING | DEMARCATING | DEMISSIVE | DEMOTISTS |
| DELAYERS | DELIVERLY | DÉMARCHE | DEMISSLY | DEMOUNT |
| DELAYING | DELIVERS | DÉMARCHES | DEMIST | DEMOUNTED |
| DELAYS | DELIVERY | DEMARK | DEMISTED | DEMOUNTING |
| DELE | DELL | DEMARKED | DEMISTER | DEMOUNTS |
| DELEBLE | DELLS | DEMARKING | DEMISTERS | DEMPSTER |
| DELED | DELOUSE | DEMARKS | DEMISTING | DEMPSTERS |
| DELEGABLE | DELOUSED | DEMAYNE | DEMISTS | DEMPT |
| DELEGACIES | DELOUSES | DEMAYNES | DEMIT | DEMULCENT |
| DELEGACY | DELOUSING | DEME | DEMITASSE | DEMULCENTS |
| DELEGATE | DELPH | DEMEAN | DEMITASSES | DEMULSIFIED |
| DELEGATED | DELPHIC | DEMEANE | DEMITS | DEMULSIFIES |
| DELEGATES | DELPHIN | DEMEANED | DEMITTED | DEMULSIFY |
| DELEGATING | DELPHINIA | DEMEANES | DEMITTING | DEMULSIFYING |
| DELEING | DELPHS | DEMEANING | DEMIURGE | DEMUR |
| DELENDA | DELS | DEMEANOR | DEMIURGES | DEMURE |
| DELES | DELTA | DEMEANORS | DEMIURGIC | DEMURED |
| DELETE | DELTAIC | DEMEANOUR | DEMIURGUS | DEMURELY |
| DELETED | DELTAS | DEMEANOURS | DEMIURGUSES | DEMURER |
| DELETES | DELTOID | DEMEANS | DEMO | DEMURES |
| DELETING | DELUBRUM | DEMENT | DEMOB | DEMUREST |
| DELETION | DELUBRUMS | DEMENTATE | DEMOBBED | DEMURING |
| DELETIONS | DELUDABLE | DEMENTATED | DEMOBBING | DEMURRAGE |
| DELETIVE | DELUDE | DEMENTATES | DEMOBS | DEMURRAGES |
| DELETORY | DELUDED | DEMENTATING | DEMOCRACIES | DEMURRAL |
| DELF | DELUDER | DEMENTED | DEMOCRACY | DEMURRALS |
| DELFS | DELUDERS | DÉMENTI | DEMOCRAT | DEMURRED |
| DELFT | DELUDES | DEMENTIA | DEMOCRATIES | DEMURRER |
| DELFTS | DELUDING | DEMENTIAS | DEMOCRATS | DEMURRERS |
| DELI | DELUGE | DEMENTING | DEMOCRATY | DEMURRING |
| DELIBATE | DELUGED | DÉMENTIS | DÉMODÉ | DEMURS |
| DELIBATED | DELUGES | DEMENTS | DEMODED | DEMY |
| DELIBATES | DELUGING | DEMERARA | DEMOLISH | DEMYSHIP |
| DELIBATING | DELUNDUNG | DEMERARAS | DEMOLISHED | DEMYSHIPS |
| DELIBLE | DELUNDUNGS | DEMERGE | DEMOLISHES | DEMYSTIFIED |

DEMYSTIFIES
DEMYSTIFY
DEMYSTIFYING
DEN
DENARIES
DENARII
DENARIUS
DENARY
DENATURE
DENATURED
DENATURES
DENATURING
DENAY
DENAYED
DENAYING
DENAYS
DENAZIFIED
DENAZIFIES
DENAZIFY
DENAZIFYING
DENDRITE
DENDRITES
DENDRITIC
DENDROID
DENDRON
DENDRONS
DENE
DENES
DENGUE
DENGUES
DENIABLE
DENIABLY
DENIAL
DENIALS
DENIED
DENIER
DENIERS
DENIES
DENIGRATE
DENIGRATED
DENIGRATES
DENIGRATING
DENIM
DENIMS
DENITRATE
DENITRATED
DENITRATES
DENITRATING
DENITRIFIED
DENITRIFIES
DENITRIFY
DENITRIFYING
DENIZEN
DENIZENED
DENIZENING
DENIZENS
DENNED
DENNET
DENNETS
DENNING
DENOTABLE
DENOTATE
DENOTATED
DENOTATES
DENOTATING
DENOTE
DENOTED
DENOTES
DENOTING
DENOUNCE

DENOUNCED
DENOUNCER
DENOUNCERS
DENOUNCES
DENOUNCING
DENS
DENSE
DENSELY
DENSENESS
DENSENESSES
DENSER
DENSEST
DENSIFIED
DENSIFIER
DENSIFIERS
DENSIFIES
DENSIFY
DENSIFYING
DENSITIES
DENSITY
DENT
DENTAL
DENTALIA
DENTALIUM
DENTALIUMS
DENTALS
DENTARIA
DENTARIAS
DENTARIES
DENTARY
DENTATE
DENTATED
DENTATION
DENTATIONS
DENTED
DENTEL
DENTELLE
DENTELLES
DENTELS
DENTEX
DENTEXES
DENTICLE
DENTICLES
DENTIFORM
DENTIL
DENTILS
DENTIN
DENTINE
DENTINES
DENTING
DENTINS
DENTIST
DENTISTRIES
DENTISTRY
DENTISTS
DENTITION
DENTITIONS
DENTOID
DENTS
DENTURE
DENTURES
DENUDATE
DENUDATED
DENUDATES
DENUDATING
DENUDE
DENUDED
DENUDES
DENUDING
DENY

DENYING
DENYINGLY
DEODAND
DEODANDS
DEODAR
DEODARS
DEODATE
DEODATES
DEODORANT
DEODORANTS
DEODORISE
DEODORISED
DEODORISES
DEODORISING
DEODORIZE
DEODORIZED
DEODORIZES
DEODORIZING
DEONTIC
DEONTICS
DEOXIDATE
DEOXIDATED
DEOXIDATES
DEOXIDATING
DEOXIDISE
DEOXIDISED
DEOXIDISES
DEOXIDISING
DEOXIDIZE
DEOXIDIZED
DEOXIDIZES
DEOXIDIZING
DEPAINT
DEPAINTED
DEPAINTING
DEPAINTS
DEPART
DEPARTED
DEPARTER
DEPARTERS
DEPARTING
DEPARTINGS
DEPARTS
DEPARTURE
DEPARTURES
DEPASTURE
DEPASTURED
DEPASTURES
DEPASTURING
DÉPÊCHE
DÉPÊCHES
DEPEINCT
DEPEINCTED
DEPEINCTING
DEPEINCTS
DEPEND
DEPENDANT
DEPENDANTS
DEPENDED
DEPENDENT
DEPENDENTS
DEPENDING
DEPENDS
DEPICT
DEPICTED
DEPICTER
DEPICTERS
DEPICTING
DEPICTION
DEPICTIONS

DEPICTIVE
DEPICTOR
DEPICTORS
DEPICTS
DEPICTURE
DEPICTURED
DEPICTURES
DEPICTURING
DEPILATE
DEPILATED
DEPILATES
DEPILATING
DEPILATOR
DEPILATORS
DEPLANE
DEPLANED
DEPLANES
DEPLANING
DEPLETE
DEPLETED
DEPLETES
DEPLETING
DEPLETION
DEPLETIONS
DEPLETIVE
DEPLETORY
DEPLORE
DEPLORED
DEPLORES
DEPLORING
DEPLOY
DEPLOYED
DEPLOYING
DEPLOYS
DEPLUME
DEPLUMED
DEPLUMES
DEPLUMING
DEPONE
DEPONED
DEPONENT
DEPONENTS
DEPONES
DEPONING
DEPORT
DEPORTED
DEPORTEE
DEPORTEES
DEPORTING
DEPORTS
DEPOSABLE
DEPOSAL
DEPOSALS
DEPOSE
DEPOSED
DEPOSER
DEPOSERS
DEPOSES
DEPOSING
DEPOSIT
DEPOSITED
DEPOSITING
DEPOSITOR
DEPOSITORS
DEPOSITS
DEPOT
DEPOTS
DEPRAVE
DEPRAVED
DEPRAVES

DEPRAVING
DEPRAVITIES
DEPRAVITY
DEPRECATE
DEPRECATED
DEPRECATES
DEPRECATING
DEPREDATE
DEPREDATED
DEPREDATES
DEPREDATING
DEPREHEND
DEPREHENDED
DEPREHENDING
DEPREHENDS
DEPRESS
DEPRESSED
DEPRESSES
DEPRESSING
DEPRESSOR
DEPRESSORS
DEPRIVAL
DEPRIVALS
DEPRIVE
DEPRIVED
DEPRIVES
DEPRIVING
DEPROGRAM
DEPROGRAMMED
DEPROGRAMMING
DEPROGRAMS
DEPSIDE
DEPSIDES
DEPTH
DEPTHLESS
DEPTHS
DEPURANT
DEPURANTS
DEPURATE
DEPURATED
DEPURATES
DEPURATING
DEPURATOR
DEPURATORS
DEPUTE
DEPUTED
DEPUTES
DEPUTIES
DEPUTING
DEPUTISE
DEPUTISED
DEPUTISES
DEPUTISING
DEPUTIZE
DEPUTIZED
DEPUTIZES
DEPUTIZING
DEPUTY
DÉRACINÉ
DERAIGN
DERAIGNED
DERAIGNING
DERAIGNS
DERAIL
DERAILED
DERAILER
DERAILERS
DERAILING
DERAILS
DERANGE

| | | | | |
|---|---|---|---|---|
| DERANGED | DERRICKING | DESERTION | DESMINES | DESSES |
| DERANGES | DERRICKS | DESERTIONS | DESMODIUM | DESTEMPER |
| DERANGING | DERRIÈRE | DESERTS | DESMODIUMS | DESTEMPERED |
| DERATE | DERRIÈRES | DESERVE | DESMOID | DESTEMPERING |
| DERATED | DERRIES | DESERVED | DESMOSOME | DESTEMPERS |
| DERATES | DERRINGER | DESERVER | DESMOSOMES | DESTINATE |
| DERATING | DERRINGERS | DESERVERS | DÉSOEUVRÉ | DESTINATED |
| DERATINGS | DERRIS | DESERVES | DESOLATE | DESTINATES |
| DERATION | DERRISES | DESERVING | DESOLATED | DESTINATING |
| DERATIONED | DERRY | DESEX | DESOLATER | DESTINE |
| DERATIONING | DERTH | DESEXED | DESOLATERS | DESTINED |
| DERATIONS | DERTHS | DESEXES | DESOLATES | DESTINES |
| DERAY | DERV | DESEXING | DESOLATING | DESTINIES |
| DERAYED | DERVISH | DESICCANT | DESOLATOR | DESTINING |
| DERAYING | DERVISHES | DESICCANTS | DESOLATORS | DESTINY |
| DERAYS | DERVS | DESICCATE | DESORB | DESTITUTE |
| DERBIES | DESALT | DESICCATED | DESORBED | DESTITUTED |
| DERBY | DESALTED | DESICCATES | DESORBING | DESTITUTES |
| DERE | DESALTING | DESICCATING | DESORBS | DESTITUTING |
| DERED | DESALTINGS | DESIGN | DESPAIR | DESTRIER |
| DERELICT | DESALTS | DESIGNATE | DESPAIRED | DESTRIERS |
| DERELICTS | DESCALE | DESIGNATED | DESPAIRING | DESTROY |
| DERES | DESCALED | DESIGNATES | DESPAIRS | DESTROYED |
| DERHAM | DESCALES | DESIGNATING | DESPATCH | DESTROYER |
| DERHAMS | DESCALING | DESIGNED | DESPATCHED | DESTROYERS |
| DERIDE | DESCANT | DESIGNER | DESPATCHES | DESTROYING |
| DERIDED | DESCANTED | DESIGNERS | DESPATCHING | DESTROYS |
| DERIDER | DESCANTING | DESIGNFUL | DESPERADO | DESTRUCT |
| DERIDERS | DESCANTS | DESIGNING | DESPERADOES | DESTRUCTED |
| DERIDES | DESCEND | DESIGNINGS | DESPERADOS | DESTRUCTING |
| DERIDING | DESCENDED | DESIGNS | DESPERATE | DESTRUCTS |
| DERING | DESCENDER | DESILVER | DESPIGHT | DESUETUDE |
| DERISIBLE | DESCENDERS | DESILVERED | DESPIGHTS | DESUETUDES |
| DERISION | DESCENDING | DESILVERING | DESPISAL | DESULPHUR |
| DERISIONS | DESCENDINGS | DESILVERS | DESPISALS | DESULPHURED |
| DERISIVE | DESCENDS | DESINE | DESPISE | DESULPHURING |
| DERISORY | DESCENT | DESINED | DESPISED | DESULPHURS |
| DERIVABLE | DESCENTS | DESINENCE | DESPISER | DESULTORY |
| DERIVABLY | DESCHOOL | DESINENCES | DESPISERS | DESYATIN |
| DERIVATE | DESCHOOLED | DESINENT | DESPISES | DESYATINS |
| DERIVATES | DESCHOOLING | DESINES | DESPISING | DESYNE |
| DERIVE | DESCHOOLINGS | DESINING | DESPITE | DESYNED |
| DERIVED | DESCHOOLS | DESIPIENT | DESPITES | DESYNES |
| DERIVES | DESCRIBE | DESIRABLE | DESPOIL | DESYNING |
| DERIVING | DESCRIBED | DESIRABLES | DESPOILED | DETACH |
| DERM | DESCRIBER | DESIRABLY | DESPOILER | DETACHED |
| DERMA | DESCRIBERS | DESIRE | DESPOILERS | DETACHES |
| DERMAL | DESCRIBES | DESIRED | DESPOILING | DETACHING |
| DERMAS | DESCRIBING | DESIRER | DESPOILS | DETAIL |
| DERMATIC | DESCRIED | DESIRERS | DESPOND | DETAILED |
| DERMATOID | DESCRIES | DESIRES | DESPONDED | DETAILING |
| DERMATOME | DESCRIVE | DESIRING | DESPONDING | DETAILS |
| DERMATOMES | DESCRIVED | DESIROUS | DESPONDINGS | DETAIN |
| DERMIC | DESCRIVES | DESIST | DESPONDS | DETAINED |
| DERMIS | DESCRIVING | DESISTED | DESPOT | DETAINEE |
| DERMISES | DESCRY | DESISTING | DESPOTAT | DETAINEES |
| DERMOID | DESCRYING | DESISTS | DESPOTATE | DETAINER |
| DERMOIDS | DESECRATE | DESK | DESPOTATES | DETAINERS |
| DERMS | DESECRATED | DESKBOUND | DESPOTATS | DETAINING |
| DERN | DESECRATES | DESKILL | DESPOTIC | DETAINS |
| DERNFUL | DESECRATING | DESKILLED | DESPOTISM | DETECT |
| DERNIER | DESELECT | DESKILLING | DESPOTISMS | DETECTED |
| DERNLY | DESELECTED | DESKILLS | DESPOTS | DETECTING |
| DERNS | DESELECTING | DESKS | DESPUMATE | DETECTION |
| DEROGATE | DESELECTS | DESKTOP | DESPUMATED | DETECTIONS |
| DEROGATED | DESERT | DESMAN | DESPUMATES | DETECTIVE |
| DEROGATES | DESERTED | DESMANS | DESPUMATING | DETECTIVES |
| DEROGATING | DESERTER | DESMID | DESSE | DETECTOR |
| DERRICK | DESERTERS | DESMIDS | DESSERT | DETECTORS |
| DERRICKED | DESERTING | DESMINE | DESSERTS | DETECTS |

DETENT
DÉTENTE
DÉTENTES
DETENTION
DETENTIONS
DETENTS
DÉTENU
DÉTENUE
DÉTENUES
DÉTENUS
DETER
DETERGE
DETERGED
DETERGENT
DETERGENTS
DETERGES
DETERGING
DETERMENT
DETERMENTS
DETERMINE
DETERMINED
DETERMINES
DETERMINING
DETERRED
DETERRENT
DETERRENTS
DETERRING
DETERS
DETERSION
DETERSIONS
DETERSIVE
DETERSIVES
DETEST
DETESTED
DETESTING
DETESTS
DETHRONE
DETHRONED
DETHRONER
DETHRONERS
DETHRONES
DETHRONING
DETHRONINGS
DETINUE
DETINUES
DETONATE
DETONATED
DETONATES
DETONATING
DETONATOR
DETONATORS
DETORSION
DETORSIONS
DETORT
DETORTED
DETORTING
DETORTION
DETORTIONS
DETORTS
DETOUR
DETOURED
DETOURING
DETOURS
DETOXIFIED
DETOXIFIES
DETOXIFY
DETOXIFYING
DETRACT
DETRACTED
DETRACTING

DETRACTINGS
DETRACTOR
DETRACTORS
DETRACTS
DETRAIN
DETRAINED
DETRAINING
DETRAINS
DÉTRAQUÉ
DÉTRAQUÉE
DÉTRAQUÉES
DÉTRAQUÉS
DETRIMENT
DETRIMENTS
DETRITAL
DETRITION
DETRITIONS
DETRITUS
DETRUDE
DETRUDED
DETRUDES
DETRUDING
DETRUSION
DETRUSIONS
DEUCE
DEUCED
DEUCEDLY
DEUCES
DEUDDARN
DEUDDARNS
DEUS
DEUTERATE
DEUTERATED
DEUTERATES
DEUTERATING
DEUTERIDE
DEUTERIDES
DEUTERIUM
DEUTERIUMS
DEUTERON
DEUTERONS
DEUTON
DEUTONS
DEVA
DEVALL
DEVALLED
DEVALLING
DEVALLS
DEVALUATE
DEVALUATED
DEVALUATES
DEVALUATING
DEVALUE
DEVALUED
DEVALUES
DEVALUING
DEVAS
DEVASTATE
DEVASTATED
DEVASTATES
DEVASTATING
DEVEL
DEVELLED
DEVELLING
DEVELOP
DEVELOPE
DEVELOPED
DEVELOPER
DEVELOPERS
DEVELOPES

DEVELOPING
DEVELOPS
DEVELS
DEVEST
DEVESTED
DEVESTING
DEVESTS
DEVIANCE
DEVIANCES
DEVIANCIES
DEVIANCY
DEVIANT
DEVIANTS
DEVIATE
DEVIATED
DEVIATES
DEVIATING
DEVIATION
DEVIATIONS
DEVIATOR
DEVIATORS
DEVIATORY
DEVICE
DEVICEFUL
DEVICES
DEVIL
DEVILDOM
DEVILDOMS
DEVILESS
DEVILESSES
DEVILET
DEVILETS
DEVILING
DEVILINGS
DEVILISH
DEVILISM
DEVILISMS
DEVILKIN
DEVILKINS
DEVILLED
DEVILLING
DEVILMENT
DEVILMENTS
DEVILRIES
DEVILRY
DEVILS
DEVILSHIP
DEVILSHIPS
DEVILTRIES
DEVILTRY
DEVIOUS
DEVIOUSLY
DEVISABLE
DEVISAL
DEVISALS
DEVISE
DEVISED
DEVISEE
DEVISEES
DEVISER
DEVISERS
DEVISES
DEVISING
DEVISOR
DEVISORS
DEVITRIFIED
DEVITRIFIES
DEVITRIFY
DEVITRIFYING
DEVLING

DEVLINGS
DEVOICE
DEVOICED
DEVOICES
DEVOICING
DEVOID
DEVOIR
DEVOIRS
DEVOLVE
DEVOLVED
DEVOLVES
DEVOLVING
DEVONPORT
DEVONPORTS
DÉVOT
DEVOTE
DEVOTED
DEVOTEDLY
DEVOTEE
DEVOTEES
DEVOTES
DEVOTING
DEVOTION
DEVOTIONS
DÉVOTS
DEVOUR
DEVOURED
DEVOURER
DEVOURERS
DEVOURING
DEVOURS
DEVOUT
DEVOUTER
DEVOUTEST
DEVOUTLY
DEVVEL
DEVVELLED
DEVVELLING
DEVVELS
DEW
DEWAN
DEWANI
DEWANIS
DEWANNIES
DEWANNY
DEWANS
DEWATER
DEWATERED
DEWATERING
DEWATERS
DEWED
DEWFULL
DEWIER
DEWIEST
DEWILY
DEWINESS
DEWINESSES
DEWING
DEWITT
DEWITTED
DEWITTING
DEWITTS
DEWLAP
DEWLAPPED
DEWLAPS
DEWLAPT
DEWPOINT
DEWPOINTS
DEWS
DEWY

DEXTER
DEXTERITIES
DEXTERITY
DEXTEROUS
DEXTERS
DEXTRAL
DEXTRALLY
DEXTRAN
DEXTRANS
DEXTRIN
DEXTRINE
DEXTRINES
DEXTRINS
DEXTRORSE
DEXTROSE
DEXTROSES
DEXTROUS
DEY
DEYS
DHAK
DHAKS
DHAL
DHALS
DHARMA
DHARMAS
DHARMSALA
DHARMSALAS
DHARNA
DHARNAS
DHOBI
DHOBIS
DHOLE
DHOLES
DHOLL
DHOLLS
DHOOLIES
DHOOLY
DHOOTI
DHOOTIS
DHOTI
DHOTIS
DHOW
DHOWS
DHURRA
DHURRAS
DHURRIE
DHURRIES
DI
DIABASE
DIABASES
DIABASIC
DIABETES
DIABETIC
DIABETICS
DIABLERIE
DIABLERIES
DIABLERY
DIABOLIC
DIABOLISE
DIABOLISED
DIABOLISES
DIABOLISING
DIABOLISM
DIABOLISMS
DIABOLIZE
DIABOLIZED
DIABOLIZES
DIABOLIZING
DIABOLO
DIABOLOGIES

DIABOLOGY
DIABOLOS
DIACHYLON
DIACHYLONS
DIACHYLUM
DIACHYLUMS
DIACID
DIACODION
DIACODIONS
DIACODIUM
DIACODIUMS
DIACONAL
DIACONATE
DIACONATES
DIACRITIC
DIACRITICS
DIACT
DIACTINAL
DIACTINE
DIACTINIC
DIADEM
DIADEMED
DIADEMS
DIADOCHI
DIADROM
DIADROMS
DIAERESES
DIAERESIS
DIAGLYPH
DIAGLYPHS
DIAGNOSE
DIAGNOSED
DIAGNOSES
DIAGNOSING
DIAGNOSIS
DIAGONAL
DIAGONALS
DIAGRAM
DIAGRAMS
DIAGRAPH
DIAGRAPHS
DIAGRID
DIAGRIDS
DIAL
DIALECT
DIALECTAL
DIALECTIC
DIALECTICS
DIALECTS
DIALIST
DIALISTS
DIALLAGE
DIALLAGES
DIALLAGIC
DIALLED
DIALLER
DIALLERS
DIALLING
DIALLINGS
DIALOG
DIALOGIC
DIALOGISE
DIALOGISED
DIALOGISES
DIALOGISING
DIALOGIST
DIALOGISTS
DIALOGITE
DIALOGITES
DIALOGIZE

DIALOGIZED
DIALOGIZES
DIALOGIZING
DIALOGS
DIALOGUE
DIALOGUED
DIALOGUES
DIALOGUING
DIALS
DIALYSE
DIALYSED
DIALYSER
DIALYSERS
DIALYSES
DIALYSING
DIALYSIS
DIALYTIC
DIALYZE
DIALYZED
DIALYZER
DIALYZERS
DIALYZES
DIALYZING
DIAMAGNET
DIAMAGNETS
DIAMANTÉ
DIAMANTÉS
DIAMETER
DIAMETERS
DIAMETRAL
DIAMETRIC
DIAMOND
DIAMONDED
DIAMONDS
DIAMYL
DIANDRIES
DIANDROUS
DIANDRY
DIANETICS®
DIANODAL
DIANOETIC
DIANTHUS
DIANTHUSES
DIAPASE
DIAPASES
DIAPASON
DIAPASONS
DIAPAUSE
DIAPAUSES
DIAPENTE
DIAPENTES
DIAPER
DIAPERED
DIAPERING
DIAPERINGS
DIAPERS
DIAPHONE
DIAPHONES
DIAPHRAGM
DIAPHRAGMS
DIAPHYSES
DIAPHYSIS
DIAPIR
DIAPIRIC
DIAPIRISM
DIAPIRISMS
DIAPIRS
DIAPYESES
DIAPYESIS
DIAPYETIC

DIAPYETICS
DIARCH
DIARCHAL
DIARCHIC
DIARCHIES
DIARCHY
DIARIAL
DIARIAN
DIARIES
DIARISE
DIARISED
DIARISES
DIARISING
DIARIST
DIARISTS
DIARIZE
DIARIZED
DIARIZES
DIARIZING
DIARRHEA
DIARRHEAL
DIARRHEAS
DIARRHEIC
DIARRHOEA
DIARRHOEAS
DIARY
DIASCOPE
DIASCOPES
DIASPORA
DIASPORAS
DIASPORE
DIASPORES
DIASTASE
DIASTASES
DIASTASIC
DIASTASIS
DIASTATIC
DIASTEMA
DIASTEMATA
DIASTER
DIASTERS
DIASTOLE
DIASTOLES
DIASTOLIC
DIASTYLE
DIASTYLES
DIATHERMIES
DIATHERMY
DIATHESES
DIATHESIS
DIATHETIC
DIATOM
DIATOMIC
DIATOMIST
DIATOMISTS
DIATOMITE
DIATOMITES
DIATOMS
DIATONIC
DIATRETUM
DIATRETUMS
DIATRIBE
DIATRIBES
DIATROPIC
DIAXON
DIAXONS
DIAZEPAM
DIAZEPAMS
DIAZEUXES
DIAZEUXIS

DIAZO
DIAZOES
DIAZOS
DIB
DIBASIC
DIBBED
DIBBER
DIBBERS
DIBBING
DIBBLE
DIBBLED
DIBBLER
DIBBLERS
DIBBLES
DIBBLING
DIBBS
DIBS
DIBUTYL
DICACIOUS
DICACITIES
DICACITY
DICAST
DICASTERIES
DICASTERY
DICASTIC
DICASTS
DICE
DICED
DICENTRA
DICENTRAS
DICER
DICERS
DICES
DICEY
DICH
DICHASIA
DICHASIAL
DICHASIUM
DICHOGAMIES
DICHOGAMY
DICHORD
DICHORDS
DICHOTOMIES
DICHOTOMY
DICHROIC
DICHROISM
DICHROISMS
DICHROITE
DICHROITES
DICHROMAT
DICHROMATS
DICHROMIC
DICHT
DICHTED
DICHTING
DICHTS
DICIER
DICIEST
DICING
DICINGS
DICK
DICKENS
DICKER
DICKERED
DICKERING
DICKERS
DICKEY
DICKEYS
DICKIE
DICKIER

DICKIES
DICKIEST
DICKS
DICKTIER
DICKTIEST
DICKTY
DICKY
DICLINISM
DICLINISMS
DICLINOUS
DICOT
DICOTS
DICROTIC
DICROTISM
DICROTISMS
DICROTOUS
DICT
DICTA
DICTATE
DICTATED
DICTATES
DICTATING
DICTATION
DICTATIONS
DICTATOR
DICTATORS
DICTATORY
DICTATRIX
DICTATRIXES
DICTATURE
DICTATURES
DICTED
DICTIER
DICTIEST
DICTING
DICTION
DICTIONS
DICTS
DICTUM
DICTY
DICTYOGEN
DICTYOGENS
DICYCLIC
DID
DIDACTIC
DIDACTICS
DIDACTYL
DIDACTYLS
DIDAKAI
DIDAKAIS
DIDAKEI
DIDAKEIS
DIDAPPER
DIDAPPERS
DIDDER
DIDDERED
DIDDERING
DIDDERS
DIDDICOI
DIDDICOIS
DIDDICOY
DIDDICOYS
DIDDLE
DIDDLED
DIDDLER
DIDDLERS
DIDDLES
DIDDLING
DIDELPHIC
DIDELPHID

| | | | | |
|---|---|---|---|---|
| DIDELPHIDS | DIETITIANS | DIGITIZE | DILDOE | DIMIDIATED |
| DIDICOI | DIETS | DIGITIZED | DILDOES | DIMIDIATES |
| DIDICOIS | DIFFER | DIGITIZER | DILDOS | DIMIDIATING |
| DIDICOY | DIFFERED | DIGITIZERS | DILEMMA | DIMINISH |
| DIDICOYS | DIFFERENT | DIGITIZES | DILEMMAS | DIMINISHED |
| DIDO | DIFFERING | DIGITIZING | DILIGENCE | DIMINISHES |
| DIDOES | DIFFERS | DIGITS | DILIGENCES | DIMINISHING |
| DIDOS | DIFFICILE | DIGLOT | DILIGENT | DIMINISHINGS |
| DIDRACHM | DIFFICULT | DIGLOTS | DILL | DIMISSORY |
| DIDRACHMA | DIFFIDENT | DIGLYPH | DILLI | DIMITIES |
| DIDRACHMAS | DIFFLUENT | DIGLYPHS | DILLIER | DIMITY |
| DIDRACHMS | DIFFORM | DIGNIFIED | DILLIES | DIMLY |
| DIDST | DIFFRACT | DIGNIFIES | DILLIEST | DIMMED |
| DIDYMIUM | DIFFRACTED | DIGNIFY | DILLING | DIMMER |
| DIDYMIUMS | DIFFRACTING | DIGNIFYING | DILLINGS | DIMMERS |
| DIDYMOUS | DIFFRACTS | DIGNITARIES | DILLIS | DIMMEST |
| DIE | DIFFUSE | DIGNITARY | DILLS | DIMMING |
| DIEB | DIFFUSED | DIGNITIES | DILLY | DIMMISH |
| DIEBACK | DIFFUSELY | DIGNITY | DILUENT | DIMNESS |
| DIEBACKS | DIFFUSER | DIGONAL | DILUENTS | DIMNESSES |
| DIEBS | DIFFUSERS | DIGRAPH | DILUTABLE | DIMORPH |
| DIED | DIFFUSES | DIGRAPHS | DILUTABLES | DIMORPHIC |
| DIEDRAL | DIFFUSING | DIGRESS | DILUTE | DIMORPHS |
| DIEDRALS | DIFFUSION | DIGRESSED | DILUTED | DIMPLE |
| DIÈDRE | DIFFUSIONS | DIGRESSES | DILUTEE | DIMPLED |
| DIÈDRES | DIFFUSIVE | DIGRESSING | DILUTEES | DIMPLES |
| DIEGESES | DIG | DIGS | DILUTER | DIMPLIER |
| DIEGESIS | DIGAMIES | DIGYNIAN | DILUTERS | DIMPLIEST |
| DIELDRIN | DIGAMIST | DIGYNOUS | DILUTES | DIMPLING |
| DIELDRINS | DIGAMISTS | DIHEDRAL | DILUTING | DIMPLY |
| DIELYTRA | DIGAMMA | DIHEDRALS | DILUTION | DIMS |
| DIELYTRAS | DIGAMMAS | DIHEDRON | DILUTIONS | DIMWIT |
| DIENE | DIGAMOUS | DIHEDRONS | DILUTOR | DIMWITS |
| DIENES | DIGAMY | DIHYBRID | DILUTORS | DIMYARIAN |
| DIERESES | DIGASTRIC | DIHYBRIDS | DILUVIA | DIN |
| DIERESIS | DIGEST | DIHYDRIC | DILUVIAL | DINAR |
| DIES | DIGESTED | DIKA | DILUVIAN | DINARCHIES |
| DIESEL | DIGESTER | DIKAS | DILUVION | DINARCHY |
| DIESELISE | DIGESTERS | DIKAST | DILUVIONS | DINARS |
| DIESELISED | DIGESTING | DIKASTS | DILUVIUM | DINDLE |
| DIESELISES | DIGESTION | DIKE | DILUVIUMS | DINDLED |
| DIESELISING | DIGESTIONS | DIKED | DIM | DINDLES |
| DIESELIZE | DIGESTIVE | DIKER | DIMBLE | DINDLING |
| DIESELIZED | DIGESTIVES | DIKERS | DIMBLES | DINE |
| DIESELIZES | DIGESTS | DIKES | DIME | DINED |
| DIESELIZING | DIGGABLE | DIKEY | DIMENSION | DINER |
| DIESELS | DIGGED | DIKIER | DIMENSIONED | DINERS |
| DIESES | DIGGER | DIKIEST | DIMENSIONING | DINES |
| DIESIS | DIGGERS | DIKING | DIMENSIONS | DINETTE |
| DIESTRUS | DIGGING | DIKTAT | DIMER | DINETTES |
| DIESTRUSES | DIGGINGS | DIKTATS | DIMERIC | DINFUL |
| DIET | DIGHT | DILATABLE | DIMERISE | DING |
| DIETARIAN | DIGHTED | DILATANCIES | DIMERISED | DINGBAT |
| DIETARIANS | DIGHTING | DILATANCY | DIMERISES | DINGBATS |
| DIETARIES | DIGHTS | DILATANT | DIMERISING | DINGE |
| DIETARY | DIGIT | DILATATOR | DIMERISM | DINGED |
| DIETED | DIGITAL | DILATATORS | DIMERISMS | DINGER |
| DIETER | DIGITALIN | DILATE | DIMERIZE | DINGERS |
| DIETERS | DIGITALINS | DILATED | DIMERIZED | DINGES |
| DIETETIC | DIGITALIS | DILATER | DIMERIZES | DINGESES |
| DIETETICS | DIGITALISES | DILATERS | DIMERIZING | DINGEY |
| DIETHYL | DIGITALS | DILATES | DIMEROUS | DINGEYS |
| DIETICIAN | DIGITATE | DILATING | DIMERS | DINGHIES |
| DIETICIANS | DIGITATED | DILATION | DIMES | DINGHY |
| DIETINE | DIGITISE | DILATIONS | DIMETER | DINGIER |
| DIETINES | DIGITISED | DILATIVE | DIMETERS | DINGIES |
| DIETING | DIGITISER | DILATOR | DIMETHYL | DINGIEST |
| DIETIST | DIGITISERS | DILATORS | DIMETHYLS | DINGINESS |
| DIETISTS | DIGITISES | DILATORY | DIMETRIC | DINGINESSES |
| DIETITIAN | DIGITISING | DILDO | DIMIDIATE | DINGING |

| | | | | |
|---|---|---|---|---|
| DINGLE | DIORITES | DIPSADES | DIRLED | DISANOINTING |
| DINGLES | DIORITIC | DIPSAS | DIRLING | DISANOINTS |
| DINGO | DIOSGENIN | DIPSO | DIRLS | DISAPPEAR |
| DINGOES | DIOSGENINS | DIPSOS | DIRNDL | DISAPPEARED |
| DINGS | DIOTA | DIPTERAL | DIRNDLS | DISAPPEARING |
| DINGUS | DIOTAS | DIPTERAN | DIRT | DISAPPEARS |
| DINGUSES | DIOXAN | DIPTERANS | DIRTED | DISAPPLIED |
| DINGY | DIOXANE | DIPTERIST | DIRTIED | DISAPPLIES |
| DINIC | DIOXANES | DIPTERISTS | DIRTIER | DISAPPLY |
| DINICS | DIOXANS | DIPTEROI | DIRTIES | DISAPPLYING |
| DINING | DIOXIDE | DIPTEROS | DIRTIEST | DISARM |
| DINK | DIOXIDES | DIPTEROSES | DIRTILY | DISARMED |
| DINKED | DIOXIN | DIPTEROUS | DIRTINESS | DISARMER |
| DINKER | DIOXINS | DIPTYCH | DIRTINESSES | DISARMERS |
| DINKEST | DIP | DIPTYCHS | DIRTING | DISARMING |
| DINKIER | DIPCHICK | DIRDAM | DIRTS | DISARMS |
| DINKIES | DIPCHICKS | DIRDAMS | DIRTY | DISARRAY |
| DINKIEST | DIPEPTIDE | DIRDUM | DIRTYING | DISARRAYED |
| DINKING | DIPEPTIDES | DIRDUMS | DISA | DISARRAYING |
| DINKS | DIPHENYL | DIRE | DISABLE | DISARRAYS |
| DINKUM | DIPHENYLS | DIRECT | DISABLED | DISAS |
| DINKY | DIPHONE | DIRECTED | DISABLES | DISASTER |
| DINMONT | DIPHONES | DIRECTER | DISABLING | DISASTERS |
| DINMONTS | DIPHTHONG | DIRECTEST | DISABUSE | DISATTIRE |
| DINNED | DIPHTHONGS | DIRECTING | DISABUSED | DISATTIRED |
| DINNER | DIPHYSITE | DIRECTION | DISABUSES | DISATTIRES |
| DINNERED | DIPHYSITES | DIRECTIONS | DISABUSING | DISATTIRING |
| DINNERING | DIPLEX | DIRECTIVE | DISACCORD | DISATTUNE |
| DINNERS | DIPLOE | DIRECTIVES | DISACCORDED | DISATTUNED |
| DINNING | DIPLOES | DIRECTLY | DISACCORDING | DISATTUNES |
| DINNLE | DIPLOGEN | DIRECTOR | DISACCORDS | DISATTUNING |
| DINNLED | DIPLOGENS | DIRECTORIES | DISADORN | DISAVOUCH |
| DINNLES | DIPLOID | DIRECTORS | DISADORNED | DISAVOUCHED |
| DINNLING | DIPLOIDIES | DIRECTORY | DISADORNING | DISAVOUCHES |
| DINOSAUR | DIPLOIDY | DIRECTRICES | DISADORNS | DISAVOUCHING |
| DINOSAURS | DIPLOMA | DIRECTRIX | DISAFFECT | DISAVOW |
| DINS | DIPLOMACIES | DIRECTRIXES | DISAFFECTED | DISAVOWAL |
| DINT | DIPLOMACY | DIRECTS | DISAFFECTING | DISAVOWALS |
| DINTED | DIPLOMAED | DIREFUL | DISAFFECTS | DISAVOWED |
| DINTING | DIPLOMAING | DIREFULLY | DISAFFIRM | DISAVOWING |
| DINTS | DIPLOMAS | DIREMPT | DISAFFIRMED | DISAVOWS |
| DIOCESAN | DIPLOMAT | DIREMPTED | DISAFFIRMING | DISBAND |
| DIOCESANS | DIPLOMATE | DIREMPTING | DISAFFIRMS | DISBANDED |
| DIOCESE | DIPLOMATED | DIREMPTS | DISAGREE | DISBANDING |
| DIOCESES | DIPLOMATES | DIRER | DISAGREED | DISBANDS |
| DIODE | DIPLOMATING | DIREST | DISAGREEING | DISBAR |
| DIODES | DIPLOMATS | DIRGE | DISAGREES | DISBARK |
| DIOECIOUS | DIPLON | DIRGES | DISALLIED | DISBARKED |
| DIOECISM | DIPLONS | DIRHAM | DISALLIES | DISBARKING |
| DIOECISMS | DIPLONT | DIRHAMS | DISALLOW | DISBARKS |
| DIOESTRUS | DIPLONTS | DIRHEM | DISALLOWED | DISBARRED |
| DIOESTRUSES | DIPLOPIA | DIRHEMS | DISALLOWING | DISBARRING |
| DIOPSIDE | DIPLOPIAS | DIRIGE | DISALLOWS | DISBARS |
| DIOPSIDES | DIPNOAN | DIRIGENT | DISALLY | DISBELIEF |
| DIOPTASE | DIPNOANS | DIRIGES | DISALLYING | DISBELIEFS |
| DIOPTASES | DIPNOOUS | DIRIGIBLE | DISANCHOR | DISBENCH |
| DIOPTER | DIPODIES | DIRIGIBLES | DISANCHORED | DISBENCHED |
| DIOPTERS | DIPODY | DIRIGISM | DISANCHORING | DISBENCHES |
| DIOPTRATE | DIPOLAR | DIRIGISME | DISANCHORS | DISBENCHING |
| DIOPTRE | DIPOLE | DIRIGISMES | DISANNEX | DISBODIED |
| DIOPTRES | DIPOLES | DIRIGISMS | DISANNEXED | DISBOSOM |
| DIOPTRIC | DIPPED | DIRIGISTE | DISANNEXES | DISBOSOMED |
| DIOPTRICS | DIPPER | DIRIMENT | DISANNEXING | DISBOSOMING |
| DIORAMA | DIPPERS | DIRK | DISANNUL | DISBOSOMS |
| DIORAMAS | DIPPIER | DIRKE | DISANNULLED | DISBOWEL |
| DIORAMIC | DIPPIEST | DIRKED | DISANNULLING | DISBOWELLED |
| DIORISM | DIPPING | DIRKES | DISANNULLINGS | DISBOWELLING |
| DIORISMS | DIPPINGS | DIRKING | DISANNULS | DISBOWELS |
| DIORISTIC | DIPPY | DIRKS | DISANOINT | DISBRANCH |
| DIORITE | DIPS | DIRL | DISANOINTED | DISBRANCHED |

| | | | | |
|---|---|---|---|---|
| DISBRANCHES | DISCIPLE | DISCUMBER | DISEUSE | DISGUSTS |
| DISBRANCHING | DISCIPLED | DISCUMBERED | DISEUSES | DISH |
| DISBUD | DISCIPLES | DISCUMBERING | DISFAME | DISHABIT |
| DISBUDDED | DISCIPLING | DISCUMBERS | DISFAMES | DISHABITED |
| DISBUDDING | DISCLAIM | DISCURE | DISFAVOR | DISHABITING |
| DISBUDS | DISCLAIMED | DISCURED | DISFAVORED | DISHABITS |
| DISBURDEN | DISCLAIMING | DISCURES | DISFAVORING | DISHABLE |
| DISBURDENED | DISCLAIMS | DISCURING | DISFAVORS | DISHABLED |
| DISBURDENING | DISCLOSE | DISCURSUS | DISFAVOUR | DISHABLES |
| DISBURDENS | DISCLOSED | DISCURSUSES | DISFAVOURED | DISHABLING |
| DISBURSAL | DISCLOSES | DISCUS | DISFAVOURING | DISHALLOW |
| DISBURSALS | DISCLOSING | DISCUSES | DISFAVOURS | DISHALLOWED |
| DISBURSE | DISCLOST | DISCUSS | DISFIGURE | DISHALLOWING |
| DISBURSED | DISCO | DISCUSSED | DISFIGURED | DISHALLOWS |
| DISBURSES | DISCOBOLI | DISCUSSES | DISFIGURES | DISHED |
| DISBURSING | DISCOER | DISCUSSING | DISFIGURING | DISHELM |
| DISC | DISCOERS | DISDAIN | DISFLESH | DISHELMED |
| DISCAGE | DISCOID | DISDAINED | DISFLESHED | DISHELMING |
| DISCAGED | DISCOIDAL | DISDAINING | DISFLESHES | DISHELMS |
| DISCAGES | DISCOLOUR | DISDAINS | DISFLESHING | DISHERIT |
| DISCAGING | DISCOLOURED | DISEASE | DISFLUENT | DISHERITED |
| DISCAL | DISCOLOURING | DISEASED | DISFOREST | DISHERITING |
| DISCALCED | DISCOLOURS | DISEASES | DISFORESTED | DISHERITS |
| DISCANDIE | DISCOMFIT | DISEASING | DISFORESTING | DISHES |
| DISCANDIED | DISCOMFITED | DISEDGE | DISFORESTS | DISHEVEL |
| DISCANDIES | DISCOMFITING | DISEDGED | DISFORM | DISHEVELLED |
| DISCANDY | DISCOMFITS | DISEDGES | DISFORMED | DISHEVELLING |
| DISCANDYING | DISCOMMON | DISEDGING | DISFORMING | DISHEVELS |
| DISCANDYINGS | DISCOMMONED | DISEMBARK | DISFORMS | DISHFUL |
| DISCANT | DISCOMMONING | DISEMBARKED | DISFROCK | DISHFULS |
| DISCANTED | DISCOMMONS | DISEMBARKING | DISFROCKED | DISHIER |
| DISCANTING | DISCORD | DISEMBARKS | DISFROCKING | DISHIEST |
| DISCANTS | DISCORDED | DISEMBODIED | DISFROCKS | DISHING |
| DISCARD | DISCORDING | DISEMBODIES | DISGAVEL | DISHINGS |
| DISCARDED | DISCORDS | DISEMBODY | DISGAVELLED | DISHOME |
| DISCARDING | DISCOS | DISEMBODYING | DISGAVELLING | DISHOMED |
| DISCARDS | DISCOUNT | DISEMPLOY | DISGAVELS | DISHOMES |
| DISCASE | DISCOUNTED | DISEMPLOYED | DISGEST | DISHOMING |
| DISCASED | DISCOUNTING | DISEMPLOYING | DISGESTED | DISHONEST |
| DISCASES | DISCOUNTS | DISEMPLOYS | DISGESTING | DISHONOR |
| DISCASING | DISCOURE | DISENABLE | DISGESTS | DISHONORED |
| DISCED | DISCOURED | DISENABLED | DISGODDED | DISHONORING |
| DISCEPT | DISCOURES | DISENABLES | DISGORGE | DISHONORS |
| DISCEPTED | DISCOURING | DISENABLING | DISGORGED | DISHONOUR |
| DISCEPTING | DISCOURSE | DISENDOW | DISGORGES | DISHONOURED |
| DISCEPTS | DISCOURSED | DISENDOWED | DISGORGING | DISHONOURING |
| DISCERN | DISCOURSES | DISENDOWING | DISGOWN | DISHONOURS |
| DISCERNED | DISCOURSING | DISENDOWS | DISGOWNED | DISHORN |
| DISCERNER | DISCOVER | DISENGAGE | DISGOWNING | DISHORNED |
| DISCERNERS | DISCOVERED | DISENGAGED | DISGOWNS | DISHORNING |
| DISCERNING | DISCOVERIES | DISENGAGES | DISGRACE | DISHORNS |
| DISCERNS | DISCOVERING | DISENGAGING | DISGRACED | DISHORSE |
| DISCERP | DISCOVERS | DISENROL | DISGRACER | DISHORSED |
| DISCERPED | DISCOVERT | DISENROLLED | DISGRACERS | DISHORSES |
| DISCERPING | DISCOVERY | DISENROLLING | DISGRACES | DISHORSING |
| DISCERPS | DISCREDIT | DISENROLS | DISGRACING | DISHOUSE |
| DISCHARGE | DISCREDITED | DISENTAIL | DISGRADE | DISHOUSED |
| DISCHARGED | DISCREDITING | DISENTAILED | DISGRADED | DISHOUSES |
| DISCHARGES | DISCREDITS | DISENTAILING | DISGRADES | DISHOUSING |
| DISCHARGING | DISCREET | DISENTAILS | DISGRADING | DISHUMOUR |
| DISCHURCH | DISCREETER | DISENTOMB | DISGUISE | DISHUMOURED |
| DISCHURCHED | DISCREETEST | DISENTOMBED | DISGUISED | DISHUMOURING |
| DISCHURCHES | DISCRETE | DISENTOMBING | DISGUISER | DISHUMOURS |
| DISCHURCHING | DISCRETER | DISENTOMBS | DISGUISERS | DISHY |
| DISCIDE | DISCRETEST | DISESTEEM | DISGUISES | DISILLUDE |
| DISCIDED | DISCROWN | DISESTEEMED | DISGUISING | DISILLUDED |
| DISCIDES | DISCROWNED | DISESTEEMING | DISGUISINGS | DISILLUDES |
| DISCIDING | DISCROWNING | DISESTEEMS | DISGUST | DISILLUDING |
| DISCINCT | DISCROWNS | DISEUR | DISGUSTED | DISIMMURE |
| DISCING | DISCS | DISEURS | DISGUSTING | DISIMMURED |

DISIMMURES
DISIMMURING
DISINFECT
DISINFECTED
DISINFECTING
DISINFECTS
DISINFEST
DISINFESTED
DISINFESTING
DISINFESTS
DISINHUME
DISINHUMED
DISINHUMES
DISINHUMING
DISINTER
DISINTERRED
DISINTERRING
DISINTERS
DISINURE
DISINURED
DISINURES
DISINURING
DISINVEST
DISINVESTED
DISINVESTING
DISINVESTS
DISJASKIT
DISJECT
DISJECTED
DISJECTING
DISJECTS
DISJOIN
DISJOINED
DISJOINING
DISJOINS
DISJOINT
DISJOINTED
DISJOINTING
DISJOINTS
DISJUNCT
DISJUNCTS
DISJUNE
DISJUNES
DISK
DISKED
DISKETTE
DISKETTES
DISKING
DISKS
DISLEAF
DISLEAFED
DISLEAFING
DISLEAFS
DISLEAL
DISLEAVE
DISLEAVED
DISLEAVES
DISLEAVING
DISLIKE
DISLIKED
DISLIKEN
DISLIKENED
DISLIKENING
DISLIKENS
DISLIKES
DISLIKING
DISLIMB
DISLIMBED
DISLIMBING
DISLIMBS

DISLIMN
DISLIMNED
DISLIMNING
DISLIMNS
DISLINK
DISLINKED
DISLINKING
DISLINKS
DISLOAD
DISLOADED
DISLOADING
DISLOADS
DISLOCATE
DISLOCATED
DISLOCATES
DISLOCATING
DISLODGE
DISLODGED
DISLODGES
DISLODGING
DISLOIGN
DISLOIGNED
DISLOIGNING
DISLOIGNS
DISLOYAL
DISLUSTRE
DISLUSTRED
DISLUSTRES
DISLUSTRING
DISMAL
DISMALITIES
DISMALITY
DISMALLER
DISMALLEST
DISMALLY
DISMALS
DISMAN
DISMANNED
DISMANNING
DISMANS
DISMANTLE
DISMANTLED
DISMANTLES
DISMANTLING
DISMASK
DISMASKED
DISMASKING
DISMASKS
DISMAST
DISMASTED
DISMASTING
DISMASTS
DISMAY
DISMAYD
DISMAYED
DISMAYFUL
DISMAYING
DISMAYL
DISMAYLED
DISMAYLING
DISMAYLS
DISMAYS
DISME
DISMEMBER
DISMEMBERED
DISMEMBERING
DISMEMBERS
DISMES
DISMISS
DISMISSAL

DISMISSALS
DISMISSED
DISMISSES
DISMISSING
DISMODED
DISMOUNT
DISMOUNTED
DISMOUNTING
DISMOUNTS
DISNEST
DISNESTED
DISNESTING
DISNESTS
DISOBEY
DISOBEYED
DISOBEYING
DISOBEYS
DISOBLIGE
DISOBLIGED
DISOBLIGES
DISOBLIGING
DISORBED
DISORDER
DISORDERED
DISORDERING
DISORDERS
DISORIENT
DISORIENTED
DISORIENTING
DISORIENTS
DISOWN
DISOWNED
DISOWNING
DISOWNS
DISPACE
DISPACED
DISPACES
DISPACING
DISPARAGE
DISPARAGED
DISPARAGES
DISPARAGING
DISPARATE
DISPARATES
DISPARITIES
DISPARITY
DISPARK
DISPARKED
DISPARKING
DISPARKS
DISPART
DISPARTED
DISPARTING
DISPARTS
DISPATCH
DISPATCHED
DISPATCHES
DISPATCHING
DISPATHIES
DISPATHY
DISPAUPER
DISPAUPERED
DISPAUPERING
DISPAUPERS
DISPEACE
DISPEACES
DISPEL
DISPELLED
DISPELLING
DISPELS

DISPENCE
DISPENCED
DISPENCES
DISPENCING
DISPEND
DISPENDED
DISPENDING
DISPENDS
DISPENSE
DISPENSED
DISPENSER
DISPENSERS
DISPENSES
DISPENSING
DISPEOPLE
DISPEOPLED
DISPEOPLES
DISPEOPLING
DISPERSAL
DISPERSALS
DISPERSE
DISPERSED
DISPERSER
DISPERSERS
DISPERSES
DISPERSING
DISPIRIT
DISPIRITED
DISPIRITING
DISPIRITS
DISPLACE
DISPLACED
DISPLACES
DISPLACING
DISPLANT
DISPLANTED
DISPLANTING
DISPLANTS
DISPLAY
DISPLAYED
DISPLAYER
DISPLAYERS
DISPLAYING
DISPLAYS
DISPLE
DISPLEASE
DISPLEASED
DISPLEASES
DISPLEASING
DISPLED
DISPLES
DISPLING
DISPLODE
DISPLODED
DISPLODES
DISPLODING
DISPLUME
DISPLUMED
DISPLUMES
DISPLUMING
DISPONDEE
DISPONDEES
DISPONE
DISPONED
DISPONEE
DISPONEES
DISPONER
DISPONERS
DISPONES
DISPONGE

DISPONGED
DISPONGES
DISPONGING
DISPONING
DISPORT
DISPORTED
DISPORTING
DISPORTS
DISPOSAL
DISPOSALS
DISPOSE
DISPOSED
DISPOSER
DISPOSERS
DISPOSES
DISPOSING
DISPOSINGS
DISPOST
DISPOSTED
DISPOSTING
DISPOSTS
DISPOSURE
DISPOSURES
DISPRAD
DISPRAISE
DISPRAISED
DISPRAISES
DISPRAISING
DISPREAD
DISPREADING
DISPREADS
DISPRED
DISPREDDEN
DISPREDDING
DISPREDS
DISPRISON
DISPRISONED
DISPRISONING
DISPRISONS
DISPRIZE
DISPRIZED
DISPRIZES
DISPRIZING
DISPROFIT
DISPROFITS
DISPROOF
DISPROOFS
DISPROOVE
DISPROOVED
DISPROOVES
DISPROOVING
DISPROVAL
DISPROVALS
DISPROVE
DISPROVED
DISPROVEN
DISPROVES
DISPROVING
DISPUNGE
DISPUNGED
DISPUNGES
DISPUNGING
DISPURSE
DISPURSED
DISPURSES
DISPURSING
DISPURVEY
DISPURVEYED
DISPURVEYING
DISPURVEYS

DISPUTANT
DISPUTANTS
DISPUTE
DISPUTED
DISPUTER
DISPUTERS
DISPUTES
DISPUTING
DISQUIET
DISQUIETED
DISQUIETING
DISQUIETS
DISRANK
DISRANKED
DISRANKING
DISRANKS
DISRATE
DISRATED
DISRATES
DISRATING
DISREGARD
DISREGARDED
DISREGARDING
DISREGARDS
DISRELISH
DISRELISHED
DISRELISHES
DISRELISHING
DISREPAIR
DISREPAIRS
DISREPUTE
DISREPUTES
DISROBE
DISROBED
DISROBES
DISROBING
DISROOT
DISROOTED
DISROOTING
DISROOTS
DISRUPT
DISRUPTED
DISRUPTER
DISRUPTERS
DISRUPTING
DISRUPTOR
DISRUPTORS
DISRUPTS
DISS
DISSEAT
DISSEATED
DISSEATING
DISSEATS
DISSECT
DISSECTED
DISSECTING
DISSECTINGS
DISSECTOR
DISSECTORS
DISSECTS
DISSEISE
DISSEISED
DISSEISES
DISSEISIN
DISSEISING
DISSEISINS
DISSEISOR
DISSEISORS
DISSEIZE
DISSEIZED

DISSEIZES
DISSEIZIN
DISSEIZING
DISSEIZINS
DISSEIZOR
DISSEIZORS
DISSEMBLE
DISSEMBLED
DISSEMBLES
DISSEMBLIES
DISSEMBLING
DISSEMBLINGS
DISSEMBLY
DISSENT
DISSENTED
DISSENTER
DISSENTERS
DISSENTING
DISSENTS
DISSERT
DISSERTED
DISSERTING
DISSERTS
DISSERVE
DISSERVED
DISSERVES
DISSERVING
DISSES
DISSEVER
DISSEVERED
DISSEVERING
DISSEVERS
DISSHIVER
DISSHIVERED
DISSHIVERING
DISSHIVERS
DISSIDENT
DISSIDENTS
DISSIGHT
DISSIGHTS
DISSIMILE
DISSIMILES
DISSIPATE
DISSIPATED
DISSIPATES
DISSIPATING
DISSOCIAL
DISSOLUTE
DISSOLUTES
DISSOLVE
DISSOLVED
DISSOLVES
DISSOLVING
DISSOLVINGS
DISSONANT
DISSUADE
DISSUADED
DISSUADER
DISSUADERS
DISSUADES
DISSUADING
DISSUNDER
DISSUNDERED
DISSUNDERING
DISSUNDERS
DISTAFF
DISTAFFS
DISTAIN
DISTAINED
DISTAINING

DISTAINS
DISTAL
DISTALLY
DISTANCE
DISTANCED
DISTANCES
DISTANCING
DISTANT
DISTANTLY
DISTASTE
DISTASTED
DISTASTES
DISTASTING
DISTEMPER
DISTEMPERED
DISTEMPERING
DISTEMPERS
DISTEND
DISTENDED
DISTENDING
DISTENDS
DISTENT
DISTHENE
DISTHENES
DISTHRONE
DISTHRONED
DISTHRONES
DISTHRONING
DISTICH
DISTICHAL
DISTICHS
DISTIL
DISTILL
DISTILLED
DISTILLER
DISTILLERS
DISTILLING
DISTILLINGS
DISTILLS
DISTILS
DISTINCT
DISTINCTER
DISTINCTEST
DISTINGUÉ
DISTORT
DISTORTED
DISTORTING
DISTORTS
DISTRACT
DISTRACTED
DISTRACTING
DISTRACTS
DISTRAIN
DISTRAINED
DISTRAINING
DISTRAINS
DISTRAINT
DISTRAINTS
DISTRAIT
DISTRAITE
DISTRESS
DISTRESSED
DISTRESSES
DISTRESSING
DISTRICT
DISTRICTED
DISTRICTING
DISTRICTS
DISTRUST
DISTRUSTED

DISTRUSTING
DISTRUSTS
DISTUNE
DISTUNED
DISTUNES
DISTUNING
DISTURB
DISTURBED
DISTURBER
DISTURBERS
DISTURBING
DISTURBS
DISTYLE
DISTYLES
DISUNION
DISUNIONS
DISUNITE
DISUNITED
DISUNITES
DISUNITIES
DISUNITING
DISUNITY
DISUSAGE
DISUSAGES
DISUSE
DISUSED
DISUSES
DISUSING
DISVALUE
DISVALUED
DISVALUES
DISVALUING
DISVOUCH
DISVOUCHED
DISVOUCHES
DISVOUCHING
DISYOKE
DISYOKED
DISYOKES
DISYOKING
DIT
DITA
DITAL
DITALS
DITAS
DITCH
DITCHED
DITCHER
DITCHERS
DITCHES
DITCHING
DITE
DITED
DITES
DITHECAL
DITHECOUS
DITHEISM
DITHEISMS
DITHEIST
DITHEISTS
DITHELETE
DITHELETES
DITHELISM
DITHELISMS
DITHER
DITHERED
DITHERER
DITHERERS
DITHERIER
DITHERIEST

DITHERING
DITHERS
DITHERY
DITHYRAMB
DITHYRAMBS
DITING
DITOKOUS
DITONE
DITONES
DITROCHEE
DITROCHEES
DITS
DITT
DITTANDER
DITTANDERS
DITTANIES
DITTANY
DITTAY
DITTAYS
DITTED
DITTIED
DITTIES
DITTING
DITTIT
DITTO
DITTOED
DITTOING
DITTOLOGIES
DITTOLOGY
DITTOS
DITTS
DITTY
DITTYING
DIURESES
DIURESIS
DIURETIC
DIURETICS
DIURNAL
DIURNALLY
DIURNALS
DIUTURNAL
DIV
DIVA
DIVAGATE
DIVAGATED
DIVAGATES
DIVAGATING
DIVALENT
DIVALENTS
DIVAN
DIVANS
DIVAS
DIVE
DIVED
DIVELLENT
DIVER
DIVERGE
DIVERGED
DIVERGENT
DIVERGES
DIVERGING
DIVERS
DIVERSE
DIVERSED
DIVERSELY
DIVERSES
DIVERSIFIED
DIVERSIFIES
DIVERSIFY
DIVERSIFYING

DIVERSING
DIVERSION
DIVERSIONS
DIVERSITIES
DIVERSITY
DIVERSLY
DIVERT
DIVERTED
DIVERTING
DIVERTIVE
DIVERTS
DIVES
DIVEST
DIVESTED
DIVESTING
DIVESTS
DIVI
DIVIDABLE
DIVIDANT
DIVIDE
DIVIDED
DIVIDEDLY
DIVIDEND
DIVIDENDS
DIVIDER
DIVIDERS
DIVIDES
DIVIDING
DIVIDINGS
DIVIDIVI
DIVIDIVIS
DIVIDUAL
DIVIDUOUS
DIVIED
DIVIING
DIVINATOR
DIVINATORS
DIVINE
DIVINED
DIVINELY
DIVINER
DIVINERS
DIVINES
DIVINEST
DIVING
DIVINGS
DIVINIFIED
DIVINIFIES
DIVINIFY
DIVINIFYING
DIVINING
DIVINISE
DIVINISED
DIVINISES
DIVINISING
DIVINITIES
DIVINITY
DIVINIZE
DIVINIZED
DIVINIZES
DIVINIZING
DIVIS
DIVISIBLE
DIVISIBLY
DIVISIM
DIVISION
DIVISIONS
DIVISIVE
DIVISOR
DIVISORS

DIVORCE
DIVORCED
DIVORCEE
DIVORCEES
DIVORCER
DIVORCERS
DIVORCES
DIVORCING
DIVORCIVE
DIVOT
DIVOTS
DIVS
DIVULGATE
DIVULGATED
DIVULGATES
DIVULGATING
DIVULGE
DIVULGED
DIVULGES
DIVULGING
DIVULSION
DIVULSIONS
DIVULSIVE
DIVVIED
DIVVIES
DIVVY
DIVVYING
DIWAN
DIWANS
DIXI
DIXIE
DIXIES
DIXY
DIZAIN
DIZAINS
DIZEN
DIZENED
DIZENING
DIZENS
DIZYGOTIC
DIZZARD
DIZZARDS
DIZZIED
DIZZIER
DIZZIES
DIZZIEST
DIZZILY
DIZZINESS
DIZZINESSES
DIZZY
DIZZYING
DJEBEL
DJEBELS
DJELLABA
DJELLABAH
DJELLABAHS
DJELLABAS
DJIBBAH
DJIBBAHS
DJINN
DJINNI
DO
DOAB
DOABLE
DOABS
DOAT
DOATED
DOATER
DOATERS
DOATING

DOATINGS
DOATS
DOB
DOBBED
DOBBER
DOBBERS
DOBBIE
DOBBIES
DOBBIN
DOBBING
DOBBINS
DOBBY
DOBCHICK
DOBCHICKS
DOBHASH
DOBHASHES
DOBS
DOC
DOCENT
DOCENTS
DOCHMIAC
DOCHMII
DOCHMIUS
DOCHMIUSES
DOCHT
DOCIBLE
DOCILE
DOCILER
DOCILEST
DOCILITIES
DOCILITY
DOCIMASIES
DOCIMASY
DOCK
DOCKAGE
DOCKAGES
DOCKED
DOCKEN
DOCKENS
DOCKER
DOCKERS
DOCKET
DOCKETED
DOCKETING
DOCKETS
DOCKING
DOCKINGS
DOCKISE
DOCKISED
DOCKISES
DOCKISING
DOCKIZE
DOCKIZED
DOCKIZES
DOCKIZING
DOCKLAND
DOCKLANDS
DOCKS
DOCKYARD
DOCKYARDS
DOCQUET
DOCQUETED
DOCQUETING
DOCQUETS
DOCS
DOCTOR
DOCTORAL
DOCTORAND
DOCTORANDS
DOCTORATE

DOCTORATED
DOCTORATES
DOCTORATING
DOCTORED
DOCTORESS
DOCTORESSES
DOCTORIAL
DOCTORING
DOCTORLY
DOCTORS
DOCTRESS
DOCTRESSES
DOCTRINAL
DOCTRINE
DOCTRINES
DOCUDRAMA
DOCUDRAMAS
DOCUMENT
DOCUMENTED
DOCUMENTING
DOCUMENTS
DOD
DODDARD
DODDED
DODDER
DODDERED
DODDERER
DODDERERS
DODDERIER
DODDERIEST
DODDERING
DODDERS
DODDERY
DODDIER
DODDIES
DODDIEST
DODDING
DODDIPOLL
DODDIPOLLS
DODDLE
DODDLES
DODDY
DODDYPOLL
DODDYPOLLS
DODECAGON
DODECAGONS
DODGE
DODGED
DODGEM
DODGEMS
DODGER
DODGERIES
DODGERS
DODGERY
DODGES
DODGIER
DODGIEST
DODGING
DODGY
DODKIN
DODKINS
DODMAN
DODMANS
DODO
DODOES
DODOS
DODS
DOE
DOEN
DOER

DOERS
DOES
DOEST
DOETH
DOFF
DOFFED
DOFFER
DOFFERS
DOFFING
DOFFS
DOG
DOGARESSA
DOGARESSAS
DOGATE
DOGATES
DOGBANE
DOGBANES
DOGBERRIES
DOGBERRY
DOGBOLT
DOGBOLTS
DOGCART
DOGCARTS
DOGDAYS
DOGE
DOGEATE
DOGEATES
DOGES
DOGESHIP
DOGESHIPS
DOGFIGHT
DOGFIGHTS
DOGFISH
DOGFISHES
DOGFOX
DOGFOXES
DOGGED
DOGGEDER
DOGGEDEST
DOGGEDLY
DOGGER
DOGGEREL
DOGGERELS
DOGGERIES
DOGGERMAN
DOGGERMEN
DOGGERS
DOGGERY
DOGGESS
DOGGESSES
DOGGIE
DOGGIER
DOGGIES
DOGGIEST
DOGGINESS
DOGGINESSES
DOGGING
DOGGINGS
DOGGISH
DOGGISHLY
DOGGO
DOGGONE
DOGGONED
DOGGREL
DOGGRELS
DOGGY
DOGHOLE
DOGHOLES
DOGIE
DOGIES

DOGMA
DOGMAS
DOGMATIC
DOGMATICS
DOGMATISE
DOGMATISED
DOGMATISES
DOGMATISING
DOGMATISM
DOGMATISMS
DOGMATIST
DOGMATISTS
DOGMATIZE
DOGMATIZED
DOGMATIZES
DOGMATIZING
DOGMATORY
DOGS
DOGSBODIES
DOGSBODY
DOGSHIP
DOGSHIPS
DOGSHORES
DOGSKIN
DOGSKINS
DOGSLEEP
DOGSLEEPS
DOGTEETH
DOGTOOTH
DOGTOWN
DOGTOWNS
DOGTROT
DOGTROTS
DOGVANE
DOGVANES
DOGWOOD
DOGWOODS
DOGY
DOH
DOHS
DOILED
DOILIES
DOILT
DOILTER
DOILTEST
DOILY
DOING
DOINGS
DOIT
DOITED
DOITIT
DOITKIN
DOITKINS
DOITS
DOJO
DOJOS
DOLCE
DOLCES
DOLDRUMS
DOLE
DOLED
DOLEFUL
DOLEFULLY
DOLENT
DOLERITE
DOLERITES
DOLERITIC
DOLES
DOLESOME
DOLIA

DOLICHOS
DOLICHOSES
DOLING
DOLIUM
DOLL
DOLLAR
DOLLARED
DOLLARS
DOLLDOM
DOLLDOMS
DOLLED
DOLLHOOD
DOLLHOODS
DOLLIED
DOLLIER
DOLLIERS
DOLLIES
DOLLINESS
DOLLINESSES
DOLLING
DOLLISH
DOLLOP
DOLLOPS
DOLLS
DOLLY
DOLLYING
DOLMA
DOLMADES
DOLMAN
DOLMANS
DOLMAS
DOLMEN
DOLMENS
DOLOMITE
DOLOMITES
DOLOMITIC
DOLORIFIC
DOLOROSO
DOLOROUS
DOLOUR
DOLOURS
DOLPHIN
DOLPHINET
DOLPHINETS
DOLPHINS
DOLT
DOLTISH
DOLTISHLY
DOLTS
DOMAIN
DOMAINAL
DOMAINS
DOMAL
DOMANIAL
DOMATIA
DOMATIUM
DOME
DOMED
DOMES
DOMESTIC
DOMESTICS
DOMETT
DOMETTS
DOMICAL
DOMICIL
DOMICILE
DOMICILED
DOMICILES
DOMICILING
DOMICILS

DOMIER
DOMIEST
DOMINANCE
DOMINANCES
DOMINANCIES
DOMINANCY
DOMINANT
DOMINANTS
DOMINATE
DOMINATED
DOMINATES
DOMINATING
DOMINATOR
DOMINATORS
DOMINEER
DOMINEERED
DOMINEERING
DOMINEERS
DOMING
DOMINICAL
DOMINIE
DOMINIES
DOMINION
DOMINIONS
DOMINO
DOMINOES
DOMINOS
DOMY
DON
DONA
DONAH
DONAHS
DONARIES
DONARY
DONAS
DONATARIES
DONATARY
DONATE
DONATED
DONATES
DONATING
DONATION
DONATIONS
DONATISM
DONATISMS
DONATIVE
DONATIVES
DONATOR
DONATORIES
DONATORS
DONATORY
DONE
DONEE
DONEES
DONENESS
DONENESSES
DONG
DONGA
DONGAS
DONGED
DONGING
DONGLE
DONGLES
DONGS
DONING
DONINGS
DONJON
DONJONS
DONKEY
DONKEYS

DONNARD
DONNART
DONNAT
DONNATS
DONNÉ
DONNE
DONNED
DONNÉE
DONNÉES
DONNERD
DONNERED
DONNERT
DONNÉS
DONNING
DONNISH
DONNISM
DONNISMS
DONNOT
DONNOTS
DONOR
DONORS
DONS
DONSHIP
DONSHIPS
DONSIE
DONSIER
DONSIEST
DONUT
DONUTS
DONZEL
DONZELS
DOO
DOOB
DOOBS
DOOCOT
DOOCOTS
DOODAD
DOODADS
DOODAH
DOODAHS
DOODLE
DOODLEBUG
DOODLEBUGS
DOODLED
DOODLER
DOODLERS
DOODLES
DOODLING
DOOK
DOOKED
DOOKET
DOOKETS
DOOKING
DOOKS
DOOL
DOOLE
DOOLES
DOOLIE
DOOLIES
DOOLS
DOOM
DOOMED
DOOMFUL
DOOMIER
DOOMIEST
DOOMING
DOOMS
DOOMSDAY
DOOMSDAYS
DOOMSMAN

DOOMSMEN
DOOMSTER
DOOMSTERS
DOOMWATCH
DOOMWATCHED
DOOMWATCHES
DOOMWATCHING
DOOMWATCHINGS
DOOMY
DOOR
DOORBELL
DOORBELLS
DOORKNOB
DOORKNOBS
DOORKNOCK
DOORKNOCKED
DOORKNOCKING
DOORKNOCKS
DOORMAT
DOORMATS
DOORN
DOORNAIL
DOORNAILS
DOORNS
DOORPOST
DOORPOSTS
DOORS
DOORSTEP
DOORSTEPPED
DOORSTEPPING
DOORSTEPPINGS
DOORSTEPS
DOORSTONE
DOORSTONES
DOORSTOP
DOORSTOPS
DOORWAY
DOORWAYS
DOOS
DOP
DOPA
DOPAMINE
DOPAMINES
DOPANT
DOPANTS
DOPAS
DOPE
DOPED
DOPER
DOPERS
DOPES
DOPEY
DOPIER
DOPIEST
DOPING
DOPINGS
DOPPED
DOPPER
DOPPERS
DOPPIE
DOPPIES
DOPPING
DOPPINGS
DOPS
DOPY
DOR
DORAD
DORADO
DORADOS
DORADS

| | | | | |
|---|---|---|---|---|
| DOREE | DOSAGE | DOTTY | DOUPS | DOWELLED |
| DOREES | DOSAGES | DOTY | DOUR | DOWELLING |
| DORHAWK | DOSE | DOUANE | DOURA | DOWELLINGS |
| DORHAWKS | DOSED | DOUANES | DOURAS | DOWELS |
| DORIDOID | DOSEH | DOUANIER | DOURER | DOWER |
| DORIDOIDS | DOSEHS | DOUANIERS | DOUREST | DOWERED |
| DORIES | DOSES | DOUAR | DOURINE | DOWERING |
| DORISE | DOSIMETER | DOUARS | DOURINES | DOWERLESS |
| DORISED | DOSIMETERS | DOUBLE | DOURNESS | DOWERS |
| DORISES | DOSIMETRIES | DOUBLED | DOURNESSES | DOWF |
| DORISING | DOSIMETRY | DOUBLER | DOUSE | DOWFNESS |
| DORIZE | DOSING | DOUBLERS | DOUSED | DOWFNESSES |
| DORIZED | DOSIOLOGIES | DOUBLES | DOUSER | DOWIE |
| DORIZES | DOSIOLOGY | DOUBLET | DOUSERS | DOWIER |
| DORIZING | DOSOLOGIES | DOUBLETON | DOUSES | DOWIEST |
| DORLACH | DOSOLOGY | DOUBLETONS | DOUSING | DOWING |
| DORLACHS | DOSS | DOUBLETS | DOUT | DOWL |
| DORM | DOSSAL | DOUBLING | DOUTED | DOWLAS |
| DORMANCIES | DOSSALS | DOUBLINGS | DOUTER | DOWLASES |
| DORMANCY | DOSSED | DOUBLOON | DOUTERS | DOWLE |
| DORMANT | DOSSEL | DOUBLOONS | DOUTING | DOWLES |
| DORMANTS | DOSSELS | DOUBLY | DOUTS | DOWLNE |
| DORMER | DOSSER | DOUBT | DOUZEPER | DOWLNES |
| DORMERS | DOSSERS | DOUBTABLE | DOUZEPERS | DOWLNEY |
| DORMICE | DOSSES | DOUBTED | DOVE | DOWLS |
| DORMIE | DOSSIER | DOUBTER | DOVECOT | DOWN |
| DORMIENT | DOSSIERS | DOUBTERS | DOVECOTE | DOWNA |
| DORMITION | DOSSIL | DOUBTFUL | DOVECOTES | DOWNBEAT |
| DORMITIONS | DOSSILS | DOUBTFULS | DOVECOTS | DOWNBEATS |
| DORMITIVE | DOSSING | DOUBTING | DOVED | DOWNBOW |
| DORMITIVES | DOST | DOUBTINGS | DOVEISH | DOWNBOWS |
| DORMITORIES | DOT | DOUBTLESS | DOVEKIE | DOWNCAST |
| DORMITORY | DOTAGE | DOUBTS | DOVEKIES | DOWNCASTS |
| DORMOUSE | DOTAGES | DOUC | DOVELET | DOWNED |
| DORMS | DOTAL | DOUCE | DOVELETS | DOWNER |
| DORMY | DOTANT | DOUCELY | DOVER | DOWNERS |
| DORNICK | DOTANTS | DOUCENESS | DOVERED | DOWNFALL |
| DORNICKS | DOTARD | DOUCENESSES | DOVERING | DOWNFALLS |
| DORP | DOTARDS | DOUCEPERE | DOVERS | DOWNFLOW |
| DORPS | DOTATION | DOUCEPERES | DOVES | DOWNFLOWS |
| DORR | DOTATIONS | DOUCER | DOVETAIL | DOWNFORCE |
| DORRED | DOTE | DOUCEST | DOVETAILED | DOWNFORCES |
| DORRING | DOTED | DOUCET | DOVETAILING | DOWNGRADE |
| DORRS | DOTER | DOUCETS | DOVETAILINGS | DOWNGRADED |
| DORS | DOTERS | DOUCEUR | DOVETAILS | DOWNGRADES |
| DORSA | DOTES | DOUCEURS | DOVIE | DOWNGRADING |
| DORSAL | DOTH | DOUCHE | DOVIER | DOWNHILL |
| DORSALLY | DOTIER | DOUCHED | DOVIEST | DOWNHILLS |
| DORSALS | DOTIEST | DOUCHES | DOVING | DOWNIER |
| DORSE | DOTING | DOUCHING | DOVISH | DOWNIEST |
| DORSEL | DOTINGS | DOUCINE | DOW | DOWNINESS |
| DORSELS | DOTISH | DOUCINES | DOWABLE | DOWNINESSES |
| DORSER | DOTS | DOUCS | DOWAGER | DOWNING |
| DORSERS | DOTTED | DOUGH | DOWAGERS | DOWNLAND |
| DORSES | DOTTEREL | DOUGHIER | DOWAR | DOWNLANDS |
| DORSIFLEX | DOTTERELS | DOUGHIEST | DOWARS | DOWNMOST |
| DORSUM | DOTTIER | DOUGHNUT | DOWD | DOWNPIPE |
| DORT | DOTTIEST | DOUGHNUTS | DOWDIER | DOWNPIPES |
| DORTED | DOTTINESS | DOUGHS | DOWDIES | DOWNPOUR |
| DORTER | DOTTINESSES | DOUGHT | DOWDIEST | DOWNPOURS |
| DORTERS | DOTTING | DOUGHTIER | DOWDILY | DOWNRIGHT |
| DORTIER | DOTTIPOLL | DOUGHTIEST | DOWDINESS | DOWNRUSH |
| DORTIEST | DOTTIPOLLS | DOUGHTILY | DOWDINESSES | DOWNRUSHES |
| DORTING | DOTTLE | DOUGHTY | DOWDS | DOWNS |
| DORTOUR | DOTTLED | DOUGHY | DOWDY | DOWNSTAGE |
| DORTOURS | DOTTLER | DOULEIA | DOWDYISH | DOWNSTAIR |
| DORTS | DOTTLES | DOULEIAS | DOWDYISM | DOWNSTAIRS |
| DORTY | DOTTLEST | DOUMA | DOWDYISMS | DOWNSWING |
| DORY | DOTTREL | DOUMAS | DOWED | DOWNSWINGS |
| DOS | DOTTRELS | DOUP | DOWEL | DOWNTIME |

| | | | | |
|---|---|---|---|---|
| DOWNTIMES | DRABBLING | DRAGONISING | DRAPERIED | DREADLY |
| DOWNTREND | DRABBLINGS | DRAGONISM | DRAPERIES | DREADS |
| DOWNTRENDS | DRABBY | DRAGONISMS | DRAPERS | DREAM |
| DOWNTURN | DRABETTE | DRAGONIZE | DRAPERY | DREAMBOAT |
| DOWNTURNS | DRABETTES | DRAGONIZED | DRAPERYING | DREAMBOATS |
| DOWNWARD | DRABLER | DRAGONIZES | DRAPES | DREAMED |
| DOWNWARDS | DRABLERS | DRAGONIZING | DRAPET | DREAMER |
| DOWNWIND | DRABLY | DRAGONNÉ | DRAPETS | DREAMERIES |
| DOWNY | DRABNESS | DRAGONS | DRAPIER | DREAMERS |
| DOWP | DRABNESSES | DRAGOON | DRAPIERS | DREAMERY |
| DOWPS | DRABS | DRAGOONED | DRAPING | DREAMFUL |
| DOWRIES | DRACHM | DRAGOONING | DRAPPED | DREAMHOLE |
| DOWRY | DRACHMA | DRAGOONS | DRAPPIE | DREAMHOLES |
| DOWS | DRACHMAE | DRAGS | DRAPPIES | DREAMIER |
| DOWSE | DRACHMAI | DRAGSMAN | DRAPPING | DREAMIEST |
| DOWSED | DRACHMAS | DRAGSMEN | DRAPPY | DREAMILY |
| DOWSER | DRACHMS | DRAGSTER | DRAPS | DREAMING |
| DOWSERS | DRACONE | DRAGSTERS | DRASTIC | DREAMINGS |
| DOWSES | DRACONES | DRAIL | DRASTICS | DREAMLESS |
| DOWSET | DRACONIAN | DRAILED | DRAT | DREAMS |
| DOWSETS | DRACONIC | DRAILING | DRATCHELL | DREAMT |
| DOWSING | DRACONISM | DRAILS | DRATCHELLS | DREAMTIME |
| DOWT | DRACONISMS | DRAIN | DRATTED | DREAMTIMES |
| DOWTS | DRACONTIC | DRAINABLE | DRAUGHT | DREAMY |
| DOXIES | DRAD | DRAINAGE | DRAUGHTED | DREAR |
| DOXOLOGIES | DRAFF | DRAINAGES | DRAUGHTER | DREARE |
| DOXOLOGY | DRAFFIER | DRAINED | DRAUGHTERS | DREARER |
| DOXY | DRAFFIEST | DRAINER | DRAUGHTIER | DREARES |
| DOYEN | DRAFFISH | DRAINERS | DRAUGHTIEST | DREAREST |
| DOYENNE | DRAFFS | DRAINING | DRAUGHTING | DREARIER |
| DOYENNES | DRAFFY | DRAINS | DRAUGHTS | DREARIEST |
| DOYENS | DRAFT | DRAISENE | DRAUGHTY | DREARILY |
| DOYLEY | DRAFTED | DRAISENES | DRAUNT | DREARING |
| DOYLEYS | DRAFTEE | DRAISINE | DRAUNTED | DREARINGS |
| DOYLIES | DRAFTEES | DRAISINES | DRAUNTING | DREARS |
| DOYLY | DRAFTER | DRAKE | DRAUNTS | DREARY |
| DOZE | DRAFTERS | DRAKES | DRAVE | DRECK |
| DOZED | DRAFTING | DRAM | DRAW | DRECKS |
| DOZEN | DRAFTS | DRAMA | DRAWABLE | DREDGE |
| DOZENED | DRAFTSMAN | DRAMAS | DRAWBACK | DREDGED |
| DOZENING | DRAFTSMEN | DRAMATIC | DRAWBACKS | DREDGER |
| DOZENS | DRAG | DRAMATICS | DRAWEE | DREDGERS |
| DOZENTH | DRAGÉE | DRAMATISE | DRAWEES | DREDGES |
| DOZENTHS | DRAGÉES | DRAMATISED | DRAWER | DREDGING |
| DOZER | DRAGGED | DRAMATISES | DRAWERS | DREE |
| DOZERS | DRAGGIER | DRAMATISING | DRAWING | DREED |
| DOZES | DRAGGING | DRAMATIST | DRAWINGS | DREEING |
| DOZIER | DRAGGLE | DRAMATISTS | DRAWL | DREES |
| DOZIEST | DRAGGLED | DRAMATIZE | DRAWLED | DREGGIER |
| DOZINESS | DRAGGLES | DRAMATIZED | DRAWLER | DREGGIEST |
| DOZINESSES | DRAGGLING | DRAMATIZES | DRAWLERS | DREGGY |
| DOZING | DRAGGY | DRAMATIZING | DRAWLING | DREGS |
| DOZINGS | DRAGHOUND | DRAMATURG | DRAWLS | DREICH |
| DOZY | DRAGHOUNDS | DRAMATURGS | DRAWN | DREICHER |
| DRAB | DRAGLINE | DRAMMACH | DRAWS | DREICHEST |
| DRABBED | DRAGLINES | DRAMMACHS | DRAY | DRENCH |
| DRABBER | DRAGOMAN | DRAMMED | DRAYAGE | DRENCHED |
| DRABBERS | DRAGOMANS | DRAMMING | DRAYAGES | DRENCHER |
| DRABBEST | DRAGON | DRAMMOCK | DRAYMAN | DRENCHERS |
| DRABBET | DRAGONESS | DRAMMOCKS | DRAYMEN | DRENCHES |
| DRABBETS | DRAGONESSES | DRAMS | DRAYS | DRENCHING |
| DRABBIER | DRAGONET | DRANK | DRAZEL | DRENT |
| DRABBIEST | DRAGONETS | DRANT | DRAZELS | DREPANIUM |
| DRABBING | DRAGONFLIES | DRANTED | DREAD | DREPANIUMS |
| DRABBISH | DRAGONFLY | DRANTING | DREADED | DRERE |
| DRABBLE | DRAGONISE | DRANTS | DREADER | DRERES |
| DRABBLED | DRAGONISED | DRAP | DREADERS | DRERYHEAD |
| DRABBLER | DRAGONISES | DRAPE | DREADFUL | DRERYHEADS |
| DRABBLERS | DRAGONISH | DRAPED | DREADING | DRESS |
| DRABBLES | | DRAPER | DREADLESS | DRESSAGE |

| | | | | |
|---|---|---|---|---|
| DRESSAGES | DRINKERS | DROLLNESSES | DROSERA | DRUG |
| DRESSED | DRINKING | DROLLS | DROSERAS | DRUGGED |
| DRESSER | DRINKINGS | DROLLY | DROSHKIES | DRUGGER |
| DRESSERS | DRINKS | DROME | DROSHKY | DRUGGERS |
| DRESSES | DRIP | DROMEDARE | DROSKIES | DRUGGET |
| DRESSIER | DRIPPED | DROMEDARES | DROSKY | DRUGGETS |
| DRESSIEST | DRIPPIER | DROMEDARIES | DROSS | DRUGGING |
| DRESSING | DRIPPIEST | DROMEDARY | DROSSES | DRUGGIST |
| DRESSINGS | DRIPPING | DROMES | DROSSIER | DRUGGISTS |
| DRESSY | DRIPPINGS | DROMIC | DROSSIEST | DRUGS |
| DREST | DRIPPY | DROMICAL | DROSSY | DRUID |
| DREVILL | DRIPS | DROMOI | DROSTDIES | DRUIDESS |
| DREVILLS | DRISHEEN | DROMON | DROSTDY | DRUIDESSES |
| DREW | DRISHEENS | DROMOND | DROSTDYS | DRUIDIC |
| DREY | DRIVABLE | DROMONDS | DROUGHT | DRUIDICAL |
| DREYS | DRIVE | DROMONS | DROUGHTIER | DRUIDISM |
| DRIB | DRIVEABLE | DROMOS | DROUGHTIEST | DRUIDISMS |
| DRIBBED | DRIVEL | DRONE | DROUGHTS | DRUIDS |
| DRIBBER | DRIVELLED | DRONED | DROUGHTY | DRUM |
| DRIBBERS | DRIVELLER | DRONES | DROUK | DRUMBEAT |
| DRIBBING | DRIVELLERS | DRONGO | DROUKED | DRUMBEATS |
| DRIBBLE | DRIVELLING | DRONGOES | DROUKING | DRUMBLE |
| DRIBBLED | DRIVELS | DRONGOS | DROUKINGS | DRUMBLED |
| DRIBBLER | DRIVEN | DRONIER | DROUKIT | DRUMBLES |
| DRIBBLERS | DRIVER | DRONIEST | DROUKS | DRUMBLING |
| DRIBBLES | DRIVERS | DRONING | DROUTH | DRUMFIRE |
| DRIBBLET | DRIVES | DRONINGLY | DROUTHIER | DRUMFIRES |
| DRIBBLETS | DRIVEWAY | DRONISH | DROUTHIEST | DRUMFISH |
| DRIBBLIER | DRIVEWAYS | DRONISHLY | DROUTHS | DRUMFISHES |
| DRIBBLIEST | DRIVING | DRONY | DROUTHY | DRUMHEAD |
| DRIBBLING | DRIZZLE | DROOK | DROVE | DRUMHEADS |
| DRIBBLY | DRIZZLED | DROOKED | DROVER | DRUMLIER |
| DRIBLET | DRIZZLES | DROOKING | DROVERS | DRUMLIEST |
| DRIBLETS | DRIZZLIER | DROOKINGS | DROVES | DRUMLIN |
| DRIBS | DRIZZLIEST | DROOKIT | DROW | DRUMLINS |
| DRICKSIE | DRIZZLING | DROOKS | DROWN | DRUMLY |
| DRICKSIER | DRIZZLY | DROOL | DROWNDED | DRUMMED |
| DRICKSIEST | DROGER | DROOLED | DROWNED | DRUMMER |
| DRIED | DROGERS | DROOLING | DROWNER | DRUMMERS |
| DRIER | DROGHER | DROOLS | DROWNERS | DRUMMING |
| DRIERS | DROGHERS | DROOME | DROWNING | DRUMMOCK |
| DRIES | DROGUE | DROOMES | DROWNINGS | DRUMMOCKS |
| DRIEST | DROGUES | DROOP | DROWNS | DRUMS |
| DRIFT | DROGUET | DROOPED | DROWSE | DRUMSTICK |
| DRIFTAGE | DROGUETS | DROOPIER | DROWSED | DRUMSTICKS |
| DRIFTAGES | DROICH | DROOPIEST | DROWSES | DRUNK |
| DRIFTED | DROICHIER | DROOPILY | DROWSIER | DRUNKARD |
| DRIFTER | DROICHIEST | DROOPING | DROWSIEST | DRUNKARDS |
| DRIFTERS | DROICHS | DROOPS | DROWSIHED | DRUNKEN |
| DRIFTIER | DROICHY | DROOPY | DROWSIHEDS | DRUNKENLY |
| DRIFTIEST | DROIL | DROP | DROWSILY | DRUNKER |
| DRIFTING | DROILED | DROPFLIES | DROWSING | DRUNKEST |
| DRIFTLESS | DROILING | DROPFLY | DROWSY | DRUNKS |
| DRIFTPIN | DROILS | DROPLET | DRUB | DRUPE |
| DRIFTPINS | DROIT | DROPLETS | DRUBBED | DRUPEL |
| DRIFTS | DROITS | DROPPED | DRUBBING | DRUPELET |
| DRIFTY | DRÔLE | DROPPER | DRUBBINGS | DRUPELETS |
| DRILL | DRÔLER | DROPPERS | DRUBS | DRUPELS |
| DRILLED | DRÔLES | DROPPING | DRUCKEN | DRUPES |
| DRILLER | DRÔLEST | DROPPINGS | DRUDGE | DRUSE |
| DRILLERS | DROLL | DROPPLE | DRUDGED | DRUSES |
| DRILLING | DROLLED | DROPPLES | DRUDGER | DRUSIER |
| DRILLINGS | DROLLER | DROPS | DRUDGERIES | DRUSIEST |
| DRILLS | DROLLERIES | DROPSICAL | DRUDGERS | DRUSY |
| DRILLSHIP | DROLLERY | DROPSIED | DRUDGERY | DRUXIER |
| DRILLSHIPS | DROLLEST | DROPSIES | DRUDGES | DRUXIEST |
| DRILY | DROLLING | DROPSTONE | DRUDGING | DRUXY |
| DRINK | DROLLINGS | DROPSTONES | DRUDGISM | DRY |
| DRINKABLE | DROLLISH | DROPSY | DRUDGISMS | DRYAD |
| DRINKER | DROLLNESS | DROPWISE | | DRYADES |

DRYADS
DRYBEAT
DRYBEATEN
DRYBEATING
DRYBEATS
DRYER
DRYERS
DRYING
DRYINGS
DRYISH
DRYLY
DRYMOUTH
DRYMOUTHS
DRYNESS
DRYNESSES
DRYSALTER
DRYSALTERS
DSO
DSOBO
DSOBOS
DSOMO
DSOMOS
DSOS
DUAD
DUADS
DUAL
DUALIN
DUALINS
DUALISM
DUALISMS
DUALIST
DUALISTIC
DUALISTS
DUALITIES
DUALITY
DUALLY
DUALS
DUAN
DUANS
DUAR
DUARCHIES
DUARCHY
DUARS
DUB
DUBBED
DUBBIN
DUBBING
DUBBINGS
DUBBINS
DUBIETIES
DUBIETY
DUBIOSITIES
DUBIOSITY
DUBIOUS
DUBIOUSLY
DUBITABLE
DUBITABLY
DUBITANCIES
DUBITANCY
DUBITATE
DUBITATED
DUBITATES
DUBITATING
DUBS
DUCAL
DUCALLY
DUCAT
DUCATOON
DUCATOONS
DUCATS

DUCDAME
DUCE
DUCES
DUCHESS
DUCHESSE
DUCHESSES
DUCHIES
DUCHY
DUCK
DUCKBILL
DUCKBILLS
DUCKED
DUCKER
DUCKERS
DUCKIER
DUCKIES
DUCKIEST
DUCKING
DUCKINGS
DUCKLING
DUCKLINGS
DUCKMOLE
DUCKMOLES
DUCKS
DUCKSHOVE
DUCKSHOVED
DUCKSHOVES
DUCKSHOVING
DUCKWEED
DUCKWEEDS
DUCKY
DUCT
DUCTED
DUCTILE
DUCTILITIES
DUCTILITY
DUCTING
DUCTLESS
DUCTS
DUD
DUDDER
DUDDERIES
DUDDERS
DUDDERY
DUDDIE
DUDDIER
DUDDIEST
DUDE
DUDEEN
DUDEENS
DUDES
DUDGEON
DUDGEONS
DUDHEEN
DUDHEENS
DUDISH
DUDISM
DUDISMS
DUDS
DUE
DUED
DUEFUL
DUEL
DUELLED
DUELLER
DUELLERS
DUELLING
DUELLINGS
DUELLIST
DUELLISTS

DUELLO
DUELLOS
DUELS
DUELSOME
DUENNA
DUENNAS
DUES
DUET
DUETS
DUETT
DUETTED
DUETTI
DUETTING
DUETTINO
DUETTINOS
DUETTIST
DUETTISTS
DUETTO
DUETTOS
DUETTS
DUFF
DUFFED
DUFFEL
DUFFELS
DUFFER
DUFFERDOM
DUFFERDOMS
DUFFERISM
DUFFERISMS
DUFFERS
DUFFEST
DUFFING
DUFFINGS
DUFFLE
DUFFLES
DUFFS
DUG
DUGONG
DUGONGS
DUGOUT
DUGOUTS
DUGS
DUIKER
DUIKERS
DUING
DUKE
DUKED
DUKEDOM
DUKEDOMS
DUKELING
DUKELINGS
DUKERIES
DUKERY
DUKES
DUKESHIP
DUKESHIPS
DUKING
DULCAMARA
DULCAMARAS
DULCET
DULCIAN
DULCIANA
DULCIANAS
DULCIANS
DULCIFIED
DULCIFIES
DULCIFY
DULCIFYING
DULCIMER
DULCIMERS

DULCITE
DULCITES
DULCITOL
DULCITOLS
DULCITUDE
DULCITUDES
DULCOSE
DULCOSES
DULE
DULES
DULIA
DULIAS
DULL
DULLARD
DULLARDS
DULLED
DULLER
DULLEST
DULLIER
DULLIEST
DULLING
DULLISH
DULLNESS
DULLNESSES
DULLS
DULLY
DULNESS
DULNESSES
DULOCRACIES
DULOCRACY
DULOSES
DULOSIS
DULOTIC
DULSE
DULSES
DULY
DUMA
DUMAIST
DUMAISTS
DUMAS
DUMB
DUMBED
DUMBER
DUMBEST
DUMBFOUND
DUMBFOUNDED
DUMBFOUNDING
DUMBFOUNDS
DUMBING
DUMBLY
DUMBNESS
DUMBNESSES
DUMBS
DUMDUM
DUMDUMS
DUMFOUND
DUMFOUNDED
DUMFOUNDING
DUMFOUNDS
DUMKA
DUMKY
DUMMERER
DUMMERERS
DUMMIED
DUMMIER
DUMMIES
DUMMIEST
DUMMINESS
DUMMINESSES
DUMMY

DUMMYING
DUMOSE
DUMOSITIES
DUMOSITY
DUMOUS
DUMP
DUMPBIN
DUMPBINS
DUMPED
DUMPER
DUMPERS
DUMPIER
DUMPIES
DUMPIEST
DUMPINESS
DUMPINESSES
DUMPING
DUMPISH
DUMPISHLY
DUMPLE
DUMPLED
DUMPLES
DUMPLING
DUMPLINGS
DUMPS
DUMPY
DUN
DUNCE
DUNCEDOM
DUNCEDOMS
DUNCERIES
DUNCERY
DUNCES
DUNCH
DUNCHED
DUNCHES
DUNCHING
DUNDER
DUNDERS
DUNE
DUNES
DUNG
DUNGAREE
DUNGAREES
DUNGED
DUNGEON
DUNGEONED
DUNGEONER
DUNGEONERS
DUNGEONING
DUNGEONS
DUNGIER
DUNGIEST
DUNGING
DUNGMERE
DUNGMERES
DUNGS
DUNGY
DUNITE
DUNITES
DUNK
DUNKED
DUNKING
DUNKS
DUNLIN
DUNLINS
DUNNAGE
DUNNAGES
DUNNAKIN
DUNNAKINS

# DUNNED

DUNNED
DUNNER
DUNNEST
DUNNIER
DUNNIES
DUNNIEST
DUNNING
DUNNINGS
DUNNISH
DUNNITE
DUNNITES
DUNNO
DUNNOCK
DUNNOCKS
DUNNY
DUNS
DUNSH
DUNSHED
DUNSHES
DUNSHING
DUNT
DUNTED
DUNTING
DUNTS
DUO
DUODECIMO
DUODECIMOS
DUODENA
DUODENAL
DUODENARY
DUODENUM
DUOLOGUE
DUOLOGUES
DUOMI
DUOMO
DUOMOS
DUOPOLIES
DUOPOLY
DUOS
DUOTONE
DUOTONES
DUP
DUPABLE
DUPE
DUPED
DUPER
DUPERIES
DUPERS
DUPERY
DUPES
DUPING
DUPION
DUPIONS
DUPLE
DUPLET
DUPLETS
DUPLEX
DUPLEXES
DUPLICAND
DUPLICANDS
DUPLICATE
DUPLICATED
DUPLICATES
DUPLICATING
DUPLICITIES
DUPLICITY
DUPLIED
DUPLIES
DUPLY
DUPLYING

DUPONDII
DUPONDIUS
DUPPED
DUPPIES
DUPPING
DUPPY
DUPS
DURA
DURABLE
DURABLES
DURABLY
DURAL
DURALS
DURALUMIN
DURALUMINS
DURAMEN
DURAMENS
DURANCE
DURANCES
DURANT
DURANTS
DURAS
DURATION
DURATIONS
DURBAR
DURBARS
DURDUM
DURDUMS
DURE
DURED
DUREFUL
DURES
DURESS
DURESSE
DURESSES
DURGAN
DURGANS
DURGIER
DURGIEST
DURGY
DURIAN
DURIANS
DURING
DURION
DURIONS
DURMAST
DURMASTS
DURN
DURNS
DURO
DUROS
DUROY
DUROYS
DURRA
DURRAS
DURRIE
DURRIES
DURST
DURUKULI
DURUKULIS
DURUM
DURUMS
DUSH
DUSHED
DUSHES
DUSHING
DUSK
DUSKED
DUSKEN
DUSKENED

DUSKENING
DUSKENS
DUSKER
DUSKEST
DUSKIER
DUSKIEST
DUSKILY
DUSKINESS
DUSKINESSES
DUSKING
DUSKISH
DUSKISHLY
DUSKLY
DUSKNESS
DUSKNESSES
DUSKS
DUSKY
DUST
DUSTBIN
DUSTBINS
DUSTED
DUSTER
DUSTERS
DUSTIER
DUSTIEST
DUSTILY
DUSTINESS
DUSTINESSES
DUSTING
DUSTLESS
DUSTMAN
DUSTMEN
DUSTPROOF
DUSTS
DUSTY
DUTCH
DUTCHES
DUTEOUS
DUTEOUSLY
DUTIABLE
DUTIED
DUTIES
DUTIFUL
DUTIFULLY
DUTY
DUUMVIR
DUUMVIRAL
DUUMVIRI
DUUMVIRS
DUVET
DUVETINE
DUVETINES
DUVETS
DUVETYN
DUVETYNE
DUVETYNES
DUVETYNS
DUX
DUXELLES
DUXES
DUYKER
DUYKERS
DVANDVA
DVANDVAS
DVORNIK
DVORNIKS
DWALE
DWALES
DWALM
DWALMED

DWALMING
DWALMS
DWAM
DWAMMED
DWAMMING
DWAMS
DWARF
DWARFED
DWARFING
DWARFISH
DWARFISM
DWARFISMS
DWARFS
DWARVES
DWAUM
DWAUMED
DWAUMING
DWAUMS
DWELL
DWELLED
DWELLER
DWELLERS
DWELLING
DWELLINGS
DWELLS
DWELT
DWINDLE
DWINDLED
DWINDLES
DWINDLING
DWINE
DWINED
DWINES
DWINING
DYABLE
DYAD
DYADIC
DYADS
DYARCHIES
DYARCHY
DYBBUK
DYBBUKS
DYE
DYEABLE
DYED
DYEING
DYEINGS
DYELINE
DYELINES
DYER
DYERS
DYES
DYESTER
DYESTERS
DYESTUFF
DYESTUFFS
DYING
DYINGLY
DYINGNESS
DYINGNESSES
DYINGS
DYKE
DYKED
DYKES
DYKEY
DYKIER
DYKIEST
DYKING
DYNAMIC
DYNAMICAL

DYNAMICS
DYNAMISE
DYNAMISED
DYNAMISES
DYNAMISING
DYNAMISM
DYNAMISMS
DYNAMIST
DYNAMISTS
DYNAMITE
DYNAMITED
DYNAMITER
DYNAMITERS
DYNAMITES
DYNAMITING
DYNAMIZE
DYNAMIZED
DYNAMIZES
DYNAMIZING
DYNAMO
DYNAMOS
DYNAMOTOR
DYNAMOTORS
DYNAST
DYNASTIC
DYNASTIES
DYNASTS
DYNASTY
DYNATRON
DYNATRONS
DYNE
DYNES
DYNODE
DYNODES
DYSCHROA
DYSCHROAS
DYSCHROIA
DYSCHROIAS
DYSCRASIA
DYSCRASIAS
DYSENTERIES
DYSENTERY
DYSGENIC
DYSGENICS
DYSLECTIC
DYSLECTICS
DYSLEXIA
DYSLEXIAS
DYSLEXIC
DYSLEXICS
DYSLOGIES
DYSLOGY
DYSMELIA
DYSMELIAS
DYSMELIC
DYSODIL
DYSODILE
DYSODILES
DYSODILS
DYSODYLE
DYSODYLES
DYSPATHIES
DYSPATHY
DYSPEPSIA
DYSPEPSIAS
DYSPEPSIES
DYSPEPSY
DYSPEPTIC
DYSPEPTICS
DYSPHAGIA

DYSPHAGIAS
DYSPHAGIC
DYSPHAGIES
DYSPHAGY
DYSPHASIA
DYSPHASIAS
DYSPHONIA
DYSPHONIAS
DYSPHONIC
DYSPHORIA
DYSPHORIAS

DYSPHORIC
DYSPLASIA
DYSPLASIAS
DYSPNEA
DYSPNEAL
DYSPNEAS
DYSPNEIC
DYSPNOEA
DYSPNOEAL
DYSPNOEAS
DYSPNOEIC

DYSPRAXIA
DYSPRAXIAS
DYSTECTIC
DYSTHESIA
DYSTHESIAS
DYSTHETIC
DYSTHYMIA
DYSTHYMIAS
DYSTHYMIC
DYSTOPIA
DYSTOPIAN

DYSTOPIAS
DYSTROPHIES
DYSTROPHY
DYSURIA
DYSURIAS
DYSURIC
DYSURIES
DYSURY
DYTISCID
DYTISCIDS
DYVOUR

DYVOURIES
DYVOURS
DYVOURY
DZEREN
DZERENS
DZIGGETAI
DZIGGETAIS
DZO
DZOS

# E

EA
EACH
EACHWHERE
EADISH
EADISHES
EAGER
EAGERLY
EAGERNESS
EAGERNESSES
EAGERS
EAGLE
EAGLES
EAGLET
EAGLETS
EAGLEWOOD
EAGLEWOODS
EAGRE
EAGRES
EALDORMAN
EALDORMEN
EALE
EALES
EAN
EANED
EANING
EANLING
EANLINGS
EANS
EAR
EARACHE
EARACHES
EARBASH
EARBASHED
EARBASHES
EARBASHING
EARBOB
EARBOBS
EARD
EARDED
EARDING
EARDROP
EARDROPS
EARDRUM
EARDRUMS
EARDS
EARED
EARFLAP
EARFLAPS
EARFUL
EARFULS
EARING
EARINGS
EARL
EARLAP
EARLAPS
EARLDOM
EARLDOMS
EARLESS
EARLIER
EARLIEST
EARLINESS
EARLINESSES
EARLOCK

EARLOCKS
EARLS
EARLY
EARMARK
EARMARKED
EARMARKING
EARMARKS
EARMUFFS
EARN
EARNED
EARNER
EARNERS
EARNEST
EARNESTLY
EARNESTS
EARNING
EARNINGS
EARNS
EARPHONE
EARPHONES
EARPICK
EARPICKS
EARPIECE
EARPIECES
EARPLUG
EARPLUGS
EARRING
EARRINGS
EARS
EARST
EARTH
EARTHBORN
EARTHED
EARTHEN
EARTHFALL
EARTHFALLS
EARTHFAST
EARTHFLAX
EARTHFLAXES
EARTHIER
EARTHIEST
EARTHING
EARTHLIER
EARTHLIES
EARTHLIEST
EARTHLING
EARTHLINGS
EARTHLY
EARTHMAN
EARTHMEN
EARTHS
EARTHWARD
EARTHWAX
EARTHWAXES
EARTHWOLF
EARTHWOLVES
EARTHWORK
EARTHWORKS
EARTHWORM
EARTHWORMS
EARTHY
EARWAX
EARWAXES

EARWIG
EARWIGGED
EARWIGGING
EARWIGGY
EARWIGS
EAS
EASE
EASED
EASEFUL
EASEL
EASELS
EASEMENT
EASEMENTS
EASES
EASIER
EASIEST
EASILY
EASINESS
EASINESSES
EASING
EASLE
EASLES
EASSEL
EASSIL
EAST
EASTED
EASTER
EASTERLIES
EASTERLY
EASTERN
EASTERNER
EASTERNERS
EASTING
EASTINGS
EASTLAND
EASTLANDS
EASTLIN
EASTLING
EASTLINGS
EASTLINS
EASTMOST
EASTS
EASTWARD
EASTWARDS
EASY
EAT
EATABLE
EATABLES
EATAGE
EATAGES
EATCHE
EATCHES
EATEN
EATER
EATERIES
EATERS
EATERY
EATH
EATHE
EATHLY
EATING
EATINGS
EATS

EAU
EAUS
EAUX
EAVES
EAVESDRIP
EAVESDRIPS
EAVESDROP
EAVESDROPPED
EAVESDROPPING
EAVESDROPPINGS
EAVESDROPS
ÉBAUCHE
ÉBAUCHES
EBB
EBBED
EBBING
EBBLESS
EBBS
EBBTIDE
EBBTIDES
EBENEZER
EBENEZERS
ÉBÉNISTE
ÉBÉNISTES
EBIONISE
EBIONISED
EBIONISES
EBIONISING
EBIONISM
EBIONISMS
EBIONITIC
EBIONIZE
EBIONIZED
EBIONIZES
EBIONIZING
EBON
EBONIES
EBONISE
EBONISED
EBONISES
EBONISING
EBONIST
EBONISTS
EBONITE
EBONITES
EBONIZE
EBONIZED
EBONIZES
EBONIZING
EBONS
EBONY
EBRIATE
EBRIATED
EBRIETIES
EBRIETY
EBRILLADE
EBRILLADES
EBRIOSE
EBRIOSITIES
EBRIOSITY
EBULLIENT
EBURNEAN
EBURNEOUS

ECAD
ECADS
ÉCARTÉ
ÉCARTÉS
ECAUDATE
ECBOLE
ECBOLES
ECBOLIC
ECBOLICS
ECCE
ECCENTRIC
ECCENTRICS
ECCLESIA
ECCLESIAL
ECCLESIAS
ECCO
ECCRINE
ECCRISES
ECCRISIS
ECCRITIC
ECCRITICS
ECDYSES
ECDYSIAST
ECDYSIASTS
ECDYSIS
ECH
ÉCHAPPÉ
ÉCHAPPÉS
ECHE
ECHED
ECHELON
ECHELONS
ECHES
ECHEVERIA
ECHEVERIAS
ECHIDNA
ECHIDNAS
ECHIDNINE
ECHIDNINES
ECHINATE
ECHINATED
ECHING
ECHINI
ECHINOID
ECHINOIDS
ECHINUS
ECHINUSES
ECHO
ECHOED
ECHOER
ECHOERS
ECHOES
ECHOGRAM
ECHOGRAMS
ECHOIC
ECHOING
ECHOISE
ECHOISED
ECHOISES
ECHOISING
ECHOISM
ECHOISMS
ECHOIST

| | | | | |
|---|---|---|---|---|
| ECHOISTS | ÉCOSSAISES | ÉCUELLE | EDIT | EEVNING |
| ECHOIZE | ECOSTATE | ÉCUELLES | EDITED | EEVNINGS |
| ECHOIZED | ECOSYSTEM | ECUMENIC | EDITING | EEVNS |
| ECHOIZES | ECOSYSTEMS | ECUMENICS | EDITION | EF |
| ECHOIZING | ECOTYPE | ECUMENISM | EDITIONS | EFF |
| ECHOLALIA | ECOTYPES | ECUMENISMS | EDITOR | EFFABLE |
| ECHOLALIAS | ÉCRASEUR | ÉCURIE | EDITORIAL | EFFACE |
| ECHOLESS | ÉCRASEURS | ÉCURIES | EDITORIALS | EFFACED |
| ECHT | ÉCRITOIRE | ECUS | EDITORS | EFFACES |
| ÉCLAIR | ÉCRITOIRES | ECZEMA | EDITRESS | EFFACING |
| ÉCLAIRS | ECRU | ECZEMAS | EDITRESSES | EFFECT |
| ECLAMPSIA | ECRUS | EDACIOUS | EDITS | EFFECTED |
| ECLAMPSIAS | ECSTASES | EDACITIES | EDUCABLE | EFFECTER |
| ECLAMPSIES | ECSTASIED | EDACITY | EDUCATE | EFFECTERS |
| ECLAMPSY | ECSTASIES | EDAPHIC | EDUCATED | EFFECTING |
| ECLAMPTIC | ECSTASIS | EDDIED | EDUCATES | EFFECTIVE |
| ÉCLAT | ECSTASISE | EDDIES | EDUCATING | EFFECTIVES |
| ÉCLATS | ECSTASISED | EDDISH | EDUCATION | EFFECTOR |
| ECLECTIC | ECSTASISES | EDDISHES | EDUCATIONS | EFFECTORS |
| ECLECTICS | ECSTASISING | EDDO | EDUCATIVE | EFFECTS |
| ECLIPSE | ECSTASIZE | EDDOES | EDUCATOR | EFFECTUAL |
| ECLIPSED | ECSTASIZED | EDDY | EDUCATORS | EFFED |
| ECLIPSES | ECSTASIZES | EDDYING | EDUCATORY | EFFEIR |
| ECLIPSING | ECSTASIZING | EDELWEISS | EDUCE | EFFEIRED |
| ECLIPTIC | ECSTASY | EDELWEISSES | EDUCED | EFFEIRING |
| ECLIPTICS | ECSTASYING | EDEMA | EDUCEMENT | EFFEIRS |
| ECLOGITE | ECSTATIC | EDEMAS | EDUCEMENTS | EFFENDI |
| ECLOGITES | ECSTATICS | EDEMATOSE | EDUCES | EFFENDIS |
| ECLOGUE | ECTASES | EDEMATOUS | EDUCIBLE | EFFERE |
| ECLOGUES | ECTASIS | EDENTAL | EDUCING | EFFERED |
| ECLOSE | ECTHYMA | EDENTATE | EDUCT | EFFERENCE |
| ECLOSED | ECTHYMAS | EDENTATES | EDUCTION | EFFERENCES |
| ECLOSES | ECTOBLAST | EDGE | EDUCTIONS | EFFERENT |
| ECLOSING | ECTOBLASTS | EDGEBONE | EDUCTOR | EFFERES |
| ECLOSION | ECTOCRINE | EDGEBONES | EDUCTORS | EFFERING |
| ECLOSIONS | ECTOCRINES | EDGED | EDUCTS | EFFETE |
| ECOCIDE | ECTODERM | EDGELESS | EDUSKUNTA | EFFETELY |
| ECOCIDES | ECTODERMS | EDGER | EDUSKUNTAS | EFFICACIES |
| ECOFREAK | ECTOGENIC | EDGERS | EE | EFFICACY |
| ECOFREAKS | ECTOGENIES | EDGES | EECH | EFFICIENT |
| ECOLOGIC | ECTOGENY | EDGEWAYS | EECHED | EFFICIENTS |
| ECOLOGIES | ECTOMORPH | EDGEWISE | EECHES | EFFIERCE |
| ECOLOGIST | ECTOMORPHS | EDGIER | EECHING | EFFIERCED |
| ECOLOGISTS | ECTOPHYTE | EDGIEST | EEK | EFFIERCES |
| ECOLOGY | ECTOPHYTES | EDGINESS | EEL | EFFIERCING |
| ECONOMIC | ECTOPIA | EDGINESSES | EELFARE | EFFIGIES |
| ECONOMICS | ECTOPIAS | EDGING | EELFARES | EFFIGY |
| ECONOMIES | ECTOPIC | EDGINGS | EELGRASS | EFFING |
| ECONOMISE | ECTOPIES | EDGY | EELGRASSES | EFFLUENCE |
| ECONOMISED | ECTOPLASM | EDH | EELIER | EFFLUENCES |
| ECONOMISES | ECTOPLASMS | EDHS | EELIEST | EFFLUENT |
| ECONOMISING | ECTOPY | EDIBILITIES | EELPOUT | EFFLUENTS |
| ECONOMISM | ECTOSARC | EDIBILITY | EELPOUTS | EFFLUVIA |
| ECONOMISMS | ECTOSARCS | EDIBLE | EELS | EFFLUVIAL |
| ECONOMIST | ECTOTHERM | EDIBLES | EELWORM | EFFLUVIUM |
| ECONOMISTS | ECTOTHERMS | EDICT | EELWORMS | EFFLUX |
| ECONOMIZE | ECTOZOA | EDICTAL | EELWRACK | EFFLUXES |
| ECONOMIZED | ECTOZOAN | EDICTALLY | EELWRACKS | EFFLUXION |
| ECONOMIZES | ECTOZOANS | EDICTS | EELY | EFFLUXIONS |
| ECONOMIZING | ECTOZOIC | EDIFICE | EEN | EFFORCE |
| ECONOMY | ECTOZOON | EDIFICES | EERIE | EFFORCED |
| ECONUT | ECTROPIC | EDIFICIAL | EERIER | EFFORCES |
| ECONUTS | ECTROPION | EDIFIED | EERIEST | EFFORCING |
| ECOPHOBIA | ECTROPIONS | EDIFIER | EERILY | EFFORT |
| ECOPHOBIAS | ECTROPIUM | EDIFIERS | EERINESS | EFFORTFUL |
| ÉCORCHÉ | ECTROPIUMS | EDIFIES | EERINESSES | EFFORTS |
| ÉCORCHÉS | ECTYPAL | EDIFY | EERY | EFFRAIDE |
| ECOSPHERE | ECTYPE | EDIFYING | EEVEN | EFFRAY |
| ECOSPHERES | ECTYPES | EDILE | EEVENS | EFFRAYS |
| ÉCOSSAISE | ECU | EDILES | EEVN | EFFS |

| | | | | |
|---|---|---|---|---|
| EFFULGE | EGMAS | EIGHTSOMES | ELANETS | ELECTRETS |
| EFFULGED | EGO | EIGHTVO | ÉLANS | ELECTRIC |
| EFFULGENT | EGOISM | EIGHTVOS | ELAPHINE | ELECTRICS |
| EFFULGES | EGOISMS | EIGHTY | ELAPSE | ELECTRIFIED |
| EFFULGING | EGOIST | EIGNE | ELAPSED | ELECTRIFIES |
| EFFUSE | EGOISTIC | EIK | ELAPSES | ELECTRIFY |
| EFFUSED | EGOISTS | EIKED | ELAPSING | ELECTRIFYING |
| EFFUSES | EGOITIES | EIKING | ELASTANCE | ELECTRISE |
| EFFUSING | EGOITY | EIKON | ELASTANCES | ELECTRISED |
| EFFUSION | EGOMANIA | EIKONS | ELASTASE | ELECTRISES |
| EFFUSIONS | EGOMANIAC | EIKS | ELASTASES | ELECTRISING |
| EFFUSIVE | EGOMANIACS | EILD | ELASTIC | ELECTRIZE |
| EFS | EGOMANIAS | EILDING | ELASTICS | ELECTRIZED |
| EFT | EGOS | EILDINGS | ELASTIN | ELECTRIZES |
| EFTEST | EGOTHEISM | EILDS | ELASTINS | ELECTRIZING |
| EFTS | EGOTHEISMS | EINE | ELASTOMER | ELECTRO |
| EFTSOONS | EGOTISE | EIRACK | ELASTOMERS | ELECTRODE |
| EGAD | EGOTISED | EIRACKS | ELATE | ELECTRODES |
| EGAL | EGOTISES | EIRENIC | ELATED | ELECTRON |
| EGALITIES | EGOTISING | EIRENICON | ELATEDLY | ELECTRONS |
| EGALITY | EGOTISM | EIRENICONS | ELATER | ELECTROS |
| EGALLY | EGOTISMS | EISEL | ELATERIN | ELECTRUM |
| EGAREMENT | EGOTIST | EISELL | ELATERINS | ELECTRUMS |
| EGAREMENTS | EGOTISTIC | EISELLS | ELATERITE | ELECTS |
| EGENCE | EGOTISTS | EISELS | ELATERITES | ELECTUARIES |
| EGENCES | EGOTIZE | EITHER | ELATERIUM | ELECTUARY |
| EGENCIES | EGOTIZED | EJACULATE | ELATERIUMS | ELEGANCE |
| EGENCY | EGOTIZES | EJACULATED | ELATERS | ELEGANCES |
| EGER | EGOTIZING | EJACULATES | ELATES | ELEGANCIES |
| EGERS | EGREGIOUS | EJACULATING | ELATING | ELEGANCY |
| EGEST | EGRESS | EJECT | ELATION | ELEGANT |
| EGESTA | EGRESSES | EJECTA | ELATIONS | ELEGANTLY |
| EGESTED | EGRESSION | EJECTED | ELATIVE | ELEGIAC |
| EGESTING | EGRESSIONS | EJECTING | ELATIVES | ELEGIACAL |
| EGESTION | EGRET | EJECTION | ELBOW | ELEGIACS |
| EGESTIONS | EGRETS | EJECTIONS | ELBOWED | ELEGIAST |
| EGESTIVE | EH | EJECTIVE | ELBOWING | ELEGIASTS |
| EGESTS | EHED | EJECTMENT | ELBOWS | ELEGIES |
| EGG | EHING | EJECTMENTS | ELCHEE | ELEGISE |
| EGGAR | EHS | EJECTOR | ELCHEES | ELEGISED |
| EGGARS | EIDENT | EJECTORS | ELCHI | ELEGISES |
| EGGCUP | EIDER | EJECTS | ELCHIS | ELEGISING |
| EGGCUPS | EIDERDOWN | EKE | ELD | ELEGIST |
| EGGED | EIDERDOWNS | EKED | ELDER | ELEGISTS |
| EGGER | EIDERS | EKES | ELDERLIES | ELEGIT |
| EGGERIES | EIDETIC | EKING | ELDERLY | ELEGITS |
| EGGERS | EIDETICS | EKISTIC | ELDERS | ELEGIZE |
| EGGERY | EIDOGRAPH | EKISTICS | ELDERSHIP | ELEGIZED |
| EGGHEAD | EIDOGRAPHS | EKKA | ELDERSHIPS | ELEGIZES |
| EGGHEADS | EIDOLA | EKKAS | ELDEST | ELEGIZING |
| EGGIER | EIDOLON | EKLOGITE | ELDIN | ELEGY |
| EGGIEST | EIGENTONE | EKLOGITES | ELDING | ELEMENT |
| EGGING | EIGENTONES | EKPWELE | ELDINGS | ELEMENTAL |
| EGGLER | EIGHT | EKPWELES | ELDINS | ELEMENTALS |
| EGGLERS | EIGHTEEN | EKUELE | ELDRITCH | ELEMENTS |
| EGGMASS | EIGHTEENS | EL | ELDS | ELEMI |
| EGGMASSES | EIGHTFOIL | ELABORATE | ELECT | ELEMIS |
| EGGNOG | EIGHTFOILS | ELABORATED | ELECTABLE | ELENCH |
| EGGNOGS | EIGHTFOLD | ELABORATES | ELECTED | ELENCHI |
| EGGS | EIGHTFOOT | ELABORATING | ELECTING | ELENCHS |
| EGGSHELL | EIGHTH | ELAEOLITE | ELECTION | ELENCHUS |
| EGGSHELLS | EIGHTHLY | ELAEOLITES | ELECTIONS | ELENCTIC |
| EGGY | EIGHTHS | ÉLAN | ELECTIVE | ELEPHANT |
| EGIS | EIGHTIES | ELANCE | ELECTIVES | ELEPHANTS |
| EGISES | EIGHTIETH | ELANCED | ELECTOR | ELEUTHERI |
| EGLANTINE | EIGHTIETHS | ELANCES | ELECTORAL | ELEVATE |
| EGLANTINES | EIGHTS | ELANCING | ELECTORS | ELEVATED |
| EGLATERE | EIGHTSMAN | ELAND | ELECTRESS | ELEVATEDS |
| EGLATERES | EIGHTSMEN | ELANDS | ELECTRESSES | ELEVATES |
| EGMA | EIGHTSOME | ELANET | ELECTRET | ELEVATING |

ELEVATION
ELEVATIONS
ELEVATOR
ELEVATORS
ELEVATORY
ELEVEN
ELEVENS
ELEVENSES
ELEVENTH
ELEVENTHS
ELEVON
ELEVONS
ELF
ELFED
ELFHOOD
ELFHOODS
ELFIN
ELFING
ELFINS
ELFISH
ELFLAND
ELFLANDS
ELFLOCKS
ELFS
ELIAD
ELIADS
ELICIT
ELICITED
ELICITING
ELICITOR
ELICITORS
ELICITS
ELIDE
ELIDED
ELIDES
ELIDING
ELIGIBLE
ELIGIBLES
ELIGIBLY
ELIMINANT
ELIMINANTS
ELIMINATE
ELIMINATED
ELIMINATES
ELIMINATING
ELISION
ELISIONS
ÉLITE
ÉLITES
ELITISM
ELITISMS
ELITIST
ELITISTS
ELIXIR
ELIXIRS
ELK
ELKHOUND
ELKHOUNDS
ELKS
ELL
ELLAGIC
ELLIPSE
ELLIPSES
ELLIPSIS
ELLIPSOID
ELLIPSOIDS
ELLIPTIC
ELLOPS
ELLOPSES
ELLS

ELLWAND
ELLWANDS
ELM
ELMEN
ELMIER
ELMIEST
ELMS
ELMWOOD
ELMWOODS
ELMY
ELOCUTE
ELOCUTED
ELOCUTES
ELOCUTING
ELOCUTION
ELOCUTIONS
ELOCUTORY
ÉLOGE
ÉLOGES
ELOGIES
ELOGIST
ELOGISTS
ELOGIUM
ELOGIUMS
ELOGY
ELOIGN
ELOIGNED
ELOIGNER
ELOIGNERS
ELOIGNING
ELOIGNS
ELOIN
ELOINED
ELOINER
ELOINERS
ELOINING
ELOINMENT
ELOINMENTS
ELOINS
ELONGATE
ELONGATED
ELONGATES
ELONGATING
ELOPE
ELOPED
ELOPEMENT
ELOPEMENTS
ELOPER
ELOPERS
ELOPES
ELOPING
ELOPS
ELOPSES
ELOQUENCE
ELOQUENCES
ELOQUENT
ELPEE
ELPEES
ELS
ELSE
ELSEWHERE
ELSEWISE
ELSHIN
ELSHINS
ELSIN
ELSINS
ELT
ELTCHI
ELTCHIS
ELTS

ELUANT
ELUANTS
ELUATE
ELUATES
ELUCIDATE
ELUCIDATED
ELUCIDATES
ELUCIDATING
ELUDE
ELUDED
ELUDER
ELUDERS
ELUDES
ELUDIBLE
ELUDING
ELUENT
ELUENTS
ELUSION
ELUSIONS
ELUSIVE
ELUSIVELY
ELUSORY
ELUTE
ELUTED
ELUTES
ELUTING
ELUTION
ELUTIONS
ELUTOR
ELUTORS
ELUTRIATE
ELUTRIATED
ELUTRIATES
ELUTRIATING
ELUVIA
ELUVIAL
ELUVIUM
ELUVIUMS
ELVAN
ELVANITE
ELVANITES
ELVANS
ELVER
ELVERS
ELVES
ELVISH
ELYTRA
ELYTRAL
ELYTRON
ELYTRUM
EM
EMACIATE
EMACIATED
EMACIATES
EMACIATING
EMALANGENI
EMANANT
EMANATE
EMANATED
EMANATES
EMANATING
EMANATION
EMANATIONS
EMANATIST
EMANATISTS
EMANATIVE
EMANATORY
EMBACE
EMBACES
EMBACING

EMBAIL
EMBAILED
EMBAILING
EMBAILS
EMBALE
EMBALED
EMBALES
EMBALING
EMBALL
EMBALLED
EMBALLING
EMBALLINGS
EMBALLS
EMBALM
EMBALMED
EMBALMER
EMBALMERS
EMBALMING
EMBALMINGS
EMBALMS
EMBANK
EMBANKED
EMBANKER
EMBANKERS
EMBANKING
EMBANKS
EMBAR
EMBARGO
EMBARGOED
EMBARGOES
EMBARGOING
EMBARK
EMBARKED
EMBARKING
EMBARKS
EMBARRASS
EMBARRASSED
EMBARRASSES
EMBARRASSING
EMBARRED
EMBARRING
EMBARRINGS
EMBARS
EMBASE
EMBASED
EMBASES
EMBASING
EMBASSADE
EMBASSADES
EMBASSAGE
EMBASSAGES
EMBASSIES
EMBASSY
EMBASTE
EMBATHE
EMBATHED
EMBATHES
EMBATHING
EMBATTLE
EMBATTLED
EMBATTLES
EMBATTLING
EMBAY
EMBAYED
EMBAYING
EMBAYLD
EMBAYMENT
EMBAYMENTS
EMBAYS
EMBED

EMBEDDED
EMBEDDING
EMBEDMENT
EMBEDMENTS
EMBEDS
EMBELLISH
EMBELLISHED
EMBELLISHES
EMBELLISHING
EMBER
EMBERS
EMBEZZLE
EMBEZZLED
EMBEZZLER
EMBEZZLERS
EMBEZZLES
EMBEZZLING
EMBITTER
EMBITTERED
EMBITTERING
EMBITTERINGS
EMBITTERS
EMBLAZE
EMBLAZED
EMBLAZES
EMBLAZING
EMBLAZON
EMBLAZONED
EMBLAZONING
EMBLAZONS
EMBLEM
EMBLEMA
EMBLEMATA
EMBLEMED
EMBLEMING
EMBLEMISE
EMBLEMISED
EMBLEMISES
EMBLEMISING
EMBLEMIZE
EMBLEMIZED
EMBLEMIZES
EMBLEMIZING
EMBLEMS
EMBLIC
EMBLICS
EMBLOOM
EMBLOOMED
EMBLOOMING
EMBLOOMS
EMBLOSSOM
EMBLOSSOMED
EMBLOSSOMING
EMBLOSSOMS
EMBODIED
EMBODIES
EMBODY
EMBODYING
EMBOG
EMBOGGED
EMBOGGING
EMBOGS
EMBOGUE
EMBOGUED
EMBOGUES
EMBOGUING
EMBOIL
EMBOILED
EMBOILING
EMBOILS

| | | | | |
|---|---|---|---|---|
| EMBOLDEN | EMBRASURE | EMCEES | ÉMIGRÉS | EMPACKETED |
| EMBOLDENED | EMBRASURES | EME | EMINENCE | EMPACKETING |
| EMBOLDENING | EMBRAVE | EMEER | EMINENCES | EMPACKETS |
| EMBOLDENS | EMBRAVED | EMEERS | EMINENCIES | EMPAESTIC |
| EMBOLI | EMBRAVES | EMEND | EMINENCY | EMPAIRE |
| EMBOLIC | EMBRAVING | EMENDABLE | EMINENT | EMPAIRED |
| EMBOLIES | EMBRAZURE | EMENDALS | EMINENTLY | EMPAIRES |
| EMBOLISM | EMBRAZURES | EMENDATE | EMIR | EMPAIRING |
| EMBOLISMS | EMBREAD | EMENDATED | EMIRATE | EMPALE |
| EMBOLUS | EMBREADED | EMENDATES | EMIRATES | EMPALED |
| EMBOLUSES | EMBREADING | EMENDATING | EMIRS | EMPALES |
| EMBOLY | EMBREADS | EMENDATOR | EMISSARIES | EMPALING |
| EMBORDER | EMBREATHE | EMENDATORS | EMISSARY | EMPANEL |
| EMBORDERED | EMBREATHED | EMENDED | EMISSILE | EMPANELLED |
| EMBORDERING | EMBREATHES | EMENDING | EMISSION | EMPANELLING |
| EMBORDERS | EMBREATHING | EMENDS | EMISSIONS | EMPANELS |
| EMBOSCATA | EMBREWE | EMERALD | EMISSIVE | EMPANOPLIED |
| EMBOSCATAS | EMBREWED | EMERALDS | EMIT | EMPANOPLIES |
| EMBOSOM | EMBREWES | EMERAUDE | EMITS | EMPANOPLY |
| EMBOSOMED | EMBREWING | EMERAUDES | EMITTED | EMPANOPLYING |
| EMBOSOMING | EMBRITTLE | EMERGE | EMITTING | EMPARE |
| EMBOSOMS | EMBRITTLED | EMERGED | EMMA | EMPARED |
| EMBOSS | EMBRITTLES | EMERGENCE | EMMARBLE | EMPARES |
| EMBOSSED | EMBRITTLING | EMERGENCES | EMMARBLED | EMPARING |
| EMBOSSER | EMBROCATE | EMERGENCIES | EMMARBLES | EMPART |
| EMBOSSERS | EMBROCATED | EMERGENCY | EMMARBLING | EMPARTED |
| EMBOSSES | EMBROCATES | EMERGENT | EMMAS | EMPARTING |
| EMBOSSING | EMBROCATING | EMERGES | EMMER | EMPARTS |
| EMBOST | EMBROGLIO | EMERGING | EMMERS | EMPATHIC |
| EMBOUND | EMBROGLIOS | EMERIED | EMMESH | EMPATHIES |
| EMBOUNDED | EMBROIDER | EMERIES | EMMESHED | EMPATHISE |
| EMBOUNDING | EMBROIDERED | EMERITI | EMMESHES | EMPATHISED |
| EMBOUNDS | EMBROIDERING | EMERITUS | EMMESHING | EMPATHISES |
| EMBOW | EMBROIDERS | EMERODS | EMMET | EMPATHISING |
| EMBOWED | EMBROIL | EMERSED | EMMETROPE | EMPATHIZE |
| EMBOWEL | EMBROILED | EMERSION | EMMETROPES | EMPATHIZED |
| EMBOWELLED | EMBROILING | EMERSIONS | EMMETS | EMPATHIZES |
| EMBOWELLING | EMBROILS | EMERY | EMMEW | EMPATHIZING |
| EMBOWELS | EMBROWN | EMERYING | EMMEWED | EMPATHY |
| EMBOWER | EMBROWNED | EMES | EMMEWING | EMPATRON |
| EMBOWERED | EMBROWNING | EMESES | EMMEWS | EMPATRONED |
| EMBOWERING | EMBROWNS | EMESIS | EMMOVE | EMPATRONING |
| EMBOWERS | EMBRUE | EMETIC | EMMOVED | EMPATRONS |
| EMBOWING | EMBRUED | EMETICAL | EMMOVES | EMPAYRE |
| EMBOWS | EMBRUES | EMETICS | EMMOVING | EMPAYRED |
| EMBOX | EMBRUING | EMETIN | EMOLLIATE | EMPAYRES |
| EMBOXED | EMBRUTE | EMETINE | EMOLLIATED | EMPAYRING |
| EMBOXES | EMBRUTED | EMETINES | EMOLLIATES | EMPEACH |
| EMBOXING | EMBRUTES | EMETINS | EMOLLIATING | EMPEACHED |
| EMBRACE | EMBRUTING | EMEU | EMOLLIENT | EMPEACHES |
| EMBRACED | EMBRYO | EMEUS | EMOLLIENTS | EMPEACHING |
| EMBRACEOR | EMBRYON | ÉMEUTE | EMOLUMENT | EMPENNAGE |
| EMBRACEORS | EMBRYONAL | ÉMEUTES | EMOLUMENTS | EMPENNAGES |
| EMBRACER | EMBRYONIC | EMICANT | EMONG | EMPEOPLE |
| EMBRACERIES | EMBRYONS | EMICATE | EMONGES | EMPEOPLED |
| EMBRACERS | EMBRYOS | EMICATED | EMONGEST | EMPEOPLES |
| EMBRACERY | EMBRYOTIC | EMICATES | EMONGST | EMPEOPLING |
| EMBRACES | EMBUS | EMICATING | EMOTE | EMPERCE |
| EMBRACING | EMBUSIED | EMICATION | EMOTED | EMPERCED |
| EMBRACIVE | EMBUSIES | EMICATIONS | EMOTES | EMPERCES |
| EMBRAID | EMBUSQUÉ | EMICTION | EMOTING | EMPERCING |
| EMBRAIDED | EMBUSQUÉS | EMICTIONS | EMOTION | EMPERIES |
| EMBRAIDING | EMBUSSED | EMICTORY | EMOTIONAL | EMPERISE |
| EMBRAIDS | EMBUSSES | EMIGRANT | EMOTIONS | EMPERISED |
| EMBRANGLE | EMBUSSING | EMIGRANTS | EMOTIVE | EMPERISES |
| EMBRANGLED | EMBUSY | EMIGRATE | EMOVE | EMPERISH |
| EMBRANGLES | EMBUSYING | EMIGRATED | EMOVED | EMPERISHED |
| EMBRANGLING | EMCEE | EMIGRATES | EMOVES | EMPERISHES |
| EMBRASOR | EMCEED | EMIGRATING | EMOVING | EMPERISHING |
| EMBRASORS | EMCEEING | ÉMIGRÉ | EMPACKET | EMPERISING |

EMPERIZE
EMPERIZED
EMPERIZES
EMPERIZING
EMPEROR
EMPERORS
EMPERY
EMPHASES
EMPHASIS
EMPHASISE
EMPHASISED
EMPHASISES
EMPHASISING
EMPHASIZE
EMPHASIZED
EMPHASIZES
EMPHASIZING
EMPHATIC
EMPHLYSES
EMPHLYSIS
EMPHYSEMA
EMPHYSEMAS
EMPIERCE
EMPIERCED
EMPIERCES
EMPIERCING
EMPIGHT
EMPIRE
EMPIRES
EMPIRIC
EMPIRICAL
EMPIRICS
EMPLACE
EMPLACED
EMPLACES
EMPLACING
EMPLANE
EMPLANED
EMPLANES
EMPLANING
EMPLASTER
EMPLASTERED
EMPLASTERING
EMPLASTERS
EMPLASTIC
EMPLASTICS
EMPLECTON
EMPLECTONS
EMPLECTUM
EMPLECTUMS
EMPLONGE
EMPLONGED
EMPLONGES
EMPLONGING
EMPLOY
EMPLOYED
EMPLOYEE
EMPLOYEES
EMPLOYER
EMPLOYERS
EMPLOYING
EMPLOYS
EMPLUME
EMPLUMED
EMPLUMES
EMPLUMING
EMPOISON
EMPOISONED
EMPOISONING
EMPOISONS

EMPOLDER
EMPOLDERED
EMPOLDERING
EMPOLDERS
EMPORIA
EMPORIUM
EMPORIUMS
EMPOWER
EMPOWERED
EMPOWERING
EMPOWERS
EMPRESS
EMPRESSE
EMPRESSES
EMPRISE
EMPRISES
EMPTIED
EMPTIER
EMPTIERS
EMPTIES
EMPTIEST
EMPTILY
EMPTINESS
EMPTINESSES
EMPTION
EMPTIONAL
EMPTIONS
EMPTY
EMPTYING
EMPTYINGS
EMPTYSES
EMPTYSIS
EMPURPLE
EMPURPLED
EMPURPLES
EMPURPLING
EMPUSA
EMPUSAS
EMPUSE
EMPUSES
EMPYEMA
EMPYEMAS
EMPYESES
EMPYESIS
EMPYREAL
EMPYREAN
EMPYREANS
EMPYREUMA
EMPYREUMATA
EMS
EMU
EMULATE
EMULATED
EMULATES
EMULATING
EMULATION
EMULATIONS
EMULATIVE
EMULATOR
EMULATORS
EMULE
EMULED
EMULES
EMULGE
EMULGED
EMULGENCE
EMULGENCES
EMULGENT
EMULGES
EMULGING

EMULING
EMULOUS
EMULOUSLY
EMULSIFIED
EMULSIFIES
EMULSIFY
EMULSIFYING
EMULSIN
EMULSINS
EMULSION
EMULSIONS
EMULSIVE
EMULSOID
EMULSOIDS
EMULSOR
EMULSORS
EMUNCTORIES
EMUNCTORY
EMUNGE
EMUNGED
EMUNGES
EMUNGING
EMURE
EMURED
EMURES
EMURING
EMUS
EMYDES
EMYS
EN
ENABLE
ENABLED
ENABLER
ENABLERS
ENABLES
ENABLING
ENACT
ENACTED
ENACTING
ENACTION
ENACTIONS
ENACTIVE
ENACTMENT
ENACTMENTS
ENACTOR
ENACTORS
ENACTS
ENACTURE
ENACTURES
ENALLAGE
ENALLAGES
ENAMEL
ENAMELLED
ENAMELLER
ENAMELLERS
ENAMELLING
ENAMELLINGS
ENAMELS
ENAMOR
ENAMORADO
ENAMORADOS
ENAMORED
ENAMORING
ENAMORS
ENAMOUR
ENAMOURED
ENAMOURING
ENAMOURS
ENARCH
ENARCHED

ENARCHES
ENARCHING
ENARM
ENARMED
ENARMING
ENARMS
ENATE
ENATION
ENATIONS
ENAUNTER
ENCAENIA
ENCAENIAS
ENCAGE
ENCAGED
ENCAGES
ENCAGING
ENCALM
ENCALMED
ENCALMING
ENCALMS
ENCAMP
ENCAMPED
ENCAMPING
ENCAMPS
ENCANTHIS
ENCANTHISES
ENCARPUS
ENCARPUSES
ENCASE
ENCASED
ENCASES
ENCASH
ENCASHED
ENCASHES
ENCASHING
ENCASING
ENCAUSTIC
ENCAUSTICS
ENCAVE
ENCAVED
ENCAVES
ENCAVING
ENCEINTE
ENCEINTES
ENCHAFE
ENCHAFED
ENCHAFES
ENCHAFING
ENCHAIN
ENCHAINED
ENCHAINING
ENCHAINS
ENCHANT
ENCHANTED
ENCHANTER
ENCHANTERS
ENCHANTING
ENCHANTS
ENCHARGE
ENCHARGED
ENCHARGES
ENCHARGING
ENCHARM
ENCHARMED
ENCHARMING
ENCHARMS
ENCHASE
ENCHASED
ENCHASES
ENCHASING

ENCHEASON
ENCHEASONS
ENCHEER
ENCHEERED
ENCHEERING
ENCHEERS
ENCHILADA
ENCHILADAS
ENCHORIAL
ENCHORIC
ENCIPHER
ENCIPHERED
ENCIPHERING
ENCIPHERS
ENCIRCLE
ENCIRCLED
ENCIRCLES
ENCIRCLING
ENCIRCLINGS
ENCLASP
ENCLASPED
ENCLASPING
ENCLASPS
ENCLAVE
ENCLAVED
ENCLAVES
ENCLAVING
ENCLISES
ENCLISIS
ENCLITIC
ENCLITICS
ENCLOSE
ENCLOSED
ENCLOSER
ENCLOSERS
ENCLOSES
ENCLOSING
ENCLOSURE
ENCLOSURES
ENCLOTHE
ENCLOTHED
ENCLOTHES
ENCLOTHING
ENCLOUD
ENCLOUDED
ENCLOUDING
ENCLOUDS
ENCODE
ENCODED
ENCODES
ENCODING
ENCOLOUR
ENCOLOURED
ENCOLOURING
ENCOLOURS
ENCOLPION
ENCOLPIONS
ENCOLPIUM
ENCOLPIUMS
ENCOLURE
ENCOLURES
ENCOMIA
ENCOMIAST
ENCOMIASTS
ENCOMION
ENCOMIUM
ENCOMIUMS
ENCOMPASS
ENCOMPASSED
ENCOMPASSES

ENCOMPASSING
ENCORE
ENCORED
ENCORES
ENCORING
ENCOUNTER
ENCOUNTERED
ENCOUNTERING
ENCOUNTERS
ENCOURAGE
ENCOURAGED
ENCOURAGES
ENCOURAGING
ENCOURAGINGS
ENCRADLE
ENCRADLED
ENCRADLES
ENCRADLING
ENCRATIES
ENCRATY
ENCREASE
ENCREASED
ENCREASES
ENCREASING
ENCRIMSON
ENCRIMSONED
ENCRIMSONING
ENCRIMSONS
ENCRINAL
ENCRINIC
ENCRINITE
ENCRINITES
ENCROACH
ENCROACHED
ENCROACHES
ENCROACHING
ENCRUST
ENCRUSTED
ENCRUSTING
ENCRUSTS
ENCRYPT
ENCRYPTED
ENCRYPTING
ENCRYPTS
ENCUMBER
ENCUMBERED
ENCUMBERING
ENCUMBERS
ENCURTAIN
ENCURTAINED
ENCURTAINING
ENCURTAINS
ENCYCLIC
ENCYCLICS
ENCYST
ENCYSTED
ENCYSTING
ENCYSTS
END
ENDAMAGE
ENDAMAGED
ENDAMAGES
ENDAMAGING
ENDAMOEBA
ENDAMOEBAE
ENDAMOEBAS
ENDANGER
ENDANGERED
ENDANGERING
ENDANGERS

ENDARCH
ENDART
ENDARTED
ENDARTING
ENDARTS
ENDEAR
ENDEARED
ENDEARING
ENDEARS
ENDEAVOUR
ENDEAVOURED
ENDEAVOURING
ENDEAVOURS
ENDECAGON
ENDECAGONS
ENDED
ENDEICTIC
ENDEIXES
ENDEIXIS
ENDEIXISES
ENDEMIAL
ENDEMIC
ENDEMICAL
ENDEMICS
ENDEMISM
ENDEMISMS
ENDENIZEN
ENDENIZENED
ENDENIZENING
ENDENIZENS
ENDERMIC
ENDERON
ENDERONS
ENDEW
ENDEWED
ENDEWING
ENDEWS
ENDGAME
ENDGAMES
ENDING
ENDINGS
ENDIRON
ENDIRONS
ENDITE
ENDITED
ENDITES
ENDITING
ENDIVE
ENDIVES
ENDLANG
ENDLESS
ENDLESSLY
ENDLONG
ENDMOST
ENDOBLAST
ENDOBLASTS
ENDOCARP
ENDOCARPS
ENDOCRINE
ENDOCRINES
ENDODERM
ENDODERMS
ENDODYNE
ENDOGAMIC
ENDOGAMIES
ENDOGAMY
ENDOGEN
ENDOGENIC
ENDOGENIES
ENDOGENS

ENDOGENY
ENDOLYMPH
ENDOLYMPHS
ENDOMIXES
ENDOMIXIS
ENDOMIXISES
ENDOMORPH
ENDOMORPHS
ENDOPHAGIES
ENDOPHAGY
ENDOPHYTE
ENDOPHYTES
ENDOPLASM
ENDOPLASMS
ENDORPHIN
ENDORPHINS
ENDORSE
ENDORSED
ENDORSEE
ENDORSEES
ENDORSER
ENDORSERS
ENDORSES
ENDORSING
ENDOSARC
ENDOSARCS
ENDOSCOPE
ENDOSCOPES
ENDOSCOPIES
ENDOSCOPY
ENDOSMOSE
ENDOSMOSES
ENDOSPERM
ENDOSPERMS
ENDOSPORE
ENDOSPORES
ENDOSS
ENDOSSED
ENDOSSES
ENDOSSING
ENDOSTEAL
ENDOSTEUM
ENDOSTEUMS
ENDOW
ENDOWED
ENDOWER
ENDOWERS
ENDOWING
ENDOWMENT
ENDOWMENTS
ENDOWS
ENDOZOA
ENDOZOIC
ENDOZOON
ENDS
ENDSHIP
ENDSHIPS
ENDUE
ENDUED
ENDUES
ENDUING
ENDUNGEON
ENDUNGEONED
ENDUNGEONING
ENDUNGEONS
ENDURABLE
ENDURABLY
ENDURANCE
ENDURANCES
ENDURE

ENDURED
ENDURER
ENDURERS
ENDURES
ENDURING
ENDWAYS
ENDWISE
ENE
ENEMA
ENEMAS
ENEMATA
ENEMIES
ENEMY
ENERGETIC
ENERGETICS
ENERGIC
ENERGID
ENERGIDS
ENERGIES
ENERGISE
ENERGISED
ENERGISES
ENERGISING
ENERGIZE
ENERGIZED
ENERGIZES
ENERGIZING
ENERGUMEN
ENERGUMENS
ENERGY
ENERVATE
ENERVATED
ENERVATES
ENERVATING
ENERVE
ENERVED
ENERVES
ENERVING
ENES
ENEW
ENEWED
ENEWING
ENEWS
ENFACE
ENFACED
ENFACES
ENFACING
ENFANT
ENFANTS
ENFEEBLE
ENFEEBLED
ENFEEBLES
ENFEEBLING
ENFELON
ENFELONED
ENFELONING
ENFELONS
ENFEOFF
ENFEOFFED
ENFEOFFING
ENFEOFFS
ENFESTED
ENFETTER
ENFETTERED
ENFETTERING
ENFETTERS
ENFIERCE
ENFIERCED
ENFIERCES
ENFIERCING

ENFILADE
ENFILADED
ENFILADES
ENFILADING
ENFILED
ENFIRE
ENFIRED
ENFIRES
ENFIRING
ENFIX
ENFIXED
ENFIXES
ENFIXING
ENFLESH
ENFLESHED
ENFLESHES
ENFLESHING
ENFLOWER
ENFLOWERED
ENFLOWERING
ENFLOWERS
ENFOLD
ENFOLDED
ENFOLDING
ENFOLDS
ENFORCE
ENFORCED
ENFORCES
ENFORCING
ENFOREST
ENFORESTED
ENFORESTING
ENFORESTS
ENFORM
ENFORMED
ENFORMING
ENFORMS
ENFRAME
ENFRAMED
ENFRAMES
ENFRAMING
ENFREE
ENFREED
ENFREEDOM
ENFREEDOMED
ENFREEDOMING
ENFREEDOMS
ENFREEING
ENFREES
ENFREEZE
ENFREEZES
ENFREEZING
ENFROSEN
ENFROZE
ENFROZEN
ENG
ENGAGÉ
ENGAGE
ENGAGED
ENGAGER
ENGAGERS
ENGAGES
ENGAGING
ENGAOL
ENGAOLED
ENGAOLING
ENGAOLS
ENGARLAND
ENGARLANDED
ENGARLANDING

ENGARLANDS
ENGENDER
ENGENDERED
ENGENDERING
ENGENDERS
ENGENDURE
ENGENDURES
ENGILD
ENGILDED
ENGILDING
ENGILDS
ENGILT
ENGINE
ENGINED
ENGINEER
ENGINEERED
ENGINEERING
ENGINEERINGS
ENGINEERS
ENGINER
ENGINERIES
ENGINERS
ENGINERY
ENGINES
ENGINING
ENGIRD
ENGIRDING
ENGIRDLE
ENGIRDLED
ENGIRDLES
ENGIRDLING
ENGIRDS
ENGIRT
ENGISCOPE
ENGISCOPES
ENGLOBE
ENGLOBED
ENGLOBES
ENGLOBING
ENGLOOM
ENGLOOMED
ENGLOOMING
ENGLOOMS
ENGLUT
ENGLUTS
ENGLUTTED
ENGLUTTING
ENGOBE
ENGOBES
ENGORE
ENGORED
ENGORES
ENGORGE
ENGORGED
ENGORGES
ENGORGING
ENGORING
ENGOULED
ENGOÛMENT
ENGOÛMENTS
ENGRACE
ENGRACED
ENGRACES
ENGRACING
ENGRAFF
ENGRAFFED
ENGRAFFING
ENGRAFFS
ENGRAFT
ENGRAFTED

ENGRAFTING
ENGRAFTS
ENGRAIL
ENGRAILED
ENGRAILING
ENGRAILS
ENGRAIN
ENGRAINED
ENGRAINER
ENGRAINERS
ENGRAINING
ENGRAINS
ENGRAM
ENGRAMMA
ENGRAMMAS
ENGRAMS
ENGRASP
ENGRASPED
ENGRASPING
ENGRASPS
ENGRAVE
ENGRAVED
ENGRAVEN
ENGRAVER
ENGRAVERIES
ENGRAVERS
ENGRAVERY
ENGRAVES
ENGRAVING
ENGRAVINGS
ENGRENAGE
ENGRENAGES
ENGRIEVE
ENGRIEVED
ENGRIEVES
ENGRIEVING
ENGROOVE
ENGROOVED
ENGROOVES
ENGROOVING
ENGROSS
ENGROSSED
ENGROSSER
ENGROSSERS
ENGROSSES
ENGROSSING
ENGS
ENGUARD
ENGUARDED
ENGUARDING
ENGUARDS
ENGULF
ENGULFED
ENGULFING
ENGULFS
ENGULPH
ENGULPHED
ENGULPHING
ENGULPHS
ENGYSCOPE
ENGYSCOPES
ENHALO
ENHALOED
ENHALOES
ENHALOING
ENHALOS
ENHANCE
ENHANCED
ENHANCES
ENHANCING

ENHANCIVE
ENHEARSE
ENHEARSED
ENHEARSES
ENHEARSING
ENHEARTEN
ENHEARTENED
ENHEARTENING
ENHEARTENS
ENHUNGER
ENHUNGERED
ENHUNGERING
ENHUNGERS
ENHYDRITE
ENHYDRITES
ENHYDROS
ENHYDROSES
ENHYDROUS
ENIAC
ENIACS
ENIGMA
ENIGMAS
ENIGMATIC
ENISLE
ENISLED
ENISLES
ENISLING
ENJAMB
ENJAMBED
ENJAMBING
ENJAMBS
ENJOIN
ENJOINED
ENJOINER
ENJOINERS
ENJOINING
ENJOINS
ENJOY
ENJOYABLE
ENJOYABLY
ENJOYED
ENJOYER
ENJOYERS
ENJOYING
ENJOYMENT
ENJOYMENTS
ENJOYS
ENKERNEL
ENKERNELLED
ENKERNELLING
ENKERNELS
ENKINDLE
ENKINDLED
ENKINDLES
ENKINDLING
ENLACE
ENLACED
ENLACES
ENLACING
ENLARD
ENLARDED
ENLARDING
ENLARDS
ENLARGE
ENLARGED
ENLARGEN
ENLARGENED
ENLARGENING
ENLARGENS
ENLARGER

ENLARGERS
ENLARGES
ENLARGING
ENLEVÉ
ENLIGHT
ENLIGHTED
ENLIGHTEN
ENLIGHTENED
ENLIGHTENING
ENLIGHTENS
ENLIGHTING
ENLIGHTS
ENLINK
ENLINKED
ENLINKING
ENLINKS
ENLIST
ENLISTED
ENLISTING
ENLISTS
ENLIT
ENLIVEN
ENLIVENED
ENLIVENER
ENLIVENERS
ENLIVENING
ENLIVENS
ENLOCK
ENLOCKED
ENLOCKING
ENLOCKS
ENLUMINE
ENLUMINED
ENLUMINES
ENLUMINING
ENMESH
ENMESHED
ENMESHES
ENMESHING
ENMEW
ENMEWED
ENMEWING
ENMEWS
ENMITIES
ENMITY
ENMOSSED
ENMOVE
ENMOVED
ENMOVES
ENMOVING
ENNEAD
ENNEADIC
ENNEADS
ENNEAGON
ENNEAGONS
ENNOBLE
ENNOBLED
ENNOBLES
ENNOBLING
ENNUI
ENNUIED
ENNUIS
ENNUYÉ
ENNUYED
ENNUYING
ENODAL
ENOMOTIES
ENOMOTY
ENORM
ENORMITIES

ENORMITY
ENORMOUS
ENOSES
ENOSIS
ENOUGH
ENOUGHS
ENOUNCE
ENOUNCED
ENOUNCES
ENOUNCING
ENOW
ENPRINT
ENPRINTS
ENQUIRE
ENQUIRED
ENQUIRER
ENQUIRERS
ENQUIRES
ENQUIRIES
ENQUIRING
ENQUIRY
ENRACE
ENRACED
ENRACES
ENRACING
ENRAGÉ
ENRAGE
ENRAGED
ENRAGES
ENRAGING
ENRANCKLE
ENRANCKLED
ENRANCKLES
ENRANCKLING
ENRANGE
ENRANGED
ENRANGES
ENRANGING
ENRANK
ENRANKED
ENRANKING
ENRANKS
ENRAPT
ENRAPTURE
ENRAPTURED
ENRAPTURES
ENRAPTURING
ENRAUNGE
ENRAUNGED
ENRAUNGES
ENRAUNGING
ENRAVISH
ENRAVISHED
ENRAVISHES
ENRAVISHING
ENRHEUM
ENRHEUMED
ENRHEUMING
ENRHEUMS
ENRICH
ENRICHED
ENRICHES
ENRICHING
ENRIDGED
ENRING
ENRINGED
ENRINGING
ENRINGS
ENRIVEN
ENROBE

ENROBED
ENROBES
ENROBING
ENROL
ENROLL
ENROLLED
ENROLLER
ENROLLERS
ENROLLING
ENROLLS
ENROLMENT
ENROLMENTS
ENROLS
ENROOT
ENROOTED
ENROOTING
ENROOTS
ENROUGH
ENROUGHED
ENROUGHING
ENROUGHS
ENROUND
ENROUNDED
ENROUNDING
ENROUNDS
ENS
ENSAMPLE
ENSAMPLED
ENSAMPLES
ENSAMPLING
ENSATE
ENSCONCE
ENSCONCED
ENSCONCES
ENSCONCING
ENSEAL
ENSEALED
ENSEALING
ENSEALS
ENSEAM
ENSEAMED
ENSEAMING
ENSEAMS
ENSEAR
ENSEARED
ENSEARING
ENSEARS
ENSEMBLE
ENSEMBLES
ENSEW
ENSEWED
ENSEWING
ENSEWS
ENSHEATH
ENSHEATHE
ENSHEATHED
ENSHEATHES
ENSHEATHING
ENSHEATHS
ENSHELL
ENSHELLED
ENSHELLING
ENSHELLS
ENSHELTER
ENSHELTERED
ENSHELTERING
ENSHELTERS
ENSHIELD
ENSHIELDED
ENSHIELDING

ENSHIELDS
ENSHRINE
ENSHRINED
ENSHRINES
ENSHRINING
ENSHROUD
ENSHROUDED
ENSHROUDING
ENSHROUDS
ENSIFORM
ENSIGN
ENSIGNCIES
ENSIGNCY
ENSIGNED
ENSIGNING
ENSIGNS
ENSILAGE
ENSILAGED
ENSILAGES
ENSILAGING
ENSILE
ENSILED
ENSILES
ENSILING
ENSKIED
ENSKIES
ENSKY
ENSKYING
ENSLAVE
ENSLAVED
ENSLAVER
ENSLAVERS
ENSLAVES
ENSLAVING
ENSNARE
ENSNARED
ENSNARES
ENSNARING
ENSNARL
ENSNARLED
ENSNARLING
ENSNARLS
ENSORCELL
ENSORCELLED
ENSORCELLING
ENSORCELLS
ENSOUL
ENSOULED
ENSOULING
ENSOULS
ENSPHERE
ENSPHERED
ENSPHERES
ENSPHERING
ENSTAMP
ENSTAMPED
ENSTAMPING
ENSTAMPS
ENSTATITE
ENSTATITES
ENSTEEP
ENSTEEPED
ENSTEEPING
ENSTEEPS
ENSTYLE
ENSTYLED
ENSTYLES
ENSTYLING
ENSUE
ENSUED

ENSUES
ENSUING
ENSURE
ENSURED
ENSURER
ENSURERS
ENSURES
ENSURING
ENSWATHE
ENSWATHED
ENSWATHES
ENSWATHING
ENSWEEP
ENSWEEPING
ENSWEEPS
ENSWEPT
ENTAIL
ENTAILED
ENTAILER
ENTAILERS
ENTAILING
ENTAILS
ENTAME
ENTAMED
ENTAMES
ENTAMING
ENTAMOEBA
ENTAMOEBAE
ENTAMOEBAS
ENTANGLE
ENTANGLED
ENTANGLES
ENTANGLING
ENTASES
ENTASIS
ENTAYLE
ENTAYLED
ENTAYLES
ENTAYLING
ENTELECHIES
ENTELECHY
ENTELLUS
ENTELLUSES
ENTENDER
ENTENDERED
ENTENDERING
ENTENDERS
ENTENTE
ENTENTES
ENTER
ENTERA
ENTERABLE
ENTERAL
ENTERATE
ENTERED
ENTERER
ENTERERS
ENTERIC
ENTERICS
ENTERING
ENTERINGS
ENTERITIS
ENTERITISES
ENTERON
ENTERS
ENTERTAIN
ENTERTAINED
ENTERTAINING
ENTERTAININGS
ENTERTAINS

ENTERTAKE
ENTERTAKEN
ENTERTAKES
ENTERTAKING
ENTERTOOK
ENTÊTÉ
ENTÊTÉE
ENTHALPIES
ENTHALPY
ENTHETIC
ENTHRAL
ENTHRALL
ENTHRALLED
ENTHRALLING
ENTHRALLS
ENTHRALS
ENTHRONE
ENTHRONED
ENTHRONES
ENTHRONING
ENTHUSE
ENTHUSED
ENTHUSES
ENTHUSING
ENTHYMEME
ENTHYMEMES
ENTIA
ENTICE
ENTICED
ENTICER
ENTICERS
ENTICES
ENTICING
ENTICINGS
ENTIRE
ENTIRELY
ENTIRES
ENTIRETIES
ENTIRETY
ENTITIES
ENTITLE
ENTITLED
ENTITLES
ENTITLING
ENTITY
ENTOBLAST
ENTOBLASTS
ENTODERM
ENTODERMS
ENTOIL
ENTOILED
ENTOILING
ENTOILS
ENTOMB
ENTOMBED
ENTOMBING
ENTOMBS
ENTOMIC
ENTOPHYTE
ENTOPHYTES
ENTOPIC
ENTOPTIC
ENTOPTICS
ENTOTIC
ENTOURAGE
ENTOURAGES
ENTOZOA
ENTOZOAL
ENTOZOIC
ENTOZOON

ENTRAIL
ENTRAILED
ENTRAILING
ENTRAILS
ENTRAIN
ENTRAINED
ENTRAINING
ENTRAINS
ENTRALL
ENTRALLES
ENTRAMMEL
ENTRAMMELLED
ENTRAMMELLING
ENTRAMMELS
ENTRANCE
ENTRANCED
ENTRANCES
ENTRANCING
ENTRANT
ENTRANTS
ENTRAP
ENTRAPPED
ENTRAPPER
ENTRAPPERS
ENTRAPPING
ENTRAPS
ENTREAT
ENTREATED
ENTREATIES
ENTREATING
ENTREATS
ENTREATY
ENTRECHAT
ENTRECHATS
ENTRECÔTE
ENTRECÔTES
ENTRÉE
ENTRÉES
ENTREMES
ENTREMETS
ENTRENCH
ENTRENCHED
ENTRENCHES
ENTRENCHING
ENTREPOT
ENTREPOTS
ENTRESOL
ENTRESOLS
ENTREZ
ENTRIES
ENTRISM
ENTRISMS
ENTRIST
ENTRISTS
ENTROLD
ENTROPIES
ENTROPION
ENTROPIONS
ENTROPIUM
ENTROPIUMS
ENTROPY
ENTRUST
ENTRUSTED
ENTRUSTING
ENTRUSTS
ENTRY
ENTRYISM
ENTRYISMS
ENTRYIST
ENTRYISTS

ENTWINE
ENTWINED
ENTWINES
ENTWINING
ENTWIST
ENTWISTED
ENTWISTING
ENTWISTS
ENUCLEATE
ENUCLEATED
ENUCLEATES
ENUCLEATING
ENUMERATE
ENUMERATED
ENUMERATES
ENUMERATING
ENUNCIATE
ENUNCIATED
ENUNCIATES
ENUNCIATING
ENURE
ENURED
ENURES
ENURESES
ENURESIS
ENURETIC
ENURETICS
ENURING
ENVASSAL
ENVASSALLED
ENVASSALLING
ENVASSALS
ENVAULT
ENVAULTED
ENVAULTING
ENVAULTS
ENVEIGLE
ENVEIGLED
ENVEIGLES
ENVEIGLING
ENVELOP
ENVELOPE
ENVELOPED
ENVELOPES
ENVELOPING
ENVELOPS
ENVENOM
ENVENOMED
ENVENOMING
ENVENOMS
ENVERMEIL
ENVERMEILED
ENVERMEILING
ENVERMEILS
ENVIABLE
ENVIABLY
ENVIED
ENVIER
ENVIERS
ENVIES
ENVIOUS
ENVIOUSLY
ENVIRON
ENVIRONED
ENVIRONING
ENVIRONS
ENVISAGE
ENVISAGED
ENVISAGES
ENVISAGING

ENVISION
ENVISIONED
ENVISIONING
ENVISIONS
ENVOI
ENVOIS
ENVOY
ENVOYS
ENVOYSHIP·
ENVOYSHIPS
ENVY
ENVYING
ENVYINGS
ENWALL
ENWALLED
ENWALLING
ENWALLOW
ENWALLOWED
ENWALLOWING
ENWALLOWS
ENWALLS
ENWHEEL
ENWHEELED
ENWHEELING
ENWHEELS
ENWIND
ENWINDING
ENWINDS
ENWOMB
ENWOMBED
ENWOMBING
ENWOMBS
ENWOUND
ENWRAP
ENWRAPPED
ENWRAPPING
ENWRAPPINGS
ENWRAPS
ENWREATHE
ENWREATHED
ENWREATHES
ENWREATHING
ENZIAN
ENZIANS
ENZONE
ENZONED
ENZONES
ENZONING
ENZOOTIC
ENZOOTICS
ENZYMATIC
ENZYME
ENZYMES
ENZYMIC
EOAN
ÉOLIENNE
ÉOLIENNES
EOLIPILE
EOLIPILES
EOLITH
EOLITHIC
EOLITHS
EON
EONISM
EONISMS
EONS
EORL
EORLS
EOSIN
EOSINS

EOTHEN
EPACRID
EPACRIDS
EPACRIS
EPACRISES
EPACT
EPACTS
EPAENETIC
EPAGOGE
EPAGOGES
EPAGOGIC
EPAINETIC
EPANODOS
EPANODOSES
EPARCH
EPARCHATE
EPARCHATES
EPARCHIES
EPARCHS
EPARCHY
ÉPATANT
EPAULE
EPAULES
EPAULET
EPAULETS
EPAULETTE
EPAULETTES
EPAXIAL
EPEDAPHIC
ÉPÉE
ÉPÉES
EPEIRA
EPEIRAS
EPEIRID
EPEIRIDS
EPEOLATRIES
EPEOLATRY
ÉPERDU
ÉPERDUE
EPERGNE
EPERGNES
EPHA
EPHAH
EPHAHS
EPHAS
EPHEBE
EPHEBI
EPHEBIC
EPHEBOS
EPHEBUS
EPHEDRA
EPHEDRAS
EPHEDRINE
EPHEDRINES
EPHELIDES
EPHELIS
EPHEMERA
EPHEMERAE
EPHEMERAL
EPHEMERALS
EPHEMERAS
EPHEMERID
EPHEMERIDES
EPHEMERIDS
EPHEMERIS
EPHEMERON
EPHIALTES
EPHOD
EPHODS
EPHOR

EPHORALTIES
EPHORALTY
EPHORS
EPIBLAST
EPIBLASTS
EPIC
EPICAL
EPICALLY
EPICALYCES
EPICALYX
EPICALYXES
EPICANTHI
EPICARP
EPICARPS
EPICEDE
EPICEDES
EPICEDIA
EPICEDIAL
EPICEDIAN
EPICEDIUM
EPICENE
EPICENES
EPICENTRE
EPICENTRES
ÉPICIER
ÉPICIERS
EPICISM
EPICISMS
EPICIST
EPICISTS
EPICLESES
EPICLESIS
EPICOTYL
EPICOTYLS
EPICRITIC
EPICS
EPICURE
EPICUREAN
EPICUREANS
EPICURES
EPICURISE
EPICURISED
EPICURISES
EPICURISING
EPICURISM
EPICURISMS
EPICURIZE
EPICURIZED
EPICURIZES
EPICURIZING
EPICYCLE
EPICYCLES
EPICYCLIC
EPIDEMIC
EPIDEMICS
EPIDERMAL
EPIDERMIC
EPIDERMIS
EPIDERMISES
EPIDOSITE
EPIDOSITES
EPIDOTE
EPIDOTES
EPIDOTIC
EPIDURAL
EPIDURALS
EPIFOCAL
EPIGAEAL
EPIGAEAN
EPIGAEOUS

EPIGAMIC
EPIGEAL
EPIGEAN
EPIGENE
EPIGEOUS
EPIGON
EPIGONE
EPIGONES
EPIGONI
EPIGONS
EPIGRAM
EPIGRAMS
EPIGRAPH
EPIGRAPHED
EPIGRAPHIES
EPIGRAPHING
EPIGRAPHS
EPIGRAPHY
EPIGYNIES
EPIGYNOUS
EPIGYNY
EPILATE
EPILATED
EPILATES
EPILATING
EPILATION
EPILATIONS
EPILATOR
EPILATORS
EPILEPSIES
EPILEPSY
EPILEPTIC
EPILEPTICS
EPILOBIUM
EPILOBIUMS
EPILOGIC
EPILOGISE
EPILOGISED
EPILOGISES
EPILOGISING
EPILOGIZE
EPILOGIZED
EPILOGIZES
EPILOGIZING
EPILOGUE
EPILOGUES
EPIMER
EPIMERIC
EPIMERS
EPINASTIC
EPINASTIES
EPINASTY
EPINICIAN
EPINICION
EPINICIONS
EPINIKIAN
EPINIKION
EPINIKIONS
EPINOSIC
EPIPHANIC
EPIPHRAGM
EPIPHRAGMS
EPIPHYSES
EPIPHYSIS
EPIPHYTAL
EPIPHYTE
EPIPHYTES
EPIPHYTIC
EPIPLOIC
EPIPLOON

EPIPLOONS
EPIPOLIC
EPIPOLISM
EPIPOLISMS
EPIRRHEMA
EPIRRHEMAS
EPISCOPAL
EPISCOPE
EPISCOPES
EPISCOPIES
EPISCOPY
EPISEMON
EPISEMONS
EPISODAL
EPISODE
EPISODES
EPISODIAL
EPISODIC
EPISOME
EPISOMES
EPISPERM
EPISPERMS
EPISPORE
EPISPORES
EPISTASES
EPISTASIS
EPISTATIC
EPISTAXES
EPISTAXIS
EPISTAXISES
EPISTEMIC
EPISTEMICS
EPISTLE
EPISTLED
EPISTLER
EPISTLERS
EPISTLES
EPISTLING
EPISTOLER
EPISTOLERS
EPISTOLET
EPISTOLETS
EPISTOLIC
EPISTYLE
EPISTYLES
EPITAPH
EPITAPHED
EPITAPHER
EPITAPHERS
EPITAPHIC
EPITAPHING
EPITAPHS
EPITASES
EPITASIS
EPITAXIAL
EPITAXIES
EPITAXY
EPITHEM
EPITHEMA
EPITHEMATA
EPITHEMS
EPITHESES
EPITHESIS
EPITHET
EPITHETED
EPITHETIC
EPITHETING
EPITHETON
EPITHETONS
EPITHETS

EPITOME
EPITOMES
EPITOMIC
EPITOMISE
EPITOMISED
EPITOMISES
EPITOMISING
EPITOMIST
EPITOMISTS
EPITOMIZE
EPITOMIZED
EPITOMIZES
EPITOMIZING
EPITONIC
EPITRITE
EPITRITES
EPIZEUXES
EPIZEUXIS
EPIZEUXISES
EPIZOA
EPIZOAN
EPIZOANS
EPIZOIC
EPIZOON
EPIZOOTIC
EPIZOOTICS
EPOCH
EPOCHA
EPOCHAL
EPOCHAS
EPOCHS
EPODE
EPODES
EPODIC
EPONYM
EPONYMOUS
EPONYMS
EPOPEE
EPOPEES
EPOPOEIA
EPOPOEIAS
EPOPT
EPOPTS
EPOS
EPOSES
EPOXIDE
EPOXIDES
EPOXIES
EPOXY
ÉPRIS
ÉPRISE
EPSILON
EPSILONS
EPSOMITE
EPSOMITES
ÉPUISÉ
ÉPUISÉE
EPULARY
EPULATION
EPULATIONS
EPULIDES
EPULIS
EPULISES
EPULOTIC
EPULOTICS
EPURATE
EPURATED
EPURATES
EPURATING
EPURATION

EPURATIONS
EPYLLION
EPYLLIONS
EQUABLE
EQUABLY
EQUAL
EQUALISE
EQUALISED
EQUALISER
EQUALISERS
EQUALISES
EQUALISING
EQUALITIES
EQUALITY
EQUALIZE
EQUALIZED
EQUALIZER
EQUALIZERS
EQUALIZES
EQUALIZING
EQUALLED
EQUALLING
EQUALLY
EQUALNESS
EQUALNESSES
EQUALS
EQUANT
EQUANTS
EQUATE
EQUATED
EQUATES
EQUATING
EQUATION
EQUATIONS
EQUATOR
EQUATORS
EQUERRIES
EQUERRY
EQUINAL
EQUINE
EQUINIA
EQUINIAS
EQUINITIES
EQUINITY
EQUINOX
EQUINOXES
EQUIP
EQUIPAGE
EQUIPAGED
EQUIPAGES
EQUIPAGING
ÉQUIPE
ÉQUIPES
EQUIPMENT
EQUIPMENTS
EQUIPOISE
EQUIPOISED
EQUIPOISES
EQUIPOISING
EQUIPPED
EQUIPPING
EQUIPS
EQUISETA
EQUISETIC
EQUISETUM
EQUISETUMS
EQUITABLE
EQUITABLY
EQUITANT
EQUITIES

EQUITY
EQUIVALVE
EQUIVOCAL
EQUIVOKE
EQUIVOKES
EQUIVOQUE
EQUIVOQUES
ER
ERA
ERADIATE
ERADIATED
ERADIATES
ERADIATING
ERADICATE
ERADICATED
ERADICATES
ERADICATING
ERAS
ERASABLE
ERASE
ERASED
ERASEMENT
ERASEMENTS
ERASER
ERASERS
ERASES
ERASING
ERASION
ERASIONS
ERASURE
ERASURES
ERATHEM
ERATHEMS
ERBIA
ERBIAS
ERBIUM
ERBIUMS
ERE
ERECT
ERECTED
ERECTER
ERECTERS
ERECTILE
ERECTING
ERECTION
ERECTIONS
ERECTIVE
ERECTLY
ERECTNESS
ERECTNESSES
ERECTOR
ERECTORS
ERECTS
ERED
ERELONG
EREMIC
EREMITAL
EREMITE
EREMITES
EREMITIC
EREMITISM
EREMITISMS
ERENOW
EREPSIN
EREPSINS
ERES
ERETHISM
ERETHISMS
ERETHITIC
EREWHILE

ERF
ERG
ERGATANER
ERGATANERS
ERGATE
ERGATES
ERGATOID
ERGO
ERGODIC
ERGOGRAM
ERGOGRAMS
ERGOGRAPH
ERGOGRAPHS
ERGOMETER
ERGOMETERS
ERGON
ERGONOMIC
ERGONOMICS
ERGONS
ERGOT
ERGOTISE
ERGOTISED
ERGOTISES
ERGOTISING
ERGOTISM
ERGOTISMS
ERGOTIZE
ERGOTIZED
ERGOTIZES
ERGOTIZING
ERGOTS
ERGS
ERIACH
ERIACHS
ERIC
ERICA
ERICAS
ERICK
ERICOID
ERICS
ERIGERON
ERIGERONS
ERING
ERINGO
ERINGOES
ERINGOS
ERINITE
ERINITES
ERIOMETER
ERIOMETERS
ERIONITE
ERIONITES
ERISTIC
ERISTICAL
ERK
ERKS
ERMELIN
ERMELINS
ERMINE
ERMINED
ERMINES
ERN
ERNE
ERNED
ERNES
ERNING
ERNS
ERODE
ERODED

| | | | | |
|---|---|---|---|---|
| ERODENT | ERUCTS | ESCAROLE | ESLOYNE | ESSE |
| ERODENTS | ERUDITE | ESCAROLES | ESLOYNED | ESSENCE |
| ERODES | ERUDITELY | ESCARP | ESLOYNES | ESSENCES |
| ERODING | ERUDITES | ESCARPED | ESLOYNING | ESSENTIAL |
| ERODIUM | ERUDITION | ESCARPING | ESNE | ESSENTIALS |
| ERODIUMS | ERUDITIONS | ESCARPS | ESNECIES | ESSES |
| EROGENIC | ERUPT | ESCHALOT | ESNECY | ESSIVE |
| EROGENOUS | ERUPTED | ESCHALOTS | ESNES | ESSIVES |
| EROSE | ERUPTING | ESCHAR | ESOPHAGI | ESSOIN |
| EROSION | ERUPTION | ESCHARS | ESOPHAGUS | ESSOINER |
| EROSIONS | ERUPTIONS | ESCHEAT | ESOTERIC | ESSOINERS |
| EROSIVE | ERUPTIVE | ESCHEATED | ESOTERICA | ESSOINS |
| EROSTRATE | ERUPTS | ESCHEATING | ESOTERIES | ESSONITE |
| EROTEMA | ERVALENTA | ESCHEATOR | ESOTERISM | ESSONITES |
| EROTEMAS | ERVALENTAS | ESCHEATORS | ESOTERISMS | ESSOYNE |
| EROTEME | ERVEN | ESCHEATS | ESOTERY | ESSOYNES |
| EROTEMES | ERYNGIUM | ESCHEW | ESPADA | ESTABLISH |
| EROTESES | ERYNGIUMS | ESCHEWED | ESPADAS | ESTABLISHED |
| EROTESIS | ERYNGO | ESCHEWING | ESPAGNOLE | ESTABLISHES |
| EROTETIC | ERYNGOES | ESCHEWS | ESPAGNOLES | ESTABLISHING |
| EROTIC | ERYNGOS | ESCLANDRE | ESPALIER | ESTACADE |
| EROTICA | ERYTHEMA | ESCLANDRES | ESPALIERED | ESTACADES |
| EROTICAL | ERYTHEMAL | ESCOLAR | ESPALIERING | ESTAFETTE |
| EROTICISM | ERYTHEMAS | ESCOLARS | ESPALIERS | ESTAFETTES |
| EROTICISMS | ERYTHRINA | ESCOPETTE | ESPARTO | ESTAMINET |
| EROTICIST | ERYTHRINAS | ESCOPETTES | ESPARTOS | ESTAMINETS |
| EROTICISTS | ERYTHRISM | ESCORT | ESPECIAL | ESTANCIA |
| EROTICS | ERYTHRISMS | ESCORTAGE | ESPERANCE | ESTANCIAS |
| EROTISM | ERYTHRITE | ESCORTAGES | ESPERANCES | ESTATE |
| EROTISMS | ERYTHRITES | ESCORTED | ESPIAL | ESTATED |
| ERR | ES | ESCORTING | ESPIALS | ESTATES |
| ERRABLE | ESCALADE | ESCORTS | ESPIED | ESTATING |
| ERRAND | ESCALADED | ESCOT | ESPIÈGLE | ESTEEM |
| ERRANDS | ESCALADES | ESCOTS | ESPIES | ESTEEMED |
| ERRANT | ESCALADING | ESCOTTED | ESPIONAGE | ESTEEMING |
| ERRANTLY | ESCALADO | ESCOTTING | ESPIONAGES | ESTEEMS |
| ERRANTRIES | ESCALADOES | ESCRIBANO | ESPLANADE | ESTER |
| ERRANTRY | ESCALATE | ESCRIBANOS | ESPLANADES | ESTERIFIED |
| ERRANTS | ESCALATED | ESCRIBE | ESPOUSAL | ESTERIFIES |
| ERRATA | ESCALATES | ESCRIBED | ESPOUSALS | ESTERIFY |
| ERRATIC | ESCALATING | ESCRIBES | ESPOUSE | ESTERIFYING |
| ERRATICAL | ESCALATOR | ESCRIBING | ESPOUSED | ESTERS |
| ERRATICS | ESCALATORS | ESCROC | ESPOUSER | ESTHESES |
| ERRATUM | ESCALIER | ESCROCS | ESPOUSERS | ESTHESIA |
| ERRED | ESCALIERS | ESCROL | ESPOUSES | ESTHESIAS |
| ERRHINE | ESCALLOP | ESCROLL | ESPOUSING | ESTHESIS |
| ERRHINES | ESCALLOPS | ESCROLLS | ESPRESSO | ESTHETE |
| ERRING | ESCALOP | ESCROLS | ESPRESSOS | ESTHETES |
| ERRINGLY | ESCALOPE | ESCROW | ESPRIT | ESTHETIC |
| ERRINGS | ESCALOPES | ESCROWS | ESPRITS | ESTHETICS |
| ERRONEOUS | ESCALOPS | ESCUAGE | ESPUMOSO | ESTIMABLE |
| ERROR | ESCAPABLE | ESCUAGES | ESPUMOSOS | ESTIMABLY |
| ERRORIST | ESCAPADE | ESCUDO | ESPY | ESTIMATE |
| ERRORISTS | ESCAPADES | ESCUDOS | ESPYING | ESTIMATED |
| ERRORS | ESCAPADO | ESCULENT | ESQUIRE | ESTIMATES |
| ERRS | ESCAPADOES | ESCULENTS | ESQUIRES | ESTIMATING |
| ERS | ESCAPE | ESEMPLASIES | ESQUISSE | ESTIMATOR |
| ERSATZ | ESCAPED | ESEMPLASY | ESQUISSES | ESTIMATORS |
| ERSATZES | ESCAPEE | ESILE | ESS | ESTIVAL |
| ERSES | ESCAPEES | ESILES | ESSAY | ESTIVATE |
| ERST | ESCAPER | ESKAR | ESSAYED | ESTIVATED |
| ERSTWHILE | ESCAPERS | ESKARS | ESSAYER | ESTIVATES |
| ERUCIFORM | ESCAPES | ESKER | ESSAYERS | ESTIVATING |
| ERUCT | ESCAPING | ESKERS | ESSAYETTE | ESTOC |
| ERUCTATE | ESCAPISM | ESKIES | ESSAYETTES | ESTOCS |
| ERUCTATED | ESCAPISMS | ESKY® | ESSAYING | ESTOILE |
| ERUCTATES | ESCAPIST | ESLOIN | ESSAYISH | ESTOILES |
| ERUCTATING | ESCAPISTS | ESLOINED | ESSAYIST | ESTOP |
| ERUCTED | ESCARGOT | ESLOINING | ESSAYISTS | ESTOPPAGE |
| ERUCTING | ESCARGOTS | ESLOINS | ESSAYS | ESTOPPAGES |

ESTOPPED
ESTOPPEL
ESTOPPELS
ESTOPPING
ESTOPS
ESTOVER
ESTOVERS
ESTRADE
ESTRADES
ESTRADIOL
ESTRADIOLS
ESTRAL
ESTRANGE
ESTRANGED
ESTRANGER
ESTRANGERS
ESTRANGES
ESTRANGING
ESTRAPADE
ESTRAPADES
ESTRAY
ESTRAYED
ESTRAYING
ESTRAYS
ESTREAT
ESTREATED
ESTREATING
ESTREATS
ESTREPE
ESTREPED
ESTREPES
ESTREPING
ESTRICH
ESTRICHES
ESTRIDGE
ESTRIDGES
ESTRILDID
ESTRILDIDS
ESTRO
ESTROGEN
ESTROGENS
ESTROS
ESTROUS
ESTRUM
ESTRUMS
ESTRUS
ESTRUSES
ESTUARIAL
ESTUARIAN
ESTUARIES
ESTUARINE
ESTUARY
ESURIENCE
ESURIENCES
ESURIENCIES
ESURIENCY
ESURIENT
ETA
ETACISM
ETACISMS
ETAERIO
ETAERIOS
ÉTAGE
ÉTAGÈRE
ÉTAGÈRES
ÉTAGES
ÉTALAGE
ÉTALAGES
ETALON
ETALONS

ÉTAPE
ÉTAPES
ETAS
ÉTAT
ÉTATISME
ÉTATISMES
ÉTATISTE
ÉTATISTES
ÉTATS
ETCH
ETCHANT
ETCHANTS
ETCHED
ETCHER
ETCHERS
ETCHES
ETCHING
ETCHINGS
ETEN
ETENS
ETERNAL
ETERNALLY
ETERNE
ETERNISE
ETERNISED
ETERNISES
ETERNISING
ETERNITIES
ETERNITY
ETERNIZE
ETERNIZED
ETERNIZES
ETERNIZING
ETESIAN
ETH
ETHAL
ETHALS
ETHANE
ETHANES
ETHANOL
ETHANOLS
ETHE
ETHENE
ETHENES
ETHER
ETHERCAP
ETHERCAPS
ETHEREAL
ETHEREOUS
ETHERIAL
ETHERIC
ETHERICAL
ETHERION
ETHERIONS
ETHERISE
ETHERISED
ETHERISES
ETHERISING
ETHERISM
ETHERISMS
ETHERIST
ETHERISTS
ETHERIZE
ETHERIZED
ETHERIZES
ETHERIZING
ETHERS
ETHIC
ETHICAL
ETHICALLY

ETHICALS
ETHICISE
ETHICISED
ETHICISES
ETHICISING
ETHICISM
ETHICISMS
ETHICIST
ETHICISTS
ETHICIZE
ETHICIZED
ETHICIZES
ETHICIZING
ETHICS
ETHIOPS
ETHIOPSES
ETHMOID
ETHMOIDAL
ETHNARCH
ETHNARCHIES
ETHNARCHS
ETHNARCHY
ETHNIC
ETHNICAL
ETHNICISM
ETHNICISMS
ETHNICITIES
ETHNICITY
ETHNICS
ETHNOCIDE
ETHNOCIDES
ETHNOLOGIES
ETHNOLOGY
ETHOLOGIC
ETHOLOGIES
ETHOLOGY
ETHOS
ETHOSES
ETHS
ETHYL
ETHYLATE
ETHYLATED
ETHYLATES
ETHYLATING
ETHYLENE
ETHYLENES
ETHYLS
ETHYNE
ETHYNES
ETIOLATE
ETIOLATED
ETIOLATES
ETIOLATING
ETIOLIN
ETIOLINS
ETIOLOGIES
ETIOLOGY
ETIQUETTE
ETIQUETTES
ETNA
ETNAS
ÉTOILE
ÉTOILES
ÉTOURDI
ÉTOURDIE
ÉTRANGER
ÉTRANGÈRE
ÉTRANGÈRES
ÉTRANGERS
ÉTRENNE

ÉTRENNES
ÉTRIER
ÉTRIERS
ETTERCAP
ETTERCAPS
ETTIN
ETTINS
ETTLE
ETTLED
ETTLES
ETTLING
ÉTUDE
ÉTUDES
ETUI
ETUIS
ETWEE
ETWEES
ETYMA
ETYMIC
ETYMOLOGIES
ETYMOLOGY
ETYMON
ETYMONS
ETYPIC
ETYPICAL
EUCAIN
EUCAINE
EUCAINES
EUCAINS
EUCALYPT
EUCALYPTI
EUCALYPTS
EUCARYON
EUCARYONS
EUCARYOT
EUCARYOTE
EUCARYOTES
EUCARYOTS
EUCHARIS
EUCHARISES
EUCHLORIC
EUCHOLOGIES
EUCHOLOGY
EUCHRE
EUCHRED
EUCHRES
EUCHRING
EUCLASE
EUCLASES
EUCRITE
EUCRITES
EUCRITIC
EUCYCLIC
EUDAEMONIES
EUDAEMONY
EUDEMONIA
EUDEMONIAS
EUDEMONIC
EUDEMONICS
EUDEMONIES
EUDEMONY
EUDIALYTE
EUDIALYTES
EUGE
EUGENIC
EUGENICS
EUGENISM
EUGENISMS
EUGENIST
EUGENISTS

EUGENOL
EUGENOLS
EUGH
EUGHEN
EUGHS
EUK
EUKARYON
EUKARYONS
EUKARYOT
EUKARYOTE
EUKARYOTES
EUKARYOTS
EUKED
EUKING
EUKS
EULACHON
EULACHONS
EULOGIA
EULOGIES
EULOGISE
EULOGISED
EULOGISES
EULOGISING
EULOGIST
EULOGISTS
EULOGIUM
EULOGIUMS
EULOGIZE
EULOGIZED
EULOGIZES
EULOGIZING
EULOGY
EUMELANIN
EUMELANINS
EUMERISM
EUMERISMS
EUNUCH
EUNUCHISE
EUNUCHISED
EUNUCHISES
EUNUCHISING
EUNUCHISM
EUNUCHISMS
EUNUCHIZE
EUNUCHIZED
EUNUCHIZES
EUNUCHIZING
EUNUCHOID
EUNUCHOIDS
EUNUCHS
EUOI
EUONYMIN
EUONYMINS
EUONYMUS
EUONYMUSES
EUOUAE
EUOUAES
EUPAD
EUPADS
EUPATRID
EUPATRIDAE
EUPATRIDS
EUPEPSIA
EUPEPSIAS
EUPEPSIES
EUPEPSY
EUPEPTIC
EUPHAUSID
EUPHAUSIDS
EUPHEMISE

| | | | | |
|---|---|---|---|---|
| EUPHEMISED | EUSTACY | EVANISHED | EVERYWHEN | EVOLUTION |
| EUPHEMISES | EUSTASIES | EVANISHES | EVES | EVOLUTIONS |
| EUPHEMISING | EUSTASY | EVANISHING | EVET | EVOLUTIVE |
| EUPHEMISM | EUSTATIC | EVANITION | EVETS | EVOLVABLE |
| EUPHEMISMS | EUSTYLE | EVANITIONS | EVHOE | EVOLVE |
| EUPHEMIZE | EUSTYLES | EVAPORATE | EVICT | EVOLVED |
| EUPHEMIZED | EUTAXIES | EVAPORATED | EVICTED | EVOLVENT |
| EUPHEMIZES | EUTAXITE | EVAPORATES | EVICTING | EVOLVES |
| EUPHEMIZING | EUTAXITES | EVAPORATING | EVICTION | EVOLVING |
| EUPHENICS | EUTAXITIC | EVAPORITE | EVICTIONS | EVOVAE |
| EUPHOBIA | EUTAXY | EVAPORITES | EVICTOR | EVOVAES |
| EUPHOBIAS | EUTECTIC | EVASIBLE | EVICTORS | EVULGATE |
| EUPHON | EUTECTICS | EVASION | EVICTS | EVULGATED |
| EUPHONIA | EUTECTOID | EVASIONS | EVIDENCE | EVULGATES |
| EUPHONIAS | EUTECTOIDS | EVASIVE | EVIDENCED | EVULGATING |
| EUPHONIC | EUTEXIA | EVASIVELY | EVIDENCES | EVULSE |
| EUPHONIES | EUTEXIAS | EVE | EVIDENCING | EVULSED |
| EUPHONISE | EUTHANASIES | EVECTION | EVIDENT | EVULSES |
| EUPHONISED | EUTHANASY | EVECTIONS | EVIDENTLY | EVULSING |
| EUPHONISES | EUTHENICS | EVEJAR | EVIDENTS | EVULSION |
| EUPHONISING | EUTHENIST | EVEJARS | EVIL | EVULSIONS |
| EUPHONIUM | EUTHENISTS | EVEN | EVILLER | EVZONE |
| EUPHONIUMS | EUTHERIAN | EVENED | EVILLEST | EVZONES |
| EUPHONIZE | EUTHERIANS | ÉVÉNEMENT | EVILLY | EWE |
| EUPHONIZED | EUTRAPELIES | ÉVÉNEMENTS | EVILNESS | EWER |
| EUPHONIZES | EUTRAPELY | EVENER | EVILNESSES | EWERS |
| EUPHONIZING | EUTROPHIC | EVENEST | EVILS | EWES |
| EUPHONS | EUTROPHIES | EVENFALL | EVINCE | EWEST |
| EUPHONY | EUTROPHY | EVENFALLS | EVINCED | EWFTES |
| EUPHORBIA | EUTROPIC | EVENING | EVINCES | EWGHEN |
| EUPHORBIAS | EUTROPIES | EVENINGS | EVINCIBLE | EWHOW |
| EUPHORIA | EUTROPOUS | EVENLY | EVINCIBLY | EWK |
| EUPHORIAS | EUTROPY | EVENNESS | EVINCING | EWKED |
| EUPHORIC | EUXENITE | EVENNESSES | EVINCIVE | EWKING |
| EUPHORIES | EUXENITES | EVENS | EVIRATE | EWKS |
| EUPHORY | EVACUANT | EVENSONG | EVIRATED | EWT |
| EUPHRASIES | EVACUANTS | EVENSONGS | EVIRATES | EWTS |
| EUPHRASY | EVACUATE | EVENT | EVIRATING | EX |
| EUPHROE | EVACUATED | EVENTER | EVITABLE | EXACT |
| EUPHROES | EVACUATES | EVENTERS | EVITATE | EXACTED |
| EUPHUISE | EVACUATING | EVENTFUL | EVITATED | EXACTER |
| EUPHUISED | EVACUATOR | EVENTIDE | EVITATES | EXACTERS |
| EUPHUISES | EVACUATORS | EVENTIDES | EVITATING | EXACTEST |
| EUPHUISING | EVACUEE | EVENTING | EVITATION | EXACTING |
| EUPHUISM | EVACUEES | EVENTINGS | EVITATIONS | EXACTION |
| EUPHUISMS | EVADABLE | EVENTS | EVITE | EXACTIONS |
| EUPHUIST | EVADE | EVENTUAL | EVITED | EXACTLY |
| EUPHUISTS | EVADED | EVENTUATE | EVITERNAL | EXACTMENT |
| EUPHUIZE | EVADES | EVENTUATED | EVITES | EXACTMENTS |
| EUPHUIZED | EVADING | EVENTUATES | EVITING | EXACTNESS |
| EUPHUIZES | EVAGATION | EVENTUATING | EVOCATE | EXACTNESSES |
| EUPHUIZING | EVAGATIONS | EVER | EVOCATED | EXACTOR |
| EUREKA | EVAGINATE | EVERGLADE | EVOCATES | EXACTORS |
| EUREKAS | EVAGINATED | EVERGLADES | EVOCATING | EXACTRESS |
| EURHYTHMIES | EVAGINATES | EVERGREEN | EVOCATION | EXACTRESSES |
| EURHYTHMY | EVAGINATING | EVERGREENS | EVOCATIONS | EXACTS |
| EURIPI | EVALUATE | EVERMORE | EVOCATIVE | EXALT |
| EURIPUS | EVALUATED | EVERSIBLE | EVOCATORY | EXALTED |
| EURIPUSES | EVALUATES | EVERSION | EVOE | EXALTING |
| EURO | EVALUATING | EVERSIONS | EVOHE | EXALTS |
| EUROPIUM | EVANESCE | EVERT | EVOKE | EXAM |
| EUROPIUMS | EVANESCED | EVERTED | EVOKED | EXAMEN |
| EUROS | EVANESCES | EVERTING | EVOKES | EXAMENS |
| EURYTHERM | EVANESCING | EVERTS | EVOKING | EXAMINANT |
| EURYTHERMS | EVANGEL | EVERY | ÉVOLUÉ | EXAMINANTS |
| EURYTHMIES | EVANGELIC | EVERYBODY | ÉVOLUÉS | EXAMINATE |
| EURYTHMY | EVANGELIES | EVERYDAY | EVOLUTE | EXAMINATES |
| EUSOL | EVANGELS | EVERYDAYS | EVOLUTED | EXAMINE |
| EUSOLS | EVANGELY | EVERYONE | EVOLUTES | EXAMINED |
| EUSTACIES | EVANISH | EVERYWAY | EVOLUTING | EXAMINEE |

EXAMINEES
EXAMINER
EXAMINERS
EXAMINES
EXAMINING
EXAMPLAR
EXAMPLARS
EXAMPLE
EXAMPLED
EXAMPLES
EXAMPLING
EXAMS
EXANIMATE
EXANTHEM
EXANTHEMA
EXANTHEMATA
EXANTHEMS
EXARATE
EXARATION
EXARATIONS
EXARCH
EXARCHATE
EXARCHATES
EXARCHIES
EXARCHIST
EXARCHISTS
EXARCHS
EXARCHY
EXCAMB
EXCAMBED
EXCAMBING
EXCAMBION
EXCAMBIONS
EXCAMBIUM
EXCAMBIUMS
EXCAMBS
EXCARNATE
EXCARNATED
EXCARNATES
EXCARNATING
EXCAUDATE
EXCAVATE
EXCAVATED
EXCAVATES
EXCAVATING
EXCAVATOR
EXCAVATORS
EXCEED
EXCEEDED
EXCEEDING
EXCEEDS
EXCEL
EXCELLED
EXCELLENT
EXCELLING
EXCELS
EXCELSIOR
EXCELSIORS
EXCENTRIC
EXCENTRICS
EXCEPT
EXCEPTANT
EXCEPTANTS
EXCEPTED
EXCEPTING
EXCEPTION
EXCEPTIONS
EXCEPTIVE
EXCEPTOR
EXCEPTORS

EXCEPTS
EXCERPT
EXCERPTA
EXCERPTED
EXCERPTING
EXCERPTINGS
EXCERPTOR
EXCERPTORS
EXCERPTS
EXCERPTUM
EXCESS
EXCESSES
EXCESSIVE
EXCHANGE
EXCHANGED
EXCHANGER
EXCHANGERS
EXCHANGES
EXCHANGING
EXCHEAT
EXCHEATS
EXCHEQUER
EXCHEQUERED
EXCHEQUERING
EXCHEQUERS
EXCIDE
EXCIDED
EXCIDES
EXCIDING
EXCIPIENT
EXCIPIENTS
EXCISABLE
EXCISE
EXCISED
EXCISEMAN
EXCISEMEN
EXCISES
EXCISING
EXCISION
EXCISIONS
EXCITABLE
EXCITANCIES
EXCITANCY
EXCITANT
EXCITANTS
EXCITE
EXCITED
EXCITER
EXCITERS
EXCITES
EXCITING
EXCITON
EXCITONS
EXCITOR
EXCITORS
EXCLAIM
EXCLAIMED
EXCLAIMING
EXCLAIMS
EXCLAVE
EXCLAVES
EXCLOSURE
EXCLOSURES
EXCLUDE
EXCLUDED
EXCLUDEE
EXCLUDEES
EXCLUDES
EXCLUDING
EXCLUSION

EXCLUSIONS
EXCLUSIVE
EXCLUSIVES
EXCLUSORY
EXCORIATE
EXCORIATED
EXCORIATES
EXCORIATING
EXCREMENT
EXCREMENTS
EXCRETA
EXCRETE
EXCRETED
EXCRETES
EXCRETING
EXCRETION
EXCRETIONS
EXCRETIVE
EXCRETORIES
EXCRETORY
EXCUBANT
EXCUDIT
EXCULPATE
EXCULPATED
EXCULPATES
EXCULPATING
EXCURRENT
EXCURSE
EXCURSED
EXCURSES
EXCURSING
EXCURSION
EXCURSIONED
EXCURSIONING
EXCURSIONS
EXCURSIVE
EXCURSUS
EXCURSUSES
EXCUSABLE
EXCUSABLY
EXCUSAL
EXCUSALS
EXCUSE
EXCUSED
EXCUSER
EXCUSERS
EXCUSES
EXCUSING
EXCUSIVE
EXEAT
EXEATS
EXECRABLE
EXECRABLY
EXECRATE
EXECRATED
EXECRATES
EXECRATING
EXECUTANT
EXECUTANTS
EXECUTE
EXECUTED
EXECUTER
EXECUTERS
EXECUTES
EXECUTING
EXECUTION
EXECUTIONS
EXECUTIVE
EXECUTIVES
EXECUTOR

EXECUTORS
EXECUTORY
EXECUTRICES
EXECUTRIES
EXECUTRIX
EXECUTRIXES
EXECUTRY
EXEDRA
EXEDRAE
EXEEM
EXEEMED
EXEEMING
EXEEMS
EXEGESES
EXEGESIS
EXEGETE
EXEGETES
EXEGETIC
EXEGETICS
EXEGETIST
EXEGETISTS
EXEME
EXEMED
EXEMES
EXEMING
EXEMPLA
EXEMPLAR
EXEMPLARS
EXEMPLARY
EXEMPLE
EXEMPLES
EXEMPLIFIED
EXEMPLIFIES
EXEMPLIFY
EXEMPLIFYING
EXEMPLUM
EXEMPT
EXEMPTED
EXEMPTING
EXEMPTION
EXEMPTIONS
EXEMPTS
EXEQUATUR
EXEQUATURS
EXEQUIAL
EXEQUIES
EXEQUY
EXERCISE
EXERCISED
EXERCISER
EXERCISERS
EXERCISES
EXERCISING
EXERGUAL
EXERGUE
EXERGUES
EXERT
EXERTED
EXERTING
EXERTION
EXERTIONS
EXERTIVE
EXERTS
EXES
EXEUNT
EXFOLIATE
EXFOLIATED
EXFOLIATES
EXFOLIATING
EXHALABLE

EXHALANT
EXHALANTS
EXHALE
EXHALED
EXHALES
EXHALING
EXHAUST
EXHAUSTED
EXHAUSTER
EXHAUSTERS
EXHAUSTING
EXHAUSTS
EXHEDRA
EXHEDRAE
EXHIBIT
EXHIBITED
EXHIBITER
EXHIBITERS
EXHIBITING
EXHIBITOR
EXHIBITORS
EXHIBITS
EXHORT
EXHORTED
EXHORTER
EXHORTERS
EXHORTING
EXHORTS
EXHUMATE
EXHUMATED
EXHUMATES
EXHUMATING
EXHUME
EXHUMED
EXHUMER
EXHUMERS
EXHUMES
EXHUMING
EXIES
EXIGEANT
EXIGEANTE
EXIGENCE
EXIGENCES
EXIGENCIES
EXIGENCY
EXIGENT
EXIGENTS
EXIGIBLE
EXIGUITIES
EXIGUITY
EXIGUOUS
EXILE
EXILED
EXILEMENT
EXILEMENTS
EXILES
EXILIAN
EXILIC
EXILING
EXILITIES
EXILITY
EXIMIOUS
EXINE
EXINES
EXIST
EXISTED
EXISTENCE
EXISTENCES
EXISTENT
EXISTING

EXISTS
EXIT
EXITANCE
EXITANCES
EXITED
EXITING
EXITS
EXOCARP
EXOCARPS
EXOCRINE
EXOCRINES
EXODE
EXODERM
EXODERMAL
EXODERMIS
EXODERMISES
EXODERMS
EXODES
EXODIC
EXODIST
EXODISTS
EXODUS
EXODUSES
EXOENZYME
EXOENZYMES
EXOERGIC
EXOGAMIC
EXOGAMIES
EXOGAMOUS
EXOGAMY
EXOGEN
EXOGENOUS
EXOGENS
EXOMION
EXOMIONS
EXOMIS
EXOMISES
EXON
EXONERATE
EXONERATED
EXONERATES
EXONERATING
EXONS
EXONYM
EXONYMS
EXOPHAGIES
EXOPHAGY
EXOPLASM
EXOPLASMS
EXOPOD
EXOPODITE
EXOPODITES
EXOPODS
EXORABLE
EXORATION
EXORATIONS
EXORCISE
EXORCISED
EXORCISER
EXORCISERS
EXORCISES
EXORCISING
EXORCISM
EXORCISMS
EXORCIST
EXORCISTS
EXORCIZE
EXORCIZED
EXORCIZER
EXORCIZERS

EXORCIZES
EXORCIZING
EXORDIA
EXORDIAL
EXORDIUM
EXORDIUMS
EXOSMOSE
EXOSMOSES
EXOSMOSIS
EXOSMOTIC
EXOSPHERE
EXOSPHERES
EXOSPORAL
EXOSPORE
EXOSPORES
EXOSTOSES
EXOSTOSIS
EXOTERIC
EXOTIC
EXOTICA
EXOTICISM
EXOTICISMS
EXOTICS
EXOTOXIC
EXOTOXIN
EXOTOXINS
EXPAND
EXPANDED
EXPANDER
EXPANDERS
EXPANDING
EXPANDOR
EXPANDORS
EXPANDS
EXPANSE
EXPANSES
EXPANSILE
EXPANSION
EXPANSIONS
EXPANSIVE
EXPAT
EXPATIATE
EXPATIATED
EXPATIATES
EXPATIATING
EXPATS
EXPECT
EXPECTANT
EXPECTANTS
EXPECTED
EXPECTER
EXPECTERS
EXPECTING
EXPECTINGS
EXPECTS
EXPEDIENT
EXPEDIENTS
EXPEDITE
EXPEDITED
EXPEDITES
EXPEDITING
EXPEL
EXPELLANT
EXPELLANTS
EXPELLED
EXPELLEE
EXPELLEES
EXPELLENT
EXPELLENTS
EXPELLING

EXPELS
EXPEND
EXPENDED
EXPENDER
EXPENDERS
EXPENDING
EXPENDS
EXPENSE
EXPENSES
EXPENSIVE
EXPERT
EXPERTED
EXPERTING
EXPERTISE
EXPERTISED
EXPERTISES
EXPERTISING
EXPERTIZE
EXPERTIZED
EXPERTIZES
EXPERTIZING
EXPERTLY
EXPERTS
EXPIABLE
EXPIATE
EXPIATED
EXPIATES
EXPIATING
EXPIATION
EXPIATIONS
EXPIATOR
EXPIATORS
EXPIATORY
EXPIRABLE
EXPIRANT
EXPIRANTS
EXPIRE
EXPIRED
EXPIRES
EXPIRIES
EXPIRING
EXPIRY
EXPISCATE
EXPISCATED
EXPISCATES
EXPISCATING
EXPLAIN
EXPLAINED
EXPLAINER
EXPLAINERS
EXPLAINING
EXPLAINS
EXPLANT
EXPLANTED
EXPLANTING
EXPLANTS
EXPLETIVE
EXPLETIVES
EXPLETORY
EXPLICATE
EXPLICATED
EXPLICATES
EXPLICATING
EXPLICIT
EXPLICITS
EXPLODE
EXPLODED
EXPLODER
EXPLODERS
EXPLODES

EXPLODING
EXPLOIT
EXPLOITED
EXPLOITER
EXPLOITERS
EXPLOITING
EXPLOITS
EXPLORE
EXPLORED
EXPLORER
EXPLORERS
EXPLORES
EXPLORING
EXPLOSION
EXPLOSIONS
EXPLOSIVE
EXPLOSIVES
EXPO
EXPONENT
EXPONENTS
EXPONIBLE
EXPORT
EXPORTED
EXPORTER
EXPORTERS
EXPORTING
EXPORTS
EXPOS
EXPOSAL
EXPOSALS
EXPOSE
EXPOSÉ
EXPOSED
EXPOSER
EXPOSERS
EXPOSÉS
EXPOSES
EXPOSING
EXPOSITOR
EXPOSITORS
EXPOSTURE
EXPOSTURES
EXPOSURE
EXPOSURES
EXPOUND
EXPOUNDED
EXPOUNDER
EXPOUNDERS
EXPOUNDING
EXPOUNDS
EXPRESS
EXPRESSED
EXPRESSES
EXPRESSING
EXPRESSLY
EXPRESSO
EXPRESSOS
EXPUGN
EXPUGNED
EXPUGNING
EXPUGNS
EXPULSE
EXPULSED
EXPULSES
EXPULSING
EXPULSION
EXPULSIONS
EXPULSIVE
EXPUNCT
EXPUNCTED

EXPUNCTING
EXPUNCTS
EXPUNGE
EXPUNGED
EXPUNGER
EXPUNGERS
EXPUNGES
EXPUNGING
EXPURGATE
EXPURGATED
EXPURGATES
EXPURGATING
EXPURGE
EXPURGED
EXPURGES
EXPURGING
EXQUISITE
EXQUISITES
EXSCIND
EXSCINDED
EXSCINDING
EXSCINDS
EXSECT
EXSECTED
EXSECTING
EXSECTION
EXSECTIONS
EXSECTS
EXSERT
EXSERTED
EXSERTILE
EXSERTING
EXSERTION
EXSERTIONS
EXSERTS
EXSICCANT
EXSICCATE
EXSICCATED
EXSICCATES
EXSICCATING
EXSUCCOUS
EXTANT
EXTASIES
EXTASY
EXTATIC
EXTEMPORE
EXTEMPORES
EXTEND
EXTENDANT
EXTENDED
EXTENDER
EXTENDERS
EXTENDING
EXTENDS
EXTENSE
EXTENSILE
EXTENSION
EXTENSIONS
EXTENSITIES
EXTENSITY
EXTENSIVE
EXTENSOR
EXTENSORS
EXTENT
EXTENTS
EXTENUATE
EXTENUATED
EXTENUATES
EXTENUATING
EXTENUATINGS

| | | | | |
|---|---|---|---|---|
| EXTERIOR | EXTORTION | EXTRICATED | EXULTANCY | EYEHOOKS |
| EXTERIORS | EXTORTIONS | EXTRICATES | EXULTANT | EYEING |
| EXTERMINE | EXTORTIVE | EXTRICATING | EXULTED | EYELASH |
| EXTERMINED | EXTORTS | EXTRINSIC | EXULTING | EYELASHES |
| EXTERMINES | EXTRA | EXTRORSE | EXULTS | EYELESS |
| EXTERMINING | EXTRACT | EXTROVERT | EXURB | EYELET |
| EXTERN | EXTRACTED | EXTROVERTED | EXURBAN | EYELETED |
| EXTERNAL | EXTRACTING | EXTROVERTING | EXURBIA | EYELETING |
| EXTERNALS | EXTRACTOR | EXTROVERTS | EXURBIAS | EYELETS |
| EXTERNAT | EXTRACTORS | EXTRUDE | EXURBS | EYELIAD |
| EXTERNATS | EXTRACTS | EXTRUDED | EXUVIAE | EYELIADS |
| EXTERNE | EXTRADITE | EXTRUDER | EXUVIAL | EYELID |
| EXTERNES | EXTRADITED | EXTRUDERS | EXUVIATE | EYELIDS |
| EXTERNS | EXTRADITES | EXTRUDES | EXUVIATED | EYELINER |
| EXTINCT | EXTRADITING | EXTRUDING | EXUVIATES | EYELINERS |
| EXTINCTED | EXTRADOS | EXTRUSION | EXUVIATING | EYES |
| EXTINE | EXTRADOSES | EXTRUSIONS | EYALET | EYESHADE |
| EXTINES | EXTRAIT | EXTRUSIVE | EYALETS | EYESHADES |
| EXTIRP | EXTRAITS | EXTRUSORY | EYAS | EYESIGHT |
| EXTIRPATE | EXTRAS | EXUBERANT | EYASES | EYESIGHTS |
| EXTIRPATED | EXTRAUGHT | EXUBERATE | EYE | EYESORE |
| EXTIRPATES | EXTRAVERT | EXUBERATED | EYEBALL | EYESORES |
| EXTIRPATING | EXTRAVERTED | EXUBERATES | EYEBALLED | EYESTALK |
| EXTIRPED | EXTRAVERTING | EXUBERATING | EYEBALLING | EYESTALKS |
| EXTIRPING | EXTRAVERTS | EXUDATE | EYEBALLS | EYESTRAIN |
| EXTIRPS | EXTREAT | EXUDATES | EYEBOLT | EYESTRAINS |
| EXTOL | EXTREATS | EXUDATION | EYEBOLTS | EYING |
| EXTOLD | EXTREME | EXUDATIONS | EYEBRIGHT | EYLIAD |
| EXTOLLED | EXTREMELY | EXUDATIVE | EYEBRIGHTS | EYLIADS |
| EXTOLLER | EXTREMER | EXUDE | EYEBROW | EYNE |
| EXTOLLERS | EXTREMES | EXUDED | EYEBROWED | EYOT |
| EXTOLLING | EXTREMEST | EXUDES | EYEBROWING | EYOTS |
| EXTOLMENT | EXTREMISM | EXUDING | EYEBROWS | EYRA |
| EXTOLMENTS | EXTREMISMS | EXUL | EYED | EYRAS |
| EXTOLS | EXTREMIST | EXULS | EYEFUL | EYRE |
| EXTORSIVE | EXTREMISTS | EXULT | EYEFULS | EYRES |
| EXTORT | EXTREMITIES | EXULTANCE | EYEGLASS | EYRIE |
| EXTORTED | EXTREMITY | EXULTANCES | EYEGLASSES | EYRIES |
| EXTORTING | EXTRICATE | EXULTANCIES | EYEHOOK | EYRY |

# F

| | | | | |
|---|---|---|---|---|
| FA | FACILITIES | FADDISMS | FAHLERZ | FAIRING |
| FAB | FACILITY | FADDIST | FAHLERZES | FAIRINGS |
| FABACEOUS | FACING | FADDISTS | FAHLORE | FAIRISH |
| FABBER | FACINGS | FADDLE | FAHLORES | FAIRLY |
| FABBEST | FAÇONNÉ | FADDLED | FAHS | FAIRNESS |
| FABLE | FAÇONNÉS | FADDLES | FAIBLE | FAIRNESSES |
| FABLED | FACSIMILE | FADDLING | FAIBLES | FAIRS |
| FABLER | FACSIMILED | FADDY | FAÏENCE | FAIRWAY |
| FABLERS | FACSIMILEING | FADE | FAIENCE | FAIRWAYS |
| FABLES | FACSIMILES | FADED | FAÏENCES | FAIRY |
| FABLIAU | FACT | FADEDLY | FAIENCES | FAIRYDOM |
| FABLIAUX | FACTION | FADEDNESS | FAIK | FAIRYDOMS |
| FABLING | FACTIONAL | FADEDNESSES | FAIKED | FAIRYHOOD |
| FABLINGS | FACTIONS | FADELESS | FAIKES | FAIRYHOODS |
| FABRIC | FACTIOUS | FADES | FAIKING | FAIRYISM |
| FABRICANT | FACTITIVE | FADEUR | FAIKS | FAIRYISMS |
| FABRICANTS | FACTIVE | FADEURS | FAIL | FAIRYLAND |
| FABRICATE | FACTOID | FADGE | FAILED | FAIRYLANDS |
| FABRICATED | FACTOIDS | FADGED | FAILING | FAIRYLIKE |
| FABRICATES | FACTOR | FADGES | FAILINGS | FAITH |
| FABRICATING | FACTORAGE | FADGING | FAILLE | FAITHED |
| FABRICKED | FACTORAGES | FADIER | FAILLES | FAITHFUL |
| FABRICKING | FACTORED | FADIEST | FAILS | FAITHING |
| FABRICS | FACTORIAL | FADING | FAILURE | FAITHLESS |
| FABULAR | FACTORIALS | FADINGS | FAILURES | FAITHS |
| FABULISE | FACTORIES | FADO | FAIN | FAITOR |
| FABULISED | FACTORING | FADOS | FAINE | FAITORS |
| FABULISES | FACTORINGS | FADS | FAINÉANCE | FAITOUR |
| FABULISING | FACTORISE | FADY | FAINÉANCES | FAITOURS |
| FABULIST | FACTORISED | FAECAL | FAINÉANCIES | FAIX |
| FABULISTS | FACTORISES | FAECES | FAINÉANCY | FAKE |
| FABULIZE | FACTORISING | FAERIE | FAINÉANT | FAKED |
| FABULIZED | FACTORIZE | FAERIES | FAINÉANTS | FAKEMENT |
| FABULIZES | FACTORIZED | FAERY | FAINED | FAKEMENTS |
| FABULIZING | FACTORIZES | FAFF | FAINER | FAKER |
| FABULOUS | FACTORIZING | FAFFED | FAINES | FAKERIES |
| FABURDEN | FACTORS | FAFFING | FAINEST | FAKERS |
| FABURDENS | FACTORY | FAFFS | FAINING | FAKERY |
| FAÇADE | FACTOTUM | FAG | FAINITES | FAKES |
| FAÇADES | FACTOTUMS | FAGACEOUS | FAINLY | FAKING |
| FACE | FACTS | FAGGED | FAINNESS | FAKIR |
| FACED | FACTUAL | FAGGERIES | FAINNESSES | FAKIRISM |
| FACELESS | FACTUM | FAGGERY | FAINS | FAKIRISMS |
| FACEMAN | FACTUMS | FAGGING | FAINT | FAKIRS |
| FACEMEN | FACTURE | FAGGINGS | FAINTED | FALAFEL |
| FACER | FACTURES | FAGGOT | FAINTER | FALAFELS |
| FACERS | FACULA | FAGGOTED | FAINTEST | FALAJ |
| FACES | FACULAE | FAGGOTING | FAINTIER | FALANGISM |
| FACET | FACULAR | FAGGOTINGS | FAINTIEST | FALANGISMS |
| FACETE | FACULTIES | FAGGOTS | FAINTING | FALANGIST |
| FACETED | FACULTY | FAGOT | FAINTINGS | FALANGISTS |
| FACETIAE | FACUNDITIES | FAGOTED | FAINTISH | FALBALA |
| FACETING | FACUNDITY | FAGOTING | FAINTLY | FALBALAS |
| FACETIOUS | FAD | FAGOTINGS | FAINTNESS | FALCADE |
| FACETS | FADABLE | FAGOTS | FAINTNESSES | FALCADES |
| FACIA | FADAISE | FAGOTTI | FAINTS | FALCATE |
| FACIAL | FADAISES | FAGOTTIST | FAINTY | FALCATED |
| FACIALLY | FADDIER | FAGOTTISTS | FAIR | FALCATION |
| FACIALS | FADDIEST | FAGOTTO | FAIRED | FALCATIONS |
| FACIAS | FADDINESS | FAGS | FAIRER | FALCES |
| FACIES | FADDINESSES | FAH | FAIREST | FALCHION |
| FACILE | FADDISH | FAHLBAND | FAIRIES | FALCHIONS |
| FACILELY | FADDISM | FAHLBANDS | FAIRILY | FALCIFORM |

FALCON
FALCONER
FALCONERS
FALCONET
FALCONETS
FALCONINE
FALCONRIES
FALCONRY
FALCONS
FALCULA
FALCULAS
FALCULATE
FALDAGE
FALDAGES
FALDERAL
FALDERALS
FALDETTA
FALDETTAS
FALDSTOOL
FALDSTOOLS
FALL
FALLACIES
FALLACY
FALLAL
FALLALERIES
FALLALERY
FALLALS
FALLEN
FALLIBLE
FALLIBLY
FALLING
FALLINGS
FALLOW
FALLOWED
FALLOWER
FALLOWEST
FALLOWING
FALLOWS
FALLS
FALSE
FALSED
FALSEHOOD
FALSEHOODS
FALSELY
FALSENESS
FALSENESSES
FALSER
FALSERS
FALSES
FALSEST
FALSETTO
FALSETTOS
FALSEWORK
FALSEWORKS
FALSIE
FALSIES
FALSIFIED
FALSIFIER
FALSIFIERS
FALSIFIES
FALSIFY
FALSIFYING
FALSING
FALSISH
FALSISM
FALSISMS
FALSITIES
FALSITY
FALTBOAT
FALTBOATS

FALTER
FALTERED
FALTERING
FALTERINGS
FALTERS
FALX
FAME
FAMED
FAMELESS
FAMES
FAMILIAL
FAMILIAR
FAMILIARS
FAMILIES
FAMILISM
FAMILISMS
FAMILY
FAMINE
FAMINES
FAMING
FAMISH
FAMISHED
FAMISHES
FAMISHING
FAMOUS
FAMOUSED
FAMOUSES
FAMOUSING
FAMOUSLY
FAMULUS
FAMULUSES
FAN
FANAL
FANALS
FANATIC
FANATICAL
FANATICS
FANCIED
FANCIER
FANCIERS
FANCIES
FANCIEST
FANCIFUL
FANCILESS
FANCY
FANCYING
FANCYWORK
FANCYWORKS
FAND
FANDANGLE
FANDANGLES
FANDANGO
FANDANGOS
FANDED
FANDING
FANDOM
FANDOMS
FANDS
FANE
FANES
FANFARADE
FANFARADES
FANFARE
FANFARED
FANFARES
FANFARING
FANFARON
FANFARONA
FANFARONAS
FANFARONS

FANFOLD
FANG
FANGED
FANGING
FANGLE
FANGLED
FANGLES
FANGLESS
FANGLING
FANGO
FANGOS
FANGS
FANION
FANIONS
FANK
FANKLE
FANKLED
FANKLES
FANKLING
FANKS
FANLIGHT
FANLIGHTS
FANNED
FANNEL
FANNELL
FANNELLS
FANNELS
FANNER
FANNERS
FANNIES
FANNING
FANNINGS
FANNY
FANON
FANONS
FANS
FANTAD
FANTADS
FANTAIL
FANTAILED
FANTAILS
FANTASIA
FANTASIAS
FANTASIED
FANTASIES
FANTASISE
FANTASISED
FANTASISES
FANTASISING
FANTASIST
FANTASISTS
FANTASIZE
FANTASIZED
FANTASIZES
FANTASIZING
FANTASM
FANTASMS
FANTASQUE
FANTASQUES
FANTAST
FANTASTIC
FANTASTICS
FANTASTRIES
FANTASTRY
FANTASTS
FANTASY
FANTASYING
FANTEEG
FANTEEGS
FANTIGUE

FANTIGUES
FANTOD
FANTODS
FANTOM
FANTOMS
FANTOOSH
FANZINE
FANZINES
FAP
FAQUIR
FAQUIRS
FAR
FARAD
FARADAY
FARADAYS
FARADIC
FARADISE
FARADISED
FARADISES
FARADISING
FARADISM
FARADISMS
FARADIZE
FARADIZED
FARADIZES
FARADIZING
FARADS
FARAND
FARANDINE
FARANDINES
FARANDOLE
FARANDOLES
FARAWAY
FARAWAYS
FARCE
FARCED
FARCES
FARCEUR
FARCEURS
FARCEUSE
FARCEUSES
FARCI
FARCICAL
FARCIED
FARCIES
FARCIFIED
FARCIFIES
FARCIFY
FARCIFYING
FARCIN
FARCING
FARCINGS
FARCINS
FARCY
FARD
FARDAGE
FARDAGES
FARDED
FARDEL
FARDELS
FARDEN
FARDENS
FARDING
FARDINGS
FARDS
FARE
FARED
FARES
FAREWELL
FAREWELLS

FARFET
FARINA
FARINAS
FARING
FARINOSE
FARL
FARLE
FARLES
FARLS
FARM
FARMED
FARMER
FARMERESS
FARMERESSES
FARMERIES
FARMERS
FARMERY
FARMHOUSE
FARMHOUSES
FARMING
FARMINGS
FARMOST
FARMS
FARMSTEAD
FARMSTEADS
FARMYARD
FARMYARDS
FARNESOL
FARNESOLS
FARNESS
FARNESSES
FARO
FAROS
FAROUCHE
FARRAGO
FARRAGOES
FARRAND
FARRANT
FARRED
FARREN
FARRENS
FARRIER
FARRIERIES
FARRIERS
FARRIERY
FARRING
FARROW
FARROWED
FARROWING
FARROWS
FARRUCA
FARRUCAS
FARS
FARSE
FARSED
FARSES
FARSING
FART
FARTED
FARTHEL
FARTHELS
FARTHER
FARTHEST
FARTHING
FARTHINGS
FARTING
FARTS
FAS
FASCES
FASCI

| | | | | |
|---|---|---|---|---|
| FASCIA | FATAL | FAUCES | FAWNERS | FEATLY |
| FASCIAL | FATALISM | FAUCET | FAWNING | FEATOUS |
| FASCIAS | FATALISMS | FAUCETS | FAWNINGLY | FEATS |
| FASCIATE | FATALIST | FAUCHION | FAWNINGS | FEATUOUS |
| FASCIATED | FATALISTS | FAUCHIONS | FAWNS | FEATURE |
| FASCICLE | FATALITIES | FAUCHON | FAWS | FEATURED |
| FASCICLED | FATALITY | FAUCHONS | FAX | FEATURELY |
| FASCICLES | FATALLY | FAUCIAL | FAXED | FEATURES |
| FASCICULE | FATE | FAUGH | FAXES | FEATURING |
| FASCICULES | FATED | FAULCHIN | FAXING | FEBLESSE |
| FASCICULI | FATEFUL | FAULCHINS | FAY | FEBLESSES |
| FASCINATE | FATEFULLY | FAULCHION | FAYALITE | FEBRICITIES |
| FASCINATED | FATES | FAULCHIONS | FAYALITES | FEBRICITY |
| FASCINATES | FATHER | FAULT | FAYED | FEBRICULA |
| FASCINATING | FATHERED | FAULTED | FAYENCE | FEBRICULAS |
| FASCINE | FATHERING | FAULTFUL | FAYENCES | FEBRICULE |
| FASCINES | FATHERLY | FAULTIER | FAYER | FEBRICULES |
| FASCIO | FATHERS | FAULTIEST | FAYEST | FEBRIFIC |
| FASCIOLA | FATHOM | FAULTILY | FAYING | FEBRIFUGE |
| FASCIOLAS | FATHOMED | FAULTING | FAYNE | FEBRIFUGES |
| FASCIOLE | FATHOMING | FAULTLESS | FAYNED | FEBRILE |
| FASCIOLES | FATHOMS | FAULTS | FAYNES | FEBRILITIES |
| FASCISM | FATIDICAL | FAULTY | FAYNING | FEBRILITY |
| FASCISMI | FATIGABLE | FAUN | FAYS | FECAL |
| FASCISMO | FATIGATE | FAUNA | FAZE | FECES |
| FASCISMS | FATIGATED | FAUNAE | FAZED | FECHT |
| FASCIST | FATIGATES | FAUNAL | FAZES | FECHTER |
| FASCISTA | FATIGATING | FAUNAS | FAZING | FECHTERS |
| FASCISTI | FATIGUE | FAUNIST | FEAGUE | FECHTING |
| FASCISTIC | FATIGUED | FAUNISTIC | FEAGUED | FECHTS |
| FASCISTS | FATIGUES | FAUNISTS | FEAGUES | FECIAL |
| FASH | FATIGUING | FAUNS | FEAGUING | FECIT |
| FASHED | FATISCENT | FAURD | FEAL | FECK |
| FASHERIES | FATLING | FAUSTIAN | FEALED | FECKLESS |
| FASHERY | FATLINGS | FAUTEUIL | FEALING | FECKLY |
| FASHES | FATLY | FAUTEUILS | FEALS | FECKS |
| FASHING | FATNESS | FAUTOR | FEALTIES | FECULA |
| FASHION | FATNESSES | FAUTORS | FEALTY | FECULAS |
| FASHIONED | FATS | FAUVETTE | FEAR | FECULENCE |
| FASHIONER | FATSO | FAUVETTES | FEARE | FECULENCES |
| FASHIONERS | FATSOES | FAUX | FEARED | FECULENCIES |
| FASHIONING | FATSOS | FAVEL | FEARES | FECULENCY |
| FASHIONS | FATSTOCK | FAVELA | FEARFUL | FECULENT |
| FASHIOUS | FATSTOCKS | FAVELAS | FEARFULLY | FECUND |
| FAST | FATTED | FAVELL | FEARING | FECUNDATE |
| FASTBACK | FATTEN | FAVEOLATE | FEARLESS | FECUNDATED |
| FASTBACKS | FATTENED | FAVISM | FEARS | FECUNDATES |
| FASTED | FATTENER | FAVISMS | FEARSOME | FECUNDATING |
| FASTEN | FATTENERS | FAVOR | FEASIBLE | FECUNDITIES |
| FASTENED | FATTENING | FAVORED | FEASIBLY | FECUNDITY |
| FASTENER | FATTENINGS | FAVORING | FEAST | FED |
| FASTENERS | FATTENS | FAVORS | FEASTED | FEDARIE |
| FASTENING | FATTER | FAVOSE | FEASTER | FEDARIES |
| FASTENINGS | FATTEST | FAVOUR | FEASTERS | FEDAYEE |
| FASTENS | FATTIER | FAVOURED | FEASTFUL | FEDAYEEN |
| FASTER | FATTIES | FAVOURER | FEASTING | FEDELINI |
| FASTERS | FATTIEST | FAVOURERS | FEASTINGS | FEDELINIS |
| FASTEST | FATTINESS | FAVOURING | FEASTS | FEDERACIES |
| FASTI | FATTINESSES | FAVOURITE | FEAT | FEDERACY |
| FASTIGIUM | FATTING | FAVOURITES | FEATED | FEDERAL |
| FASTIGIUMS | FATTISH | FAVOURS | FEATEOUS | FEDERALS |
| FASTING | FATTRELS | FAVOUS | FEATHER | FEDERARIE |
| FASTINGS | FATTY | FAVRILE | FEATHERED | FEDERARIES |
| FASTISH | FATUITIES | FAVRILES | FEATHERIER | FEDERARY |
| FASTLY | FATUITOUS | FAVUS | FEATHERIEST | FEDERATE |
| FASTNESS | FATUITY | FAVUSES | FEATHERING | FEDERATED |
| FASTNESSES | FATUOUS | FAW | FEATHERINGS | FEDERATES |
| FASTS | FAUBOURG | FAWN | FEATHERS | FEDERATING |
| FASTUOUS | FAUBOURGS | FAWNED | FEATHERY | FEDORA |
| FAT | FAUCAL | FAWNER | FEATING | FEDORAS |

FEDS
FEE
FÉE
FEEBLE
FEEBLED
FEEBLER
FEEBLES
FEEBLEST
FEEBLING
FEEBLISH
FEEBLY
FEED
FEEDBACK
FEEDBACKS
FEEDER
FEEDERS
FEEDING
FEEDINGS
FEEDLOT
FEEDLOTS
FEEDS
FEEDSTOCK
FEEDSTOCKS
FEEDSTUFF
FEEDSTUFFS
FEEING
FEEL
FEELER
FEELERS
FEELING
FEELINGLY
FEELINGS
FEELS
FEER
FEERED
FÉERIE
FÉERIES
FEERIN
FEERING
FEERINGS
FEERINS
FEERS
FEES
FEESE
FEESED
FEESES
FEESING
FEET
FEETLESS
FEEZE
FEEZED
FEEZES
FEEZING
FEGARIES
FEGARY
FEGS
FEHM
FEHME
FEHMIC
FEIGN
FEIGNED
FEIGNEDLY
FEIGNING
FEIGNINGS
FEIGNS
FEINT
FEINTED
FEINTER
FEINTEST
FEINTING

FEINTS
FEIS
FEISEANNA
FEISTIER
FEISTIEST
FEISTY
FELAFEL
FELAFELS
FELDGRAU
FELDGRAUS
FELDSHER
FELDSHERS
FELDSPAR
FELDSPARS
FELDSPATH
FELDSPATHS
FELICIFIC
FELICITER
FELICITIES
FELICITY
FELINE
FELINES
FELINITIES
FELINITY
FELL
FELLA
FELLABLE
FELLAH
FELLAHÎN
FELLAHS
FELLAS
FELLATE
FELLATED
FELLATES
FELLATING
FELLATIO
FELLATION
FELLATIONS
FELLATIOS
FELLED
FELLER
FELLERS
FELLEST
FELLIES
FELLING
FELLNESS
FELLNESSES
FELLOE
FELLOES
FELLOW
FELLOWLY
FELLOWS
FELLS
FELLY
FELON
FELONIES
FELONIOUS
FELONOUS
FELONRIES
FELONRY
FELONS
FELONY
FELSITE
FELSITES
FELSITIC
FELSPAR
FELSPARS
FELSTONE
FELSTONES
FELT

FELTED
FELTER
FELTERED
FELTERING
FELTERS
FELTING
FELTINGS
FELTS
FELUCCA
FELUCCAS
FELWORT
FELWORTS
FEMAL
FEMALE
FEMALES
FEMALITIES
FEMALITY
FEMALS
FEME
FEMERALL
FEMERALLS
FEMES
FEMETARIES
FEMETARY
FEMINAL
FEMINEITIES
FEMINEITY
FEMININE
FEMININES
FEMINISE
FEMINISED
FEMINISES
FEMINISING
FEMINISM
FEMINISMS
FEMINIST
FEMINISTS
FEMINITIES
FEMINITY
FEMINIZE
FEMINIZED
FEMINIZES
FEMINIZING
FEMITER
FEMITERS
FEMME
FEMMES
FEMORA
FEMORAL
FEMUR
FEMURS
FEN
FENCE
FENCED
FENCELESS
FENCER
FENCERS
FENCES
FENCIBLE
FENCIBLES
FENCING
FENCINGS
FEND
FENDED
FENDER
FENDERS
FENDIER
FENDIEST
FENDING
FENDS

FENDY
FENESTRA
FENESTRAL
FENESTRALS
FENESTRAS
FENITAR
FENITARS
FENKS
FENLAND
FENLANDS
FENMAN
FENMEN
FENNEC
FENNECS
FENNEL
FENNELS
FENNIER
FENNIEST
FENNISH
FENNY
FENS
FENT
FENTS
FENUGREEK
FENUGREEKS
FEOD
FEODAL
FEODARIES
FEODARY
FEODS
FEOFF
FEOFFED
FEOFFEE
FEOFFEES
FEOFFER
FEOFFERS
FEOFFING
FEOFFMENT
FEOFFMENTS
FEOFFOR
FEOFFORS
FEOFFS
FERACIOUS
FERACITIES
FERACITY
FERAL
FERALISED
FERALIZED
FERE
FERER
FERES
FEREST
FERETORIES
FERETORY
FERIAL
FERINE
FERITIES
FERITY
FERLIED
FERLIER
FERLIES
FERLIEST
FERLY
FERLYING
FERM
FERMATA
FERMATAS
FERMENT
FERMENTED
FERMENTING

FERMENTS
FERMI
FERMION
FERMIONS
FERMIS
FERMIUM
FERMIUMS
FERMS
FERN
FERNBIRD
FERNBIRDS
FERNERIES
FERNERY
FERNIER
FERNIEST
FERNING
FERNINGS
FERNS
FERNSHAW
FERNSHAWS
FERNTICLE
FERNTICLES
FERNY
FEROCIOUS
FEROCITIES
FEROCITY
FERRATE
FERRATES
FERREL
FERRELS
FERREOUS
FERRET
FERRETED
FERRETER
FERRETERS
FERRETING
FERRETS
FERRETY
FERRIAGE
FERRIAGES
FERRIC
FERRIED
FERRIES
FERRITE
FERRITES
FERRITIC
FERROTYPE
FERROTYPES
FERROUS
FERRUGO
FERRUGOS
FERRULE
FERRULES
FERRY
FERRYING
FERRYMAN
FERRYMEN
FERTILE
FERTILELY
FERTILER
FERTILEST
FERTILISE
FERTILISED
FERTILISES
FERTILISING
FERTILITIES
FERTILITY
FERTILIZE
FERTILIZED
FERTILIZES

FERTILIZING
FERULA
FERULAS
FERULE
FERULES
FERVENCIES
FERVENCY
FERVENT
FERVENTER
FERVENTEST
FERVENTLY
FERVID
FERVIDER
FERVIDEST
FERVIDITIES
FERVIDITY
FERVIDLY
FERVOROUS
FERVOUR
FERVOURS
FESCUE
FESCUES
FESS
FESSE
FESSES
FEST
FESTA
FESTAL
FESTALLY
FESTALS
FESTAS
FESTER
FESTERED
FESTERING
FESTERS
FESTILOGIES
FESTILOGY
FESTINATE
FESTINATED
FESTINATES
FESTINATING
FESTIVAL
FESTIVALS
FESTIVE
FESTIVELY
FESTIVITIES
FESTIVITY
FESTIVOUS
FESTOLOGIES
FESTOLOGY
FESTOON
FESTOONED
FESTOONING
FESTOONS
FESTS
FET
FETA
FETAL
FETAS
FETCH
FETCHED
FETCHES
FETCHING
FÊTE
FÊTED
FÊTES
FETIAL
FETICH
FETICHE
FETICHES

FETICHISE
FETICHISED
FETICHISES
FETICHISING
FETICHISM
FETICHISMS
FETICHIST
FETICHISTS
FETICHIZE
FETICHIZED
FETICHIZES
FETICHIZING
FETICIDAL
FETICIDE
FETICIDES
FETID
FETIDER
FETIDEST
FETIDNESS
FETIDNESSES
FÊTING
FETISH
FETISHES
FETISHISE
FETISHISED
FETISHISES
FETISHISING
FETISHISM
FETISHISMS
FETISHIST
FETISHISTS
FETISHIZE
FETISHIZED
FETISHIZES
FETISHIZING
FETLOCK
FETLOCKED
FETLOCKS
FETOR
FETORS
FETOSCOPIES
FETOSCOPY
FETS
FETT
FETTA
FETTAS
FETTED
FETTER
FETTERED
FETTERING
FETTERS
FETTING
FETTLE
FETTLED
FETTLER
FETTLERS
FETTLES
FETTLING
FETTLINGS
FETTS
FETTUCINE
FETTUCINES
FETTUCINI
FETTUCINIS
FETUS
FETUSES
FETWA
FETWAS
FEU
FEUAR

FEUARS
FEUD
FEUDAL
FEUDALISE
FEUDALISED
FEUDALISES
FEUDALISING
FEUDALISM
FEUDALISMS
FEUDALIST
FEUDALISTS
FEUDALITIES
FEUDALITY
FEUDALIZE
FEUDALIZED
FEUDALIZES
FEUDALIZING
FEUDALLY
FEUDARIES
FEUDARY
FEUDATORIES
FEUDATORY
FEUDED
FEUDING
FEUDINGS
FEUDIST
FEUDISTS
FEUDS
FEUED
FEUILLETÉ
FEUILLETÉS
FEUING
FEUS
FEUTRE
FEUTRED
FEUTRES
FEUTRING
FEVER
FEVERED
FEVERFEW
FEVERFEWS
FEVERING
FEVERISH
FEVEROUS
FEVERS
FEW
FEWER
FEWEST
FEWMET
FEWMETS
FEWNESS
FEWNESSES
FEWTER
FEWTERED
FEWTERING
FEWTERS
FEWTRILS
FEY
FEYED
FEYER
FEYEST
FEYING
FEYS
FEZ
FEZES
FEZZED
FEZZES
FIACRE
FIACRES
FIANCÉ

FIANCÉE
FIANCÉES
FIANCÉS
FIAR
FIARS
FIASCO
FIASCOES
FIASCOS
FIAT
FIATED
FIATING
FIATS
FIAUNT
FIAUNTS
FIB
FIBBED
FIBBER
FIBBERIES
FIBBERS
FIBBERY
FIBBING
FIBER
FIBERS
FIBRE
FIBRED
FIBRELESS
FIBRES
FIBRIFORM
FIBRIL
FIBRILLA
FIBRILLAE
FIBRILLAR
FIBRILS
FIBRIN
FIBRINOUS
FIBRINS
FIBRO
FIBROCYTE
FIBROCYTES
FIBROID
FIBROIDS
FIBROIN
FIBROINS
FIBROLINE
FIBROLINES
FIBROLITE
FIBROLITES
FIBROMA
FIBROMAS
FIBROMATA
FIBROS
FIBROSE
FIBROSED
FIBROSES
FIBROSING
FIBROSIS
FIBROTIC
FIBROUS
FIBS
FIBSTER
FIBSTERS
FIBULA
FIBULAR
FIBULAS
FICHE
FICHES
FICHU
FICHUS
FICKLE
FICKLED

FICKLER
FICKLES
FICKLEST
FICKLING
FICO
FICOS
FICTILE
FICTION
FICTIONAL
FICTIONS
FICTIVE
FICTOR
FICTORS
FID
FIDDIOUS
FIDDIOUSED
FIDDIOUSES
FIDDIOUSING
FIDDLE
FIDDLED
FIDDLER
FIDDLERS
FIDDLES
FIDDLEY
FIDDLEYS
FIDDLIER
FIDDLIEST
FIDDLING
FIDDLY
FIDEISM
FIDEISMS
FIDEISTIC
FIDELITIES
FIDELITY
FIDGE
FIDGED
FIDGES
FIDGET
FIDGETED
FIDGETING
FIDGETS
FIDGETY
FIDGING
FIDIBUS
FIDIBUSES
FIDS
FIDUCIAL
FIDUCIARIES
FIDUCIARY
FIE
FIEF
FIEFS
FIELD
FIELDED
FIELDER
FIELDERS
FIELDFARE
FIELDFARES
FIELDING
FIELDINGS
FIELDMICE
FIELDS
FIELDSMAN
FIELDSMEN
FIELDWARD
FIELDWARDS
FIELDWORK
FIELDWORKS
FIEND
FIENDISH

| | | | | |
|---|---|---|---|---|
| FIENDS | FIGURING | FILIBEGS | FILTERED | FINED |
| FIENT | FIGURIST | FILICIDE | FILTERING | FINEER |
| FIENTS | FIGURISTS | FILICIDES | FILTERS | FINEERED |
| FIERCE | FIGWORT | FILIFORM | FILTH | FINEERING |
| FIERCELY | FIGWORTS | FILIGRAIN | FILTHIER | FINEERS |
| FIERCER | FIKE | FILIGRAINS | FILTHIEST | FINEISH |
| FIERCEST | FIKED | FILIGRANE | FILTHILY | FINELESS |
| FIERE | FIKERIES | FILIGRANES | FILTHS | FINELY |
| FIERES | FIKERY | FILIGREE | FILTHY | FINENESS |
| FIERIER | FIKES | FILIGREED | FILTRABLE | FINENESSES |
| FIERIEST | FIKIER | FILIGREES | FILTRATE | FINER |
| FIERILY | FIKIEST | FILING | FILTRATED | FINERIES |
| FIERINESS | FIKING | FILINGS | FILTRATES | FINERS |
| FIERINESSES | FIKISH | FILIOQUE | FILTRATING | FINERY |
| FIERY | FIKY | FILIOQUES | FIMBLE | FINES |
| FIESTA | FIL | FILL | FIMBLES | FINESSE |
| FIESTAS | FILABEG | FILLE | FIMBRIA | FINESSED |
| FIFE | FILABEGS | FILLED | FIMBRIAS | FINESSER |
| FIFED | FILACEOUS | FILLER | FIMBRIATE | FINESSERS |
| FIFER | FILACER | FILLERS | FIMBRIATED | FINESSES |
| FIFERS | FILACERS | FILLES | FIMBRIATES | FINESSING |
| FIFES | FILAGREE | FILLET | FIMBRIATING | FINESSINGS |
| FIFING | FILAGREES | FILLETED | FIN | FINEST |
| FIFTEEN | FILAMENT | FILLETING | FINABLE | FINGAN |
| FIFTEENER | FILAMENTS | FILLETS | FINAGLE | FINGANS |
| FIFTEENERS | FILANDER | FILLIBEG | FINAGLED | FINGER |
| FIFTEENS | FILANDERS | FILLIBEGS | FINAGLES | FINGERED |
| FIFTEENTH | FILAR | FILLIES | FINAGLING | FINGERING |
| FIFTEENTHS | FILARIA | FILLING | FINAL | FINGERINGS |
| FIFTH | FILARIAL | FILLINGS | FINALE | FINGERS |
| FIFTHLY | FILARIAS | FILLIP | FINALES | FINGERTIP |
| FIFTHS | FILASSE | FILLIPED | FINALISE | FINGERTIPS |
| FIFTIES | FILASSES | FILLIPEEN | FINALISED | FINIAL |
| FIFTIETH | FILATORIES | FILLIPEENS | FINALISES | FINIALS |
| FIFTIETHS | FILATORY | FILLIPING | FINALISING | FINICAL |
| FIFTY | FILATURE | FILLIPS | FINALISM | FINICALLY |
| FIFTYISH | FILATURES | FILLISTER | FINALISMS | FINICKIER |
| FIG | FILAZER | FILLISTERS | FINALIST | FINICKIEST |
| FIGGED | FILAZERS | FILLS | FINALISTS | FINICKING |
| FIGGERIES | FILBERD | FILLY | FINALITIES | FINICKINGS |
| FIGGERY | FILBERDS | FILM | FINALITY | FINICKY |
| FIGGING | FILBERT | FILMABLE | FINALIZE | FINIKIN |
| FIGHT | FILBERTS | FILMDOM | FINALIZED | FINING |
| FIGHTABLE | FILCH | FILMDOMS | FINALIZES | FININGS |
| FIGHTBACK | FILCHED | FILMED | FINALIZING | FINIS |
| FIGHTBACKS | FILCHER | FILMGOER | FINALLY | FINISH |
| FIGHTER | FILCHERS | FILMGOERS | FINALS | FINISHED |
| FIGHTERS | FILCHES | FILMIC | FINANCE | FINISHER |
| FIGHTING | FILCHING | FILMIER | FINANCED | FINISHERS |
| FIGHTINGS | FILCHINGS | FILMIEST | FINANCES | FINISHES |
| FIGHTS | FILE | FILMINESS | FINANCIAL | FINISHING |
| FIGMENT | FILED | FILMINESSES | FINANCIER | FINISHINGS |
| FIGMENTS | FILEMOT | FILMING | FINANCIERED | FINITE |
| FIGO | FILEMOTS | FILMISH | FINANCIERING | FINITELY |
| FIGOS | FILER | FILMLAND | FINANCIERS | FINITUDE |
| FIGS | FILERS | FILMLANDS | FINANCING | FINITUDES |
| FIGULINE | FILES | FILMS | FINBACK | FINJAN |
| FIGULINES | FILET | FILMSET | FINBACKS | FINJANS |
| FIGURABLE | FILETS | FILMSETS | FINCH | FINK |
| FIGURAL | FILFOT | FILMSETTING | FINCHED | FINKED |
| FIGURANT | FILFOTS | FILMSETTINGS | FINCHES | FINKING |
| FIGURANTE | FILIAL | FILMY | FIND | FINKS |
| FIGURANTES | FILIALLY | FILOPLUME | FINDER | FINLESS |
| FIGURANTS | FILIATE | FILOPLUMES | FINDERS | FINNAC |
| FIGURATE | FILIATED | FILOPODIA | FINDING | FINNACK |
| FIGURE | FILIATES | FILOSE | FINDINGS | FINNACKS |
| FIGURED | FILIATING | FILOSELLE | FINDRAM | FINNACS |
| FIGURES | FILIATION | FILOSELLES | FINDRAMS | FINNAN |
| FIGURINE | FILIATIONS | FILS | FINDS | FINNANS |
| FIGURINES | FILIBEG | FILTER | FINE | FINNED |

| | | | | |
|---|---|---|---|---|
| FINNER | FIREPLACES | FIRTHS | FISTFULS | FIXATIVES |
| FINNERS | FIREPOT | FISC | FISTIANA | FIXATURE |
| FINNESKO | FIREPOTS | FISCAL | FISTIANAS | FIXATURES |
| FINNIER | FIREPROOF | FISCALS | FISTIC | FIXED |
| FINNIEST | FIREPROOFED | FISCS | FISTICAL | FIXEDLY |
| FINNOCHIO | FIREPROOFING | FISGIG | FISTICUFF | FIXEDNESS |
| FINNOCHIOS | FIREPROOFINGS | FISGIGS | FISTICUFFS | FIXEDNESSES |
| FINNOCK | FIREPROOFS | FISH | FISTIER | FIXER |
| FINNOCKS | FIRER | FISHABLE | FISTIEST | FIXERS |
| FINNSKO | FIRERS | FISHBALL | FISTING | FIXES |
| FINNY | FIRES | FISHBALLS | FISTMELE | FIXING |
| FINO | FIRESHIP | FISHCAKE | FISTMELES | FIXINGS |
| FINOCCHIO | FIRESHIPS | FISHCAKES | FISTS | FIXITIES |
| FINOCCHIOS | FIRESIDE | FISHED | FISTULA | FIXITY |
| FINOCHIO | FIRESIDES | FISHER | FISTULAE | FIXIVE |
| FINOCHIOS | FIRESTONE | FISHERIES | FISTULAR | FIXTURE |
| FINOS | FIRESTONES | FISHERMAN | FISTULAS | FIXTURES |
| FINS | FIRETHORN | FISHERMEN | FISTULOSE | FIXURE |
| FINSKO | FIRETHORNS | FISHERS | FISTULOUS | FIXURES |
| FIORD | FIREWEED | FISHERY | FISTY | FIZ |
| FIORDS | FIREWEEDS | FISHES | FIT | FIZGIG |
| FIORIN | FIREWOMAN | FISHEYE | FITCH | FIZGIGS |
| FIORINS | FIREWOMEN | FISHEYES | FITCHÉ | FIZZ |
| FIORITURA | FIREWOOD | FISHFUL | FITCHÉE | FIZZED |
| FIORITURE | FIREWOODS | FISHGIG | FITCHES | FIZZEN |
| FIPPENCE | FIREWORK | FISHGIGS | FITCHET | FIZZENS |
| FIPPENCES | FIREWORKS | FISHIER | FITCHETS | FIZZER |
| FIPPLE | FIREWORM | FISHIEST | FITCHEW | FIZZERS |
| FIPPLES | FIREWORMS | FISHIFIED | FITCHEWS | FIZZES |
| FIR | FIRING | FISHIFIES | FITCHY | FIZZGIG |
| FIRE | FIRINGS | FISHIFY | FITFUL | FIZZGIGS |
| FIREARM | FIRK | FISHIFYING | FITFULLY | FIZZIER |
| FIREARMS | FIRKED | FISHINESS | FITLIER | FIZZIEST |
| FIREBALL | FIRKIN | FISHINESSES | FITLIEST | FIZZING |
| FIREBALLS | FIRKING | FISHING | FITLY | FIZZINGS |
| FIREBRAND | FIRKINS | FISHINGS | FITMENT | FIZZLE |
| FIREBRANDS | FIRKS | FISHSKIN | FITMENTS | FIZZLED |
| FIREBRAT | FIRLOT | FISHSKINS | FITNESS | FIZZLES |
| FIREBRATS | FIRLOTS | FISHWIFE | FITNESSES | FIZZLING |
| FIREBRICK | FIRM | FISHWIVES | FITS | FIZZY |
| FIREBRICKS | FIRMAMENT | FISHY | FITT | FJORD |
| FIREBUG | FIRMAMENTS | FISHYBACK | FITTE | FJORDS |
| FIREBUGS | FIRMAN | FISHYBACKS | FITTED | FLAB |
| FIRECREST | FIRMANS | FISK | FITTER | FLABBIER |
| FIRECRESTS | FIRMED | FISKED | FITTERS | FLABBIEST |
| FIRED | FIRMER | FISKING | FITTES | FLABBY |
| FIREDAMP | FIRMERS | FISKS | FITTEST | FLABELLA |
| FIREDAMPS | FIRMEST | FISNOMIE | FITTING | FLABELLUM |
| FIREDOG | FIRMING | FISNOMIES | FITTINGLY | FLABELLUMS |
| FIREDOGS | FIRMLESS | FISSILE | FITTINGS | FLABS |
| FIREFLIES | FIRMLY | FISSILITIES | FITTS | FLACCID |
| FIREFLOAT | FIRMNESS | FISSILITY | FIVE | FLACCIDER |
| FIREFLOATS | FIRMNESSES | FISSION | FIVEFOLD | FLACCIDEST |
| FIREFLY | FIRMS | FISSIONS | FIVEPENCE | FLACCIDLY |
| FIREGUARD | FIRMWARE | FISSIPED | FIVEPENCES | FLACK |
| FIREGUARDS | FIRMWARES | FISSIPEDE | FIVEPENNY | FLACKER |
| FIREHOUSE | FIRN | FISSIPEDES | FIVEPIN | FLACKERED |
| FIREHOUSES | FIRNS | FISSIPEDS | FIVEPINS | FLACKERING |
| FIRELESS | FIRRIER | FISSIVE | FIVER | FLACKERS |
| FIRELIGHT | FIRRIEST | FISSLE | FIVERS | FLACKET |
| FIRELIGHTS | FIRRING | FISSLED | FIVES | FLACKETS |
| FIRELOCK | FIRRINGS | FISSLES | FIX | FLACKS |
| FIRELOCKS | FIRRY | FISSLING | FIXABLE | FLACON |
| FIREMAN | FIRS | FISSURE | FIXATE | FLACONS |
| FIREMARK | FIRST | FISSURED | FIXATED | FLAFF |
| FIREMARKS | FIRSTLING | FISSURES | FIXATES | FLAFFED |
| FIREMEN | FIRSTLINGS | FISSURING | FIXATING | FLAFFER |
| FIREPAN | FIRSTLY | FIST | FIXATION | FLAFFERED |
| FIREPANS | FIRSTS | FISTED | FIXATIONS | FLAFFERING |
| FIREPLACE | FIRTH | FISTFUL | FIXATIVE | FLAFFERS |

| | | | | |
|---|---|---|---|---|
| FLAFFING | FLAMIER | FLASHCUBE | FLAUGHTERING | FLECKERED |
| FLAFFS | FLAMIEST | FLASHCUBES | FLAUGHTERS | FLECKERING |
| FLAG | FLAMINES | FLASHED | FLAUGHTING | FLECKERS |
| FLAGELLA | FLAMING | FLASHER | FLAUGHTS | FLECKING |
| FLAGELLUM | FLAMINGLY | FLASHERS | FLAUNCH | FLECKLESS |
| FLAGEOLET | FLAMINGO | FLASHES | FLAUNCHED | FLECKS |
| FLAGEOLETS | FLAMINGOES | FLASHEST | FLAUNCHES | FLECTION |
| FLAGGED | FLAMINGOS | FLASHIER | FLAUNCHING | FLECTIONS |
| FLAGGIER | FLAMM | FLASHIEST | FLAUNCHINGS | FLED |
| FLAGGIEST | FLAMMABLE | FLASHILY | FLAUNE | FLEDGE |
| FLAGGING | FLAMMED | FLASHING | FLAUNES | FLEDGED |
| FLAGGINGS | FLAMMING | FLASHINGS | FLAUNT | FLEDGES |
| FLAGGY | FLAMMS | FLASHY | FLAUNTED | FLEDGIER |
| FLAGITATE | FLAMMULE | FLASK | FLAUNTER | FLEDGIEST |
| FLAGITATED | FLAMMULES | FLASKET | FLAUNTERS | FLEDGING |
| FLAGITATES | FLAMS | FLASKETS | FLAUNTIER | FLEDGLING |
| FLAGITATING | FLAMY | FLASKS | FLAUNTIEST | FLEDGLINGS |
| FLAGON | FLAN | FLAT | FLAUNTING | FLEDGY |
| FLAGONS | FLANCH | FLATBACK | FLAUNTS | FLEE |
| FLAGPOLE | FLANCHED | FLATBACKS | FLAUNTY | FLEECE |
| FLAGPOLES | FLANCHES | FLATBOAT | FLAUTIST | FLEECED |
| FLAGRANCE | FLANCHING | FLATBOATS | FLAUTISTS | FLEECER |
| FLAGRANCES | FLANCHINGS | FLATFISH | FLAVIN | FLEECERS |
| FLAGRANCIES | FLÂNERIE | FLATFISHES | FLAVINE | FLEECES |
| FLAGRANCY | FLÂNERIES | FLATHEAD | FLAVINES | FLEECH |
| FLAGRANT | FLÂNEUR | FLATHEADS | FLAVINS | FLEECHED |
| FLAGS | FLÂNEURS | FLATIRON | FLAVONE | FLEECHES |
| FLAGSHIP | FLANGE | FLATIRONS | FLAVONES | FLEECHING |
| FLAGSHIPS | FLANGED | FLATLET | FLAVOROUS | FLEECHINGS |
| FLAGSTAFF | FLANGES | FLATLETS | FLAVOUR | FLEECIER |
| FLAGSTAFFS | FLANGING | FLATLING | FLAVOURED | FLEECIEST |
| FLAGSTICK | FLANK | FLATLINGS | FLAVOURING | FLEECING |
| FLAGSTICKS | FLANKED | FLATLONG | FLAVOURINGS | FLEECY |
| FLAGSTONE | FLANKER | FLATLY | FLAVOURS | FLEEING |
| FLAGSTONES | FLANKERED | FLATMATE | FLAW | FLEER |
| FLAIL | FLANKERING | FLATMATES | FLAWED | FLEERED |
| FLAILED | FLANKERS | FLATNESS | FLAWIER | FLEERER |
| FLAILING | FLANKING | FLATNESSES | FLAWIEST | FLEERERS |
| FLAILS | FLANKS | FLATS | FLAWING | FLEERING |
| FLAIR | FLANNEL | FLATTED | FLAWLESS | FLEERINGS |
| FLAIRS | FLANNELLED | FLATTEN | FLAWN | FLEERS |
| FLAK | FLANNELLING | FLATTENED | FLAWNS | FLEES |
| FLAKE | FLANNELLY | FLATTENING | FLAWS | FLEET |
| FLAKED | FLANNELS | FLATTENS | FLAWY | FLEETED |
| FLAKES | FLANNEN | FLATTER | FLAX | FLEETER |
| FLAKIER | FLANNENS | FLATTERED | FLAXEN | FLEETEST |
| FLAKIEST | FLANS | FLATTERER | FLAXES | FLEETING |
| FLAKINESS | FLAP | FLATTERERS | FLAXIER | FLEETLY |
| FLAKINESSES | FLAPJACK | FLATTERIES | FLAXIEST | FLEETNESS |
| FLAKING | FLAPJACKS | FLATTERING | FLAXY | FLEETNESSES |
| FLAKS | FLAPPABLE | FLATTERS | FLAY | FLEETS |
| FLAKY | FLAPPED | FLATTERY | FLAYED | FLEG |
| FLAM | FLAPPER | FLATTEST | FLAYER | FLEGGED |
| FLAMBÉ | FLAPPERS | FLATTING | FLAYERS | FLEGGING |
| FLAMBEAU | FLAPPING | FLATTINGS | FLAYING | FLEGS |
| FLAMBEAUS | FLAPPINGS | FLATTISH | FLAYS | FLEME |
| FLAMBEAUX | FLAPS | FLATULENT | FLEA | FLEMES |
| FLAMBÉED | FLAPTRACK | FLATUOUS | FLEAM | FLEMING |
| FLAME | FLAPTRACKS | FLATUS | FLEAMS | FLEMISH |
| FLAMED | FLARE | FLATUSES | FLEAS | FLEMISHED |
| FLAMELESS | FLARED | FLATWARE | FLEASOME | FLEMISHES |
| FLAMELET | FLARES | FLATWARES | FLÈCHE | FLEMISHING |
| FLAMELETS | FLARIER | FLATWAYS | FLÈCHES | FLEMIT |
| FLAMEN | FLARIEST | FLATWISE | FLECHETTE | FLENCH |
| FLAMENCO | FLARING | FLATWORM | FLÉCHETTE | FLENCHED |
| FLAMENCOS | FLARINGLY | FLATWORMS | FLECHETTES | FLENCHES |
| FLAMENS | FLARY | FLAUGHT | FLÉCHETTES | FLENCHING |
| FLAMES | FLASER | FLAUGHTED | FLECK | FLENSE |
| FLAMFEW | FLASERS | FLAUGHTER | FLECKED | FLENSED |
| FLAMFEWS | FLASH | FLAUGHTERED | FLECKER | FLENSES |

| | | | | |
|---|---|---|---|---|
| FLENSING | FLICKER | FLIRTING | FLOGGINGS | FLORIGENS |
| FLESH | FLICKERED | FLIRTINGS | FLOGS | FLORIN |
| FLESHED | FLICKERING | FLIRTISH | FLONG | FLORINS |
| FLESHER | FLICKERS | FLIRTS | FLONGS | FLORIST |
| FLESHERS | FLICKING | FLIRTY | FLOOD | FLORISTIC |
| FLESHES | FLICKS | FLISK | FLOODED | FLORISTICS |
| FLESHHOOD | FLICS | FLISKED | FLOODGATE | FLORISTRIES |
| FLESHHOODS | FLIER | FLISKIER | FLOODGATES | FLORISTRY |
| FLESHIER | FLIERS | FLISKIEST | FLOODING | FLORISTS |
| FLESHIEST | FLIES | FLISKING | FLOODINGS | FLORS |
| FLESHING | FLIEST | FLISKS | FLOODLIT | FLORUIT |
| FLESHINGS | FLIGHT | FLISKY | FLOODMARK | FLORUITS |
| FLESHLESS | FLIGHTED | FLIT | FLOODMARKS | FLORY |
| FLESHLIER | FLIGHTIER | FLITCH | FLOODS | FLOSCULAR |
| FLESHLIEST | FLIGHTIEST | FLITCHES | FLOODTIDE | FLOSCULE |
| FLESHLING | FLIGHTILY | FLITE | FLOODTIDES | FLOSCULES |
| FLESHLINGS | FLIGHTING | FLITED | FLOODWALL | FLOSH |
| FLESHLY | FLIGHTS | FLITES | FLOODWALLS | FLOSHES |
| FLESHMENT | FLIGHTY | FLITING | FLOODWAY | FLOSS |
| FLESHMENTS | FLIMP | FLITS | FLOODWAYS | FLOSSES |
| FLESHWORM | FLIMPED | FLITT | FLOOR | FLOSSIER |
| FLESHWORMS | FLIMPING | FLITTED | FLOORED | FLOSSIEST |
| FLESHY | FLIMPS | FLITTER | FLOORER | FLOSSY |
| FLETCH | FLIMSIER | FLITTERED | FLOORERS | FLOTA |
| FLETCHED | FLIMSIES | FLITTERING | FLOORHEAD | FLOTAGE |
| FLETCHER | FLIMSIEST | FLITTERN | FLOORHEADS | FLOTAGES |
| FLETCHERS | FLIMSILY | FLITTERNS | FLOORING | FLOTANT |
| FLETCHES | FLIMSY | FLITTERS | FLOORINGS | FLOTAS |
| FLETCHING | FLINCH | FLITTING | FLOORS | FLOTATION |
| FLETTON | FLINCHED | FLITTINGS | FLOOSIE | FLOTATIONS |
| FLETTONS | FLINCHER | FLIVVER | FLOOSIES | FLOTE |
| FLEURET | FLINCHERS | FLIVVERS | FLOOSY | FLOTEL |
| FLEURETS | FLINCHES | FLIX | FLOOZIE | FLOTELS |
| FLEURETTE | FLINCHING | FLIXED | FLOOZIES | FLOTES |
| FLEURETTES | FLINCHINGS | FLIXES | FLOOZY | FLOTILLA |
| FLEURON | FLINDER | FLIXING | FLOP | FLOTILLAS |
| FLEURONS | FLINDERS | FLOAT | FLOPHOUSE | FLOTSAM |
| FLEURY | FLING | FLOATABLE | FLOPHOUSES | FLOTSAMS |
| FLEW | FLINGER | FLOATAGE | FLOPPED | FLOUNCE |
| FLEWED | FLINGERS | FLOATAGES | FLOPPIER | FLOUNCED |
| FLEWS | FLINGING | FLOATANT | FLOPPIEST | FLOUNCES |
| FLEX | FLINGS | FLOATANTS | FLOPPILY | FLOUNCING |
| FLEXED | FLINT | FLOATED | FLOPPING | FLOUNCINGS |
| FLEXES | FLINTIER | FLOATEL | FLOPPY | FLOUNDER |
| FLEXIBLE | FLINTIEST | FLOATELS | FLOPS | FLOUNDERED |
| FLEXIBLY | FLINTIFIED | FLOATER | FLOR | FLOUNDERING |
| FLEXILE | FLINTIFIES | FLOATERS | FLORA | FLOUNDERS |
| FLEXING | FLINTIFY | FLOATIER | FLORAE | FLOUR |
| FLEXION | FLINTIFYING | FLOATIEST | FLORAL | FLOURED |
| FLEXIONS | FLINTILY | FLOATING | FLORALLY | FLOURIER |
| FLEXITIME | FLINTLOCK | FLOATINGS | FLORAS | FLOURIEST |
| FLEXITIMES | FLINTLOCKS | FLOATS | FLOREAT | FLOURING |
| FLEXOR | FLINTS | FLOATY | FLOREATED | FLOURISH |
| FLEXORS | FLINTY | FLOCCI | FLORENCE | FLOURISHED |
| FLEXUOSE | FLIP | FLOCCOSE | FLORENCES | FLOURISHES |
| FLEXUOUS | FLIPFLOP | FLOCCULAR | FLORET | FLOURISHING |
| FLEXURAL | FLIPFLOPS | FLOCCULE | FLORETS | FLOURISHY |
| FLEXURE | FLIPPANCIES | FLOCCULES | FLORIATED | FLOURS |
| FLEXURES | FLIPPANCY | FLOCCULI | FLORID | FLOURY |
| FLEY | FLIPPANT | FLOCCULUS | FLORIDEAN | FLOUSE |
| FLEYED | FLIPPED | FLOCCUS | FLORIDEANS | FLOUSED |
| FLEYING | FLIPPER | FLOCK | FLORIDER | FLOUSES |
| FLEYS | FLIPPERS | FLOCKED | FLORIDEST | FLOUSH |
| FLIC | FLIPPEST | FLOCKING | FLORIDITIES | FLOUSHED |
| FLICHTER | FLIPPING | FLOCKS | FLORIDITY | FLOUSHES |
| FLICHTERED | FLIPS | FLOE | FLORIDLY | FLOUSHING |
| FLICHTERING | FLIRT | FLOES | FLORIER | FLOUSING |
| FLICHTERS | FLIRTED | FLOG | FLORIEST | FLOUT |
| FLICK | FLIRTIER | FLOGGED | FLORIFORM | FLOUTED |
| FLICKED | FLIRTIEST | FLOGGING | FLORIGEN | FLOUTING |

| | | | | |
|---|---|---|---|---|
| FLOUTS | FLUIDIFY | FLURRYING | FLYLEAF | FODDER |
| FLOW | FLUIDIFYING | FLUS | FLYLEAVES | FODDERED |
| FLOWAGE | FLUIDISE | FLUSH | FLYMAKER | FODDERER |
| FLOWAGES | FLUIDISED | FLUSHED | FLYMAKERS | FODDERERS |
| FLOWED | FLUIDISES | FLUSHER | FLYOVER | FODDERING |
| FLOWER | FLUIDISING | FLUSHERS | FLYOVERS | FODDERINGS |
| FLOWERAGE | FLUIDITIES | FLUSHES | FLYPAPER | FODDERS |
| FLOWERAGES | FLUIDITY | FLUSHEST | FLYPAPERS | FOE |
| FLOWERED | FLUIDIZE | FLUSHIER | FLYPE | FOEDARIE |
| FLOWERER | FLUIDIZED | FLUSHIEST | FLYPED | FOEDARIES |
| FLOWERERS | FLUIDIZES | FLUSHING | FLYPES | FOEDERATI |
| FLOWERET | FLUIDIZING | FLUSHINGS | FLYPING | FOEHN |
| FLOWERETS | FLUIDNESS | FLUSHNESS | FLYSCH | FOEHNS |
| FLOWERIER | FLUIDNESSES | FLUSHNESSES | FLYSCHES | FOEMAN |
| FLOWERIEST | FLUIDS | FLUSHY | FLYTE | FOEMEN |
| FLOWERING | FLUIER | FLUSTER | FLYTED | FOEN |
| FLOWERINGS | FLUIEST | FLUSTERED | FLYTES | FOES |
| FLOWERPOT | FLUKE | FLUSTERING | FLYTING | FOETAL |
| FLOWERPOTS | FLUKED | FLUSTERS | FLYTINGS | FOETICIDE |
| FLOWERS | FLUKES | FLUSTERY | FLYTRAP | FOETICIDES |
| FLOWERY | FLUKEY | FLUSTRATE | FLYTRAPS | FOETID |
| FLOWING | FLUKIER | FLUSTRATED | FLYWAY | FOETIDER |
| FLOWINGLY | FLUKIEST | FLUSTRATES | FLYWAYS | FOETIDEST |
| FLOWMETER | FLUKING | FLUSTRATING | FLYWEIGHT | FOETOR |
| FLOWMETERS | FLUKY | FLUTE | FLYWEIGHTS | FOETORS |
| FLOWN | FLUME | FLUTED | FLYWHEEL | FOETUS |
| FLOWS | FLUMES | FLUTER | FLYWHEELS | FOETUSES |
| FLU | FLUMMERIES | FLUTERS | FOAL | FOG |
| FLUATE | FLUMMERY | FLUTES | FOALED | FOGASH |
| FLUATES | FLUMMOX | FLUTIER | FOALFOOT | FOGASHES |
| FLUB | FLUMMOXED | FLUTIEST | FOALFOOTS | FOGBOUND |
| FLUBBED | FLUMMOXES | FLUTINA | FOALING | FOGEY |
| FLUBBING | FLUMMOXING | FLUTINAS | FOALS | FOGEYS |
| FLUBS | FLUMP | FLUTING | FOAM | FOGGAGE |
| FLUCTUANT | FLUMPED | FLUTINGS | FOAMED | FOGGAGED |
| FLUCTUATE | FLUMPING | FLUTIST | FOAMIER | FOGGAGES |
| FLUCTUATED | FLUMPS | FLUTISTS | FOAMIEST | FOGGAGING |
| FLUCTUATES | FLUNG | FLUTTER | FOAMILY | FOGGED |
| FLUCTUATING | FLUNK | FLUTTERED | FOAMINESS | FOGGER |
| FLUE | FLUNKED | FLUTTERING | FOAMINESSES | FOGGERS |
| FLUELLIN | FLUNKEY | FLUTTERS | FOAMING | FOGGIER |
| FLUELLINS | FLUNKEYS | FLUTY | FOAMINGLY | FOGGIEST |
| FLUENCE | FLUNKIES | FLUVIAL | FOAMINGS | FOGGILY |
| FLUENCES | FLUNKING | FLUVIATIC | FOAMLESS | FOGGINESS |
| FLUENCIES | FLUNKS | FLUX | FOAMS | FOGGINESSES |
| FLUENCY | FLUNKY | FLUXED | FOAMY | FOGGING |
| FLUENT | FLUOR | FLUXES | FOB | FOGGY |
| FLUENTLY | FLUORESCE | FLUXING | FOBBED | FOGHORN |
| FLUENTS | FLUORESCED | FLUXION | FOBBING | FOGHORNS |
| FLUES | FLUORESCES | FLUXIONAL | FOBS | FOGIES |
| FLUEWORK | FLUORESCING | FLUXIONS | FOCAL | FOGLE |
| FLUEWORKS | FLUORIC | FLUXIVE | FOCALISE | FOGLES |
| FLUEY | FLUORIDE | FLY | FOCALISED | FOGLESS |
| FLUFF | FLUORIDES | FLYABLE | FOCALISES | FOGMAN |
| FLUFFED | FLUORINE | FLYAWAY | FOCALISING | FOGMEN |
| FLUFFIER | FLUORINES | FLYBANE | FOCALIZE | FOGRAM |
| FLUFFIEST | FLUORITE | FLYBANES | FOCALIZED | FOGRAMITE |
| FLUFFING | FLUORITES | FLYBELT | FOCALIZES | FOGRAMITES |
| FLUFFS | FLUOROSES | FLYBELTS | FOCALIZING | FOGRAMITIES |
| FLUFFY | FLUOROSIS | FLYBLOW | FOCALLY | FOGRAMITY |
| FLUGEL | FLUORS | FLYBLOWS | FOCI | FOGRAMS |
| FLUGELMAN | FLUORSPAR | FLYBOAT | FOCIMETER | FOGS |
| FLUGELMEN | FLUORSPARS | FLYBOATS | FOCIMETERS | FOGY |
| FLUGELS | FLURR | FLYBOOK | FOCUS | FOGYDOM |
| FLUID | FLURRED | FLYBOOKS | FOCUSED | FOGYDOMS |
| FLUIDAL | FLURRIED | FLYER | FOCUSES | FOGYISH |
| FLUIDIC | FLURRIES | FLYERS | FOCUSING | FOGYISM |
| FLUIDICS | FLURRING | FLYEST | FOCUSSED | FOGYISMS |
| FLUIDIFIED | FLURRS | FLYING | FOCUSSES | FOH |
| FLUIDIFIES | FLURRY | FLYINGS | FOCUSSING | FÖHN |

FÖHNS
FOIBLE
FOIBLES
FOIL
FOILED
FOILING
FOILINGS
FOILS
FOIN
FOINED
FOINING
FOININGLY
FOINS
FOISON
FOISONS
FOIST
FOISTED
FOISTER
FOISTERS
FOISTING
FOISTS
FOLACIN
FOLACINS
FOLATE
FOLD
FOLDABLE
FOLDAWAY
FOLDBOAT
FOLDBOATS
FOLDED
FOLDER
FOLDEROL
FOLDEROLS
FOLDERS
FOLDING
FOLDINGS
FOLDS
FOLIA
FOLIAGE
FOLIAGED
FOLIAGES
FOLIAR
FOLIATE
FOLIATED
FOLIATES
FOLIATING
FOLIATION
FOLIATIONS
FOLIATURE
FOLIATURES
FOLIE
FOLIES
FOLIO
FOLIOED
FOLIOING
FOLIOLATE
FOLIOLE
FOLIOLES
FOLIOLOSE
FOLIOS
FOLIOSE
FOLIUM
FOLK
FOLKLAND
FOLKLANDS
FOLKLORE
FOLKLORES
FOLKLORIC
FOLKMOOT
FOLKMOOTS

FOLKROCK
FOLKROCKS
FOLKS
FOLKSIER
FOLKSIEST
FOLKSY
FOLKWAY
FOLKWAYS
FOLLICLE
FOLLICLES
FOLLIED
FOLLIES
FOLLOW
FOLLOWED
FOLLOWER
FOLLOWERS
FOLLOWING
FOLLOWINGS
FOLLOWS
FOLLY
FOLLYING
FOMENT
FOMENTED
FOMENTER
FOMENTERS
FOMENTING
FOMENTS
FOMES
FOMITES
FON
FOND
FONDA
FONDANT
FONDANTS
FONDAS
FONDED
FONDER
FONDEST
FONDING
FONDLE
FONDLED
FONDLER
FONDLERS
FONDLES
FONDLING
FONDLINGS
FONDLY
FONDNESS
FONDNESSES
FONDS
FONDUE
FONDUES
FONE
FONLY
FONNED
FONNING
FONS
FONT
FONTAL
FONTANEL
FONTANELS
FONTANGE
FONTANGES
FONTICULI
FONTLET
FONTLETS
FONTS
FOOD
FOODFUL
FOODIE

FOODIES
FOODLESS
FOODS
FOODSTUFF
FOODSTUFFS
FOOL
FOOLED
FOOLERIES
FOOLERY
FOOLHARDY
FOOLING
FOOLINGS
FOOLISH
FOOLISHER
FOOLISHEST
FOOLISHLY
FOOLPROOF
FOOLS
FOOLSCAP
FOOLSCAPS
FOOT
FOOTAGE
FOOTAGES
FOOTBALL
FOOTBALLS
FOOTBAR
FOOTBARS
FOOTBOARD
FOOTBOARDS
FOOTBOY
FOOTBOYS
FOOTCLOTH
FOOTCLOTHS
FOOTED
FOOTER
FOOTERS
FOOTFALL
FOOTFALLS
FOOTFAULT
FOOTFAULTED
FOOTFAULTING
FOOTFAULTS
FOOTGEAR
FOOTGEARS
FOOTHILL
FOOTHILLS
FOOTHOLD
FOOTHOLDS
FOOTIER
FOOTIEST
FOOTING
FOOTINGS
FOOTLE
FOOTLED
FOOTLES
FOOTLESS
FOOTLIGHT
FOOTLIGHTS
FOOTLING
FOOTLINGS
FOOTLOOSE
FOOTMAN
FOOTMARK
FOOTMARKS
FOOTMEN
FOOTMUFF
FOOTMUFFS
FOOTNOTE
FOOTNOTES
FOOTPACE

FOOTPACES
FOOTPAD
FOOTPADS
FOOTPAGE
FOOTPAGES
FOOTPATH
FOOTPATHS
FOOTPLATE
FOOTPLATES
FOOTPOST
FOOTPOSTS
FOOTPRINT
FOOTPRINTS
FOOTRA
FOOTRAS
FOOTREST
FOOTRESTS
FOOTROT
FOOTROTS
FOOTRULE
FOOTRULES
FOOTS
FOOTSLOG
FOOTSLOGGED
FOOTSLOGGING
FOOTSLOGGINGS
FOOTSLOGS
FOOTSORE
FOOTSTALK
FOOTSTALKS
FOOTSTEP
FOOTSTEPS
FOOTSTOOL
FOOTSTOOLS
FOOTWAY
FOOTWAYS
FOOTWEAR
FOOTWEARS
FOOTWORK
FOOTWORKS
FOOTWORN
FOOTY
FOOZLE
FOOZLED
FOOZLER
FOOZLERS
FOOZLES
FOOZLING
FOOZLINGS
FOP
FOPLING
FOPLINGS
FOPPERIES
FOPPERY
FOPPISH
FOPPISHLY
FOPS
FOR
FORA
FORAGE
FORAGED
FORAGER
FORAGERS
FORAGES
FORAGING
FORAMEN
FORAMINA
FORAMINAL
FORANE
FORASMUCH

FORAY
FORAYED
FORAYER
FORAYERS
FORAYING
FORAYS
FORBAD
FORBADE
FORBEAR
FORBEARING
FORBEARS
FORBID
FORBIDDAL
FORBIDDALS
FORBIDDEN
FORBIDDER
FORBIDDERS
FORBIDDING
FORBIDDINGS
FORBIDS
FORBODE
FORBODES
FORBORE
FORBORNE
FORBY
FORBYE
FORÇAT
FORÇATS
FORCE
FORCED
FORCEDLY
FORCEFUL
FORCELESS
FORCEMEAT
FORCEMEATS
FORCEPS
FORCEPSES
FORCER
FORCERS
FORCES
FORCIBLE
FORCIBLY
FORCING
FORCIPATE
FORCIPES
FORD
FORDABLE
FORDED
FORDID
FORDING
FORDO
FORDOES
FORDOING
FORDONE
FORDS
FORE
FOREANENT
FOREARM
FOREARMED
FOREARMING
FOREARMS
FOREBEAR
FOREBEARS
FOREBITT
FOREBITTS
FOREBODE
FOREBODED
FOREBODER
FOREBODERS
FOREBODES

FOREBODING
FOREBODINGS
FOREBY
FORECABIN
FORECABINS
FORECAR
FORECARS
FORECAST
FORECASTED
FORECASTING
FORECASTS
FORECLOSE
FORECLOSED
FORECLOSES
FORECLOSING
FORECLOTH
FORECLOTHS
FORECOURT
FORECOURTS
FOREDATE
FOREDATED
FOREDATES
FOREDATING
FOREDECK
FOREDECKS
FOREDOOM
FOREDOOMED
FOREDOOMING
FOREDOOMS
FOREFEEL
FOREFEELING
FOREFEELS
FOREFEET
FOREFELT
FOREFOOT
FOREFRONT
FOREFRONTS
FOREGLEAM
FOREGLEAMS
FOREGO
FOREGOER
FOREGOERS
FOREGOES
FOREGOING
FOREGOINGS
FOREGONE
FOREGUT
FOREGUTS
FOREHAND
FOREHANDS
FOREHEAD
FOREHEADS
FOREHENT
FOREHENTING
FOREHENTS
FOREIGN
FOREIGNER
FOREIGNERS
FOREJUDGE
FOREJUDGED
FOREJUDGES
FOREJUDGING
FOREKING
FOREKINGS
FOREKNEW
FOREKNOW
FOREKNOWING
FOREKNOWN
FOREKNOWS
FOREL

FORELAID
FORELAIN
FORELAND
FORELANDS
FORELAY
FORELAYING
FORELAYS
FORELEG
FORELEGS
FORELEND
FORELENDING
FORELENDS
FORELENT
FORELIE
FORELIES
FORELIFT
FORELIFTED
FORELIFTING
FORELIFTS
FORELIMB
FORELIMBS
FORELOCK
FORELOCKS
FORELS
FORELYING
FOREMAN
FOREMAST
FOREMASTS
FOREMEAN
FOREMEANING
FOREMEANS
FOREMEANT
FOREMEN
FOREMOST
FORENAME
FORENAMED
FORENAMES
FORENIGHT
FORENIGHTS
FORENOON
FORENOONS
FORENSIC
FORENSICS
FOREPART
FOREPARTS
FOREPAST
FOREPAW
FOREPAWS
FOREPEAK
FOREPEAKS
FOREPLAN
FOREPLANNED
FOREPLANNING
FOREPLANS
FOREPLAY
FOREPLAYS
FOREPOINT
FOREPOINTED
FOREPOINTING
FOREPOINTS
FORERAN
FOREREACH
FOREREACHED
FOREREACHES
FOREREACHING
FOREREAD
FOREREADING
FOREREADINGS
FOREREADS
FORERUN

FORERUNNING
FORERUNS
FORES
FORESAID
FORESAIL
FORESAILS
FORESAW
FORESAY
FORESAYING
FORESAYS
FORESEE
FORESEEING
FORESEEN
FORESEES
FORESHEW
FORESHEWED
FORESHEWING
FORESHEWN
FORESHEWS
FORESHIP
FORESHIPS
FORESHOCK
FORESHOCKS
FORESHORE
FORESHORES
FORESHOW
FORESHOWED
FORESHOWING
FORESHOWN
FORESHOWS
FORESIDE
FORESIDES
FORESIGHT
FORESIGHTS
FORESKIN
FORESKINS
FORESKIRT
FORESKIRTS
FORESLACK
FORESLACKED
FORESLACKING
FORESLACKS
FORESLOW
FORESLOWED
FORESLOWING
FORESLOWS
FORESPEAK
FORESPEAKING
FORESPEAKS
FORESPEND
FORESPENDING
FORESPENDS
FORESPENT
FORESPOKE
FORESPOKEN
FOREST
FORESTAGE
FORESTAGES
FORESTAIR
FORESTAIRS
FORESTAL
FORESTALL
FORESTALLED
FORESTALLING
FORESTALLINGS
FORESTALLS
FORESTAY
FORESTAYS
FORESTEAL
FORESTED

FORESTER
FORESTERS
FORESTINE
FORESTING
FORESTRIES
FORESTRY
FORESTS
FORETASTE
FORETASTED
FORETASTES
FORETASTING
FORETAUGHT
FORETEACH
FORETEACHES
FORETEACHING
FORETEETH
FORETELL
FORETELLING
FORETELLS
FORETHINK
FORETHINKING
FORETHINKS
FORETHOUGHT
FORETHOUGHTS
FORETIME
FORETIMES
FORETOKEN
FORETOKENED
FORETOKENING
FORETOKENINGS
FORETOKENS
FORETOLD
FORETOOTH
FORETOP
FORETOPS
FOREVER
FOREVERS
FOREWARD
FOREWARDS
FOREWARN
FOREWARNED
FOREWARNING
FOREWARNINGS
FOREWARNS
FOREWEIGH
FOREWEIGHED
FOREWEIGHING
FOREWEIGHS
FOREWENT
FOREWIND
FOREWINDS
FOREWING
FOREWINGS
FOREWOMAN
FOREWOMEN
FOREWORD
FOREWORDS
FORFAIR
FORFAIRED
FORFAIRING
FORFAIRN
FORFAIRS
FORFAULT
FORFAULTS
FORFEIT
FORFEITED
FORFEITER
FORFEITERS
FORFEITING
FORFEITS

FORFEND
FORFENDED
FORFENDING
FORFENDS
FORFEX
FORFEXES
FORFICATE
FORGAT
FORGATHER
FORGATHERED
FORGATHERING
FORGATHERS
FORGAVE
FORGE
FORGEABLE
FORGED
FORGEMAN
FORGEMEN
FORGER
FORGERIES
FORGERS
FORGERY
FORGES
FORGET
FORGETFUL
FORGETIVE
FORGETS
FORGETTER
FORGETTERS
FORGETTING
FORGETTINGS
FORGING
FORGINGS
FORGIVE
FORGIVEN
FORGIVES
FORGIVING
FORGO
FORGOES
FORGOING
FORGONE
FORGOT
FORGOTTEN
FORHAILE
FORHAILED
FORHAILES
FORHAILING
FORHENT
FORHENTING
FORHENTS
FORHOO
FORHOOED
FORHOOIE
FORHOOIED
FORHOOIEING
FORHOOIES
FORHOOING
FORHOOS
FORHOW
FORHOWED
FORHOWING
FORHOWS
FORINSEC
FORINT
FORINTS
FORJASKIT
FORJESKIT
FORJUDGE
FORJUDGED
FORJUDGES

| | | | | |
|---|---|---|---|---|
| FORJUDGING | FORMER | FORSAKES | FORTILAGES | FOSSETTE |
| FORK | FORMERLY | FORSAKING | FORTING | FOSSETTES |
| FORKED | FORMERS | FORSAKINGS | FORTIS | FOSSICK |
| FORKEDLY | FORMES | FORSAY | FORTITUDE | FOSSICKED |
| FORKER | FORMIATE | FORSAYING | FORTITUDES | FOSSICKER |
| FORKERS | FORMIATES | FORSAYS | FORTLET | FOSSICKERS |
| FORKHEAD | FORMIC | FORSLACK | FORTLETS | FOSSICKING |
| FORKHEADS | FORMICANT | FORSLACKED | FORTNIGHT | FOSSICKINGS |
| FORKIER | FORMICARIES | FORSLACKING | FORTNIGHTS | FOSSICKS |
| FORKIEST | FORMICARY | FORSLACKS | FORTRESS | FOSSIL |
| FORKINESS | FORMICATE | FORSLOE | FORTRESSED | FOSSILISE |
| FORKINESSES | FORMING | FORSLOED | FORTRESSES | FOSSILISED |
| FORKING | FORMINGS | FORSLOEING | FORTRESSING | FOSSILISES |
| FORKS | FORMLESS | FORSLOES | FORTS | FOSSILISING |
| FORKTAIL | FORMOL | FORSLOW | FORTUITIES | FOSSILIZE |
| FORKTAILS | FORMOLS | FORSLOWED | FORTUITY | FOSSILIZED |
| FORKY | FORMS | FORSLOWING | FORTUNATE | FOSSILIZES |
| FORLANA | FORMULA | FORSLOWS | FORTUNE | FOSSILIZING |
| FORLANAS | FORMULAE | FORSOOK | FORTUNED | FOSSILS |
| FORLEND | FORMULAIC | FORSOOTH | FORTUNES | FOSSOR |
| FORLENDING | FORMULAR | FORSPEAK | FORTUNING | FOSSORIAL |
| FORLENDS | FORMULARIES | FORSPEAKING | FORTUNIZE | FOSSORS |
| FORLENT | FORMULARY | FORSPEAKS | FORTUNIZED | FOSSULA |
| FORLESE | FORMULAS | FORSPEND | FORTUNIZES | FOSSULAS |
| FORLESES | FORMULATE | FORSPENDING | FORTUNIZING | FOSSULATE |
| FORLESING | FORMULATED | FORSPENDS | FORTY | FOSTER |
| FORLORE | FORMULATES | FORSPENT | FORTYISH | FOSTERAGE |
| FORLORN | FORMULATING | FORSPOKE | FORUM | FOSTERAGES |
| FORLORNER | FORMULISE | FORSPOKEN | FORUMS | FOSTERED |
| FORLORNEST | FORMULISED | FORSWATT | FORWANDER | FOSTERER |
| FORLORNLY | FORMULISES | FORSWEAR | FORWANDERED | FOSTERERS |
| FORLORNS | FORMULISING | FORSWEARING | FORWANDERING | FOSTERING |
| FORM | FORMULISM | FORSWEARS | FORWANDERS | FOSTERINGS |
| FORMABLE | FORMULISMS | FORSWINK | FORWARD | FOSTERS |
| FORMAL | FORMULIST | FORSWINKED | FORWARDED | FOSTRESS |
| FORMALIN | FORMULISTS | FORSWINKING | FORWARDER | FOSTRESSES |
| FORMALINS | FORMULIZE | FORSWINKS | FORWARDERS | FOTHER |
| FORMALISE | FORMULIZED | FORSWONCK | FORWARDEST | FOTHERED |
| FORMALISED | FORMULIZES | FORSWORE | FORWARDING | FOTHERING |
| FORMALISES | FORMULIZING | FORSWORN | FORWARDINGS | FOTHERS |
| FORMALISING | FORMWORK | FORSWUNK | FORWARDLY | FOU |
| FORMALISM | FORMWORKS | FORSYTHIA | FORWARDS | FOUAT |
| FORMALISMS | FORNENST | FORSYTHIAS | FORWARN | FOUATS |
| FORMALIST | FORNENT | FORT | FORWARNED | FOUD |
| FORMALISTS | FORNICAL | FORTALICE | FORWARNING | FOUDRIE |
| FORMALITIES | FORNICATE | FORTALICES | FORWARNS | FOUDRIES |
| FORMALITY | FORNICATED | FORTE | FORWASTE | FOUDS |
| FORMALIZE | FORNICATES | FORTED | FORWASTED | FOUER |
| FORMALIZED | FORNICATING | FORTES | FORWASTES | FOUEST |
| FORMALIZES | FORNIX | FORTH | FORWASTING | FOUET |
| FORMALIZING | FORNIXES | FORTHCAME | FORWEARIED | FOUETS |
| FORMALLY | FORPET | FORTHCOME | FORWEARIES | FOUETTÉ |
| FORMANT | FORPETS | FORTHCOMES | FORWEARY | FOUETTÉS |
| FORMANTS | FORPINE | FORTHCOMING | FORWEARYING | FOUGADE |
| FORMAT | FORPINED | FORTHINK | FORWENT | FOUGADES |
| FORMATE | FORPINES | FORTHINKING | FORWHY | FOUGASSE |
| FORMATED | FORPINING | FORTHINKS | FORWORN | FOUGASSES |
| FORMATES | FORPIT | FORTHOUGHT | FORZANDI | FOUGHT |
| FORMATING | FORPITS | FORTHWITH | FORZANDO | FOUGHTEN |
| FORMATION | FORRAD | FORTHY | FORZANDOS | FOUGHTIER |
| FORMATIONS | FORRADER | FORTIES | FORZATI | FOUGHTIEST |
| FORMATIVE | FORRAY | FORTIETH | FORZATO | FOUGHTY |
| FORMATIVES | FORRAYED | FORTIETHS | FORZATOS | FOUL |
| FORMATS | FORRAYING | FORTIFIED | FOSS | FOULARD |
| FORMATTED | FORRAYS | FORTIFIER | FOSSA | FOULARDS |
| FORMATTER | FORREN | FORTIFIERS | FOSSAE | FOULDER |
| FORMATTERS | FORRIT | FORTIFIES | FOSSAS | FOULDERED |
| FORMATTING | FORSAID | FORTIFY | FOSSE | FOULDERING |
| FORME | FORSAKE | FORTIFYING | FOSSED | FOULDERS |
| FORMED | FORSAKEN | FORTILAGE | FOSSES | FOULÉ |

FOULED
FOULER
FOULÉS
FOULEST
FOULING
FOULLY
FOULMART
FOULMARTS
FOULNESS
FOULNESSES
FOULS
FOUMART
FOUMARTS
FOUND
FOUNDED
FOUNDER
FOUNDERED
FOUNDERING
FOUNDERS
FOUNDING
FOUNDINGS
FOUNDLING
FOUNDLINGS
FOUNDRESS
FOUNDRESSES
FOUNDRIES
FOUNDRY
FOUNDS
FOUNT
FOUNTAIN
FOUNTAINED
FOUNTAINING
FOUNTAINS
FOUNTFUL
FOUNTS
FOUR
FOURFOLD
FOURGON
FOURGONS
FOURPENCE
FOURPENCES
FOURPENNIES
FOURPENNY
FOURS
FOURSCORE
FOURSES
FOURSOME
FOURSOMES
FOURTEEN
FOURTEENS
FOURTH
FOURTHLY
FOURTHS
FOUS
FOUSSA
FOUSSAS
FOUTER
FOUTERS
FOUTH
FOUTHS
FOUTRA
FOUTRAS
FOUTRE
FOUTRES
FOVEA
FOVEAE
FOVEAL
FOVEATE
FOVEOLA
FOVEOLAS

FOVEOLE
FOVEOLES
FOWL
FOWLED
FOWLER
FOWLERS
FOWLING
FOWLINGS
FOWLS
FOWTH
FOWTHS
FOX
FOXBERRIES
FOXBERRY
FOXED
FOXES
FOXGLOVE
FOXGLOVES
FOXHOLE
FOXHOLES
FOXHOUND
FOXHOUNDS
FOXIER
FOXIEST
FOXINESS
FOXINESSES
FOXING
FOXINGS
FOXSHARK
FOXSHARKS
FOXSHIP
FOXSHIPS
FOXTROT
FOXTROTS
FOXTROTTED
FOXTROTTING
FOXY
FOY
FOYER
FOYERS
FOYLE
FOYLED
FOYLES
FOYLING
FOYNE
FOYNED
FOYNES
FOYNING
FOYS
FOZIER
FOZIEST
FOZINESS
FOZINESSES
FOZY
FRA
FRAB
FRABBED
FRABBING
FRABBIT
FRABJOUS
FRABS
FRACAS
FRACK
FRACT
FRACTED
FRACTING
FRACTION
FRACTIONS
FRACTIOUS
FRACTS

FRACTURE
FRACTURED
FRACTURES
FRACTURING
FRAE
FRAENA
FRAENUM
FRAGILE
FRAGILELY
FRAGILER
FRAGILEST
FRAGILITIES
FRAGILITY
FRAGMENT
FRAGMENTED
FRAGMENTING
FRAGMENTS
FRAGOR
FRAGORS
FRAGRANCE
FRAGRANCED
FRAGRANCES
FRAGRANCIES
FRAGRANCING
FRAGRANCY
FRAGRANT
FRAÎCHEUR
FRAÎCHEURS
FRAIL
FRAILER
FRAILEST
FRAILISH
FRAILLY
FRAILNESS
FRAILNESSES
FRAILS
FRAILTEE
FRAILTEES
FRAILTIES
FRAILTY
FRAIM
FRAIMS
FRAISE
FRAISED
FRAISES
FRAISING
FRAME
FRAMED
FRAMER
FRAMERS
FRAMES
FRAMEWORK
FRAMEWORKS
FRAMING
FRAMINGS
FRAMPAL
FRAMPLER
FRAMPLERS
FRAMPOLD
FRANC
FRANCHISE
FRANCHISED
FRANCHISES
FRANCHISING
FRANCIUM
FRANCIUMS
FRANCO
FRANCOLIN
FRANCOLINS
FRANCS

FRANGIBLE
FRANION
FRANIONS
FRANK
FRANKED
FRANKER
FRANKEST
FRANKING
FRANKLIN
FRANKLINS
FRANKLY
FRANKNESS
FRANKNESSES
FRANKS
FRANTIC
FRANTICLY
FRANZIER
FRANZIEST
FRANZY
FRAP
FRAPPANT
FRAPPÉ
FRAPPED
FRAPPÉE
FRAPPING
FRAPS
FRAS
FRASS
FRASSES
FRATCH
FRATCHES
FRATCHETY
FRATCHIER
FRATCHIEST
FRATCHING
FRATCHY
FRATE
FRATER
FRATERIES
FRATERNAL
FRATERS
FRATERY
FRATI
FRATRIES
FRATRY
FRAU
FRAUD
FRAUDFUL
FRAUDS
FRAUDSMAN
FRAUDSMEN
FRAUDSTER
FRAUDSTERS
FRAUGHT
FRAUGHTED
FRAUGHTER
FRAUGHTEST
FRAUGHTING
FRAUGHTS
FRÄULEIN
FRÄULEINS
FRAUS
FRAUTAGE
FRAUTAGES
FRAY
FRAYED
FRAYING
FRAYINGS
FRAYS
FRAZIL

FRAZILS
FRAZZLE
FRAZZLED
FRAZZLES
FRAZZLING
FREAK
FREAKED
FREAKFUL
FREAKIER
FREAKIEST
FREAKING
FREAKISH
FREAKS
FREAKY
FRECKLE
FRECKLED
FRECKLES
FRECKLIER
FRECKLIEST
FRECKLING
FRECKLINGS
FRECKLY
FREDAINE
FREDAINES
FREE
FREEBEE
FREEBEES
FREEBIE
FREEBIES
FREEBOOTIES
FREEBOOTY
FREEBORN
FREED
FREEDMAN
FREEDMEN
FREEDOM
FREEDOMS
FREEHOLD
FREEHOLDS
FREEING
FREELOAD
FREELOADED
FREELOADING
FREELOADINGS
FREELOADS
FREELY
FREEMAN
FREEMASON
FREEMASONS
FREEMEN
FREENESS
FREENESSES
FREER
FREERS
FREES
FREESHEET
FREESHEETS
FREESIA
FREESIAS
FREEST
FREESTONE
FREESTONES
FREESTYLE
FREESTYLES
FREET
FREETIER
FREETIEST
FREETS
FREETY
FREEWAY

FREEWAYS
FREEWOMAN
FREEWOMEN
FREEZABLE
FREEZE
FREEZER
FREEZERS
FREEZES
FREEZING
FREEZINGS
FREIGHT
FREIGHTED
FREIGHTER
FREIGHTERS
FREIGHTING
FREIGHTS
FREIT
FREITIER
FREITIEST
FREITS
FREITY
FREMD
FREMDS
FREMIT
FREMITS
FREMITUS
FREMITUSES
FRENA
FRENCH
FRENETIC
FRENETICS
FRENNE
FRENNES
FRENUM
FRENZICAL
FRENZIED
FRENZIES
FRENZY
FRENZYING
FREON
FREONS
FREQUENCE
FREQUENCES
FREQUENCIES
FREQUENCY
FREQUENT
FREQUENTED
FREQUENTER
FREQUENTERS
FREQUENTEST
FREQUENTING
FREQUENTS
FRÈRE
FRÈRES
FRESCADE
FRESCADES
FRESCO
FRESCOED
FRESCOER
FRESCOERS
FRESCOES
FRESCOING
FRESCOINGS
FRESCOIST
FRESCOISTS
FRESCOS
FRESH
FRESHED

FRESHEN
FRESHENED
FRESHENER
FRESHENERS
FRESHENING
FRESHENS
FRESHER
FRESHERS
FRESHES
FRESHEST
FRESHET
FRESHETS
FRESHING
FRESHISH
FRESHLY
FRESHMAN
FRESHMEN
FRESHNESS
FRESHNESSES
FRET
FRETFUL
FRETFULLY
FRETS
FRETSAW
FRETSAWS
FRETTED
FRETTIER
FRETTIEST
FRETTING
FRETTINGS
FRETTY
FRETWORK
FRETWORKS
FRIABLE
FRIAND
FRIANDE
FRIANDES
FRIANDS
FRIAR
FRIARBIRD
FRIARBIRDS
FRIARIES
FRIARLY
FRIARS
FRIARY
FRIBBLE
FRIBBLED
FRIBBLER
FRIBBLERS
FRIBBLES
FRIBBLING
FRIBBLISH
FRICADEL
FRICADELS
FRICASSEE
FRICASSEED
FRICASSEEING
FRICASSEES
FRICATIVE
FRICATIVES
FRICHT
FRICHTED
FRICHTING
FRICHTS
FRICTION
FRICTIONS
FRIDGE
FRIDGED

FRIDGES
FRIDGING
FRIED
FRIEDCAKE
FRIEDCAKES
FRIEND
FRIENDED
FRIENDING
FRIENDINGS
FRIENDLIER
FRIENDLIES
FRIENDLIEST
FRIENDLY
FRIENDS
FRIER
FRIERS
FRIES
FRIEZE
FRIEZED
FRIEZES
FRIEZING
FRIG
FRIGATE
FRIGATES
FRIGATOON
FRIGATOONS
FRIGES
FRIGGED
FRIGGER
FRIGGERS
FRIGGING
FRIGGINGS
FRIGHT
FRIGHTED
FRIGHTEN
FRIGHTENED
FRIGHTENING
FRIGHTENS
FRIGHTFUL
FRIGHTING
FRIGHTS
FRIGID
FRIGIDER
FRIGIDEST
FRIGIDITIES
FRIGIDITY
FRIGIDLY
FRIGOT
FRIGOTS
FRIGS
FRIJOL
FRIJOLE
FRIJOLES
FRIKKADEL
FRIKKADELS
FRILL
FRILLED
FRILLIER
FRILLIES
FRILLIEST
FRILLING
FRILLINGS
FRILLS
FRILLY
FRINGE
FRINGED
FRINGES
FRINGIER

FRINGIEST
FRINGING
FRINGY
FRIPON
FRIPONS
FRIPPER
FRIPPERER
FRIPPERERS
FRIPPERIES
FRIPPERS
FRIPPERY
FRIS
FRISES
FRISETTE
FRISETTES
FRISEUR
FRISEURS
FRISK
FRISKA
FRISKAS
FRISKED
FRISKER
FRISKERS
FRISKET
FRISKETS
FRISKFUL
FRISKIER
FRISKIEST
FRISKILY
FRISKING
FRISKINGS
FRISKS
FRISKY
FRISSON
FRISSONS
FRIST
FRISTED
FRISTING
FRISTS
FRISURE
FRISURES
FRIT
FRITFLIES
FRITFLY
FRITH
FRITHBORH
FRITHBORHS
FRITHGILD
FRITHGILDS
FRITHS
FRITS
FRITTED
FRITTER
FRITTERED
FRITTERER
FRITTERERS
FRITTERING
FRITTERS
FRITTING
FRITURE
FRITURES
FRIVOL
FRIVOLITIES
FRIVOLITY
FRIVOLLED
FRIVOLLING
FRIVOLOUS
FRIVOLS

FRIZ
FRIZE
FRIZES
FRIZING
FRIZZ
FRIZZANTE
FRIZZED
FRIZZES
FRIZZIER
FRIZZIEST
FRIZZING
FRIZZLE
FRIZZLED
FRIZZLES
FRIZZLIER
FRIZZLIEST
FRIZZLING
FRIZZLY
FRIZZY
FRO
FROCK
FROCKED
FROCKING
FROCKINGS
FROCKLESS
FROCKS
FROG
FROGBIT
FROGBITS
FROGGED
FROGGERIES
FROGGERY
FROGGIER
FROGGIEST
FROGGING
FROGGINGS
FROGGY
FROGLET
FROGLETS
FROGLING
FROGLINGS
FROGMAN
FROGMEN
FROGMOUTH
FROGMOUTHS
FROGS
FROISE
FROISES
FROLIC
FROLICKED
FROLICKING
FROLICS
FROM
FROMENTIES
FROMENTY
FROND
FRONDAGE
FRONDAGES
FRONDED
FRONDENT
FRONDEUR
FRONDEURS
FRONDOSE
FRONDS
FRONT
FRONTAGE
FRONTAGER
FRONTAGERS

| | | | | |
|---|---|---|---|---|
| FRONTAGES | FROWARD | FRUITIVE | FUCK | FUGUES |
| FRONTAL | FROWARDLY | FRUITLESS | FUCKED | FUGUIST |
| FRONTALS | FROWARDS | FRUITLET | FUCKER | FUGUISTS |
| FRONTED | FROWIE | FRUITLETS | FUCKERS | FULCRA |
| FRONTIER | FROWIER | FRUITS | FUCKING | FULCRATE |
| FRONTIERED | FROWIEST | FRUITWOOD | FUCKINGS | FULCRUM |
| FRONTIERING | FROWN | FRUITWOODS | FUCKS | FULCRUMS |
| FRONTIERS | FROWNED | FRUITY | FUCOID | FULFIL |
| FRONTING | FROWNING | FRUMENTIES | FUCOIDAL | FULFILLED |
| FRONTLESS | FROWNS | FRUMENTY | FUCOIDS | FULFILLER |
| FRONTLET | FROWS | FRUMP | FUCUS | FULFILLERS |
| FRONTLETS | FROWSIER | FRUMPED | FUCUSED | FULFILLING |
| FRONTMAN | FROWSIEST | FRUMPIER | FUCUSES | FULFILLINGS |
| FRONTMEN | FROWST | FRUMPIEST | FUD | FULFILS |
| FRONTON | FROWSTED | FRUMPING | FUDDLE | FULGENCIES |
| FRONTONS | FROWSTER | FRUMPISH | FUDDLED | FULGENCY |
| FRONTOON | FROWSTERS | FRUMPLE | FUDDLER | FULGENT |
| FRONTOONS | FROWSTIER | FRUMPLED | FUDDLERS | FULGENTLY |
| FRONTS | FROWSTIEST | FRUMPLES | FUDDLES | FULGID |
| FRONTWARD | FROWSTING | FRUMPLING | FUDDLING | FULGOR |
| FRONTWARDS | FROWSTS | FRUMPS | FUDDLINGS | FULGOROUS |
| FRONTWAYS | FROWSTY | FRUMPY | FUDGE | FULGORS |
| FRONTWISE | FROWSY | FRUSH | FUDGED | FULGOUR |
| FRORE | FROWY | FRUSHED | FUDGES | FULGOURS |
| FROREN | FROWZIER | FRUSHES | FUDGING | FULGURAL |
| FRORN | FROWZIEST | FRUSHING | FUDS | FULGURANT |
| FRORNE | FROWZY | FRUST | FUEL | FULGURATE |
| FRORY | FROZE | FRUSTA | FUELLED | FULGURATED |
| FROST | FROZEN | FRUSTRATE | FUELLER | FULGURATES |
| FROSTBIT | FRUCTED | FRUSTRATED | FUELLERS | FULGURATING |
| FROSTBITE | FRUCTIFIED | FRUSTRATES | FUELLING | FULGURITE |
| FROSTBITES | FRUCTIFIES | FRUSTRATING | FUELS | FULGURITES |
| FROSTBITING | FRUCTIFY | FRUSTS | FUERO | FULGUROUS |
| FROSTBITTEN | FRUCTIFYING | FRUSTULE | FUEROS | FULHAM |
| FROSTED | FRUCTOSE | FRUSTULES | FUFF | FULHAMS |
| FROSTIER | FRUCTOSES | FRUSTUM | FUFFED | FULL |
| FROSTIEST | FRUCTUARIES | FRUSTUMS | FUFFIER | FULLAGE |
| FROSTILY | FRUCTUARY | FRUTEX | FUFFIEST | FULLAGES |
| FROSTING | FRUCTUATE | FRUTICES | FUFFING | FULLAM |
| FROSTINGS | FRUCTUATED | FRUTICOSE | FUFFS | FULLAMS |
| FROSTLESS | FRUCTUATES | FRUTIFIED | FUFFY | FULLAN |
| FROSTS | FRUCTUATING | FRUTIFIES | FUG | FULLANS |
| FROSTWORK | FRUCTUOUS | FRUTIFY | FUGACIOUS | FULLED |
| FROSTWORKS | FRUGAL | FRUTIFYING | FUGACITIES | FULLER |
| FROSTY | FRUGALIST | FRY | FUGACITY | FULLERS |
| FROTH | FRUGALISTS | FRYER | FUGAL | FULLEST |
| FROTHED | FRUGALITIES | FRYERS | FUGALLY | FULLING |
| FROTHERIES | FRUGALITY | FRYING | FUGATO | FULLISH |
| FROTHERY | FRUGALLY | FRYINGS | FUGATOS | FULLNESS |
| FROTHIER | FRUICT | FUB | FUGGED | FULLNESSES |
| FROTHIEST | FRUICTS | FUBBED | FUGGIER | FULLS |
| FROTHILY | FRUIT | FUBBERIES | FUGGIEST | FULLY |
| FROTHING | FRUITAGE | FUBBERY | FUGGING | FULMAR |
| FROTHLESS | FRUITAGES | FUBBIER | FUGGY | FULMARS |
| FROTHS | FRUITED | FUBBIEST | FUGHETTA | FULMINANT |
| FROTHY | FRUITER | FUBBING | FUGHETTAS | FULMINANTS |
| FROTTAGE | FRUITERER | FUBBY | FUGIE | FULMINATE |
| FROTTAGES | FRUITERERS | FUBS | FUGIES | FULMINATED |
| FROTTEUR | FRUITERIES | FUBSIER | FUGITIVE | FULMINATES |
| FROTTEURS | FRUITERS | FUBSIEST | FUGITIVES | FULMINATING |
| FROUGHIER | FRUITERY | FUBSY | FUGLE | FULMINE |
| FROUGHIEST | FRUITFUL | FUCHSIA | FUGLED | FULMINED |
| FROUGHY | FRUITIER | FUCHSIAS | FUGLEMAN | FULMINES |
| FROUNCE | FRUITIEST | FUCHSINE | FUGLEMEN | FULMINING |
| FROUNCED | FRUITING | FUCHSINES | FUGLES | FULMINOUS |
| FROUNCES | FRUITINGS | FUCHSITE | FUGLING | FULNESS |
| FROUNCING | FRUITION | FUCHSITES | FUGS | FULNESSES |
| FROW | FRUITIONS | FUCI | FUGUE | FULSOME |

| | | | | |
|---|---|---|---|---|
| FULSOMELY | FUNDS | FURANS | FURNISHED | FUSELAGES |
| FULSOMER | FUNDUS | FURBELOW | FURNISHER | FUSES |
| FULSOMEST | FUNEBRAL | FURBELOWED | FURNISHERS | FUSHION |
| FULVID | FUNÈBRE | FURBELOWING | FURNISHES | FUSHIONS |
| FULVOUS | FUNEBRIAL | FURBELOWS | FURNISHING | FUSIBLE |
| FUM | FUNERAL | FURBISH | FURNISHINGS | FUSIFORM |
| FUMADO | FUNERALS | FURBISHED | FURNITURE | FUSIL |
| FUMADOES | FUNERARY | FURBISHER | FURNITURES | FUSILE |
| FUMADOS | FUNEREAL | FURBISHERS | FUROL | FUSILEER |
| FUMAGE | FUNEST | FURBISHES | FUROLE | FUSILEERS |
| FUMAGES | FUNFAIR | FURBISHING | FUROLES | FUSILIER |
| FUMAROLE | FUNFAIRS | FURCAL | FUROLS | FUSILIERS |
| FUMAROLES | FUNG | FURCATE | FUROR | FUSILLADE |
| FUMATORIA | FUNGAL | FURCATED | FURORE | FUSILLADES |
| FUMATORIES | FUNGI | FURCATION | FURORES | FUSILS |
| FUMATORY | FUNGIBLES | FURCATIONS | FURORS | FUSING |
| FUMBLE | FUNGICIDE | FURCULA | FURPHIES | FUSION |
| FUMBLED | FUNGICIDES | FURCULAR | FURPHY | FUSIONISM |
| FUMBLER | FUNGIFORM | FURCULAS | FURR | FUSIONISMS |
| FUMBLERS | FUNGOID | FURDER | FURRED | FUSIONIST |
| FUMBLES | FUNGOIDAL | FUREUR | FURRIER | FUSIONISTS |
| FUMBLING | FUNGOSITIES | FUREURS | FURRIERIES | FUSIONS |
| FUME | FUNGOSITY | FURFAIR | FURRIERS | FUSS |
| FUMED | FUNGOUS | FURFAIRS | FURRIERY | FUSSED |
| FUMEROLE | FUNGS | FURFUR | FURRIEST | FUSSER |
| FUMEROLES | FUNGUS | FURFURAL | FURRING | FUSSERS |
| FUMES | FUNGUSES | FURFURALS | FURRINGS | FUSSES |
| FUMET | FUNICLE | FURFURAN | FURROW | FUSSIER |
| FUMETS | FUNICLES | FURFURANS | FURROWED | FUSSIEST |
| FUMETTE | FUNICULAR | FURFUROL | FURROWING | FUSSILY |
| FUMETTES | FUNICULI | FURFUROLE | FURROWS | FUSSINESS |
| FUMETTI | FUNICULUS | FURFUROLES | FURROWY | FUSSINESSES |
| FUMETTO | FUNK | FURFUROLS | FURRS | FUSSING |
| FUMIER | FUNKED | FURFUROUS | FURRY | FUSSY |
| FUMIEST | FUNKHOLE | FURFURS | FURS | FUST |
| FUMIGANT | FUNKHOLES | FURIBUND | FURTH | FUSTED |
| FUMIGANTS | FUNKIA | FURIES | FURTHER | FUSTET |
| FUMIGATE | FUNKIAS | FURIOSITIES | FURTHERED | FUSTETS |
| FUMIGATED | FUNKIER | FURIOSITY | FURTHERER | FUSTIAN |
| FUMIGATES | FUNKIEST | FURIOSO | FURTHERERS | FUSTIANS |
| FUMIGATING | FUNKINESS | FURIOSOS | FURTHERING | FUSTIC |
| FUMIGATOR | FUNKINESSES | FURIOUS | FURTHERS | FUSTICS |
| FUMIGATORS | FUNKING | FURIOUSLY | FURTHEST | FUSTIER |
| FUMING | FUNKS | FURL | FURTIVE | FUSTIEST |
| FUMITORIES | FUNKY | FURLANA | FURTIVELY | FUSTIGATE |
| FUMITORY | FUNNED | FURLANAS | FURTIVER | FUSTIGATED |
| FUMOSITIES | FUNNEL | FURLED | FURTIVEST | FUSTIGATES |
| FUMOSITY | FUNNELLED | FURLING | FURUNCLE | FUSTIGATING |
| FUMOUS | FUNNELLING | FURLONG | FURUNCLES | FUSTILUGS |
| FUMS | FUNNELS | FURLONGS | FURY | FUSTILY |
| FUMY | FUNNIER | FURLOUGH | FURZE | FUSTINESS |
| FUN | FUNNIES | FURLOUGHED | FURZES | FUSTINESSES |
| FUNCTION | FUNNIEST | FURLOUGHING | FURZIER | FUSTING |
| FUNCTIONED | FUNNILY | FURLOUGHS | FURZIEST | FUSTOC |
| FUNCTIONING | FUNNINESS | FURLS | FURZY | FUSTOCS |
| FUNCTIONS | FUNNINESSES | FURMENTIES | FUSAIN | FUSTS |
| FUND | FUNNING | FURMENTY | FUSAINS | FUSTY |
| FUNDABLE | FUNNY | FURMETIES | FUSAROL | FUTCHEL |
| FUNDAMENT | FUNS | FURMETY | FUSAROLE | FUTCHELS |
| FUNDAMENTS | FUR | FURMITIES | FUSAROLES | FUTHARK |
| FUNDED | FURACIOUS | FURMITY | FUSAROLS | FUTHARKS |
| FUNDER | FURACITIES | FURNACE | FUSC | FUTHORC |
| FUNDERS | FURACITY | FURNACED | FUSCOUS | FUTHORCS |
| FUNDI | FURAL | FURNACES | FUSE | FUTHORK |
| FUNDING | FURALS | FURNACING | FUSED | FUTHORKS |
| FUNDINGS | FURAN | FURNIMENT | FUSEE | FUTILE |
| FUNDIS | FURANE | FURNIMENTS | FUSEES | FUTILELY |
| FUNDLESS | FURANES | FURNISH | FUSELAGE | FUTILER |

FUTILEST
FUTILITIES
FUTILITY
FUTON
FUTONS
FUTTOCK
FUTTOCKS
FUTURE
FUTURES
FUTURISM

FUTURISMS
FUTURIST
FUTURISTS
FUTURITIES
FUTURITY
FUZE
FUZEE
FUZEES
FUZES
FUZZ

FUZZED
FUZZES
FUZZIER
FUZZIEST
FUZZILY
FUZZINESS
FUZZINESSES
FUZZING
FUZZLE
FUZZLED

FUZZLES
FUZZLING
FUZZY
FY
FYKE
FYKED
FYKES
FYKING
FYLE
FYLES

FYLFOT
FYLFOTS
FYNBOS
FYNBOSES
FYRD
FYRDS
FYTTE
FYTTES

# G

GAB
GABARDINE
GABARDINES
GABBARD
GABBARDS
GABBART
GABBARTS
GABBED
GABBER
GABBERS
GABBIER
GABBIEST
GABBING
GABBLE
GABBLED
GABBLER
GABBLERS
GABBLES
GABBLING
GABBLINGS
GABBRO
GABBROIC
GABBROID
GABBROS
GABBY
GABELLE
GABELLER
GABELLERS
GABELLES
GABERDINE
GABERDINES
GABFEST
GABFESTS
GABIES
GABION
GABIONADE
GABIONADES
GABIONAGE
GABIONAGES
GABIONED
GABIONS
GABLE
GABLED
GABLES
GABLET
GABLETS
GABNASH
GABNASHES
GABS
GABY
GAD
GADABOUT
GADABOUTS
GADDED
GADDER
GADDERS
GADDING
GADE
GADES
GADFLIES
GADFLY
GADGE
GADGES

GADGET
GADGETEER
GADGETEERS
GADGETRIES
GADGETRY
GADGETS
GADGIE
GADGIES
GADI
GADIS
GADJE
GADJES
GADLING
GADLINGS
GADOID
GADOIDS
GADROON
GADROONED
GADROONS
GADS
GADSMAN
GADSMEN
GADSO
GADSOS
GADWALL
GADWALLS
GADZOOKS
GAE
GAED
GAELICISE
GAELICISED
GAELICISES
GAELICISING
GAELICISM
GAELICISMS
GAELICIZE
GAELICIZED
GAELICIZES
GAELICIZING
GAES
GAFF
GAFFE
GAFFED
GAFFER
GAFFERS
GAFFES
GAFFING
GAFFINGS
GAFFS
GAG
GAGA
GAGAKU
GAGAKUS
GAGE
GAGED
GAGES
GAGGED
GAGGER
GAGGERS
GAGGING
GAGGLE
GAGGLED
GAGGLES

GAGGLING
GAGGLINGS
GAGING
GAGMAN
GAGMEN
GAGS
GAGSTER
GAGSTERS
GAHNITE
GAHNITES
GAID
GAIDS
GAIETIES
GAIETY
GAILLARD
GAILLARDE
GAILY
GAIN
GAINABLE
GAINED
GAINER
GAINERS
GAINEST
GAINFUL
GAINFULLY
GAINING
GAININGS
GAINLESS
GAINLIER
GAINLIEST
GAINLY
GAINS
GAINSAID
GAINSAY
GAINSAYER
GAINSAYERS
GAINSAYING
GAINSAYINGS
GAINSAYS
GAIR
GAIRFOWL
GAIRFOWLS
GAIRS
GAIT
GAITED
GAITER
GAITERS
GAITS
GAITT
GAITTS
GAJO
GAJOS
GAL
GALA
GALABEA
GALABEAH
GALABEAHS
GALABEAS
GALABIA
GALABIAH
GALABIAHS
GALABIAS
GALABIEH

GALABIEHS
GALABIYA
GALABIYAH
GALABIYAHS
GALABIYAS
GALABIYEH
GALABIYEHS
GALACTIC
GALACTOSE
GALACTOSES
GALAGE
GALAGES
GALAH
GALAHS
GALANGA
GALANGAL
GALANGALS
GALANGAS
GALANT
GALANTINE
GALANTINES
GALAPAGO
GALAPAGOS
GALAS
GALATEA
GALATEAS
GALAXIES
GALAXY
GALBANUM
GALBANUMS
GALDRAGON
GALDRAGONS
GALE
GALEA
GALEAS
GALEATE
GALEATED
GALENA
GALENAS
GALENGALE
GALENGALES
GALENITE
GALENITES
GALENOID
GALÈRE
GALÈRES
GALES
GALILEE
GALILEES
GALINGALE
GALINGALES
GALIONGEE
GALIONGEES
GALIOT
GALIOTS
GALIPOT
GALIPOTS
GALL
GALLABEA
GALLABEAH
GALLABEAHS
GALLABEAS
GALLABIA

GALLABIAH
GALLABIAHS
GALLABIAS
GALLABIEH
GALLABIEHS
GALLABIYA
GALLABIYAS
GALLANT
GALLANTER
GALLANTEST
GALLANTLY
GALLANTRIES
GALLANTRY
GALLANTS
GALLATE
GALLATES
GALLEASS
GALLEASSES
GALLED
GALLEON
GALLEONS
GALLERIED
GALLERIES
GALLERY
GALLERYING
GALLET
GALLETED
GALLETING
GALLETS
GALLEY
GALLEYS
GALLIARD
GALLIARDS
GALLIASS
GALLIASSES
GALLICISE
GALLICISED
GALLICISES
GALLICISING
GALLICISM
GALLICISMS
GALLICIZE
GALLICIZED
GALLICIZES
GALLICIZING
GALLIED
GALLIES
GALLINAZO
GALLINAZOS
GALLING
GALLINGLY
GALLINULE
GALLINULES
GALLIOT
GALLIOTS
GALLIPOT
GALLIPOTS
GALLISE
GALLISED
GALLISES
GALLISING
GALLISISE
GALLISISED

| | | | | |
|---|---|---|---|---|
| GALLISISES | GALOSHES | GAMBOLS | GAN | GANTRY |
| GALLISISING | GALOSHING | GAMBREL | GANCH | GANTS |
| GALLISIZE | GALOWSES | GAMBRELS | GANCHED | GAOL |
| GALLISIZED | GALRAVAGE | GAMBROON | GANCHES | GAOLED |
| GALLISIZES | GALRAVAGED | GAMBROONS | GANCHING | GAOLER |
| GALLISIZING | GALRAVAGES | GAMBS | GANDER | GAOLERESS |
| GALLIUM | GALRAVAGING | GAME | GANDERISM | GAOLERESSES |
| GALLIUMS | GALS | GAMED | GANDERISMS | GAOLERS |
| GALLIVANT | GALTONIA | GAMELAN | GANDERS | GAOLING |
| GALLIVANTED | GALTONIAS | GAMELANS | GANE | GAOLS |
| GALLIVANTING | GALUMPH | GAMELY | GANG | GAP |
| GALLIVANTS | GALUMPHED | GAMENESS | GANGBOARD | GAPE |
| GALLIVAT | GALUMPHER | GAMENESSES | GANGBOARDS | GAPED |
| GALLIVATS | GALUMPHERS | GAMER | GANGED | GAPER |
| GALLIWASP | GALUMPHING | GAMES | GANGER | GAPERS |
| GALLIWASPS | GALUMPHS | GAMESIER | GANGERS | GAPES |
| GALLIZE | GALUT | GAMESIEST | GANGING | GAPESEED |
| GALLIZED | GALUTH | GAMESOME | GANGINGS | GAPESEEDS |
| GALLIZES | GALUTHS | GAMEST | GANGLAND | GAPEWORM |
| GALLIZING | GALUTS | GAMESTER | GANGLANDS | GAPEWORMS |
| GALLON | GALVANIC | GAMESTERS | GANGLIA | GAPING |
| GALLONAGE | GALVANISE | GAMESY | GANGLIAR | GAPINGLY |
| GALLONAGES | GALVANISED | GAMETAL | GANGLIATE | GAPINGS |
| GALLONS | GALVANISES | GAMETE | GANGLIER | GAPO |
| GALLOON | GALVANISING | GAMETES | GANGLIEST | GAPOS |
| GALLOONED | GALVANISM | GAMETIC | GANGLING | GAPPED |
| GALLOONS | GALVANISMS | GAMIC | GANGLION | GAPPIER |
| GALLOP | GALVANIST | GAMIER | GANGLIONS | GAPPIEST |
| GALLOPADE | GALVANISTS | GAMIEST | GANGLY | GAPPING |
| GALLOPADED | GALVANIZE | GAMIN | GANGPLANK | GAPPY |
| GALLOPADES | GALVANIZED | GAMINE | GANGPLANKS | GAPS |
| GALLOPADING | GALVANIZES | GAMINERIE | GANGREL | GAR |
| GALLOPED | GALVANIZING | GAMINERIES | GANGRELS | GARAGE |
| GALLOPER | GAM | GAMINES | GANGRENE | GARAGED |
| GALLOPERS | GAMASH | GAMING | GANGRENED | GARAGES |
| GALLOPHIL | GAMASHES | GAMINGS | GANGRENES | GARAGING |
| GALLOPHILS | GAMB | GAMINS | GANGRENING | GARAGINGS |
| GALLOPING | GAMBA | GAMMA | GANGS | GARB |
| GALLOPS | GAMBADO | GAMMADION | GANGSMAN | GARBAGE |
| GALLOW | GAMBADOES | GAMMADIONS | GANGSMEN | GARBAGES |
| GALLOWED | GAMBADOS | GAMMAS | GANGSTER | GARBANZO |
| GALLOWING | GAMBAS | GAMMATION | GANGSTERS | GARBANZOS |
| GALLOWS | GAMBESON | GAMMATIONS | GANGUE | GARBE |
| GALLOWSES | GAMBESONS | GAMME | GANGUES | GARBED |
| GALLS | GAMBET | GAMMED | GANGWAY | GARBES |
| GALLUMPH | GAMBETS | GAMMER | GANGWAYS | GARBING |
| GALLUMPHED | GAMBIER | GAMMERS | GANISTER | GARBLE |
| GALLUMPHING | GAMBIERS | GAMMES | GANISTERS | GARBLED |
| GALLUMPHS | GAMBIR | GAMMIER | GANJA | GARBLER |
| GALLUS | GAMBIRS | GAMMIEST | GANJAS | GARBLERS |
| GALLUSES | GAMBIST | GAMMING | GANNET | GARBLES |
| GALLY | GAMBISTS | GAMMOCK | GANNETRIES | GARBLING |
| GALLYING | GAMBIT | GAMMOCKED | GANNETRY | GARBLINGS |
| GALOCHE | GAMBITED | GAMMOCKING | GANNETS | GARBO |
| GALOCHED | GAMBITING | GAMMOCKS | GANNISTER | GARBOARD |
| GALOCHES | GAMBITS | GAMMON | GANNISTERS | GARBOARDS |
| GALOCHING | GAMBLE | GAMMONED | GANOID | GARBOIL |
| GALOOT | GAMBLED | GAMMONER | GANOIDS | GARBOILS |
| GALOOTS | GAMBLER | GAMMONERS | GANOIN | GARBOS |
| GALOP | GAMBLERS | GAMMONING | GANOINS | GARBS |
| GALOPED | GAMBLES | GAMMONINGS | GANT | GARÇON |
| GALOPIN | GAMBLING | GAMMONS | GANTED | GARÇONS |
| GALOPING | GAMBLINGS | GAMMY | GANTING | GARDA |
| GALOPINS | GAMBOGE | GAMP | GANTLET | GARDAI |
| GALOPPED | GAMBOGES | GAMPISH | GANTLETS | GARDANT |
| GALOPPING | GAMBOGIAN | GAMPS | GANTLINE | GARDANTS |
| GALOPS | GAMBOGIC | GAMS | GANTLINES | GARDEN |
| GALORE | GAMBOL | GAMUT | GANTLOPE | GARDENED |
| GALOSH | GAMBOLLED | GAMUTS | GANTLOPES | GARDENER |
| GALOSHED | GAMBOLLING | GAMY | GANTRIES | GARDENERS |

| | | | | |
|---|---|---|---|---|
| GARDENIA | GARNISHEED | GARUM | GASPIEST | GAUCHER |
| GARDENIAS | GARNISHEEING | GARUMS | GASPINESS | GAUCHERIE |
| GARDENING | GARNISHEES | GARVIE | GASPINESSES | GAUCHERIES |
| GARDENINGS | GARNISHER | GARVIES | GASPING | GAUCHESCO |
| GARDENS | GARNISHERS | GARVOCK | GASPINGLY | GAUCHEST |
| GARDEROBE | GARNISHES | GARVOCKS | GASPINGS | GAUCHO |
| GARDEROBES | GARNISHING | GAS | GASPS | GAUCHOS |
| GARDYLOO | GARNISHINGS | GASAHOL | GASPY | GAUCIE |
| GARDYLOOS | GARNISHRIES | GASAHOLS | GASSED | GAUCIER |
| GARE | GARNISHRY | GASALIER | GASSES | GAUCIEST |
| GAREFOWL | GARNITURE | GASALIERS | GASSIER | GAUCY |
| GAREFOWLS | GARNITURES | GASCON | GASSIEST | GAUD |
| GARFISH | GAROTTE | GASCONADE | GASSINESS | GAUDEAMUS |
| GARFISHES | GAROTTED | GASCONADED | GASSINESSES | GAUDEAMUSES |
| GARGANEY | GAROTTER | GASCONADES | GASSING | GAUDED |
| GARGANEYS | GAROTTERS | GASCONADING | GASSINGS | GAUDERIES |
| GARGARISE | GAROTTES | GASCONISM | GASSY | GAUDERY |
| GARGARISED | GAROTTING | GASCONISMS | GAST | GAUDGIE |
| GARGARISES | GAROTTINGS | GASCONS | GASTED | GAUDGIES |
| GARGARISING | GARPIKE | GASEITIES | GASTFULL | GAUDIER |
| GARGARISM | GARPIKES | GASEITY | GASTING | GAUDIES |
| GARGARISMS | GARRAN | GASELIER | GASTNESS | GAUDIEST |
| GARGARIZE | GARRANS | GASELIERS | GASTNESSE | GAUDILY |
| GARGARIZED | GARRE | GASEOUS | GASTNESSES | GAUDINESS |
| GARGARIZES | GARRED | GASES | GASTRAEA | GAUDINESSES |
| GARGARIZING | GARRES | GASFIELD | GASTRAEAS | GAUDING |
| GARGET | GARRET | GASFIELDS | GASTRAEUM | GAUDS |
| GARGETS | GARRETED | GASH | GASTRAEUMS | GAUDY |
| GARGLE | GARRETEER | GASHED | GASTRIC | GAUFER |
| GARGLED | GARRETEERS | GASHES | GASTRIN | GAUFERS |
| GARGLES | GARRETS | GASHFUL | GASTRINS | GAUFRE |
| GARGLING | GARRIGUE | GASHING | GASTRITIS | GAUFRES |
| GARGOYLE | GARRIGUES | GASHLY | GASTRITISES | GAUGE |
| GARGOYLES | GARRING | GASIFIED | GASTROPOD | GAUGEABLE |
| GARIAL | GARRISON | GASIFIER | GASTROPODS | GAUGED |
| GARIALS | GARRISONED | GASIFIERS | GASTRULA | GAUGER |
| GARIBALDI | GARRISONING | GASIFIES | GASTRULAE | GAUGERS |
| GARIBALDIS | GARRISONS | GASIFORM | GASTRULAS | GAUGES |
| GARIGUE | GARRON | GASIFY | GASTS | GAUGING |
| GARIGUES | GARRONS | GASIFYING | GAT | GAUGINGS |
| GARISH | GARROT | GASKET | GATE | GAUJE |
| GARISHED | GARROTE | GASKETS | GÂTEAU | GAUJES |
| GARISHES | GARROTED | GASKIN | GÂTEAUS | GAULEITER |
| GARISHING | GARROTES | GASKINS | GÂTEAUX | GAULEITERS |
| GARISHLY | GARROTING | GASLIGHT | GATECRASH | GAULT |
| GARJAN | GARROTS | GASLIGHTS | GATECRASHED | GAULTER |
| GARJANS | GARROTTE | GASLIT | GATECRASHES | GAULTERS |
| GARLAND | GARROTTED | GASMAN | GATECRASHING | GAULTS |
| GARLANDED | GARROTTER | GASMEN | GATED | GAUM |
| GARLANDING | GARROTTERS | GASOGENE | GATEFOLD | GAUMED |
| GARLANDRIES | GARROTTES | GASOGENES | GATEFOLDS | GAUMIER |
| GARLANDRY | GARROTTING | GASOHOL | GATELEG | GAUMIEST |
| GARLANDS | GARROTTINGS | GASOHOLS | GATELESS | GAUMING |
| GARLIC | GARRULITIES | GASOLENE | GATES | GAUMLESS |
| GARLICKY | GARRULITY | GASOLENES | GATEWAY | GAUMS |
| GARLICS | GARRULOUS | GASOLIER | GATEWAYS | GAUMY |
| GARMENT | GARRYA | GASOLIERS | GATH | GAUN |
| GARMENTED | GARRYAS | GASOLINE | GATHER | GAUNCH |
| GARMENTING | GARRYOWEN | GASOLINES | GATHERED | GAUNCHED |
| GARMENTS | GARRYOWENS | GASOMETER | GATHERER | GAUNCHES |
| GARNER | GARS | GASOMETERS | GATHERERS | GAUNCHING |
| GARNERED | GART | GASOMETRIES | GATHERING | GAUNT |
| GARNERING | GARTER | GASOMETRY | GATHERINGS | GAUNTED |
| GARNERS | GARTERED | GASP | GATHERS | GAUNTER |
| GARNET | GARTERING | GASPED | GATHS | GAUNTEST |
| GARNETS | GARTERS | GASPER | GATING | GAUNTING |
| GARNI | GARTH | GASPEREAU | GATINGS | GAUNTLET |
| GARNISH | GARTHS | GASPEREAUS | GATS | GAUNTLETS |
| GARNISHED | GARUDA | GASPERS | GAU | GAUNTLY |
| GARNISHEE | GARUDAS | GASPIER | GAUCHE | GAUNTNESS |

GAUNTNESSES
GAUNTREE
GAUNTREES
GAUNTRIES
GAUNTRY
GAUNTS
GAUP
GAUPED
GAUPER
GAUPERS
GAUPING
GAUPS
GAUPUS
GAUPUSES
GAUR
GAURS
GAUS
GAUSS
GAUSSES
GAUSSIAN
GAUZE
GAUZES
GAUZIER
GAUZIEST
GAUZINESS
GAUZINESSES
GAUZY
GAVAGE
GAVAGES
GAVE
GAVEL
GAVELKIND
GAVELKINDS
GAVELMAN
GAVELMEN
GAVELOCK
GAVELOCKS
GAVELS
GAVIAL
GAVIALS
GAVOTTE
GAVOTTES
GAWCIER
GAWCIEST
GAWCY
GAWD
GAWDS
GAWK
GAWKED
GAWKER
GAWKERS
GAWKIER
GAWKIES
GAWKIEST
GAWKIHOOD
GAWKIHOODS
GAWKINESS
GAWKINESSES
GAWKING
GAWKS
GAWKY
GAWP
GAWPED
GAWPER
GAWPERS
GAWPING
GAWPS
GAWPUS
GAWPUSES
GAWSIER

GAWSIEST
GAWSY
GAY
GAYAL
GAYALS
GAYER
GAYEST
GAYNESS
GAYNESSES
GAYS
GAYSOME
GAZAL
GAZALS
GAZE
GAZEBO
GAZEBOES
GAZEBOS
GAZED
GAZEFUL
GAZEL
GAZELLE
GAZELLES
GAZELS
GAZEMENT
GAZEMENTS
GAZER
GAZERS
GAZES
GAZETTE
GAZETTED
GAZETTEER
GAZETTEERED
GAZETTEERING
GAZETTEERS
GAZETTES
GAZETTING
GAZIER
GAZIEST
GAZING
GAZOGENE
GAZOGENES
GAZON
GAZONS
GAZOO
GAZOOKA
GAZOOKAS
GAZOON
GAZOONS
GAZOOS
GAZPACHO
GAZPACHOS
GAZUMP
GAZUMPED
GAZUMPING
GAZUMPS
GAZY
GEAL
GEALED
GEALING
GEALOUS
GEALOUSIES
GEALOUSY
GEALS
GEAN
GEANS
GEAR
GEARBOX
GEARBOXES
GEARE
GEARED

GEARES
GEARING
GEARINGS
GEARLESS
GEARS
GEASON
GEAT
GEATS
GEBUR
GEBURS
GECK
GECKED
GECKING
GECKO
GECKOES
GECKOS
GECKS
GED
GEDS
GEE
GEEBUNG
GEEBUNGS
GEED
GEEING
GEES
GEESE
GEEZER
GEEZERS
GEFUFFLE
GEFUFFLED
GEFUFFLES
GEFUFFLING
GEISHA
GEISHAS
GEIST
GEISTS
GEIT
GEITS
GEL
GELADA
GELADAS
GELASTIC
GELATI
GELATIN
GELATINE
GELATINES
GELATINS
GELATION
GELATIONS
GELATO
GELD
GELDED
GELDER
GELDERS
GELDING
GELDINGS
GELDS
GELID
GELIDER
GELIDEST
GELIDITIES
GELIDITY
GELIDLY
GELIDNESS
GELIDNESSES
GELIGNITE
GELIGNITES
GELLED
GELLING
GELLY

GELOSIES
GELOSY
GELS
GELSEMINE
GELSEMINES
GELSEMIUM
GELSEMIUMS
GELT
GELTS
GEM
GEMATRIA
GEMATRIAS
GEMEL
GEMELS
GEMINATE
GEMINATED
GEMINATES
GEMINATING
GEMINI
GEMINIES
GEMINOUS
GEMINY
GEMMA
GEMMAE
GEMMAN
GEMMATE
GEMMATED
GEMMATES
GEMMATING
GEMMATION
GEMMATIONS
GEMMATIVE
GEMMED
GEMMEN
GEMMEOUS
GEMMERIES
GEMMERY
GEMMIER
GEMMIEST
GEMMING
GEMMOLOGIES
GEMMOLOGY
GEMMULE
GEMMULES
GEMMY
GEMOLOGIES
GEMOLOGY
GEMONY
GEMOT
GEMOTS
GEMS
GEMSBOK
GEMSBOKS
GEMSTONE
GEMSTONES
GEMÜTLICH
GEN
GENA
GENAL
GENAPPE
GENAPPES
GENAS
GENDARME
GENDARMES
GENDER
GENDERED
GENDERING
GENDERS
GENE
GENEALOGIES

GENEALOGY
GENERA
GENERABLE
GENERAL
GENERALE
GENERALIA
GENERALLED
GENERALLING
GENERALLY
GENERALS
GENERANT
GENERANTS
GENERATE
GENERATED
GENERATES
GENERATING
GENERATOR
GENERATORS
GENERIC
GENERICAL
GENERICS
GENEROUS
GENES
GENESES
GENESIS
GENET
GENETIC
GENETICAL
GENETICS
GENETRICES
GENETRIX
GENETRIXES
GENETS
GENETTE
GENETTES
GENEVA
GENEVAS
GENIAL
GENIALISE
GENIALISED
GENIALISES
GENIALISING
GENIALITIES
GENIALITY
GENIALIZE
GENIALIZED
GENIALIZES
GENIALIZING
GENIALLY
GENIC
GENIE
GENIES
GENII
GENIP
GENIPAP
GENIPAPS
GENIPS
GENISTA
GENISTAS
GENITAL
GENITALIA
GENITALIC
GENITALS
GENITIVAL
GENITIVE
GENITIVES
GENITOR
GENITORS
GENITRICES
GENITRIX

GENITRIXES
GENITURE
GENITURES
GENIUS
GENIUSES
GENIZAH
GENIZAHS
GENNET
GENNETS
GENOA
GENOAS
GENOCIDAL
GENOCIDE
GENOCIDES
GENOM
GENOME
GENOMES
GENOMS
GENOTYPE
GENOTYPES
GENOTYPIC
GENRE
GENRES
GENS
GENSDARMES
GENT
GENTEEL
GENTEELER
GENTEELEST
GENTEELLY
GENTES
GENTIAN
GENTIANS
GENTIER
GENTIEST
GENTILE
GENTILES
GENTILIC
GENTILISE
GENTILISED
GENTILISES
GENTILISH
GENTILISING
GENTILISM
GENTILISMS
GENTILITIES
GENTILITY
GENTILIZE
GENTILIZED
GENTILIZES
GENTILIZING
GENTLE
GENTLED
GENTLEMAN
GENTLEMEN
GENTLER
GENTLES
GENTLEST
GENTLING
GENTLY
GENTOO
GENTOOS
GENTRICE
GENTRICES
GENTRIES
GENTRIFIED
GENTRIFIES
GENTRIFY
GENTRIFYING
GENTRY

GENTS
GENTY
GENU
GENUFLECT
GENUFLECTED
GENUFLECTING
GENUFLECTS
GENUINE
GENUINELY
GENUS
GENUSES
GEO
GEOCARPIC
GEOCARPIES
GEOCARPY
GEODE
GEODES
GEODESIC
GEODESIES
GEODESIST
GEODESISTS
GEODESY
GEODETIC
GEODETICS
GEODIC
GEOGENIES
GEOGENY
GEOGNOSES
GEOGNOSIES
GEOGNOSIS
GEOGNOST
GEOGNOSTS
GEOGNOSY
GEOGONIC
GEOGONIES
GEOGONY
GEOGRAPHIES
GEOGRAPHY
GEOID
GEOIDAL
GEOIDS
GEOLATRIES
GEOLATRY
GEOLOGER
GEOLOGERS
GEOLOGIAN
GEOLOGIANS
GEOLOGIC
GEOLOGIES
GEOLOGISE
GEOLOGISED
GEOLOGISES
GEOLOGISING
GEOLOGIST
GEOLOGISTS
GEOLOGIZE
GEOLOGIZED
GEOLOGIZES
GEOLOGIZING
GEOLOGY
GEOMANCER
GEOMANCERS
GEOMANCIES
GEOMANCY
GEOMANTIC
GEOMETER
GEOMETERS
GEOMETRIC
GEOMETRID
GEOMETRIDS

GEOMETRIES
GEOMETRY
GEOMYOID
GEOPHAGIES
GEOPHAGY
GEOPHILIC
GEOPHONE
GEOPHONES
GEOPHYTE
GEOPHYTES
GEOPHYTIC
GEOPONIC
GEOPONICS
GEORDIE
GEORDIES
GEORGETTE
GEORGETTES
GEORGIC
GEORGICS
GEOS
GEOSPHERE
GEOSPHERES
GEOSTATIC
GEOSTATICS
GEOTACTIC
GEOTAXES
GEOTAXIS
GEOTROPIC
GERAH
GERAHS
GERANIOL
GERANIOLS
GERANIUM
GERANIUMS
GERBE
GERBERA
GERBERAS
GERBES
GERBIL
GERBILLE
GERBILLES
GERBILS
GERE
GERENT
GERENTS
GERENUK
GERENUKS
GERES
GERFALCON
GERFALCONS
GERIATRIC
GERIATRICS
GERIATRIES
GERIATRY
GERLE
GERLES
GERM
GERMAIN
GERMAINE
GERMAINES
GERMAINS
GERMAN
GERMANDER
GERMANDERS
GERMANE
GERMANELY
GERMANIUM
GERMANIUMS
GERMANS
GERMED

GERMEN
GERMENS
GERMICIDE
GERMICIDES
GERMIN
GERMINAL
GERMINANT
GERMINATE
GERMINATED
GERMINATES
GERMINATING
GERMING
GERMINS
GERMS
GERNE
GERNED
GERNES
GERNING
GERONTIC
GEROPIGA
GEROPIGAS
GERUND
GERUNDIAL
GERUNDIVE
GERUNDIVES
GERUNDS
GESNERIA
GESNERIAS
GESSAMINE
GESSAMINES
GESSE
GESSED
GESSES
GESSING
GESSO
GESSOES
GEST
GESTALT
GESTALTS
GESTANT
GESTATE
GESTATED
GESTATES
GESTATING
GESTATION
GESTATIONS
GESTATIVE
GESTATORY
GESTE
GESTES
GESTIC
GESTS
GESTURAL
GESTURE
GESTURED
GESTURES
GESTURING
GET
GETA
GETAS
GETAWAY
GETAWAYS
GETS
GETTABLE
GETTER
GETTERED
GETTERING
GETTERINGS
GETTERS
GETTING

GETTINGS
GEUM
GEUMS
GEWGAW
GEWGAWS
GEY
GEYAN
GEYER
GEYEST
GEYSER
GEYSERITE
GEYSERITES
GEYSERS
GHARIAL
GHARIALS
GHARRI
GHARRIES
GHARRIS
GHARRY
GHAST
GHASTED
GHASTFUL
GHASTFULL
GHASTING
GHASTLIER
GHASTLIEST
GHASTLY
GHASTNESS
GHASTNESSES
GHASTS
GHAT
GHATS
GHAUT
GHAUTS
GHAZAL
GHAZALS
GHAZEL
GHAZELS
GHAZI
GHAZIS
GHEE
GHEES
GHERAO
GHERAOED
GHERAOING
GHERAOS
GHERKIN
GHERKINS
GHESSE
GHESSED
GHESSES
GHESSING
GHEST
GHETTO
GHETTOES
GHETTOISE
GHETTOISED
GHETTOISES
GHETTOISING
GHETTOIZE
GHETTOIZED
GHETTOIZES
GHETTOIZING
GHETTOS
GHI
GHILGAI
GHILGAIS
GHILLIE
GHILLIED
GHILLIES

GHILLYING
GHIS
GHOST
GHOSTED
GHOSTIER
GHOSTIEST
GHOSTING
GHOSTLIER
GHOSTLIEST
GHOSTLY
GHOSTS
GHOSTY
GHOUL
GHOULISH
GHOULS
GHYLL
GHYLLS
GI
GIAMBEUX
GIANT
GIANTESS
GIANTESSES
GIANTHOOD
GIANTHOODS
GIANTISM
GIANTISMS
GIANTLIER
GIANTLIEST
GIANTLY
GIANTRIES
GIANTRY
GIANTS
GIANTSHIP
GIANTSHIPS
GIAOUR
GIAOURS
GIB
GIBBED
GIBBER
GIBBERED
GIBBERING
GIBBERISH
GIBBERISHES
GIBBERS
GIBBET
GIBBETED
GIBBETING
GIBBETS
GIBBING
GIBBON
GIBBONS
GIBBOSE
GIBBOSITIES
GIBBOSITY
GIBBOUS
GIBBOUSLY
GIBBSITE
GIBBSITES
GIBE
GIBED
GIBEL
GIBELS
GIBER
GIBERS
GIBES
GIBING
GIBINGLY
GIBLET
GIBLETS
GIBS

GIBUS
GIBUSES
GID
GIDDIED
GIDDIER
GIDDIES
GIDDIEST
GIDDILY
GIDDINESS
GIDDINESSES
GIDDY
GIDDYING
GIDGEE
GIDGEES
GIDJEE
GIDJEES
GIDS
GIE
GIED
GIEING
GIEN
GIES
GIF
GIFT
GIFTED
GIFTEDLY
GIFTING
GIFTS
GIG
GIGA
GIGAHERTZ
GIGAHERTZES
GIGANTEAN
GIGANTIC
GIGANTISM
GIGANTISMS
GIGAS
GIGAWATT
GIGAWATTS
GIGGED
GIGGING
GIGGIT
GIGGITED
GIGGITING
GIGGITS
GIGGLE
GIGGLED
GIGGLER
GIGGLERS
GIGGLES
GIGGLIER
GIGGLIEST
GIGGLING
GIGGLINGS
GIGGLY
GIGLET
GIGLETS
GIGLOT
GIGLOTS
GIGMAN
GIGMANITIES
GIGMANITY
GIGMEN
GIGOLO
GIGOLOS
GIGOT
GIGOTS
GIGS
GIGUE
GIGUES

GILA
GILAS
GILBERT
GILBERTS
GILCUP
GILCUPS
GILD
GILDED
GILDEN
GILDER
GILDERS
GILDING
GILDINGS
GILDS
GILET
GILETS
GILGAI
GILGAIS
GILGIE
GILGIES
GILL
GILLAROO
GILLAROOS
GILLED
GILLET
GILLETS
GILLFLIRT
GILLFLIRTS
GILLIE
GILLIED
GILLIES
GILLING
GILLION
GILLIONS
GILLS
GILLY
GILLYING
GILLYVOR
GILLYVORS
GILPEY
GILPEYS
GILPIES
GILPY
GILRAVAGE
GILRAVAGED
GILRAVAGES
GILRAVAGING
GILT
GILTCUP
GILTCUPS
GILTS
GILTWOOD
GIMBAL
GIMBALS
GIMCRACK
GIMCRACKS
GIMLET
GIMLETED
GIMLETING
GIMLETS
GIMMAL
GIMMALLED
GIMMALS
GIMME
GIMMER
GIMMERS
GIMMES
GIMMICK
GIMMICKIER
GIMMICKIEST

GIMMICKRIES
GIMMICKRY
GIMMICKS
GIMMICKY
GIMMOR
GIMMORS
GIMP
GIMPED
GIMPING
GIMPS
GIN
GING
GINGAL
GINGALL
GINGALLS
GINGALS
GINGELLIES
GINGELLY
GINGER
GINGERADE
GINGERADES
GINGERED
GINGERING
GINGERLY
GINGEROUS
GINGERS
GINGERY
GINGHAM
GINGHAMS
GINGILI
GINGILIS
GINGIVAL
GINGKO
GINGKOES
GINGLE
GINGLED
GINGLES
GINGLING
GINGLYMI
GINGLYMUS
GINGS
GINHOUSE
GINHOUSES
GINK
GINKGO
GINKGOES
GINKS
GINN
GINNED
GINNEL
GINNELS
GINNER
GINNERIES
GINNERS
GINNERY
GINNING
GINS
GINSENG
GINSENGS
GINSHOP
GINSHOPS
GIO
GIOCOSO
GIOS
GIP
GIPPIES
GIPPO
GIPPOS
GIPPY
GIPS

GIPSEN
GIPSENS
GIPSIED
GIPSIES
GIPSY
GIPSYING
GIRAFFE
GIRAFFES
GIRAFFID
GIRAFFINE
GIRAFFOID
GIRANDOLA
GIRANDOLAS
GIRANDOLE
GIRANDOLES
GIRASOL
GIRASOLE
GIRASOLES
GIRASOLS
GIRD
GIRDED
GIRDER
GIRDERS
GIRDING
GIRDINGS
GIRDLE
GIRDLED
GIRDLER
GIRDLERS
GIRDLES
GIRDLING
GIRDS
GIRKIN
GIRKINS
GIRL
GIRLHOOD
GIRLHOODS
GIRLIE
GIRLIES
GIRLISH
GIRLISHLY
GIRLOND
GIRLONDS
GIRLS
GIRLY
GIRN
GIRNED
GIRNEL
GIRNELS
GIRNIE
GIRNIER
GIRNIEST
GIRNING
GIRNS
GIRO
GIRON
GIRONS
GIROS
GIROSOL
GIROSOLS
GIRR
GIRRS
GIRT
GIRTED
GIRTH
GIRTHED
GIRTHING
GIRTHLINE
GIRTHLINES
GIRTHS

GIRTING
GIRTLINE
GIRTLINES
GIRTS
GIS
GISARME
GISARMES
GISM
GISMO
GISMOS
GISMS
GIST
GISTS
GIT
GITANA
GITANAS
GITANO
GITANOS
GITE
GITES
GITS
GITTERN
GITTERNED
GITTERNING
GITTERNS
GIUST
GIUSTED
GIUSTING
GIUSTO
GIUSTS
GIVE
GIVEAWAY
GIVEAWAYS
GIVED
GIVEN
GIVENNESS
GIVENNESSES
GIVER
GIVERS
GIVES
GIVING
GIVINGS
GIZMO
GIZMOS
GIZZ
GIZZARD
GIZZARDS
GIZZEN
GIZZENED
GIZZENING
GIZZENS
GIZZES
GJU
GJUS
GLABELLA
GLABELLAE
GLABELLAR
GLABRATE
GLABROUS
GLACÉ
GLACÉED
GLACÉING
GLACÉS
GLACIAL
GLACIALS
GLACIATE
GLACIATED
GLACIATES
GLACIATING
GLACIER

GLACIERS
GLACIS
GLACISES
GLAD
GLADDED
GLADDEN
GLADDENED
GLADDENING
GLADDENS
GLADDER
GLADDEST
GLADDIE
GLADDIES
GLADDING
GLADDON
GLADDONS
GLADE
GLADES
GLADFUL
GLADIATE
GLADIATOR
GLADIATORS
GLADIER
GLADIEST
GLADIOLE
GLADIOLES
GLADIOLI
GLADIOLUS
GLADIOLUSES
GLADIUS
GLADIUSES
GLADLY
GLADNESS
GLADNESSES
GLADS
GLADSOME
GLADY
GLAIK
GLAIKET
GLAIKIT
GLAIKS
GLAIR
GLAIRED
GLAIREOUS
GLAIRIER
GLAIRIEST
GLAIRIN
GLAIRING
GLAIRINS
GLAIRS
GLAIRY
GLAIVE
GLAIVED
GLAIVES
GLAM
GLAMOR
GLAMORED
GLAMORING
GLAMORISE
GLAMORISED
GLAMORISES
GLAMORISING
GLAMORIZE
GLAMORIZED
GLAMORIZES
GLAMORIZING
GLAMOROUS
GLAMORS
GLAMOUR
GLAMOURED

GLAMOURING
GLAMOURS
GLANCE
GLANCED
GLANCES
GLANCING
GLANCINGS
GLAND
GLANDERED
GLANDERS
GLANDES
GLANDS
GLANDULAR
GLANDULE
GLANDULES
GLANS
GLARE
GLAREAL
GLARED
GLAREOUS
GLARES
GLARIER
GLARIEST
GLARING
GLARINGLY
GLARY
GLASNOST
GLASNOSTS
GLASS
GLASSED
GLASSEN
GLASSES
GLASSFUL
GLASSFULS
GLASSIER
GLASSIEST
GLASSIFIED
GLASSIFIES
GLASSIFY
GLASSIFYING
GLASSILY
GLASSINE
GLASSINES
GLASSING
GLASSLIKE
GLASSMAN
GLASSMEN
GLASSWARE
GLASSWARES
GLASSWORK
GLASSWORKS
GLASSWORT
GLASSWORTS
GLASSY
GLAUCOMA
GLAUCOMAS
GLAUCOUS
GLAUM
GLAUMED
GLAUMING
GLAUMS
GLAUR
GLAURIER
GLAURIEST
GLAURS
GLAURY
GLAZE
GLAZED
GLAZEN
GLAZER

GLAZERS
GLAZES
GLAZIER
GLAZIERS
GLAZIEST
GLAZING
GLAZINGS
GLAZY
GLEAM
GLEAMED
GLEAMIER
GLEAMIEST
GLEAMING
GLEAMINGS
GLEAMS
GLEAMY
GLEAN
GLEANED
GLEANER
GLEANERS
GLEANING
GLEANINGS
GLEANS
GLEAVE
GLEAVES
GLEBE
GLEBES
GLEBOUS
GLEBY
GLED
GLEDE
GLEDES
GLEDGE
GLEDGED
GLEDGES
GLEDGING
GLEDS
GLEE
GLEED
GLEEDS
GLEEFUL
GLEEING
GLEEK
GLEEKED
GLEEKING
GLEEKS
GLEEMAN
GLEEMEN
GLEES
GLEESOME
GLEET
GLEETED
GLEETIER
GLEETIEST
GLEETING
GLEETS
GLEETY
GLEG
GLEGGER
GLEGGEST
GLEI
GLEIS
GLEN
GLENGARRIES
GLENGARRY
GLENOID
GLENOIDAL
GLENOIDS
GLENS
GLENT

GLENTED
GLENTING
GLENTS
GLEY
GLEYED
GLEYING
GLEYS
GLIA
GLIADIN
GLIADINE
GLIADINES
GLIADINS
GLIAL
GLIAS
GLIB
GLIBBED
GLIBBER
GLIBBERY
GLIBBEST
GLIBBING
GLIBLY
GLIBNESS
GLIBNESSES
GLIBS
GLID
GLIDDER
GLIDDERY
GLIDDEST
GLIDE
GLIDED
GLIDER
GLIDERS
GLIDES
GLIDING
GLIDINGLY
GLIDINGS
GLIFF
GLIFFING
GLIFFINGS
GLIFFS
GLIFT
GLIFTS
GLIKE
GLIKES
GLIM
GLIMMER
GLIMMERED
GLIMMERING
GLIMMERINGS
GLIMMERS
GLIMMERY
GLIMPSE
GLIMPSED
GLIMPSES
GLIMPSING
GLIMS
GLINT
GLINTED
GLINTING
GLINTS
GLIOMA
GLIOMAS
GLIOMATA
GLIOSES
GLIOSIS
GLISK
GLISKS
GLISSADE
GLISSADED
GLISSADES

GLISSADING
GLISSANDO
GLISSANDOS
GLISTEN
GLISTENED
GLISTENING
GLISTENS
GLISTER
GLISTERED
GLISTERING
GLISTERS
GLIT
GLITCH
GLITCHES
GLITS
GLITTER
GLITTERED
GLITTERING
GLITTERINGS
GLITTERS
GLITTERY
GLITZ
GLITZES
GLITZIER
GLITZIEST
GLITZY
GLOAMING
GLOAMINGS
GLOAT
GLOATED
GLOATING
GLOATS
GLOB
GLOBAL
GLOBALISE
GLOBALISED
GLOBALISES
GLOBALISING
GLOBALIZE
GLOBALIZED
GLOBALIZES
GLOBALIZING
GLOBALLY
GLOBATE
GLOBATED
GLOBE
GLOBED
GLOBES
GLOBIN
GLOBING
GLOBINS
GLOBOID
GLOBOIDS
GLOBOSE
GLOBOSES
GLOBOSITIES
GLOBOSITY
GLOBOUS
GLOBS
GLOBULAR
GLOBULE
GLOBULES
GLOBULET
GLOBULETS
GLOBULIN
GLOBULINS
GLOBULITE
GLOBULITES
GLOBULOUS
GLOBY

GLODE
GLOGG
GLOGGS
GLOIRE
GLOIRES
GLOM
GLOMERATE
GLOMERATED
GLOMERATES
GLOMERATING
GLOMERULE
GLOMERULES
GLOMERULI
GLOMMED
GLOMMING
GLOMS
GLONOIN
GLONOINS
GLOOM
GLOOMED
GLOOMFUL
GLOOMIER
GLOOMIEST
GLOOMILY
GLOOMING
GLOOMINGS
GLOOMS
GLOOMY
GLORIA
GLORIAS
GLORIED
GLORIES
GLORIFIED
GLORIFIES
GLORIFY
GLORIFYING
GLORIOLE
GLORIOLES
GLORIOSA
GLORIOSAS
GLORIOUS
GLORY
GLORYBOX
GLORYBOXES
GLORYING
GLOSS
GLOSSA
GLOSSAE
GLOSSAL
GLOSSARIES
GLOSSARY
GLOSSAS
GLOSSATOR
GLOSSATORS
GLOSSED
GLOSSEME
GLOSSEMES
GLOSSER
GLOSSERS
GLOSSES
GLOSSIER
GLOSSIES
GLOSSIEST
GLOSSILY
GLOSSINA
GLOSSINAS
GLOSSING
GLOSSITIS
GLOSSITISES
GLOSSY

GLOTTAL
GLOTTIC
GLOTTIDES
GLOTTIS
GLOTTISES
GLOUT
GLOUTED
GLOUTING
GLOUTS
GLOVE
GLOVED
GLOVER
GLOVERS
GLOVES
GLOVING
GLOW
GLOWED
GLOWER
GLOWERED
GLOWERING
GLOWERS
GLOWING
GLOWINGLY
GLOWLAMP
GLOWLAMPS
GLOWS
GLOXINIA
GLOXINIAS
GLOZE
GLOZED
GLOZES
GLOZING
GLOZINGS
GLUCAGON
GLUCAGONS
GLUCINA
GLUCINAS
GLUCINIUM
GLUCINIUMS
GLUCINUM
GLUCINUMS
GLUCOSE
GLUCOSES
GLUCOSIC
GLUCOSIDE
GLUCOSIDES
GLUE
GLUED
GLUER
GLUERS
GLUES
GLUEY
GLUEYNESS
GLUEYNESSES
GLUG
GLUGGED
GLUGGING
GLUGS
GLÜHWEIN
GLÜHWEINS
GLUIER
GLUIEST
GLUING
GLUISH
GLUM
GLUME
GLUMELLA
GLUMELLAS
GLUMES
GLUMLY

GLUMMER
GLUMMEST
GLUMNESS
GLUMNESSES
GLUMPIER
GLUMPIEST
GLUMPISH
GLUMPS
GLUMPY
GLUON
GLUONS
GLUT
GLUTAEAL
GLUTAEI
GLUTAEUS
GLUTAMATE
GLUTAMATES
GLUTAMINE
GLUTAMINES
GLUTEAL
GLUTEI
GLUTELIN
GLUTELINS
GLUTEN
GLUTENOUS
GLUTENS
GLUTEUS
GLUTINOUS
GLUTS
GLUTTED
GLUTTING
GLUTTON
GLUTTONIES
GLUTTONS
GLUTTONY
GLYCERIC
GLYCERIDE
GLYCERIDES
GLYCERIN
GLYCERINE
GLYCERINES
GLYCERINS
GLYCEROL
GLYCEROLS
GLYCERYL
GLYCERYLS
GLYCIN
GLYCINE
GLYCINES
GLYCINS
GLYCOCOLL
GLYCOCOLLS
GLYCOGEN
GLYCOGENS
GLYCOL
GLYCOLIC
GLYCOLLIC
GLYCOLS
GLYCONIC
GLYCONICS
GLYCOSE
GLYCOSES
GLYCOSIDE
GLYCOSIDES
GLYCOSYL
GLYCOSYLS
GLYPH
GLYPHIC
GLYPHS
GLYPTIC

GLYPTICS
GMELINITE
GMELINITES
GNAR
GNARL
GNARLED
GNARLIER
GNARLIEST
GNARLING
GNARLS
GNARLY
GNARR
GNARRED
GNARRING
GNARRS
GNARS
GNASH
GNASHED
GNASHER
GNASHERS
GNASHES
GNASHING
GNAT
GNATHAL
GNATHIC
GNATHITE
GNATHITES
GNATHONIC
GNATLING
GNATLINGS
GNATS
GNAW
GNAWED
GNAWER
GNAWERS
GNAWING
GNAWN
GNAWS
GNEISS
GNEISSES
GNEISSIC
GNEISSOID
GNEISSOSE
GNOCCHI
GNOCCHIS
GNOMAE
GNOME
GNOMES
GNOMIC
GNOMISH
GNOMIST
GNOMISTS
GNOMON
GNOMONIC
GNOMONICS
GNOMONS
GNOSES
GNOSIS
GNOSTIC
GNOSTICAL
GNU
GNUS
GO
GOA
GOAD
GOADED
GOADING
GOADS
GOADSMAN
GOADSMEN

| | | | | |
|---|---|---|---|---|
| GOADSTER | GODDAM | GOFFERINGS | GOLDSTONES | GOMUTO |
| GOADSTERS | GODDAMN | GOFFERS | GOLDY | GOMUTOS |
| GOAF | GODDAMNED | GOFFING | GOLE | GON |
| GOAFS | GODDED | GOFFS | GOLEM | GONAD |
| GOAL | GODDESS | GOG | GOLEMS | GONADIAL |
| GOALED | GODDESSES | GOGGLE | GOLES | GONADIC |
| GOALIE | GODDING | GOGGLED | GOLF | GONADS |
| GOALIES | GODET | GOGGLER | GOLFED | GONDELAY |
| GOALING | GODETIA | GOGGLERS | GOLFER | GONDELAYS |
| GOALLESS | GODETIAS | GOGGLES | GOLFERS | GONDOLA |
| GOALMOUTH | GODETS | GOGGLIER | GOLFIANA | GONDOLAS |
| GOALMOUTHS | GODFATHER | GOGGLIEST | GOLFIANAS | GONDOLIER |
| GOALPOST | GODFATHERS | GOGGLING | GOLFING | GONDOLIERS |
| GOALPOSTS | GODHEAD | GOGGLINGS | GOLFINGS | GONE |
| GOALS | GODHEADS | GOGGLY | GOLFS | GONENESS |
| GOANNA | GODHOOD | GOGLET | GOLIARD | GONENESSES |
| GOANNAS | GODHOODS | GOGLETS | GOLIARDIC | GONER |
| GOARY | GODLESS | GOGO | GOLIARDIES | GONERS |
| GOAS | GODLESSLY | GOGS | GOLIARDS | GONFALON |
| GOAT | GODLIER | GOIER | GOLIARDY | GONFALONS |
| GOATEE | GODLIEST | GOIEST | GOLIAS | GONFANON |
| GOATEED | GODLIKE | GOING | GOLIASED | GONFANONS |
| GOATEES | GODLILY | GOINGS | GOLIASES | GONG |
| GOATFISH | GODLINESS | GOITER | GOLIASING | GONGED |
| GOATFISHES | GODLINESSES | GOITERS | GOLLAN | GONGING |
| GOATHERD | GODLING | GOITRE | GOLLAND | GONGS |
| GOATHERDS | GODLINGS | GOITRED | GOLLANDS | GONGSTER |
| GOATIER | GODLY | GOITRES | GOLLANS | GONGSTERS |
| GOATIEST | GODMOTHER | GOITROUS | GOLLAR | GONIA |
| GOATISH | GODMOTHERS | GOLD | GOLLARED | GONIATITE |
| GOATLING | GODOWN | GOLDARN | GOLLARING | GONIATITES |
| GOATLINGS | GODOWNS | GOLDCREST | GOLLARS | GONIDIA |
| GOATS | GODPARENT | GOLDCRESTS | GOLLIES | GONIDIAL |
| GOATSKIN | GODPARENTS | GOLDEN | GOLLIWOG | GONIDIC |
| GOATSKINS | GODROON | GOLDENED | GOLLIWOGS | GONIDIUM |
| GOATWEED | GODROONS | GOLDENER | GOLLOP | GONION |
| GOATWEEDS | GODS | GOLDENEST | GOLLOPED | GONK |
| GOATY | GODSEND | GOLDENING | GOLLOPING | GONKS |
| GOB | GODSENDS | GOLDENLY | GOLLOPS | GONNA |
| GOBANG | GODSHIP | GOLDENROD | GOLLY | GONOCOCCI |
| GOBANGS | GODSHIPS | GOLDENRODS | GOLLYWOG | GONOCYTE |
| GOBBELINE | GODSO | GOLDENS | GOLLYWOGS | GONOCYTES |
| GOBBELINES | GODSON | GOLDER | GOLOMYNKA | GONOPHORE |
| GOBBET | GODSONS | GOLDEST | GOLOMYNKAS | GONOPHORES |
| GOBBETS | GODSOS | GOLDEYE | GOLOSH | GONORRHEA |
| GOBBI | GODSPEED | GOLDEYES | GOLOSHED | GONORRHEAS |
| GOBBLE | GODSPEEDS | GOLDFIELD | GOLOSHES | GONS |
| GOBBLED | GODWARD | GOLDFIELDS | GOLOSHING | GOO |
| GOBBLER | GODWARDS | GOLDFINCH | GOLP | GOOBER |
| GOBBLERS | GODWIT | GOLDFINCHES | GOLPE | GOOBERS |
| GOBBLES | GODWITS | GOLDFINNIES | GOLPES | GOOD |
| GOBBLING | GOE | GOLDFINNY | GOLPS | GOODFACED |
| GOBBO | GOEL | GOLDFISH | GOMBEEN | GOODIER |
| GOBIES | GOELS | GOLDFISHES | GOMBEENS | GOODIES |
| GOBIOID | GOER | GOLDIER | GOMBO | GOODIEST |
| GOBLET | GOERS | GOLDIEST | GOMBOS | GOODINESS |
| GOBLETS | GOES | GOLDISH | GOMBRO | GOODINESSES |
| GOBLIN | GOETHITE | GOLDLESS | GOMBROS | GOODISH |
| GOBLINS | GOETHITES | GOLDS | GOMERAL | GOODLIER |
| GOBO | GOETIC | GOLDSINNIES | GOMERALS | GOODLIEST |
| GOBOES | GOETIES | GOLDSINNY | GOMERIL | GOODLY |
| GOBONY | GOETY | GOLDSIZE | GOMERILS | GOODMAN |
| GOBOS | GOEY | GOLDSIZES | GOMOKU | GOODMEN |
| GOBS | GOFER | GOLDSMITH | GOMOKUS | GOODNESS |
| GOBURRA | GOFERS | GOLDSMITHS | GOMPA | GOODNESSES |
| GOBURRAS | GOFF | GOLDSPINK | GOMPAS | GOODNIGHT |
| GOBY | GOFFED | GOLDSPINKS | GOMPHOSES | GOODNIGHTS |
| GOD | GOFFER | GOLDSTICK | GOMPHOSIS | GOODS |
| GODCHILD | GOFFERED | GOLDSTICKS | GOMUTI | GOODSIRE |
| GODCHILDREN | GOFFERING | GOLDSTONE | GOMUTIS | GOODSIRES |

| | | | | |
|---|---|---|---|---|
| GOODTIME | GOOSES | GORMIER | GOTHICIZED | GOWANY |
| GOODWIFE | GOOSEY | GORMIEST | GOTHICIZES | GOWD |
| GOODWILL | GOOSEYS | GORMING | GOTHICIZING | GOWDER |
| GOODWILLS | GOOSIER | GORMLESS | GÖTHITE | GOWDEST |
| GOODWIVES | GOOSIES | GORMS | GÖTHITES | GOWDS |
| GOODY | GOOSIEST | GORMY | GOTTA | GOWDSPINK |
| GOODYEAR | GOOSING | GORSE | GOTTEN | GOWDSPINKS |
| GOODYEARS | GOOSY | GORSEDD | GOUACHE | GOWF |
| GOOEY | GOPAK | GORSEDDS | GOUACHES | GOWFED |
| GOOF | GOPAKS | GORSES | GOUGE | GOWFER |
| GOOFBALL | GOPHER | GORSIER | GOUGED | GOWFERS |
| GOOFBALLS | GOPHERED | GORSIEST | GOUGÈRE | GOWFING |
| GOOFED | GOPHERING | GORSOON | GOUGÈRES | GOWFS |
| GOOFIER | GOPHERS | GORSOONS | GOUGES | GOWK |
| GOOFIEST | GOPURA | GORSY | GOUGING | GOWKS |
| GOOFILY | GOPURAM | GORY | GOUJEERS | GOWL |
| GOOFINESS | GOPURAMS | GOS | GOUJONS | GOWLAND |
| GOOFINESSES | GOPURAS | GOSH | GOUK | GOWLANDS |
| GOOFING | GORAL | GOSHAWK | GOUKS | GOWLED |
| GOOFS | GORALS | GOSHAWKS | GOULASH | GOWLING |
| GOOFY | GORAMIES | GOSLARITE | GOULASHES | GOWLS |
| GOOGLE | GORAMY | GOSLARITES | GOURAMI | GOWN |
| GOOGLED | GORBLIMEY | GOSLET | GOURAMIS | GOWNBOY |
| GOOGLES | GORBLIMY | GOSLETS | GOURD | GOWNBOYS |
| GOOGLIES | GORCOCK | GOSLING | GOURDE | GOWNED |
| GOOGLING | GORCOCKS | GOSLINGS | GOURDES | GOWNING |
| GOOGLY | GORCROW | GOSPEL | GOURDIER | GOWNMAN |
| GOOGOL | GORCROWS | GOSPELISE | GOURDIEST | GOWNMEN |
| GOOGOLS | GORE | GOSPELISED | GOURDS | GOWNS |
| GOOIER | GORED | GOSPELISES | GOURDY | GOWNSMAN |
| GOOIEST | GORES | GOSPELISING | GOURMAND | GOWNSMEN |
| GOOK | GORGE | GOSPELIZE | GOURMANDS | GOWPEN |
| GOOKS | GORGED | GOSPELIZED | GOURMET | GOWPENFUL |
| GOOL | GORGEOUS | GOSPELIZES | GOURMETS | GOWPENFULS |
| GOOLD | GORGERIN | GOSPELIZING | GOUSTIER | GOWPENS |
| GOOLDS | GORGERINS | GOSPELLED | GOUSTIEST | GOY |
| GOOLEY | GORGES | GOSPELLER | GOUSTROUS | GOYIM |
| GOOLEYS | GORGET | GOSPELLERS | GOUSTY | GOYISCH |
| GOOLIE | GORGETS | GOSPELLING | GOUT | GOYISH |
| GOOLIES | GORGIA | GOSPELS | GOUTFLIES | GOZZAN |
| GOOLS | GORGIAS | GOSPODAR | GOUTFLY | GOZZANS |
| GOOLY | GORGING | GOSPODARS | GOUTIER | GRAAL |
| GOON | GORGIO | GOSSAMER | GOUTIEST | GRAALS |
| GOONEY | GORGIOS | GOSSAMERS | GOUTINESS | GRAB |
| GOONEYS | GORGON | GOSSAMERY | GOUTINESSES | GRABBED |
| GOONS | GORGONEIA | GOSSAN | GOUTS | GRABBER |
| GOOP | GORGONIAN | GOSSANS | GOUTTE | GRABBERS |
| GOOPIER | GORGONIANS | GOSSE | GOUTTES | GRABBING |
| GOOPIEST | GORGONISE | GOSSES | GOUTWEED | GRABBLE |
| GOOPS | GORGONISED | GOSSIB | GOUTWEEDS | GRABBLED |
| GOOPY | GORGONISES | GOSSIBS | GOUTWORT | GRABBLER |
| GOOR | GORGONISING | GOSSIP | GOUTWORTS | GRABBLERS |
| GOOROO | GORGONIZE | GOSSIPED | GOUTY | GRABBLES |
| GOOROOS | GORGONIZED | GOSSIPING | GOV | GRABBLING |
| GOORS | GORGONIZES | GOSSIPINGS | GOVERN | GRABEN |
| GOOS | GORGONIZING | GOSSIPRIES | GOVERNALL | GRABENS |
| GOOSANDER | GORGONS | GOSSIPRY | GOVERNALLS | GRABS |
| GOOSANDERS | GORIER | GOSSIPS | GOVERNED | GRACE |
| GOOSE | GORIEST | GOSSIPY | GOVERNESS | GRACED |
| GOOSED | GORILLA | GOSSOON | GOVERNESSED | GRACEFUL |
| GOOSEFOOT | GORILLAS | GOSSOONS | GOVERNESSES | GRACELESS |
| GOOSEFOOTS | GORILLIAN | GOSSYPINE | GOVERNESSING | GRACES |
| GOOSEGOB | GORILLINE | GOSSYPOL | GOVERNING | GRACILE |
| GOOSEGOBS | GORILY | GOSSYPOLS | GOVERNOR | GRACILITIES |
| GOOSEGOG | GORING | GOT | GOVERNORS | GRACILITY |
| GOOSEGOGS | GORINGS | GOTHICISE | GOVERNS | GRACING |
| GOOSEHERD | GORM | GOTHICISED | GOVS | GRACIOSO |
| GOOSEHERDS | GORMAND | GOTHICISES | GOWAN | GRACIOSOS |
| GOOSERIES | GORMANDS | GOTHICISING | GOWANED | GRACIOUS |
| GOOSERY | GORMED | GOTHICIZE | GOWANS | GRACIOUSES |

GRACKLE
GRACKLES
GRADABLE
GRADABLES
GRADATE
GRADATED
GRADATES
GRADATIM
GRADATING
GRADATION
GRADATIONS
GRADATORY
GRADDAN
GRADDANED
GRADDANING
GRADDANS
GRADE
GRADED
GRADELY
GRADER
GRADERS
GRADES
GRADIENT
GRADIENTS
GRADIN
GRADINE
GRADINES
GRADING
GRADINI
GRADINO
GRADINS
GRADUAL
GRADUALLY
GRADUALS
GRADUAND
GRADUANDS
GRADUATE
GRADUATED
GRADUATES
GRADUATING
GRADUATOR
GRADUATORS
GRADUS
GRADUSES
GRAFF
GRAFFED
GRAFFING
GRAFFITI
GRAFFITIS
GRAFFITO
GRAFFS
GRAFT
GRAFTED
GRAFTER
GRAFTERS
GRAFTING
GRAFTINGS
GRAFTS
GRAIL
GRAILE
GRAILES
GRAILS
GRAIN
GRAINAGE
GRAINAGES
GRAINE
GRAINED
GRAINER
GRAINERS
GRAINES

GRAINIER
GRAINIEST
GRAINING
GRAININGS
GRAINS
GRAINY
GRAIP
GRAIPS
GRAITH
GRAITHED
GRAITHING
GRAITHLY
GRAITHS
GRAKLE
GRAKLES
GRALLOCH
GRALLOCHED
GRALLOCHING
GRALLOCHS
GRAM
GRAMA
GRAMARIES
GRAMARY
GRAMARYE
GRAMARYES
GRAMAS
GRAMASH
GRAMASHES
GRAME
GRAMERCIES
GRAMERCY
GRAMES
GRAMMAR
GRAMMARS
GRAMMATIC
GRAMME
GRAMMES
GRAMOCHE
GRAMOCHES
GRAMPUS
GRAMPUSES
GRAMS
GRAN
GRANARIES
GRANARY
GRAND
GRANDAD
GRANDADDIES
GRANDADDY
GRANDADS
GRANDAM
GRANDAMS
GRANDDAD
GRANDDADS
GRANDE
GRANDEE
GRANDEES
GRANDER
GRANDEST
GRANDEUR
GRANDEURS
GRANDIOSE
GRANDLY
GRANDMA
GRANDMAMA
GRANDMAMAS
GRANDMAS
GRANDNESS
GRANDNESSES
GRANDPA

GRANDPAPA
GRANDPAPAS
GRANDPAS
GRANDS
GRANDSIRE
GRANDSIRES
GRANDSON
GRANDSONS
GRANFER
GRANFERS
GRANGE
GRANGER
GRANGERS
GRANGES
GRANITE
GRANITES
GRANITIC
GRANITISE
GRANITISED
GRANITISES
GRANITISING
GRANITITE
GRANITITES
GRANITIZE
GRANITIZED
GRANITIZES
GRANITIZING
GRANITOID
GRANIVORE
GRANIVORES
GRANNAM
GRANNAMS
GRANNIE
GRANNIES
GRANNY
GRANS
GRANT
GRANTABLE
GRANTED
GRANTEE
GRANTEES
GRANTER
GRANTERS
GRANTING
GRANTOR
GRANTORS
GRANTS
GRANULAR
GRANULARY
GRANULATE
GRANULATED
GRANULATES
GRANULATING
GRANULE
GRANULES
GRANULITE
GRANULITES
GRANULOMA
GRANULOMAS
GRANULOMATA
GRANULOSE
GRANULOUS
GRAPE
GRAPED
GRAPELESS
GRAPERIES
GRAPERY
GRAPES
GRAPESEED
GRAPESEEDS

GRAPESHOT
GRAPESHOTS
GRAPETREE
GRAPETREES
GRAPEVINE
GRAPEVINES
GRAPEY
GRAPH
GRAPHED
GRAPHEME
GRAPHEMES
GRAPHEMIC
GRAPHEMICS
GRAPHIC
GRAPHICAL
GRAPHICLY
GRAPHICS
GRAPHING
GRAPHITE
GRAPHITES
GRAPHITIC
GRAPHIUM
GRAPHIUMS
GRAPHS
GRAPIER
GRAPIEST
GRAPING
GRAPLE
GRAPLES
GRAPNEL
GRAPNELS
GRAPPA
GRAPPAS
GRAPPLE
GRAPPLED
GRAPPLES
GRAPPLING
GRAPY
GRASP
GRASPABLE
GRASPED
GRASPER
GRASPERS
GRASPING
GRASPLESS
GRASPS
GRASS
GRASSED
GRASSER
GRASSERS
GRASSES
GRASSHOOK
GRASSHOOKS
GRASSIER
GRASSIEST
GRASSING
GRASSINGS
GRASSLAND
GRASSLANDS
GRASSUM
GRASSUMS
GRASSY
GRASTE
GRAT
GRATE
GRATED
GRATEFUL
GRATER
GRATERS
GRATES

GRATICULE
GRATICULES
GRATIFIED
GRATIFIER
GRATIFIERS
GRATIFIES
GRATIFY
GRATIFYING
GRATING
GRATINGLY
GRATINGS
GRATIS
GRATITUDE
GRATITUDES
GRATTOIR
GRATTOIRS
GRATUITIES
GRATUITY
GRATULANT
GRATULATE
GRATULATED
GRATULATES
GRATULATING
GRAUPEL
GRAUPELS
GRAVAMEN
GRAVAMINA
GRAVE
GRAVED
GRAVEL
GRAVELESS
GRAVELLED
GRAVELLING
GRAVELLY
GRAVELS
GRAVELY
GRAVEN
GRAVENESS
GRAVENESSES
GRAVER
GRAVERS
GRAVES
GRAVEST
GRAVEYARD
GRAVEYARDS
GRAVID
GRAVIDITIES
GRAVIDITY
GRAVIES
GRAVING
GRAVINGS
GRAVITAS
GRAVITASES
GRAVITATE
GRAVITATED
GRAVITATES
GRAVITATING
GRAVITIES
GRAVITON
GRAVITONS
GRAVITY
GRAVURE
GRAVURES
GRAVY
GRAY
GRAYED
GRAYER
GRAYEST
GRAYFLIES
GRAYFLY

| | | | | |
|---|---|---|---|---|
| GRAYING | GREENERIES | GREMLIN | GRIEFFUL | GRIMNESSES |
| GRAYLE | GREENERY | GREMLINS | GRIEFLESS | GRIMOIRE |
| GRAYLES | GREENEST | GREN | GRIEFS | GRIMOIRES |
| GRAYLING | GREENFLIES | GRENADE | GRIESIE | GRIMY |
| GRAYLINGS | GREENFLY | GRENADES | GRIESLY | GRIN |
| GRAYS | GREENGAGE | GRENADIER | GRIESY | GRIND |
| GRAYWACKE | GREENGAGES | GRENADIERS | GRIEVANCE | GRINDED |
| GRAYWACKES | GREENHAND | GRENADINE | GRIEVANCES | GRINDER |
| GRAZE | GREENHANDS | GRENADINES | GRIEVE | GRINDERIES |
| GRAZED | GREENHORN | GRENNED | GRIEVED | GRINDERS |
| GRAZER | GREENHORNS | GRENNING | GRIEVER | GRINDERY |
| GRAZERS | GREENIER | GRENS | GRIEVERS | GRINDING |
| GRAZES | GREENIEST | GRESE | GRIEVES | GRINDINGS |
| GRAZIER | GREENING | GRESES | GRIEVING | GRINDS |
| GRAZIERS | GREENINGS | GRESSING | GRIEVOUS | GRINGO |
| GRAZING | GREENISH | GRESSINGS | GRIFF | GRINGOS |
| GRAZINGS | GREENLET | GREVE | GRIFFE | GRINNED |
| GRAZIOSO | GREENLETS | GREVES | GRIFFES | GRINNER |
| GREASE | GREENLY | GREW | GRIFFIN | GRINNERS |
| GREASED | GREENMAIL | GREWED | GRIFFINS | GRINNING |
| GREASER | GREENMAILS | GREWHOUND | GRIFFON | GRINS |
| GREASERS | GREENNESS | GREWHOUNDS | GRIFFONS | GRIOT |
| GREASES | GREENNESSES | GREWING | GRIFFS | GRIOTS |
| GREASIER | GREENROOM | GREWS | GRIFT | GRIP |
| GREASIEST | GREENROOMS | GREY | GRIFTED | GRIPE |
| GREASILY | GREENS | GREYBEARD | GRIFTER | GRIPED |
| GREASING | GREENSAND | GREYBEARDS | GRIFTERS | GRIPER |
| GREASY | GREENSANDS | GREYED | GRIFTING | GRIPERS |
| GREAT | GREENTH | GREYER | GRIFTS | GRIPES |
| GREATCOAT | GREENTHS | GREYEST | GRIG | GRIPING |
| GREATCOATS | GREENWEED | GREYHEN | GRIGGED | GRIPINGLY |
| GREATEN | GREENWEEDS | GREYHENS | GRIGGING | GRIPLE |
| GREATENED | GREENWOOD | GREYHOUND | GRIGRI | GRIPPE |
| GREATENING | GREENWOODS | GREYHOUNDS | GRIGRIS | GRIPPED |
| GREATENS | GREENY | GREYING | GRIGS | GRIPPER |
| GREATER | GREES | GREYISH | GRIKE | GRIPPERS |
| GREATEST | GREESE | GREYLY | GRIKES | GRIPPES |
| GREATLY | GREESES | GREYNESS | GRILL | GRIPPIER |
| GREATNESS | GREESING | GREYNESSES | GRILLADE | GRIPPIEST |
| GREATNESSES | GREESINGS | GREYS | GRILLADES | GRIPPING |
| GREATS | GREET | GREYWACKE | GRILLAGE | GRIPPLE |
| GREAVE | GREETE | GREYWACKES | GRILLAGES | GRIPPLES |
| GREAVED | GREETED | GRIBBLE | GRILLE | GRIPPY |
| GREAVES | GREETES | GRIBBLES | GRILLED | GRIPS |
| GREAVING | GREETING | GRICE | GRILLES | GRIPSACK |
| GREBE | GREETINGS | GRICER | GRILLING | GRIPSACKS |
| GREBES | GREETS | GRICERS | GRILLINGS | GRIS |
| GRECE | GREFFIER | GRICES | GRILLS | GRISAILLE |
| GRECES | GREFFIERS | GRICING | GRILSE | GRISAILLES |
| GRECIAN | GREGALE | GRICINGS | GRILSES | GRISE |
| GRECIANS | GREGALES | GRID | GRIM | GRISED |
| GRECQUE | GREGARIAN | GRIDDLE | GRIMACE | GRISELY |
| GRECQUES | GREGARINE | GRIDDLES | GRIMACED | GRISEOUS |
| GREE | GREGARINES | GRIDE | GRIMACES | GRISES |
| GREECE | GREGATIM | GRIDED | GRIMACING | GRISETTE |
| GREECES | GRÈGE | GRIDELIN | GRIMALKIN | GRISETTES |
| GREED | GREGO | GRIDELINS | GRIMALKINS | GRISGRIS |
| GREEDIER | GREGORIES | GRIDES | GRIME | GRISING |
| GREEDIEST | GREGORY | GRIDING | GRIMED | GRISKIN |
| GREEDILY | GREGOS | GRIDIRON | GRIMES | GRISKINS |
| GREEDS | GREIGE | GRIDIRONED | GRIMIER | GRISLED |
| GREEDY | GREIN | GRIDIRONING | GRIMIEST | GRISLIER |
| GREEGREE | GREINED | GRIDIRONS | GRIMILY | GRISLIEST |
| GREEGREES | GREINING | GRIDLOCK | GRIMINESS | GRISLY |
| GREEING | GREINS | GRIDLOCKS | GRIMINESSES | GRISON |
| GREEN | GREISEN | GRIDS | GRIMING | GRISONS |
| GREENBACK | GREISENS | GRIECE | GRIMLY | GRIST |
| GREENBACKS | GREISLY | GRIECED | GRIMMER | GRISTLE |
| GREENED | GREMIAL | GRIECES | GRIMMEST | GRISTLES |
| GREENER | GREMIALS | GRIEF | GRIMNESS | GRISTLIER |

| | | | | |
|---|---|---|---|---|
| GRISTLIEST | GROMWELL | GROUCHIER | GROWLIER | GRUMMET |
| GRISTLY | GROMWELLS | GROUCHIEST | GROWLIEST | GRUMMETS |
| GRISTS | GRONE | GROUCHILY | GROWLING | GRUMNESS |
| GRISY | GRONED | GROUCHING | GROWLINGS | GRUMNESSES |
| GRIT | GRONEFULL | GROUCHY | GROWLS | GRUMOSE |
| GRITH | GRONES | GROUF | GROWLY | GRUMOUS |
| GRITHS | GRONING | GROUFS | GROWN | GRUMPH |
| GRITS | GROOF | GROUND | GROWS | GRUMPHED |
| GRITSTONE | GROOFS | GROUNDAGE | GROWTH | GRUMPHIE |
| GRITSTONES | GROOLY | GROUNDAGES | GROWTHIST | GRUMPHIES |
| GRITTED | GROOM | GROUNDED | GROWTHISTS | GRUMPHING |
| GRITTER | GROOMED | GROUNDEN | GROWTHS | GRUMPHS |
| GRITTERS | GROOMING | GROUNDER | GROYNE | GRUMPIER |
| GRITTEST | GROOMS | GROUNDERS | GROYNES | GRUMPIEST |
| GRITTIER | GROOMSMAN | GROUNDING | GRUB | GRUMPILY |
| GRITTIEST | GROOMSMEN | GROUNDINGS | GRUBBED | GRUMPY |
| GRITTING | GROOVE | GROUNDMAN | GRUBBER | GRUNGIER |
| GRITTY | GROOVED | GROUNDMEN | GRUBBERS | GRUNGIEST |
| GRIVET | GROOVES | GROUNDS | GRUBBIER | GRUNGY |
| GRIVETS | GROOVIER | GROUNDSEL | GRUBBIEST | GRUNION |
| GRIZE | GROOVIEST | GROUNDSELS | GRUBBING | GRUNIONS |
| GRIZES | GROOVING | GROUP | GRUBBLE | GRUNT |
| GRIZZLE | GROOVY | GROUPAGE | GRUBBLED | GRUNTED |
| GRIZZLED | GROPE | GROUPAGES | GRUBBLES | GRUNTER |
| GRIZZLER | GROPED | GROUPED | GRUBBLING | GRUNTERS |
| GRIZZLERS | GROPER | GROUPER | GRUBBY | GRUNTING |
| GRIZZLES | GROPERS | GROUPERS | GRUBS | GRUNTINGS |
| GRIZZLIER | GROPES | GROUPIE | GRUDGE | GRUNTLE |
| GRIZZLIES | GROPING | GROUPIES | GRUDGED | GRUNTLED |
| GRIZZLIEST | GROPINGLY | GROUPING | GRUDGEFUL | GRUNTLES |
| GRIZZLING | GROSBEAK | GROUPINGS | GRUDGES | GRUNTLING |
| GRIZZLY | GROSBEAKS | GROUPIST | GRUDGING | GRUNTS |
| GROAN | GROSCHEN | GROUPISTS | GRUDGINGS | GRUPPETTI |
| GROANED | GROSCHENS | GROUPLET | GRUE | GRUPPETTO |
| GROANER | GROSER | GROUPLETS | GRUED | GRUTCH |
| GROANERS | GROSERS | GROUPS | GRUEING | GRUTCHED |
| GROANFUL | GROSERT | GROUPY | GRUEL | GRUTCHES |
| GROANING | GROSERTS | GROUSE | GRUELLED | GRUTCHING |
| GROANINGS | GROSET | GROUSED | GRUELLING | GRUTTEN |
| GROANS | GROSETS | GROUSER | GRUELLINGS | GRYCE |
| GROAT | GROSGRAIN | GROUSERS | GRUELS | GRYCES |
| GROATS | GROSGRAINS | GROUSES | GRUES | GRYDE |
| GROCER | GROSS | GROUSING | GRUESOME | GRYDED |
| GROCERIES | GROSSART | GROUT | GRUESOMER | GRYDES |
| GROCERS | GROSSARTS | GROUTED | GRUESOMEST | GRYDING |
| GROCERY | GROSSED | GROUTIER | GRUFF | GRYESLY |
| GROCKLE | GROSSER | GROUTIEST | GRUFFER | GRYESY |
| GROCKLES | GROSSES | GROUTING | GRUFFEST | GRYFON |
| GROG | GROSSEST | GROUTINGS | GRUFFISH | GRYFONS |
| GROGGED | GROSSING | GROUTS | GRUFFLY | GRYKE |
| GROGGERIES | GROSSLY | GROUTY | GRUFFNESS | GRYKES |
| GROGGERY | GROSSNESS | GROVE | GRUFFNESSES | GRYPE |
| GROGGIER | GROSSNESSES | GROVEL | GRUFTED | GRYPES |
| GROGGIEST | GROSSULAR | GROVELLED | GRUING | GRYPHON |
| GROGGING | GROSSULARS | GROVELLER | GRUM | GRYPHONS |
| GROGGY | GROT | GROVELLERS | GRUMBLE | GRYPT |
| GROGRAM | GROTESQUE | GROVELLING | GRUMBLED | GRYSBOK |
| GROGRAMS | GROTESQUER | GROVELS | GRUMBLER | GRYSBOKS |
| GROGS | GROTESQUES | GROVES | GRUMBLERS | GRYSELY |
| GROIN | GROTESQUEST | GROW | GRUMBLES | GRYSIE |
| GROINED | GROTS | GROWER | GRUMBLIER | GU |
| GROINING | GROTTIER | GROWERS | GRUMBLIEST | GUACAMOLE |
| GROININGS | GROTTIEST | GROWING | GRUMBLING | GUACAMOLES |
| GROINS | GROTTO | GROWINGS | GRUMBLINGS | GUACHARO |
| GROMA | GROTTOES | GROWL | GRUMBLY | GUACHAROS |
| GROMAS | GROTTOS | GROWLED | GRUME | GUACO |
| GROMET | GROTTY | GROWLER | GRUMES | GUACOS |
| GROMETS | GROUCH | GROWLERIES | GRUMLY | GUAIACUM |
| GROMMET | GROUCHED | GROWLERS | GRUMMER | GUAIACUMS |
| GROMMETS | GROUCHES | GROWLERY | GRUMMEST | GUAN |

| | | | | |
|---|---|---|---|---|
| GUANA | GUDEMEN | GUIDESHIP | GULCHES | GUMMOSITIES |
| GUANACO | GUDESIRE | GUIDESHIPS | GULCHING | GUMMOSITY |
| GUANACOS | GUDESIRES | GUIDING | GULDEN | GUMMOUS |
| GUANAS | GUDEWIFE | GUIDINGS | GULDENS | GUMMY |
| GUANAZOLO | GUDEWIVES | GUIDON | GULE | GUMNUT |
| GUANAZOLOS | GUDGEON | GUIDONS | GULES | GUMNUTS |
| GUANIN | GUDGEONED | GUILD | GULF | GUMP |
| GUANINE | GUDGEONING | GUILDER | GULFED | GUMPED |
| GUANINES | GUDGEONS | GUILDERS | GULFIER | GUMPHION |
| GUANINS | GUE | GUILDHALL | GULFIEST | GUMPHIONS |
| GUANO | GUENON | GUILDHALLS | GULFING | GUMPING |
| GUANOS | GUENONS | GUILDRIES | GULFS | GUMPS |
| GUANS | GUERDON | GUILDRY | GULFY | GUMPTION |
| GUAR | GUERDONED | GUILDS | GULL | GUMPTIONS |
| GUARANÁ | GUERDONING | GUILE | GULLABLE | GUMPTIOUS |
| GUARANÁS | GUERDONS | GUILED | GULLED | GUMS |
| GUARANI | GUEREZA | GUILEFUL | GULLER | GUMSHIELD |
| GUARANIES | GUEREZAS | GUILELESS | GULLERIES | GUMSHIELDS |
| GUARANTEE | GUÉRIDON | GUILER | GULLERS | GUMSHOE |
| GUARANTEED | GUÉRIDONS | GUILERS | GULLERY | GUMSHOED |
| GUARANTEEING | GUERILLA | GUILES | GULLET | GUMSHOEING |
| GUARANTEES | GUERILLAS | GUILING | GULLETS | GUMSHOES |
| GUARANTIED | GUERNSEY | GUILLEMOT | GULLEY | GUN |
| GUARANTIES | GUERNSEYS | GUILLEMOTS | GULLEYED | GUNBOAT |
| GUARANTOR | GUERRILLA | GUILLOCHE | GULLEYING | GUNBOATS |
| GUARANTORS | GUERRILLAS | GUILLOCHED | GULLEYS | GUNCOTTON |
| GUARANTY | GUES | GUILLOCHES | GULLIBLE | GUNCOTTONS |
| GUARANTYING | GUESS | GUILLOCHING | GULLIED | GUNDIES |
| GUARD | GUESSABLE | GUILT | GULLIES | GUNDY |
| GUARDABLE | GUESSED | GUILTIER | GULLING | GUNFIGHT |
| GUARDAGE | GUESSER | GUILTIEST | GULLISH | GUNFIGHTING |
| GUARDAGES | GUESSERS | GUILTILY | GULLS | GUNFIGHTS |
| GUARDANT | GUESSES | GUILTLESS | GULLY | GUNFIRE |
| GUARDANTS | GUESSING | GUILTS | GULLYING | GUNFIRES |
| GUARDED | GUESSINGS | GUILTY | GULOSITIES | GUNFLINT |
| GUARDEDLY | GUEST | GUIMBARD | GULOSITY | GUNFLINTS |
| GUARDEE | GUESTED | GUIMBARDS | GULP | GUNFOUGHT |
| GUARDEES | GUESTEN | GUIMP | GULPED | GUNGE |
| GUARDIAN | GUESTENED | GUIMPE | GULPER | GUNGES |
| GUARDIANS | GUESTENING | GUIMPED | GULPERS | GUNGIER |
| GUARDING | GUESTENS | GUIMPES | GULPH | GUNGIEST |
| GUARDLESS | GUESTING | GUIMPING | GULPHED | GUNGY |
| GUARDS | GUESTS | GUIMPS | GULPHING | GUNITE |
| GUARDSMAN | GUESTWISE | GUINEA | GULPHS | GUNITES |
| GUARDSMEN | GUFF | GUINEAS | GULPING | GUNK |
| GUARISH | GUFFAW | GUIPURE | GULPS | GUNKS |
| GUARISHED | GUFFAWED | GUIPURES | GULY | GUNLAYER |
| GUARISHES | GUFFAWING | GUIRO | GUM | GUNLAYERS |
| GUARISHING | GUFFAWS | GUIROS | GUMBO | GUNMAKER |
| GUARS | GUFFS | GUISARD | GUMBOIL | GUNMAKERS |
| GUAVA | GUGGLE | GUISARDS | GUMBOILS | GUNMAN |
| GUAVAS | GUGGLED | GUISE | GUMBOOT | GUNMEN |
| GUAYULE | GUGGLES | GUISED | GUMBOOTS | GUNMETAL |
| GUAYULES | GUGGLING | GUISER | GUMBOS | GUNMETALS |
| GUB | GUICHET | GUISERS | GUMDROP | GUNNAGE |
| GUBBAH | GUICHETS | GUISES | GUMDROPS | GUNNAGES |
| GUBBAHS | GUID | GUISING | GUMMA | GUNNED |
| GUBBINS | GUIDABLE | GUITAR | GUMMATA | GUNNEL |
| GUBS | GUIDAGE | GUITARIST | GUMMATOUS | GUNNELS |
| GUCK | GUIDAGES | GUITARISTS | GUMMED | GUNNER |
| GUCKIER | GUIDANCE | GUITARS | GUMMIER | GUNNERA |
| GUCKIEST | GUIDANCES | GUIZER | GUMMIEST | GUNNERAS |
| GUCKS | GUIDE | GUIZERS | GUMMINESS | GUNNERIES |
| GUCKY | GUIDED | GULA | GUMMINESSES | GUNNERS |
| GUDDLE | GUIDELESS | GULAG | GUMMING | GUNNERY |
| GUDDLED | GUIDELINE | GULAGS | GUMMINGS | GUNNIES |
| GUDDLES | GUIDELINES | GULAR | GUMMITE | GUNNING |
| GUDDLING | GUIDER | GULAS | GUMMITES | GUNNINGS |
| GUDE | GUIDERS | GULCH | GUMMOSES | GUNNY |
| GUDEMAN | GUIDES | GULCHED | GUMMOSIS | GUNPLAY |

GUNPLAYS
GUNPORT
GUNPORTS
GUNPOWDER
GUNPOWDERS
GUNROOM
GUNROOMS
GUNRUNNER
GUNRUNNERS
GUNS
GUNSEL
GUNSELS
GUNSHIP
GUNSHIPS
GUNSHOT
GUNSHOTS
GUNSMITH
GUNSMITHS
GUNSTICK
GUNSTICKS
GUNSTOCK
GUNSTOCKS
GUNSTONE
GUNSTONES
GUNTER
GUNTERS
GUNWALE
GUNWALES
GUNYAH
GUNYAHS
GUP
GUPPIES
GUPPY
GUPS
GUR
GURAMI
GURAMIS
GURDWARA
GURDWARAS
GURGE
GURGES
GURGLE
GURGLED
GURGLES
GURGLING
GURGOYLE
GURGOYLES
GURJUN
GURJUNS
GURL
GURLED
GURLET
GURLETS
GURLIER
GURLIEST
GURLING
GURLS
GURLY
GURN
GURNARD
GURNARDS
GURNED

GURNET
GURNETS
GURNEY
GURNEYS
GURNING
GURNS
GURRAH
GURRAHS
GURRIES
GURRY
GURS
GURU
GURUDOM
GURUDOMS
GURUISM
GURUISMS
GURUS
GURUSHIP
GURUSHIPS
GUS
GUSH
GUSHED
GUSHER
GUSHERS
GUSHES
GUSHIER
GUSHIEST
GUSHING
GUSHINGLY
GUSHY
GUSLA
GUSLAR
GUSLARS
GUSLAS
GUSLE
GUSLES
GUSLI
GUSLIS
GUSSET
GUSSETED
GUSSETING
GUSSETS
GUST
GUSTABLE
GUSTABLES
GUSTATION
GUSTATIONS
GUSTATIVE
GUSTATORY
GUSTED
GUSTFUL
GUSTIER
GUSTIEST
GUSTINESS
GUSTINESSES
GUSTING
GUSTO
GUSTOS
GUSTS
GUSTY
GUT
GUTBUCKET

GUTBUCKETS
GUTCHER
GUTCHERS
GUTLESS
GUTS
GUTSIER
GUTSIEST
GUTSINESS
GUTSINESSES
GUTSY
GUTTA
GUTTAE
GUTTAS
GUTTATE
GUTTATED
GUTTATES
GUTTATING
GUTTATION
GUTTATIONS
GUTTED
GUTTER
GUTTERED
GUTTERING
GUTTERINGS
GUTTERS
GUTTIES
GUTTING
GUTTLE
GUTTLED
GUTTLES
GUTTLING
GUTTURAL
GUTTURALS
GUTTY
GUTZER
GUTZERS
GUY
GUYED
GUYING
GUYLE
GUYLED
GUYLER
GUYLERS
GUYLES
GUYLING
GUYOT
GUYOTS
GUYS
GUYSE
GUYSES
GUZZLE
GUZZLED
GUZZLER
GUZZLERS
GUZZLES
GUZZLING
GWINIAD
GWINIADS
GWYNIAD
GWYNIADS
GYAL
GYALS

GYBE
GYBED
GYBES
GYBING
GYELD
GYELDS
GYLDEN
GYM
GYMBAL
GYMBALS
GYMKHANA
GYMKHANAS
GYMMAL
GYMMALS
GYMNASIA
GYMNASIAL
GYMNASIC
GYMNASIEN
GYMNASIUM
GYMNASIUMS
GYMNAST
GYMNASTIC
GYMNASTICS
GYMNASTS
GYMNIC
GYMNOSOPH
GYMNOSOPHS
GYMP
GYMPED
GYMPING
GYMPS
GYMS
GYNAE
GYNAECEUM
GYNAECEUMS
GYNAECOID
GYNAES
GYNANDRIES
GYNANDRY
GYNECIUM
GYNECIUMS
GYNIES
GYNNEY
GYNNEYS
GYNNIES
GYNNY
GYNOCRACIES
GYNOCRACY
GYNOECIUM
GYNOECIUMS
GYNOPHORE
GYNOPHORES
GYNY
GYP
GYPPED
GYPPIE
GYPPIES
GYPPING
GYPPO
GYPPOS
GYPPY
GYPS

GYPSEOUS
GYPSIED
GYPSIES
GYPSUM
GYPSUMS
GYPSY
GYPSYDOM
GYPSYDOMS
GYPSYING
GYPSYISM
GYPSYISMS
GYPSYWORT
GYPSYWORTS
GYRAL
GYRALLY
GYRANT
GYRATE
GYRATED
GYRATES
GYRATING
GYRATION
GYRATIONS
GYRATORY
GYRE
GYRED
GYRES
GYRFALCON
GYRFALCONS
GYRI
GYRING
GYRO
GYROCAR
GYROCARS
GYRODYNE
GYRODYNES
GYROIDAL
GYROMANCIES
GYROMANCY
GYRON
GYRONNY
GYRONS
GYROPLANE
GYROPLANES
GYROS
GYROSCOPE
GYROSCOPES
GYROSE
GYROSTAT
GYROSTATS
GYROUS
GYROVAGUE
GYROVAGUES
GYRUS
GYRUSES
GYTE
GYTES
GYTRASH
GYTRASHES
GYVE
GYVED
GYVES
GYVING

# H

HA
HAAF
HAAFS
HAANEPOOT
HAANEPOOTS
HAAR
HAARS
HABANERA
HABANERAS
HABDABS
HABERDINE
HABERDINES
HABERGEON
HABERGEONS
HABILABLE
HABILE
HABIT
HABITABLE
HABITABLY
HABITANS
HABITANT
HABITANTS
HABITAT
HABITATS
HABITED
HABITING
HABITS
HABITUAL
HABITUALS
HABITUATE
HABITUATED
HABITUATES
HABITUATING
HABITUDE
HABITUDES
HABITUÉ
HABITUÉS
HABITUS
HABLE
HABOOB
HABOOBS
HACEK
HACEKS
HACHIS
HACHURE
HACHURED
HACHURES
HACHURING
HACIENDA
HACIENDAS
HACK
HACKAMORE
HACKAMORES
HACKBERRIES
HACKBERRY
HACKBOLT
HACKBOLTS
HACKBUT
HACKBUTS
HACKED
HACKEE
HACKEES
HACKER

HACKERIES
HACKERS
HACKERY
HACKETTE
HACKETTES
HACKING
HACKINGS
HACKLE
HACKLED
HACKLER
HACKLERS
HACKLES
HACKLET
HACKLETS
HACKLIER
HACKLIEST
HACKLING
HACKLY
HACKNEY
HACKNEYED
HACKNEYING
HACKNEYS
HACKS
HACQUETON
HACQUETONS
HAD
HADAL
HADDEN
HADDIE
HADDIES
HADDING
HADDOCK
HADDOCKS
HADE
HADED
HADES
HADING
HADITH
HADITHS
HADJ
HADJES
HADJI
HADJIS
HADROME
HADROMES
HADRON
HADRONIC
HADRONS
HADROSAUR
HADROSAURS
HADS
HADST
HAE
HAECCEITIES
HAECCEITY
HAEING
HAEM
HAEMAL
HAEMATIC
HAEMATIN
HAEMATINS
HAEMATITE
HAEMATITES

HAEMATOID
HAEMATOMA
HAEMATOMAS
HAEMIC
HAEMIN
HAEMINS
HAEMOCYTE
HAEMOCYTES
HAEMONIES
HAEMONY
HAEMOSTAT
HAEMOSTATS
HAEMS
HAET
HAETS
HAFF
HAFFET
HAFFETS
HAFFIT
HAFFITS
HAFFLIN
HAFFLINS
HAFFS
HAFNIUM
HAFNIUMS
HAFT
HAFTED
HAFTING
HAFTS
HAG
HAGBERRIES
HAGBERRY
HAGBOLT
HAGBOLTS
HAGBUT
HAGBUTS
HAGDEN
HAGDENS
HAGDON
HAGDONS
HAGDOWN
HAGDOWNS
HAGFISH
HAGFISHES
HAGG
HAGGARD
HAGGARDLY
HAGGARDS
HAGGED
HAGGING
HAGGIS
HAGGISES
HAGGISH
HAGGISHLY
HAGGLE
HAGGLED
HAGGLER
HAGGLERS
HAGGLES
HAGGLING
HAGGS
HAGIARCHIES
HAGIARCHY

HAGIOLOGIES
HAGIOLOGY
HAGLET
HAGLETS
HAGS
HAH
HAHNIUM
HAHNIUMS
HAICK
HAICKS
HAIDUK
HAIDUKS
HAIK
HAIKAI
HAIKS
HAIKU
HAIL
HAILED
HAILER
HAILERS
HAILIER
HAILIEST
HAILING
HAILS
HAILSHOT
HAILSHOTS
HAILSTONE
HAILSTONES
HAILY
HAIN
HAINCH
HAINCHED
HAINCHES
HAINCHING
HAINED
HAINING
HAININGS
HAINS
HAIQUE
HAIQUES
HAIR
HAIRBELL
HAIRBELLS
HAIRCLOTH
HAIRCLOTHS
HAIRCUT
HAIRCUTS
HAIRED
HAIRIER
HAIRIEST
HAIRINESS
HAIRINESSES
HAIRING
HAIRLESS
HAIRLIKE
HAIRLINE
HAIRLINES
HAIRPIN
HAIRPINS
HAIRS
HAIRST
HAIRSTED
HAIRSTING

HAIRSTS
HAIRSTYLE
HAIRSTYLES
HAIRY
HAITH
HAJ
HAJES
HAJI
HAJIS
HAJJ
HAJJES
HAJJI
HAJJIS
HAKA
HAKAM
HAKAMS
HAKAS
HAKE
HAKES
HAKIM
HAKIMS
HALAL
HALALLED
HALALLING
HALALS
HALATION
HALATIONS
HALAVAH
HALAVAHS
HALBERD
HALBERDS
HALBERT
HALBERTS
HALCYON
HALCYONS
HALE
HALED
HALENESS
HALENESSES
HALER
HALERS
HALES
HALEST
HALF
HALFA
HALFAS
HALFEN
HALFLIN
HALFLING
HALFLINGS
HALFLINS
HALFPACE
HALFPACES
HALFPENCE
HALFPENNIES
HALFPENNY
HALFWAY
HALIBUT
HALIBUTS
HALICORE
HALICORES
HALIDE
HALIDES

| | | | | |
|---|---|---|---|---|
| HALIDOM | HALO | HAMFATTERING | HANDBILL | HANDSEL |
| HALIDOMS | HALOBIONT | HAMFATTERS | HANDBILLS | HANDSELLED |
| HALIEUTIC | HALOBIONTS | HAMING | HANDBOOK | HANDSELLING |
| HALIEUTICS | HALOED | HAMLET | HANDBOOKS | HANDSELS |
| HALIMOT | HALOES | HAMLETS | HANDCAR | HANDSET |
| HALIMOTE | HALOGEN | HAMMAL | HANDCARS | HANDSETS |
| HALIMOTES | HALOGENS | HAMMALS | HANDCLAP | HANDSHAKE |
| HALIMOTS | HALOID | HAMMAM | HANDCLAPS | HANDSHAKES |
| HALING | HALOIDS | HAMMAMS | HANDCLASP | HANDSOME |
| HALIOTIS | HALOING | HAMMED | HANDCLASPS | HANDSOMER |
| HALITE | HALOPHILE | HAMMER | HANDCRAFT | HANDSOMEST |
| HALITES | HALOPHILIES | HAMMERED | HANDCRAFTS | HANDSPIKE |
| HALITOSES | HALOPHILY | HAMMERER | HANDCUFF | HANDSPIKES |
| HALITOSIS | HALOPHOBE | HAMMERERS | HANDCUFFED | HANDSTAFF |
| HALITOUS | HALOPHOBES | HAMMERING | HANDCUFFING | HANDSTAFFS |
| HALITUS | HALOPHYTE | HAMMERINGS | HANDCUFFS | HANDSTAND |
| HALITUSES | HALOPHYTES | HAMMERKOP | HANDED | HANDSTANDS |
| HALL | HALOS | HAMMERKOPS | HANDER | HANDSTAVES |
| HALLAL | HALOTHANE | HAMMERMAN | HANDERS | HANDSTURN |
| HALLALI | HALOTHANES | HAMMERMEN | HANDFAST | HANDSTURNS |
| HALLALIS | HALSE | HAMMERS | HANDFASTED | HANDTOWEL |
| HALLALLED | HALSED | HAMMIER | HANDFASTING | HANDTOWELS |
| HALLALLING | HALSER | HAMMIEST | HANDFASTINGS | HANDWORK |
| HALLALOO | HALSERS | HAMMILY | HANDFASTS | HANDWORKS |
| HALLALOOS | HALSES | HAMMING | HANDFUL | HANDY |
| HALLALS | HALSING | HAMMOCK | HANDFULS | HANDYMAN |
| HALLAN | HALT | HAMMOCKS | HANDGRIP | HANDYMEN |
| HALLANS | HALTED | HAMMY | HANDGRIPS | HANDYWORK |
| HALLIAN | HALTER | HAMOSE | HANDHOLD | HANDYWORKS |
| HALLIANS | HALTERED | HAMOUS | HANDHOLDS | HANEPOOT |
| HALLIARD | HALTERES | HAMPER | HANDICAP | HANEPOOTS |
| HALLIARDS | HALTERING | HAMPERED | HANDICAPPED | HANG |
| HALLING | HALTERS | HAMPERING | HANDICAPPING | HANGABLE |
| HALLINGS | HALTING | HAMPERS | HANDICAPS | HANGAR |
| HALLION | HALTINGLY | HAMPSTER | HANDIER | HANGARS |
| HALLIONS | HALTINGS | HAMPSTERS | HANDIEST | HANGBIRD |
| HALLMARK | HALTS | HAMS | HANDILY | HANGBIRDS |
| HALLMARKED | HALVA | HAMSTER | HANDINESS | HANGDOG |
| HALLMARKING | HALVAH | HAMSTERS | HANDINESSES | HANGDOGS |
| HALLMARKS | HALVAHS | HAMSTRING | HANDING | HANGED |
| HALLO | HALVAS | HAMSTRINGED | HANDIWORK | HANGER |
| HALLOA | HALVE | HAMSTRINGING | HANDIWORKS | HANGERS |
| HALLOAED | HALVED | HAMSTRINGS | HANDJAR | HANGFIRE |
| HALLOAING | HALVER | HAMSTRUNG | HANDJARS | HANGFIRES |
| HALLOAS | HALVERS | HAMULAR | HANDLE | HANGING |
| HALLOED | HALVES | HAMULATE | HANDLEBAR | HANGINGS |
| HALLOES | HALVING | HAMULI | HANDLEBARS | HANGMAN |
| HALLOING | HALYARD | HAMULUS | HANDLED | HANGMEN |
| HALLOO | HALYARDS | HAMZA | HANDLER | HANGNAIL |
| HALLOOED | HAM | HAMZAH | HANDLERS | HANGNAILS |
| HALLOOING | HAMADRYAD | HAMZAHS | HANDLES | HANGNEST |
| HALLOOS | HAMADRYADES | HAMZAS | HANDLESS | HANGNESTS |
| HALLOS | HAMADRYADS | HAN | HANDLING | HANGOUT |
| HALLOW | HAMAL | HANAP | HANDLINGS | HANGOUTS |
| HALLOWED | HAMALS | HANAPER | HANDLIST | HANGOVER |
| HALLOWING | HAMARTIA | HANAPERS | HANDLISTS | HANGOVERS |
| HALLOWS | HAMARTIAS | HANAPS | HANDMADE | HANGS |
| HALLS | HAMATE | HANCE | HANDMAID | HANJAR |
| HALLSTAND | HAMBLE | HANCES | HANDMAIDS | HANJARS |
| HALLSTANDS | HAMBLED | HANCH | HANDOUT | HANK |
| HALLUCES | HAMBLES | HANCHED | HANDOUTS | HANKED |
| HALLUX | HAMBLING | HANCHES | HANDOVER | HANKER |
| HALLWAY | HAMBURGER | HANCHING | HANDOVERS | HANKERED |
| HALLWAYS | HAMBURGERS | HAND | HANDPLAY | HANKERING |
| HALLYON | HAME | HANDBAG | HANDPLAYS | HANKERINGS |
| HALLYONS | HAMED | HANDBAGS | HANDRAIL | HANKERS |
| HALM | HAMES | HANDBALL | HANDRAILS | HANKIE |
| HALMA | HAMEWITH | HANDBALLS | HANDS | HANKIES |
| HALMAS | HAMFATTER | HANDBELL | HANDSAW | HANKING |
| HALMS | HAMFATTERED | HANDBELLS | HANDSAWS | HANKS |

| | | | | |
|---|---|---|---|---|
| HANKY | HARBOUR | HAREBELL | HARMONICA | HARRYING |
| HANSEL | HARBOURED | HAREBELLS | HARMONICAS | HARSH |
| HANSELLED | HARBOURER | HARED | HARMONICS | HARSHEN |
| HANSELLING | HARBOURERS | HAREEM | HARMONIES | HARSHENED |
| HANSELS | HARBOURING | HAREEMS | HARMONISE | HARSHENING |
| HANSOM | HARBOURS | HARELD | HARMONISED | HARSHENS |
| HANSOMS | HARD | HARELDS | HARMONISES | HARSHER |
| HANTLE | HARDBACK | HAREM | HARMONISING | HARSHEST |
| HANTLES | HARDBACKS | HAREMS | HARMONIST | HARSHLY |
| HANUMAN | HARDBAKE | HARES | HARMONISTS | HARSHNESS |
| HANUMANS | HARDBAKES | HAREWOOD | HARMONIUM | HARSHNESSES |
| HAOMA | HARDBEAM | HAREWOODS | HARMONIUMS | HARSLET |
| HAOMAS | HARDBEAMS | HARICOT | HARMONIZE | HARSLETS |
| HAP | HARDBOARD | HARICOTS | HARMONIZED | HART |
| HAPHAZARD | HARDBOARDS | HARIGALDS | HARMONIZES | HARTAL |
| HAPHAZARDS | HARDCORE | HARIGALS | HARMONIZING | HARTALS |
| HAPLESS | HARDCORES | HARIM | HARMONY | HARTBEES |
| HAPLESSLY | HARDEN | HARIMS | HARMOST | HARTBEESES |
| HAPLOID | HARDENED | HARING | HARMOSTIES | HARTELY |
| HAPLOIDIES | HARDENER | HARIOLATE | HARMOSTS | HARTEN |
| HAPLOIDY | HARDENERS | HARIOLATED | HARMOSTY | HARTENED |
| HAPLOLOGIES | HARDENING | HARIOLATES | HARMOTOME | HARTENING |
| HAPLOLOGY | HARDENINGS | HARIOLATING | HARMOTOMES | HARTENS |
| HAPLY | HARDENS | HARISH | HARMS | HARTLESSE |
| HAPPED | HARDER | HARK | HARN | HARTS |
| HAPPEN | HARDEST | HARKED | HARNESS | HARTSHORN |
| HAPPENED | HARDFACE | HARKEN | HARNESSED | HARTSHORNS |
| HAPPENING | HARDFACES | HARKENED | HARNESSES | HARUSPEX |
| HAPPENINGS | HARDGRASS | HARKENING | HARNESSING | HARUSPICES |
| HAPPENS | HARDGRASSES | HARKENS | HARNS | HARUSPICIES |
| HAPPIED | HARDHACK | HARKING | HARO | HARUSPICY |
| HAPPIER | HARDHACKS | HARKS | HAROS | HARVEST |
| HAPPIES | HARDHEAD | HARL | HAROSET | HARVESTED |
| HAPPIEST | HARDHEADS | HARLED | HAROSETH | HARVESTER |
| HAPPILY | HARDIER | HARLEQUIN | HAROSETHS | HARVESTERS |
| HAPPINESS | HARDIEST | HARLEQUINED | HAROSETS | HARVESTING |
| HAPPINESSES | HARDIHEAD | HARLEQUINING | HARP | HARVESTS |
| HAPPING | HARDIHEADS | HARLEQUINS | HARPED | HAS |
| HAPPY | HARDIHOOD | HARLING | HARPER | HASH |
| HAPPYING | HARDIHOODS | HARLINGS | HARPERS | HASHED |
| HAPS | HARDILY | HARLOT | HARPIES | HASHEESH |
| HAPTERON | HARDIMENT | HARLOTRIES | HARPING | HASHEESHES |
| HAPTERONS | HARDIMENTS | HARLOTRY | HARPINGS | HASHES |
| HAPTIC | HARDINESS | HARLOTS | HARPIST | HASHIER |
| HAPTICS | HARDINESSES | HARLS | HARPISTS | HASHIEST |
| HAQUETON | HARDISH | HARM | HARPOON | HASHING |
| HAQUETONS | HARDLINE | HARMALA | HARPOONED | HASHISH |
| HARAM | HARDLINER | HARMALAS | HARPOONER | HASHISHES |
| HARAMS | HARDLINERS | HARMALIN | HARPOONERS | HASHY |
| HARANGUE | HARDLY | HARMALINE | HARPOONING | HASK |
| HARANGUED | HARDNESS | HARMALINES | HARPOONS | HASKS |
| HARANGUER | HARDNESSES | HARMALINS | HARPS | HASLET |
| HARANGUERS | HARDNOSED | HARMAN | HARPY | HASLETS |
| HARANGUES | HARDOKE | HARMANS | HARQUEBUS | HASP |
| HARANGUING | HARDOKES | HARMATTAN | HARQUEBUSES | HASPED |
| HARASS | HARDPARTS | HARMATTANS | HARRIDAN | HASPING |
| HARASSED | HARDS | HARMDOING | HARRIDANS | HASPS |
| HARASSER | HARDSHELL | HARMDOINGS | HARRIED | HASSAR |
| HARASSERS | HARDSHIP | HARMED | HARRIER | HASSARS |
| HARASSES | HARDSHIPS | HARMEL | HARRIERS | HASSLE |
| HARASSING | HARDTACK | HARMELS | HARRIES | HASSLED |
| HARASSINGS | HARDTACKS | HARMFUL | HARROW | HASSLES |
| HARBINGER | HARDTOP | HARMFULLY | HARROWED | HASSLING |
| HARBINGERED | HARDTOPS | HARMIN | HARROWING | HASSOCK |
| HARBINGERING | HARDWARE | HARMINE | HARROWS | HASSOCKS |
| HARBINGERS | HARDWARES | HARMINES | HARRUMPH | HASSOCKY |
| HARBOR | HARDWOOD | HARMING | HARRUMPHED | HAST |
| HARBORED | HARDWOODS | HARMINS | HARRUMPHING | HASTA |
| HARBORING | HARDY | HARMLESS | HARRUMPHS | HASTATE |
| HARBORS | HARE | HARMONIC | HARRY | HASTATED |

| | | | | |
|---|---|---|---|---|
| HASTE | HATPINS | HAUTE | HAWSE | HAZILY |
| HASTED | HATRACK | HAUTEUR | HAWSED | HAZINESS |
| HASTEN | HATRACKS | HAUTEURS | HAWSEHOLE | HAZINESSES |
| HASTENED | HATRED | HAÜYNE | HAWSEHOLES | HAZING |
| HASTENER | HATREDS | HAÜYNES | HAWSEPIPE | HAZINGS |
| HASTENERS | HATS | HAVE | HAWSEPIPES | HAZY |
| HASTENING | HATSTAND | HAVELOCK | HAWSER | HE |
| HASTENS | HATSTANDS | HAVELOCKS | HAWSERS | HEAD |
| HASTES | HATTED | HAVEN | HAWSES | HEADACHE |
| HASTIER | HATTER | HAVENED | HAWSING | HEADACHES |
| HASTIEST | HATTERED | HAVENING | HAWTHORN | HEADACHIER |
| HASTILY | HATTERING | HAVENS | HAWTHORNS | HEADACHIEST |
| HASTINESS | HATTERS | HAVEOUR | HAY | HEADACHY |
| HASTINESSES | HATTING | HAVEOURS | HAYBAND | HEADBAND |
| HASTING | HATTINGS | HAVER | HAYBANDS | HEADBANDS |
| HASTINGS | HATTOCK | HAVERED | HAYBOX | HEADBOARD |
| HASTY | HATTOCKS | HAVEREL | HAYBOXES | HEADBOARDS |
| HAT | HAUBERK | HAVERELS | HAYCOCK | HEADCASE |
| HATABLE | HAUBERKS | HAVERING | HAYCOCKS | HEADCASES |
| HATBAND | HAUD | HAVERINGS | HAYED | HEADCHAIR |
| HATBANDS | HAUDING | HAVERS | HAYFIELD | HEADCHAIRS |
| HATBOX | HAUDS | HAVERSACK | HAYFIELDS | HEADCLOTH |
| HATBOXES | HAUGH | HAVERSACKS | HAYFORK | HEADCLOTHS |
| HATBRUSH * | HAUGHS | HAVERSINE | HAYFORKS | HEADED |
| HATBRUSHES | HAUGHT | HAVERSINES | HAYING | HEADER |
| HATCH | HAUGHTIER | HAVES | HAYINGS | HEADERS |
| HATCHBACK | HAUGHTIEST | HAVILDAR | HAYLE | HEADFAST |
| HATCHBACKS | HAUGHTILY | HAVILDARS | HAYLES | HEADFASTS |
| HATCHED | HAUGHTY | HAVING | HAYLOFT | HEADFRAME |
| HATCHEL | HAUL | HAVINGS | HAYLOFTS | HEADFRAMES |
| HATCHELLED | HAULAGE | HAVIOUR | HAYMAKER | HEADGEAR |
| HATCHELLING | HAULAGES | HAVIOURS | HAYMAKERS | HEADGEARS |
| HATCHELS | HAULD | HAVOC | HAYMAKING | HEADHUNT |
| HATCHER | HAULDS | HAVOCKED | HAYMAKINGS | HEADHUNTED |
| HATCHERIES | HAULED | HAVOCKING | HAYMOW | HEADHUNTING |
| HATCHERS | HAULER | HAVOCS | HAYMOWS | HEADHUNTINGS |
| HATCHERY | HAULERS | HAW | HAYRICK | HEADHUNTS |
| HATCHES | HAULIER | HAWBUCK | HAYRICKS | HEADIER |
| HATCHET | HAULIERS | HAWBUCKS | HAYS | HEADIEST |
| HATCHETS | HAULING | HAWED | HAYSEED | HEADILY |
| HATCHETY | HAULM | HAWFINCH | HAYSEEDS | HEADINESS |
| HATCHING | HAULMS | HAWFINCHES | HAYSEL | HEADINESSES |
| HATCHINGS | HAULS | HAWING | HAYSELS | HEADING |
| HATCHLING | HAULST | HAWK | HAYSTACK | HEADINGS |
| HATCHLINGS | HAULT | HAWKBELL | HAYSTACKS | HEADLAMP |
| HATCHMENT | HAUNCH | HAWKBELLS | HAYWARD | HEADLAMPS |
| HATCHMENTS | HAUNCHED | HAWKBIT | HAYWARDS | HEADLAND |
| HATCHWAY | HAUNCHES | HAWKBITS | HAYWIRE | HEADLANDS |
| HATCHWAYS | HAUNCHING | HAWKED | HAYWIRES | HEADLESS |
| HATE | HAUNT | HAWKER | HAZARD | HEADLIGHT |
| HATEABLE | HAUNTED | HAWKERS | HAZARDED | HEADLIGHTS |
| HATED | HAUNTER | HAWKEY | HAZARDING | HEADLINE |
| HATEFUL | HAUNTERS | HAWKEYS | HAZARDIZE | HEADLINED |
| HATEFULLY | HAUNTING | HAWKIE | HAZARDIZES | HEADLINER |
| HATELESS | HAUNTINGS | HAWKIES | HAZARDOUS | HEADLINERS |
| HATER | HAUNTS | HAWKING | HAZARDRIES | HEADLINES |
| HATERENT | HAURIANT | HAWKINGS | HAZARDRY | HEADLINING |
| HATERENTS | HAURIENT | HAWKISH | HAZARDS | HEADLOCK |
| HATERS | HAUSE | HAWKISHLY | HAZE | HEADLOCKS |
| HATES | HAUSED | HAWKIT | HAZED | HEADLONG |
| HATFUL | HAUSES | HAWKS | HAZEL | HEADMAN |
| HATFULS | HAUSFRAU | HAWKSBILL | HAZELLY | HEADMARK |
| HATGUARD | HAUSFRAUS | HAWKSBILLS | HAZELNUT | HEADMARKS |
| HATGUARDS | HAUSING | HAWKWEED | HAZELNUTS | HEADMEN |
| HATH | HAUSTELLA | HAWKWEEDS | HAZELS | HEADMOST |
| HATING | HAUSTORIA | HAWM | HAZER | HEADNOTE |
| HATLESS | HAUT | HAWMED | HAZERS | HEADNOTES |
| HATPEG | HAUTBOIS | HAWMING | HAZES | HEADPEACE |
| HATPEGS | HAUTBOY | HAWMS | HAZIER | HEADPEACES |
| HATPIN | HAUTBOYS | HAWS | HAZIEST | HEADPHONE |

HEADPHONES
HEADPIECE
HEADPIECES
HEADRACE
HEADRACES
HEADRAIL
HEADRAILS
HEADREACH
HEADREACHED
HEADREACHES
HEADREACHING
HEADREST
HEADRESTS
HEADRIG
HEADRIGS
HEADRING
HEADRINGS
HEADROOM
HEADROOMS
HEADROPE
HEADROPES
HEADS
HEADSCARF
HEADSCARVES
HEADSET
HEADSETS
HEADSHAKE
HEADSHAKES
HEADSHIP
HEADSHIPS
HEADSMAN
HEADSMEN
HEADSTALL
HEADSTALLS
HEADSTICK
HEADSTICKS
HEADSTOCK
HEADSTOCKS
HEADSTONE
HEADSTONES
HEADWAY
HEADWAYS
HEADWORD
HEADWORDS
HEADWORK
HEADWORKS
HEADY
HEAL
HEALABLE
HEALD
HEALDED
HEALDING
HEALDS
HEALED
HEALER
HEALERS
HEALING
HEALINGLY
HEALINGS
HEALS
HEALSOME
HEALTH
HEALTHFUL
HEALTHIER
HEALTHIEST
HEALTHILY
HEALTHS
HEALTHY
HEAME
HEAP

HEAPED
HEAPIER
HEAPIEST
HEAPING
HEAPS
HEAPSTEAD
HEAPSTEADS
HEAPY
HEAR
HEARD
HEARDS
HEARE
HEARER
HEARERS
HEARES
HEARIE
HEARING
HEARINGS
HEARKEN
HEARKENED
HEARKENER
HEARKENERS
HEARKENING
HEARKENS
HEARS
HEARSAY
HEARSAYS
HEARSE
HEARSED
HEARSES
HEARSIER
HEARSIEST
HEARSING
HEARSY
HEART
HEARTACHE
HEARTACHES
HEARTBURN
HEARTBURNS
HEARTED
HEARTEN
HEARTENED
HEARTENING
HEARTENS
HEARTFELT
HEARTH
HEARTHS
HEARTIER
HEARTIES
HEARTIEST
HEARTIKIN
HEARTIKINS
HEARTILY
HEARTING
HEARTLAND
HEARTLANDS
HEARTLESS
HEARTLET
HEARTLETS
HEARTLING
HEARTLINGS
HEARTLY
HEARTPEA
HEARTPEAS
HEARTS
HEARTSEED
HEARTSEEDS
HEARTSOME
HEARTWOOD
HEARTWOODS

HEARTY
HEAST
HEASTE
HEASTES
HEASTS
HEAT
HEATED
HEATER
HEATERS
HEATH
HEATHBIRD
HEATHBIRDS
HEATHCOCK
HEATHCOCKS
HEATHEN
HEATHENRIES
HEATHENRY
HEATHENS
HEATHER
HEATHERS
HEATHERY
HEATHIER
HEATHIEST
HEATHS
HEATHY
HEATING
HEATINGS
HEATS
HEATSPOT
HEATSPOTS
HEAUME
HEAUMES
HEAVE
HEAVED
HEAVEN
HEAVENLIER
HEAVENLIEST
HEAVENLY
HEAVENS
HEAVER
HEAVERS
HEAVES
HEAVIER
HEAVIES
HEAVIEST
HEAVILY
HEAVINESS
HEAVINESSES
HEAVING
HEAVINGS
HEAVY
HEBDOMAD
HEBDOMADS
HEBE
HEBEN
HEBENON
HEBENONS
HEBENS
HEBES
HEBETANT
HEBETATE
HEBETATED
HEBETATES
HEBETATING
HEBETUDE
HEBETUDES
HEBONA
HEBONAS
HECATOMB
HECATOMBS

HECH
HECHT
HECHTING
HECHTS
HECK
HECKLE
HECKLED
HECKLER
HECKLERS
HECKLES
HECKLING
HECKLINGS
HECKS
HECOGENIN
HECOGENINS
HECTARE
HECTARES
HECTIC
HECTICAL
HECTICS
HECTOGRAM
HECTOGRAMS
HECTOR
HECTORED
HECTORER
HECTORERS
HECTORING
HECTORINGS
HECTORISM
HECTORISMS
HECTORLY
HECTORS
HEDDLE
HEDDLED
HEDDLES
HEDDLING
HEDERAL
HEDERATED
HEDGE
HEDGEBILL
HEDGEBILLS
HEDGED
HEDGEHOG
HEDGEHOGS
HEDGEPIG
HEDGEPIGS
HEDGER
HEDGEROW
HEDGEROWS
HEDGERS
HEDGES
HEDGIER
HEDGIEST
HEDGING
HEDGINGS
HEDGY
HEDONIC
HEDONICS
HEDONISM
HEDONISMS
HEDONIST
HEDONISTS
HEDYPHANE
HEDYPHANES
HEED
HEEDED
HEEDFUL
HEEDFULLY
HEEDINESS
HEEDINESSES

HEEDING
HEEDLESS
HEEDS
HEEDY
HEEHAW
HEEHAWED
HEEHAWING
HEEHAWS
HEEL
HEELED
HEELER
HEELERS
HEELING
HEELINGS
HEELS
HEEZE
HEEZED
HEEZES
HEEZIE
HEEZIES
HEEZING
HEFT
HEFTE
HEFTED*
HEFTIER
HEFTIEST
HEFTING
HEFTS
HEFTY
HEGEMONIC
HEGEMONIES
HEGEMONY
HEGIRA
HEGIRAS
HEID
HEIDS
HEIFER
HEIFERS
HEIGH
HEIGHT
HEIGHTEN
HEIGHTENED
HEIGHTENING
HEIGHTENS
HEIGHTS
HEIL
HEINOUS
HEINOUSLY
HEIR
HEIRDOM
HEIRDOMS
HEIRED
HEIRESS
HEIRESSES
HEIRING
HEIRLESS
HEIRLOOM
HEIRLOOMS
HEIRS
HEIRSHIP
HEIRSHIPS
HEIST
HEISTED
HEISTER
HEISTERS
HEISTING
HEISTS
HEJAB
HEJABS
HEJIRA

| | | | | |
|---|---|---|---|---|
| HEJIRAS | HELLIER | HEMIHEDRY | HENOTIC | HERBAR |
| HEJRA | HELLIERS | HEMINA | HENPECK | HERBARIA |
| HEJRAS | HELLING | HEMINAS | HENPECKED | HERBARIAN |
| HELCOID | HELLION | HEMIOLA | HENPECKING | HERBARIANS |
| HELD | HELLIONS | HEMIOLAS | HENPECKS | HERBARIES |
| HELE | HELLISH | HEMIOLIA | HENRIES | HERBARIUM |
| HELED | HELLISHLY | HEMIOLIAS | HENRY | HERBARIUMS |
| HELES | HELLO | HEMIOLIC | HENRYS | HERBARS |
| HELIAC | HELLOED | HEMIONE | HENS | HERBARY |
| HELIACAL | HELLOES | HEMIONES | HENT | HERBELET |
| HELIBUS | HELLOING | HEMIONUS | HENTING | HERBELETS |
| HELIBUSES | HELLOS | HEMIONUSES | HENTS | HERBICIDE |
| HELICAL | HELLOVA | HEMIOPIA | HEP | HERBICIDES |
| HELICALLY | HELLS | HEMIOPIAS | HEPAR | HERBIER |
| HELICES | HELLUVA | HEMIOPIC | HEPARIN | HERBIEST |
| HELICOID | HELLWARD | HEMIOPSIA | HEPARINS | HERBIST |
| HELICTITE | HELLWARDS | HEMIOPSIAS | HEPARS | HERBISTS |
| HELICTITES | HELM | HEMISPACE | HEPATIC | HERBIVORA |
| HELIDROME | HELMED | HEMISPACES | HEPATICAL | HERBIVORE |
| HELIDROMES | HELMET | HEMISTICH | HEPATICS | HERBIVORES |
| HELIMAN | HELMETED | HEMISTICHS | HEPATISE | HERBIVORIES |
| HELIMEN | HELMETS | HEMITROPE | HEPATISED | HERBIVORY |
| HELING | HELMING | HEMITROPES | HEPATISES | HERBLESS |
| HELIODOR | HELMINTH | HEMLOCK | HEPATISING | HERBLET |
| HELIODORS | HELMINTHS | HEMLOCKS | HEPATITE | HERBLETS |
| HELIOLOGIES | HELMLESS | HEMMED | HEPATITES | HERBORISE |
| HELIOLOGY | HELMS | HEMMING | HEPATITIS | HERBORISED |
| HELIOSES | HELMSMAN | HEMP | HEPATITISES | HERBORISES |
| HELIOSIS | HELMSMEN | HEMPEN | HEPATIZE | HERBORISING |
| HELIOSTAT | HELOT | HEMPIER | HEPATIZED | HERBORIST |
| HELIOSTATS | HELOTAGE | HEMPIES | HEPATIZES | HERBORISTS |
| HELIOTYPE | HELOTAGES | HEMPIEST | HEPATIZING | HERBORIZE |
| HELIOTYPES | HELOTISM | HEMPS | HEPPER | HERBORIZED |
| HELIOTYPIES | HELOTISMS | HEMPY | HEPPEST | HERBORIZES |
| HELIOTYPY | HELOTRIES | HEMS | HEPS | HERBORIZING |
| HELIOZOAN | HELOTRY | HEN | HEPSTER | HERBOSE |
| HELIOZOANS | HELOTS | HENBANE | HEPSTERS | HERBOUS |
| HELIOZOIC | HELP | HENBANES | HEPT | HERBS |
| HELIPAD | HELPABLE | HENCE | HEPTAD | HERBY |
| HELIPADS | HELPED | HENCHMAN | HEPTADS | HERCOGAMIES |
| HELIPILOT | HELPER | HENCHMEN | HEPTAGLOT | HERCOGAMY |
| HELIPILOTS | HELPERS | HEND | HEPTAGLOTS | HERCULEAN |
| HELIPORT | HELPFUL | HENDED | HEPTAGON | HERCYNITE |
| HELIPORTS | HELPING | HENDIADYS | HEPTAGONS | HERCYNITES |
| HELISCOOP | HELPINGS | HENDIADYSES | HEPTANE | HERD |
| HELISCOOPS | HELPLESS | HENDING | HEPTANES | HERDBOY |
| HELISTOP | HELPLINE | HENDS | HEPTAPODIES | HERDBOYS |
| HELISTOPS | HELPLINES | HENEQUEN | HEPTAPODY | HERDED |
| HELIUM | HELPMATE | HENEQUENS | HEPTARCH | HERDEN |
| HELIUMS | HELPMATES | HENEQUIN | HEPTARCHIES | HERDENS |
| HELIX | HELPMEET | HENEQUINS | HEPTARCHS | HERDESS |
| HELIXES | HELPMEETS | HENGE | HEPTARCHY | HERDESSES |
| HELL | HELPS | HENGES | HER | HERDIC |
| HELLEBORE | HELVE | HENIQUIN | HERALD | HERDICS |
| HELLEBORES | HELVED | HENIQUINS | HERALDED | HERDING |
| HELLED | HELVES | HENNA | HERALDIC | HERDMAN |
| HELLENISE | HELVETIUM | HENNAED | HERALDING | HERDMEN |
| HELLENISED | HELVETIUMS | HENNAS | HERALDRIES | HERDS |
| HELLENISES | HELVING | HENNED | HERALDRY | HERDSMAN |
| HELLENISING | HEM | HENNER | HERALDS | HERDSMEN |
| HELLENIZE | HEMAL | HENNERIES | HERB | HERDWICK |
| HELLENIZED | HEMATITE | HENNERS | HERBAGE | HERDWICKS |
| HELLENIZES | HEMATITES | HENNERY | HERBAGED | HERE |
| HELLENIZING | HEME | HENNIER | HERBAGES | HEREABOUT |
| HELLER | HEMES | HENNIES | HERBAL | HEREABOUTS |
| HELLERS | HEMIALGIA | HENNIEST | HERBALISM | HEREAFTER |
| HELLHOUND | HEMIALGIAS | HENNIN | HERBALISMS | HEREAFTERS |
| HELLHOUNDS | HEMICYCLE | HENNING | HERBALIST | HEREAT |
| HELLICAT | HEMICYCLES | HENNINS | HERBALISTS | HEREAWAY |
| HELLICATS | HEMIHEDRIES | HENNY | HERBALS | HEREBY |

| | | | | |
|---|---|---|---|---|
| HEREDITIES | HEROICS | HESITATOR | HEWINGS | HIBERNISES |
| HEREDITY | HEROIN | HESITATORS | HEWN | HIBERNISING |
| HEREFROM | HEROINE | HESP | HEWS | HIBERNIZE |
| HEREIN | HEROINES | HESPED | HEX | HIBERNIZED |
| HERENESS | HEROINS | HESPERID | HEXACHORD | HIBERNIZES |
| HERENESSES | HEROISE | HESPERIDS | HEXACHORDS | HIBERNIZING |
| HEREOF | HEROISED | HESPING | HEXACT | HIBISCUS |
| HEREON | HEROISES | HESPS | HEXACTS | HIBISCUSES |
| HERESIES | HEROISING | HESSIAN | HEXAD | HIC |
| HERESY | HEROISM | HESSIANS | HEXADIC | HICATEE |
| HERETIC | HEROISMS | HESSONITE | HEXADS | HICATEES |
| HERETICAL | HEROIZE | HESSONITES | HEXAFOIL | HICCATEE |
| HERETICS | HEROIZED | HEST | HEXAFOILS | HICCATEES |
| HERETO | HEROIZES | HESTERNAL | HEXAGLOT | HICCOUGH |
| HEREUNDER | HEROIZING | HESTS | HEXAGON | HICCOUGHED |
| HEREUNTO | HERON | HET | HEXAGONAL | HICCOUGHING |
| HEREUPON | HERONRIES | HETAERA | HEXAGONS | HICCOUGHS |
| HEREWITH | HERONRY | HETAERAE | HEXAGRAM | HICCUP |
| HERIED | HERONS | HETAERAS | HEXAGRAMS | HICCUPED |
| HERIES | HERONSEW | HETAERIA | HEXAHEDRA | HICCUPING |
| HERIOT | HERONSEWS | HETAERIAS | HEXAMETER | HICCUPS |
| HERIOTS | HERONSHAW | HETAERISM | HEXAMETERS | HICCUPY |
| HÉRISSÉ | HERONSHAWS | HETAERISMS | HEXANE | HICK |
| HERISSON | HEROON | HETAERIST | HEXANES | HICKEY |
| HERISSONS | HEROONS | HETAERISTS | HEXAPLA | HICKEYS |
| HERITABLE | HEROSHIP | HETAIRA | HEXAPLAR | HICKORIES |
| HERITABLY | HEROSHIPS | HETAIRAI | HEXAPLAS | HICKORY |
| HERITAGE | HERPES | HETAIRIA | HEXAPLOID | HICKS |
| HERITAGES | HERPETIC | HETAIRIAS | HEXAPLOIDS | HICKWALL |
| HERITOR | HERPETOID | HETAIRISM | HEXAPOD | HICKWALLS |
| HERITORS | HERRIED | HETAIRISMS | HEXAPODIES | HID |
| HERITRESS | HERRIES | HETAIRIST | HEXAPODS | HIDAGE |
| HERITRESSES | HERRIMENT | HETAIRISTS | HEXAPODY | HIDAGES |
| HERITRICES | HERRIMENTS | HETE | HEXARCH | HIDALGA |
| HERITRIX | HERRING | HETERODOX | HEXASTICH | HIDALGAS |
| HERITRIXES | HERRINGER | HETERONYM | HEXASTICHS | HIDALGO |
| HERKOGAMIES | HERRINGERS | HETERONYMS | HEXASTYLE | HIDALGOS |
| HERKOGAMY | HERRINGS | HETEROPOD | HEXASTYLES | HIDDEN |
| HERL | HERRY | HETEROPODS | HEXED | HIDDENITE |
| HERLING | HERRYING | HETEROSES | HEXENE | HIDDENITES |
| HERLINGS | HERRYMENT | HETEROSIS | HEXENES | HIDDENLY |
| HERLS | HERRYMENTS | HETEROTIC | HEXES | HIDDER |
| HERM | HERS | HETES | HEXING | HIDDERS |
| HERMA | HERSALL | HETHER | HEXINGS | HIDE |
| HERMAE | HERSALLS | HETING | HEXOSE | HIDED |
| HERMANDAD | HERSE | HETMAN | HEXOSES | HIDEOSITIES |
| HERMANDADS | HERSED | HETMANATE | HEXYLENE | HIDEOSITY |
| HERMETIC | HERSEEMED | HETMANATES | HEXYLENES | HIDEOUS |
| HERMETICS | HERSEEMS | HETMANS | HEY | HIDEOUSLY |
| HERMIT | HERSELF | HETS | HEYDAY | HIDEOUT |
| HERMITAGE | HERSES | HEUCH | HEYDAYS | HIDEOUTS |
| HERMITAGES | HERSHIP | HEUCHS | HEYDUCK | HIDES |
| HERMITESS | HERSHIPS | HEUGH | HEYDUCKS | HIDING |
| HERMITESSES | HERTZ | HEUGHS | HEYED | HIDINGS |
| HERMITS | HERTZES | HEUREKA | HEYING | HIDLING |
| HERMS | HERY | HEUREKAS | HEYS | HIDLINGS |
| HERN | HERYE | HEURETIC | HI | HIDLINS |
| HERNIA | HERYED | HEURETICS | HIANT | HIDROSES |
| HERNIAL | HERYES | HEURISM | HIATUS | HIDROSIS |
| HERNIAS | HERYING | HEURISMS | HIATUSES | HIDROTIC |
| HERNIATED | HES | HEURISTIC | HIBACHI | HIDROTICS |
| HERNS | HESITANCE | HEURISTICS | HIBACHIS | HIE |
| HERNSHAW | HESITANCES | HEVEA | HIBAKUSHA | HIED |
| HERNSHAWS | HESITANCIES | HEVEAS | HIBERNAL | HIEING |
| HERO | HESITANCY | HEW | HIBERNATE | HIELAMAN |
| HEROE | HESITANT | HEWED | HIBERNATED | HIELAMANS |
| HEROES | HESITATE | HEWER | HIBERNATES | HIEMAL |
| HEROIC | HESITATED | HEWERS | HIBERNATING | HIEMS |
| HEROICAL | HESITATES | HEWGH | HIBERNISE | HIERACIUM |
| HEROICLY | HESITATING | HEWING | HIBERNISED | HIERACIUMS |

| | | | | |
|---|---|---|---|---|
| HIERARCH | HIGHWAY | HINDBERRIES | HIPPYDOMS | HISTOID |
| HIERARCHIES | HIGHWAYS | HINDBERRY | HIPS | HISTOLOGIES |
| HIERARCHS | HIJACK | HINDER | HIPSTER | HISTOLOGY |
| HIERARCHY | HIJACKED | HINDERED | HIPSTERS | HISTONE |
| HIERATIC | HIJACKER | HINDERER | HIPT | HISTONES |
| HIERATICA | HIJACKERS | HINDERERS | HIRABLE | HISTORIAN |
| HIERATICAS | HIJACKING | HINDERING | HIRCINE | HISTORIANS |
| HIEROCRAT | HIJACKS | HINDERS | HIRCOSITIES | HISTORIC |
| HIEROCRATS | HIJINKS | HINDFEET | HIRCOSITY | HISTORIED |
| HIERODULE | HIJRA | HINDFOOT | HIRE | HISTORIES |
| HIERODULES | HIJRAH | HINDHEAD | HIREABLE | HISTORIFIED |
| HIEROGRAM | HIJRAHS | HINDHEADS | HIRED | HISTORIFIES |
| HIEROGRAMS | HIJRAS | HINDLEG | HIRELING | HISTORIFY |
| HIEROLOGIES | HIKE | HINDLEGS | HIRELINGS | HISTORIFYING |
| HIEROLOGY | HIKED | HINDMOST | HIRER | HISTORISM |
| HIERURGIES | HIKER | HINDRANCE | HIRERS | HISTORISMS |
| HIERURGY | HIKERS | HINDRANCES | HIRES | HISTORY |
| HIES | HIKES | HINDS | HIRING | HISTORYING |
| HIGGLE | HIKING | HINDSIGHT | HIRINGS | HISTRIO |
| HIGGLED | HILA | HINDSIGHTS | HIRLING | HISTRION |
| HIGGLER | HILAR | HINDWARD | HIRLINGS | HISTRIONS |
| HIGGLERS | HILARIOUS | HING | HIRPLE | HISTRIOS |
| HIGGLES | HILARITIES | HINGE | HIRPLED | HISTS |
| HIGGLING | HILARITY | HINGED | HIRPLES | HIT |
| HIGGLINGS | HILCH | HINGES | HIRPLING | HITCH |
| HIGH | HILCHED | HINGING | HIRRIENT | HITCHED |
| HIGHBALL | HILCHES | HINGS | HIRRIENTS | HITCHER |
| HIGHBALLED | HILCHING | HINNIED | HIRSEL | HITCHERS |
| HIGHBALLING | HILD | HINNIES | HIRSELLED | HITCHES |
| HIGHBALLS | HILDING | HINNY | HIRSELLING | HITCHIER |
| HIGHBOY | HILDINGS | HINNYING | HIRSELS | HITCHIEST |
| HIGHBOYS | HILI | HINS | HIRSLE | HITCHILY |
| HIGHBROW | HILL | HINT | HIRSLED | HITCHING |
| HIGHBROWS | HILLED | HINTED | HIRSLES | HITCHY |
| HIGHED | HILLFOLK | HINTING | HIRSLING | HITHE |
| HIGHER | HILLIER | HINTINGLY | HIRSTIE | HITHER |
| HIGHERED | HILLIEST | HINTS | HIRSUTE | HITHERED |
| HIGHERING | HILLINESS | HIP | HIRUDIN | HITHERING |
| HIGHERS | HILLINESSES | HIPPARCH | HIRUDINS | HITHERS |
| HIGHEST | HILLING | HIPPARCHS | HIRUNDINE | HITHERTO |
| HIGHING | HILLMEN | HIPPED | HIS | HITHES |
| HIGHISH | HILLO | HIPPER | HISH | HITS |
| HIGHJACK | HILLOCK | HIPPEST | HISHED | HITTER |
| HIGHJACKED | HILLOCKS | HIPPIATRIES | HISHES | HITTERS |
| HIGHJACKING | HILLOCKY | HIPPIATRY | HISHING | HITTING |
| HIGHJACKS | HILLOED | HIPPIC | HISN | HIVE |
| HIGHLAND | HILLOES | HIPPIE | HISPID | HIVED |
| HIGHLANDS | HILLOING | HIPPIEDOM | HISPIDITIES | HIVELESS |
| HIGHLIGHT | HILLOS | HIPPIEDOMS | HISPIDITY | HIVELIKE |
| HIGHLIGHTED | HILLS | HIPPIER | HISS | HIVER |
| HIGHLIGHTING | HILLSIDE | HIPPIES | HISSED | HIVERS |
| HIGHLIGHTS | HILLSIDES | HIPPIEST | HISSES | HIVES |
| HIGHLY | HILLTOP | HIPPING | HISSING | HIVEWARD |
| HIGHMAN | HILLTOPS | HIPPINGS | HISSINGLY | HIVEWARDS |
| HIGHMEN | HILLY | HIPPISH | HISSINGS | HIVING |
| HIGHMOST | HILT | HIPPO | HIST | HIYA |
| HIGHNESS | HILTED | HIPPOCRAS | HISTAMINE | HIZEN |
| HIGHNESSES | HILTING | HIPPOCRASES | HISTAMINES | HIZENS |
| HIGHROAD | HILTS | HIPPODAME | HISTED | HIZZ |
| HIGHROADS | HILUM | HIPPODAMES | HISTIDINE | HIZZED |
| HIGHS | HILUS | HIPPOLOGIES | HISTIDINES | HIZZES |
| HIGHT | HIM | HIPPOLOGY | HISTIE | HIZZING |
| HIGHTAIL | HIMATIA | HIPPOS | HISTING | HO |
| HIGHTAILED | HIMATION | HIPPURIC | HISTIOID | HOA |
| HIGHTAILING | HIMATIONS | HIPPURITE | HISTOGEN | HOACTZIN |
| HIGHTAILS | HIMSEEMED | HIPPURITES | HISTOGENIES | HOACTZINS |
| HIGHTH | HIMSEEMS | HIPPUS | HISTOGENS | HOAED |
| HIGHTHS | HIMSELF | HIPPUSES | HISTOGENY | HOAING |
| HIGHTING | HIN | HIPPY | HISTOGRAM | HOAR |
| HIGHTS | HIND | HIPPYDOM | HISTOGRAMS | HOARD |

| | | | | |
|---|---|---|---|---|
| HOARDED | HOBJOBBER | HOERS | HOISTING | HOLLOAED |
| HOARDER | HOBJOBBERS | HOES | HOISTINGS | HOLLOAING |
| HOARDERS | HOBJOBBING | HOG | HOISTMAN | HOLLOAS |
| HOARDING | HOBJOBBINGS | HOGAN | HOISTMEN | HOLLOED |
| HOARDINGS | HOBJOBS | HOGANS | HOISTS | HOLLOES |
| HOARDS | HOBNAIL | HOGBACK | HOISTWAY | HOLLOING |
| HOARED | HOBNAILED | HOGBACKS | HOISTWAYS | HOLLOS |
| HOARHEAD | HOBNAILING | HOGEN | HOKE | HOLLOW |
| HOARHEADS | HOBNAILS | HOGENS | HOKED | HOLLOWARE |
| HOARHOUND | HOBNOB | HOGG | HOKES | HOLLOWARES |
| HOARHOUNDS | HOBNOBBED | HOGGED | HOKEY | HOLLOWED |
| HOARIER | HOBNOBBING | HOGGER | HOKIER | HOLLOWER |
| HOARIEST | HOBNOBBY | HOGGEREL | HOKIEST | HOLLOWEST |
| HOARILY | HOBNOBS | HOGGERELS | HOKING | HOLLOWING |
| HOARINESS | HOBO | HOGGERIES | HOKKU | HOLLOWLY |
| HOARINESSES | HOBODOM | HOGGERS | HOKUM | HOLLOWS |
| HOARING | HOBODOMS | HOGGERY | HOKUMS | HOLLY |
| HOARS | HOBOED | HOGGET | HOLD | HOLLYHOCK |
| HOARSE | HOBOES | HOGGETS | HOLDBACK | HOLLYHOCKS |
| HOARSELY | HOBOING | HOGGIN | HOLDBACKS | HOLM |
| HOARSEN | HOBOISM | HOGGING | HOLDEN | HOLMIA |
| HOARSENED | HOBOISMS | HOGGINGS | HOLDER | HOLMIAS |
| HOARSENING | HOBS | HOGGINS | HOLDERBAT | HOLMIC |
| HOARSENS | HOC | HOGGISH | HOLDERBATS | HOLMIUM |
| HOARSER | HOCK | HOGGISHLY | HOLDERS | HOLMIUMS |
| HOARSEST | HOCKED | HOGGS | HOLDFAST | HOLMS |
| HOARY | HOCKER | HOGH | HOLDFASTS | HOLOCAUST |
| HOAS | HOCKERS | HOGHOOD | HOLDING | HOLOCAUSTS |
| HOAST | HOCKEY | HOGHOODS | HOLDINGS | HOLOCRINE |
| HOASTED | HOCKEYS | HOGHS | HOLDOVER | HOLOGRAM |
| HOASTING | HOCKING | HOGS | HOLDOVERS | HOLOGRAMS |
| HOASTMAN | HOCKS | HOGSHEAD | HOLDS | HOLOGRAPH |
| HOASTMEN | HOCUS | HOGSHEADS | HOLE | HOLOGRAPHED |
| HOASTS | HOCUSED | HOGTIE | HOLED | HOLOGRAPHING |
| HOATZIN | HOCUSES | HOGTIED | HOLES | HOLOGRAPHS |
| HOATZINS | HOCUSING | HOGTIES | HOLESOM | HOLOPHOTE |
| HOAX | HOCUSSED | HOGTYING | HOLESOME | HOLOPHOTES |
| HOAXED | HOCUSSES | HOGWARD | HOLEY | HOLOPHYTE |
| HOAXER | HOCUSSING | HOGWARDS | HOLIBUT | HOLOPHYTES |
| HOAXERS | HOD | HOGWASH | HOLIBUTS | HOLOPTIC |
| HOAXES | HODDED | HOGWASHES | HOLIDAY | HOLOTYPE |
| HOAXING | HODDEN | HOGWEED | HOLIDAYED | HOLOTYPES |
| HOB | HODDENS | HOGWEEDS | HOLIDAYING | HOLOTYPIC |
| HOBBIES | HODDING | HOH | HOLIDAYS | HOLOZOIC |
| HOBBISH | HODDLE | HOHED | HOLIER | HOLP |
| HOBBIT | HODDLED | HOHING | HOLIES | HOLPEN |
| HOBBITRIES | HODDLES | HOHS | HOLIEST | HOLS |
| HOBBITRY | HODDLING | HOI | HOLILY | HOLSTER |
| HOBBITS | HODIERNAL | HOICK | HOLINESS | HOLSTERED |
| HOBBLE | HODJA | HOICKED | HOLINESSES | HOLSTERS |
| HOBBLED | HODJAS | HOICKING | HOLING | HOLT |
| HOBBLER | HODMAN | HOICKS | HOLINGS | HOLTS |
| HOBBLERS | HODMANDOD | HOICKSED | HOLISM | HOLY |
| HOBBLES | HODMANDODS | HOICKSES | HOLISMS | HOLYDAM |
| HOBBLING | HODMEN | HOICKSING | HOLIST | HOLYDAME |
| HOBBLINGS | HODOGRAPH | HOIDEN | HOLISTIC | HOLYDAMES |
| HOBBY | HODOGRAPHS | HOIDENS | HOLISTS | HOLYDAMS |
| HOBBYISM | HODOMETER | HOIK | HOLLA | HOLYSTONE |
| HOBBYISMS | HODOMETERS | HOIKED | HOLLAND | HOLYSTONED |
| HOBBYIST | HODOMETRIES | HOIKING | HOLLANDS | HOLYSTONES |
| HOBBYISTS | HODOMETRY | HOIKS | HOLLAS | HOLYSTONING |
| HOBBYLESS | HODOSCOPE | HOING | HOLLER | HOMAGE |
| HOBDAY | HODOSCOPES | HOISE | HOLLERED | HOMAGED |
| HOBDAYED | HODS | HOISED | HOLLERING | HOMAGER |
| HOBDAYING | HOE | HOISES | HOLLERS | HOMAGERS |
| HOBDAYS | HOED | HOISING | HOLLIDAM | HOMAGES |
| HOBGOBLIN | HOEDOWN | HOIST | HOLLIDAMS | HOMAGING |
| HOBGOBLINS | HOEDOWNS | HOISTED | HOLLIES | HOMALOID |
| HOBJOB | HOEING | HOISTER | HOLLO | HOMALOIDS |
| HOBJOBBED | HOER | HOISTERS | HOLLOA | HOMBRE |

| | | | | |
|---|---|---|---|---|
| HOMBRES | HOMOGAMY | HONEYCOMBED | HOOFED | HOOTER |
| HOME | HOMOGENIES | HONEYCOMBING | HOOFER | HOOTERS |
| HOMEBOUND | HOMOGENY | HONEYCOMBS | HOOFERS | HOOTING |
| HOMECRAFT | HOMOGRAFT | HONEYED | HOOFING | HOOTNANNIES |
| HOMECRAFTS | HOMOGRAFTS | HONEYING | HOOFLESS | HOOTNANNY |
| HOMED | HOMOGRAPH | HONEYLESS | HOOFPRINT | HOOTS |
| HOMEFELT | HOMOGRAPHS | HONEYMOON | HOOFPRINTS | HOOVE |
| HOMELAND | HOMOLOG | HONEYMOONED | HOOFROT | HOOVED |
| HOMELANDS | HOMOLOGIES | HONEYMOONING | HOOFROTS | HOOVEN |
| HOMELESS | HOMOLOGS | HONEYMOONS | HOOFS | HOOVER |
| HOMELIER | HOMOLOGUE | HONEYPOT | HOOK | HOOVERED |
| HOMELIEST | HOMOLOGUES | HONEYPOTS | HOOKA | HOOVERING |
| HOMELIKE | HOMOLOGY | HONEYS | HOOKAH | HOOVERS |
| HOMELILY | HOMOMORPH | HONG | HOOKAHS | HOOVES |
| HOMELY | HOMOMORPHS | HONGING | HOOKAS | HOOVING |
| HOMELYN | HOMONYM | HONGS | HOOKED | HOP |
| HOMELYNS | HOMONYMIC | HONIED | HOOKER | HOPBIND |
| HOMEMAKER | HOMONYMIES | HONING | HOOKERS | HOPBINDS |
| HOMEMAKERS | HOMONYMS | HONK | HOOKEY | HOPBINE |
| HOMEOMERIES | HOMONYMY | HONKED | HOOKEYS | HOPBINES |
| HOMEOMERY | HOMOPHILE | HONKER | HOOKIER | HOPDOG |
| HOMEOPATH | HOMOPHILES | HONKERS | HOOKIES | HOPDOGS |
| HOMEOPATHS | HOMOPHOBE | HONKIE | HOOKIEST | HOPE |
| HOMEOSES | HOMOPHOBES | HONKIES | HOOKING | HOPED |
| HOMEOSIS | HOMOPHONE | HONKING | HOOKS | HOPEFUL |
| HOMER | HOMOPHONES | HONKS | HOOKY | HOPEFULLY |
| HOMERS | HOMOPHONIES | HONKY | HOOLACHAN | HOPEFULS |
| HOMES | HOMOPHONY | HONOR | HOOLACHANS | HOPELESS |
| HOMESICK | HOMOPHYLIES | HONORAND | HOOLEY | HOPER |
| HOMESPUN | HOMOPHYLY | HONORANDS | HOOLEYS | HOPERS |
| HOMESPUNS | HOMOPLASIES | HONORARIA | HOOLICAN | HOPES |
| HOMESTALL | HOMOPLASY | HONORARIES | HOOLICANS | HOPING |
| HOMESTALLS | HOMOPOLAR | HONORARY | HOOLIER | HOPINGLY |
| HOMESTEAD | HOMOS | HONORED | HOOLIEST | HOPLITE |
| HOMESTEADS | HOMOTAXES | HONORIFIC | HOOLIGAN | HOPLITES |
| HOMEWARD | HOMOTAXIC | HONORIFICS | HOOLIGANS | HOPLOLOGIES |
| HOMEWARDS | HOMOTAXIS | HONORING | HOOLOCK | HOPLOLOGY |
| HOMEWORK | HOMOTONIC | HONORS | HOOLOCKS | HOPPED |
| HOMEWORKS | HOMOTONIES | HONOUR | HOOLY | HOPPER |
| HOMEY | HOMOTONY | HONOURED | HOOP | HOPPERS |
| HOMICIDAL | HOMOTYPAL | HONOURER | HOOPED | HOPPIER |
| HOMICIDE | HOMOTYPE | HONOURERS | HOOPER | HOPPIEST |
| HOMICIDES | HOMOTYPES | HONOURING | HOOPERS | HOPPING |
| HOMIER | HOMOTYPIC | HONOURS | HOOPING | HOPPINGS |
| HOMIEST | HOMOTYPIES | HONS | HOOPOE | HOPPLE |
| HOMILETIC | HOMOTYPY | HOO | HOOPOES | HOPPLED |
| HOMILETICS | HOMOUSIAN | HOOCH | HOOPS | HOPPLES |
| HOMILIES | HOMOUSIANS | HOOCHES | HOORAH | HOPPLING |
| HOMILIST | HOMUNCLE | HOOD | HOORAHED | HOPPY |
| HOMILISTS | HOMUNCLES | HOODED | HOORAHING | HOPS |
| HOMILY | HOMUNCULE | HOODING | HOORAHS | HOPSACK |
| HOMING | HOMUNCULES | HOODLESS | HOORAY | HOPSACKS |
| HOMINGS | HOMUNCULI | HOODLUM | HOORAYED | HORAL |
| HOMINID | HOMY | HOODLUMS | HOORAYING | HORARY |
| HOMINIDS | HON | HOODMAN | HOORAYS | HORDE |
| HOMINIES | HOND | HOODMEN | HOORD | HORDED |
| HOMINOID | HONDS | HOODOO | HOORDS | HORDEIN |
| HOMINOIDS | HONE | HOODOOED | HOOROO | HORDEINS |
| HOMINY | HONED | HOODOOING | HOOSEGOW | HORDEOLUM |
| HOMME | HONES | HOODOOS | HOOSEGOWS | HORDEOLUMS |
| HOMMES | HONEST | HOODS | HOOSGOW | HORDES |
| HOMMOCK | HONESTER | HOODWINK | HOOSGOWS | HORDING |
| HOMMOCKS | HONESTEST | HOODWINKED | HOOSH | HORDOCK |
| HOMO | HONESTIES | HOODWINKING | HOOSHED | HORDOCKS |
| HOMODONT | HONESTLY | HOODWINKS | HOOSHES | HORE |
| HOMODYNE | HONESTY | HOOEY | HOOSHING | HOREHOUND |
| HOMOEOSES | HONEY | HOOEYS | HOOT | HOREHOUNDS |
| HOMOEOSIS | HONEYBUN | HOOF | HOOTCH | HORIZON |
| HOMOGAMIC | HONEYBUNS | HOOFBEAT | HOOTCHES | HORIZONS |
| HOMOGAMIES | HONEYCOMB | HOOFBEATS | HOOTED | HORKEY |

| | | | | |
|---|---|---|---|---|
| HORKEYS | HOROSCOPE | HOSANNAS | HOTELIERS | HOUSELS |
| HORME | HOROSCOPES | HOSE | HOTELS | HOUSEMAID |
| HORMES | HOROSCOPIES | HOSED | HOTEN | HOUSEMAIDS |
| HORMONAL | HOROSCOPY | HOSEMAN | HOTFOOT | HOUSEMAN |
| HORMONE | HORRENT | HOSEMEN | HOTHEAD | HOUSEMEN |
| HORMONES | HORRIBLE | HOSEN | HOTHEADED | HOUSES |
| HORMONIC | HORRIBLY | HOSEPIPE | HOTHEADS | HOUSETOP |
| HORN | HORRID | HOSEPIPES | HOTHOUSE | HOUSETOPS |
| HORNBEAK | HORRIDER | HOSES | HOTHOUSES | HOUSEWIFE |
| HORNBEAKS | HORRIDEST | HOSIER | HOTLY | HOUSEWIVES |
| HORNBEAM | HORRIDLY | HOSIERIES | HOTNESS | HOUSEWORK |
| HORNBEAMS | HORRIFIC | HOSIERS | HOTNESSES | HOUSEWORKS |
| HORNBILL | HORRIFIED | HOSIERY | HOTPOT | HOUSING |
| HORNBILLS | HORRIFIES | HOSING | HOTPOTS | HOUSINGS |
| HORNBOOK | HORRIFY | HOSPICE | HOTS | HOUSLING |
| HORNBOOKS | HORRIFYING | HOSPICES | HOTSHOT | HOUT |
| HORNBUG | HORROR | HOSPITAGE | HOTSHOTS | HOUTS |
| HORNBUGS | HORRORS | HOSPITAGES | HOTTED | HOVE |
| HORNED | HORS | HOSPITAL | HOTTENTOT | HOVED |
| HORNER | HORSE | HOSPITALE | HOTTENTOTS | HOVEL |
| HORNERS | HORSEBACK | HOSPITALES | HOTTER | HOVELED |
| HORNET | HORSEBACKS | HOSPITALS | HOTTERED | HOVELING |
| HORNETS | HORSECAR | HOSPITIA | HOTTERING | HOVELLED |
| HORNFELS | HORSECARS | HOSPITIUM | HOTTERS | HOVELLER |
| HORNFELSES | HORSED | HOSPODAR | HOTTEST | HOVELLERS |
| HORNFUL | HORSEFLIES | HOSPODARS | HOTTIE | HOVELLING |
| HORNFULS | HORSEFLY | HOSS | HOTTIES | HOVELS |
| HORNGELD | HORSEHAIR | HOSSES | HOTTING | HOVEN |
| HORNGELDS | HORSEHAIRS | HOST | HOTTISH | HOVER |
| HORNIER | HORSEHIDE | HOSTA | HOUDAH | HOVERED |
| HORNIEST | HORSEHIDES | HOSTAGE | HOUDAHS | HOVERING |
| HORNINESS | HORSELESS | HOSTAGES | HOUDAN | HOVERPORT |
| HORNINESSES | HORSEMAN | HOSTAS | HOUDANS | HOVERPORTS |
| HORNING | HORSEMEAT | HOSTED | HOUF | HOVERS |
| HORNINGS | HORSEMEATS | HOSTEL | HOUFED | HOVES |
| HORNISH | HORSEMEN | HOSTELER | HOUFF | HOVING |
| HORNIST | HORSEMINT | HOSTELERS | HOUFFED | HOW |
| HORNISTS | HORSEMINTS | HOSTELLER | HOUFFING | HOWBE |
| HORNITO | HORSEPLAY | HOSTELLERS | HOUFFS | HOWBEIT |
| HORNITOS | HORSEPLAYS | HOSTELRIES | HOUFING | HOWDAH |
| HORNLESS | HORSEPOND | HOSTELRY | HOUFS | HOWDAHS |
| HORNLET | HORSEPONDS | HOSTELS | HOUGH | HOWDIE |
| HORNLETS | HORSES | HOSTESS | HOUGHED | HOWDIES |
| HORNPIPE | HORSESHOE | HOSTESSED | HOUGHING | HOWDY |
| HORNPIPES | HORSESHOES | HOSTESSES | HOUGHS | HOWE |
| HORNS | HORSETAIL | HOSTESSING | HOUND | HOWES |
| HORNSTONE | HORSETAILS | HOSTILE | HOUNDED | HOWEVER |
| HORNSTONES | HORSEWAY | HOSTILELY | HOUNDING | HOWF |
| HORNTAIL | HORSEWAYS | HOSTILITIES | HOUNDS | HOWFED |
| HORNTAILS | HORSEWHIP | HOSTILITY | HOUR | HOWFF |
| HORNWORK | HORSEWHIPPED | HOSTING | HOURI | HOWFFED |
| HORNWORKS | HORSEWHIPPING | HOSTINGS | HOURIS | HOWFFING |
| HORNWORM | HORSEWHIPS | HOSTLER | HOURLONG | HOWFFS |
| HORNWORMS | HORSIER | HOSTLERS | HOURLY | HOWFING |
| HORNWORT | HORSIEST | HOSTLESSE | HOURPLATE | HOWFS |
| HORNWORTS | HORSINESS | HOSTRIES | HOURPLATES | HOWITZER |
| HORNWRACK | HORSINESSES | HOSTRY | HOURS | HOWITZERS |
| HORNWRACKS | HORSING | HOSTS | HOUSE | HOWK |
| HORNY | HORSINGS | HOT | HOUSEBOY | HOWKED |
| HORNYHEAD | HORSON | HOTBED | HOUSEBOYS | HOWKER |
| HORNYHEADS | HORSONS | HOTBEDS | HOUSED | HOWKERS |
| HOROLOGE | HORST | HOTCH | HOUSEFUL | HOWKING |
| HOROLOGER | HORSTS | HOTCHED | HOUSEFULS | HOWKS |
| HOROLOGERS | HORSY | HOTCHES | HOUSEHOLD | HOWL |
| HOROLOGES | HORTATION | HOTCHING | HOUSEHOLDS | HOWLED |
| HOROLOGIC | HORTATIONS | HOTCHPOT | HOUSEL | HOWLER |
| HOROLOGIES | HORTATIVE | HOTCHPOTS | HOUSELESS | HOWLERS |
| HOROLOGY | HORTATORY | HOTE | HOUSELLED | HOWLET |
| HOROMETRIES | HOS | HOTEL | HOUSELLING | HOWLETS |
| HOROMETRY | HOSANNA | HOTELIER | HOUSELLINGS | HOWLING |

HOWLINGS
HOWLS
HOWRE
HOWRES
HOWS
HOWSO
HOWSOEVER
HOWTOWDIE
HOWTOWDIES
HOWZAT
HOX
HOXED
HOXES
HOXING
HOY
HOYA
HOYAS
HOYDEN
HOYDENISH
HOYDENISM
HOYDENISMS
HOYDENS
HOYED
HOYING
HOYS
HUANACO
HUANACOS
HUB
HUBBIES
HUBBUB
HUBBUBOO
HUBBUBOOS
HUBBUBS
HUBBY
HUBRIS
HUBRISES
HUBRISTIC
HUBS
HUCK
HUCKABACK
HUCKABACKS
HUCKLE
HUCKLES
HUCKS
HUCKSTER
HUCKSTERED
HUCKSTERIES
HUCKSTERING
HUCKSTERS
HUCKSTERY
HUDDEN
HUDDLE
HUDDLED
HUDDLES
HUDDLING
HUDDUP
HUE
HUED
HUELESS
HUER
HUERS
HUES
HUFF
HUFFED
HUFFIER
HUFFIEST
HUFFILY
HUFFINESS
HUFFINESSES
HUFFING

HUFFISH
HUFFISHLY
HUFFKIN
HUFFKINS
HUFFS
HUFFY
HUG
HUGE
HUGELY
HUGENESS
HUGENESSES
HUGEOUS
HUGEOUSLY
HUGER
HUGEST
HUGGABLE
HUGGED
HUGGING
HUGS
HUGY
HUH
HUIA
HUIAS
HUISSIER
HUISSIERS
HUITAIN
HUITAINS
HULA
HULAS
HULE
HULES
HULK
HULKIER
HULKIEST
HULKING
HULKS
HULKY
HULL
HULLED
HULLIER
HULLIEST
HULLING
HULLO
HULLOED
HULLOES
HULLOING
HULLOS
HULLS
HULLY
HUM
HUMA
HUMAN
HUMANE
HUMANELY
HUMANER
HUMANEST
HUMANISE
HUMANISED
HUMANISES
HUMANISING
HUMANISM
HUMANISMS
HUMANIST
HUMANISTS
HUMANITIES
HUMANITY
HUMANIZE
HUMANIZED
HUMANIZES
HUMANIZING

HUMANKIND
HUMANLIKE
HUMANLY
HUMANNESS
HUMANNESSES
HUMANOID
HUMANOIDS
HUMANS
HUMAS
HUMBLE
HUMBLED
HUMBLER
HUMBLES
HUMBLESSE
HUMBLESSES
HUMBLEST
HUMBLING
HUMBLINGS
HUMBLY
HUMBUG
HUMBUGGED
HUMBUGGER
HUMBUGGERS
HUMBUGGING
HUMBUGS
HUMBUZZ
HUMBUZZES
HUMDINGER
HUMDINGERS
HUMDRUM
HUMDRUMS
HUMECT
HUMECTANT
HUMECTANTS
HUMECTATE
HUMECTATED
HUMECTATES
HUMECTATING
HUMECTED
HUMECTING
HUMECTIVE
HUMECTIVES
HUMECTS
HUMEFIED
HUMEFIES
HUMEFY
HUMEFYING
HUMERAL
HUMERALS
HUMERI
HUMERUS
HUMF
HUMFED
HUMFING
HUMFS
HUMHUM
HUMHUMS
HUMIC
HUMID
HUMIDER
HUMIDEST
HUMIDIFIED
HUMIDIFIES
HUMIDIFY
HUMIDIFYING
HUMIDITIES
HUMIDITY
HUMIDLY
HUMIDNESS
HUMIDNESSES

HUMIDOR
HUMIDORS
HUMIFIED
HUMIFIES
HUMIFY
HUMIFYING
HUMILIANT
HUMILIATE
HUMILIATED
HUMILIATES
HUMILIATING
HUMILITIES
HUMILITY
HUMITE
HUMITES
HUMLIE
HUMLIES
HUMMABLE
HUMMAUM
HUMMAUMS
HUMMED
HUMMEL
HUMMELLED
HUMMELLER
HUMMELLERS
HUMMELLING
HUMMELS
HUMMER
HUMMERS
HUMMING
HUMMINGS
HUMMOCK
HUMMOCKED
HUMMOCKS
HUMMOCKY
HUMMUM
HUMMUMS
HUMMUS
HUMMUSES
HUMOGEN
HUMOGENS
HUMOR
HUMORAL
HUMORALLY
HUMORED
HUMORESK
HUMORESKS
HUMORING
HUMORIST
HUMORISTS
HUMOROUS
HUMORS
HUMOUR
HUMOURED
HUMOURING
HUMOURS
HUMOUS
HUMP
HUMPBACK
HUMPBACKS
HUMPED
HUMPEN
HUMPENS
HUMPH
HUMPHED
HUMPHING
HUMPHS
HUMPIER
HUMPIES
HUMPIEST

HUMPING
HUMPS
HUMPTIES
HUMPTY
HUMPY
HUMS
HUMSTRUM
HUMSTRUMS
HUMUS
HUMUSES
HUMUSY
HUNCH
HUNCHBACK
HUNCHBACKS
HUNCHED
HUNCHES
HUNCHING
HUNDRED
HUNDREDER
HUNDREDERS
HUNDREDOR
HUNDREDORS
HUNDREDS
HUNDREDTH
HUNDREDTHS
HUNG
HUNGER
HUNGERED
HUNGERFUL
HUNGERING
HUNGERLY
HUNGERS
HUNGRIER
HUNGRIEST
HUNGRILY
HUNGRY
HUNK
HUNKER
HUNKERED
HUNKERING
HUNKERS
HUNKIER
HUNKIES
HUNKIEST
HUNKS
HUNKSES
HUNKY
HUNT
HUNTED
HUNTER
HUNTERS
HUNTING
HUNTINGS
HUNTRESS
HUNTRESSES
HUNTS
HUNTSMAN
HUNTSMEN
HUP
HUPPED
HUPPING
HUPS
HURCHEON
HURCHEONS
HURDEN
HURDENS
HURDIES
HURDLE
HURDLED
HURDLER

HURDLERS
HURDLES
HURDLING
HURDLINGS
HURDS
HURL
HURLED
HURLER
HURLERS
HURLEY
HURLEYS
HURLIES
HURLING
HURLINGS
HURLS
HURLY
HURRA
HURRAED
HURRAH
HURRAHED
HURRAHING
HURRAHS
HURRAING
HURRAS
HURRAY
HURRAYED
HURRAYING
HURRAYS
HURRICANE
HURRICANES
HURRICANO
HURRICANOES
HURRIED
HURRIEDLY
HURRIES
HURRY
HURRYING
HURRYINGS
HURST
HURSTS
HURT
HURTER
HURTERS
HURTFUL
HURTFULLY
HURTING
HURTLE
HURTLED
HURTLES
HURTLESS
HURTLING
HURTS
HUSBAND
HUSBANDED
HUSBANDING
HUSBANDLY
HUSBANDRIES
HUSBANDRY
HUSBANDS
HUSH
HUSHABIED
HUSHABIES
HUSHABY
HUSHABYING
HUSHED
HUSHER
HUSHERED
HUSHERING
HUSHERS
HUSHES

HUSHIER
HUSHIEST
HUSHING
HUSHY
HUSK
HUSKED
HUSKER
HUSKERS
HUSKIER
HUSKIES
HUSKIEST
HUSKILY
HUSKINESS
HUSKINESSES
HUSKING
HUSKINGS
HUSKS
HUSKY
HUSO
HUSOS
HUSS
HUSSAR
HUSSARS
HUSSES
HUSSIES
HUSSIF
HUSSIFS
HUSSY
HUSTINGS
HUSTLE
HUSTLED
HUSTLER
HUSTLERS
HUSTLES
HUSTLING
HUSTLINGS
HUSWIFE
HUSWIVES
HUT
HUTCH
HUTCHED
HUTCHES
HUTCHING
HUTIA
HUTIAS
HUTMENT
HUTMENTS
HUTS
HUTTED
HUTTING
HUTTINGS
HUZOOR
HUZOORS
HUZZA
HUZZAED
HUZZAING
HUZZAS
HUZZIES
HUZZY
HWYL
HWYLS
HYACINE
HYACINES
HYACINTH
HYACINTHS
HYAENA
HYAENAS
HYALINE
HYALINES
HYALINISE

HYALINISED
HYALINISES
HYALINISING
HYALINIZE
HYALINIZED
HYALINIZES
HYALINIZING
HYALITE
HYALITES
HYALOID
HYALONEMA
HYALONEMAS
HYBRID
HYBRIDISE
HYBRIDISED
HYBRIDISES
HYBRIDISING
HYBRIDISM
HYBRIDISMS
HYBRIDITIES
HYBRIDITY
HYBRIDIZE
HYBRIDIZED
HYBRIDIZES
HYBRIDIZING
HYBRIDOMA
HYBRIDOMAS
HYBRIDOUS
HYBRIDS
HYBRIS
HYBRISES
HYDATHODE
HYDATHODES
HYDATID
HYDATIDS
HYDATOID
HYDRA
HYDRAEMIA
HYDRAEMIAS
HYDRANGEA
HYDRANGEAS
HYDRANT
HYDRANTH
HYDRANTHS
HYDRANTS
HYDRAS
HYDRATE
HYDRATED
HYDRATES
HYDRATING
HYDRATION
HYDRATIONS
HYDRAULIC
HYDRAULICKED
HYDRAULICKING
HYDRAULICS
HYDRAZINE
HYDRAZINES
HYDREMIA
HYDREMIAS
HYDRIA
HYDRIAE
HYDRIAS
HYDRIC
HYDRIDE
HYDRIDES
HYDRIODIC
HYDRO
HYDROCELE
HYDROCELES

HYDROFOIL
HYDROFOILS
HYDROGEN
HYDROGENS
HYDROID
HYDROIDS
HYDROLOGIES
HYDROLOGY
HYDROLYSE
HYDROLYSED
HYDROLYSES
HYDROLYSING
HYDROLYTE
HYDROLYTES
HYDROLYZE
HYDROLYZED
HYDROLYZES
HYDROLYZING
HYDROMEL
HYDROMELS
HYDRONAUT
HYDRONAUTS
HYDROPIC
HYDROPSIES
HYDROPSY
HYDROPTIC
HYDROPULT
HYDROPULTS
HYDROS
HYDROSKI
HYDROSKIS
HYDROSOMA
HYDROSOMATA
HYDROSOME
HYDROSOMES
HYDROSTAT
HYDROSTATS
HYDROUS
HYDROVANE
HYDROVANES
HYDROXIDE
HYDROXIDES
HYDROXY
HYDROXYL
HYDROXYLS
HYDROZOA
HYDROZOAN
HYDROZOANS
HYDROZOON
HYDYNE
HYDYNES
HYE
HYED
HYEING
HYEN
HYENA
HYENAS
HYENS
HYES
HYETAL
HYETOLOGIES
HYETOLOGY
HYGIENE
HYGIENES
HYGIENIC
HYGIENICS
HYGIENIST
HYGIENISTS
HYGRISTOR
HYGRISTORS

HYGRODEIK
HYGRODEIKS
HYGROLOGIES
HYGROLOGY
HYGROPHIL
HYGROSTAT
HYGROSTATS
HYING
HYKE
HYKES
HYLDING
HYLDINGS
HYLE
HYLEG
HYLEGS
HYLES
HYLIC
HYLICISM
HYLICISMS
HYLICIST
HYLICISTS
HYLISM
HYLISMS
HYLIST
HYLISTS
HYLOBATE
HYLOBATES
HYLOIST
HYLOISTS
HYLOPHYTE
HYLOPHYTES
HYLOZOISM
HYLOZOISMS
HYLOZOIST
HYLOZOISTS
HYMEN
HYMENAEAL
HYMENAEAN
HYMENAL
HYMENEAL
HYMENEALS
HYMENEAN
HYMENIA
HYMENIAL
HYMENIUM
HYMENIUMS
HYMENS
HYMN
HYMNAL
HYMNALS
HYMNARIES
HYMNARY
HYMNED
HYMNIC
HYMNING
HYMNIST
HYMNISTS
HYMNODIES
HYMNODIST
HYMNODISTS
HYMNODY
HYMNOLOGIES
HYMNOLOGY
HYMNS
HYNDE
HYNDES
HYOID
HYOSCINE
HYOSCINES
HYP

HYPALGIA
HYPALGIAS
HYPALLAGE
HYPALLAGES
HYPATE
HYPATES
HYPE
HYPED
HYPER
HYPERBOLA
HYPERBOLAS
HYPERBOLE
HYPERBOLES
HYPERCUBE
HYPERCUBES
HYPEREMIA
HYPEREMIAS
HYPERGAMIES
HYPERGAMY
HYPERMART
HYPERMARTS
HYPERON
HYPERONS
HYPEROPIA
HYPEROPIAS
HYPERS
HYPES
HYPHA
HYPHAE
HYPHAL
HYPHEN
HYPHENATE

HYPHENATED
HYPHENATES
HYPHENATING
HYPHENED
HYPHENIC
HYPHENING
HYPHENISE
HYPHENISED
HYPHENISES
HYPHENISING
HYPHENISM
HYPHENISMS
HYPHENIZE
HYPHENIZED
HYPHENIZES
HYPHENIZING
HYPHENS
HYPING
HYPINOSES
HYPINOSIS
HYPNA
HYPNIC
HYPNICS
HYPNOGENIES
HYPNOGENY
HYPNOID
HYPNOIDAL
HYPNOLOGIES
HYPNOLOGY
HYPNONE
HYPNONES
HYPNOSES

HYPNOSIS
HYPNOTEE
HYPNOTEES
HYPNOTIC
HYPNOTICS
HYPNOTISE
HYPNOTISED
HYPNOTISES
HYPNOTISING
HYPNOTISM
HYPNOTISMS
HYPNOTIST
HYPNOTISTS
HYPNOTIZE
HYPNOTIZED
HYPNOTIZES
HYPNOTIZING
HYPNOTOID
HYPNUM
HYPNUMS
HYPO
HYPOBLAST
HYPOBLASTS
HYPOBOLE
HYPOBOLES
HYPOCAUST
HYPOCAUSTS
HYPOCIST
HYPOCISTS
HYPOCOTYL
HYPOCOTYLS
HYPOCRISIES

HYPOCRISY
HYPOCRITE
HYPOCRITES
HYPODERM
HYPODERMA
HYPODERMAS
HYPODERMS
HYPOGAEA
HYPOGAEAL
HYPOGAEAN
HYPOGAEUM
HYPOGEA
HYPOGEAL
HYPOGEAN
HYPOGENE
HYPOGEOUS
HYPOGEUM
HYPOGYNIES
HYPOGYNY
HYPOID
HYPOMANIA
HYPOMANIAS
HYPOMANIC
HYPONASTIES
HYPONASTY
HYPONYM
HYPONYMS
HYPOS
HYPOSTYLE
HYPOSTYLES
HYPOTAXES
HYPOTAXIS

HYPOTHEC
HYPOTHECS
HYPOTONIA
HYPOTONIAS
HYPOTONIC
HYPOXEMIA
HYPOXEMIAS
HYPOXEMIC
HYPOXIA
HYPOXIAS
HYPOXIC
HYPPED
HYPPING
HYPS
HYPURAL
HYRACES
HYRACOID
HYRAX
HYRAXES
HYSON
HYSONS
HYSSOP
HYSSOPS
HYSTERIA
HYSTERIAS
HYSTERIC
HYSTERICS
HYSTEROID
HYTHE
HYTHES

# I

| | | | | |
|---|---|---|---|---|
| IAIDO | ICICLES | IDEALIZERS | IDIOTICON | IGAPOS |
| IAIDOS | ICIER | IDEALIZES | IDIOTICONS | IGARAPÉ |
| IAMB | ICIEST | IDEALIZING | IDIOTISH | IGARAPÉS |
| IAMBI | ICILY | IDEALLESS | IDIOTISM | IGLOO |
| IAMBIC | ICINESS | IDEALLY | IDIOTISMS | IGLOOS |
| IAMBICS | ICINESSES | IDEALOGUE | IDIOTS | IGNARO |
| IAMBIST | ICING | IDEALOGUES | IDLE | IGNAROES |
| IAMBISTS | ICINGS | IDEALS | IDLED | IGNAROS |
| IAMBS | ICKER | IDEAS | IDLEHOOD | IGNEOUS |
| IAMBUS | ICKERS | IDEATE | IDLEHOODS | IGNESCENT |
| IAMBUSES | ICKIER | IDEATED | IDLENESS | IGNESCENTS |
| IANTHINE | ICKIEST | IDEATES | IDLENESSES | IGNITABLE |
| IATRIC | ICKY | IDEATING | IDLER | IGNITE |
| IATRICAL | ICON | IDEATION | IDLERS | IGNITED |
| IATROGENIES | ICONIC | IDEATIONS | IDLES | IGNITER |
| IATROGENY | ICONISE | IDEATIVE | IDLESSE | IGNITERS |
| IBEX | ICONISED | IDÉE | IDLESSES | IGNITES |
| IBEXES | ICONISES | IDÉES | IDLEST | IGNITIBLE |
| IBICES | ICONISING | IDEM | IDLING | IGNITING |
| IBIDEM | ICONIZE | IDENTIC | IDLY | IGNITION |
| IBIS | ICONIZED | IDENTICAL | IDOCRASE | IGNITIONS |
| IBISES | ICONIZES | IDENTIFIED | IDOCRASES | IGNITRON |
| IBUPROFEN | ICONIZING | IDENTIFIES | IDOL | IGNITRONS |
| IBUPROFENS | ICONOLOGIES | IDENTIFY | IDOLATER | IGNOBLE |
| ICE | ICONOLOGY | IDENTIFYING | IDOLATERS | IGNOBLED |
| ICEBERG | ICONOSTAS | IDENTIKIT | IDOLATRIES | IGNOBLER |
| ICEBERGS | ICONOSTASES | IDENTIKITS | IDOLATRY | IGNOBLES |
| ICEBLINK | ICONS | IDENTITIES | IDOLISE | IGNOBLEST |
| ICEBLINKS | ICTAL | IDENTITY | IDOLISED | IGNOBLING |
| ICEBOX | ICTERIC | IDEOGRAM | IDOLISER | IGNOBLY |
| ICEBOXES | ICTERICAL | IDEOGRAMS | IDOLISERS | IGNOMIES |
| ICED | ICTERICALS | IDEOGRAPH | IDOLISES | IGNOMINIES |
| ICEMAN | ICTERICS | IDEOGRAPHS | IDOLISING | IGNOMINY |
| ICEMEN | ICTERINE | IDEOLOGIC | IDOLISM | IGNOMY |
| ICEPACK | ICTERUS | IDEOLOGIES | IDOLISMS | IGNORABLE |
| ICEPACKS | ICTERUSES | IDEOLOGUE | IDOLIST | IGNORAMUS |
| ICEPLANT | ICTIC | IDEOLOGUES | IDOLISTS | IGNORAMUSES |
| ICEPLANTS | ICTUS | IDEOLOGY | IDOLIZE | IGNORANCE |
| ICER | ICTUSES | IDEOPHONE | IDOLIZED | IGNORANCES |
| ICERS | ICY | IDEOPHONES | IDOLIZER | IGNORANT |
| ICES | ID | IDES | IDOLIZERS | IGNORANTS |
| ICH | IDANT | IDIOBLAST | IDOLIZES | IGNORE |
| ICHABOD | IDANTS | IDIOBLASTS | IDOLIZING | IGNORED |
| ICHED | IDE | IDIOCIES | IDOLS | IGNORER |
| ICHES | IDEA | IDIOCY | IDS | IGNORERS |
| ICHING | IDEAED | IDIOGRAPH | IDYL | IGNORES |
| ICHNEUMON | IDEAL | IDIOGRAPHS | IDYLL | IGNORING |
| ICHNEUMONS | IDEALESS | IDIOLECT | IDYLLIAN | IGUANA |
| ICHNITE | IDEALISE | IDIOLECTS | IDYLLIC | IGUANAS |
| ICHNITES | IDEALISED | IDIOM | IDYLLIST | IGUANID |
| ICHNOLITE | IDEALISER | IDIOMATIC | IDYLLISTS | IGUANIDS |
| ICHNOLITES | IDEALISERS | IDIOMS | IDYLLS | IHRAM |
| ICHNOLOGIES | IDEALISES | IDIOPATHIES | IDYLS | IHRAMS |
| ICHNOLOGY | IDEALISING | IDIOPATHY | IF | IKAT |
| ICHOR | IDEALISM | IDIOPHONE | IFF | IKATS |
| ICHOROUS | IDEALISMS | IDIOPHONES | IFFIER | IKEBANA |
| ICHORS | IDEALIST | IDIOPLASM | IFFIEST | IKEBANAS |
| ICHTHIC | IDEALISTS | IDIOPLASMS | IFFINESS | IKON |
| ICHTHYOID | IDEALITIES | IDIOT | IFFINESSES | IKONS |
| ICHTHYOIDS | IDEALITY | IDIOTCIES | IFFY | ILEA |
| ICHTHYS | IDEALIZE | IDIOTCY | IFS | ILEAC |
| ICHTHYSES | IDEALIZED | IDIOTIC | IGAD | ILEITIS |
| ICICLE | IDEALIZER | IDIOTICAL | IGAPO | ILEITISES |

ILEUM
ILEUS
ILEUSES
ILEX
ILEXES
ILIA
ILIAC
ILICES
ILIUM
ILK
ILKA
ILKADAY
ILKADAYS
ILKS
ILL
ILLAPSE
ILLAPSED
ILLAPSES
ILLAPSING
ILLATION
ILLATIONS
ILLATIVE
ILLATIVES
ILLEGAL
ILLEGALLY
ILLEGIBLE
ILLEGIBLY
ILLIAD
ILLIADS
ILLIBERAL
ILLICIT
ILLICITLY
ILLIMITED
ILLINIUM
ILLINIUMS
ILLIPE
ILLIPES
ILLIQUID
ILLISION
ILLISIONS
ILLITE
ILLITES
ILLNESS
ILLNESSES
ILLOGIC
ILLOGICAL
ILLOGICS
ILLS
ILLTH
ILLTHS
ILLUDE
ILLUDED
ILLUDES
ILLUDING
ILLUME
ILLUMED
ILLUMES
ILLUMINE
ILLUMINED
ILLUMINER
ILLUMINERS
ILLUMINES
ILLUMING
ILLUMINING
ILLUPI
ILLUPIS
ILLUSION
ILLUSIONS
ILLUSIVE
ILLUSORY

ILLY
ILMENITE
ILMENITES
IMAGE
IMAGEABLE
IMAGED
IMAGELESS
IMAGERIES
IMAGERY
IMAGES
IMAGINAL
IMAGINARY
IMAGINE
IMAGINED
IMAGINER
IMAGINERS
IMAGINES
IMAGING
IMAGINGS
IMAGINING
IMAGININGS
IMAGINIST
IMAGINISTS
IMAGISM
IMAGISMS
IMAGIST
IMAGISTIC
IMAGISTS
IMAGO
IMAGOES
IMAGOS
IMAM
IMAMATE
IMAMATES
IMAMS
IMARI
IMARIS
IMAUM
IMAUMS
IMBALANCE
IMBALANCES
IMBAR
IMBARK
IMBARKED
IMBARKING
IMBARKS
IMBARRED
IMBARRING
IMBARS
IMBASE
IMBASED
IMBASES
IMBASING
IMBATHE
IMBATHED
IMBATHES
IMBATHING
IMBECILE
IMBECILES
IMBECILIC
IMBED
IMBEDDED
IMBEDDING
IMBEDS
IMBIBE
IMBIBED
IMBIBER
IMBIBERS
IMBIBES
IMBIBING

IMBITTER
IMBITTERED
IMBITTERING
IMBITTERS
IMBODIED
IMBODIES
IMBODY
IMBODYING
IMBORDER
IMBORDERED
IMBORDERING
IMBORDERS
IMBOSK
IMBOSKED
IMBOSKING
IMBOSKS
IMBOSOM
IMBOSOMED
IMBOSOMING
IMBOSOMS
IMBOSS
IMBOSSED
IMBOSSES
IMBOSSING
IMBOWER
IMBOWERED
IMBOWERING
IMBOWERS
IMBRANGLE
IMBRANGLED
IMBRANGLES
IMBRANGLING
IMBRAST
IMBREX
IMBRICATE
IMBRICATED
IMBRICATES
IMBRICATING
IMBRICES
IMBROGLIO
IMBROGLIOS
IMBROWN
IMBROWNED
IMBROWNING
IMBROWNS
IMBRUE
IMBRUED
IMBRUES
IMBRUING
IMBRUTE
IMBRUTED
IMBRUTES
IMBRUTING
IMBUE
IMBUED
IMBUES
IMBUING
IMBURSE
IMBURSED
IMBURSES
IMBURSING
IMIDE
IMIDES
IMINE
IMINES
IMITABLE
IMITANCIES
IMITANCY
IMITANT
IMITANTS

IMITATE
IMITATED
IMITATES
IMITATING
IMITATION
IMITATIONS
IMITATIVE
IMITATOR
IMITATORS
IMMANACLE
IMMANACLED
IMMANACLES
IMMANACLING
IMMANE
IMMANELY
IMMANENCE
IMMANENCES
IMMANENCIES
IMMANENCY
IMMANENT
IMMANITIES
IMMANITY
IMMANTLE
IMMANTLED
IMMANTLES
IMMANTLING
IMMASK
IMMASKED
IMMASKING
IMMASKS
IMMATURE
IMMATURED
IMMEDIACIES
IMMEDIACY
IMMEDIATE
IMMENSE
IMMENSELY
IMMENSER
IMMENSEST
IMMENSITIES
IMMENSITY
IMMERGE
IMMERGED
IMMERGES
IMMERGING
IMMERSE
IMMERSED
IMMERSES
IMMERSING
IMMERSION
IMMERSIONS
IMMESH
IMMESHED
IMMESHES
IMMESHING
IMMEW
IMMEWED
IMMEWING
IMMEWS
IMMIGRANT
IMMIGRANTS
IMMIGRATE
IMMIGRATED
IMMIGRATES
IMMIGRATING
IMMINENCE
IMMINENCES
IMMINENCIES
IMMINENCY
IMMINENT

IMMINGLE
IMMINGLED
IMMINGLES
IMMINGLING
IMMISSION
IMMISSIONS
IMMIT
IMMITS
IMMITTED
IMMITTING
IMMIX
IMMIXED
IMMIXES
IMMIXING
IMMOBILE
IMMODEST
IMMODESTIES
IMMODESTY
IMMOLATE
IMMOLATED
IMMOLATES
IMMOLATING
IMMOLATOR
IMMOLATORS
IMMOMENT
IMMORAL
IMMORALLY
IMMORTAL
IMMORTALS
IMMOVABLE
IMMOVABLY
IMMUNE
IMMUNES
IMMUNISE
IMMUNISED
IMMUNISES
IMMUNISING
IMMUNITIES
IMMUNITY
IMMUNIZE
IMMUNIZED
IMMUNIZES
IMMUNIZING
IMMUNOGEN
IMMUNOGENS
IMMURE
IMMURED
IMMURES
IMMURING
IMMUTABLE
IMMUTABLY
IMP
IMPACABLE
IMPACT
IMPACTED
IMPACTING
IMPACTION
IMPACTIONS
IMPACTITE
IMPACTITES
IMPACTS
IMPAINT
IMPAINTED
IMPAINTING
IMPAINTS
IMPAIR
IMPAIRED
IMPAIRING
IMPAIRS
IMPALA

| | | | | |
|---|---|---|---|---|
| IMPALAS | IMPEDANCES | IMPLEACHING | IMPOLITIC | IMPRESTING |
| IMPALE | IMPEDE | IMPLEAD | IMPONE | IMPRESTS |
| IMPALED | IMPEDED | IMPLEADED | IMPONED | IMPRIMIS |
| IMPALES | IMPEDES | IMPLEADER | IMPONENT | IMPRINT |
| IMPALING | IMPEDING | IMPLEADERS | IMPONENTS | IMPRINTED |
| IMPANATE | IMPEL | IMPLEADING | IMPONES | IMPRINTING |
| IMPANEL | IMPELLED | IMPLEADS | IMPONING | IMPRINTINGS |
| IMPANELLED | IMPELLENT | IMPLEDGE | IMPORT | IMPRINTS |
| IMPANELLING | IMPELLENTS | IMPLEDGED | IMPORTANT | IMPRISON |
| IMPANELS | IMPELLER | IMPLEDGES | IMPORTED | IMPRISONED |
| IMPANNEL | IMPELLERS | IMPLEDGING | IMPORTER | IMPRISONING |
| IMPANNELLED | IMPELLING | IMPLEMENT | IMPORTERS | IMPRISONS |
| IMPANNELLING | IMPELS | IMPLEMENTED | IMPORTING | IMPROBITIES |
| IMPANNELS | IMPEND | IMPLEMENTING | IMPORTS | IMPROBITY |
| IMPARITIES | IMPENDED | IMPLEMENTS | IMPORTUNE | IMPROMPTU |
| IMPARITY | IMPENDENT | IMPLETE | IMPORTUNED | IMPROMPTUS |
| IMPARK | IMPENDING | IMPLETED | IMPORTUNES | IMPROPER |
| IMPARKED | IMPENDS | IMPLETES | IMPORTUNING | IMPROVE |
| IMPARKING | IMPERATOR | IMPLETING | IMPORTUNINGS | IMPROVED |
| IMPARKS | IMPERATORS | IMPLETION | IMPOSABLE | IMPROVER |
| IMPARL | IMPERFECT | IMPLETIONS | IMPOSE | IMPROVERS |
| IMPARLED | IMPERFECTS | IMPLEX | IMPOSED | IMPROVES |
| IMPARLING | IMPERIAL | IMPLEXES | IMPOSER | IMPROVING |
| IMPARLS | IMPERIALS | IMPLEXION | IMPOSERS | IMPROVISE |
| IMPART | IMPERIL | IMPLEXIONS | IMPOSES | IMPROVISED |
| IMPARTED | IMPERILLED | IMPLICATE | IMPOSING | IMPROVISES |
| IMPARTER | IMPERILLING | IMPLICATED | IMPOST | IMPROVISING |
| IMPARTERS | IMPERILS | IMPLICATES | IMPOSTER | IMPRUDENT |
| IMPARTIAL | IMPERIOUS | IMPLICATING | IMPOSTERS | IMPS |
| IMPARTING | IMPERIUM | IMPLICIT | IMPOSTOR | IMPUDENCE |
| IMPARTS | IMPERIUMS | IMPLIED | IMPOSTORS | IMPUDENCES |
| IMPASSE | IMPETICOS | IMPLIEDLY | IMPOSTS | IMPUDENT |
| IMPASSES | IMPETICOSSED | IMPLIES | IMPOSTUME | IMPUGN |
| IMPASSION | IMPETICOSSES | IMPLODE | IMPOSTUMES | IMPUGNED |
| IMPASSIONED | IMPETICOSSING | IMPLODED | IMPOSTURE | IMPUGNER |
| IMPASSIONING | IMPETIGINES | IMPLODENT | IMPOSTURES | IMPUGNERS |
| IMPASSIONS | IMPETIGO | IMPLODENTS | IMPOT | IMPUGNING |
| IMPASSIVE | IMPETIGOS | IMPLODES | IMPOTENCE | IMPUGNS |
| IMPASTE | IMPETRATE | IMPLODING | IMPOTENCES | IMPULSE |
| IMPASTED | IMPETRATED | IMPLORE | IMPOTENCIES | IMPULSES |
| IMPASTES | IMPETRATES | IMPLORED | IMPOTENCY | IMPULSION |
| IMPASTING | IMPETRATING | IMPLORER | IMPOTENT | IMPULSIONS |
| IMPASTO | IMPETUOUS | IMPLORERS | IMPOTS | IMPULSIVE |
| IMPASTOED | IMPETUS | IMPLORES | IMPOUND | IMPULSORY |
| IMPASTOS | IMPETUSES | IMPLORING | IMPOUNDED | IMPUNITIES |
| IMPATIENS | IMPI | IMPLOSION | IMPOUNDER | IMPUNITY |
| IMPATIENT | IMPIETIES | IMPLOSIONS | IMPOUNDERS | IMPURE |
| IMPAVE | IMPIETY | IMPLOSIVE | IMPOUNDING | IMPURELY |
| IMPAVED | IMPING | IMPLOSIVES | IMPOUNDS | IMPURER |
| IMPAVES | IMPINGE | IMPLUNGE | IMPRECATE | IMPUREST |
| IMPAVID | IMPINGED | IMPLUNGED | IMPRECATED | IMPURITIES |
| IMPAVIDLY | IMPINGENT | IMPLUNGES | IMPRECATES | IMPURITY |
| IMPAVING | IMPINGES | IMPLUNGING | IMPRECATING | IMPURPLE |
| IMPAWN | IMPINGING | IMPLUVIA | IMPRECISE | IMPURPLED |
| IMPAWNED | IMPIOUS | IMPLUVIUM | IMPREGN | IMPURPLES |
| IMPAWNING | IMPIOUSLY | IMPLY | IMPREGNED | IMPURPLING |
| IMPAWNS | IMPIS | IMPLYING | IMPREGNING | IMPUTABLE |
| IMPEACH | IMPISH | IMPOCKET | IMPREGNS | IMPUTABLY |
| IMPEACHED | IMPISHLY | IMPOCKETED | IMPRESA | IMPUTE |
| IMPEACHER | IMPLANT | IMPOCKETING | IMPRESARI | IMPUTED |
| IMPEACHERS | IMPLANTED | IMPOCKETS | IMPRESAS | IMPUTER |
| IMPEACHES | IMPLANTING | IMPOLDER | IMPRESE | IMPUTERS |
| IMPEACHING | IMPLANTS | IMPOLDERED | IMPRESES | IMPUTES |
| IMPEARL | IMPLATE | IMPOLDERING | IMPRESS | IMPUTING |
| IMPEARLED | IMPLATED | IMPOLDERS | IMPRESSE | IMSHI |
| IMPEARLING | IMPLATES | IMPOLICIES | IMPRESSED | IMSHY |
| IMPEARLS | IMPLATING | IMPOLICY | IMPRESSES | IN |
| IMPECCANT | IMPLEACH | IMPOLITE | IMPRESSING | INABILITIES |
| IMPED | IMPLEACHED | IMPOLITER | IMPREST | INABILITY |
| IMPEDANCE | IMPLEACHES | IMPOLITEST | IMPRESTED | INACTION |

INACTIONS
INACTIVE
INAIDABLE
INAMORATA
INAMORATAS
INAMORATO
INAMORATOS
INANE
INANELY
INANENESS
INANENESSES
INANER
INANES
INANEST
INANIMATE
INANITIES
INANITION
INANITIONS
INANITY
INAPT
INAPTLY
INAPTNESS
INAPTNESSES
INARABLE
INARCH
INARCHED
INARCHES
INARCHING
INARM
INARMED
INARMING
INARMS
INAUDIBLE
INAUDIBLY
INAUGURAL
INAUGURALS
INAURATE
INBEING
INBEINGS
INBENT
INBOARD
INBORN
INBREAK
INBREAKS
INBREATHE
INBREATHED
INBREATHES
INBREATHING
INBRED
INBREED
INBREEDING
INBREEDINGS
INBREEDS
INBRING
INBRINGING
INBRINGINGS
INBRINGS
INBROUGHT
INBURNING
INBURST
INBURSTS
INBY
INBYE
INCAGE
INCAGED
INCAGES
INCAGING
INCAPABLE
INCAPABLES
INCAPABLY

INCARNATE
INCARNATED
INCARNATES
INCARNATING
INCASE
INCASED
INCASES
INCASING
INCAUTION
INCAUTIONS
INCAVE
INCAVED
INCAVES
INCAVI
INCAVING
INCAVO
INCEDE
INCEDED
INCEDES
INCEDING
INCENSE
INCENSED
INCENSER
INCENSERS
INCENSES
INCENSING
INCENSOR
INCENSORIES
INCENSORS
INCENSORY
INCENTIVE
INCENTIVES
INCENTRE
INCENTRES
INCEPT
INCEPTED
INCEPTING
INCEPTION
INCEPTIONS
INCEPTIVE
INCEPTIVES
INCEPTOR
INCEPTORS
INCEPTS
INCERTAIN
INCESSANT
INCEST
INCESTS
INCH
INCHASE
INCHASED
INCHASES
INCHASING
INCHED
INCHES
INCHING
INCHMEAL
INCHOATE
INCHOATED
INCHOATES
INCHOATING
INCHPIN
INCHPINS
INCIDENCE
INCIDENCES
INCIDENT
INCIDENTS
INCIPIENT
INCIPIT
INCISE

INCISED
INCISES
INCISING
INCISION
INCISIONS
INCISIVE
INCISOR
INCISORS
INCISORY
INCISURE
INCISURES
INCITANT
INCITANTS
INCITE
INCITED
INCITER
INCITERS
INCITES
INCITING
INCIVIL
INCIVISM
INCIVISMS
INCLASP
INCLASPED
INCLASPING
INCLASPS
INCLE
INCLEMENT
INCLES
INCLINE
INCLINED
INCLINES
INCLINING
INCLININGS
INCLIP
INCLIPPED
INCLIPPING
INCLIPS
INCLOSE
INCLOSED
INCLOSER
INCLOSERS
INCLOSES
INCLOSING
INCLOSURE
INCLOSURES
INCLUDE
INCLUDED
INCLUDES
INCLUDING
INCLUSION
INCLUSIONS
INCLUSIVE
INCOGNITA
INCOGNITAS
INCOGNITO
INCOGNITOS
INCOME
INCOMER
INCOMERS
INCOMES
INCOMING
INCOMINGS
INCOMMODE
INCOMMODED
INCOMMODES
INCOMMODING
INCONDITE
INCONIE
INCONNU

INCONNUE
INCONNUES
INCONNUS
INCONY
INCORPSE
INCORPSED
INCORPSES
INCORPSING
INCORRECT
INCORRUPT
INCREASE
INCREASED
INCREASER
INCREASERS
INCREASES
INCREASING
INCREASINGS
INCREATE
INCREMATE
INCREMATED
INCREMATES
INCREMATING
INCREMENT
INCREMENTS
INCROSS
INCROSSED
INCROSSES
INCROSSING
INCRUST
INCRUSTED
INCRUSTING
INCRUSTS
INCUBATE
INCUBATED
INCUBATES
INCUBATING
INCUBATOR
INCUBATORS
INCUBI
INCUBOUS
INCUBUS
INCUBUSES
INCUDES
INCULCATE
INCULCATED
INCULCATES
INCULCATING
INCULPATE
INCULPATED
INCULPATES
INCULPATING
INCULT
INCUMBENT
INCUMBENTS
INCUNABLE
INCUNABLES
INCUR
INCURABLE
INCURABLES
INCURABLY
INCURIOUS
INCURRED
INCURRENT
INCURRING
INCURS
INCURSION
INCURSIONS
INCURSIVE
INCURVATE
INCURVATED

INCURVATES
INCURVATING
INCURVE
INCURVED
INCURVES
INCURVING
INCURVITIES
INCURVITY
INCUS
INCUSE
INCUSED
INCUSES
INCUSING
INCUT
INDABA
INDABAS
INDAGATE
INDAGATED
INDAGATES
INDAGATING
INDAGATOR
INDAGATORS
INDART
INDARTED
INDARTING
INDARTS
INDEBTED
INDECENCIES
INDECENCY
INDECENT
INDECORUM
INDECORUMS
INDEED
INDELIBLE
INDELIBLY
INDEMNIFIED
INDEMNIFIES
INDEMNIFY
INDEMNIFYING
INDEMNITIES
INDEMNITY
INDENE
INDENES
INDENT
INDENTED
INDENTER
INDENTERS
INDENTING
INDENTION
INDENTIONS
INDENTS
INDENTURE
INDENTURED
INDENTURES
INDENTURING
INDEW
INDEWED
INDEWING
INDEWS
INDEX
INDEXED
INDEXER
INDEXERS
INDEXES
INDEXICAL
INDEXING
INDEXINGS
INDEXLESS
INDICAN
INDICANS

| | | | | |
|---|---|---|---|---|
| INDICANT | INDORSED | INDWELT | INFANTA | INFINITE |
| INDICANTS | INDORSES | INEARTH | INFANTAS | INFINITES |
| INDICATE | INDORSING | INEARTHED | INFANTE | INFINITIES |
| INDICATED | INDRAFT | INEARTHING | INFANTED | INFINITY |
| INDICATES | INDRAFTS | INEARTHS | INFANTES | INFIRM |
| INDICATING | INDRAUGHT | INEBRIANT | INFANTILE | INFIRMARIES |
| INDICATOR | INDRAUGHTS | INEBRIANTS | INFANTINE | INFIRMARY |
| INDICATORS | INDRAWN | INEBRIATE | INFANTING | INFIRMER |
| INDICES | INDRENCH | INEBRIATED | INFANTRIES | INFIRMEST |
| INDICIA | INDRENCHED | INEBRIATES | INFANTRY | INFIRMITIES |
| INDICIUM | INDRENCHES | INEBRIATING | INFANTS | INFIRMITY |
| INDICT | INDRENCHING | INEBRIETIES | INFARCT | INFIRMLY |
| INDICTED | INDRI | INEBRIETY | INFARCTS | INFIX |
| INDICTEE | INDRIS | INEBRIOUS | INFARE | INFIXED |
| INDICTEES | INDRISES | INEDIBLE | INFARES | INFIXES |
| INDICTING | INDUBIOUS | INEDITED | INFATUATE | INFIXING |
| INDICTION | INDUCE | INEFFABLE | INFATUATED | INFLAME |
| INDICTIONS | INDUCED | INEFFABLY | INFATUATES | INFLAMED |
| INDICTS | INDUCER | INELASTIC | INFATUATING | INFLAMER |
| INDIGENCE | INDUCERS | INELEGANT | INFAUST | INFLAMERS |
| INDIGENCES | INDUCES | INEPT | INFECT | INFLAMES |
| INDIGENCIES | INDUCIAE | INEPTER | INFECTED | INFLAMING |
| INDIGENCY | INDUCIBLE | INEPTEST | INFECTING | INFLATE |
| INDIGENE | INDUCING | INEPTLY | INFECTION | INFLATED |
| INDIGENES | INDUCT | INEPTNESS | INFECTIONS | INFLATES |
| INDIGENT | INDUCTED | INEPTNESSES | INFECTIVE | INFLATING |
| INDIGEST | INDUCTILE | INEQUABLE | INFECTOR | INFLATION |
| INDIGESTS | INDUCTING | INEQUITIES | INFECTORS | INFLATIONS |
| INDIGN | INDUCTION | INEQUITY | INFECTS | INFLATIVE |
| INDIGNANT | INDUCTIONS | INERM | INFECUND | INFLATOR |
| INDIGNIFIED | INDUCTIVE | INERRABLE | INFEFT | INFLATORS |
| INDIGNIFIES | INDUCTOR | INERRABLY | INFEFTED | INFLATUS |
| INDIGNIFY | INDUCTORS | INERRANCIES | INFEFTING | INFLATUSES |
| INDIGNIFYING | INDUCTS | INERRANCY | INFEFTS | INFLECT |
| INDIGNITIES | INDUE | INERRANT | INFELT | INFLECTED |
| INDIGNITY | INDUED | INERT | INFER | INFLECTING |
| INDIGO | INDUES | INERTER | INFERABLE | INFLECTS |
| INDIGOES | INDUING | INERTEST | INFERE | INFLEXED |
| INDIGOS | INDULGE | INERTIA | INFERENCE | INFLEXION |
| INDIGOTIN | INDULGED | INERTIAL | INFERENCES | INFLEXIONS |
| INDIGOTINS | INDULGENT | INERTIAS | INFERIAE | INFLEXURE |
| INDIRECT | INDULGER | INERTLY | INFERIOR | INFLEXURES |
| INDIRUBIN | INDULGERS | INERTNESS | INFERIORS | INFLICT |
| INDIRUBINS | INDULGES | INERTNESSES | INFERNAL | INFLICTED |
| INDISPOSE | INDULGING | INERUDITE | INFERNO | INFLICTING |
| INDISPOSED | INDULINE | INESSIVE | INFERNOS | INFLICTS |
| INDISPOSES | INDULINES | INESSIVES | INFERRED | INFLOW |
| INDISPOSING | INDULT | INEXACT | INFERRING | INFLOWING |
| INDITE | INDULTS | INEXACTLY | INFERS | INFLOWS |
| INDITED | INDUNA | INEXPERT | INFERTILE | INFLUENCE |
| INDITER | INDUNAS | INFALL | INFEST | INFLUENCED |
| INDITERS | INDURATE | INFALLS | INFESTED | INFLUENCES |
| INDITES | INDURATED | INFAME | INFESTING | INFLUENCING |
| INDITING | INDURATES | INFAMED | INFESTS | INFLUENT |
| INDIUM | INDURATING | INFAMES | INFICETE | INFLUENTS |
| INDIUMS | INDUSIA | INFAMIES | INFIDEL | INFLUENZA |
| INDOCIBLE | INDUSIAL | INFAMING | INFIDELS | INFLUENZAS |
| INDOCILE | INDUSIATE | INFAMISE | INFIELD | INFLUX |
| INDOL | INDUSIUM | INFAMISED | INFIELDER | INFLUXES |
| INDOLE | INDUSTRIES | INFAMISES | INFIELDERS | INFLUXION |
| INDOLENCE | INDUSTRY | INFAMISING | INFIELDS | INFLUXIONS |
| INDOLENCES | INDUVIAE | INFAMIZE | INFILL | INFO |
| INDOLENCIES | INDUVIAL | INFAMIZED | INFILLED | INFOLD |
| INDOLENCY | INDUVIATE | INFAMIZES | INFILLING | INFOLDED |
| INDOLENT | INDWELL | INFAMIZING | INFILLINGS | INFOLDING |
| INDOLES | INDWELLER | INFAMOUS | INFILLS | INFOLDS |
| INDOLS | INDWELLERS | INFAMY | INFILTER | INFORCE |
| INDOOR | INDWELLING | INFANCIES | INFILTERED | INFORCED |
| INDOORS | INDWELLINGS | INFANCY | INFILTERING | INFORCES |
| INDORSE | INDWELLS | INFANT | INFILTERS | INFORCING |

| | | | | |
|---|---|---|---|---|
| INFORM | INGLOBE | INHAUSTING | INJECT | INLAND |
| INFORMAL | INGLOBED | INHAUSTS | INJECTED | INLANDER |
| INFORMANT | INGLOBES | INHEARSE | INJECTING | INLANDERS |
| INFORMANTS | INGLOBING | INHEARSED | INJECTION | INLANDS |
| INFORMED | INGLUVIAL | INHEARSES | INJECTIONS | INLAY |
| INFORMER | INGLUVIES | INHEARSING | INJECTOR | INLAYER |
| INFORMERS | INGO | INHERCE | INJECTORS | INLAYERS |
| INFORMING | INGOES | INHERCED | INJECTS | INLAYING |
| INFORMS | INGOING | INHERCES | INJELLIED | INLAYINGS |
| INFORTUNE | INGOINGS | INHERCING | INJELLIES | INLAYS |
| INFORTUNES | INGOT | INHERE | INJELLY | INLET |
| INFOS | INGOTS | INHERED | INJELLYING | INLETS |
| INFRA | INGOWES | INHERENCE | INJOINT | INLIER |
| INFRACT | INGRAFT | INHERENCES | INJOINTED | INLIERS |
| INFRACTED | INGRAFTED | INHERENCIES | INJOINTING | INLIEST |
| INFRACTING | INGRAFTING | INHERENCY | INJOINTS | INLOCK |
| INFRACTOR | INGRAFTS | INHERENT | INJUNCT | INLOCKED |
| INFRACTORS | INGRAIN | INHERES | INJUNCTED | INLOCKING |
| INFRACTS | INGRAINED | INHERING | INJUNCTING | INLOCKS |
| INFRINGE | INGRAINING | INHERIT | INJUNCTS | INLY |
| INFRINGED | INGRAINS | INHERITED | INJURANT | INLYING |
| INFRINGES | INGRAM | INHERITING | INJURANTS | INMATE |
| INFRINGING | INGRATE | INHERITOR | INJURE | INMATES |
| INFULA | INGRATES | INHERITORS | INJURED | INMESH |
| INFULAE | INGRESS | INHERITS | INJURER | INMESHED |
| INFURIATE | INGRESSES | INHESION | INJURERS | INMESHES |
| INFURIATED | INGROOVE | INHESIONS | INJURES | INMESHING |
| INFURIATES | INGROOVED | INHIBIT | INJURIES | INMOST |
| INFURIATING | INGROOVES | INHIBITED | INJURING | INN |
| INFUSCATE | INGROOVING | INHIBITING | INJURIOUS | INNARDS |
| INFUSE | INGROSS | INHIBITOR | INJURY | INNATE |
| INFUSED | INGROSSED | INHIBITORS | INJUSTICE | INNATELY |
| INFUSER | INGROSSES | INHIBITS | INJUSTICES | INNATIVE |
| INFUSERS | INGROSSING | INHOLDER | INK | INNED |
| INFUSES | INGROUP | INHOLDERS | INKBERRIES | INNER |
| INFUSIBLE | INGROUPS | INHOOP | INKBERRY | INNERMOST |
| INFUSING | INGROWING | INHOOPED | INKED | INNERS |
| INFUSION | INGROWN | INHOOPING | INKER | INNERVATE |
| INFUSIONS | INGROWTH | INHOOPS | INKERS | INNERVATED |
| INFUSIVE | INGROWTHS | INHUMAN | INKHOLDER | INNERVATES |
| INFUSORIA | INGRUM | INHUMANE | INKHOLDERS | INNERVATING |
| INFUSORY | INGUINAL | INHUMANLY | INKHORN | INNERVE |
| INGAN | INGULF | INHUMATE | INKHORNS | INNERVED |
| INGANS | INGULFED | INHUMATED | INKIER | INNERVES |
| INGATE | INGULFING | INHUMATES | INKIEST | INNERVING |
| INGATES | INGULFS | INHUMATING | INKINESS | INNHOLDER |
| INGENER | INGULPH | INHUME | INKINESSES | INNHOLDERS |
| INGENERS | INGULPHED | INHUMED | INKING | INNING |
| INGENIOUS | INGULPHING | INHUMES | INKLE | INNINGS |
| INGENIUM | INGULPHS | INHUMING | INKLED | INNKEEPER |
| INGENIUMS | INHABIT | INIA | INKLES | INNKEEPERS |
| INGÉNU | INHABITED | INIMICAL | INKLING | INNOCENCE |
| INGÉNUE | INHABITING | INION | INKLINGS | INNOCENCES |
| INGÉNUES | INHABITOR | INIQUITIES | INKPOT | INNOCENCIES |
| INGENUITIES | INHABITORS | INIQUITY | INKPOTS | INNOCENCY |
| INGENUITY | INHABITS | INISLE | INKS | INNOCENT |
| INGENUOUS | INHALANT | INISLED | INKSPOT | INNOCENTS |
| INGÉNUS | INHALANTS | INISLES | INKSPOTS | INNOCUITIES |
| INGEST | INHALATOR | INISLING | INKSTAND | INNOCUITY |
| INGESTA | INHALATORS | INITIAL | INKSTANDS | INNOCUOUS |
| INGESTED | INHALE | INITIALLED | INKSTONE | INNOVATE |
| INGESTING | INHALED | INITIALLING | INKSTONES | INNOVATED |
| INGESTION | INHALER | INITIALLY | INKWELL | INNOVATES |
| INGESTIONS | INHALERS | INITIALS | INKWELLS | INNOVATING |
| INGESTIVE | INHALES | INITIATE | INKY | INNOVATOR |
| INGESTS | INHALING | INITIATED | INLACE | INNOVATORS |
| INGINE | INHARMONIES | INITIATES | INLACED | INNOXIOUS |
| INGINES | INHARMONY | INITIATING | INLACES | INNS |
| INGLE | INHAUST | INITIATOR | INLACING | INNUENDO |
| INGLES | INHAUSTED | INITIATORS | INLAID | INNUENDOED |

| | | | | |
|---|---|---|---|---|
| INNUENDOES | INSANER | INSHELLED | INSOULED | INSTINCTS |
| INNUENDOING | INSANEST | INSHELLING | INSOULING | INSTITUTE |
| INNUENDOS | INSANIE | INSHELLS | INSOULS | INSTITUTED |
| INNYARD | INSANIES | INSHELTER | INSPAN | INSTITUTES |
| INNYARDS | INSANITIES | INSHELTERED | INSPANNED | INSTITUTING |
| INOCULATE | INSANITY | INSHELTERING | INSPANNING | INSTRESS |
| INOCULATED | INSATIATE | INSHELTERS | INSPANS | INSTRESSED |
| INOCULATES | INSATIETIES | INSHIP | INSPECT | INSTRESSES |
| INOCULATING | INSATIETY | INSHIPPED | INSPECTED | INSTRESSING |
| INOCULUM | INSCAPE | INSHIPPING | INSPECTING | INSTRUCT |
| INOCULUMS | INSCAPES | INSHIPS | INSPECTOR | INSTRUCTED |
| INODOROUS | INSCIENCE | INSHORE | INSPECTORS | INSTRUCTING |
| INOPINATE | INSCIENCES | INSHRINE | INSPECTS | INSTRUCTS |
| INORB | INSCIENT | INSHRINED | INSPHERE | INSUCKEN |
| INORBED | INSCONCE | INSHRINES | INSPHERED | INSULA |
| INORBING | INSCONCED | INSHRINING | INSPHERES | INSULAE |
| INORBS | INSCONCES | INSIDE | INSPHERING | INSULANCE |
| INORGANIC | INSCONCING | INSIDER | INSPIRE | INSULANCES |
| INORNATE | INSCRIBE | INSIDERS | INSPIRED | INSULANT |
| INOSITOL | INSCRIBED | INSIDES | INSPIRER | INSULANTS |
| INOSITOLS | INSCRIBER | INSIDIOUS | INSPIRERS | INSULAR |
| INOTROPIC | INSCRIBERS | INSIGHT | INSPIRES | INSULARLY |
| INPAYMENT | INSCRIBES | INSIGHTS | INSPIRING | INSULAS |
| INPAYMENTS | INSCRIBING | INSIGNE | INSPIRIT | INSULATE |
| INPHASE | INSCROLL | INSIGNES | INSPIRITED | INSULATED |
| INPOURING | INSCROLLED | INSIGNIA | INSPIRITING | INSULATES |
| INPOURINGS | INSCROLLING | INSIGNIAS | INSPIRITS | INSULATING |
| INPUT | INSCROLLS | INSINCERE | INSPYRE | INSULATOR |
| INPUTS | INSCULP | INSINEW | INSPYRED | INSULATORS |
| INPUTTER | INSCULPED | INSINEWED | INSPYRES | INSULIN |
| INPUTTERS | INSCULPING | INSINEWING | INSPYRING | INSULINS |
| INPUTTING | INSCULPS | INSINEWS | INSTABLE | INSULSE |
| INQILAB | INSCULPT | INSINUATE | INSTAL | INSULSITIES |
| INQILABS | INSEAM | INSINUATED | INSTALL | INSULSITY |
| INQUERE | INSEAMED | INSINUATES | INSTALLED | INSULT |
| INQUERED | INSEAMING | INSINUATING | INSTALLING | INSULTANT |
| INQUERES | INSEAMS | INSIPID | INSTALLS | INSULTED |
| INQUERING | INSECT | INSIPIDLY | INSTALS | INSULTER |
| INQUEST | INSECTARIES | INSIPIENT | INSTANCE | INSULTERS |
| INQUESTS | INSECTARY | INSIST | INSTANCED | INSULTING |
| INQUIET | INSECTILE | INSISTED | INSTANCES | INSULTS |
| INQUIETED | INSECTION | INSISTENT | INSTANCIES | INSURABLE |
| INQUIETING | INSECTIONS | INSISTING | INSTANCING | INSURANCE |
| INQUIETLY | INSECTS | INSISTS | INSTANCY | INSURANCES |
| INQUIETS | INSECTY | INSISTURE | INSTANT | INSURANT |
| INQUILINE | INSECURE | INSISTURES | INSTANTER | INSURANTS |
| INQUILINES | INSEEM | INSNARE | INSTANTLY | INSURE |
| INQUINATE | INSEEMED | INSNARED | INSTANTS | INSURED |
| INQUINATED | INSEEMING | INSNARES | INSTAR | INSURER |
| INQUINATES | INSEEMS | INSNARING | INSTARRED | INSURERS |
| INQUINATING | INSELBERG | INSOLATE | INSTARRING | INSURES |
| INQUIRE | INSELBERGE | INSOLATED | INSTARS | INSURGENT |
| INQUIRED | INSENSATE | INSOLATES | INSTATE | INSURGENTS |
| INQUIRER | INSERT | INSOLATING | INSTATED | INSURING |
| INQUIRERS | INSERTED | INSOLE | INSTATES | INSWATHE |
| INQUIRES | INSERTER | INSOLENCE | INSTATING | INSWATHED |
| INQUIRIES | INSERTERS | INSOLENCES | INSTEAD | INSWATHES |
| INQUIRING | INSERTING | INSOLENT | INSTEP | INSWATHING |
| INQUIRY | INSERTION | INSOLES | INSTEPS | INSWING |
| INQUORATE | INSERTIONS | INSOLUBLE | INSTIGATE | INSWINGER |
| INRO | INSERTS | INSOLUBLY | INSTIGATED | INSWINGERS |
| INROAD | INSET | INSOLVENT | INSTIGATES | INSWINGS |
| INROADS | INSETS | INSOLVENTS | INSTIGATING | INTACT |
| INRUSH | INSETTING | INSOMNIA | INSTIL | INTAGLIO |
| INRUSHES | INSHALLAH | INSOMNIAC | INSTILL | INTAGLIOED |
| INRUSHING | INSHEATHE | INSOMNIACS | INSTILLED | INTAGLIOING |
| INRUSHINGS | INSHEATHED | INSOMNIAS | INSTILLING | INTAGLIOS |
| INS | INSHEATHES | INSOMUCH | INSTILLS | INTAKE |
| INSANE | INSHEATHING | INSOOTH | INSTILS | INTAKES |
| INSANELY | INSHELL | INSOUL | INSTINCT | INTARSI |

| | | | | |
|---|---|---|---|---|
| INTARSIA | INTERCEPTS | INTERJOIN | INTERNS | INTESTATE |
| INTARSIAS | INTERCITY | INTERJOINED | INTERPAGE | INTESTATES |
| INTARSIO | INTERCOM | INTERJOINING | INTERPAGED | INTESTINE |
| INTARSIOS | INTERCOMS | INTERJOINS | INTERPAGES | INTESTINES |
| INTEGER | INTERCROP | INTERKNIT | INTERPAGING | INTHRAL |
| INTEGERS | INTERCROPPED | INTERKNITS | INTERPLAY | INTHRALL |
| INTEGRAL | INTERCROPPING | INTERKNITTED | INTERPLAYS | INTHRALLED |
| INTEGRALS | INTERCROPS | INTERKNITTING | INTERPONE | INTHRALLING |
| INTEGRAND | INTERCUT | INTERLACE | INTERPONED | INTHRALLS |
| INTEGRANDS | INTERCUTS | INTERLACED | INTERPONES | INTHRALS |
| INTEGRANT | INTERCUTTING | INTERLACES | INTERPONING | INTIL |
| INTEGRATE | INTERDASH | INTERLACING | INTERPOSE | INTIMA |
| INTEGRATED | INTERDASHED | INTERLAID | INTERPOSED | INTIMACIES |
| INTEGRATES | INTERDASHES | INTERLARD | INTERPOSES | INTIMACY |
| INTEGRATING | INTERDASHING | INTERLARDED | INTERPOSING | INTIMAE |
| INTEGRITIES | INTERDEAL | INTERLARDING | INTERPRET | INTIMATE |
| INTEGRITY | INTERDEALING | INTERLARDS | INTERPRETED | INTIMATED |
| INTELLECT | INTERDEALS | INTERLAY | INTERPRETING | INTIMATES |
| INTELLECTS | INTERDEALT | INTERLAYING | INTERPRETS | INTIMATING |
| INTENABLE | INTERDICT | INTERLAYS | INTERRED | INTIME |
| INTEND | INTERDICTED | INTERLEAF | INTERREGES | INTIMISM |
| INTENDANT | INTERDICTING | INTERLEAVES | INTERREX | INTIMISMS |
| INTENDANTS | INTERDICTS | INTERLINE | INTERRING | INTIMIST |
| INTENDED | INTERDINE | INTERLINED | INTERRUPT | INTIMISTE |
| INTENDEDS | INTERDINED | INTERLINES | INTERRUPTED | INTIMISTES |
| INTENDER | INTERDINES | INTERLINING | INTERRUPTING | INTIMISTS |
| INTENDERED | INTERDINING | INTERLININGS | INTERRUPTS | INTIMITIES |
| INTENDERING | INTERESS | INTERLINK | INTERS | INTIMITY |
| INTENDERS | INTERESSE | INTERLINKED | INTERSECT | INTINE |
| INTENDING | INTERESSED | INTERLINKING | INTERSECTED | INTINES |
| INTENDS | INTERESSES | INTERLINKS | INTERSECTING | INTIRE |
| INTENIBLE | INTERESSING | INTERLOCK | INTERSECTS | INTITULE |
| INTENSATE | INTEREST | INTERLOCKED | INTERSERT | INTITULED |
| INTENSATED | INTERESTED | INTERLOCKING | INTERSERTED | INTITULES |
| INTENSATES | INTERESTING | INTERLOCKS | INTERSERTING | INTITULING |
| INTENSATING | INTERESTS | INTERLOPE | INTERSERTS | INTO |
| INTENSE | INTERFACE | INTERLOPED | INTERSEX | INTOED |
| INTENSELY | INTERFACED | INTERLOPES | INTERSEXES | INTOMB |
| INTENSER | INTERFACES | INTERLOPING | INTERTIE | INTOMBED |
| INTENSEST | INTERFACING | INTERLUDE | INTERTIES | INTOMBING |
| INTENSIFIED | INTERFACINGS | INTERLUDED | INTERVAL | INTOMBS |
| INTENSIFIES | INTERFERE | INTERLUDES | INTERVALE | INTONATE |
| INTENSIFY | INTERFERED | INTERLUDING | INTERVALES | INTONATED |
| INTENSIFYING | INTERFERES | INTERMENT | INTERVALS | INTONATES |
| INTENSION | INTERFERING | INTERMENTS | INTERVEIN | INTONATING |
| INTENSIONS | INTERFLOW | INTERMIT | INTERVEINED | INTONATOR |
| INTENSITIES | INTERFLOWED | INTERMITS | INTERVEINING | INTONATORS |
| INTENSITY | INTERFLOWING | INTERMITTED | INTERVEINS | INTONE |
| INTENSIVE | INTERFLOWS | INTERMITTING | INTERVENE | INTONED |
| INTENSIVES | INTERFOLD | INTERMIX | INTERVENED | INTONER |
| INTENT | INTERFOLDED | INTERMIXED | INTERVENES | INTONERS |
| INTENTION | INTERFOLDING | INTERMIXES | INTERVENING | INTONES |
| INTENTIONS | INTERFOLDS | INTERMIXING | INTERVIEW | INTONING |
| INTENTIVE | INTERFUSE | INTERMURE | INTERVIEWED | INTONINGS |
| INTENTLY | INTERFUSED | INTERMURED | INTERVIEWING | INTORSION |
| INTENTS | INTERFUSES | INTERMURES | INTERVIEWS | INTORSIONS |
| INTER | INTERFUSING | INTERMURING | INTERWAR | INTORTED |
| INTERACT | INTERGREW | INTERN | INTERWIND | INTORTION |
| INTERACTED | INTERGROW | INTERNAL | INTERWINDING | INTORTIONS |
| INTERACTING | INTERGROWING | INTERNALS | INTERWINDS | INTOWN |
| INTERACTS | INTERGROWN | INTERNE | INTERWORK | INTRA |
| INTERBANK | INTERGROWS | INTERNED | INTERWORKED | INTRADOS |
| INTERBRED | INTERIM | INTERNEE | INTERWORKING | INTRADOSES |
| INTERCEDE | INTERIMS | INTERNEES | INTERWORKS | INTRANT |
| INTERCEDED | INTERIOR | INTERNES | INTERWOUND | INTRANTS |
| INTERCEDES | INTERIORS | INTERNING | INTERWOVE | INTREAT |
| INTERCEDING | INTERJECT | INTERNIST | INTERZONE | INTREATED |
| INTERCEPT | INTERJECTED | INTERNISTS | INTERZONES | INTREATING |
| INTERCEPTED | INTERJECTING | INTERNODE | INTESTACIES | INTREATS |
| INTERCEPTING | INTERJECTS | INTERNODES | INTESTACY | INTRENCH |

| | | | | |
|---|---|---|---|---|
| INTRENCHED | INTUMESCES | INVECTIVES | INVOCATES | IODINES |
| INTRENCHES | INTUMESCING | INVEIGH | INVOCATING | IODISE |
| INTRENCHING | INTUSE | INVEIGHED | INVOICE | IODISED |
| INTREPID | INTUSES | INVEIGHING | INVOICED | IODISES |
| INTRICACIES | INTWINE | INVEIGHS | INVOICES | IODISING |
| INTRICACY | INTWINED | INVEIGLE | INVOICING | IODISM |
| INTRICATE | INTWINES | INVEIGLED | INVOKE | IODISMS |
| INTRIGANT | INTWINING | INVEIGLER | INVOKED | IODIZE |
| INTRIGANTS | INTWIST | INVEIGLERS | INVOKES | IODIZED |
| INTRIGUE | INTWISTED | INVEIGLES | INVOKING | IODIZES |
| INTRIGUED | INTWISTING | INVEIGLING | INVOLUCEL | IODIZING |
| INTRIGUER | INTWISTS | INVENIT | INVOLUCELS | IODOFORM |
| INTRIGUERS | INULA | INVENT | INVOLUCRA | IODOFORMS |
| INTRIGUES | INULAS | INVENTED | INVOLUCRE | IODOPHILE |
| INTRIGUING | INULASE | INVENTING | INVOLUCRES | IODOUS |
| INTRINCE | INULASES | INVENTION | INVOLUTE | IODURET |
| INTRINSIC | INULIN | INVENTIONS | INVOLUTED | IODURETS |
| INTRO | INULINS | INVENTIVE | INVOLUTES | IODYRITE |
| INTRODUCE | INUMBRATE | INVENTOR | INVOLUTING | IODYRITES |
| INTRODUCED | INUMBRATED | INVENTORIED | INVOLVE | IOLITE |
| INTRODUCES | INUMBRATES | INVENTORIES | INVOLVED | IOLITES |
| INTRODUCING | INUMBRATING | INVENTORS | INVOLVES | ION |
| INTROIT | INUNCTION | INVENTORY | INVOLVING | IONIC |
| INTROITS | INUNCTIONS | INVENTORYING | INWALL | IONISE |
| INTROITUS | INUNDANT | INVENTS | INWALLED | IONISED |
| INTROITUSES | INUNDATE | INVERSE | INWALLING | IONISER |
| INTROJECT | INUNDATED | INVERSED | INWALLS | IONISERS |
| INTROJECTED | INUNDATES | INVERSELY | INWARD | IONISES |
| INTROJECTING | INUNDATING | INVERSES | INWARDLY | IONISING |
| INTROJECTS | INURBANE | INVERSING | INWARDS | IONIUM |
| INTROLD | INURE | INVERSION | INWEAVE | IONIUMS |
| INTROMIT | INURED | INVERSIONS | INWEAVES | IONIZE |
| INTROMITS | INUREMENT | INVERSIVE | INWEAVING | IONIZED |
| INTROMITTED | INUREMENTS | INVERT | INWICK | IONIZER |
| INTROMITTING | INURES | INVERTASE | INWICKED | IONIZERS |
| INTRON | INURING | INVERTASES | INWICKING | IONIZES |
| INTRONS | INURN | INVERTED | INWICKS | IONIZING |
| INTRORSE | INURNED | INVERTER | INWIND | IONOMER |
| INTROS | INURNING | INVERTERS | INWINDING | IONOMERS |
| INTROVERT | INURNS | INVERTIN | INWINDS | IONONE |
| INTROVERTED | INUSITATE | INVERTING | INWIT | IONONES |
| INTROVERTING | INUST | INVERTINS | INWITH | IONOPAUSE |
| INTROVERTS | INUSTION | INVERTOR | INWITS | IONOPAUSES |
| INTRUDE | INUSTIONS | INVERTORS | INWORK | IONOPHORE |
| INTRUDED | INUTILITIES | INVERTS | INWORKED | IONOPHORES |
| INTRUDER | INUTILITY | INVEST | INWORKING | IONS |
| INTRUDERS | INVADE | INVESTED | INWORKINGS | IOS |
| INTRUDES | INVADED | INVESTING | INWORKS | IOTA |
| INTRUDING | INVADER | INVESTOR | INWORN | IOTACISM |
| INTRUSION | INVADERS | INVESTORS | INWOUND | IOTACISMS |
| INTRUSIONS | INVADES | INVESTS | INWOVE | IOTAS |
| INTRUSIVE | INVADING | INVEXED | INWOVEN | IPECAC |
| INTRUSIVES | INVALID | INVIABLE | INWRAP | IPECACS |
| INTRUST | INVALIDED | INVIDIOUS | INWRAPPED | IPOMOEA |
| INTRUSTED | INVALIDING | INVIOLATE | INWRAPPING | IPOMOEAS |
| INTRUSTING | INVALIDINGS | INVIOUS | INWRAPS | IRACUND |
| INTRUSTS | INVALIDLY | INVISIBLE | INWREATHE | IRADE |
| INTUBATE | INVALIDS | INVISIBLES | INWREATHED | IRADES |
| INTUBATED | INVARIANT | INVISIBLY | INWREATHES | IRASCIBLE |
| INTUBATES | INVARIANTS | INVITE | INWREATHING | IRASCIBLY |
| INTUBATING | INVASION | INVITED | INWROUGHT | IRATE |
| INTUIT | INVASIONS | INVITEE | INYALA | IRATELY |
| INTUITED | INVASIVE | INVITEES | INYALAS | IRATER |
| INTUITING | INVEAGLE | INVITER | IO | IRATEST |
| INTUITION | INVEAGLED | INVITERS | IODATE | IRE |
| INTUITIONS | INVEAGLES | INVITES | IODATES | IREFUL |
| INTUITIVE | INVEAGLING | INVITING | IODIC | IREFULLY |
| INTUITS | INVECKED | INVITINGS | IODIDE | IRENIC |
| INTUMESCE | INVECTED | INVOCATE | IODIDES | IRENICAL |
| INTUMESCED | INVECTIVE | INVOCATED | IODINE | IRENICISM |

| | | | | |
|---|---|---|---|---|
| IRENICISMS | IRONIZED | ISCHAEMIA | ISOCLINE | ISOMERIC |
| IRENICON | IRONIZES | ISCHAEMIAS | ISOCLINES | ISOMERISE |
| IRENICONS | IRONIZING | ISCHAEMIC | ISOCLINIC | ISOMERISED |
| IRENICS | IRONS | ISCHEMIA | ISOCLINICS | ISOMERISES |
| IRENOLOGIES | IRONSMITH | ISCHEMIAS | ISOCRACIES | ISOMERISING |
| IRENOLOGY | IRONSMITHS | ISCHEMIC | ISOCRACY | ISOMERISM |
| IRES | IRONSTONE | ISCHIA | ISOCRATIC | ISOMERISMS |
| IRID | IRONSTONES | ISCHIADIC | ISOCRYMAL | ISOMERIZE |
| IRIDAL | IRONWARE | ISCHIAL | ISOCRYMALS | ISOMERIZED |
| IRIDEAL | IRONWARES | ISCHIATIC | ISOCRYME | ISOMERIZES |
| IRIDES | IRONWOOD | ISCHIUM | ISOCRYMES | ISOMERIZING |
| IRIDIAL | IRONWOODS | ISCHURIA | ISOCYCLIC | ISOMEROUS |
| IRIDIAN | IRONWORK | ISCHURIAS | ISODICON | ISOMERS |
| IRIDIC | IRONWORKS | ISENERGIC | ISODICONS | ISOMETRIC |
| IRIDISE | IRONY | ISH | ISODOMA | ISOMETRICS |
| IRIDISED | IRRADIANT | ISHES | ISODOMON | ISOMETRIES |
| IRIDISES | IRRADIATE | ISINGLASS | ISODOMONS | ISOMETRY |
| IRIDISING | IRRADIATED | ISINGLASSES | ISODOMOUS | ISOMORPH |
| IRIDIUM | IRRADIATES | ISLAND | ISODOMUM | ISOMORPHS |
| IRIDIUMS | IRRADIATING | ISLANDED | ISODONT | ISONIAZID |
| IRIDIZE | IRREALITIES | ISLANDER | ISODONTAL | ISONIAZIDS |
| IRIDIZED | IRREALITY | ISLANDERS | ISODONTS | ISONOMIC |
| IRIDIZES | IRREGULAR | ISLANDING | ISOETES | ISONOMIES |
| IRIDIZING | IRREGULARS | ISLANDS | ISOGAMETE | ISONOMOUS |
| IRIDOLOGIES | IRRELATED | ISLE | ISOGAMETES | ISONOMY |
| IRIDOLOGY | IRRIGABLE | ISLED | ISOGAMIC | ISOPLETH |
| IRIDOTOMIES | IRRIGATE | ISLEMAN | ISOGAMIES | ISOPLETHS |
| IRIDOTOMY | IRRIGATED | ISLEMEN | ISOGAMOUS | ISOPOD |
| IRIDS | IRRIGATES | ISLES | ISOGAMY | ISOPODAN |
| IRIS | IRRIGATING | ISLESMAN | ISOGENIES | ISOPODOUS |
| IRISATE | IRRIGATOR | ISLESMEN | ISOGENOUS | ISOPODS |
| IRISATED | IRRIGATORS | ISLET | ISOGENY | ISOPOLITIES |
| IRISATES | IRRIGUOUS | ISLETS | ISOGLOSS | ISOPOLITY |
| IRISATING | IRRISION | ISLING | ISOGLOSSES | ISOPRENE |
| IRISATION | IRRISIONS | ISM | ISOGON | ISOPRENES |
| IRISATIONS | IRRISORY | ISMATIC | ISOGONAL | ISOPROPYL |
| IRISCOPE | IRRITABLE | ISMATICAL | ISOGONALS | ISOPROPYLS |
| IRISCOPES | IRRITABLY | ISMIER | ISOGONIC | ISOSCELES |
| IRISED | IRRITANCIES | ISMIEST | ISOGONICS | ISOSPIN |
| IRISES | IRRITANCY | ISMS | ISOGONS | ISOSPINS |
| IRISING | IRRITANT | ISMY | ISOGRAM | ISOSPORIES |
| IRITIC | IRRITANTS | ISOBAR | ISOGRAMS | ISOSPORY |
| IRITIS | IRRITATE | ISOBARE | ISOHEL | ISOSTASIES |
| IRITISES | IRRITATED | ISOBARES | ISOHELS | ISOSTASY |
| IRK | IRRITATES | ISOBARIC | ISOHYET | ISOSTATIC |
| IRKED | IRRITATING | ISOBARS | ISOHYETAL | ISOSTERIC |
| IRKING | IRRITATOR | ISOBASE | ISOHYETALS | ISOTACTIC |
| IRKS | IRRITATORS | ISOBASES | ISOHYETS | ISOTHERAL |
| IRKSOME | IRRUPT | ISOBATH | ISOKONT | ISOTHERALS |
| IRKSOMELY | IRRUPTED | ISOBATHIC | ISOKONTAN | ISOTHERE |
| IROKO | IRRUPTING | ISOBATHS | ISOKONTANS | ISOTHERES |
| IROKOS | IRRUPTION | ISOBRONT | ISOKONTS | ISOTHERM |
| IRON | IRRUPTIONS | ISOBRONTS | ISOLABLE | ISOTHERMS |
| IRONBARK | IRRUPTIVE | ISOCHASM | ISOLATE | ISOTONE |
| IRONBARKS | IRRUPTS | ISOCHASMS | ISOLATED | ISOTONES |
| IRONED | IS | ISOCHEIM | ISOLATES | ISOTONIC |
| IRONER | ISABEL | ISOCHEIMS | ISOLATING | ISOTOPE |
| IRONERS | ISABELLA | ISOCHIMAL | ISOLATION | ISOTOPES |
| IRONIC | ISABELLAS | ISOCHIMALS | ISOLATIONS | ISOTOPIC |
| IRONICAL | ISABELS | ISOCHIME | ISOLATIVE | ISOTOPIES |
| IRONIES | ISAGOGE | ISOCHIMES | ISOLATOR | ISOTOPY |
| IRONING | ISAGOGES | ISOCHOR | ISOLATORS | ISOTRON |
| IRONINGS | ISAGOGIC | ISOCHORE | ISOLINE | ISOTRONS |
| IRONISE | ISAGOGICS | ISOCHORES | ISOLINES | ISOTROPIC |
| IRONISED | ISALLOBAR | ISOCHORIC | ISOLOGOUS | ISOTROPIES |
| IRONISES | ISALLOBARS | ISOCHORS | ISOLOGUE | ISOTROPY |
| IRONISING | ISATIN | ISOCHRONE | ISOLOGUES | ISOTYPE |
| IRONIST | ISATINE | ISOCHRONES | ISOMER | ISOTYPES |
| IRONISTS | ISATINES | ISOCLINAL | ISOMERE | ISSEI |
| IRONIZE | ISATINS | ISOCLINALS | ISOMERES | ISSEIS |

| | | | | |
|---|---|---|---|---|
| ISSUABLE | ITACISMS | ITCHWEED | ITERATES | IVORIED |
| ISSUABLY | ITALIC | ITCHWEEDS | ITERATING | IVORIES |
| ISSUANCE | ITALICISE | ITCHY | ITERATION | IVORIST |
| ISSUANCES | ITALICISED | ITEM | ITERATIONS | IVORISTS |
| ISSUANT | ITALICISES | ITEMED | ITERATIVE | IVORY |
| ISSUE | ITALICISING | ITEMING | ITERUM | IVRESSE |
| ISSUED | ITALICIZE | ITEMISE | ITINERACIES | IVRESSES |
| ISSUELESS | ITALICIZED | ITEMISED | ITINERACY | IVY |
| ISSUER | ITALICIZES | ITEMISES | ITINERANT | IWIS |
| ISSUERS | ITALICIZING | ITEMISING | ITINERANTS | IXIA |
| ISSUES | ITALICS | ITEMIZE | ITINERARIES | IXIAS |
| ISSUING | ITAS | ITEMIZED | ITINERARY | IXTLE |
| ISTHMIAN | ITCH | ITEMIZES | ITINERATE | IXTLES |
| ISTHMUS | ITCHED | ITEMIZING | ITINERATED | IZARD |
| ISTHMUSES | ITCHES | ITEMS | ITINERATES | IZARDS |
| ISTLE | ITCHIER | ITERANCE | ITINERATING | IZZARD |
| ISTLES | ITCHIEST | ITERANCES | ITS | IZZARDS |
| IT | ITCHINESS | ITERANT | ITSELF | IZZET |
| ITA | ITCHINESSES | ITERATE | IVIED | IZZETS |
| ITACISM | ITCHING | ITERATED | IVIES | |

# J

JAB
JABBED
JABBER
JABBERED
JABBERER
JABBERERS
JABBERING
JABBERINGS
JABBERS
JABBING
JABBLE
JABBLED
JABBLES
JABBLING
JABERS
JABIRU
JABIRUS
JABORANDI
JABORANDIS
JABOT
JABOTS
JABS
JACAMAR
JACAMARS
JACANA
JAÇANA
JACANAS
JAÇANAS
JACARANDA
JACARANDAS
JACCHUS
JACCHUSES
JACENT
JACINTH
JACINTHS
JACK
JACKAL
JACKALLED
JACKALLING
JACKALS
JACKAROO
JACKAROOED
JACKAROOING
JACKAROOS
JACKASS
JACKASSES
JACKBOOT
JACKBOOTED
JACKBOOTING
JACKBOOTS
JACKDAW
JACKDAWS
JACKED
JACKEROO
JACKEROOED
JACKEROOING
JACKEROOS
JACKET
JACKETED
JACKETING
JACKETS
JACKING
JACKMAN

JACKMEN
JACKPOT
JACKPOTS
JACKS
JACKSIE
JACKSIES
JACKSMITH
JACKSMITHS
JACKSY
JACOBUS
JACOBUSES
JACONET
JACONETS
JACQUARD
JACQUARDS
JACTATION
JACTATIONS
JACULATE
JACULATED
JACULATES
JACULATING
JACULATOR
JACULATORS
JACUZZI
JACUZZIS
JADE
JADED
JADEDLY
JADEITE
JADEITES
JADERIES
JADERY
JADES
JADING
JADISH
JAEGER
JAEGERS
JAG
JÄGER
JÄGERS
JAGGED
JAGGEDLY
JAGGER
JAGGERIES
JAGGERS
JAGGERY
JAGGIER
JAGGIEST
JAGGING
JAGGY
JAGHIR
JAGHIRDAR
JAGHIRDARS
JAGHIRE
JAGHIRES
JAGHIRS
JAGIR
JAGIRS
JAGS
JAGUAR
JAGUARS
JAIL
JAILED

JAILER
JAILERESS
JAILERESSES
JAILERS
JAILHOUSE
JAILHOUSES
JAILING
JAILOR
JAILORESS
JAILORESSES
JAILORS
JAILS
JAK
JAKE
JAKES
JAKESES
JAKS
JALAP
JALAPIC
JALAPIN
JALAPINS
JALAPS
JALOPIES
JALOPPIES
JALOPPY
JALOPY
JALOUSE
JALOUSED
JALOUSES
JALOUSIE
JALOUSIED
JALOUSIES
JALOUSING
JAM
JAMADAR
JAMADARS
JAMB
JAMBE
JAMBEAU
JAMBEAUX
JAMBEE
JAMBEES
JAMBER
JAMBERS
JAMBES
JAMBEUX
JAMBIER
JAMBIERS
JAMBIYA
JAMBIYAH
JAMBIYAHS
JAMBIYAS
JAMBO
JAMBOK
JAMBOKKED
JAMBOKKING
JAMBOKS
JAMBOLAN
JAMBOLANA
JAMBOLANAS
JAMBOLANS
JAMBONE
JAMBONES

JAMBOOL
JAMBOOLS
JAMBOREE
JAMBOREES
JAMBOS
JAMBS
JAMBU
JAMBUL
JAMBULS
JAMBUS
JAMDANI
JAMDANIS
JAMES
JAMESES
JAMJAR
JAMJARS
JAMMED
JAMMER
JAMMERS
JAMMIER
JAMMIEST
JAMMING
JAMMY
JAMPAN
JAMPANEE
JAMPANEES
JAMPANI
JAMPANIS
JAMPANS
JAMPOT
JAMPOTS
JAMS
JANE
JANES
JANGLE
JANGLED
JANGLER
JANGLERS
JANGLES
JANGLIER
JANGLIEST
JANGLING
JANGLINGS
JANGLY
JANISSARIES
JANISSARY
JANITOR
JANITORS
JANITRESS
JANITRESSES
JANITRIX
JANITRIXES
JANIZAR
JANIZARIES
JANIZARS
JANIZARY
JANKER
JANKERS
JANN
JANNOCK
JANNOCKS
JANNS
JANSKIES

JANSKY
JANTEE
JANTIER
JANTIES
JANTIEST
JANTY
JAP
JAPAN
JAPANNED
JAPANNER
JAPANNERS
JAPANNING
JAPANS
JAPE
JAPED
JAPES
JAPING
JAPONICA
JAPONICAS
JAPPED
JAPPING
JAPS
JAR
JARARACA
JARARACAS
JARARAKA
JARARAKAS
JARFUL
JARFULS
JARGON
JARGONED
JARGONEER
JARGONEERS
JARGONING
JARGONISE
JARGONISED
JARGONISES
JARGONISING
JARGONIST
JARGONISTS
JARGONIZE
JARGONIZED
JARGONIZES
JARGONIZING
JARGONS
JARGOON
JARGOONS
JARK
JARKMAN
JARKMEN
JARKS
JARL
JARLS
JAROOL
JAROOLS
JAROSITE
JAROSITES
JARRAH
JARRAHS
JARRED
JARRING
JARRINGLY
JARRINGS

JARS
JARTA
JARTAS
JARUL
JARULS
JARVEY
JARVEYS
JARVIE
JARVIES
JASEY
JASEYS
JASIES
JASMINE
JASMINES
JASP
JASPÉ
JASPER
JASPERISE
JASPERISED
JASPERISES
JASPERISING
JASPERIZE
JASPERIZED
JASPERIZES
JASPERIZING
JASPEROUS
JASPERS
JASPERY
JASPES
JASPIDEAN
JASPIS
JASPISES
JASPS
JASY
JATAKA
JATAKAS
JATO
JATOS
JAUNCE
JAUNCED
JAUNCES
JAUNCING
JAUNDICE
JAUNDICED
JAUNDICES
JAUNDICING
JAUNSE
JAUNSED
JAUNSES
JAUNSING
JAUNT
JAUNTED
JAUNTEE
JAUNTIE
JAUNTIER
JAUNTIES
JAUNTIEST
JAUNTILY
JAUNTING
JAUNTS
JAUNTY
JAUP
JAUPED
JAUPING
JAUPS
JAVEL
JAVELIN
JAVELINS
JAVELS
JAW

JAWAN
JAWANS
JAWARI
JAWARIS
JAWBATION
JAWBATIONS
JAWBONE
JAWBONED
JAWBONES
JAWBONING
JAWBONINGS
JAWBOX
JAWBOXES
JAWED
JAWFALL
JAWFALLS
JAWHOLE
JAWHOLES
JAWING
JAWINGS
JAWS
JAY
JAYS
JAYWALK
JAYWALKED
JAYWALKER
JAYWALKERS
JAYWALKING
JAYWALKINGS
JAYWALKS
JAZERANT
JAZERANTS
JAZIES
JAZY
JAZZ
JAZZED
JAZZES
JAZZIER
JAZZIEST
JAZZILY
JAZZINESS
JAZZINESSES
JAZZING
JAZZMAN
JAZZMEN
JAZZY
JEALOUS
JEALOUSE
JEALOUSED
JEALOUSES
JEALOUSIES
JEALOUSING
JEALOUSLY
JEALOUSY
JEAN
JEANETTE
JEANETTES
JEANS
JEAT
JEATS
JEBEL
JEBELS
JEE
JEED
JEEING
JEEL
JEELED
JEELIE
JEELIED
JEELIEING

JEELIES
JEELING
JEELS
JEELY
JEELYING
JEEP
JEEPERS
JEEPNEY
JEEPNEYS
JEEPS
JEER
JEERED
JEERER
JEERERS
JEERING
JEERINGLY
JEERINGS
JEERS
JEES
JEFF
JEFFED
JEFFING
JEFFS
JEHAD
JEHADS
JEJUNA
JEJUNE
JEJUNELY
JEJUNITIES
JEJUNITY
JEJUNUM
JELAB
JELABS
JELL
JELLABA
JELLABAS
JELLED
JELLIED
JELLIES
JELLIFIED
JELLIFIES
JELLIFORM
JELLIFY
JELLIFYING
JELLING
JELLO
JELLOS
JELLS
JELLY
JELLYBEAN
JELLYBEANS
JELLYFISH
JELLYFISHES
JELLYING
JELUTONG
JELUTONGS
JEMADAR
JEMADARS
JEMIDAR
JEMIDARS
JEMIMA
JEMIMAS
JEMMIER
JEMMIES
JEMMIEST
JEMMINESS
JEMMINESSES
JEMMY
JENNET
JENNETING

JENNETINGS
JENNETS
JENNIES
JENNY
JEOFAIL
JEOFAILS
JEOPARD
JEOPARDED
JEOPARDER
JEOPARDERS
JEOPARDIED
JEOPARDIES
JEOPARDING
JEOPARDS
JEOPARDY
JEOPARDYING
JEQUIRITIES
JEQUIRITY
JERBIL
JERBILS
JERBOA
JERBOAS
JEREED
JEREEDS
JEREMIAD
JEREMIADS
JERFALCON
JERFALCONS
JERID
JERIDS
JERK
JERKED
JERKER
JERKERS
JERKIER
JERKIES
JERKIEST
JERKIN
JERKINESS
JERKINESSES
JERKING
JERKINGS
JERKINS
JERKS
JERKY
JEROBOAM
JEROBOAMS
JERQUE
JERQUED
JERQUER
JERQUERS
JERQUES
JERQUING
JERQUINGS
JERRICAN
JERRICANS
JERRIES
JERRY
JERRYCAN
JERRYCANS
JERSEY
JERSEYS
JESS
JESSAMIES
JESSAMINE
JESSAMINES
JESSAMY
JESSANT
JESSED
JESSERANT

JESSERANTS
JESSES
JESSIE
JESSIES
JEST
JESTBOOK
JESTBOOKS
JESTED
JESTEE
JESTEES
JESTER
JESTERS
JESTFUL
JESTING
JESTINGLY
JESTINGS
JESTS
JÉSUS
JET
JETÉ
JETÉS
JETFOIL
JETFOILS
JETLINER
JETLINERS
JETON
JETONS
JETPLANE
JETPLANES
JETS
JETSAM
JETSAMS
JETSOM
JETSOMS
JETSON
JETSONS
JETSTREAM
JETSTREAMS
JETTATURA
JETTATURAS
JETTED
JETTIER
JETTIES
JETTIEST
JETTINESS
JETTINESSES
JETTING
JETTISON
JETTISONED
JETTISONING
JETTISONS
JETTON
JETTONS
JETTY
JEU
JEUNE
JEUX
JEWEL
JEWELFISH
JEWELFISHES
JEWELLED
JEWELLER
JEWELLERIES
JEWELLERS
JEWELLERY
JEWELLING
JEWELRIES
JEWELRY
JEWELS
JEWFISH

| | | | | |
|---|---|---|---|---|
| JEWFISHES | JILLFLIRT | JIRGA | JOCKTELEGS | JOINTURING |
| JEZAIL | JILLFLIRTS | JIRGAS | JOCO | JOIST |
| JEZAILS | JILLS | JIRKINET | JOCOROUS | JOISTED |
| JHALA | JILT | JIRKINETS | JOCOSE | JOISTING |
| JHALAS | JILTED | JISM | JOCOSELY | JOISTS |
| JIAO | JILTING | JISMS | JOCOSITIES | JOJOBA |
| JIAOS | JILTS | JISSOM | JOCOSITY | JOJOBAS |
| JIB | JIMCRACK | JISSOMS | JOCULAR | JOKE |
| JIBBAH | JIMCRACKS | JITNEY | JOCULARLY | JOKED |
| JIBBAHS | JIMINY | JITNEYS | JOCULATOR | JOKER |
| JIBBED | JIMJAM | JITTER | JOCULATORS | JOKERS |
| JIBBER | JIMJAMS | JITTERBUG | JOCUND | JOKES |
| JIBBERED | JIMMIED | JITTERBUGGED | JOCUNDITIES | JOKESMITH |
| JIBBERING | JIMMIES | JITTERBUGGING | JOCUNDITY | JOKESMITHS |
| JIBBERS | JIMMY | JITTERBUGS | JOCUNDLY | JOKESOME |
| JIBBING | JIMMYING | JITTERED | JODEL | JOKEY |
| JIBBINGS | JIMP | JITTERING | JODELLED | JOKIER |
| JIBE | JIMPER | JITTERS | JODELLING | JOKIEST |
| JIBED | JIMPEST | JITTERY | JODELS | JOKING |
| JIBER | JIMPIER | JIVE | JODHPURS | JOKINGLY |
| JIBERS | JIMPIEST | JIVED | JOE | JOKOL |
| JIBES | JIMPLY | JIVER | JOES | JOKY |
| JIBING | JIMPNESS | JIVERS | JOEY | JOLE |
| JIBS | JIMPNESSES | JIVES | JOEYS | JOLED |
| JICKAJOG | JIMPY | JIVING | JOG | JOLES |
| JICKAJOGS | JINGAL | JIZ | JOGGED | JOLING |
| JIFF | JINGALS | JIZZ | JOGGER | JOLL |
| JIFFIES | JINGBANG | JIZZES | JOGGERS | JOLLED |
| JIFFS | JINGBANGS | JO | JOGGING | JOLLIED |
| JIFFY | JINGLE | JOANNA | JOGGINGS | JOLLIER |
| JIG | JINGLED | JOANNAS | JOGGLE | JOLLIES |
| JIGAJIG | JINGLER | JOANNES | JOGGLED | JOLLIEST |
| JIGAJIGS | JINGLERS | JOANNESES | JOGGLES | JOLLIFIED |
| JIGAJOG | JINGLES | JOB | JOGGLING | JOLLIFIES |
| JIGAJOGS | JINGLET | JOBATION | JOGS | JOLLIFY |
| JIGAMAREE | JINGLETS | JOBATIONS | JOGTROT | JOLLIFYING |
| JIGAMAREES | JINGLIER | JOBBED | JOGTROTS | JOLLILY |
| JIGGED | JINGLIEST | JOBBER | JOHANNES | JOLLIMENT |
| JIGGER | JINGLING | JOBBERIES | JOHANNESES | JOLLIMENTS |
| JIGGERED | JINGLINGS | JOBBERS | JOHN | JOLLINESS |
| JIGGERING | JINGLY | JOBBERY | JOHNNIE | JOLLINESSES |
| JIGGERS | JINGO | JOBBING | JOHNNIES | JOLLING |
| JIGGING | JINGOES | JOBBINGS | JOHNNY | JOLLITIES |
| JIGGINGS | JINGOISH | JOBCENTRE | JOHNS | JOLLITY |
| JIGGISH | JINGOISM | JOBCENTRES | JOIN | JOLLS |
| JIGGLE | JINGOISMS | JOBE | JOINDER | JOLLY |
| JIGGLED | JINGOIST | JOBED | JOINDERS | JOLLYBOAT |
| JIGGLES | JINGOISTS | JOBERNOWL | JOINED | JOLLYBOATS |
| JIGGLING | JINJILI | JOBERNOWLS | JOINER | JOLLYHEAD |
| JIGGUMBOB | JINJILIS | JOBES | JOINERIES | JOLLYHEADS |
| JIGGUMBOBS | JINK | JOBING | JOINERS | JOLLYING |
| JIGJIG | JINKED | JOBLESS | JOINERY | JOLT |
| JIGJIGS | JINKER | JOBS | JOINING | JOLTED |
| JIGOT | JINKERS | JOBSWORTH | JOININGS | JOLTER |
| JIGOTS | JINKING | JOBSWORTHS | JOINS | JOLTERS |
| JIGS | JINKS | JOCK | JOINT | JOLTHEAD |
| JIGSAW | JINN | JOCKETTE | JOINTED | JOLTHEADS |
| JIGSAWED | JINNEE | JOCKETTES | JOINTER | JOLTIER |
| JIGSAWING | JINNI | JOCKEY | JOINTERS | JOLTIEST |
| JIGSAWN | JINNS | JOCKEYED | JOINTING | JOLTING |
| JIGSAWS | JINX | JOCKEYING | JOINTLESS | JOLTINGLY |
| JIHAD | JINXED | JOCKEYISM | JOINTLY | JOLTS |
| JIHADS | JINXES | JOCKEYISMS | JOINTNESS | JOLTY |
| JILGIE | JINXING | JOCKEYS | JOINTNESSES | JOMO |
| JILGIES | JIRBLE | JOCKO | JOINTRESS | JOMOS |
| JILL | JIRBLED | JOCKOS | JOINTRESSES | JONCANOE |
| JILLAROO | JIRBLES | JOCKS | JOINTS | JONCANOES |
| JILLAROOS | JIRBLING | JOCKSTRAP | JOINTURE | JONGLEUR |
| JILLET | JIRD | JOCKSTRAPS | JOINTURED | JONGLEURS |
| JILLETS | JIRDS | JOCKTELEG | JOINTURES | JONQUIL |

JONQUILS
JONTIES
JONTY
JOOK
JOOKED
JOOKERIES
JOOKERY
JOOKING
JOOKS
JOR
JORAM
JORAMS
JORDAN
JORDANS
JORDELOO
JORDELOOS
JORS
JORUM
JORUMS
JOSEPH
JOSEPHS
JOSH
JOSHED
JOSHER
JOSHERS
JOSHES
JOSHING
JOSKIN
JOSKINS
JOSS
JOSSER
JOSSERS
JOSSES
JOSTLE
JOSTLED
JOSTLES
JOSTLING
JOSTLINGS
JOT
JOTA
JOTAS
JOTS
JOTTED
JOTTER
JOTTERS
JOTTING
JOTTINGS
JOTUN
JÖTUNN
JÖTUNNS
JOTUNS
JOUGS
JOUISANCE
JOUISANCES
JOUK
JOUKED
JOUKERIES
JOUKERY
JOUKING
JOUKS
JOULE
JOULED
JOULES
JOULING
JOUNCE
JOUNCED
JOUNCES
JOUNCING
JOUR
JOURNAL

JOURNALLED
JOURNALLING
JOURNALS
JOURNEY
JOURNEYED
JOURNEYER
JOURNEYERS
JOURNEYING
JOURNEYS
JOURNO
JOURNOS
JOURS
JOUST
JOUSTED
JOUSTER
JOUSTERS
JOUSTING
JOUSTS
JOVIAL
JOVIALITIES
JOVIALITY
JOVIALLY
JOW
JOWAR
JOWARI
JOWARIS
JOWARS
JOWED
JOWING
JOWL
JOWLED
JOWLER
JOWLERS
JOWLING
JOWLS
JOWS
JOY
JOYANCE
JOYANCES
JOYED
JOYFUL
JOYFULLER
JOYFULLEST
JOYFULLY
JOYING
JOYLESS
JOYLESSLY
JOYOUS
JOYOUSLY
JOYS
JUBA
JUBAS
JUBATE
JUBBAH
JUBBAHS
JUBE
JUBES
JUBILANCE
JUBILANCES
JUBILANCIES
JUBILANCY
JUBILANT
JUBILATE
JUBILATED
JUBILATES
JUBILATING
JUBILEE
JUBILEES
JUD
JUDAS

JUDASES
JUDDER
JUDDERED
JUDDERING
JUDDERS
JUDGE
JUDGED
JUDGEMENT
JUDGEMENTS
JUDGES
JUDGESHIP
JUDGESHIPS
JUDGING
JUDGMENT
JUDGMENTS
JUDICABLE
JUDICATOR
JUDICATORS
JUDICIAL
JUDICIARIES
JUDICIARY
JUDICIOUS
JUDIES
JUDO
JUDOGI
JUDOGIS
JUDOIST
JUDOISTS
JUDOKA
JUDOKAS
JUDOS
JUDS
JUDY
JUG
JUGA
JUGAL
JUGALS
JUGATE
JUGFUL
JUGFULS
JUGGED
JUGGING
JUGGINS
JUGGINSES
JUGGLE
JUGGLED
JUGGLER
JUGGLERIES
JUGGLERS
JUGGLERY
JUGGLES
JUGGLING
JUGGLINGS
JUGS
JUGULAR
JUGULARS
JUGULATE
JUGULATED
JUGULATES
JUGULATING
JUGUM
JUICE
JUICED
JUICELESS
JUICER
JUICERS
JUICES
JUICIER
JUICIEST
JUICINESS

JUICINESSES
JUICING
JUICY
JUJU
JUJUBE
JUJUBES
JUJUS
JUKE
JUKED
JUKES
JUKING
JULEP
JULEPS
JULIENNE
JULIENNES
JUMAR
JUMARRED
JUMARRING
JUMARS
JUMART
JUMARTS
JUMBAL
JUMBALS
JUMBIE
JUMBIES
JUMBLE
JUMBLED
JUMBLER
JUMBLERS
JUMBLES
JUMBLIER
JUMBLIEST
JUMBLING
JUMBLY
JUMBO
JUMBOISE
JUMBOISED
JUMBOISES
JUMBOISING
JUMBOIZE
JUMBOIZED
JUMBOIZES
JUMBOIZING
JUMBOS
JUMBUCK
JUMBUCKS
JUMBY
JUMELLE
JUMELLES
JUMP
JUMPED
JUMPER
JUMPERS
JUMPIER
JUMPIEST
JUMPILY
JUMPINESS
JUMPINESSES
JUMPING
JUMPS
JUMPY
JUNCATE
JUNCATES
JUNCO
JUNCOES
JUNCOS
JUNCTION
JUNCTIONS
JUNCTURE
JUNCTURES

JUNCUS
JUNCUSES
JUNEATING
JUNEATINGS
JUNGLE
JUNGLES
JUNGLI
JUNGLIER
JUNGLIEST
JUNGLIS
JUNGLY
JUNIOR
JUNIORITIES
JUNIORITY
JUNIORS
JUNIPER
JUNIPERS
JUNK
JUNKANOO
JUNKANOOS
JUNKED
JUNKER
JUNKERDOM
JUNKERDOMS
JUNKERISM
JUNKERISMS
JUNKERS
JUNKET
JUNKETED
JUNKETING
JUNKETINGS
JUNKETS
JUNKIE
JUNKIER
JUNKIES
JUNKIEST
JUNKING
JUNKMAN
JUNKMEN
JUNKS
JUNKY
JUNTA
JUNTAS
JUNTO
JUNTOS
JUPATI
JUPATIS
JUPON
JUPONS
JURA
JURAL
JURALLY
JURANT
JURANTS
JURAT
JURATORY
JURATS
JURE
JURIDIC
JURIDICAL
JURIES
JURIST
JURISTIC
JURISTS
JUROR
JURORS
JURY
JURYMAN
JURYMAST
JURYMASTS

JURYMEN
JURYWOMAN
JURYWOMEN
JUS
JUSSIVE
JUSSIVES
JUST
JUSTED
JUSTER
JUSTEST
JUSTICE

JUSTICER
JUSTICERS
JUSTICES
JUSTICIAR
JUSTICIARS
JUSTIFIED
JUSTIFIER
JUSTIFIERS
JUSTIFIES
JUSTIFY
JUSTIFYING

JUSTING
JUSTLE
JUSTLED
JUSTLES
JUSTLING
JUSTLY
JUSTNESS
JUSTNESSES
JUSTS
JUT
JUTE

JUTES
JUTS
JUTTED
JUTTIED
JUTTIES
JUTTING
JUTTINGLY
JUTTY
JUTTYING
JUVENAL
JUVENALS

JUVENILE
JUVENILES
JUVENILIA
JUXTAPOSE
JUXTAPOSED
JUXTAPOSES
JUXTAPOSING
JYMOLD
JYNX
JYNXES

# K

KA
KAAMA
KAAMAS
KABAB
KABABS
KABALA
KABALAS
KABAYA
KABAYAS
KABBALA
KABBALAH
KABBALAHS
KABBALAS
KABELE
KABELES
KABELJOU
KABELJOUS
KABELJOUW
KABELJOUWS
KABOB
KABOBS
KABUKI
KABUKIS
KACCHA
KACCHAS
KACHA
KACHAHRI
KACHAHRIS
KACHCHA
KACHERI
KACHERIS
KACHINA
KACHINAS
KADE
KADES
KADI
KADIS
KAE
KAED
KAEING
KAES
KAFFIYEH
KAFFIYEHS
KAFILA
KAFILAS
KAFTAN
KAFTANS
KAGO
KAGOOL
KAGOOLS
KAGOS
KAGOUL
KAGOULE
KAGOULES
KAGOULS
KAHAL
KAHALS
KAI
KAIAK
KAIAKS
KAID
KAIDS
KAIE

KAIES
KAIF
KAIFS
KAIKAI
KAIKAIED
KAIKAIING
KAIKAIS
KAIL
KAILS
KAILYAIRD
KAILYAIRDS
KAILYARD
KAILYARDS
KAIM
KAIMAKAM
KAIMAKAMS
KAIMS
KAIN
KAING
KAINITE
KAINITES
KAINS
KAIS
KAISER
KAISERDOM
KAISERDOMS
KAISERIN
KAISERINS
KAISERISM
KAISERISMS
KAISERS
KAJAWAH
KAJAWAHS
KAKA
KAKAPO
KAKAPOS
KAKAS
KAKEMONO
KAKEMONOS
KAKI
KAKIEMON
KAKIEMONS
KAKIS
KAKODYL
KAKODYLS
KALAMDAN
KALAMDANS
KALAMKARI
KALAMKARIS
KALE
KALENDAR
KALENDARED
KALENDARING
KALENDARS
KALENDS
KALES
KALI
KALIAN
KALIANS
KALIF
KALIFS
KALINITE
KALINITES

KALIS
KALIUM
KALIUMS
KALLITYPE
KALLITYPES
KALMIA
KALMIAS
KALONG
KALONGS
KALOTYPE
KALOTYPES
KALPA
KALPAK
KALPAKS
KALPAS
KALPIS
KALPISES
KALUMPIT
KALUMPITS
KALYPTRA
KALYPTRAS
KAM
KAMACITE
KAMACITES
KAMALA
KAMALAS
KAME
KAMEES
KAMEESES
KAMEEZ
KAMEEZES
KAMELA
KAMELAS
KAMERAD
KAMERADED
KAMERADING
KAMERADS
KAMES
KAMI
KAMICHI
KAMICHIS
KAMIK
KAMIKAZE
KAMIKAZES
KAMIKS
KAMILA
KAMILAS
KAMIS
KAMISES
KAMME
KAMPONG
KAMPONGS
KAMSEEN
KAMSEENS
KAMSIN
KAMSINS
KANA
KANAKA
KANAKAS
KANAS
KANDIES
KANDY
KANEH

KANEHS
KANG
KANGA
KANGAROO
KANGAROOED
KANGAROOING
KANGAROOS
KANGAS
KANGHA
KANGHAS
KANGS
KANS
KANSES
KANT
KANTAR
KANTARS
KANTED
KANTELA
KANTELAS
KANTELE
KANTELES
KANTEN
KANTENS
KANTHA
KANTHAS
KANTIKOY
KANTIKOYED
KANTIKOYING
KANTIKOYS
KANTING
KANTS
KANZU
KANZUS
KAOLIANG
KAOLIANGS
KAOLIN
KAOLINE
KAOLINES
KAOLINISE
KAOLINISED
KAOLINISES
KAOLINISING
KAOLINITE
KAOLINITES
KAOLINIZE
KAOLINIZED
KAOLINIZES
KAOLINIZING
KAOLINS
KAON
KAONS
KAPOK
KAPOKS
KAPPA
KAPPAS
KAPUT
KAPUTT
KARA
KARABINER
KARABINERS
KARAISM
KARAISMS
KARAIT

KARAITS
KARAKA
KARAKAS
KARAKUL
KARAKULS
KARAS
KARAT
KARATE
KARATEIST
KARATEISTS
KARATEKA
KARATEKAS
KARATES
KARATS
KARITE
KARITES
KARMA
KARMAS
KARMIC
KAROSS
KAROSSES
KARRI
KARRIS
KARSEY
KARSEYS
KARSIES
KARST
KARSTS
KARSY
KART
KARTING
KARTINGS
KARTS
KARYOLOGIES
KARYOLOGY
KARYOSOME
KARYOSOMES
KARZIES
KARZY
KAS
KASBA
KASBAH
KASBAHS
KASBAS
KASHMIR
KASHMIRS
KAT
KATABASES
KATABASIS
KATABATIC
KATABOLIC
KATAKANA
KATAKANAS
KATANA
KATANAS
KATHAK
KATHAKALI
KATHAKALIS
KATHAKS
KATHARSES
KATHARSIS
KATHODE
KATHODES

KATI
KATION
KATIONS
KATIS
KATORGA
KATORGAS
KATS
KATTI
KATTIS
KATYDID
KATYDIDS
KAUGH
KAUGHS
KAURI
KAURIS
KAVA
KAVAS
KAVASS
KAVASSES
KAW
KAWED
KAWING
KAWS
KAY
KAYAK
KAYAKS
KAYLE
KAYLES
KAYO
KAYOE
KAYOED
KAYOEING
KAYOES
KAYOING
KAYOS
KAYS
KAZATZKA
KAZATZKAS
KAZI
KAZIS
KAZOO
KAZOOS
KEA
KEAS
KEASAR
KEASARS
KEB
KEBAB
KEBABS
KEBBED
KEBBIE
KEBBIES
KEBBING
KEBBOCK
KEBBOCKS
KEBBUCK
KEBBUCKS
KEBELE
KEBELES
KEBLAH
KEBLAHS
KEBOB
KEBOBS
KEBS
KECK
KECKED
KECKING
KECKLE
KECKLED
KECKLES

KECKLING
KECKLINGS
KECKS
KECKSES
KECKSIES
KECKSY
KED
KEDDAH
KEDDAHS
KEDGE
KEDGED
KEDGER
KEDGEREE
KEDGEREES
KEDGERS
KEDGES
KEDGIER
KEDGIEST
KEDGING
KEDGY
KEDS
KEECH
KEECHES
KEEK
KEEKED
KEEKER
KEEKERS
KEEKING
KEEKS
KEEL
KEELAGE
KEELAGES
KEELBOAT
KEELBOATS
KEELED
KEELER
KEELERS
KEELHAUL
KEELHAULED
KEELHAULING
KEELHAULINGS
KEELHAULS
KEELIE
KEELIES
KEELING
KEELINGS
KEELIVINE
KEELIVINES
KEELMAN
KEELMEN
KEELS
KEELSON
KEELSONS
KEELYVINE
KEELYVINES
KEEN
KEENED
KEENER
KEENERS
KEENEST
KEENING
KEENINGS
KEENLY
KEENNESS
KEENNESSES
KEENS
KEEP
KEEPER
KEEPERS
KEEPING

KEEPINGS
KEEPNET
KEEPNETS
KEEPS
KEEPSAKE
KEEPSAKES
KEEPSAKY
KEESHOND
KEESHONDS
KEEVE
KEEVES
KEF
KEFFEL
KEFFELS
KEFFIYEH
KEFFIYEHS
KEFIR
KEFIRS
KEFS
KEFUFFLE
KEFUFFLED
KEFUFFLES
KEFUFFLING
KEG
KEGS
KEIGHT
KEIR
KEIRS
KEITLOA
KEITLOAS
KEKSYE
KEKSYES
KELIM
KELIMS
KELL
KELLAUT
KELLAUTS
KELLIES
KELLS
KELLY
KELOID
KELOIDAL
KELOIDS
KELP
KELPER
KELPERS
KELPIE
KELPIES
KELPS
KELPY
KELSON
KELSONS
KELT
KELTER
KELTERS
KELTIE
KELTIES
KELTS
KELTY
KELVIN
KELVINS
KEMB
KEMBED
KEMBING
KEMBO
KEMBOED
KEMBOING
KEMBOS
KEMBS
KEMP

KEMPED
KEMPER
KEMPERS
KEMPING
KEMPINGS
KEMPLE
KEMPLES
KEMPS
KEMPT
KEN
KENAF
KENAFS
KENDO
KENDOS
KENNED
KENNEL
KENNELLED
KENNELLING
KENNELS
KENNER
KENNERS
KENNET
KENNETS
KENNING
KENNINGS
KENOSES
KENOSIS
KENOTIC
KENS
KENSPECK
KENT
KENTED
KENTING
KENTLEDGE
KENTLEDGES
KENTS
KEP
KEPHALIC
KEPHALICS
KEPHIR
KEPHIRS
KEPI
KEPIS
KEPPING
KEPPIT
KEPS
KEPT
KERAMIC
KERAMICS
KERATIN
KERATINS
KERATITIS
KERATITISES
KERATOID
KERATOSE
KERATOSES
KERATOSIS
KERB
KERBS
KERBSIDE
KERBSIDES
KERBSTONE
KERBSTONES
KERCHIEF
KERCHIEFED
KERCHIEFING
KERCHIEFS
KERF
KERFS
KERFUFFLE

KERFUFFLED
KERFUFFLES
KERFUFFLING
KERMES
KERMESITE
KERMESITES
KERMESS
KERMESSE
KERMESSES
KERMIS
KERMISES
KERN
KERNE
KERNED
KERNEL
KERNELLED
KERNELLING
KERNELLY
KERNELS
KERNES
KERNING
KERNISH
KERNITE
KERNITES
KERNS
KEROGEN
KEROGENS
KEROSENE
KEROSENES
KEROSINE
KEROSINES
KERRIA
KERRIAS
KERSEY
KERSEYS
KERVE
KERVED
KERVES
KERVING
KERYGMA
KERYGMAS
KESAR
KESARS
KESH
KESHES
KEST
KESTING
KESTREL
KESTRELS
KESTS
KET
KETA
KETAS
KETCH
KETCHES
KETCHING
KETCHUP
KETCHUPS
KETONE
KETONES
KETOSE
KETOSES
KETOSIS
KETS
KETTLE
KETTLEFUL
KETTLEFULS
KETTLES
KEVEL
KEVELS

KEX
KEXES
KEY
KEYBOARD
KEYBOARDED
KEYBOARDING
KEYBOARDS
KEYBUGLE
KEYBUGLES
KEYED
KEYHOLE
KEYHOLES
KEYING
KEYLESS
KEYNOTE
KEYNOTED
KEYNOTES
KEYNOTING
KEYS
KEYSTONE
KEYSTONED
KEYSTONES
KEYSTONING
KEYSTROKE
KEYSTROKES
KGOTLA
KGOTLAS
KHADDAR
KHADDARS
KHADI
KHADIS
KHAKI
KHAKIS
KHALAT
KHALATS
KHALIF
KHALIFA
KHALIFAH
KHALIFAHS
KHALIFAS
KHALIFAT
KHALIFATE
KHALIFATES
KHALIFATS
KHALIFS
KHAMSIN
KHAMSINS
KHAN
KHANATE
KHANATES
KHANGA
KHANGAS
KHANJAR
KHANJARS
KHANS
KHANSAMA
KHANSAMAH
KHANSAMAHS
KHANSAMAS
KHANUM
KHANUMS
KHARIF
KHARIFS
KHAT
KHATS
KHAYA
KHAYAS
KHEDA
KHEDAS
KHEDIVA

KHEDIVAL
KHEDIVAS
KHEDIVATE
KHEDIVATES
KHEDIVE
KHEDIVES
KHEDIVIAL
KHILAFAT
KHILAFATS
KHILAT
KHILATS
KHILIM
KHILIMS
KHODJA
KHODJAS
KHOJA
KHOJAS
KHOR
KHORS
KHOTBAH
KHOTBAHS
KHOTBEH
KHOTBEHS
KHUD
KHUDS
KHURTA
KHURTAS
KHUSKHUS
KHUSKHUSES
KHUTBAH
KHUTBAHS
KIANG
KIANGS
KIAUGH
KIAUGHS
KIBBLE
KIBBLED
KIBBLES
KIBBLING
KIBBUTZ
KIBBUTZIM
KIBE
KIBES
KIBITKA
KIBITKAS
KIBITZ
KIBITZED
KIBITZER
KIBITZERS
KIBITZES
KIBITZING
KIBLAH
KIBLAHS
KIBOSH
KIBOSHED
KIBOSHES
KIBOSHING
KICK
KICKABLE
KICKBACK
KICKBACKS
KICKDOWN
KICKDOWNS
KICKED
KICKER
KICKERS
KICKING
KICKS
KICKSHAW
KICKSHAWS

KICKSHAWSES
KID
KIDDED
KIDDER
KIDDERS
KIDDIED
KIDDIER
KIDDIERS
KIDDIES
KIDDING
KIDDLE
KIDDLES
KIDDUSH
KIDDUSHES
KIDDY
KIDDYING
KIDDYWINK
KIDDYWINKS
KIDEL
KIDELS
KIDGE
KIDLING
KIDLINGS
KIDNAP
KIDNAPPED
KIDNAPPER
KIDNAPPERS
KIDNAPPING
KIDNAPS
KIDNEY
KIDNEYS
KIDOLOGIES
KIDOLOGY
KIDS
KIER
KIERIE
KIERIES
KIERS
KIESERITE
KIESERITES
KIEVE
KIEVES
KIF
KIFS
KIGHT
KIGHTS
KIKE
KIKES
KIKUMON
KIKUMONS
KIKUYU
KIKUYUS
KILD
KILDERKIN
KILDERKINS
KILERG
KILERGS
KILEY
KILEYS
KILIM
KILIMS
KILL
KILLADAR
KILLADARS
KILLAS
KILLASES
KILLCOW
KILLCOWS
KILLCROP
KILLCROPS

KILLDEE
KILLDEER
KILLDEERS
KILLDEES
KILLED
KILLER
KILLERS
KILLICK
KILLICKS
KILLING
KILLINGS
KILLJOY
KILLJOYS
KILLOCK
KILLOCKS
KILLOGIE
KILLOGIES
KILLS
KILLUT
KILLUTS
KILN
KILNED
KILNING
KILNS
KILO
KILOBAR
KILOBARS
KILOBIT
KILOBITS
KILOBYTE
KILOBYTES
KILOGRAM
KILOGRAMS
KILOHERTZ
KILOHERTZES
KILOJOULE
KILOJOULES
KILOMETRE
KILOMETRES
KILOS
KILOTON
KILOTONNE
KILOTONNES
KILOTONS
KILOVOLT
KILOVOLTS
KILOWATT
KILOWATTS
KILP
KILPS
KILT
KILTED
KILTER
KILTERS
KILTIE
KILTIES
KILTING
KILTS
KILTY
KIMBO
KIMBOED
KIMBOING
KIMBOS
KIMMER
KIMMERS
KIMONO
KIMONOS
KIN
KINA
KINAKINA

KINAKINAS
KINAS
KINASE
KINASES
KINCHIN
KINCHINS
KINCOB
KINCOBS
KIND
KINDA
KINDED
KINDER
KINDEST
KINDING
KINDLE
KINDLED
KINDLER
KINDLERS
KINDLES
KINDLESS
KINDLIER
KINDLIEST
KINDLILY
KINDLING
KINDLINGS
KINDLY
KINDNESS
KINDNESSES
KINDRED
KINDREDS
KINDS
KINE
KINEMA
KINEMAS
KINEMATIC
KINEMATICS
KINESES
KINESICS
KINESIS
KINETIC
KINETICAL
KINETICS
KINFOLK
KINFOLKS
KING
KINGCRAFT
KINGCRAFTS
KINGCUP
KINGCUPS
KINGDOM
KINGDOMED
KINGDOMS
KINGED
KINGFISH
KINGFISHES
KINGHOOD
KINGHOODS
KINGING
KINGLE
KINGLES
KINGLESS
KINGLET
KINGLETS
KINGLIER
KINGLIEST
KINGLING
KINGLINGS
KINGLY
KINGMAKER
KINGMAKERS

KINGPOST
KINGPOSTS
KINGS
KINGSHIP
KINGSHIPS
KINGWOOD
KINGWOODS
KININ
KININS
KINK
KINKAJOU
KINKAJOUS
KINKED
KINKIER
KINKIEST
KINKING
KINKLE
KINKLES
KINKS
KINKY
KINLESS
KINO
KINONE
KINONES
KINOS
KINRED
KINREDS
KINS
KINSFOLK
KINSFOLKS
KINSHIP
KINSHIPS
KINSMAN
KINSMEN
KINSWOMAN
KINSWOMEN
KINTLEDGE
KINTLEDGES
KIOSK
KIOSKS
KIP
KIPE
KIPES
KIPP
KIPPAGE
KIPPAGES
KIPPED
KIPPER
KIPPERED
KIPPERER
KIPPERERS
KIPPERING
KIPPERS
KIPPING
KIPPS
KIPS
KIR
KIRBEH
KIRBEHS
KIRBIGRIP
KIRBIGRIPS
KIRI
KIRIMON
KIRIMONS
KIRIS
KIRK
KIRKED
KIRKING
KIRKINGS
KIRKS

KIRKTON
KIRKTONS
KIRKTOWN
KIRKTOWNS
KIRKWARD
KIRKYAIRD
KIRKYAIRDS
KIRKYARD
KIRKYARDS
KIRMESS
KIRMESSES
KIRN
KIRNS
KIRPAN
KIRPANS
KIRS
KIRSCH
KIRSCHES
KIRTLE
KIRTLED
KIRTLES
KISAN
KISANS
KISH
KISHES
KISMET
KISMETS
KISS
KISSABLE
KISSED
KISSER
KISSERS
KISSES
KISSING
KIST
KISTED
KISTING
KISTS
KISTVAEN
KISTVAENS
KIT
KITCHEN
KITCHENED
KITCHENER
KITCHENERS
KITCHENING
KITCHENS
KITE
KITED
KITES
KITH
KITHARA
KITHARAS
KITHE
KITHED
KITHES
KITHING
KITHS
KITING
KITLING
KITLINGS
KITS
KITSCH
KITSCHES
KITSCHIER
KITSCHIEST
KITSCHILY
KITSCHY
KITTED
KITTEN

KITTENED
KITTENING
KITTENISH
KITTENS
KITTENY
KITTIES
KITTING
KITTIWAKE
KITTIWAKES
KITTLE
KITTLED
KITTLER
KITTLES
KITTLEST
KITTLIER
KITTLIEST
KITTLING
KITTLY
KITTUL
KITTULS
KITTY
KIWI
KIWIS
KLANG
KLANGS
KLAVIER
KLAVIERS
KLAXON
KLAXONS
KLENDUSIC
KLEPHT
KLEPHTIC
KLEPHTISM
KLEPHTISMS
KLEPHTS
KLINKER
KLINKERS
KLINOSTAT
KLINOSTATS
KLIPDAS
KLIPDASES
KLONDIKE
KLONDIKED
KLONDIKES
KLONDIKING
KLONDYKE
KLONDYKED
KLONDYKER
KLONDYKERS
KLONDYKES
KLONDYKING
KLOOF
KLOOFS
KLUDGE
KLUDGES
KLUTZ
KLUTZES
KLYSTRON
KLYSTRONS
KNACK
KNACKER
KNACKERED
KNACKERIES
KNACKERING
KNACKERS
KNACKERY
KNACKIER
KNACKIEST
KNACKISH
KNACKS

KNACKY
KNAG
KNAGGIER
KNAGGIEST
KNAGGY
KNAGS
KNAP
KNAPPED
KNAPPER
KNAPPERS
KNAPPING
KNAPPLE
KNAPPLED
KNAPPLES
KNAPPLING
KNAPS
KNAPSACK
KNAPSACKS
KNAPSCAL
KNAPSCALS
KNAPSCULL
KNAPSCULLS
KNAPSKULL
KNAPSKULLS
KNAPWEED
KNAPWEEDS
KNAR
KNARL
KNARLS
KNARRED
KNARRING
KNARS
KNAVE
KNAVERIES
KNAVERY
KNAVES
KNAVESHIP
KNAVESHIPS
KNAVISH
KNAVISHLY
KNAWEL
KNAWELS
KNEAD
KNEADED
KNEADER
KNEADERS
KNEADING
KNEADS
KNEE
KNEED
KNEEHOLE
KNEEHOLES
KNEEING
KNEEL
KNEELED
KNEELER
KNEELERS
KNEELING
KNEELS
KNEES
KNELL
KNELLED
KNELLING
KNELLS
KNELT
KNEVELL
KNEVELLED
KNEVELLING
KNEVELLS
KNEW

KNICKER
KNICKERED
KNICKERS
KNICKS
KNIFE
KNIFED
KNIFELESS
KNIFES
KNIFING
KNIFINGS
KNIGHT
KNIGHTAGE
KNIGHTAGES
KNIGHTED
KNIGHTING
KNIGHTLIER
KNIGHTLIEST
KNIGHTLY
KNIGHTS
KNISH
KNISHES
KNIT
KNITCH
KNITCHES
KNITS
KNITTED
KNITTER
KNITTERS
KNITTING
KNITTINGS
KNITTLE
KNITTLES
KNITWEAR
KNITWEARS
KNIVE
KNIVED
KNIVES
KNIVING
KNOB
KNOBBED
KNOBBER
KNOBBERS
KNOBBIER
KNOBBIEST
KNOBBLE
KNOBBLED
KNOBBLES
KNOBBLIER
KNOBBLIEST
KNOBBLING
KNOBBLY
KNOBBY
KNOBS
KNOCK
KNOCKED
KNOCKER
KNOCKERS
KNOCKING
KNOCKINGS
KNOCKOUT
KNOCKOUTS
KNOCKS
KNOLL
KNOLLED
KNOLLING
KNOLLS
KNOP
KNOPS
KNOSP
KNOSPS

KNOT
KNOTGRASS
KNOTGRASSES
KNOTLESS
KNOTS
KNOTTED
KNOTTER
KNOTTERS
KNOTTIER
KNOTTIEST
KNOTTING
KNOTTINGS
KNOTTY
KNOTWEED
KNOTWEEDS
KNOTWORK
KNOTWORKS
KNOUT
KNOUTED
KNOUTING
KNOUTS
KNOW
KNOWABLE
KNOWE
KNOWER
KNOWERS
KNOWES
KNOWING
KNOWINGLY
KNOWLEDGE
KNOWLEDGED
KNOWLEDGES
KNOWLEDGING
KNOWN
KNOWS
KNUB
KNUBBIER
KNUBBIEST
KNUBBLE
KNUBBLED
KNUBBLES
KNUBBLIER
KNUBBLIEST
KNUBBLING
KNUBBLY
KNUBBY
KNUBS
KNUCKLE
KNUCKLED
KNUCKLES
KNUCKLING
KNUR
KNURL
KNURLED
KNURLIER
KNURLIEST
KNURLING
KNURLINGS
KNURLS
KNURLY
KNURR
KNURRS
KNURS
KNUT
KNUTS
KO
KOA
KOALA
KOALAS
KOAN

KOANS
KOAS
KOB
KOBAN
KOBANG
KOBANGS
KOBANS
KOBOLD
KOBOLDS
KOBS
KOFF
KOFFS
KOFTA
KOFTAS
KOFTGAR
KOFTGARI
KOFTGARIS
KOFTGARS
KOFTWORK
KOFTWORKS
KOHL
KOHLRABI
KOHLRABIS
KOHLS
KOINE
KOINES
KOKRA
KOKRAS
KOKUM
KOKUMS
KOLA
KOLAS
KOLINSKIES
KOLINSKY
KOLKHOZ
KOLKHOZES
KOLO
KOLOS
KOMISSAR
KOMISSARS
KOMITAJI
KOMITAJIS
KON
KOND
KONFYT
KONFYTS
KONIMETER
KONIMETERS
KONIOLOGIES
KONIOLOGY
KONISCOPE
KONISCOPES
KONK
KONKED
KONKING
KONKS
KONNING
KONS
KOODOO
KOODOOS
KOOK
KOOKED
KOOKIE
KOOKIER
KOOKIEST
KOOKING
KOOKS
KOOKY
KOOLAH
KOOLAHS

KOP
KOPECK
KOPECKS
KOPJE
KOPJES
KOPPA
KOPPAS
KOPPIE
KOPPIES
KOPS
KORA
KORAS
KORFBALL
KORFBALLS
KORKIR
KORKIRS
KORMA
KORMAS
KORORA
KORORAS
KORUNA
KORUNAS
KOS
KOSES
KOSHER
KOSHERS
KOSMOS
KOSMOSES
KOSS
KOSSES
KOTO
KOTOS
KOTOW
KOTOWED
KOTOWING
KOTOWS
KOTTABOS
KOTTABOSES
KOTWAL
KOTWALS
KOULAN
KOULANS
KOUMISS
KOUMISSES
KOURBASH
KOURBASHED
KOURBASHES
KOURBASHING
KOUSKOUS
KOUSKOUSES
KOW
KOWHAI
KOWHAIS
KOWS
KOWTOW
KOWTOWED
KOWTOWING
KOWTOWS
KRAAL
KRAALED
KRAALING
KRAALS
KRAFT
KRAFTS
KRAIT
KRAITS
KRAKEN
KRAKENS
KRAKOWIAK
KRAKOWIAKS

KRAMERIA
KRAMERIAS
KRANG
KRANGS
KRANS
KRANSES
KRANTZ
KRANTZES
KRANZ
KRANZES
KRAUT
KRAUTS
KREASOTE
KREASOTED
KREASOTES
KREASOTING
KREATINE
KREATINES
KREESE
KREESED
KREESES
KREESING
KREMLIN
KREMLINS
KRENG
KRENGS
KREOSOTE
KREOSOTED
KREOSOTES
KREOSOTING
KREPLACH
KREUTZER
KREUTZERS
KRILL
KRILLS
KRIMMER
KRIMMERS
KRIS
KRISED
KRISES
KRISING
KROMESKIES
KROMESKY
KRONA
KRONE
KRONEN
KRONER
KRONOR
KRONUR
KRUMHORN
KRUMHORNS
KRUMMHORN
KRUMMHORNS
KRYOMETER
KRYOMETERS
KRYPSES
KRYPSIS
KRYPTON
KRYPTONS
KSAR
KSARS
KUCHCHA
KUDOS
KUDOSES
KUDU
KUDUS
KUDZU
KUDZUS
KUFFIAH
KUFFIAHS

KUFFIEH
KUFFIEHS
KUFFIYEH
KUFFIYEHS
KUFIAH
KUFIAHS
KUFIYA
KUFIYAH
KUFIYAHS
KUFIYAS
KUKRI
KUKRIS
KUKU
KUKUS
KULAK
KULAKS
KULAN
KULANS
KUMARA
KUMARAS
KUMARI
KUMARIS
KUMISS
KUMISSES
KÜMMEL
KÜMMELS
KUMQUAT
KUMQUATS
KUNKAR
KUNKARS
KUNKUR
KUNKURS
KURBASH
KURBASHED
KURBASHES
KURBASHING
KURGAN
KURGANS
KURRAJONG
KURRAJONGS
KURRE
KURRES
KURSAAL
KURSAALS
KURTA
KURTAS
KURTOSES
KURTOSIS
KURVEY
KURVEYED
KURVEYING
KURVEYOR
KURVEYORS
KURVEYS
KUTCH
KUTCHA
KUTCHES
KVASS
KVASSES
KVETCH
KVETCHED
KVETCHER
KVETCHERS
KVETCHES
KVETCHING
KWACHA
KWACHAS
KWELA
KWELAS
KY

KYANG
KYANGS
KYANISE
KYANISED
KYANISES
KYANISING
KYANITE
KYANITES
KYANIZE
KYANIZED
KYANIZES
KYANIZING

KYAT
KYATS
KYBOSH
KYBOSHED
KYBOSHES
KYBOSHING
KYDST
KYE
KYLE
KYLES
KYLEY
KYLEYS

KYLICES
KYLIE
KYLIES
KYLIN
KYLINS
KYLIX
KYLLOSES
KYLLOSIS
KYLOE
KYLOES
KYMOGRAM
KYMOGRAMS

KYMOGRAPH
KYMOGRAPHS
KYND
KYNDE
KYNDED
KYNDES
KYNDING
KYNDS
KYNE
KYPHOSES
KYPHOSIS
KYPHOTIC

KYRIELLE
KYRIELLES
KYTE
KYTES
KYTHE
KYTHED
KYTHES
KYTHING

# L

LA
LAAGER
LAAGERED
LAAGERING
LAAGERS
LAB
LABARA
LABARUM
LABARUMS
LABDA
LABDACISM
LABDACISMS
LABDANUM
LABDANUMS
LABDAS
LABEL
LABELLA
LABELLED
LABELLING
LABELLOID
LABELLUM
LABELS
LABIA
LABIAL
LABIALISE
LABIALISED
LABIALISES
LABIALISING
LABIALISM
LABIALISMS
LABIALIZE
LABIALIZED
LABIALIZES
LABIALIZING
LABIALLY
LABIALS
LABIATE
LABIATES
LABILE
LABILITIES
LABILITY
LABIS
LABISES
LABIUM
LABLAB
LABLABS
LABOR
LABORED
LABORING
LABORIOUS
LABORS
LABOUR
LABOURED
LABOURER
LABOURERS
LABOURING
LABOURISM
LABOURISMS
LABOURIST
LABOURISTS
LABOURS
LABRA
LABRET

LABRETS
LABRID
LABRIDS
LABROID
LABROIDS
LABROSE
LABRUM
LABRYS
LABRYSES
LABS
LABURNUM
LABURNUMS
LABYRINTH
LABYRINTHS
LAC
LACCOLITE
LACCOLITES
LACCOLITH
LACCOLITHS
LACE
LACEBARK
LACEBARKS
LACED
LACERABLE
LACERANT
LACERATE
LACERATED
LACERATES
LACERATING
LACERTIAN
LACERTINE
LACES
LACET
LACETS
LACEY
LACHES
LACHESES
LACHRYMAL
LACHRYMALS
LACIER
LACIEST
LACING
LACINGS
LACINIA
LACINIAE
LACINIATE
LACK
LACKADAY
LACKED
LACKER
LACKERED
LACKERING
LACKERS
LACKEY
LACKEYED
LACKEYING
LACKEYS
LACKING
LACKLAND
LACKLANDS
LACKS
LACMUS
LACMUSES

LACONIC
LACONICAL
LACONISM
LACONISMS
LACQUER
LACQUERED
LACQUERER
LACQUERERS
LACQUERING
LACQUERINGS
LACQUERS
LACQUEY
LACQUEYED
LACQUEYING
LACQUEYS
LACRIMAL
LACRIMALS
LACROSSE
LACROSSES
LACRYMAL
LACRYMALS
LACS
LACTASE
LACTASES
LACTATE
LACTATED
LACTATES
LACTATING
LACTATION
LACTATIONS
LACTEAL
LACTEALS
LACTEOUS
LACTIC
LACTIFIC
LACTONE
LACTONES
LACTOSE
LACTOSES
LACUNA
LACUNAE
LACUNAL
LACUNAR
LACUNARIA
LACUNARS
LACUNARY
LACUNATE
LACUNOSE
LACY
LAD
LADANUM
LADANUMS
LADDER
LADDERED
LADDERING
LADDERS
LADDERY
LADDIE
LADDIES
LADE
LADED
LADEN
LADES

LADIES
LADIFIED
LADIFIES
LADIFY
LADIFYING
LADING
LADINGS
LADLE
LADLED
LADLEFUL
LADLEFULS
LADLES
LADLING
LADRONE
LADRONES
LADS
LADY
LADYBIRD
LADYBIRDS
LADYBUG
LADYBUGS
LADYCOW
LADYCOWS
LADYFIED
LADYFIES
LADYFLIES
LADYFLY
LADYFY
LADYFYING
LADYHOOD
LADYHOODS
LADYISH
LADYISM
LADYISMS
LADYKIN
LADYKINS
LADYLIKE
LADYSHIP
LADYSHIPS
LAER
LAERS
LAESIE
LAETARE
LAETARES
LAEVIGATE
LAEVIGATED
LAEVIGATES
LAEVIGATING
LAEVULOSE
LAEVULOSES
LAG
LAGAN
LAGANS
LAGENA
LAGENAS
LAGER
LAGERS
LAGGARD
LAGGARDS
LAGGED
LAGGEN
LAGGENS
LAGGER

LAGGERS
LAGGIN
LAGGING
LAGGINGLY
LAGGINGS
LAGGINS
LAGNIAPPE
LAGNIAPPES
LAGOMORPH
LAGOMORPHS
LAGOON
LAGOONAL
LAGOONS
LAGRIMOSO
LAGS
LAGUNE
LAGUNES
LAH
LAHAR
LAHARS
LAHS
LAIC
LAICAL
LAICISE
LAICISED
LAICISES
LAICISING
LAICITIES
LAICITY
LAICIZE
LAICIZED
LAICIZES
LAICIZING
LAICS
LAID
LAIDED
LAIDING
LAIDLY
LAIDS
LAIGH
LAIGHER
LAIGHEST
LAIGHS
LAIK
LAIKA
LAIKAS
LAIKED
LAIKING
LAIKS
LAIN
LAIR
LAIRAGE
LAIRAGES
LAIRD
LAIRDS
LAIRDSHIP
LAIRDSHIPS
LAIRED
LAIRIER
LAIRIEST
LAIRING
LAIRISE
LAIRISED

LAIRISES
LAIRISING
LAIRIZE
LAIRIZED
LAIRIZES
LAIRIZING
LAIRS
LAIRY
LAISSE
LAISSES
LAITANCE
LAITANCES
LAITH
LAITIES
LAITY
LAKE
LAKED
LAKELET
LAKELETS
LAKER
LAKERS
LAKES
LAKH
LAKHS
LAKIER
LAKIEST
LAKIN
LAKING
LAKINS
LAKISH
LAKY
LALANG
LALANGS
LALDIE
LALDIES
LALDY
LALLAN
LALLANS
LALLATION
LALLATIONS
LALLING
LALLINGS
LALLYGAG
LALLYGAGGED
LALLYGAGGING
LALLYGAGS
LAM
LAMA
LAMAISTIC
LAMANTIN
LAMANTINS
LAMAS
LAMASERAI
LAMASERAIS
LAMASERIES
LAMASERY
LAMB
LAMBAST
LAMBASTE
LAMBASTED
LAMBASTES
LAMBASTING
LAMBASTS
LAMBDA
LAMBDAS
LAMBDOID
LAMBED
LAMBENCIES
LAMBENCY
LAMBENT

LAMBENTLY
LAMBER
LAMBERS
LAMBERT
LAMBERTS
LAMBIE
LAMBIES
LAMBING
LAMBITIVE
LAMBITIVES
LAMBKIN
LAMBKINS
LAMBLING
LAMBLINGS
LAMBOYS
LAMBS
LAMBSKIN
LAMBSKINS
LAME
LAMED
LAMELLA
LAMELLAE
LAMELLAR
LAMELLATE
LAMELLOID
LAMELLOSE
LAMELY
LAMENESS
LAMENESSES
LAMENT
LAMENTED
LAMENTING
LAMENTINGS
LAMENTS
LAMER
LAMES
LAMEST
LAMETER
LAMETERS
LAMIA
LAMIAE
LAMIAS
LAMIGER
LAMIGERS
LAMINA
LAMINABLE
LAMINAE
LAMINAR
LAMINARY
LAMINATE
LAMINATED
LAMINATES
LAMINATING
LAMINATOR
LAMINATORS
LAMING
LAMINGTON
LAMINGTONS
LAMINITIS
LAMINITISES
LAMISH
LAMITER
LAMITERS
LAMMED
LAMMER
LAMMERS
LAMMIE
LAMMIES
LAMMIGER
LAMMIGERS

LAMMING
LAMMINGS
LAMMY
LAMP
LAMPAD
LAMPADARIES
LAMPADARY
LAMPADIST
LAMPADISTS
LAMPADS
LAMPAS
LAMPASES
LAMPASSE
LAMPASSES
LAMPED
LAMPERN
LAMPERNS
LAMPHOLE
LAMPHOLES
LAMPING
LAMPION
LAMPIONS
LAMPLIGHT
LAMPLIGHTS
LAMPOON
LAMPOONED
LAMPOONER
LAMPOONERS
LAMPOONING
LAMPOONS
LAMPPOST
LAMPPOSTS
LAMPREY
LAMPREYS
LAMPS
LAMPSHADE
LAMPSHADES
LAMPUKA
LAMPUKAS
LAMPUKI
LAMPUKIS
LAMS
LANA
LANAS
LANATE
LANCE
LANCED
LANCEGAY
LANCEGAYS
LANCELET
LANCELETS
LANCEOLAR
LANCER
LANCERS
LANCES
LANCET
LANCETED
LANCETS
LANCH
LANCHED
LANCHES
LANCHING
LANCIFORM
LANCINATE
LANCINATED
LANCINATES
LANCINATING
LANCING
LAND
LANDAMMAN

LANDAMMANS
LANDAU
LANDAULET
LANDAULETS
LANDAUS
LANDDAMNE
LANDDAMNED
LANDDAMNES
LANDDAMNING
LANDDROS
LANDDROSES
LANDDROST
LANDDROSTS
LANDE
LANDED
LANDER
LANDERS
LANDES
LANDFALL
LANDFALLS
LANDFILL
LANDFILLS
LANDFORCE
LANDFORCES
LANDFORM
LANDFORMS
LANDGRAVE
LANDGRAVES
LANDING
LANDINGS
LANDLADIES
LANDLADY
LÄNDLER
LÄNDLERS
LANDLESS
LANDLOPER
LANDLOPERS
LANDLORD
LANDLORDS
LANDMAN
LANDMARK
LANDMARKS
LANDMASS
LANDMASSES
LANDMEN
LANDOWNER
LANDOWNERS
LANDRACE
LANDRACES
LANDRAIL
LANDRAILS
LANDS
LANDSCAPE
LANDSCAPED
LANDSCAPES
LANDSCAPING
LANDSKIP
LANDSKIPS
LANDSLIDE
LANDSLIDES
LANDSLIP
LANDSLIPS
LANDSMAN
LANDSMEN
LANDWARD
LANDWARDS
LANDWIND
LANDWINDS
LANE
LANES

LANEWAY
LANEWAYS
LANG
LANGAHA
LANGAHAS
LANGER
LANGEST
LANGLAUF
LANGLAUFS
LANGOUSTE
LANGOUSTES
LANGRAGE
LANGRAGES
LANGREL
LANGRELS
LANGRIDGE
LANGRIDGES
LANGSPEL
LANGSPELS
LANGSPIEL
LANGSPIELS
LANGUAGE
LANGUAGED
LANGUAGES
LANGUAGING
LANGUE
LANGUED
LANGUES
LANGUET
LANGUETS
LANGUETTE
LANGUETTES
LANGUID
LANGUIDLY
LANGUISH
LANGUISHED
LANGUISHES
LANGUISHING
LANGUISHINGS
LANGUOR
LANGUORS
LANGUR
LANGURS
LANIARD
LANIARDS
LANIARY
LANK
LANKED
LANKER
LANKEST
LANKIER
LANKIEST
LANKINESS
LANKINESSES
LANKING
LANKLY
LANKNESS
LANKNESSES
LANKS
LANKY
LANNER
LANNERET
LANNERETS
LANNERS
LANOLIN
LANOLINE
LANOLINES
LANOLINS
LANOSE
LANT

LANTANA
LANTANAS
LANTERLOO
LANTERLOOS
LANTERN
LANTERNED
LANTERNING
LANTERNS
LANTHANUM
LANTHANUMS
LANTHORN
LANTHORNS
LANTS
LANTSKIP
LANTSKIPS
LANUGO
LANUGOS
LANX
LANYARD
LANYARDS
LAP
LAPDOG
LAPDOGS
LAPEL
LAPELLED
LAPELS
LAPFUL
LAPFULS
LAPIDARIES
LAPIDARY
LAPIDATE
LAPIDATED
LAPIDATES
LAPIDATING
LAPIDEOUS
LAPIDIFIC
LAPIDIFIED
LAPIDIFIES
LAPIDIFY
LAPIDIFYING
LAPILLI
LAPIS
LAPISES
LAPJE
LAPJES
LAPPED
LAPPEL
LAPPELS
LAPPER
LAPPERED
LAPPERING
LAPPERS
LAPPET
LAPPETED
LAPPETS
LAPPIE
LAPPIES
LAPPING
LAPPINGS
LAPS
LAPSABLE
LAPSANG
LAPSANGS
LAPSE
LAPSED
LAPSES
LAPSING
LAPSTONE
LAPSTONES
LAPSTREAK

LAPSTREAKS
LAPSUS
LAPSUSES
LAPTOP
LAPTOPS
LAPWING
LAPWINGS
LAPWORK
LAPWORKS
LAQUEARIA
LAR
LARBOARD
LARBOARDS
LARCENER
LARCENERS
LARCENIES
LARCENIST
LARCENISTS
LARCENOUS
LARCENY
LARCH
LARCHEN
LARCHES
LARD
LARDALITE
LARDALITES
LARDED
LARDER
LARDERER
LARDERERS
LARDERS
LARDIER
LARDIEST
LARDING
LARDON
LARDONS
LARDOON
LARDOONS
LARDS
LARDY
LARE
LARES
LARGE
LARGELY
LARGEN
LARGENED
LARGENESS
LARGENESSES
LARGENING
LARGENS
LARGER
LARGES
LARGESS
LARGESSE
LARGESSES
LARGEST
LARGHETTO
LARGHETTOS
LARGISH
LARGITION
LARGITIONS
LARGO
LARGOS
LARIAT
LARIATS
LARINE
LARK
LARKED
LARKER
LARKERS

LARKIER
LARKIEST
LARKINESS
LARKINESSES
LARKING
LARKISH
LARKS
LARKSPUR
LARKSPURS
LARKY
LARMIER
LARMIERS
LARN
LARNAKES
LARNAX
LARNED
LARNING
LARNS
LAROID
LARRIGAN
LARRIGANS
LARRIKIN
LARRIKINS
LARRUP
LARRUPED
LARRUPING
LARRUPS
LARUM
LARUMS
LARVA
LARVAE
LARVAL
LARVATE
LARVATED
LARVICIDE
LARVICIDES
LARVIFORM
LARVIKITE
LARVIKITES
LARYNGAL
LARYNGEAL
LARYNGES
LARYNX
LARYNXES
LAS
LASAGNA
LASAGNAS
LASAGNE
LASAGNES
LASCAR
LASCARS
LASE
LASED
LASER
LASERS
LASERWORT
LASERWORTS
LASES
LASH
LASHED
LASHER
LASHERS
LASHES
LASHING
LASHINGS
LASHKAR
LASHKARS
LASING
LASINGS
LASKET

LASKETS
LASQUE
LASQUES
LASS
LASSES
LASSIE
LASSIES
LASSITUDE
LASSITUDES
LASSLORN
LASSO
LASSOCK
LASSOCKS
LASSOED
LASSOES
LASSOING
LASSOS
LASSU
LASSUS
LAST
LASTAGE
LASTAGES
LASTED
LASTER
LASTERS
LASTING
LASTINGLY
LASTINGS
LASTLY
LASTS
LAT
LATCH
LATCHED
LATCHES
LATCHET
LATCHETS
LATCHING
LATCHKEY
LATCHKEYS
LATE
LATED
LATEEN
LATELY
LATEN
LATENCE
LATENCES
LATENCIES
LATENCY
LATENED
LATENESS
LATENESSES
LATENING
LATENS
LATENT
LATENTLY
LATER
LATERAL
LATERALLY
LATERALS
LATERITE
LATERITES
LATESCENT
LATEST
LATESTS
LATEWAKE
LATEWAKES
LATEX
LATEXES
LATH
LATHE

LATHED
LATHEE
LATHEES
LATHEN
LATHER
LATHERED
LATHERING
LATHERS
LATHERY
LATHES
LATHI
LATHIER
LATHIEST
LATHING
LATHINGS
LATHIS
LATHS
LATHY
LATHYRISM
LATHYRISMS
LATHYRUS
LATHYRUSES
LATICES
LATICLAVE
LATICLAVES
LATIFONDI
LATISH
LATITANCIES
LATITANCY
LATITANT
LATITAT
LATITATS
LATITUDE
LATITUDES
LATKE
LATKES
LATRANT
LATRATION
LATRATIONS
LATRIA
LATRIAS
LATRINE
LATRINES
LATROCINIES
LATROCINY
LATRON
LATRONS
LATS
LATTEN
LATTENS
LATTER
LATTERLY
LATTICE
LATTICED
LATTICES
LATTICING
LATTICINI
LATTICINO
LAUCH
LAUCHING
LAUCHS
LAUD
LAUDABLE
LAUDABLY
LAUDANUM
LAUDANUMS
LAUDATION
LAUDATIONS
LAUDATIVE
LAUDATIVES

| | | | | |
|---|---|---|---|---|
| LAUDATORIES | LAVATERAS | LAX | LEA | LEAKINESSES |
| LAUDATORY | LAVATION | LAXATIVE | LEACH | LEAKING |
| LAUDED | LAVATIONS | LAXATIVES | LEACHATE | LEAKS |
| LAUDER | LAVATORIES | LAXATOR | LEACHATES | LEAKY |
| LAUDERS | LAVATORY | LAXATORS | LEACHED | LEAL |
| LAUDING | LAVE | LAXER | LEACHES | LEALTIES |
| LAUDS | LAVED | LAXES | LEACHIER | LEALTY |
| LAUF | LAVEER | LAXEST | LEACHIEST | LEAM |
| LAUFS | LAVEERED | LAXISM | LEACHING | LEAMED |
| LAUGH | LAVEERING | LAXISMS | LEACHINGS | LEAMING |
| LAUGHABLE | LAVEERS | LAXIST | LEACHOUR | LEAMS |
| LAUGHABLY | LAVEMENT | LAXISTS | LEACHOURS | LEAN |
| LAUGHED | LAVEMENTS | LAXITIES | LEACHY | LEANED |
| LAUGHER | LAVENDER | LAXITY | LEAD | LEANER |
| LAUGHERS | LAVENDERED | LAXLY | LEADED | LEANEST |
| LAUGHFUL | LAVENDERING | LAXNESS | LEADEN | LEANING |
| LAUGHIER | LAVENDERS | LAXNESSES | LEADENED | LEANINGS |
| LAUGHIEST | LAVER | LAY | LEADENING | LEANLY |
| LAUGHING | LAVEROCK | LAYABOUT | LEADENLY | LEANNESS |
| LAUGHINGS | LAVEROCKED | LAYABOUTS | LEADENS | LEANNESSES |
| LAUGHS | LAVEROCKING | LAYAWAY | LEADER | LEANS |
| LAUGHSOME | LAVEROCKS | LAYAWAYS | LEADERS | LEANT |
| LAUGHTER | LAVERS | LAYBACK | LEADIER | LEANY |
| LAUGHTERS | LAVES | LAYBACKED | LEADIEST | LEAP |
| LAUGHY | LAVING | LAYBACKING | LEADING | LEAPED |
| LAUNCE | LAVISH | LAYBACKS | LEADINGS | LEAPER |
| LAUNCED | LAVISHED | LAYER | LEADLESS | LEAPEROUS |
| LAUNCES | LAVISHER | LAYERED | LEADS | LEAPERS |
| LAUNCH | LAVISHES | LAYERING | LEADSMAN | LEAPING |
| LAUNCHED | LAVISHEST | LAYERINGS | LEADSMEN | LEAPOROUS |
| LAUNCHER | LAVISHING | LAYERS | LEADY | LEAPROUS |
| LAUNCHERS | LAVISHLY | LAYETTE | LEAF | LEAPS |
| LAUNCHES | LAVOLT | LAYETTES | LEAFAGE | LEAPT |
| LAUNCHING | LAVOLTA | LAYING | LEAFAGES | LEAR |
| LAUNCING | LAVOLTAS | LAYINGS | LEAFBUD | LEARE |
| LAUND | LAVOLTED | LAYLOCK | LEAFBUDS | LEARED |
| LAUNDER | LAVOLTING | LAYLOCKS | LEAFED | LEARES |
| LAUNDERED | LAVOLTS | LAYMAN | LEAFERIES | LEARIER |
| LAUNDERER | LAVRA | LAYMEN | LEAFERY | LEARIEST |
| LAUNDERERS | LAVRAS | LAYPERSON | LEAFIER | LEARING |
| LAUNDERING | LAVS | LAYPERSONS | LEAFIEST | LEARN |
| LAUNDERS | LAW | LAYS | LEAFINESS | LEARNABLE |
| LAUNDRESS | LAWED | LAYSTALL | LEAFINESSES | LEARNED |
| LAUNDRESSES | LAWER | LAYSTALLS | LEAFING | LEARNEDLY |
| LAUNDRIES | LAWEST | LAYTIME | LEAFLESS | LEARNER |
| LAUNDRY | LAWFUL | LAYTIMES | LEAFLET | LEARNERS |
| LAUNDS | LAWFULLY | LAZAR | LEAFLETED | LEARNING |
| LAURA | LAWING | LAZARET | LEAFLETING | LEARNINGS |
| LAURAS | LAWINGS | LAZARETS | LEAFLETS | LEARNS |
| LAUREATE | LAWK | LAZARETTO | LEAFLETTED | LEARNT |
| LAUREATED | LAWKS | LAZARETTOS | LEAFLETTING | LEARS |
| LAUREATES | LAWLAND | LAZARS | LEAFS | LEARY |
| LAUREATING | LAWLANDS | LAZE | LEAFY | LEAS |
| LAUREL | LAWLESS | LAZED | LEAGUE | LEASABLE |
| LAURELLED | LAWLESSLY | LAZES | LEAGUED | LEASE |
| LAURELS | LAWMAN | LAZIER | LEAGUER | LEASEBACK |
| LAUWINE | LAWMEN | LAZIEST | LEAGUERED | LEASEBACKS |
| LAUWINES | LAWMONGER | LAZILY | LEAGUERING | LEASED |
| LAV | LAWMONGERS | LAZINESS | LEAGUERS | LEASEHOLD |
| LAVA | LAWN | LAZINESSES | LEAGUES | LEASEHOLDS |
| LAVABO | LAWNIER | LAZING | LEAGUING | LEASER |
| LAVABOES | LAWNIEST | LAZULITE | LEAK | LEASERS |
| LAVABOS | LAWNS | LAZULITES | LEAKAGE | LEASES |
| LAVAFORM | LAWNY | LAZURITE | LEAKAGES | LEASH |
| LAVAGE | LAWS | LAZURITES | LEAKED | LEASHED |
| LAVAGES | LAWSUIT | LAZY | LEAKER | LEASHES |
| LAVALIERE | LAWSUITS | LAZZARONE | LEAKERS | LEASHING |
| LAVALIERES | LAWYER | LAZZARONI | LEAKIER | LEASING |
| LAVAS | LAWYERLY | LAZZI | LEAKIEST | LEASINGS |
| LAVATERA | LAWYERS | LAZZO | LEAKINESS | LEASOW |

LEASOWE
LEASOWED
LEASOWES
LEASOWING
LEASOWS
LEAST
LEASTS
LEASTWAYS
LEASTWISE
LEASURE
LEASURES
LEAT
LEATHER
LEATHERED
LEATHERING
LEATHERINGS
LEATHERN
LEATHERS
LEATHERY
LEATS
LEAVE
LEAVED
LEAVEN
LEAVENED
LEAVENING
LEAVENINGS
LEAVENOUS
LEAVENS
LEAVES
LEAVIER
LEAVIEST
LEAVING
LEAVINGS
LEAVY
LEAZE
LEAZES
LEBBEK
LEBBEKS
LECANORA
LECANORAS
LECH
LECHED
LECHER
LECHERED
LECHERIES
LECHERING
LECHEROUS
LECHERS
LECHERY
LECHES
LECHING
LECHWE
LECHWES
LECITHIN
LECITHINS
LECTERN
LECTERNS
LECTIN
LECTINS
LECTION
LECTIONS
LECTOR
LECTORATE
LECTORATES
LECTORS
LECTRESS
LECTRESSES
LECTURE
LECTURED
LECTURER

LECTURERS
LECTURES
LECTURING
LECTURN
LECTURNS
LECYTHI
LECYTHUS
LED
LEDDEN
LEDDENS
LEDGE
LEDGER
LEDGERED
LEDGERING
LEDGERS
LEDGES
LEDGIER
LEDGIEST
LEDGY
LEDUM
LEDUMS
LEE
LEEAR
LEEARS
LEECH
LEECHDOM
LEECHDOMS
LEECHED
LEECHEE
LEECHEES
LEECHES
LEECHING
LEED
LEEING
LEEK
LEEKS
LEEP
LEEPED
LEEPING
LEEPS
LEER
LEERED
LEERIER
LEERIEST
LEERING
LEERINGLY
LEERINGS
LEERS
LEERY
LEES
LEESE
LEESES
LEESING
LEET
LEETLE
LEETS
LEEWARD
LEEWARDS
LEEWAY
LEEWAYS
LEFT
LEFTE
LEFTIE
LEFTIES
LEFTISM
LEFTISMS
LEFTIST
LEFTISTS
LEFTS
LEFTWARD

LEFTWARDS
LEFTY
LEG
LEGACIES
LEGACY
LEGAL
LEGALESE
LEGALESES
LEGALISE
LEGALISED
LEGALISES
LEGALISING
LEGALISM
LEGALISMS
LEGALIST
LEGALISTS
LEGALITIES
LEGALITY
LEGALIZE
LEGALIZED
LEGALIZES
LEGALIZING
LEGALLY
LEGATARIES
LEGATARY
LEGATE
LEGATEE
LEGATEES
LEGATES
LEGATINE
LEGATION
LEGATIONS
LEGATO
LEGATOR
LEGATORS
LEGATOS
LEGEND
LEGENDARIES
LEGENDARY
LEGENDIST
LEGENDISTS
LEGENDRIES
LEGENDRY
LEGENDS
LEGER
LEGERING
LEGERINGS
LEGERITIES
LEGERITY
LEGERS
LEGES
LEGGE
LEGGED
LEGGER
LEGGERS
LEGGES
LEGGIER
LEGGIEST
LEGGINESS
LEGGINESSES
LEGGING
LEGGINGS
LEGGISM
LEGGISMS
LEGGY
LEGHORN
LEGHORNS
LEGIBLE
LEGIBLY
LEGION

LEGIONARIES
LEGIONARY
LEGIONED
LEGIONS
LEGISLATE
LEGISLATED
LEGISLATES
LEGISLATING
LEGIST
LEGISTS
LEGIT
LEGITIM
LEGITIMS
LEGLAN
LEGLANS
LEGLEN
LEGLENS
LEGLESS
LEGLET
LEGLETS
LEGLIN
LEGLINS
LEGROOM
LEGROOMS
LEGS
LEGUME
LEGUMES
LEGUMIN
LEGUMINS
LEGWORK
LEGWORKS
LEHR
LEHRJAHRE
LEHRS
LEI
LEIDGER
LEIDGERS
LEIGER
LEIGERS
LEIPOA
LEIPOAS
LEIR
LEIRED
LEIRING
LEIRS
LEIS
LEISH
LEISHER
LEISHEST
LEISLER
LEISLERS
LEISTER
LEISTERED
LEISTERING
LEISTERS
LEISURE
LEISURED
LEISURELY
LEISURES
LEISURING
LEITMOTIF
LEITMOTIFS
LEITMOTIV
LEITMOTIVS
LEK
LEKE
LEKKED
LEKKING
LEKKINGS
LEKS

LEKYTHOI
LEKYTHOS
LEMAN
LEMANS
LEME
LEMED
LEMEL
LEMELS
LEMES
LEMING
LEMMA
LEMMAS
LEMMATA
LEMMING
LEMMINGS
LEMON
LEMONADE
LEMONADES
LEMONED
LEMONING
LEMONS
LEMONY
LEMPIRA
LEMPIRAS
LEMUR
LEMURES
LEMURIAN
LEMURIANS
LEMURINE
LEMURINES
LEMUROID
LEMUROIDS
LEMURS
LEND
LENDER
LENDERS
LENDING
LENDINGS
LENDS
LENES
LENG
LENGED
LENGER
LENGEST
LENGING
LENGS
LENGTH
LENGTHEN
LENGTHENED
LENGTHENING
LENGTHENS
LENGTHFUL
LENGTHIER
LENGTHIEST
LENGTHILY
LENGTHS
LENGTHY
LENIENCE
LENIENCES
LENIENCIES
LENIENCY
LENIENT
LENIENTLY
LENIENTS
LENIFIED
LENIFIES
LENIFY
LENIFYING
LENIS
LENITIES

LENITION
LENITIONS
LENITIVE
LENITIVES
LENITY
LENO
LENOS
LENS
LENSES
LENT
LENTANDO
LENTEN
LENTI
LENTIC
LENTICEL
LENTICELS
LENTICLE
LENTICLES
LENTIFORM
LENTIGINES
LENTIGO
LENTIL
LENTILS
LENTISK
LENTISKS
LENTO
LENTOID
LENTOR
LENTORS
LENTOS
LENTOUS
LENVOY
LENVOYS
LEONE
LEONES
LEONINE
LEOPARD
LEOPARDS
LEOTARD
LEOTARDS
LEP
LEPER
LEPERS
LEPID
LEPIDOTE
LEPORINE
LEPPED
LEPPING
LEPRA
LEPRAS
LEPROSE
LEPROSERIES
LEPROSERY
LEPROSIES
LEPROSITIES
LEPROSITY
LEPROSY
LEPROUS
LEPS
LEPTA
LEPTOME
LEPTOMES
LEPTON
LEPTONIC
LEPTONS
LEPTOSOME
LEPTOSOMES
LEPTOTENE
LEPTOTENES
LERE

LERED
LERES
LERING
LERNAEAN
LERNEAN
LES
LESBIAN
LESBIANS
LESBIC
LESES
LESION
LESIONS
LESS
LESSEE
LESSEES
LESSEN
LESSENED
LESSENING
LESSENS
LESSER
LESSES
LESSON
LESSONED
LESSONING
LESSONINGS
LESSONS
LESSOR
LESSORS
LEST
LESTED
LESTING
LESTS
LET
LETCH
LETCHED
LETCHES
LETCHING
LETHAL
LETHALITIES
LETHALITY
LETHALLY
LETHARGIC
LETHARGIES
LETHARGY
LETHEAN
LETHEE
LETHEES
LETHIED
LETS
LETTABLE
LETTED
LETTER
LETTERED
LETTERER
LETTERERS
LETTERING
LETTERINGS
LETTERN
LETTERNS
LETTERS
LETTING
LETTINGS
LETTRE
LETTRES
LETTUCE
LETTUCES
LEU
LEUCAEMIA
LEUCAEMIAS
LEUCAEMIC

LEUCH
LEUCHEN
LEUCIN
LEUCINE
LEUCINES
LEUCINS
LEUCITE
LEUCITES
LEUCITIC
LEUCOCYTE
LEUCOCYTES
LEUCOMA
LEUCOMAS
LEUCOTOME
LEUCOTOMES
LEUCOTOMIES
LEUCOTOMY
LEUGH
LEUGHEN
LEUKAEMIA
LEUKAEMIAS
LEV
LEVA
LEVANT
LEVANTED
LEVANTER
LEVANTERS
LEVANTINE
LEVANTINES
LEVANTING
LEVANTS
LEVATOR
LEVATORS
LEVE
LEVEE
LEVEED
LEVEEING
LEVEES
LEVEL
LEVELLED
LEVELLER
LEVELLERS
LEVELLEST
LEVELLING
LEVELLINGS
LEVELS
LEVER
LEVERAGE
LEVERAGES
LEVERED
LEVERET
LEVERETS
LEVERING
LEVERS
LEVIABLE
LEVIATHAN
LEVIATHANS
LEVIED
LEVIES
LEVIGABLE
LEVIGATE
LEVIGATED
LEVIGATES
LEVIGATING
LEVIN
LEVINS
LEVIRATE
LEVIRATES
LEVIS
LEVITATE

LEVITATED
LEVITATES
LEVITATING
LEVITE
LEVITES
LEVITIC
LEVITICAL
LEVITIES
LEVITY
LEVULOSE
LEVULOSES
LEVY
LEVYING
LEW
LEWD
LEWDER
LEWDEST
LEWDLY
LEWDNESS
LEWDNESSES
LEWDSBIES
LEWDSBY
LEWDSTER
LEWDSTERS
LEWIS
LEWISES
LEWISITE
LEWISITES
LEWISSON
LEWISSONS
LEX
LEXEME
LEXEMES
LEXES
LEXICAL
LEXICALLY
LEXICON
LEXICONS
LEXIGRAM
LEXIGRAMS
LEXIS
LEXISES
LEY
LEYS
LEZ
LEZES
LEZZ
LEZZES
LEZZIES
LEZZY
LI
LIABILITIES
LIABILITY
LIABLE
LIAISE
LIAISED
LIAISES
LIAISING
LIAISON
LIAISONS
LIANA
LIANAS
LIANE
LIANES
LIANG
LIANGS
LIANOID
LIAR
LIARD
LIARDS

LIARS
LIART
LIB
LIBANT
LIBATE
LIBATED
LIBATES
LIBATING
LIBATION
LIBATIONS
LIBATORY
LIBBARD
LIBBARDS
LIBBED
LIBBER
LIBBERS
LIBBING
LIBECCHIO
LIBECCHIOS
LIBECCIO
LIBECCIOS
LIBEL
LIBELLANT
LIBELLANTS
LIBELLED
LIBELLEE
LIBELLEES
LIBELLER
LIBELLERS
LIBELLING
LIBELLINGS
LIBELLOUS
LIBELS
LIBER
LIBERAL
LIBERALLY
LIBERALS
LIBERATE
LIBERATED
LIBERATES
LIBERATING
LIBERATOR
LIBERATORS
LIBERS
LIBERTIES
LIBERTINE
LIBERTINES
LIBERTY
LIBIDINAL
LIBIDO
LIBIDOS
LIBKEN
LIBKENS
LIBRA
LIBRAE
LIBRAIRE
LIBRAIRES
LIBRAIRIE
LIBRAIRIES
LIBRARIAN
LIBRARIANS
LIBRARIES
LIBRARY
LIBRAS
LIBRATE
LIBRATED
LIBRATES
LIBRATING
LIBRATION
LIBRATIONS

LIBRATORY
LIBRETTI
LIBRETTO
LIBRETTOS
LIBS
LICE
LICENCE
LICENCED
LICENCES
LICENCING
LICENSE
LICENSED
LICENSEE
LICENSEES
LICENSER
LICENSERS
LICENSES
LICENSING
LICENSOR
LICENSORS
LICENSURE
LICENSURES
LICH
LICHANOS
LICHANOSES
LICHEE
LICHEES
LICHEN
LICHENED
LICHENIN
LICHENINS
LICHENISM
LICHENISMS
LICHENIST
LICHENISTS
LICHENOID
LICHENOSE
LICHENOUS
LICHENS
LICHES
LICHGATE
LICHGATES
LICHI
LICHIS
LICHT
LICHTED
LICHTER
LICHTEST
LICHTING
LICHTLIED
LICHTLIES
LICHTLY
LICHTLYING
LICHTS
LICHWAKE
LICHWAKES
LICHWAY
LICHWAYS
LICIT
LICITLY
LICK
LICKED
LICKER
LICKERISH
LICKERS
LICKING
LICKINGS
LICKPENNIES
LICKPENNY
LICKS

LICORICE
LICORICES
LICTOR
LICTORS
LID
LIDDED
LIDGER
LIDGERS
LIDLESS
LIDO
LIDOCAINE
LIDOCAINES
LIDOS
LIDS
LIE
LIED
LIEDER
LIEF
LIEFER
LIEFEST
LIEFS
LIEGE
LIEGEDOM
LIEGEDOMS
LIEGELESS
LIEGEMAN
LIEGEMEN
LIEGER
LIEGERS
LIEGES
LIEN
LIENAL
LIENS
LIENTERIC
LIENTERIES
LIENTERY
LIER
LIERNE
LIERNES
LIERS
LIES
LIEU
LIEUS
LIEVE
LIEVER
LIEVEST
LIFE
LIFEBELT
LIFEBELTS
LIFEBOAT
LIFEBOATS
LIFEFUL
LIFEGUARD
LIFEGUARDS
LIFEHOLD
LIFELESS
LIFELIKE
LIFELONG
LIFER
LIFERS
LIFESOME
LIFESPAN
LIFESPANS
LIFETIME
LIFETIMES
LIFT
LIFTABLE
LIFTED
LIFTER
LIFTERS

LIFTING
LIFTS
LIFULL
LIG
LIGAMENT
LIGAMENTS
LIGAN
LIGAND
LIGANDS
LIGANS
LIGATE
LIGATED
LIGATES
LIGATING
LIGATION
LIGATIONS
LIGATURE
LIGATURED
LIGATURES
LIGATURING
LIGER
LIGERS
LIGGE
LIGGED
LIGGEN
LIGGER
LIGGERS
LIGGES
LIGGING.
LIGGINGS
LIGHT
LIGHTED
LIGHTEN
LIGHTENED
LIGHTENING
LIGHTENINGS
LIGHTENS
LIGHTER
LIGHTERS
LIGHTEST
LIGHTFAST
LIGHTFUL
LIGHTING
LIGHTINGS
LIGHTISH
LIGHTLESS
LIGHTLIED
LIGHTLIES
LIGHTLY
LIGHTLYING
LIGHTNESS
LIGHTNESSES
LIGHTNING
LIGHTNINGS
LIGHTS
LIGHTSHIP
LIGHTSHIPS
LIGHTSOME
LIGNAGE
LIGNAGES
LIGNALOES
LIGNE
LIGNEOUS
LIGNES
LIGNIFIED
LIGNIFIES
LIGNIFORM
LIGNIFY
LIGNIFYING
LIGNIN

LIGNINS
LIGNITE
LIGNITES
LIGNITIC
LIGNUM
LIGNUMS
LIGROIN
LIGROINS
LIGS
LIGULA
LIGULAE
LIGULAR
LIGULAS
LIGULATE
LIGULE
LIGULES
LIGULOID
LIGURE
LIGURES
LIKABLE
LIKE
LIKEABLE
LIKED
LIKELIER
LIKELIEST
LIKELY
LIKEN
LIKENED
LIKENESS
LIKENESSES
LIKENING
LIKENS
LIKER
LIKERS
LIKES
LIKEWAKE
LIKEWAKES
LIKEWALK
LIKEWALKS
LIKEWISE
LIKIN
LIKING
LIKINGS
LIKINS
LILAC
LILACS
LILANGENI
LILIED
LILIES
LILL
LILLED
LILLING
LILLS
LILO
LILOS
LILT
LILTED
LILTING
LILTS
LILY
LIMA
LIMACEL
LIMACELS
LIMACEOUS
LIMACES
LIMACINE
LIMAÇON
LIMAÇONS
LIMAIL
LIMAILS

LIMAS
LIMATION
LIMATIONS
LIMAX
LIMB
LIMBATE
LIMBEC
LIMBECK
LIMBECKS
LIMBECS
LIMBED
LIMBER
LIMBERED
LIMBERING
LIMBERS
LIMBIC
LIMBING
LIMBLESS
LIMBMEAL
LIMBO
LIMBOS
LIMBOUS
LIMBS
LIME
LIMED
LIMEKILN
LIMEKILNS
LIMELIGHT
LIMELIGHTED
LIMELIGHTING
LIMELIGHTS
LIMELIT
LIMEN
LIMENS
LIMEPIT
LIMEPITS
LIMERICK
LIMERICKS
LIMES
LIMESTONE
LIMESTONES
LIMEWASH
LIMEWASHES
LIMEWATER
LIMEWATERS
LIMEY
LIMEYS
LIMIER
LIMIEST
LIMINAL
LIMINESS
LIMINESSES
LIMING
LIMINGS
LIMIT
LIMITABLE
LIMITARY
LIMITED
LIMITEDLY
LIMITEDS
LIMITER
LIMITERS
LIMITES
LIMITING
LIMITINGS
LIMITLESS
LIMITS
LIMMA
LIMMAS
LIMMER

LIMMERS
LIMN
LIMNAEID
LIMNAEIDS
LIMNED
LIMNER
LIMNERS
LIMNETIC
LIMNING
LIMNOLOGIES
LIMNOLOGY
LIMNS
LIMONITE
LIMONITES
LIMONITIC
LIMOSES
LIMOSIS
LIMOUS
LIMOUSINE
LIMOUSINES
LIMP
LIMPED
LIMPER
LIMPEST
LIMPET
LIMPETS
LIMPID
LIMPIDITIES
LIMPIDITY
LIMPIDLY
LIMPING
LIMPINGLY
LIMPINGS
LIMPKIN
LIMPKINS
LIMPS
LIMULI
LIMULUS
LIMULUSES
LIMY
LIN
LINAGE
LINAGES
LINALOOL
LINALOOLS
LINCH
LINCHES
LINCHET
LINCHETS
LINCHPIN
LINCHPINS
LINCRUSTA
LINCRUSTAS
LINCTURE
LINCTURES
LINCTUS
LINCTUSES
LIND
LINDANE
LINDANES
LINDEN
LINDENS
LINDS
LINDWORM
LINDWORMS
LINE
LINEAGE
LINEAGES
LINEAL
LINEALITIES

LINEALITY
LINEALLY
LINEAMENT
LINEAMENTS
LINEAR
LINEARITIES
LINEARITY
LINEARLY
LINEATE
LINEATED
LINEATION
LINEATIONS
LINED
LINEMAN
LINEMEN
LINEN
LINENS
LINEOLATE
LINER
LINERS
LINES
LINESMAN
LINESMEN
LINEY
LING
LINGA
LINGAM
LINGAMS
LINGAS
LINGEL
LINGELS
LINGER
LINGERED
LINGERER
LINGERERS
LINGERIE
LINGERIES
LINGERING
LINGERINGS
LINGERS
LINGIER
LINGIEST
LINGLE
LINGLES
LINGO
LINGOES
LINGOT
LINGOTS
LINGS
LINGSTER
LINGSTERS
LINGUA
LINGUAE
LINGUAL
LINGUALLY
LINGUAS
LINGUINE
LINGUINI
LINGUIST
LINGUISTS
LINGULA
LINGULAE
LINGULAR
LINGULAS
LINGULATE
LINGY
LINHAY
LINHAYS
LINIER
LINIEST

LINIMENT
LINIMENTS
LININ
LINING
LININGS
LININS
LINK
LINKAGE
LINKAGES
LINKBOY
LINKBOYS
LINKED
LINKING
LINKMAN
LINKMEN
LINKS
LINKSTER
LINKSTERS
LINKWORK
LINKWORKS
LINN
LINNED
LINNET
LINNETS
LINNEY
LINNEYS
LINNIES
LINNING
LINNS
LINNY
LINO
LINOCUT
LINOCUTS
LINOLEUM
LINOLEUMS
LINOS
LINS
LINSANG
LINSANGS
LINSEED
LINSEEDS
LINSEY
LINSEYS
LINSTOCK
LINSTOCKS
LINT
LINTEL
LINTELLED
LINTELS
LINTER
LINTERS
LINTIE
LINTIER
LINTIES
LINTIEST
LINTS
LINTSEED
LINTSEEDS
LINTSTOCK
LINTSTOCKS
LINTWHITE
LINTWHITES
LINTY
LINY
LION
LIONCEL
LIONCELLE
LIONCELLES
LIONCELS
LIONEL

LIONELS
LIONESS
LIONESSES
LIONET
LIONETS
LIONISE
LIONISED
LIONISES
LIONISING
LIONISM
LIONISMS
LIONIZE
LIONIZED
LIONIZES
LIONIZING
LIONLY
LIONS
LIP
LIPARITE
LIPARITES
LIPASE
LIPASES
LIPECTOMIES
LIPECTOMY
LIPGLOSS
LIPGLOSSES
LIPID
LIPIDE
LIPIDES
LIPIDS
LIPLESS
LIPOGRAM
LIPOGRAMS
LIPOID
LIPOIDS
LIPOMA
LIPOMATA
LIPOSOMAL
LIPOSOME
LIPOSOMES
LIPPED
LIPPEN
LIPPENED
LIPPENING
LIPPENS
LIPPIE
LIPPIER
LIPPIES
LIPPIEST
LIPPING
LIPPITUDE
LIPPITUDES
LIPPY
LIPS
LIPSALVE
LIPSALVES
LIPSTICK
LIPSTICKED
LIPSTICKING
LIPSTICKS
LIQUABLE
LIQUATE
LIQUATED
LIQUATES
LIQUATING
LIQUATION
LIQUATIONS
LIQUEFIED
LIQUEFIER
LIQUEFIERS

LIQUEFIES
LIQUEFY
LIQUEFYING
LIQUESCE
LIQUESCED
LIQUESCES
LIQUESCING
LIQUEUR
LIQUEURED
LIQUEURING
LIQUEURS
LIQUID
LIQUIDATE
LIQUIDATED
LIQUIDATES
LIQUIDATING
LIQUIDISE
LIQUIDISED
LIQUIDISES
LIQUIDISING
LIQUIDITIES
LIQUIDITY
LIQUIDIZE
LIQUIDIZED
LIQUIDIZES
LIQUIDIZING
LIQUIDLY
LIQUIDS
LIQUIDUS
LIQUIDUSES
LIQUOR
LIQUORED
LIQUORICE
LIQUORICES
LIQUORING
LIQUORISH
LIQUORS
LIRA
LIRAS
LIRE
LIRIPIPE
LIRIPIPES
LIRIPOOP
LIRIPOOPS
LIRK
LIRKED
LIRKING
LIRKS
LIS
LISK
LISKS
LISLE
LISLES
LISP
LISPED
LISPER
LISPERS
LISPING
LISPINGLY
LISPINGS
LISPOUND
LISPOUNDS
LISPS
LISPUND
LISPUNDS
LISSES
LISSOM
LISSOME
LIST
LISTED

| | | | | |
|---|---|---|---|---|
| LISTEL | LITHOCYSTS | LIVENS | LOAFING | LOBLOLLY |
| LISTELS | LITHOID | LIVER | LOAFINGS | LOBO |
| LISTEN | LITHOIDAL | LIVERIED | LOAFS | LOBOS |
| LISTENED | LITHOLOGIES | LIVERIES | LOAM | LOBOSE |
| LISTENER | LITHOLOGY | LIVERISH | LOAMED | LOBOTOMIES |
| LISTENERS | LITHOPONE | LIVERS | LOAMIER | LOBOTOMY |
| LISTENING | LITHOPONES | LIVERWORT | LOAMIEST | LOBS |
| LISTENS | LITHOS | LIVERWORTS | LOAMINESS | LOBSCOUSE |
| LISTER | LITHOTOME | LIVERY | LOAMINESSES | LOBSCOUSES |
| LISTERS | LITHOTOMES | LIVERYMAN | LOAMING | LOBSTER |
| LISTETH | LITHOTOMIES | LIVERYMEN | LOAMS | LOBSTERS |
| LISTFUL | LITHOTOMY | LIVES | LOAMY | LOBULAR |
| LISTING | LITHS | LIVESTOCK | LOAN | LOBULATE |
| LISTINGS | LITIGABLE | LIVESTOCKS | LOANABLE | LOBULATED |
| LISTLESS | LITIGANT | LIVEWARE | LOANED | LOBULE |
| LISTS | LITIGANTS | LIVEWARES | LOANING | LOBULES |
| LIT | LITIGATE | LIVID | LOANINGS | LOBULI |
| LITANIES | LITIGATED | LIVIDER | LOANS | LOBULUS |
| LITANY | LITIGATES | LIVIDEST | LOAST | LOBUS |
| LITCHI | LITIGATING | LIVIDITIES | LOATH | LOBWORM |
| LITCHIS | LITIGIOUS | LIVIDITY | LOATHE | LOBWORMS |
| LITE | LITING | LIVIDNESS | LOATHED | LOCAL |
| LITED | LITMUS | LIVIDNESSES | LOATHER | LOCALE |
| LITER | LITMUSES | LIVING | LOATHERS | LOCALES |
| LITERACIES | LITOTES | LIVINGS | LOATHES | LOCALISE |
| LITERACY | LITRE | LIVOR | LOATHEST | LOCALISED |
| LITERAL | LITRES | LIVORS | LOATHFUL | LOCALISER |
| LITERALLY | LITTEN | LIVRAISON | LOATHIER | LOCALISERS |
| LITERALS | LITTER | LIVRAISONS | LOATHIEST | LOCALISES |
| LITERARY | LITTERED | LIVRE | LOATHING | LOCALISING |
| LITERATE | LITTERING | LIVRES | LOATHINGS | LOCALISM |
| LITERATES | LITTERS | LIXIVIAL | LOATHLY | LOCALISMS |
| LITERATI | LITTERY | LIXIVIATE | LOATHSOME | LOCALIST |
| LITERATIM | LITTLE | LIXIVIATED | LOATHY | LOCALISTS |
| LITERATO | LITTLEANE | LIXIVIATES | LOAVE | LOCALITIES |
| LITERATOR | LITTLEANES | LIXIVIATING | LOAVED | LOCALITY |
| LITERATORS | LITTLER | LIXIVIOUS | LOAVES | LOCALIZE |
| LITERATUS | LITTLES | LIXIVIUM | LOAVING | LOCALIZED |
| LITEROSE | LITTLEST | LIXIVIUMS | LOB | LOCALIZER |
| LITERS | LITTLIN | LIZARD | LOBAR | LOCALIZERS |
| LITES | LITTLING | LIZARDS | LOBATE | LOCALIZES |
| LITH | LITTLINGS | LLAMA | LOBATION | LOCALIZING |
| LITHARGE | LITTLINS | LLAMAS | LOBATIONS | LOCALLY |
| LITHARGES | LITTORAL | LLANERO | LOBBED | LOCALS |
| LITHATE | LITTORALS | LLANEROS | LOBBIED | LOCATE |
| LITHATES | LITURGIC | LLANO | LOBBIES | LOCATED |
| LITHE | LITURGICS | LLANOS | LOBBING | LOCATES |
| LITHED | LITURGIES | LO | LOBBY | LOCATING |
| LITHELY | LITURGIST | LOACH | LOBBYER | LOCATION |
| LITHENESS | LITURGISTS | LOACHES | LOBBYERS | LOCATIONS |
| LITHENESSES | LITURGY | LOAD | LOBBYING | LOCATIVE |
| LITHER | LITUUS | LOADED | LOBBYINGS | LOCATIVES |
| LITHERLY | LITUUSES | LOADEN | LOBBYIST | LOCELLATE |
| LITHES | LIVABLE | LOADENED | LOBBYISTS | LOCH |
| LITHESOME | LIVE | LOADENING | LOBE | LOCHAN |
| LITHEST | LIVEABLE | LOADENS | LOBECTOMIES | LOCHANS |
| LITHIA | LIVED | LOADER | LOBECTOMY | LOCHIA |
| LITHIAS | LIVELIER | LOADERS | LOBED | LOCHIAL |
| LITHIASES | LIVELIEST | LOADING | LOBELET | LOCHS |
| LITHIASIS | LIVELILY | LOADINGS | LOBELETS | LOCI |
| LITHIC | LIVELOD | LOADS | LOBELIA | LOCK |
| LITHING | LIVELODS | LOADSTAR | LOBELIAS | LOCKAGE |
| LITHISTID | LIVELONG | LOADSTARS | LOBELINE | LOCKAGES |
| LITHISTIDS | LIVELONGS | LOADSTONE | LOBELINES | LOCKAWAY |
| LITHITE | LIVELOOD | LOADSTONES | LOBES | LOCKAWAYS |
| LITHITES | LIVELOODS | LOAF | LOBI | LOCKED |
| LITHIUM | LIVELY | LOAFED | LOBING | LOCKER |
| LITHIUMS | LIVEN | LOAFER | LOBINGS | LOCKERS |
| LITHO | LIVENED | LOAFERISH | LOBIPED | LOCKET |
| LITHOCYST | LIVENING | LOAFERS | LOBLOLLIES | LOCKETS |

LOCKFAST
LOCKFUL
LOCKFULS
LOCKHOUSE
LOCKHOUSES
LOCKING
LOCKMAN
LOCKMEN
LOCKOUT
LOCKOUTS
LOCKPICK
LOCKPICKS
LOCKRAM
LOCKRAMS
LOCKS
LOCKSMAN
LOCKSMEN
LOCKSMITH
LOCKSMITHS
LOCKSTEP
LOCKSTEPS
LOCO
LOCOED
LOCOES
LOCOFOCO
LOCOFOCOS
LOCOMAN
LOCOMEN
LOCOMOTE
LOCOMOTED
LOCOMOTES
LOCOMOTING
LOCOMOTOR
LOCOMOTORS
LOCOS
LOCULAR
LOCULATE
LOCULE
LOCULES
LOCULI
LOCULUS
LOCUM
LOCUMS
LOCUPLETE
LOCUS
LOCUST
LOCUSTA
LOCUSTAE
LOCUSTED
LOCUSTING
LOCUSTS
LOCUTION
LOCUTIONS
LOCUTORIES
LOCUTORY
LODE
LODEN
LODENS
LODES
LODESMAN
LODESMEN
LODESTAR
LODESTARS
LODESTONE
LODESTONES
LODGE
LODGED
LODGEMENT
LODGEMENTS
LODGEPOLE

LODGEPOLES
LODGER
LODGERS
LODGES
LODGING
LODGINGS
LODGMENT
LODGMENTS
LODICULA
LODICULAE
LODICULE
LODICULES
LOESS
LOESSES
LOFT
LOFTED
LOFTER
LOFTERS
LOFTIER
LOFTIEST
LOFTILY
LOFTINESS
LOFTINESSES
LOFTING
LOFTS
LOFTY
LOG
LOGAN
LOGANS
LOGAOEDIC
LOGARITHM
LOGARITHMS
LOGBOARD
LOGBOARDS
LOGE
LOGES
LOGGAT
LOGGATS
LOGGED
LOGGER
LOGGERS
LOGGIA
LOGGIAS
LOGGIE
LOGGING
LOGGINGS
LOGIA
LOGIC
LOGICAL
LOGICALLY
LOGICIAN
LOGICIANS
LOGICISE
LOGICISED
LOGICISES
LOGICISING
LOGICIZE
LOGICIZED
LOGICIZES
LOGICIZING
LOGICS
LOGIE
LOGIES
LOGION
LOGISTIC
LOGISTICS
LOGJUICE
LOGJUICES
LOGLINE
LOGLINES

LOGLOG
LOGLOGS
LOGO
LOGOGRAM
LOGOGRAMS
LOGOGRAPH
LOGOGRAPHS
LOGOGRIPH
LOGOGRIPHS
LOGOMACHIES
LOGOMACHY
LOGORRHEA
LOGORRHEAS
LOGOS
LOGOTHETE
LOGOTHETES
LOGOTYPE
LOGOTYPES
LOGS
LOGWOOD
LOGWOODS
LOID
LOIDED
LOIDING
LOIDS
LOIN
LOINS
LOIPE
LOIPES
LOIR
LOIRS
LOITER
LOITERED
LOITERER
LOITERERS
LOITERING
LOITERINGS
LOITERS
LOKE
LOKES
LOKSHEN
LOLL
LOLLED
LOLLER
LOLLERS
LOLLIES
LOLLING
LOLLINGLY
LOLLIPOP
LOLLIPOPS
LOLLOP
LOLLOPED
LOLLOPING
LOLLOPS
LOLLS
LOLLY
LOLLYGAG
LOLLYGAGGED
LOLLYGAGGING
LOLLYGAGS
LOLOG
LOLOGS
LOMA
LOMAS
LOME
LOMENT
LOMENTA
LOMENTS
LOMENTUM
LOMES

LOMPISH
LONE
LONELIER
LONELIEST
LONELY
LONENESS
LONENESSES
LONER
LONERS
LONESOME
LONESOMES
LONG
LONGA
LONGAEVAL
LONGAN
LONGANS
LONGAS
LONGBOAT
LONGBOATS
LONGBOW
LONGBOWS
LONGCLOTH
LONGCLOTHS
LONGE
LONGED
LONGEING
LONGER
LONGERON
LONGERONS
LONGES
LONGEST
LONGEVAL
LONGEVITIES
LONGEVITY
LONGEVOUS
LONGHAND
LONGHANDS
LONGHORN
LONGHORNS
LONGICORN
LONGICORNS
LONGING
LONGINGLY
LONGINGS
LONGISH
LONGITUDE
LONGITUDES
LONGLY
LONGNESS
LONGNESSES
LONGS
LONGSHIP
LONGSHIPS
LONGSHORE
LONGSOME
LONGUEUR
LONGUEURS
LONGWALL
LONGWALLS
LONGWAYS
LONGWISE
LONICERA
LONICERAS
LOO
LOOBIER
LOOBIES
LOOBIEST
LOOBILY
LOOBY
LOOED

LOOF
LOOFA
LOOFAH
LOOFAHS
LOOFAS
LOOFED
LOOFFUL
LOOFFULS
LOOFING
LOOFS
LOOING
LOOK
LOOKED
LOOKER
LOOKERS
LOOKING
LOOKINGS
LOOKOUT
LOOKOUTS
LOOKS
LOOM
LOOMED
LOOMING
LOOMS
LOON
LOONIE
LOONIER
LOONIES
LOONIEST
LOONING
LOONINGS
LOONS
LOONY
LOOP
LOOPED
LOOPER
LOOPERS
LOOPHOLE
LOOPHOLED
LOOPHOLES
LOOPHOLING
LOOPIER
LOOPIEST
LOOPING
LOOPINGS
LOOPS
LOOPY
LOOR
LOORD
LOORDS
LOOS
LOOSE
LOOSED
LOOSELY
LOOSEN
LOOSENED
LOOSENER
LOOSENERS
LOOSENESS
LOOSENESSES
LOOSENING
LOOSENS
LOOSER
LOOSES
LOOSEST
LOOSING
LOOT
LOOTED
LOOTEN
LOOTER

| | | | | |
|---|---|---|---|---|
| LOOTERS | LORICS | LOUDEN | LOUVER | LOWLILY |
| LOOTING | LORIES | LOUDENED | LOUVERED | LOWLINESS |
| LOOTS | LORIKEET | LOUDENING | LOUVERS | LOWLINESSES |
| LOOVES | LORIKEETS | LOUDENS | LOUVRE | LOWLY |
| LOP | LORIMER | LOUDER | LOUVRED | LOWN |
| LOPE | LORIMERS | LOUDEST | LOUVRES | LOWND |
| LOPED | LORINER | LOUDISH | LOVABLE | LOWNDED |
| LOPER | LORINERS | LOUDLY | LOVAGE | LOWNDING |
| LOPERS | LORING | LOUDMOUTH | LOVAGES | LOWNDS |
| LOPES | LORINGS | LOUDMOUTHS | LOVAT | LOWNE |
| LOPGRASS | LORIOT | LOUDNESS | LOVATS | LOWNED |
| LOPGRASSES | LORIOTS | LOUDNESSES | LOVE | LOWNES |
| LOPHODONT | LORIS | LOUGH | LOVEABLE | LOWNESS |
| LOPING | LORISES | LOUGHS | LOVEBIRD | LOWNESSES |
| LOPPED | LORN | LOUIS | LOVEBIRDS | LOWNING |
| LOPPER | LORRELL | LOUN | LOVEBITE | LOWNS |
| LOPPERED | LORRELLS | LOUND | LOVEBITES | LOWS |
| LOPPERING | LORRIES | LOUNDED | LOVED | LOWSE |
| LOPPERS | LORRY | LOUNDER | LOVELESS | LOWSER |
| LOPPING | LORY | LOUNDERED | LOVELIER | LOWSES |
| LOPPINGS | LOS | LOUNDERING | LOVELIES | LOWSEST |
| LOPS | LOSABLE | LOUNDERINGS | LOVELIEST | LOWSING |
| LOQUACITIES | LOSE | LOUNDERS | LOVELIGHT | LOWSIT |
| LOQUACITY | LOSED | LOUNDING | LOVELIGHTS | LOWT |
| LOQUAT | LOSEL | LOUNDS | LOVELILY | LOWTED |
| LOQUATS | LOSELS | LOUNED | LOVELOCK | LOWTING |
| LOQUITUR | LOSEN | LOUNGE | LOVELOCKS | LOWTS |
| LOR | LOSER | LOUNGED | LOVELORN | LOWVELD |
| LORAL | LOSERS | LOUNGER | LOVELY | LOWVELDS |
| LORAN | LOSES | LOUNGERS | LOVER | LOX |
| LORANS | LOSH | LOUNGES | LOVERED | LOXES |
| LORATE | LOSING | LOUNGING | LOVERLESS | LOXODROME |
| LORCHA | LOSINGLY | LOUNGINGS | LOVERLY | LOXODROMES |
| LORCHAS | LOSINGS | LOUNING | LOVERS | LOXODROMIES |
| LORD | LOSS | LOUNS | LOVES | LOXODROMY |
| LORDED | LOSSES | LOUP | LOVESICK | LOXYGEN |
| LORDING | LOSSIER | LOUPE | LOVESOME | LOXYGENS |
| LORDINGS | LOSSIEST | LOUPED | LOVEY | LOY |
| LORDKIN | LOSSY | LOUPEN | LOVEYS | LOYAL |
| LORDKINS | LOST | LOUPES | LOVING | LOYALIST |
| LORDLESS | LOT | LOUPING | LOVINGLY | LOYALISTS |
| LORDLIER | LOTA | LOUPIT | LOVINGS | LOYALLER |
| LORDLIEST | LOTAH | LOUPS | LOW | LOYALLEST |
| LORDLING | LOTAHS | LOUR | LOWAN | LOYALLY |
| LORDLINGS | LOTAS | LOURE | LOWANS | LOYALTIES |
| LORDLY | LOTE | LOURED | LOWBOY | LOYALTY |
| LORDOSES | LOTES | LOURES | LOWBOYS | LOYS |
| LORDOSIS | LOTH | LOURIER | LOWE | LOZELL |
| LORDOTIC | LOTHEFULL | LOURIEST | LOWED | LOZELLS |
| LORDS | LOTHER | LOURING | LOWER | LOZEN |
| LORDSHIP | LOTHEST | LOURINGLY | LOWERED | LOZENGE |
| LORDSHIPS | LOTHFULL | LOURINGS | LOWERIER | LOZENGED |
| LORDY | LOTIC | LOURS | LOWERIEST | LOZENGES |
| LORE | LOTION | LOURY | LOWERING | LOZENGY |
| LOREL | LOTIONS | LOUSE | LOWERINGS | LOZENS |
| LORELS | LOTO | LOUSED | LOWERMOST | LUAU |
| LORES | LOTOS | LOUSES | LOWERS | LUAUS |
| LORETTE | LOTOSES | LOUSIER | LOWERY | LUBBARD |
| LORETTES | LOTS | LOUSIEST | LOWES | LUBBARDS |
| LORGNETTE | LOTTED | LOUSILY | LOWEST | LUBBER |
| LORGNETTES | LOTTERIES | LOUSINESS | LOWING | LUBBERLY |
| LORGNON | LOTTERY | LOUSINESSES | LOWINGS | LUBBERS |
| LORGNONS | LOTTING | LOUSING | LOWLAND | LUBFISH |
| LORIC | LOTTO | LOUSY | LOWLANDER | LUBFISHES |
| LORICA | LOTTOS | LOUT | LOWLANDERS | LUBRA |
| LORICAE | LOTUS | LOUTED | LOWLANDS | LUBRAS |
| LORICATE | LOTUSES | LOUTING | LOWLIER | LUBRIC |
| LORICATED | LOUCHE | LOUTISH | LOWLIEST | LUBRICAL |
| LORICATES | LOUCHELY | LOUTISHLY | LOWLIHEAD | LUBRICANT |
| LORICATING | LOUD | LOUTS | LOWLIHEADS | LUBRICANTS |

LUBRICATE
LUBRICATED
LUBRICATES
LUBRICATING
LUBRICITIES
LUBRICITY
LUBRICOUS
LUCARNE
LUCARNES
LUCE
LUCENCIES
LUCENCY
LUCENT
LUCERN
LUCERNE
LUCERNES
LUCERNS
LUCES
LUCID
LUCIDER
LUCIDEST
LUCIDITIES
LUCIDITY
LUCIDLY
LUCIDNESS
LUCIDNESSES
LUCIFER
LUCIFERIN
LUCIFERINS
LUCIFERS
LUCIGEN
LUCIGENS
LUCK
LUCKEN
LUCKIE
LUCKIER
LUCKIES
LUCKIEST
LUCKILY
LUCKINESS
LUCKINESSES
LUCKLESS
LUCKS
LUCKY
LUCRATIVE
LUCRE
LUCRES
LUCTATION
LUCTATIONS
LUCUBRATE
LUCUBRATED
LUCUBRATES
LUCUBRATING
LUCULENT
LUCUMA
LUCUMAS
LUCUMO
LUCUMONES
LUCUMOS
LUD
LUDIC
LUDICROUS
LUDO
LUDOS
LUDS
LUDSHIP
LUDSHIPS
LUES
LUETIC
LUFF

LUFFA
LUFFAS
LUFFED
LUFFING
LUFFS
LUG
LUGE
LUGED
LUGEING
LUGEINGS
LUGES
LUGGAGE
LUGGAGES
LUGGED
LUGGER
LUGGERS
LUGGIE
LUGGIES
LUGGING
LUGING
LUGINGS
LUGS
LUGSAIL
LUGSAILS
LUGWORM
LUGWORMS
LUIT
LUITEN
LUKE
LUKEWARM
LULL
LULLABIED
LULLABIES
LULLABY
LULLABYING
LULLED
LULLING
LULLS
LULU
LULUS
LUM
LUMBAGO
LUMBAGOS
LUMBANG
LUMBANGS
LUMBAR
LUMBER
LUMBERED
LUMBERER
LUMBERERS
LUMBERING
LUMBERINGS
LUMBERLY
LUMBERMAN
LUMBERMEN
LUMBERS
LUMBRICAL
LUMBRICALS
LUMBRICI
LUMBRICUS
LUMBRICUSES
LUMEN
LUMENAL
LUMENS
LUMINA
LUMINAIRE
LUMINAIRES
LUMINAL
LUMINANCE
LUMINANCES

LUMINANT
LUMINANTS
LUMINARIES
LUMINARY
LUMINE
LUMINED
LUMINES
LUMINESCE
LUMINESCED
LUMINESCES
LUMINESCING
LUMINING
LUMINIST
LUMINISTS
LUMINOUS
LUMME
LUMMIER
LUMMIEST
LUMMOX
LUMMOXES
LUMMY
LUMP
LUMPED
LUMPEN
LUMPENLY
LUMPER
LUMPERS
LUMPFISH
LUMPFISHES
LUMPIER
LUMPIEST
LUMPILY
LUMPINESS
LUMPINESSES
LUMPING
LUMPISH
LUMPISHLY
LUMPKIN
LUMPKINS
LUMPS
LUMPY
LUMS
LUNACIES
LUNACY
LUNANAUT
LUNANAUTS
LUNAR
LUNARIAN
LUNARIANS
LUNARIES
LUNARIST
LUNARISTS
LUNARNAUT
LUNARNAUTS
LUNARS
LUNARY
LUNATE
LUNATED
LUNATIC
LUNATICS
LUNATION
LUNATIONS
LUNCH
LUNCHED
LUNCHEON
LUNCHEONED
LUNCHEONING
LUNCHEONS
LUNCHER
LUNCHERS

LUNCHES
LUNCHING
LUNE
LUNES
LUNETTE
LUNETTES
LUNG
LUNGE
LUNGED
LUNGEING
LUNGES
LUNGFUL
LUNGFULS
LUNGI
LUNGIE
LUNGIES
LUNGING
LUNGIS
LUNGS
LUNGWORT
LUNGWORTS
LUNISOLAR
LUNITIDAL
LUNKER
LUNKERS
LUNKHEAD
LUNKHEADS
LUNT
LUNTED
LUNTING
LUNTS
LUNULA
LUNULAR
LUNULAS
LUNULATE
LUNULATED
LUNULE
LUNULES
LUNYIE
LUNYIES
LUPIN
LUPINE
LUPINES
LUPINS
LUPPEN
LUPULIN
LUPULINE
LUPULINIC
LUPULINS
LUPUS
LUPUSES
LUR
LURCH
LURCHED
LURCHER
LURCHERS
LURCHES
LURCHING
LURDAN
LURDANE
LURDANES
LURDANS
LURDEN
LURDENS
LURE
LURED
LURES
LURGI
LURGIES
LURGIS

LURGY
LURID
LURIDER
LURIDEST
LURIDLY
LURIDNESS
LURIDNESSES
LURING
LURK
LURKED
LURKER
LURKERS
LURKING
LURKINGS
LURKS
LURRIES
LURRY
LURS
LUSCIOUS
LUSH
LUSHED
LUSHER
LUSHERS
LUSHES
LUSHEST
LUSHIER
LUSHIEST
LUSHING
LUSHLY
LUSHNESS
LUSHNESSES
LUSHY
LUSK
LUSKED
LUSKING
LUSKISH
LUSKS
LUST
LUSTED
LUSTER
LUSTERED
LUSTERING
LUSTERS
LUSTFUL
LUSTFULLY
LUSTICK
LUSTIER
LUSTIEST
LUSTIHEAD
LUSTIHEADS
LUSTIHOOD
LUSTIHOODS
LUSTILY
LUSTINESS
LUSTINESSES
LUSTING
LUSTIQUE
LUSTLESS
LUSTRA
LUSTRAL
LUSTRATE
LUSTRATED
LUSTRATES
LUSTRATING
LUSTRE
LUSTRED
LUSTRES
LUSTRINE
LUSTRINES
LUSTRING

LUSTRINGS
LUSTROUS
LUSTRUM
LUSTRUMS
LUSTS
LUSTY
LUTANIST
LUTANISTS
LUTE
LUTEAL
LUTECIUM
LUTECIUMS
LUTED
LUTEIN
LUTEINISE
LUTEINISED
LUTEINISES
LUTEINISING
LUTEINIZE
LUTEINIZED
LUTEINIZES
LUTEINIZING
LUTEINS
LUTENIST
LUTENISTS
LUTEOLIN
LUTEOLINS
LUTEOLOUS
LUTEOUS
LUTER
LUTERS
LUTES
LUTESCENT
LUTETIUM
LUTETIUMS
LUTHERN
LUTHERNS

LUTHIER
LUTHIERS
LUTING
LUTINGS
LUTIST
LUTISTS
LUTTEN
LUTZ
LUTZES
LUX
LUXATE
LUXATED
LUXATES
LUXATING
LUXATION
LUXATIONS
LUXE
LUXES
LUXMETER
LUXMETERS
LUXURIANT
LUXURIATE
LUXURIATED
LUXURIATES
LUXURIATING
LUXURIES
LUXURIOUS
LUXURIST
LUXURISTS
LUXURY
LUZ
LUZERN
LUZERNS
LUZZES
LYAM
LYAMS
LYART

LYCÉE
LYCÉES
LYCEUM
LYCEUMS
LYCHEE
LYCHEES
LYCHGATE
LYCHGATES
LYCHNIS
LYCHNISES
LYCOPOD
LYCOPODS
LYDDITE
LYDDITES
LYE
LYES
LYFULL
LYING
LYINGLY
LYINGS
LYKEWAKE
LYKEWAKES
LYKEWALK
LYKEWALKS
LYM
LYME
LYMES
LYMITER
LYMITERS
LYMPH
LYMPHAD
LYMPHADS
LYMPHATIC
LYMPHATICS
LYMPHOID
LYMPHOMA
LYMPHOMAS

LYMPHS
LYMS
LYNAGE
LYNAGES
LYNCEAN
LYNCH
LYNCHED
LYNCHES
LYNCHET
LYNCHETS
LYNCHING
LYNCHPIN
LYNCHPINS
LYNE
LYNES
LYNX
LYNXES
LYOMEROUS
LYOPHIL
LYOPHILE
LYOPHILIC
LYOPHOBE
LYOPHOBIC
LYRATE
LYRATED
LYRE
LYRES
LYRIC
LYRICAL
LYRICALLY
LYRICISM
LYRICISMS
LYRICIST
LYRICISTS
LYRICS
LYRIFORM
LYRISM

LYRISMS
LYRIST
LYRISTS
LYSE
LYSED
LYSERGIDE
LYSERGIDES
LYSES
LYSIGENIC
LYSIMETER
LYSIMETERS
LYSIN
LYSINE
LYSINES
LYSING
LYSINS
LYSIS
LYSOL
LYSOLS
LYSOSOME
LYSOSOMES
LYSOZYME
LYSOZYMES
LYSSA
LYSSAS
LYTE
LYTED
LYTES
LYTHE
LYTHES
LYTING
LYTTA
LYTTAS

# M

MA
MAAR
MAARS
MAC
MACABRE
MACACO
MACACOS
MACADAM
MACADAMIA
MACADAMIAS
MACADAMS
MACAHUBA
MACAHUBAS
MACAQUE
MACAQUES
MACARISE
MACARISED
MACARISES
MACARISING
MACARISM
MACARISMS
MACARIZE
MACARIZED
MACARIZES
MACARIZING
MACARONI
MACARONIC
MACARONICS
MACARONIES
MACARONIS
MACAROON
MACAROONS
MACAW
MACAWS
MACCHIE
MACE
MACED
MACÉDOINE
MACÉDOINES
MACER
MACERATE
MACERATED
MACERATES
MACERATING
MACERATOR
MACERATORS
MACERS
MACES
MACHAIR
MACHAIRS
MACHAN
MACHANS
MACHETE
MACHETES
MACHINATE
MACHINATED
MACHINATES
MACHINATING
MACHINE
MACHINED
MACHINERIES
MACHINERY
MACHINES

MACHINING
MACHINIST
MACHINISTS
MACHISMO
MACHISMOS
MACHMETER
MACHMETERS
MACHO
MACHOS
MACHREE
MACHREES
MACHZOR
MACHZORIM
MACING
MACINTOSH
MACINTOSHES
MACK
MACKEREL
MACKERELS
MACKINAW
MACKINAWS
MACKLE
MACKLED
MACKLES
MACKLING
MACKS
MACLE
MACLED
MACLES
MACOYA
MACOYAS
MACRAMÉ
MACRAMÉS
MACRAMI
MACRAMIS
MACRO
MACROBIAN
MACROCODE
MACROCODES
MACROCOPIES
MACROCOPY
MACROCOSM
MACROCOSMS
MACROCYTE
MACROCYTES
MACRODOME
MACRODOMES
MACROLOGIES
MACROLOGY
MACRON
MACRONS
MACROPOD
MACROPODS
MACROS
MACRURAL
MACRUROUS
MACS
MACTATION
MACTATIONS
MACULA
MACULAE
MACULAR
MACULATE

MACULATED
MACULATES
MACULATING
MACULE
MACULES
MACULOSE
MAD
MADAM
MADAME
MADAMED
MADAMING
MADAMS
MADAROSES
MADAROSIS
MADBRAIN
MADCAP
MADCAPS
MADDED
MADDEN
MADDENED
MADDENING
MADDENS
MADDER
MADDERS
MADDEST
MADDING
MADDINGLY
MADE
MADEFIED
MADEFIES
MADEFY
MADEFYING
MADELEINE
MADELEINES
MADERISE
MADERISED
MADERISES
MADERISING
MADERIZE
MADERIZED
MADERIZES
MADERIZING
MADGE
MADGES
MADHOUSE
MADHOUSES
MADID
MADLING
MADLINGS
MADLY
MADMAN
MADMEN
MADNESS
MADNESSES
MADOQUA
MADOQUAS
MADRAS
MADRASA
MADRASAH
MADRASAHS
MADRASAS
MADRASES
MADRASSA

MADRASSAH
MADRASSAHS
MADRASSAS
MADREPORE
MADREPORES
MADRIGAL
MADRIGALS
MADROÑA
MADROÑAS
MADROÑO
MADROÑOS
MADS
MADWOMAN
MADWOMEN
MADWORT
MADWORTS
MADZOON
MADZOONS
MAE
MAELSTROM
MAELSTROMS
MAENAD
MAENADIC
MAENADS
MAESTOSO
MAESTRI
MAESTRO
MAESTROS
MAFFIA
MAFFIAS
MAFFICK
MAFFICKED
MAFFICKER
MAFFICKERS
MAFFICKING
MAFFICKINGS
MAFFICKS
MAFFLED
MAFFLIN
MAFFLING
MAFFLINGS
MAFFLINS
MAFIA
MAFIAS
MAFIOSI
MAFIOSO
MAG
MAGAZINE
MAGAZINES
MAGDALEN
MAGDALENE
MAGDALENES
MAGDALENS
MAGE
MAGENTA
MAGENTAS
MAGES
MAGESHIP
MAGESHIPS
MAGG
MAGGED
MAGGING
MAGGOT

MAGGOTS
MAGGOTY
MAGGS
MAGI
MAGIAN
MAGIANISM
MAGIANISMS
MAGIANS
MAGIC
MAGICAL
MAGICALLY
MAGICIAN
MAGICIANS
MAGICKED
MAGICKING
MAGICS
MAGILP
MAGILPS
MAGISM
MAGISMS
MAGISTER
MAGISTERIES
MAGISTERS
MAGISTERY
MAGISTRAL
MAGISTRALS
MAGLEV
MAGMA
MAGMAS
MAGMATA
MAGMATIC
MAGNALIUM
MAGNALIUMS
MAGNATE
MAGNATES
MAGNES
MAGNESES
MAGNESIA
MAGNESIAN
MAGNESIAS
MAGNESITE
MAGNESITES
MAGNESIUM
MAGNESIUMS
MAGNET
MAGNETIC
MAGNETICS
MAGNETISE
MAGNETISED
MAGNETISES
MAGNETISING
MAGNETISM
MAGNETISMS
MAGNETIST
MAGNETISTS
MAGNETITE
MAGNETITES
MAGNETIZE
MAGNETIZED
MAGNETIZES
MAGNETIZING
MAGNETO
MAGNETON

MAGNETONS
MAGNETOS
MAGNETRON
MAGNETRONS
MAGNETS
MAGNIFIC
MAGNIFICO
MAGNIFICOES
MAGNIFIED
MAGNIFIER
MAGNIFIERS
MAGNIFIES
MAGNIFY
MAGNIFYING
MAGNITUDE
MAGNITUDES
MAGNOLIA
MAGNOLIAS
MAGNOX
MAGNOXES
MAGNUM
MAGNUMS
MAGOT
MAGOTS
MAGPIE
MAGPIES
MAGS
MAGSMAN
MAGSMEN
MAGUEY
MAGUEYS
MAGUS
MAGYAR
MAHARAJA
MAHARAJAH
MAHARAJAHS
MAHARAJAS
MAHARANEE
MAHARANEES
MAHARANI
MAHARANIS
MAHARISHI
MAHARISHIS
MAHATMA
MAHATMAS
MAHLSTICK
MAHLSTICKS
MAHMAL
MAHMALS
MAHOE
MAHOES
MAHOGANIES
MAHOGANY
MAHONIA
MAHONIAS
MAHOUT
MAHOUTS
MAHSEER
MAHSEERS
MAHSIR
MAHSIRS
MAHUA
MAHUAS
MAHWA
MAHWAS
MAHZOR
MAHZORIM
MAID
MAIDAN
MAIDANS

MAIDED
MAIDEN
MAIDENISH
MAIDENLY
MAIDENS
MAIDHOOD
MAIDHOODS
MAIDING
MAIDISH
MAIDISM
MAIDISMS
MAIDLESS
MAIDS
MAIEUTIC
MAIEUTICS
MAIGRE
MAIGRES
MAIK
MAIKO
MAIKOS
MAIKS
MAIL
MAILABLE
MAILE
MAILED
MAILER
MAILERS
MAILES
MAILING
MAILINGS
MAILLOT
MAILLOTS
MAILMAN
MAILMEN
MAILMERGE
MAILMERGED
MAILMERGES
MAILMERGING
MAILS
MAIM
MAIMED
MAIMING
MAIMINGS
MAIMS
MAIN
MAINBOOM
MAINBOOMS
MAINBRACE
MAINBRACES
MAINDOOR
MAINDOORS
MAINED
MAINER
MAINEST
MAINFRAME
MAINFRAMES
MAINING
MAINLAND
MAINLANDS
MAINLINE
MAINLINED
MAINLINER
MAINLINERS
MAINLINES
MAINLINING
MAINLININGS
MAINLY
MAINMAST
MAINMASTS
MAINOR

MAINORS
MAINOUR
MAINOURS
MAINPRISE
MAINPRISES
MAINS
MAINSAIL
MAINSAILS
MAINSHEET
MAINSHEETS
MAINSTAY
MAINSTAYS
MAINTAIN
MAINTAINED
MAINTAINING
MAINTAINS
MAINTOP
MAINTOPS
MAINYARD
MAINYARDS
MAIOLICA
MAIOLICAS
MAIRE
MAIRES
MAISE
MAISES
MAIST
MAISTER
MAISTERED
MAISTERING
MAISTERS
MAISTRIES
MAISTRING
MAISTRINGS
MAISTRY
MAIZE
MAIZES
MAJESTIC
MAJESTIES
MAJESTY
MAJOLICA
MAJOLICAS
MAJOR
MAJORAT
MAJORATS
MAJORED
MAJORETTE
MAJORETTES
MAJORING
MAJORITIES
MAJORITY
MAJORS
MAJORSHIP
MAJORSHIPS
MAJUSCULE
MAJUSCULES
MAK
MAKABLE
MAKAR
MAKARS
MAKE
MAKEABLE
MAKEBATE
MAKEBATES
MAKELESS
MAKER
MAKERS
MAKES
MAKESHIFT
MAKESHIFTS

MAKIMONO
MAKIMONOS
MAKING
MAKINGS
MAKO
MAKOS
MAKS
MAL
MALACHITE
MALACHITES
MALACIA
MALACIAS
MALADIES
MALADROIT
MALADY
MALAGUEÑA
MALAGUEÑAS
MALAISE
MALAISES
MALAMUTE
MALAMUTES
MALANDER
MALANDERS
MALAPERT
MALAR
MALARIA
MALARIAL
MALARIAN
MALARIAS
MALARIOUS
MALARKEY
MALARKEYS
MALARKIES
MALARKY
MALARS
MALATE
MALATES
MALAX
MALAXAGE
MALAXAGES
MALAXATE
MALAXATED
MALAXATES
MALAXATING
MALAXATOR
MALAXATORS
MALAXED
MALAXES
MALAXING
MALE
MALEATE
MALEATES
MALEDICT
MALEDICTED
MALEDICTING
MALEDICTS
MALEFIC
MALEFICE
MALEFICES
MALEIC
MALEMUTE
MALEMUTES
MALENGINE
MALENGINES
MALES
MALFORMED
MALGRADO
MALGRE
MALGRES
MALI

MALIC
MALICE
MALICED
MALICES
MALICHO
MALICHOS
MALICING
MALICIOUS
MALIGN
MALIGNANT
MALIGNANTS
MALIGNED
MALIGNER
MALIGNERS
MALIGNING
MALIGNITIES
MALIGNITY
MALIGNLY
MALIGNS
MALINGER
MALINGERED
MALINGERIES
MALINGERING
MALINGERS
MALINGERY
MALIS
MALISON
MALISONS
MALIST
MALKIN
MALKINS
MALL
MALLAM
MALLAMS
MALLANDER
MALLANDERS
MALLARD
MALLARDS
MALLEABLE
MALLEATE
MALLEATED
MALLEATES
MALLEATING
MALLECHO
MALLECHOS
MALLED
MALLEE
MALLEES
MALLEI
MALLEMUCK
MALLEMUCKS
MALLENDER
MALLENDERS
MALLEOLAR
MALLEOLI
MALLEOLUS
MALLEOLUSES
MALLET
MALLETS
MALLEUS
MALLEUSES
MALLING
MALLOW
MALLOWS
MALLS
MALM
MALMAG
MALMAGS
MALMS
MALMSEY

| | | | | |
|---|---|---|---|---|
| MALMSEYS | MAMMEE | MANCUSES | MANES | MANICURED |
| MALODOUR | MAMMEES | MAND | MANET | MANICURES |
| MALODOURS | MAMMER | MANDALA | MANEUVER | MANICURING |
| MALONATE | MAMMERED | MANDALAS | MANEUVERED | MANIES |
| MALONATES | MAMMERING | MANDAMUS | MANEUVERING | MANIFEST |
| MALS | MAMMERS | MANDAMUSES | MANEUVERS | MANIFESTED |
| MALSTICK | MAMMET | MANDARIN | MANFUL | MANIFESTING |
| MALSTICKS | MAMMETRIES | MANDARINE | MANFULLY | MANIFESTO |
| MALT | MAMMETRY | MANDARINES | MANGABEY | MANIFESTOED |
| MALTALENT | MAMMETS | MANDARINS | MANGABEYS | MANIFESTOES |
| MALTALENTS | MAMMIES | MANDATARIES | MANGAL | MANIFESTOING |
| MALTASE | MAMMIFER | MANDATARY | MANGALS | MANIFESTOS |
| MALTASES | MAMMIFERS | MANDATE | MANGANATE | MANIFESTS |
| MALTED | MAMMIFORM | MANDATED | MANGANATES | MANIFOLD |
| MALTHA | MAMMILLA | MANDATES | MANGANESE | MANIFOLDED |
| MALTHAS | MAMMILLAE | MANDATING | MANGANESES | MANIFOLDING |
| MALTIER | MAMMOCK | MANDATOR | MANGANIC | MANIFOLDS |
| MALTIEST | MAMMOCKED | MANDATORIES | MANGANITE | MANIFORM |
| MALTING | MAMMOCKING | MANDATORS | MANGANITES | MANIHOC |
| MALTINGS | MAMMOCKS | MANDATORY | MANGANOUS | MANIHOCS |
| MALTMAN | MAMMOGRAM | MANDIBLE | MANGE | MANIKIN |
| MALTMEN | MAMMOGRAMS | MANDIBLES | MANGEL | MANIKINS |
| MALTOSE | MAMMON | MANDILION | MANGELS | MANILA |
| MALTOSES | MAMMONISH | MANDILIONS | MANGER | MANILAS |
| MALTREAT | MAMMONISM | MANDIOC | MANGERS | MANILLA |
| MALTREATED | MAMMONISMS | MANDIOCA | MANGES | MANILLAS |
| MALTREATING | MAMMONIST | MANDIOCAS | MANGETOUT | MANILLE |
| MALTREATS | MAMMONISTS | MANDIOCCA | MANGETOUTS | MANILLES |
| MALTS | MAMMONITE | MANDIOCCAS | MANGEY | MANIOC |
| MALTSTER | MAMMONITES | MANDIOCS | MANGIER | MANIOCS |
| MALTSTERS | MAMMONS | MANDIR | MANGIEST | MANIPLE |
| MALTWORM | MAMMOTH | MANDIRA | MANGINESS | MANIPLES |
| MALTWORMS | MAMMOTHS | MANDIRAS | MANGINESSES | MANIPLIES |
| MALTY | MAMMY | MANDIRS | MANGLE | MANIPULAR |
| MALVA | MAMS | MANDOLA | MANGLED | MANIPULARS |
| MALVAS | MAMSELLE | MANDOLAS | MANGLER | MANITO |
| MALVASIA | MAMSELLES | MANDOLIN | MANGLERS | MANITOS |
| MALVASIAS | MAN | MANDOLINE | MANGLES | MANITOU |
| MALVESIE | MANA | MANDOLINES | MANGLING | MANITOUS |
| MALVESIES | MANACLE | MANDOLINS | MANGO | MANJACK |
| MALVOISIE | MANACLED | MANDOM | MANGOES | MANJACKS |
| MALVOISIES | MANACLES | MANDOMS | MANGOLD | MANKIER |
| MAM | MANACLING | MANDORA | MANGOLDS | MANKIEST |
| MAMA | MANAGE | MANDORAS | MANGONEL | MANKIND |
| MAMAS | MANAGED | MANDORLA | MANGONELS | MANKINDS |
| MAMBA | MANAGER | MANDORLAS | MANGOSTAN | MANKY |
| MAMBAS | MANAGERS | MANDRAKE | MANGOSTANS | MANLIER |
| MAMBO | MANAGES | MANDRAKES | MANGOUSTE | MANLIEST |
| MAMBOED | MANAGING | MANDREL | MANGOUSTES | MANLINESS |
| MAMBOING | MANAKIN | MANDRELS | MANGROVE | MANLINESSES |
| MAMBOS | MANAKINS | MANDRIL | MANGROVES | MANLY |
| MAMELON | MAÑANA | MANDRILL | MANGY | MANNA |
| MAMELONS | MAÑANAS | MANDRILLS | MANHANDLE | MANNAS |
| MAMELUCO | MANAS | MANDRILS | MANHANDLED | MANNED |
| MAMELUCOS | MANATEE | MANDUCATE | MANHANDLES | MANNEQUIN |
| MAMILLA | MANATEES | MANDUCATED | MANHANDLING | MANNEQUINS |
| MAMILLAE | MANATI | MANDUCATES | MANHOLE | MANNER |
| MAMILLAR | MANATIS | MANDUCATING | MANHOLES | MANNERED |
| MAMILLARY | MANCANDO | MANDYLION | MANHOOD | MANNERISM |
| MAMILLATE | MANCHE | MANDYLIONS | MANHOODS | MANNERISMS |
| MAMMA | MANCHES | MANE | MANHUNT | MANNERIST |
| MAMMAE | MANCHET | MANED | MANHUNTS | MANNERISTS |
| MAMMAL | MANCHETS | MANÈGE | MANIA | MANNERLY |
| MAMMALIAN | MANCIPATE | MANÈGED | MANIAC | MANNERS |
| MAMMALOGIES | MANCIPATED | MANÈGES | MANIACAL | MANNIKIN |
| MAMMALOGY | MANCIPATES | MANÈGING | MANIACS | MANNIKINS |
| MAMMALS | MANCIPATING | MANEH | MANIAS | MANNING |
| MAMMARY | MANCIPLE | MANEHS | MANIC | MANNISH |
| MAMMAS | MANCIPLES | MANELESS | MANICALLY | MANNITE |
| MAMMATE | MANCUS | MANENT | MANICURE | MANNITES |

MANNITOL
MANNITOLS
MANNOSE
MANNOSES
MANOAO
MANOAOS
MANOEUVRE
MANOEUVRED
MANOEUVRES
MANOEUVRING
MANOMETER
MANOMETERS
MANOMETRIES
MANOMETRY
MANOR
MANORIAL
MANORS
MANPACK
MANPACKS
MANPOWER
MANPOWERS
MANQUÉ
MANRED
MANREDS
MANRENT
MANRENTS
MANRIDER
MANRIDERS
MANS
MANSARD
MANSARDS
MANSE
MANSES
MANSHIFT
MANSHIFTS
MANSION
MANSIONS
MANSONRIES
MANSONRY
MANSUETE
MANSWORN
MANTA
MANTAS
MANTEAU
MANTEAUS
MANTEAUX
MANTEEL
MANTEELS
MANTEL
MANTELET
MANTELETS
MANTELS
MANTIC
MANTICORA
MANTICORAS
MANTICORE
MANTICORES
MANTID
MANTIDS
MANTIES
MANTILLA
MANTILLAS
MANTIS
MANTISES
MANTISSA
MANTISSAS
MANTLE
MANTLED
MANTLES
MANTLET

MANTLETS
MANTLING
MANTLINGS
MANTO
MANTOES
MANTOS
MANTRA
MANTRAM
MANTRAMS
MANTRAP
MANTRAPS
MANTRAS
MANTUA
MANTUAS
MANTY
MANUAL
MANUALLY
MANUALS
MANUBRIA
MANUBRIAL
MANUBRIUM
MANUKA
MANUKAS
MANUL
MANULS
MANUMIT
MANUMITS
MANUMITTED
MANUMITTING
MANURANCE
MANURANCES
MANURE
MANURED
MANURER
MANURERS
MANURES
MANURIAL
MANURING
MANURINGS
MANUS
MANY
MANYFOLD
MANYPLIES
MANZANITA
MANZANITAS
MANZELLO
MANZELLOS
MAORMOR
MAORMORS
MAP
MAPLE
MAPLES
MAPPED
MAPPEMOND
MAPPEMONDS
MAPPER
MAPPERIES
MAPPERS
MAPPERY
MAPPING
MAPPIST
MAPPISTS
MAPS
MAPSTICK
MAPSTICKS
MAPWISE
MAQUETTE
MAQUETTES
MAQUI
MAQUIS

MAQUISARD
MAQUISARDS
MAR
MARA
MARABOU
MARABOUS
MARABOUT
MARABOUTS
MARACA
MARACAS
MARAGING
MARAGINGS
MARAH
MARAHS
MARAS
MARASMIC
MARASMUS
MARASMUSES
MARATHON
MARATHONS
MARAUD
MARAUDED
MARAUDER
MARAUDERS
MARAUDING
MARAUDS
MARAVEDI
MARAVEDIS
MARBLE
MARBLED
MARBLER
MARBLERS
MARBLES
MARBLIER
MARBLIEST
MARBLING
MARBLINGS
MARBLY
MARC
MARCASITE
MARCASITES
MARCATO
MARCEL
MARCELLA
MARCELLAS
MARCELLED
MARCELLING
MARCELS
MARCH
MARCHED
MARCHER
MARCHERS
MARCHES
MARCHESA
MARCHESAS
MARCHESE
MARCHESES
MARCHESI
MARCHING
MARCHMAN
MARCHMEN
MARCHPANE
MARCHPANES
MARCONI
MARCONIED
MARCONIING
MARCONIS
MARCS
MARD
MARDIED

MARDIER
MARDIES
MARDIEST
MARDY
MARDYING
MARE
MAREMMA
MAREMMAS
MARES
MARESCHAL
MARESCHALLED
MARESCHALLING
MARESCHALS
MARG
MARGARIC
MARGARIN
MARGARINE
MARGARINES
MARGARINS
MARGARITA
MARGARITAS
MARGARITE
MARGARITES
MARGAY
MARGAYS
MARGE
MARGENT
MARGENTED
MARGENTING
MARGENTS
MARGES
MARGIN
MARGINAL
MARGINALS
MARGINATE
MARGINED
MARGINING
MARGINS
MARGOSA
MARGOSAS
MARGRAVE
MARGRAVES
MARGS
MARIA
MARIACHI
MARIACHIS
MARIALITE
MARIALITES
MARID
MARIDS
MARIGOLD
MARIGOLDS
MARIGRAM
MARIGRAMS
MARIGRAPH
MARIGRAPHS
MARIHUANA
MARIHUANAS
MARIJUANA
MARIJUANAS
MARIMBA
MARIMBAS
MARINA
MARINADE
MARINADED
MARINADES
MARINADING
MARINAS
MARINATE
MARINATED

MARINATES
MARINATING
MARINE
MARINER
MARINERS
MARINES
MARINIÈRE
MARIPOSA
MARIPOSAS
MARISCHAL
MARISCHALLED
MARISCHALLING
MARISCHALS
MARISH
MARISHES
MARITAGE
MARITAGES
MARITAL
MARITALLY
MARITIME
MARJORAM
MARJORAMS
MARK
MARKED
MARKEDLY
MARKER
MARKERS
MARKET
MARKETED
MARKETEER
MARKETEERS
MARKETER
MARKETERS
MARKETING
MARKETINGS
MARKETS
MARKHOR
MARKHORS
MARKING
MARKINGS
MARKKA
MARKKAA
MARKKAS
MARKMAN
MARKMEN
MARKS
MARKSMAN
MARKSMEN
MARL
MARLE
MARLED
MARLES
MARLIER
MARLIEST
MARLIN
MARLINE
MARLINES
MARLING
MARLINGS
MARLINS
MARLS
MARLSTONE
MARLSTONES
MARLY
MARM
MARMALADE
MARMALADES
MARMARISE
MARMARISED
MARMARISES

| | | | | |
|---|---|---|---|---|
| MARMARISING | MARSH | MARZIPANS | MASOOLAHS | MASTICATED |
| MARMARIZE | MARSHAL | MAS | MASQUE | MASTICATES |
| MARMARIZED | MARSHALCIES | MASCARA | MASQUER | MASTICATING |
| MARMARIZES | MARSHALCY | MASCARAS | MASQUERS | MASTICH |
| MARMARIZING | MARSHALLED | MASCARON | MASQUES | MASTICHS |
| MARMITE | MARSHALLING | MASCARONS | MASS | MASTICOT |
| MARMITES | MARSHALLINGS | MASCLE | MASSA | MASTICOTS |
| MARMOREAL | MARSHALS | MASCLED | MASSACRE | MASTICS |
| MARMOSE | MARSHES | MASCLES | MASSACRED | MASTIER |
| MARMOSES | MARSHIER | MASCON | MASSACRES | MASTIEST |
| MARMOSET | MARSHIEST | MASCONS | MASSACRING | MASTIFF |
| MARMOSETS | MARSHLAND | MASCOT | MASSAGE | MASTIFFS |
| MARMOT | MARSHLANDS | MASCOTS | MASSAGED | MASTING |
| MARMOTS | MARSHWORT | MASCULINE | MASSAGES | MASTITIS |
| MARMS | MARSHWORTS | MASCULINES | MASSAGING | MASTITISES |
| MAROCAIN | MARSHY | MASCULY | MASSAGIST | MASTLESS |
| MAROCAINS | MARSUPIA | MASE | MASSAGISTS | MASTODON |
| MAROON | MARSUPIAL | MASED | MASSAS | MASTODONS |
| MAROONED | MARSUPIALS | MASER | MASSÉ | MASTOID |
| MAROONER | MARSUPIUM | MASERS | MASSED | MASTOIDAL |
| MAROONERS | MARSUPIUMS | MASES | MASSES | MASTOIDS |
| MAROONING | MART | MASH | MASSÉS | MASTS |
| MAROONINGS | MARTAGON | MASHALLAH | MASSETER | MASTY |
| MAROONS | MARTAGONS | MASHED | MASSETERS | MASU |
| MAROQUIN | MARTED | MASHER | MASSEUR | MASULA |
| MAROQUINS | MARTEL | MASHERS | MASSEURS | MASULAS |
| MAROR | MARTELLED | MASHES | MASSEUSE | MASURIUM |
| MARORS | MARTELLING | MASHIE | MASSEUSES | MASURIUMS |
| MARPLOT | MARTELLO | MASHIER | MASSICOT | MASUS |
| MARPLOTS | MARTELLOS | MASHIES | MASSICOTS | MAT |
| MARQUE | MARTELS | MASHIEST | MASSIER | MATACHIN |
| MARQUEE | MARTEN | MASHING | MASSIEST | MATACHINS |
| MARQUEES | MARTENOT | MASHINGS | MASSIF | MATADOR |
| MARQUES | MARTENOTS | MASHLAM | MASSIFS | MATADORE |
| MARQUESS | MARTENS | MASHLAMS | MASSINESS | MATADORES |
| MARQUESSES | MARTIAL | MASHLIM | MASSINESSES | MATADORS |
| MARQUETRIES | MARTIALLY | MASHLIMS | MASSING | MATAMATA |
| MARQUETRY | MARTIN | MASHLIN | MASSIVE | MATAMATAS |
| MARQUIS | MARTINET | MASHLINS | MASSIVELY | MATCH |
| MARQUISE | MARTINETS | MASHLOCH | MASSOOLA | MATCHABLE |
| MARQUISES | MARTING | MASHLOCHS | MASSOOLAS | MATCHBOX |
| MARRAM | MARTINI | MASHLUM | MASSY | MATCHBOXES |
| MARRAMS | MARTINIS | MASHLUMS | MASSYMORE | MATCHED |
| MARRED | MARTINS | MASHMAN | MASSYMORES | MATCHER |
| MARRELS | MARTLET | MASHMEN | MAST | MATCHERS |
| MARRIAGE | MARTLETS | MASHY | MASTABA | MATCHES |
| MARRIAGES | MARTS | MASING | MASTABAS | MATCHING |
| MARRIED | MARTYR | MASJID | MASTED | MATCHLESS |
| MARRIER | MARTYRDOM | MASJIDS | MASTER | MATCHLOCK |
| MARRIERS | MARTYRDOMS | MASK | MASTERATE | MATCHLOCKS |
| MARRIES | MARTYRED | MASKED | MASTERATES | MATCHWOOD |
| MARRING | MARTYRIES | MASKER | MASTERDOM | MATCHWOODS |
| MARROW | MARTYRING | MASKERS | MASTERDOMS | MATE |
| MARROWED | MARTYRISE | MASKING | MASTERED | MATÉ |
| MARROWFAT | MARTYRISED | MASKS | MASTERFUL | MATED |
| MARROWFATS | MARTYRISES | MASLIN | MASTERIES | MATELASSÉ |
| MARROWING | MARTYRISING | MASLINS | MASTERING | MATELASSÉS |
| MARROWISH | MARTYRIZE | MASOCHISM | MASTERINGS | MATELESS |
| MARROWS | MARTYRIZED | MASOCHISMS | MASTERLY | MATELOT |
| MARROWSKIED | MARTYRIZES | MASOCHIST | MASTERS | MATELOTE |
| MARROWSKIES | MARTYRIZING | MASOCHISTS | MASTERY | MATELOTES |
| MARROWSKY | MARTYRS | MASON | MASTFUL | MATELOTS |
| MARROWSKYING | MARTYRY | MASONED | MASTHEAD | MATER |
| MARROWY | MARVEL | MASONIC | MASTHEADED | MATERIAL |
| MARRUM | MARVELLED | MASONING | MASTHEADING | MATERIALS |
| MARRUMS | MARVELLING | MASONRIED | MASTHEADS | MATÉRIEL |
| MARRY | MARVELS | MASONRIES | MASTHOUSE | MATÉRIELS |
| MARRYING | MARYBUD | MASONRY | MASTHOUSES | MATERNAL |
| MARRYINGS | MARYBUDS | MASONS | MASTIC | MATERNITIES |
| MARS | MARZIPAN | MASOOLAH | MASTICATE | MATERNITY |

MATERS
MATES
MATÉS
MATESHIP
MATESHIPS
MATEY
MATFELON
MATFELONS
MATGRASS
MATGRASSES
MATH
MATHESES
MATHESIS
MATHS
MATICO
MATICOS
MATIER
MATIEST
MATIN
MATINAL
MATINEE
MATINÉE
MATINEES
MATINÉES
MATING
MATINS
MATLO
MATLOS
MATLOW
MATLOWS
MATRASS
MATRASSES
MATRIARCH
MATRIARCHS
MATRIC
MATRICE
MATRICES
MATRICIDE
MATRICIDES
MATRICS
MATRICULA
MATRICULAS
MATRILINIES
MATRILINY
MATRIMONIES
MATRIMONY
MATRIX
MATRIXES
MATRON
MATRONAGE
MATRONAGES
MATRONAL
MATRONISE
MATRONISED
MATRONISES
MATRONISING
MATRONIZE
MATRONIZED
MATRONIZES
MATRONIZING
MATRONLY
MATRONS
MATROSS
MATROSSES
MATS
MATT
MATTAMORE
MATTAMORES
MATTE
MATTED

MATTER
MATTERED
MATTERFUL
MATTERING
MATTERS
MATTERY
MATTES
MATTIE
MATTIES
MATTING
MATTINGS
MATTINS
MATTOCK
MATTOCKS
MATTOID
MATTOIDS
MATTRESS
MATTRESSES
MATURABLE
MATURATE
MATURATED
MATURATES
MATURATING
MATURE
MATURED
MATURELY
MATURER
MATURES
MATUREST
MATURING
MATURITIES
MATURITY
MATUTINAL
MATUTINE
MATWEED
MATWEEDS
MATY
MATZA
MATZAH
MATZAHS
MATZAS
MATZO
MATZOH
MATZOON
MATZOONS
MATZOS
MATZOT
MATZOTH
MAUD
MAUDLIN
MAUDS
MAUGRE
MAUGRES
MAUL
MAULED
MAULERS
MAULGRE
MAULGRES
MAULING
MAULS
MAULSTICK
MAULSTICKS
MAULVI
MAULVIS
MAUMET
MAUMETRIES
MAUMETRY
MAUMETS
MAUN
MAUND

MAUNDED
MAUNDER
MAUNDERED
MAUNDERER
MAUNDERERS
MAUNDERING
MAUNDERINGS
MAUNDERS
MAUNDIES
MAUNDING
MAUNDS
MAUNDY
MAUNNA
MAUSOLEAN
MAUSOLEUM
MAUSOLEUMS
MAUTHER
MAUTHERS
MAUVAIS
MAUVAISE
MAUVE
MAUVEIN
MAUVEINE
MAUVEINES
MAUVEINS
MAUVER
MAUVES
MAUVEST
MAUVIN
MAUVINE
MAUVINES
MAUVINS
MAVERICK
MAVERICKED
MAVERICKING
MAVERICKS
MAVIN
MAVINS
MAVIS
MAVISES
MAW
MAWBOUND
MAWK
MAWKIER
MAWKIEST
MAWKIN
MAWKINS
MAWKISH
MAWKISHLY
MAWKS
MAWKY
MAWMET
MAWMETRIES
MAWMETRY
MAWMETS
MAWPUS
MAWPUSES
MAWR
MAWRS
MAWS
MAWSEED
MAWSEEDS
MAWTHER
MAWTHERS
MAX
MAXES
MAXI
MAXILLA
MAXILLAE
MAXILLARIES

MAXILLARY
MAXILLULA
MAXILLULAE
MAXIM
MAXIMA
MAXIMAL
MAXIMALLY
MAXIMIN
MAXIMINS
MAXIMISE
MAXIMISED
MAXIMISES
MAXIMISING
MAXIMIST
MAXIMISTS
MAXIMIZE
MAXIMIZED
MAXIMIZES
MAXIMIZING
MAXIMS
MAXIMUM
MAXIS
MAXIXE
MAXIXES
MAXWELL
MAXWELLS
MAY
MAYA
MAYAS
MAYBE
MAYBES
MAYDAY
MAYDAYS
MAYED
MAYEST
MAYFLIES
MAYFLOWER
MAYFLOWERS
MAYFLY
MAYHAP
MAYHEM
MAYHEMS
MAYING
MAYINGS
MAYOR
MAYORAL
MAYORALTIES
MAYORALTY
MAYORESS
MAYORESSES
MAYORS
MAYORSHIP
MAYORSHIPS
MAYPOLE
MAYPOLES
MAYS
MAYST
MAYSTER
MAYSTERS
MAYWEED
MAYWEEDS
MAZARD
MAZARDS
MAZARINE
MAZARINES
MAZE
MAZED
MAZEFUL
MAZEMENT
MAZEMENTS

MAZER
MAZERS
MAZES
MAZHBI
MAZHBIS
MAZIER
MAZIEST
MAZILY
MAZINESS
MAZINESSES
MAZING
MAZOUT
MAZOUTS
MAZUMA
MAZUMAS
MAZURKA
MAZURKAS
MAZUT
MAZUTS
MAZY
MAZZARD
MAZZARDS
ME
MEACOCK
MEACOCKS
MEAD
MEADOW
MEADOWS
MEADOWY
MEADS
MEAGRE
MEAGRELY
MEAGRER
MEAGRES
MEAGREST
MEAL
MEALED
MEALER
MEALERS
MEALIE
MEALIER
MEALIES
MEALIEST
MEALINESS
MEALINESSES
MEALING
MEALS
MEALY
MEAN
MEANDER
MEANDERED
MEANDERING
MEANDERS
MEANDRIAN
MEANDROUS
MEANE
MEANED
MEANER
MEANES
MEANEST
MEANIE
MEANIES
MEANING
MEANINGLY
MEANINGS
MEANLY
MEANNESS
MEANNESSES
MEANS
MEANT

MEANTIME
MEANTIMES
MEANWHILE
MEANWHILES
MEANY
MEARE
MEARES
MEASE
MEASED
MEASES
MEASING
MEASLE
MEASLED
MEASLES
MEASLIER
MEASLIEST
MEASLING
MEASLY
MEASURE
MEASURED
MEASURER
MEASURERS
MEASURES
MEASURING
MEASURINGS
MEAT
MEATAL
MEATH
MEATHE
MEATHEAD
MEATHEADS
MEATHES
MEATHS
MEATIER
MEATIEST
MEATINESS
MEATINESSES
MEATLESS
MEATS
MEATUS
MEATUSES
MEATY
MEAWES
MEAZEL
MEAZELS
MEBOS
MEBOSES
MECHANIC
MECHANICS
MECHANISE
MECHANISED
MECHANISES
MECHANISING
MECHANISM
MECHANISMS
MECHANIST
MECHANISTS
MECHANIZE
MECHANIZED
MECHANIZES
MECHANIZING
MECONATE
MECONATES
MECONIC
MECONIN
MECONINS
MECONIUM
MECONIUMS
MEDAEWART
MEDAEWARTS

MEDAL
MEDALET
MEDALETS
MEDALLED
MEDALLIC
MEDALLING
MEDALLION
MEDALLIONED
MEDALLIONING
MEDALLIONS
MEDALLIST
MEDALLISTS
MEDALS
MEDDLE
MEDDLED
MEDDLER
MEDDLERS
MEDDLES
MEDDLING
MEDDLINGS
MEDFLIES
MEDFLY
MEDIA
MEDIACIES
MEDIACY
MEDIAE
MEDIAEVAL
MEDIAL
MEDIALLY
MEDIALS
MEDIAN
MEDIANS
MEDIANT
MEDIANTS
MEDIATE
MEDIATED
MEDIATELY
MEDIATES
MEDIATING
MEDIATION
MEDIATIONS
MEDIATISE
MEDIATISED
MEDIATISES
MEDIATISING
MEDIATIVE
MEDIATIZE
MEDIATIZED
MEDIATIZES
MEDIATIZING
MEDIATOR
MEDIATORS
MEDIATORY
MEDIATRICES
MEDIATRIX
MEDIC
MEDICABLE
MEDICAID
MEDICAIDS
MEDICAL
MEDICALLY
MEDICALS
MEDICARE
MEDICARES
MEDICATE
MEDICATED
MEDICATES
MEDICATING
MEDICINAL
MEDICINE

MEDICINED
MEDICINER
MEDICINERS
MEDICINES
MEDICINING
MEDICK
MEDICKS
MEDICO
MEDICOS
MEDICS
MEDIEVAL
MEDII
MEDINA
MEDINAS
MEDIOCRE
MEDITATE
MEDITATED
MEDITATES
MEDITATING
MEDIUM
MEDIUMS
MEDIUS
MEDIUSES
MEDLAR
MEDLARS
MEDLE
MEDLED
MEDLES
MEDLEY
MEDLEYS
MEDLING
MEDRESSEH
MEDRESSEHS
MEDULLA
MEDULLAE
MEDULLAR
MEDULLARY
MEDULLAS
MEDULLATE
MEDUSA
MEDUSAE
MEDUSAN
MEDUSANS
MEDUSAS
MEDUSOID
MEDUSOIDS
MEED
MEEDS
MEEK
MEEKEN
MEEKENED
MEEKENING
MEEKENS
MEEKER
MEEKEST
MEEKLY
MEEKNESS
MEEKNESSES
MEER
MEERCAT
MEERCATS
MEERED
MEERING
MEERKAT
MEERKATS
MEERS
MEET
MEETER
MEETEST
MEETING

MEETINGS
MEETLY
MEETNESS
MEETNESSES
MEETS
MEGABAR
MEGABARS
MEGABIT
MEGABITS
MEGABYTE
MEGABYTES
MEGACURIE
MEGACURIES
MEGACYCLE
MEGACYCLES
MEGADEATH
MEGADEATHS
MEGADYNE
MEGADYNES
MEGAFARAD
MEGAFARADS
MEGAFAUNA
MEGAFAUNAE
MEGAFAUNAS
MEGAFLORA
MEGAFLORAE
MEGAFLORAS
MEGAFOG
MEGAFOGS
MEGAGAUSS
MEGAGAUSSES
MEGAHERTZ
MEGAHERTZES
MEGAJOULE
MEGAJOULES
MEGALITH
MEGALITHS
MEGAPHONE
MEGAPHONED
MEGAPHONES
MEGAPHONING
MEGAPODE
MEGAPODES
MEGARA
MEGARAD
MEGARADS
MEGARON
MEGARONS
MEGASCOPE
MEGASCOPES
MEGASPORE
MEGASPORES
MEGASS
MEGASSE
MEGASSES
MEGASTORE
MEGASTORES
MEGATON
MEGATONNE
MEGATONNES
MEGATONS
MEGAVOLT
MEGAVOLTS
MEGAWATT
MEGAWATTS
MEGILP
MEGILPS
MEGOHM
MEGOHMS
MEGRIM

MEGRIMS
MEIN
MEINED
MEINEY
MEINEYS
MEINIE
MEINIES
MEINING
MEINS
MEINT
MEINY
MEIOFAUNA
MEIONITE
MEIONITES
MEIOSES
MEIOSIS
MEIOTIC
MEITH
MEITHS
MEKOMETER
MEKOMETERS
MEL
MELAMINE
MELAMINES
MELAMPODE
MELAMPODES
MÉLANGE
MÉLANGES
MELANIC
MELANIN
MELANINS
MELANISM
MELANISMS
MELANITE
MELANITES
MELANO
MELANOMA
MELANOMAS
MELANOMATA
MELANOS
MELANOSES
MELANOSIS
MELANOTIC
MELANOUS
MELANURIA
MELANURIAS
MELANURIC
MELAPHYRE
MELAPHYRES
MELATONIN
MELATONINS
MELD
MELDED
MELDER
MELDERS
MELDING
MELDS
MÊLÉE
MÊLÉES
MELIC
MELICS
MELILITE
MELILITES
MELILOT
MELILOTS
MELINITE
MELINITES
MELIORATE
MELIORATED
MELIORATES

MELIORATING
MELIORISM
MELIORISMS
MELIORIST
MELIORISTS
MELIORITIES
MELIORITY
MELISMA
MELISMAS
MELISMATA
MELL
MELLAY
MELLAYS
MELLED
MELLING
MELLITE
MELLITES
MELLITIC
MELLOW
MELLOWED
MELLOWER
MELLOWEST
MELLOWING
MELLOWLY
MELLOWS
MELLOWY
MELLS
MELOCOTON
MELOCOTONS
MELODEON
MELODEONS
MELODIC
MELODICS
MELODIES
MELODION
MELODIONS
MELODIOUS
MELODISE
MELODISED
MELODISES
MELODISING
MELODIST
MELODISTS
MELODIZE
MELODIZED
MELODIZES
MELODIZING
MELODRAMA
MELODRAMAS
MELODRAME
MELODRAMES
MELODY
MELOMANIA
MELOMANIAS
MELOMANIC
MELON
MELONS
MELS
MELT
MELTDOWN
MELTDOWNS
MELTED
MELTING
MELTINGLY
MELTINGS
MELTITH
MELTITHS
MELTON
MELTONS
MELTS

MEMBER
MEMBERED
MEMBERS
MEMBRAL
MEMBRANE
MEMBRANES
MEMENTO
MEMENTOES
MEMENTOS
MEMO
MEMOIR
MEMOIRISM
MEMOIRISMS
MEMOIRIST
MEMOIRISTS
MEMOIRS
MEMORABLE
MEMORABLY
MEMORANDA
MEMORIAL
MEMORIALS
MEMORIES
MEMORISE
MEMORISED
MEMORISES
MEMORISING
MEMORITER
MEMORIZE
MEMORIZED
MEMORIZES
MEMORIZING
MEMORY
MEMOS
MEN
MENACE
MENACED
MENACER
MENACERS
MENACES
MENACING
MENADIONE
MENADIONES
MÉNAGE
MENAGERIE
MENAGERIES
MÉNAGES
MENARCHE
MENARCHES
MEND
MENDACITIES
MENDACITY
MENDED
MENDER
MENDERS
MENDICANT
MENDICANTS
MENDICITIES
MENDICITY
MENDING
MENDINGS
MENDS
MENE
MENED
MENEER
MENEERS
MENES
MENFOLK
MENFOLKS
MENG
MENGE

MENGED
MENGES
MENGING
MENGS
MENHADEN
MENHADENS
MENHIR
MENHIRS
MENIAL
MENIALS
MENING
MENINGEAL
MENINGES
MENINX
MENISCI
MENISCOID
MENISCUS
MENISCUSES
MENOLOGIES
MENOLOGY
MENOMINEE
MENOMINEES
MENOPAUSE
MENOPAUSES
MENOPOME
MENOPOMES
MENORAH
MENORAHS
MENORRHEA
MENORRHEAS
MENSAL
MENSCH
MENSCHES
MENSE
MENSED
MENSEFUL
MENSELESS
MENSES
MENSH
MENSHED
MENSHES
MENSHING
MENSING
MENSTRUA
MENSTRUAL
MENSTRUUM
MENSTRUUMS
MENSUAL
MENSURAL
MENSWEAR
MENSWEARS
MENT
MENTAL
MENTALISM
MENTALISMS
MENTALIST
MENTALISTS
MENTALITIES
MENTALITY
MENTALLY
MENTATION
MENTATIONS
MENTHOL
MENTHOLS
MENTICIDE
MENTICIDES
MENTION
MENTIONED
MENTIONING
MENTIONS

MENTOR
MENTORIAL
MENTORING
MENTORINGS
MENTORS
MENTUM
MENTUMS
MENU
MENUISIER
MENUISIERS
MENUS
MEOW
MEOWED
MEOWING
MEOWS
MEPACRINE
MEPACRINES
MEPHITIC
MEPHITIS
MEPHITISES
MEPHITISM
MEPHITISMS
MERC
MERCAPTAN
MERCAPTANS
MERCAT
MERCATS
MERCENARIES
MERCENARY
MERCER
MERCERIES
MERCERISE
MERCERISED
MERCERISES
MERCERISING
MERCERIZE
MERCERIZED
MERCERIZES
MERCERIZING
MERCERS
MERCERY
MERCHANT
MERCHANTED
MERCHANTING
MERCHANTINGS
MERCHANTS
MERCHET
MERCHETS
MERCHILD
MERCHILDREN
MERCIABLE
MERCIES
MERCIFIDE
MERCIFIED
MERCIFIES
MERCIFUL
MERCIFY
MERCIFYING
MERCILESS
MERCS
MERCURATE
MERCURATED
MERCURATES
MERCURATING
MERCURIAL
MERCURIALS
MERCURIC
MERCURIES
MERCUROUS
MERCURY

MERCY
MERE
MERED
MEREL
MERELL
MERELLS
MERELS
MERELY
MERER
MERES
MERESMAN
MERESMEN
MEREST
MERESTONE
MERESTONES
MERFOLK
MERFOLKS
MERGANSER
MERGANSERS
MERGE
MERGED
MERGENCE
MERGENCES
MERGER
MERGERS
MERGES
MERGING
MERI
MERICARP
MERICARPS
MERIDIAN
MERIDIANS
MERIL
MERILS
MERIMAKE
MERIMAKES
MERING
MERINGUE
MERINGUES
MERINO
MERINOS
MERIS
MERISM
MERISMS
MERISTEM
MERISTEMS
MERISTIC
MERIT
MERITED
MERITING
MERITS
MERK
MERKIN
MERKINS
MERKS
MERL
MERLE
MERLES
MERLIN
MERLING
MERLINGS
MERLINS
MERLON
MERLONS
MERLS
MERMAID
MERMAIDEN
MERMAIDENS
MERMAIDS
MERMAN

MERMEN
MEROGONIES
MEROGONY
MEROISTIC
MEROME
MEROMES
MEROPIDAN
MEROPIDANS
MEROSOME
MEROSOMES
MEROZOITE
MEROZOITES
MERPEOPLE
MERPEOPLES
MERRIER
MERRIES
MERRIEST
MERRILY
MERRIMENT
MERRIMENTS
MERRINESS
MERRINESSES
MERRY
MERRYMAN
MERRYMEN
MERSALYL
MERSALYLS
MERSE
MERSES
MERSION
MERSIONS
MERYCISM
MERYCISMS
MES
MESA
MESAIL
MESAILS
MESAL
MESALLY
MESARAIC
MESARCH
MESAS
MESCAL
MESCALIN
MESCALINS
MESCALISM
MESCALISMS
MESCALS
MESDAMES
MESE
MESEEMED
MESEEMS
MESEL
MESELED
MESELS
MESENTERA
MESENTERIES
MESENTERY
MESES
MESH
MESHED
MESHES
MESHIER
MESHIEST
MESHING
MESHINGS
MESHUGA
MESHUGGA
MESHUGGE
MESHY

MESIAL
MESIALLY
MESIAN
MESIC
MESMERIC
MESMERISE
MESMERISED
MESMERISES
MESMERISING
MESMERISM
MESMERISMS
MESMERIST
MESMERISTS
MESMERIZE
MESMERIZED
MESMERIZES
MESMERIZING
MESNE
MESOBLAST
MESOBLASTS
MESOCARP
MESOCARPS
MESODERM
MESODERMS
MESOGLOEA
MESOGLOEAS
MESOLITE
MESOLITES
MESOMORPH
MESOMORPHS
MESON
MESONIC
MESONS
MESOPHYLL
MESOPHYLLS
MESOPHYTE
MESOPHYTES
MESOTRON
MESOTRONS
MESPRISE
MESPRISES
MESPRIZE
MESPRIZES
MESQUIN
MESQUINE
MESQUIT
MESQUITE
MESQUITES
MESQUITS
MESS
MESSAGE
MESSAGED
MESSAGES
MESSAGING
MESSAN
MESSANS
MESSED
MESSENGER
MESSENGERS
MESSES
MESSIER
MESSIEST
MESSIEURS
MESSILY
MESSINESS
MESSINESSES
MESSING
MESSMATE
MESSMATES
MESSUAGE

MESSUAGES
MESSY
MESTEE
MESTEES
MESTIZA
MESTIZAS
MESTIZO
MESTIZOS
MESTO
MET
METABASES
METABASIS
METABATIC
METABOLIC
METAGE
METAGES
MÉTAIRIE
MÉTAIRIES
METAL
METALLED
METALLIC
METALLINE
METALLING
METALLINGS
METALLISE
METALLISED
METALLISES
METALLISING
METALLIST
METALLISTS
METALLIZE
METALLIZED
METALLIZES
METALLIZING
METALLOID
METALLOIDS
METALLY
METALS
METAMER
METAMERE
METAMERES
METAMERIC
METAMERS
METANOIA
METANOIAS
METAPHASE
METAPHASES
METAPHOR
METAPHORS
METAPLASM
METAPLASMS
METATARSI
MÉTAYAGE
MÉTAYAGES
MÉTAYER
MÉTAYERS
METAZOA
METAZOAN
METAZOANS
METAZOIC
METAZOON
METCAST
METCASTS
METE
METED
METEOR
METEORIC
METEORISM
METEORISMS
METEORIST

METEORISTS
METEORITE
METEORITES
METEOROID
METEOROIDS
METEOROUS
METEORS
METER
METERED
METERING
METERS
METES
METESTICK
METESTICKS
METEWAND
METEWANDS
METEYARD
METEYARDS
METHADON
METHADONE
METHADONES
METHADONS
METHANE
METHANES
METHANOL
METHANOLS
METHEGLIN
METHEGLINS
METHINK
METHINKS
METHOD
METHODIC
METHODISE
METHODISED
METHODISES
METHODISING
METHODIST
METHODISTS
METHODIZE
METHODIZED
METHODIZES
METHODIZING
METHODS
METHOUGHT
METHS
METHYL
METHYLATE
METHYLATED
METHYLATES
METHYLATING
METHYLENE
METHYLENES
METHYLIC
METHYLS
METHYSES
METHYSIS
METHYSTIC
METIC
METICAL
METICALS
METICS
MÉTIER
MÉTIERS
METIF
METIFS
METING
MÉTIS
MÉTISSE
MÉTISSES
METOL

METOLS
METONYM
METONYMIC
METONYMIES
METONYMS
METONYMY
METOPE
METOPES
METOPIC
METOPISM
METOPISMS
METOPON
METOPONS
METOPRYL
METOPRYLS
METRE
METRED
METRES
METRIC
METRICAL
METRICATE
METRICATED
METRICATES
METRICATING
METRICIAN
METRICIANS
METRICISE
METRICISED
METRICISES
METRICISING
METRICIST
METRICISTS
METRICIZE
METRICIZED
METRICIZES
METRICIZING
METRICS
METRIFIER
METRIFIERS
METRING
METRIST
METRISTS
METRITIS
METRITISES
METRO
MÉTRO
METROLOGIES
METROLOGY
METRONOME
METRONOMES
METROS
MÉTROS
METTLE
METTLED
METTLES
MEU
MEUNIÈRE
MEUS
MEUSE
MEUSED
MEUSES
MEUSING
MEVE
MEVED
MEVES
MEVING
MEW
MEWED
MEWING
MEWL

MEWLED
MEWLING
MEWLS
MEWS
MEWSED
MEWSES
MEWSING
MEYNT
MEZAIL
MEZAILS
MÉZÉ
MEZE
MEZEREON
MEZEREONS
MEZEREUM
MEZEREUMS
MÉZÉS
MEZES
MEZUZA
MEZUZAH
MEZUZAHS
MEZUZOTH
MEZZANINE
MEZZANINES
MEZZO
MEZZOS
MEZZOTINT
MEZZOTINTS
MGANGA
MGANGAS
MHO
MHORR
MHORRS
MHOS
MI
MIAOW
MIAOWED
MIAOWING
MIAOWS
MIASM
MIASMA
MIASMAL
MIASMAS
MIASMATA
MIASMATIC
MIASMIC
MIASMOUS
MIASMS
MIAUL
MIAULED
MIAULING
MIAULS
MICA
MICACEOUS
MICAS
MICATE
MICATED
MICATES
MICATING
MICE
MICELLA
MICELLAR
MICELLAS
MICELLE
MICELLES
MICHE
MICHED
MICHER
MICHERS
MICHES

MICHING
MICHINGS
MICK
MICKEY
MICKEYED
MICKEYING
MICKEYS
MICKIES
MICKLE
MICKLES
MICKS
MICKY
MICO
MICOS
MICRO
MICROBAR
MICROBARS
MICROBE
MICROBES
MICROBIAL
MICROBIAN
MICROBIC
MICROCARD
MICROCARDS
MICROCHIP
MICROCHIPS
MICROCODE
MICROCODES
MICROCOPIES
MICROCOPY
MICROCOSM
MICROCOSMS
MICROCYTE
MICROCYTES
MICRODOT
MICRODOTS
MICROFILM
MICROFILMED
MICROFILMING
MICROFILMS
MICROFORM
MICROFORMS
MICROGRAM
MICROGRAMS
MICROLITE
MICROLITES
MICROLITH
MICROLITHS
MICROLOGIES
MICROLOGY
MICRON
MICRONS
MICROPSIA
MICROPSIAS
MICROPYLE
MICROPYLES
MICROS
MICROSOME
MICROSOMES
MICROTOME
MICROTOMES
MICROTOMIES
MICROTOMY
MICROTONE
MICROTONES
MICROWAVE
MICROWAVES
MICROWIRE
MICROWIRES
MICRURGIES

MICRURGY
MICTION
MICTIONS
MICTURATE
MICTURATED
MICTURATES
MICTURATING
MID
MIDBRAIN
MIDBRAINS
MIDDAY
MIDDAYS
MIDDEN
MIDDENS
MIDDEST
MIDDIES
MIDDLE
MIDDLED
MIDDLEMAN
MIDDLEMEN
MIDDLES
MIDDLING
MIDDLINGS
MIDDY
MIDFIELD
MIDFIELDS
MIDGE
MIDGES
MIDGET
MIDGETS
MIDI
MIDINETTE
MIDINETTES
MIDIRON
MIDIRONS
MIDIS
MIDLAND
MIDLANDS
MIDMOST
MIDMOSTS
MIDNIGHT
MIDNIGHTS
MIDNOON
MIDNOONS
MIDRIB
MIDRIBS
MIDRIFF
MIDRIFFS
MIDS
MIDSHIP
MIDSHIPS
MIDST
MIDSTREAM
MIDSTREAMS
MIDSTS
MIDSUMMER
MIDSUMMERS
MIDWAY
MIDWAYS
MIDWIFE
MIDWIFED
MIDWIFERIES
MIDWIFERY
MIDWIFES
MIDWIFING
MIDWIVE
MIDWIVED
MIDWIVES
MIDWIVING
MIEN

MIENS
MIEVE
MIEVED
MIEVES
MIEVING
MIFF
MIFFED
MIFFIER
MIFFIEST
MIFFINESS
MIFFINESSES
MIFFING
MIFFS
MIFFY
MIFTY
MIGHT
MIGHTEST
MIGHTFUL
MIGHTIER
MIGHTIEST
MIGHTILY
MIGHTS
MIGHTST
MIGHTY
MIGNON
MIGNONNE
MIGRAINE
MIGRAINES
MIGRANT
MIGRANTS
MIGRATE
MIGRATED
MIGRATES
MIGRATING
MIGRATION
MIGRATIONS
MIGRATOR
MIGRATORS
MIGRATORY
MIHRAB
MIHRABS
MIKADO
MIKADOS
MIKE
MIKES
MIKRON
MIKRONS
MIL
MILADI
MILADIES
MILADIS
MILADY
MILAGE
MILAGES
MILCH
MILD
MILDEN
MILDENED
MILDENING
MILDENS
MILDER
MILDEST
MILDEW
MILDEWED
MILDEWING
MILDEWS
MILDEWY
MILDLY
MILDNESS
MILDNESSES

MILDS
MILE
MILEAGE
MILEAGES
MILER
MILERS
MILES
MILESTONE
MILESTONES
MILFOIL
MILFOILS
MILIARIA
MILIARIAS
MILIARY
MILIEU
MILIEUS
MILIEUX
MILITANCIES
MILITANCY
MILITANT
MILITANTS
MILITAR
MILITARIA
MILITARIES
MILITARY
MILITATE
MILITATED
MILITATES
MILITATING
MILITIA
MILITIAS
MILK
MILKED
MILKEN
MILKER
MILKERS
MILKFISH
MILKFISHES
MILKIER
MILKIEST
MILKILY
MILKINESS
MILKINESSES
MILKING
MILKINGS
MILKLESS
MILKLIKE
MILKMAID
MILKMAIDS
MILKMAN
MILKMEN
MILKS
MILKWOOD
MILKWOODS
MILKWORT
MILKWORTS
MILKY
MILL
MILLDAM
MILLDAMS
MILLE
MILLED
MILLENARIES
MILLENARY
MILLENNIA
MILLEPED
MILLEPEDE
MILLEPEDES
MILLEPEDS
MILLEPORE

| | | | | |
|---|---|---|---|---|
| MILLEPORES | MIM | MINDSETS | MINIMIZE | MINSTREL |
| MILLER | MIMBAR | MINE | MINIMIZED | MINSTRELS |
| MILLERITE | MIMBARS | MINED | MINIMIZES | MINT |
| MILLERITES | MIME | MINEOLA | MINIMIZING | MINTAGE |
| MILLERS | MIMED | MINEOLAS | MINIMS | MINTAGES |
| MILLES | MIMER | MINER | MINIMUM | MINTED |
| MILLET | MIMERS | MINERAL | MINIMUS | MINTER |
| MILLETS | MIMES | MINERALS | MINIMUSES | MINTERS |
| MILLIARD | MIMESES | MINERS | MINING | MINTIER |
| MILLIARDS | MIMESIS | MINES | MININGS | MINTIEST |
| MILLIARE | MIMESTER | MINETTE | MINION | MINTING |
| MILLIARES | MIMESTERS | MINETTES | MINIONS | MINTS |
| MILLIARIES | MIMETIC | MINEVER | MINIPILL | MINTY |
| MILLIARY | MIMETICAL | MINEVERS | MINIPILLS | MINUEND |
| MILLIBAR | MIMETITE | MING | MINIS | MINUENDS |
| MILLIBARS | MIMETITES | MINGED | MINISCULE | MINUET |
| MILLIÈME | MIMIC | MINGIER | MINISCULES | MINUETS |
| MILLIÈMES | MIMICAL | MINGIEST | MINISH | MINUS |
| MILLIME | MIMICKED | MINGINESS | MINISHED | MINUSCULE |
| MILLIMES | MIMICKER | MINGINESSES | MINISHES | MINUSCULES |
| MILLINER | MIMICKERS | MINGING | MINISHING | MINUSES |
| MILLINERIES | MIMICKING | MINGLE | MINISKIRT | MINUTE |
| MILLINERS | MIMICRIES | MINGLED | MINISKIRTS | MINUTED |
| MILLINERY | MIMICRY | MINGLER | MINISKIS | MINUTELY |
| MILLING | MIMICS | MINGLERS | MINISTER | MINUTEMAN |
| MILLINGS | MIMING | MINGLES | MINISTERED | MINUTEMEN |
| MILLION | MIMMER | MINGLING | MINISTERING | MINUTER |
| MILLIONS | MIMMEST | MINGLINGS | MINISTERS | MINUTES |
| MILLIONTH | MIMMICK | MINGS | MINISTRIES | MINUTEST |
| MILLIONTHS | MIMMICKED | MINGY | MINISTRY | MINUTIA |
| MILLIPED | MIMMICKING | MINI | MINISUB | MINUTIAE |
| MILLIPEDE | MIMMICKS | MINIATE | MINISUBS | MINUTING |
| MILLIPEDES | MIMOSA | MINIATED | MINIUM | MINUTIOSE |
| MILLIPEDS | MIMOSAS | MINIATES | MINIUMS | MINX |
| MILLOCRAT | MIMULUS | MINIATING | MINIVER | MINXES |
| MILLOCRATS | MIMULUSES | MINIATION | MINIVERS | MINY |
| MILLPOND | MINA | MINIATIONS | MINIVET | MINYAN |
| MILLPONDS | MINACIOUS | MINIATURE | MINIVETS | MINYANIM |
| MILLRACE | MINACITIES | MINIATURED | MINK | MINYANS |
| MILLRACES | MINACITY | MINIATURES | MINKE | MIOSES |
| MILLRIND | MINAE | MINIATURING | MINKES | MIOSIS |
| MILLRINDS | MINAR | MINIBUS | MINKS | MIR |
| MILLS | MINARET | MINIBUSES | MINNEOLA | MIRABELLE |
| MILLSTONE | MINARETS | MINICAB | MINNEOLAS | MIRABELLES |
| MILLSTONES | MINARS | MINICABS | MINNICK | MIRABILIA |
| MILLTAIL | MINAS | MINICAR | MINNICKED | MIRABILIS |
| MILLTAILS | MINATORY | MINICARS | MINNICKING | MIRABILISES |
| MILO | MINBAR | MINIDRESS | MINNICKS | MIRABLE |
| MILOMETER | MINBARS | MINIDRESSES | MINNIE | MIRACLE |
| MILOMETERS | MINCE | MINIER | MINNIES | MIRACLES |
| MILOR | MINCED | MINIEST | MINNOCK | MIRADOR |
| MILORD | MINCEMEAT | MINIFIED | MINNOCKED | MIRADORS |
| MILORDS | MINCEMEATS | MINIFIES | MINNOCKING | MIRAGE |
| MILORS | MINCER | MINIFY | MINNOCKS | MIRAGES |
| MILOS | MINCERS | MINIFYING | MINNOW | MIRBANE |
| MILREIS | MINCES | MINIKIN | MINNOWS | MIRBANES |
| MILS | MINCING | MINIKINS | MINO | MIRE |
| MILSEY | MINCINGLY | MINIM | MINOR | MIRED |
| MILSEYS | MINCINGS | MINIMA | MINORESS | MIREPOIX |
| MILT | MIND | MINIMAL | MINORESSES | MIRES |
| MILTED | MINDED | MINIMENT | MINORITE | MIRIER |
| MILTER | MINDER | MINIMENTS | MINORITES | MIRIEST |
| MILTERS | MINDERS | MINIMISE | MINORITIES | MIRIFIC |
| MILTING | MINDFUL | MINIMISED | MINORITY | MIRIFICAL |
| MILTONIA | MINDFULLY | MINIMISES | MINORS | MIRINESS |
| MILTONIAS | MINDING | MINIMISING | MINORSHIP | MIRINESSES |
| MILTS | MINDINGS | MINIMISM | MINORSHIPS | MIRING |
| MILTZ | MINDLESS | MINIMISMS | MINOS | MIRITI |
| MILTZES | MINDS | MINIMIST | MINSTER | MIRITIS |
| MILVINE | MINDSET | MINIMISTS | MINSTERS | MIRK |

MIRKER
MIRKEST
MIRKIER
MIRKIEST
MIRKS
MIRKSOME
MIRKY
MIRLIER
MIRLIEST
MIRLIGOES
MIRLITON
MIRLITONS
MIRLY
MIRROR
MIRRORED
MIRRORING
MIRRORS
MIRS
MIRTH
MIRTHFUL
MIRTHLESS
MIRTHS
MIRY
MIS
MISADVISE
MISADVISED
MISADVISES
MISADVISING
MISAIM
MISAIMED
MISAIMING
MISAIMS
MISALLEGE
MISALLEGED
MISALLEGES
MISALLEGING
MISALLIED
MISALLOT
MISALLOTS
MISALLOTTED
MISALLOTTING
MISANDRIES
MISANDRY
MISAPPLIED
MISAPPLIES
MISAPPLY
MISAPPLYING
MISARRAY
MISARRAYS
MISASSIGN
MISASSIGNED
MISASSIGNING
MISASSIGNS
MISAUNTER
MISAUNTERS
MISAVISED
MISBECAME
MISBECOME
MISBECOMES
MISBECOMING
MISBEGOT
MISBEHAVE
MISBEHAVED
MISBEHAVES
MISBEHAVING
MISBELIEF
MISBELIEFS
MISBESEEM
MISBESEEMED
MISBESEEMING

MISBESEEMS
MISBESTOW
MISBESTOWED
MISBESTOWING
MISBESTOWS
MISBIRTH
MISBIRTHS
MISBORN
MISCALL
MISCALLED
MISCALLING
MISCALLS
MISCARRIED
MISCARRIES
MISCARRY
MISCARRYING
MISCAST
MISCASTING
MISCASTS
MISCEGEN
MISCEGENE
MISCEGENES
MISCEGENS
MISCEGINE
MISCEGINES
MISCHANCE
MISCHANCED
MISCHANCES
MISCHANCING
MISCHANCY
MISCHARGE
MISCHARGED
MISCHARGES
MISCHARGING
MISCHIEF
MISCHIEFED
MISCHIEFING
MISCHIEFS
MISCIBLE
MISCOLOUR
MISCOLOURED
MISCOLOURING
MISCOLOURS
MISCOPIED
MISCOPIES
MISCOPY
MISCOPYING
MISCOUNT
MISCOUNTED
MISCOUNTING
MISCOUNTS
MISCREANT
MISCREANTS
MISCREATE
MISCREDIT
MISCREDITED
MISCREDITING
MISCREDITS
MISCREED
MISCREEDS
MISCUE
MISCUED
MISCUEING
MISCUES
MISCUING
MISDATE
MISDATED
MISDATES
MISDATING
MISDEAL

MISDEALING
MISDEALS
MISDEALT
MISDEED
MISDEEDS
MISDEEM
MISDEEMED
MISDEEMING
MISDEEMINGS
MISDEEMS
MISDEMEAN
MISDEMEANED
MISDEMEANING
MISDEMEANS
MISDEMPT
MISDESERT
MISDESERTS
MISDID
MISDIET
MISDIETS
MISDIGHT
MISDIRECT
MISDIRECTED
MISDIRECTING
MISDIRECTS
MISDO
MISDOER
MISDOERS
MISDOES
MISDOING
MISDOINGS
MISDONE
MISDONNE
MISDOUBT
MISDOUBTED
MISDOUBTING
MISDOUBTS
MISDRAW
MISDRAWING
MISDRAWINGS
MISDRAWN
MISDRAWS
MISDREAD
MISDREADS
MISDREW
MISE
MISEASE
MISEASES
MISEMPLOY
MISEMPLOYED
MISEMPLOYING
MISEMPLOYS
MISENTRIES
MISENTRY
MISER
MISERABLE
MISERABLES
MISERABLY
MISERE
MISÈRE
MISERERE
MISERERES
MISÈRES
MISERIES
MISERLY
MISERS
MISERY
MISES
MISESTEEM
MISESTEEMED

MISESTEEMING
MISESTEEMS
MISFAITH
MISFAITHS
MISFALL
MISFALLEN
MISFALLING
MISFALLS
MISFALNE
MISFARE
MISFARED
MISFARES
MISFARING
MISFARINGS
MISFEASOR
MISFEASORS
MISFEIGN
MISFEIGNED
MISFEIGNING
MISFEIGNS
MISFELL
MISFILE
MISFILED
MISFILES
MISFILING
MISFIRE
MISFIRED
MISFIRES
MISFIRING
MISFIT
MISFITS
MISFITTED
MISFITTING
MISFORM
MISFORMED
MISFORMING
MISFORMS
MISGAVE
MISGIVE
MISGIVEN
MISGIVES
MISGIVING
MISGIVINGS
MISGO
MISGOES
MISGOING
MISGONE
MISGOTTEN
MISGOVERN
MISGOVERNED
MISGOVERNING
MISGOVERNS
MISGRAFF
MISGRAFFED
MISGRAFFING
MISGRAFFS
MISGRAFT
MISGRAFTED
MISGRAFTING
MISGRAFTS
MISGROWTH
MISGROWTHS
MISGUGGLE
MISGUGGLED
MISGUGGLES
MISGUGGLING
MISGUIDE
MISGUIDED
MISGUIDER
MISGUIDERS

MISGUIDES
MISGUIDING
MISHANDLE
MISHANDLED
MISHANDLES
MISHANDLING
MISHANTER
MISHANTERS
MISHAP
MISHAPPED
MISHAPPEN
MISHAPPENED
MISHAPPENING
MISHAPPENS
MISHAPPING
MISHAPS
MISHAPT
MISHEAR
MISHEARD
MISHEARING
MISHEARS
MISHIT
MISHITS
MISHITTING
MISHMASH
MISHMASHES
MISHMEE
MISHMEES
MISHMI
MISHMIS
MISINFORM
MISINFORMED
MISINFORMING
MISINFORMS
MISINTEND
MISINTENDED
MISINTENDING
MISINTENDS
MISJOIN
MISJOINED
MISJOINING
MISJOINS
MISJUDGE
MISJUDGED
MISJUDGES
MISJUDGING
MISKEN
MISKENNED
MISKENNING
MISKENS
MISKENT
MISKNEW
MISKNOW
MISKNOWING
MISKNOWN
MISKNOWS
MISLAID
MISLAY
MISLAYING
MISLAYS
MISLEAD
MISLEADER
MISLEADERS
MISLEADING
MISLEADS
MISLEARED
MISLED
MISLEEKE
MISLEEKED
MISLEEKES

MISLEEKING
MISLETOE
MISLETOES
MISLIGHT
MISLIGHTED
MISLIGHTING
MISLIGHTS
MISLIKE
MISLIKED
MISLIKER
MISLIKERS
MISLIKES
MISLIKING
MISLIKINGS
MISLIPPEN
MISLIPPENED
MISLIPPENING
MISLIPPENS
MISLIT
MISLIVE
MISLIVED
MISLIVES
MISLIVING
MISLUCK
MISLUCKED
MISLUCKING
MISLUCKS
MISMADE
MISMAKE
MISMAKES
MISMAKING
MISMANAGE
MISMANAGED
MISMANAGES
MISMANAGING
MISMARRIED
MISMARRIES
MISMARRY
MISMARRYING
MISMATCH
MISMATCHED
MISMATCHES
MISMATCHING
MISMATE
MISMATED
MISMATES
MISMATING
MISMETRE
MISMETRED
MISMETRES
MISMETRING
MISNAME
MISNAMED
MISNAMES
MISNAMING
MISNOMER
MISNOMERED
MISNOMERING
MISNOMERS
MISO
MISOCLERE
MISOGAMIES
MISOGAMY
MISOGYNIES
MISOGYNY
MISOLOGIES
MISOLOGY
MISONEISM
MISONEISMS
MISONEIST

MISONEISTS
MISORDER
MISORDERED
MISORDERING
MISORDERS
MISOS
MISPICKEL
MISPICKELS
MISPLACE
MISPLACED
MISPLACES
MISPLACING
MISPLAY
MISPLAYED
MISPLAYING
MISPLAYS
MISPLEAD
MISPLEADED
MISPLEADING
MISPLEADINGS
MISPLEADS
MISPLEASE
MISPLEASED
MISPLEASES
MISPLEASING
MISPOINT
MISPOINTED
MISPOINTING
MISPOINTS
MISPRAISE
MISPRAISED
MISPRAISES
MISPRAISING
MISPRINT
MISPRINTED
MISPRINTING
MISPRINTS
MISPRISE
MISPRISED
MISPRISES
MISPRISING
MISPRIZE
MISPRIZED
MISPRIZES
MISPRIZING
MISPROUD
MISQUOTE
MISQUOTED
MISQUOTES
MISQUOTING
MISRATE
MISRATED
MISRATES
MISRATING
MISREAD
MISREADING
MISREADINGS
MISREADS
MISRECKON
MISRECKONED
MISRECKONING
MISRECKONINGS
MISRECKONS
MISREGARD
MISREGARDS
MISRELATE
MISRELATED
MISRELATES
MISRELATING
MISREPORT

MISREPORTED
MISREPORTING
MISREPORTS
MISRULE
MISRULED
MISRULES
MISRULING
MISS
MISSA
MISSABLE
MISSAID
MISSAL
MISSALS
MISSAS
MISSAW
MISSAY
MISSAYING
MISSAYINGS
MISSAYS
MISSED
MISSEE
MISSEEING
MISSEEM
MISSEEMED
MISSEEMING
MISSEEMINGS
MISSEEMS
MISSEEN
MISSEES
MISSEL
MISSELS
MISSEND
MISSENDING
MISSENDS
MISSENT
MISSES
MISSET
MISSETS
MISSETTING
MISSHAPE
MISSHAPED
MISSHAPEN
MISSHAPES
MISSHAPING
MISSHOOD
MISSHOODS
MISSIER
MISSIES
MISSIEST
MISSILE
MISSILERIES
MISSILERY
MISSILES
MISSILRIES
MISSILRY
MISSING
MISSINGLY
MISSION
MISSIONED
MISSIONER
MISSIONERS
MISSIONING
MISSIONS
MISSIS
MISSISES
MISSISH
MISSIVE
MISSIVES
MISSPEAK
MISSPEAKING

MISSPEAKS
MISSPELL
MISSPELLED
MISSPELLING
MISSPELLINGS
MISSPELLS
MISSPELT
MISSPEND
MISSPENDING
MISSPENDS
MISSPENT
MISSPOKE
MISSPOKEN
MISSTATE
MISSTATED
MISSTATES
MISSTATING
MISSTEP
MISSTEPPED
MISSTEPPING
MISSTEPS
MISSUIT
MISSUITED
MISSUITING
MISSUITS
MISSUS
MISSUSES
MISSY
MIST
MISTAKE
MISTAKEN
MISTAKES
MISTAKING
MISTAKINGS
MISTAUGHT
MISTEACH
MISTEACHES
MISTEACHING
MISTED
MISTELL
MISTELLING
MISTELLS
MISTEMPER
MISTEMPERED
MISTEMPERING
MISTEMPERS
MISTER
MISTERED
MISTERIES
MISTERING
MISTERM
MISTERMED
MISTERMING
MISTERMS
MISTERS
MISTERY
MISTFUL
MISTHINK
MISTHINKING
MISTHINKS
MISTHOUGHT
MISTHOUGHTS
MISTICO
MISTICOS
MISTIER
MISTIEST
MISTIGRIS
MISTIGRISES
MISTILY
MISTIME

MISTIMED
MISTIMES
MISTIMING
MISTINESS
MISTINESSES
MISTING
MISTINGS
MISTITLE
MISTITLED
MISTITLES
MISTITLING
MISTLE
MISTLED
MISTLES
MISTLETOE
MISTLETOES
MISTLING
MISTOLD
MISTOOK
MISTRAL
MISTRALS
MISTREAT
MISTREATED
MISTREATING
MISTREATS
MISTRESS
MISTRESSED
MISTRESSES
MISTRESSING
MISTRIAL
MISTRIALS
MISTRUST
MISTRUSTED
MISTRUSTING
MISTRUSTS
MISTRYST
MISTRYSTED
MISTRYSTING
MISTRYSTS
MISTS
MISTUNE
MISTUNED
MISTUNES
MISTUNING
MISTY
MISUSAGE
MISUSAGES
MISUSE
MISUSED
MISUSER
MISUSERS
MISUSES
MISUSING
MISUST
MISWEEN
MISWEENED
MISWEENING
MISWEENS
MISWEND
MISWENDING
MISWENDS
MISWENT
MISWORD
MISWORDED
MISWORDING
MISWORDINGS
MISWORDS
MISWRITE
MISWRITES
MISWRITING

| | | | | |
|---|---|---|---|---|
| MISWRITTEN | MIXES | MOBILISED | MODENA | MODULES |
| MISWROTE | MIXIER | MOBILISES | MODENAS | MODULI |
| MISYOKE | MIXIEST | MOBILISING | MODERATE | MODULO |
| MISYOKED | MIXING | MOBILITIES | MODERATED | MODULUS |
| MISYOKES | MIXT | MOBILITY | MODERATES | MODUS |
| MISYOKING | MIXTION | MOBILIZE | MODERATING | MOE |
| MITCH | MIXTIONS | MOBILIZED | MODERATO | MOELLON |
| MITCHED | MIXTURE | MOBILIZES | MODERATOR | MOELLONS |
| MITCHES | MIXTURES | MOBILIZING | MODERATORS | MOES |
| MITCHING | MIXY | MOBLE | MODERATOS | MOFETTE |
| MITE | MIZ | MOBLED | MODERN | MOFETTES |
| MITER | MIZEN | MOBLES | MODERNER | MOFUSSIL |
| MITERED | MIZENS | MOBLING | MODERNEST | MOFUSSILS |
| MITERING | MIZES | MOBOCRACIES | MODERNISE | MOG |
| MITERS | MIZMAZE | MOBOCRACY | MODERNISED | MOGGAN |
| MITES | MIZMAZES | MOBOCRAT | MODERNISES | MOGGANS |
| MITHER | MIZZ | MOBOCRATS | MODERNISING | MOGGIE |
| MITHERED | MIZZEN | MOBS | MODERNISM | MOGGIES |
| MITHERING | MIZZENS | MOBSMAN | MODERNISMS | MOGGY |
| MITHERS | MIZZES | MOBSMEN | MODERNIST | MOGS |
| MITICIDAL | MIZZLE | MOBSTER | MODERNISTS | MOGUL |
| MITICIDE | MIZZLED | MOBSTERS | MODERNITIES | MOGULS |
| MITICIDES | MIZZLES | MOCASSIN | MODERNITY | MOHAIR |
| MITIER | MIZZLIER | MOCASSINS | MODERNIZE | MOHAIRS |
| MITIEST | MIZZLIEST | MOCCASIN | MODERNIZED | MOHAWK |
| MITIGABLE | MIZZLING | MOCCASINS | MODERNIZES | MOHAWKS |
| MITIGANT | MIZZLINGS | MOCHA | MODERNIZING | MOHEL |
| MITIGATE | MIZZLY | MOCHAS | MODERNLY | MOHELS |
| MITIGATED | MIZZONITE | MOCHELL | MODERNS | MOHR |
| MITIGATES | MIZZONITES | MOCHELLS | MODES | MOHRS |
| MITIGATING | MNA | MOCK | MODEST | MOHUR |
| MITIGATOR | MNAS | MOCKABLE | MODESTER | MOHURS |
| MITIGATORS | MNEME | MOCKADO | MODESTEST | MOIDER |
| MITOGEN | MNEMES | MOCKADOES | MODESTIES | MOIDERED |
| MITOGENIC | MNEMIC | MOCKAGE | MODESTLY | MOIDERING |
| MITOGENS | MNEMON | MOCKAGES | MODESTY | MOIDERS |
| MITOSES | MNEMONIC | MOCKED | MODI | MOIDORE |
| MITOSIS | MNEMONICS | MOCKER | MODICUM | MOIDORES |
| MITOTIC | MNEMONIST | MOCKERIES | MODICUMS | MOIETIES |
| MITRAILLE | MNEMONISTS | MOCKERS | MODIFIED | MOIETY |
| MITRAILLES | MNEMONS | MOCKERY | MODIFIER | MOIL |
| MITRAL | MO | MOCKING | MODIFIERS | MOILED |
| MITRE | MOA | MOCKINGLY | MODIFIES | MOILER |
| MITRED | MOAN | MOCKINGS | MODIFY | MOILERS |
| MITRES | MOANED | MOCKS | MODIFYING | MOILING |
| MITRIFORM | MOANER | MOCOCK | MODII | MOILS |
| MITRING | MOANERS | MOCOCKS | MODILLION | MOINEAU |
| MITT | MOANFUL | MOCUCK | MODILLIONS | MOINEAUS |
| MITTEN | MOANFULLY | MOCUCKS | MODIOLAR | MOIRE |
| MITTENED | MOANING | MOCUDDUM | MODIOLI | MOIRÉ |
| MITTENS | MOANS | MOCUDDUMS | MODIOLUS | MOIRES |
| MITTIMUS | MOAS | MOD | MODIOLUSES | MOIRÉS |
| MITTIMUSES | MOAT | MODAL | MODISH | MOIST |
| MITTS | MOATED | MODALISM | MODISHLY | MOISTED |
| MITY | MOATING | MODALISMS | MODIST | MOISTEN |
| MITZVAH | MOATS | MODALIST | MODISTE | MOISTENED |
| MITZVAHS | MOB | MODALISTS | MODISTES | MOISTENING |
| MITZVOTH | MOBBED | MODALITIES | MODISTS | MOISTENS |
| MIURUS | MOBBIE | MODALITY | MODIUS | MOISTER |
| MIURUSES | MOBBIES | MODALLY | MODIWORT | MOISTEST |
| MIX | MOBBING | MODE | MODIWORTS | MOISTIFIED |
| MIXABLE | MOBBISH | MODEL | MODS | MOISTIFIES |
| MIXED | MOBBLE | MODELLED | MODULAR | MOISTIFY |
| MIXEDLY | MOBBLED | MODELLER | MODULATE | MOISTIFYING |
| MIXEDNESS | MOBBLES | MODELLERS | MODULATED | MOISTING |
| MIXEDNESSES | MOBBLING | MODELLING | MODULATES | MOISTLY |
| MIXEN | MOBBY | MODELLINGS | MODULATING | MOISTNESS |
| MIXENS | MOBILE | MODELS | MODULATOR | MOISTNESSES |
| MIXER | MOBILES | MODEM | MODULATORS | MOISTS |
| MIXERS | MOBILISE | MODEMS | MODULE | MOISTURE |

MOISTURES
MOIT
MOITHER
MOITHERED
MOITHERING
MOITHERS
MOITS
MOKADDAM
MOKADDAMS
MOKE
MOKES
MOKI
MOKIS
MOKO
MOKOS
MOLAL
MOLALITIES
MOLALITY
MOLAR
MOLARITIES
MOLARITY
MOLARS
MOLASSES
MOLD
MOLDED
MOLDING
MOLDS
MOLDWARP
MOLDWARPS
MOLE
MOLECAST
MOLECASTS
MOLECULAR
MOLECULE
MOLECULES
MOLEHILL
MOLEHILLS
MOLERAT
MOLERATS
MOLES
MOLESKIN
MOLESKINS
MOLEST
MOLESTED
MOLESTER
MOLESTERS
MOLESTFUL
MOLESTING
MOLESTS
MOLIES
MOLIMEN
MOLIMENS
MOLINE
MOLINES
MOLL
MOLLA
MOLLAH
MOLLAHS
MOLLAS
MOLLIE
MOLLIES
MOLLIFIED
MOLLIFIER
MOLLIFIERS
MOLLIFIES
MOLLIFY
MOLLIFYING
MOLLITIES
MOLLS
MOLLUSC

MOLLUSCAN
MOLLUSCS
MOLLUSK
MOLLUSKS
MOLLY
MOLLYMAWK
MOLLYMAWKS
MOLOCH
MOLOCHISE
MOLOCHISED
MOLOCHISES
MOLOCHISING
MOLOCHIZE
MOLOCHIZED
MOLOCHIZES
MOLOCHIZING
MOLOCHS
MOLOSSI
MOLOSSUS
MOLT
MOLTED
MOLTEN
MOLTENLY
MOLTING
MOLTO
MOLTS
MOLY
MOLYBDATE
MOLYBDATES
MOLYBDIC
MOLYBDOUS
MOM
MOME
MOMENT
MOMENTA
MOMENTANY
MOMENTARY
MOMENTLY
MOMENTOUS
MOMENTS
MOMES
MOMMA
MOMMAS
MOMMET
MOMMETS
MOMMIES
MOMMY
MOMS
MONA
MONACHAL
MONACHISM
MONACHISMS
MONACHIST
MONACID
MONACT
MONACTINE
MONAD
MONADES
MONADIC
MONADICAL
MONADISM
MONADISMS
MONADS
MONAL
MONALS
MONANDRIES
MONANDRY
MONARCH
MONARCHAL

MONARCHIC
MONARCHIES
MONARCHS
MONARCHY
MONARDA
MONARDAS
MONAS
MONASES
MONASTERIES
MONASTERY
MONASTIC
MONASTICS
MONATOMIC
MONAUL
MONAULS
MONAURAL
MONAXIAL
MONAXON
MONAXONIC
MONAXONS
MONAZITE
MONAZITES
MONDAIN
MONDAINE
MONDAINES
MONDAINS
MONDIAL
MONECIOUS
MONER
MONERA
MONERGISM
MONERGISMS
MONERON
MONERS
MONETARY
MONETH
MONETHS
MONETISE
MONETISED
MONETISES
MONETISING
MONETIZE
MONETIZED
MONETIZES
MONETIZING
MONEY
MONEYED
MONEYER
MONEYERS
MONEYLESS
MONEYS
MONEYWORT
MONEYWORTS
MONG
MONGCORN
MONGCORNS
MONGER
MONGERIES
MONGERING
MONGERINGS
MONGERS
MONGERY
MONGOL
MONGOLISM
MONGOLISMS
MONGOLOID
MONGOLOIDS
MONGOLS
MONGOOSE
MONGOOSES

MONGREL
MONGRELLY
MONGRELS
MONGS
MONIAL
MONIALS
MONICKER
MONICKERS
MONIED
MONIES
MONIKER
MONIKERS
MONILIA
MONILIAS
MONIMENT
MONIMENTS
MONIPLIES
MONISM
MONISMS
MONIST
MONISTIC
MONISTS
MONITION
MONITIONS
MONITIVE
MONITOR
MONITORED
MONITORING
MONITORS
MONITORY
MONITRESS
MONITRESSES
MONK
MONKERIES
MONKERY
MONKEY
MONKEYED
MONKEYING
MONKEYISH
MONKEYISM
MONKEYISMS
MONKEYS
MONKFISH
MONKFISHES
MONKHOOD
MONKHOODS
MONKISH
MONKS
MONKSHOOD
MONKSHOODS
MONO
MONOACID
MONOAMINE
MONOAMINES
MONOBASIC
MONOCARP
MONOCARPS
MONOCEROS
MONOCEROSES
MONOCHORD
MONOCHORDS
MONOCLE
MONOCLED
MONOCLES
MONOCLINE
MONOCLINES
MONOCOQUE
MONOCOQUES
MONOCOT
MONOCOTS

MONOCRACIES
MONOCRACY
MONOCRAT
MONOCRATS
MONOCULAR
MONOCYTE
MONOCYTES
MONODIC
MONODICAL
MONODIES
MONODIST
MONODISTS
MONODONT
MONODRAMA
MONODRAMAS
MONODY
MONOECISM
MONOECISMS
MONOFIL
MONOFILS
MONOGAMIC
MONOGAMIES
MONOGAMY
MONOGENIES
MONOGENY
MONOGLOT
MONOGLOTS
MONOGONIES
MONOGONY
MONOGRAM
MONOGRAMS
MONOGRAPH
MONOGRAPHED
MONOGRAPHING
MONOGRAPHS
MONOGYNIES
MONOGYNY
MONOHULL
MONOHULLS
MONOLATER
MONOLATERS
MONOLATRIES
MONOLATRY
MONOLITH
MONOLITHS
MONOLOGIC
MONOLOGIES
MONOLOGUE
MONOLOGUES
MONOLOGY
MONOMACHIES
MONOMACHY
MONOMANIA
MONOMANIAS
MONOMARK
MONOMARKS
MONOMER
MONOMERIC
MONOMERS
MONOMETER
MONOMETERS
MONOMIAL
MONOMIALS
MONOMODE
MONOPHAGIES
MONOPHAGY
MONOPHASE
MONOPHONIES
MONOPHONY
MONOPITCH

MONOPLANE
MONOPLANES
MONOPODE
MONOPODES
MONOPODIA
MONOPOLE
MONOPOLES
MONOPOLIES
MONOPOLY
MONOPSONIES
MONOPSONY
MONOPTERA
MONOPTOTE
MONOPTOTES
MONORAIL
MONORAILS
MONORCHID
MONORHINE
MONORHYME
MONORHYMES
MONOS
MONOSES
MONOSIES
MONOSIS
MONOSTICH
MONOSTICHS
MONOSTYLE
MONOSY
MONOTINT
MONOTINTS
MONOTONE
MONOTONED
MONOTONES
MONOTONIC
MONOTONIES
MONOTONING
MONOTONY
MONOTREME
MONOTREMES
MONOTROCH
MONOTROCHS
MONOTYPE
MONOTYPES
MONOTYPIC
MONOXIDE
MONOXIDES
MONOXYLON
MONOXYLONS
MONSIEUR
MONSOON
MONSOONAL
MONSOONS
MONSTER
MONSTERA
MONSTERAS
MONSTERS
MONSTROUS
MONTAGE
MONTAGES
MONTANE
MONTANT
MONTANTO
MONTANTOS
MONTANTS
MONTARIA
MONTARIAS
MONTE
MONTEITH
MONTEITHS
MONTEM

MONTEMS
MONTERO
MONTEROS
MONTES
MONTH
MONTHLIES
MONTHLING
MONTHLINGS
MONTHLY
MONTHS
MONTICLE
MONTICLES
MONTICULE
MONTICULES
MONTRE
MONTRES
MONTURE
MONTURES
MONUMENT
MONUMENTED
MONUMENTING
MONUMENTS
MONY
MONYPLIES
MONZONITE
MONZONITES
MOO
MOOCH
MOOCHED
MOOCHER
MOOCHERS
MOOCHES
MOOCHING
MOOD
MOODIED
MOODIER
MOODIES
MOODIEST
MOODILY
MOODINESS
MOODINESSES
MOODS
MOODY
MOODYING
MOOED
MOOI
MOOING
MOOKTAR
MOOKTARS
MOOL
MOOLA
MOOLAH
MOOLAHS
MOOLAS
MOOLED
MOOLI
MOOLIES
MOOLING
MOOLIS
MOOLS
MOOLY
MOON
MOONBEAM
MOONBEAMS
MOONBLIND
MOONCALF
MOONCALVES
MOONED
MOONER
MOONERS

MOONEYE
MOONEYES
MOONFACE
MOONFACES
MOONIER
MOONIES
MOONIEST
MOONING
MOONISH
MOONLESS
MOONLET
MOONLETS
MOONLIGHT
MOONLIGHTS
MOONLIT
MOONQUAKE
MOONQUAKES
MOONRAKER
MOONRAKERS
MOONRISE
MOONRISES
MOONS
MOONSAIL
MOONSAILS
MOONSCAPE
MOONSCAPES
MOONSEED
MOONSEEDS
MOONSET
MOONSETS
MOONSHEE
MOONSHEES
MOONSHINE
MOONSHINES
MOONSHINY
MOONSHOT
MOONSHOTS
MOONSTONE
MOONSTONES
MOONWORT
MOONWORTS
MOONY
MOOP
MOOPED
MOOPING
MOOPS
MOOR
MOORAGE
MOORAGES
MOORCOCK
MOORCOCKS
MOORED
MOORFOWL
MOORFOWLS
MOORHEN
MOORHENS
MOORIER
MOORIEST
MOORILL
MOORILLS
MOORING
MOORINGS
MOORISH
MOORLAND
MOORLANDS
MOORLOG
MOORLOGS
MOORMAN
MOORMEN
MOORS

MOORVA
MOORVAS
MOORY
MOOS
MOOSE
MOOSEYARD
MOOSEYARDS
MOOT
MOOTABLE
MOOTED
MOOTER
MOOTERS
MOOTEST
MOOTING
MOOTINGS
MOOTMAN
MOOTMEN
MOOTS
MOOVE
MOOVED
MOOVES
MOOVING
MOP
MOPANE
MOPANES
MOPBOARD
MOPBOARDS
MOPE
MOPED
MOPEDS
MOPEHAWK
MOPEHAWKS
MOPER
MOPERS
MOPES
MOPIER
MOPIEST
MOPING
MOPINGLY
MOPISH
MOPISHLY
MOPOKE
MOPOKES
MOPPED
MOPPER
MOPPERS
MOPPET
MOPPETS
MOPPIER
MOPPIEST
MOPPING
MOPPY
MOPS
MOPSIES
MOPSTICK
MOPSTICKS
MOPSY
MOPUS
MOPUSES
MOPY
MOQUETTE
MOQUETTES
MOR
MORA
MORACEOUS
MORAINAL
MORAINE
MORAINES
MORAINIC
MORAL

MORALE
MORALES
MORALISE
MORALISED
MORALISER
MORALISERS
MORALISES
MORALISING
MORALISM
MORALISMS
MORALIST
MORALISTS
MORALITIES
MORALITY
MORALIZE
MORALIZED
MORALIZER
MORALIZERS
MORALIZES
MORALIZING
MORALL
MORALLED
MORALLER
MORALLERS
MORALLING
MORALLS
MORALLY
MORALS
MORAS
MORASS
MORASSES
MORASSY
MORAT
MORATORIA
MORATORY
MORATS
MORAY
MORAYS
MORBID
MORBIDITIES
MORBIDITY
MORBIDLY
MORBIFIC
MORBILLI
MORBUS
MORBUSES
MORCEAU
MORCEAUX
MORDACITIES
MORDACITY
MORDANCIES
MORDANCY
MORDANT
MORDANTED
MORDANTING
MORDANTLY
MORDANTS
MORDENT
MORDENTS
MORE
MOREEN
MOREENS
MOREISH
MOREL
MORELLO
MORELLOS
MORELS
MORENDO
MOREOVER
MORES

| | | | | |
|---|---|---|---|---|
| MORGANITE | MORRICE | MORTISE | MOTEN | MOTORING |
| MORGANITES | MORRICES | MORTISED | MOTES | MOTORISE |
| MORGAY | MORRION | MORTISER | MOTET | MOTORISED |
| MORGAYS | MORRIONS | MORTISERS | MOTETS | MOTORISES |
| MORGEN | MORRIS | MORTISES | MOTETT | MOTORISING |
| MORGENS | MORRISED | MORTISING | MOTETTIST | MOTORIST |
| MORGUE | MORRISES | MORTLING | MOTETTISTS | MOTORISTS |
| MORGUES | MORRISING | MORTLINGS | MOTETTS | MOTORIUM |
| MORIA | MORRO | MORTMAIN | MOTEY | MOTORIUMS |
| MORIAS | MORROS | MORTMAINS | MOTH | MOTORIZE |
| MORIBUND | MORROW | MORTS | MOTHBALL | MOTORIZED |
| MORICHE | MORROWS | MORTUARIES | MOTHBALLED | MOTORIZES |
| MORICHES | MORS | MORTUARY | MOTHBALLING | MOTORIZING |
| MORION | MORSAL | MORULA | MOTHBALLS | MOTORMAN |
| MORIONS | MORSE | MORULAR | MOTHED | MOTORMEN |
| MORISCO | MORSEL | MORULAS | MOTHER | MOTORS |
| MORISCOES | MORSELLED | MORWONG | MOTHERED | MOTORWAY |
| MORISCOS | MORSELLING | MORWONGS | MOTHERING | MOTORWAYS |
| MORISH | MORSELS | MOSAIC | MOTHERINGS | MOTORY |
| MORKIN | MORSES | MOSAICISM | MOTHERLY | MOTOSCAFI |
| MORKINS | MORSURE | MOSAICISMS | MOTHERS | MOTOSCAFO |
| MORLING | MORSURES | MOSAICIST | MOTHERY | MOTS |
| MORLINGS | MORT | MOSAICISTS | MOTHIER | MOTSER |
| MORMAOR | MORTAL | MOSAICS | MOTHIEST | MOTSERS |
| MORMAORS | MORTALISE | MOSCHATEL | MOTHS | MOTT |
| MORN | MORTALISED | MOSCHATELS | MOTHY | MOTTE |
| MORNAY | MORTALISES | MOSE | MOTIER | MOTTES |
| MORNAYS | MORTALISING | MOSED | MOTIEST | MOTTIER |
| MORNE | MORTALITIES | MOSES | MOTIF | MOTTIEST |
| MORNÉ | MORTALITY | MOSEY | MOTIFS | MOTTLE |
| MORNED | MORTALIZE | MOSEYED | MOTILE | MOTTLED |
| MORNES | MORTALIZED | MOSEYING | MOTILES | MOTTLES |
| MORNING | MORTALIZES | MOSEYS | MOTILITIES | MOTTLING |
| MORNINGS | MORTALIZING | MOSHAV | MOTILITY | MOTTLINGS |
| MORNS | MORTALLY | MOSHAVIM | MOTION | MOTTO |
| MOROCCO | MORTALS | MOSING | MOTIONAL | MOTTOED |
| MOROCCOS | MORTAR | MOSKONFYT | MOTIONED | MOTTOES |
| MORON | MORTARED | MOSKONFYTS | MOTIONING | MOTTS |
| MORONIC | MORTARING | MOSLINGS | MOTIONIST | MOTTY |
| MORONS | MORTARS | MOSQUE | MOTIONISTS | MOTUCA |
| MOROSE | MORTBELL | MOSQUES | MOTIONS | MOTUCAS |
| MOROSELY | MORTBELLS | MOSQUITO | MOTIVATE | MOTZA |
| MOROSER | MORTCLOTH | MOSQUITOES | MOTIVATED | MOTZAS |
| MOROSEST | MORTCLOTHS | MOSQUITOS | MOTIVATES | MOU |
| MOROSITIES | MORTGAGE | MOSS | MOTIVATING | MOUCH |
| MOROSITY | MORTGAGED | MOSSED | MOTIVE | MOUCHARD |
| MORPH | MORTGAGEE | MOSSES | MOTIVED | MOUCHARDS |
| MORPHEAN | MORTGAGEES | MOSSIE | MOTIVES | MOUCHED |
| MORPHEME | MORTGAGER | MOSSIER | MOTIVIC | MOUCHER |
| MORPHEMES | MORTGAGERS | MOSSIES | MOTIVING | MOUCHERS |
| MORPHEMIC | MORTGAGES | MOSSIEST | MOTIVITIES | MOUCHES |
| MORPHEMICS | MORTGAGING | MOSSINESS | MOTIVITY | MOUCHING |
| MORPHETIC | MORTGAGOR | MOSSINESSES | MOTLEY | MOUCHOIR |
| MORPHEW | MORTGAGORS | MOSSING | MOTLEYER | MOUCHOIRS |
| MORPHEWS | MORTICE | MOSSLAND | MOTLEYEST | MOUDIWART |
| MORPHIA | MORTICED | MOSSLANDS | MOTLEYS | MOUDIWARTS |
| MORPHIAS | MORTICER | MOSSPLANT | MOTLIER | MOUDIWORT |
| MORPHIC | MORTICERS | MOSSPLANTS | MOTLIEST | MOUDIWORTS |
| MORPHINE | MORTICES | MOSSY | MOTMOT | MOUE |
| MORPHINES | MORTICIAN | MOST | MOTMOTS | MOUES |
| MORPHO | MORTICIANS | MOSTLY | MOTOCROSS | MOUFFLON |
| MORPHOS | MORTICING | MOSTST | MOTOCROSSES | MOUFFLONS |
| MORPHOSES | MORTIFIC | MOSTWHAT | MOTOR | MOUFLON |
| MORPHOSIS | MORTIFIED | MOT | MOTORABLE | MOUFLONS |
| MORPHOTIC | MORTIFIER | MOTE | MOTORAIL | MOUGHT |
| MORPHS | MORTIFIERS | MOTED | MOTORAILS | MOUILLÉ |
| MORRA | MORTIFIES | MOTEL | MOTORCADE | MOUJIK |
| MORRAS | MORTIFY | MOTELIER | MOTORCADES | MOUJIKS |
| MORRHUA | MORTIFYING | MOTELIERS | MOTORED | MOULAGE |
| MORRHUAS | MORTIFYINGS | MOTELS | MOTORIAL | MOULAGES |

| | | | | |
|---|---|---|---|---|
| MOULD | MOUSERY | MOVINGLY | MUCHEL | MUDÉJAR |
| MOULDABLE | MOUSES | MOVY | MUCHELL | MUDÉJARES |
| MOULDED | MOUSEY | MOW | MUCHELLS | MUDIR |
| MOULDER | MOUSIE | MOWA | MUCHELS | MUDIRIA |
| MOULDERED | MOUSIER | MOWAS | MUCHES | MUDIRIAS |
| MOULDERING | MOUSIES | MOWBURN | MUCHLY | MUDIRIEH |
| MOULDERS | MOUSIEST | MOWBURNED | MUCHNESS | MUDIRIEHS |
| MOULDIER | MOUSING | MOWBURNING | MUCHNESSES | MUDIRS |
| MOULDIEST | MOUSINGS | MOWBURNS | MUCIC | MUDLARK |
| MOULDING | MOUSLE | MOWBURNT | MUCID | MUDLARKED |
| MOULDINGS | MOUSLED | MOWDIWART | MUCIGEN | MUDLARKING |
| MOULDS | MOUSLES | MOWDIWARTS | MUCIGENS | MUDLARKS |
| MOULDWARP | MOUSLING | MOWDIWORT | MUCILAGE | MUDPACK |
| MOULDWARPS | MOUSMÉ | MOWDIWORTS | MUCILAGES | MUDPACKS |
| MOULDY | MOUSMEE | MOWED | MUCIN | MUDRA |
| MOULIN | MOUSMEES | MOWER | MUCINS | MUDRAS |
| MOULINET | MOUSMÉS | MOWERS | MUCK | MUDS |
| MOULINETS | MOUSSAKA | MOWING | MUCKED | MUDSCOW |
| MOULINS | MOUSSAKAS | MOWINGS | MUCKENDER | MUDSCOWS |
| MOULS | MOUSSE | MOWN | MUCKENDERS | MUDSTONE |
| MOULT | MOUSSES | MOWRA | MUCKER | MUDSTONES |
| MOULTED | MOUST | MOWRAS | MUCKERED | MUDWORT |
| MOULTEN | MOUSTACHE | MOWS | MUCKERING | MUDWORTS |
| MOULTING | MOUSTACHES | MOXA | MUCKERS | MUEDDIN |
| MOULTINGS | MOUSTED | MOXAS | MUCKIER | MUEDDINS |
| MOULTS | MOUSTING | MOXIE | MUCKIEST | MUESLI |
| MOUND | MOUSTS | MOXIES | MUCKINESS | MUESLIS |
| MOUNDED | MOUSY | MOY | MUCKINESSES | MUEZZIN |
| MOUNDING | MOUTAN | MOYA | MUCKING | MUEZZINS |
| MOUNDS | MOUTANS | MOYAS | MUCKLE | MUFF |
| MOUNSEER | MOUTER | MOYGASHEL | MUCKLES | MUFFED |
| MOUNSEERS | MOUTERED | MOYGASHELS | MUCKLUCK | MUFFETTEE |
| MOUNT | MOUTERER | MOYITIES | MUCKLUCKS | MUFFETTEES |
| MOUNTAIN | MOUTERERS | MOYITY | MUCKS | MUFFIN |
| MOUNTAINS | MOUTERING | MOYL | MUCKY | MUFFINEER |
| MOUNTANT | MOUTERS | MOYLE | MUCLUC | MUFFINEERS |
| MOUNTANTS | MOUTH | MOYLED | MUCLUCS | MUFFING |
| MOUNTED | MOUTHABLE | MOYLES | MUCOID | MUFFINS |
| MOUNTER | MOUTHED | MOYLING | MUCOR | MUFFLE |
| MOUNTERS | MOUTHER | MOYLS | MUCORS | MUFFLED |
| MOUNTIE | MOUTHERS | MOYS | MUCOSA | MUFFLER |
| MOUNTIES | MOUTHFUL | MOZ | MUCOSAE | MUFFLERS |
| MOUNTING | MOUTHFULS | MOZE | MUCOSITIES | MUFFLES |
| MOUNTINGS | MOUTHIER | MOZED | MUCOSITY | MUFFLING |
| MOUNTS | MOUTHIEST | MOZES | MUCOUS | MUFFS |
| MOUNTY | MOUTHING | MOZETTA | MUCRO | MUFLON |
| MOUP | MOUTHLESS | MOZETTAS | MUCRONATE | MUFLONS |
| MOUPED | MOUTHS | MOZING | MUCRONES | MUFTI |
| MOUPING | MOUTHWASH | MOZZ | MUCROS | MUFTIS |
| MOUPS | MOUTHWASHES | MOZZES | MUCULENT | MUG |
| MOURN | MOUTHY | MOZZETTA | MUCUS | MUGEARITE |
| MOURNED | MOUTON | MOZZETTAS | MUCUSES | MUGEARITES |
| MOURNER | MOUTONS | MOZZIE | MUD | MUGFUL |
| MOURNERS | MOVABLE | MOZZIES | MUDDED | MUGFULS |
| MOURNFUL | MOVABLES | MOZZLE | MUDDIED | MUGGED |
| MOURNING | MOVABLY | MOZZLES | MUDDIER | MUGGER |
| MOURNINGS | MOVE | MPRET | MUDDIES | MUGGERS |
| MOURNIVAL | MOVEABLE | MPRETS | MUDDIEST | MUGGIER |
| MOURNIVALS | MOVEABLES | MRIDAMGAM | MUDDILY | MUGGIEST |
| MOURNS | MOVEABLY | MRIDAMGAMS | MUDDINESS | MUGGINESS |
| MOUS | MOVED | MRIDANG | MUDDINESSES | MUGGINESSES |
| MOUSAKA | MOVELESS | MRIDANGA | MUDDING | MUGGING |
| MOUSAKAS | MOVEMENT | MRIDANGAM | MUDDLE | MUGGINGS |
| MOUSE | MOVEMENTS | MRIDANGAMS | MUDDLED | MUGGINS |
| MOUSED | MOVER | MRIDANGAS | MUDDLER | MUGGINSES |
| MOUSEKIN | MOVERS | MRIDANGS | MUDDLERS | MUGGISH |
| MOUSEKINS | MOVES | MU | MUDDLES | MUGGY |
| MOUSER | MOVIE | MUCATE | MUDDLING | MUGS |
| MOUSERIES | MOVIES | MUCATES | MUDDY | MUGSHOT |
| MOUSERS | MOVING | MUCH | MUDDYING | MUGSHOTS |

MUGWORT
MUGWORTS
MUGWUMP
MUGWUMPS
MUID
MUIDS
MUIL
MUILS
MUIR
MUIRS
MUIST
MUISTED
MUISTING
MUISTS
MUJAHEDIN
MUJAHIDIN
MUJIK
MUJIKS
MUKHTAR
MUKHTARS
MUKLUK
MUKLUKS
MULATTA
MULATTAS
MULATTO
MULATTOS
MULBERRIES
MULBERRY
MULCH
MULCHED
MULCHES
MULCHING
MULCT
MULCTED
MULCTING
MULCTS
MULE
MULES
MULETEER
MULETEERS
MULEY
MULEYS
MULGA
MULGAS
MULISH
MULISHLY
MULL
MULLAH
MULLAHS
MULLED
MULLEIN
MULLEINS
MULLER
MULLERS
MULLET
MULLETS
MULLEY
MULLEYS
MULLIGAN
MULLIGANS
MULLING
MULLION
MULLIONED
MULLIONS
MULLOCK
MULLOCKS
MULLOWAY
MULLOWAYS
MULLS
MULMUL

MULMULL
MULMULLS
MULMULS
MULSE
MULSES
MULSH
MULSHED
MULSHES
MULSHING
MULTEITIES
MULTEITY
MULTIFID
MULTIFIL
MULTIFILS
MULTIFOIL
MULTIFOILS
MULTIFORM
MULTIFORMS
MULTIHULL
MULTIHULLS
MULTIPARA
MULTIPARAE
MULTIPARAS
MULTIPED
MULTIPEDE
MULTIPEDES
MULTIPEDS
MULTIPLE
MULTIPLES
MULTIPLET
MULTIPLETS
MULTIPLEX
MULTIPLEXED
MULTIPLEXES
MULTIPLEXING
MULTIPLIED
MULTIPLIES
MULTIPLY
MULTIPLYING
MULTITUDE
MULTITUDES
MULTUM
MULTUMS
MULTURE
MULTURED
MULTURER
MULTURERS
MULTURES
MULTURING
MUM
MUMBLE
MUMBLED
MUMBLER
MUMBLERS
MUMBLES
MUMBLING
MUMBLINGS
MUMCHANCE
MUMCHANCES
MUMM
MUMMED
MUMMER
MUMMERIES
MUMMERS
MUMMERY
MUMMIA
MUMMIAS
MUMMIED
MUMMIES
MUMMIFIED

MUMMIFIES
MUMMIFORM
MUMMIFY
MUMMIFYING
MUMMING
MUMMINGS
MUMMOCK
MUMMOCKS
MUMMS
MUMMY
MUMMYING
MUMP
MUMPED
MUMPER
MUMPERS
MUMPING
MUMPISH
MUMPISHLY
MUMPS
MUMPSIMUS
MUMPSIMUSES
MUMS
MUMSIER
MUMSIEST
MUMSY
MUN
MUNCH
MUNCHED
MUNCHER
MUNCHERS
MUNCHES
MUNCHING
MUNDANE
MUNDANELY
MUNDANER
MUNDANEST
MUNDANITIES
MUNDANITY
MUNDIC
MUNDICS
MUNDIFIED
MUNDIFIES
MUNDIFY
MUNDIFYING
MUNDUNGUS
MUNDUNGUSES
MUNGCORN
MUNGCORNS
MUNGO
MUNGOOSE
MUNGOOSES
MUNGOS
MUNICIPAL
MUNIFIED
MUNIFIES
MUNIFY
MUNIFYING
MUNIMENT
MUNIMENTS
MUNITE
MUNITED
MUNITES
MUNITING
MUNITION
MUNITIONED
MUNITIONING
MUNITIONS
MUNNION
MUNNIONS
MUNSHI

MUNSHIS
MUNSTER
MUNSTERS
MUNTIN
MUNTING
MUNTINGS
MUNTINS
MUNTJAC
MUNTJACS
MUNTJAK
MUNTJAKS
MUON
MUONIC
MUONIUM
MUONIUMS
MUONS
MUQADDAM
MUQADDAMS
MURAENA
MURAENAS
MURAGE
MURAGES
MURAL
MURALIST
MURALISTS
MURALS
MURDER
MURDERED
MURDERER
MURDERERS
MURDERESS
MURDERESSES
MURDERING
MURDEROUS
MURDERS
MURE
MURED
MURENA
MURENAS
MURES
MUREX
MUREXES
MURGEON
MURGEONED
MURGEONING
MURGEONS
MURIATE
MURIATED
MURIATES
MURIATIC
MURICATE
MURICATED
MURICES
MURIFORM
MURINE
MURINES
MURING
MURK
MURKER
MURKEST
MURKIER
MURKIEST
MURKILY
MURKINESS
MURKINESSES
MURKISH
MURKS
MURKSOME
MURKY
MURL

MURLAIN
MURLAINS
MURLAN
MURLANS
MURLED
MURLIER
MURLIEST
MURLIN
MURLING
MURLINS
MURLS
MURLY
MURMUR
MURMURED
MURMURER
MURMURERS
MURMURING
MURMURINGS
MURMUROUS
MURMURS
MURPHIES
MURPHY
MURRA
MURRAIN
MURRAINED
MURRAINS
MURRAM
MURRAMS
MURRAS
MURRAY
MURRAYS
MURRE
MURRELET
MURRELETS
MURREN
MURRENS
MURRES
MURREY
MURREYS
MURRHA
MURRHAS
MURRHINE
MURRIES
MURRIN
MURRINE
MURRINS
MURRION
MURRIONS
MURRY
MURTHER
MURTHERED
MURTHERER
MURTHERERS
MURTHERING
MURTHERS
MURVA
MURVAS
MUS
MUSACEOUS
MUSANG
MUSANGS
MUSCADEL
MUSCADELS
MUSCADIN
MUSCADINE
MUSCADINES
MUSCADINS
MUSCARINE
MUSCARINES
MUSCAT

| | | | | |
|---|---|---|---|---|
| MUSCATEL | MUSINGLY | MUSTELINES | MUTT | MYCOPHAGIES |
| MUSCATELS | MUSINGS | MUSTER | MUTTER | MYCOPHAGY |
| MUSCATS | MUSIT | MUSTERED | MUTTERED | MYCORHIZA |
| MUSCID | MUSITS | MUSTERER | MUTTERER | MYCORHIZAS |
| MUSCIDS | MUSIVE | MUSTERERS | MUTTERERS | MYCOSES |
| MUSCLE | MUSK | MUSTERING | MUTTERING | MYCOSIS |
| MUSCLED | MUSKED | MUSTERS | MUTTERINGS | MYCOTIC |
| MUSCLES | MUSKEG· | MUSTH | MUTTERS | MYCOTOXIN |
| MUSCLING | MUSKEGS | MUSTHS | MUTTON | MYCOTOXINS |
| MUSCLINGS | MUSKET | MUSTIER | MUTTONS | MYDRIASES |
| MUSCOID | MUSKETEER | MUSTIEST | MUTTONY | MYDRIASIS |
| MUSCOLOGIES | MUSKETEERS | MUSTING | MUTTS | MYDRIATIC |
| MUSCOLOGY | MUSKETOON | MUSTS | MUTUAL | MYDRIATICS |
| MUSCONE | MUSKETOONS | MUSTY | MUTUALISE | MYELIN |
| MUSCONES | MUSKETRIES | MUTABLE | MUTUALISED | MYELINS |
| MUSCOSE | MUSKETRY | MUTABLY | MUTUALISES | MYELITIS |
| MUSCOVADO | MUSKETS | MUTAGEN | MUTUALISING | MYELITISES |
| MUSCOVADOS | MUSKIER | MUTAGENIC | MUTUALISM | MYELOID |
| MUSCOVITE | MUSKIEST | MUTAGENS | MUTUALISMS | MYELOMA |
| MUSCOVITES | MUSKILY | MUTANDA | MUTUALITIES | MYELOMAS |
| MUSCULAR | MUSKINESS | MUTANDUM | MUTUALITY | MYELON |
| MUSCULOUS | MUSKINESSES | MUTANT | MUTUALIZE | MYELONS |
| MUSE | MUSKING | MUTANTS | MUTUALIZED | MYGALE |
| MUSED | MUSKLE | MUTATE | MUTUALIZES | MYGALES |
| MUSEFUL | MUSKLES | MUTATED | MUTUALIZING | MYIASES |
| MUSEFULLY | MUSKONE | MUTATES | MUTUALLY | MYIASIS |
| MUSEOLOGIES | MUSKONES | MUTATING | MUTUCA | MYLODON |
| MUSEOLOGY | MUSKS | MUTATION | MUTUCAS | MYLODONS |
| MUSER | MUSKY | MUTATIONS | MUTULE | MYLODONT |
| MUSERS | MUSLIN | MUTATIVE | MUTULES | MYLODONTS |
| MUSES | MUSLINED | MUTATORY | MUTUUM | MYLOHYOID |
| MUSET | MUSLINET | MUTCH | MUTUUMS | MYLOHYOIDS |
| MUSETS | MUSLINETS | MUTCHES | MUX | MYLONITE |
| MUSETTE | MUSLINS | MUTCHKIN | MUXED | MYLONITES |
| MUSETTES | MUSMON | MUTCHKINS | MUXES | MYLONITIC |
| MUSEUM | MUSMONS | MUTE | MUXING | MYNA |
| MUSEUMS | MUSQUASH | MUTED | MUZHIK | MYNAH |
| MUSH | MUSQUASHES | MUTELY | MUZHIKS | MYNAHS |
| MUSHA | MUSROL | MUTENESS | MUZZIER | MYNAS |
| MUSHED | MUSROLS | MUTENESSES | MUZZIEST | MYNHEER |
| MUSHER | MUSS | MUTER | MUZZILY | MYNHEERS |
| MUSHERS | MUSSE | MUTES | MUZZINESS | MYOBLAST |
| MUSHES | MUSSED | MUTEST | MUZZINESSES | MYOBLASTS |
| MUSHIER | MUSSEL | MUTICOUS | MUZZLE | MYOFIBRIL |
| MUSHIEST | MUSSELLED | MUTILATE | MUZZLED | MYOFIBRILS |
| MUSHILY | MUSSELS | MUTILATED | MUZZLER | MYOGEN |
| MUSHINESS | MUSSES | MUTILATES | MUZZLERS | MYOGENIC |
| MUSHINESSES | MUSSIER | MUTILATING | MUZZLES | MYOGENS |
| MUSHING | MUSSIEST | MUTILATOR | MUZZLING | MYOGLOBIN |
| MUSHROOM | MUSSINESS | MUTILATORS | MUZZY | MYOGLOBINS |
| MUSHROOMED | MUSSINESSES | MUTINE | MVULE | MYOGRAM |
| MUSHROOMING | MUSSING | MUTINED | MVULES | MYOGRAMS |
| MUSHROOMS | MUSSITATE | MUTINEER | MY | MYOGRAPH |
| MUSHY | MUSSITATED | MUTINEERED | MYAL | MYOGRAPHIES |
| MUSIC | MUSSITATES | MUTINEERING· | MYALGIA | MYOGRAPHS |
| MUSICAL | MUSSITATING | MUTINEERS | MYALGIAS | MYOGRAPHY |
| MUSICALE | MUSSY | MUTINES | MYALGIC | MYOID |
| MUSICALES | MUST | MUTING | MYALISM | MYOLOGIES |
| MUSICALLY | MUSTACHE | MUTINIED | MYALISMS | MYOLOGIST |
| MUSICALS | MUSTACHES | MUTINIES | MYALL | MYOLOGISTS |
| MUSICIAN | MUSTACHIO | MUTINING | MYALLS | MYOLOGY |
| MUSICIANS | MUSTACHIOS | MUTINOUS | MYCELIA | MYOMA |
| MUSICKED | MUSTANG | MUTINY | MYCELIAL | MYOMANCIES |
| MUSICKER | MUSTANGS | MUTINYING | MYCELIUM | MYOMANCY |
| MUSICKERS | MUSTARD | MUTISM | MYCETES | MYOMANTIC |
| MUSICKING | MUSTARDS | MUTISMS | MYCETOMA | MYOMAS |
| MUSICS | MUSTED | MUTON | MYCETOMAS | MYOPE |
| MUSIMON | MUSTEE | MUTONS | MYCOLOGIC | MYOPES |
| MUSIMONS | MUSTEES | MUTOSCOPE | MYCOLOGIES | MYOPIA |
| MUSING | MUSTELINE | MUTOSCOPES | MYCOLOGY | MYOPIAS |

MYOPIC
MYOPICS
MYOPS
MYOPSES
MYOSES
MYOSIN
MYOSINS
MYOSIS
MYOSITIC
MYOSITIS
MYOSITISES
MYOSOTE
MYOSOTES
MYOSOTIS
MYOSOTISES
MYOTIC
MYOTICS
MYOTUBE
MYOTUBES
MYRBANE
MYRBANES
MYRIAD
MYRIADS

MYRIADTH
MYRIADTHS
MYRIAPOD
MYRIAPODS
MYRINGA
MYRINGAS
MYRIOPOD
MYRIOPODS
MYRIORAMA
MYRIORAMAS
MYRISTIC
MYRMECOID
MYRMIDON
MYRMIDONS
MYROBALAN
MYROBALANS
MYRRH
MYRRHIC
MYRRHINE
MYRRHOL
MYRRHOLS
MYRRHS
MYRTLE

MYRTLES
MYSELF
MYSTAGOGIES
MYSTAGOGY
MYSTERIES
MYSTERY
MYSTIC
MYSTICAL
MYSTICISM
MYSTICISMS
MYSTICS
MYSTIFIED
MYSTIFIER
MYSTIFIERS
MYSTIFIES
MYSTIFY
MYSTIFYING
MYSTIQUE
MYSTIQUES
MYTH
MYTHIC
MYTHICAL
MYTHICISE

MYTHICISED
MYTHICISES
MYTHICISING
MYTHICISM
MYTHICISMS
MYTHICIST
MYTHICISTS
MYTHICIZE
MYTHICIZED
MYTHICIZES
MYTHICIZING
MYTHISE
MYTHISED
MYTHISES
MYTHISING
MYTHISM
MYTHISMS
MYTHIST
MYTHISTS
MYTHIZE
MYTHIZED
MYTHIZES
MYTHIZING

MYTHOLOGIES
MYTHOLOGY
MYTHOMANE
MYTHOMANES
MYTHOPOET
MYTHOPOETS
MYTHOS
MYTHOSES
MYTHS
MYTHUS
MYTHUSES
MYTILOID
MYXEDEMA
MYXEDEMAS
MYXOEDEMA
MYXOEDEMAS
MYXOMA
MYXOMATA
MYXOVIRUS
MYXOVIRUSES
MZUNGU
MZUNGUS

# N

NA
NAAM
NAAMS
NAAN
NAANS
NAARTJE
NAARTJES
NAB
NABBED
NABBER
NABBERS
NABBING
NABK
NABKS
NABLA
NABLAS
NABOB
NABOBS
NABS
NACARAT
NACARATS
NACELLE
NACELLES
NACH
NACHE
NACHES
NACHTMAAL
NACHTMAALS
NACKET
NACKETS
NACRE
NACREOUS
NACRES
NACRITE
NACRITES
NACROUS
NADA
NADAS
NADIR
NADIRS
NAE
NAEBODIES
NAEBODY
NAETHING
NAETHINGS
NAEVE
NAEVES
NAEVI
NAEVOID
NAEVUS
NAFF
NAFFING
NAFFS
NAG
NAGA
NAGANA
NAGANAS
NAGAPIE
NAGAPIES
NAGARI
NAGARIS
NAGAS
NAGGED

NAGGER
NAGGERS
NAGGIER
NAGGIEST
NAGGING
NAGGY
NAGMAAL
NAGMAALS
NAGOR
NAGORS
NAGS
NAHAL
NAHALS
NAIAD
NAIADES
NAIADS
NAIANT
NAÏF
NAÏFER
NAÏFEST
NAIK
NAIKS
NAIL
NAILED
NAILER
NAILERIES
NAILERS
NAILERY
NAILING
NAILINGS
NAILS
NAIN
NAINSELL
NAINSELLS
NAINSOOK
NAINSOOKS
NAIRA
NAIRAS
NAISSANT
NAÏVE
NAÏVELY
NAÏVER
NAÏVEST
NAÏVETÉ
NAÏVETÉS
NAÏVETIES
NAÏVETY
NAKED
NAKEDER
NAKEDEST
NAKEDLY
NAKEDNESS
NAKEDNESSES
NAKER
NAKERS
NALA
NALAS
NALLA
NALLAH
NALLAHS
NALLAS
NALOXONE
NALOXONES

NAM
NAMABLE
NAMASKAR
NAMASKARS
NAMASTE
NAMASTES
NAME
NAMEABLE
NAMED
NAMELESS
NAMELY
NAMER
NAMERS
NAMES
NAMESAKE
NAMESAKES
NAMING
NAMINGS
NAMS
NAN
NANA
NANAS
NANCE
NANCES
NANCIES
NANCY
NANDINE
NANDINES
NANDOO
NANDOOS
NANDU
NANDUS
NANISM
NANISMS
NANKEEN
NANKEENS
NANKIN
NANKINS
NANNA
NANNAS
NANNIED
NANNIES
NANNY
NANNYING
NANNYISH
NANOGRAM
NANOGRAMS
NANOMETRE
NANOMETRES
NANS
NAOI
NAOS
NAOSES
NAP
NAPA
NAPALM
NAPALMS
NAPAS
NAPE
NAPERIES
NAPERY
NAPES
NAPHTHA

NAPHTHAS
NAPHTHOL
NAPHTHOLS
NAPIFORM
NAPKIN
NAPKINS
NAPLESS
NAPOLEON
NAPOLEONS
NAPOO
NAPOOED
NAPOOING
NAPOOS
NAPPA
NAPPAS
NAPPE
NAPPED
NAPPER
NAPPERS
NAPPES
NAPPIER
NAPPIES
NAPPIEST
NAPPINESS
NAPPINESSES
NAPPING
NAPPY
NAPRON
NAPRONS
NAPS
NARAS
NARASES
NARCISSI
NARCISSUS
NARCISSUSES
NARCOSES
NARCOSIS
NARCOTIC
NARCOTICS
NARCOTINE
NARCOTINES
NARCOTISE
NARCOTISED
NARCOTISES
NARCOTISING
NARCOTISM
NARCOTISMS
NARCOTIST
NARCOTISTS
NARCOTIZE
NARCOTIZED
NARCOTIZES
NARCOTIZING
NARD
NARDED
NARDING
NARDOO
NARDOOS
NARDS
NARE
NARES
NARGHILE
NARGHILES

NARGHILIES
NARGHILLIES
NARGHILLY
NARGHILY
NARGILE
NARGILEH
NARGILEHS
NARGILES
NARGILIES
NARGILLIES
NARGILLY
NARGILY
NARIAL
NARICORN
NARICORNS
NARINE
NARK
NARKED
NARKIER
NARKIEST
NARKING
NARKS
NARKY
NARQUOIS
NARRAS
NARRASES
NARRATE
NARRATED
NARRATES
NARRATING
NARRATION
NARRATIONS
NARRATIVE
NARRATIVES
NARRATOR
NARRATORS
NARRATORY
NARRE
NARROW
NARROWED
NARROWER
NARROWEST
NARROWING
NARROWINGS
NARROWLY
NARROWS
NARTHEX
NARTHEXES
NARTJIE
NARTJIES
NARWHAL
NARWHALS
NARY
NAS
NASAL
NASALISE
NASALISED
NASALISES
NASALISING
NASALITIES
NASALITY
NASALIZE
NASALIZED

| | | | | |
|---|---|---|---|---|
| NASALIZES | NATTIER | NAVELWORTS | NEATER | NECKLINES |
| NASALIZING | NATTIEST | NAVES | NEATEST | NECKS |
| NASALLY | NATTILY | NAVETTE | NEATH | NECKTIE |
| NASALS | NATTINESS | NAVETTES | NEATLY | NECKTIES |
| NASARD | NATTINESSES | NAVEW | NEATNESS | NECKVERSE |
| NASARDS | NATTY | NAVEWS | NEATNESSES | NECKVERSES |
| NASCENCE | NATURA | NAVICERT | NEB | NECKWEAR |
| NASCENCES | NATURAE | NAVICERTS | NEBBED | NECKWEARS |
| NASCENCIES | NATURAL | NAVICULA | NEBBICH | NECKWEED |
| NASCENCY | NATURALLY | NAVICULAR | NEBBICHS | NECKWEEDS |
| NASCENT | NATURALS | NAVICULARS | NEBBING | NECROLOGIES |
| NASEBERRIES | NATURE | NAVICULAS | NEBBISH | NECROLOGY |
| NASEBERRY | NATURED | NAVIES | NEBBISHE | NECROPSIES |
| NASHGAB | NATURES | NAVIGABLE | NEBBISHER | NECROPSY |
| NASHGABS | NATURING | NAVIGATE | NEBBISHERS | NECROSE |
| NASION | NATURISM | NAVIGATED | NEBBISHES | NECROSED |
| NASIONS | NATURISMS | NAVIGATES | NEBBUK | NECROSES |
| NASTALIK | NATURIST | NAVIGATING | NEBBUKS | NECROSING |
| NASTALIKS | NATURISTS | NAVIGATOR | NEBECK | NECROSIS |
| NASTIC | NAUGHT | NAVIGATORS | NEBECKS | NECROTIC |
| NASTIER | NAUGHTIER | NAVVIED | NEBEK | NECROTISE |
| NASTIES | NAUGHTIES | NAVVIES | NEBEKS | NECROTISED |
| NASTIEST | NAUGHTIEST | NAVVY | NEBEL | NECROTISES |
| NASTILY | NAUGHTILY | NAVVYING | NEBELS | NECROTISING |
| NASTINESS | NAUGHTS | NAVY | NEBISH | NECROTIZE |
| NASTINESSES | NAUGHTY | NAWAB | NEBISHES | NECROTIZED |
| NASTY | NAUMACHIA | NAWABS | NEBRIS | NECROTIZES |
| NASUTE | NAUMACHIAE | NAY | NEBRISES | NECROTIZING |
| NASUTES | NAUMACHIAS | NAYS | NEBS | NECROTOMIES |
| NAT | NAUMACHIES | NAYTHLES | NEBULA | NECROTOMY |
| NATAL | NAUMACHY | NAYWARD | NEBULAE | NECTAR |
| NATALITIES | NAUNT | NAYWARDS | NEBULAR | NECTAREAL |
| NATALITY | NAUNTS | NAYWORD | NEBULE | NECTAREAN |
| NATANT | NAUPLII | NAYWORDS | NEBULÉ | NECTARED |
| NATATION | NAUPLIOID | NAZE | NEBULES | NECTARIAL |
| NATATIONS | NAUPLIUS | NAZES | NEBULISE | NECTARIES |
| NATATORY | NAUSEA | NAZIR | NEBULISED | NECTARINE |
| NATCH | NAUSEANT | NAZIRS | NEBULISER | NECTARINES |
| NATCHES | NAUSEANTS | NE | NEBULISERS | NECTAROUS |
| NATES | NAUSEAS | NEAFE | NEBULISES | NECTARS |
| NATHELESS | NAUSEATE | NEAFES | NEBULISING | NECTARY |
| NATHEMO | NAUSEATED | NEAFFE | NEBULIUM | NED |
| NATHEMORE | NAUSEATES | NEAFFES | NEBULIUMS | NEDDIES |
| NATHLESS | NAUSEATING | NEAL | NEBULIZE | NEDDY |
| NATIFORM | NAUSEOUS | NEALED | NEBULIZED | NEDS |
| NATION | NAUTCH | NEALING | NEBULIZER | NÉE |
| NATIONAL | NAUTCHES | NEALS | NEBULIZERS | NEED |
| NATIONALS | NAUTIC | NEANIC | NEBULIZES | NEEDED |
| NATIONS | NAUTICAL | NEAP | NEBULIZING | NEEDER |
| NATIVE | NAUTICS | NEAPED | NEBULOUS | NEEDERS |
| NATIVELY | NAUTILI | NEAPING | NEBULY | NEEDFUL |
| NATIVES | NAUTILUS | NEAPS | NECESSARIES | NEEDFULLY |
| NATIVISM | NAUTILUSES | NEAPTIDE | NECESSARY | NEEDIER |
| NATIVISMS | NAVAID | NEAPTIDES | NECESSITIES | NEEDIEST |
| NATIVIST | NAVAIDS | NEAR | NECESSITY | NEEDILY |
| NATIVISTS | NAVAL | NEARED | NECK | NEEDINESS |
| NATIVITIES | NAVALISM | NEARER | NECKATEE | NEEDINESSES |
| NATIVITY | NAVALISMS | NEAREST | NECKATEES | NEEDING |
| NATRIUM | NAVARCH | NEARING | NECKBEEF | NEEDLE |
| NATRIUMS | NAVARCHIES | NEARLY | NECKBEEFS | NEEDLED |
| NATROLITE | NAVARCHS | NEARNESS | NECKED | NEEDLEFUL |
| NATROLITES | NAVARCHY | NEARNESSES | NECKGEAR | NEEDLEFULS |
| NATRON | NAVARHO | NEARS | NECKGEARS | NEEDLER |
| NATRONS | NAVARHOS | NEARSIDE | NECKING | NEEDLERS |
| NATS | NAVARIN | NEARSIDES | NECKINGS | NEEDLES |
| NATTER | NAVARINS | NEAT | NECKLACE | NEEDLESS |
| NATTERED | NAVE | NEATEN | NECKLACES | NEEDLIER |
| NATTERING | NAVEL | NEATENED | NECKLET | NEEDLIEST |
| NATTERS | NAVELS | NEATENING | NECKLETS | NEEDLING |
| NATTERY | NAVELWORT | NEATENS | NECKLINE | NEEDLY |

NEEDMENT
NEEDMENTS
NEEDS
NEEDY
NEELD
NEELDS
NEELE
NEELES
NEEM
NEEMS
NEEP
NEEPS
NEESBERRIES
NEESBERRY
NEESE
NEESED
NEESES
NEESING
NEEZE
NEEZED
NEEZES
NEEZING
NEF
NEFANDOUS
NEFARIOUS
NEFAST
NEFS
NEGATE
NEGATED
NEGATES
NEGATING
NEGATION
NEGATIONS
NEGATIVE
NEGATIVED
NEGATIVES
NEGATIVING
NEGATORY
NEGATRON
NEGATRONS
NEGLECT
NEGLECTED
NEGLECTER
NEGLECTERS
NEGLECTING
NEGLECTS
NÉGLIGÉ
NEGLIGEE
NEGLIGEES
NEGLIGENT
NÉGLIGÉS
NÉGOCIANT
NÉGOCIANTS
NEGOTIATE
NEGOTIATED
NEGOTIATES
NEGOTIATING
NEGRESS
NEGRESSES
NEGRITUDE
NEGRITUDES
NEGRO
NEGROES
NEGROHEAD
NEGROHEADS
NEGROID
NEGROIDAL
NEGROIDS
NEGROISM
NEGROISMS

NEGROPHIL
NEGROPHILS
NEGUS
NEGUSES
NEIF
NEIFS
NEIGH
NEIGHBOR
NEIGHBORED
NEIGHBORING
NEIGHBORS
NEIGHBOUR
NEIGHBOURED
NEIGHBOURING
NEIGHBOURS
NEIGHED
NEIGHING
NEIGHS
NEIST
NEITHER
NEIVE
NEIVES
NEK
NEKS
NEKTON
NEKTONS
NELIES
NELIS
NELLIES
NELLY
NELSON
NELSONS
NELUMBIUM
NELUMBIUMS
NELUMBO
NELUMBOS
NEMATIC
NEMATODE
NEMATODES
NEMATOID
NEMERTEAN
NEMERTEANS
NEMERTIAN
NEMERTIANS
NEMERTINE
NEMERTINES
NEMESES
NEMESIA
NEMESIAS
NEMESIS
NEMN
NEMNED
NEMNING
NEMNS
NEMOPHILA
NEMOPHILAS
NEMORAL
NEMOROUS
NEMPT
NENE
NENES
NENUPHAR
NENUPHARS
NEOBLAST
NEOBLASTS
NEODYMIUM
NEODYMIUMS
NEOLITH
NEOLITHS
NEOLOGIAN

NEOLOGIANS
NEOLOGIC
NEOLOGIES
NEOLOGISE
NEOLOGISED
NEOLOGISES
NEOLOGISING
NEOLOGISM
NEOLOGISMS
NEOLOGIST
NEOLOGISTS
NEOLOGIZE
NEOLOGIZED
NEOLOGIZES
NEOLOGIZING
NEOLOGY
NEOMYCIN
NEOMYCINS
NEON
NEONATAL
NEONATE
NEONATES
NEONOMIAN
NEONOMIANS
NEONS
NEOPAGAN
NEOPAGANS
NEOPHILE
NEOPHILES
NEOPHILIA
NEOPHILIAS
NEOPHOBIA
NEOPHOBIAS
NEOPHYTE
NEOPHYTES
NEOPHYTIC
NEOPLASM
NEOPLASMS
NEOPRENE
NEOPRENES
NEOTEINIA
NEOTEINIAS
NEOTEINIC
NEOTENIC
NEOTENIES
NEOTENOUS
NEOTENY
NEOTERIC
NEOTERISE
NEOTERISED
NEOTERISES
NEOTERISING
NEOTERISM
NEOTERISMS
NEOTERIST
NEOTERISTS
NEOTERIZE
NEOTERIZED
NEOTERIZES
NEOTERIZING
NEP
NEPENTHE
NEPENTHES
NEPER
NEPERS
NEPHALISM
NEPHALISMS
NEPHALIST
NEPHALISTS
NEPHELINE

NEPHELINES
NEPHELITE
NEPHELITES
NEPHEW
NEPHEWS
NEPHOGRAM
NEPHOGRAMS
NEPHOLOGIES
NEPHOLOGY
NEPHRALGIES
NEPHRALGY
NEPHRIC
NEPHRIDIA
NEPHRITE
NEPHRITES
NEPHRITIC
NEPHRITICS
NEPHRITIS
NEPHRITISES
NEPHROID
NEPHRON
NEPHRONS
NEPHROSES
NEPHROSIS
NEPHROTIC
NEPIONIC
NEPIT
NEPITS
NEPOTIC
NEPOTISM
NEPOTISMS
NEPOTIST
NEPOTISTS
NEPS
NEPTUNIUM
NEPTUNIUMS
NERD
NERDS
NEREID
NEREIDS
NERINE
NERINES
NERITE
NERITES
NERITIC
NERKA
NERKAS
NEROLI
NEROLIS
NERVAL
NERVATE
NERVATION
NERVATIONS
NERVATURE
NERVATURES
NERVE
NERVED
NERVELESS
NERVELET
NERVELETS
NERVER
NERVERS
NERVES
NERVIER
NERVIEST
NERVINE
NERVINES
NERVINESS
NERVINESSES
NERVING

NERVOUS
NERVOUSLY
NERVULAR
NERVULE
NERVULES
NERVURE
NERVURES
NERVY
NESCIENCE
NESCIENCES
NESCIENT
NESH
NESHNESS
NESHNESSES
NESS
NESSES
NEST
NESTED
NESTER
NESTERS
NESTING
NESTLE
NESTLED
NESTLES
NESTLING
NESTLINGS
NESTS
NET
NETBALL
NETBALLS
NETE
NETES
NETFUL
NETFULS
NETHELESS
NETHER
NETS
NETSUKE
NETSUKES
NETT
NETTED
NETTIER
NETTIEST
NETTING
NETTINGS
NETTLE
NETTLED
NETTLES
NETTLING
NETTS
NETTY
NETWORK
NETWORKED
NETWORKING
NETWORKS
NEUK
NEUKS
NEUM
NEUME
NEUMES
NEUMS
NEURAL
NEURALGIA
NEURALGIAS
NEURALGIC
NEURATION
NEURATIONS
NEURILITIES
NEURILITY
NEURINE

NEURINES
NEURISM
NEURISMS
NEURITE
NEURITES
NEURITIC
NEURITICS
NEURITIS
NEURITISES
NEUROGLIA
NEUROGLIAS
NEUROGRAM
NEUROGRAMS
NEUROLOGIES
NEUROLOGY
NEUROMA
NEUROMAS
NEURON
NEURONAL
NEURONE
NEURONES
NEURONS
NEUROPATH
NEUROPATHS
NEUROSES
NEUROSIS
NEUROTIC
NEUROTICS
NEUROTOMIES
NEUROTOMY
NEUSTON
NEUSTONS
NEUTER
NEUTERED
NEUTERING
NEUTERS
NEUTRAL
NEUTRALLY
NEUTRALS
NEUTRETTO
NEUTRETTOS
NEUTRINO
NEUTRINOS
NEUTRON
NEUTRONS
NÉVÉ
NEVEL
NEVELLED
NEVELLING
NEVELS
NEVER
NEVERMORE
NÉVÉS
NEW
NEWBORN
NEWCOME
NEWCOMER
NEWCOMERS
NEWED
NEWEL
NEWELL
NEWELLED
NEWELLS
NEWELS
NEWER
NEWEST
NEWFANGLE
NEWING
NEWISH
NEWLY

NEWMARKET
NEWMARKETS
NEWNESS
NEWNESSES
NEWS
NEWSAGENT
NEWSAGENTS
NEWSBOY
NEWSBOYS
NEWSCAST
NEWSCASTS
NEWSED
NEWSES
NEWSFLASH
NEWSFLASHES
NEWSGIRL
NEWSGIRLS
NEWSHAWK
NEWSHAWKS
NEWSHOUND
NEWSHOUNDS
NEWSIER
NEWSIES
NEWSIEST
NEWSINESS
NEWSINESSES
NEWSING
NEWSMAN
NEWSMEN
NEWSPAPER
NEWSPAPERS
NEWSPEAK
NEWSPEAKS
NEWSPRINT
NEWSPRINTS
NEWSREEL
NEWSREELS
NEWSROOM
NEWSROOMS
NEWSTRADE
NEWSTRADES
NEWSWOMAN
NEWSWOMEN
NEWSY
NEWT
NEWTON
NEWTONS
NEWTS
NEXT
NEXTLY
NEXTNESS
NEXTNESSES
NEXUS
NEXUSES
NGAIO
NGAIOS
NGWEE
NIACIN
NIACINS
NIAISERIE
NIAISERIES
NIB
NIBBED
NIBBING
NIBBLE
NIBBLED
NIBBLER
NIBBLERS
NIBBLES
NIBBLING

NIBBLINGS
NIBLICK
NIBLICKS
NIBS
NICCOLITE
NICCOLITES
NICE
NICEISH
NICELY
NICENESS
NICENESSES
NICER
NICEST
NICETIES
NICETY
NICHE
NICHED
NICHER
NICHERED
NICHERING
NICHERS
NICHES
NICHING
NICK
NICKAR
NICKARS
NICKED
NICKEL
NICKELIC
NICKELINE
NICKELINES
NICKELISE
NICKELISED
NICKELISES
NICKELISING
NICKELIZE
NICKELIZED
NICKELIZES
NICKELIZING
NICKELLED
NICKELLING
NICKELOUS
NICKELS
NICKER
NICKERED
NICKERING
NICKERS
NICKING
NICKNAME
NICKNAMED
NICKNAMES
NICKNAMING
NICKS
NICKSTICK
NICKSTICKS
NICKUM
NICKUMS
NICOL
NICOLS
NICOMPOOP
NICOMPOOPS
NICOTIAN
NICOTIANA
NICOTIANAS
NICOTIANS
NICOTINE
NICOTINES
NICOTINIC
NICTATE
NICTATED

NICTATES
NICTATING
NICTATION
NICTATIONS
NICTITATE
NICTITATED
NICTITATES
NICTITATING
NID
NIDAL
NIDATION
NIDATIONS
NIDDERING
NIDDERINGS
NIDE
NIDERING
NIDERINGS
NIDERLING
NIDERLINGS
NIDES
NIDGET
NIDGETS
NIDI
NIDIFIED
NIDIFIES
NIDIFY
NIDIFYING
NIDING
NIDINGS
NIDOR
NIDOROUS
NIDORS
NIDS
NIDUS
NIE
NIECE
NIECES
NIED
NIEF
NIEFS
NIELLATED
NIELLI
NIELLIST
NIELLISTS
NIELLO
NIELLOED
NIELLOING
NIELLOS
NIES
NIEVE
NIEVEFUL
NIEVEFULS
NIEVES
NIFE
NIFES
NIFF
NIFFED
NIFFER
NIFFERED
NIFFERING
NIFFERS
NIFFIER
NIFFIEST
NIFFING
NIFFNAFF
NIFFNAFFED
NIFFNAFFING
NIFFNAFFS
NIFFS
NIFFY

NIFTIER
NIFTIEST
NIFTINESS
NIFTINESSES
NIFTY
NIGELLA
NIGELLAS
NIGER
NIGERS
NIGGARD
NIGGARDED
NIGGARDING
NIGGARDLY
NIGGARDS
NIGGER
NIGGERDOM
NIGGERDOMS
NIGGERED
NIGGERING
NIGGERISH
NIGGERISM
NIGGERISMS
NIGGERS
NIGGERY
NIGGLE
NIGGLED
NIGGLER
NIGGLERS
NIGGLES
NIGGLIER
NIGGLIEST
NIGGLING
NIGGLINGS
NIGGLY
NIGH
NIGHED
NIGHEST
NIGHING
NIGHLY
NIGHNESS
NIGHNESSES
NIGHS
NIGHT
NIGHTCAP
NIGHTCAPS
NIGHTED
NIGHTFALL
NIGHTFALLS
NIGHTFIRE
NIGHTFIRES
NIGHTGEAR
NIGHTGEARS
NIGHTGOWN
NIGHTGOWNS
NIGHTHAWK
NIGHTHAWKS
NIGHTIE
NIGHTIES
NIGHTJAR
NIGHTJARS
NIGHTLESS
NIGHTLONG
NIGHTLY
NIGHTMARE
NIGHTMARES
NIGHTMARY
NIGHTS
NIGHTSPOT
NIGHTSPOTS
NIGHTWARD

NIGHTWEAR
NIGHTWEARS
NIGHTY
NIGRICANT
NIGRIFIED
NIGRIFIES
NIGRIFY
NIGRIFYING
NIGRITUDE
NIGRITUDES
NIGROSINE
NIGROSINES
NIHIL
NIHILISM
NIHILISMS
NIHILIST
NIHILISTS
NIHILITIES
NIHILITY
NIHILS
NIL
NILGAI
NILGAIS
NILGAU
NILGAUS
NILL
NILLED
NILLING
NILLS
NILS
NIM
NIMBED
NIMBI
NIMBLE
NIMBLER
NIMBLESSE
NIMBLESSES
NIMBLEST
NIMBLY
NIMBUS
NIMBUSED
NIMBUSES
NIMIETIES
NIMIETY
NIMIOUS
NIMMED
NIMMER
NIMMERS
NIMMING
NIMONIC
NIMS
NINCOM
NINCOMS
NINCUM
NINCUMS
NINE
NINEFOLD
NINEHOLES
NINEPENCE
NINEPENCES
NINEPENNIES
NINEPENNY
NINEPINS
NINES
NINESCORE
NINESCORES
NINETEEN
NINETEENS
NINETIES
NINETIETH

NINETIETHS
NINETY
NINJA
NINJAS
NINNIES
NINNY
NINON
NINONS
NINTH
NINTHLY
NINTHS
NIOBATE
NIOBATES
NIOBIC
NIOBITE
NIOBITES
NIOBIUM
NIOBIUMS
NIOBOUS
NIP
NIPPED
NIPPER
NIPPERED
NIPPERING
NIPPERKIN
NIPPERKINS
NIPPERS
NIPPIER
NIPPIEST
NIPPING
NIPPINGLY
NIPPLE
NIPPLED
NIPPLES
NIPPLING
NIPPY
NIPS
NIPTER
NIPTERS
NIRL
NIRLED
NIRLIE
NIRLIER
NIRLIEST
NIRLING
NIRLIT
NIRLS
NIRLY
NIRVANA
NIRVANAS
NIS
NISBERRIES
NISBERRY
NISEI
NISEIS
NISI
NISSE
NISSES
NISUS
NISUSES
NIT
NITERIE
NITERIES
NITERY
NITHING
NITHINGS
NITID
NITON
NITONS
NITRATE

NITRATED
NITRATES
NITRATINE
NITRATINES
NITRATING
NITRATION
NITRATIONS
NITRE
NITRES
NITRIC
NITRIDE
NITRIDED
NITRIDES
NITRIDING
NITRIDINGS
NITRIFIED
NITRIFIES
NITRIFY
NITRIFYING
NITRILE
NITRILES
NITRITE
NITRITES
NITROGEN
NITROGENS
NITROUS
NITROXYL
NITROXYLS
NITRY
NITRYL
NITRYLS
NITS
NITTIER
NITTIEST
NITTY
NITWIT
NITWITS
NITWITTED
NIVAL
NIVEOUS
NIX
NIXES
NIXIE
NIXIES
NIXY
NIZAM
NIZAMS
NO
NOB
NOBBIER
NOBBIEST
NOBBILY
NOBBINESS
NOBBINESSES
NOBBLE
NOBBLED
NOBBLER
NOBBLERS
NOBBLES
NOBBLING
NOBBUT
NOBBY
NOBELIUM
NOBELIUMS
NOBILESSE
NOBILESSES
NOBILIARY
NOBILITIES
NOBILITY
NOBLE

NOBLEMAN
NOBLEMEN
NOBLENESS
NOBLENESSES
NOBLER
NOBLES
NOBLESSE
NOBLESSES
NOBLEST
NOBLY
NOBODIES
NOBODY
NOBS
NOCAKE
NOCAKES
NOCENT
NOCENTLY
NOCENTS
NOCHEL
NOCHELLED
NOCHELLING
NOCHELS
NOCK
NOCKED
NOCKET
NOCKETS
NOCKING
NOCKS
NOCTILUCA
NOCTILUCAS
NOCTUA
NOCTUARIES
NOCTUARY
NOCTUAS
NOCTUID
NOCTUIDS
NOCTULE
NOCTULES
NOCTURN
NOCTURNAL
NOCTURNALS
NOCTURNE
NOCTURNES
NOCTURNS
NOCUOUS
NOCUOUSLY
NOD
NODAL
NODALISE
NODALISED
NODALISES
NODALISING
NODALITIES
NODALITY
NODALIZE
NODALIZED
NODALIZES
NODALIZING
NODATED
NODATION
NODATIONS
NODDED
NODDER
NODDERS
NODDIES
NODDING
NODDINGS
NODDLE
NODDLED
NODDLES

NODDLING
NODDY
NODE
NODES
NODI
NODICAL
NODOSE
NODOSITIES
NODOSITY
NODOUS
NODS
NODULAR
NODULATED
NODULE
NODULED
NODULES
NODULOSE
NODULOUS
NODUS
NOËL
NOËLS
NOES
NOESES
NOESIS
NOETIC
NOG
NOGAKU
NOGGIN
NOGGING
NOGGINGS
NOGGINS
NOGS
NOH
NOHOW
NOHOWISH
NOIL
NOILS
NOINT
NOINTED
NOINTING
NOINTS
NOISE
NOISED
NOISEFUL
NOISELESS
NOISES
NOISETTE
NOISETTES
NOISIER
NOISIEST
NOISILY
NOISINESS
NOISINESSES
NOISING
NOISOME
NOISOMELY
NOISY
NOLE
NOLES
NOLITION
NOLITIONS
NOLL
NOLLS
NOM
NOMA
NOMAD
NOMADE
NOMADES
NOMADIC
NOMADIES

| | | | | |
|---|---|---|---|---|
| NOMADISE | NONESUCHES | NOOSPHERES | NOSED | NOTCHBACKS |
| NOMADISED | NONET | NOPAL | NOSEGAY | NOTCHED |
| NOMADISES | NONETS | NOPALS | NOSEGAYS | NOTCHEL |
| NOMADISING | NONETTE | NOPE | NOSELESS | NOTCHELLED |
| NOMADISM | NONETTES | NOR | NOSELITE | NOTCHELLING |
| NOMADISMS | NONETTI | NORI | NOSELITES | NOTCHELS |
| NOMADIZE | NONETTO | NORIA | NOSER | NOTCHES |
| NOMADIZED | NONETTOS | NORIAS | NOSERS | NOTCHIER |
| NOMADIZES | NONG | NORIMON | NOSES | NOTCHIEST |
| NOMADIZING | NONGS | NORIMONS | NOSEY | NOTCHING |
| NOMADS | NONILLION | NORIS | NOSEYS | NOTCHINGS |
| NOMADY | NONILLIONS | NORITE | NOSH | NOTCHY |
| NOMARCH | NONJURING | NORITES | NOSHED | NOTE |
| NOMARCHIES | NONJUROR | NORK | NOSHES | NOTEBOOK |
| NOMARCHS | NONJURORS | NORKS | NOSHING | NOTEBOOKS |
| NOMARCHY | NONNIES | NORLAND | NOSIER | NOTED |
| NOMAS | NONNY | NORLANDS | NOSIES | NOTEDLY |
| NOMBRIL | NONPAREIL | NORM | NOSIEST | NOTEDNESS |
| NOMBRILS | NONPAREILS | NORMA | NOSILY | NOTEDNESSES |
| NOME | NONPAROUS | NORMAL | NOSINESS | NOTELESS |
| NOMEN | NONPLUS | NORMALCIES | NOSINESSES | NOTELET |
| NOMES | NONPLUSES | NORMALCY | NOSING | NOTELETS |
| NOMIC | NONPLUSSED | NORMALISE | NOSINGS | NOTEPAPER |
| NOMINA | NONPLUSSES | NORMALISED | NOSOLOGIES | NOTEPAPERS |
| NOMINABLE | NONPLUSSING | NORMALISES | NOSOLOGY | NOTER |
| NOMINAL | NONPOLAR | NORMALISING | NOSTALGIA | NOTERS |
| NOMINALLY | NONSENSE | NORMALITIES | NOSTALGIAS | NOTES |
| NOMINALS | NONSENSES | NORMALITY | NOSTALGIC | NOTHING |
| NOMINATE | NONSUCH | NORMALIZE | NOSTOC | NOTHINGS |
| NOMINATED | NONSUCHES | NORMALIZED | NOSTOCS | NOTICE |
| NOMINATES | NONSUIT | NORMALIZES | NOSTOI | NOTICED |
| NOMINATING | NONSUITED | NORMALIZING | NOSTOLOGIES | NOTICES |
| NOMINATOR | NONSUITING | NORMALLY | NOSTOLOGY | NOTICING |
| NOMINATORS | NONSUITS | NORMALS | NOSTOS | NOTIFIED |
| NOMINEE | NONUPLE | NORMAN | NOSTRIL | NOTIFIER |
| NOMINEES | NONUPLET | NORMANS | NOSTRILS | NOTIFIERS |
| NOMISM | NONUPLETS | NORMAS | NOSTRUM | NOTIFIES |
| NOMISMS | NOODLE | NORMATIVE | NOSTRUMS | NOTIFY |
| NOMISTIC | NOODLED | NORMS | NOSY | NOTIFYING |
| NOMOCRACIES | NOODLEDOM | NORSEL | NOT | NOTING |
| NOMOCRACY | NOODLEDOMS | NORSELLED | NOTABILIA | NOTION |
| NOMOGENIES | NOODLES | NORSELLER | NOTABLE | NOTIONAL |
| NOMOGENY | NOODLING | NORSELLERS | NOTABLES | NOTIONIST |
| NOMOGRAM | NOOK | NORSELLING | NOTABLY | NOTIONISTS |
| NOMOGRAMS | NOOKIE | NORSELS | NOTAEUM | NOTIONS |
| NOMOGRAPH | NOOKIER | NORTH | NOTAEUMS | NOTITIA |
| NOMOGRAPHS | NOOKIES | NORTHED | NOTAL | NOTITIAS |
| NOMOI | NOOKIEST | NORTHER | NOTANDA | NOTOCHORD |
| NOMOLOGIES | NOOKS | NORTHERED | NOTANDUM | NOTOCHORDS |
| NOMOLOGY | NOOKY | NORTHERING | NOTAPHILIES | NOTORIETIES |
| NOMOS | NOOLOGIES | NORTHERLIES | NOTAPHILY | NOTORIETY |
| NOMOTHETE | NOOLOGY | NORTHERLY | NOTARIAL | NOTORIOUS |
| NOMOTHETES | NOOMETRIES | NORTHERN | NOTARIES | NOTORNIS |
| NOMS | NOOMETRY | NORTHERNS | NOTARISE | NOTORNISES |
| NON | NOON | NORTHERS | NOTARISED | NOTOUR |
| NONAGE | NOONDAY | NORTHING | NOTARISES | NOTT |
| NONAGED | NOONDAYS | NORTHINGS | NOTARISING | NOTUM |
| NONAGES | NOONED | NORTHLAND | NOTARIZE | NOTUMS |
| NONAGON | NOONING | NORTHLANDS | NOTARIZED | NOUGAT |
| NONAGONS | NOONINGS | NORTHMOST | NOTARIZES | NOUGATS |
| NONANE | NOONS | NORTHS | NOTARIZING | NOUGHT |
| NONANES | NOONTIDE | NORTHWARD | NOTARY | NOUGHTS |
| NONARY | NOONTIDES | NORTHWARDS | NOTATE | NOUL |
| NONCE | NOOP | NORWARD | NOTATED | NOULD |
| NONCES | NOOPS | NORWARDS | NOTATES | NOULDE |
| NONE | NOOSE | NOSE | NOTATING | NOULE |
| NONENTITIES | NOOSED | NOSEAN | NOTATION | NOULES |
| NONENTITY | NOOSES | NOSEANS | NOTATIONS | NOULS |
| NONES | NOOSING | NOSEBAG | NOTCH | NOUMENA |
| NONESUCH | NOOSPHERE | NOSEBAGS | NOTCHBACK | NOUMENAL |

NOUMENON
NOUN
NOUNAL
NOUNIER
NOUNIEST
NOUNS
NOUNY
NOUP
NOUPS
NOURICE
NOURICES
NOURISH
NOURISHED
NOURISHER
NOURISHERS
NOURISHES
NOURISHING
NOURITURE
NOURITURES
NOURSLE
NOURSLED
NOURSLES
NOURSLING
NOUS
NOUSELL
NOUSELLED
NOUSELLING
NOUSELLS
NOUSES
NOUSLE
NOUSLED
NOUSLES
NOUSLING
NOUT
NOUVEAU
NOUVELLE
NOUVELLES
NOVA
NOVAE
NOVALIA
NOVAS
NOVATION
NOVATIONS
NOVEL
NOVELDOM
NOVELDOMS
NOVELESE
NOVELESES
NOVELETTE
NOVELETTES
NOVELISE
NOVELISED
NOVELISER
NOVELISERS
NOVELISES
NOVELISH
NOVELISING
NOVELISM
NOVELISMS
NOVELIST
NOVELISTS
NOVELIZE
NOVELIZED
NOVELIZER
NOVELIZERS
NOVELIZES
NOVELIZING
NOVELLA
NOVELLAE
NOVELLAS

NOVELLE
NOVELS
NOVELTIES
NOVELTY
NOVENA
NOVENARIES
NOVENARY
NOVENAS
NOVENNIAL
NOVERCAL
NOVERINT
NOVERINTS
NOVICE
NOVICES
NOVICIATE
NOVICIATES
NOVITIATE
NOVITIATES
NOVITIES
NOVITY
NOVODAMUS
NOVODAMUSES
NOVUM
NOVUMS
NOW
NOWADAYS
NOWAY
NOWAYS
NOWED
NOWHENCE
NOWHERE
NOWHERES
NOWHITHER
NOWISE
NOWL
NOWLS
NOWN
NOWNESS
NOWNESSES
NOWS
NOWT
NOWTS
NOWY
NOXAL
NOXIOUS
NOXIOUSLY
NOY
NOYADE
NOYADES
NOYANCE
NOYANCES
NOYAU
NOYAUS
NOYED
NOYES
NOYESES
NOYING
NOYOUS
NOYS
NOYSOME
NOZZLE
NOZZLES
NTH
NU
NUANCE
NUANCED
NUANCES
NUANCING
NUB
NUBBED

NUBBIER
NUBBIEST
NUBBIN
NUBBING
NUBBINS
NUBBLE
NUBBLED
NUBBLES
NUBBLIER
NUBBLIEST
NUBBLING
NUBBLY
NUBBY
NUBECULA
NUBECULAE
NUBIA
NUBIAS
NUBIFORM
NUBILE
NUBILITIES
NUBILITY
NUBILOUS
NUBS
NUCELLAR
NUCELLI
NUCELLUS
NUCELLUSES
NUCHA
NUCHAL
NUCHAS
NUCLEAL
NUCLEAR
NUCLEARY
NUCLEASE
NUCLEASES
NUCLEATE
NUCLEATED
NUCLEATES
NUCLEATING
NUCLEI
NUCLEIDE
NUCLEIDES
NUCLEIN
NUCLEINS
NUCLEOLAR
NUCLEOLE
NUCLEOLES
NUCLEOLI
NUCLEOLUS
NUCLEON
NUCLEONS
NUCLEUS
NUCLIDE
NUCLIDES
NUCULE
NUCULES
NUDATION
NUDATIONS
NUDE
NUDELY
NUDENESS
NUDENESSES
NUDER
NUDES
NUDEST
NUDGE
NUDGED
NUDGES
NUDGING
NUDICAUL

NUDIE
NUDIES
NUDISM
NUDISMS
NUDIST
NUDISTS
NUDITIES
NUDITY
NUGAE
NUGATORY
NUGGAR
NUGGARS
NUGGET
NUGGETS
NUGGETY
NUISANCE
NUISANCER
NUISANCERS
NUISANCES
NUKE
NUKED
NUKES
NUKING
NULL
NULLA
NULLAH
NULLAHS
NULLAS
NULLED
NULLIFIED
NULLIFIER
NULLIFIERS
NULLIFIES
NULLIFY
NULLIFYING
NULLING
NULLINGS
NULLIPARA
NULLIPARAE
NULLIPARAS
NULLIPORE
NULLIPORES
NULLITIES
NULLITY
NULLNESS
NULLNESSES
NULLS
NUMB
NUMBAT
NUMBATS
NUMBED
NUMBER
NUMBERED
NUMBERER
NUMBERERS
NUMBERING
NUMBERS
NUMBEST
NUMBING
NUMBLES
NUMBS
NUMBSKULL
NUMBSKULLS
NUMDAH
NUMDAHS
NUMEN
NUMERABLE
NUMERABLY
NUMERACIES
NUMERACY

NUMERAIRE
NUMERAIRES
NUMERAL
NUMERALLY
NUMERALS
NUMERARY
NUMERATE
NUMERATED
NUMERATES
NUMERATING
NUMERATOR
NUMERATORS
NUMERIC
NUMERICAL
NUMEROUS
NUMINA
NUMINOUS
NUMMARY
NUMMULAR
NUMMULARY
NUMMULINE
NUMMULITE
NUMMULITES
NUMNAH
NUMNAHS
NUMSKULL
NUMSKULLS
NUN
NUNATAK
NUNATAKER
NUNATAKS
NUNCHEON
NUNCHEONS
NUNCIO
NUNCIOS
NUNCLE
NUNCLES
NUNCUPATE
NUNCUPATED
NUNCUPATES
NUNCUPATING
NUNDINAL
NUNDINE
NUNDINES
NUNHOOD
NUNHOODS
NUNNATION
NUNNATIONS
NUNNERIES
NUNNERY
NUNNISH
NUNS
NUNSHIP
NUNSHIPS
NUPTIAL
NUPTIALS
NUR
NURAGHE
NURAGHI
NURAGHIC
NURD
NURDS
NURHAG
NURHAGS
NURL
NURLED
NURLING
NURLS
NURR
NURRS

| | | | | |
|---|---|---|---|---|
| NURS | NURTURING | NUTMEGGY | NUTTINGS | NYLGHAUS |
| NURSE | NUS | NUTMEGS | NUTTY | NYLON |
| NURSED | NUT | NUTPECKER | NUZZER | NYLONS |
| NURSELIKE | NUTANT | NUTPECKERS | NUZZERS | NYMPH |
| NURSELING | NUTARIAN | NUTRIA | NUZZLE | NYMPHAE |
| NURSELINGS | NUTARIANS | NUTRIAS | NUZZLED | NYMPHAEA |
| NURSEMAID | NUTATE | NUTRIENT | NUZZLES | NYMPHAEUM |
| NURSEMAIDS | NUTATED | NUTRIENTS | NUZZLING | NYMPHAEUMS |
| NURSER | NUTATES | NUTRIMENT | NY | NYMPHAL |
| NURSERIES | NUTATING | NUTRIMENTS | NYAFF | NYMPHALID |
| NURSERS | NUTATION | NUTRITION | NYAFFED | NYMPHALIDS |
| NURSERY | NUTATIONS | NUTRITIONS | NYAFFING | NYMPHEAN |
| NURSES | NUTCASE | NUTRITIVE | NYAFFS | NYMPHET |
| NURSING | NUTCASES | NUTS | NYALA | NYMPHETS |
| NURSLE | NUTHATCH | NUTSHELL | NYALAS | NYMPHIC |
| NURSLED | NUTHATCHES | NUTSHELLS | NYANZA | NYMPHICAL |
| NURSLES | NUTHOUSE | NUTTED | NYANZAS | NYMPHISH |
| NURSLING | NUTHOUSES | NUTTER | NYAS | NYMPHLY |
| NURSLINGS | NUTJOBBER | NUTTERIES | NYASES | NYMPHO |
| NURTURAL | NUTJOBBERS | NUTTERS | NYCTALOPES | NYMPHOS |
| NURTURANT | NUTLET | NUTTERY | NYCTALOPS | NYMPHS |
| NURTURE | NUTLETS | NUTTIER | NYE | NYS |
| NURTURED | NUTMEAL | NUTTIEST | NYED | NYSTAGMIC |
| NURTURER | NUTMEALS | NUTTINESS | NYES | NYSTAGMUS |
| NURTURERS | NUTMEG | NUTTINESSES | NYING | NYSTAGMUSES |
| NURTURES | NUTMEGGED | NUTTING | NYLGHAU | |

# O

OAF
OAFISH
OAFS
OAK
OAKEN
OAKENSHAW
OAKENSHAWS
OAKER
OAKERS
OAKIER
OAKIEST
OAKLING
OAKLINGS
OAKS
OAKUM
OAKUMS
OAKY
OAR
OARAGE
OARAGES
OARED
OARIER
OARIEST
OARING
OARLESS
OARS
OARSMAN
OARSMEN
OARSWOMAN
OARSWOMEN
OARWEED
OARWEEDS
OARY
OASES
OASIS
OAST
OASTS
OAT
OATCAKE
OATCAKES
OATEN
OATH
OATHABLE
OATHS
OATMEAL
OATMEALS
OATS
OAVES
OB
OBANG
OBANGS
OBBLIGATI
OBBLIGATO
OBBLIGATOS
OBCONIC
OBCONICAL
OBCORDATE
OBDURACIES
OBDURACY
OBDURATE
OBDURATED
OBDURATES
OBDURATING

OBDURE
OBDURED
OBDURES
OBDURING
OBEAH
OBEAHED
OBEAHING
OBEAHISM
OBEAHISMS
OBEAHS
OBECHE
OBECHES
OBEDIENCE
OBEDIENCES
OBEDIENT
OBEISANCE
OBEISANCES
OBEISANT
OBEISM
OBEISMS
OBELI
OBELION
OBELIONS
OBELISCAL
OBELISE
OBELISED
OBELISES
OBELISING
OBELISK
OBELISKS
OBELIZE
OBELIZED
OBELIZES
OBELIZING
OBELUS
OBESE
OBESENESS
OBESENESSES
OBESER
OBESEST
OBESITIES
OBESITY
OBEY
OBEYED
OBEYER
OBEYERS
OBEYING
OBEYS
OBFUSCATE
OBFUSCATED
OBFUSCATES
OBFUSCATING
OBI
OBIA
OBIAS
OBIED
OBIING
OBIISM
OBIISMS
OBIIT
OBIS
OBIT
OBITAL

OBITER
OBITS
OBITUAL
OBITUARIES
OBITUARY
OBJECT
OBJECTED
OBJECTIFIED
OBJECTIFIES
OBJECTIFY
OBJECTIFYING
OBJECTING
OBJECTION
OBJECTIONS
OBJECTIVE
OBJECTIVES
OBJECTOR
OBJECTORS
OBJECTS
OBJET
OBJETS
OBJURE
OBJURED
OBJURES
OBJURGATE
OBJURGATED
OBJURGATES
OBJURGATING
OBJURING
OBLAST
OBLASTS
OBLATE
OBLATES
OBLATION
OBLATIONS
OBLATORY
OBLIGANT
OBLIGANTS
OBLIGATE
OBLIGATED
OBLIGATES
OBLIGATING
OBLIGE
OBLIGED
OBLIGEE
OBLIGEES
OBLIGES
OBLIGING
OBLIGOR
OBLIGORS
OBLIQUE
OBLIQUED
OBLIQUELY
OBLIQUER
OBLIQUES
OBLIQUEST
OBLIQUID
OBLIQUING
OBLIQUITIES
OBLIQUITY
OBLIVION
OBLIVIONS
OBLIVIOUS

OBLONG
OBLONGS
OBLOQUIES
OBLOQUY
OBNOXIOUS
OBOE
OBOES
OBOIST
OBOISTS
OBOL
OBOLARY
OBOLI
OBOLS
OBOLUS
OBOVATE
OBOVATELY
OBOVOID
OBREPTION
OBREPTIONS
OBS
OBSCENE
OBSCENELY
OBSCENER
OBSCENEST
OBSCENITIES
OBSCENITY
OBSCURANT
OBSCURANTS
OBSCURE
OBSCURED
OBSCURELY
OBSCURER
OBSCURERS
OBSCURES
OBSCUREST
OBSCURING
OBSCURITIES
OBSCURITY
OBSECRATE
OBSECRATED
OBSECRATES
OBSECRATING
OBSEQUENT
OBSEQUIAL
OBSEQUIE
OBSEQUIES
OBSEQUY
OBSERVANT
OBSERVANTS
OBSERVE
OBSERVED
OBSERVER
OBSERVERS
OBSERVES
OBSERVING
OBSESS
OBSESSED
OBSESSES
OBSESSING
OBSESSION
OBSESSIONS
OBSESSIVE
OBSIDIAN

OBSIDIANS
OBSIGN
OBSIGNATE
OBSIGNATED
OBSIGNATES
OBSIGNATING
OBSIGNED
OBSIGNING
OBSIGNS
OBSOLESCE
OBSOLESCED
OBSOLESCES
OBSOLESCING
OBSOLETE
OBSTACLE
OBSTACLES
OBSTETRIC
OBSTETRICS
OBSTINACIES
OBSTINACY
OBSTINATE
OBSTRUCT
OBSTRUCTED
OBSTRUCTING
OBSTRUCTS
OBSTRUENT
OBSTRUENTS
OBTAIN
OBTAINED
OBTAINER
OBTAINERS
OBTAINING
OBTAINS
OBTECT
OBTECTED
OBTEMPER
OBTEMPERED
OBTEMPERING
OBTEMPERS
OBTEND
OBTENDED
OBTENDING
OBTENDS
OBTENTION
OBTENTIONS
OBTEST
OBTESTED
OBTESTING
OBTESTS
OBTRUDE
OBTRUDED
OBTRUDER
OBTRUDERS
OBTRUDES
OBTRUDING
OBTRUDINGS
OBTRUSION
OBTRUSIONS
OBTRUSIVE
OBTUND
OBTUNDED
OBTUNDENT
OBTUNDENTS

| | | | | |
|---|---|---|---|---|
| OBTUNDING | OCCULTED | OCHROUS | OCTOSTYLE | ODOMETER |
| OBTUNDS | OCCULTING | OCHRY | OCTOSTYLES | ODOMETERS |
| OBTURATE | OCCULTISM | OCKER | OCTROI | ODOMETRIES |
| OBTURATED | OCCULTISMS | OCKERISM | OCTROIS | ODOMETRY |
| OBTURATES | OCCULTIST | OCKERISMS | OCTUOR | ODONATIST |
| OBTURATING | OCCULTISTS | OCKERS | OCTUORS | ODONATISTS |
| OBTURATOR | OCCULTLY | OCOTILLO | OCTUPLE | ODONTALGIES |
| OBTURATORS | OCCULTS | OCOTILLOS | OCTUPLED | ODONTALGY |
| OBTUSE | OCCUPANCE | OCREA | OCTUPLES | ODONTIC |
| OBTUSELY | OCCUPANCES | OCREAE | OCTUPLET | ODONTIST |
| OBTUSER | OCCUPANCIES | OCREATE | OCTUPLETS | ODONTISTS |
| OBTUSEST | OCCUPANCY | OCTACHORD | OCTUPLING | ODONTOID |
| OBTUSITIES | OCCUPANT | OCTACHORDS | OCULAR | ODONTOMA |
| OBTUSITY | OCCUPANTS | OCTAD | OCULARIST | ODONTOMAS |
| OBUMBRATE | OCCUPATE | OCTADIC | OCULARISTS | ODONTOMATA |
| OBUMBRATED | OCCUPATED | OCTADS | OCULARLY | ODOR |
| OBUMBRATES | OCCUPATES | OCTAGON | OCULARS | ODORANT |
| OBUMBRATING | OCCUPATING | OCTAGONAL | OCULATE | ODORATE |
| OBVENTION | OCCUPIED | OCTAGONS | OCULATED | ODOROUS |
| OBVENTIONS | OCCUPIER | OCTAHEDRA | OCULI | ODOROUSLY |
| OBVERSE | OCCUPIERS | OCTAL | OCULIST | ODORS |
| OBVERSELY | OCCUPIES | OCTAMETER | OCULISTS | ODOUR |
| OBVERSES | OCCUPY | OCTAMETERS | OCULUS | ODOURED |
| OBVERSION | OCCUPYING | OCTANE | OD | ODOURLESS |
| OBVERSIONS | OCCUR | OCTANES | ODA | ODOURS |
| OBVERT | OCCURRED | OCTANT | ODAL | ODS |
| OBVERTED | OCCURRENT | OCTANTAL | ODALIQUE | ODSO |
| OBVERTING | OCCURRENTS | OCTANTS | ODALIQUES | ODSOS |
| OBVERTS | OCCURRING | OCTAPLA | ODALISK | ODYL |
| OBVIATE | OCCURS | OCTAPLAS | ODALISKS | ODYLE |
| OBVIATED | OCEAN | OCTAPLOID | ODALISQUE | ODYLES |
| OBVIATES | OCEANAUT | OCTAPLOIDS | ODALISQUES | ODYLISM |
| OBVIATING | OCEANAUTS | OCTAPODIC | ODALLER | ODYLISMS |
| OBVIATION | OCEANIC | OCTAPODIES | ODALLERS | ODYLS |
| OBVIATIONS | OCEANID | OCTAPODY | ODALS | ODYSSEY |
| OBVIOUS | OCEANIDES | OCTAROON | ODAS | ODYSSEYS |
| OBVIOUSLY | OCEANIDS | OCTAROONS | ODD | ODZOOKS |
| OBVOLUTE | OCEANS | OCTASTICH | ODDBALL | OE |
| OBVOLUTED | OCELLAR | OCTASTICHS | ODDBALLS | OECIST |
| OBVOLVENT | OCELLATE | OCTASTYLE | ODDER | OECISTS |
| OCA | OCELLATED | OCTASTYLES | ODDEST | OECOLOGIES |
| OCARINA | OCELLI | OCTAVAL | ODDISH | OECOLOGY |
| OCARINAS | OCELLUS | OCTAVE | ODDITIES | OECUMENIC |
| OCAS | OCELOID | OCTAVES | ODDITY | OEDEMA |
| OCCAMIES | OCELOT | OCTAVO | ODDLY | OEDEMAS |
| OCCAMY | OCELOTS | OCTAVOS | ODDMENT | OEILLADE |
| OCCASION | OCH | OCTENNIAL | ODDMENTS | OEILLADES |
| OCCASIONED | OCHE | OCTET | ODDNESS | OENANTHIC |
| OCCASIONING | OCHER | OCTETS | ODDNESSES | OENOLOGIES |
| OCCASIONS | OCHERED | OCTETT | ODDS | OENOLOGY |
| OCCIDENT | OCHERING | OCTETTE | ODDSMAN | OENOMANCIES |
| OCCIDENTS | OCHEROUS | OCTETTES | ODDSMEN | OENOMANCY |
| OCCIPITAL | OCHERS | OCTETTS | ODE | OENOMANIA |
| OCCIPITALS | OCHERY | OCTILLION | ODEA | OENOMANIAS |
| OCCIPUT | OCHES | OCTILLIONS | ODEON | OENOMEL |
| OCCIPUTS | OCHIDORE | OCTOFID | ODEONS | OENOMELS |
| OCCLUDE | OCHIDORES | OCTOHEDRA | ODES | OENOMETER |
| OCCLUDED | OCHLOCRAT | OCTONARIES | ODEUM | OENOMETERS |
| OCCLUDENT | OCHLOCRATS | OCTONARII | ODEUMS | OENOPHIL |
| OCCLUDENTS | OCHONE | OCTONARY | ODIC | OENOPHILE |
| OCCLUDES | OCHRE | OCTOPI | ODIOUS | OENOPHILES |
| OCCLUDING | OCHREA | OCTOPLOID | ODIOUSLY | OENOPHILIES |
| OCCLUSAL | OCHREAE | OCTOPLOIDS | ODISM | OENOPHILS |
| OCCLUSION | OCHREATE | OCTOPOD | ODISMS | OENOPHILY |
| OCCLUSIONS | OCHRED | OCTOPODES | ODIST | OERLIKON |
| OCCLUSIVE | OCHREOUS | OCTOPODS | ODISTS | OERLIKONS |
| OCCLUSIVES | OCHRES | OCTOPUS | ODIUM | OERSTED |
| OCCLUSOR | OCHREY | OCTOPUSES | ODIUMS | OERSTEDS |
| OCCLUSORS | OCHRING | OCTOROON | ODOGRAPH | OES |
| OCCULT | OCHROID | OCTOROONS | ODOGRAPHS | OESOPHAGI |

OESTRAL
OESTROGEN
OESTROGENS
OESTROUS
OESTRUM
OESTRUMS
OESTRUS
OESTRUSES
OEUVRE
OEUVRES
OF
OFAY
OFAYS
OFF
OFFAL
OFFALS
OFFBEAT
OFFCUT
OFFCUTS
OFFED
OFFENCE
OFFENCES
OFFEND
OFFENDED
OFFENDER
OFFENDERS
OFFENDING
OFFENDS
OFFENSE
OFFENSES
OFFENSIVE
OFFENSIVES
OFFER
OFFERABLE
OFFERED
OFFEREE
OFFEREES
OFFERER
OFFERERS
OFFERING
OFFERINGS
OFFEROR
OFFERORS
OFFERS
OFFERTORIES
OFFERTORY
OFFHAND
OFFHANDED
OFFICE
OFFICER
OFFICERED
OFFICERING
OFFICERS
OFFICES
OFFICIAL
OFFICIALS
OFFICIANT
OFFICIANTS
OFFICIATE
OFFICIATED
OFFICIATES
OFFICIATING
OFFICINAL
OFFICIOUS
OFFING
OFFINGS
OFFISH
OFFLOAD
OFFLOADED
OFFLOADING

OFFLOADS
OFFPEAK
OFFPRINT
OFFPRINTS
OFFPUT
OFFPUTS
OFFS
OFFSADDLE
OFFSADDLED
OFFSADDLES
OFFSADDLING
OFFSCUM
OFFSCUMS
OFFSEASON
OFFSEASONS
OFFSET
OFFSETS
OFFSETTING
OFFSHOOT
OFFSHOOTS
OFFSHORE
OFFSIDE
OFFSIDER
OFFSIDERS
OFFSIDES
OFFSPRING
OFFSPRINGS
OFFTAKE
OFFTAKES
OFLAG
OFLAGS
OFT
OFTEN
OFTENER
OFTENEST
OFTENNESS
OFTENNESSES
OFTTIMES
OGAM
OGAMIC
OGAMS
OGDOAD
OGDOADS
OGEE
OGEES
OGGIN
OGGINS
OGHAM
OGHAMIC
OGHAMS
OGIVAL
OGIVE
OGIVES
OGLE
OGLED
OGLER
OGLERS
OGLES
OGLING
OGLINGS
OGMIC
OGRE
OGREISH
OGRES
OGRESS
OGRESSES
OGRISH
OH
OHM
OHMIC

OHMMETER
OHMMETERS
OHMS
OHO
OHONE
OHOS
OI
OIDIA
OIDIUM
OIK
OIKIST
OIKISTS
OIKS
OIL
OILCAN
OILCANS
OILCLOTH
OILCLOTHS
OILED
OILER
OILERIES
OILERS
OILERY
OILIER
OILIEST
OILILY
OILINESS
OILINESSES
OILING
OILLET
OILLETS
OILNUT
OILNUTS
OILS
OILSKIN
OILSKINS
OILSTONE
OILSTONES
OILY
OINT
OINTED
OINTING
OINTMENT
OINTMENTS
OINTS
OITICICA
OITICICAS
OJIME
OJIMES
OKAPI
OKAPIS
OKAY
OKAYED
OKAYING
OKAYS
OKE
OKES
OKIMONO
OKIMONOS
OKRA
OKRAS
OLD
OLDEN
OLDENED
OLDENING
OLDENS
OLDER
OLDEST
OLDIE
OLDIES

OLDISH
OLDNESS
OLDNESSES
OLDS
OLDSQUAW
OLDSQUAWS
OLDSTER
OLDSTERS
OLDY
OLÉ
OLEACEOUS
OLEANDER
OLEANDERS
OLEARIA
OLEARIAS
OLEASTER
OLEASTERS
OLEATE
OLEATES
OLECRANAL
OLECRANON
OLECRANONS
OLEFIANT
OLEFIN
OLEFINE
OLEFINES
OLEFINS
OLEIC
OLEIN
OLEINS
OLENT
OLEO
OLEOGRAPH
OLEOGRAPHS
OLEOS
OLEUM
OLEUMS
OLFACT
OLFACTED
OLFACTING
OLFACTION
OLFACTIONS
OLFACTIVE
OLFACTORY
OLFACTS
OLIBANUM
OLIBANUMS
OLID
OLIGAEMIA
OLIGAEMIAS
OLIGARCH
OLIGARCHIES
OLIGARCHS
OLIGARCHY
OLIGIST
OLIGISTS
OLIGOPOLIES
OLIGOPOLY
OLIO
OLIOS
OLIPHANT
OLIPHANTS
OLITORIES
OLITORY
OLIVARY
OLIVE
OLIVENITE
OLIVENITES
OLIVER
OLIVERS

OLIVES
OLIVET
OLIVETS
OLIVINE
OLIVINES
OLLA
OLLAMH
OLLAMHS
OLLAS
OLLAV
OLLAVS
OLM
OLMS
OLOGIES
OLOGY
OLOROSO
OLOROSOS
OLPAE
OLPE
OLPES
OLYCOOK
OLYCOOKS
OLYKOEK
OLYKOEKS
OLYMPIAD
OLYMPIADS
OLYMPICS
OM
OMADHAUN
OMADHAUNS
OMASA
OMASAL
OMASUM
OMBRE
OMBRÉ
OMBRELLA
OMBRELLAS
OMBRES
OMBROPHIL
OMBROPHILS
OMBU
OMBÚ
OMBUDSMAN
OMBUDSMEN
OMBÚS
OMBUS
OMEGA
OMEGAS
OMELET
OMELETS
OMELETTE
OMELETTES
OMEN
OMENED
OMENING
OMENS
OMENTA
OMENTAL
OMENTUM
OMER
OMERS
OMERTÀ
OMERTÀS
OMICRON
OMICRONS
OMINOUS
OMINOUSLY
OMISSIBLE
OMISSION
OMISSIONS

| | | | | |
|---|---|---|---|---|
| OMISSIVE | ONCOGENS | ONSIDE | OOM | OPAQUEST |
| OMIT | ONCOLOGIES | ONSIDES | OOMIAC | OPAQUING |
| OMITS | ONCOLOGY | ONSLAUGHT | OOMIACK | OPE |
| OMITTANCE | ONCOME | ONSLAUGHTS | OOMIACKS | OPED |
| OMITTANCES | ONCOMES | ONST | OOMIACS | OPEN |
| OMITTED | ONCOMETER | ONSTEAD | OOMIAK | OPENABLE |
| OMITTER | ONCOMETERS | ONSTEADS | OOMIAKS | OPENED |
| OMITTERS | ONCOMING | ONTO | OOMPAH | OPENER |
| OMITTING | ONCOMINGS | ONTOGENIC | OOMPAHED | OPENERS |
| OMLAH | ONCOST | ONTOGENIES | OOMPAHING | OPENEST |
| OMLAHS | ONCOSTMAN | ONTOGENY | OOMPAHS | OPENING |
| OMMATEA | ONCOSTMEN | ONTOLOGIC | OOMPH | OPENINGS |
| OMMATEUM | ONCOSTS | ONTOLOGIES | OOMPHS | OPENLY |
| OMMATIDIA | ONCOTOMIES | ONTOLOGY | OOMS | OPENNESS |
| OMNEITIES | ONCOTOMY | ONUS | OON | OPENNESSES |
| OMNEITY | ONCUS | ONUSES | OONS | OPENS |
| OMNIANA | ONDATRA | ONWARD | OONT | OPERA |
| OMNIBUS | ONDATRAS | ONWARDLY | OONTS | OPERABLE |
| OMNIBUSES | ONDINE | ONWARDS | OOP | OPERAND |
| OMNIETIES | ONDINES | ONYCHA | OOPED | OPERANDS |
| OMNIETY | ONDING | ONYCHAS | OOPHORON | OPERANT |
| OMNIFIC | ONDINGS | ONYCHIA | OOPHORONS | OPERANTS |
| OMNIFIED | ONE | ONYCHIAS | OOPHYTE | OPERAS |
| OMNIFIES | ONEFOLD | ONYCHITE | OOPHYTES | OPERATE |
| OMNIFORM | ONEIRIC | ONYCHITES | OOPING | OPERATED |
| OMNIFY | ONELY | ONYCHITIS | OOPS | OPERATES |
| OMNIFYING | ONENESS | ONYCHITISES | OOR | OPERATIC |
| OMNIUM | ONENESSES | ONYCHIUM | OORIAL | OPERATING |
| OMNIUMS | ONER | ONYCHIUMS | OORIALS | OPERATION |
| OMNIVORE | ONEROUS | ONYMOUS | OORIE | OPERATIONS |
| OMNIVORES | ONEROUSLY | ONYX | OORIER | OPERATIVE |
| OMNIVORIES | ONERS | ONYXES | OORIEST | OPERATIVES |
| OMNIVORY | ONES | OO | OOS | OPERATOR |
| OMOHYOID | ONESELF | OOBIT | OOSE | OPERATORS |
| OMOHYOIDS | ONEYER | OOBITS | OOSES | OPERCULA |
| OMOPHAGIA | ONEYERS | OOCYTE | OOSIER | OPERCULAR |
| OMOPHAGIAS | ONEYRE | OOCYTES | OOSIEST | OPERCULUM |
| OMOPHAGIC | ONEYRES | OODLES | OOSPHERE | OPERETTA |
| OMOPHAGIES | ONFALL | OODLINS | OOSPHERES | OPERETTAS |
| OMOPHAGY | ONFALLS | OOF | OOSPORE | OPEROSE |
| OMOPLATE | ONFLOW | OOFS | OOSPORES | OPEROSELY |
| OMOPLATES | ONFLOWS | OOFTISH | OOSY | OPEROSITIES |
| OMPHACITE | ONGOING | OOFTISHES | OOZE | OPEROSITY |
| OMPHACITES | ONGOINGS | OOGAMIES | OOZED | OPES |
| OMPHALIC | ONION | OOGAMOUS | OOZES | OPHIDIAN |
| OMPHALOID | ONIONED | OOGAMY | OOZIER | OPHIDIANS |
| OMPHALOS | ONIONING | OOGENESES | OOZIEST | OPHIOLITE |
| OMPHALOSES | ONIONS | OOGENESIS | OOZILY | OPHIOLITES |
| OMRAH | ONIONY | OOGENETIC | OOZINESS | OPHIOLOGIES |
| OMRAHS | ONIRIC | OOGENIES | OOZINESSES | OPHIOLOGY |
| OMS | ONISCOID | OOGENY | OOZING | OPHITE |
| ON | ONKUS | OOGONIA | OOZY | OPHITES |
| ONAGER | ONLOOKER | OOGONIAL | OP | OPHITIC |
| ONAGERS | ONLOOKERS | OOGONIUM | OPACITIES | OPHIURAN |
| ONANISM | ONLOOKING | OOH | OPACITY | OPHIURANS |
| ONANISMS | ONLY | OOHED | OPACOUS | OPHIURID |
| ONANIST | ONNED | OOHING | OPAH | OPHIURIDS |
| ONANISTIC | ONNING | OOHS | OPAHS | OPHIUROID |
| ONANISTS | ONOMASTIC | OOIDAL | OPAL | OPHIUROIDS |
| ONBOARD | ONOMASTICS | OOLAKAN | OPALED | OPIATE |
| ONCE | ONRUSH | OOLAKANS | OPALINE | OPIATED |
| ONCER | ONRUSHES | OOLITE | OPALINES | OPIATES |
| ONCERS | ONS | OOLITES | OPALISED | OPIATING |
| ONCES | ONSET | OOLITIC | OPALIZED | OPIFICER |
| ONCIDIUM | ONSETS | OOLOGIES | OPALS | OPIFICERS |
| ONCIDIUMS | ONSETTER | OOLOGIST | OPAQUE | OPINABLE |
| ONCOGEN | ONSETTERS | OOLOGISTS | OPAQUED | OPINE |
| ONCOGENE | ONSETTING | OOLOGY | OPAQUELY | OPINED |
| ONCOGENES | ONSETTINGS | OOLONG | OPAQUER | OPINES |
| ONCOGENIC | ONSHORE | OOLONGS | OPAQUES | OPING |

OPINICUS
OPINICUSES
OPINING
OPINION
OPINIONED
OPINIONS
OPIOID
OPIUM
OPIUMS
OPOBALSAM
OPOBALSAMS
OPODELDOC
OPODELDOCS
OPOPANAX
OPOPANAXES
OPORICE
OPORICES
OPOSSUM
OPOSSUMS
OPPIDAN
OPPIDANS
OPPILATE
OPPILATED
OPPILATES
OPPILATING
OPPONENCIES
OPPONENCY
OPPONENT
OPPONENTS
OPPORTUNE
OPPOSABLE
OPPOSE
OPPOSED
OPPOSER
OPPOSERS
OPPOSES
OPPOSING
OPPOSITE
OPPOSITES
OPPRESS
OPPRESSED
OPPRESSES
OPPRESSING
OPPRESSOR
OPPRESSORS
OPPUGN
OPPUGNANT
OPPUGNANTS
OPPUGNED
OPPUGNER
OPPUGNERS
OPPUGNING
OPPUGNS
OPS
OPSIMATH
OPSIMATHIES
OPSIMATHS
OPSIMATHY
OPSOMANIA
OPSOMANIAS
OPSONIC
OPSONIN
OPSONINS
OPSONIUM
OPSONIUMS
OPT
OPTANT
OPTANTS
OPTATIVE
OPTATIVES

OPTED
OPTIC
OPTICAL
OPTICALLY
OPTICIAN
OPTICIANS
OPTICS
OPTIMA
OPTIMAL
OPTIMATE
OPTIMATES
OPTIME
OPTIMES
OPTIMISE
OPTIMISED
OPTIMISES
OPTIMISING
OPTIMISM
OPTIMISMS
OPTIMIST
OPTIMISTS
OPTIMIZE
OPTIMIZED
OPTIMIZES
OPTIMIZING
OPTIMUM
OPTING
OPTION
OPTIONAL
OPTIONS
OPTOLOGIES
OPTOLOGY
OPTOMETER
OPTOMETERS
OPTOMETRIES
OPTOMETRY
OPTOPHONE
OPTOPHONES
OPTS
OPULENCE
OPULENCES
OPULENT
OPULENTLY
OPULUS
OPULUSES
OPUNTIA
OPUNTIAS
OPUS
OPUSCLE
OPUSCLES
OPUSCULA
OPUSCULE
OPUSCULES
OPUSCULUM
OPUSES
OR
ORACH
ORACHE
ORACHES
ORACIES
ORACLE
ORACLED
ORACLES
ORACLING
ORACULAR
ORACULOUS
ORACY
ORAGIOUS
ORAL
ORALLY

ORALS
ORANG
ORANGE
ORANGEADE
ORANGEADES
ORANGER
ORANGERIES
ORANGERY
ORANGES
ORANGEST
ORANGS
ORANT
ORANTS
ORARIA
ORARIAN
ORARIANS
ORARION
ORARIONS
ORARIUM
ORARIUMS
ORATE
ORATED
ORATES
ORATING
ORATION
ORATIONS
ORATOR
ORATORIAL
ORATORIAN
ORATORIANS
ORATORIES
ORATORIO
ORATORIOS
ORATORS
ORATORY
ORATRESS
ORATRESSES
ORATRIX
ORATRIXES
ORB
ORBED
ORBICULAR
ORBIER
ORBIEST
ORBING
ORBIT
ORBITA
ORBITAL
ORBITALS
ORBITAS
ORBITED
ORBITER
ORBITERS
ORBITIES
ORBITING
ORBITS
ORBITY
ORBS
ORBY
ORC
ORCEIN
ORCEINS
ORCHARD
ORCHARDS
ORCHAT
ORCHATS
ORCHEL
ORCHELLA
ORCHELLAS
ORCHELS

ORCHESES
ORCHESIS
ORCHESTIC
ORCHESTICS
ORCHESTRA
ORCHESTRAS
ORCHID
ORCHIDIST
ORCHIDISTS
ORCHIDS
ORCHIL
ORCHILLA
ORCHILLAS
ORCHILS
ORCHIS
ORCHISES
ORCHITIC
ORCHITIS
ORCHITISES
ORCIN
ORCINE
ORCINES
ORCINOL
ORCINOLS
ORCINS
ORCS
ORD
ORDAIN
ORDAINED
ORDAINER
ORDAINERS
ORDAINING
ORDAINS
ORDALIAN
ORDALIUM
ORDALIUMS
ORDEAL
ORDEALS
ORDER
ORDERED
ORDERER
ORDERERS
ORDERING
ORDERINGS
ORDERLESS
ORDERLIES
ORDERLY
ORDERS
ORDINAIRE
ORDINAIRES
ORDINAL
ORDINALS
ORDINANCE
ORDINANCES
ORDINAND
ORDINANDS
ORDINANT
ORDINANTS
ORDINAR
ORDINARIES
ORDINARS
ORDINARY
ORDINATE
ORDINATED
ORDINATES
ORDINATING
ORDINEE
ORDINEES
ORDNANCE
ORDNANCES

ORDS
ORDURE
ORDURES
ORDUROUS
ORE
OREAD
OREADES
OREADS
ORECROWE
ORECROWED
ORECROWES
ORECROWING
ORECTIC
OREGANO
OREGANOS
OREIDE
OREIDES
OREOLOGIES
OREOLOGY
OREPEARCH
OREPEARCHED
OREPEARCHES
OREPEARCHING
ORES
ORESTUNCK
OREWEED
OREWEEDS
OREXIS
OREXISES
ORF
ORFE
ORFES
ORFS
ORGAN
ORGANA
ORGANDIE
ORGANDIES
ORGANELLE
ORGANELLES
ORGANIC
ORGANICAL
ORGANISE
ORGANISED
ORGANISER
ORGANISERS
ORGANISES
ORGANISING
ORGANISM
ORGANISMS
ORGANIST
ORGANISTS
ORGANITIES
ORGANITY
ORGANIZE
ORGANIZED
ORGANIZER
ORGANIZERS
ORGANIZES
ORGANIZING
ORGANON
ORGANS
ORGANUM
ORGANZA
ORGANZAS
ORGANZINE
ORGANZINES
ORGASM
ORGASMED
ORGASMIC
ORGASMING

ORGASMS
ORGASTIC
ORGEAT
ORGEATS
ORGIA
ORGIAS
ORGIAST
ORGIASTIC
ORGIASTS
ORGIC
ORGIES
ORGILLOUS
ORGONE
ORGONES
ORGUE
ORGUES
ORGULOUS
ORGY
ORIBI
ORIBIS
ORICALCHE
ORICALCHES
ORICHALC
ORICHALCS
ORIEL
ORIELLED
ORIELS
ORIENCIES
ORIENCY
ORIENT
ORIENTAL
ORIENTALS
ORIENTATE
ORIENTATED
ORIENTATES
ORIENTATING
ORIENTED
ORIENTEER
ORIENTEERED
ORIENTEERING
ORIENTEERINGS
ORIENTEERS
ORIENTING
ORIENTS
ORIFEX
ORIFEXES
ORIFICE
ORIFICES
ORIFICIAL
ORIFLAMME
ORIFLAMMES
ORIGAMI
ORIGAMIS
ORIGAN
ORIGANE
ORIGANES
ORIGANS
ORIGANUM
ORIGANUMS
ORIGIN
ORIGINAL
ORIGINALS
ORIGINATE
ORIGINATED
ORIGINATES
ORIGINATING
ORIGINS
ORILLION
ORILLIONS
ORIOLE

ORIOLES
ORISON
ORISONS
ORLE
ORLEANS
ORLEANSES
ORLES
ORLOP
ORLOPS
ORMER
ORMERS
ORMOLU
ORMOLUS
ORNAMENT
ORNAMENTED
ORNAMENTING
ORNAMENTS
ORNATE
ORNATELY
ORNATER
ORNATEST
ORNERY
ORNIS
ORNISES
ORNITHIC
ORNITHOID
OROGEN
OROGENIC
OROGENIES
OROGENS
OROGENY
OROGRAPHIES
OROGRAPHY
OROIDE
OROIDES
OROLOGIES
OROLOGIST
OROLOGISTS
OROLOGY
OROPESA
OROPESAS
OROROTUND
OROTUND
ORPHAN
ORPHANAGE
ORPHANAGES
ORPHANED
ORPHANING
ORPHANISM
ORPHANISMS
ORPHANS
ORPHARION
ORPHARIONS
ORPHREY
ORPHREYS
ORPIMENT
ORPIMENTS
ORPIN
ORPINE
ORPINES
ORPINS
ORRA
ORRERIES
ORRERY
ORRIS
ORRISES
ORS
ORSEILLE
ORSEILLES
ORSELLIC

ORT
ORTANIQUE
ORTANIQUES
ORTHIAN
ORTHICON
ORTHICONS
ORTHO
ORTHOAXES
ORTHOAXIS
ORTHODOX
ORTHODOXIES
ORTHODOXY
ORTHOEPIC
ORTHOEPIES
ORTHOEPY
ORTHOPEDIES
ORTHOPEDY
ORTHOPOD
ORTHOPODS
ORTHOPTIC
ORTHOPTICS
ORTHOS
ORTHOSES
ORTHOSIS
ORTHOTIC
ORTHOTICS
ORTHOTIST
ORTHOTISTS
ORTHOTONE
ORTHROS
ORTHROSES
ORTOLAN
ORTOLANS
ORTS
ORVAL
ORVALS
ORYX
ORYXES
OS
OSCHEAL
OSCILLATE
OSCILLATED
OSCILLATES
OSCILLATING
OSCINE
OSCININE
OSCITANCIES
OSCITANCY
OSCITANT
OSCITATE
OSCITATED
OSCITATES
OSCITATING
OSCULA
OSCULANT
OSCULAR
OSCULATE
OSCULATED
OSCULATES
OSCULATING
OSCULE
OSCULES
OSCULUM
OSCULUMS
OSHAC
OSHACS
OSIER
OSIERED
OSIERIES
OSIERS

OSIERY
OSMATE
OSMATES
OSMETERIA
OSMIATE
OSMIATES
OSMIC
OSMIOUS
OSMIUM
OSMIUMS
OSMOMETER
OSMOMETERS
OSMOMETRIES
OSMOMETRY
OSMOSE
OSMOSED
OSMOSES
OSMOSING
OSMOSIS
OSMOTIC
OSMOUS
OSMUND
OSMUNDA
OSMUNDAS
OSMUNDS
OSNABURG
OSNABURGS
OSPREY
OSPREYS
OSSA
OSSARIUM
OSSARIUMS
OSSEIN
OSSEINS
OSSELET
OSSELETS
OSSEOUS
OSSETER
OSSETERS
OSSIA
OSSICLE
OSSICLES
OSSICULAR
OSSIFIC
OSSIFIED
OSSIFIES
OSSIFRAGA
OSSIFRAGAS
OSSIFRAGE
OSSIFRAGES
OSSIFY
OSSIFYING
OSSUARIES
OSSUARY
OSTEAL
OSTEITIS
OSTEITISES
OSTENSIVE
OSTENSORIES
OSTENSORY
OSTENT
OSTENTS
OSTEODERM
OSTEODERMS
OSTEOGENIES
OSTEOGENY
OSTEOID
OSTEOLOGIES
OSTEOLOGY
OSTEOMA

OSTEOMAS
OSTEOPATH
OSTEOPATHS
OSTEOTOME
OSTEOTOMES
OSTEOTOMIES
OSTEOTOMY
OSTIA
OSTIAL
OSTIARIES
OSTIARY
OSTIATE
OSTINATO
OSTINATOS
OSTIOLATE
OSTIOLE
OSTIOLES
OSTIUM
OSTLER
OSTLERESS
OSTLERESSES
OSTLERS
OSTRACA
OSTRACEAN
OSTRACISE
OSTRACISED
OSTRACISES
OSTRACISING
OSTRACISM
OSTRACISMS
OSTRACIZE
OSTRACIZED
OSTRACIZES
OSTRACIZING
OSTRACOD
OSTRACODS
OSTRACON
OSTRAKA
OSTRAKON
OSTREGER
OSTREGERS
OSTRICH
OSTRICHES
OTALGIA
OTALGIAS
OTALGIES
OTALGY
OTARIES
OTARINE
OTARY
OTHER
OTHERNESS
OTHERNESSES
OTHERS
OTHERWISE
OTIC
OTIOSE
OTIOSITIES
OTIOSITY
OTITIS
OTITISES
OTOCYST
OTOCYSTS
OTOLITH
OTOLITHS
OTOLOGIES
OTOLOGIST
OTOLOGISTS
OTOLOGY
OTORRHOEA

| | | | | |
|---|---|---|---|---|
| OTORRHOEAS | OUPS | OUTBREEDING | OUTDRIVES | OUTFOOTS |
| OTOSCOPE | OUR | OUTBREEDINGS | OUTDRIVING | OUTFOUGHT |
| OTOSCOPES | OURALI | OUTBREEDS | OUTDROVE | OUTFOX |
| OTTAR | OURALIS | OUTBROKE | OUTDRUNK | OUTFOXED |
| OTTARS | OURARI | OUTBROKEN | OUTDURE | OUTFOXES |
| OTTAVA | OURARIS | OUTBURN | OUTDURED | OUTFOXING |
| OTTAVAS | OUREBI | OUTBURNED | OUTDURES | OUTFROWN |
| OTTAVINO | OUREBIS | OUTBURNING | OUTDURING | OUTFROWNED |
| OTTAVINOS | OURIE | OUTBURNS | OUTDWELL | OUTFROWNING |
| OTTER | OURIER | OUTBURNT | OUTDWELLED | OUTFROWNS |
| OTTERED | OURIEST | OUTBURST | OUTDWELLING | OUTGAS |
| OTTERING | OURN | OUTBURSTING | OUTDWELLS | OUTGASSED |
| OTTERS | OUROBOROS | OUTBURSTS | OUTDWELT | OUTGASSES |
| OTTO | OUROBOROSES | OUTBY | OUTEAT | OUTGASSING |
| OTTOMAN | OUROLOGIES | OUTBYE | OUTEATEN | OUTGASSINGS |
| OTTOMANS | OUROLOGY | OUTCAST | OUTEATING | OUTGATE |
| OTTOS | OUROSCOPIES | OUTCASTE | OUTEATS | OUTGATES |
| OTTRELITE | OUROSCOPY | OUTCASTED | OUTED | OUTGAVE |
| OTTRELITES | OURS | OUTCASTES | OUTEDGE | OUTGIVE |
| OU | OURSELF | OUTCASTING | OUTEDGES | OUTGIVEN |
| OUABAIN | OURSELVES | OUTCASTS | OUTER | OUTGIVES |
| OUABAINS | OUSEL | OUTCLASS | OUTERMOST | OUTGIVING |
| OUAKARI | OUSELS | OUTCLASSED | OUTERS | OUTGIVINGS |
| OUAKARIS | OUST | OUTCLASSES | OUTERWEAR | OUTGLARE |
| OUBIT | OUSTED | OUTCLASSING | OUTERWEARS | OUTGLARED |
| OUBITS | OUSTER | OUTCOME | OUTFACE | OUTGLARES |
| OUBLIETTE | OUSTERS | OUTCOMES | OUTFACED | OUTGLARING |
| OUBLIETTES | OUSTING | OUTCRAFTIED | OUTFACES | OUTGO |
| OUCH | OUSTITI | OUTCRAFTIES | OUTFACING | OUTGOER |
| OUCHES | OUSTITIS | OUTCRAFTY | OUTFALL | OUTGOERS |
| OUCHT | OUSTS | OUTCRAFTYING | OUTFALLS | OUTGOES |
| OUCHTS | OUT | OUTCRIED | OUTFIELD | OUTGOING |
| OUGHLIED | OUTACT | OUTCRIES | OUTFIELDS | OUTGOINGS |
| OUGHLIES | OUTACTED | OUTCROP | OUTFIGHT | OUTGONE |
| OUGHLY | OUTACTING | OUTCROPPED | OUTFIGHTING | OUTGREW |
| OUGHLYING | OUTACTS | OUTCROPPING | OUTFIGHTS | OUTGROW |
| OUGHT | OUTAGE | OUTCROPS | OUTFIT | OUTGROWING |
| OUGHTNESS | OUTAGES | OUTCROSS | OUTFITS | OUTGROWN |
| OUGHTNESSES | OUTATE | OUTCROSSED | OUTFITTED | OUTGROWS |
| OUGHTS | OUTBACK | OUTCROSSES | OUTFITTER | OUTGROWTH |
| OUGLIE | OUTBACKER | OUTCROSSING | OUTFITTERS | OUTGROWTHS |
| OUGLIED | OUTBACKERS | OUTCROSSINGS | OUTFITTING | OUTGUARD |
| OUGLIEING | OUTBACKS | OUTCRY | OUTFITTINGS | OUTGUARDS |
| OUGLIES | OUTBAR | OUTCRYING | OUTFLANK | OUTGUN |
| OUIJA | OUTBARRED | OUTDANCE | OUTFLANKED | OUTGUNNED |
| OUIJAS | OUTBARRING | OUTDANCED | OUTFLANKING | OUTGUNNING |
| OUISTITI | OUTBARS | OUTDANCES | OUTFLANKS | OUTGUNS |
| OUISTITIS | OUTBID | OUTDANCING | OUTFLASH | OUTGUSH |
| OUK | OUTBIDDING | OUTDARE | OUTFLASHED | OUTGUSHED |
| OUKS | OUTBIDS | OUTDARED | OUTFLASHES | OUTGUSHES |
| OULACHON | OUTBOARD | OUTDARES | OUTFLASHING | OUTGUSHING |
| OULACHONS | OUTBOUND | OUTDARING | OUTFLEW | OUTHAUL |
| OULAKAN | OUTBOUNDS | OUTDATE | OUTFLIES | OUTHAULER |
| OULAKANS | OUTBOX | OUTDATED | OUTFLING | OUTHAULERS |
| OULK | OUTBOXED | OUTDATES | OUTFLINGS | OUTHAULS |
| OULKS | OUTBOXES | OUTDATING | OUTFLOW | OUTHER |
| OULONG | OUTBOXING | OUTDID | OUTFLOWED | OUTHIRE |
| OULONGS | OUTBRAG | OUTDO | OUTFLOWING | OUTHIRED |
| OUNCE | OUTBRAGGED | OUTDOES | OUTFLOWINGS | OUTHIRES |
| OUNCES | OUTBRAGGING | OUTDOING | OUTFLOWN | OUTHIRING |
| OUNDIER | OUTBRAGS | OUTDONE | OUTFLOWS | OUTHIT |
| OUNDIEST | OUTBRAVE | OUTDOOR | OUTFLUSH | OUTHITS |
| OUNDY | OUTBRAVED | OUTDOORS | OUTFLUSHED | OUTHITTING |
| OUP | OUTBRAVES | OUTDOORSY | OUTFLUSHES | OUTHOUSE |
| OUPED | OUTBRAVING | OUTDRANK | OUTFLUSHING | OUTHOUSES |
| OUPH | OUTBREAK | OUTDRINK | OUTFLY | OUTHYRE |
| OUPHE | OUTBREAKING | OUTDRINKING | OUTFLYING | OUTHYRED |
| OUPHES | OUTBREAKS | OUTDRINKS | OUTFOOT | OUTHYRES |
| OUPHS | OUTBRED | OUTDRIVE | OUTFOOTED | OUTHYRING |
| OUPING | OUTBREED | OUTDRIVEN | OUTFOOTING | OUTING |

| | | | | |
|---|---|---|---|---|
| OUTINGS | OUTLOOK | OUTPORT | OUTRELIEF | OUTSHOTS |
| OUTJEST | OUTLOOKED | OUTPORTS | OUTRELIEFS | OUTSIDE |
| OUTJESTED | OUTLOOKING | OUTPOST | OUTREMER | OUTSIDER |
| OUTJESTING | OUTLOOKS | OUTPOSTS | OUTREMERS | OUTSIDERS |
| OUTJESTS | OUTLUSTRE | OUTPOUR | OUTRIDDEN | OUTSIDES |
| OUTJET | OUTLUSTRED | OUTPOURED | OUTRIDE | OUTSIGHT |
| OUTJETS | OUTLUSTRES | OUTPOURER | OUTRIDER | OUTSIGHTS |
| OUTJUMP | OUTLUSTRING | OUTPOURERS | OUTRIDERS | OUTSIT |
| OUTJUMPED | OUTLYING | OUTPOURING | OUTRIDES | OUTSITS |
| OUTJUMPING | OUTMAN | OUTPOURINGS | OUTRIDING | OUTSITTING |
| OUTJUMPS | OUTMANNED | OUTPOURS | OUTRIGGER | OUTSIZE |
| OUTJUT | OUTMANNING | OUTPOWER | OUTRIGGERS | OUTSIZED |
| OUTJUTS | OUTMANS | OUTPOWERED | OUTRIGHT | OUTSIZES |
| OUTLAID | OUTMANTLE | OUTPOWERING | OUTRIVAL | OUTSKIRT |
| OUTLAIN | OUTMANTLED | OUTPOWERS | OUTRIVALLED | OUTSKIRTS |
| OUTLAND | OUTMANTLES | OUTPRAY | OUTRIVALLING | OUTSLEEP |
| OUTLANDER | OUTMANTLING | OUTPRAYED | OUTRIVALS | OUTSLEEPING |
| OUTLANDERS | OUTMARCH | OUTPRAYING | OUTROAR | OUTSLEEPS |
| OUTLANDS | OUTMARCHED | OUTPRAYS | OUTROARED | OUTSLEPT |
| OUTLASH | OUTMARCHES | OUTPRICE | OUTROARING | OUTSMART |
| OUTLASHES | OUTMARCHING | OUTPRICED | OUTROARS | OUTSMARTED |
| OUTLAST | OUTMATCH | OUTPRICES | OUTRODE | OUTSMARTING |
| OUTLASTED | OUTMATCHED | OUTPRICING | OUTROOP | OUTSMARTS |
| OUTLASTING | OUTMATCHES | OUTPRIZE | OUTROOPER | OUTSOAR |
| OUTLASTS | OUTMATCHING | OUTPRIZED | OUTROOPERS | OUTSOARED |
| OUTLAUNCE | OUTMODE | OUTPRIZES | OUTROOPS | OUTSOARING |
| OUTLAUNCED | OUTMODED | OUTPRIZING | OUTROOT | OUTSOARS |
| OUTLAUNCES | OUTMODES | OUTPUT | OUTROOTED | OUTSOLD |
| OUTLAUNCH | OUTMODING | OUTPUTS | OUTROOTING | OUTSOLE |
| OUTLAUNCHED | OUTMOST | OUTPUTTING | OUTROOTS | OUTSOLES |
| OUTLAUNCHES | OUTMOVE | OUTRACE | OUTROPE | OUTSPAN |
| OUTLAUNCHING | OUTMOVED | OUTRACED | OUTROPER | OUTSPANNED |
| OUTLAUNCING | OUTMOVES | OUTRACES | OUTROPERS | OUTSPANNING |
| OUTLAW | OUTMOVING | OUTRACING | OUTROPES | OUTSPANS |
| OUTLAWED | OUTNAME | OUTRAGE | OUTRUN | OUTSPEAK |
| OUTLAWING | OUTNAMED | OUTRAGED | OUTRUNNER | OUTSPEAKING |
| OUTLAWRIES | OUTNAMES | OUTRAGES | OUTRUNNERS | OUTSPEAKS |
| OUTLAWRY | OUTNAMING | OUTRAGING | OUTRUNNING | OUTSPEND |
| OUTLAWS | OUTNESS | OUTRAIGNE | OUTRUNS | OUTSPENDING |
| OUTLAY | OUTNESSES | OUTRAIGNED | OUTRUSH | OUTSPENDS |
| OUTLAYING | OUTNIGHT | OUTRAIGNES | OUTRUSHED | OUTSPENT |
| OUTLAYS | OUTNIGHTED | OUTRAIGNING | OUTRUSHES | OUTSPOKE |
| OUTLEAP | OUTNIGHTING | OUTRAN | OUTRUSHING | OUTSPOKEN |
| OUTLEAPED | OUTNIGHTS | OUTRANCE | OUTS | OUTSPORT |
| OUTLEAPING | OUTNUMBER | OUTRANCES | OUTSAIL | OUTSPORTED |
| OUTLEAPS | OUTNUMBERED | OUTRANK | OUTSAILED | OUTSPORTING |
| OUTLEAPT | OUTNUMBERING | OUTRANKED | OUTSAILING | OUTSPORTS |
| OUTLEARN | OUTNUMBERS | OUTRANKING | OUTSAILS | OUTSPRANG |
| OUTLEARNED | OUTPACE | OUTRANKS | OUTSAT | OUTSPREAD |
| OUTLEARNING | OUTPACED | OUTRATE | OUTSCOLD | OUTSPREADING |
| OUTLEARNS | OUTPACES | OUTRATED | OUTSCOLDED | OUTSPREADS |
| OUTLEARNT | OUTPACING | OUTRATES | OUTSCOLDING | OUTSPRING |
| OUTLER | OUTPART | OUTRATING | OUTSCOLDS | OUTSPRINGING |
| OUTLERS | OUTPARTS | OUTRÉ | OUTSCORN | OUTSPRINGS |
| OUTLET | OUTPEEP | OUTREACH | OUTSCORNED | OUTSPRUNG |
| OUTLETS | OUTPEEPED | OUTREACHED | OUTSCORNING | OUTSTAND |
| OUTLIE | OUTPEEPING | OUTREACHES | OUTSCORNS | OUTSTANDING |
| OUTLIED | OUTPEEPS | OUTREACHING | OUTSELL | OUTSTANDS |
| OUTLIER | OUTPEER | OUTRED | OUTSELLING | OUTSTARE |
| OUTLIERS | OUTPEERED | OUTREDDED | OUTSELLS | OUTSTARED |
| OUTLIES | OUTPEERING | OUTREDDEN | OUTSET | OUTSTARES |
| OUTLINE | OUTPEERS | OUTREDDENED | OUTSETS | OUTSTARING |
| OUTLINEAR | OUTPLAY | OUTREDDENING | OUTSHINE | OUTSTAY |
| OUTLINED | OUTPLAYED | OUTREDDENS | OUTSHINES | OUTSTAYED |
| OUTLINES | OUTPLAYING | OUTREDDING | OUTSHINING | OUTSTAYING |
| OUTLINING | OUTPLAYS | OUTREDS | OUTSHONE | OUTSTAYS |
| OUTLIVE | OUTPOINT | OUTREIGN | OUTSHOOT | OUTSTEP |
| OUTLIVED | OUTPOINTED | OUTREIGNED | OUTSHOOTING | OUTSTEPPED |
| OUTLIVES | OUTPOINTING | OUTREIGNING | OUTSHOOTS | OUTSTEPPING |
| OUTLIVING | OUTPOINTS | OUTREIGNS | OUTSHOT | OUTSTEPS |

| | | | | |
|---|---|---|---|---|
| OUTSTOOD | OUTVIES | OUTWORKERS | OVERAWES | OVERCARRYING |
| OUTSTRAIN | OUTVOICE | OUTWORKING | OVERAWING | OVERCAST |
| OUTSTRAINED | OUTVOICED | OUTWORKS | OVERBEAR | OVERCASTING |
| OUTSTRAINING | OUTVOICES | OUTWORN | OVERBEARING | OVERCASTINGS |
| OUTSTRAINS | OUTVOICING | OUTWORTH | OVERBEARS | OVERCASTS |
| OUTSTRIKE | OUTVOTE | OUTWORTHED | OVERBEAT | OVERCATCH |
| OUTSTRIKES | OUTVOTED | OUTWORTHING | OVERBEATEN | OVERCATCHES |
| OUTSTRIKING | OUTVOTER | OUTWORTHS | OVERBEATING | OVERCATCHING |
| OUTSTRIP | OUTVOTERS | OUTWOUND | OVERBEATS | OVERCAUGHT |
| OUTSTRIPPED | OUTVOTES | OUTWREST | OVERBID | OVERCHECK |
| OUTSTRIPPING | OUTVOTING | OUTWRESTED | OVERBIDDING | OVERCHECKS |
| OUTSTRIPS | OUTVYING | OUTWRESTING | OVERBIDDINGS | OVERCLAD |
| OUTSTRUCK | OUTWALK | OUTWRESTS | OVERBIDS | OVERCLOUD |
| OUTSUM | OUTWALKED | OUTWROUGHT | OVERBITE | OVERCLOUDED |
| OUTSUMMED | OUTWALKING | OUVERT | OVERBITES | OVERCLOUDING |
| OUTSUMMING | OUTWALKS | OUVERTE | OVERBLEW | OVERCLOUDS |
| OUTSUMS | OUTWARD | OUVRAGE | OVERBLOW | OVERCLOY |
| OUTSWEAR | OUTWARDLY | OUVRAGES | OVERBLOWING | OVERCLOYED |
| OUTSWEARING | OUTWARDS | OUVRIER | OVERBLOWN | OVERCLOYING |
| OUTSWEARS | OUTWATCH | OUVRIÈRE | OVERBLOWS | OVERCLOYS |
| OUTSWELL | OUTWATCHED | OUVRIÈRES | OVERBOARD | OVERCOAT |
| OUTSWELLED | OUTWATCHES | OUVRIERS | OVERBOIL | OVERCOATS |
| OUTSWELLING | OUTWATCHING | OUZEL | OVERBOILED | OVERCOME |
| OUTSWELLS | OUTWEAR | OUZELS | OVERBOILING | OVERCOMES |
| OUTSWING | OUTWEARIED | OUZO | OVERBOILS | OVERCOMING |
| OUTSWINGS | OUTWEARIES | OUZOS | OVERBOLD | OVERCOUNT |
| OUTSWOLLEN | OUTWEARING | OVA | OVERBOOK | OVERCOUNTED |
| OUTSWORE | OUTWEARS | OVAL | OVERBOOKED | OVERCOUNTING |
| OUTSWORN | OUTWEARY | OVALBUMIN | OVERBOOKING | OVERCOUNTS |
| OUTTAKE | OUTWEARYING | OVALBUMINS | OVERBOOKS | OVERCOVER |
| OUTTAKEN | OUTWEED | OVALLY | OVERBORE | OVERCOVERED |
| OUTTAKES | OUTWEEDED | OVALS | OVERBORNE | OVERCOVERING |
| OUTTAKING | OUTWEEDING | OVARIAN | OVERBOUGHT | OVERCOVERS |
| OUTTALK | OUTWEEDS | OVARIES | OVERBOUND | OVERCRAW |
| OUTTALKED | OUTWEEP | OVARIOLE | OVERBOUNDED | OVERCRAWED |
| OUTTALKING | OUTWEEPING | OVARIOLES | OVERBOUNDING | OVERCRAWING |
| OUTTALKS | OUTWEEPS | OVARIOUS | OVERBOUNDS | OVERCRAWS |
| OUTTELL | OUTWEIGH | OVARITIS | OVERBROW | OVERCROP |
| OUTTELLING | OUTWEIGHED | OVARITISES | OVERBROWED | OVERCROPPED |
| OUTTELLS | OUTWEIGHING | OVARY | OVERBROWING | OVERCROPPING |
| OUTTHINK | OUTWEIGHS | OVATE | OVERBROWS | OVERCROPS |
| OUTTHINKING | OUTWELL | OVATED | OVERBUILD | OVERCROW |
| OUTTHINKS | OUTWELLED | OVATES | OVERBUILDING | OVERCROWD |
| OUTTHOUGHT | OUTWELLING | OVATING | OVERBUILDS | OVERCROWDED |
| OUTTOLD | OUTWELLS | OVATION | OVERBUILT | OVERCROWDING |
| OUTTONGUE | OUTWENT | OVATIONS | OVERBULK | OVERCROWDS |
| OUTTONGUED | OUTWEPT | OVATOR | OVERBULKED | OVERCROWED |
| OUTTONGUES | OUTWICK | OVATORS | OVERBULKING | OVERCROWING |
| OUTTONGUING | OUTWICKED | OVEN | OVERBULKS | OVERCROWS |
| OUTTOOK | OUTWICKING | OVENS | OVERBURN | OVERDATED |
| OUTTOP | OUTWICKS | OVENWARE | OVERBURNED | OVERDID |
| OUTTOPPED | OUTWIN | OVENWARES | OVERBURNING | OVERDIGHT |
| OUTTOPPING | OUTWIND | OVENWOOD | OVERBURNS | OVERDO |
| OUTTOPS | OUTWINDING | OVENWOODS | OVERBURNT | OVERDOER |
| OUTTRAVEL | OUTWINDS | OVER | OVERBUSIED | OVERDOERS |
| OUTTRAVELLED | OUTWING | OVERACT | OVERBUSIES | OVERDOES |
| OUTTRAVELLING | OUTWINGED | OVERACTED | OVERBUSY | OVERDOING |
| OUTTRAVELS | OUTWINGING | OVERACTING | OVERBUSYING | OVERDONE |
| OUTTURN | OUTWINGS | OVERACTS | OVERBUY | OVERDOSE |
| OUTTURNS | OUTWINNING | OVERALL | OVERBUYING | OVERDOSED |
| OUTVALUE | OUTWINS | OVERALLED | OVERBUYS | OVERDOSES |
| OUTVALUED | OUTWIT | OVERALLS | OVERBY | OVERDOSING |
| OUTVALUES | OUTWITH | OVERARCH | OVERCALL | OVERDRAFT |
| OUTVALUING | OUTWITS | OVERARCHED | OVERCALLED | OVERDRAFTS |
| OUTVENOM | OUTWITTED | OVERARCHES | OVERCALLING | OVERDRAW |
| OUTVENOMED | OUTWITTING | OVERARCHING | OVERCALLS | OVERDRAWING |
| OUTVENOMING | OUTWON | OVERARM | OVERCAME | OVERDRAWN |
| OUTVENOMS | OUTWORE | OVERATE | OVERCARRIED | OVERDRAWS |
| OUTVIE | OUTWORK | OVERAWE | OVERCARRIES | OVERDRESS |
| OUTVIED | OUTWORKER | OVERAWED | OVERCARRY | OVERDRESSED |

OVERDRESSES
OVERDRESSING
OVERDREW
OVERDRIVE
OVERDRIVEN
OVERDRIVES
OVERDRIVING
OVERDROVE
OVERDUE
OVERDUST
OVERDUSTED
OVERDUSTING
OVERDUSTS
OVERDYE
OVERDYED
OVERDYEING
OVERDYES
OVEREAT
OVEREATEN
OVEREATING
OVEREATS
OVERED
OVEREXERT
OVEREXERTED
OVEREXERTING
OVEREXERTS
OVEREYE
OVEREYED
OVEREYEING
OVEREYES
OVEREYING
OVERFALL
OVERFALLEN
OVERFALLING
OVERFALLS
OVERFAR
OVERFED
OVERFEED
OVERFEEDING
OVERFEEDS
OVERFELL
OVERFILL
OVERFILLED
OVERFILLING
OVERFILLS
OVERFINE
OVERFIRE
OVERFIRED
OVERFIRES
OVERFIRING
OVERFISH
OVERFISHED
OVERFISHES
OVERFISHING
OVERFLEW
OVERFLIES
OVERFLOW
OVERFLOWED
OVERFLOWING
OVERFLOWINGS
OVERFLOWN
OVERFLOWS
OVERFLUSH
OVERFLUSHED
OVERFLUSHES
OVERFLUSHING
OVERFLY
OVERFLYING
OVERFOLD
OVERFOLDED

OVERFOLDING
OVERFOLDS
OVERFOND
OVERFREE
OVERFULL
OVERGALL
OVERGALLED
OVERGALLING
OVERGALLS
OVERGANG
OVERGANGED
OVERGANGING
OVERGANGS
OVERGAVE
OVERGET
OVERGETS
OVERGETTING
OVERGIVE
OVERGIVEN
OVERGIVES
OVERGIVING
OVERGLAZE
OVERGLAZED
OVERGLAZES
OVERGLAZING
OVERGLOOM
OVERGLOOMED
OVERGLOOMING
OVERGLOOMS
OVERGO
OVERGOES
OVERGOING
OVERGOINGS
OVERGONE
OVERGORGE
OVERGORGED
OVERGORGES
OVERGORGING
OVERGOT
OVERGRAIN
OVERGRAINED
OVERGRAINING
OVERGRAINS
OVERGRASS
OVERGRASSED
OVERGRASSES
OVERGRASSING
OVERGRAZE
OVERGRAZED
OVERGRAZES
OVERGRAZING
OVERGRAZINGS
OVERGREAT
OVERGREEN
OVERGREENED
OVERGREENING
OVERGREENS
OVERGREW
OVERGROW
OVERGROWING
OVERGROWN
OVERGROWS
OVERHAILE
OVERHAILED
OVERHAILES
OVERHAILING
OVERHAIR
OVERHAIRS
OVERHALE
OVERHALED

OVERHALES
OVERHALING
OVERHAND
OVERHANDED
OVERHANDING
OVERHANDS
OVERHANG
OVERHANGING
OVERHANGS
OVERHAPPY
OVERHASTE
OVERHASTES
OVERHASTY
OVERHAUL
OVERHAULED
OVERHAULING
OVERHAULS
OVERHEAD
OVERHEADS
OVERHEAR
OVERHEARD
OVERHEARING
OVERHEARS
OVERHEAT
OVERHEATED
OVERHEATING
OVERHEATS
OVERHELD
OVERHENT
OVERHENTING
OVERHENTS
OVERHIT
OVERHITS
OVERHITTING
OVERHOLD
OVERHOLDING
OVERHOLDS
OVERHUNG
OVERING
OVERINKED
OVERISSUE
OVERISSUED
OVERISSUES
OVERISSUING
OVERJOY
OVERJOYED
OVERJOYING
OVERJOYS
OVERJUMP
OVERJUMPED
OVERJUMPING
OVERJUMPS
OVERKEEP
OVERKEEPING
OVERKEEPS
OVERKEPT
OVERKEST
OVERKILL
OVERKILLS
OVERKIND
OVERKING
OVERKINGS
OVERKNEE
OVERLADE
OVERLADED
OVERLADEN
OVERLADES
OVERLADING
OVERLAID
OVERLAIN

OVERLAND
OVERLANDED
OVERLANDING
OVERLANDS
OVERLAP
OVERLAPPED
OVERLAPPING
OVERLAPS
OVERLARD
OVERLARDED
OVERLARDING
OVERLARDS
OVERLAY
OVERLAYING
OVERLAYINGS
OVERLAYS
OVERLEAF
OVERLEAP
OVERLEAPED
OVERLEAPING
OVERLEAPS
OVERLEAPT
OVERLEND
OVERLENDING
OVERLENDS
OVERLENT
OVERLIE
OVERLIER
OVERLIERS
OVERLIES
OVERLIVE
OVERLIVED
OVERLIVES
OVERLIVING
OVERLOAD
OVERLOADED
OVERLOADING
OVERLOADS
OVERLONG
OVERLOOK
OVERLOOKED
OVERLOOKING
OVERLOOKS
OVERLORD
OVERLORDED
OVERLORDING
OVERLORDS
OVERLUSTY
OVERLY
OVERLYING
OVERMAN
OVERMANNED
OVERMANNING
OVERMANS
OVERMAST
OVERMASTED
OVERMASTING
OVERMASTS
OVERMATCH
OVERMATCHED
OVERMATCHES
OVERMATCHING
OVERMEN
OVERMERRY
OVERMOUNT
OVERMOUNTED
OVERMOUNTING
OVERMOUNTS
OVERMUCH
OVERNAME

OVERNAMED
OVERNAMES
OVERNAMING
OVERNEAT
OVERNET
OVERNETS
OVERNETTED
OVERNETTING
OVERNICE
OVERNIGHT
OVERNIGHTS
OVERPAGE
OVERPAID
OVERPAINT
OVERPAINTED
OVERPAINTING
OVERPAINTS
OVERPART
OVERPARTED
OVERPARTING
OVERPARTS
OVERPASS
OVERPASSED
OVERPASSES
OVERPASSING
OVERPAST
OVERPAY
OVERPAYING
OVERPAYS
OVERPEDAL
OVERPEDALLED
OVERPEDALLING
OVERPEDALS
OVERPEER
OVERPEERED
OVERPEERING
OVERPEERS
OVERPERCH
OVERPERCHED
OVERPERCHES
OVERPERCHING
OVERPITCH
OVERPITCHED
OVERPITCHES
OVERPITCHING
OVERPLAST
OVERPLAY
OVERPLAYED
OVERPLAYING
OVERPLAYS
OVERPLIED
OVERPLIES
OVERPLUS
OVERPLUSES
OVERPLY
OVERPLYING
OVERPOISE
OVERPOISED
OVERPOISES
OVERPOISING
OVERPOST
OVERPOSTED
OVERPOSTING
OVERPOSTS
OVERPOWER
OVERPOWERED
OVERPOWERING
OVERPOWERS
OVERPRESS
OVERPRESSED

| | | | | |
|---|---|---|---|---|
| OVERPRESSES | OVERRULES | OVERSLIPPING | OVERSTUFFED | OVERTOPS |
| OVERPRESSING | OVERRULING | OVERSLIPS | OVERSTUFFING | OVERTOWER |
| OVERPRINT | OVERRUN | OVERSMAN | OVERSTUFFS | OVERTOWERED |
| OVERPRINTED | OVERRUNNING | OVERSMEN | OVERSTUNK | OVERTOWERING |
| OVERPRINTING | OVERRUNS | OVERSOLD | OVERSWAM | OVERTOWERS |
| OVERPRINTS | OVERS | OVERSOUL | OVERSWAY | OVERTRAIN |
| OVERPRIZE | OVERSAIL | OVERSOULS | OVERSWAYED | OVERTRAINED |
| OVERPRIZED | OVERSAILED | OVERSOW | OVERSWAYING | OVERTRAINING |
| OVERPRIZES | OVERSAILING | OVERSOWED | OVERSWAYS | OVERTRAINS |
| OVERPRIZING | OVERSAILS | OVERSOWING | OVERSWEAR | OVERTRICK |
| OVERPROOF | OVERSAW | OVERSOWN | OVERSWEARING | OVERTRICKS |
| OVERPROUD | OVERSCORE | OVERSOWS | OVERSWEARS | OVERTRIP |
| OVERRACK | OVERSCORED | OVERSPEND | OVERSWELL | OVERTRIPPED |
| OVERRACKED | OVERSCORES | OVERSPENDING | OVERSWELLED | OVERTRIPPING |
| OVERRACKING | OVERSCORING | OVERSPENDS | OVERSWELLING | OVERTRIPS |
| OVERRACKS | OVERSEA | OVERSPENT | OVERSWELLS | OVERTRUMP |
| OVERRAKE | OVERSEAS | OVERSPILL | OVERSWIM | OVERTRUMPED |
| OVERRAKED | OVERSEE | OVERSPILLS | OVERSWIMMING | OVERTRUMPING |
| OVERRAKES | OVERSEEING | OVERSPIN | OVERSWIMS | OVERTRUMPS |
| OVERRAKING | OVERSEEN | OVERSPINS | OVERSWOLLEN | OVERTRUST |
| OVERRAN | OVERSEER | OVERSTAFF | OVERSWORE | OVERTRUSTED |
| OVERRANK | OVERSEERS | OVERSTAFFED | OVERSWORN | OVERTRUSTING |
| OVERRASH | OVERSEES | OVERSTAFFING | OVERSWUM | OVERTRUSTS |
| OVERRATE | OVERSELL | OVERSTAFFS | OVERT | OVERTURE |
| OVERRATED | OVERSELLING | OVERSTAIN | OVERTAKE | OVERTURED |
| OVERRATES | OVERSELLS | OVERSTAINED | OVERTAKEN | OVERTURES |
| OVERRATING | OVERSET | OVERSTAINING | OVERTAKES | OVERTURING |
| OVERRAUGHT | OVERSETS | OVERSTAINS | OVERTAKING | OVERTURN |
| OVERREACH | OVERSETTING | OVERSTAND | OVERTALK | OVERTURNED |
| OVERREACHED | OVERSEW | OVERSTANDING | OVERTALKED | OVERTURNING |
| OVERREACHES | OVERSEWED | OVERSTANDS | OVERTALKING | OVERTURNS |
| OVERREACHING | OVERSEWING | OVERSTANK | OVERTALKS | OVERUSE |
| OVERREACT | OVERSEWN | OVERSTARE | OVERTASK | OVERUSED |
| OVERREACTED | OVERSEWS | OVERSTARED | OVERTASKED | OVERUSES |
| OVERREACTING | OVERSEXED | OVERSTARES | OVERTASKING | OVERUSING |
| OVERREACTS | OVERSHADE | OVERSTARING | OVERTASKS | OVERVALUE |
| OVERREAD | OVERSHADED | OVERSTATE | OVERTAX | OVERVALUED |
| OVERREADING | OVERSHADES | OVERSTATED | OVERTAXED | OVERVALUES |
| OVERREADS | OVERSHADING | OVERSTATES | OVERTAXES | OVERVALUING |
| OVERRED | OVERSHINE | OVERSTATING | OVERTAXING | OVERVEIL |
| OVERREDDED | OVERSHINES | OVERSTAY | OVERTEEM | OVERVEILED |
| OVERREDDING | OVERSHINING | OVERSTAYED | OVERTEEMED | OVERVEILING |
| OVERREDS | OVERSHIRT | OVERSTAYING | OVERTEEMING | OVERVEILS |
| OVERREN | OVERSHIRTS | OVERSTAYS | OVERTEEMS | OVERVIEW |
| OVERRENNING | OVERSHOE | OVERSTEER | OVERTHREW | OVERVIEWS |
| OVERRENS | OVERSHOES | OVERSTEERED | OVERTHROW | OVERWASH |
| OVERRIDDEN | OVERSHONE | OVERSTEERING | OVERTHROWING | OVERWASHES |
| OVERRIDE | OVERSHOOT | OVERSTEERS | OVERTHROWN | OVERWATCH |
| OVERRIDER | OVERSHOOTING | OVERSTEP | OVERTHROWS | OVERWATCHED |
| OVERRIDERS | OVERSHOOTS | OVERSTEPPED | OVERTIME | OVERWATCHES |
| OVERRIDES | OVERSHOT | OVERSTEPPING | OVERTIMED | OVERWATCHING |
| OVERRIDING | OVERSIDE | OVERSTEPS | OVERTIMER | OVERWEAR |
| OVERRIPE | OVERSIGHT | OVERSTINK | OVERTIMERS | OVERWEARIED |
| OVERRIPEN | OVERSIGHTS | OVERSTINKING | OVERTIMES | OVERWEARIES |
| OVERRIPENED | OVERSIZE | OVERSTINKS | OVERTIMING | OVERWEARING |
| OVERRIPENING | OVERSIZED | OVERSTOCK | OVERTIRE | OVERWEARS |
| OVERRIPENS | OVERSIZES | OVERSTOCKED | OVERTIRED | OVERWEARY |
| OVERROAST | OVERSIZING | OVERSTOCKING | OVERTIRES | OVERWEARYING |
| OVERROASTED | OVERSKIP | OVERSTOCKS | OVERTIRING | OVERWEEN |
| OVERROASTING | OVERSKIPPED | OVERSTOOD | OVERTLY | OVERWEENED |
| OVERROASTS | OVERSKIPPING | OVERSTREW | OVERTOIL | OVERWEENING |
| OVERRODE | OVERSKIPS | OVERSTREWED | OVERTOILED | OVERWEENINGS |
| OVERRUFF | OVERSKIRT | OVERSTREWING | OVERTOILING | OVERWEENS |
| OVERRUFFED | OVERSKIRTS | OVERSTREWN | OVERTOILS | OVERWEIGH |
| OVERRUFFING | OVERSLEEP | OVERSTREWS | OVERTONE | OVERWEIGHED |
| OVERRUFFS | OVERSLEEPING | OVERSTUDIED | OVERTONES | OVERWEIGHING |
| OVERRULE | OVERSLEEPS | OVERSTUDIES | OVERTOOK | OVERWEIGHS |
| OVERRULED | OVERSLEPT | OVERSTUDY | OVERTOP | OVERWENT |
| OVERRULER | OVERSLIP | OVERSTUDYING | OVERTOPPED | OVERWHELM |
| OVERRULERS | OVERSLIPPED | OVERSTUFF | OVERTOPPING | OVERWHELMED |

OVERWHELMING
OVERWHELMINGS
OVERWHELMS
OVERWIND
OVERWINDING
OVERWINDS
OVERWING
OVERWINGED
OVERWINGING
OVERWINGS
OVERWISE
OVERWORD
OVERWORDS
OVERWORE
OVERWORK
OVERWORKED
OVERWORKING
OVERWORKS
OVERWORN
OVERWOUND
OVERWREST
OVERWRESTED
OVERWRESTING
OVERWRESTS
OVERWRITE
OVERWRITES
OVERWRITING
OVERWRITTEN
OVERWROTE
OVERWROUGHT
OVERYEAR
OVERYEARED
OVERYEARING
OVERYEARS
OVIBOS
OVIBOSES
OVIBOVINE
OVICIDE
OVICIDES
OVIDUCAL
OVIDUCT
OVIDUCTAL
OVIDUCTS
OVIFEROUS
OVIFORM
OVIGEROUS
OVINE
OVIPARITIES
OVIPARITY
OVIPAROUS

OVIPOSIT
OVIPOSITED
OVIPOSITING
OVIPOSITS
OVISAC
OVISACS
OVIST
OVISTS
OVOID
OVOIDAL
OVOIDS
OVOLI
OVOLO
OVOTESTES
OVOTESTIS
OVULAR
OVULATE
OVULATED
OVULATES
OVULATING
OVULATION
OVULATIONS
OVULE
OVULES
OVUM
OW
OWCHE
OWCHES
OWE
OWED
OWELTIES
OWELTY
OWER
OWERBY
OWERLOUP
OWERLOUPEN
OWERLOUPING
OWERLOUPIT
OWERLOUPS
OWES
OWING
OWL
OWLED
OWLER
OWLERIES
OWLERS
OWLERY
OWLET
OWLETS
OWLIER

OWLIEST
OWLING
OWLISH
OWLS
OWLY
OWN
OWNED
OWNER
OWNERLESS
OWNERS
OWNERSHIP
OWNERSHIPS
OWNING
OWNS
OWRE
OWRECOME
OWRECOMES
OWRES
OWREWORD
OWREWORDS
OWRIE
OWRIER
OWRIEST
OWSEN
OWT
OWTS
OX
OXALATE
OXALATES
OXALIC
OXALIS
OXALISES
OXAZINE
OXAZINES
OXBLOOD
OXBLOODS
OXEN
OXER
OXERS
OXGANG
OXGANGS
OXGATE
OXGATES
OXHEAD
OXHEADS
OXIDANT
OXIDANTS
OXIDASE
OXIDASES
OXIDATE

OXIDATED
OXIDATES
OXIDATING
OXIDATION
OXIDATIONS
OXIDE
OXIDES
OXIDISE
OXIDISED
OXIDISER
OXIDISERS
OXIDISES
OXIDISING
OXIDIZE
OXIDIZED
OXIDIZER
OXIDIZERS
OXIDIZES
OXIDIZING
OXIME
OXIMES
OXIMETER
OXIMETERS
OXLAND
OXLANDS
OXLIP
OXLIPS
OXONIUM
OXONIUMS
OXSLIP
OXSLIPS
OXTAIL
OXTAILS
OXTER
OXTERED
OXTERING
OXTERS
OXYGEN
OXYGENATE
OXYGENATED
OXYGENATES
OXYGENATING
OXYGENISE
OXYGENISED
OXYGENISES
OXYGENISING
OXYGENIZE
OXYGENIZED
OXYGENIZES
OXYGENIZING

OXYGENOUS
OXYGENS
OXYGRENS
OXYMEL
OXYMELS
OXYMORON
OXYMORONS
OXYTOCIC
OXYTOCICS
OXYTOCIN
OXYTOCINS
OXYTONE
OXYTONES
OY
OYE
OYER
OYERS
OYES
OYESES
OYEZ
OYEZES
OYS
OYSTER
OYSTERS
OYSTRIGE
OYSTRIGES
OZAENA
OZAENAS
OZEKI
OZEKIS
OZOCERITE
OZOCERITES
OZOKERITE
OZOKERITES
OZONATION
OZONATIONS
OZONE
OZONES
OZONISE
OZONISED
OZONISER
OZONISERS
OZONISES
OZONISING
OZONIZE
OZONIZED
OZONIZER
OZONIZERS
OZONIZES
OZONIZING

# P

PA
PABOUCHE
PABOUCHES
PABULAR
PABULOUS
PABULUM
PABULUMS
PACA
PACABLE
PACAS
PACATION
PACATIONS
PACE
PACED
PACEMAKER
PACEMAKERS
PACER
PACERS
PACES
PACEY
PACHA
PACHAK
PACHAKS
PACHALIC
PACHALICS
PACHAS
PACHINKO
PACHINKOS
PACHISI
PACHISIS
PACHYDERM
PACHYDERMS
PACIER
PACIEST
PACIFIC
PACIFICAL
PACIFIED
PACIFIER
PACIFIERS
PACIFIES
PACIFISM
PACIFISMS
PACIFIST
PACIFISTS
PACIFY
PACIFYING
PACING
PACK
PACKAGE
PACKAGED
PACKAGER
PACKAGERS
PACKAGES
PACKAGING
PACKAGINGS
PACKED
PACKER
PACKERS
PACKET
PACKETED
PACKETING
PACKETS
PACKFONG

PACKFONGS
PACKING
PACKINGS
PACKMAN
PACKMEN
PACKS
PACKSHEET
PACKSHEETS
PACKSTAFF
PACKSTAFFS
PACKWAY
PACKWAYS
PACO
PACOS
PACT
PACTA
PACTION
PACTIONAL
PACTIONED
PACTIONING
PACTIONS
PACTS
PACTUM
PACY
PAD
PADANG
PADANGS
PADAUK
PADAUKS
PADDED
PADDER
PADDERS
PADDIES
PADDING
PADDINGS
PADDLE
PADDLED
PADDLER
PADDLERS
PADDLES
PADDLING
PADDLINGS
PADDOCK
PADDOCKS
PADDY
PADELLA
PADELLAS
PADEMELON
PADEMELONS
PADERERO
PADEREROES
PADEREROS
PADISHAH
PADISHAHS
PADLE
PADLES
PADLOCK
PADLOCKED
PADLOCKING
PADLOCKS
PADMA
PADMAS
PADOUK

PADOUKS
PADRE
PADRES
PADRONE
PADRONI
PADS
PADUASOY
PADUASOYS
PADYMELON
PADYMELONS
PAEAN
PAEANS
PAEDERAST
PAEDERASTS
PAEDEUTIC
PAEDEUTICS
PAEDIATRIES
PAEDIATRY
PAEDOLOGIES
PAEDOLOGY
PAELLA
PAELLAS
PAENULA
PAENULAE
PAENULAS
PAEON
PAEONIC
PAEONICS
PAEONIES
PAEONS
PAEONY
PAGAN
PAGANISE
PAGANISED
PAGANISES
PAGANISH
PAGANISING
PAGANISM
PAGANISMS
PAGANIZE
PAGANIZED
PAGANIZES
PAGANIZING
PAGANS
PAGE
PAGEANT
PAGEANTRIES
PAGEANTRY
PAGEANTS
PAGED
PAGEHOOD
PAGEHOODS
PAGER
PAGERS
PAGES
PAGINAL
PAGINATE
PAGINATED
PAGINATES
PAGINATING
PAGING
PAGINGS
PAGLE

PAGLES
PAGOD
PAGODA
PAGODAS
PAGODS
PAGRI
PAGRIS
PAGURIAN
PAGURIANS
PAGURID
PAGURIDS
PAH
PAHOEHOE
PAHOEHOES
PAHS
PAID
PAIDEUTIC
PAIDEUTICS
PAIDLE
PAIDLES
PAIGLE
PAIGLES
PAIK
PAIKED
PAIKING
PAIKS
PAIL
PAILFUL
PAILFULS
PAILLASSE
PAILLASSES
PAILLETTE
PAILLETTES
PAILLON
PAILLONS
PAILS
PAIN
PAINED
PAINFUL
PAINFULLER
PAINFULLEST
PAINFULLY
PAINIM
PAINIMS
PAINING
PAINLESS
PAINS
PAINT
PAINTABLE
PAINTED
PAINTER
PAINTERLY
PAINTERS
PAINTIER
PAINTIEST
PAINTING
PAINTINGS
PAINTRESS
PAINTRESSES
PAINTS
PAINTURE
PAINTURES
PAINTY

PAIOCK
PAIOCKE
PAIOCKES
PAIOCKS
PAIR
PAIRE
PAIRED
PAIRES
PAIRIAL
PAIRIALS
PAIRING
PAIRINGS
PAIRS
PAIRWISE
PAIS
PAISA
PAISANO
PAISANOS
PAISAS
PAISE
PAISLEY
PAISLEYS
PAITRICK
PAITRICKS
PAJAMAS
PAJOCK
PAJOCKE
PAJOCKES
PAJOCKS
PAKAPOO
PAKAPOOS
PAKEHA
PAKEHAS
PAKFONG
PAKFONGS
PAKKA
PAKORA
PAKORAS
PAKTONG
PAKTONGS
PAL
PALABRA
PALABRAS
PALACE
PALACES
PALADIN
PALADINS
PALAESTRA
PALAESTRAE
PALAESTRAS
PALAFITTE
PALAFITTES
PALAMA
PALAMAE
PALAMATE
PALAMINO
PALAMINOS
PALAMPORE
PALAMPORES
PALANKEEN
PALANKEENS
PALANQUIN
PALANQUINS

PALAS
PALASES
PALATABLE
PALATABLY
PALATAL
PALATALS
PALATE
PALATED
PALATES
PALATIAL
PALATINE
PALATINES
PALATING
PALAVER
PALAVERED
PALAVERER
PALAVERERS
PALAVERING
PALAVERS
PALAY
PALAYS
PALAZZI
PALAZZO
PALE
PALEA
PALEAE
PALEBUCK
PALEBUCKS
PALED
PALEFACE
PALEFACES
PALELY
PALEMPORE
PALEMPORES
PALENESS
PALENESSES
PALER
PALES
PALEST
PALESTRA
PALESTRAE
PALESTRAS
PALET
PALETOT
PALETOTS
PALETS
PALETTE
PALETTES
PALEWISE
PALFREY
PALFREYED
PALFREYS
PALIER
PALIEST
PALIFORM
PALILALIA
PALILALIAS
PALILLOGIES
PALILLOGY
PALIMONIES
PALIMONY
PALING
PALINGS
PALINODE
PALINODES
PALINODIES
PALINODY
PALISADE
PALISADED
PALISADES

PALISADING
PALISADO
PALISADOED
PALISADOES
PALISADOING
PALISH
PALKEE
PALKEES
PALKI
PALKIS
PALL
PALLA
PALLADIC
PALLADIUM
PALLADIUMS
PALLADOUS
PALLAE
PALLAH
PALLAHS
PALLED
PALLET
PALLETED
PALLETISE
PALLETISED
PALLETISES
PALLETISING
PALLETIZE
PALLETIZED
PALLETIZES
PALLETIZING
PALLETS
PALLIA
PALLIAL
PALLIARD
PALLIARDS
PALLIASSE
PALLIASSES
PALLIATE
PALLIATED
PALLIATES
PALLIATING
PALLID
PALLIDER
PALLIDEST
PALLIDITIES
PALLIDITY
PALLIDLY
PALLIER
PALLIEST
PALLING
PALLIUM
PALLONE
PALLONES
PALLOR
PALLORS
PALLS
PALLY
PALM
PALMAR
PALMARIAN
PALMARY
PALMATE
PALMATED
PALMATELY
PALMATION
PALMATIONS
PALMED
PALMER
PALMERS
PALMETTE

PALMETTES
PALMETTO
PALMETTOES
PALMETTOS
PALMFUL
PALMFULS
PALMHOUSE
PALMHOUSES
PALMIE
PALMIER
PALMIES
PALMIEST
PALMIET
PALMIETS
PALMING
PALMIPED
PALMIPEDE
PALMIPEDES
PALMIPEDS
PALMIST
PALMISTRIES
PALMISTRY
PALMISTS
PALMITATE
PALMITATES
PALMITIN
PALMITINS
PALMS
PALMY
PALMYRA
PALMYRAS
PALOLO
PALOLOS
PALOMINO
PALOMINOS
PALOOKA
PALOOKAS
PALP
PALPABLE
PALPABLY
PALPAL
PALPATE
PALPATED
PALPATES
PALPATING
PALPATION
PALPATIONS
PALPEBRAL
PALPED
PALPI
PALPING
PALPITANT
PALPITATE
PALPITATED
PALPITATES
PALPITATING
PALPS
PALPUS
PALS
PALSGRAVE
PALSGRAVES
PALSIED
PALSIER
PALSIES
PALSIEST
PALSTAFF
PALSTAFFS
PALSTAVE
PALSTAVES
PALSY

PALSYING
PALTER
PALTERED
PALTERER
PALTERERS
PALTERING
PALTERS
PALTRIER
PALTRIEST
PALTRILY
PALTRY
PALUDAL
PALUDIC
PALUDINAL
PALUDINE
PALUDISM
PALUDISMS
PALUDOSE
PALUDOUS
PALUSTRAL
PALY
PAM
PAMPA
PAMPAS
PAMPASES
PAMPEAN
PAMPER
PAMPERED
PAMPERER
PAMPERERS
PAMPERING
PAMPERO
PAMPEROS
PAMPERS
PAMPHLET
PAMPHLETS
PAMS
PAN
PANACEA
PANACEAN
PANACEAS
PANACHAEA
PANACHAEAS
PANACHE
PANACHES
PANADA
PANADAS
PANAMA
PANAMAS
PANARIES
PANARY
PANATELLA
PANATELLAS
PANAX
PANAXES
PANCAKE
PANCAKED
PANCAKES
PANCAKING
PANCE
PANCES
PANCHAX
PANCHAXES
PANCHAYAT
PANCHAYATS
PANCHEON
PANCHEONS
PANCHION
PANCHIONS
PANCOSMIC

PANCRATIC
PANCREAS
PANCREASES
PAND
PANDA
PANDAR
PANDARED
PANDARING
PANDARS
PANDAS
PANDATION
PANDATIONS
PANDECT
PANDECTS
PANDEMIA
PANDEMIAN
PANDEMIAS
PANDEMIC
PANDEMICS
PANDER
PANDERED
PANDERESS
PANDERESSES
PANDERING
PANDERISM
PANDERISMS
PANDERLY
PANDEROUS
PANDERS
PANDIED
PANDIES
PANDIT
PANDITS
PANDOOR
PANDOORS
PANDORA
PANDORAS
PANDORE
PANDORES
PANDOUR
PANDOURS
PANDOWDIES
PANDOWDY
PANDS
PANDURA
PANDURAS
PANDURATE
PANDY
PANDYING
PANE
PANED
PANEGOISM
PANEGOISMS
PANEGYRIC
PANEGYRICS
PANEGYRIES
PANEGYRY
PANEITIES
PANEITY
PANEL
PANELLED
PANELLING
PANELLINGS
PANELLIST
PANELLISTS
PANELS
PANES
PANETTONE
PANETTONI
PANFUL

PANFULS
PANG
PANGA
PANGAMIC
PANGAMIES
PANGAMY
PANGAS
PANGED
PANGEN
PANGENE
PANGENES
PANGENS
PANGING
PANGLESS
PANGOLIN
PANGOLINS
PANGRAM
PANGRAMS
PANGS
PANHANDLE
PANHANDLED
PANHANDLES
PANHANDLING
PANIC
PANICK
PANICKED
PANICKING
PANICKS
PANICKY
PANICLE
PANICLED
PANICLES
PANICS
PANIM
PANIMS
PANING
PANISC
PANISCS
PANISK
PANISKS
PANISLAM
PANISLAMS
PANLOGISM
PANLOGISMS
PANMICTIC
PANMIXIA
PANMIXIAS
PANMIXIS
PANMIXISES
PANNAGE
PANNAGES
PANNE
PANNED
PANNELLED
PANNES
PANNICK
PANNICKS
PANNICLE
PANNICLES
PANNIER
PANNIERED
PANNIERS
PANNIKEL
PANNIKELL
PANNIKELLS
PANNIKELS
PANNIKIN
PANNIKINS
PANNING
PANNINGS

PANNOSE
PANNUS
PANNUSES
PANOCHA
PANOCHAS
PANOISTIC
PANOPLIED
PANOPLIES
PANOPLY
PANOPTIC
PANORAMA
PANORAMAS
PANORAMIC
PANS
PANSEXUAL
PANSIED
PANSIES
PANSOPHIC
PANSOPHIES
PANSOPHY
PANSPERMIES
PANSPERMY
PANSY
PANT
PANTABLE
PANTABLES
PANTAGAMIES
PANTAGAMY
PANTALEON
PANTALEONS
PANTALETS
PANTALON
PANTALONS
PANTALOON
PANTALOONS
PANTED
PANTER
PANTERS
PANTHEISM
PANTHEISMS
PANTHEIST
PANTHEISTS
PANTHENOL
PANTHENOLS
PANTHER
PANTHERS
PANTIES
PANTIHOSE
PANTILE
PANTILED
PANTILES
PANTILING
PANTILINGS
PANTINE
PANTINES
PANTING
PANTINGLY
PANTINGS
PANTLER
PANTLERS
PANTO
PANTOFFLE
PANTOFFLES
PANTOFLE
PANTOFLES
PANTOMIME
PANTOMIMES
PANTON
PANTONS
PANTOS

PANTOUFLE
PANTOUFLES
PANTOUM
PANTOUMS
PANTRIES
PANTRY
PANTRYMAN
PANTRYMEN
PANTS
PANTUN
PANTUNS
PANZER
PANZERS
PAOLI
PAOLO
PAP
PAPA
PAPABLE
PAPACIES
PAPACY
PAPAIN
PAPAINS
PAPAL
PAPALISE
PAPALISED
PAPALISES
PAPALISING
PAPALISM
PAPALISMS
PAPALIST
PAPALISTS
PAPALIZE
PAPALIZED
PAPALIZES
PAPALIZING
PAPALLY
PAPARAZZI
PAPARAZZO
PAPAS
PAPAW
PAPAWS
PAPAYA
PAPAYAS
PAPE
PAPER
PAPERBACK
PAPERBACKED
PAPERBACKING
PAPERBACKS
PAPERED
PAPERER
PAPERERS
PAPERING
PAPERINGS
PAPERLESS
PAPERS
PAPERWARE
PAPERWARES
PAPERWORK
PAPERWORKS
PAPERY
PAPES
PAPETERIE
PAPETERIES
PAPILIO
PAPILIOS
PAPILLA
PAPILLAE
PAPILLAR
PAPILLARY

PAPILLATE
PAPILLOMA
PAPILLOMAS
PAPILLON
PAPILLONS
PAPILLOSE
PAPILLOTE
PAPILLOTES
PAPILLOUS
PAPILLULE
PAPILLULES
PAPISH
PAPISHER
PAPISHERS
PAPISHES
PAPISM
PAPISMS
PAPIST
PAPISTIC
PAPISTRIES
PAPISTRY
PAPISTS
PAPOOSE
PAPOOSES
PAPPADOM
PAPPADOMS
PAPPED
PAPPIER
PAPPIES
PAPPIEST
PAPPING
PAPPOOSE
PAPPOOSES
PAPPOSE
PAPPOUS
PAPPUS
PAPPUSES
PAPPY
PAPRIKA
PAPRIKAS
PAPS
PAPULA
PAPULAE
PAPULAR
PAPULE
PAPULES
PAPULOSE
PAPULOUS
PAPYRI
PAPYRUS
PAR
PARA
PARABASES
PARABASIS
PARABEMA
PARABEMATA
PARABLE
PARABLED
PARABLES
PARABLING
PARABOLA
PARABOLAS
PARABOLE
PARABOLES
PARABOLIC
PARABRAKE
PARABRAKES
PARACHUTE
PARACHUTED
PARACHUTES

PARACHUTING
PARACLETE
PARACLETES
PARACME
PARACMES
PARACUSES
PARACUSIS
PARADE
PARADED
PARADES
PARADIGM
PARADIGMS
PARADING
PARADISAL
PARADISE
PARADISES
PARADISIC
PARADOS
PARADOSES
PARADOX
PARADOXAL
PARADOXER
PARADOXERS
PARADOXES
PARADOXIES
PARADOXY
PARADROP
PARADROPS
PARAFFIN
PARAFFINE
PARAFFINED
PARAFFINES
PARAFFINING
PARAFFINS
PARAFFINY
PARAFFLE
PARAFFLES
PARAFLE
PARAFLES
PARAFOIL
PARAFOILS
PARAGE
PARAGES
PARAGOGE
PARAGOGES
PARAGOGIC
PARAGOGUE
PARAGOGUES
PARAGON
PARAGONED
PARAGONING
PARAGONS
PARAGRAM
PARAGRAMS
PARAGRAPH
PARAGRAPHED
PARAGRAPHING
PARAGRAPHS
PARAKEET
PARAKEETS
PARALALIA
PARALALIAS
PARALEGAL
PARALEGALS
PARALEXIA
PARALEXIAS
PARALLAX
PARALLAXES
PARALLEL
PARALLELED

PARALLELING
PARALLELS
PARALOGIA
PARALOGIAS
PARALOGIES
PARALOGY
PARALYSE
PARALYSED
PARALYSER
PARALYSERS
PARALYSES
PARALYSING
PARALYSIS
PARALYTIC
PARALYTICS
PARALYZE
PARALYZED
PARALYZER
PARALYZERS
PARALYZES
PARALYZING
PARAMATTA
PARAMATTAS
PARAMECIA
PARAMEDIC
PARAMEDICS
PARAMENT
PARAMENTS
PARAMESE
PARAMESES
PARAMETER
PARAMETERS
PARAMO
PARAMORPH
PARAMORPHS
PARAMOS
PARAMOUNT
PARAMOUNTS
PARAMOUR
PARAMOURS
PARANETE
PARANETES
PARANG
PARANGS
PARANOEA
PARANOEAS
PARANOEIC
PARANOEICS
PARANOIA
PARANOIAC
PARANOIACS
PARANOIAS
PARANOIC
PARANOICS
PARANOID
PARANYM
PARANYMPH
PARANYMPHS
PARANYMS
PARAPET
PARAPETED
PARAPETS
PARAPH
PARAPHED
PARAPHING
PARAPHS
PARAPODIA
PARAQUAT
PARAQUATS
PARAQUITO

PARAQUITOS
PARARHYME
PARARHYMES
PARAS
PARASANG
PARASANGS
PARASCEVE
PARASCEVES
PARASITE
PARASITES
PARASITIC
PARASOL
PARASOLS
PARATAXES
PARATAXIS
PARATHA
PARATHAS
PARATONIC
PARAVAIL
PARAVANE
PARAVANES
PARAVANT
PARAVAUNT
PARAZOA
PARAZOAN
PARAZOANS
PARAZOON
PARBOIL
PARBOILED
PARBOILING
PARBOILS
PARBREAK
PARBREAKED
PARBREAKING
PARBREAKS
PARBUCKLE
PARBUCKLED
PARBUCKLES
PARBUCKLING
PARCEL
PARCELLED
PARCELLING
PARCELS
PARCENARIES
PARCENARY
PARCENER
PARCENERS
PARCH
PARCHED
PARCHEDLY
PARCHES
PARCHESI
PARCHESIS
PARCHING
PARCHMENT
PARCHMENTS
PARCIMONIES
PARCIMONY
PARCLOSE
PARCLOSES
PARD
PARDAL
PARDALE
PARDALES
PARDALIS
PARDALISES
PARDALS
PARDED
PARDI
PARDIE

PARDINE
PARDNER
PARDNERS
PARDON
PARDONED
PARDONER
PARDONERS
PARDONING
PARDONINGS
PARDONS
PARDS
PARDY
PARE
PARECIOUS
PARED
PAREGORIC
PAREGORICS
PAREIRA
PAREIRAS
PARELLA
PARELLAS
PARELLE
PARELLES
PARENESES
PARENESIS
PARENT
PARENTAGE
PARENTAGES
PARENTAL
PARENTED
PARENTING
PARENTINGS
PARENTS
PAREO
PAREOS
PARER
PARERGA
PARERGON
PARERS
PARES
PARESES
PARESIS
PARETIC
PAREU
PAREUS
PARFAIT
PARFAITS
PARFLECHE
PARFLECHES
PARGANA
PARGANAS
PARGASITE
PARGASITES
PARGE
PARGED
PARGES
PARGET
PARGETED
PARGETER
PARGETERS
PARGETING
PARGETINGS
PARGETS
PARGETTED
PARGETTING
PARGETTINGS
PARGING
PARHELIA
PARHELIC
PARHELION

PARHYPATE
PARHYPATES
PARIAH
PARIAHS
PARIAL
PARIALS
PARIETAL
PARIETALS
PARING
PARINGS
PARISCHAN
PARISCHANS
PARISH
PARISHEN
PARISHENS
PARISHES
PARISON
PARISONS
PARITIES
PARITOR
PARITORS
PARITY
PARK
PARKA
PARKAS
PARKED
PARKEE
PARKEES
PARKER
PARKERS
PARKI
PARKIER
PARKIEST
PARKIN
PARKING
PARKINGS
PARKINS
PARKIS
PARKISH
PARKLAND
PARKLANDS
PARKLIKE
PARKLY
PARKS
PARKWARD
PARKWARDS
PARKWAY
PARKWAYS
PARKY
PARLANCE
PARLANCES
PARLANDO
PARLAY
PARLAYED
PARLAYING
PARLAYS
PARLE
PARLED
PARLES
PARLEY
PARLEYED
PARLEYING
PARLEYS
PARLEYVOO
PARLEYVOOED
PARLEYVOOING
PARLEYVOOS
PARLIES
PARLING
PARLOUR

PARLOURS
PARLOUS
PARLY
PAROCHIAL
PAROCHIN
PAROCHINE
PAROCHINES
PAROCHINS
PARODIC
PARODICAL
PARODIED
PARODIES
PARODIST
PARODISTS
PARODY
PARODYING
PAROEMIA
PAROEMIAC
PAROEMIACS
PAROEMIAL
PAROEMIAS
PAROICOUS
PAROL
PAROLE
PAROLED
PAROLEE
PAROLEES
PAROLES
PAROLING
PARONYM
PARONYMIES
PARONYMS
PARONYMY
PAROQUET
PAROQUETS
PAROTIC
PAROTID
PAROTIDS
PAROTIS
PAROTISES
PAROTITIS
PAROTITISES
PAROUSIA
PAROUSIAS
PAROXYSM
PAROXYSMS
PARPANE
PARPANES
PARPEN
PARPEND
PARPENDS
PARPENS
PARPENT
PARPENTS
PARPOINT
PARPOINTS
PARQUET
PARQUETED
PARQUETING
PARQUETRIES
PARQUETRY
PARQUETS
PARQUETTED
PARQUETTING
PARR
PARRAKEET
PARRAKEETS
PARRAL
PARRALS
PARREL

| | | | | |
|---|---|---|---|---|
| PARRELS | PARTIBLE | PASHED | PASSLESS | PATACA |
| PARRHESIA | PARTICLE | PASHES | PASSMAN | PATACAS |
| PARRHESIAS | PARTICLES | PASHIM | PASSMEN | PATAGIA |
| PARRICIDE | PARTIED | PASHIMS | PASSMENT | PATAGIAL |
| PARRICIDES | PARTIES | PASHING | PASSMENTED | PATAGIUM |
| PARRIED | PARTIM | PASHM | PASSMENTING | PATAMAR |
| PARRIES | PARTING | PASHMINA | PASSMENTS | PATAMARS |
| PARRITCH | PARTINGS | PASHMINAS | PASSOUT | PATBALL |
| PARRITCHES | PARTIS | PASHMS | PASSPORT | PATBALLS |
| PARROCK | PARTISAN | PASPALUM | PASSPORTS | PATCH |
| PARROCKED | PARTISANS | PASPALUMS | PASSUS | PATCHABLE |
| PARROCKING | PARTITA | PASPIES | PASSUSES | PATCHED |
| PARROCKS | PARTITAS | PASPY | PASSWORD | PATCHER |
| PARROQUET | PARTITE | PASQUILER | PASSWORDS | PATCHERIES |
| PARROQUETS | PARTITION | PASQUILERS | PAST | PATCHERS |
| PARROT | PARTITIONED | PASS | PASTA | PATCHERY |
| PARROTED | PARTITIONING | PASSABLE | PASTANCE | PATCHES |
| PARROTER | PARTITIONS | PASSABLY | PASTANCES | PATCHIER |
| PARROTERS | PARTITIVE | PASSADE | PASTAS | PATCHIEST |
| PARROTING | PARTITIVES | PASSADES | PASTE | PATCHILY |
| PARROTRIES | PARTITURA | PASSADO | PASTED | PATCHING |
| PARROTRY | PARTITURAS | PASSADOES | PASTEL | PATCHINGS |
| PARROTS | PARTIZAN | PASSADOS | PASTELS | PATCHOCKE |
| PARROTY | PARTIZANS | PASSAGE | PASTER | PATCHOCKES |
| PARRS | PARTLET | PASSAGED | PASTERN | PATCHOULI |
| PARRY | PARTLETS | PASSAGES | PASTERNS | PATCHOULIES |
| PARRYING | PARTLY | PASSAGING | PASTERS | PATCHOULIS |
| PARS | PARTNER | PASSAMENT | PASTES | PATCHOULY |
| PARSE | PARTNERED | PASSAMENTED | PASTICCI | PATCHWORK |
| PARSEC | PARTNERING | PASSAMENTING | PASTICCIO | PATCHWORKS |
| PARSECS | PARTNERS | PASSAMENTS | PASTICHE | PATCHY |
| PARSED | PARTON | PASSANT | PASTICHES | PÂTÉ |
| PARSER | PARTONS | PASSÉ | PASTIER | PATE |
| PARSERS | PARTOOK | PASSED | PASTIES | PATED |
| PARSES | PARTRIDGE | PASSÉE | PASTIEST | PATELLA |
| PARSIMONIES | PARTRIDGES | PASSEMENT | PASTIL | PATELLAE |
| PARSIMONY | PARTS | PASSEMENTED | PASTILLE | PATELLAR |
| PARSING | PARTURE | PASSEMENTING | PASTILLES | PATELLAS |
| PARSINGS | PARTURES | PASSEMENTS | PASTILS | PATELLATE |
| PARSLEY | PARTWORK | PASSENGER | PASTIME | PATEN |
| PARSLEYS | PARTWORKS | PASSENGERS | PASTIMES | PATENCIES |
| PARSNEP | PARTY | PASSEPIED | PASTINESS | PATENCY |
| PARSNEPS | PARTYING | PASSEPIEDS | PASTINESSES | PATENS |
| PARSNIP | PARTYISM | PASSER | PASTING | PATENT |
| PARSNIPS | PARTYISMS | PASSERINE | PASTINGS | PATENTED |
| PARSON | PARULIS | PASSERINES | PASTIS | PATENTEE |
| PARSONAGE | PARULISES | PASSERS | PASTISES | PATENTEES |
| PARSONAGES | PARURE | PASSES | PASTOR | PATENTING |
| PARSONIC | PARURES | PASSIBLE | PASTORAL | PATENTLY |
| PARSONISH | PARVENU | PASSIBLY | PASTORALE | PATENTOR |
| PARSONS | PARVENUS | PASSIM | PASTORALES | PATENTORS |
| PART | PARVIS | PASSING | PASTORALS | PATENTS |
| PARTAKE | PARVISE | PASSINGS | PASTORATE | PATER |
| PARTAKEN | PARVISES | PASSION | PASTORATES | PATERA |
| PARTAKER | PAS | PASSIONAL | PASTORLY | PATERAE |
| PARTAKERS | PASCAL | PASSIONALS | PASTORS | PATERCOVE |
| PARTAKES | PASCALS | PASSIONED | PASTRAMI | PATERCOVES |
| PARTAKING | PASCHAL | PASSIONING | PASTRAMIS | PATERERO |
| PARTAKINGS | PASCUAL | PASSIONS | PASTRIES | PATEREROES |
| PARTAN | PASEAR | PASSIVE | PASTRY | PATEREROS |
| PARTANS | PASEARED | PASSIVELY | PASTS | PATERNAL |
| PARTED | PASEARING | PASSIVES | PASTURAGE | PATERNITIES |
| PARTER | PASEARS | PASSIVISM | PASTURAGES | PATERNITY |
| PARTERRE | PASEO | PASSIVISMS | PASTURAL | PATERS |
| PARTERRES | PASEOS | PASSIVIST | PASTURE | PATES |
| PARTERS | PASH | PASSIVISTS | PASTURED | PÂTÉS |
| PARTI | PASHA | PASSIVITIES | PASTURES | PATH |
| PARTIAL | PASHALIK | PASSIVITY | PASTURING | PATHED |
| PARTIALLY | PASHALIKS | PASSKEY | PASTY | PATHETIC |
| PARTIALS | PASHAS | PASSKEYS | PAT | PATHETICS |

PATHIC
PATHICS
PATHING
PATHLESS
PATHOGEN
PATHOGENIES
PATHOGENS
PATHOGENY
PATHOLOGIES
PATHOLOGY
PATHOS
PATHOSES
PATHS
PATHWAY
PATHWAYS
PATIBLE
PATIENCE
PATIENCES
PATIENT
PATIENTED
PATIENTING
PATIENTLY
PATIENTS
PATIN
PATINA
PATINAS
PATINATED
PATINE
PATINED
PATINES
PATINS
PATIO
PATIOS
PATLY
PATNESS
PATNESSES
PATOIS
PATONCE
PATRIAL
PATRIALS
PATRIARCH
PATRIARCHS
PATRIATE
PATRIATED
PATRIATES
PATRIATING
PATRICIAN
PATRICIANS
PATRICIDE
PATRICIDES
PATRICK
PATRICKS
PATRICO
PATRICOES
PATRILINIES
PATRILINY
PATRIMONIES
PATRIMONY
PATRIOT
PATRIOTIC
PATRIOTS
PATRISTIC
PATRISTICS
PATROL
PATROLLED
PATROLLER
PATROLLERS
PATROLLING
PATROLMAN
PATROLMEN

PATROLOGIES
PATROLOGY
PATROLS
PATRON
PATRONAGE
PATRONAGED
PATRONAGES
PATRONAGING
PATRONAL
PATRONESS
PATRONESSES
PATRONISE
PATRONISED
PATRONISES
PATRONISING
PATRONIZE
PATRONIZED
PATRONIZES
PATRONIZING
PATRONNE
PATRONNES
PATRONS
PATROON
PATROONS
PATS
PATSIES
PATSY
PATTE
PATTÉ
PATTED
PATTÉE
PATTEN
PATTENED
PATTENING
PATTENS
PATTER
PATTERED
PATTERER
PATTERERS
PATTERING
PATTERN
PATTERNED
PATTERNING
PATTERNS
PATTERS
PATTES
PATTIES
PATTING
PATTLE
PATTLES
PATTY
PATULIN
PATULINS
PATULOUS
PATZER
PATZERS
PAUA
PAUAS
PAUCITIES
PAUCITY
PAUGHTIER
PAUGHTIEST
PAUGHTY
PAUL
PAULDRON
PAULDRONS
PAULOWNIA
PAULOWNIAS
PAULS
PAUNCE

PAUNCES
PAUNCH
PAUNCHED
PAUNCHES
PAUNCHIER
PAUNCHIEST
PAUNCHING
PAUNCHY
PAUPER
PAUPERESS
PAUPERESSES
PAUPERISE
PAUPERISED
PAUPERISES
PAUPERISING
PAUPERISM
PAUPERISMS
PAUPERIZE
PAUPERIZED
PAUPERIZES
PAUPERIZING
PAUPERS
PAUSAL
PAUSE
PAUSED
PAUSEFUL
PAUSELESS
PAUSER
PAUSERS
PAUSES
PAUSING
PAUSINGLY
PAUSINGS
PAVAGE
PAVAGES
PAVAN
PAVANE
PAVANES
PAVANS
PAVE
PAVED
PAVEMENT
PAVEMENTED
PAVEMENTING
PAVEMENTS
PAVEN
PAVENS
PAVER
PAVERS
PAVES
PAVID
PAVILION
PAVILIONED
PAVILIONING
PAVILIONS
PAVIN
PAVING
PAVINGS
PAVINS
PAVIOR
PAVIORS
PAVIOUR
PAVIOURS
PAVIS
PAVISE
PAVISES
PAVLOVA
PAVLOVAS
PAVONAZZO
PAVONAZZOS

PAVONE
PAVONES
PAVONIAN
PAVONINE
PAW
PAWA
PAWAS
PAWAW
PAWAWS
PAWED
PAWING
PAWK
PAWKIER
PAWKIEST
PAWKILY
PAWKINESS
PAWKINESSES
PAWKS
PAWKY
PAWL
PAWLS
PAWN
PAWNCE
PAWNCES
PAWNED
PAWNEE
PAWNEES
PAWNER
PAWNERS
PAWNING
PAWNS
PAWNSHOP
PAWNSHOPS
PAWPAW
PAWPAWS
PAWS
PAX
PAXES
PAXIUBA
PAXIUBAS
PAXWAX
PAXWAXES
PAY
PAYABLE
PAYED
PAYEE
PAYEES
PAYER
PAYERS
PAYING
PAYINGS
PAYMASTER
PAYMASTERS
PAYMENT
PAYMENTS
PAYNIM
PAYNIMRIES
PAYNIMRY
PAYNIMS
PAYOLA
PAYOLAS
PAYROLL
PAYROLLS
PAYS
PAYSAGE
PAYSAGES
PAYSAGIST
PAYSAGISTS
PAYSD
PAZAZZ

PAZAZZES
PEA
PEABERRIES
PEABERRY
PEACE
PEACEABLE
PEACEABLY
PEACED
PEACEFUL
PEACELESS
PEACENIK
PEACENIKS
PEACES
PEACETIME
PEACETIMES
PEACH
PEACHED
PEACHER
PEACHERS
PEACHES
PEACHIER
PEACHIEST
PEACHING
PEACHY
PEACING
PEACOCK
PEACOCKED
PEACOCKING
PEACOCKS
PEACOCKY
PEACOD
PEACODS
PEAG
PEAGS
PEAK
PEAKED
PEAKIER
PEAKIEST
PEAKING
PEAKS
PEAKY
PEAL
PEALED
PEALING
PEALS
PEAN
PEANED
PEANING
PEANS
PEANUT
PEANUTS
PEAPOD
PEAPODS
PEAR
PEARCE
PEARCED
PEARCES
PEARCING
PEARE
PEARES
PEARL
PEARLED
PEARLER
PEARLERS
PEARLIER
PEARLIES
PEARLIEST
PEARLIN
PEARLING
PEARLINGS

PEARLINS
PEARLISED
PEARLITE
PEARLITES
PEARLITIC
PEARLIZED
PEARLS
PEARLY
PEARMAIN
PEARMAINS
PEARS
PEARST
PEART
PEARTLY
PEAS
PEASANT
PEASANTRIES
PEASANTRY
PEASANTS
PEASANTY
PEASCOD
PEASCODS
PEASE
PEASECOD
PEASECODS
PEASED
PEASES
PEASEWEEP
PEASEWEEPS
PEASING
PEASON
PEAT
PEATARIES
PEATARY
PEATERIES
PEATERY
PEATIER
PEATIEST
PEATMAN
PEATMEN
PEATS
PEATSHIP
PEATSHIPS
PEATY
PEAVEY
PEAVEYS
PEAVIES
PEAVY
PEAZE
PEAZED
PEAZES
PEAZING
PEBA
PEBAS
PEBBLE
PEBBLED
PEBBLES
PEBBLIER
PEBBLIEST
PEBBLING
PEBBLINGS
PEBBLY
PÉBRINE
PÉBRINES
PEC
PECAN
PECANS
PECCABLE
PECCANCIES
PECCANCY

PECCANT
PECCANTLY
PECCARIES
PECCARY
PECCAVI
PECCAVIS
PECH
PECHED
PECHING
PECHS
PECK
PECKE
PECKED
PECKER
PECKERS
PECKES
PECKING
PECKINGS
PECKISH
PECKS
PECS
PECTEN
PECTIC
PECTIN
PECTINAL
PECTINATE
PECTINEAL
PECTINES
PECTINS
PECTISE
PECTISED
PECTISES
PECTISING
PECTIZE
PECTIZED
PECTIZES
PECTIZING
PECTOLITE
PECTOLITES
PECTORAL
PECTORALS
PECTOSE
PECTOSES
PECULATE
PECULATED
PECULATES
PECULATING
PECULATOR
PECULATORS
PECULIAR
PECULIARS
PECULIUM
PECULIUMS
PECUNIARY
PECUNIOUS
PED
PEDAGOGIC
PEDAGOGICS
PEDAGOGIES
PEDAGOGUE
PEDAGOGUED
PEDAGOGUES
PEDAGOGUING
PEDAGOGY
PEDAL
PEDALIER
PEDALIERS
PEDALLED
PEDALLER
PEDALLERS

PEDALLING
PEDALLINGS
PEDALO
PEDALOES
PEDALOS
PEDALS
PEDANT
PEDANTIC
PEDANTISE
PEDANTISED
PEDANTISES
PEDANTISING
PEDANTISM
PEDANTISMS
PEDANTIZE
PEDANTIZED
PEDANTIZES
PEDANTIZING
PEDANTRIES
PEDANTRY
PEDANTS
PEDATE
PEDATELY
PEDATIFID
PEDDER
PEDDERS
PEDDLE
PEDDLED
PEDDLER
PEDDLERS
PEDDLES
PEDDLING
PEDDLINGS
PEDERASTIES
PEDERASTY
PEDERERO
PEDEREROES
PEDEREROS
PEDESES
PEDESIS
PEDESTAL
PEDESTALLED
PEDESTALLING
PEDESTALS
PEDETIC
PEDICAB
PEDICABS
PEDICEL
PEDICELS
PEDICLE
PEDICLED
PEDICLES
PEDICULAR
PEDICULUS
PEDICULUSES
PEDICURE
PEDICURED
PEDICURES
PEDICURING
PEDIGREE
PEDIGREED
PEDIGREES
PEDIMENT
PEDIMENTS
PEDIPALP
PEDIPALPI
PEDIPALPS
PEDLAR
PEDLARIES
PEDLARS

PEDLARY
PEDOLOGIES
PEDOLOGY
PEDOMETER
PEDOMETERS
PEDRAIL
PEDRAILS
PEDRERO
PEDREROES
PEDREROS
PEDRO
PEDROS
PEDS
PEDUNCLE
PEDUNCLES
PEE
PEECE
PEECES
PEED
PEEING
PEEK
PEEKABO
PEEKABOO
PEEKABOOS
PEEKABOS
PEEKED
PEEKING
PEEKS
PEEL
PEELED
PEELER
PEELERS
PEELING
PEELINGS
PEELS
PEEN
PEENED
PEENGE
PEENGED
PEENGEING
PEENGES
PEENGING
PEENING
PEENS
PEEOY
PEEOYS
PEEP
PEEPE
PEEPED
PEEPER
PEEPERS
PEEPES
PEEPING
PEEPS
PEEPUL
PEEPULS
PEER
PEERAGE
PEERAGES
PEERED
PEERESS
PEERESSES
PEERIE
PEERIER
PEERIES
PEERIEST
PEERING
PEERLESS
PEERS
PEERY

PEES
PEESWEEP
PEESWEEPS
PEETWEET
PEETWEETS
PEEVE
PEEVED
PEEVER
PEEVERS
PEEVES
PEEVING
PEEVISH
PEEVISHLY
PEEWEE
PEEWEES
PEEWIT
PEEWITS
PEG
PEGASUS
PEGASUSES
PEGBOARD
PEGBOARDS
PEGGED
PEGGIES
PEGGING
PEGGINGS
PEGGY
PEGH
PEGHED
PEGHING
PEGHS
PEGMATITE
PEGMATITES
PEGS
PEIGNOIR
PEIGNOIRS
PEIN
PEINCT
PEINCTED
PEINCTING
PEINCTS
PEINED
PEINING
PEINS
PEIRASTIC
PEISE
PEISED
PEISES
PEISHWA
PEISHWAH
PEISHWAHS
PEISHWAS
PEISING
PEIZE
PEIZED
PEIZES
PEIZING
PEJORATE
PEJORATED
PEJORATES
PEJORATING
PEKAN
PEKANS
PEKE
PEKES
PEKOE
PEKOES
PELA
PELAGE
PELAGES

| | | | | |
|---|---|---|---|---|
| PELAGIAN | PELORIZED | PENCRAFT | PENK | PENSIVE |
| PELAGIANS | PELORUS | PENCRAFTS | PENKNIFE | PENSIVELY |
| PELAGIC | PELORUSES | PEND | PENKNIVES | PENSTEMON |
| PELAS | PELORY | PENDANT | PENKS | PENSTEMONS |
| PELE | PELOTA | PENDANTS | PENLIGHT | PENSTOCK |
| PELERINE | PELOTAS | PENDED | PENLIGHTS | PENSTOCKS |
| PELERINES | PELT | PENDENCIES | PENMAN | PENSUM |
| PELES | PELTA | PENDENCY | PENMEN | PENSUMS |
| PELF | PELTAE | PENDENT | PENNA | PENT |
| PELFS | PELTAS | PENDENTLY | PENNAE | PENTACLE |
| PELHAM | PELTAST | PENDENTS | PENNAL | PENTACLES |
| PELHAMS | PELTASTS | PENDICLE | PENNALISM | PENTACT |
| PELICAN | PELTATE | PENDICLER | PENNALISMS | PENTACTS |
| PELICANS | PELTED | PENDICLERS | PENNALS | PENTAD |
| PELISSE | PELTER | PENDICLES | PENNANT | PENTADIC |
| PELISSES | PELTERED | PENDING | PENNANTS | PENTADS |
| PELITE | PELTERING | PENDRAGON | PENNATE | PENTAGON |
| PELITES | PELTERS | PENDRAGONS | PENNATULA | PENTAGONS |
| PELITIC | PELTING | PENDS | PENNATULAE | PENTAGRAM |
| PELL | PELTINGLY | PENDULAR | PENNATULAS | PENTAGRAMS |
| PELLACH | PELTINGS | PENDULATE | PENNE | PENTALOGIES |
| PELLACHS | PELTRIES | PENDULATED | PENNED | PENTALOGY |
| PELLACK | PELTRY | PENDULATES | PENNEECH | PENTALPHA |
| PELLACKS | PELTS | PENDULATING | PENNEECHS | PENTALPHAS |
| PELLAGRA | PELVES | PENDULINE | PENNEECK | PENTAMERIES |
| PELLAGRAS | PELVIC | PENDULOUS | PENNEECKS | PENTAMERY |
| PELLAGRIN | PELVIFORM | PENDULUM | PENNER | PENTANE |
| PELLAGRINS | PELVIS | PENDULUMS | PENNERS | PENTANES |
| PELLET | PELVISES | PENE | PENNES | PENTANGLE |
| PELLETED | PEMBROKE | PENED | PENNIED | PENTANGLES |
| PELLETIFIED | PEMBROKES | PENEPLAIN | PENNIES | PENTAPODIES |
| PELLETIFIES | PEMICAN | PENEPLAINS | PENNIFORM | PENTAPODY |
| PELLETIFY | PEMICANS | PENEPLANE | PENNILESS | PENTARCH |
| PELLETIFYING | PEMMICAN | PENEPLANES | PENNILL | PENTARCHIES |
| PELLETING | PEMMICANS | PENES | PENNILLION | PENTARCHS |
| PELLETISE | PEMOLINE | PENETRANT | PENNINE | PENTARCHY |
| PELLETISED | PEMOLINES | PENETRANTS | PENNINES | PENTEL® |
| PELLETISES | PEMPHIGUS | PENETRATE | PENNING | PENTELS® |
| PELLETISING | PEMPHIGUSES | PENETRATED | PENNINITE | PENTENE |
| PELLETIZE | PEN | PENETRATES | PENNINITES | PENTENES |
| PELLETIZED | PENAL | PENETRATING | PENNON | PENTHIA |
| PELLETIZES | PENALISE | PENFOLD | PENNONCEL | PENTHIAS |
| PELLETIZING | PENALISED | PENFOLDS | PENNONCELS | PENTHOUSE |
| PELLETS | PENALISES | PENFUL | PENNONED | PENTHOUSED |
| PELLICLE | PENALISING | PENFULS | PENNONS | PENTHOUSES |
| PELLICLES | PENALIZE | PENGUIN | PENNY | PENTHOUSING |
| PELLITORIES | PENALIZED | PENGUINRIES | PENNYFEE | PENTICE |
| PELLITORY | PENALIZES | PENGUINRY | PENNYFEES | PENTICED |
| PELLOCK | PENALIZING | PENGUINS | PENNYLAND | PENTICES |
| PELLOCKS | PENALLY | PENHOLDER | PENNYLANDS | PENTICING |
| PELLS | PENALTIES | PENHOLDERS | PENOLOGIES | PENTISE |
| PELLUCID | PENALTY | PENI | PENOLOGY | PENTISED |
| PELMA | PENANCE | PENIAL | PENONCEL | PENTISES |
| PELMANISM | PENANCED | PENIE | PENONCELS | PENTISING |
| PELMANISMS | PENANCES | PENIES | PENS | PENTODE |
| PELMAS | PENANCING | PENILE | PENSÉE | PENTODES |
| PELMATIC | PENATES | PENILLION | PENSÉES | PENTOMIC |
| PELMET | PENCE | PENING | PENSEL | PENTOSAN |
| PELMETS | PENCEL | PENINSULA | PENSELS | PENTOSANE |
| PELOID | PENCELS | PENINSULAS | PENSIL | PENTOSANES |
| PELOIDS | PENCES | PENIS | PENSILE | PENTOSANS |
| PELOLOGIES | PENCHANT | PENISES | PENSILITIES | PENTOSE |
| PELOLOGY | PENCHANTS | PENISTONE | PENSILITY | PENTOSES |
| PELORIA | PENCIL | PENISTONES | PENSILS | PENTOXIDE |
| PELORIAS | PENCILLED | PENITENCE | PENSION | PENTOXIDES |
| PELORIC | PENCILLER | PENITENCES | PENSIONED | PENTROOF |
| PELORIES | PENCILLERS | PENITENCIES | PENSIONER | PENTROOFS |
| PELORISED | PENCILLING | PENITENCY | PENSIONERS | PENTS |
| PELORISM | PENCILLINGS | PENITENT | PENSIONING | PENTYLENE |
| PELORISMS | PENCILS | PENITENTS | PENSIONS | PENTYLENES |

| | | | | |
|---|---|---|---|---|
| PENUCHE | PEPTIC | PERCOLATED | PERFORATED | PERIDIUM |
| PENUCHES | PEPTICITIES | PERCOLATES | PERFORATES | PERIDIUMS |
| PENUCHI | PEPTICITY | PERCOLATING | PERFORATING | PERIDOT |
| PENUCHIS | PEPTICS | PERCOLIN | PERFORCE | PERIDOTE |
| PENUCHLE | PEPTIDE | PERCOLINS | PERFORM | PERIDOTES |
| PENUCHLES | PEPTIDES | PERCUSS | PERFORMED | PERIDOTIC |
| PENULT | PEPTISE | PERCUSSED | PERFORMER | PERIDOTS |
| PENULTIMA | PEPTISED | PERCUSSES | PERFORMERS | PERIDROME |
| PENULTIMAS | PEPTISES | PERCUSSING | PERFORMING | PERIDROMES |
| PENULTS | PEPTISING | PERCUSSOR | PERFORMINGS | PERIGEAL |
| PENUMBRA | PEPTIZE | PERCUSSORS | PERFORMS | PERIGEAN |
| PENUMBRAL | PEPTIZED | PERDENDO | PERFUME | PERIGEE |
| PENUMBRAS | PEPTIZES | PERDIE | PERFUMED | PERIGEES |
| PENURIES | PEPTIZING | PERDITION | PERFUMER | PERIGON |
| PENURIOUS | PEPTONE | PERDITIONS | PERFUMERIES | PERIGONE |
| PENURY | PEPTONES | PERDU | PERFUMERS | PERIGONES |
| PENWOMAN | PEPTONISE | PERDUE | PERFUMERY | PERIGONS |
| PENWOMEN | PEPTONISED | PERDUES | PERFUMES | PERIGYNIES |
| PEON | PEPTONISES | PERDURE | PERFUMING | PERIGYNY |
| PEONAGE | PEPTONISING | PERDURED | PERFUMY | PERIKARYA |
| PEONAGES | PEPTONIZE | PERDURES | PERFUSATE | PERIL |
| PEONIES | PEPTONIZED | PERDURING | PERFUSATES | PERILLED |
| PEONISM | PEPTONIZES | PERDUS | PERFUSE | PERILLING |
| PEONISMS | PEPTONIZING | PERDY | PERFUSED | PERILOUS |
| PEONS | PER | PÈRE | PERFUSES | PERILS |
| PEONY | PERACUTE | PEREGAL | PERFUSING | PERILUNE |
| PEOPLE | PERAEA | PEREGALS | PERFUSION | PERILUNES |
| PEOPLED | PERAEON | PEREGRINE | PERFUSIONS | PERILYMPH |
| PEOPLES | PERAEONS | PEREGRINES | PERFUSIVE | PERILYMPHS |
| PEOPLING | PERAEOPOD | PEREIA | PERGOLA | PERIMETER |
| PEP | PERAEOPODS | PEREION | PERGOLAS | PERIMETERS |
| PEPERINO | PERAI | PEREIOPOD | PERGUNNAH | PERIMETRIES |
| PEPERINOS | PERAIS | PEREIOPODS | PERGUNNAHS | PERIMETRY |
| PEPEROMIA | PERCALE | PEREIRA | PERHAPS | PERIMORPH |
| PEPEROMIAS | PERCALES | PEREIRAS | PERI | PERIMORPHS |
| PEPERONI | PERCALINE | PERENNATE | PERIAGUA | PERINAEAL |
| PEPERONIS | PERCALINES | PERENNATED | PERIAGUAS | PERINAEUM |
| PEPFUL | PERCASE | PERENNATES | PERIAKTOI | PERINAEUMS |
| PEPLOS | PERCE | PERENNATING | PERIAKTOS | PERINATAL |
| PEPLOSES | PERCEABLE | PERENNIAL | PERIANTH | PERINEAL |
| PEPLUM | PERCEANT | PERENNIALS | PERIANTHS | PERINEUM |
| PEPLUMS | PERCED | PERENNITIES | PERIAPT | PERINEUMS |
| PEPLUS | PERCEIVE | PERENNITY | PERIAPTS | PERIOD |
| PEPLUSES | PERCEIVED | PÈRES | PERIBLAST | PERIODATE |
| PEPO | PERCEIVER | PERFAY | PERIBLASTS | PERIODATES |
| PEPOS | PERCEIVERS | PERFECT | PERIBLEM | PERIODED |
| PEPPED | PERCEIVES | PERFECTA | PERIBLEMS | PERIODIC |
| PEPPER | PERCEIVING | PERFECTAS | PERIBOLI | PERIODING |
| PEPPERED | PERCEIVINGS | PERFECTED | PERIBOLOI | PERIODS |
| PEPPERER | PERCEN | PERFECTER | PERIBOLOS | PERIOST |
| PEPPERERS | PERCENTAL | PERFECTERS | PERIBOLUS | PERIOSTS |
| PEPPERING | PERCEPT | PERFECTEST | PERICARP | PERIOTIC |
| PEPPERINGS | PERCEPTS | PERFECTI | PERICARPS | PERIOTICS |
| PEPPERONI | PERCES | PERFECTING | PERICLASE | PERIPATUS |
| PEPPERONIS | PERCH | PERFECTLY | PERICLASES | PERIPATUSES |
| PEPPERS | PERCHANCE | PERFECTO | PERICLINE | PERIPETIA |
| PEPPERY | PERCHED | PERFECTOR | PERICLINES | PERIPETIAS |
| PEPPIER | PERCHER | PERFECTORS | PERICON | PERIPETIES |
| PEPPIEST | PERCHERON | PERFECTOS | PERICONES | PERIPETY |
| PEPPING | PERCHERONS | PERFECTS | PERICOPE | PERIPHERIES |
| PEPPY | PERCHERS | PERFERVID | PERICOPES | PERIPHERY |
| PEPS | PERCHES | PERFERVOR | PERICRANIES | PERIPLAST |
| PEPSIN | PERCHING | PERFERVORS | PERICRANY | PERIPLASTS |
| PEPSINATE | PERCHINGS | PERFET | PERICYCLE | PERIPLUS |
| PEPSINATED | PERCIFORM | PERFIDIES | PERICYCLES | PERIPLUSES |
| PEPSINATES | PERCINE | PERFIDY | PERIDERM | PERIPROCT |
| PEPSINATING | PERCING | PERFORANS | PERIDERMS | PERIPROCTS |
| PEPSINE | PERCOCT | PERFORANSES | PERIDIA | PERIPTERIES |
| PEPSINES | PERCOID | PERFORANT | PERIDIAL | PERIPTERY |
| PEPSINS | PERCOLATE | PERFORATE | PERIDINIA | PERIQUE |

PERIQUES
PERIS
PERISARC
PERISARCS
PERISCIAN
PERISCIANS
PERISCOPE
PERISCOPES
PERISH
PERISHED
PERISHER
PERISHERS
PERISHES
PERISHING
PERISPERM
PERISPERMS
PERISTOME
PERISTOMES
PERISTYLE
PERISTYLES
PERITI
PERITRICH
PERITRICHA
PERITUS
PERIWIG
PERIWIGGED
PERIWIGGING
PERIWIGS
PERJINK
PERJURE
PERJURED
PERJURER
PERJURERS
PERJURES
PERJURIES
PERJURING
PERJUROUS
PERJURY
PERK
PERKED
PERKIER
PERKIEST
PERKILY
PERKIN
PERKINESS
PERKINESSES
PERKING
PERKINS
PERKS
PERKY
PERLITE
PERLITES
PERLITIC
PERLOUS
PERM
PERMALLOY
PERMALLOYS
PERMANENT
PERMEABLE
PERMEABLY
PERMEANCE
PERMEANCES
PERMEASE
PERMEASES
PERMEATE
PERMEATED
PERMEATES
PERMEATING
PERMED
PERMING

PERMIT
PERMITS
PERMITTED
PERMITTER
PERMITTERS
PERMITTING
PERMS
PERMUTATE
PERMUTATED
PERMUTATES
PERMUTATING
PERMUTE
PERMUTED
PERMUTES
PERMUTING
PERN
PERNANCIES
PERNANCY
PERNS
PERONE
PERONEAL
PERONES
PERONEUS
PERONEUSES
PERORATE
PERORATED
PERORATES
PERORATING
PEROXIDE
PEROXIDED
PEROXIDES
PEROXIDING
PERPEND
PERPENDED
PERPENDING
PERPENDS
PERPENT
PERPENTS
PERPETUAL
PERPETUALS
PERPLEX
PERPLEXED
PERPLEXES
PERPLEXING
PERRADIAL
PERRADII
PERRADIUS
PERRIER
PERRIERS
PERRIES
PERRON
PERRONS
PERRUQUE
PERRUQUES
PERRY
PERSANT
PERSAUNT
PERSE
PERSECUTE
PERSECUTED
PERSECUTES
PERSECUTING
PERSEITIES
PERSEITY
PERSELINE
PERSELINES
PERSES
PERSEVERE
PERSEVERED
PERSEVERES

PERSEVERING
PERSICO
PERSICOS
PERSICOT
PERSICOTS
PERSIENNE
PERSIENNES
PERSIMMON
PERSIMMONS
PERSING
PERSIST
PERSISTED
PERSISTING
PERSISTS
PERSON
PERSONA
PERSONAE
PERSONAGE
PERSONAGES
PERSONAL
PERSONAS
PERSONATE
PERSONATED
PERSONATES
PERSONATING
PERSONATINGS
PERSONIFIED
PERSONIFIES
PERSONIFY
PERSONIFYING
PERSONISE
PERSONISED
PERSONISES
PERSONISING
PERSONIZE
PERSONIZED
PERSONIZES
PERSONIZING
PERSONNEL
PERSONNELS
PERSONS
PERSPIRE
PERSPIRED
PERSPIRES
PERSPIRING
PERST
PERSUADE
PERSUADED
PERSUADER
PERSUADERS
PERSUADES
PERSUADING
PERSUE
PERSUED
PERSUES
PERSUING
PERSWADE
PERSWADED
PERSWADES
PERSWADING
PERT
PERTAIN
PERTAINED
PERTAINING
PERTAINS
PERTAKE
PERTAKEN
PERTAKES
PERTAKING
PERTER

PERTEST
PERTHITE
PERTHITES
PERTHITIC
PERTINENT
PERTINENTS
PERTLY
PERTNESS
PERTNESSES
PERTOOK
PERTS
PERTURB
PERTURBED
PERTURBER
PERTURBERS
PERTURBING
PERTURBS
PERTUSATE
PERTUSE
PERTUSED
PERTUSION
PERTUSIONS
PERTUSSAL
PERTUSSIS
PERTUSSISES
PERUKE
PERUKED
PERUKES
PERUSAL
PERUSALS
PERUSE
PERUSED
PERUSER
PERUSERS
PERUSES
PERUSING
PERV
PERVADE
PERVADED
PERVADES
PERVADING
PERVASION
PERVASIONS
PERVASIVE
PERVE
PERVED
PERVERSE
PERVERSER
PERVERSEST
PERVERT
PERVERTED
PERVERTER
PERVERTERS
PERVERTING
PERVERTS
PERVES
PERVIATE
PERVIATED
PERVIATES
PERVIATING
PERVICACIES
PERVICACY
PERVING
PERVIOUS
PERVS
PESADE
PESADES
PESANT
PESANTE
PESANTS

PESAUNT
PESAUNTS
PESETA
PESETAS
PESEWA
PESEWAS
PESHWA
PESHWAS
PESKIER
PESKIEST
PESKILY
PESKY
PESO
PESOS
PESSARIES
PESSARY
PESSIMISM
PESSIMISMS
PESSIMIST
PESSIMISTS
PEST
PESTER
PESTERED
PESTERER
PESTERERS
PESTERING
PESTEROUS
PESTERS
PESTFUL
PESTHOUSE
PESTHOUSES
PESTICIDE
PESTICIDES
PESTILENT
PESTLE
PESTLED
PESTLES
PESTLING
PESTO
PESTOLOGIES
PESTOLOGY
PESTOS
PESTS
PET
PETAL
PETALINE
PETALISM
PETALISMS
PETALLED
PETALODIES
PETALODY
PETALOID
PETALOUS
PETALS
PÉTANQUE
PÉTANQUES
PETAR
PETARA
PETARAS
PETARD
PETARDS
PETARIES
PETARS
PETARY
PETASUS
PETASUSES
PETAURINE
PETAURIST
PETAURISTS
PETCHARIES

PETCHARY
PETCOCK
PETCOCKS
PETECHIA
PETECHIAE
PETECHIAL
PETER
PETERED
PETERING
PETERMAN
PETERMEN
PETERS
PETERSHAM
PETERSHAMS
PETHER
PETHERS
PETHIDINE
PETHIDINES
PÉTILLANT
PETIOLAR
PETIOLATE
PETIOLE
PETIOLED
PETIOLES
PETIOLULE
PETIOLULES
PETIT
PETITE
PETITION
PETITIONED
PETITIONING
PETITIONINGS
PETITIONS
PETITORY
PETRARIES
PETRARY
PETRE
PETREL
PETRELS
PETRES
PETRIFIC
PETRIFIED
PETRIFIES
PETRIFY
PETRIFYING
PETROGRAM
PETROGRAMS
PETROL
PETROLAGE
PETROLAGES
PETROLEUM
PETROLEUMS
PETROLEUR
PETROLEURS
PETROLIC
PETROLLED
PETROLLING
PETROLOGIES
PETROLOGY
PETROLS
PETRONEL
PETRONELS
PETROSAL
PETROSALS
PETROUS
PETS
PETTED
PETTEDLY
PETTER
PETTERS

PETTICOAT
PETTICOATS
PETTIER
PETTIES
PETTIEST
PETTIFOG
PETTIFOGGED
PETTIFOGGING
PETTIFOGGINGS
PETTIFOGS
PETTILY
PETTINESS
PETTINESSES
PETTING
PETTINGS
PETTISH
PETTISHLY
PETTITOES
PETTLE
PETTLED
PETTLES
PETTLING
PETTY
PETULANCE
PETULANCES
PETULANCIES
PETULANCY
PETULANT
PETUNIA
PETUNIAS
PETUNTSE
PETUNTSES
PETUNTZE
PETUNTZES
PEW
PEWEE
PEWEES
PEWIT
PEWITS
PEWS
PEWTER
PEWTERER
PEWTERERS
PEWTERS
PEYOTE
PEYOTES
PEYOTISM
PEYOTISMS
PEYOTIST
PEYOTISTS
PEYSE
PEYSED
PEYSES
PEYSING
PEZANT
PEZANTS
PEZIZOID
PFENNIG
PFENNIGE
PFENNIGS
PFENNING
PFENNINGS
PHACOID
PHACOIDAL
PHACOLITE
PHACOLITES
PHACOLITH
PHACOLITHS
PHAEIC
PHAEISM

PHAEISMS
PHAENOGAM
PHAENOGAMS
PHAETON
PHAETONS
PHAGE
PHAGEDENA
PHAGEDENAS
PHAGES
PHAGOCYTE
PHAGOCYTES
PHALANGAL
PHALANGE
PHALANGER
PHALANGERS
PHALANGES
PHALANGID
PHALANGIDS
PHALANX
PHALANXES
PHALAROPE
PHALAROPES
PHALLI
PHALLIC
PHALLIN
PHALLINS
PHALLISM
PHALLISMS
PHALLOID
PHALLUS
PHALLUSES
PHANG
PHANGED
PHANGING
PHANGS
PHANSIGAR
PHANSIGARS
PHANTASIED
PHANTASIES
PHANTASIM
PHANTASIMS
PHANTASM
PHANTASMA
PHANTASMATA
PHANTASMS
PHANTASY
PHANTASYING
PHANTOM
PHANTOMS
PHANTOMY
PHANTOSME
PHANTOSMES
PHARAONIC
PHARE
PHARES
PHARISAIC
PHARMACIES
PHARMACY
PHAROS
PHAROSES
PHARYNGAL
PHARYNGES
PHARYNX
PHARYNXES
PHASE
PHASED
PHASELESS
PHASES
PHASIC
PHASING

PHASIS
PHASMID
PHASMIDS
PHATIC
PHEASANT
PHEASANTS
PHEAZAR
PHEAZARS
PHEER
PHEERE
PHEERES
PHEERS
PHEESE
PHEESED
PHEESES
PHEESING
PHEEZE
PHEEZED
PHEEZES
PHEEZING
PHELLEM
PHELLEMS
PHELLOGEN
PHELLOGENS
PHELLOID
PHELONION
PHELONIONS
PHENACITE
PHENACITES
PHENAKISM
PHENAKISMS
PHENAKITE
PHENAKITES
PHENATE
PHENATES
PHENE
PHENES
PHENETIC
PHENETICS
PHENGITE
PHENGITES
PHENIC
PHENOGAM
PHENOGAMS
PHENOL
PHENOLATE
PHENOLATES
PHENOLIC
PHENOLOGIES
PHENOLOGY
PHENOLS
PHENOMENA
PHENOTYPE
PHENOTYPED
PHENOTYPES
PHENOTYPING
PHENYL
PHENYLIC
PHENYLS
PHEON
PHEONS
PHEROMONE
PHEROMONES
PHESE
PHESED
PHESES
PHESING
PHEW
PHI
PHIAL

PHIALLED
PHIALLING
PHIALS
PHILABEG
PHILABEGS
PHILAMOT
PHILAMOTS
PHILANDER
PHILANDERED
PHILANDERING
PHILANDERS
PHILATELIES
PHILATELY
PHILHORSE
PHILHORSES
PHILIBEG
PHILIBEGS
PHILIPPIC
PHILIPPICS
PHILLABEG
PHILLABEGS
PHILLIBEG
PHILLIBEGS
PHILOGYNIES
PHILOGYNY
PHILOLOGIES
PHILOLOGY
PHILOMATH
PHILOMATHS
PHILOMOT
PHILOMOTS
PHILOPENA
PHILOPENAS
PHILTER
PHILTERS
PHILTRE
PHILTRES
PHIMOSES
PHIMOSIS
PHINNOCK
PHINNOCKS
PHIS
PHISNOMIES
PHISNOMY
PHIZ
PHIZOG
PHIZOGS
PHIZZES
PHLEBITIS
PHLEBITISES
PHLEGM
PHLEGMIER
PHLEGMIEST
PHLEGMON
PHLEGMONS
PHLEGMS
PHLEGMY
PHLOEM
PHLOEMS
PHLOMIS
PHLOMISES
PHLOX
PHLOXES
PHLYCTENA
PHLYCTENAE
PHO
PHOBIA
PHOBIAS
PHOBIC
PHOBISM

| | | | | |
|---|---|---|---|---|
| PHOBISMS | PHONY | PHOTOTYPES | PHYLLOME | PIASSAVAS |
| PHOBIST | PHONYING | PHOTOTYPIES | PHYLLOMES | PIASTRE |
| PHOBISTS | PHOOEY | PHOTOTYPING | PHYLLOPOD | PIASTRES |
| PHOCA | PHORMINGES | PHOTOTYPY | PHYLLOPODS | PIAZZA |
| PHOCAE | PHORMINX | PHOTS | PHYLLOS | PIAZZAS |
| PHOCAS | PHORMIUM | PHRASAL | PHYLOGENIES | PIAZZIAN |
| PHOCINE | PHORMIUMS | PHRASE | PHYLOGENY | PIBROCH |
| PHOEBE | PHOS | PHRASED | PHYLUM | PIBROCHS |
| PHOEBES | PHOSGENE | PHRASEMAN | PHYSALIA | PIC |
| PHOENIX | PHOSGENES | PHRASEMEN | PHYSALIAS | PICA |
| PHOENIXES | PHOSPHATE | PHRASER | PHYSALIS | PICADOR |
| PHOH | PHOSPHATED | PHRASERS | PHYSALISES | PICADORS |
| PHOLADES | PHOSPHATES | PHRASES | PHYSIC | PICAMAR |
| PHOLAS | PHOSPHATING | PHRASIER | PHYSICAL | PICAMARS |
| PHON | PHOSPHENE | PHRASIEST | PHYSICALS | PICARIAN |
| PHONAL | PHOSPHENES | PHRASING | PHYSICIAN | PICARIANS |
| PHONATE | PHOSPHIDE | PHRASINGS | PHYSICIANS | PICAROON |
| PHONATED | PHOSPHIDES | PHRASY | PHYSICISM | PICAROONS |
| PHONATES | PHOSPHINE | PHRATRIES | PHYSICISMS | PICAS |
| PHONATING | PHOSPHINES | PHRATRY | PHYSICIST | PICAYUNE |
| PHONATION | PHOSPHITE | PHREATIC | PHYSICISTS | PICAYUNES |
| PHONATIONS | PHOSPHITES | PHRENESES | PHYSICKED | PICCADILL |
| PHONATORY | PHOSPHOR | PHRENESIS | PHYSICKING | PICCADILLS |
| PHONE | PHOSPHORS | PHRENETIC | PHYSICKY | PICCANIN |
| PHONECARD | PHOT | PHRENETICS | PHYSICS | PICCANINS |
| PHONECARDS | PHOTIC | PHRENIC | PHYSIO | PICCOLO |
| PHONED | PHOTICS | PHRENISM | PHYSIOS | PICCOLOS |
| PHONEME | PHOTISM | PHRENISMS | PHYSIQUE | PICE |
| PHONEMES | PHOTISMS | PHRENITIC | PHYSIQUES | PICENE |
| PHONEMIC | PHOTO | PHRENITIS | PHYTOGENIES | PICENES |
| PHONEMICS | PHOTOCALL | PHRENITISES | PHYTOGENY | PICEOUS |
| PHONES | PHOTOCALLS | PHRENSIES | PHYTOLOGIES | PICHURIM |
| PHONETIC | PHOTOCELL | PHRENSY | PHYTOLOGY | PICHURIMS |
| PHONETICS | PHOTOCELLS | PHRENTICK | PHYTON | PICINE |
| PHONETISM | PHOTOCOPIED | PHTHALATE | PHYTONS | PICK |
| PHONETISMS | PHOTOCOPIES | PHTHALATES | PHYTOSES | PICKABACK |
| PHONETIST | PHOTOCOPY | PHTHALEIN | PHYTOSIS | PICKABACKS |
| PHONETISTS | PHOTOCOPYING | PHTHALEINS | PHYTOTOMIES | PICKAPACK |
| PHONEY | PHOTOCOPYINGS | PHTHALIC | PHYTOTOMY | PICKAPACKS |
| PHONEYED | PHOTOED | PHTHALIN | PHYTOTRON | PICKAXE |
| PHONEYING | PHOTOFIT | PHTHALINS | PHYTOTRONS | PICKAXES |
| PHONEYS | PHOTOFITS | PHTHISES | PI | PICKBACK |
| PHONIC | PHOTOGEN | PHTHISIC | PIA | PICKBACKS |
| PHONICS | PHOTOGENE | PHTHISICS | PIACEVOLE | PICKED |
| PHONIED | PHOTOGENES | PHTHISIS | PIACULAR | PICKEER |
| PHONIER | PHOTOGENIES | PHUT | PIAFFE | PICKEERED |
| PHONIES | PHOTOGENS | PHUTS | PIAFFED | PICKEERER |
| PHONIEST | PHOTOGENY | PHYCOCYAN | PIAFFER | PICKEERERS |
| PHONINESS | PHOTOGRAM | PHYCOCYANS | PIAFFERS | PICKEERING |
| PHONINESSES | PHOTOGRAMS | PHYCOLOGIES | PIAFFES | PICKEERS |
| PHONING | PHOTOING | PHYCOLOGY | PIAFFING | PICKER |
| PHONMETER | PHOTOLYSE | PHYLA | PIANETTE | PICKEREL |
| PHONMETERS | PHOTOLYSED | PHYLAE | PIANETTES | PICKERELS |
| PHONOGRAM | PHOTOLYSES | PHYLARCH | PIANINO | PICKERIES |
| PHONOGRAMS | PHOTOLYSING | PHYLARCHIES | PIANINOS | PICKERS |
| PHONOLITE | PHOTON | PHYLARCHS | PIANISM | PICKERY |
| PHONOLITES | PHOTONICS | PHYLARCHY | PIANISMS | PICKET |
| PHONOLOGIES | PHOTONS | PHYLE | PIANIST | PICKETED |
| PHONOLOGY | PHOTOPHIL | PHYLES | PIANISTE | PICKETER |
| PHONON | PHOTOPHILS | PHYLETIC | PIANISTES | PICKETERS |
| PHONONS | PHOTOPIA | PHYLLARIES | PIANISTIC | PICKETING |
| PHONOPORE | PHOTOPIAS | PHYLLARY | PIANISTS | PICKETS |
| PHONOPORES | PHOTOPIC | PHYLLITE | PIANO | PICKIER |
| PHONOTYPE | PHOTOPSIA | PHYLLITES | PIANOS | PICKIEST |
| PHONOTYPED | PHOTOPSIAS | PHYLLO | PIARIST | PICKING |
| PHONOTYPES | PHOTOPSIES | PHYLLODE | PIARISTS | PICKINGS |
| PHONOTYPIES | PHOTOPSY | PHYLLODES | PIAS | PICKLE |
| PHONOTYPING | PHOTOS | PHYLLODIES | PIASSABA | PICKLED |
| PHONOTYPY | PHOTOTYPE | PHYLLODY | PIASSABAS | PICKLER |
| PHONS | PHOTOTYPED | PHYLLOID | PIASSAVA | PICKLERS |

| | | | | |
|---|---|---|---|---|
| PICKLES | PIECEMEAL | PIG | PIGSWILLS | PILFERY |
| PICKLING | PIECEMEALED | PIGBOAT | PIGTAIL | PILGRIM |
| PICKLOCK | PIECEMEALING | PIGBOATS | PIGTAILS | PILGRIMER |
| PICKLOCKS | PIECEMEALS | PIGEON | PIGWASH | PILGRIMERS |
| PICKMAW | PIECEN | PIGEONED | PIGWASHES | PILGRIMS |
| PICKMAWS | PIECENED | PIGEONING | PIGWEED | PILHORSE |
| PICKS | PIECENER | PIGEONRIES | PIGWEEDS | PILHORSES |
| PICKY | PIECENERS | PIGEONRY | PIKA | PILI |
| PICNIC | PIECENING | PIGEONS | PIKADELL | PILIFORM |
| PICNICKED | PIECENS | PIGFEED | PIKADELLS | PILING |
| PICNICKER | PIECER | PIGFEEDS | PIKAS | PILIS |
| PICNICKERS | PIECERS | PIGGERIES | PIKE | PILL |
| PICNICKING | PIECES | PIGGERY | PIKED | PILLAGE |
| PICNICKY | PIECING | PIGGIE | PIKELET | PILLAGED |
| PICNICS | PIECRUST | PIGGIER | PIKELETS | PILLAGER |
| PICOCURIE | PIECRUSTS | PIGGIES | PIKEMAN | PILLAGERS |
| PICOCURIES | PIED | PIGGIEST | PIKEMEN | PILLAGES |
| PICOT | PIEDISH | PIGGIN | PIKER | PILLAGING |
| PICOTÉ | PIEDISHES | PIGGING | PIKERS | PILLAR |
| PICOTED | PIEDMONT | PIGGINGS | PIKES | PILLARIST |
| PICOTEE | PIEDMONTS | PIGGINS | PIKESTAFF | PILLARISTS |
| PICOTEES | PIEDNESS | PIGGISH | PIKESTAFFS | PILLARS |
| PICOTING | PIEDNESSES | PIGGISHLY | PIKING | PILLAU |
| PICOTITE | PIEING | PIGGY | PIKUL | PILLAUS |
| PICOTITES | PIEMAN | PIGGYBACK | PIKULS | PILLED |
| PICOTS | PIEMEN | PIGGYBACKS | PILA | PILLHEAD |
| PICQUET | PIEND | PIGHEADED | PILAFF | PILLHEADS |
| PICQUETED | PIENDS | PIGHT | PILAFFS | PILLICOCK |
| PICQUETING | PIEPOWDER | PIGHTED | PILASTER | PILLICOCKS |
| PICQUETS | PIEPOWDERS | PIGHTING | PILASTERS | PILLING |
| PICRA | PIER | PIGHTLE | PILAU | PILLION |
| PICRAS | PIERAGE | PIGHTLES | PILAUS | PILLIONED |
| PICRATE | PIERAGES | PIGHTS | PILAW | PILLIONING |
| PICRATES | PIERCE | PIGLET | PILAWS | PILLIONS |
| PICRIC | PIERCED | PIGLETS | PILCH | PILLOCK |
| PICRITE | PIERCER | PIGLING | PILCHARD | PILLOCKS |
| PICRITES | PIERCERS | PIGLINGS | PILCHARDS | PILLORIED |
| PICS | PIERCES | PIGMEAN | PILCHER | PILLORIES |
| PICTARNIE | PIERCING | PIGMEAT | PILCHERS | PILLORISE |
| PICTARNIES | PIERID | PIGMEATS | PILCHES | PILLORISED |
| PICTOGRAM | PIERIDINE | PIGMENT | PILCORN | PILLORISES |
| PICTOGRAMS | PIERIDS | PIGMENTAL | PILCORNS | PILLORISING |
| PICTORIAL | PIERROT | PIGMENTED | PILCROW | PILLORIZE |
| PICTORIALS | PIERROTS | PIGMENTS | PILCROWS | PILLORIZED |
| PICTURAL | PIERS | PIGMIES | PILE | PILLORIZES |
| PICTURALS | PIERST | PIGMY | PILEA | PILLORIZING |
| PICTURE | PIERT | PIGNERATE | PILEATE | PILLORY |
| PICTURED | PIES | PIGNERATED | PILEATED | PILLORYING |
| PICTURES | PIET | PIGNERATES | PILED | PILLOW |
| PICTURING | PIETÀ | PIGNERATING | PILEI | PILLOWED |
| PICUL | PIETÀS | PIGNORATE | PILEOUS | PILLOWING |
| PICULS | PIETIES | PIGNORATED | PILER | PILLOWS |
| PIDDLE | PIETISM | PIGNORATES | PILERS | PILLOWY |
| PIDDLED | PIETISMS | PIGNORATING | PILES | PILLS |
| PIDDLER | PIETIST | PIGPEN | PILEUM | PILLWORM |
| PIDDLERS | PIETISTIC | PIGPENS | PILEUS | PILLWORMS |
| PIDDLES | PIETISTS | PIGS | PILEWORK | PILLWORT |
| PIDDLING | PIETS | PIGSCONCE | PILEWORKS | PILLWORTS |
| PIDDOCK | PIETY | PIGSCONCES | PILEWORT | PILOSE |
| PIDDOCKS | PIEZO | PIGSKIN | PILEWORTS | PILOSITIES |
| PIDGEON | PIFFERARI | PIGSKINS | PILFER | PILOSITY |
| PIDGEONS | PIFFERARO | PIGSNEY | PILFERAGE | PILOT |
| PIDGIN | PIFFERO | PIGSNEYS | PILFERAGES | PILOTAGE |
| PIDGINS | PIFFEROS | PIGSNIE | PILFERED | PILOTAGES |
| PIE | PIFFLE | PIGSNIES | PILFERER | PILOTED |
| PIEBALD | PIFFLED | PIGSNY | PILFERERS | PILOTING |
| PIEBALDS | PIFFLER | PIGSTIES | PILFERIES | PILOTLESS |
| PIECE | PIFFLERS | PIGSTY | PILFERING | PILOTS |
| PIECED | PIFFLES | PIGSWILL | PILFERINGS | PILOUS |
| PIECELESS | PIFFLING | PIGSWILLS | PILFERS | PILOW |

PILOWS
PILSENER
PILSENERS
PILSNER
PILSNERS
PILULA
PILULAR
PILULAS
PILULE
PILULES
PILUM
PILUS
PIMENT
PIMENTO
PIMENTOS
PIMENTS
PIMIENTO
PIMIENTOS
PIMP
PIMPED
PIMPERNEL
PIMPERNELS
PIMPING
PIMPLE
PIMPLED
PIMPLES
PIMPLIER
PIMPLIEST
PIMPLY
PIMPS
PIN
PIÑA
PINACOID
PINACOIDS
PINAFORE
PINAFORED
PINAFORES
PINAKOID
PINAKOIDS
PIÑAS
PINASTER
PINASTERS
PINBALL
PINBALLS
PINCASE
PINCASES
PINCER
PINCERED
PINCERING
PINCERS
PINCH
PINCHBECK
PINCHBECKS
PINCHCOCK
PINCHCOCKS
PINCHED
PINCHER
PINCHERS
PINCHES
PINCHFIST
PINCHFISTS
PINCHGUT
PINCHGUTS
PINCHING
PINCHINGS
PINDAREE
PINDAREES
PINDARI
PINDARIS
PINDER

PINDERS
PINE
PINEAL
PINEAPPLE
PINEAPPLES
PINED
PINERIES
PINERY
PINES
PINETA
PINETUM
PINEY
PINFISH
PINFISHES
PINFOLD
PINFOLDED
PINFOLDING
PINFOLDS
PING
PINGED
PINGER
PINGERS
PINGING
PINGLE
PINGLED
PINGLER
PINGLERS
PINGLES
PINGLING
PINGO
PINGOES
PINGOS
PINGS
PINGUEFIED
PINGUEFIES
PINGUEFY
PINGUEFYING
PINGUID
PINGUIN
PINGUINS
PINHEAD
PINHEADS
PINHOLE
PINHOLES
PINIER
PINIES
PINIEST
PINING
PINION
PINIONED
PINIONING
PINIONS
PINITE
PINITES
PINK
PINKED
PINKER
PINKERTON
PINKERTONS
PINKEST
PINKIE
PINKIER
PINKIES
PINKIEST
PINKINESS
PINKINESSES
PINKING
PINKINGS
PINKISH
PINKNESS

PINKNESSES
PINKO
PINKOES
PINKOS
PINKROOT
PINKROOTS
PINKS
PINKY
PINNA
PINNACE
PINNACES
PINNACLE
PINNACLED
PINNACLES
PINNACLING
PINNAE
PINNATE
PINNATED
PINNATELY
PINNED
PINNER
PINNERS
PINNET
PINNETS
PINNIE
PINNIES
PINNING
PINNINGS
PINNIPED
PINNIPEDE
PINNIPEDES
PINNIPEDS
PINNOCK
PINNOCKS
PINNOED
PINNULA
PINNULAS
PINNULATE
PINNULE
PINNULES
PINNY
PINOCHLE
PINOCHLES
PINOCLE
PINOCLES
PINOLE
PINOLES
PIÑON
PIÑONS
PINOT
PINOTS
PINS
PINT
PINTA
PINTABLE
PINTABLES
PINTADO
PINTADOS
PINTAIL
PINTAILED
PINTAILS
PINTAS
PINTLE
PINTLES
PINTO
PINTOS
PINTS
PINXIT
PINY
PIOLET

PIOLETS
PION
PIONED
PIONEER
PIONEERED
PIONEERING
PIONEERS
PIONER
PIONERS
PIONEY
PIONEYS
PIONIC
PIONIES
PIONING
PIONINGS
PIONS
PIONY
PIOTED
PIOUS
PIOUSLY
PIOY
PIOYE
PIOYES
PIOYS
PIP
PIPA
PIPAGE
PIPAGES
PIPAL
PIPALS
PIPAS
PIPE
PIPECLAY
PIPECLAYED
PIPECLAYING
PIPECLAYS
PIPED
PIPEFISH
PIPEFISHES
PIPEFUL
PIPEFULS
PIPELESS
PIPELIKE
PIPELINE
PIPELINES
PIPER
PIPERIC
PIPERINE
PIPERINES
PIPERONAL
PIPERONALS
PIPERS
PIPES
PIPESTONE
PIPESTONES
PIPETTE
PIPETTED
PIPETTES
PIPETTING
PIPEWORK
PIPEWORKS
PIPEWORT
PIPEWORTS
PIPI
PIPIER
PIPIEST
PIPING
PIPINGS
PIPIS
PIPIT

PIPITS
PIPKIN
PIPKINS
PIPLESS
PIPPED
PIPPIER
PIPPIEST
PIPPIN
PIPPING
PIPPINS
PIPPY
PIPS
PIPSQUEAK
PIPSQUEAKS
PIPUL
PIPULS
PIPY
PIQUANCIES
PIQUANCY
PIQUANT
PIQUANTLY
PIQUE
PIQUED
PIQUES
PIQUET
PIQUETED
PIQUETING
PIQUETS
PIQUING
PIR
PIRACIES
PIRACY
PIRAGUA
PIRAGUAS
PIRAI
PIRAIS
PIRAÑA
PIRAÑAS
PIRANHA
PIRANHAS
PIRARUCU
PIRARUCUS
PIRATE
PIRATED
PIRATES
PIRATIC
PIRATICAL
PIRATING
PIRAYA
PIRAYAS
PIRL
PIRLICUE
PIRLICUED
PIRLICUES
PIRLICUING
PIRLS
PIRN
PIRNIE
PIRNIES
PIRNIT
PIRNS
PIROGUE
PIROGUES
PIROSHKI
PIROUETTE
PIROUETTED
PIROUETTES
PIROUETTING
PIROZHKI
PIRS

PIS
PISCARIES
PISCARY
PISCATOR
PISCATORS
PISCATORY
PISCATRIX
PISCATRIXES
PISCIFORM
PISCINA
PISCINAE
PISCINAS
PISCINE
PISCINES
PISÉ
PISÉS
PISH
PISHED
PISHES
PISHING
PISHOGUE
PISHOGUES
PISIFORM
PISIFORMS
PISKIES
PISKY
PISMIRE
PISMIRES
PISOLITE
PISOLITES
PISOLITIC
PISS
PISSED
PISSES
PISSING
PISSOIR
PISSOIRS
PISTACHIO
PISTACHIOS
PISTAREEN
PISTAREENS
PISTE
PISTES
PISTIL
PISTILS
PISTOL
PISTOLE
PISTOLEER
PISTOLEERS
PISTOLES
PISTOLET
PISTOLETS
PISTOLLED
PISTOLLING
PISTOLS
PISTON
PISTONS
PIT
PITA
PITAPAT
PITAPATS
PITAPATTED
PITAPATTING
PITARA
PITARAH
PITARAHS
PITARAS
PITAS
PITCH
PITCHED

PITCHER
PITCHERS
PITCHES
PITCHFORK
PITCHFORKED
PITCHFORKING
PITCHFORKS
PITCHIER
PITCHIEST
PITCHING
PITCHINGS
PITCHMAN
PITCHMEN
PITCHPINE
PITCHPINES
PITCHPIPE
PITCHPIPES
PITCHY
PITEOUS
PITEOUSLY
PITFALL
PITFALLS
PITH
PITHBALL
PITHBALLS
PITHEAD
PITHEADS
PITHECOID
PITHED
PITHFUL
PITHIER
PITHIEST
PITHILY
PITHINESS
PITHINESSES
PITHING
PITHLESS
PITHLIKE
PITHOI
PITHOS
PITHS
PITHY
PITIABLE
PITIABLY
PITIED
PITIER
PITIERS
PITIES
PITIFUL
PITIFULLY
PITILESS
PITMAN
PITMEN
PITON
PITONS
PITS
PITTA
PITTANCE
PITTANCES
PITTAS
PITTED
PITTEN
PITTER
PITTERED
PITTERING
PITTERS
PITTING
PITTINGS
PITTITE
PITTITES

PITUITA
PITUITARY
PITUITAS
PITUITE
PITUITES
PITUITRIN
PITUITRINS
PITURI
PITURIS
PITY
PITYING
PITYINGLY
PITYROID
PIÙ
PIUM
PIUMS
PIUPIU
PIUPIUS
PIVOT
PIVOTAL
PIVOTALLY
PIVOTED
PIVOTER
PIVOTERS
PIVOTING
PIVOTINGS
PIVOTS
PIX
PIXEL
PIXELS
PIXES
PIXIE
PIXIES
PIXILATED
PIXY
PIZAZZ
PIZAZZES
PIZE
PIZES
PIZZA
PIZZAIOLA
PIZZAS
PIZZERIA
PIZZERIAS
PIZZICATO
PIZZICATOS
PIZZLE
PIZZLES
PLACABLE
PLACABLY
PLACARD
PLACARDED
PLACARDING
PLACARDS
PLACATE
PLACATED
PLACATES
PLACATING
PLACATION
PLACATIONS
PLACATORY
PLACCAT
PLACCATE
PLACCATES
PLACCATS
PLACE
PLACEBO
PLACEBOS
PLACED
PLACELESS

PLACEMAN
PLACEMEN
PLACEMENT
PLACEMENTS
PLACENTA
PLACENTAE
PLACENTAL
PLACENTALS
PLACENTAS
PLACER
PLACERS
PLACES
PLACET
PLACETS
PLACID
PLACIDER
PLACIDEST
PLACIDITIES
PLACIDITY
PLACIDLY
PLACING
PLACINGS
PLACIT
PLACITA
PLACITORY
PLACITS
PLACITUM
PLACK
PLACKET
PLACKETS
PLACKLESS
PLACKS
PLACODERM
PLACODERMS
PLACOID
PLAFOND
PLAFONDS
PLAGAL
PLAGE
PLAGES
PLAGIARIES
PLAGIARY
PLAGIUM
PLAGIUMS
PLAGUE
PLAGUED
PLAGUES
PLAGUEY
PLAGUIER
PLAGUIEST
PLAGUILY
PLAGUING
PLAGUY
PLAICE
PLAICES
PLAID
PLAIDED
PLAIDING
PLAIDINGS
PLAIDMAN
PLAIDMEN
PLAIDS
PLAIN
PLAINANT
PLAINANTS
PLAINED
PLAINER
PLAINEST
PLAINFUL
PLAINING

PLAININGS
PLAINISH
PLAINLY
PLAINNESS
PLAINNESSES
PLAINS
PLAINSMAN
PLAINSMEN
PLAINSONG
PLAINSONGS
PLAINT
PLAINTFUL
PLAINTIFF
PLAINTIFFS
PLAINTIVE
PLAINTS
PLAINWORK
PLAINWORKS
PLAISTER
PLAISTERS
PLAIT
PLAITED
PLAITER
PLAITERS
PLAITING
PLAITINGS
PLAITS
PLAN
PLANAR
PLANARIAN
PLANARIANS
PLANATION
PLANATIONS
PLANCH
PLANCHED
PLANCHES
PLANCHET
PLANCHETS
PLANCHING
PLANE
PLANED
PLANER
PLANERS
PLANES
PLANET
PLANETARY
PLANETIC
PLANETOID
PLANETOIDS
PLANETS
PLANGENCIES
PLANGENCY
PLANGENT
PLANING
PLANISH
PLANISHED
PLANISHER
PLANISHERS
PLANISHES
PLANISHING
PLANK
PLANKED
PLANKING
PLANKINGS
PLANKS
PLANKTON
PLANKTONS
PLANLESS
PLANNED
PLANNER

PLANNERS
PLANNING
PLANS
PLANT
PLANTA
PLANTABLE
PLANTAGE
PLANTAGES
PLANTAIN
PLANTAINS
PLANTAR
PLANTAS
PLANTED
PLANTER
PLANTERS
PLANTING
PLANTINGS
PLANTLESS
PLANTLET
PLANTLETS
PLANTLING
PLANTLINGS
PLANTS
PLANTSMAN
PLANTSMEN
PLANTULE
PLANTULES
PLANULA
PLANULAE
PLANULAR
PLANULOID
PLANURIA
PLANURIAS
PLANURIES
PLANURY
PLANXTIES
PLANXTY
PLAP
PLAPPED
PLAPPING
PLAPS
PLAQUE
PLAQUES
PLAQUETTE
PLAQUETTES
PLASH
PLASHED
PLASHES
PLASHET
PLASHETS
PLASHIER
PLASHIEST
PLASHING
PLASHINGS
PLASHY
PLASM
PLASMA
PLASMAS
PLASMATIC
PLASMIC
PLASMID
PLASMIDS
PLASMIN
PLASMINS
PLASMODIA
PLASMS
PLAST
PLASTE
PLASTER
PLASTERED

PLASTERER
PLASTERERS
PLASTERING
PLASTERINGS
PLASTERS
PLASTERY
PLASTIC
PLASTICS
PLASTID
PLASTIDS
PLASTIQUE
PLASTIQUES
PLASTISOL
PLASTISOLS
PLASTRAL
PLASTRON
PLASTRONS
PLAT
PLATAN
PLATANE
PLATANES
PLATANNA
PLATANNAS
PLATANS
PLATBAND
PLATBANDS
PLATE
PLATEASM
PLATEASMS
PLATEAU
PLATEAUED
PLATEAUING
PLATEAUS
PLATEAUX
PLATED
PLATEFUL
PLATEFULS
PLATELET
PLATELETS
PLATEMAN
PLATEMARK
PLATEMARKS
PLATEMEN
PLATEN
PLATENS
PLATER
PLATERS
PLATES
PLATFORM
PLATFORMED
PLATFORMING
PLATFORMINGS
PLATFORMS
PLATIER
PLATIEST
PLATINA
PLATINAS
PLATING
PLATINGS
PLATINIC
PLATINISE
PLATINISED
PLATINISES
PLATINISING
PLATINIZE
PLATINIZED
PLATINIZES
PLATINIZING
PLATINOID
PLATINOIDS

PLATINOUS
PLATINUM
PLATINUMS
PLATITUDE
PLATITUDES
PLATONIC
PLATOON
PLATOONS
PLATS
PLATTED
PLATTER
PLATTERS
PLATTING
PLATTINGS
PLATY
PLATYPUS
PLATYPUSES
PLATYSMA
PLATYSMAS
PLAUDIT
PLAUDITE
PLAUDITS
PLAUSIBLE
PLAUSIBLY
PLAUSIVE
PLAUSTRAL
PLAY
PLAYA
PLAYABLE
PLAYAS
PLAYBACK
PLAYBACKS
PLAYBILL
PLAYBILLS
PLAYBOOK
PLAYBOOKS
PLAYBOY
PLAYBOYS
PLAYBUS
PLAYBUSES
PLAYED
PLAYER
PLAYERS
PLAYFUL
PLAYFULLY
PLAYGIRL
PLAYGIRLS
PLAYGROUP
PLAYGROUPS
PLAYHOUSE
PLAYHOUSES
PLAYING
PLAYLET
PLAYLETS
PLAYMATE
PLAYMATES
PLAYROOM
PLAYROOMS
PLAYS
PLAYSOME
PLAYSUIT
PLAYSUITS
PLAYTHING
PLAYTHINGS
PLAYTIME
PLAYTIMES
PLAZA
PLAZAS
PLEA
PLEACH

PLEACHED
PLEACHES
PLEACHING
PLEAD
PLEADABLE
PLEADED
PLEADER
PLEADERS
PLEADING
PLEADINGS
PLEADS
PLEAED
PLEAING
PLEAS
PLEASANCE
PLEASANCES
PLEASANT
PLEASANTER
PLEASANTEST
PLEASE
PLEASED
PLEASEMAN
PLEASEMEN
PLEASER
PLEASERS
PLEASES
PLEASETH
PLEASING
PLEASINGS
PLEASURE
PLEASURED
PLEASURER
PLEASURERS
PLEASURES
PLEASURING
PLEAT
PLEATED
PLEATING
PLEATS
PLEB
PLEBBIER
PLEBBIEST
PLEBBY
PLEBEAN
PLEBEIAN
PLEBEIANS
PLEBIFIED
PLEBIFIES
PLEBIFY
PLEBIFYING
PLEBS
PLECTRA
PLECTRE
PLECTRES
PLECTRON
PLECTRONS
PLECTRUM
PLECTRUMS
PLED
PLEDGE
PLEDGED
PLEDGEE
PLEDGEES
PLEDGEOR
PLEDGEORS
PLEDGER
PLEDGERS
PLEDGES
PLEDGET
PLEDGETS

PLEDGING
PLEDGOR
PLEDGORS
PLEIOMERIES
PLEIOMERY
PLENARILY
PLENARTIES
PLENARTY
PLENARY
PLENILUNE
PLENILUNES
PLENIPO
PLENIPOES
PLENIPOS
PLENISH
PLENISHED
PLENISHES
PLENISHING
PLENISHINGS
PLENIST
PLENISTS
PLENITUDE
PLENITUDES
PLENTEOUS
PLENTIES
PLENTIFUL
PLENTY
PLENUM
PLENUMS
PLEON
PLEONASM
PLEONASMS
PLEONAST
PLEONASTE
PLEONASTES
PLEONASTS
PLEONEXIA
PLEONEXIAS
PLEONS
PLEOPOD
PLEOPODS
PLEROMA
PLEROMAS
PLEROME
PLEROMES
PLESH
PLESHES
PLESSOR
PLESSORS
PLETHORA
PLETHORAS
PLETHORIC
PLEUCH
PLEUCHS
PLEUGH
PLEUGHS
PLEURA
PLEURAE
PLEURAL
PLEURISIES
PLEURISY
PLEURITIC
PLEURITICS
PLEURITIS
PLEURITISES
PLEURON
PLEXIFORM
PLEXOR
PLEXORS
PLEXURE

| | | | | |
|---|---|---|---|---|
| PLEXURES | PLONKED | PLUCKIEST | PLUMMIEST | PLURISIES |
| PLEXUS | PLONKER | PLUCKILY | PLUMMY | PLUS |
| PLEXUSES | PLONKERS | PLUCKING | PLUMOSE | PLUSAGE |
| PLIABLE | PLONKING | PLUCKS | PLUMOUS | PLUSAGES |
| PLIABLY | PLONKS | PLUCKY | PLUMP | PLUSED |
| PLIANCIES | PLOOK | PLUFF | PLUMPED | PLUSES |
| PLIANCY | PLOOKIE | PLUFFED | PLUMPEN | PLUSH |
| PLIANT | PLOOKIER | PLUFFIER | PLUMPENED | PLUSHER |
| PLIANTLY | PLOOKIEST | PLUFFIEST | PLUMPENING | PLUSHES |
| PLICA | PLOOKS | PLUFFING | PLUMPENS | PLUSHEST |
| PLICAE | PLOP | PLUFFS | PLUMPER | PLUSHIER |
| PLICAL | PLOPPED | PLUFFY | PLUMPERS | PLUSHIEST |
| PLICATE | PLOPPING | PLUG | PLUMPEST | PLUSHY |
| PLICATED | PLOPS | PLUGGED | PLUMPIE | PLUSING |
| PLICATELY | PLOSION | PLUGGER | PLUMPING | PLUSSAGE |
| PLICATES | PLOSIONS | PLUGGERS | PLUMPISH | PLUSSAGES |
| PLICATING | PLOSIVE | PLUGGING | PLUMPLY | PLUSSED |
| PLICATION | PLOSIVES | PLUGGINGS | PLUMPNESS | PLUSSES |
| PLICATIONS | PLOT | PLUGS | PLUMPNESSES | PLUSSING |
| PLICATURE | PLOTFUL | PLUM | PLUMPS | PLUTEAL |
| PLICATURES | PLOTLESS | PLUMAGE | PLUMPY | PLUTEUS |
| PLIÉ | PLOTS | PLUMAGED | PLUMS | PLUTEUSES |
| PLIED | PLOTTED | PLUMAGES | PLUMULA | PLUTOCRAT |
| PLIER | PLOTTER | PLUMATE | PLUMULAE | PLUTOCRATS |
| PLIERS | PLOTTERED | PLUMB | PLUMULAR | PLUTOLOGIES |
| PLIÉS | PLOTTERING | PLUMBAGO | PLUMULATE | PLUTOLOGY |
| PLIES | PLOTTERS | PLUMBAGOS | PLUMULE | PLUTON |
| PLIGHT | PLOTTIE | PLUMBATE | PLUMULES | PLUTONIUM |
| PLIGHTED | PLOTTIES | PLUMBATES | PLUMULOSE | PLUTONIUMS |
| PLIGHTER | PLOTTING | PLUMBED | PLUMY | PLUTONOMIES |
| PLIGHTERS | PLOTTINGS | PLUMBEOUS | PLUNDER | PLUTONOMY |
| PLIGHTFUL | PLOTTY | PLUMBER | PLUNDERED | PLUTONS |
| PLIGHTING | PLOUGH | PLUMBERIES | PLUNDERER | PLUVIAL |
| PLIGHTS | PLOUGHBOY | PLUMBERS | PLUNDERERS | PLUVIALS |
| PLIM | PLOUGHBOYS | PLUMBERY | PLUNDERING | PLUVIOSE |
| PLIMMED | PLOUGHED | PLUMBIC | PLUNDERS | PLUVIOUS |
| PLIMMING | PLOUGHER | PLUMBING | PLUNGE | PLY |
| PLIMS | PLOUGHERS | PLUMBINGS | PLUNGED | PLYING |
| PLIMSOLE | PLOUGHING | PLUMBISM | PLUNGER | PLYWOOD |
| PLIMSOLES | PLOUGHINGS | PLUMBISMS | PLUNGERS | PLYWOODS |
| PLIMSOLL | PLOUGHMAN | PLUMBITE | PLUNGES | PNEUMA |
| PLIMSOLLS | PLOUGHMEN | PLUMBITES | PLUNGING | PNEUMAS |
| PLINK | PLOUGHS | PLUMBLESS | PLUNGINGS | PNEUMATIC |
| PLINKED | PLOUK | PLUMBOUS | PLUNK | PNEUMATICS |
| PLINKING | PLOUKIE | PLUMBS | PLUNKED | PNEUMONIA |
| PLINKS | PLOUKIER | PLUMBUM | PLUNKER | PNEUMONIAS |
| PLINTH | PLOUKIEST | PLUMBUMS | PLUNKERS | PNEUMONIC |
| PLINTHS | PLOUKS | PLUMCOT | PLUNKING | PNEUMONICS |
| PLISKIE | PLOUTER | PLUMCOTS | PLUNKS | PO |
| PLISKIES | PLOUTERED | PLUMDAMAS | PLURAL | POA |
| PLISSÉ | PLOUTERING | PLUMDAMASES | PLURALISE | POACEOUS |
| PLOAT | PLOUTERS | PLUME | PLURALISED | POACH |
| PLOATED | PLOVER | PLUMED | PLURALISES | POACHED |
| PLOATING | PLOVERS | PLUMELESS | PLURALISING | POACHER |
| PLOATS | PLOVERY | PLUMELET | PLURALISM | POACHERS |
| PLOD | PLOW | PLUMELETS | PLURALISMS | POACHES |
| PLODDED | PLOWED | PLUMERIES | PLURALIST | POACHIER |
| PLODDER | PLOWING | PLUMERY | PLURALISTS | POACHIEST |
| PLODDERS | PLOWS | PLUMES | PLURALITIES | POACHING |
| PLODDING | PLOWTER | PLUMIER | PLURALITY | POACHINGS |
| PLODDINGS | PLOWTERED | PLUMIEST | PLURALIZE | POACHY |
| PLODS | PLOWTERING | PLUMING | PLURALIZED | POAKA |
| PLONG | PLOWTERS | PLUMIPED | PLURALIZES | POAKAS |
| PLONGD | PLOY | PLUMIST | PLURALIZING | POAKE |
| PLONGE | PLOYS | PLUMISTS | PLURALLY | POAKES |
| PLONGED | PLUCK | PLUMMET | PLURALS | POAS |
| PLONGES | PLUCKED | PLUMMETED | PLURIPARA | POCHARD |
| PLONGING | PLUCKER | PLUMMETING | PLURIPARAE | POCHARDS |
| PLONGS | PLUCKERS | PLUMMETS | PLURIPARAS | POCHAY |
| PLONK | PLUCKIER | PLUMMIER | PLURISIE | POCHAYED |

POCHAYING
POCHAYS
POCHETTE
POCHETTES
POCHOIR
POCHOIRS
POCK
POCKARD
POCKARDS
POCKED
POCKET
POCKETED
POCKETFUL
POCKETFULS
POCKETING
POCKETS
POCKIER
POCKIEST
POCKMANKIES
POCKMANKY
POCKMARK
POCKMARKS
POCKPIT
POCKPITS
POCKS
POCKY
POCO
POD
PODAGRA
PODAGRAL
PODAGRAS
PODAGRIC
PODAGROUS
PODAL
PODALIC
PODDED
PODDIER
PODDIEST
PODDING
PODDY
PODESTA
PODESTAS
PODEX
PODEXES
PODGE
PODGES
PODGIER
PODGIEST
PODGINESS
PODGINESSES
PODGY
PODIA
PODIAL
PODIATRIES
PODIATRY
PODITE
PODITES
PODIUM
PODLEY
PODLEYS
PODOLOGIES
PODOLOGY
PODS
PODSOL
PODSOLIC
PODSOLS
PODZOL
PODZOLS
POEM
POEMATIC

POEMS
POENOLOGIES
POENOLOGY
POESIED
POESIES
POESY
POESYING
POET
POETASTER
POETASTERS
POETASTRIES
POETASTRY
POETESS
POETESSES
POETIC
POETICAL
POETICISE
POETICISED
POETICISES
POETICISING
POETICISM
POETICISMS
POETICIZE
POETICIZED
POETICIZES
POETICIZING
POETICS
POETICULE
POETICULES
POETISE
POETISED
POETISES
POETISING
POETIZE
POETIZED
POETIZES
POETIZING
POETRESSE
POETRESSES
POETRIES
POETRY
POETS
POETSHIP
POETSHIPS
POFFLE
POFFLES
POGGE
POGGES
POGROM
POGROMS
POH
POI
POIGNADO
POIGNADOS
POIGNANCIES
POIGNANCY
POIGNANT
POILU
POILUS
POINADO
POINADOS
POINCIANA
POINCIANAS
POIND
POINDED
POINDER
POINDERS
POINDING
POINDINGS
POINDS

POINT
POINTE
POINTED
POINTEDLY
POINTEL
POINTELS
POINTER
POINTERS
POINTES
POINTIER
POINTIEST
POINTILLÉ
POINTING
POINTINGS
POINTLESS
POINTS
POINTSMAN
POINTSMEN
POINTY
POIS
POISE
POISED
POISER
POISERS
POISES
POISING
POISON
POISONED
POISONER
POISONERS
POISONING
POISONOUS
POISONS
POISSON
POISSONS
POITREL
POITRELS
POKAL
POKALS
POKE
POKEBERRIES
POKEBERRY
POKED
POKEFUL
POKEFULS
POKER
POKERISH
POKERS
POKES
POKEWEED
POKEWEEDS
POKIER
POKIEST
POKING
POKY
POLACCA
POLACCAS
POLACRE
POLACRES
POLAR
POLARISE
POLARISED
POLARISER
POLARISERS
POLARISES
POLARISING
POLARITIES
POLARITY
POLARIZE
POLARIZED

POLARIZER
POLARIZERS
POLARIZES
POLARIZING
POLARON
POLARONS
POLARS
POLDER
POLDERED
POLDERING
POLDERS
POLE
POLECAT
POLECATS
POLED
POLEMARCH
POLEMARCHS
POLEMIC
POLEMICAL
POLEMICS
POLEMISE
POLEMISED
POLEMISES
POLEMISING
POLEMIST
POLEMISTS
POLEMIZE
POLEMIZED
POLEMIZES
POLEMIZING
POLENTA
POLENTAS
POLER
POLERS
POLES
POLEY
POLEYN
POLEYNS
POLEYS
POLIANITE
POLIANITES
POLICE
POLICED
POLICEMAN
POLICEMEN
POLICES
POLICIES
POLICING
POLICY
POLING
POLINGS
POLIO
POLIOS
POLISH
POLISHED
POLISHER
POLISHERS
POLISHES
POLISHING
POLISHINGS
POLITE
POLITELY
POLITER
POLITESSE
POLITESSES
POLITEST
POLITIC
POLITICAL
POLITICK
POLITICKED

POLITICKING
POLITICKINGS
POLITICKS
POLITICLY
POLITICO
POLITICOES
POLITICOS
POLITICS
POLITIES
POLITIQUE
POLITIQUES
POLITY
POLK
POLKA
POLKAS
POLKED
POLKING
POLKS
POLL
POLLACK
POLLACKS
POLLAN
POLLANS
POLLARD
POLLARDED
POLLARDING
POLLARDS
POLLED
POLLEN
POLLENED
POLLENING
POLLENS
POLLENT
POLLER
POLLERS
POLLEX
POLLICAL
POLLICES
POLLICIE
POLLICIES
POLLICY
POLLIES
POLLINATE
POLLINATED
POLLINATES
POLLINATING
POLLING
POLLINGS
POLLINIA
POLLINIC
POLLINIUM
POLLIWIG
POLLIWIGS
POLLIWOG
POLLIWOGS
POLLMAN
POLLMEN
POLLOCK
POLLOCKS
POLLS
POLLSTER
POLLSTERS
POLLUSION
POLLUSIONS
POLLUTANT
POLLUTANTS
POLLUTE
POLLUTED
POLLUTER
POLLUTERS

| | | | | |
|---|---|---|---|---|
| POLLUTES | POLYGENIES | POLYPOID | POMOERIUM | PONENT |
| POLLUTING | POLYGENY | POLYPOSES | POMOERIUMS | PONES |
| POLLUTION | POLYGLOT | POLYPOSIS | POMOLOGIES | PONEY |
| POLLUTIONS | POLYGLOTS | POLYPOUS | POMOLOGY | PONEYS |
| POLLUTIVE | POLYGLOTT | POLYPS | POMP | PONG |
| POLLY | POLYGLOTTS | POLYPTYCH | POMPADOUR | PONGED |
| POLLYANNA | POLYGON | POLYPTYCHS | POMPADOURS | PONGEE |
| POLLYANNAS | POLYGONAL | POLYPUS | POMPANO | PONGEES |
| POLLYWIG | POLYGONIES | POLYS | POMPANOS | PONGID |
| POLLYWIGS | POLYGONS | POLYSEME | POMPELO | PONGIDS |
| POLLYWOG | POLYGONUM | POLYSEMES | POMPELOS | PONGIER |
| POLLYWOGS | POLYGONUMS | POLYSEMIES | POMPEY | PONGIEST |
| POLO | POLYGONY | POLYSEMY | POMPEYED | PONGING |
| POLOIST | POLYGRAPH | POLYSOME | POMPEYING | PONGO |
| POLOISTS | POLYGRAPHS | POLYSOMES | POMPEYS | PONGOES |
| POLONAISE | POLYGYNIES | POLYSOMIES | POMPHOLYX | PONGOS |
| POLONAISES | POLYGYNY | POLYSOMY | POMPHOLYXES | PONGS |
| POLONIE | POLYHEDRA | POLYSTYLE | POMPIER | PONGY |
| POLONIES | POLYLEMMA | POLYTENE | POMPION | PONIARD |
| POLONISE | POLYLEMMAS | POLYTHENE | POMPIONS | PONIARDED |
| POLONISED | POLYMASTIES | POLYTHENES | POMPOM | PONIARDING |
| POLONISES | POLYMASTY | POLYTONAL | POMPOMS | PONIARDS |
| POLONISING | POLYMATH | POLYTYPIC | POMPON | PONIED |
| POLONISM | POLYMATHIES | POLYURIA | POMPONS | PONIES |
| POLONISMS | POLYMATHS | POLYURIAS | POMPOON | PONK |
| POLONIUM | POLYMATHY | POLYVINYL | POMPOONS | PONKED |
| POLONIUMS | POLYMER | POLYVINYLS | POMPOSITIES | PONKING |
| POLONIZE | POLYMERIC | POLYWATER | POMPOSITY | PONKS |
| POLONIZED | POLYMERIES | POLYWATERS | POMPOUS | PONS |
| POLONIZES | POLYMERS | POLYZOA | POMPOUSLY | PONTAGE |
| POLONIZING | POLYMERY | POLYZOAN | POMPS | PONTAGES |
| POLONY | POLYMORPH | POLYZOANS | POMROY | PONTAL |
| POLOS | POLYMORPHS | POLYZOARIES | POMROYS | PONTES |
| POLT | POLYNIA | POLYZOARY | POMS | PONTIANAC |
| POLTED | POLYNIAS | POLYZOIC | POMWATER | PONTIANACS |
| POLTFEET | POLYNYA | POLYZONAL | POMWATERS | PONTIANAK |
| POLTFOOT | POLYNYAS | POLYZOOID | PONCE | PONTIANAKS |
| POLTING | POLYOMINO | POLYZOON | PONCEAU | PONTIC |
| POLTROON | POLYOMINOS | POM | PONCEAUS | PONTIE |
| POLTROONS | POLYONYM | POMACE | PONCEAUX | PONTIES |
| POLTS | POLYONYMIES | POMACEOUS | PONCED | PONTIFEX |
| POLVERINE | POLYONYMS | POMACES | PONCES | PONTIFF |
| POLVERINES | POLYONYMY | POMADE | PONCHO | PONTIFFS |
| POLY | POLYP | POMADED | PONCHOS | PONTIFIC |
| POLYACID | POLYPARIES | POMADES | PONCING | PONTIFICE |
| POLYACT | POLYPARY | POMADING | POND | PONTIFICES |
| POLYAMIDE | POLYPE | POMANDER | PONDAGE | PONTIFIED |
| POLYAMIDES | POLYPES | POMANDERS | PONDAGES | PONTIFIES |
| POLYANDRIES | POLYPHAGIES | POMATO | PONDED | PONTIFY |
| POLYANDRY | POLYPHAGY | POMATOES | PONDER | PONTIFYING |
| POLYARCH | POLYPHASE | POMATUM | PONDERAL | PONTIL |
| POLYARCHIES | POLYPHON | POMATUMS | PONDERATE | PONTILE |
| POLYARCHY | POLYPHONE | POMBE | PONDERATED | PONTILS |
| POLYAXIAL | POLYPHONES | POMBES | PONDERATES | PONTLEVIS |
| POLYAXON | POLYPHONIES | POME | PONDERATING | PONTLEVISES |
| POLYAXONS | POLYPHONS | POMELO | PONDERED | PONTON |
| POLYBASIC | POLYPHONY | POMELOS | PONDERER | PONTONEER |
| POLYCONIC | POLYPI | POMEROY | PONDERERS | PONTONEERS |
| POLYESTER | POLYPIDE | POMEROYS | PONDERING | PONTONIER |
| POLYESTERS | POLYPIDES | POMES | PONDEROUS | PONTONIERS |
| POLYGALA | POLYPIDOM | POMFRET | PONDERS | PONTONS |
| POLYGALAS | POLYPIDOMS | POMFRETS | PONDING | PONTOON |
| POLYGAM | POLYPINE | POMMEL | PONDOK | PONTOONED |
| POLYGAMIC | POLYPITE | POMMELE | PONDOKKIE | PONTOONER |
| POLYGAMIES | POLYPITES | POMMELLED | PONDOKKIES | PONTOONERS |
| POLYGAMS | POLYPLOID | POMMELLING | PONDOKS | PONTOONING |
| POLYGAMY | POLYPOD | POMMELS | PONDS | PONTOONS |
| POLYGENE | POLYPODIES | POMMETTY | PONDWEED | PONTY |
| POLYGENES | POLYPODS | POMMIES | PONDWEEDS | PONY |
| POLYGENIC | POLYPODY | POMMY | PONE | PONYING |

POO
POOCH
POOCHES
POOD
POODLE
POODLES
POODS
POOED
POOF
POOFIER
POOFIEST
POOFS
POOFTAH
POOFTAHS
POOFTER
POOFTERS
POOFY
POOGYE
POOGYEE
POOGYEES
POOGYES
POOH
POOING
POOJA
POOJAH
POOJAHS
POOJAS
POOK
POOKA
POOKAS
POOKING
POOKIT
POOKS
POOL
POOLED
POOLING
POOLS
POOLSIDE
POOLSIDES
POON
POONAC
POONACS
POONS
POONTANG
POONTANGS
POOP
POOPED
POOPING
POOPS
POOR
POORER
POOREST
POORHOUSE
POORHOUSES
POORISH
POORLIER
POORLIEST
POORLY
POORNESS
POORNESSES
POORT
POORTITH
POORTITHS
POORTS
POORWILL
POORWILLS
POOS
POOT
POOTED
POOTER

POOTERS
POOTING
POOTS
POOVE
POOVERIES
POOVERY
POOVES
POOVIER
POOVIEST
POOVY
POP
POPADUM
POPADUMS
POPCORN
POPCORNS
POPE
POPEDOM
POPEDOMS
POPEHOOD
POPEHOODS
POPELING
POPELINGS
POPERIES
POPERIN
POPERINS
POPERY
POPES
POPESHIP
POPESHIPS
POPINJAY
POPINJAYS
POPISH
POPISHLY
POPJOY
POPJOYED
POPJOYING
POPJOYS
POPLAR
POPLARS
POPLIN
POPLINS
POPLITEAL
POPLITIC
POPOVER
POPOVERS
POPPA
POPPADUM
POPPADUMS
POPPAS
POPPED
POPPER
POPPERING
POPPERINGS
POPPERS
POPPET
POPPETS
POPPIED
POPPIES
POPPING
POPPIT
POPPITS
POPPLE
POPPLED
POPPLES
POPPLIER
POPPLIEST
POPPLING
POPPLY
POPPY
POPPYCOCK

POPPYCOCKS
POPRIN
POPRINS
POPS
POPSIES
POPSY
POPULACE
POPULACES
POPULAR
POPULARLY
POPULARS
POPULATE
POPULATED
POPULATES
POPULATING
POPULISM
POPULISMS
POPULIST
POPULISTS
POPULOUS
PORAL
PORBEAGLE
PORBEAGLES
PORCELAIN
PORCELAINS
PORCH
PORCHES
PORCINE
PORCPISCE
PORCPISCES
PORCUPINE
PORCUPINES
PORE
PORED
PORER
PORERS
PORES
PORGE
PORGED
PORGES
PORGIE
PORGIES
PORGING
PORGY
PORIER
PORIEST
PORIFER
PORIFERAL
PORIFERAN
PORIFERS
PORINESS
PORINESSES
PORING
PORISM
PORISMS
PORISTIC
PORK
PORKER
PORKERS
PORKIER
PORKIEST
PORKLING
PORKLINGS
PORKS
PORKY
PORN
PORNO
PORNOMAG
PORNOMAGS
PORNOS

PORNS
POROGAMIC
POROGAMIES
POROGAMY
POROMERIC
POROSCOPE
POROSCOPES
POROSCOPIES
POROSCOPY
POROSE
POROSES
POROSIS
POROSITIES
POROSITY
POROUS
PORPESS
PORPESSE
PORPESSES
PORPHYRIA
PORPHYRIAS
PORPHYRIES
PORPHYRIO
PORPHYRIOS
PORPHYRY
PORPOISE
PORPOISED
PORPOISES
PORPOISING
PORPORATE
PORRECT
PORRECTED
PORRECTING
PORRECTS
PORRENGER
PORRENGERS
PORRIDGE
PORRIDGES
PORRIGO
PORRIGOS
PORRINGER
PORRINGERS
PORT
PORTA
PORTABLE
PORTABLES
PORTAGE
PORTAGES
PORTAGUE
PORTAGUES
PORTAL
PORTALS
PORTANCE
PORTANCES
PORTAS
PORTASES
PORTATE
PORTATILE
PORTATIVE
PORTATIVES
PORTED
PORTEND
PORTENDED
PORTENDING
PORTENDS
PORTENT
PORTENTS
PORTEOUS
PORTEOUSES
PORTER
PORTERAGE

PORTERAGES
PORTERESS
PORTERESSES
PORTERLY
PORTERS
PORTESS
PORTESSE
PORTESSES
PORTFOLIO
PORTFOLIOS
PORTHOLE
PORTHOLES
PORTHORS
PORTHORSES
PORTHOS
PORTHOSES
PORTHOUSE
PORTHOUSES
PORTICO
PORTICOED
PORTICOES
PORTICOS
PORTIER
PORTIÈRE
PORTIÈRES
PORTIEST
PORTIGUE
PORTIGUES
PORTING
PORTION
PORTIONED
PORTIONER
PORTIONERS
PORTIONING
PORTIONS
PORTLAND
PORTLANDS
PORTLAST
PORTLASTS
PORTLIER
PORTLIEST
PORTLY
PORTMAN
PORTMEN
PORTOISE
PORTOISES
PORTOLAN
PORTOLANI
PORTOLANO
PORTOLANOS
PORTOLANS
PORTOUS
PORTOUSES
PORTRAIT
PORTRAITED
PORTRAITING
PORTRAITS
PORTRAY
PORTRAYAL
PORTRAYALS
PORTRAYED
PORTRAYER
PORTRAYERS
PORTRAYING
PORTRAYS
PORTREEVE
PORTREEVES
PORTRESS
PORTRESSES
PORTS

PORTULACA
PORTULACAS
PORTULAN
PORTULANS
PORTY
PORWIGGLE
PORWIGGLES
PORY
POS
POSADA
POSADAS
POSAUNE
POSAUNES
POSE
POSÉ
POSEABLE
POSED
POSER
POSERS
POSES
POSEUR
POSEURS
POSEUSE
POSEUSES
POSH
POSHED
POSHER
POSHES
POSHEST
POSHING
POSHLY
POSHNESS
POSHNESSES
POSHTEEN
POSHTEENS
POSIES
POSIGRADE
POSING
POSINGLY
POSINGS
POSIT
POSITED
POSITING
POSITION
POSITIONED
POSITIONING
POSITIONS
POSITIVE
POSITIVES
POSITON
POSITONS
POSITRON
POSITRONS
POSITS
POSNET
POSNETS
POSOLOGIES
POSOLOGY
POSS
POSSE
POSSED
POSSER
POSSERS
POSSES
POSSESS
POSSESSED
POSSESSES
POSSESSING
POSSESSOR
POSSESSORS

POSSET
POSSETED
POSSETING
POSSETS
POSSIBLE
POSSIBLES
POSSIBLY
POSSIE
POSSIES
POSSING
POSSUM
POSSUMED
POSSUMING
POSSUMS
POST
POSTAGE
POSTAGES
POSTAL
POSTALS
POSTCARD
POSTCARDED
POSTCARDING
POSTCARDS
POSTCODE
POSTCODED
POSTCODES
POSTCODING
POSTDATE
POSTDATED
POSTDATES
POSTDATING
POSTED
POSTEEN
POSTEENS
POSTER
POSTERED
POSTERING
POSTERIOR
POSTERIORS
POSTERITIES
POSTERITY
POSTERN
POSTERNS
POSTERS
POSTFACE
POSTFACES
POSTFIX
POSTFIXED
POSTFIXES
POSTFIXING
POSTHASTE
POSTHASTES
POSTHORSE
POSTHORSES
POSTHOUSE
POSTHOUSES
POSTICHE
POSTICHES
POSTICOUS
POSTIE
POSTIES
POSTIL
POSTILION
POSTILIONS
POSTILLED
POSTILLER
POSTILLERS
POSTILLING
POSTILS
POSTING

POSTINGS
POSTLUDE
POSTLUDES
POSTMAN
POSTMARK
POSTMARKS
POSTMEN
POSTPONE
POSTPONED
POSTPONER
POSTPONERS
POSTPONES
POSTPONING
POSTS
POSTULANT
POSTULANTS
POSTULATA
POSTULATE
POSTULATED
POSTULATES
POSTULATING
POSTURAL
POSTURE
POSTURED
POSTURER
POSTURERS
POSTURES
POSTURING
POSTURIST
POSTURISTS
POSTWOMAN
POSTWOMEN
POSY
POT
POTABLE
POTABLES
POTAGE
POTAGES
POTAMIC
POTASH
POTASHED
POTASHES
POTASHING
POTASS
POTASSA
POTASSAS
POTASSES
POTASSIC
POTASSIUM
POTASSIUMS
POTATION
POTATIONS
POTATO
POTATOES
POTATORY
POTCH
POTCHE
POTCHED
POTCHER
POTCHERS
POTCHES
POTCHING
POTE
POTED
POTEEN
POTEENS
POTENCE
POTENCÉ
POTENCES
POTENCÉS

POTENCIES
POTENCY
POTENT
POTENTATE
POTENTATES
POTENTIAL
POTENTIALS
POTENTISE
POTENTISED
POTENTISES
POTENTISING
POTENTIZE
POTENTIZED
POTENTIZES
POTENTIZING
POTENTLY
POTENTS
POTES
POTFUL
POTFULS
POTGUN
POTGUNS
POTHECARIES
POTHECARY
POTHEEN
POTHEENS
POTHER
POTHERED
POTHERING
POTHERS
POTHERY
POTHOLE
POTHOLER
POTHOLERS
POTHOLES
POTHOLING
POTHOLINGS
POTHOOK
POTHOOKS
POTHOUSE
POTHOUSES
POTICARIES
POTICARY
POTICHE
POTICHES
POTIN
POTING
POTINS
POTION
POTIONS
POTLACH
POTLACHES
POTLATCH
POTLATCHES
POTOMETER
POTOMETERS
POTOROO
POTOROOS
POTS
POTSHERD
POTSHERDS
POTSTONE
POTSTONES
POTT
POTTAGE
POTTAGES
POTTED
POTTER
POTTERED
POTTERER

POTTERERS
POTTERIES
POTTERING
POTTERINGS
POTTERS
POTTERY
POTTIER
POTTIES
POTTIEST
POTTINESS
POTTINESSES
POTTING
POTTINGAR
POTTINGARS
POTTINGER
POTTINGERS
POTTLE
POTTLES
POTTO
POTTOS
POTTS
POTTY
POUCH
POUCHED
POUCHES
POUCHFUL
POUCHFULS
POUCHIER
POUCHIEST
POUCHING
POUCHY
POUDER
POUDERS
POUDRE
POUDRES
POUF
POUFED
POUFFE
POUFFES
POUFS
POUFTAH
POUFTAHS
POUFTER
POUFTERS
POUK
POUKE
POUKES
POUKING
POUKIT
POUKS
POULAINE
POULAINES
POULARD
POULARDS
POULDER
POULDERS
POULDRE
POULDRES
POULDRON
POULDRONS
POULE
POULES
POULP
POULPE
POULPES
POULPS
POULT
POULTER
POULTERER
POULTERERS

POULTERS
POULTICE
POULTICED
POULTICES
POULTICING
POULTRIES
POULTRY
POULTS
POUNCE
POUNCED
POUNCES
POUNCET
POUNCETS
POUNCHING
POUNCING
POUND
POUNDAGE
POUNDAGES
POUNDAL
POUNDALS
POUNDED
POUNDER
POUNDERS
POUNDING
POUNDS
POUPE
POUPED
POUPES
POUPING
POUPT
POUR
POURABLE
POURBOIRE
POURBOIRES
POURED
POURER
POURERS
POURIE
POURIES
POURING
POURINGS
POURPOINT
POURPOINTS
POURS
POURSEW
POURSEWED
POURSEWING
POURSEWS
POURSUE
POURSUED
POURSUES
POURSUING
POURSUIT
POURSUITS
POURSUITT
POURSUITTS
POURTRAHED
POURTRAY
POURTRAYD
POURTRAYED
POURTRAYING
POURTRAYS
POUSOWDIE
POUSOWDIES
POUSSE
POUSSES
POUSSETTE
POUSSETTED
POUSSETTES
POUSSETTING

POUSSIN
POUSSINS
POUT
POUTED
POUTER
POUTERS
POUTHER
POUTHERED
POUTHERING
POUTHERS
POUTIER
POUTIEST
POUTING
POUTINGLY
POUTINGS
POUTS
POUTY
POVERTIES
POVERTY
POW
POWAN
POWANS
POWDER
POWDERED
POWDERIER
POWDERIEST
POWDERING
POWDERS
POWDERY
POWELLISE
POWELLISED
POWELLISES
POWELLISING
POWELLITE
POWELLITES
POWELLIZE
POWELLIZED
POWELLIZES
POWELLIZING
POWER
POWERBOAT
POWERBOATS
POWERED
POWERFUL
POWERING
POWERLESS
POWERPLAY
POWERPLAYS
POWERS
POWIN
POWINS
POWN
POWND
POWNDED
POWNDING
POWNDS
POWNEY
POWNEYS
POWNIE
POWNIES
POWNS
POWNY
POWRE
POWRED
POWRES
POWRING
POWS
POWSOWDIES
POWSOWDY
POWTER

POWTERED
POWTERING
POWTERS
POWWAW
POWWOW
POWWOWED
POWWOWING
POWWOWS
POX
POXED
POXES
POXIER
POXIEST
POXING
POXVIRUS
POXVIRUSES
POXY
POYNANT
POYNT
POYNTED
POYNTING
POYNTS
POYSE
POYSED
POYSES
POYSING
POYSON
POYSONED
POYSONING
POYSONS
POZ
POZZ
POZZIES
POZZOLANA
POZZOLANAS
POZZY
PRAAM
PRAAMS
PRABBLE
PRABBLES
PRACTIC
PRACTICAL
PRACTICALS
PRACTICE
PRACTICED
PRACTICES
PRACTICING
PRACTICK
PRACTICKS
PRACTICS
PRACTICUM
PRACTICUMS
PRACTIQUE
PRACTIQUES
PRACTISE
PRACTISED
PRACTISER
PRACTISERS
PRACTISES
PRACTISING
PRACTIVE
PRACTOLOL
PRACTOLOLS
PRAD
PRADS
PRAEAMBLE
PRAEAMBLES
PRAECOCES
PRAEDIAL
PRAEDIALS

PRAEFECT
PRAEFECTS
PRAELUDIA
PRAENOMEN
PRAENOMENS
PRAENOMINA
PRAESES
PRAESIDIA
PRAETOR
PRAETORS
PRAGMATIC
PRAGMATICS
PRAHU
PRAHUS
PRAIRIE
PRAIRIED
PRAIRIES
PRAISE
PRAISEACH
PRAISEACHS
PRAISED
PRAISEFUL
PRAISER
PRAISERS
PRAISES
PRAISING
PRAISINGS
PRALINE
PRALINES
PRAM
PRAMS
PRANA
PRANAS
PRANAYAMA
PRANAYAMAS
PRANCE
PRANCED
PRANCER
PRANCERS
PRANCES
PRANCING
PRANCINGS
PRANCK
PRANCKE
PRANCKED
PRANCKES
PRANCKING
PRANCKS
PRANDIAL
PRANG
PRANGED
PRANGING
PRANGS
PRANK
PRANKED
PRANKFUL
PRANKIER
PRANKIEST
PRANKING
PRANKINGS
PRANKISH
PRANKLE
PRANKLED
PRANKLES
PRANKLING
PRANKS
PRANKSOME
PRANKSTER
PRANKSTERS
PRANKY

PRASE
PRASES
PRAT
PRATE
PRATED
PRATER
PRATERS
PRATES
PRATFALL
PRATFALLEN
PRATFALLING
PRATFALLS
PRATFELL
PRATIE
PRATIES
PRATING
PRATINGLY
PRATINGS
PRATIQUE
PRATIQUES
PRATS
PRATTED
PRATTING
PRATTLE
PRATTLED
PRATTLER
PRATTLERS
PRATTLES
PRATTLING
PRATY
PRAU
PRAUNCE
PRAUNCED
PRAUNCES
PRAUNCING
PRAUS
PRAVITIES
PRAVITY
PRAWLE
PRAWLES
PRAWLIN
PRAWLINS
PRAWN
PRAWNED
PRAWNING
PRAWNS
PRAXES
PRAXIS
PRAY
PRAYED
PRAYER
PRAYERFUL
PRAYERS
PRAYING
PRAYINGLY
PRAYINGS
PRAYS
PRE
PREACE
PREACED
PREACES
PREACH
PREACHED
PREACHER
PREACHERS
PREACHES
PREACHIER
PREACHIEST
PREACHIFIED
PREACHIFIES

PREACHIFY
PREACHIFYING
PREACHILY
PREACHING
PREACHINGS
PREACHY
PREACING
PREAMBLE
PREAMBLED
PREAMBLES
PREAMBLING
PREASE
PREASED
PREASES
PREASING
PREASSE
PREASSED
PREASSES
PREASSING
PREBEND
PREBENDAL
PREBENDS
PREBIOTIC
PRECAST
PRECATIVE
PRECATORY
PRECEDE
PRECEDED
PRECEDENT
PRECEDENTS
PRECEDES
PRECEDING
PRECEESE
PRECENTOR
PRECENTORS
PRECEPIT
PRECEPITS
PRECEPT
PRECEPTOR
PRECEPTORS
PRECEPTS
PRECESS
PRECESSED
PRECESSES
PRECESSING
PRÉCIEUSE
PRÉCIEUSES
PRECINCT
PRECINCTS
PRECIOUS
PRECIOUSES
PRECIPICE
PRECIPICES
PRÉCIS
PRECISE
PRÉCISED
PRECISELY
PRECISER
PRÉCISES
PRECISEST
PRECISIAN
PRECISIANS
PRÉCISING
PRECISION
PRECISIONS
PRECISIVE
PRECLUDE
PRECLUDED
PRECLUDES
PRECLUDING

PRECOCIAL
PRECOCITIES
PRECOCITY
PRECONISE
PRECONISED
PRECONISES
PRECONISING
PRECONIZE
PRECONIZED
PRECONIZES
PRECONIZING
PRECOOK
PRECOOKED
PRECOOKING
PRECOOKS
PRECURRER
PRECURRERS
PRECURSE
PRECURSES
PRECURSOR
PRECURSORS
PREDACITIES
PREDACITY
PREDATE
PREDATED
PREDATES
PREDATING
PREDATION
PREDATIONS
PREDATIVE
PREDATOR
PREDATORS
PREDATORY
PREDEFINE
PREDEFINED
PREDEFINES
PREDEFINING
PREDELLA
PREDELLAS
PREDESIGN
PREDESIGNED
PREDESIGNING
PREDESIGNS
PREDEVOTE
PREDIAL
PREDIALS
PREDICANT
PREDICANTS
PREDICATE
PREDICATED
PREDICATES
PREDICATING
PREDICT
PREDICTED
PREDICTING
PREDICTOR
PREDICTORS
PREDICTS
PREDIED
PREDIES
PREDIGEST
PREDIGESTED
PREDIGESTING
PREDIGESTS
PREDIKANT
PREDIKANTS
PREDILECT
PREDOOM
PREDOOMED
PREDOOMING

PREDOOMS
PREDY
PREDYING
PREE
PREED
PREEING
PREEMIE
PREEMIES
PREEN
PREENED
PREENING
PREENS
PREES
PREEVE
PREEVED
PREEVES
PREEVING
PREFAB
PREFABS
PREFACE
PREFACED
PREFACES
PREFACIAL
PREFACING
PREFADE
PREFADED
PREFADES
PREFADING
PREFARD
PREFATORY
PREFECT
PREFECTS
PREFER
PREFERRED
PREFERRER
PREFERRERS
PREFERRING
PREFERS
PREFIGURE
PREFIGURED
PREFIGURES
PREFIGURING
PREFIX
PREFIXED
PREFIXES
PREFIXING
PREFIXION
PREFIXIONS
PREFLIGHT
PREFORM
PREFORMED
PREFORMING
PREFORMS
PREGGERS
PREGNABLE
PREGNANCE
PREGNANCES
PREGNANCIES
PREGNANCY
PREGNANT
PREHALLUCES
PREHALLUX
PREHEAT
PREHEATED
PREHEATING
PREHEATS
PREHEND
PREHENDED
PREHENDING
PREHENDS

PREHENSOR
PREHENSORS
PREHNITE
PREHNITES
PREHUMAN
PREIF
PREIFE
PREIFES
PREIFS
PREJINK
PREJUDGE
PREJUDGED
PREJUDGES
PREJUDGING
PREJUDICE
PREJUDICED
PREJUDICES
PREJUDICING
PREJUDIZE
PREJUDIZES
PRELACIES
PRELACY
PRELATE
PRELATES
PRELATESS
PRELATESSES
PRELATIAL
PRELATIC
PRELATIES
PRELATION
PRELATIONS
PRELATISE
PRELATISED
PRELATISES
PRELATISH
PRELATISING
PRELATISM
PRELATISMS
PRELATIST
PRELATISTS
PRELATIZE
PRELATIZED
PRELATIZES
PRELATIZING
PRELATURE
PRELATURES
PRELATY
PRELECT
PRELECTED
PRELECTING
PRELECTOR
PRELECTORS
PRELECTS
PRELIM
PRELIMS
PRELUDE
PRELUDED
PRELUDES
PRELUDI
PRELUDIAL
PRELUDING
PRELUDIO
PRELUSION
PRELUSIONS
PRELUSIVE
PRELUSORY
PREMATURE
PREMED
PREMEDIC
PREMEDICS

PREMEDS
PREMIA
PREMIE
PREMIER
PREMIÈRE
PREMIÈRED
PREMIÈRES
PREMIÈRING
PREMIERS
PREMIES
PREMISE
PREMISED
PREMISES
PREMISING
PREMISS
PREMISSES
PREMIUM
PREMIUMS
PREMIX
PREMIXED
PREMIXES
PREMIXING
PREMOLAR
PREMOLARS
PREMONISH
PREMONISHED
PREMONISHES
PREMONISHING
PREMORSE
PREMOSAIC
PREMOTION
PREMOTIONS
PREMOVE
PREMOVED
PREMOVES
PREMOVING
PREMY
PRENASAL
PRENASALS
PRENATAL
PRENOTION
PRENOTIONS
PRENT
PRENTICE
PRENTICES
PRENTS
PRENUBILE
PRENZIE
PREOCCUPIED
PREOCCUPIES
PREOCCUPY
PREOCCUPYING
PREOPTION
PREOPTIONS
PREORAL
PREORALLY
PREORDAIN
PREORDAINED
PREORDAINING
PREORDAINS
PREORDER
PREORDERED
PREORDERING
PREORDERS
PREP
PREPACK
PREPACKED
PREPACKING
PREPACKS
PREPAID

| | | | | |
|---|---|---|---|---|
| PREPARE | PRESENCE | PRETENDED | PREXES | PRIESTS |
| PREPARED | PRESENCES | PRETENDER | PREXIES | PRIEVE |
| PREPARER | PRESENT | PRETENDERS | PREXY | PRIEVED |
| PREPARERS | PRESENTED | PRETENDING | PREY | PRIEVES |
| PREPARES | PRESENTEE | PRETENDS | PREYED | PRIEVING |
| PREPARING | PRESENTEES | PRETENSE | PREYFUL | PRIG |
| PREPAY | PRESENTER | PRETENSES | PREYING | PRIGGED |
| PREPAYING | PRESENTERS | PRETERIST | PREYS | PRIGGER |
| PREPAYS | PRESENTING | PRETERISTS | PREZZIE | PRIGGERIES |
| PREPENSE | PRESENTLY | PRETERIT | PREZZIES | PRIGGERS |
| PREPENSED | PRESENTS | PRETERITE | PRIAL | PRIGGERY |
| PREPENSES | PRESERVE | PRETERITES | PRIALS | PRIGGING |
| PREPENSING | PRESERVED | PRETERITS | PRIAPIC | PRIGGINGS |
| PREPOLLEX | PRESERVER | PRETERM | PRIAPISM | PRIGGISH |
| PREPOLLICES | PRESERVERS | PRETERMIT | PRIAPISMS | PRIGGISM |
| PREPOTENT | PRESERVES | PRETERMITS | PRIBBLE | PRIGGISMS |
| PREPPED | PRESERVING | PRETERMITTED | PRIBBLES | PRIGS |
| PREPPIER | PRESES | PRETERMITTING | PRICE | PRILL |
| PREPPIES | PRESET | PRETEXT | PRICED | PRILLED |
| PREPPIEST | PRESETS | PRETEXTS | PRICELESS | PRILLING |
| PREPPING | PRESETTING | PRETTIER | PRICER | PRILLS |
| PREPPY | PRESIDE | PRETTIES | PRICERS | PRIM |
| PREPS | PRESIDED | PRETTIEST | PRICES | PRIMA |
| PREPUCE | PRESIDENT | PRETTIFIED | PRICEY | PRIMACIES |
| PREPUCES | PRESIDENTS | PRETTIFIES | PRICIER | PRIMACY |
| PREPUTIAL | PRESIDES | PRETTIFY | PRICIEST | PRIMAEVAL |
| PREQUEL | PRESIDIA | PRETTIFYING | PRICINESS | PRIMAGE |
| PREQUELS | PRESIDIAL | PRETTILY | PRICINESSES | PRIMAGES |
| PRERECORD | PRESIDING | PRETTY | PRICING | PRIMAL |
| PRERECORDED | PRESIDIO | PRETTYISH | PRICK | PRIMALITIES |
| PRERECORDING | PRESIDIOS | PRETTYISM | PRICKED | PRIMALITY |
| PRERECORDS | PRESIDIUM | PRETTYISMS | PRICKER | PRIMALLY |
| PREROSION | PRESIDIUMS | PRETZEL | PRICKERS | PRIMARIES |
| PREROSIONS | PRESS | PRETZELS | PRICKET | PRIMARILY |
| PRERUPT | PRESSED | PREVAIL | PRICKETS | PRIMARY |
| PRESA | PRESSER | PREVAILED | PRICKING | PRIMATAL |
| PRESAGE | PRESSERS | PREVAILING | PRICKINGS | PRIMATE |
| PRESAGED | PRESSES | PREVAILS | PRICKLE | PRIMATES |
| PRESAGER | PRESSFAT | PREVALENT | PRICKLED | PRIMATIAL |
| PRESAGERS | PRESSFATS | PREVE | PRICKLES | PRIMATIC |
| PRESAGES | PRESSFUL | PREVED | PRICKLIER | PRIME |
| PRESAGING | PRESSFULS | PREVENE | PRICKLIEST | PRIMED |
| PRESBYOPE | PRESSING | PREVENED | PRICKLING | PRIMELY |
| PRESBYOPES | PRESSINGS | PREVENES | PRICKLINGS | PRIMENESS |
| PRESBYOPIES | PRESSION | PREVENING | PRICKLY | PRIMENESSES |
| PRESBYOPY | PRESSIONS | PREVENT | PRICKS | PRIMER |
| PRESBYTE | PRESSMAN | PREVENTED | PRICKWOOD | PRIMERO |
| PRESBYTER | PRESSMEN | PREVENTER | PRICKWOODS | PRIMEROS |
| PRESBYTERS | PRESSOR | PREVENTERS | PRICY | PRIMERS |
| PRESBYTES | PRESSURE | PREVENTING | PRIDE | PRIMES |
| PRESCHOOL | PRESSURED | PREVENTS | PRIDED | PRIMEUR |
| PRESCIENT | PRESSURES | PREVERB | PRIDEFUL | PRIMEURS |
| PRESCIND | PRESSURING | PREVERBAL | PRIDELESS | PRIMEVAL |
| PRESCINDED | PREST | PREVERBS | PRIDES | PRIMINE |
| PRESCINDING | PRESTED | PREVES | PRIDIAN | PRIMINES |
| PRESCINDS | PRESTIGE | PREVIEW | PRIDING | PRIMING |
| PRESCIOUS | PRESTIGES | PREVIEWED | PRIED | PRIMINGS |
| PRESCRIBE | PRESTING | PREVIEWING | PRIEF | PRIMIPARA |
| PRESCRIBED | PRESTO | PREVIEWS | PRIEFE | PRIMIPARAE |
| PRESCRIBES | PRESTOS | PREVING | PRIEFES | PRIMIPARAS |
| PRESCRIBING | PRESTS | PREVIOUS | PRIEFS | PRIMITIAE |
| PRESCRIPT | PRESUME | PREVISE | PRIER | PRIMITIAL |
| PRESCRIPTS | PRESUMED | PREVISED | PRIERS | PRIMITIAS |
| PRESCUTA | PRESUMER | PREVISES | PRIES | PRIMITIVE |
| PRESCUTUM | PRESUMERS | PREVISING | PRIEST | PRIMITIVES |
| PRESE | PRESUMES | PREVISION | PRIESTED | PRIMLY |
| PRESELECT | PRESUMING | PREVISIONS | PRIESTESS | PRIMMED |
| PRESELECTED | PRETENCE | PREWYN | PRIESTESSES | PRIMMER |
| PRESELECTING | PRETENCES | PREWYNS | PRIESTING | PRIMMEST |
| PRESELECTS | PRETEND | PREX | PRIESTLY | PRIMMING |

PRIMNESS
PRIMNESSES
PRIMO
PRIMORDIA
PRIMOS
PRIMP
PRIMPED
PRIMPING
PRIMPS
PRIMROSE
PRIMROSED
PRIMROSES
PRIMROSING
PRIMROSY
PRIMS
PRIMSIE
PRIMULA
PRIMULAS
PRIMULINE
PRIMULINES
PRIMUS
PRIMUSES
PRIMY
PRINCE
PRINCED
PRINCEDOM
PRINCEDOMS
PRINCEKIN
PRINCEKINS
PRINCELET
PRINCELETS
PRINCELIER
PRINCELIEST
PRINCELY
PRINCES
PRINCESS
PRINCESSE
PRINCESSES
PRINCING
PRINCIPAL
PRINCIPALS
PRINCIPIA
PRINCIPLE
PRINCIPLED
PRINCIPLES
PRINCIPLING
PRINCOCK
PRINCOCKS
PRINCOX
PRINCOXES
PRINK
PRINKED
PRINKING
PRINKS
PRINT
PRINTABLE
PRINTED
PRINTER
PRINTERS
PRINTING
PRINTINGS
PRINTLESS
PRINTS
PRION
PRIONS
PRIOR
PRIORATE
PRIORATES
PRIORESS
PRIORESSES

PRIORIES
PRIORITIES
PRIORITY
PRIORS
PRIORSHIP
PRIORSHIPS
PRIORY
PRISAGE
PRISAGES
PRISE
PRISED
PRISER
PRISERS
PRISES
PRISING
PRISM
PRISMATIC
PRISMOID
PRISMOIDS
PRISMS
PRISMY
PRISON
PRISONED
PRISONER
PRISONERS
PRISONING
PRISONOUS
PRISONS
PRISSIER
PRISSIEST
PRISSY
PRISTINE
PRITHEE
PRIVACIES
PRIVACY
PRIVADO
PRIVADOES
PRIVADOS
PRIVATE
PRIVATEER
PRIVATEERED
PRIVATEERING
PRIVATEERINGS
PRIVATEERS
PRIVATELY
PRIVATES
PRIVATION
PRIVATIONS
PRIVATISE
PRIVATISED
PRIVATISES
PRIVATISING
PRIVATIVE
PRIVATIVES
PRIVATIZE
PRIVATIZED
PRIVATIZES
PRIVATIZING
PRIVET
PRIVETS
PRIVIER
PRIVIES
PRIVIEST
PRIVILEGE
PRIVILEGED
PRIVILEGES
PRIVILEGING
PRIVILY
PRIVITIES
PRIVITY

PRIVY
PRIZABLE
PRIZE
PRIZED
PRIZER
PRIZERS
PRIZES
PRIZING
PRO
PROA
PROAS
PROBABLE
PROBABLES
PROBABLY
PROBALL
PROBAND
PROBANDS
PROBANG
PROBANGS
PROBATE
PROBATED
PROBATES
PROBATING
PROBATION
PROBATIONS
PROBATIVE
PROBATORY
PROBE
PROBED
PROBES
PROBING
PROBIT
PROBITIES
PROBITS
PROBITY
PROBLEM
PROBLEMS
PROBOSCIDES
PROBOSCIS
PROBOSCISES
PROCACITIES
PROCACITY
PROCAINE
PROCAINES
PROCARYON
PROCARYONS
PROCEDURE
PROCEDURES
PROCEED
PROCEEDED
PROCEEDER
PROCEEDERS
PROCEEDING
PROCEEDINGS
PROCEEDS
PROCERITIES
PROCERITY
PROCESS
PROCESSED
PROCESSES
PROCESSING
PROCESSOR
PROCESSORS
PROCIDENT
PROCINCT
PROCINCTS
PROCLAIM
PROCLAIMED
PROCLAIMING
PROCLAIMS

PROCLISES
PROCLISIS
PROCLITIC
PROCLITICS
PROCLIVE
PROCONSUL
PROCONSULS
PROCREANT
PROCREANTS
PROCREATE
PROCREATED
PROCREATES
PROCREATING
PROCTAL
PROCTITIS
PROCTITISES
PROCTOR
PROCTORS
PROCURACIES
PROCURACY
PROCURE
PROCURED
PROCURER
PROCURERS
PROCURES
PROCURESS
PROCURESSES
PROCUREUR
PROCUREURS
PROCURING
PROD
PRODDED
PRODDING
PRODIGAL
PRODIGALS
PRODIGIES
PRODIGY
PRODITOR
PRODITORS
PRODITORY
PRODNOSE
PRODNOSED
PRODNOSES
PRODNOSING
PRODROMAL
PRODROME
PRODROMES
PRODROMI
PRODROMIC
PRODROMUS
PRODS
PRODUCE
PRODUCED
PRODUCER
PRODUCERS
PRODUCES
PRODUCING
PRODUCT
PRODUCTS
PROEM
PROEMBRYO
PROEMBRYOS
PROEMIAL
PROEMS
PROENZYME
PROENZYMES
PROF
PROFACE
PROFANE
PROFANED

PROFANELY
PROFANER
PROFANERS
PROFANES
PROFANING
PROFANITIES
PROFANITY
PROFESS
PROFESSED
PROFESSES
PROFESSING
PROFESSOR
PROFESSORS
PROFFER
PROFFERED
PROFFERER
PROFFERERS
PROFFERING
PROFFERS
PROFILE
PROFILED
PROFILER
PROFILERS
PROFILES
PROFILING
PROFILIST
PROFILISTS
PROFIT
PROFITED
PROFITEER
PROFITEERED
PROFITEERING
PROFITEERINGS
PROFITEERS
PROFITER
PROFITERS
PROFITING
PROFITINGS
PROFITS
PROFLUENT
PROFORMA
PROFORMAS
PROFOUND
PROFOUNDER
PROFOUNDEST
PROFOUNDS
PROFS
PROFUSE
PROFUSELY
PROFUSER
PROFUSERS
PROFUSION
PROFUSIONS
PROG
PROGENIES
PROGENY
PROGERIA
PROGERIAS
PROGESTIN
PROGESTINS
PROGGED
PROGGING
PROGGINS
PROGGINSES
PROGNOSES
PROGNOSIS
PROGRADE
PROGRADED
PROGRADES
PROGRADING

PROGRAM
PROGRAMME
PROGRAMMED
PROGRAMMES
PROGRAMMING
PROGRAMMINGS
PROGRAMS
PROGRESS
PROGRESSED
PROGRESSES
PROGRESSING
PROGS
PROHIBIT
PROHIBITED
PROHIBITING
PROHIBITS
PROIGN
PROIGNED
PROIGNING
PROIGNS
PROIN
PROINE
PROINED
PROINES
PROINING
PROINS
PROJECT
PROJECTED
PROJECTING
PROJECTINGS
PROJECTOR
PROJECTORS
PROJECTS
PROKARYON
PROKARYONS
PROKARYOT
PROKARYOTS
PROKE
PROKED
PROKER
PROKERS
PROKES
PROKING
PROLACTIN
PROLACTINS
PROLAMIN
PROLAMINE
PROLAMINES
PROLAMINS
PROLAPSE
PROLAPSED
PROLAPSES
PROLAPSING
PROLAPSUS
PROLAPSUSES
PROLATE
PROLATED
PROLATELY
PROLATES
PROLATING
PROLATION
PROLATIONS
PROLATIVE
PROLE
PROLED
PROLEG
PROLEGS
PROLEPSES
PROLEPSIS
PROLEPTIC

PROLER
PROLERS
PROLES
PROLETARIES
PROLETARY
PROLICIDE
PROLICIDES
PROLIFIC
PROLINE
PROLINES
PROLING
PROLIX
PROLIXITIES
PROLIXITY
PROLIXLY
PROLL
PROLLED
PROLLER
PROLLERS
PROLLING
PROLLS
PROLOGISE
PROLOGISED
PROLOGISES
PROLOGISING
PROLOGIZE
PROLOGIZED
PROLOGIZES
PROLOGIZING
PROLOGUE
PROLOGUED
PROLOGUES
PROLOGUING
PROLONG
PROLONGE
PROLONGED
PROLONGER
PROLONGERS
PROLONGES
PROLONGING
PROLONGS
PROLUSION
PROLUSIONS
PROLUSORY
PROM
PROMACHOS
PROMACHOES
PROMENADE
PROMENADED
PROMENADES
PROMENADING
PROMETAL
PROMETALS
PROMINENT
PROMISE
PROMISED
PROMISEE
PROMISEES
PROMISER
PROMISERS
PROMISES
PROMISING
PROMISOR
PROMISORS
PROMISSOR
PROMISSORS
PROMMER
PROMMERS
PROMO
PROMOS

PROMOTE
PROMOTED
PROMOTER
PROMOTERS
PROMOTES
PROMOTING
PROMOTION
PROMOTIONS
PROMOTIVE
PROMOTOR
PROMOTORS
PROMPT
PROMPTED
PROMPTER
PROMPTERS
PROMPTEST
PROMPTING
PROMPTINGS
PROMPTLY
PROMPTS
PROMPTURE
PROMPTURES
PROMS
PROMULGE
PROMULGED
PROMULGES
PROMULGING
PROMUSCES
PROMUSCIDES
PROMUSCIS
PROMUSCISES
PRONAOI
PRONAOS
PRONATE
PRONATED
PRONATES
PRONATING
PRONATION
PRONATIONS
PRONATOR
PRONATORS
PRONE
PRONELY
PRONENESS
PRONENESSES
PRONER
PRONES
PRONEST
PRONEUR
PRONEURS
PRONG
PRONGBUCK
PRONGBUCKS
PRONGED
PRONGHORN
PRONGHORNS
PRONGING
PRONGS
PRONOTA
PRONOTAL
PRONOTUM
PRONOUN
PRONOUNCE
PRONOUNCED
PRONOUNCES
PRONOUNCING
PRONOUNCINGS
PRONOUNS
PRONTO
PRONUCLEI

PROO
PROOEMION
PROOEMIONS
PROOEMIUM
PROOEMIUMS
PROOF
PROOFED
PROOFING
PROOFINGS
PROOFLESS
PROOFS
PROOTIC
PROOTICS
PROP
PROPAGATE
PROPAGATED
PROPAGATES
PROPAGATING
PROPAGE
PROPAGED
PROPAGES
PROPAGING
PROPAGULE
PROPAGULES
PROPALE
PROPALED
PROPALES
PROPALING
PROPANE
PROPANES
PROPEL
PROPELLED
PROPELLER
PROPELLERS
PROPELLING
PROPELS
PROPEND
PROPENDED
PROPENDING
PROPENDS
PROPENE
PROPENES
PROPENSE
PROPER
PROPERDIN
PROPERDINS
PROPERLY
PROPERS
PROPERTIED
PROPERTIES
PROPERTY
PROPERTYING
PROPHASE
PROPHASES
PROPHECIES
PROPHECY
PROPHESIED
PROPHESIES
PROPHESY
PROPHESYING
PROPHESYINGS
PROPHET
PROPHETIC
PROPHETS
PROPHYLL
PROPHYLLS
PROPINE
PROPINED
PROPINES
PROPINING

PROPODEON
PROPODEONS
PROPODEUM
PROPODEUMS
PROPOLIS
PROPOLISES
PROPONE
PROPONED
PROPONENT
PROPONENTS
PROPONES
PROPONING
PROPOSAL
PROPOSALS
PROPOSE
PROPOSED
PROPOSER
PROPOSERS
PROPOSES
PROPOSING
PROPOUND
PROPOUNDED
PROPOUNDING
PROPOUNDS
PROPPED
PROPPING
PROPRIETIES
PROPRIETY
PROPS
PROPTOSES
PROPTOSIS
PROPYL
PROPYLA
PROPYLAEA
PROPYLENE
PROPYLENES
PROPYLIC
PROPYLITE
PROPYLITES
PROPYLON
PROPYLS
PRORATE
PRORATED
PRORATES
PRORATING
PRORATION
PRORATIONS
PRORE
PRORECTOR
PRORECTORS
PRORES
PROROGATE
PROROGATED
PROROGATES
PROROGATING
PROROGUE
PROROGUED
PROROGUES
PROROGUING
PROS
PROSAIC
PROSAICAL
PROSAISM
PROSAISMS
PROSAIST
PROSAISTS
PROSATEUR
PROSATEURS
PROSCRIBE
PROSCRIBED

PROSCRIBES
PROSCRIBING
PROSCRIPT
PROSCRIPTS
PROSE
PROSECTOR
PROSECTORS
PROSECUTE
PROSECUTED
PROSECUTES
PROSECUTING
PROSED
PROSELYTE
PROSELYTED
PROSELYTES
PROSELYTING
PROSEMAN
PROSEMEN
PROSER
PROSERS
PROSES
PROSEUCHA
PROSEUCHAE
PROSEUCHE
PROSIER
PROSIEST
PROSILY
PROSIMIAN
PROSIMIANS
PROSINESS
PROSINESSES
PROSING
PROSINGS
PROSIT
PROSODIAL
PROSODIAN
PROSODIANS
PROSODIC
PROSODIES
PROSODIST
PROSODISTS
PROSODY
PROSOPON
PROSOPONS
PROSPECT
PROSPECTED
PROSPECTING
PROSPECTINGS
PROSPECTS
PROSPER
PROSPERED
PROSPERING
PROSPERS
PROSTATE
PROSTATES
PROSTATIC
PROSTRATE
PROSTRATED
PROSTRATES
PROSTRATING
PROSTYLE
PROSTYLES
PROSY
PROTAMINE
PROTAMINES
PROTANDRIES
PROTANDRY
PROTANOPE
PROTANOPES
PROTASES

PROTASIS
PROTATIC
PROTEA
PROTEAN
PROTEAS
PROTEASE
PROTEASES
PROTECT
PROTECTED
PROTECTING
PROTECTOR
PROTECTORS
PROTECTS
PROTÉGÉ
PROTÉGÉE
PROTÉGÉES
PROTÉGÉS
PROTEID
PROTEIDS
PROTEIN
PROTEINIC
PROTEINS
PROTEND
PROTENDED
PROTENDING
PROTENDS
PROTENSE
PROTENSES
PROTEST
PROTESTED
PROTESTER
PROTESTERS
PROTESTING
PROTESTOR
PROTESTORS
PROTESTS
PROTEUS
PROTEUSES
PROTHALLI
PROTHESES
PROTHESIS
PROTHETIC
PROTHORACES
PROTHORAX
PROTHORAXES
PROTHYL
PROTHYLE
PROTHYLES
PROTHYLS
PROTIST
PROTISTIC
PROTISTS
PROTIUM
PROTIUMS
PROTOCOL
PROTOCOLLED
PROTOCOLLING
PROTOCOLS
PROTOGINE
PROTOGINES
PROTOGYNIES
PROTOGYNY
PROTON
PROTONEMA
PROTONEMATA
PROTONIC
PROTONS
PROTOSTAR
PROTOSTARS
PROTOTYPE

PROTOTYPED
PROTOTYPES
PROTOTYPING
PROTOXIDE
PROTOXIDES
PROTOZOA
PROTOZOAN
PROTOZOANS
PROTOZOIC
PROTOZOON
PROTRACT
PROTRACTED
PROTRACTING
PROTRACTS
PROTRUDE
PROTRUDED
PROTRUDES
PROTRUDING
PROTYL
PROTYLE
PROTYLES
PROTYLS
PROUD
PROUDER
PROUDEST
PROUDISH
PROUDLY
PROUDNESS
PROUDNESSES
PROUL
PROULED
PROULER
PROULERS
PROULING
PROULS
PROUSTITE
PROUSTITES
PROVABLE
PROVABLY
PROVAND
PROVANDS
PROVANT
PROVE
PROVEABLE
PROVEABLY
PROVED
PROVEDOR
PROVEDORE
PROVEDORES
PROVEDORS
PROVEN
PROVEND
PROVENDER
PROVENDERED
PROVENDERING
PROVENDERS
PROVENDS
PROVER
PROVERB
PROVERBED
PROVERBING
PROVERBS
PROVERS
PROVES
PROVIANT
PROVIANTS
PROVIDE
PROVIDED
PROVIDENT
PROVIDER

PROVIDERS
PROVIDES
PROVIDING
PROVIDOR
PROVIDORS
PROVINCE
PROVINCES
PROVINE
PROVINED
PROVINES
PROVING
PROVINING
PROVIRAL
PROVIRUS
PROVIRUSES
PROVISION
PROVISIONED
PROVISIONING
PROVISIONS
PROVISO
PROVISOES
PROVISOR
PROVISORS
PROVISORY
PROVISOS
PROVOCANT
PROVOCANTS
PROVOKE
PROVOKED
PROVOKER
PROVOKERS
PROVOKES
PROVOKING
PROVOST
PROVOSTRIES
PROVOSTRY
PROVOSTS
PROW
PROWESS
PROWESSED
PROWESSES
PROWEST
PROWL
PROWLED
PROWLER
PROWLERS
PROWLING
PROWLINGS
PROWLS
PROWS
PROXIES
PROXIMAL
PROXIMATE
PROXIMITIES
PROXIMITY
PROXIMO
PROXY
PROYN
PROYNE
PROYNED
PROYNES
PROYNING
PROYNS
PROZYMITE
PROZYMITES
PRUDE
PRUDENCE
PRUDENCES
PRUDENT
PRUDENTLY

PRUDERIES
PRUDERY
PRUDES
PRUDISH
PRUDISHLY
PRUH
PRUINA
PRUINAS
PRUINE
PRUINES
PRUINOSE
PRUNE
PRUNED
PRUNELLA
PRUNELLAS
PRUNELLE
PRUNELLES
PRUNELLO
PRUNELLOS
PRUNER
PRUNERS
PRUNES
PRUNING
PRUNINGS
PRUNT
PRUNTED
PRUNTS
PRURIENCE
PRURIENCES
PRURIENCIES
PRURIENCY
PRURIENT
PRURIGO
PRURIGOS
PRURITIC
PRURITUS
PRURITUSES
PRUSSIATE
PRUSSIATES
PRUSSIC
PRY
PRYER
PRYERS
PRYING
PRYINGLY
PRYINGS
PRYS
PRYSE
PRYSED
PRYSES
PRYSING
PRYTANEA
PRYTANEUM
PRYTHEE
PSALM
PSALMIST
PSALMISTS
PSALMODIC
PSALMODIES
PSALMODY
PSALMS
PSALTER
PSALTERIA
PSALTERIES
PSALTERS
PSALTERY
PSALTRESS
PSALTRESSES
PSAMMITE
PSAMMITES

PSAMMITIC
PSELLISM
PSELLISMS
PSEPHISM
PSEPHISMS
PSEPHITE
PSEPHITES
PSEPHITIC
PSEUD
PSEUDAXES
PSEUDAXIS
PSEUDERIES
PSEUDERY
PSEUDISH
PSEUDO
PSEUDONYM
PSEUDONYMS
PSEUDOPOD
PSEUDOPODS
PSEUDS
PSHAW
PSHAWED
PSHAWING
PSHAWS
PSI
PSILOSES
PSILOSIS
PSILOTIC
PSIONIC
PSIS
PSOAS
PSOASES
PSORA
PSORAS
PSORIASES
PSORIASIS
PSORIATIC
PSORIC
PSST
PST
PSYCH
PSYCHE
PSYCHED
PSYCHES
PSYCHIC
PSYCHICAL
PSYCHICS
PSYCHING
PSYCHISM
PSYCHISMS
PSYCHIST
PSYCHISTS
PSYCHO
PSYCHOGAS
PSYCHOGASES
PSYCHOID
PSYCHOIDS
PSYCHOS
PSYCHOSES
PSYCHOSIS
PSYCHOTIC
PSYCHOTICS
PSYCHS
PSYOP
PSYOPS
PSYWAR
PSYWARS
PTARMIC
PTARMICS
PTARMIGAN

PTARMIGANS
PTERIA
PTERIN
PTERINS
PTERION
PTEROPOD
PTEROPODS
PTEROSAUR
PTEROSAURS
PTERYGIA
PTERYGIAL
PTERYGIUM
PTERYGOID
PTERYGOIDS
PTERYLA
PTERYLAE
PTILOSES
PTILOSIS
PTISAN
PTISANS
PTOMAINE
PTOMAINES
PTOSES
PTOSIS
PTYALIN
PTYALINS
PTYALISE
PTYALISED
PTYALISES
PTYALISING
PTYALISM
PTYALISMS
PTYALIZE
PTYALIZED
PTYALIZES
PTYALIZING
PTYXES
PTYXIS
PTYXISES
PUB
PUBERAL
PUBERTAL
PUBERTIES
PUBERTY
PUBES
PUBESCENT
PUBIC
PUBIS
PUBISES
PUBLIC
PUBLICAN
PUBLICANS
PUBLICISE
PUBLICISED
PUBLICISES
PUBLICISING
PUBLICIST
PUBLICISTS
PUBLICITIES
PUBLICITY
PUBLICIZE
PUBLICIZED
PUBLICIZES
PUBLICIZING
PUBLICLY
PUBLICS
PUBLISH
PUBLISHED
PUBLISHER
PUBLISHERS

PUBLISHES
PUBLISHING
PUBS
PUCCOON
PUCCOONS
PUCE
PUCELAGE
PUCELAGES
PUCELLE
PUCELLES
PUCES
PUCK
PUCKA
PUCKER
PUCKERED
PUCKERING
PUCKERS
PUCKERY
PUCKFIST
PUCKFISTS
PUCKISH
PUCKS
PUD
PUDDEN
PUDDENING
PUDDENINGS
PUDDENS
PUDDER
PUDDERED
PUDDERING
PUDDERS
PUDDIES
PUDDING
PUDDINGS
PUDDINGY
PUDDLE
PUDDLED
PUDDLER
PUDDLERS
PUDDLES
PUDDLIER
PUDDLIEST
PUDDLING
PUDDLINGS
PUDDLY
PUDDOCK
PUDDOCKS
PUDDY
PUDENCIES
PUDENCY
PUDENDA
PUDENDAL
PUDENDOUS
PUDENDUM
PUDENT
PUDGE
PUDGES
PUDGIER
PUDGIEST
PUDGINESS
PUDGINESSES
PUDGY
PUDIBUND
PUDIC
PUDICITIES
PUDICITY
PUDOR
PUDORS
PUDS
PUDSEY

PUDSIER
PUDSIEST
PUDSY
PUEBLO
PUEBLOS
PUER
PUERED
PUERILE
PUERILISM
PUERILISMS
PUERILITIES
PUERILITY
PUERING
PUERPERAL
PUERS
PUFF
PUFFBALL
PUFFBALLS
PUFFED
PUFFER
PUFFERIES
PUFFERS
PUFFERY
PUFFIER
PUFFIEST
PUFFILY
PUFFIN
PUFFINESS
PUFFINESSES
PUFFING
PUFFINGLY
PUFFINGS
PUFFINS
PUFFS
PUFFY
PUG
PUGGAREE
PUGGAREES
PUGGED
PUGGERIES
PUGGERY
PUGGIER
PUGGIES
PUGGIEST
PUGGING
PUGGINGS
PUGGISH
PUGGREE
PUGGREES
PUGGY
PUGH
PUGIL
PUGILISM
PUGILISMS
PUGILIST
PUGILISTS
PUGILS
PUGNACITIES
PUGNACITY
PUGS
PUH
PUIR
PUIRER
PUIREST
PUISNE
PUISNES
PUISNY
PUISSANCE
PUISSANCES
PUISSANT

PUISSAUNT
PUJA
PUJAS
PUKE
PUKED
PUKER
PUKERS
PUKES
PUKING
PUKKA
PULDRON
PULDRONS
PULE
PULED
PULER
PULERS
PULES
PULICIDE
PULICIDES
PULIER
PULIEST
PULING
PULINGLY
PULINGS
PULK
PULKA
PULKAS
PULKHA
PULKHAS
PULKS
PULL
PULLED
PULLER
PULLERS
PULLET
PULLETS
PULLEY
PULLEYS
PULLING
PULLOVER
PULLOVERS
PULLS
PULLULATE
PULLULATED
PULLULATES
PULLULATING
PULMO
PULMONARY
PULMONATE
PULMONATES
PULMONES
PULMONIC
PULMONICS
PULP
PULPBOARD
PULPBOARDS
PULPED
PULPER
PULPERS
PULPIER
PULPIEST
PULPIFIED
PULPIFIES
PULPIFY
PULPIFYING
PULPILY
PULPINESS
PULPINESSES
PULPING
PULPIT

PULPITED
PULPITEER
PULPITEERS
PULPITER
PULPITERS
PULPITRIES
PULPITRY
PULPITS
PULPITUM
PULPITUMS
PULPMILL
PULPMILLS
PULPOUS
PULPS
PULPSTONE
PULPSTONES
PULPWOOD
PULPWOODS
PULPY
PULQUE
PULQUES
PULSAR
PULSARS
PULSATE
PULSATED
PULSATES
PULSATILE
PULSATING
PULSATION
PULSATIONS
PULSATIVE
PULSATOR
PULSATORS
PULSATORY
PULSE
PULSED
PULSEJET
PULSEJETS
PULSELESS
PULSES
PULSIDGE
PULSIDGES
PULSIFIC
PULSING
PULSOJET
PULSOJETS
PULTAN
PULTANS
PULTON
PULTONS
PULTOON
PULTOONS
PULTUN
PULTUNS
PULTURE
PULTURES
PULU
PULUS
PULVER
PULVERED
PULVERINE
PULVERINES
PULVERING
PULVERISE
PULVERISED
PULVERISES
PULVERISING
PULVERIZE
PULVERIZED
PULVERIZES

PULVERIZING
PULVEROUS
PULVERS
PULVIL
PULVILIO
PULVILIOS
PULVILLAR
PULVILLE
PULVILLED
PULVILLES
PULVILLI
PULVILLING
PULVILLIO
PULVILLIOS
PULVILLUS
PULVILS
PULVINAR
PULVINARS
PULVINATE
PULVINI
PULVINULE
PULVINULES
PULVINUS
PULWAR
PULWARS
PULY
PUMA
PUMAS
PUMELO
PUMELOS
PUMICATE
PUMICATED
PUMICATES
PUMICATING
PUMICE
PUMICED
PUMICEOUS
PUMICES
PUMICING
PUMIE
PUMIES
PUMMEL
PUMMELLED
PUMMELLING
PUMMELS
PUMP
PUMPED
PUMPER
PUMPERS
PUMPING
PUMPION
PUMPIONS
PUMPKIN
PUMPKINS
PUMPS
PUMY
PUN
PUNA
PUNALUA
PUNALUAN
PUNALUAS
PUNAS
PUNCE
PUNCES
PUNCH
PUNCHED
PUNCHEON
PUNCHEONS
PUNCHER
PUNCHERS

PUNCHES
PUNCHIER
PUNCHIEST
PUNCHING
PUNCHY
PUNCTA
PUNCTATE
PUNCTATED
PUNCTATOR
PUNCTATORS
PUNCTILIO
PUNCTILIOS
PUNCTO
PUNCTOS
PUNCTUAL
PUNCTUATE
PUNCTUATED
PUNCTUATES
PUNCTUATING
PUNCTULE
PUNCTULES
PUNCTUM
PUNCTURE
PUNCTURED
PUNCTURES
PUNCTURING
PUNDIT
PUNDITRIES
PUNDITRY
PUNDITS
PUNDONOR
PUNDONORES
PUNGENCE
PUNGENCES
PUNGENCIES
PUNGENCY
PUNGENT
PUNGENTLY
PUNIER
PUNIEST
PUNILY
PUNINESS
PUNINESSES
PUNISH
PUNISHED
PUNISHER
PUNISHERS
PUNISHES
PUNISHING
PUNITION
PUNITIONS
PUNITIVE
PUNITORY
PUNK
PUNKA
PUNKAH
PUNKAHS
PUNKAS
PUNKINESS
PUNKINESSES
PUNKS
PUNNED
PUNNER
PUNNERS
PUNNET
PUNNETS
PUNNING
PUNNINGS
PUNS
PUNSTER

PUNSTERS
PUNT
PUNTED
PUNTEE
PUNTEES
PUNTER
PUNTERS
PUNTIES
PUNTING
PUNTO
PUNTOS
PUNTS
PUNTSMAN
PUNTSMEN
PUNTY
PUNY
PUP
PUPA
PUPAE
PUPAL
PUPARIA
PUPARIAL
PUPARIUM
PUPAS
PUPATE
PUPATED
PUPATES
PUPATING
PUPATION
PUPATIONS
PUPFISH
PUPFISHES
PUPIL
PUPILAGE
PUPILAGES
PUPILARY
PUPILATE
PUPILLAGE
PUPILLAGES
PUPILLARY
PUPILLATE
PUPILS
PUPPED
PUPPET
PUPPETEER
PUPPETEERS
PUPPETRIES
PUPPETRY
PUPPETS
PUPPIED
PUPPIES
PUPPING
PUPPODUM
PUPPODUMS
PUPPY
PUPPYDOM
PUPPYDOMS
PUPPYHOOD
PUPPYHOODS
PUPPYING
PUPPYISH
PUPPYISM
PUPPYISMS
PUPS
PUPUNHA
PUPUNHAS
PUR
PURBLIND
PURCHASE
PURCHASED

PURCHASER
PURCHASERS
PURCHASES
PURCHASING
PURDAH
PURDAHS
PURDONIUM
PURDONIUMS
PURE
PURED
PURÉE
PURÉED
PURÉEING
PURÉES
PURELY
PURENESS
PURENESSES
PURER
PURES
PUREST
PURFLE
PURFLED
PURFLES
PURFLING
PURFLINGS
PURFLY
PURGATION
PURGATIONS
PURGATIVE
PURGATIVES
PURGATORIES
PURGATORY
PURGE
PURGED
PURGER
PURGERS
PURGES
PURGING
PURGINGS
PURI
PURIFIED
PURIFIER
PURIFIERS
PURIFIES
PURIFY
PURIFYING
PURIM
PURIMS
PURIN
PURINE
PURINES
PURING
PURINS
PURIS
PURISM
PURISMS
PURIST
PURISTIC
PURISTS
PURITAN
PURITANIC
PURITANS
PURITIES
PURITY
PURL
PURLED
PURLER
PURLERS
PURLICUE
PURLICUED

PURLICUES
PURLICUING
PURLIEU
PURLIEUS
PURLIN
PURLINE
PURLINES
PURLING
PURLINGS
PURLINS
PURLOIN
PURLOINED
PURLOINER
PURLOINERS
PURLOINING
PURLOINS
PURLS
PURPIE
PURPIES
PURPLE
PURPLED
PURPLER
PURPLES
PURPLEST
PURPLING
PURPLISH
PURPLY
PURPORT
PURPORTED
PURPORTING
PURPORTS
PURPOSE
PURPOSED
PURPOSELY
PURPOSES
PURPOSING
PURPOSIVE
PURPURA
PURPURAS
PURPURE
PURPUREAL
PURPURES
PURPURIC
PURPURIN
PURPURINS
PURPY
PURR
PURRED
PURRING
PURRINGLY
PURRINGS
PURRS
PURS
PURSE
PURSED
PURSEFUL
PURSEFULS
PURSER
PURSERS
PURSES
PURSEW
PURSEWED
PURSEWING
PURSEWS
PURSIER
PURSIEST
PURSINESS
PURSINESSES
PURSING
PURSLAIN

PURSLAINS
PURSLANE
PURSLANES
PURSUABLE
PURSUAL
PURSUALS
PURSUANCE
PURSUANCES
PURSUANT
PURSUE
PURSUED
PURSUER
PURSUERS
PURSUES
PURSUING
PURSUINGS
PURSUIT
PURSUITS
PURSY
PURTIER
PURTIEST
PURTRAID
PURTRAYD
PURTY
PURULENCE
PURULENCES
PURULENCIES
PURULENCY
PURULENT
PURVEY
PURVEYED
PURVEYING
PURVEYOR
PURVEYORS
PURVEYS
PURVIEW
PURVIEWS
PUS
PUSES
PUSH
PUSHED
PUSHER
PUSHERS
PUSHES
PUSHFUL
PUSHFULLY
PUSHIER
PUSHIEST
PUSHINESS
PUSHINESSES
PUSHING
PUSHINGLY
PUSHROD
PUSHRODS
PUSHY
PUSLE
PUSLED
PUSLES
PUSLING
PUSS
PUSSEL
PUSSELS
PUSSES
PUSSIES
PUSSY
PUSSYFOOT
PUSSYFOOTED
PUSSYFOOTING
PUSSYFOOTS
PUSTULANT

PUSTULANTS
PUSTULAR
PUSTULATE
PUSTULATED
PUSTULATES
PUSTULATING
PUSTULE
PUSTULES
PUSTULOUS
PUT
PUTAMEN
PUTAMINA
PUTATIVE
PUTCHER
PUTCHERS
PUTCHOCK
PUTCHOCKS
PUTCHUK
PUTCHUKS
PUTEAL
PUTEALS
PUTELI
PUTELIS
PUTID
PUTLOCK
PUTLOCKS
PUTLOG
PUTLOGS
PUTOIS
PUTREFIED
PUTREFIES
PUTREFY
PUTREFYING
PUTRID
PUTRIDER
PUTRIDEST
PUTRIDITIES
PUTRIDITY
PUTRIDLY
PUTS
PUTSCH
PUTSCHES
PUTT
PUTTED
PUTTEE
PUTTEES
PUTTEN
PUTTER
PUTTERED
PUTTERING
PUTTERS
PUTTI
PUTTIE
PUTTIED
PUTTIER
PUTTIERS
PUTTIES
PUTTING
PUTTINGS
PUTTO
PUTTOCK
PUTTOCKS
PUTTS
PUTTY
PUTTYING
PUTURE
PUTURES
PUTZ
PUTZES
PUY

PUYS
PUZEL
PUZELS
PUZZEL
PUZZELS
PUZZLE
PUZZLED
PUZZLEDOM
PUZZLEDOMS
PUZZLER
PUZZLERS
PUZZLES
PUZZLING
PUZZOLANA
PUZZOLANAS
PYAEMIA
PYAEMIAS
PYAEMIC
PYAT
PYATS
PYCNIC
PYCNIDIA
PYCNIDIUM
PYCNIDIUMS
PYCNITE
PYCNITES
PYCNON
PYCNONS
PYE
PYEBALD
PYEBALDS
PYEING
PYELITIC
PYELITIS
PYELITISES
PYELOGRAM
PYELOGRAMS
PYEMIA
PYEMIAS
PYENGADU
PYENGADUS
PYES
PYET
PYETS
PYGAL
PYGALS
PYGARG
PYGARGS
PYGIDIA
PYGIDIAL
PYGIDIUM
PYGIDIUMS
PYGMAEAN
PYGMEAN
PYGMIES
PYGMOID
PYGMY
PYGOSTYLE
PYGOSTYLES
PYJAMAED
PYJAMAS
PYKNIC
PYKNOSOME
PYKNOSOMES
PYLON
PYLONS
PYLORIC
PYLORUS
PYLORUSES
PYNE

PYNED
PYNES
PYNING
PYOGENIC
PYOID
PYONER
PYONERS
PYONINGS
PYORRHOEA
PYORRHOEAS
PYOT
PYOTS
PYRACANTH
PYRACANTHS
PYRAL
PYRALID
PYRALIDS
PYRALIS
PYRALISES
PYRAMID
PYRAMIDAL
PYRAMIDED
PYRAMIDES
PYRAMIDIC
PYRAMIDING
PYRAMIDON
PYRAMIDONS
PYRAMIDS
PYRAMIS
PYRAMISES
PYRE
PYRENE
PYRENEITE
PYRENEITES
PYRENES
PYRENOID
PYRENOIDS
PYRES
PYRETHRIN
PYRETHRINS
PYRETHRUM
PYRETHRUMS
PYRETIC
PYREXIA
PYREXIAL
PYREXIAS
PYREXIC
PYRIDINE
PYRIDINES
PYRIDOXIN
PYRIDOXINS
PYRIFORM
PYRITE
PYRITES
PYRITIC
PYRITICAL
PYRITISE
PYRITISED
PYRITISES
PYRITISING
PYRITIZE
PYRITIZED
PYRITIZES
PYRITIZING
PYRITOUS
PYRO
PYROCLAST
PYROCLASTS
PYROGEN
PYROGENIC

PYROGENS
PYROLATER
PYROLATERS
PYROLATRIES
PYROLATRY
PYROLYSE
PYROLYSED
PYROLYSES
PYROLYSING
PYROLYSIS
PYROLYTIC
PYROLYZE
PYROLYZED
PYROLYZES
PYROLYZING

PYROMANCIES
PYROMANCY
PYROMANIA
PYROMANIAS
PYROMETER
PYROMETERS
PYROMETRIES
PYROMETRY
PYROPE
PYROPES
PYROPHONE
PYROPHONES
PYROPUS
PYROPUSES
PYROS

PYROSCOPE
PYROSCOPES
PYROSES
PYROSIS
PYROSOME
PYROSOMES
PYROSTAT
PYROSTATS
PYROXENE
PYROXENES
PYROXENIC
PYROXYLE
PYROXYLES
PYROXYLIC
PYROXYLIN

PYROXYLINS
PYRRHIC
PYRRHICS
PYRRHOUS
PYRROLE
PYRROLES
PYRUVATE
PYRUVATES
PYTHIUM
PYTHIUMS
PYTHON
PYTHONESS
PYTHONESSES
PYTHONIC
PYTHONS

PYURIA
PYURIAS
PYX
PYXED
PYXES
PYXIDES
PYXIDIA
PYXIDIUM
PYXING
PYXIS
PZAZZ
PZAZZES

# Q

| | | | | |
|---|---|---|---|---|
| QADI | QUADRUPLY | QUALE | QUARKS | QUASI |
| QADIS | QUADS | QUALIA | QUARREL | QUASSIA |
| QALAMDAN | QUAERE | QUALIFIED | QUARRELLED | QUASSIAS |
| QALAMDANS | QUAERED | QUALIFIER | QUARRELLING | QUAT |
| QANAT | QUAEREING | QUALIFIERS | QUARRELLINGS | QUATCH |
| QANATS | QUAERES | QUALIFIES | QUARRELS | QUATCHED |
| QAT | QUAERITUR | QUALIFY | QUARRIED | QUATCHES |
| QATS | QUAESITUM | QUALIFYING | QUARRIER | QUATCHING |
| QIBLA | QUAESITUMS | QUALIFYINGS | QUARRIERS | QUATORZE |
| QIBLAS | QUAESTOR | QUALITIED | QUARRIES | QUATORZES |
| QIGONG | QUAESTORS | QUALITIES | QUARRY | QUATRAIN |
| QIGONGS | QUAFF | QUALITY | QUARRYING | QUATRAINS |
| QINTAR | QUAFFED | QUALM | QUARRYMAN | QUATS |
| QINTARS | QUAFFER | QUALMIER | QUARRYMEN | QUAVER |
| QUA | QUAFFERS | QUALMIEST | QUART | QUAVERED |
| QUACK | QUAFFING | QUALMING | QUARTAN | QUAVERER |
| QUACKED | QUAFFS | QUALMISH | QUARTANS | QUAVERERS |
| QUACKERIES | QUAG | QUALMLESS | QUARTE | QUAVERING |
| QUACKERY | QUAGGA | QUALMS | QUARTER | QUAVERINGS |
| QUACKING | QUAGGAS | QUALMY | QUARTERED | QUAVERS |
| QUACKLE | QUAGGIER | QUAMASH | QUARTERING | QUAVERY |
| QUACKLED | QUAGGIEST | QUAMASHES | QUARTERINGS | QUAY |
| QUACKLES | QUAGGY | QUANDANG | QUARTERLIES | QUAYAGE |
| QUACKLING | QUAGMIRE | QUANDANGS | QUARTERLY | QUAYAGES |
| QUACKS | QUAGMIRED | QUANDARIES | QUARTERN | QUAYD |
| QUAD | QUAGMIRES | QUANDARY | QUARTERNS | QUAYS |
| QUADDED | QUAGMIRIER | QUANDONG | QUARTERS | QUAYSIDE |
| QUADDING | QUAGMIRIEST | QUANDONGS | QUARTES | QUAYSIDES |
| QUADRANS | QUAGMIRING | QUANGO | QUARTET | QUEACH |
| QUADRANT | QUAGMIRY | QUANGOS | QUARTETS | QUEACHES |
| QUADRANTES | QUAGS | QUANNET | QUARTETT | QUEACHY |
| QUADRANTS | QUAHAUG | QUANNETS | QUARTETTE | QUEAN |
| QUADRAT | QUAHAUGS | QUANT | QUARTETTES | QUEANS |
| QUADRATE | QUAHOG | QUANTA | QUARTETTI | QUEASIER |
| QUADRATED | QUAHOGS | QUANTAL | QUARTETTO | QUEASIEST |
| QUADRATES | QUAICH | QUANTED | QUARTETTS | QUEASILY |
| QUADRATIC | QUAICHS | QUANTIC | QUARTIC | QUEASY |
| QUADRATICS | QUAIGH | QUANTICAL | QUARTICS | QUEAZIER |
| QUADRATING | QUAIGHS | QUANTICS | QUARTIER | QUEAZIEST |
| QUADRATS | QUAIL | QUANTIFIED | QUARTIERS | QUEAZY |
| QUADRATUS | QUAILED | QUANTIFIES | QUARTILE | QUEBRACHO |
| QUADRATUSES | QUAILING | QUANTIFY | QUARTILES | QUEBRACHOS |
| QUADRELLA | QUAILINGS | QUANTIFYING | QUARTO | QUEECHY |
| QUADRELLAS | QUAILS | QUANTING | QUARTOS | QUEEN |
| QUADRIC | QUAINT | QUANTISE | QUARTS | QUEENDOM |
| QUADRIFID | QUAINTER | QUANTISED | QUARTZ | QUEENDOMS |
| QUADRIGA | QUAINTEST | QUANTISES | QUARTZES | QUEENED |
| QUADRIGAE | QUAINTLY | QUANTISING | QUARTZIER | QUEENHOOD |
| QUADRILLE | QUAIR | QUANTITIES | QUARTZIEST | QUEENHOODS |
| QUADRILLED | QUAIRS | QUANTITY | QUARTZITE | QUEENING |
| QUADRILLES | QUAKE | QUANTIZE | QUARTZITES | QUEENINGS |
| QUADRILLING | QUAKED | QUANTIZED | QUARTZOSE | QUEENITE |
| QUADROON | QUAKES | QUANTIZES | QUARTZY | QUEENITES |
| QUADROONS | QUAKIER | QUANTIZING | QUASAR | QUEENLESS |
| QUADRUMAN | QUAKIEST | QUANTONG | QUASARS | QUEENLET |
| QUADRUMANS | QUAKINESS | QUANTONGS | QUASH | QUEENLETS |
| QUADRUPED | QUAKINESSES | QUANTS | QUASHED | QUEENLIER |
| QUADRUPEDS | QUAKING | QUANTUM | QUASHEE | QUEENLIEST |
| QUADRUPLE | QUAKINGLY | QUARENDEN | QUASHEES | QUEENLY |
| QUADRUPLED | QUAKINGS | QUARENDENS | QUASHES | QUEENS |
| QUADRUPLES | QUAKY | QUARENDER | QUASHIE | QUEENSHIP |
| QUADRUPLIES | QUALAMDAN | QUARENDERS | QUASHIES | QUEENSHIPS |
| QUADRUPLING | QUALAMDANS | QUARK | QUASHING | QUEER |

| | | | | |
|---|---|---|---|---|
| QUEERDOM | QUESTIONS | QUICKSTEPPING | QUILLMAN | QUINTETTES |
| QUEERDOMS | QUESTOR | QUICKSTEPS | QUILLMEN | QUINTETTI |
| QUEERED | QUESTORS | QUID | QUILLON | QUINTETTO |
| QUEERER | QUESTRIST | QUIDAM | QUILLONS | QUINTETTS |
| QUEEREST | QUESTRISTS | QUIDAMS | QUILLS | QUINTIC |
| QUEERING | QUESTS | QUIDDANIES | QUILLWORT | QUINTILE |
| QUEERISH | QUETCH | QUIDDANY | QUILLWORTS | QUINTILES |
| QUEERITIES | QUETCHED | QUIDDIT | QUILT | QUINTROON |
| QUEERITY | QUETCHES | QUIDDITIES | QUILTED | QUINTROONS |
| QUEERLY | QUETCHING | QUIDDITS | QUILTER | QUINTS |
| QUEERNESS | QUETHE | QUIDDITY | QUILTERS | QUINTUPLE |
| QUEERNESSES | QUETHES | QUIDDLE | QUILTING | QUINTUPLED |
| QUEERS | QUETHING | QUIDDLED | QUILTINGS | QUINTUPLES |
| QUEEST | QUETSCH | QUIDDLER | QUILTS | QUINTUPLING |
| QUEESTS | QUETSCHES | QUIDDLERS | QUIM | QUINZE |
| QUEINT | QUETZAL | QUIDDLES | QUIMS | QUINZES |
| QUELCH | QUETZALS | QUIDDLING | QUIN | QUIP |
| QUELCHED | QUEUE | QUIDNUNC | QUINA | QUIPO |
| QUELCHES | QUEUED | QUIDNUNCS | QUINARY | QUIPOS |
| QUELCHING | QUEUEING | QUIDS | QUINAS | QUIPPED |
| QUELEA | QUEUEINGS | QUIESCE | QUINATE | QUIPPING |
| QUELEAS | QUEUES | QUIESCED | QUINCE | QUIPPISH |
| QUELL | QUEUING | QUIESCENT | QUINCES | QUIPS |
| QUELLED | QUEUINGS | QUIESCES | QUINCHE | QUIPSTER |
| QUELLER | QUEY | QUIESCING | QUINCHED | QUIPSTERS |
| QUELLERS | QUEYN | QUIET | QUINCHES | QUIPU |
| QUELLING | QUEYNIE | QUIETED | QUINCHING | QUIPUS |
| QUELLS | QUEYNIES | QUIETEN | QUINCUNX | QUIRE |
| QUEME | QUEYNS | QUIETENED | QUINCUNXES | QUIRED |
| QUEMED | QUEYS | QUIETENING | QUINE | QUIRES |
| QUEMES | QUIBBLE | QUIETENINGS | QUINELLA | QUIRING |
| QUEMING | QUIBBLED | QUIETENS | QUINELLAS | QUIRISTER |
| QUENA | QUIBBLER | QUIETER | QUINES | QUIRISTERS |
| QUENAS | QUIBBLERS | QUIETERS | QUINIC | QUIRK |
| QUENCH | QUIBBLES | QUIETEST | QUINIDINE | QUIRKED |
| QUENCHED | QUIBBLING | QUIETING | QUINIDINES | QUIRKIER |
| QUENCHER | QUIBBLINGS | QUIETINGS | QUINIE | QUIRKIEST |
| QUENCHERS | QUIBLIN | QUIETISM | QUINIES | QUIRKING |
| QUENCHES | QUIBLINS | QUIETISMS | QUININE | QUIRKISH |
| QUENCHING | QUICH | QUIETIST | QUININES | QUIRKS |
| QUENCHINGS | QUICHE | QUIETISTS | QUINNAT | QUIRKY |
| QUENELLE | QUICHED | QUIETIVE | QUINNATS | QUIRT |
| QUENELLES | QUICHES | QUIETIVES | QUINOA | QUIRTED |
| QUEP | QUICHING | QUIETLY | QUINOAS | QUIRTING |
| QUERCETUM | QUICK | QUIETNESS | QUINOL | QUIRTS |
| QUERCETUMS | QUICKBEAM | QUIETNESSES | QUINOLINE | QUISLING |
| QUERIED | QUICKBEAMS | QUIETS | QUINOLINES | QUISLINGS |
| QUERIES | QUICKEN | QUIETSOME | QUINOLS | QUIST |
| QUERIMONIES | QUICKENED | QUIETUDE | QUINONE | QUISTS |
| QUERIMONY | QUICKENER | QUIETUDES | QUINONES | QUIT |
| QUERIST | QUICKENERS | QUIETUS | QUINQUINA | QUITCH |
| QUERISTS | QUICKENING | QUIETUSES | QUINQUINAS | QUITCHED |
| QUERN | QUICKENINGS | QUIFF | QUINS | QUITCHES |
| QUERNS | QUICKENS | QUIFFS | QUINSIED | QUITCHING |
| QUERULOUS | QUICKER | QUIGHT | QUINSIES | QUITE |
| QUERY | QUICKEST | QUIGHTED | QUINSY | QUITED |
| QUERYING | QUICKIE | QUIGHTING | QUINT | QUITES |
| QUERYINGS | QUICKIES | QUIGHTS | QUINTA | QUITING |
| QUEST | QUICKLIME | QUILL | QUINTAIN | QUITS |
| QUESTANT | QUICKLIMES | QUILLAI | QUINTAINS | QUITTAL |
| QUESTANTS | QUICKLY | QUILLAIA | QUINTAL | QUITTALS |
| QUESTED | QUICKNESS | QUILLAIAS | QUINTALS | QUITTANCE |
| QUESTER | QUICKNESSES | QUILLAIS | QUINTAN | QUITTANCED |
| QUESTERS | QUICKS | QUILLAJA | QUINTAS | QUITTANCES |
| QUESTING | QUICKSAND | QUILLAJAS | QUINTE | QUITTANCING |
| QUESTINGS | QUICKSANDS | QUILLED | QUINTES | QUITTED |
| QUESTION | QUICKSET | QUILLET | QUINTET | QUITTER |
| QUESTIONED | QUICKSETS | QUILLETS | QUINTETS | QUITTERS |
| QUESTIONING | QUICKSTEP | QUILLING | QUINTETT | QUITTING |
| QUESTIONINGS | QUICKSTEPPED | QUILLINGS | QUINTETTE | QUITTOR |

QUITTORS
QUIVER
QUIVERED
QUIVERFUL
QUIVERFULS
QUIVERING
QUIVERINGS
QUIVERISH
QUIVERS
QUIVERY
QUIXOTIC
QUIXOTISM
QUIXOTISMS
QUIXOTRIES
QUIXOTRY
QUIZ
QUIZZED
QUIZZER
QUIZZERIES
QUIZZERS
QUIZZERY

QUIZZES
QUIZZICAL
QUIZZIFIED
QUIZZIFIES
QUIZZIFY
QUIZZIFYING
QUIZZING
QUIZZINGS
QUOAD
QUOD
QUODDED
QUODDING
QUODLIBET
QUODLIBETS
QUODLIN
QUODLINS
QUODS
QUOIF
QUOIFED
QUOIFING
QUOIFS

QUOIN
QUOINED
QUOINING
QUOINS
QUOIST
QUOISTS
QUOIT
QUOITED
QUOITER
QUOITERS
QUOITING
QUOITS
QUOKKA
QUOKKAS
QUOLL
QUOLLS
QUONDAM
QUONK
QUONKED
QUONKING
QUONKS

QUOOKE
QUOP
QUOPPED
QUOPPING
QUOPS
QUORATE
QUORUM
QUORUMS
QUOTA
QUOTABLE
QUOTABLY
QUOTAS
QUOTATION
QUOTATIONS
QUOTATIVE
QUOTATIVES
QUOTE
QUOTED
QUOTER
QUOTERS
QUOTES

QUOTH
QUOTHA
QUOTIDIAN
QUOTIDIANS
QUOTIENT
QUOTIENTS
QUOTING
QUOTITION
QUOTITIONS
QUOTUM
QUOTUMS
QUYTE
QUYTED
QUYTES
QUYTING
QWERTIES
QWERTY
QWERTYS

# R

| | | | | |
|---|---|---|---|---|
| RABANNA | RACAHOUT | RACING | RADIALITIES | RADON |
| RABANNAS | RACAHOUTS | RACINGS | RADIALITY | RADONS |
| RABAT | RACCAHOUT | RACISM | RADIALIZE | RADS |
| RABATINE | RACCAHOUTS | RACISMS | RADIALIZED | RADULA |
| RABATINES | RACCOON | RACIST | RADIALIZES | RADULAE |
| RABATMENT | RACCOONS | RACISTS | RADIALIZING | RADULAR |
| RABATMENTS | RACE | RACK | RADIALLY | RADULATE |
| RABATO | RACED | RACKED | RADIALS | RAFALE |
| RABATOES | RACEGOER | RACKER | RADIAN | RAFALES |
| RABATS | RACEGOERS | RACKERS | RADIANCE | RAFF |
| RABATTE | RACEGOING | RACKET | RADIANCES | RAFFIA |
| RABATTED | RACEGOINGS | RACKETED | RADIANCIES | RAFFIAS |
| RABATTES | RACEHORSE | RACKETEER | RADIANCY | RAFFINATE |
| RABATTING | RACEHORSES | RACKETEERED | RADIANS | RAFFINATES |
| RABATTINGS | RACEMATE | RACKETEERING | RADIANT | RAFFINOSE |
| RABBET | RACEMATES | RACKETEERINGS | RADIANTLY | RAFFINOSES |
| RABBETED | RACEME | RACKETEERS | RADIANTS | RAFFISH |
| RABBETING | RACEMED | RACKETER | RADIATE | RAFFISHLY |
| RABBETS | RACEMES | RACKETERS | RADIATED | RAFFLE |
| RABBI | RACEMIC | RACKETING | RADIATELY | RAFFLED |
| RABBIN | RACEMISE | RACKETRIES | RADIATES | RAFFLER |
| RABBINATE | RACEMISED | RACKETRY | RADIATING | RAFFLERS |
| RABBINATES | RACEMISES | RACKETS | RADIATION | RAFFLES |
| RABBINIC | RACEMISING | RACKETT | RADIATIONS | RAFFLING |
| RABBINISM | RACEMISM | RACKETTS | RADIATIVE | RAFFS |
| RABBINISMS | RACEMISMS | RACKETY | RADIATOR | RAFT |
| RABBINIST | RACEMIZE | RACKING | RADIATORS | RAFTED |
| RABBINISTS | RACEMIZED | RACKINGS | RADIATORY | RAFTER |
| RABBINITE | RACEMIZES | RACKS | RADICAL | RAFTERED |
| RABBINITES | RACEMIZING | RACKWORK | RADICALLY | RAFTERING |
| RABBINS | RACEMOSE | RACKWORKS | RADICALS | RAFTERINGS |
| RABBIS | RACER | RACLETTE | RADICANT | RAFTERS |
| RABBIT | RACERS | RACLETTES | RADICATE | RAFTING |
| RABBITED | RACES | RACLOIR | RADICATED | RAFTMAN |
| RABBITER | RACEWAY | RACLOIRS | RADICATES | RAFTMEN |
| RABBITERS | RACEWAYS | RACON | RADICATING | RAFTS |
| RABBITING | RACH | RACONS | RADICEL | RAFTSMAN |
| RABBITRIES | RACHE | RACONTEUR | RADICELS | RAFTSMEN |
| RABBITRY | RACHES | RACONTEURS | RADICES | RAG |
| RABBITS | RACHIAL | RACOON | RADICLE | RAGA |
| RABBITY | RACHIDES | RACOONS | RADICLES | RAGAS |
| RABBLE | RACHIDIAL | RACQUET | RADICULAR | RAGBOLT |
| RABBLED | RACHIDIAN | RACQUETS | RADICULE | RAGBOLTS |
| RABBLER | RACHILLA | RACY | RADICULES | RAGDE |
| RABBLERS | RACHILLAS | RAD | RADII | RAGE |
| RABBLES | RACHIS | RADAR | RADIO | RAGED |
| RABBLING | RACHISES | RADARS | RADIOED | RAGEE |
| RABBLINGS | RACHITIC | RADDLE | RADIOGRAM | RAGEES |
| RABBONI | RACHITIS | RADDLED | RADIOGRAMS | RAGEFUL |
| RABBONIS | RACHITISES | RADDLEMAN | RADIOING | RAGER |
| RABI | RACIAL | RADDLEMEN | RADIOLOGIES | RAGERS |
| RABIC | RACIALISM | RADDLES | RADIOLOGY | RAGES |
| RABID | RACIALISMS | RADDLING | RADIONICS | RAGG |
| RABIDER | RACIALIST | RADDOCKE | RADIOS | RAGGED |
| RABIDEST | RACIALISTS | RADDOCKES | RADISH | RAGGEDER |
| RABIDITIES | RACIALLY | RADE | RADISHES | RAGGEDEST |
| RABIDITY | RACIATION | RADIAL | RADIUM | RAGGEDLY |
| RABIDLY | RACIATIONS | RADIALE | RADIUMS | RAGGEDY |
| RABIDNESS | RACIER | RADIALIA | RADIUS | RAGGEE |
| RABIDNESSES | RACIEST | RADIALISE | RADIUSES | RAGGEES |
| RABIES | RACILY | RADIALISED | RADIX | RAGGERIES |
| RABIS | RACINESS | RADIALISES | RADOME | RAGGERY |
| RACA | RACINESSES | RADIALISING | RADOMES | RAGGIER |

| | | | | |
|---|---|---|---|---|
| RAGGIES | RAILING | RAIYAT | RAMEES | RAMULAR |
| RAGGIEST | RAILINGLY | RAIYATS | RAMEKIN | RAMULI |
| RAGGING | RAILINGS | RAJ | RAMEKINS | RAMULOSE |
| RAGGINGS | RAILLERIES | RAJA | RAMENTA | RAMULOUS |
| RAGGLE | RAILLERY | RAJAH | RAMENTUM | RAMULUS |
| RAGGLED | RAILLESS | RAJAHS | RAMEOUS | RAMUS |
| RAGGLES | RAILLIES | RAJAHSHIP | RAMEQUIN | RAN |
| RAGGLING | RAILLY | RAJAHSHIPS | RAMEQUINS | RANA |
| RAGGS | RAILMAN | RAJAS | RAMFEEZLE | RANARIAN |
| RAGGY | RAILMEN | RAJASHIP | RAMFEEZLED | RANARIUM |
| RAGI | RAILROAD | RAJASHIPS | RAMFEEZLES | RANARIUMS |
| RAGING | RAILROADED | RAJES | RAMFEEZLING | RANAS |
| RAGINGLY | RAILROADING | RAKE | RAMI | RANCE |
| RAGINI | RAILROADS | RAKED | RAMIE | RANCED |
| RAGINIS | RAILS | RAKEE | RAMIES | RANCEL |
| RAGIS | RAILWAY | RAKEES | RAMIFIED | RANCELS |
| RAGLAN | RAILWAYS | RAKEHELL | RAMIFIES | RANCES |
| RAGLANS | RAIMENT | RAKEHELLS | RAMIFORM | RANCH |
| RAGMAN | RAIMENTS | RAKEHELLY | RAMIFY | RANCHED |
| RAGMANS | RAIN | RAKER | RAMIFYING | RANCHER |
| RAGMEN | RAINBAND | RAKERIES | RAMIS | RANCHERIA |
| RAGMENT | RAINBANDS | RAKERS | RAMMED | RANCHERIAS |
| RAGMENTS | RAINBOW | RAKERY | RAMMER | RANCHERO |
| RAGOUT | RAINBOWED | RAKES | RAMMERS | RANCHEROS |
| RAGOUTED | RAINBOWS | RAKESHAME | RAMMIES | RANCHERS |
| RAGOUTING | RAINBOWY | RAKESHAMES | RAMMING | RANCHES |
| RAGOUTS | RAINCHECK | RAKI | RAMMISH | RANCHING |
| RAGS | RAINCHECKS | RAKING | RAMMY | RANCHINGS |
| RAGSTONE | RAINCOAT | RAKINGS | RAMOSE | RANCHMAN |
| RAGSTONES | RAINCOATS | RAKIS | RAMOUS | RANCHMEN |
| RAGTIME | RAINDROP | RAKISH | RAMP | RANCHO |
| RAGTIMER | RAINDROPS | RAKISHLY | RAMPAGE | RANCHOS |
| RAGTIMERS | RAINE | RAKSHAS | RAMPAGED | RANCID |
| RAGTIMES | RAINED | RAKSHASA | RAMPAGES | RANCIDER |
| RAGULED | RAINES | RAKSHASAS | RAMPAGING | RANCIDEST |
| RAGULY | RAINFALL | RAKSHASES | RAMPANCIES | RANCIDITIES |
| RAGWEED | RAINFALLS | RALE | RAMPANCY | RANCIDITY |
| RAGWEEDS | RAINIER | RÂLE | RAMPANT | RANCING |
| RAGWHEEL | RAINIEST | RALES | RAMPANTLY | RANCOR |
| RAGWHEELS | RAININESS | RÂLES | RAMPART | RANCOROUS |
| RAGWORK | RAININESSES | RALLIED | RAMPARTED | RANCORS |
| RAGWORKS | RAINING | RALLIER | RAMPARTING | RANCOUR |
| RAGWORM | RAINLESS | RALLIERS | RAMPARTS | RANCOURS |
| RAGWORMS | RAINPROOF | RALLIES | RAMPAUGE | RAND |
| RAGWORT | RAINPROOFED | RALLINE | RAMPAUGED | RANDAN |
| RAGWORTS | RAINPROOFING | RALLY | RAMPAUGES | RANDANS |
| RAH | RAINPROOFS | RALLYE | RAMPAUGING | RANDED |
| RAHED | RAINS | RALLYES | RAMPED | RANDEM |
| RAHING | RAINSTORM | RALLYING | RAMPER | RANDEMS |
| RAHS | RAINSTORMS | RALLYINGS | RAMPERS | RANDIE |
| RAID | RAINTIGHT | RALLYIST | RAMPICK | RANDIER |
| RAIDED | RAINY | RALLYISTS | RAMPICKED | RANDIES |
| RAIDER | RAIRD | RAM | RAMPICKS | RANDIEST |
| RAIDERS | RAIRDS | RAMAKIN | RAMPIKE | RANDING |
| RAIDING | RAISABLE | RAMAKINS | RAMPIKES | RANDOM |
| RAIDS | RAISE | RAMAL | RAMPING | RANDOMISE |
| RAIK | RAISEABLE | RAMATE | RAMPION | RANDOMISED |
| RAIKED | RAISED | RAMBLE | RAMPIONS | RANDOMISES |
| RAIKING | RAISER | RAMBLED | RAMPIRE | RANDOMISING |
| RAIKS | RAISERS | RAMBLER | RAMPIRED | RANDOMIZE |
| RAIL | RAISES | RAMBLERS | RAMPIRES | RANDOMIZED |
| RAILBUS | RAISIN | RAMBLES | RAMPS | RANDOMIZES |
| RAILBUSES | RAISING | RAMBLING | RAMPSMAN | RANDOMIZING |
| RAILCARD | RAISINGS | RAMBLINGS | RAMPSMEN | RANDOMLY |
| RAILCARDS | RAISINS | RAMBUTAN | RAMROD | RANDOMS |
| RAILE | RAISONNÉ | RAMBUTANS | RAMRODS | RANDON |
| RAILED | RAIT | RAMCAT | RAMS | RANDONS |
| RAILER | RAITED | RAMCATS | RAMSON | RANDS |
| RAILERS | RAITING | RAMEAL | RAMSONS | RANDY |
| RAILES | RAITS | RAMEE | RAMSTAM | RANEE |

RANEES
RANG
RANGE
RANGED
RANGELAND
RANGELANDS
RANGER
RANGERS
RANGES
RANGIER
RANGIEST
RANGINESS
RANGINESSES
RANGING
RANGY
RANI
RANIFORM
RANINE
RANIS
RANK
RANKE
RANKED
RANKER
RANKERS
RANKES
RANKEST
RANKING
RANKINGS
RANKLE
RANKLED
RANKLES
RANKLING
RANKLY
RANKNESS
RANKNESSES
RANKS
RANSACK
RANSACKED
RANSACKER
RANSACKERS
RANSACKING
RANSACKS
RANSEL
RANSELS
RANSHAKLE
RANSHAKLED
RANSHAKLES
RANSHAKLING
RANSOM
RANSOMED
RANSOMER
RANSOMERS
RANSOMING
RANSOMS
RANT
RANTED
RANTER
RANTERISM
RANTERISMS
RANTERS
RANTING
RANTINGLY
RANTIPOLE
RANTIPOLED
RANTIPOLES
RANTIPOLING
RANTS
RANULA
RANULAS
RANUNCULI

RANZEL
RANZELMAN
RANZELMEN
RANZELS
RAP
RAPACIOUS
RAPACITIES
RAPACITY
RAPE
RAPED
RAPER
RAPERS
RAPES
RAPHANIA
RAPHANIAS
RAPHE
RAPHES
RAPHIA
RAPHIAS
RAPHIDE
RAPHIDES
RAPHIS
RAPID
RAPIDER
RAPIDEST
RAPIDITIES
RAPIDITY
RAPIDLY
RAPIDNESS
RAPIDNESSES
RAPIDS
RAPIER
RAPIERS
RAPINE
RAPINES
RAPING
RAPIST
RAPISTS
RAPLOCH
RAPLOCHS
RAPPAREE
RAPPAREES
RAPPED
RAPPEE
RAPPEES
RAPPEL
RAPPELLED
RAPPELLING
RAPPELS
RAPPER
RAPPERS
RAPPING
RAPPINGS
RAPPORT
RAPPORTS
RAPS
RAPT
RAPTOR
RAPTORIAL
RAPTORS
RAPTURE
RAPTURED
RAPTURES
RAPTURING
RAPTURISE
RAPTURISED
RAPTURISES
RAPTURISING
RAPTURIST
RAPTURISTS

RAPTURIZE
RAPTURIZED
RAPTURIZES
RAPTURIZING
RAPTUROUS
RARE
RAREBIT
RAREBITS
RAREFIED
RAREFIES
RAREFY
RAREFYING
RARELY
RARENESS
RARENESSES
RARER
RAREST
RARING
RARITIES
RARITY
RAS
RASCAILLE
RASCAILLES
RASCAL
RASCALDOM
RASCALDOMS
RASCALISM
RASCALISMS
RASCALITIES
RASCALITY
RASCALLIEST
RASCALLY
RASCALS
RASCHEL
RASCHELS
RASE
RASED
RASES
RASH
RASHED
RASHER
RASHERS
RASHES
RASHEST
RASHING
RASHLY
RASHNESS
RASHNESSES
RASING
RASORIAL
RASP
RASPATORIES
RASPATORY
RASPBERRIES
RASPBERRY
RASPED
RASPER
RASPERS
RASPIER
RASPIEST
RASPING
RASPINGLY
RASPINGS
RASPS
RASPY
RASSE
RASSES
RAST
RASTA
RASTAFARI

RASTER
RASTERS
RASTRUM
RASTRUMS
RASURE
RASURES
RAT
RATA
RATABLE
RATABLY
RATAFIA
RATAFIAS
RATAN
RATANS
RATAPLAN
RATAPLANS
RATAS
RATBAG
RATBAGS
RATCH
RATCHES
RATCHET
RATCHETS
RATE
RATEABLE
RATEABLY
RATED
RATEL
RATELS
RATEPAYER
RATEPAYERS
RATER
RATERS
RATES
RATFINK
RATFINKS
RATH
RATHE
RATHER
RATHEREST
RATHERIPE
RATHERIPES
RATHERISH
RATHEST
RATHRIPE
RATHRIPES
RATHS
RATIFIED
RATIFIER
RATIFIERS
RATIFIES
RATIFY
RATIFYING
RATINE
RATINES
RATING
RATINGS
RATIO
RATION
RATIONAL
RATIONALE
RATIONALES
RATIONALS
RATIONED
RATIONING
RATIONS
RATIOS
RATITE
RATLIN
RATLINE

RATLINES
RATLING
RATLINGS
RATLINS
RATOON
RATOONED
RATOONER
RATOONERS
RATOONING
RATOONS
RATPACK
RATPACKS
RATPROOF
RATS
RATSBANE
RATSBANES
RATTAN
RATTANS
RATTED
RATTEEN
RATTEENS
RATTEN
RATTENED
RATTENING
RATTENINGS
RATTENS
RATTER
RATTERIES
RATTERS
RATTERY
RATTIER
RATTIEST
RATTING
RATTINGS
RATTISH
RATTLE
RATTLEBAG
RATTLEBAGS
RATTLED
RATTLER
RATTLERS
RATTLES
RATTLIN
RATTLINE
RATTLINES
RATTLING
RATTLINGS
RATTLINS
RATTLY
RATTON
RATTONS
RATTY
RATU
RATUS
RAUCID
RAUCLE
RAUCLER
RAUCLEST
RAUCOUS
RAUCOUSLY
RAUGHT
RAUN
RAUNCH
RAUNCHED
RAUNCHES
RAUNCHIER
RAUNCHIEST
RAUNCHING
RAUNCHY
RAUNGE

RAUNGED
RAUNGES
RAUNGING
RAUNS
RAVAGE
RAVAGED
RAVAGER
RAVAGERS
RAVAGES
RAVAGING
RAVE
RAVED
RAVEL
RAVELIN
RAVELINS
RAVELLED
RAVELLING
RAVELLINGS
RAVELMENT
RAVELMENTS
RAVELS
RAVEN
RAVENED
RAVENER
RAVENERS
RAVENING
RAVENOUS
RAVENS
RAVER
RAVERS
RAVES
RAVIN
RAVINE
RAVINED
RAVINES
RAVING
RAVINGLY
RAVINGS
RAVINING
RAVINS
RAVIOLI
RAVIOLIS
RAVISH
RAVISHED
RAVISHER
RAVISHERS
RAVISHES
RAVISHING
RAW
RAWBONE
RAWBONED
RAWER
RAWEST
RAWHEAD
RAWHEADS
RAWHIDE
RAWHIDES
RAWING
RAWINGS
RAWISH
RAWLY
RAWN
RAWNESS
RAWNESSES
RAWNS
RAWS
RAX
RAXED
RAXES
RAXING

RAY
RAYAH
RAYAHS
RAYED
RAYING
RAYLE
RAYLED
RAYLES
RAYLESS
RAYLET
RAYLETS
RAYLING
RAYNE
RAYNES
RAYON
RAYONS
RAYS
RAZE
RAZED
RAZEE
RAZEED
RAZEEING
RAZEES
RAZES
RAZING
RAZMATAZ
RAZMATAZES
RAZMATAZZ
RAZMATAZZES
RAZOR
RAZORABLE
RAZORS
RAZURE
RAZURES
RAZZ
RAZZED
RAZZES
RAZZIA
RAZZIAS
RAZZING
RAZZLE
RAZZLES
RAZZMATAZ
RAZZMATAZES
RE
REABSORB
REABSORBED
REABSORBING
REABSORBS
REACH
REACHABLE
REACHED
REACHER
REACHERS
REACHES
REACHING
REACHLESS
REACQUIRE
REACQUIRED
REACQUIRES
REACQUIRING
REACT
REACTANCE
REACTANCES
REACTANT
REACTANTS
REACTED
REACTING
REACTION
REACTIONS

REACTIVE
REACTOR
REACTORS
REACTS
REACTUATE
REACTUATED
REACTUATES
REACTUATING
READ
READABLE
READABLY
READAPT
READAPTED
READAPTING
READAPTS
READDRESS
READDRESSED
READDRESSES
READDRESSING
READER
READERS
READIED
READIER
READIES
READIEST
READILY
READINESS
READINESSES
READING
READINGS
READJUST
READJUSTED
READJUSTING
READJUSTS
READMIT
READMITS
READMITTED
READMITTING
READOPT
READOPTED
READOPTING
READOPTS
READS
READVANCE
READVANCED
READVANCES
READVANCING
READVISE
READVISED
READVISES
READVISING
READY
READYING
REAEDIFIED
REAEDIFIES
REAEDIFY
REAEDIFYE
REAEDIFYED
REAEDIFYES
REAEDIFYING
REAFFIRM
REAFFIRMED
REAFFIRMING
REAFFIRMS
REAGENCIES
REAGENCY
REAGENT
REAGENTS
REAK
REAKED

REAKING
REAKS
REAL
REALER
REALEST
REALGAR
REALGARS
REALIA
REALIGN
REALIGNED
REALIGNING
REALIGNS
REALISE
REALISED
REALISER
REALISERS
REALISES
REALISING
REALISM
REALISMS
REALIST
REALISTIC
REALISTS
REALITIES
REALITY
REALIZE
REALIZED
REALIZER
REALIZERS
REALIZES
REALIZING
REALLIE
REALLIED
REALLIES
REALLOT
REALLOTS
REALLOTTED
REALLOTTING
REALLY
REALLYING
REALM
REALMLESS
REALMS
REALNESS
REALNESSES
REALS
REALTIE
REALTIES
REALTIME
REALTOR
REALTORS
REALTY
REAM
REAME
REAMED
REAMEND
REAMENDED
REAMENDING
REAMENDS
REAMER
REAMERS
REAMES
REAMIER
REAMIEST
REAMING
REAMS
REAMY
REAN
REANIMATE
REANIMATED

REANIMATES
REANIMATING
REANNEX
REANNEXED
REANNEXES
REANNEXING
REANS
REANSWER
REANSWERED
REANSWERING
REANSWERS
REAP
REAPED
REAPER
REAPERS
REAPING
REAPPAREL
REAPPARELLED
REAPPARELLING
REAPPARELS
REAPPEAR
REAPPEARED
REAPPEARING
REAPPEARS
REAPPLIED
REAPPLIES
REAPPLY
REAPPLYING
REAPPOINT
REAPPOINTED
REAPPOINTING
REAPPOINTS
REAPS
REAR
REARED
REARER
REARERS
REARHORSE
REARHORSES
REARING
REARISE
REARISEN
REARISES
REARISING
REARLY
REARM
REARMED
REARMICE
REARMING
REARMOST
REARMOUSE
REARMS
REAROSE
REAROUSAL
REAROUSALS
REAROUSE
REAROUSED
REAROUSES
REAROUSING
REARRANGE
REARRANGED
REARRANGES
REARRANGING
REARREST
REARRESTED
REARRESTING
REARRESTS
REARS
REARWARD
REARWARDS

REASCEND
REASCENDED
REASCENDING
REASCENDS
REASCENT
REASCENTS
REASON
REASONED
REASONER
REASONERS
REASONING
REASONINGS
REASONS
REASSERT
REASSERTED
REASSERTING
REASSERTS
REASSESS
REASSESSED
REASSESSES
REASSESSING
REASSIGN
REASSIGNED
REASSIGNING
REASSIGNS
REASSUME
REASSUMED
REASSUMES
REASSUMING
REASSURE
REASSURED
REASSURER
REASSURERS
REASSURES
REASSURING
REAST
REASTED
REASTIER
REASTIEST
REASTING
REASTS
REASTY
REATA
REATAS
REATE
REATES
REATTACH
REATTACHED
REATTACHES
REATTACHING
REATTAIN
REATTAINED
REATTAINING
REATTAINS
REATTEMPT
REATTEMPTED
REATTEMPTING
REATTEMPTS
REAVE
REAVER
REAVERS
REAVES
REAVING
REAWAKE
REAWAKED
REAWAKEN
REAWAKENED
REAWAKENING
REAWAKENINGS
REAWAKENS

REAWAKES
REAWAKING
REAWOKE
REAWOKEN
REBACK
REBACKED
REBACKING
REBACKS
REBAPTISE
REBAPTISED
REBAPTISES
REBAPTISING
REBAPTISM
REBAPTISMS
REBAPTIZE
REBAPTIZED
REBAPTIZES
REBAPTIZING
REBATE
REBATED
REBATER
REBATERS
REBATES
REBATING
REBATO
REBATOES
REBEC
REBECK
REBECKS
REBECS
REBEL
REBELDOM
REBELDOMS
REBELLED
REBELLER
REBELLERS
REBELLING
REBELLION
REBELLIONS
REBELLOW
REBELLOWED
REBELLOWING
REBELLOWS
REBELS
REBID
REBIDDEN
REBIDDING
REBIDS
REBIND
REBINDING
REBINDS
REBIRTH
REBIRTHS
REBIT
REBITE
REBITES
REBITING
REBITTEN
REBLOOM
REBLOOMED
REBLOOMING
REBLOOMS
REBLOSSOM
REBLOSSOMED
REBLOSSOMING
REBLOSSOMS
REBOANT
REBOATION
REBOATIONS
REBOIL

REBOILED
REBOILING
REBOILS
REBORE
REBORED
REBORES
REBORING
REBORN
REBOUND
REBOUNDED
REBOUNDING
REBOUNDS
REBRACE
REBRACED
REBRACES
REBRACING
REBUFF
REBUFFED
REBUFFING
REBUFFS
REBUILD
REBUILDING
REBUILDS
REBUILT
REBUKABLE
REBUKE
REBUKED
REBUKEFUL
REBUKER
REBUKERS
REBUKES
REBUKING
REBURIAL
REBURIALS
REBURIED
REBURIES
REBURY
REBURYING
REBUS
REBUSES
REBUT
REBUTMENT
REBUTMENTS
REBUTS
REBUTTAL
REBUTTALS
REBUTTED
REBUTTER
REBUTTERS
REBUTTING
REBUTTON
REBUTTONED
REBUTTONING
REBUTTONS
RECAL
RECALESCE
RECALESCED
RECALESCES
RECALESCING
RECALL
RECALLED
RECALLING
RECALLS
RECALMENT
RECALMENTS
RECALS
RECANT
RECANTED
RECANTER
RECANTERS

RECANTING
RECANTS
RECAP
RECAPPED
RECAPPING
RECAPS
RECAPTION
RECAPTIONS
RECAPTOR
RECAPTORS
RECAPTURE
RECAPTURED
RECAPTURES
RECAPTURING
RECAST
RECASTING
RECASTS
RECATCH
RECATCHES
RECATCHING
RECAUGHT
RECCE
RECCED
RECCEED
RECCEING
RECCES
RECCIED
RECCIES
RECCO
RECCOS
RECCY
RECCYING
RECEDE
RECEDED
RECEDES
RECEDING
RECEIPT
RECEIPTED
RECEIPTING
RECEIPTS
RECEIVAL
RECEIVALS
RECEIVE
RECEIVED
RECEIVER
RECEIVERS
RECEIVES
RECEIVING
RECEIVINGS
RECENCIES
RECENCY
RECENSE
RECENSED
RECENSES
RECENSING
RECENSION
RECENSIONS
RECENT
RECENTER
RECENTEST
RECENTLY
RECENTRE
RECENTRED
RECENTRES
RECENTRING
RECEPT
RECEPTION
RECEPTIONS
RECEPTIVE
RECEPTOR

RECEPTORS
RECEPTS
RECESS
RECESSED
RECESSES
RECESSING
RECESSION
RECESSIONS
RECESSIVE
RECESSIVES
RECHARGE
RECHARGED
RECHARGES
RECHARGING
RECHART
RECHARTED
RECHARTER
RECHARTERED
RECHARTERING
RECHARTERS
RECHARTING
RECHARTS
RECHATE
RECHATES
RÉCHAUFFÉ
RÉCHAUFFÉS
RECHEAT
RECHEATED
RECHEATING
RECHEATS
RECHECK
RECHECKED
RECHECKING
RECHECKS
RECHERCHÉ
RECHIE
RECHLESSE
RECIPE
RECIPES
RECIPIENT
RECIPIENTS
RECISION
RECISIONS
RÉCIT
RECITAL
RECITALS
RECITE
RECITED
RECITER
RECITERS
RECITES
RECITING
RÉCITS
RECK
RECKAN
RECKED
RECKING
RECKLESS
RECKLING
RECKLINGS
RECKON
RECKONED
RECKONER
RECKONERS
RECKONING
RECKONINGS
RECKONS
RECKS
RECLAIM
RECLAIMED

RECLAIMER
RECLAIMERS
RECLAIMING
RECLAIMS
RÉCLAME
RÉCLAMES
RECLIMB
RECLIMBED
RECLIMBING
RECLIMBS
RECLINATE
RECLINE
RECLINED
RECLINER
RECLINERS
RECLINES
RECLINING
RECLOSE
RECLOSED
RECLOSES
RECLOSING
RECLOTHE
RECLOTHED
RECLOTHES
RECLOTHING
RECLUSE
RECLUSELY
RECLUSES
RECLUSION
RECLUSIONS
RECLUSIVE
RECLUSORIES
RECLUSORY
RECOGNISE
RECOGNISED
RECOGNISES
RECOGNISING
RECOGNIZE
RECOGNIZED
RECOGNIZES
RECOGNIZING
RECOIL
RECOILED
RECOILER
RECOILERS
RECOILING
RECOILS
RECOINAGE
RECOINAGES
RECOLLECT
RECOLLECTED
RECOLLECTING
RECOLLECTS
RÉCOLLET
RÉCOLLETS
RECOMBINE
RECOMBINED
RECOMBINES
RECOMBINING
RECOMFORT
RECOMFORTED
RECOMFORTING
RECOMFORTS
RECOMMEND
RECOMMENDED
RECOMMENDING
RECOMMENDS
RECOMMIT
RECOMMITS
RECOMMITTED

RECOMMITTING
RECOMPACT
RECOMPACTED
RECOMPACTING
RECOMPACTS
RECOMPOSE
RECOMPOSED
RECOMPOSES
RECOMPOSING
RECONCILE
RECONCILED
RECONCILES
RECONCILING
RECONDITE
RECONFIRM
RECONFIRMED
RECONFIRMING
RECONFIRMS
RECONNECT
RECONNECTED
RECONNECTING
RECONNECTS
RECONQUER
RECONQUERED
RECONQUERING
RECONQUERS
RECONVENE
RECONVENED
RECONVENES
RECONVENING
RECONVERT
RECONVERTED
RECONVERTING
RECONVERTS
RECONVEY
RECONVEYED
RECONVEYING
RECONVEYS
RECORD
RECORDED
RECORDER
RECORDERS
RECORDING
RECORDINGS
RECORDIST
RECORDISTS
RECORDS
RECOUNT
RECOUNTAL
RECOUNTALS
RECOUNTED
RECOUNTING
RECOUNTS
RECOUP
RECOUPED
RECOUPING
RECOUPS
RECOURE
RECOURED
RECOURES
RECOURING
RECOURSE
RECOURSED
RECOURSES
RECOURSING
RECOVER
RECOVERED
RECOVEREE
RECOVEREES
RECOVERER

RECOVERERS
RECOVERIES
RECOVERING
RECOVEROR
RECOVERORS
RECOVERS
RECOVERY
RECOWER
RECOWERED
RECOWERING
RECOWERS
RECOYLE
RECOYLED
RECOYLES
RECOYLING
RECREANCE
RECREANCES
RECREANCIES
RECREANCY
RECREANT
RECREANTS
RECREATE
RECREATED
RECREATES
RECREATING
RECREMENT
RECREMENTS
RECROSS
RECROSSED
RECROSSES
RECROSSING
RECRUIT
RECRUITAL
RECRUITALS
RECRUITED
RECRUITER
RECRUITERS
RECRUITING
RECRUITS
RECTA
RECTAL
RECTALLY
RECTANGLE
RECTANGLES
RECTI
RECTIFIED
RECTIFIER
RECTIFIERS
RECTIFIES
RECTIFY
RECTIFYING
RECTION
RECTIONS
RECTITIC
RECTITIS
RECTITISES
RECTITUDE
RECTITUDES
RECTO
RECTOR
RECTORAL
RECTORATE
RECTORATES
RECTORESS
RECTORESSES
RECTORIAL
RECTORIALS
RECTORIES
RECTORS
RECTORY

RECTOS
RECTRESS
RECTRESSES
RECTRICES
RECTRIX
RECTUM
RECTUMS
RECTUS
RECUILE
RECUILED
RECUILES
RECUILING
RECULE
RECULED
RECULES
RECULING
RECUMBENT
RECUR
RECURE
RECURED
RECURES
RECURING
RECURRED
RECURRENT
RECURRING
RECURS
RECURSION
RECURSIONS
RECURSIVE
RECURVE
RECURVED
RECURVES
RECURVING
RECUSANCE
RECUSANCES
RECUSANCIES
RECUSANCY
RECUSANT
RECUSANTS
RECUSE
RECUSED
RECUSES
RECUSING
RECYCLE
RECYCLED
RECYCLES
RECYCLING
RED
REDACT
REDACTED
REDACTING
REDACTION
REDACTIONS
REDACTOR
REDACTORS
REDACTS
REDAN
REDANS
REDARGUE
REDARGUED
REDARGUES
REDARGUING
REDBACK
REDBACKS
REDBREAST
REDBREASTS
REDBRICK
REDCOAT
REDCOATS
REDD

REDDEN
REDDENDA
REDDENDO
REDDENDOS
REDDENDUM
REDDENED
REDDENING
REDDENS
REDDER
REDDERS
REDDEST
REDDIER
REDDIEST
REDDING
REDDINGS
REDDISH
REDDLE
REDDLED
REDDLEMAN
REDDLEMEN
REDDLES
REDDLING
REDDS
REDDY
REDE
REDEAL
REDEALING
REDEALS
REDEALT
REDECRAFT
REDECRAFTS
REDEEM
REDEEMED
REDEEMER
REDEEMERS
REDEEMING
REDEEMS
REDEFINE
REDEFINED
REDEFINES
REDEFINING
REDELESS
REDELIVER
REDELIVERED
REDELIVERING
REDELIVERS
REDEPLOY
REDEPLOYED
REDEPLOYING
REDEPLOYS
REDES
REDESCEND
REDESCENDED
REDESCENDING
REDESCENDS
REDESIGN
REDESIGNED
REDESIGNING
REDESIGNS
REDEVELOP
REDEVELOPED
REDEVELOPING
REDEVELOPS
REDEYE
REDEYES
REDFISH
REDFISHES
REDHANDED
REDIA
REDIAE

| | | | | |
|---|---|---|---|---|
| REDID | REDRIVE | REEDSTOP | REFERENCED | REFLOATING |
| REDING | REDRIVEN | REEDSTOPS | REFERENCES | REFLOATS |
| REDINGOTE | REDRIVES | REEDY | REFERENCING | REFLOW |
| REDINGOTES | REDRIVING | REEF | REFERENDA | REFLOWED |
| REDIP | REDROVE | REEFED | REFERENT | REFLOWER |
| REDIPPED | REDS | REEFER | REFERENTS | REFLOWERED |
| REDIPPING | REDSEAR | REEFERS | REFERRAL | REFLOWERING |
| REDIPS | REDSHANK | REEFING | REFERRALS | REFLOWERINGS |
| REDIRECT | REDSHANKS | REEFINGS | REFERRED | REFLOWERS |
| REDIRECTED | REDSHARE | REEFS | REFERRING | REFLOWING |
| REDIRECTING | REDSHIRE | REEK | REFERS | REFLOWINGS |
| REDIRECTS | REDSHORT | REEKED | REFFED | REFLOWS |
| REDISTIL | REDSKIN | REEKIE | REFFING | REFLUENCE |
| REDISTILLED | REDSKINS | REEKIER | REFFO | REFLUENCES |
| REDISTILLING | REDSTART | REEKIEST | REFFOS | REFLUENT |
| REDISTILS | REDSTARTS | REEKING | REFIGURE | REFLUX |
| REDIVIDE | REDSTREAK | REEKS | REFIGURED | REFLUXED |
| REDIVIDED | REDSTREAKS | REEKY | REFIGURES | REFLUXES |
| REDIVIDES | REDTOP | REEL | REFIGURING | REFLUXING |
| REDIVIDING | REDTOPS | REELED | REFILL | REFOOT |
| REDIVIVUS | REDUCE | REELER | REFILLED | REFOOTED |
| REDLEG | REDUCED | REELERS | REFILLING | REFOOTING |
| REDLEGS | REDUCER | REELING | REFILLS | REFOOTS |
| REDLY | REDUCERS | REELINGLY | REFINE | REFORM |
| REDNECK | REDUCES | REELINGS | REFINED | REFORMADE |
| REDNECKS | REDUCIBLE | REELMAN | REFINEDLY | REFORMADES |
| REDNESS | REDUCING | REELMEN | REFINER | REFORMADO |
| REDNESSES | REDUCTANT | REELS | REFINERIES | REFORMADOES |
| REDO | REDUCTANTS | REEN | REFINERS | REFORMADOS |
| REDOES | REDUCTASE | REENS | REFINERY | REFORMED |
| REDOING | REDUCTASES | REES | REFINES | REFORMER |
| REDOLENCE | REDUCTION | REEST | REFINING | REFORMERS |
| REDOLENCES | REDUCTIONS | REESTED | REFININGS | REFORMING |
| REDOLENCIES | REDUCTIVE | REESTIER | REFIT | REFORMISM |
| REDOLENCY | REDUIT | REESTIEST | REFITMENT | REFORMISMS |
| REDOLENT | REDUITS | REESTING | REFITMENTS | REFORMIST |
| REDONE | REDUNDANT | REESTS | REFITS | REFORMISTS |
| REDOUBLE | REDWATER | REESTY | REFITTED | REFORMS |
| REDOUBLED | REDWATERS | REEVE | REFITTING | REFORTIFIED |
| REDOUBLES | REDWING | REEVED | REFITTINGS | REFORTIFIES |
| REDOUBLING | REDWINGS | REEVES | REFLAG | REFORTIFY |
| REDOUBT | REDWOOD | REEVING | REFLAGGED | REFORTIFYING |
| REDOUBTED | REDWOODS | REF | REFLAGGING | REFOUND |
| REDOUBTING | REE | REFACE | REFLAGS | REFOUNDED |
| REDOUBTS | REEBOK | REFACED | REFLATE | REFOUNDER |
| REDOUND | REEBOKS | REFACES | REFLATED | REFOUNDERS |
| REDOUNDED | REECH | REFACING | REFLATES | REFOUNDING |
| REDOUNDING | REECHED | REFASHION | REFLATING | REFOUNDS |
| REDOUNDINGS | REECHES | REFASHIONED | REFLATION | REFRACT |
| REDOUNDS | REECHIE | REFASHIONING | REFLATIONS | REFRACTED |
| REDOWA | REECHIER | REFASHIONS | REFLECT | REFRACTING |
| REDOWAS | REECHIEST | REFECT | REFLECTED | REFRACTOR |
| REDOX | REECHING | REFECTED | REFLECTER | REFRACTORS |
| REDPOLL | REECHY | REFECTING | REFLECTERS | REFRACTS |
| REDPOLLS | REED | REFECTION | REFLECTING | REFRAIN |
| REDRAFT | REEDE | REFECTIONS | REFLECTOR | REFRAINED |
| REDRAFTED | REEDED | REFECTORIES | REFLECTORS | REFRAINING |
| REDRAFTING | REEDEN | REFECTORY | REFLECTS | REFRAINS |
| REDRAFTS | REEDER | REFECTS | REFLET | REFRAME |
| REDRAW | REEDERS | REFEL | REFLETS | REFRAMED |
| REDRAWING | REEDES | REFELLED | REFLEX | REFRAMES |
| REDRAWN | REEDIER | REFELLING | REFLEXED | REFRAMING |
| REDRAWS | REEDIEST | REFELS | REFLEXES | REFREEZE |
| REDRESS | REEDINESS | REFER | REFLEXING | REFREEZES |
| REDRESSED | REEDINESSES | REFERABLE | REFLEXION | REFREEZING |
| REDRESSER | REEDING | REFEREE | REFLEXIONS | REFRESH |
| REDRESSERS | REEDINGS | REFEREED | REFLEXIVE | REFRESHED |
| REDRESSES | REEDLING | REFEREEING | REFLEXLY | REFRESHEN |
| REDRESSING | REEDLINGS | REFEREES | REFLOAT | REFRESHENED |
| REDREW | REEDS | REFERENCE | REFLOATED | REFRESHENING |

REFRESHENS
REFRESHER
REFRESHERS
REFRESHES
REFRESHING
REFRINGE
REFRINGED
REFRINGES
REFRINGING
REFROZE
REFROZEN
REFS
REFT
REFUEL
REFUELLED
REFUELLING
REFUELS
REFUGE
REFUGED
REFUGEE
REFUGEES
REFUGES
REFUGIA
REFUGING
REFUGIUM
REFULGENT
REFUND
REFUNDED
REFUNDER
REFUNDERS
REFUNDING
REFUNDS
REFURBISH
REFURBISHED
REFURBISHES
REFURBISHING
REFURNISH
REFURNISHED
REFURNISHES
REFURNISHING
REFUSABLE
REFUSAL
REFUSALS
REFUSE
REFUSED
REFUSENIK
REFUSENIKS
REFUSER
REFUSERS
REFUSES
REFUSING
REFUSION
REFUSIONS
REFUSNIK
REFUSNIKS
REFUTABLE
REFUTABLY
REFUTAL
REFUTALS
REFUTE
REFUTED
REFUTER
REFUTERS
REFUTES
REFUTING
REGAIN
REGAINED
REGAINER
REGAINERS
REGAINING

REGAINS
REGAL
REGALE
REGALED
REGALES
REGALIA
REGALIAN
REGALIAS
REGALING
REGALISM
REGALISMS
REGALIST
REGALISTS
REGALITIES
REGALITY
REGALLY
REGALS
REGAR
REGARD
REGARDANT
REGARDED
REGARDER
REGARDERS
REGARDFUL
REGARDING
REGARDS
REGARS
REGATHER
REGATHERED
REGATHERING
REGATHERS
REGATTA
REGATTAS
REGAVE
REGELATE
REGELATED
REGELATES
REGELATING
REGENCE
REGENCES
REGENCIES
REGENCY
REGENT
REGENTS
REGEST
REGESTS
REGGAE
REGGAES
REGICIDAL
REGICIDE
REGICIDES
RÉGIE
RÉGIES
RÉGIME
REGIMEN
REGIMENS
REGIMENT
REGIMENTED
REGIMENTING
REGIMENTS
RÉGIMES
REGIMINAL
REGINA
REGINAE
REGINAL
REGINAS
REGION
REGIONAL
REGIONARY
REGIONS

REGISSEUR
REGISSEURS
REGISTER
REGISTERED
REGISTERING
REGISTERS
REGISTRAR
REGISTRARS
REGISTRIES
REGISTRY
REGIUS
REGIVE
REGIVEN
REGIVES
REGIVING
REGLET
REGLETS
REGMA
REGMATA
REGNAL
REGNANT
REGOLITH
REGOLITHS
REGORGE
REGORGED
REGORGES
REGORGING
REGRADE
REGRADED
REGRADES
REGRADING
REGRANT
REGRANTED
REGRANTING
REGRANTS
REGRATE
REGRATED
REGRATER
REGRATERS
REGRATES
REGRATING
REGRATINGS
REGRATOR
REGRATORS
REGREDE
REGREDED
REGREDES
REGREDING
REGREET
REGREETED
REGREETING
REGREETS
REGRESS
REGRESSED
REGRESSES
REGRESSING
REGRET
REGRETFUL
REGRETS
REGRETTED
REGRETTING
REGRIND
REGRINDING
REGRINDS
REGROUND
REGROUP
REGROUPED
REGROUPING
REGROUPS
REGROWTH

REGROWTHS
REGUERDON
REGUERDONED
REGUERDONING
REGUERDONS
REGULA
REGULAE
REGULAR
REGULARLY
REGULARS
REGULATE
REGULATED
REGULATES
REGULATING
REGULATOR
REGULATORS
REGULINE
REGULISE
REGULISED
REGULISES
REGULISING
REGULIZE
REGULIZED
REGULIZES
REGULIZING
REGULO®
REGULOS®
REGULUS
REGULUSES
REGUR
REGURS
REH
REHANDLE
REHANDLED
REHANDLES
REHANDLING
REHANDLINGS
REHASH
REHASHED
REHASHES
REHASHING
REHEAR
REHEARD
REHEARING
REHEARINGS
REHEARS
REHEARSAL
REHEARSALS
REHEARSE
REHEARSED
REHEARSER
REHEARSERS
REHEARSES
REHEARSING
REHEARSINGS
REHEAT
REHEATED
REHEATER
REHEATERS
REHEATING
REHEATS
REHEEL
REHEELED
REHEELING
REHEELS
REHOBOAM
REHOBOAMS
REHOUSE
REHOUSED
REHOUSES

REHOUSING
REHOUSINGS
REHS
REIF
REIFIED
REIFIES
REIFS
REIFY
REIFYING
REIGN
REIGNED
REIGNING
REIGNS
REIK
REIKS
REILLUME
REILLUMED
REILLUMES
REILLUMING
REIMBURSE
REIMBURSED
REIMBURSES
REIMBURSING
REIMPLANT
REIMPLANTED
REIMPLANTING
REIMPLANTS
REIMPORT
REIMPORTED
REIMPORTING
REIMPORTS
REIMPOSE
REIMPOSED
REIMPOSES
REIMPOSING
REIN
REINDEER
REINDEERS
REINED
REINETTE
REINETTES
REINFORCE
REINFORCED
REINFORCES
REINFORCING
REINFORM
REINFORMED
REINFORMING
REINFORMS
REINFUND
REINFUNDED
REINFUNDING
REINFUNDS
REINFUSE
REINFUSED
REINFUSES
REINFUSING
REINHABIT
REINHABITED
REINHABITING
REINHABITS
REINING
REINLESS
REINS
REINSERT
REINSERTED
REINSERTING
REINSERTS
REINSMAN
REINSMEN

| | | | | |
|---|---|---|---|---|
| REINSPECT | REJECTIVE | RELAXED | RELIGIOSO | REMAKING |
| REINSPECTED | REJECTOR | RELAXES | RELIGIOUS | REMAN |
| REINSPECTING | REJECTORS | RELAXIN | RELIGIOUSES | REMAND |
| REINSPECTS | REJECTS | RELAXING | RELINE | REMANDED |
| REINSPIRE | REJIG | RELAXINS | RELINED | REMANDING |
| REINSPIRED | REJIGGED | RELAY | RELINES | REMANDS |
| REINSPIRES | REJIGGER | RELAYED | RELINING | REMANENCE |
| REINSPIRING | REJIGGERED | RELAYING | RELIQUARIES | REMANENCES |
| REINSTALL | REJIGGERING | RELAYS | RELIQUARY | REMANENCIES |
| REINSTALLED | REJIGGERS | RELEASE | RELIQUE | REMANENCY |
| REINSTALLING | REJIGGING | RELEASED | RELIQUES | REMANENT |
| REINSTALLS | REJIGS | RELEASEE | RELIQUIAE | REMANENTS |
| REINSTATE | REJOICE | RELEASEES | RELISH | REMANET |
| REINSTATED | REJOICED | RELEASER | RELISHED | REMANETS |
| REINSTATES | REJOICER | RELEASERS | RELISHES | REMANIÉ |
| REINSTATING | REJOICERS | RELEASES | RELISHING | REMANIÉS |
| REINSURE | REJOICES | RELEASING | RELIT | REMANNED |
| REINSURED | REJOICING | RELEASOR | RELIVE | REMANNING |
| REINSURER | REJOICINGS | RELEASORS | RELIVED | REMANS |
| REINSURERS | REJOIN | RELEGABLE | RELIVER | REMARK |
| REINSURES | REJOINDER | RELEGATE | RELIVERED | REMARKED |
| REINSURING | REJOINDERS | RELEGATED | RELIVERING | REMARKER |
| REINTER | REJOINED | RELEGATES | RELIVERS | REMARKERS |
| REINTERRED | REJOINING | RELEGATING | RELIVES | REMARKING |
| REINTERRING | REJOINS | RELENT | RELIVING | REMARKS |
| REINTERS | REJÓN | RELENTED | RELLISH | REMARQUÉ |
| REINVEST | REJONEO | RELENTING | RELLISHED | REMARQUED |
| REINVESTED | REJONEOS | RELENTINGS | RELLISHES | REMARQUÉS |
| REINVESTING | REJONES | RELENTS | RELLISHING | REMARRIED |
| REINVESTS | REJOURN | RELET | RELOAD | REMARRIES |
| REINVOLVE | REJOURNED | RELETS | RELOADED | REMARRY |
| REINVOLVED | REJOURNING | RELETTING | RELOADING | REMARRYING |
| REINVOLVES | REJOURNS | RELEVANCE | RELOADS | REMATCH |
| REINVOLVING | REJUDGE | RELEVANCES | RELOCATE | REMATCHED |
| REIRD | REJUDGED | RELEVANCIES | RELOCATED | REMATCHES |
| REIRDS | REJUDGES | RELEVANCY | RELOCATES | REMATCHING |
| REIS | REJUDGING | RELEVANT | RELOCATING | REMBLAI |
| REISES | REKE | RELIABLE | RELUCENT | REMBLAIS |
| REISSUE | REKED | RELIABLY | RELUCT | REMBLE |
| REISSUED | REKES | RELIANCE | RELUCTANT | REMBLED |
| REISSUES | REKINDLE | RELIANCES | RELUCTATE | REMBLES |
| REISSUING | REKINDLED | RELIANT | RELUCTATED | REMBLING |
| REIST | REKINDLES | RELIC | RELUCTATES | REMEAD |
| REISTAFEL | REKINDLING | RELICS | RELUCTATING | REMEADS |
| REISTAFELS | REKING | RELICT | RELUCTED | REMEASURE |
| REISTED | RELÂCHE | RELICTS | RELUCTING | REMEASURED |
| REISTIER | RELÂCHES | RELIDE | RELUCTS | REMEASURES |
| REISTIEST | RELAID | RELIE | RELUME | REMEASURING |
| REISTING | RELAPSE | RELIED | RELUMED | REMEDE |
| REISTS | RELAPSED | RELIEF | RELUMES | REMEDES |
| REISTY | RELAPSER | RELIEFS | RELUMINE | REMEDIAL |
| REITER | RELAPSERS | RELIER | RELUMINED | REMEDIAT |
| REITERANT | RELAPSES | RELIERS | RELUMINES | REMEDIATE |
| REITERATE | RELAPSING | RELIES | RELUMING | REMEDIED |
| REITERATED | RELATE | RELIEVE | RELUMINING | REMEDIES |
| REITERATES | RELATED | RELIEVED | RELY | REMEDY |
| REITERATING | RELATER | RELIEVER | RELYING | REMEDYING |
| REITERS | RELATERS | RELIEVERS | REM | REMEID |
| REIVE | RELATES | RELIEVES | REMADE | REMEIDS |
| REIVER | RELATING | RELIEVING | REMADES | REMEMBER |
| REIVERS | RELATION | RELIEVO | REMAIN | REMEMBERED |
| REIVES | RELATIONS | RELIEVOS | REMAINDER | REMEMBERING |
| REIVING | RELATIVAL | RELIGHT | REMAINDERED | REMEMBERS |
| REJECT | RELATIVE | RELIGHTED | REMAINDERING | REMEN |
| REJECTED | RELATIVES | RELIGHTING | REMAINDERS | REMENS |
| REJECTER | RELATOR | RELIGHTS | REMAINED | REMERCIED |
| REJECTERS | RELATORS | RELIGIEUX | REMAINING | REMERCIES |
| REJECTING | RELAX | RELIGION | REMAINS | REMERCY |
| REJECTION | RELAXANT | RELIGIONS | REMAKE | REMERCYING |
| REJECTIONS | RELAXANTS | RELIGIOSE | REMAKES | REMERGE |

REMERGED
REMERGES
REMERGING
REMEX
REMIGATE
REMIGATED
REMIGATES
REMIGATING
REMIGES
REMIGIAL
REMIGRATE
REMIGRATED
REMIGRATES
REMIGRATING
REMIND
REMINDED
REMINDER
REMINDERS
REMINDFUL
REMINDING
REMINDS
REMINISCE
REMINISCED
REMINISCES
REMINISCING
REMISE
REMISED
REMISES
REMISING
REMISS
REMISSION
REMISSIONS
REMISSIVE
REMISSLY
REMISSORY
REMIT
REMITMENT
REMITMENTS
REMITS
REMITTAL
REMITTALS
REMITTED
REMITTEE
REMITTEES
REMITTENT
REMITTER
REMITTERS
REMITTING
REMITTOR
REMITTORS
REMNANT
REMNANTS
REMODEL
REMODELLED
REMODELLING
REMODELS
REMODIFIED
REMODIFIES
REMODIFY
REMODIFYING
REMONTANT
REMONTANTS
REMORA
REMORAS
REMORSE
REMORSES
REMOTE
REMOTELY
REMOTER
REMOTES

REMOTEST
REMOTION
REMOTIONS
REMOUD
REMOULADE
RÉMOULADE
REMOULADES
RÉMOULADES
REMOULD
REMOULDED
REMOULDING
REMOULDS
REMOUNT
REMOUNTED
REMOUNTING
REMOUNTS
REMOVABLE
REMOVABLY
REMOVAL
REMOVALS
REMOVE
REMOVED
REMOVER
REMOVERS
REMOVES
REMOVING
REMS
REMUAGE
REMUAGES
REMUDA
REMUDAS
REMUEUR
REMUEURS
REMURMUR
REMURMURED
REMURMURING
REMURMURS
REN
RENAGUE
RENAGUED
RENAGUES
RENAGUING
RENAL
RENAME
RENAMED
RENAMES
RENAMING
RENASCENT
RENAY
RENAYED
RENAYING
RENAYS
RENCONTRE
RENCONTRES
REND
RENDER
RENDERED
RENDERER
RENDERERS
RENDERING
RENDERINGS
RENDERS
RENDING
RENDITION
RENDITIONS
RENDS
RENDZINA
RENDZINAS
RENEGADE
RENEGADED

RENEGADES
RENEGADING
RENEGADO
RENEGADOS
RENEGATE
RENEGATES
RENEGE
RENEGED
RENEGER
RENEGERS
RENEGES
RENEGING
RENEGUE
RENEGUED
RENEGUER
RENEGUERS
RENEGUES
RENEGUING
RENEW
RENEWABLE
RENEWAL
RENEWALS
RENEWED
RENEWER
RENEWERS
RENEWING
RENEWINGS
RENEWS
RENEY
RENEYED
RENEYING
RENEYS
RENFIERST
RENFORCE
RENFORCED
RENFORCES
RENFORCING
RENFORST
RENGA
RENGAS
RENIED
RENIES
RENIFORM
RENIG
RENIGGED
RENIGGING
RENIGS
RENIN
RENINS
RENITENCIES
RENITENCY
RENITENT
RENMINBI
RENMINBIS
RENNE
RENNED
RENNES
RENNET
RENNETS
RENNIN
RENNING
RENNINGS
RENNINS
RENOUNCE
RENOUNCED
RENOUNCER
RENOUNCERS
RENOUNCES
RENOUNCING
RENOVATE

RENOVATED
RENOVATES
RENOVATING
RENOVATOR
RENOVATORS
RENOWN
RENOWNED
RENOWNER
RENOWNERS
RENOWNING
RENOWNS
RENS
RENT
RENTABLE
RENTAL
RENTALLER
RENTALLERS
RENTALS
RENTBOY
RENTBOYS
RENTE
RENTED
RENTER
RENTERS
RENTES
RENTIER
RENTIERS
RENTING
RENTS
RENUMBER
RENUMBERED
RENUMBERING
RENUMBERS
RENVERSE
RENVERSED
RENVERSES
RENVERSING
RENVERST
RENVOI
RENVOIS
RENVOY
RENVOYS
RENY
RENYING
REOCCUPIED
REOCCUPIES
REOCCUPY
REOCCUPYING
REOFFEND
REOFFENDED
REOFFENDING
REOFFENDS
REOPEN
REOPENED
REOPENER
REOPENERS
REOPENING
REOPENS
REORDAIN
REORDAINED
REORDAINING
REORDAINS
REORDER
REORDERED
REORDERING
REORDERS
REORIENT
REORIENTED
REORIENTING
REORIENTS

REP
REPACK
REPACKED
REPACKING
REPACKS
REPAID
REPAINT
REPAINTED
REPAINTING
REPAINTINGS
REPAINTS
REPAIR
REPAIRED
REPAIRER
REPAIRERS
REPAIRING
REPAIRMAN
REPAIRMEN
REPAIRS
REPAND
REPAPER
REPAPERED
REPAPERING
REPAPERS
REPARABLE
REPARABLY
REPARTEE
REPARTEED
REPARTEEING
REPARTEES
REPASS
REPASSAGE
REPASSAGES
REPASSED
REPASSES
REPASSING
REPAST
REPASTED
REPASTING
REPASTS
REPASTURE
REPASTURES
REPAY
REPAYABLE
REPAYING
REPAYMENT
REPAYMENTS
REPAYS
REPEAL
REPEALED
REPEALER
REPEALERS
REPEALING
REPEALS
REPEAT
REPEATED
REPEATER
REPEATERS
REPEATING
REPEATINGS
REPEATS
REPECHAGE
REPEL
REPELLANT
REPELLANTS
REPELLED
REPELLENT
REPELLENTS
REPELLER
REPELLERS

REPELLING
REPELS
REPENT
REPENTANT
REPENTANTS
REPENTED
REPENTER
REPENTERS
REPENTING
REPENTS
REPEOPLE
REPEOPLED
REPEOPLES
REPEOPLING
REPERCUSS
REPERCUSSED
REPERCUSSES
REPERCUSSING
REPERTORIES
REPERTORY
REPERUSAL
REPERUSALS
REPERUSE
REPERUSED
REPERUSES
REPERUSING
REPETEND
REPETENDS
REPHRASE
REPHRASED
REPHRASES
REPHRASING
REPINE
REPINED
REPINER
REPINERS
REPINES
REPINING
REPININGS
REPIQUE
REPIQUED
REPIQUES
REPIQUING
REPLA
REPLACE
REPLACED
REPLACER
REPLACERS
REPLACES
REPLACING
REPLAN
REPLANNED
REPLANNING
REPLANS
REPLANT
REPLANTED
REPLANTING
REPLANTS
REPLAY
REPLAYED
REPLAYING
REPLAYS
REPLENISH
REPLENISHED
REPLENISHES
REPLENISHING
REPLETE
REPLETED
REPLETES
REPLETING

REPLETION
REPLETIONS
REPLEVIED
REPLEVIES
REPLEVIN
REPLEVINED
REPLEVINING
REPLEVINS
REPLEVY
REPLEVYING
REPLICA
REPLICAS
REPLICATE
REPLICATED
REPLICATES
REPLICATING
REPLIED
REPLIER
REPLIERS
REPLIES
REPLUM
REPLY
REPLYING
REPOINT
REPOINTED
REPOINTING
REPOINTS
REPONE
REPONED
REPONES
REPONING
REPORT
REPORTAGE
REPORTAGES
REPORTED
REPORTER
REPORTERS
REPORTING
REPORTINGS
REPORTS
REPOSAL
REPOSALL
REPOSALLS
REPOSALS
REPOSE
REPOSED
REPOSEDLY
REPOSEFUL
REPOSES
REPOSING
REPOSIT
REPOSITED
REPOSITING
REPOSITOR
REPOSITORS
REPOSITS
REPOSSESS
REPOSSESSED
REPOSSESSES
REPOSSESSING
REPOST
REPOSTED
REPOSTING
REPOSTS
REPOSURE
REPOSURES
REPOT
REPOTS
REPOTTED
REPOTTING

REPOTTINGS
REPOUSSÉ
REPOUSSÉS
REPP
REPPED
REPPING
REPPINGS
REPPS
REPREEVE
REPREEVED
REPREEVES
REPREEVING
REPREHEND
REPREHENDED
REPREHENDING
REPREHENDS
REPRESENT
REPRESENTED
REPRESENTING
REPRESENTS
REPRESS
REPRESSED
REPRESSES
REPRESSING
REPRESSOR
REPRESSORS
REPRIEFE
REPRIEFES
REPRIEVAL
REPRIEVALS
REPRIEVE
REPRIEVED
REPRIEVES
REPRIEVING
REPRIMAND
REPRIMANDED
REPRIMANDING
REPRIMANDS
REPRIME
REPRIMED
REPRIMES
REPRIMING
REPRINT
REPRINTED
REPRINTING
REPRINTS
REPRISAL
REPRISALS
REPRISE
REPRISED
REPRISES
REPRISING
REPRIVE
REPRIVED
REPRIVES
REPRIVING
REPRIZE
REPRIZED
REPRIZES
REPRIZING
REPRO
REPROACH
REPROACHED
REPROACHES
REPROACHING
REPROBACIES
REPROBACY
REPROBATE
REPROBATED
REPROBATES

REPROBATING
REPROCESS
REPROCESSED
REPROCESSES
REPROCESSING
REPRODUCE
REPRODUCED
REPRODUCES
REPRODUCING
REPROOF
REPROOFED
REPROOFING
REPROOFS
REPROS
REPROVAL
REPROVALS
REPROVE
REPROVED
REPROVER
REPROVERS
REPROVES
REPROVING
REPROVINGS
REPRYVE
REPRYVED
REPRYVES
REPRYVING
REPS
REPTANT
REPTATION
REPTATIONS
REPTILE
REPTILES
REPTILIAN
REPTILOID
REPUBLIC
REPUBLICS
REPUBLISH
REPUBLISHED
REPUBLISHES
REPUBLISHING
REPUDIATE
REPUDIATED
REPUDIATES
REPUDIATING
REPUGN
REPUGNANT
REPUGNED
REPUGNING
REPUGNS
REPULP
REPULPED
REPULPING
REPULPS
REPULSE
REPULSED
REPULSES
REPULSING
REPULSION
REPULSIONS
REPULSIVE
REPURE
REPURED
REPURES
REPURIFIED
REPURIFIES
REPURIFY
REPURIFYING
REPURING
REPUTABLE

REPUTABLY
REPUTE
REPUTED
REPUTEDLY
REPUTES
REPUTING
REPUTINGS
REQUERE
REQUERED
REQUERES
REQUERING
REQUEST
REQUESTED
REQUESTER
REQUESTERS
REQUESTING
REQUESTS
REQUICKEN
REQUICKENED
REQUICKENING
REQUICKENS
REQUIEM
REQUIEMS
REQUIGHT
REQUIGHTED
REQUIGHTING
REQUIGHTS
REQUIRE
REQUIRED
REQUIRER
REQUIRERS
REQUIRES
REQUIRING
REQUIRINGS
REQUISITE
REQUISITES
REQUIT
REQUITAL
REQUITALS
REQUITE
REQUITED
REQUITER
REQUITERS
REQUITES
REQUITING
REQUITS
REQUITTED
REQUITTING
REQUOTE
REQUOTED
REQUOTES
REQUOTING
REQUOYLE
REQUOYLED
REQUOYLES
REQUOYLING
RERADIATE
RERADIATED
RERADIATES
RERADIATING
RERAIL
RERAILED
RERAILING
RERAILS
RERAN
REREAD
REREADING
REREADS
REREBRACE
REREBRACES

| | | | | |
|---|---|---|---|---|
| REREDORSE | RESEATS | RESHUFFLING | RESISTIVE | RESPECTING |
| REREDORSES | RÉSEAU | RESIANCE | RESISTOR | RESPECTS |
| REREDOS | RÉSEAUS | RESIANCES | RESISTORS | RESPELL |
| REREDOSES | RÉSEAUX | RESIANT | RESISTS | RESPELLED |
| REREDOSSE | RESECT | RESIANTS | RESIT | RESPELLING |
| REREDOSSES | RESECTED | RESIDE | RESITS | RESPELLS |
| REREMICE | RESECTING | RESIDED | RESITTING | RESPELT |
| REREMOUSE | RESECTION | RESIDENCE | RESKEW | RESPIRE |
| REREVISE | RESECTIONS | RESIDENCES | RESKEWED | RESPIRED |
| REREVISED | RESECTS | RESIDENCIES | RESKEWING | RESPIRES |
| REREVISES | RESEDA | RESIDENCY | RESKEWS | RESPIRING |
| REREVISING | RESEDAS | RESIDENT | RESKUE | RESPITE |
| REREWARD | RESEIZE | RESIDENTS | RESKUED | RESPITED |
| REREWARDS | RESEIZED | RESIDER | RESKUES | RESPITES |
| REROUTE | RESEIZES | RESIDERS | RESKUING | RESPITING |
| REROUTED | RESEIZING | RESIDES | RESNATRON | RESPLEND |
| REROUTEING | RESELECT | RESIDING | RESNATRONS | RESPLENDED |
| REROUTES | RESELECTED | RESIDUA | RESOLD | RESPLENDING |
| REROUTING | RESELECTING | RESIDUAL | RESOLE | RESPLENDS |
| RERUN | RESELECTS | RESIDUALS | RESOLED | RESPOKE |
| RERUNNING | RESELL | RESIDUARY | RESOLES | RESPOKEN |
| RERUNS | RESELLING | RESIDUE | RESOLING | RESPOND |
| RES | RESELLS | RESIDUES | RESOLUBLE | RESPONDED |
| RESAID | RESEMBLE | RESIDUOUS | RESOLUTE | RESPONDER |
| RESALE | RESEMBLED | RESIDUUM | RESOLUTES | RESPONDERS |
| RESALES | RESEMBLER | RESIGN | RESOLVE | RESPONDING |
| RESALGAR | RESEMBLERS | RESIGNED | RESOLVED | RESPONDS |
| RESALGARS | RESEMBLES | RESIGNER | RESOLVENT | RESPONSA |
| RESALUTE | RESEMBLING | RESIGNERS | RESOLVENTS | RESPONSE |
| RESALUTED | RESENT | RESIGNING | RESOLVER | RESPONSER |
| RESALUTES | RESENTED | RESIGNS | RESOLVERS | RESPONSERS |
| RESALUTING | RESENTER | RESILE | RESOLVES | RESPONSES |
| RESAT | RESENTERS | RESILED | RESOLVING | RESPONSOR |
| RESAY | RESENTFUL | RESILES | RESONANCE | RESPONSORS |
| RESAYING | RESENTING | RESILIENT | RESONANCES | RESPONSUM |
| RESAYS | RESENTIVE | RESILING | RESONANT | RESPONSUMS |
| RESCALE | RESENTS | RESIN | RESONATE | RESPRAY |
| RESCALED | RESERPINE | RESINATA | RESONATED | RESPRAYED |
| RESCALES | RESERPINES | RESINATAS | RESONATES | RESPRAYING |
| RESCALING | RESERVE | RESINATE | RESONATING | RESPRAYS |
| RESCIND | RESERVED | RESINATES | RESONATOR | RESSALDAR |
| RESCINDED | RESERVES | RESINED | RESONATORS | RESSALDARS |
| RESCINDING | RESERVING | RESINER | RESORB | REST |
| RESCINDS | RESERVIST | RESINERS | RESORBED | RESTAFF |
| RESCORE | RESERVISTS | RESINIFIED | RESORBENT | RESTAFFED |
| RESCORED | RESERVOIR | RESINIFIES | RESORBING | RESTAFFING |
| RESCORES | RESERVOIRED | RESINIFY | RESORBS | RESTAFFS |
| RESCORING | RESERVOIRING | RESINIFYING | RESORCIN | RESTAGE |
| RESCRIPT | RESERVOIRS | RESINING | RESORCINS | RESTAGED |
| RESCRIPTED | RESET | RESINISE | RESORT | RESTAGES |
| RESCRIPTING | RESETS | RESINISED | RESORTED | RESTAGING |
| RESCRIPTS | RESETTED | RESINISES | RESORTER | RESTART |
| RESCUABLE | RESETTER | RESINISING | RESORTERS | RESTARTED |
| RESCUE | RESETTERS | RESINIZE | RESORTING | RESTARTER |
| RESCUED | RESETTING | RESINIZED | RESORTS | RESTARTERS |
| RESCUER | RESETTLE | RESINIZES | RESOUND | RESTARTING |
| RESCUERS | RESETTLED | RESINIZING | RESOUNDED | RESTARTS |
| RESCUES | RESETTLES | RESINOID | RESOUNDING | RESTATE |
| RESCUING | RESETTLING | RESINOIDS | RESOUNDS | RESTATED |
| RESEAL | RESHAPE | RESINOSES | RESOURCE | RESTATES |
| RESEALED | RESHAPED | RESINOSIS | RESOURCED | RESTATING |
| RESEALING | RESHAPES | RESINOUS | RESOURCES | RESTED |
| RESEALS | RESHAPING | RESINS | RESOURCING | RESTEM |
| RESEARCH | RESHIP | RESIST | RESPEAK | RESTEMMED |
| RESEARCHED | RESHIPPED | RESISTANT | RESPEAKING | RESTEMMING |
| RESEARCHES | RESHIPPING | RESISTANTS | RESPEAKS | RESTEMS |
| RESEARCHING | RESHIPS | RESISTED | RESPECT | RESTER |
| RESEAT | RESHUFFLE | RESISTENT | RESPECTED | RESTERS |
| RESEATED | RESHUFFLED | RESISTENTS | RESPECTER | RESTFUL |
| RESEATING | RESHUFFLES | RESISTING | RESPECTERS | RESTFULLER |

RESTFULLEST
RESTFULLY
RESTIER
RESTIEST
RESTIFF
RESTIFORM
RESTING
RESTINGS
RESTITUTE
RESTITUTED
RESTITUTES
RESTITUTING
RESTIVE
RESTIVELY
RESTLESS
RESTOCK
RESTOCKED
RESTOCKING
RESTOCKS
RESTORE
RESTORED
RESTORER
RESTORERS
RESTORES
RESTORING
RESTRAIN
RESTRAINED
RESTRAINING
RESTRAININGS
RESTRAINS
RESTRAINT
RESTRAINTS
RESTRICT
RESTRICTED
RESTRICTING
RESTRICTS
RESTRING
RESTRINGE
RESTRINGED
RESTRINGES
RESTRINGING
RESTRINGS
RESTRUNG
RESTS
RESTY
RESTYLE
RESTYLED
RESTYLES
RESTYLING
RESUBMIT
RESUBMITS
RESUBMITTED
RESUBMITTING
RESULT
RESULTANT
RESULTANTS
RESULTED
RESULTFUL
RESULTING
RESULTS
RESUMABLE
RESUME
RÉSUMÉ
RESUMED
RESUMES
RÉSUMÉS
RESUMING
RESUPINE
RESURGE
RESURGED

RESURGENT
RESURGES
RESURGING
RESURRECT
RESURRECTED
RESURRECTING
RESURRECTS
RESURVEY
RESURVEYED
RESURVEYING
RESURVEYS
RET
RETABLE
RETABLES
RETAIL
RETAILED
RETAILER
RETAILERS
RETAILING
RETAILS
RETAIN
RETAINED
RETAINER
RETAINERS
RETAINING
RETAINS
RETAKE
RETAKEN
RETAKER
RETAKERS
RETAKES
RETAKING
RETAKINGS
RETALIATE
RETALIATED
RETALIATES
RETALIATING
RETAMA
RETAMAS
RETARD
RETARDANT
RETARDANTS
RETARDATE
RETARDATES
RETARDED
RETARDER
RETARDERS
RETARDING
RETARDS
RETCH
RETCHED
RETCHES
RETCHING
RETCHLESS
RETE
RETELL
RETELLER
RETELLERS
RETELLING
RETELLS
RETENE
RETENES
RETENTION
RETENTIONS
RETENTIVE
RETES
RETEXTURE
RETEXTURED
RETEXTURES
RETEXTURING

RETHINK
RETHINKING
RETHINKS
RETHOUGHT
RETIAL
RETIARII
RETIARIUS
RETIARIUSES
RETIARY
RETICENCE
RETICENCES
RETICENCIES
RETICENCY
RETICENT
RETICLE
RETICLES
RETICULAR
RETICULE
RETICULES
RETICULUM
RETICULUMS
RETIE
RETIED
RETIES
RETIFORM
RETILE
RETILED
RETILES
RETILING
RETINA
RETINAE
RETINAL
RETINAS
RETINITE
RETINITES
RETINITIS
RETINITISES
RETINOL
RETINOLS
RETINUE
RETINUES
RETINULA
RETINULAE
RETINULAR
RETIRACIES
RETIRACY
RETIRAL
RETIRALS
RETIRE
RETIRED
RETIREDLY
RETIREE
RETIREES
RETIRER
RETIRERS
RETIRES
RETIRING
RETITLE
RETITLED
RETITLES
RETITLING
RETOLD
RETOOK
RETOOL
RETOOLED
RETOOLING
RETOOLS
RETORSION
RETORSIONS
RETORT

RETORTED
RETORTER
RETORTERS
RETORTING
RETORTION
RETORTIONS
RETORTIVE
RETORTS
RETOUCH
RETOUCHED
RETOUCHER
RETOUCHERS
RETOUCHES
RETOUCHING
RETOUR
RETOURED
RETOURING
RETOURS
RETRACE
RETRACED
RETRACES
RETRACING
RETRACT
RETRACTED
RETRACTING
RETRACTOR
RETRACTORS
RETRACTS
RETRAICT
RETRAICTS
RETRAIN
RETRAINED
RETRAINING
RETRAINS
RETRAIT
RETRAITE
RETRAITES
RETRAITS
RETRAITT
RETRAITTS
RETRAL
RETRALLY
RETRATE
RETRATED
RETRATES
RETRATING
RETREAD
RETREADED
RETREADING
RETREADS
RETREAT
RETREATED
RETREATING
RETREATS
RETREE
RETREES
RETRENCH
RETRENCHED
RETRENCHES
RETRENCHING
RETRIAL
RETRIALS
RETRIBUTE
RETRIBUTED
RETRIBUTES
RETRIBUTING
RETRIED
RETRIES
RETRIEVAL
RETRIEVALS

RETRIEVE
RETRIEVED
RETRIEVER
RETRIEVERS
RETRIEVES
RETRIEVING
RETRIEVINGS
RETRIM
RETRIMMED
RETRIMMING
RETRIMS
RETRO
RETROACT
RETROACTED
RETROACTING
RETROACTS
RETROCEDE
RETROCEDED
RETROCEDES
RETROCEDING
RETROD
RETRODDEN
RETROFIT
RETROFITS
RETROFITTED
RETROFITTING
RETROFITTINGS
RETROFLEX
RETROJECT
RETROJECTED
RETROJECTING
RETROJECTS
RETRORSE
RETROS
RETROUSSÉ
RETROVERT
RETROVERTED
RETROVERTING
RETROVERTS
RETRY
RETRYING
RETS
RETSINA
RETSINAS
RETTED
RETTERIES
RETTERY
RETTING
RETUND
RETUNDED
RETUNDING
RETUNDS
RETUNE
RETUNED
RETUNES
RETUNING
RETURF
RETURFED
RETURFING
RETURFS
RETURN
RETURNED
RETURNEE
RETURNEES
RETURNING
RETURNS
RETUSE
RETYING
REUNIFIED
REUNIFIES

REUNIFY
REUNIFYING
REUNION
REUNIONS
REUNITE
REUNITED
REUNITES
REUNITING
REURGE
REURGED
REURGES
REURGING
REUSABLE
REUSE
REUSED
REUSES
REUSING
REUTTER
REUTTERED
REUTTERING
REUTTERS
REV
REVALENTA
REVALENTAS
REVALUE
REVALUED
REVALUES
REVALUING
REVAMP
REVAMPED
REVAMPING
REVAMPS
REVANCHE
REVANCHES
REVEAL
REVEALED
REVEALER
REVEALERS
REVEALING
REVEALINGS
REVEALS
REVEILLE
REVEILLES
REVEL
REVELATOR
REVELATORS
REVELLED
REVELLER
REVELLERS
REVELLING
REVELLINGS
REVELRIES
REVELRY
REVELS
REVENANT
REVENANTS
REVENGE
REVENGED
REVENGER
REVENGERS
REVENGES
REVENGING
REVENGINGS
REVENGIVE
REVENUE
REVENUED
REVENUES
REVERABLE
REVERB
REVERBED

REVERBING
REVERBS
REVERE
REVERED
REVERENCE
REVERENCED
REVERENCES
REVERENCING
REVEREND
REVERENDS
REVERENT
REVERER
REVERERS
REVERES
REVERIE
REVERIES
REVERING
REVERIST
REVERISTS
REVERS
REVERSAL
REVERSALS
REVERSE
REVERSED
REVERSELY
REVERSER
REVERSERS
REVERSES
REVERSI
REVERSING
REVERSINGS
REVERSION
REVERSIONS
REVERSIS
REVERSISES
REVERSO
REVERSOS
REVERT
REVERTED
REVERTING
REVERTIVE
REVERTS
REVERY
REVEST
REVESTED
REVESTING
REVESTRIES
REVESTRY
REVESTS
REVET
REVETMENT
REVETMENTS
REVETS
REVETTED
REVETTING
RÊVEUR
RÊVEURS
RÊVEUSE
RÊVEUSES
REVICTUAL
REVICTUALLED
REVICTUALLING
REVICTUALS
REVIE
REVIED
REVIES
REVIEW
REVIEWAL
REVIEWALS
REVIEWED

REVIEWER
REVIEWERS
REVIEWING
REVIEWS
REVILE
REVILED
REVILER
REVILERS
REVILES
REVILING
REVILINGS
REVISABLE
REVISAL
REVISALS
REVISE
REVISED
REVISER
REVISERS
REVISES
REVISING
REVISION
REVISIONS
REVISIT
REVISITED
REVISITING
REVISITS
REVISOR
REVISORS
REVISORY
REVIVABLE
REVIVABLY
REVIVAL
REVIVALS
REVIVE
REVIVED
REVIVER
REVIVERS
REVIVES
REVIVIFIED
REVIVIFIES
REVIVIFY
REVIVIFYING
REVIVING
REVIVINGS
REVIVOR
REVIVORS
REVOCABLE
REVOCABLY
REVOKE
REVOKED
REVOKES
REVOKING
REVOLT
REVOLTED
REVOLTER
REVOLTERS
REVOLTING
REVOLTS
REVOLUTE
REVOLVE
REVOLVED
REVOLVER
REVOLVERS
REVOLVES
REVOLVING
REVOLVINGS
REVS
REVUE
REVUES
REVULSION

REVULSIONS
REVULSIVE
REVVED
REVVING
REVYING
REW
REWARD
REWARDED
REWARDER
REWARDERS
REWARDFUL
REWARDING
REWARDS
REWAREWA
REWAREWAS
REWEIGH
REWEIGHED
REWEIGHING
REWEIGHS
REWIND
REWINDING
REWINDS
REWIRE
REWIRED
REWIRES
REWIRING
REWORD
REWORDED
REWORDING
REWORDS
REWORK
REWORKED
REWORKING
REWORKS
REWOUND
REWRAP
REWRAPPED
REWRAPPING
REWRAPS
REWRITE
REWRITES
REWRITING
REWRITTEN
REWROTE
REWS
REWTH
REWTHS
REX
REYNARD
REYNARDS
RHABDOID
RHABDOIDS
RHABDOM
RHABDOMS
RHABDUS
RHABDUSES
RHACHIDES
RHACHIS
RHACHISES
RHACHITIS
RHACHITISES
RHAMPHOID
RHAPHE
RHAPHES
RHAPHIDE
RHAPHIDES
RHAPHIS
RHAPONTIC
RHAPONTICS
RHAPSODE

RHAPSODES
RHAPSODIC
RHAPSODIES
RHAPSODY
RHATANIES
RHATANY
RHEA
RHEAS
RHEMATIC
RHENIUM
RHENIUMS
RHEOCHORD
RHEOCHORDS
RHEOCORD
RHEOCORDS
RHEOLOGIC
RHEOLOGIES
RHEOLOGY
RHEOMETER
RHEOMETERS
RHEOSTAT
RHEOSTATS
RHEOTAXES
RHEOTAXIS
RHEOTOME
RHEOTOMES
RHEOTROPE
RHEOTROPES
RHESUS
RHESUSES
RHETOR
RHETORIC
RHETORICS
RHETORISE
RHETORISED
RHETORISES
RHETORISING
RHETORIZE
RHETORIZED
RHETORIZES
RHETORIZING
RHETORS
RHEUM
RHEUMATIC
RHEUMATICS
RHEUMATIZ
RHEUMATIZES
RHEUMATIZZES
RHEUMED
RHEUMS
RHEUMY
RHEXES
RHEXIS
RHEXISES
RHIES
RHIME
RHIMES
RHINAL
RHINE
RHINES
RHINITIS
RHINITISES
RHINO
RHINOLITH
RHINOLITHS
RHINOLOGIES
RHINOLOGY
RHINOS
RHIPIDATE
RHIPIDION

| | | | | |
|---|---|---|---|---|
| RHIPIDIONS | RHOTACISE | RIATAS | RICH | RIDDLE |
| RHIPIDIUM | RHOTACISED | RIB | RICHED | RIDDLED |
| RHIPIDIUMS | RHOTACISES | RIBALD | RICHEN | RIDDLER |
| RHIZIC | RHOTACISING | RIBALDRIES | RICHENED | RIDDLERS |
| RHIZINE | RHOTACISM | RIBALDRY | RICHENING | RIDDLES |
| RHIZINES | RHOTACISMS | RIBALDS | RICHENS | RIDDLING |
| RHIZOBIA | RHOTACIZE | RIBAND | RICHER | RIDDLINGS |
| RHIZOBIUM | RHOTACIZED | RIBANDED | RICHES | RIDE |
| RHIZOCARP | RHOTACIZES | RIBANDING | RICHESSE | RIDEABLE |
| RHIZOCARPS | RHOTACIZING | RIBANDS | RICHESSES | RIDENT |
| RHIZOCAUL | RHOTIC | RIBATTUTA | RICHEST | RIDER |
| RHIZOCAULS | RHUBARB | RIBATTUTAS | RICHING | RIDERED |
| RHIZOID | RHUBARBS | RIBAUD | RICHLY | RIDERLESS |
| RHIZOIDAL | RHUBARBY | RIBAUDRED | RICHNESS | RIDERS |
| RHIZOIDS | RHUMB | RIBAUDRIES | RICHNESSES | RIDES |
| RHIZOME | RHUMBA | RIBAUDRY | RICHT | RIDGE |
| RHIZOMES | RHUMBAED | RIBAUDS | RICHTED | RIDGEBACK |
| RHIZOPI | RHUMBAING | RIBBAND | RICHTER | RIDGEBACKS |
| RHIZOPOD | RHUMBAS | RIBBANDED | RICHTEST | RIDGED |
| RHIZOPODS | RHUMBS | RIBBANDING | RICHTING | RIDGEL |
| RHIZOPUS | RHUS | RIBBANDS | RICHTS | RIDGELS |
| RHIZOPUSES | RHUSES | RIBBED | RICIER | RIDGES |
| RHO | RHY | RIBBIER | RICIEST | RIDGEWAY |
| RHODAMINE | RHYME | RIBBIEST | RICIN | RIDGEWAYS |
| RHODAMINES | RHYMED | RIBBING | RICING | RIDGIER |
| RHODANATE | RHYMELESS | RIBBINGS | RICINS | RIDGIEST |
| RHODANATES | RHYMER | RIBBON | RICK | RIDGIL |
| RHODANIC | RHYMERS | RIBBONED | RICKED | RIDGILS |
| RHODANISE | RHYMES | RIBBONING | RICKER | RIDGING |
| RHODANISED | RHYMESTER | RIBBONRIES | RICKERS | RIDGINGS |
| RHODANISES | RHYMESTERS | RIBBONRY | RICKETILY | RIDGLING |
| RHODANISING | RHYMING | RIBBONS | RICKETS | RIDGLINGS |
| RHODANIZE | RHYMIST | RIBBONY | RICKETTY | RIDGY |
| RHODANIZED | RHYMISTS | RIBBY | RICKETY | RIDICULE |
| RHODANIZES | RHYNE | RIBCAGE | RICKING | RIDICULED |
| RHODANIZING | RHYNES | RIBCAGES | RICKLE | RIDICULER |
| RHODIC | RHYOLITE | RIBIBE | RICKLES | RIDICULERS |
| RHODIUM | RHYOLITES | RIBIBES | RICKLY | RIDICULES |
| RHODIUMS | RHYOLITIC | RIBIBLE | RICKS | RIDICULING |
| RHODOLITE | RHYTA | RIBIBLES | RICKSHA | RIDING |
| RHODOLITES | RHYTHM | RIBLESS | RICKSHAS | RIDINGS |
| RHODONITE | RHYTHMAL | RIBLET | RICKSHAW | RIDOTTO |
| RHODONITES | RHYTHMED | RIBLETS | RICKSHAWS | RIDOTTOS |
| RHODOPSIN | RHYTHMI | RIBLIKE | RICKSTAND | RIDS |
| RHODOPSINS | RHYTHMIC | RIBOSE | RICKSTANDS | RIEL |
| RHODORA | RHYTHMICS | RIBOSES | RICKSTICK | RIELS |
| RHODORAS | RHYTHMISE | RIBOSOMAL | RICKSTICKS | RIEM |
| RHODOUS | RHYTHMISED | RIBOSOME | RICKYARD | RIEMPIE |
| RHOEADINE | RHYTHMISES | RIBOSOMES | RICKYARDS | RIEMPIES |
| RHOEADINES | RHYTHMISING | RIBS | RICOCHET | RIEMS |
| RHOMB | RHYTHMIST | RIBSTON | RICOCHETED | RIEVE |
| RHOMBI | RHYTHMISTS | RIBSTONE | RICOCHETING | RIEVER |
| RHOMBIC | RHYTHMIZE | RIBSTONES | RICOCHETS | RIEVERS |
| RHOMBOI | RHYTHMIZED | RIBSTONS | RICOCHETTED | RIEVES |
| RHOMBOID | RHYTHMIZES | RIBWORK | RICOCHETTING | RIEVING |
| RHOMBOIDS | RHYTHMIZING | RIBWORKS | RICOTTA | RIFE |
| RHOMBOS | RHYTHMS | RIBWORT | RICOTTAS | RIFELY |
| RHOMBS | RHYTHMUS | RIBWORTS | RICTAL | RIFENESS |
| RHOMBUS | RHYTHMUSES | RICE | RICTUS | RIFENESSES |
| RHOMBUSES | RHYTINA | RICED | RICTUSES | RIFER |
| RHONCHAL | RHYTINAS | RICER | RICY | RIFEST |
| RHONCHI | RHYTON | RICERCAR | RID | RIFF |
| RHONCHIAL | RIA | RICERCARE | RIDABLE | RIFFLE |
| RHONCHUS | RIAL | RICERCARES | RIDDANCE | RIFFLED |
| RHONE | RIALS | RICERCARS | RIDDANCES | RIFFLER |
| RHONES | RIANCIES | RICERCATA | RIDDED | RIFFLERS |
| RHOPALIC | RIANCY | RICERCATAS | RIDDEN | RIFFLES |
| RHOPALISM | RIANT | RICERS | RIDDER | RIFFLING |
| RHOPALISMS | RIAS | RICES | RIDDERS | RIFFS |
| RHOS | RIATA | RICEY | RIDDING | RIFLE |

| | | | | |
|---|---|---|---|---|
| RIFLED | RIGIDIZES | RIN | RIOTER | RISALDARS |
| RIFLEMAN | RIGIDIZING | RIND | RIOTERS | RISE |
| RIFLEMEN | RIGIDLY | RINDED | RIOTING | RISEN |
| RIFLER | RIGIDNESS | RINDIER | RIOTINGS | RISER |
| RIFLERS | RIGIDNESSES | RINDIEST | RIOTISE | RISERS |
| RIFLES | RIGIDS | RINDING | RIOTISES | RISES |
| RIFLING | RIGLIN | RINDLESS | RIOTIZE | RISHI |
| RIFLINGS | RIGLING | RINDS | RIOTIZES | RISHIS |
| RIFT | RIGLINGS | RINDY | RIOTOUS | RISIBLE |
| RIFTE | RIGLINS | RINE | RIOTOUSLY | RISING |
| RIFTED | RIGMAROLE | RINES | RIOTRIES | RISINGS |
| RIFTIER | RIGMAROLES | RING | RIOTRY | RISK |
| RIFTIEST | RIGOL | RINGBIT | RIOTS | RISKED |
| RIFTING | RIGOLL | RINGBITS | RIP | RISKER |
| RIFTLESS | RIGOLLS | RINGBONE | RIPARIAL | RISKERS |
| RIFTS | RIGOLS | RINGBONES | RIPARIAN | RISKFUL |
| RIFTY | RIGOR | RINGED | RIPARIANS | RISKIER |
| RIG | RIGORISM | RINGENT | RIPE | RISKIEST |
| RIGADOON | RIGORISMS | RINGER | RIPECK | RISKILY |
| RIGADOONS | RIGORIST | RINGERS | RIPECKS | RISKINESS |
| RIGG | RIGORISTS | RINGGIT | RIPED | RISKINESSES |
| RIGGALD | RIGOROUS | RINGGITS | RIPELY | RISKING |
| RIGGALDS | RIGORS | RINGHALS | RIPEN | RISKS |
| RIGGED | RIGOUR | RINGHALSES | RIPENED | RISKY |
| RIGGER | RIGOURS | RINGING | RIPENESS | RISOLUTO |
| RIGGERS | RIGS | RINGINGLY | RIPENESSES | RISOTTO |
| RIGGING | RIGWIDDIE | RINGINGS | RIPENING | RISOTTOS |
| RIGGINGS | RIGWIDDIES | RINGLESS | RIPENS | RISP |
| RIGGISH | RIGWOODIE | RINGLET | RIPER | RISPED |
| RIGGS | RIGWOODIES | RINGLETED | RIPERS | RISPETTI |
| RIGHT | RIJSTAFEL | RINGLETS | RIPES | RISPETTO |
| RIGHTABLE | RIJSTAFELS | RINGMAN | RIPEST | RISPING |
| RIGHTED | RILE | RINGMEN | RIPIENI | RISPINGS |
| RIGHTEN | RILED | RINGS | RIPIENIST | RISPS |
| RIGHTENED | RILES | RINGSIDE | RIPIENISTS | RISQUE |
| RIGHTENING | RILEY | RINGSIDER | RIPIENO | RISQUÉ |
| RIGHTENS | RILIEVI | RINGSIDERS | RIPIENOS | RISQUES |
| RIGHTEOUS | RILIEVO | RINGSIDES | RIPING | RISSOLE |
| RIGHTER | RILING | RINGSTAND | RIPOSTE | RISSOLES |
| RIGHTERS | RILL | RINGSTANDS | RIPOSTED | RISUS |
| RIGHTEST | RILLE | RINGSTER | RIPOSTES | RISUSES |
| RIGHTFUL | RILLED | RINGSTERS | RIPOSTING | RIT |
| RIGHTING | RILLES | RINGTAIL | RIPP | RITE |
| RIGHTINGS | RILLET | RINGTAILS | RIPPED | RITELESS |
| RIGHTIST | RILLETS | RINGWAY | RIPPER | RITENUTO |
| RIGHTISTS | RILLETTES | RINGWAYS | RIPPERS | RITENUTOS |
| RIGHTLESS | RILLING | RINGWISE | RIPPIER | RITES |
| RIGHTLY | RILLMARK | RINGWORK | RIPPIERS | RITORNEL |
| RIGHTNESS | RILLMARKS | RINGWORKS | RIPPING | RITORNELL |
| RIGHTNESSES | RILLS | RINGWORM | RIPPINGLY | RITORNELLS |
| RIGHTO | RIM | RINGWORMS | RIPPLE | RITORNELS |
| RIGHTOS | RIMA | RINK | RIPPLED | RITS |
| RIGHTS | RIMAE | RINKED | RIPPLER | RITT |
| RIGHTWARD | RIME | RINKHALS | RIPPLERS | RITTED |
| RIGHTWARDS | RIMED | RINKHALSES | RIPPLES | RITTER |
| RIGID | RIMER | RINKING | RIPPLET | RITTERS |
| RIGIDER | RIMERS | RINKS | RIPPLETS | RITTING |
| RIGIDEST | RIMES | RINNING | RIPPLIER | RITTS |
| RIGIDIFIED | RIMIER | RINS | RIPPLIEST | RITUAL |
| RIGIDIFIES | RIMIEST | RINSABLE | RIPPLING | RITUALISE |
| RIGIDIFY | RIMING | RINSE | RIPPLINGS | RITUALISED |
| RIGIDIFYING | RIMLESS | RINSED | RIPPLY | RITUALISES |
| RIGIDISE | RIMMED | RINSER | RIPPS | RITUALISING |
| RIGIDISED | RIMMING | RINSERS | RIPRAP | RITUALISM |
| RIGIDISES | RIMOSE | RINSES | RIPRAPS | RITUALISMS |
| RIGIDISING | RIMOUS | RINSIBLE | RIPS | RITUALIST |
| RIGIDITIES | RIMS | RINSING | RIPT | RITUALISTS |
| RIGIDITY | RIMU | RINSINGS | RIPTIDE | RITUALIZE |
| RIGIDIZE | RIMUS | RIOT | RIPTIDES | RITUALIZED |
| RIGIDIZED | RIMY | RIOTED | RISALDAR | RITUALIZES |

| | | | | |
|---|---|---|---|---|
| RITUALIZING | RIVIÈRES | ROARIEST | ROCKAWAY | ROE |
| RITUALLY | RIVING | ROARING | ROCKAWAYS | ROEBUCK |
| RITUALS | RIVLIN | ROARINGLY | ROCKCRESS | ROEBUCKS |
| RITZIER | RIVLINS | ROARINGS | ROCKCRESSES | ROED |
| RITZIEST | RIVO | ROARS | ROCKED | ROEMER |
| RITZY | RIVOS | ROARY | ROCKER | ROEMERS |
| RIVA | RIVULET | ROAST | ROCKERIES | ROENTGEN |
| RIVAGE | RIVULETS | ROASTED | ROCKERS | ROENTGENS |
| RIVAGES | RIYAL | ROASTER | ROCKERY | ROES |
| RIVAL | RIYALS | ROASTERS | ROCKET | ROESTONE |
| RIVALESS | RIZ | ROASTING | ROCKETED | ROESTONES |
| RIVALESSES | RIZARD | ROASTINGS | ROCKETEER | ROGATION |
| RIVALISE | RIZARDS | ROASTS | ROCKETEERS | ROGATIONS |
| RIVALISED | RIZZAR | ROATE | ROCKETER | ROGATORY |
| RIVALISES | RIZZARED | ROATED | ROCKETERS | ROGER |
| RIVALISING | RIZZARING | ROATES | ROCKETING | ROGERED |
| RIVALITIES | RIZZARS | ROATING | ROCKETRIES | ROGERING |
| RIVALITY | RIZZART | ROB | ROCKETRY | ROGERINGS |
| RIVALIZE | RIZZARTS | ROBALO | ROCKETS | ROGERS |
| RIVALIZED | RIZZER | ROBALOS | ROCKIER | ROGUE |
| RIVALIZES | RIZZERED | ROBBED | ROCKIERS | ROGUED |
| RIVALIZING | RIZZERING | ROBBER | ROCKIEST | ROGUERIES |
| RIVALLED | RIZZERS | ROBBERIES | ROCKILY | ROGUERY |
| RIVALLESS | RIZZOR | ROBBERS | ROCKINESS | ROGUES |
| RIVALLING | RIZZORED | ROBBERY | ROCKINESSES | ROGUESHIP |
| RIVALRIES | RIZZORING | ROBBING | ROCKING | ROGUESHIPS |
| RIVALRY | RIZZORS | ROBE | ROCKINGS | ROGUING |
| RIVALS | ROACH | ROBED | ROCKLAY | ROGUISH |
| RIVALSHIP | ROACHED | ROBES | ROCKLAYS | ROGUISHLY |
| RIVALSHIPS | ROACHES | ROBIN | ROCKLING | ROGUY |
| RIVAS | ROACHING | ROBING | ROCKLINGS | ROIL |
| RIVE | ROAD | ROBINGS | ROCKS | ROILED |
| RIVED | ROADBLOCK | ROBINIA | ROCKWATER | ROILIER |
| RIVEL | ROADBLOCKS | ROBINIAS | ROCKWATERS | ROILIEST |
| RIVELLED | ROADHOUSE | ROBINS | ROCKWEED | ROILING |
| RIVELLING | ROADHOUSES | ROBLE | ROCKWEEDS | ROILS |
| RIVELS | ROADIE | ROBLES | ROCKWORK | ROILY |
| RIVEN | ROADIES | ROBORANT | ROCKWORKS | ROIN |
| RIVER | ROADING | ROBORANTS | ROCKY | ROINED |
| RIVERAIN | ROADINGS | ROBOT | ROCOCO | ROINING |
| RIVERAINS | ROADLESS | ROBOTIC | ROCOCOS | ROINISH |
| RIVERED | ROADMAN | ROBOTICS | ROCQUET | ROINS |
| RIVERET | ROADMEN | ROBOTISE | ROCQUETS | ROIST |
| RIVERETS | ROADS | ROBOTISED | ROCS | ROISTED |
| RIVERINE | ROADSHOW | ROBOTISES | ROD | ROISTER |
| RIVERLESS | ROADSHOWS | ROBOTISING | RODDED | ROISTERED |
| RIVERLIKE | ROADSIDE | ROBOTIZE | RODDING | ROISTERER |
| RIVERMAN | ROADSIDES | ROBOTIZED | RODDINGS | ROISTERERS |
| RIVERMEN | ROADSMAN | ROBOTIZES | RODE | ROISTERING |
| RIVERS | ROADSMEN | ROBOTIZING | RODED | ROISTERS |
| RIVERSIDE | ROADSTEAD | ROBOTS | RODENT | ROISTING |
| RIVERSIDES | ROADSTEADS | ROBS | RODENTS | ROISTS |
| RIVERWAY | ROADSTER | ROBURITE | RODEO | ROK |
| RIVERWAYS | ROADSTERS | ROBURITES | RODEOS | ROKE |
| RIVERWEED | ROADWAY | ROBUST | RODES | ROKED |
| RIVERWEEDS | ROADWAYS | ROBUSTA | RODEWAY | ROKELAY |
| RIVERY | ROAM | ROBUSTAS | RODEWAYS | ROKELAYS |
| RIVES | ROAMED | ROBUSTER | RODFISHER | ROKER |
| RIVET | ROAMER | ROBUSTEST | RODFISHERS | ROKERS |
| RIVETED | ROAMERS | ROBUSTLY | RODING | ROKES |
| RIVETER | ROAMING | ROC | RODINGS | ROKIER |
| RIVETERS | ROAMS | ROCAILLE | RODLESS | ROKIEST |
| RIVETING | ROAN | ROCAILLES | RODLIKE | ROKING |
| RIVETINGS | ROANS | ROCAMBOLE | RODMAN | ROKS |
| RIVETS | ROAR | ROCAMBOLES | RODMEN | ROKY |
| RIVETTED | ROARED | ROCH | RODS | ROLAG |
| RIVETTING | ROARER | ROCHES | RODSMAN | ROLAGS |
| RIVIERA | ROARERS | ROCHET | RODSMEN | RÔLE |
| RIVIERAS | ROARIE | ROCHETS | RODSTER | ROLE |
| RIVIÈRE | ROARIER | ROCK | RODSTERS | RÔLES |

ROLES
ROLL
ROLLABLE
ROLLED
ROLLER
ROLLERS
ROLLICK
ROLLICKED
ROLLICKING
ROLLICKINGS
ROLLICKS
ROLLING
ROLLINGS
ROLLMOP
ROLLMOPS
ROLLOCK
ROLLOCKS
ROLLS
ROM
ROMA
ROMAGE
ROMAGES
ROMAIKA
ROMAIKAS
ROMAL
ROMALS
ROMAN
ROMANCE
ROMANCED
ROMANCER
ROMANCERS
ROMANCES
ROMANCING
ROMANCINGS
ROMANS
ROMANTIC
ROMANTICS
ROMAS
ROMAUNT
ROMAUNTS
ROMNEYA
ROMNEYAS
ROMP
ROMPED
ROMPER
ROMPERS
ROMPING
ROMPINGLY
ROMPISH
ROMPISHLY
ROMPS
RONCADOR
RONCADORS
RONDACHE
RONDACHES
RONDAVEL
RONDAVELS
RONDE
RONDEAU
RONDEAUX
RONDEL
RONDELS
RONDES
RONDINO
RONDINOS
RONDO
RONDOS
RONDURE
RONDURES
RONE

RONEO
RONEOED
RONEOING
RONEOS
RONES
RONG
RONGGENG
RONGGENGS
RONNE
RONNING
RONT
RONTE
RONTES
RÖNTGEN
RÖNTGENS
RONTS
RONYON
RONYONS
ROO
ROOD
ROODS
ROOF
ROOFED
ROOFER
ROOFERS
ROOFIER
ROOFIEST
ROOFING
ROOFINGS
ROOFLESS
ROOFS
ROOFY
ROOINEK
ROOINEKS
ROOK
ROOKED
ROOKERIES
ROOKERY
ROOKIE
ROOKIES
ROOKING
ROOKISH
ROOKS
ROOKY
ROOM
ROOMED
ROOMER
ROOMERS
ROOMETTE
ROOMETTES
ROOMFUL
ROOMFULS
ROOMIER
ROOMIEST
ROOMILY
ROOMINESS
ROOMINESSES
ROOMING
ROOMS
ROOMSOME
ROOMY
ROON
ROONS
ROOP
ROOPED
ROOPIER
ROOPIEST
ROOPING
ROOPIT
ROOPS

ROOPY
ROOS
ROOSA
ROOSAS
ROOSE
ROOSED
ROOSES
ROOSING
ROOST
ROOSTED
ROOSTER
ROOSTERS
ROOSTING
ROOSTS
ROOT
ROOTAGE
ROOTAGES
ROOTED
ROOTEDLY
ROOTER
ROOTERS
ROOTHOLD
ROOTHOLDS
ROOTIER
ROOTIES
ROOTIEST
ROOTING
ROOTINGS
ROOTLE
ROOTLED
ROOTLES
ROOTLESS
ROOTLET
ROOTLETS
ROOTLIKE
ROOTLING
ROOTS
ROOTSTOCK
ROOTSTOCKS
ROOTY
ROPABLE
ROPE
ROPEABLE
ROPED
ROPER
ROPERIES
ROPERS
ROPERY
ROPES
ROPEWAY
ROPEWAYS
ROPEWORK
ROPEWORKS
ROPEY
ROPIER
ROPIEST
ROPILY
ROPINESS
ROPINESSES
ROPING
ROPINGS
ROPY
ROQUE
ROQUES
ROQUET
ROQUETED
ROQUETING
ROQUETS
ROQUETTE
ROQUETTES

RORAL
RORE
RORES
RORIC
RORID
RORIE
RORIER
RORIEST
RORQUAL
RORQUALS
RORT
RORTER
RORTERS
RORTIER
RORTIEST
RORTS
RORTY
RORY
ROSACE
ROSACEA
ROSACEAS
ROSACEOUS
ROSACES
ROSAKER
ROSAKERS
ROSALIA
ROSALIAS
ROSARIAN
ROSARIANS
ROSARIES
ROSARIUM
ROSARIUMS
ROSARY
ROSCID
ROSE
ROSÉ
ROSEAL
ROSEATE
ROSED
ROSEFISH
ROSEFISHES
ROSELESS
ROSELIKE
ROSELLA
ROSELLAS
ROSELLE
ROSELLES
ROSEMARIES
ROSEMARY
ROSEOLA
ROSEOLAS
ROSERIES
ROSERY
ROSES
ROSÉS
ROSET
ROSETED
ROSETING
ROSETS
ROSETTE
ROSETTED
ROSETTES
ROSETTY
ROSETY
ROSEWOOD
ROSEWOODS
ROSIED
ROSIER
ROSIERE
ROSIERES

ROSIERS
ROSIES
ROSIEST
ROSILY
ROSIN
ROSINATE
ROSINATES
ROSINED
ROSINESS
ROSINESSES
ROSING
ROSINING
ROSINS
ROSINY
ROSIT
ROSITED
ROSITING
ROSITS
ROSMARINE
ROSMARINES
ROSOGLIO
ROSOGLIOS
ROSOLIO
ROSOLIOS
ROSSER
ROSSERS
ROST
ROSTED
ROSTELLAR
ROSTELLUM
ROSTELLUMS
ROSTER
ROSTERED
ROSTERING
ROSTERINGS
ROSTERS
ROSTING
ROSTRA
ROSTRAL
ROSTRATE
ROSTRATED
ROSTRUM
ROSTRUMS
ROSTS
ROSULA
ROSULAS
ROSULATE
ROSY
ROSYING
ROT
ROTA
ROTAL
ROTAPLANE
ROTAPLANES
ROTARIES
ROTARY
ROTAS
ROTATABLE
ROTATE
ROTATED
ROTATES
ROTATING
ROTATION
ROTATIONS
ROTATIVE
ROTATOR
ROTATORS
ROTATORY
ROTAVATE
ROTAVATED

| | | | | |
|---|---|---|---|---|
| ROTAVATES | ROTURIER | ROUNDHAND | ROUTINIST | ROYALISED |
| ROTAVATING | ROTURIERS | ROUNDHANDS | ROUTINISTS | ROYALISES |
| ROTAVATOR | ROUBLE | ROUNDING | ROUTINIZE | ROYALISING |
| ROTAVATORS | ROUBLES | ROUNDINGS | ROUTINIZED | ROYALISM |
| ROTAVIRUS | ROUCOU | ROUNDISH | ROUTINIZES | ROYALISMS |
| ROTAVIRUSES | ROUCOUS | ROUNDLE | ROUTINIZING | ROYALIST |
| ROTCH | ROUÉ | ROUNDLES | ROUTOUS | ROYALISTS |
| ROTCHE | ROUÉS | ROUNDLET | ROUTOUSLY | ROYALIZE |
| ROTCHES | ROUGE | ROUNDLETS | ROUTS | ROYALIZED |
| ROTCHIE | ROUGED | ROUNDLY | ROUX | ROYALIZES |
| ROTCHIES | ROUGES | ROUNDNESS | ROVE | ROYALIZING |
| ROTE | ROUGH | ROUNDNESSES | ROVED | ROYALLER |
| ROTED | ROUGHAGE | ROUNDS | ROVER | ROYALLEST |
| ROTENONE | ROUGHAGES | ROUNDSMAN | ROVERS | ROYALLY |
| ROTENONES | ROUGHCAST | ROUNDSMEN | ROVES | ROYALS |
| ROTES | ROUGHCASTED | ROUNDURE | ROVING | ROYALTIES |
| ROTGRASS | ROUGHCASTING | ROUNDURES | ROVINGLY | ROYALTY |
| ROTGRASSES | ROUGHCASTS | ROUP | ROVINGS | ROYNE |
| ROTGUT | ROUGHED | ROUPED | ROW | ROYNED |
| ROTGUTS | ROUGHEN | ROUPIER | ROWABLE | ROYNES |
| ROTHER | ROUGHENED | ROUPIEST | ROWAN | ROYNING |
| ROTHERS | ROUGHENING | ROUPING | ROWANS | ROYNISH |
| ROTI | ROUGHENS | ROUPIT | ROWBOAT | ROYST |
| ROTIFER | ROUGHER | ROUPS | ROWBOATS | ROYSTED |
| ROTIFERAL | ROUGHERS | ROUPY | ROWDEDOW | ROYSTER |
| ROTIFERS | ROUGHEST | ROUSANT | ROWDEDOWS | ROYSTERED |
| ROTING | ROUGHIE | ROUSE | ROWDIER | ROYSTERER |
| ROTIS | ROUGHIES | ROUSED | ROWDIES | ROYSTERERS |
| ROTL | ROUGHING | ROUSEMENT | ROWDIEST | ROYSTERING |
| ROTLS | ROUGHISH | ROUSEMENTS | ROWDILY | ROYSTERS |
| ROTOGRAPH | ROUGHLY | ROUSER | ROWDINESS | ROYSTING |
| ROTOGRAPHED | ROUGHNECK | ROUSERS | ROWDINESSES | ROYSTS |
| ROTOGRAPHING | ROUGHNECKS | ROUSES | ROWDY | ROZELLE |
| ROTOGRAPHS | ROUGHNESS | ROUSING | ROWDYDOW | ROZELLES |
| ROTOLO | ROUGHNESSES | ROUSINGLY | ROWDYDOWS | ROZET |
| ROTOLOS | ROUGHS | ROUSSETTE | ROWDYISH | ROZETED |
| ROTOR | ROUGHT | ROUSSETTES | ROWDYISM | ROZETING |
| ROTORS | ROUGHY | ROUST | ROWDYISMS | ROZETS |
| ROTOVATE | ROUGING | ROUSTED | ROWED | ROZIT |
| ROTOVATED | ROUL | ROUSTER | ROWEL | ROZITED |
| ROTOVATES | ROULADE | ROUSTERS | ROWELLED | ROZITING |
| ROTOVATING | ROULADES | ROUSTING | ROWELLING | ROZITS |
| ROTOVATOR | ROULE | ROUSTS | ROWELS | ROZZER |
| ROTOVATORS | ROULEAU | ROUT | ROWEN | ROZZERS |
| ROTS | ROULEAUS | ROUTE | ROWENS | RUB |
| ROTTAN | ROULEAUX | ROUTED | ROWER | RUBAIYAT |
| ROTTANS | ROULES | ROUTEING | ROWERS | RUBAIYATS |
| ROTTED | ROULETTE | ROUTEMAN | ROWING | RUBATI |
| ROTTEN | ROULETTES | ROUTEMEN | ROWINGS | RUBATO |
| ROTTENER | ROULS | ROUTER | ROWLOCK | RUBATOS |
| ROTTENEST | ROUM | ROUTERS | ROWLOCKS | RUBBED |
| ROTTENLY | ROUMING | ROUTES | ROWME | RUBBER |
| ROTTENS | ROUMINGS | ROUTH | ROWMES | RUBBERED |
| ROTTER | ROUMS | ROUTHIE | ROWND | RUBBERING |
| ROTTERS | ROUNCE | ROUTHIER | ROWNDED | RUBBERISE |
| ROTTING | ROUNCES | ROUTHIEST | ROWNDELL | RUBBERISED |
| ROTULA | ROUNCEVAL | ROUTHS | ROWNDELLS | RUBBERISES |
| ROTULAS | ROUNCEVALS | ROUTINE | ROWNDING | RUBBERISING |
| ROTUND | ROUNCIES | ROUTINEER | ROWNDS | RUBBERIZE |
| ROTUNDA | ROUNCY | ROUTINEERS | ROWS | RUBBERIZED |
| ROTUNDAS | ROUND | ROUTINELY | ROWT | RUBBERIZES |
| ROTUNDATE | ROUNDARCH | ROUTINES | ROWTED | RUBBERIZING |
| ROTUNDED | ROUNDED | ROUTING | ROWTH | RUBBERS |
| ROTUNDER | ROUNDEL | ROUTINGS | ROWTHS | RUBBERY |
| ROTUNDEST | ROUNDELAY | ROUTINISE | ROWTING | RUBBET |
| ROTUNDING | ROUNDELAYS | ROUTINISED | ROWTS | RUBBING |
| ROTUNDITIES | ROUNDELS | ROUTINISES | ROYAL | RUBBINGS |
| ROTUNDITY | ROUNDER | ROUTINISING | ROYALET | RUBBISH |
| ROTUNDLY | ROUNDERS | ROUTINISM | ROYALETS | RUBBISHED |
| ROTUNDS | ROUNDEST | ROUTINISMS | ROYALISE | RUBBISHES |

| | | | | |
|---|---|---|---|---|
| RUBBISHING | RUCHINGS | RUELLIA | RUINOUS | RUMMEST |
| RUBBISHLY | RUCK | RUELLIAS | RUINOUSLY | RUMMIER |
| RUBBISHY | RUCKED | RUES | RUINS | RUMMIES |
| RUBBIT | RUCKING | RUFESCENT | RUKH | RUMMIEST |
| RUBBLE | RUCKLE | RUFF | RUKHS | RUMMILY |
| RUBBLES | RUCKLED | RUFFE | RULABLE | RUMMINESS |
| RUBBLIER | RUCKLES | RUFFED | RULE | RUMMINESSES |
| RUBBLIEST | RUCKLING | RUFFES | RULED | RUMMISH |
| RUBBLY | RUCKS | RUFFIAN | RULELESS | RUMMY |
| RUBDOWN | RUCKSACK | RUFFIANED | RULER | RUMOR |
| RUBDOWNS | RUCKSACKS | RUFFIANING | RULERED | RUMORED |
| RUBE | RUCKUS | RUFFIANLY | RULERING | RUMORING |
| RUBEFIED | RUCKUSES | RUFFIANS | RULERS | RUMOROUS |
| RUBEFIES | RUCS | RUFFIN | RULERSHIP | RUMORS |
| RUBEFY | RUCTATION | RUFFING | RULERSHIPS | RUMOUR |
| RUBEFYING | RUCTATIONS | RUFFINS | RULES | RUMOURED |
| RUBELLA | RUCTION | RUFFLE | RULESSE | RUMOURER |
| RUBELLAN | RUCTIONS | RUFFLED | RULIER | RUMOURERS |
| RUBELLANS | RUD | RUFFLER | RULIEST | RUMOURING |
| RUBELLAS | RUDAS | RUFFLERS | RULING | RUMOURS |
| RUBELLITE | RUDASES | RUFFLES | RULINGS | RUMP |
| RUBELLITES | RUDBECKIA | RUFFLING | RULLION | RUMPED |
| RUBEOLA | RUDBECKIAS | RUFFLINGS | RULLIONS | RUMPING |
| RUBEOLAS | RUDD | RUFFS | RULLOCK | RUMPLE |
| RUBES | RUDDED | RUFOUS | RULLOCKS | RUMPLED |
| RUBESCENT | RUDDER | RUG | RULY | RUMPLES |
| RUBICELLE | RUDDERS | RUGATE | RUM | RUMPLESS |
| RUBICELLES | RUDDIED | RUGBIES | RUMAL | RUMPLING |
| RUBICON | RUDDIER | RUGBY | RUMALS | RUMPS |
| RUBICONED | RUDDIES | RUGGED | RUMBA | RUMPUS |
| RUBICONING | RUDDIEST | RUGGEDER | RUMBAED | RUMPUSES |
| RUBICONS | RUDDILY | RUGGEDEST | RUMBAING | RUMS |
| RUBICUND | RUDDINESS | RUGGEDISE | RUMBAS | RUN |
| RUBIDIUM | RUDDINESSES | RUGGEDISED | RUMBELOW | RUNABOUT |
| RUBIDIUMS | RUDDING | RUGGEDISES | RUMBELOWS | RUNABOUTS |
| RUBIED | RUDDLE | RUGGEDISING | RUMBLE | RUNAGATE |
| RUBIER | RUDDLED | RUGGEDIZE | RUMBLED | RUNAGATES |
| RUBIES | RUDDLEMAN | RUGGEDIZED | RUMBLER | RUNAROUND |
| RUBIEST | RUDDLEMEN | RUGGEDIZES | RUMBLERS | RUNAROUNDS |
| RUBIFIED | RUDDLES | RUGGEDIZING | RUMBLES | RUNAWAY |
| RUBIFIES | RUDDLING | RUGGEDLY | RUMBLIER | RUNAWAYS |
| RUBIFY | RUDDOCK | RUGGER | RUMBLIEST | RUNCH |
| RUBIFYING | RUDDOCKS | RUGGERS | RUMBLING | RUNCHES |
| RUBIN | RUDDS | RUGGIER | RUMBLINGS | RUNCIBLE |
| RUBINE | RUDDY | RUGGIEST | RUMBLY | RUNCINATE |
| RUBINEOUS | RUDDYING | RUGGING | RUMBO | RUND |
| RUBINES | RUDE | RUGGINGS | RUMBOS | RUNDALE |
| RUBINS | RUDELY | RUGGY | RUME | RUNDALES |
| RUBIOUS | RUDENESS | RUGOSE | RUMEN | RUNDLE |
| RUBLE | RUDENESSES | RUGOSELY | RUMES | RUNDLED |
| RUBLES | RUDER | RUGOSITIES | RUMINA | RUNDLES |
| RUBRIC | RUDERAL | RUGOSITY | RUMINANT | RUNDLET |
| RUBRICAL | RUDERALS | RUGOUS | RUMINANTS | RUNDLETS |
| RUBRICATE | RUDERIES | RUGS | RUMINATE | RUNDOWN |
| RUBRICATED | RUDERY | RUGULOSE | RUMINATED | RUNDOWNS |
| RUBRICATES | RUDESBIES | RUIN | RUMINATES | RUNDS |
| RUBRICATING | RUDESBY | RUINABLE | RUMINATING | RUNE |
| RUBRICIAN | RUDEST | RUINATE | RUMINATOR | RUNED |
| RUBRICIANS | RUDIMENT | RUINATED | RUMINATORS | RUNES |
| RUBRICS | RUDIMENTS | RUINATES | RUMKIN | RUNFLAT |
| RUBS | RUDISH | RUINATING | RUMKINS | RUNG |
| RUBSTONE | RUDS | RUINATION | RUMLY | RUNGS |
| RUBSTONES | RUE | RUINATIONS | RUMMAGE | RUNIC |
| RUBY | RUED | RUINED | RUMMAGED | RUNKLE |
| RUBYING | RUEFUL | RUINER | RUMMAGER | RUNKLED |
| RUC | RUEFULLY | RUINERS | RUMMAGERS | RUNKLES |
| RUCHE | RUEING | RUING | RUMMAGES | RUNKLING |
| RUCHED | RUEINGS | RUINGS | RUMMAGING | RUNLET |
| RUCHES | RUELLE | RUINING | RUMMER | RUNLETS |
| RUCHING | RUELLES | RUININGS | RUMMERS | RUNNABLE |

RUNNEL
RUNNELS
RUNNER
RUNNERS
RUNNET
RUNNETS
RUNNIER
RUNNIEST
RUNNING
RUNNINGLY
RUNNINGS
RUNNION
RUNNIONS
RUNNY
RUNRIG
RUNRIGS
RUNS
RUNT
RUNTED
RUNTIER
RUNTIEST
RUNTISH
RUNTS
RUNTY
RUNWAY
RUNWAYS
RUPEE
RUPEES
RUPIA
RUPIAH
RUPIAHS
RUPIAS
RUPTURE
RUPTURED
RUPTURES
RUPTURING
RURAL
RURALISE
RURALISED
RURALISES
RURALISING
RURALISM

RURALISMS
RURALIST
RURALISTS
RURALITIES
RURALITY
RURALIZE
RURALIZED
RURALIZES
RURALIZING
RURALLY
RURALNESS
RURALNESSES
RURALS
RURP
RURPS
RUSA
RUSALKA
RUSALKAS
RUSAS
RUSCUS
RUSCUSES
RUSE
RUSÉ
RUSES
RUSH
RUSHED
RUSHEN
RUSHER
RUSHERS
RUSHES
RUSHIER
RUSHIEST
RUSHINESS
RUSHINESSES
RUSHING
RUSHLIGHT
RUSHLIGHTS
RUSHY
RUSINE
RUSK
RUSKS
RUSMA

RUSMAS
RUSSEL
RUSSELS
RUSSET
RUSSETED
RUSSETING
RUSSETINGS
RUSSETS
RUSSETY
RUSSIA
RUSSIAS
RUST
RUSTED
RUSTIC
RUSTICAL
RUSTICALS
RUSTICATE
RUSTICATED
RUSTICATES
RUSTICATING
RUSTICIAL
RUSTICISE
RUSTICISED
RUSTICISES
RUSTICISING
RUSTICISM
RUSTICISMS
RUSTICITIES
RUSTICITY
RUSTICIZE
RUSTICIZED
RUSTICIZES
RUSTICIZING
RUSTICS
RUSTIER
RUSTIEST
RUSTILY
RUSTINESS
RUSTINESSES
RUSTING
RUSTINGS
RUSTLE

RUSTLED
RUSTLER
RUSTLERS
RUSTLES
RUSTLESS
RUSTLING
RUSTLINGS
RUSTRE
RUSTRED
RUSTRES
RUSTS
RUSTY
RUT
RUTABAGA
RUTABAGAS
RUTACEOUS
RUTH
RUTHENIC
RUTHENIUM
RUTHENIUMS
RUTHFUL
RUTHFULLY
RUTHLESS
RUTHS
RUTILANT
RUTILATED
RUTILE
RUTILES
RUTIN
RUTINS
RUTS
RUTTED
RUTTER
RUTTERS
RUTTIER
RUTTIEST
RUTTING
RUTTINGS
RUTTISH
RUTTY
RYA
RYAL

RYALS
RYAS
RYBAT
RYBATS
RYBAUDRYE
RYBAUDRYES
RYBAULD
RYBAULDS
RYE
RYEPECK
RYEPECKS
RYES
RYFE
RYKE
RYKED
RYKES
RYKING
RYMME
RYMMED
RYMMES
RYMMING
RYND
RYNDS
RYOKAN
RYOKANS
RYOT
RYOTS
RYOTWARI
RYOTWARIS
RYPE
RYPECK
RYPECKS
RYPER
RYTHME
RYTHMED
RYTHMES
RYTHMING
RYVE
RYVED
RYVES
RYVING

# S

SAB
SABADILLA
SABADILLAS
SABATON
SABATONS
SABBAT
SABBATIC
SABBATINE
SABBATISE
SABBATISED
SABBATISES
SABBATISING
SABBATISM
SABBATISMS
SABBATIZE
SABBATIZED
SABBATIZES
SABBATIZING
SABBATS
SABELLA
SABELLAS
SABER
SABERED
SABERING
SABERS
SABIN
SABINS
SABLE
SABLED
SABLES
SABLING
SABOT
SABOTAGE
SABOTAGED
SABOTAGES
SABOTAGING
SABOTEUR
SABOTEURS
SABOTIER
SABOTIERS
SABOTS
SABRA
SABRAS
SABRE
SABRED
SABRES
SABRING
SABS
SABULOSE
SABULOUS
SABURRA
SABURRAL
SABURRAS
SAC
SACCADE
SACCADES
SACCADIC
SACCATE
SACCHARIC
SACCHARIN
SACCHARINS
SACCIFORM
SACCOI

SACCOS
SACCOSES
SACCULAR
SACCULE
SACCULES
SACCULI
SACCULUS
SACELLA
SACELLUM
SACHEM
SACHEMDOM
SACHEMDOMS
SACHEMS
SACHET
SACHETS
SACK
SACKAGE
SACKAGES
SACKBUT
SACKBUTS
SACKCLOTH
SACKCLOTHS
SACKED
SACKFUL
SACKFULS
SACKING
SACKINGS
SACKLESS
SACKS
SACLESS
SACQUE
SACQUES
SACRA
SACRAL
SACRALISE
SACRALISED
SACRALISES
SACRALISING
SACRALIZE
SACRALIZED
SACRALIZES
SACRALIZING
SACRAMENT
SACRAMENTED
SACRAMENTING
SACRAMENTS
SACRARIA
SACRARIUM
SACRED
SACREDLY
SACRIFICE
SACRIFICED
SACRIFICES
SACRIFICING
SACRIFIDE
SACRIFIED
SACRIFIES
SACRIFY
SACRIFYING
SACRILEGE
SACRILEGES
SACRING
SACRINGS

SACRIST
SACRISTAN
SACRISTANS
SACRISTIES
SACRISTS
SACRISTY
SACRUM
SACS
SAD
SADDEN
SADDENED
SADDENING
SADDENS
SADDER
SADDEST
SADDHU
SADDHUS
SADDISH
SADDLE
SADDLED
SADDLER
SADDLERIES
SADDLERS
SADDLERY
SADDLES
SADDLING
SADHU
SADHUS
SADISM
SADISMS
SADIST
SADISTIC
SADISTS
SADLY
SADNESS
SADNESSES
SAE
SAECULUM
SAECULUMS
SAETER
SAETERS
SAFARI
SAFARIED
SAFARIING
SAFARIS
SAFE
SAFED
SAFEGUARD
SAFEGUARDED
SAFEGUARDING
SAFEGUARDINGS
SAFEGUARDS
SAFELY
SAFENESS
SAFENESSES
SAFER
SAFES
SAFEST
SAFETIES
SAFETY
SAFFIAN
SAFFIANS
SAFFLOWER

SAFFLOWERS
SAFFRON
SAFFRONED
SAFFRONS
SAFFRONY
SAFING
SAFRANIN
SAFRANINE
SAFRANINES
SAFRANINS
SAFROLE
SAFROLES
SAG
SAGA
SAGACIOUS
SAGACITIES
SAGACITY
SAGAMAN
SAGAMEN
SAGAMORE
SAGAMORES
SAGAPENUM
SAGAPENUMS
SAGAS
SAGATHIES
SAGATHY
SAGE
SAGEBRUSH
SAGEBRUSHES
SAGELY
SAGENE
SAGENES
SAGENESS
SAGENESSES
SAGENITE
SAGENITES
SAGENITIC
SAGER
SAGES
SAGEST
SAGGAR
SAGGARD
SAGGARDS
SAGGARS
SAGGED
SAGGER
SAGGERS
SAGGIER
SAGGIEST
SAGGING
SAGGINGS
SAGGY
SAGIER
SAGIEST
SAGINATE
SAGINATED
SAGINATES
SAGINATING
SAGITTA
SAGITTAL
SAGITTARIES
SAGITTARY
SAGITTAS

SAGITTATE
SAGO
SAGOIN
SAGOINS
SAGOS
SAGOUIN
SAGOUINS
SAGS
SAGUARO
SAGUAROS
SAGUIN
SAGUINS
SAGUM
SAGY
SAHIB
SAHIBA
SAHIBAH
SAHIBAHS
SAHIBAS
SAHIBS
SAI
SAIBLING
SAIBLINGS
SAIC
SAICE
SAICES
SAICK
SAICKS
SAICS
SAID
SAIDEST
SAIDS
SAIDST
SAIGA
SAIGAS
SAIKEI
SAIKEIS
SAIKLESS
SAIL
SAILABLE
SAILBOARD
SAILBOARDS
SAILED
SAILER
SAILERS
SAILIER
SAILIEST
SAILING
SAILINGS
SAILLESS
SAILOR
SAILORING
SAILORINGS
SAILORLY
SAILORS
SAILPLANE
SAILPLANES
SAILS
SAILY
SAIM
SAIMIRI
SAIMIRIS
SAIMS

SAIN
SAINE
SAINED
SAINFOIN
SAINFOINS
SAINING
SAINS
SAINT
SAINTDOM
SAINTDOMS
SAINTED
SAINTESS
SAINTESSES
SAINTFOIN
SAINTFOINS
SAINTHOOD
SAINTHOODS
SAINTING
SAINTISH
SAINTISM
SAINTISMS
SAINTLIER
SAINTLIEST
SAINTLIKE
SAINTLING
SAINTLINGS
SAINTLY
SAINTS
SAINTSHIP
SAINTSHIPS
SAIQUE
SAIQUES
SAIR
SAIRED
SAIRER
SAIREST
SAIRING
SAIRS
SAIS
SAIST
SAITH
SAITHE
SAITHES
SAITHS
SAJOU
SAJOUS
SAKE
SAKER
SAKERET
SAKERETS
SAKERS
SAKES
SAKI
SAKIA
SAKIAS
SAKIEH
SAKIEHS
SAKIS
SAKIYEH
SAKIYEHS
SAKKOI
SAKKOS
SAKKOSES
SAKSAUL
SAKSAULS
SAL
SALAAM
SALAAMED
SALAAMING
SALAAMS

SALABLE
SALABLY
SALACIOUS
SALACITIES
SALACITY
SALAD
SALADE
SALADES
SALADING
SALADINGS
SALADS
SALAL
SALALS
SALAME
SALAMI
SALAMIS
SALAMON
SALAMONS
SALANGANE
SALANGANES
SALARIAT
SALARIATS
SALARIED
SALARIES
SALARY
SALARYING
SALBAND
SALBANDS
SALCHOW
SALCHOWS
SALE
SALEABLE
SALEABLY
SALEP
SALEPS
SALERATUS
SALERATUSES
SALES
SALESGIRL
SALESGIRLS
SALESLADIES
SALESLADY
SALESMAN
SALESMEN
SALET
SALETS
SALEWD
SALEWORK
SALEWORKS
SALFERN
SALFERNS
SALIAUNCE
SALIAUNCES
SALIC
SALICES
SALICET
SALICETA
SALICETS
SALICETUM
SALICETUMS
SALICIN
SALICINE
SALICINES
SALICINS
SALICYLIC
SALIENCE
SALIENCES
SALIENCIES
SALIENCY
SALIENT

SALIENTLY
SALIENTS
SALIFIED
SALIFIES
SALIFY
SALIFYING
SALIGOT
SALIGOTS
SALIMETER
SALIMETERS
SALINA
SALINAS
SALINE
SALINES
SALINITIES
SALINITY
SALIVA
SALIVAL
SALIVARY
SALIVAS
SALIVATE
SALIVATED
SALIVATES
SALIVATING
SALIX
SALLAD
SALLADS
SALLAL
SALLALS
SALLE
SALLEE
SALLEES
SALLES
SALLET
SALLETS
SALLIED
SALLIES
SALLOW
SALLOWED
SALLOWER
SALLOWEST
SALLOWING
SALLOWISH
SALLOWS
SALLOWY
SALLY
SALLYING
SALLYPORT
SALLYPORTS
SALMI
SALMIS
SALMON
SALMONET
SALMONETS
SALMONID
SALMONIDS
SALMONOID
SALMONOIDS
SALMONS
SALON
SALONS
SALOON
SALOONIST
SALOONISTS
SALOONS
SALOOP
SALOOPS
SALOP
SALOPETTE
SALOPETTES

SALOPIAN
SALOPS
SALP
SALPIAN
SALPIANS
SALPICON
SALPICONS
SALPIFORM
SALPINGES
SALPINX
SALPINXES
SALPS
SALS
SALSA
SALSAED
SALSAFIES
SALSAFY
SALSAING
SALSAS
SALSE
SALSES
SALSIFIES
SALSIFY
SALT
SALTANDO
SALTANT
SALTANTS
SALTATE
SALTATED
SALTATES
SALTATING
SALTATION
SALTATIONS
SALTATO
SALTATORY
SALTED
SALTER
SALTERN
SALTERNS
SALTERS
SALTEST
SALTIER
SALTIERS
SALTIEST
SALTILY
SALTINESS
SALTINESSES
SALTING
SALTINGS
SALTIRE
SALTIRES
SALTISH
SALTISHLY
SALTLESS
SALTLY
SALTNESS
SALTNESSES
SALTO
SALTOED
SALTOING
SALTOS
SALTPETER
SALTPETERS
SALTPETRE
SALTPETRES
SALTS
SALTUS
SALTUSES
SALTY
SALUBRITIES

SALUBRITY
SALUE
SALUED
SALUES
SALUING
SALUKI
SALUKIS
SALUTARY
SALUTE
SALUTED
SALUTER
SALUTERS
SALUTES
SALUTING
SALVABLE
SALVAGE
SALVAGED
SALVAGES
SALVAGING
SALVARSAN
SALVARSANS
SALVATION
SALVATIONS
SALVATORIES
SALVATORY
SALVE
SALVED
SALVER
SALVERS
SALVES
SALVETE
SALVETES
SALVIA
SALVIAS
SALVIFIC
SALVING
SALVINGS
SALVO
SALVOES
SALVOR
SALVORS
SALVOS
SAM
SAMAAN
SAMAANS
SAMAN
SAMANS
SAMARA
SAMARAS
SAMARIUM
SAMARIUMS
SAMBA
SAMBAL
SAMBALS
SAMBAR
SAMBARS
SAMBAS
SAMBO
SAMBOS
SAMBUCA
SAMBUCAS
SAMBUR
SAMBURS
SAME
SAMEL
SAMELY
SAMEN
SAMENESS
SAMENESSES
SAMES

SAMEY
SAMFOO
SAMFOOS
SAMFU
SAMFUS
SAMIEL
SAMIELS
SAMIER
SAMIEST
SAMISEN
SAMISENS
SAMITE
SAMITES
SAMIZDAT
SAMIZDATS
SAMLET
SAMLETS
SAMLOR
SAMLORS
SAMNITIS
SAMNITISES
SAMOSA
SAMOSAS
SAMOVAR
SAMOVARS
SAMP
SAMPAN
SAMPANS
SAMPHIRE
SAMPHIRES
SAMPI
SAMPIRE
SAMPIRES
SAMPIS
SAMPLE
SAMPLED
SAMPLER
SAMPLERIES
SAMPLERS
SAMPLERY
SAMPLES
SAMPLING
SAMPLINGS
SAMPS
SAMSHOO
SAMSHOOS
SAMSHU
SAMSHUS
SAMURAI
SAN
SANATIVE
SANATORIA
SANATORY
SANBENITO
SANBENITOS
SANCHO
SANCHOS
SANCTIFIED
SANCTIFIES
SANCTIFY
SANCTIFYING
SANCTIFYINGS
SANCTION
SANCTIONED
SANCTIONING
SANCTIONS
SANCTITIES
SANCTITY
SANCTUARIES
SANCTUARY

SANCTUM
SANCTUMS
SAND
SANDAL
SANDALLED
SANDALS
SANDARAC
SANDARACH
SANDARACHS
SANDARACS
SANDBAG
SANDBAGGED
SANDBAGGING
SANDBAGS
SANDBANK
SANDBANKS
SANDED
SANDER
SANDERS
SANDERSES
SANDHI
SANDHIS
SANDIER
SANDIEST
SANDINESS
SANDINESSES
SANDING
SANDINGS
SANDIVER
SANDIVERS
SANDLING
SANDLINGS
SANDMAN
SANDMEN
SANDPAPER
SANDPAPERED
SANDPAPERING
SANDPAPERS
SANDPIPER
SANDPIPERS
SANDS
SANDSTONE
SANDSTONES
SANDWICH
SANDWICHED
SANDWICHES
SANDWICHING
SANDWORT
SANDWORTS
SANDY
SANDYISH
SANE
SANELY
SANENESS
SANENESSES
SANER
SANEST
SANG
SANGAR
SANGAREE
SANGAREES
SANGARS
SANGFROID
SANGFROIDS
SANGLIER
SANGLIERS
SANGRIA
SANGRIAS
SANGS
SANGUIFIED

SANGUIFIES
SANGUIFY
SANGUIFYING
SANGUINE
SANGUINED
SANGUINES
SANGUINING
SANICLE
SANICLES
SANIDINE
SANIDINES
SANIES
SANIFIED
SANIFIES
SANIFY
SANIFYING
SANIOUS
SANITARIA
SANITARY
SANITATE
SANITATED
SANITATES
SANITATING
SANITIES
SANITISE
SANITISED
SANITISES
SANITISING
SANITIZE
SANITIZED
SANITIZES
SANITIZING
SANITY
SANJAK
SANJAKS
SANK
SANKO
SANKOS
SANNUP
SANNUPS
SANNYASI
SANNYASIN
SANNYASINS
SANNYASIS
SANPAN
SANPANS
SANS
SANSA
SANSAS
SANSEI
SANSEIS
SANSERIF
SANSERIFS
SANTAL
SANTALIN
SANTALINS
SANTALS
SANTIR
SANTIRS
SANTOLINA
SANTOLINAS
SANTON
SANTONICA
SANTONICAS
SANTONIN
SANTONINS
SANTONS
SANTOUR
SANTOURS
SANTUR

SANTURS
SAOUARI
SAOUARIS
SAP
SAPAJOU
SAPAJOUS
SAPAN
SAPANS
SAPEGO
SAPEGOES
SAPELE
SAPELES
SAPFUL
SAPHEAD
SAPHEADED
SAPHEADS
SAPID
SAPIDITIES
SAPIDITY
SAPIDLESS
SAPIENCE
SAPIENCES
SAPIENT
SAPIENTLY
SAPLESS
SAPLING
SAPLINGS
SAPODILLA
SAPODILLAS
SAPOGENIN
SAPOGENINS
SAPONIFIED
SAPONIFIES
SAPONIFY
SAPONIFYING
SAPONIN
SAPONINS
SAPONITE
SAPONITES
SAPOR
SAPOROUS
SAPORS
SAPOTA
SAPOTAS
SAPPAN
SAPPANS
SAPPED
SAPPER
SAPPERS
SAPPHIC
SAPPHICS
SAPPHIRE
SAPPHIRED
SAPPHIRES
SAPPHISM
SAPPHISMS
SAPPHIST
SAPPHISTS
SAPPIER
SAPPIEST
SAPPINESS
SAPPINESSES
SAPPING
SAPPLES
SAPPY
SAPRAEMIA
SAPRAEMIAS
SAPRAEMIC
SAPROBE
SAPROBES

SAPROLITE
SAPROLITES
SAPROPEL
SAPROPELS
SAPROZOIC
SAPS
SAPSAGO
SAPSAGOS
SAPSUCKER
SAPSUCKERS
SAPUCAIA
SAPUCAIAS
SAPWOOD
SAPWOODS
SAR
SARABAND
SARABANDS
SARAFAN
SARAFANS
SARANGI
SARANGIS
SARBACANE
SARBACANES
SARCASM
SARCASMS
SARCASTIC
SARCENET
SARCENETS
SARCOCARP
SARCOCARPS
SARCODE
SARCODES
SARCODIC
SARCOID
SARCOIDS
SARCOLOGIES
SARCOLOGY
SARCOMA
SARCOMAS
SARCOMATA
SARCOMERE
SARCOMERES
SARCONET
SARCONETS
SARCOPTIC
SARCOUS
SARD
SARDANA
SARDANAS
SARDEL
SARDELLE
SARDELLES
SARDELS
SARDINE
SARDINES
SARDIUS
SARDIUSES
SARDONIAN
SARDONIC
SARDONYX
SARDONYXES
SARDS
SARED
SAREE
SAREES
SARGASSO
SARGASSOS
SARGE
SARGES
SARGO

SARGOS
SARGUS
SARGUSES
SARI
SARIN
SARING
SARINS
SARIS
SARK
SARKFUL
SARKFULS
SARKIER
SARKIEST
SARKING
SARKINGS
SARKS
SARKY
SARMENT
SARMENTA
SARMENTS
SARMENTUM
SARNEY
SARNEYS
SARNIE
SARNIES
SAROD
SARODS
SARONG
SARONGS
SARONIC
SAROS
SAROSES
SARPANCH
SARPANCHES
SARRASIN
SARRASINS
SARRAZIN
SARRAZINS
SARS
SARSA
SARSAS
SARSDEN
SARSDENS
SARSEN
SARSENET
SARSENETS
SARSENS
SARSNET
SARSNETS
SARTOR
SARTORIAL
SARTORIAN
SARTORII
SARTORIUS
SARTORIUSES
SARTORS
SARUS
SARUSES
SARZA
SARZAS
SASARARA
SASARARAS
SASH
SASHAY
SASHAYED
SASHAYING
SASHAYS
SASHED
SASHES
SASHIMI

SASHIMIS
SASHING
SASIN
SASINE
SASINES
SASINS
SASKATOON
SASKATOONS
SASQUATCH
SASQUATCHES
SASS
SASSABIES
SASSABY
SASSAFRAS
SASSAFRASES
SASSARARA
SASSARARAS
SASSE
SASSED
SASSES
SASSIER
SASSIEST
SASSING
SASSOLIN
SASSOLINS
SASSOLITE
SASSOLITES
SASSY
SASTRUGA
SASTRUGI
SAT
SATANIC
SATANICAL
SATANISM
SATANISMS
SATANITIES
SATANITY
SATARA
SATARAS
SATCHEL
SATCHELS
SATE
SATED
SATEDNESS
SATEDNESSES
SATEEN
SATEENS
SATELESS
SATELLES
SATELLITE
SATELLITED
SATELLITES
SATELLITING
SATES
SATI
SATIABLE
SATIATE
SATIATED
SATIATES
SATIATING
SATIATION
SATIATIONS
SATIETIES
SATIETY
SATIN
SATINED
SATINET
SATINETS
SATINETTA
SATINETTAS

SATINETTE
SATINETTES
SATING
SATINING
SATINS
SATINWOOD
SATINWOODS
SATINY
SATIRE
SATIRES
SATIRIC
SATIRICAL
SATIRISE
SATIRISED
SATIRISES
SATIRISING
SATIRIST
SATIRISTS
SATIRIZE
SATIRIZED
SATIRIZES
SATIRIZING
SATIS
SATISFIED
SATISFIER
SATISFIERS
SATISFIES
SATISFY
SATISFYING
SATIVE
SATORI
SATORIS
SATRAP
SATRAPAL
SATRAPIC
SATRAPIES
SATRAPS
SATRAPY
SATSUMA
SATSUMAS
SATURABLE
SATURANT
SATURANTS
SATURATE
SATURATED
SATURATES
SATURATING
SATURATOR
SATURATORS
SATURNIC
SATURNINE
SATURNISM
SATURNISMS
SATURNIST
SATURNISTS
SATYR
SATYRA
SATYRAL
SATYRALS
SATYRAS
SATYRESS
SATYRESSES
SATYRIC
SATYRICAL
SATYRID
SATYRIDS
SATYRISK
SATYRISKS
SATYRS
SAUBA

SAUBAS
SAUCE
SAUCED
SAUCEPAN
SAUCEPANS
SAUCER
SAUCERFUL
SAUCERFULS
SAUCERS
SAUCES
SAUCH
SAUCHS
SAUCIER
SAUCIEST
SAUCILY
SAUCINESS
SAUCINESSES
SAUCING
SAUCISSE
SAUCISSES
SAUCISSON
SAUCISSONS
SAUCY
SAUFGARD
SAUFGARDS
SAUGER
SAUGERS
SAUGH
SAUGHS
SAUL
SAULGE
SAULGES
SAULIE
SAULIES
SAULS
SAULT
SAULTS
SAUNA
SAUNAS
SAUNT
SAUNTED
SAUNTER
SAUNTERED
SAUNTERER
SAUNTERERS
SAUNTERING
SAUNTERINGS
SAUNTERS
SAUNTING
SAUNTS
SAUREL
SAURELS
SAURIAN
SAURIANS
SAURIES
SAUROID
SAUROPOD
SAUROPODS
SAURY
SAUSAGE
SAUSAGES
SAUT
SAUTÉ
SAUTÉD
SAUTED
SAUTÉED
SAUTÉING
SAUTÉS
SAUTING
SAUTOIR

SAUTOIRS
SAUTS
SAVABLE
SAVAGE
SAVAGED
SAVAGEDOM
SAVAGEDOMS
SAVAGELY
SAVAGER
SAVAGERIES
SAVAGERY
SAVAGES
SAVAGEST
SAVAGING
SAVAGISM
SAVAGISMS
SAVANNA
SAVANNAH
SAVANNAHS
SAVANNAS
SAVANT
SAVANTS
SAVARIN
SAVARINS
SAVATE
SAVATES
SAVE
SAVED
SAVEGARD
SAVEGARDED
SAVEGARDING
SAVEGARDS
SAVELOY
SAVELOYS
SAVER
SAVERS
SAVES
SAVEY
SAVEYED
SAVEYING
SAVEYS
SAVIN
SAVINE
SAVINES
SAVING
SAVINGLY
SAVINGS
SAVINS
SAVIOUR
SAVIOURS
SAVOR
SAVORED
SAVORIES
SAVORING
SAVOROUS
SAVORS
SAVORY
SAVOUR
SAVOURED
SAVOURIES
SAVOURILY
SAVOURING
SAVOURLY
SAVOURS
SAVOURY
SAVOY
SAVOYS
SAVVEY
SAVVEYED
SAVVEYING

SAVVEYS
SAVVIED
SAVVIES
SAVVY
SAVVYING
SAW
SAWAH
SAWAHS
SAWDER
SAWDERED
SAWDERING
SAWDERS
SAWDUST
SAWDUSTED
SAWDUSTING
SAWDUSTS
SAWDUSTY
SAWED
SAWER
SAWERS
SAWING
SAWINGS
SAWN
SAWNEY
SAWNEYS
SAWPIT
SAWPITS
SAWS
SAWYER
SAWYERS
SAX
SAXATILE
SAXAUL
SAXAULS
SAXES
SAXHORN
SAXHORNS
SAXIFRAGE
SAXIFRAGES
SAXITOXIN
SAXITOXINS
SAXONIES
SAXONITE
SAXONITES
SAXONY
SAXOPHONE
SAXOPHONES
SAY
SAYABLE
SAYED
SAYEDS
SAYER
SAYERS
SAYEST
SAYID
SAYIDS
SAYING
SAYINGS
SAYNE
SAYON
SAYONARA
SAYONARAS
SAYONS
SAYS
SAYST
SAYYID
SAYYIDS
SAZ
SAZERAC®
SAZERACS®

SAZES
SAZHEN
SAZHENS
SAZZES
SBIRRI
SBIRRO
SCAB
SCABBARD
SCABBARDED
SCABBARDING
SCABBARDS
SCABBED
SCABBIER
SCABBIEST
SCABBING
SCABBLE
SCABBLED
SCABBLES
SCABBLING
SCABBY
SCABIES
SCABIOUS
SCABIOUSES
SCABRID
SCABROUS
SCABS
SCAD
SCADS
SCAFF
SCAFFIE
SCAFFIES
SCAFFOLD
SCAFFOLDED
SCAFFOLDING
SCAFFOLDINGS
SCAFFOLDS
SCAFFS
SCAG
SCAGLIA
SCAGLIAS
SCAGLIOLA
SCAGLIOLAS
SCAGS
SCAIL
SCAILED
SCAILING
SCAILS
SCAITH
SCAITHED
SCAITHING
SCAITHS
SCALA
SCALABLE
SCALADE
SCALADES
SCALADO
SCALADOS
SCALAE
SCALAR
SCALARS
SCALAWAG
SCALAWAGS
SCALD
SCALDED
SCALDER
SCALDERS
SCALDFISH
SCALDFISHES
SCALDIC
SCALDING

SCALDINGS
SCALDINI
SCALDINO
SCALDS
SCALE
SCALED
SCALELESS
SCALELIKE
SCALENE
SCALER
SCALERS
SCALES
SCALIER
SCALIEST
SCALINESS
SCALINESSES
SCALING
SCALINGS
SCALL
SCALLAWAG
SCALLAWAGS
SCALLED
SCALLION
SCALLIONS
SCALLOP
SCALLOPED
SCALLOPING
SCALLOPS
SCALLS
SCALLYWAG
SCALLYWAGS
SCALP
SCALPED
SCALPEL
SCALPELS
SCALPER
SCALPERS
SCALPING
SCALPLESS
SCALPRUM
SCALPRUMS
SCALPS
SCALY
SCAM
SCAMBLE
SCAMBLED
SCAMBLER
SCAMBLERS
SCAMBLES
SCAMBLING
SCAMBLINGS
SCAMEL
SCAMELS
SCAMMONIES
SCAMMONY
SCAMP
SCAMPED
SCAMPER
SCAMPERED
SCAMPERING
SCAMPERS
SCAMPI
SCAMPING
SCAMPINGS
SCAMPIS
SCAMPISH
SCAMPS
SCAMS
SCAN
SCAND

SCANDAL
SCANDALLED
SCANDALLING
SCANDALS
SCANDENT
SCANDIUM
SCANDIUMS
SCANNED
SCANNER
SCANNERS
SCANNING
SCANNINGS
SCANS
SCANSION
SCANSIONS
SCANT
SCANTED
SCANTER
SCANTEST
SCANTIER
SCANTIES
SCANTIEST
SCANTILY
SCANTING
SCANTITIES
SCANTITY
SCANTLE
SCANTLED
SCANTLES
SCANTLING
SCANTLINGS
SCANTLY
SCANTNESS
SCANTNESSES
SCANTS
SCANTY
SCAPA
SCAPAED
SCAPAING
SCAPAS
SCAPE
SCAPED
SCAPEGOAT
SCAPEGOATED
SCAPEGOATING
SCAPEGOATINGS
SCAPEGOATS
SCAPELESS
SCAPEMENT
SCAPEMENTS
SCAPES
SCAPHOID
SCAPHOIDS
SCAPHOPOD
SCAPHOPODS
SCAPI
SCAPING
SCAPOLITE
SCAPOLITES
SCAPPLE
SCAPPLED
SCAPPLES
SCAPPLING
SCAPULA
SCAPULAE
SCAPULAR
SCAPULARIES
SCAPULARS
SCAPULARY
SCAPULAS

SCAPUS
SCAR
SCARAB
SCARABEE
SCARABEES
SCARABOID
SCARABOIDS
SCARABS
SCARCE
SCARCELY
SCARCER
SCARCEST
SCARCITIES
SCARCITY
SCARE
SCARECROW
SCARECROWS
SCARED
SCAREDER
SCAREDEST
SCARER
SCARERS
SCARES
SCAREY
SCARF
SCARFED
SCARFING
SCARFINGS
SCARFISH
SCARFISHES
SCARFS
SCARFSKIN
SCARFSKINS
SCARIER
SCARIEST
SCARIFIED
SCARIFIER
SCARIFIERS
SCARIFIES
SCARIFY
SCARIFYING
SCARING
SCARIOUS
SCARLESS
SCARLET
SCARLETED
SCARLETING
SCARLETS
SCARMOGE
SCARMOGES
SCARP
SCARPED
SCARPER
SCARPERED
SCARPERING
SCARPERS
SCARPETTI
SCARPETTO
SCARPINES
SCARPING
SCARPINGS
SCARPS
SCARRE
SCARRED
SCARRES
SCARRIER
SCARRIEST
SCARRING
SCARRINGS
SCARRY

SCARS
SCART
SCARTED
SCARTH
SCARTHS
SCARTING
SCARTS
SCARVES
SCARY
SCAT
SCATCH
SCATCHES
SCATH
SCATHE
SCATHED
SCATHEFUL
SCATHES
SCATHING
SCATHS
SCATOLE
SCATOLES
SCATOLOGIES
SCATOLOGY
SCATS
SCATT
SCATTED
SCATTER
SCATTERED
SCATTERER
SCATTERERS
SCATTERING
SCATTERINGS
SCATTERS
SCATTERY
SCATTIER
SCATTIEST
SCATTING
SCATTS
SCATTY
SCAUD
SCAUDED
SCAUDING
SCAUDS
SCAUP
SCAUPER
SCAUPERS
SCAUPS
SCAUR
SCAURED
SCAURIES
SCAURING
SCAURS
SCAURY
SCAVAGE
SCAVAGER
SCAVAGERS
SCAVAGES
SCAVENGE
SCAVENGED
SCAVENGER
SCAVENGERED
SCAVENGERING
SCAVENGERINGS
SCAVENGERS
SCAVENGES
SCAVENGING
SCAVENGINGS
SCAW
SCAWS
SCAZON

SCAZONS
SCAZONTIC
SCAZONTICS
SCEAT
SCEATT
SCEATTAS
SCEDULE
SCEDULES
SCELERAT
SCELERATE
SCELERATES
SCELERATS
SCENA
SCENARIES
SCENARIO
SCENARIOS
SCENARISE
SCENARISED
SCENARISES
SCENARISING
SCENARIST
SCENARISTS
SCENARIZE
SCENARIZED
SCENARIZES
SCENARIZING
SCENARY
SCEND
SCENDED
SCENDING
SCENDS
SCENE
SCENED
SCENERIES
SCENERY
SCENES
SCENIC
SCENICAL
SCENING
SCENT
SCENTED
SCENTFUL
SCENTING
SCENTINGS
SCENTLESS
SCENTS
SCEPSIS
SCEPSISES
SCEPTIC
SCEPTICAL
SCEPTICS
SCEPTRAL
SCEPTRE
SCEPTRED
SCEPTRES
SCEPTRY
SCERNE
SCERNED
SCERNES
SCERNING
SCHAPPE
SCHAPPED
SCHAPPEING
SCHAPPES
SCHAPSKA
SCHAPSKAS
SCHECHITA
SCHECHITAS
SCHEDULE
SCHEDULED

SCHEDULES
SCHEDULING
SCHEELITE
SCHEELITES
SCHELLUM
SCHELLUMS
SCHELM
SCHELMS
SCHEMA
SCHEMATA
SCHEMATIC
SCHEME
SCHEMED
SCHEMER
SCHEMERS
SCHEMES
SCHEMING
SCHEMINGS
SCHERZI
SCHERZO
SCHERZOS
SCHIAVONE
SCHIAVONES
SCHIEDAM
SCHIEDAMS
SCHILLER
SCHILLERS
SCHILLING
SCHILLINGS
SCHIMMEL
SCHIMMELS
SCHISM
SCHISMA
SCHISMAS
SCHISMS
SCHIST
SCHISTOSE
SCHISTOUS
SCHISTS
SCHIZO
SCHIZOID
SCHIZOIDS
SCHIZONT
SCHIZONTS
SCHIZOPOD
SCHIZOPODS
SCHIZOS
SCHLÄGER
SCHLÄGERS
SCHLEMIEL
SCHLEMIELS
SCHLEMIHL
SCHLEMIHLS
SCHLEP
SCHLEPP
SCHLEPPED
SCHLEPPIER
SCHLEPPIEST
SCHLEPPING
SCHLEPPS
SCHLEPPY
SCHLEPS
SCHLICH
SCHLICHS
SCHLIEREN
SCHLOCK
SCHLOCKS
SCHLOSS
SCHLOSSES
SCHMALTZ

SCHMALTZES
SCHMALTZIER
SCHMALTZIEST
SCHMALTZY
SCHMELZ
SCHMELZES
SCHMO
SCHMOCK
SCHMOCKS
SCHMOE
SCHMOES
SCHMOOZE
SCHMOOZED
SCHMOOZES
SCHMOOZING
SCHMUCK
SCHMUCKS
SCHMUTTER
SCHMUTTERS
SCHNAPPER
SCHNAPPERS
SCHNAPPS
SCHNAPS
SCHNAPSES
SCHNAUZER
SCHNAUZERS
SCHNELL
SCHNITZEL
SCHNITZELS
SCHNOOK
SCHNOOKS
SCHNORKEL
SCHNORKELS
SCHNORR
SCHNORRED
SCHNORRER
SCHNORRERS
SCHNORRING
SCHNORRS
SCHNOZZLE
SCHNOZZLES
SCHOLAR
SCHOLARCH
SCHOLARCHS
SCHOLARLY
SCHOLARS
SCHOLIA
SCHOLIAST
SCHOLIASTS
SCHOLION
SCHOLIUM
SCHOOL
SCHOOLBAG
SCHOOLBAGS
SCHOOLBOY
SCHOOLBOYS
SCHOOLE
SCHOOLED
SCHOOLERIES
SCHOOLERY
SCHOOLES
SCHOOLING
SCHOOLINGS
SCHOOLMAN
SCHOOLMEN
SCHOOLS
SCHOONER
SCHOONERS
SCHORL

SCHORLS
SCHOUT
SCHOUTS
SCHTICK
SCHTICKS
SCHTIK
SCHTIKS
SCHTOOK
SCHTOOKS
SCHTOOM
SCHTUCK
SCHTUCKS
SCHUIT
SCHUITS
SCHUL
SCHULS
SCHUSS
SCHUSSED
SCHUSSES
SCHUSSING
SCHUYT
SCHUYTS
SCHWA
SCHWAS
SCIAENID
SCIAENOID
SCIAMACHIES
SCIAMACHY
SCIARID
SCIARIDS
SCIATIC
SCIATICA
SCIATICAL
SCIATICAS
SCIENCE
SCIENCED
SCIENCES
SCIENT
SCIENTER
SCIENTIAL
SCIENTISE
SCIENTISED
SCIENTISES
SCIENTISING
SCIENTISM
SCIENTISMS
SCIENTIST
SCIENTISTS
SCIENTIZE
SCIENTIZED
SCIENTIZES
SCIENTIZING
SCILICET
SCILLA
SCILLAS
SCIMITAR
SCIMITARS
SCINCOID
SCINTILLA
SCINTILLAS
SCIOLISM
SCIOLISMS
SCIOLIST
SCIOLISTS
SCIOLOUS
SCIOLTO
SCION
SCIONS
SCIOSOPHIES
SCIOSOPHY

| | | | | |
|---|---|---|---|---|
| SCIROC | SCLIMMING | SCOOTED | SCOTERS | SCOWPING |
| SCIROCCO | SCLIMS | SCOOTER | SCOTIA | SCOWPS |
| SCIROCCOS | SCOFF | SCOOTERS | SCOTIAS | SCOWRER |
| SCIROCS | SCOFFED | SCOOTING | SCOTOMA | SCOWRERS |
| SCIRRHOID | SCOFFER | SCOOTS | SCOTOMAS | SCOWRIE |
| SCIRRHOUS | SCOFFERS | SCOPA | SCOTOMATA | SCOWRIES |
| SCIRRHUS | SCOFFING | SCOPAE | SCOTOMIES | SCOWS |
| SCIRRHUSES | SCOFFINGS | SCOPATE | SCOTOMY | SCOWTH |
| SCISSEL | SCOFFLAW | SCOPE | SCOTOPIA | SCOWTHER |
| SCISSELS | SCOFFLAWS | SCOPES | SCOTOPIAS | SCOWTHERED |
| SCISSIL | SCOFFS | SCOPULA | SCOTOPIC | SCOWTHERING |
| SCISSILE | SCOG | SCOPULAS | SCOTS | SCOWTHERS |
| SCISSILS | SCOGGED | SCOPULATE | SCOUG | SCOWTHS |
| SCISSION | SCOGGING | SCORBUTIC | SCOUGED | SCRAB |
| SCISSIONS | SCOGS | SCORCH | SCOUGING | SCRABBED |
| SCISSOR | SCOINSON | SCORCHED | SCOUGS | SCRABBING |
| SCISSORED | SCOINSONS | SCORCHER | SCOUNDREL | SCRABBLE |
| SCISSORER | SCOLD | SCORCHERS | SCOUNDRELS | SCRABBLED |
| SCISSORERS | SCOLDED | SCORCHES | SCOUP | SCRABBLER |
| SCISSORING | SCOLDER | SCORCHING | SCOUPED | SCRABBLERS |
| SCISSORS | SCOLDERS | SCORCHINGS | SCOUPING | SCRABBLES |
| SCISSURE | SCOLDING | SCORDATO | SCOUPS | SCRABBLING |
| SCISSURES | SCOLDINGS | SCORE | SCOUR | SCRABS |
| SCIURINE | SCOLDS | SCORED | SCOURED | SCRAE |
| SCIUROID | SCOLECES | SCORELINE | SCOURER | SCRAES |
| SCLAFF | SCOLECID | SCORELINES | SCOURERS | SCRAG |
| SCLAFFED | SCOLECITE | SCORER | SCOURGE | SCRAGGED |
| SCLAFFING | SCOLECITES | SCORERS | SCOURGED | SCRAGGIER |
| SCLAFFS | SCOLECOID | SCORES | SCOURGER | SCRAGGIEST |
| SCLATE | SCOLEX | SCORIA | SCOURGERS | SCRAGGILY |
| SCLATED | SCOLICES | SCORIAC | SCOURGES | SCRAGGING |
| SCLATES | SCOLIOMA | SCORIAE | SCOURGING | SCRAGGLIER |
| SCLATING | SCOLIOMAS | SCORIFIED | SCOURIE | SCRAGGLIEST |
| SCLAUNDER | SCOLIOSES | SCORIFIER | SCOURIES | SCRAGGLY |
| SCLAUNDERS | SCOLIOSIS | SCORIFIERS | SCOURING | SCRAGGY |
| SCLAVE | SCOLIOTIC | SCORIFIES | SCOURINGS | SCRAGS |
| SCLAVES | SCOLLOP | SCORIFY | SCOURS | SCRAICH |
| SCLERA | SCOLLOPED | SCORIFYING | SCOURSE | SCRAICHED |
| SCLERAL | SCOLLOPING | SCORING | SCOURSED | SCRAICHING |
| SCLERAS | SCOLLOPS | SCORINGS | SCOURSES | SCRAICHS |
| SCLERE | SCOLYTOID | SCORIOUS | SCOURSING | SCRAIGH |
| SCLEREID | SCOMBROID | SCORN | SCOUSE | SCRAIGHED |
| SCLEREIDES | SCOMFISH | SCORNED | SCOUSES | SCRAIGHING |
| SCLEREIDS | SCOMFISHED | SCORNER | SCOUT | SCRAIGHS |
| SCLEREMA | SCOMFISHES | SCORNERS | SCOUTED | SCRAM |
| SCLEREMAS | SCOMFISHING | SCORNFUL | SCOUTER | SCRAMBLE |
| SCLERES | SCONCE | SCORNING | SCOUTERS | SCRAMBLED |
| SCLERITE | SCONCED | SCORNINGS | SCOUTH | SCRAMBLER |
| SCLERITES | SCONCES | SCORNS | SCOUTHER | SCRAMBLERS |
| SCLERITIS | SCONCHEON | SCORODITE | SCOUTHERED | SCRAMBLES |
| SCLERITISES | SCONCHEONS | SCORODITES | SCOUTHERING | SCRAMBLING |
| SCLEROID | SCONCING | SCORPER | SCOUTHERINGS | SCRAMBLINGS |
| SCLEROMA | SCONE | SCORPERS | SCOUTHERS | SCRAMJET |
| SCLEROMAS | SCONES | SCORPIO | SCOUTHERY | SCRAMJETS |
| SCLEROSE | SCONTION | SCORPIOID | SCOUTHS | SCRAMMED |
| SCLEROSED | SCONTIONS | SCORPION | SCOUTING | SCRAMMING |
| SCLEROSES | SCOOG | SCORPIONS | SCOUTINGS | SCRAMS |
| SCLEROSING | SCOOGED | SCORPIOS | SCOUTS | SCRAN |
| SCLEROSIS | SCOOGING | SCORSE | SCOW | SCRANCH |
| SCLEROTAL | SCOOGS | SCORSED | SCOWDER | SCRANCHED |
| SCLEROTALS | SCOOP | SCORSER | SCOWDERED | SCRANCHES |
| SCLEROTIA | SCOOPED | SCORSERS | SCOWDERING | SCRANCHING |
| SCLEROTIC | SCOOPER | SCORSES | SCOWDERINGS | SCRANNEL |
| SCLEROTICS | SCOOPERS | SCORSING | SCOWDERS | SCRANNY |
| SCLEROUS | SCOOPFUL | SCOT | SCOWL | SCRANS |
| SCLIFF | SCOOPFULS | SCOTCH | SCOWLED | SCRAP |
| SCLIFFS | SCOOPING | SCOTCHED | SCOWLING | SCRAPE |
| SCLIM | SCOOPINGS | SCOTCHES | SCOWLS | SCRAPED |
| SCLIMMED | SCOOPS | SCOTCHING | SCOWP | SCRAPER |
| | SCOOT | SCOTER | SCOWPED | SCRAPERS |

SCRAPES
SCRAPIE
SCRAPIES
SCRAPING
SCRAPINGS
SCRAPPED
SCRAPPIER
SCRAPPIEST
SCRAPPILY
SCRAPPING
SCRAPPLE
SCRAPPLES
SCRAPPY
SCRAPS
SCRAT
SCRATCH
SCRATCHED
SCRATCHER
SCRATCHERS
SCRATCHES
SCRATCHIER
SCRATCHIEST
SCRATCHING
SCRATCHINGS
SCRATCHY
SCRATS
SCRATTED
SCRATTING
SCRATTLE
SCRATTLED
SCRATTLES
SCRATTLING
SCRAUCH
SCRAUCHED
SCRAUCHING
SCRAUCHS
SCRAUGH
SCRAUGHED
SCRAUGHING
SCRAUGHS
SCRAW
SCRAWL
SCRAWLED
SCRAWLER
SCRAWLERS
SCRAWLIER
SCRAWLIEST
SCRAWLING
SCRAWLINGS
SCRAWLS
SCRAWLY
SCRAWM
SCRAWMED
SCRAWMING
SCRAWMS
SCRAWNIER
SCRAWNIEST
SCRAWNY
SCRAWS
SCRAY
SCRAYE
SCRAYES
SCRAYS
SCREAK
SCREAKED
SCREAKIER
SCREAKIEST
SCREAKING
SCREAKS
SCREAKY

SCREAM
SCREAMED
SCREAMER
SCREAMERS
SCREAMING
SCREAMS
SCREE
SCREECH
SCREECHED
SCREECHER
SCREECHERS
SCREECHES
SCREECHIER
SCREECHIEST
SCREECHING
SCREECHY
SCREED
SCREEDED
SCREEDER
SCREEDERS
SCREEDING
SCREEDINGS
SCREEDS
SCREEN
SCREENED
SCREENER
SCREENERS
SCREENING
SCREENINGS
SCREENS
SCREES
SCREEVE
SCREEVED
SCREEVER
SCREEVERS
SCREEVES
SCREEVING
SCREEVINGS
SCREICH
SCREICHED
SCREICHING
SCREICHS
SCREIGH
SCREIGHED
SCREIGHING
SCREIGHS
SCREW
SCREWBALL
SCREWBALLS
SCREWED
SCREWER
SCREWERS
SCREWIER
SCREWIEST
SCREWING
SCREWINGS
SCREWS
SCREWTOP
SCREWTOPS
SCREWY
SCRIBABLE
SCRIBAL
SCRIBBLE
SCRIBBLED
SCRIBBLER
SCRIBBLERS
SCRIBBLES
SCRIBBLIER
SCRIBBLIEST
SCRIBBLING

SCRIBBLINGS
SCRIBBLY
SCRIBE
SCRIBED
SCRIBER
SCRIBERS
SCRIBES
SCRIBING
SCRIBINGS
SCRIBISM
SCRIBISMS
SCRIECH
SCRIECHED
SCRIECHING
SCRIECHS
SCRIED
SCRIENE
SCRIENES
SCRIES
SCRIEVE
SCRIEVED
SCRIEVES
SCRIEVING
SCRIGGLE
SCRIGGLED
SCRIGGLES
SCRIGGLIER
SCRIGGLIEST
SCRIGGLING
SCRIGGLY
SCRIKE
SCRIKED
SCRIKES
SCRIKING
SCRIM
SCRIMMAGE
SCRIMMAGED
SCRIMMAGES
SCRIMMAGING
SCRIMP
SCRIMPED
SCRIMPIER
SCRIMPIEST
SCRIMPILY
SCRIMPING
SCRIMPLY
SCRIMPS
SCRIMPY
SCRIMS
SCRIMSHAW
SCRIMSHAWED
SCRIMSHAWING
SCRIMSHAWS
SCRIMURE
SCRIMURES
SCRINE
SCRINES
SCRIP
SCRIPPAGE
SCRIPPAGES
SCRIPS
SCRIPT
SCRIPTED
SCRIPTING
SCRIPTORY
SCRIPTS
SCRIPTURE
SCRIPTURES
SCRITCH
SCRITCHED

SCRITCHES
SCRITCHING
SCRIVE
SCRIVED
SCRIVENER
SCRIVENERS
SCRIVES
SCRIVING
SCROBE
SCROBES
SCRODDLED
SCROFULA
SCROFULAS
SCROG
SCROGGIE
SCROGGIER
SCROGGIEST
SCROGGY
SCROGS
SCROLL
SCROLLED
SCROLLERIES
SCROLLERY
SCROLLING
SCROLLS
SCROOGE
SCROOGED
SCROOGES
SCROOGING
SCROOP
SCROOPED
SCROOPING
SCROOPS
SCROTAL
SCROTUM
SCROTUMS
SCROUGE
SCROUGED
SCROUGER
SCROUGERS
SCROUGES
SCROUGING
SCROUNGE
SCROUNGED
SCROUNGER
SCROUNGERS
SCROUNGES
SCROUNGING
SCROUNGINGS
SCROW
SCROWDGE
SCROWDGED
SCROWDGES
SCROWDGING
SCROWL
SCROWLE
SCROWLED
SCROWLES
SCROWLING
SCROWLS
SCROWS
SCROYLE
SCROYLES
SCRUB
SCRUBBED
SCRUBBER
SCRUBBERS
SCRUBBIER
SCRUBBIEST
SCRUBBING

SCRUBBINGS
SCRUBBY
SCRUBLAND
SCRUBLANDS
SCRUBS
SCRUFF
SCRUFFIER
SCRUFFIEST
SCRUFFS
SCRUFFY
SCRUM
SCRUMMAGE
SCRUMMAGED
SCRUMMAGES
SCRUMMAGING
SCRUMMED
SCRUMMIER
SCRUMMIEST
SCRUMMING
SCRUMMY
SCRUMP
SCRUMPED
SCRUMPIES
SCRUMPING
SCRUMPS
SCRUMPY
SCRUMS
SCRUNCH
SCRUNCHED
SCRUNCHES
SCRUNCHIER
SCRUNCHIEST
SCRUNCHING
SCRUNCHY
SCRUNT
SCRUNTS
SCRUNTY
SCRUPLE
SCRUPLED
SCRUPLER
SCRUPLERS
SCRUPLES
SCRUPLING
SCRUTABLE
SCRUTATOR
SCRUTATORS
SCRUTINIES
SCRUTINY
SCRUTO
SCRUTOIRE
SCRUTOIRES
SCRUTOS
SCRUZE
SCRUZED
SCRUZES
SCRUZING
SCRY
SCRYDE
SCRYER
SCRYERS
SCRYING
SCRYINGS
SCRYNE
SCRYNES
SCUBA
SCUBAS
SCUCHIN
SCUCHINS
SCUCHION
SCUCHIONS

SCUD
SCUDDALER
SCUDDALERS
SCUDDED
SCUDDER
SCUDDERS
SCUDDING
SCUDDLE
SCUDDLED
SCUDDLES
SCUDDLING
SCUDI
SCUDLER
SCUDLERS
SCUDO
SCUDS
SCUFF
SCUFFED
SCUFFIER
SCUFFIEST
SCUFFING
SCUFFLE
SCUFFLED
SCUFFLER
SCUFFLERS
SCUFFLES
SCUFFLING
SCUFFS
SCUFFY
SCUFT
SCUFTS
SCUG
SCUGGED
SCUGGING
SCUGS
SCUL
SCULK
SCULKED
SCULKING
SCULKS
SCULL
SCULLE
SCULLED
SCULLER
SCULLERIES
SCULLERS
SCULLERY
SCULLES
SCULLING
SCULLINGS
SCULLION
SCULLIONS
SCULLS
SCULP
SCULPED
SCULPIN
SCULPING
SCULPINS
SCULPS
SCULPSIT
SCULPT
SCULPTED
SCULPTING
SCULPTOR
SCULPTORS
SCULPTS
SCULPTURE
SCULPTURED
SCULPTURES
SCULPTURING

SCULPTURINGS
SCULS
SCUM
SCUMBAG
SCUMBAGS
SCUMBER
SCUMBERED
SCUMBERING
SCUMBERS
SCUMBLE
SCUMBLED
SCUMBLES
SCUMBLING
SCUMBLINGS
SCUMFISH
SCUMFISHED
SCUMFISHES
SCUMFISHING
SCUMMED
SCUMMER
SCUMMERS
SCUMMIER
SCUMMIEST
SCUMMING
SCUMMINGS
SCUMMY
SCUMS
SCUNCHEON
SCUNCHEONS
SCUNGE
SCUNGED
SCUNGES
SCUNGIER
SCUNGIEST
SCUNGING
SCUNGY
SCUNNER
SCUNNERED
SCUNNERING
SCUNNERS
SCUP
SCUPPAUG
SCUPPAUGS
SCUPPER
SCUPPERED
SCUPPERING
SCUPPERS
SCUPS
SCUR
SCURF
SCURFIER
SCURFIEST
SCURFS
SCURFY
SCURRED
SCURRIED
SCURRIER
SCURRIERS
SCURRIES
SCURRIL
SCURRILE
SCURRING
SCURRIOUR
SCURRIOURS
SCURRY
SCURRYING
SCURS
SCURVIER
SCURVIES
SCURVIEST

SCURVILY
SCURVY
SCUSE
SCUSED
SCUSES
SCUSING
SCUT
SCUTA
SCUTAGE
SCUTAGES
SCUTAL
SCUTATE
SCUTCH
SCUTCHED
SCUTCHEON
SCUTCHEONS
SCUTCHER
SCUTCHERS
SCUTCHES
SCUTCHING
SCUTCHINGS
SCUTE
SCUTELLA
SCUTELLAR
SCUTELLUM
SCUTES
SCUTIFORM
SCUTIGER
SCUTIGERS
SCUTS
SCUTTER
SCUTTERED
SCUTTERING
SCUTTERS
SCUTTLE
SCUTTLED
SCUTTLER
SCUTTLERS
SCUTTLES
SCUTTLING
SCUTUM
SCYBALA
SCYBALOUS
SCYBALUM
SCYE
SCYES
SCYPHI
SCYPHUS
SCYTALE
SCYTALES
SCYTHE
SCYTHED
SCYTHEMAN
SCYTHEMEN
SCYTHER
SCYTHERS
SCYTHES
SCYTHING
SDAINE
SDAINED
SDAINES
SDAINING
SDAYN
SDAYNED
SDAYNING
SDAYNS
SDEIGNE
SDEIGNED
SDEIGNES
SDEIGNING

SDEIN
SDEINED
SDEINING
SDEINS
SEA
SEABED
SEABEDS
SEABERRIES
SEABERRY
SEABOARD
SEABOARDS
SEABORNE
SEACOAST
SEACOASTS
SEACRAFT
SEACRAFTS
SEACUNNIES
SEACUNNY
SEADROME
SEADROMES
SEAFARER
SEAFARERS
SEAFARING
SEAFARINGS
SEAFOOD
SEAFOODS
SEAGULL
SEAGULLS
SEAHORSE
SEAHORSES
SEAL
SEALANT
SEALANTS
SEALCH
SEALCHS
SEALED
SEALER
SEALERIES
SEALERS
SEALERY
SEALGH
SEALGHS
SEALING
SEALINGS
SEALS
SEALSKIN
SEALSKINS
SEALYHAM
SEALYHAMS
SEAM
SEAMAN
SEAMANLY
SEAMARK
SEAMARKS
SEAME
SEAMED
SEAMEN
SEAMER
SEAMERS
SEAMES
SEAMIER
SEAMIEST
SEAMINESS
SEAMINESSES
SEAMING
SEAMLESS
SEAMOUNT
SEAMOUNTS
SEAMS
SEAMSTER

SEAMSTERS
SEAMY
SEAN
SÉANCE
SÉANCES
SEANED
SEANING
SEANNACHIES
SEANNACHY
SEANS
SEAPLANE
SEAPLANES
SEAPORT
SEAPORTS
SEAQUAKE
SEAQUAKES
SEAR
SEARAT
SEARATS
SEARCE
SEARCED
SEARCES
SEARCH
SEARCHED
SEARCHER
SEARCHERS
SEARCHES
SEARCHING
SEARCING
SEARE
SEARED
SEARER
SEAREST
SEARING
SEARINGS
SEARNESS
SEARNESSES
SEARS
SEAS
SEASATYRE
SEASATYRES
SEASCAPE
SEASCAPES
SEASE
SEASED
SEASES
SEASHELL
SEASHELLS
SEASHORE
SEASHORES
SEASICK
SEASICKER
SEASICKEST
SEASIDE
SEASIDES
SEASING
SEASON
SEASONAL
SEASONED
SEASONER
SEASONERS
SEASONING
SEASONINGS
SEASONS
SEASURE
SEASURES
SEAT
SEATED
SEATER
SEATERS

| | | | | |
|---|---|---|---|---|
| SEATING | SECONDER | SECURES | SEEDCAKES | SEES |
| SEATINGS | SECONDERS | SECUREST | SEEDED | SEESAW |
| SEATLESS | SECONDES | SECURING | SEEDER | SEESAWED |
| SEATS | SECONDI | SECURITAN | SEEDERS | SEESAWING |
| SEAWARD | SECONDING | SECURITANS | SEEDIER | SEESAWS |
| SEAWARDLY | SECONDLY | SECURITIES | SEEDIEST | SEETHE |
| SEAWARDS | SECONDO | SECURITY | SEEDILY | SEETHED |
| SEAWAY | SECONDS | SED | SEEDINESS | SEETHER |
| SEAWAYS | SECRECIES | SEDAN | SEEDINESSES | SEETHERS |
| SEAWEED | SECRECY | SEDANS | SEEDING | SEETHES |
| SEAWEEDS | SECRET | SEDATE | SEEDINGS | SEETHING |
| SEAWORTHY | SECRETA | SEDATED | SEEDLESS | SEETHINGS |
| SEAZE | SECRETAGE | SEDATELY | SEEDLING | SEEWING |
| SEAZED | SECRETAGES | SEDATER | SEEDLINGS | SEG |
| SEAZES | SECRETARIES | SEDATES | SEEDLIP | SEGAR |
| SEAZING | SECRETARY | SEDATEST | SEEDLIPS | SEGARS |
| SEBACEOUS | SECRETE | SEDATING | SEEDNESS | SEGGAR |
| SEBACIC | SECRETED | SEDATION | SEEDNESSES | SEGGARS |
| SEBATE | SECRETES | SEDATIONS | SEEDS | SEGHOL |
| SEBATES | SECRETIN | SEDATIVE | SEEDSMAN | SEGHOLATE |
| SEBESTEN | SECRETING | SEDATIVES | SEEDSMEN | SEGHOLATES |
| SEBESTENS | SECRETINS | SEDENT | SEEDY | SEGHOLS |
| SEBIFIC | SECRETION | SEDENTARY | SEEING | SEGMENT |
| SEBUM | SECRETIONS | SEDERUNT | SEEINGS | SEGMENTAL |
| SEBUMS | SECRETIVE | SEDERUNTS | SEEK | SEGMENTED |
| SEBUNDIES | SECRETLY | SEDES | SEEKER | SEGMENTING |
| SEBUNDY | SECRETORY | SEDGE | SEEKERS | SEGMENTS |
| SEC | SECRETS | SEDGED | SEEKING | SEGNO |
| SECANT | SECS | SEDGELAND | SEEKS | SEGNOS |
| SECANTS | SECT | SEDGELANDS | SEEL | SEGO |
| SECATEUR | SECTARIAL | SEDGES | SEELD | SEGOL |
| SECATEURS | SECTARIAN | SEDGIER | SEELED | SEGOLATE |
| SECCO | SECTARIANS | SEDGIEST | SEELIER | SEGOLATES |
| SECCOS | SECTARIES | SEDGY | SEELIEST | SEGOLS |
| SECEDE | SECTARY | SEDILE | SEELING | SEGOS |
| SECEDED | SECTATOR | SEDILIA | SEELINGS | SEGREANT |
| SECEDER | SECTATORS | SEDIMENT | SEELS | SEGREGATE |
| SECEDERS | SECTILE | SEDIMENTED | SEELY | SEGREGATED |
| SECEDES | SECTILITIES | SEDIMENTING | SEEM | SEGREGATES |
| SECEDING | SECTILITY | SEDIMENTS | SEEMED | SEGREGATING |
| SECERN | SECTION | SEDITION | SEEMELESS | SEGS |
| SECERNED | SECTIONAL | SEDITIONS | SEEMER | SEGUE |
| SECERNENT | SECTIONED | SEDITIOUS | SEEMERS | SEGUED |
| SECERNENTS | SECTIONING | SEDUCE | SEEMING | SEGUEING |
| SECERNING | SECTIONS | SEDUCED | SEEMINGLY | SEGUES |
| SECERNS | SECTOR | SEDUCER | SEEMINGS | SEI |
| SECESH | SECTORAL | SEDUCERS | SEEMLESS | SEICENTO |
| SECESHER | SECTORED | SEDUCES | SEEMLESSE | SEICENTOS |
| SECESHERS | SECTORIAL | SEDUCING | SEEMLIER | SEICHE |
| SECESHES | SECTORIALS | SEDUCINGS | SEEMLIEST | SEICHES |
| SECESSION | SECTORING | SEDUCTION | SEEMLIHED | SEIF |
| SECESSIONS | SECTORS | SEDUCTIONS | SEEMLIHEDS | SEIFS |
| SECKEL | SECTS | SEDUCTIVE | SEEMLY | SEIGNEUR |
| SECKELS | SECULAR | SEDUCTOR | SEEMLYHED | SEIGNEURS |
| SECLUDE | SECULARLY | SEDUCTORS | SEEMLYHEDS | SEIGNIOR |
| SECLUDED | SECULARS | SEDULITIES | SEEMS | SEIGNIORIES |
| SECLUDES | SECULUM | SEDULITY | SEEN | SEIGNIORS |
| SECLUDING | SECULUMS | SEDULOUS | SEEP | SEIGNIORY |
| SECLUSION | SECUND | SEDUM | SEEPAGE | SEIGNORAL |
| SECLUSIONS | SECUNDINE | SEDUMS | SEEPAGES | SEIGNORIES |
| SECLUSIVE | SECUNDINES | SEE | SEEPED | SEIGNORY |
| SECODONT | SECUNDUM | SEEABLE | SEEPIER | SEIL |
| SECODONTS | SECURABLE | SEECATCH | SEEPIEST | SEILED |
| SECOND | SECURANCE | SEECATCHIE | SEEPING | SEILING |
| SECONDARIES | SECURANCES | SEED | SEEPS | SEILS |
| SECONDARY | SECURE | SEEDBED | SEEPY | SEINE |
| SECONDE | SECURED | SEEDBEDS | SEER | SEINED |
| SECONDED | SECURELY | SEEDBOX | SEERESS | SEINER |
| SECONDEE | SECURER | SEEDBOXES | SEERESSES | SEINERS |
| SECONDEES | SECURERS | SEEDCAKE | SEERS | SEINES |

SEINING
SEININGS
SEIS
SEISE
SEISED
SEISES
SEISIN
SEISING
SEISINS
SEISM
SEISMAL
SEISMIC
SEISMICAL
SEISMISM
SEISMISMS
SEISMS
SEITIES
SEITY
SEIZABLE
SEIZE
SEIZED
SEIZER
SEIZERS
SEIZES
SEIZIN
SEIZING
SEIZINGS
SEIZINS
SEIZURE
SEIZURES
SEJANT
SEJEANT
SEKOS
SEKOSES
SEKT
SEKTS
SEL
SELACHIAN
SELACHIANS
SELADANG
SELADANGS
SELAH
SELAHS
SELCOUTH
SELD
SELDOM
SELDSEEN
SELDSHOWN
SELE
SELECT
SELECTED
SELECTING
SELECTION
SELECTIONS
SELECTIVE
SELECTOR
SELECTORS
SELECTS
SELENATE
SELENATES
SELENIC
SELENIDE
SELENIDES
SELENIOUS
SELENITE
SELENITES
SELENITIC
SELENIUM
SELENIUMS
SELENOUS

SELES
SELF
SELFED
SELFHOOD
SELFHOODS
SELFING
SELFISH
SELFISHLY
SELFISM
SELFISMS
SELFIST
SELFISTS
SELFLESS
SELFNESS
SELFNESSES
SELFS
SELICTAR
SELICTARS
SELKIE
SELKIES
SELL
SELLABLE
SELLE
SELLER
SELLERS
SELLES
SELLING
SELLOTAPE
SELLOTAPED
SELLOTAPES
SELLOTAPING
SELLS
SELS
SELTZER
SELTZERS
SELVA
SELVAGE
SELVAGED
SELVAGEE
SELVAGEES
SELVAGES
SELVAGING
SELVAS
SELVEDGE
SELVEDGED
SELVEDGES
SELVEDGING
SELVES
SEMANTEME
SEMANTEMES
SEMANTIC
SEMANTICS
SEMANTRA
SEMANTRON
SEMAPHORE
SEMAPHORED
SEMAPHORES
SEMAPHORING
SEMATIC
SEMBLABLE
SEMBLABLES
SEMBLABLY
SEMBLANCE
SEMBLANCES
SEMBLANT
SEMBLANTS
SEMBLE
SEMBLED
SEMBLES
SEMBLING

SEMÉ
SEMÉE
SEMEIA
SEMEION
SEMEIOTIC
SEMEIOTICS
SEMEME
SEMEMES
SEMEN
SEMENS
SEMESTER
SEMESTERS
SEMESTRAL
SEMI
SEMIANGLE
SEMIANGLES
SEMIBREVE
SEMIBREVES
SEMIBULL
SEMIBULLS
SEMICOLON
SEMICOLONS
SEMICOMA
SEMICOMAS
SEMIE
SEMIES
SEMIFINAL
SEMIFINALS
SEMIFLUID
SEMIFLUIDS
SEMILOG
SEMILUNE
SEMILUNES
SEMINAL
SEMINALLY
SEMINAR
SEMINARIES
SEMINARS
SEMINARY
SEMINATE
SEMINATED
SEMINATES
SEMINATING
SEMIOLOGIES
SEMIOLOGY
SEMIOTIC
SEMIOTICS
SEMIPED
SEMIPEDS
SEMIPLUME
SEMIPLUMES
SEMIS
SEMISES
SEMITAR
SEMITARS
SEMITAUR
SEMITAURS
SEMITONE
SEMITONES
SEMITONIC
SEMIVOWEL
SEMIVOWELS
SEMMIT
SEMMITS
SEMOLINA
SEMOLINAS
SEMPER
SEMPITERN
SEMPLE
SEMPLER

SEMPLEST
SEMPLICE
SEMPRE
SEMPSTER
SEMPSTERS
SEMSEM
SEMSEMS
SEMUNCIA
SEMUNCIAE
SEMUNCIAL
SEMUNCIAS
SEN
SENARIES
SENARII
SENARIUS
SENARY
SENATE
SENATES
SENATOR
SENATORS
SEND
SENDAL
SENDALS
SENDED
SENDER
SENDERS
SENDING
SENDINGS
SENDS
SENECIO
SENECIOS
SENEGA
SENEGAS
SENESCENT
SENESCHAL
SENESCHALS
SENGREEN
SENGREENS
SENILE
SENILELY
SENILITIES
SENILITY
SENIOR
SENIORITIES
SENIORITY
SENIORS
SENNA
SENNACHIE
SENNACHIES
SENNAS
SENNET
SENNETS
SENNIGHT
SENNIGHTS
SENNIT
SENNITS
SENS
SENSA
SENSATION
SENSATIONS
SENSE
SENSED
SENSEFUL
SENSELESS
SENSES
SENSIBLE
SENSIBLER
SENSIBLES
SENSIBLEST
SENSIBLY

SENSILE
SENSILLA
SENSILLUM
SENSING
SENSINGS
SENSISM
SENSISMS
SENSIST
SENSISTS
SENSITISE
SENSITISED
SENSITISES
SENSITISING
SENSITIVE
SENSITIVES
SENSITIZE
SENSITIZED
SENSITIZES
SENSITIZING
SENSOR
SENSORIAL
SENSORIES
SENSORIUM
SENSORIUMS
SENSORS
SENSORY
SENSUAL
SENSUALLY
SENSUALTIES
SENSUALTY
SENSUISM
SENSUISMS
SENSUIST
SENSUISTS
SENSUM
SENSUOUS
SENT
SENTED
SENTENCE
SENTENCED
SENTENCER
SENTENCERS
SENTENCES
SENTENCING
SENTIENCE
SENTIENCES
SENTIENCIES
SENTIENCY
SENTIENT
SENTIENTS
SENTIMENT
SENTIMENTS
SENTINEL
SENTINELLED
SENTINELLING
SENTINELS
SENTING
SENTRIES
SENTRY
SENTS
SENVIES
SENVY
SENZA
SEPAD
SEPADDED
SEPADDING
SEPADS
SEPAL
SEPALINE
SEPALODIES

| | | | | |
|---|---|---|---|---|
| SEPALODY | SEPTUPLE | SERENADERS | SERICON | SEROTYPINGS |
| SEPALOID | SEPTUPLED | SERENADES | SERICONS | SEROUS |
| SEPALOUS | SEPTUPLES | SERENADING | SERIEMA | SEROW |
| SEPALS | SEPTUPLET | SERENATA | SERIEMAS | SEROWS |
| SEPARABLE | SEPTUPLETS | SERENATAS | SERIES | SERPENT |
| SEPARABLY | SEPTUPLING | SERENATE | SERIF | SERPENTED |
| SEPARATE | SEPULCHRE | SERENATES | SERIFS | SERPENTING |
| SEPARATED | SEPULCHRED | SERENE | SERIGRAPH | SERPENTRIES |
| SEPARATES | SEPULCHRES | SERENED | SERIGRAPHS | SERPENTRY |
| SEPARATING | SEPULCHRING | SERENELY | SERIN | SERPENTS |
| SEPARATOR | SEPULTURE | SERENER | SERINETTE | SERPIGINES |
| SEPARATORS | SEPULTURED | SERENES | SERINETTES | SERPIGO |
| SEPARATUM | SEPULTURES | SERENESS | SERING | SERPIGOES |
| SEPARATUMS | SEPULTURING | SERENESSES | SERINGA | SERPULA |
| SEPHEN | SEQUACITIES | SERENEST | SERINGAS | SERPULAE |
| SEPHENS | SEQUACITY | SERENING | SERINS | SERPULITE |
| SEPIA | SEQUEL | SERENITIES | SERIOUS | SERPULITES |
| SEPIAS | SEQUELA | SERENITY | SERIOUSLY | SERR |
| SEPIMENT | SEQUELAE | SERER | SERIPH | SERRA |
| SEPIMENTS | SEQUELS | SERES | SERIPHS | SERRAE |
| SEPIOLITE | SEQUENCE | SEREST | SERJEANCIES | SERRAN |
| SEPIOLITES | SEQUENCED | SERF | SERJEANCY | SERRANID |
| SEPIOST | SEQUENCES | SERFAGE | SERJEANT | SERRANIDS |
| SEPIOSTS | SEQUENCING | SERFAGES | SERJEANTIES | SERRANOID |
| SEPIUM | SEQUENT | SERFDOM | SERJEANTS | SERRANOIDS |
| SEPIUMS | SEQUENTS | SERFDOMS | SERJEANTY | SERRANS |
| SEPOY | SEQUESTER | SERFHOOD | SERK | SERRAS |
| SEPOYS | SEQUESTERED | SERFHOODS | SERKALI | SERRATE |
| SEPPUKU | SEQUESTERING | SERFISH | SERKALIS | SERRATED |
| SEPPUKUS | SEQUESTERS | SERFS | SERKS | SERRATES |
| SEPS | SEQUIN | SERFSHIP | SERMON | SERRATING |
| SEPSES | SEQUINS | SERFSHIPS | SERMONED | SERRATION |
| SEPSIS | SEQUOIA | SERGE | SERMONEER | SERRATIONS |
| SEPT | SEQUOIAS | SERGEANCIES | SERMONEERS | SERRATURE |
| SEPTA | SERA | SERGEANCY | SERMONER | SERRATURES |
| SEPTAL | SÉRAC | SERGEANT | SERMONERS | SERRATUS |
| SEPTARIA | SÉRACS | SERGEANTS | SERMONET | SERRATUSES |
| SEPTARIAN | SERAFILE | SERGES | SERMONETS | SERRE |
| SEPTARIUM | SERAFILES | SERIAL | SERMONIC | SERRED |
| SEPTATE | SERAGLIO | SERIALISE | SERMONING | SERREFILE |
| SEPTATION | SERAGLIOS | SERIALISED | SERMONINGS | SERREFILES |
| SEPTATIONS | SERAI | SERIALISES | SERMONISE | SERRES |
| SEPTEMFID | SERAIL | SERIALISING | SERMONISED | SERRICORN |
| SEPTEMVIR | SERAILS | SERIALISM | SERMONISES | SERRIED |
| SEPTEMVIRI | SERAIS | SERIALISMS | SERMONISH | SERRIES |
| SEPTEMVIRS | SERAL | SERIALIST | SERMONISING | SERRING |
| SEPTENARIES | SERANG | SERIALISTS | SERMONIZE | SERRS |
| SEPTENARY | SERANGS | SERIALITIES | SERMONIZED | SERRULATE |
| SEPTENNIA | SERAPE | SERIALITY | SERMONIZES | SERRY |
| SEPTET | SERAPES | SERIALIZE | SERMONIZING | SERRYING |
| SEPTETS | SERAPH | SERIALIZED | SERMONS | SERUEWE |
| SEPTETT | SERAPHIC | SERIALIZES | SEROLOGIES | SERUEWED |
| SEPTETTE | SERAPHIM | SERIALIZING | SEROLOGY | SERUEWES |
| SEPTETTES | SERAPHIMS | SERIALLY | SERON | SERUEWING |
| SEPTETTS | SERAPHIN | SERIALS | SERONS | SERUM |
| SEPTIC | SERAPHINE | SERIATE | SEROON | SERUMS |
| SEPTICITIES | SERAPHINES | SERIATED | SEROONS | SERVAL |
| SEPTICITY | SERAPHINS | SERIATELY | SEROSA | SERVALS |
| SEPTIFORM | SERAPHS | SERIATES | SEROSAE | SERVANT |
| SEPTIMAL | SERASKIER | SERIATIM | SEROSAS | SERVANTED |
| SEPTIME | SERASKIERS | SERIATING | SEROSITIES | SERVANTING |
| SEPTIMES | SERDAB | SERIATION | SEROSITY | SERVANTRIES |
| SEPTIMOLE | SERDABS | SERIATIONS | SEROTINE | SERVANTRY |
| SEPTIMOLES | SERE | SERIC | SEROTINES | SERVANTS |
| SEPTLEVA | SERED | SERICEOUS | SEROTONIN | SERVE |
| SEPTLEVAS | SEREIN | SERICIN | SEROTONINS | SERVED |
| SEPTS | SEREINS | SERICINS | SEROTYPE | SERVER |
| SEPTUM | SERENADE | SERICITE | SEROTYPED | SERVERIES |
| SEPTUOR | SERENADED | SERICITES | SEROTYPES | SERVERS |
| SEPTUORS | SERENADER | SERICITIC | SEROTYPING | SERVERY |

SERVES
SERVEWE
SERVEWED
SERVEWES
SERVEWING
SERVICE
SERVICED
SERVICES
SERVICING
SERVIENT
SERVIETTE
SERVIETTES
SERVILE
SERVILELY
SERVILES
SERVILISM
SERVILISMS
SERVILITIES
SERVILITY
SERVING
SERVINGS
SERVITOR
SERVITORS
SERVITUDE
SERVITUDES
SERVO
SESAME
SESAMES
SESAMOID
SESAMOIDS
SESE
SESELI
SESELIS
SESEY
SESS
SESSA
SESSES
SESSILE
SESSION
SESSIONAL
SESSIONS
SESSPOOL
SESSPOOLS
SESTERCE
SESTERCES
SESTERTIA
SESTET
SESTETS
SESTETT
SESTETTE
SESTETTES
SESTETTO
SESTETTOS
SESTETTS
SESTINA
SESTINAS
SESTINE
SESTINES
SESTON
SESTONS
SET
SETA
SETACEOUS
SETAE
SETBACK
SETBACKS
SETNESS
SETNESSES
SETON
SETONS

SETOSE
SETS
SETT
SETTEE
SETTEES
SETTER
SETTERED
SETTERING
SETTERS
SETTING
SETTINGS
SETTLE
SETTLED
SETTLER
SETTLERS
SETTLES
SETTLING
SETTLINGS
SETTLOR
SETTLORS
SETTS
SETUALE
SETUALES
SETWALL
SETWALLS
SEVEN
SEVENFOLD
SEVENS
SEVENTEEN
SEVENTEENS
SEVENTH
SEVENTHLY
SEVENTHS
SEVENTIES
SEVENTY
SEVER
SEVERABLE
SEVERAL
SEVERALLY
SEVERALS
SEVERALTIES
SEVERALTY
SEVERANCE
SEVERANCES
SEVERE
SEVERED
SEVERELY
SEVERER
SEVEREST
SEVERIES
SEVERING
SEVERITIES
SEVERITY
SEVERS
SEVERY
SEW
SEWAGE
SEWAGES
SEWED
SEWEL
SEWELLEL
SEWELLELS
SEWELS
SEWEN
SEWENS
SEWER
SEWERAGE
SEWERAGES
SEWERED
SEWERING

SEWERINGS
SEWERS
SEWIN
SEWING
SEWINGS
SEWINS
SEWN
SEWS
SEX
SEXED
SEXENNIAL
SEXER
SEXERS
SEXES
SEXFID
SEXFOIL
SEXFOILS
SEXIER
SEXIEST
SEXINESS
SEXINESSES
SEXING
SEXISM
SEXISMS
SEXIST
SEXISTS
SEXLESS
SEXOLOGIES
SEXOLOGY
SEXPOT
SEXPOTS
SEXT
SEXTAN
SEXTANS
SEXTANSES
SEXTANT
SEXTANTAL
SEXTANTS
SEXTET
SEXTETS
SEXTETT
SEXTETTE
SEXTETTES
SEXTETTS
SEXTILE
SEXTILES
SEXTOLET
SEXTOLETS
SEXTON
SEXTONESS
SEXTONESSES
SEXTONS
SEXTS
SEXTUOR
SEXTUORS
SEXTUPLE
SEXTUPLED
SEXTUPLES
SEXTUPLET
SEXTUPLETS
SEXTUPLING
SEXUAL
SEXUALISE
SEXUALISED
SEXUALISES
SEXUALISING
SEXUALISM
SEXUALISMS
SEXUALIST
SEXUALISTS

SEXUALITIES
SEXUALITY
SEXUALIZE
SEXUALIZED
SEXUALIZES
SEXUALIZING
SEXUALLY
SEXVALENT
SEXY
SEY
SEYEN
SEYENS
SEYS
SEYSURE
SEYSURES
SEZ
SFERICS
SFORZANDI
SFORZANDO
SFORZANDOS
SFORZATI
SFORZATO
SFORZATOS
SFUMATO
SFUMATOS
SGRAFFITI
SGRAFFITO
SH
SHABBIER
SHABBIEST
SHABBILY
SHABBLE
SHABBLES
SHABBY
SHABRACK
SHABRACKS
SHACK
SHACKLE
SHACKLED
SHACKLES
SHACKLING
SHACKS
SHAD
SHADBERRIES
SHADBERRY
SHADBUSH
SHADBUSHES
SHADDOCK
SHADDOCKS
SHADE
SHADED
SHADELESS
SHADES
SHADIER
SHADIEST
SHADILY
SHADINESS
SHADINESSES
SHADING
SHADINGS
SHADOOF
SHADOOFS
SHADOW
SHADOWED
SHADOWER
SHADOWERS
SHADOWIER
SHADOWIEST
SHADOWING
SHADOWINGS

SHADOWS
SHADOWY
SHADS
SHADUF
SHADUFS
SHADY
SHAFT
SHAFTED
SHAFTER
SHAFTERS
SHAFTING
SHAFTINGS
SHAFTLESS
SHAFTS
SHAG
SHAGEARED
SHAGGED
SHAGGIER
SHAGGIEST
SHAGGILY
SHAGGING
SHAGGY
SHAGREEN
SHAGREENS
SHAGROON
SHAGROONS
SHAGS
SHAH
SHAHS
SHAIKH
SHAIKHS
SHAIRN
SHAIRNS
SHAITAN
SHAITANS
SHAKABLE
SHAKE
SHAKEABLE
SHAKED
SHAKEN
SHAKER
SHAKERISM
SHAKERISMS
SHAKERS
SHAKES
SHAKIER
SHAKIEST
SHAKILY
SHAKINESS
SHAKINESSES
SHAKING
SHAKINGS
SHAKO
SHAKOES
SHAKOS
SHAKT
SHAKUDO
SHAKUDOS
SHAKY
SHALE
SHALED
SHALES
SHALIER
SHALIEST
SHALING
SHALL
SHALLI
SHALLIS
SHALLON
SHALLONS

| | | | | |
|---|---|---|---|---|
| SHALLOON | SHAMPOOING | SHARK | SHAWL | SHED |
| SHALLOONS | SHAMPOOS | SHARKED | SHAWLED | SHEDDER |
| SHALLOP | SHAMROCK | SHARKER | SHAWLING | SHEDDERS |
| SHALLOPS | SHAMROCKS | SHARKERS | SHAWLINGS | SHEDDING |
| SHALLOT | SHAMS | SHARKING | SHAWLLESS | SHEDDINGS |
| SHALLOTS | SHAMUS | SHARKINGS | SHAWLS | SHEDS |
| SHALLOW | SHAMUSES | SHARKS | SHAWM | SHEEL |
| SHALLOWED | SHAN | SHARKSKIN | SHAWMS | SHEELED |
| SHALLOWER | SHANACHIE | SHARKSKINS | SHAWS | SHEELING |
| SHALLOWEST | SHANACHIES | SHARN | SHAY | SHEELS |
| SHALLOWING | SHAND | SHARNIER | SHAYA | SHEEN |
| SHALLOWINGS | SHANDIES | SHARNIEST | SHAYAS | SHEENED |
| SHALLOWLY | SHANDRIES | SHARNS | SHAYS | SHEENIER |
| SHALLOWS | SHANDRY | SHARNY | SHCHI | SHEENIES |
| SHALM | SHANDS | SHARP | SHCHIS | SHEENIEST |
| SHALMS | SHANDY | SHARPED | SHE | SHEENING |
| SHALOM | SHANGHAI | SHARPEN | SHEA | SHEENS |
| SHALOT | SHANGHAIED | SHARPENED | SHEADING | SHEENY |
| SHALOTS | SHANGHAIING | SHARPENER | SHEADINGS | SHEEP |
| SHALT | SHANGHAIS | SHARPENERS | SHEAF | SHEEPDOG |
| SHALWAR | SHANK | SHARPENING | SHEAFED | SHEEPDOGS |
| SHALWARS | SHANKED | SHARPENS | SHEAFIER | SHEEPFOLD |
| SHALY | SHANKING | SHARPER | SHEAFIEST | SHEEPFOLDS |
| SHAM | SHANKS | SHARPERS | SHEAFING | SHEEPIER |
| SHAMA | SHANNIES | SHARPEST | SHEAFS | SHEEPIEST |
| SHAMAN | SHANNY | SHARPIE | SHEAFY | SHEEPISH |
| SHAMANIC | SHANS | SHARPIES | SHEAL | SHEEPMEAT |
| SHAMANISM | SHANTIES | SHARPING | SHEALED | SHEEPMEATS |
| SHAMANISMS | SHANTUNG | SHARPINGS | SHEALING | SHEEPSKIN |
| SHAMANIST | SHANTUNGS | SHARPISH | SHEALINGS | SHEEPSKINS |
| SHAMANISTS | SHANTY | SHARPLY | SHEALS | SHEEPWALK |
| SHAMANS | SHANTYMAN | SHARPNESS | SHEAR | SHEEPWALKS |
| SHAMAS | SHANTYMEN | SHARPNESSES | SHEARED | SHEEPY |
| SHAMATEUR | SHAPABLE | SHARPS | SHEARER | SHEER |
| SHAMATEURS | SHAPE | SHASH | SHEARERS | SHEERED |
| SHAMBLE | SHAPEABLE | SHASHES | SHEARING | SHEERER |
| SHAMBLED | SHAPED | SHASHLIK | SHEARINGS | SHEEREST |
| SHAMBLES | SHAPELESS | SHASHLIKS | SHEARLING | SHEERING |
| SHAMBLING | SHAPELIER | SHASTER | SHEARLINGS | SHEERLY |
| SHAMBLINGS | SHAPELIEST | SHASTERS | SHEARMAN | SHEERS |
| SHAMBOLIC | SHAPELY | SHASTRA | SHEARMEN | SHEET |
| SHAME | SHAPEN | SHASTRAS | SHEARS | SHEETED |
| SHAMED | SHAPER | SHAT | SHEAS | SHEETIER |
| SHAMEFAST | SHAPERS | SHATTER | SHEATH | SHEETIEST |
| SHAMEFUL | SHAPES | SHATTERED | SHEATHE | SHEETING |
| SHAMELESS | SHAPING | SHATTERING | SHEATHED | SHEETINGS |
| SHAMER | SHAPINGS | SHATTERS | SHEATHES | SHEETS |
| SHAMERS | SHAPS | SHATTERY | SHEATHIER | SHEETY |
| SHAMES | SHARD | SHAUCHLE | SHEATHIEST | SHEHITA |
| SHAMIANA | SHARDED | SHAUCHLED | SHEATHING | SHEHITAH |
| SHAMIANAH | SHARDS | SHAUCHLES | SHEATHINGS | SHEHITAHS |
| SHAMIANAHS | SHARE | SHAUCHLIER | SHEATHS | SHEHITAS |
| SHAMIANAS | SHARECROP | SHAUCHLIEST | SHEATHY | SHEIK |
| SHAMING | SHARECROPPED | SHAUCHLING | SHEAVE | SHEIKDOM |
| SHAMISEN | SHARECROPPING | SHAUCHLY | SHEAVED | SHEIKDOMS |
| SHAMISENS | SHARECROPS | SHAVE | SHEAVES | SHEIKH |
| SHAMMED | SHARED | SHAVED | SHEAVING | SHEIKHDOM |
| SHAMMER | SHAREMAN | SHAVELING | SHEBANG | SHEIKHDOMS |
| SHAMMERS | SHAREMEN | SHAVELINGS | SHEBANGS | SHEIKHS |
| SHAMMIES | SHARER | SHAVEN | SHEBEEN | SHEIKS |
| SHAMMING | SHARERS | SHAVER | SHEBEENED | SHEILA |
| SHAMMY | SHARES | SHAVERS | SHEBEENER | SHEILAS |
| SHAMOY | SHARESMAN | SHAVES | SHEBEENERS | SHEILING |
| SHAMOYED | SHARESMEN | SHAVIE | SHEBEENING | SHEILINGS |
| SHAMOYING | SHARIA | SHAVIES | SHEBEENINGS | SHEKEL |
| SHAMOYS | SHARIAS | SHAVING | SHEBEENS | SHEKELS |
| SHAMPOO | SHARIAT | SHAVINGS | SHECHITA | SHELDDUCK |
| SHAMPOOED | SHARIATS | SHAW | SHECHITAH | SHELDDUCKS |
| SHAMPOOER | SHARING | SHAWED | SHECHITAHS | SHELDRAKE |
| SHAMPOOERS | SHARINGS | SHAWING | SHECHITAS | SHELDRAKES |

SHELDUCK
SHELDUCKS
SHELF
SHELFED
SHELFIER
SHELFIEST
SHELFING
SHELFROOM
SHELFROOMS
SHELFS
SHELFY
SHELL
SHELLAC
SHELLACKED
SHELLACKING
SHELLACKINGS
SHELLACS
SHELLBACK
SHELLBACKS
SHELLBARK
SHELLBARKS
SHELLDUCK
SHELLDUCKS
SHELLED
SHELLER
SHELLERS
SHELLFIRE
SHELLFIRES
SHELLFISH
SHELLFISHES
SHELLFUL
SHELLFULS
SHELLIER
SHELLIEST
SHELLING
SHELLINGS
SHELLS
SHELLWORK
SHELLWORKS
SHELLY
SHELTER
SHELTERED
SHELTERER
SHELTERERS
SHELTERING
SHELTERINGS
SHELTERS
SHELTERY
SHELTIE
SHELTIES
SHELTY
SHELVE
SHELVED
SHELVES
SHELVIER
SHELVIEST
SHELVING
SHELVINGS
SHELVY
SHEMOZZLE
SHEMOZZLED
SHEMOZZLES
SHEMOZZLING
SHEND
SHENDING
SHENDS
SHENT
SHEPHERD
SHEPHERDED
SHEPHERDING

SHEPHERDS
SHERBET
SHERBETS
SHERD
SHERDS
SHERE
SHEREEF
SHEREEFS
SHERIA
SHERIAS
SHERIAT
SHERIATS
SHERIF
SHERIFF
SHERIFFS
SHERIFIAN
SHERIFS
SHERRIES
SHERRIS
SHERRISES
SHERRY
SHES
SHET
SHETLAND
SHETS
SHETTING
SHEUCH
SHEUCHED
SHEUCHING
SHEUCHS
SHEUGH
SHEUGHED
SHEUGHING
SHEUGHS
SHEVA
SHEVAS
SHEW
SHEWBREAD
SHEWBREADS
SHEWED
SHEWEL
SHEWELS
SHEWING
SHEWN
SHEWS
SHIATSU
SHIATSUS
SHIBUICHI
SHIBUICHIS
SHICKER
SHICKERED
SHICKERS
SHICKSA
SHICKSAS
SHIDDER
SHIDDERS
SHIED
SHIEL
SHIELD
SHIELDED
SHIELDER
SHIELDERS
SHIELDING
SHIELDS
SHIELDUCK
SHIELDUCKS
SHIELED
SHIELING
SHIELINGS
SHIELS

SHIER
SHIERS
SHIES
SHIEST
SHIFT
SHIFTED
SHIFTER
SHIFTERS
SHIFTIER
SHIFTIEST
SHIFTILY
SHIFTING
SHIFTINGS
SHIFTLESS
SHIFTS
SHIFTY
SHIGELLA
SHIGELLAS
SHIITAKE
SHIKAR
SHIKAREE
SHIKAREES
SHIKARI
SHIKARIS
SHIKARS
SHIKSA
SHIKSAS
SHIKSE
SHIKSES
SHILL
SHILLABER
SHILLABERS
SHILLED
SHILLELAH
SHILLELAHS
SHILLING
SHILLINGS
SHILLS
SHILPIT
SHILY
SHIM
SHIMMER
SHIMMERED
SHIMMERING
SHIMMERINGS
SHIMMERS
SHIMMERY
SHIMMIED
SHIMMIES
SHIMMY
SHIMMYING
SHIMOZZLE
SHIMOZZLES
SHIMS
SHIN
SHINDIES
SHINDIG
SHINDIGS
SHINDY
SHINE
SHINED
SHINELESS
SHINER
SHINERS
SHINES
SHINESS
SHINESSES
SHINGLE
SHINGLED
SHINGLER

SHINGLERS
SHINGLES
SHINGLIER
SHINGLIEST
SHINGLING
SHINGLINGS
SHINGLY
SHINIER
SHINIEST
SHININESS
SHININESSES
SHINING
SHININGLY
SHINNE
SHINNED
SHINNES
SHINNIED
SHINNIES
SHINNING
SHINNY
SHINNYING
SHINS
SHINTIES
SHINTY
SHINY
SHIP
SHIPBOARD
SHIPBOARDS
SHIPFUL
SHIPFULS
SHIPLAP
SHIPLAPPED
SHIPLAPPING
SHIPLAPS
SHIPLESS
SHIPMAN
SHIPMATE
SHIPMATES
SHIPMEN
SHIPMENT
SHIPMENTS
SHIPPED
SHIPPEN
SHIPPENS
SHIPPER
SHIPPERS
SHIPPING
SHIPPINGS
SHIPPO
SHIPPON
SHIPPONS
SHIPPOS
SHIPPOUND
SHIPPOUNDS
SHIPS
SHIPSHAPE
SHIPWRECK
SHIPWRECKED
SHIPWRECKING
SHIPWRECKS
SHIPYARD
SHIPYARDS
SHIR
SHIRALEE
SHIRALEES
SHIRE
SHIREMAN
SHIREMEN
SHIRES
SHIRK

SHIRKED
SHIRKER
SHIRKERS
SHIRKING
SHIRKS
SHIRR
SHIRRA
SHIRRAS
SHIRRED
SHIRRING
SHIRRINGS
SHIRRS
SHIRS
SHIRT
SHIRTED
SHIRTIER
SHIRTIEST
SHIRTING
SHIRTINGS
SHIRTLESS
SHIRTS
SHIRTY
SHIT
SHITE
SHITES
SHITING
SHITS
SHITTAH
SHITTAHS
SHITTIER
SHITTIEST
SHITTIM
SHITTIMS
SHITTING
SHITTY
SHIV
SHIVAREE
SHIVAREED
SHIVAREEING
SHIVAREES
SHIVE
SHIVER
SHIVERED
SHIVERING
SHIVERINGS
SHIVERS
SHIVERY
SHIVES
SHIVOO
SHIVOOS
SHIVS
SHIVVED
SHIVVING
SHLEMIEL
SHLEMIELS
SHLEP
SHLEPPED
SHLEPPING
SHLEPS
SHLIMAZEL
SHLIMAZELS
SHLOCK
SHLOCKS
SHMOOSE
SHMOOSED
SHMOOSES
SHMOOSING
SHMOOZE
SHMOOZED
SHMOOZES

| | | | | |
|---|---|---|---|---|
| SHMOOZING | SHOGUNS | SHORESMAN | SHOUTERS | SHRADDHAS |
| SHOAL | SHOJI | SHORESMEN | SHOUTHER | SHRANK |
| SHOALED | SHOJIS | SHOREWARD | SHOUTHERED | SHRAPNEL |
| SHOALER | SHOLA | SHOREWARDS | SHOUTHERING | SHRAPNELS |
| SHOALEST | SHOLAS | SHORING | SHOUTHERS | SHRED |
| SHOALIER | SHONE | SHORINGS | SHOUTING | SHREDDED |
| SHOALIEST | SHOO | SHORN | SHOUTINGS | SHREDDER |
| SHOALING | SHOOED | SHORT | SHOUTS | SHREDDERS |
| SHOALINGS | SHOOGIE | SHORTAGE | SHOVE | SHREDDIER |
| SHOALNESS | SHOOGIED | SHORTAGES | SHOVED | SHREDDIEST |
| SHOALNESSES | SHOOGIEING | SHORTCAKE | SHOVEL | SHREDDING |
| SHOALS | SHOOGIES | SHORTCAKES | SHOVELER | SHREDDINGS |
| SHOALWISE | SHOOGLE | SHORTCUT | SHOVELERS | SHREDDY |
| SHOALY | SHOOGLED | SHORTCUTS | SHOVELFUL | SHREDLESS |
| SHOAT | SHOOGLES | SHORTED | SHOVELFULS | SHREDS |
| SHOATS | SHOOGLIER | SHORTEN | SHOVELLED | SHREEK |
| SHOCHET | SHOOGLIEST | SHORTENED | SHOVELLER | SHREEKED |
| SHOCHETIM | SHOOGLING | SHORTENER | SHOVELLERS | SHREEKING |
| SHOCK | SHOOGLY | SHORTENERS | SHOVELLING | SHREEKS |
| SHOCKED | SHOOING | SHORTENING | SHOVELS | SHREIK |
| SHOCKER | SHOOK | SHORTENINGS | SHOVER | SHREIKED |
| SHOCKERS | SHOOKS | SHORTENS | SHOVERS | SHREIKING |
| SHOCKING | SHOOL | SHORTER | SHOVES | SHREIKS |
| SHOCKS | SHOOLED | SHORTEST | SHOVING | SHREW |
| SHOD | SHOOLING | SHORTFALL | SHOW | SHREWD |
| SHODDIER | SHOOLS | SHORTFALLS | SHOWBIZ | SHREWDER |
| SHODDIES | SHOON | SHORTGOWN | SHOWBIZZES | SHREWDEST |
| SHODDIEST | SHOOS | SHORTGOWNS | SHOWBIZZY | SHREWDLY |
| SHODDILY | SHOOT | SHORTHAND | SHOWBREAD | SHREWED |
| SHODDY | SHOOTABLE | SHORTHANDS | SHOWBREADS | SHREWING |
| SHODER | SHOOTER | SHORTIE | SHOWCARD | SHREWISH |
| SHODERS | SHOOTERS | SHORTIES | SHOWCARDS | SHREWMICE |
| SHOE | SHOOTING | SHORTING | SHOWCASE | SHREWS |
| SHOEBILL | SHOOTINGS | SHORTISH | SHOWCASED | SHRIECH |
| SHOEBILLS | SHOOTIST | SHORTLY | SHOWCASES | SHRIECHED |
| SHOEBLACK | SHOOTISTS | SHORTNESS | SHOWCASING | SHRIECHES |
| SHOEBLACKS | SHOOTS | SHORTNESSES | SHOWED | SHRIECHING |
| SHOED | SHOP | SHORTS | SHOWER | SHRIEK |
| SHOEHORN | SHOPBOARD | SHORTY | SHOWERED | SHRIEKED |
| SHOEHORNED | SHOPBOARDS | SHOT | SHOWERFUL | SHRIEKER |
| SHOEHORNING | SHOPE | SHOTE | SHOWERIER | SHRIEKERS |
| SHOEHORNS | SHOPFUL | SHOTES | SHOWERIEST | SHRIEKING |
| SHOEING | SHOPFULS | SHOTFIRER | SHOWERING | SHRIEKINGS |
| SHOEINGS | SHOPHAR | SHOTFIRERS | SHOWERINGS | SHRIEKS |
| SHOELESS | SHOPHARS | SHOTGUN | SHOWERS | SHRIEVAL |
| SHOEMAKER | SHOPHROTH | SHOTGUNS | SHOWERY | SHRIEVE |
| SHOEMAKERS | SHOPMAN | SHOTMAKER | SHOWGHE | SHRIEVED |
| SHOER | SHOPMEN | SHOTMAKERS | SHOWGHES | SHRIEVES |
| SHOERS | SHOPPED | SHOTPROOF | SHOWGIRL | SHRIEVING |
| SHOES | SHOPPER | SHOTS | SHOWGIRLS | SHRIFT |
| SHOESHINE | SHOPPERS | SHOTT | SHOWIER | SHRIFTS |
| SHOESHINES | SHOPPIER | SHOTTED | SHOWIEST | SHRIGHT |
| SHOFAR | SHOPPIEST | SHOTTEN | SHOWILY | SHRIGHTS |
| SHOFARS | SHOPPING | SHOTTING | SHOWINESS | SHRIKE |
| SHOFROTH | SHOPPINGS | SHOTTLE | SHOWINESSES | SHRIKED |
| SHOG | SHOPPY | SHOTTLES | SHOWING | SHRIKES |
| SHOGGED | SHOPS | SHOTTS | SHOWINGS | SHRIKING |
| SHOGGING | SHOPWORN | SHOUGH | SHOWMAN | SHRILL |
| SHOGGLE | SHORAN | SHOUGHS | SHOWMANLY | SHRILLED |
| SHOGGLED | SHORANS | SHOULD | SHOWMEN | SHRILLER |
| SHOGGLES | SHORE | SHOULDER | SHOWN | SHRILLEST |
| SHOGGLIER | SHORED | SHOULDERED | SHOWPIECE | SHRILLING |
| SHOGGLIEST | SHORELESS | SHOULDERING | SHOWPIECES | SHRILLINGS |
| SHOGGLING | SHORELINE | SHOULDERINGS | SHOWPLACE | SHRILLS |
| SHOGGLY | SHORELINES | SHOULDERS | SHOWPLACES | SHRILLY |
| SHOGS | SHOREMAN | SHOULDEST | SHOWROOM | SHRIMP |
| SHOGUN | SHOREMEN | SHOULDST | SHOWROOMS | SHRIMPED |
| SHOGUNAL | SHORER | SHOUT | SHOWS | SHRIMPER |
| SHOGUNATE | SHORERS | SHOUTED | SHOWY | SHRIMPERS |
| SHOGUNATES | SHORES | SHOUTER | SHRADDHA | SHRIMPING |

SHRIMPINGS
SHRIMPS
SHRINAL
SHRINE
SHRINED
SHRINES
SHRINING
SHRINK
SHRINKAGE
SHRINKAGES
SHRINKER
SHRINKERS
SHRINKING
SHRINKS
SHRITCH
SHRITCHED
SHRITCHES
SHRITCHING
SHRIVE
SHRIVED
SHRIVEL
SHRIVELLED
SHRIVELLING
SHRIVELS
SHRIVEN
SHRIVER
SHRIVERS
SHRIVES
SHRIVING
SHRIVINGS
SHROFF
SHROFFAGE
SHROFFAGES
SHROFFED
SHROFFING
SHROFFS
SHROUD
SHROUDED
SHROUDIER
SHROUDIEST
SHROUDING
SHROUDINGS
SHROUDS
SHROUDY
SHROVE
SHROVED
SHROVES
SHROVING
SHROW
SHROWD
SHROWED
SHROWING
SHROWS
SHRUB
SHRUBBED
SHRUBBERIES
SHRUBBERY
SHRUBBIER
SHRUBBIEST
SHRUBBING
SHRUBBY
SHRUBLESS
SHRUBS
SHRUG
SHRUGGED
SHRUGGING
SHRUGS
SHRUNK
SHRUNKEN
SHTCHI

SHTCHIS
SHTETL
SHTETLS
SHTICK
SHTICKS
SHTOOK
SHTOOKS
SHTOOM
SHTUCK
SHTUCKS
SHTUM
SHTUMM
SHUBUNKIN
SHUBUNKINS
SHUCK
SHUCKED
SHUCKER
SHUCKERS
SHUCKING
SHUCKINGS
SHUCKS
SHUDDER
SHUDDERED
SHUDDERING
SHUDDERINGS
SHUDDERS
SHUDDERY
SHUFFLE
SHUFFLED
SHUFFLER
SHUFFLERS
SHUFFLES
SHUFFLING
SHUFFLINGS
SHUFTI
SHUFTIES
SHUFTIS
SHUFTY
SHUL
SHULS
SHUN
SHUNLESS
SHUNNED
SHUNNING
SHUNS
SHUNT
SHUNTED
SHUNTER
SHUNTERS
SHUNTING
SHUNTINGS
SHUNTS
SHUSH
SHUSHED
SHUSHES
SHUSHING
SHUT
SHUTS
SHUTTER
SHUTTERED
SHUTTERING
SHUTTERINGS
SHUTTERS
SHUTTING
SHUTTLE
SHUTTLED
SHUTTLES
SHUTTLING
SHWA
SHWAS

SHY
SHYER
SHYERS
SHYEST
SHYING
SHYISH
SHYLY
SHYNESS
SHYNESSES
SHYSTER
SHYSTERS
SI
SIAL
SIALIC
SIALOGRAM
SIALOGRAMS
SIALOID
SIALOLITH
SIALOLITHS
SIALON
SIALONS
SIALS
SIAMANG
SIAMANGS
SIAMESE
SIAMESED
SIAMESES
SIAMESING
SIAMEZE
SIAMEZED
SIAMEZES
SIAMEZING
SIB
SIBB
SIBBS
SIBILANCE
SIBILANCES
SIBILANCIES
SIBILANCY
SIBILANT
SIBILANTS
SIBILATE
SIBILATED
SIBILATES
SIBILATING
SIBILOUS
SIBLING
SIBLINGS
SIBS
SIBSHIP
SIBSHIPS
SIBYL
SIBYLS
SIC
SICCAN
SICCAR
SICCATIVE
SICCATIVES
SICCED
SICCING
SICCITIES
SICCITY
SICE
SICES
SICH
SICILIANA
SICILIANE
SICILIANO
SICILIANOS
SICK

SICKED
SICKEN
SICKENED
SICKENER
SICKENERS
SICKENING
SICKENINGS
SICKENS
SICKER
SICKERLY
SICKEST
SICKIE
SICKIES
SICKING
SICKISH
SICKISHLY
SICKLE
SICKLED
SICKLEMAN
SICKLEMEN
SICKLES
SICKLIED
SICKLIER
SICKLIES
SICKLIEST
SICKLILY
SICKLY
SICKLYING
SICKMAN
SICKMEN
SICKNESS
SICKNESSES
SICKNURSE
SICKNURSES
SICKROOM
SICKROOMS
SICKS
SICLIKE
SICS
SIDA
SIDALCEA
SIDALCEAS
SIDAS
SIDDHA
SIDDHAS
SIDDHI
SIDDHIS
SIDDUR
SIDDURIM
SIDE
SIDEARM
SIDEARMS
SIDEBOARD
SIDEBOARDS
SIDEBURNS
SIDECAR
SIDECARS
SIDED
SIDELIGHT
SIDELIGHTS
SIDELING
SIDELOCK
SIDELOCKS
SIDELONG
SIDER
SIDERAL
SIDEREAL
SIDERITE
SIDERITES
SIDERITIC

SIDEROSES
SIDEROSIS
SIDERS
SIDES
SIDESMAN
SIDESMEN
SIDESWIPE
SIDESWIPES
SIDEWALK
SIDEWALKS
SIDEWARD
SIDEWARDS
SIDEWAY
SIDEWAYS
SIDEWISE
SIDHA
SIDHAS
SIDING
SIDINGS
SIDLE
SIDLED
SIDLES
SIDLING
SIEGE
SIEGED
SIEGER
SIEGERS
SIEGES
SIEGING
SIELD
SIEMENS
SIEN
SIENNA
SIENNAS
SIENS
SIENT
SIENTS
SIERRA
SIERRAN
SIERRAS
SIESTA
SIESTAS
SIETH
SIETHS
SIEVE
SIEVED
SIEVERT
SIEVERTS
SIEVES
SIEVING
SIFAKA
SIFAKAS
SIFFLE
SIFFLED
SIFFLES
SIFFLING
SIFT
SIFTED
SIFTER
SIFTERS
SIFTING
SIFTINGLY
SIFTINGS
SIFTS
SIGH
SIGHED
SIGHER
SIGHERS
SIGHFUL
SIGHING

| | | | | |
|---|---|---|---|---|
| SIGHINGLY | SIGNER | SILENTS | SILKY | SIMARRES |
| SIGHS | SIGNERS | SILENUS | SILL | SIMARS |
| SIGHT | SIGNET | SILENUSES | SILLABUB | SIMAS |
| SIGHTED | SIGNETED | SILER | SILLABUBS | SIMI |
| SIGHTER | SIGNETS | SILERS | SILLADAR | SIMIAL |
| SIGHTERS | SIGNEUR | SILES | SILLADARS | SIMIAN |
| SIGHTING | SIGNEURIE | SILESIA | SILLER | SIMIANS |
| SIGHTLESS | SIGNEURIES | SILESIAS | SILLERS | SIMILAR |
| SIGHTLIER | SIGNIEUR | SILEX | SILLIER | SIMILARLY |
| SIGHTLIEST | SIGNIEURS | SILEXES | SILLIES | SIMILE |
| SIGHTLY | SIGNIFICS | SILICA | SILLIEST | SIMILES |
| SIGHTS | SIGNIFIED | SILICANE | SILLILY | SIMILISE |
| SIGHTSAW | SIGNIFIER | SILICANES | SILLINESS | SIMILISED |
| SIGHTSEE | SIGNIFIERS | SILICAS | SILLINESSES | SIMILISES |
| SIGHTSEEING | SIGNIFIES | SILICATE | SILLOCK | SIMILISING |
| SIGHTSEEINGS | SIGNIFY | SILICATED | SILLOCKS | SIMILIZE |
| SIGHTSEEN | SIGNIFYING | SILICATES | SILLS | SIMILIZED |
| SIGHTSEER | SIGNING | SILICATING | SILLY | SIMILIZES |
| SIGHTSEERS | SIGNIOR | SILICEOUS | SILO | SIMILIZING |
| SIGHTSEES | SIGNIORS | SILICIC | SILOED | SIMILOR |
| SIGIL | SIGNLESS | SILICIDE | SILOING | SIMILORS |
| SIGILLARY | SIGNOR | SILICIDES | SILOS | SIMIOUS |
| SIGILLATE | SIGNORA | SILICIFIED | SILPHIA | SIMIS |
| SIGILS | SIGNORAS | SILICIFIES | SILPHIUM | SIMITAR |
| SIGISBEI | SIGNORE | SILICIFY | SILPHIUMS | SIMITARS |
| SIGISBEO | SIGNORES | SILICIFYING | SILT | SIMKIN |
| SIGLA | SIGNORI | SILICIOUS | SILTATION | SIMKINS |
| SIGMA | SIGNORIA | SILICIUM | SILTATIONS | SIMMER |
| SIGMAS | SIGNORIAL | SILICIUMS | SILTED | SIMMERED |
| SIGMATE | SIGNORIAS | SILICLE | SILTIER | SIMMERING |
| SIGMATED | SIGNORIES | SILICLES | SILTIEST | SIMMERS |
| SIGMATES | SIGNORINA | SILICON | SILTING | SIMNEL |
| SIGMATIC | SIGNORINAS | SILICONE | SILTS | SIMNELS |
| SIGMATING | SIGNORS | SILICONES | SILTSTONE | SIMONIAC' |
| SIGMATION | SIGNORY | SILICONS | SILTSTONES | SIMONIACS |
| SIGMATIONS | SIGNPOST | SILICOSES | SILTY | SIMONIES |
| SIGMATISM | SIGNPOSTED | SILICOSIS | SILURID | SIMONIOUS |
| SIGMATISMS | SIGNPOSTING | SILICOTIC | SILURIDS | SIMONIST |
| SIGMATRON | SIGNPOSTS | SILICOTICS | SILURIST | SIMONISTS |
| SIGMATRONS | SIGNS | SILICULA | SILURISTS | SIMONY |
| SIGMOID | SIKA | SILICULAS | SILUROID | SIMOOM |
| SIGMOIDAL | SIKAS | SILICULE | SILUROIDS | SIMOOMS |
| SIGN | SIKE | SILICULES | SILVA | SIMOON |
| SIGNAL | SIKES | SILING | SILVAE | SIMOONS |
| SIGNALISE | SILAGE | SILIQUA | SILVAN | SIMORG |
| SIGNALISED | SILAGED | SILIQUAS | SILVANS | SIMORGS |
| SIGNALISES | SILAGES | SILIQUE | SILVAS | SIMP |
| SIGNALISING | SILAGING | SILIQUES | SILVATIC | SIMPAI |
| SIGNALIZE | SILANE | SILIQUOSE | SILVER | SIMPAIS |
| SIGNALIZED | SILANES | SILK | SILVERED | SIMPATICO |
| SIGNALIZES | SILASTIC | SILKED | SILVERIER | SIMPER |
| SIGNALIZING | SILASTICS | SILKEN | SILVERIEST | SIMPERED |
| SIGNALLED | SILD | SILKENED | SILVERING | SIMPERER |
| SIGNALLER | SILDS | SILKENING | SILVERINGS | SIMPERERS |
| SIGNALLERS | SILE | SILKENS | SILVERISE | SIMPERING |
| SIGNALLING | SILED | SILKIE | SILVERISED | SIMPERS |
| SIGNALLINGS | SILEN | SILKIER | SILVERISES | SIMPKIN |
| SIGNALLY | SILENCE | SILKIES | SILVERISING | SIMPKINS |
| SIGNALMAN | SILENCED | SILKIEST | SILVERIZE | SIMPLE |
| SIGNALMEN | SILENCER | SILKILY | SILVERIZED | SIMPLED |
| SIGNALS | SILENCERS | SILKINESS | SILVERIZES | SIMPLER |
| SIGNARIES | SILENCES | SILKINESSES | SILVERIZING | SIMPLERS |
| SIGNARY | SILENCING | SILKING | SILVERLY | SIMPLES |
| SIGNATORIES | SILENE | SILKS | SILVERN | SIMPLESSE |
| SIGNATORY | SILENES | SILKTAIL | SILVERS | SIMPLESSES |
| SIGNATURE | SILENS | SILKTAILS | SILVERY | SIMPLEST |
| SIGNATURES | SILENT | SILKWEED | SIM | SIMPLETON |
| SIGNBOARD | SILENTER | SILKWEEDS | SIMA | SIMPLETONS |
| SIGNBOARDS | SILENTEST | SILKWORM | SIMAR | SIMPLEX |
| SIGNED | SILENTLY | SILKWORMS | SIMARRE | SIMPLICES |

| | | | | |
|---|---|---|---|---|
| SIMPLIFIED | SING | SINOEKETE | SIRENE | SIT |
| SIMPLIFIES | SINGABLE | SINOEKETES | SIRENES | SITAR |
| SIMPLIFY | SINGALONG | SINOPIA | SIRENIAN | SITARS |
| SIMPLIFYING | SINGALONGS | SINOPIAS | SIRENIANS | SITATUNGA |
| SIMPLING | SINGE | SINOPIS | SIRENIC | SITATUNGAS |
| SIMPLINGS | SINGED | SINOPISES | SIRENS | SITCOM |
| SIMPLISM | SINGEING | SINOPITE | SIRES | SITCOMS |
| SIMPLISMS | SINGER | SINOPITES | SIRGANG | SITDOWN |
| SIMPLIST | SINGERS | SINS | SIRGANGS | SITDOWNS |
| SIMPLISTE | SINGES | SINSYNE | SIRI | SITE |
| SIMPLISTS | SINGING | SINTER | SIRIASES | SITED |
| SIMPLY | SINGINGLY | SINTERED | SIRIASIS | SITES |
| SIMPS | SINGINGS | SINTERING | SIRIH | SITFAST |
| SIMS | SINGLE | SINTERS | SIRIHS | SITFASTS |
| SIMULACRA | SINGLED | SINTERY | SIRING | SITH |
| SIMULACRE | SINGLES | SINUATE | SIRIS | SITHE |
| SIMULACRES | SINGLET | SINUATED | SIRKAR | SITHED |
| SIMULANT | SINGLETON | SINUATELY | SIRKARS | SITHEN |
| SIMULANTS | SINGLETONS | SINUATION | SIRLOIN | SITHENCE |
| SIMULAR | SINGLETS | SINUATIONS | SIRLOINS | SITHENS |
| SIMULARS | SINGLING | SINUITIS | SIRNAME | SITHES |
| SIMULATE | SINGLINGS | SINUITISES | SIRNAMED | SITHING |
| SIMULATED | SINGLY | SINUOSE | SIRNAMES | SITING |
| SIMULATES | SINGS | SINUOSITIES | SIRNAMING | SITIOLOGIES |
| SIMULATING | SINGSONG | SINUOSITY | SIROC | SITIOLOGY |
| SIMULATOR | SINGSONGED | SINUOUS | SIROCCO | SITOLOGIES |
| SIMULATORS | SINGSONGING | SINUOUSLY | SIROCCOS | SITOLOGY |
| SIMULCAST | SINGSONGS | SINUS | SIROCS | SITREP |
| SIMULCASTED | SINGSPIEL | SINUSES | SIRRAH | SITREPS |
| SIMULCASTING | SINGSPIELS | SINUSITIS | SIRRAHS | SITS |
| SIMULCASTS | SINGULAR | SINUSITISES | SIRRED | SITTAR |
| SIMULIUM | SINGULARS | SINUSOID | SIRREE | SITTARS |
| SIMULIUMS | SINGULT | SINUSOIDS | SIRREES | SITTER |
| SIMURG | SINGULTS | SIP | SIRRING | SITTERS |
| SIMURGH | SINGULTUS | SIPE | SIRS | SITTINE |
| SIMURGHS | SINGULTUSES | SIPED | SIRUP | SITTING |
| SIMURGS | SINICAL | SIPES | SIRUPED | SITTINGS |
| SIN | SINICISE | SIPHON | SIRUPING | SITUATE |
| SINAPISM | SINICISED | SIPHONAGE | SIRUPS | SITUATED |
| SINAPISMS | SINICISES | SIPHONAGES | SIRVENTE | SITUATES |
| SINCE | SINICISING | SIPHONAL | SIRVENTES | SITUATING |
| SINCERE | SINICIZE | SIPHONATE | SIS | SITUATION |
| SINCERELY | SINICIZED | SIPHONED | SISAL | SITUATIONS |
| SINCERER | SINICIZES | SIPHONET | SISALS | SITULA |
| SINCEREST | SINICIZING | SIPHONETS | SISERARIES | SITULAE |
| SINCERITIES | SINING | SIPHONIC | SISERARY | SITUS |
| SINCERITY | SINISTER | SIPHONING | SISES | SITUTUNGA |
| SINCIPUT | SINISTRAL | SIPHONS | SISKIN | SITUTUNGAS |
| SINCIPUTS | SINISTRALS | SIPHUNCLE | SISKINS | SITZKRIEG |
| SIND | SINK | SIPHUNCLES | SISS | SITZKRIEGS |
| SINDED | SINKAGE | SIPING | SISSERARIES | SIVER |
| SINDING | SINKAGES | SIPPED | SISSERARY | SIVERS |
| SINDINGS | SINKER | SIPPER | SISSES | SIWASH |
| SINDON | SINKERS | SIPPERS | SISSIER | SIWASHES |
| SINDONS | SINKIER | SIPPET | SISSIES | SIX |
| SINDS | SINKIEST | SIPPETS | SISSIEST | SIXAINE |
| SINE | SINKING | SIPPING | SISSOO | SIXAINES |
| SINECURE | SINKINGS | SIPPLE | SISSOOS | SIXER |
| SINECURES | SINKS | SIPPLED | SISSY | SIXERS |
| SINED | SINKY | SIPPLES | SIST | SIXES |
| SINES | SINLESS | SIPPLING | SISTED | SIXFOLD |
| SINEW | SINLESSLY | SIPS | SISTER | SIXPENCE |
| SINEWED | SINNED | SIR | SISTERED | SIXPENCES |
| SINEWING | SINNER | SIRCAR | SISTERING | SIXPENNIES |
| SINEWLESS | SINNERED | SIRCARS | SISTERLY | SIXPENNY |
| SINEWS | SINNERING | SIRDAR | SISTERS | SIXSCORE |
| SINEWY | SINNERS | SIRDARS | SISTING | SIXSCORES |
| SINFONIA | SINNET | SIRE | SISTRA | SIXTE |
| SINFONIAS | SINNETS | SIRED | SISTRUM | SIXTEEN |
| SINFUL | SINNING | SIREN | SISTS | SIXTEENER |

| | | | | |
|---|---|---|---|---|
| SIXTEENERS | SKATOLE | SKELP | SKIDPANS | SKINNED |
| SIXTEENMO | SKATOLES | SKELPED | SKIDS | SKINNER |
| SIXTEENMOS | SKATOLOGIES | SKELPING | SKIED | SKINNERS |
| SIXTEENS | SKATOLOGY | SKELPINGS | SKIER | SKINNIER |
| SIXTEENTH | SKATS | SKELPS | SKIERS | SKINNIEST |
| SIXTEENTHS | SKATT | SKELTER | SKIES | SKINNING |
| SIXTES | SKATTS | SKELTERED | SKIEY | SKINNY |
| SIXTH | SKAW | SKELTERING | SKIEYER | SKINS |
| SIXTHLY | SKAWS | SKELTERS | SKIEYEST | SKINT |
| SIXTHS | SKEAN | SKENE | SKIFF | SKINTER |
| SIXTIES | SKEANS | SKENES | SKIFFED | SKINTEST |
| SIXTIETH | SKEAR | SKEO | SKIFFING | SKIO |
| SIXTIETHS | SKEARED | SKEOS | SKIFFLE | SKIOS |
| SIXTY | SKEARIER | SKEP | SKIFFLES | SKIP |
| SIZABLE | SKEARIEST | SKEPFUL | SKIFFS | SKIPJACK |
| SIZAR | SKEARING | SKEPFULS | SKIING | SKIPJACKS |
| SIZARS | SKEARS | SKEPPED | SKIINGS | SKIPPED |
| SIZARSHIP | SKEARY | SKEPPING | SKIJORING | SKIPPER |
| SIZARSHIPS | SKEDADDLE | SKEPS | SKIJORINGS | SKIPPERED |
| SIZE | SKEDADDLED | SKEPSIS | SKILFUL | SKIPPERING |
| SIZEABLE | SKEDADDLES | SKEPSISES | SKILFULLY | SKIPPERINGS |
| SIZED | SKEDADDLING | SKEPTIC | SKILL | SKIPPERS |
| SIZEL | SKEELIER | SKEPTICS | SKILLED | SKIPPET |
| SIZELS | SKEELIEST | SKER | SKILLESS | SKIPPETS |
| SIZER | SKEELY | SKERRED | SKILLET | SKIPPING |
| SIZERS | SKEER | SKERRICK | SKILLETS | SKIPPINGS |
| SIZES | SKEERED | SKERRICKS | SKILLIER | SKIPS |
| SIZIER | SKEERIER | SKERRIES | SKILLIES | SKIRL |
| SIZIEST | SKEERIEST | SKERRING | SKILLIEST | SKIRLED |
| SIZINESS | SKEERING | SKERRY | SKILLING | SKIRLING |
| SIZINESSES | SKEERS | SKERS | SKILLINGS | SKIRLINGS |
| SIZING | SKEERY | SKETCH | SKILLION | SKIRLS |
| SIZINGS | SKEESICKS | SKETCHED | SKILLIONS | SKIRMISH |
| SIZY | SKEET | SKETCHER | SKILLS | SKIRMISHED |
| SIZZLE | SKEETER | SKETCHERS | SKILLY | SKIRMISHES |
| SIZZLED | SKEETERS | SKETCHES | SKIM | SKIRMISHING |
| SIZZLER | SKEETS | SKETCHIER | SKIMMED | SKIRMISHINGS |
| SIZZLERS | SKEG | SKETCHIEST | SKIMMER | SKIRR |
| SIZZLES | SKEGGER | SKETCHILY | SKIMMERS | SKIRRED |
| SIZZLING | SKEGGERS | SKETCHING | SKIMMIA | SKIRRET |
| SIZZLINGS | SKEGS | SKETCHY | SKIMMIAS | SKIRRETS |
| SJAMBOK | SKEIGH | SKEW | SKIMMING | SKIRRING |
| SJAMBOKKED | SKEIGHER | SKEWBALD | SKIMMINGS | SKIRRS |
| SJAMBOKKING | SKEIGHEST | SKEWBALDS | SKIMP | SKIRT |
| SJAMBOKS | SKEIN | SKEWED | SKIMPED | SKIRTED |
| SKA | SKEINS | SKEWER | SKIMPIER | SKIRTER |
| SKAIL | SKELDER | SKEWERED | SKIMPIEST | SKIRTERS |
| SKAILED | SKELDERED | SKEWERING | SKIMPILY | SKIRTING |
| SKAILING | SKELDERING | SKEWERS | SKIMPING | SKIRTINGS |
| SKAILS | SKELDERS | SKEWEST | SKIMPS | SKIRTLESS |
| SKAITH | SKELETAL | SKEWING | SKIMPY | SKIRTS |
| SKAITHED | SKELETON | SKEWS | SKIMS | SKIS |
| SKAITHING | SKELETONS | SKI | SKIN | SKIT |
| SKAITHS | SKELF | SKIABLE | SKINFLICK | SKITE |
| SKALD | SKELFS | SKIAGRAM | SKINFLICKS | SKITED |
| SKALDIC | SKELLIE | SKIAGRAMS | SKINFLINT | SKITES |
| SKALDS | SKELLIED | SKIAGRAPH | SKINFLINTS | SKITING |
| SKART | SKELLIER | SKIAGRAPHS | SKINFOOD | SKITS |
| SKARTH | SKELLIES | SKIAMACHIES | SKINFOODS | SKITTER |
| SKARTHS | SKELLIEST | SKIAMACHY | SKINFUL | SKITTERED |
| SKARTS | SKELLOCH | SKIASCOPIES | SKINFULS | SKITTERING |
| SKAS | SKELLOCHED | SKIASCOPY | SKINHEAD | SKITTERS |
| SKAT | SKELLOCHING | SKIATRON | SKINHEADS | SKITTISH |
| SKATE | SKELLOCHS | SKIATRONS | SKINK | SKITTLE |
| SKATED | SKELLUM | SKID | SKINKED | SKITTLED |
| SKATER | SKELLUMS | SKIDDED | SKINKER | SKITTLES |
| SKATERS | SKELLY | SKIDDING | SKINKERS | SKITTLING |
| SKATES | SKELLYING | SKIDOO | SKINKING | SKIVE |
| SKATING | SKELM | SKIDOOS | SKINKS | SKIVED |
| SKATINGS | SKELMS | SKIDPAN | SKINLESS | SKIVER |

| | | | | |
|---|---|---|---|---|
| SKIVERED | SKRIMPING | SKYLARKS | SLAGGING | SLASHED |
| SKIVERING | SKRIMPS | SKYLIGHT | SLAGGY | SLASHER |
| SKIVERS | SKRUMP | SKYLIGHTS | SLAGS | SLASHERS |
| SKIVES | SKRUMPED | SKYLINE | SLAID | SLASHES |
| SKIVIE | SKRUMPING | SKYLINES | SLAIN | SLASHING |
| SKIVIER | SKRUMPS | SKYMAN | SLÀINTE | SLASHINGS |
| SKIVIEST | SKRY | SKYMEN | SLAIRG | SLAT |
| SKIVING | SKRYER | SKYR | SLAIRGED | SLATE |
| SKIVINGS | SKRYERS | SKYRE | SLAIRGING | SLATED |
| SKIVVIES | SKRYING | SKYRED | SLAIRGS | SLATER |
| SKIVVY | SKUA | SKYRES | SLAISTER | SLATERS |
| SKIVY | SKUAS | SKYRING | SLAISTERED | SLATES |
| SKLATE | SKUDLER | SKYROCKET | SLAISTERIES | SLATHER |
| SKLATED | SKUDLERS | SKYROCKETED | SLAISTERING | SLATHERED |
| SKLATES | SKUG | SKYROCKETING | SLAISTERS | SLATHERING |
| SKLATING | SKUGGED | SKYROCKETS | SLAISTERY | SLATHERS |
| SKLENT | SKUGGING | SKYRS | SLAKE | SLATIER |
| SKLENTED | SKUGS | SKYSAIL | SLAKED | SLATIEST |
| SKLENTING | SKULK | SKYSAILS | SLAKELESS | SLATINESS |
| SKLENTS | SKULKED | SKYSCAPE | SLAKES | SLATINESSES |
| SKLIFF | SKULKER | SKYSCAPES | SLAKING | SLATING |
| SKLIFFS | SKULKERS | SKYTE | SLALOM | SLATINGS |
| SKLIM | SKULKING | SKYTED | SLALOMED | SLATS |
| SKLIMMED | SKULKINGS | SKYTES | SLALOMING | SLATTED |
| SKLIMMING | SKULKS | SKYTING | SLALOMS | SLATTER |
| SKLIMS | SKULL | SKYWARD | SLAM | SLATTERED |
| SKOAL | SKULLCAP | SKYWARDS | SLAMMAKIN | SLATTERING |
| SKOFF | SKULLCAPS | SKYWAY | SLAMMAKINS | SLATTERN |
| SKOFFED | SKULLS | SKYWAYS | SLAMMED | SLATTERNS |
| SKOFFING | SKULPIN | SLAB | SLAMMER | SLATTERS |
| SKOFFS | SKULPINS | SLABBED | SLAMMERS | SLATTERY |
| SKOKIAAN | SKUMMER | SLABBER | SLAMMING | SLATTING |
| SKOKIAANS | SKUMMERED | SLABBERED | SLAMS | SLATY |
| SKOL | SKUMMERING | SLABBERER | SLANDER | SLAUGHTER |
| SKOLIA | SKUMMERS | SLABBERERS | SLANDERED | SLAUGHTERED |
| SKOLION | SKUNK | SLABBERING | SLANDERER | SLAUGHTERING |
| SKOLLIE | SKUNKED | SLABBERS | SLANDERERS | SLAUGHTERS |
| SKOLLIES | SKUNKING | SLABBERY | SLANDERING | SLAVE |
| SKOLLY | SKUNKS | SLABBIER | SLANDERS | SLAVED |
| SKRAN | SKURRIED | SLABBIEST | SLANE | SLAVER |
| SKRANS | SKURRIES | SLABBING | SLANES | SLAVERED |
| SKREAKIER | SKURRY | SLABBY | SLANG | SLAVERER |
| SKREAKIEST | SKURRYING | SLABS | SLANGED | SLAVERERS |
| SKREAKY | SKUTTLE | SLABSTONE | SLANGIER | SLAVERIES |
| SKREEN | SKUTTLED | SLABSTONES | SLANGIEST | SLAVERING |
| SKREENE | SKUTTLES | SLACK | SLANGILY | SLAVERS |
| SKREENES | SKUTTLING | SLACKED | SLANGING | SLAVERY |
| SKREENS | SKY | SLACKEN | SLANGINGS | SLAVES |
| SKREIGH | SKYBORN | SLACKENED | SLANGISH | SLAVEY |
| SKREIGHED | SKYCLAD | SLACKENING | SLANGS | SLAVEYS |
| SKREIGHING | SKYER | SLACKENINGS | SLANGULAR | SLAVING |
| SKREIGHS | SKYERS | SLACKENS | SLANGY | SLAVISH |
| SKRIECH | SKYEY | SLACKER | SLANT | SLAVISHLY |
| SKRIECHED | SKYIER | SLACKERS | SLANTED | SLAVOCRAT |
| SKRIECHING | SKYIEST | SLACKEST | SLANTING | SLAVOCRATS |
| SKRIECHS | SKYING | SLACKING | SLANTLY | SLAW |
| SKRIED | SKYISH | SLACKLY | SLANTS | SLAWS |
| SKRIEGH | SKYJACK | SLACKNESS | SLANTWAYS | SLAY |
| SKRIEGHED | SKYJACKED | SLACKNESSES | SLANTWISE | SLAYED |
| SKRIEGHING | SKYJACKER | SLACKS | SLAP | SLAYER |
| SKRIEGHS | SKYJACKERS | SLADANG | SLAPJACK | SLAYERS |
| SKRIES | SKYJACKING | SLADANGS | SLAPJACKS | SLAYING |
| SKRIK | SKYJACKINGS | SLADE | SLAPPED | SLAYS |
| SKRIKS | SKYJACKS | SLADES | SLAPPER | SLEAVE |
| SKRIMMAGE | SKYLAB | SLAE | SLAPPERS | SLEAVED |
| SKRIMMAGED | SKYLABS | SLAES | SLAPPING | SLEAVES |
| SKRIMMAGES | SKYLARK | SLAG | SLAPS | SLEAVING |
| SKRIMMAGING | SKYLARKED | SLAGGED | SLAPSTICK | SLEAZE |
| SKRIMP | SKYLARKING | SLAGGIER | SLAPSTICKS | SLEAZES |
| SKRIMPED | SKYLARKINGS | SLAGGIEST | SLASH | SLEAZIER |

SLEAZIEST
SLEAZILY
SLEAZY
SLED
SLEDDED
SLEDDING
SLEDDINGS
SLEDED
SLEDGE
SLEDGED
SLEDGER
SLEDGERS
SLEDGES
SLEDGING
SLEDGINGS
SLEDS
SLEE
SLEECH
SLEECHES
SLEECHIER
SLEECHIEST
SLEECHY
SLEEK
SLEEKED
SLEEKEN
SLEEKENED
SLEEKENING
SLEEKENS
SLEEKER
SLEEKERS
SLEEKEST
SLEEKIER
SLEEKIEST
SLEEKING
SLEEKINGS
SLEEKIT
SLEEKLY
SLEEKNESS
SLEEKNESSES
SLEEKS
SLEEKY
SLEEP
SLEEPER
SLEEPERS
SLEEPERY
SLEEPIER
SLEEPIEST
SLEEPILY
SLEEPING
SLEEPINGS
SLEEPLESS
SLEEPRY
SLEEPS
SLEEPY
SLEER
SLEEST
SLEET
SLEETED
SLEETIER
SLEETIEST
SLEETING
SLEETS
SLEETY
SLEEVE
SLEEVED
SLEEVER
SLEEVERS
SLEEVES
SLEEVING
SLEEVINGS

SLEEZIER
SLEEZIEST
SLEEZY
SLEIDED
SLEIGH
SLEIGHED
SLEIGHING
SLEIGHINGS
SLEIGHS
SLEIGHT
SLEIGHTS
SLENDER
SLENDERER
SLENDEREST
SLENDERLY
SLEPT
SLEUTH
SLEUTHED
SLEUTHING
SLEUTHS
SLEW
SLEWED
SLEWING
SLEWS
SLEY
SLEYS
SLICE
SLICED
SLICER
SLICERS
SLICES
SLICING
SLICINGS
SLICK
SLICKED
SLICKEN
SLICKENED
SLICKENING
SLICKENS
SLICKER
SLICKERS
SLICKEST
SLICKING
SLICKINGS
SLICKLY
SLICKNESS
SLICKNESSES
SLICKS
SLID
SLIDDEN
SLIDDER
SLIDDERED
SLIDDERING
SLIDDERS
SLIDDERY
SLIDE
SLIDED
SLIDER
SLIDERS
SLIDES
SLIDING
SLIDINGLY
SLIDINGS
SLIER
SLIEST
SLIGHT
SLIGHTED
SLIGHTER
SLIGHTEST
SLIGHTING

SLIGHTISH
SLIGHTLY
SLIGHTS
SLILY
SLIM
SLIME
SLIMED
SLIMES
SLIMIER
SLIMIEST
SLIMILY
SLIMINESS
SLIMINESSES
SLIMING
SLIMLINE
SLIMLY
SLIMMED
SLIMMER
SLIMMERS
SLIMMEST
SLIMMING
SLIMMINGS
SLIMMISH
SLIMNESS
SLIMNESSES
SLIMS
SLIMSIER
SLIMSIEST
SLIMSY
SLIMY
SLING
SLINGER
SLINGERS
SLINGING
SLINGS
SLINGSHOT
SLINGSHOTS
SLINK
SLINKER
SLINKERS
SLINKIER
SLINKIEST
SLINKING
SLINKS
SLINKSKIN
SLINKSKINS
SLINKWEED
SLINKWEEDS
SLINKY
SLIP
SLIPE
SLIPES
SLIPFORM
SLIPPAGE
SLIPPAGES
SLIPPED
SLIPPER
SLIPPERED
SLIPPERIER
SLIPPERIEST
SLIPPERING
SLIPPERS
SLIPPERY
SLIPPIER
SLIPPIEST
SLIPPING
SLIPPY
SLIPRAIL
SLIPRAILS
SLIPS

SLIPSHOD
SLIPSLOP
SLIPSLOPS
SLIPT
SLIPWARE
SLIPWARES
SLIPWAY
SLIPWAYS
SLISH
SLISHES
SLIT
SLITHER
SLITHERED
SLITHERIER
SLITHERIEST
SLITHERING
SLITHERS
SLITHERY
SLITS
SLITTER
SLITTERS
SLITTING
SLIVE
SLIVED
SLIVEN
SLIVER
SLIVERED
SLIVERING
SLIVERS
SLIVES
SLIVING
SLIVOVIC
SLIVOVICA
SLIVOVICAS
SLIVOVICS
SLIVOVITZ
SLIVOVITZES
SLIVOWITZ
SLIVOWITZES
SLOAN
SLOANS
SLOB
SLOBBER
SLOBBERED
SLOBBERING
SLOBBERS
SLOBBERY
SLOBBIER
SLOBBIEST
SLOBBY
SLOBLAND
SLOBLANDS
SLOBS
SLOCKEN
SLOCKENED
SLOCKENING
SLOCKENS
SLOE
SLOEBUSH
SLOEBUSHES
SLOES
SLOETHORN
SLOETHORNS
SLOETREE
SLOETREES
SLOG
SLOGAN
SLOGANEER
SLOGANEERED
SLOGANEERING

SLOGANEERINGS
SLOGANEERS
SLOGANISE
SLOGANISED
SLOGANISES
SLOGANISING
SLOGANISINGS
SLOGANIZE
SLOGANIZED
SLOGANIZES
SLOGANIZING
SLOGANIZINGS
SLOGANS
SLOGGED
SLOGGER
SLOGGERS
SLOGGING
SLOGS
SLOID
SLOIDS
SLOKEN
SLOKENED
SLOKENING
SLOKENS
SLOOM
SLOOMED
SLOOMIER
SLOOMIEST
SLOOMING
SLOOMS
SLOOMY
SLOOP
SLOOPS
SLOOT
SLOOTS
SLOP
SLOPE
SLOPED
SLOPES
SLOPEWISE
SLOPIER
SLOPIEST
SLOPING
SLOPINGLY
SLOPPED
SLOPPIER
SLOPPIEST
SLOPPILY
SLOPPING
SLOPPY
SLOPS
SLOPWORK
SLOPWORKS
SLOPY
SLOSH
SLOSHED
SLOSHES
SLOSHIER
SLOSHIEST
SLOSHING
SLOSHY
SLOT
SLOTH
SLOTHED
SLOTHFUL
SLOTHING
SLOTHS
SLOTS
SLOTTED
SLOTTER

SLOTTERS
SLOTTING
SLOUCH
SLOUCHED
SLOUCHER
SLOUCHERS
SLOUCHES
SLOUCHIER
SLOUCHIEST
SLOUCHING
SLOUCHY
SLOUGH
SLOUGHED
SLOUGHIER
SLOUGHIEST
SLOUGHING
SLOUGHS
SLOUGHY
SLOVE
SLOVEN
SLOVENLIER
SLOVENLIEST
SLOVENLY
SLOVENRIES
SLOVENRY
SLOVENS
SLOW
SLOWBACK
SLOWBACKS
SLOWCOACH
SLOWCOACHES
SLOWED
SLOWER
SLOWEST
SLOWING
SLOWINGS
SLOWISH
SLOWLY
SLOWNESS
SLOWNESSES
SLOWPOKE
SLOWPOKES
SLOWS
SLOYD
SLOYDS
SLUB
SLUBB
SLUBBED
SLUBBER
SLUBBERED
SLUBBERING
SLUBBERINGS
SLUBBERS
SLUBBIER
SLUBBIEST
SLUBBING
SLUBBINGS
SLUBBS
SLUBBY
SLUBS
SLUDGE
SLUDGES
SLUDGIER
SLUDGIEST
SLUDGY
SLUE
SLUED
SLUEING
SLUES
SLUG

SLUGFEST
SLUGFESTS
SLUGGABED
SLUGGABEDS
SLUGGARD
SLUGGARDS
SLUGGED
SLUGGER
SLUGGERS
SLUGGING
SLUGGISH
SLUGHORN
SLUGHORNE
SLUGHORNES
SLUGHORNS
SLUGS
SLUICE
SLUICED
SLUICES
SLUICIER
SLUICIEST
SLUICING
SLUICY
SLUING
SLUIT
SLUITS
SLUM
SLUMBER
SLUMBERED
SLUMBERER
SLUMBERERS
SLUMBERING
SLUMBERINGS
SLUMBERS
SLUMBERY
SLUMBROUS
SLUMBRY
SLUMMED
SLUMMER
SLUMMERS
SLUMMIER
SLUMMIEST
SLUMMING
SLUMMINGS
SLUMMOCK
SLUMMOCKED
SLUMMOCKING
SLUMMOCKS
SLUMMY
SLUMP
SLUMPED
SLUMPIER
SLUMPIEST
SLUMPING
SLUMPS
SLUMPY
SLUMS
SLUNG
SLUNK
SLUR
SLURB
SLURBS
SLURP
SLURPED
SLURPING
SLURPS
SLURRED
SLURRIES
SLURRING
SLURRY

SLURS
SLUSE
SLUSES
SLUSH
SLUSHED
SLUSHES
SLUSHIER
SLUSHIEST
SLUSHING
SLUSHY
SLUT
SLUTS
SLUTTERIES
SLUTTERY
SLUTTISH
SLY
SLYBOOTS
SLYER
SLYEST
SLYISH
SLYLY
SLYNESS
SLYNESSES
SLYPE
SLYPES
SMA
SMACK
SMACKED
SMACKER
SMACKERS
SMACKING
SMACKINGS
SMACKS
SMAIK
SMAIKS
SMALL
SMALLAGE
SMALLAGES
SMALLED
SMALLER
SMALLEST
SMALLING
SMALLISH
SMALLNESS
SMALLNESSES
SMALLPOX
SMALLPOXES
SMALLS
SMALM
SMALMED
SMALMIER
SMALMIEST
SMALMILY
SMALMING
SMALMS
SMALMY
SMALT
SMALTI
SMALTITE
SMALTITES
SMALTO
SMALTOS
SMALTS
SMARAGD
SMARAGDS
SMARM
SMARMED
SMARMIER
SMARMIEST
SMARMILY

SMARMING
SMARMS
SMARMY
SMART
SMARTARSE
SMARTARSES
SMARTASS
SMARTASSES
SMARTED
SMARTEN
SMARTENED
SMARTENING
SMARTENS
SMARTER
SMARTEST
SMARTIE
SMARTIES
SMARTING
SMARTLY
SMARTNESS
SMARTNESSES
SMARTS
SMARTY
SMASH
SMASHED
SMASHER
SMASHEROO
SMASHEROOS
SMASHERS
SMASHES
SMASHING
SMASHINGS
SMATCH
SMATCHED
SMATCHES
SMATCHING
SMATTER
SMATTERED
SMATTERER
SMATTERERS
SMATTERING
SMATTERINGS
SMATTERS
SMEAR
SMEARED
SMEARIER
SMEARIEST
SMEARILY
SMEARING
SMEARS
SMEARY
SMEATH
SMEATHS
SMECTIC
SMEDDUM
SMEDDUMS
SMEE
SMEECH
SMEECHED
SMEECHES
SMEECHING
SMEEK
SMEEKED
SMEEKING
SMEEKS
SMEES
SMEETH
SMEETHS
SMEGMA
SMEGMAS

SMELL
SMELLED
SMELLER
SMELLERS
SMELLIER
SMELLIEST
SMELLING
SMELLINGS
SMELLS
SMELLY
SMELT
SMELTED
SMELTER
SMELTERIES
SMELTERS
SMELTERY
SMELTING
SMELTINGS
SMELTS
SMEUSE
SMEUSES
SMEW
SMEWS
SMICKER
SMICKERED
SMICKERING
SMICKERINGS
SMICKERS
SMICKET
SMICKETS
SMICKLY
SMIDDIES
SMIDDY
SMIDGEN
SMIDGENS
SMIDGEON
SMIDGEONS
SMIDGIN
SMIDGINS
SMIGHT
SMIGHTING
SMIGHTS
SMILAX
SMILAXES
SMILE
SMILED
SMILEFUL
SMILELESS
SMILER
SMILERS
SMILES
SMILET
SMILETS
SMILING
SMILINGLY
SMILINGS
SMILODON
SMILODONS
SMIR
SMIRCH
SMIRCHED
SMIRCHES
SMIRCHING
SMIRK
SMIRKED
SMIRKIER
SMIRKIEST
SMIRKING
SMIRKS
SMIRKY

| | | | | |
|---|---|---|---|---|
| SMIRR | SMOOCHES | SMOYLES | SNAGGY | SNARLIER |
| SMIRRED | SMOOCHING | SMOYLING | SNAGS | SNARLIEST |
| SMIRRIER | SMOOR | SMUDGE | SNAIL | SNARLING |
| SMIRRIEST | SMOORED | SMUDGED | SNAILED | SNARLINGS |
| SMIRRING | SMOORING | SMUDGER | SNAILERIES | SNARLS |
| SMIRRS | SMOORS | SMUDGERS | SNAILERY | SNARLY |
| SMIRRY | SMOOT | SMUDGES | SNAILIER | SNARRED |
| SMIRS | SMOOTED | SMUDGIER | SNAILIEST | SNARRING |
| SMIT | SMOOTH | SMUDGIEST | SNAILING | SNARS |
| SMITE | SMOOTHE | SMUDGILY | SNAILS | SNARY |
| SMITER | SMOOTHED | SMUDGING | SNAILY | SNASH |
| SMITERS | SMOOTHEN | SMUDGY | SNAKE | SNASHED |
| SMITES | SMOOTHENED | SMUG | SNAKEBIRD | SNASHES |
| SMITH | SMOOTHENING | SMUGGED | SNAKEBIRDS | SNASHING |
| SMITHED | SMOOTHENS | SMUGGER | SNAKEBITE | SNASTE |
| SMITHERIES | SMOOTHER | SMUGGEST | SNAKEBITES | SNASTES |
| SMITHERS | SMOOTHERS | SMUGGING | SNAKED | SNATCH |
| SMITHERY | SMOOTHES | SMUGGLE | SNAKELIKE | SNATCHED |
| SMITHIED | SMOOTHEST | SMUGGLED | SNAKEROOT | SNATCHER |
| SMITHIES | SMOOTHIE | SMUGGLER | SNAKEROOTS | SNATCHERS |
| SMITHING | SMOOTHIES | SMUGGLERS | SNAKES | SNATCHES |
| SMITHS | SMOOTHING | SMUGGLES | SNAKESKIN | SNATCHIER |
| SMITHY | SMOOTHINGS | SMUGGLING | SNAKESKINS | SNATCHIEST |
| SMITHYING | SMOOTHISH | SMUGGLINGS | SNAKEWEED | SNATCHILY |
| SMITING | SMOOTHLY | SMUGLY | SNAKEWEEDS | SNATCHING |
| SMITS | SMOOTHS | SMUGNESS | SNAKEWISE | SNATCHY |
| SMITTED | SMOOTING | SMUGNESSES | SNAKEWOOD | SNATH |
| SMITTEN | SMOOTS | SMUGS | SNAKEWOODS | SNATHE |
| SMITTING | SMØRBRØD | SMUR | SNAKIER | SNATHES |
| SMITTLE | SMØRBRØDS | SMURRED | SNAKIEST | SNATHS |
| SMOCK | SMORE | SMURRIER | SNAKILY | SNAZZIER |
| SMOCKED | SMORED | SMURRIEST | SNAKINESS | SNAZZIEST |
| SMOCKING | SMORES | SMURRING | SNAKINESSES | SNAZZY |
| SMOCKINGS | SMORING | SMURRY | SNAKING | SNEAD |
| SMOCKS | SMORZANDO | SMURS | SNAKISH | SNEADS |
| SMOG | SMORZATO | SMUT | SNAKY | SNEAK |
| SMOGGIER | SMOTE | SMUTCH | SNAP | SNEAKED |
| SMOGGIEST | SMOTHER | SMUTCHED | SNAPHANCE | SNEAKER |
| SMOGGY | SMOTHERED | SMUTCHES | SNAPHANCES | SNEAKERS |
| SMOGS | SMOTHERER | SMUTCHING | SNAPPED | SNEAKEUP |
| SMOILE | SMOTHERERS | SMUTS | SNAPPER | SNEAKEUPS |
| SMOILED | SMOTHERING | SMUTTED | SNAPPERED | SNEAKIER |
| SMOILES | SMOTHERINGS | SMUTTIER | SNAPPERING | SNEAKIEST |
| SMOILING | SMOTHERS | SMUTTIEST | SNAPPERS | SNEAKILY |
| SMOKABLE | SMOTHERY | SMUTTILY | SNAPPIER | SNEAKING |
| SMOKE | SMOUCH | SMUTTING | SNAPPIEST | SNEAKISH |
| SMOKED | SMOUCHED | SMUTTY | SNAPPILY | SNEAKS |
| SMOKELESS | SMOUCHES | SMYTRIE | SNAPPING | SNEAKSBIES |
| SMOKER | SMOUCHING | SMYTRIES | SNAPPINGS | SNEAKSBY |
| SMOKERS | SMOULDER | SNAB | SNAPPISH | SNEAKY |
| SMOKES | SMOULDERED | SNABBLE | SNAPPY | SNEAP |
| SMOKIER | SMOULDERING | SNABBLED | SNAPS | SNEAPED |
| SMOKIES | SMOULDERINGS | SNABBLES | SNAPSHOT | SNEAPING |
| SMOKIEST | SMOULDERS | SNABBLING | SNAPSHOTS | SNEAPS |
| SMOKILY | SMOULDRY | SNABS | SNAR | SNEATH |
| SMOKINESS | SMOUS | SNACK | SNARE | SNEATHS |
| SMOKINESSES | SMOUSE | SNACKED | SNARED | SNEB |
| SMOKING | SMOUSED | SNACKING | SNARER | SNEBBE |
| SMOKINGS | SMOUSER | SNACKS | SNARERS | SNEBBED |
| SMOKO | SMOUSERS | SNAFFLE | SNARES | SNEBBES |
| SMOKOS | SMOUSES | SNAFFLED | SNARIER | SNEBBING |
| SMOKY | SMOUSING | SNAFFLES | SNARIEST | SNEBS |
| SMOLDER | SMOUT | SNAFFLING | SNARING | SNECK |
| SMOLDERED | SMOUTED | SNAFU | SNARINGS | SNECKED |
| SMOLDERING | SMOUTING | SNAFUS | SNARK | SNECKING |
| SMOLDERS | SMOUTS | SNAG | SNARKS | SNECKS |
| SMOLT | SMOWT | SNAGGED | SNARL | SNED |
| SMOLTS | SMOWTS | SNAGGIER | SNARLED | SNEDDED |
| SMOOCH | SMOYLE | SNAGGIEST | SNARLER | SNEDDING |
| SMOOCHED | SMOYLED | SNAGGING | SNARLERS | SNEDS |

SNEE
SNEED
SNEEING
SNEER
SNEERED
SNEERER
SNEERERS
SNEERIER
SNEERIEST
SNEERING
SNEERINGS
SNEERS
SNEERY
SNEES
SNEESH
SNEESHAN
SNEESHANS
SNEESHES
SNEESHIN
SNEESHING
SNEESHINGS
SNEESHINS
SNEEZE
SNEEZED
SNEEZER
SNEEZERS
SNEEZES
SNEEZIER
SNEEZIEST
SNEEZING
SNEEZINGS
SNEEZY
SNELL
SNELLED
SNELLER
SNELLEST
SNELLING
SNELLS
SNELLY
SNIB
SNIBBED
SNIBBING
SNIBS
SNICK
SNICKED
SNICKER
SNICKERED
SNICKERING
SNICKERS
SNICKET
SNICKETS
SNICKING
SNICKS
SNIDE
SNIDELY
SNIDENESS
SNIDENESSES
SNIDER
SNIDES
SNIDEST
SNIFF
SNIFFED
SNIFFER
SNIFFERS
SNIFFIER
SNIFFIEST
SNIFFILY
SNIFFING
SNIFFINGS
SNIFFLE

SNIFFLED
SNIFFLER
SNIFFLERS
SNIFFLES
SNIFFLING
SNIFFS
SNIFFY
SNIFT
SNIFTED
SNIFTER
SNIFTERED
SNIFTERING
SNIFTERS
SNIFTIER
SNIFTIEST
SNIFTING
SNIFTS
SNIFTY
SNIG
SNIGGED
SNIGGER
SNIGGERED
SNIGGERER
SNIGGERERS
SNIGGERING
SNIGGERINGS
SNIGGERS
SNIGGING
SNIGGLE
SNIGGLED
SNIGGLER
SNIGGLERS
SNIGGLES
SNIGGLING
SNIGGLINGS
SNIGS
SNIP
SNIPE
SNIPED
SNIPER
SNIPERS
SNIPES
SNIPIER
SNIPIEST
SNIPING
SNIPINGS
SNIPPED
SNIPPER
SNIPPERS
SNIPPET
SNIPPETS
SNIPPETY
SNIPPIER
SNIPPIEST
SNIPPING
SNIPPINGS
SNIPPY
SNIPS
SNIPY
SNIRT
SNIRTLE
SNIRTLED
SNIRTLES
SNIRTLING
SNIRTS
SNITCH
SNITCHED
SNITCHER
SNITCHERS
SNITCHES

SNITCHING
SNIVEL
SNIVELLED
SNIVELLER
SNIVELLERS
SNIVELLING
SNIVELLY
SNIVELS
SNOB
SNOBBERIES
SNOBBERY
SNOBBIER
SNOBBIEST
SNOBBISH
SNOBBISM
SNOBBISMS
SNOBBY
SNOBLING
SNOBLINGS
SNOBS
SNOD
SNODDED
SNODDING
SNODDIT
SNODS
SNOEK
SNOEKS
SNOG
SNOGGED
SNOGGING
SNOGS
SNOKE
SNOKED
SNOKES
SNOKING
SNOOD
SNOODED
SNOODING
SNOODS
SNOOK
SNOOKED
SNOOKER
SNOOKERED
SNOOKERING
SNOOKERS
SNOOKING
SNOOKS
SNOOL
SNOOLED
SNOOLING
SNOOLS
SNOOP
SNOOPED
SNOOPER
SNOOPERS
SNOOPING
SNOOPS
SNOOT
SNOOTED
SNOOTFUL
SNOOTFULS
SNOOTIER
SNOOTIEST
SNOOTING
SNOOTS
SNOOTY
SNOOZE
SNOOZED
SNOOZER
SNOOZERS

SNOOZES
SNOOZING
SNOOZLE
SNOOZLED
SNOOZLES
SNOOZLING
SNORE
SNORED
SNORER
SNORERS
SNORES
SNORING
SNORINGS
SNORKEL
SNORKELS
SNORT
SNORTED
SNORTER
SNORTERS
SNORTIER
SNORTIEST
SNORTING
SNORTINGS
SNORTS
SNORTY
SNOT
SNOTS
SNOTTED
SNOTTER
SNOTTERED
SNOTTERIES
SNOTTERING
SNOTTERS
SNOTTERY
SNOTTIER
SNOTTIES
SNOTTIEST
SNOTTILY
SNOTTING
SNOTTY
SNOUT
SNOUTED
SNOUTIER
SNOUTIEST
SNOUTING
SNOUTS
SNOUTY
SNOW
SNOWBALL
SNOWBALLED
SNOWBALLING
SNOWBALLS
SNOWCAP
SNOWCAPS
SNOWDRIFT
SNOWDRIFTS
SNOWDROP
SNOWDROPS
SNOWED
SNOWFALL
SNOWFALLS
SNOWFLAKE
SNOWFLAKES
SNOWFLECK
SNOWFLECKS
SNOWFLICK
SNOWFLICKS
SNOWIER
SNOWIEST
SNOWILY

SNOWINESS
SNOWINESSES
SNOWING
SNOWISH
SNOWK
SNOWKED
SNOWKING
SNOWKS
SNOWLESS
SNOWLIKE
SNOWLINE
SNOWLINES
SNOWMAN
SNOWMEN
SNOWS
SNOWSCAPE
SNOWSCAPES
SNOWSLIP
SNOWSLIPS
SNOWSTORM
SNOWSTORMS
SNOWY
SNUB
SNUBBE
SNUBBED
SNUBBER
SNUBBERS
SNUBBES
SNUBBIER
SNUBBIEST
SNUBBING
SNUBBINGS
SNUBBISH
SNUBBY
SNUBS
SNUCK
SNUDGE
SNUDGED
SNUDGES
SNUDGING
SNUFF
SNUFFBOX
SNUFFBOXES
SNUFFED
SNUFFER
SNUFFERS
SNUFFIER
SNUFFIEST
SNUFFING
SNUFFINGS
SNUFFLE
SNUFFLED
SNUFFLER
SNUFFLERS
SNUFFLES
SNUFFLING
SNUFFLINGS
SNUFFS
SNUFFY
SNUG
SNUGGED
SNUGGER
SNUGGERIES
SNUGGERY
SNUGGEST
SNUGGING
SNUGGLE
SNUGGLED
SNUGGLES
SNUGGLING

SNUGLY
SNUGNESS
SNUGNESSES
SNUGS
SNUSH
SNUSHED
SNUSHES
SNUSHING
SNUZZLE
SNUZZLED
SNUZZLES
SNUZZLING
SO
SOAK
SOAKAGE
SOAKAGES
SOAKAWAY
SOAKAWAYS
SOAKED
SOAKEN
SOAKER
SOAKERS
SOAKING
SOAKINGLY
SOAKINGS
SOAKS
SOAP
SOAPBERRIES
SOAPBERRY
SOAPBOX
SOAPBOXES
SOAPED
SOAPIE
SOAPIER
SOAPIES
SOAPIEST
SOAPILY
SOAPINESS
SOAPINESSES
SOAPING
SOAPLESS
SOAPS
SOAPSTONE
SOAPSTONES
SOAPWORT
SOAPWORTS
SOAPY
SOAR
SOARAWAY
SOARE
SOARED
SOARES
SOARING
SOARINGLY
SOARINGS
SOARS
SOB
SOBBED
SOBBING
SOBBINGLY
SOBBINGS
SOBEIT
SOBER
SOBERED
SOBERER
SOBEREST
SOBERING
SOBERISE
SOBERISED
SOBERISES

SOBERISING
SOBERIZE
SOBERIZED
SOBERIZES
SOBERIZING
SOBERLY
SOBERNESS
SOBERNESSES
SOBERS
SOBOLE
SOBOLES
SOBRIETIES
SOBRIETY
SOBRIQUET
SOBRIQUETS
SOBS
SOC
SOCAGE
SOCAGER
SOCAGERS
SOCAGES
SOCCAGE
SOCCAGES
SOCCER
SOCCERS
SOCIABLE
SOCIABLES
SOCIABLY
SOCIAL
SOCIALISE
SOCIALISED
SOCIALISES
SOCIALISING
SOCIALISM
SOCIALISMS
SOCIALIST
SOCIALISTS
SOCIALITE
SOCIALITES
SOCIALITIES
SOCIALITY
SOCIALIZE
SOCIALIZED
SOCIALIZES
SOCIALIZING
SOCIALLY
SOCIALS
SOCIATE
SOCIATES
SOCIATIVE
SOCIETAL
SOCIETARY
SOCIETIES
SOCIETY
SOCIOGRAM
SOCIOGRAMS
SOCIOLOGIES
SOCIOLOGY
SOCIOPATH
SOCIOPATHS
SOCK
SOCKED
SOCKER
SOCKERS
SOCKET
SOCKETED
SOCKETING
SOCKETS
SOCKEYE
SOCKEYES

SOCKING
SOCKO
SOCKS
SOCLE
SOCLES
SOCMAN
SOCMEN
SOCS
SOD
SODA
SODAIC
SODAIN
SODAINE
SODALITE
SODALITES
SODALITIES
SODALITY
SODAMIDE
SODAMIDES
SODAS
SODDED
SODDEN
SODDENED
SODDENING
SODDENS
SODDIER
SODDIEST
SODDING
SODDY
SODGER
SODGERS
SODIC
SODIUM
SODIUMS
SODOMIES
SODOMISE
SODOMISED
SODOMISES
SODOMISING
SODOMITE
SODOMITES
SODOMITIC
SODOMIZE
SODOMIZED
SODOMIZES
SODOMIZING
SODOMY
SODS
SOEVER
SOFA
SOFAR
SOFARS
SOFAS
SOFFIONI
SOFFIT
SOFFITS
SOFT
SOFTA
SOFTAS
SOFTBACK
SOFTBACKS
SOFTBALL
SOFTBALLS
SOFTED
SOFTEN
SOFTENED
SOFTENER
SOFTENERS
SOFTENING
SOFTENINGS

SOFTENS
SOFTER
SOFTEST
SOFTHEAD
SOFTHEADS
SOFTIE
SOFTIES
SOFTING
SOFTISH
SOFTLING
SOFTLINGS
SOFTLY
SOFTNESS
SOFTNESSES
SOFTS
SOFTWARE
SOFTWARES
SOFTWOOD
SOFTWOODS
SOFTY
SOG
SOGER
SOGERS
SOGGED
SOGGIER
SOGGIEST
SOGGILY
SOGGINESS
SOGGINESSES
SOGGING
SOGGINGS
SOGGY
SOGS
SOH
SOHS
SOIGNÉ
SOIGNÉE
SOIL
SOILED
SOILIER
SOILIEST
SOILINESS
SOILINESSES
SOILING
SOILINGS
SOILLESS
SOILS
SOILURE
SOILURES
SOILY
SOIRÉE
SOIRÉES
SOJA
SOJAS
SOJOURN
SOJOURNED
SOJOURNER
SOJOURNERS
SOJOURNING
SOJOURNINGS
SOJOURNS
SOKE
SOKEMAN
SOKEMANRIES
SOKEMANRY
SOKEMEN
SOKEN
SOKENS
SOKES
SOL

SOLA
SOLACE
SOLACED
SOLACES
SOLACING
SOLACIOUS
SOLAH
SOLAHS
SOLAN
SOLAND
SOLANDER
SOLANDERS
SOLANDS
SOLANINE
SOLANINES
SOLANO
SOLANOS
SOLANS
SOLANUM
SOLANUMS
SOLAR
SOLARISE
SOLARISED
SOLARISES
SOLARISING
SOLARISM
SOLARISMS
SOLARIST
SOLARISTS
SOLARIUM
SOLARIUMS
SOLARIZE
SOLARIZED
SOLARIZES
SOLARIZING
SOLARS
SOLAS
SOLATION
SOLATIONS
SOLATIUM
SOLATIUMS
SOLD
SOLDADO
SOLDADOS
SOLDAN
SOLDANS
SOLDE
SOLDER
SOLDERED
SOLDERER
SOLDERERS
SOLDERING
SOLDERINGS
SOLDERS
SOLDES
SOLDI
SOLDIER
SOLDIERED
SOLDIERIES
SOLDIERING
SOLDIERINGS
SOLDIERLY
SOLDIERS
SOLDIERY
SOLDO
SOLDS
SOLE
SOLECISE
SOLECISED
SOLECISES

SOLECISING
SOLECISM
SOLECISMS
SOLECIST
SOLECISTS
SOLECIZE
SOLECIZED
SOLECIZES
SOLECIZING
SOLED
SOLEIN
SOLELY
SOLEMN
SOLEMNER
SOLEMNESS
SOLEMNESSES
SOLEMNEST
SOLEMNIFIED
SOLEMNIFIES
SOLEMNIFY
SOLEMNIFYING
SOLEMNISE
SOLEMNISED
SOLEMNISES
SOLEMNISING
SOLEMNITIES
SOLEMNITY
SOLEMNIZE
SOLEMNIZED
SOLEMNIZES
SOLEMNIZING
SOLEMNLY
SOLEN
SOLENESS
SOLENESSES
SOLENETTE
SOLENETTES
SOLENODON
SOLENODONS
SOLENOID
SOLENOIDS
SOLENS
SOLER
SOLERA
SOLERAS
SOLERS
SOLES
SOLEUS
SOLEUSES
SOLFATARA
SOLFATARAS
SOLFEGGI
SOLFEGGIO
SOLFERINO
SOLFERINOS
SOLI
SOLICIT
SOLICITED
SOLICITIES
SOLICITING
SOLICITINGS
SOLICITOR
SOLICITORS
SOLICITS
SOLICITY
SOLID
SOLIDARE
SOLIDARES
SOLIDARY
SOLIDATE

SOLIDATED
SOLIDATES
SOLIDATING
SOLIDER
SOLIDEST
SOLIDI
SOLIDIFIED
SOLIDIFIES
SOLIDIFY
SOLIDIFYING
SOLIDISH
SOLIDISM
SOLIDISMS
SOLIDIST
SOLIDISTS
SOLIDITIES
SOLIDITY
SOLIDLY
SOLIDNESS
SOLIDNESSES
SOLIDS
SOLIDUM
SOLIDUMS
SOLIDUS
SOLILOQUIES
SOLILOQUY
SOLING
SOLIPED
SOLIPEDS
SOLIPSISM
SOLIPSISMS
SOLIPSIST
SOLIPSISTS
SOLITAIRE
SOLITAIRES
SOLITARIES
SOLITARY
SOLITO
SOLITON
SOLITONS
SOLITUDE
SOLITUDES
SOLIVE
SOLIVES
SOLLAR
SOLLARS
SOLLER
SOLLERET
SOLLERETS
SOLLERS
SOLO
SOLOED
SOLOING
SOLOIST
SOLOISTS
SOLONCHAK
SOLONCHAKS
SOLONETS
SOLONETSES
SOLONETZ
SOLONETZES
SOLOS
SOLS
SOLSTICE
SOLSTICES
SOLUBLE
SOLUM
SOLUMS
SOLUS
SOLUTE

SOLUTES
SOLUTION
SOLUTIONED
SOLUTIONING
SOLUTIONS
SOLUTIVE
SOLVABLE
SOLVATE
SOLVATED
SOLVATES
SOLVATING
SOLVATION
SOLVATIONS
SOLVE
SOLVED
SOLVENCIES
SOLVENCY
SOLVENT
SOLVENTS
SOLVER
SOLVERS
SOLVES
SOLVING
SOMA
SOMAS
SOMASCOPE
SOMASCOPES
SOMATIC
SOMATISM
SOMATISMS
SOMATIST
SOMATISTS
SOMBRE
SOMBRED
SOMBRELY
SOMBRER
SOMBRERO
SOMBREROS
SOMBRES
SOMBREST
SOMBRING
SOMBROUS
SOME
SOMEBODIES
SOMEBODY
SOMEDAY
SOMEDEAL
SOMEDELE
SOMEGATE
SOMEHOW
SOMEONE
SOMEONES
SOMEPLACE
SOMERSET
SOMERSETS
SOMERSETTED
SOMERSETTING
SOMETHING
SOMETHINGS
SOMETIME
SOMETIMES
SOMEWAY
SOMEWAYS
SOMEWHAT
SOMEWHATS
SOMEWHEN
SOMEWHERE
SOMEWHILE
SOMEWHY
SOMEWISE

SOMITAL
SOMITE
SOMITES
SOMITIC
SOMMELIER
SOMMELIERS
SOMNIAL
SOMNIFIC
SOMNOLENT
SON
SONANCE
SONANCES
SONANCIES
SONANCY
SONANT
SONANTS
SONAR
SONARS
SONATA
SONATAS
SONATINA
SONATINAS
SONCE
SONCES
SONDAGE
SONDAGES
SONDE
SONDELI
SONDELIS
SONDES
SONE
SONERI
SONERIS
SONES
SONG
SONGBIRD
SONGBIRDS
SONGBOOK
SONGBOOKS
SONGCRAFT
SONGCRAFTS
SONGFEST
SONGFESTS
SONGFUL
SONGFULLY
SONGLESS
SONGMAN
SONGMEN
SONGS
SONGSMITH
SONGSMITHS
SONGSTER
SONGSTERS
SONIC
SONICS
SONLESS
SONNE
SONNES
SONNET
SONNETARY
SONNETED
SONNETEER
SONNETEERED
SONNETEERING
SONNETEERINGS
SONNETEERS
SONNETING
SONNETINGS
SONNETISE
SONNETISED

SONNETISES
SONNETISING
SONNETIST
SONNETISTS
SONNETIZE
SONNETIZED
SONNETIZES
SONNETIZING
SONNETRIES
SONNETRY
SONNETS
SONNIES
SONNY
SONOBUOY
SONOBUOYS
SONOGRAPH
SONOGRAPHS
SONORANT
SONORANTS
SONORITIES
SONORITY
SONOROUS
SONS
SONSE
SONSES
SONSHIP
SONSHIPS
SONSIE
SONSIER
SONSIEST
SONSY
SONTAG
SONTAGS
SONTIES
SONUANCE
SONUANCES
SOOGEE
SOOGEED
SOOGEEING
SOOGEES
SOOGIE
SOOGIED
SOOGIEING
SOOGIES
SOOJEY
SOOJEYS
SOOK
SOOKS
SOOLE
SOOLED
SOOLES
SOOLING
SOOM
SOOMED
SOOMING
SOOMS
SOON
SOONER
SOONEST
SOOP
SOOPED
SOOPING
SOOPINGS
SOOPS
SOOPSTAKE
SOOT
SOOTE
SOOTED
SOOTERKIN
SOOTERKINS

SOOTES
SOOTFLAKE
SOOTFLAKES
SOOTH
SOOTHE
SOOTHED
SOOTHER
SOOTHERED
SOOTHERING
SOOTHERS
SOOTHES
SOOTHEST
SOOTHFAST
SOOTHFUL
SOOTHING
SOOTHINGS
SOOTHLICH
SOOTHLY
SOOTHS
SOOTHSAID
SOOTHSAY
SOOTHSAYING
SOOTHSAYINGS
SOOTHSAYS
SOOTIER
SOOTIEST
SOOTILY
SOOTINESS
SOOTINESSES
SOOTING
SOOTLESS
SOOTS
SOOTY
SOP
SOPH
SOPHA
SOPHAS
SOPHERIC
SOPHERIM
SOPHIA
SOPHIAS
SOPHIC
SOPHICAL
SOPHISM
SOPHISMS
SOPHIST
SOPHISTER
SOPHISTERS
SOPHISTIC
SOPHISTICS
SOPHISTRIES
SOPHISTRY
SOPHISTS
SOPHOMORE
SOPHOMORES
SOPHS
SOPITE
SOPITED
SOPITES
SOPITING
SOPOR
SOPORIFIC
SOPORIFICS
SOPOROSE
SOPOROUS
SOPORS
SOPPED
SOPPIER
SOPPIEST
SOPPILY

SOPPINESS
SOPPINESSES
SOPPING
SOPPINGS
SOPPY
SOPRA
SOPRANI
SOPRANINI
SOPRANINO
SOPRANINOS
SOPRANIST
SOPRANISTS
SOPRANO
SOPRANOS
SOPS
SORA
SORAGE
SORAGES
SORAL
SORAS
SORB
SORBARIA
SORBARIAS
SORBATE
SORBATES
SORBED
SORBENT
SORBENTS
SORBET
SORBETS
SORBING
SORBITOL
SORBITOLS
SORBO
SORBOS
SORBS
SORBUS
SORBUSES
SORCERER
SORCERERS
SORCERESS
SORCERESSES
SORCERIES
SORCEROUS
SORCERY
SORD
SORDA
SORDES
SORDID
SORDIDER
SORDIDEST
SORDIDLY
SORDINE
SORDINES
SORDINI
SORDINO
SORDO
SORDOR
SORDORS
SORDS
SORE
SORED
SOREDIA
SOREDIAL
SOREDIATE
SOREDIUM
SOREE
SOREES
SOREHEAD
SOREHEADS

SOREHON
SOREHONS
SOREL
SORELL
SORELLS
SORELS
SORELY
SORENESS
SORENESSES
SORER
SORES
SOREST
SOREX
SOREXES
SORGHO
SORGHOS
SORGHUM
SORGHUMS
SORGO
SORGOS
SORI
SORICINE
SORICOID
SORING
SORITES
SORITIC
SORITICAL
SORN
SORNED
SORNER
SORNERS
SORNING
SORNINGS
SORNS
SOROBAN
SOROBANS
SOROCHE
SOROCHES
SORORAL
SORORATE
SORORATES
SORORIAL
SORORISE
SORORISED
SORORISES
SORORISING
SORORITIES
SORORITY
SORORIZE
SORORIZED
SORORIZES
SORORIZING
SOROSES
SOROSIS
SOROSISES
SORPTION
SORPTIONS
SORRA
SORRAS
SORREL
SORRELS
SORRIER
SORRIEST
SORRILY
SORRINESS
SORRINESSES
SORROW
SORROWED
SORROWER
SORROWERS

SORROWFUL
SORROWING
SORROWINGS
SORROWS
SORRY
SORRYISH
SORT
SORTABLE
SORTANCE
SORTANCES
SORTATION
SORTATIONS
SORTED
SORTER
SORTERS
SORTES
SORTIE
SORTIED
SORTIEING
SORTIES
SORTILEGE
SORTILEGES
SORTILEGIES
SORTILEGY
SORTING
SORTINGS
SORTITION
SORTITIONS
SORTMENT
SORTMENTS
SORTS
SORUS
SOS
SOSS
SOSSED
SOSSES
SOSSING
SOSSINGS
SOSTENUTO
SOT
SOTERIAL
SOTS
SOTTED
SOTTING
SOTTINGS
SOTTISH
SOTTISHLY
SOTTISIER
SOTTISIERS
SOU
SOUARI
SOUARIS
SOUBISE
SOUBISES
SOUBRETTE
SOUBRETTES
SOUCE
SOUCED
SOUCES
SOUCHONG
SOUCHONGS
SOUCING
SOUCT
SOUFFLE
SOUFFLÉ
SOUFFLES
SOUFFLÉS
SOUGH
SOUGHED
SOUGHING

SOUGHS
SOUGHT
SOUK
SOUKS
SOUL
SOULDAN
SOULDANS
SOULDIER
SOULDIERED
SOULDIERING
SOULDIERS
SOULED
SOULFUL
SOULFULLY
SOULLESS
SOULS
SOUM
SOUMED
SOUMING
SOUMINGS
SOUMS
SOUND
SOUNDED
SOUNDER
SOUNDERS
SOUNDEST
SOUNDING
SOUNDINGS
SOUNDLESS
SOUNDLY
SOUNDNESS
SOUNDNESSES
SOUNDS
SOUP
SOUPÇON
SOUPÇONS
SOUPER
SOUPERS
SOUPIER
SOUPIEST
SOUPLE
SOUPLED
SOUPLES
SOUPLING
SOUPS
SOUPSPOON
SOUPSPOONS
SOUPY
SOUR
SOURCE
SOURCED
SOURCES
SOURCING
SOURCINGS
SOURDINE
SOURDINES
SOURDOUGH
SOURDOUGHS
SOURED
SOURER
SOUREST
SOURING
SOURINGS
SOURISH
SOURISHLY
SOURLY
SOURNESS
SOURNESSES
SOUROCK
SOUROCKS

SOURPUSS
SOURPUSSES
SOURS
SOURSE
SOURSES
SOUS
SOUSE
SOUSED
SOUSES
SOUSEWIFE
SOUSEWIVES
SOUSING
SOUSINGS
SOUSLIK
SOUSLIKS
SOUT
SOUTACHE
SOUTACHES
SOUTANE
SOUTANES
SOUTAR
SOUTARS
SOUTENEUR
SOUTENEURS
SOUTER
SOUTERLY
SOUTERS
SOUTH
SOUTHED
SOUTHER
SOUTHERED
SOUTHERING
SOUTHERLY
SOUTHERN
SOUTHERNS
SOUTHERS
SOUTHING
SOUTHINGS
SOUTHLAND
SOUTHLANDS
SOUTHMOST
SOUTHPAW
SOUTHPAWS
SOUTHRON
SOUTHRONS
SOUTHS
SOUTHSAID
SOUTHSAY
SOUTHSAYING
SOUTHSAYS
SOUTHWARD
SOUTHWARDS
SOUTS
SOUVENIR
SOUVENIRED
SOUVENIRING
SOUVENIRS
SOV
SOVENANCE
SOVENANCES
SOVEREIGN
SOVEREIGNS
SOVIET
SOVIETIC
SOVIETISE
SOVIETISED
SOVIETISES
SOVIETISING
SOVIETISM
SOVIETISMS

SOVIETIZE
SOVIETIZED
SOVIETIZES
SOVIETIZING
SOVIETS
SOVRAN
SOVRANS
SOVRANTIES
SOVRANTY
SOVS
SOW
SOWANS
SOWAR
SOWARREE
SOWARREES
SOWARRIES
SOWARRY
SOWARS
SOWCE
SOWCED
SOWCES
SOWCING
SOWED
SOWENS
SOWER
SOWERS
SOWF
SOWFED
SOWFF
SOWFFED
SOWFFING
SOWFFS
SOWFING
SOWFS
SOWING
SOWINGS
SOWL
SOWLE
SOWLED
SOWLES
SOWLING
SOWLS
SOWM
SOWMED
SOWMING
SOWMS
SOWN
SOWND
SOWNDED
SOWNDING
SOWNDS
SOWNE
SOWNES
SOWP
SOWPS
SOWS
SOWSE
SOWSED
SOWSES
SOWSING
SOWSSE
SOWSSED
SOWSSES
SOWSSING
SOWTER
SOWTERS
SOWTH
SOWTHED
SOWTHING
SOWTHS

SOX
SOY
SOYA
SOYAS
SOYLE
SOYLED
SOYLES
SOYS
SOZZLE
SOZZLED
SOZZLES
SOZZLIER
SOZZLIEST
SOZZLING
SOZZLY
SPA
SPACE
SPACED
SPACELESS
SPACEMAN
SPACEMEN
SPACER
SPACERS
SPACES
SPACESHIP
SPACESHIPS
SPACEY
SPACIAL
SPACIER
SPACIEST
SPACING
SPACINGS
SPACIOUS
SPACY
SPADASSIN
SPADASSINS
SPADE
SPADED
SPADEFUL
SPADEFULS
SPADEMAN
SPADEMEN
SPADER
SPADERS
SPADES
SPADESMAN
SPADESMEN
SPADEWORK
SPADEWORKS
SPADGER
SPADGERS
SPADICES
SPADILLE
SPADILLES
SPADILLIO
SPADILLIOS
SPADILLO
SPADILLOS
SPADING
SPADIX
SPADO
SPADOES
SPADONES
SPADOS
SPADROON
SPADROONS
SPAE
SPAED
SPAEING
SPAEMAN

SPAEMEN
SPAER
SPAERS
SPAES
SPAEWIFE
SPAEWIVES
SPAGERIC
SPAGERICS
SPAGERIST
SPAGERISTS
SPAGHETTI
SPAGHETTIS
SPAGIRIC
SPAGIRICS
SPAGIRIST
SPAGIRISTS
SPAGYRIC
SPAGYRICS
SPAGYRIST
SPAGYRISTS
SPAHEE
SPAHEES
SPAHI
SPAHIS
SPAIN
SPAINED
SPAING
SPAINGS
SPAINING
SPAINS
SPAIRGE
SPAIRGED
SPAIRGES
SPAIRGING
SPAKE
SPALD
SPALDS
SPALE
SPALES
SPALL
SPALLE
SPALLED
SPALLES
SPALLING
SPALLS
SPALPEEN
SPALPEENS
SPALT
SPALTED
SPALTING
SPALTS
SPAMMIER
SPAMMIEST
SPAMMY
SPAN
SPANAEMIA
SPANAEMIAS
SPANAEMIC
SPANCEL
SPANCELLED
SPANCELLING
SPANCELS
SPANDREL
SPANDRELS
SPANDRIL
SPANDRILS
SPANE
SPANED
SPANES
SPANG

SPANGED
SPANGHEW
SPANGHEWED
SPANGHEWING
SPANGHEWS
SPANGING
SPANGLE
SPANGLED
SPANGLER
SPANGLERS
SPANGLES
SPANGLET
SPANGLETS
SPANGLIER
SPANGLIEST
SPANGLING
SPANGLINGS
SPANGLY
SPANGS
SPANIEL
SPANIELLED
SPANIELLING
SPANIELS
SPANING
SPANK
SPANKED
SPANKER
SPANKERS
SPANKING
SPANKINGS
SPANKS
SPANLESS
SPANNED
SPANNER
SPANNERS
SPANNING
SPANS
SPANSULE
SPANSULES
SPAR
SPARABLE
SPARABLES
SPARAXIS
SPARAXISES
SPARD
SPARE
SPARED
SPARELESS
SPARELY
SPARENESS
SPARENESSES
SPARER
SPARERS
SPARES
SPAREST
SPARGE
SPARGED
SPARGER
SPARGERS
SPARGES
SPARGING
SPARID
SPARIDS
SPARING
SPARINGLY
SPARK
SPARKE
SPARKED
SPARKES
SPARKING

| | | | | |
|---|---|---|---|---|
| SPARKISH | SPÄTLESEN | SPEARING | SPEECH | SPELIKINS |
| SPARKLE | SPÄTLESES | SPEARMAN | SPEECHED | SPELK |
| SPARKLED | SPATS | SPEARMEN | SPEECHES | SPELKS |
| SPARKLER | SPATTED | SPEARMINT | SPEECHFUL | SPELL |
| SPARKLERS | SPATTEE | SPEARMINTS | SPEECHIFIED | SPELLABLE |
| SPARKLES | SPATTEES | SPEARS | SPEECHIFIES | SPELLBIND |
| SPARKLESS | SPATTER | SPEARWORT | SPEECHIFY | SPELLBINDING |
| SPARKLET | SPATTERED | SPEARWORTS | SPEECHIFYING | SPELLBINDS |
| SPARKLETS | SPATTERING | SPEARY | SPEECHING | SPELLBOUND |
| SPARKLIES | SPATTERS | SPEAT | SPEED | SPELLDOWN |
| SPARKLING | SPATTING | SPEATS | SPEEDBALL | SPELLDOWNS |
| SPARKLINGS | SPATULA | SPEC | SPEEDBALLS | SPELLED |
| SPARKLY | SPATULAR | SPECCIES | SPEEDED | SPELLER |
| SPARKS | SPATULAS | SPECCY | SPEEDER | SPELLERS |
| SPARLING | SPATULATE | SPECIAL | SPEEDERS | SPELLFUL |
| SPARLINGS | SPATULE | SPECIALLY | SPEEDFUL | SPELLICAN |
| SPAROID | SPATULES | SPECIALS | SPEEDIER | SPELLICANS |
| SPAROIDS | SPAUL | SPECIALTIES | SPEEDIEST | SPELLIKIN |
| SPARRE | SPAULD | SPECIALTY | SPEEDILY | SPELLIKINS |
| SPARRED | SPAULDS | SPECIATE | SPEEDING | SPELLING |
| SPARRER | SPAULS | SPECIATED | SPEEDINGS | SPELLINGS |
| SPARRERS | SPAVIE | SPECIATES | SPEEDLESS | SPELLS |
| SPARRES | SPAVIES | SPECIATING | SPEEDO | SPELT |
| SPARRING | SPAVIN | SPECIE | SPEEDOS | SPELTER |
| SPARRINGS | SPAVINED | SPECIES | SPEEDS | SPELTERS |
| SPARROW | SPAVINS | SPECIFIC | SPEEDSTER | SPELTS |
| SPARROWS | SPAW | SPECIFICS | SPEEDSTERS | SPENCE |
| SPARRY | SPAWL | SPECIFIED | SPEEDWAY | SPENCER |
| SPARS | SPAWLED | SPECIFIES | SPEEDWAYS | SPENCERS |
| SPARSE | SPAWLING | SPECIFY | SPEEDWELL | SPENCES |
| SPARSEDLY | SPAWLS | SPECIFYING | SPEEDWELLS | SPEND |
| SPARSELY | SPAWN | SPECIMEN | SPEEDY | SPENDABLE |
| SPARSER | SPAWNED | SPECIMENS | SPEEL | SPENDALL |
| SPARSEST | SPAWNER | SPECIOUS | SPEELED | SPENDALLS |
| SPARSITIES | SPAWNERS | SPECK | SPEELER | SPENDER |
| SPARSITY | SPAWNING | SPECKED | SPEELERS | SPENDERS |
| SPART | SPAWNINGS | SPECKIER | SPEELING | SPENDING |
| SPARTAN | SPAWNS | SPECKIEST | SPEELS | SPENDINGS |
| SPARTEINE | SPAWS | SPECKING | SPEER | SPENDS |
| SPARTEINES | SPAY | SPECKLE | SPEERED | SPENT |
| SPARTERIE | SPAYAD | SPECKLED | SPEERING | SPEOS |
| SPARTERIES | SPAYADS | SPECKLES | SPEERINGS | SPEOSES |
| SPARTH | SPAYD | SPECKLESS | SPEERS | SPERLING |
| SPARTHE | SPAYDS | SPECKLING | SPEIR | SPERLINGS |
| SPARTHES | SPAYED | SPECKS | SPEIRED | SPERM |
| SPARTHS | SPAYING | SPECKY | SPEIRING | SPERMARIA |
| SPARTS | SPAYS | SPECS | SPEIRINGS | SPERMARIES |
| SPAS | SPEAK | SPECTACLE | SPEIRS | SPERMARY |
| SPASM | SPEAKABLE | SPECTACLES | SPEISS | SPERMATIA |
| SPASMATIC | SPEAKER | SPECTATE | SPEISSES | SPERMATIC |
| SPASMED | SPEAKERS | SPECTATED | SPEKBOOM | SPERMATICS |
| SPASMIC | SPEAKING | SPECTATES | SPEKBOOMS | SPERMATID |
| SPASMING | SPEAKINGS | SPECTATING | SPELAEAN | SPERMATIDS |
| SPASMODIC | SPEAKS | SPECTATOR | SPELD | SPERMIC |
| SPASMS | SPEAL | SPECTATORS | SPELDED | SPERMOUS |
| SPASTIC | SPEALS | SPECTER | SPELDER | SPERMS |
| SPASTICS | SPEAN | SPECTERS | SPELDERED | SPERRE |
| SPAT | SPEANED | SPECTRA | SPELDERING | SPERRED |
| SPATE | SPEANING | SPECTRAL | SPELDERS | SPERRES |
| SPATES | SPEANS | SPECTRE | SPELDIN | SPERRING |
| SPATFALL | SPEAR | SPECTRES | SPELDING | SPERSE |
| SPATFALLS | SPEARED | SPECTRUM | SPELDINGS | SPERSED |
| SPATHE | SPEARFISH | SPECULA | SPELDINS | SPERSES |
| SPATHED | SPEARFISHES | SPECULAR | SPELDRIN | SPERSING |
| SPATHES | SPEARHEAD | SPECULATE | SPELDRING | SPERST |
| SPATHIC | SPEARHEADED | SPECULATED | SPELDRINGS | SPERTHE |
| SPATHOSE | SPEARHEADING | SPECULATES | SPELDRINS | SPERTHES |
| SPATIAL | SPEARHEADS | SPECULATING | SPELDS | SPET |
| SPATIALLY | SPEARIER | SPECULUM | SPELEAN | SPETCH |
| SPÄTLESE | SPEARIEST | SPED | SPELIKIN | SPETCHES |

| | | | | |
|---|---|---|---|---|
| SPETS | SPICAS | SPIKES | SPINETTES | SPIREAS |
| SPETSNAZ | SPICATE | SPIKIER | SPINIER | SPIRED |
| SPETSNAZES | SPICATED | SPIKIEST | SPINIEST | SPIRELESS |
| SPETTING | SPICCATO | SPIKILY | SPINIFEX | SPIREME |
| SPETZNAZ | SPICCATOS | SPIKINESS | SPINIFEXES | SPIREMES |
| SPETZNAZES | SPICE | SPIKINESSES | SPINIFORM | SPIRES |
| SPEW | SPICED | SPIKING | SPININESS | SPIREWISE |
| SPEWED | SPICER | SPIKS | SPININESSES | SPIRIC |
| SPEWER | SPICERIES | SPIKY | SPINK | SPIRICS |
| SPEWERS | SPICERS | SPILE | SPINKS | SPIRIER |
| SPEWIER | SPICERY | SPILED | SPINNAKER | SPIRIEST |
| SPEWIEST | SPICES | SPILES | SPINNAKERS | SPIRILLA |
| SPEWINESS | SPICIER | SPILIKIN | SPINNER | SPIRILLAR |
| SPEWINESSES | SPICIEST | SPILIKINS | SPINNERET | SPIRILLUM |
| SPEWING | SPICILEGE | SPILING | SPINNERETS | SPIRING |
| SPEWS | SPICILEGES | SPILINGS | SPINNERIES | SPIRIT |
| SPEWY | SPICILY | SPILITE | SPINNERS | SPIRITED |
| SPHACELUS | SPICINESS | SPILITES | SPINNERY | SPIRITFUL |
| SPHACELUSES | SPICINESSES | SPILITIC | SPINNET | SPIRITING |
| SPHAER | SPICING | SPILL | SPINNETS | SPIRITINGS |
| SPHAERE | SPICK | SPILLAGE | SPINNEY | SPIRITISM |
| SPHAERES | SPICKER | SPILLAGES | SPINNEYS | SPIRITISMS |
| SPHAERITE | SPICKEST | SPILLED | SPINNIES | SPIRITIST |
| SPHAERITES | SPICKNEL | SPILLER | SPINNING | SPIRITISTS |
| SPHAERS | SPICKNELS | SPILLERS | SPINNINGS | SPIRITOSO |
| SPHAGNOUS | SPICKS | SPILLIKIN | SPINNY | SPIRITOUS |
| SPHEAR | SPICS | SPILLIKINS | SPINODE | SPIRITS |
| SPHEARE | SPICULA | SPILLING | SPINODES | SPIRITUAL |
| SPHEARES | SPICULAR | SPILLINGS | SPINOSE | SPIRITUALS |
| SPHEARS | SPICULAS | SPILLOVER | SPINOSITIES | SPIRITUEL |
| SPHENDONE | SPICULATE | SPILLOVERS | SPINOSITY | SPIRITUS |
| SPHENDONES | SPICULE | SPILLS | SPINOUS | SPIRITUSES |
| SPHENE | SPICULES | SPILLWAY | SPINOUT | SPIRITY |
| SPHENES | SPICULUM | SPILLWAYS | SPINOUTS | SPIRLING |
| SPHENIC | SPICY | SPILOSITE | SPINS | SPIRLINGS |
| SPHENODON | SPIDE | SPILOSITES | SPINSTER | SPIROID |
| SPHENODONS | SPIDER | SPILT | SPINSTERS | SPIRT |
| SPHENOID | SPIDERIER | SPILTH | SPINTEXT | SPIRTED |
| SPHENOIDS | SPIDERIEST | SPILTHS | SPINTEXTS | SPIRTING |
| SPHERAL | SPIDERS | SPIN | SPINULATE | SPIRTLE |
| SPHERE | SPIDERY | SPINA | SPINULE | SPIRTLES |
| SPHERED | SPIE | SPINACH | SPINULES | SPIRTS |
| SPHERES | SPIED | SPINACHES | SPINULOSE | SPIRY |
| SPHERIC | SPIEL | SPINAE | SPINULOUS | SPIT |
| SPHERICAL | SPIELED | SPINAGE | SPINY | SPITAL |
| SPHERICS | SPIELER | SPINAGES | SPIRACLE | SPITALS |
| SPHERIER | SPIELERS | SPINAL | SPIRACLES | SPITCHER |
| SPHERIEST | SPIELING | SPINAR | SPIRACULA | SPITE |
| SPHERING | SPIELS | SPINARS | SPIRAEA | SPITED |
| SPHEROID | SPIES | SPINAS | SPIRAEAS | SPITEFUL |
| SPHEROIDS | SPIFF | SPINATE | SPIRAL | SPITEFULLER |
| SPHERULAR | SPIFFIER | SPINDLE | SPIRALISM | SPITEFULLEST |
| SPHERULE | SPIFFIEST | SPINDLED | SPIRALISMS | SPITES |
| SPHERULES | SPIFFING | SPINDLES | SPIRALIST | SPITFIRE |
| SPHERY | SPIFFY | SPINDLIER | SPIRALISTS | SPITFIRES |
| SPHINCTER | SPIGHT | SPINDLIEST | SPIRALITIES | SPITING |
| SPHINCTERS | SPIGHTED | SPINDLING | SPIRALITY | SPITS |
| SPHINGES | SPIGHTING | SPINDLINGS | SPIRALLED | SPITTED |
| SPHINGID | SPIGHTS | SPINDLY | SPIRALLING | SPITTEN |
| SPHINGIDS | SPIGNEL | SPINDRIFT | SPIRALLY | SPITTER |
| SPHINX | SPIGNELS | SPINDRIFTS | SPIRALS | SPITTERS |
| SPHINXES | SPIGOT | SPINE | SPIRANT | SPITTING |
| SPHYGMIC | SPIGOTS | SPINED | SPIRANTS | SPITTINGS |
| SPHYGMOID | SPIK | SPINEL | SPIRASTER | SPITTLE |
| SPHYGMUS | SPIKE | SPINELESS | SPIRASTERS | SPITTLES |
| SPHYGMUSES | SPIKED | SPINELS | SPIRATED | SPITTOON |
| SPIAL | SPIKELET | SPINES | SPIRATION | SPITTOONS |
| SPIALS | SPIKELETS | SPINET | SPIRATIONS | SPITZ |
| SPIC | SPIKENARD | SPINETS | SPIRE | SPITZES |
| SPICA | SPIKENARDS | SPINETTE | SPIREA | SPIV |

| | | | | |
|---|---|---|---|---|
| SPIVS | SPLINED | SPOILSMEN | SPOOL | SPORTSMEN |
| SPIVVERIES | SPLINES | SPOILT | SPOOLED | SPORTY |
| SPIVVERY | SPLINING | SPOKE | SPOOLER | SPORULAR |
| SPIVVIER | SPLINT | SPOKEN | SPOOLERS | SPORULATE |
| SPIVVIEST | SPLINTED | SPOKES | SPOOLING | SPORULATED |
| SPIVVY | SPLINTER | SPOKESMAN | SPOOLS | SPORULATES |
| SPLASH | SPLINTERED | SPOKESMEN | SPOOM | SPORULATING |
| SPLASHED | SPLINTERING | SPOKEWISE | SPOOMED | SPORULE |
| SPLASHER | SPLINTERS | SPOLIATE | SPOOMING | SPORULES |
| SPLASHERS | SPLINTERY | SPOLIATED | SPOOMS | SPOSH |
| SPLASHES | SPLINTING | SPOLIATES | SPOON | SPOSHES |
| SPLASHIER | SPLINTS | SPOLIATING | SPOONBILL | SPOSHY |
| SPLASHIEST | SPLIT | SPOLIATOR | SPOONBILLS | SPOT |
| SPLASHILY | SPLITS | SPOLIATORS | SPOONED | SPOTLESS |
| SPLASHING | SPLITTED | SPONDAIC | SPOONEY | SPOTLIGHT |
| SPLASHINGS | SPLITTER | SPONDEE | SPOONEYS | SPOTLIGHTED |
| SPLASHY | SPLITTERS | SPONDEES | SPOONFUL | SPOTLIGHTING |
| SPLAT | SPLITTING | SPONDULIX | SPOONFULS | SPOTLIGHTS |
| SPLATCH | SPLODGE | SPONDYL | SPOONIER | SPOTLIT |
| SPLATCHED | SPLODGED | SPONDYLS | SPOONIES | SPOTS |
| SPLATCHES | SPLODGES | SPONGE | SPOONIEST | SPOTTE |
| SPLATCHING | SPLODGIER | SPONGED | SPOONILY | SPOTTED |
| SPLATS | SPLODGIEST | SPONGEOUS | SPOONING | SPOTTER |
| SPLATTED | SPLODGILY | SPONGER | SPOONMEAT | SPOTTERS |
| SPLATTER | SPLODGING | SPONGERS | SPOONMEATS | SPOTTES |
| SPLATTERED | SPLODGY | SPONGES | SPOONS | SPOTTIER |
| SPLATTERING | SPLORE | SPONGIER | SPOONWAYS | SPOTTIEST |
| SPLATTERS | SPLORES | SPONGIEST | SPOONWISE | SPOTTILY |
| SPLATTING | SPLOSH | SPONGILY | SPOONY | SPOTTING |
| SPLATTINGS | SPLOSHED | SPONGIN | SPOOR | SPOTTINGS |
| SPLAY | SPLOSHES | SPONGING | SPOORED | SPOTTY |
| SPLAYED | SPLOSHING | SPONGINS | SPOORER | SPOUSAGE |
| SPLAYING | SPLOTCH | SPONGIOSE | SPOORERS | SPOUSAGES |
| SPLAYS | SPLOTCHED | SPONGIOUS | SPOORING | SPOUSAL |
| SPLEEN | SPLOTCHES | SPONGOID | SPOORS | SPOUSALS |
| SPLEENFUL | SPLOTCHIER | SPONGY | SPORADIC | SPOUSE |
| SPLEENISH | SPLOTCHIEST | SPONSAL | SPORANGIA | SPOUSED |
| SPLEENS | SPLOTCHING | SPONSALIA | SPORE | SPOUSES |
| SPLEENY | SPLOTCHY | SPONSIBLE | SPORES | SPOUSING |
| SPLENDENT | SPLURGE | SPONSING | SPORIDESM | SPOUT |
| SPLENDID | SPLURGED | SPONSINGS | SPORIDESMS | SPOUTED |
| SPLENDOR | SPLURGES | SPONSION | SPORIDIA | SPOUTER |
| SPLENDORS | SPLURGIER | SPONSIONS | SPORIDIAL | SPOUTERS |
| SPLENDOUR | SPLURGIEST | SPONSON | SPORIDIUM | SPOUTIER |
| SPLENDOURS | SPLURGING | SPONSONS | SPOROCARP | SPOUTIEST |
| SPLENETIC | SPLURGY | SPONSOR | SPOROCARPS | SPOUTING |
| SPLENETICS | SPLUTTER | SPONSORED | SPOROCYST | SPOUTLESS |
| SPLENIA | SPLUTTERED | SPONSORING | SPOROCYSTS | SPOUTS |
| SPLENIAL | SPLUTTERING | SPONSORS | SPOROGENIES | SPOUTY |
| SPLENIC | SPLUTTERINGS | SPONTOON | SPOROGENY | SPRACK |
| SPLENII | SPLUTTERS | SPONTOONS | SPOROPHYL | SPRACKLE |
| SPLENITIS | SPLUTTERY | SPOOF | SPOROPHYLS | SPRACKLED |
| SPLENITISES | SPODE | SPOOFED | SPORRAN | SPRACKLES |
| SPLENIUM | SPODES | SPOOFER | SPORRANS | SPRACKLING |
| SPLENIUMS | SPODIUM | SPOOFERIES | SPORT | SPRAD |
| SPLENIUS | SPODIUMS | SPOOFERS | SPORTABLE | SPRAG |
| SPLENIUSES | SPODUMENE | SPOOFERY | SPORTANCE | SPRAGGED |
| SPLENT | SPODUMENES | SPOOFING | SPORTANCES | SPRAGGING |
| SPLENTED | SPOFFISH | SPOOFS | SPORTED | SPRAGS |
| SPLENTING | SPOFFY | SPOOK | SPORTER | SPRAICKLE |
| SPLENTS | SPOIL | SPOOKED | SPORTERS | SPRAICKLED |
| SPLEUCHAN | SPOILAGE | SPOOKERIES | SPORTFUL | SPRAICKLES |
| SPLEUCHANS | SPOILAGES | SPOOKERY | SPORTIER | SPRAICKLING |
| SPLICE | SPOILED | SPOOKIER | SPORTIEST | SPRAID |
| SPLICED | SPOILER | SPOOKIEST | SPORTILY | SPRAIN |
| SPLICES | SPOILERS | SPOOKILY | SPORTING | SPRAINED |
| SPLICING | SPOILFUL | SPOOKING | SPORTIVE | SPRAINING |
| SPLIFF | SPOILING | SPOOKISH | SPORTLESS | SPRAINS |
| SPLIFFS | SPOILS | SPOOKS | SPORTS | SPRAINT |
| SPLINE | SPOILSMAN | SPOOKY | SPORTSMAN | SPRAINTS |

SPRANG
SPRANGLE
SPRANGLED
SPRANGLES
SPRANGLING
SPRAT
SPRATS
SPRATTLE
SPRATTLED
SPRATTLES
SPRATTLING
SPRAUCHLE
SPRAUCHLED
SPRAUCHLES
SPRAUCHLING
SPRAUNCIER
SPRAUNCIEST
SPRAUNCY
SPRAWL
SPRAWLED
SPRAWLER
SPRAWLERS
SPRAWLIER
SPRAWLIEST
SPRAWLING
SPRAWLS
SPRAWLY
SPRAY
SPRAYED
SPRAYER
SPRAYERS
SPRAYEY
SPRAYIER
SPRAYIEST
SPRAYING
SPRAYS
SPREAD
SPREADER
SPREADERS
SPREADING
SPREADINGS
SPREADS
SPREAGH
SPREAGHS
SPREATHE
SPREATHED
SPREATHES
SPREATHING
SPREAZE
SPREAZED
SPREAZES
SPREAZING
SPRECHERIES
SPRECHERY
SPRECKLED
SPRED
SPREDD
SPREDDE
SPREDDEN
SPREDDES
SPREDDING
SPREDDS
SPREDS
SPREE
SPREED
SPREEING
SPREES
SPREETHE
SPREETHED
SPREETHES

SPREETHING
SPREEZE
SPREEZED
SPREEZES
SPREEZING
SPRENT
SPRIG
SPRIGGED
SPRIGGIER
SPRIGGIEST
SPRIGGING
SPRIGGY
SPRIGHT
SPRIGHTED
SPRIGHTING
SPRIGHTLIER
SPRIGHTLIEST
SPRIGHTLY
SPRIGHTS
SPRIGS
SPRING
SPRINGAL
SPRINGALD
SPRINGALDS
SPRINGALS
SPRINGBOK
SPRINGBOKS
SPRINGE
SPRINGED
SPRINGER
SPRINGERS
SPRINGES
SPRINGIER
SPRINGIEST
SPRINGILY
SPRINGING
SPRINGINGS
SPRINGLE
SPRINGLES
SPRINGLET
SPRINGLETS
SPRINGS
SPRINGY
SPRINKLE
SPRINKLED
SPRINKLER
SPRINKLERS
SPRINKLES
SPRINKLING
SPRINKLINGS
SPRINT
SPRINTED
SPRINTER
SPRINTERS
SPRINTING
SPRINTINGS
SPRINTS
SPRIT
SPRITE
SPRITEFUL
SPRITELY
SPRITES
SPRITS
SPRITSAIL
SPRITSAILS
SPRITZER
SPRITZERS
SPRITZIG
SPRITZIGS
SPROCKET

SPROCKETS
SPROD
SPRODS
SPROG
SPROGS
SPRONG
SPROUT
SPROUTED
SPROUTING
SPROUTINGS
SPROUTS
SPRUCE
SPRUCED
SPRUCELY
SPRUCER
SPRUCES
SPRUCEST
SPRUCING
SPRUE
SPRUES
SPRUG
SPRUGS
SPRUIK
SPRUIKED
SPRUIKER
SPRUIKERS
SPRUIKING
SPRUIKS
SPRUIT
SPRUITS
SPRUNG
SPRUSH
SPRUSHED
SPRUSHES
SPRUSHING
SPRY
SPRYER
SPRYEST
SPRYLY
SPRYNESS
SPRYNESSES
SPUD
SPUDDED
SPUDDIER
SPUDDIEST
SPUDDING
SPUDDINGS
SPUDDY
SPUDS
SPUE
SPUED
SPUEING
SPUES
SPUILZIE
SPUILZIED
SPUILZIEING
SPUILZIES
SPUING
SPULE
SPULEBANE
SPULEBANES
SPULEBONE
SPULEBONES
SPULES
SPULYE
SPULYED
SPULYEING
SPULYES
SPULYIE
SPULYIED

SPULYIEING
SPULYIES
SPULZIE
SPULZIED
SPULZIEING
SPULZIES
SPUME
SPUMED
SPUMES
SPUMIER
SPUMIEST
SPUMING
SPUMOUS
SPUMY
SPUN
SPUNGE
SPUNGES
SPUNK
SPUNKED
SPUNKIE
SPUNKIER
SPUNKIES
SPUNKIEST
SPUNKING
SPUNKS
SPUNKY
SPUR
SPURGE
SPURGES
SPURIAE
SPURIOUS
SPURLESS
SPURLING
SPURLINGS
SPURN
SPURNE
SPURNED
SPURNER
SPURNERS
SPURNES
SPURNING
SPURNINGS
SPURNS
SPURRED
SPURRER
SPURRERS
SPURREY
SPURREYS
SPURRIER
SPURRIERS
SPURRIES
SPURRIEST
SPURRING
SPURRINGS
SPURRY
SPURS
SPURT
SPURTED
SPURTING
SPURTLE
SPURTLES
SPURTS
SPUTA
SPUTNIK
SPUTNIKS
SPUTTER
SPUTTERED
SPUTTERER
SPUTTERERS
SPUTTERING

SPUTTERINGS
SPUTTERS
SPUTTERY
SPUTUM
SPY
SPYAL
SPYALS
SPYGLASS
SPYGLASSES
SPYING
SPYINGS
SPYMASTER
SPYMASTERS
SPYRE
SPYRES
SQUAB
SQUABASH
SQUABASHED
SQUABASHES
SQUABASHING
SQUABBED
SQUABBER
SQUABBEST
SQUABBIER
SQUABBIEST
SQUABBING
SQUABBISH
SQUABBLE
SQUABBLED
SQUABBLER
SQUABBLERS
SQUABBLES
SQUABBLING
SQUABBY
SQUABS
SQUACCO
SQUACCOS
SQUAD
SQUADDIES
SQUADDY
SQUADRON
SQUADRONE
SQUADRONED
SQUADRONES
SQUADRONING
SQUADRONS
SQUADS
SQUAIL
SQUAILED
SQUAILER
SQUAILERS
SQUAILING
SQUAILINGS
SQUAILS
SQUALID
SQUALIDER
SQUALIDEST
SQUALIDLY
SQUALL
SQUALLED
SQUALLER
SQUALLERS
SQUALLIER
SQUALLIEST
SQUALLING
SQUALLINGS
SQUALLS
SQUALLY
SQUALOID
SQUALOR

| | | | | |
|---|---|---|---|---|
| SQUALORS | SQUAWKINGS | SQUIDGE | SQUIRMIER | STACKED |
| SQUAMA | SQUAWKS | SQUIDGED | SQUIRMIEST | STACKER |
| SQUAMAE | SQUAWKY | SQUIDGES | SQUIRMING | STACKERS |
| SQUAMATE | SQUAWMAN | SQUIDGIER | SQUIRMS | STACKET |
| SQUAME | SQUAWMEN | SQUIDGIEST | SQUIRMY | STACKETS |
| SQUAMELLA | SQUAWS | SQUIDGING | SQUIRR | STACKING |
| SQUAMELLAS | SQUEAK | SQUIDGY | SQUIRRED | STACKINGS |
| SQUAMES | SQUEAKED | SQUIDS | SQUIRREL | STACKS |
| SQUAMOSAL | SQUEAKER | SQUIER | SQUIRRELLED | STACKYARD |
| SQUAMOSALS | SQUEAKERIES | SQUIERS | SQUIRRELLING | STACKYARDS |
| SQUAMOSE | SQUEAKERS | SQUIFF | SQUIRRELS | STACTE |
| SQUAMOUS | SQUEAKERY | SQUIFFER | SQUIRRELY | STACTES |
| SQUAMULA | SQUEAKIER | SQUIFFERS | SQUIRRING | STADDA |
| SQUAMULAS | SQUEAKIEST | SQUIFFIER | SQUIRRS | STADDAS |
| SQUAMULE | SQUEAKILY | SQUIFFIEST | SQUIRT | STADDLE |
| SQUAMULES | SQUEAKING | SQUIFFY | SQUIRTED | STADDLES |
| SQUANDER | SQUEAKINGS | SQUIGGLE | SQUIRTER | STADE |
| SQUANDERED | SQUEAKS | SQUIGGLED | SQUIRTERS | STADES |
| SQUANDERING | SQUEAKY | SQUIGGLES | SQUIRTING | STADIA |
| SQUANDERINGS | SQUEAL | SQUIGGLIER | SQUIRTINGS | STADIAL |
| SQUANDERS | SQUEALED | SQUIGGLIEST | SQUIRTS | STADIALS |
| SQUARE | SQUEALER | SQUIGGLING | SQUISH | STADIAS |
| SQUARED | SQUEALERS | SQUIGGLY | SQUISHED | STADIUM |
| SQUARELY | SQUEALING | SQUILGEE | SQUISHES | STADIUMS |
| SQUARER | SQUEALINGS | SQUILGEED | SQUISHIER | STAFF |
| SQUARERS | SQUEALS | SQUILGEEING | SQUISHIEST | STAFFAGE |
| SQUARES | SQUEAMISH | SQUILGEES | SQUISHING | STAFFAGES |
| SQUAREST | SQUEEDGE | SQUILL | SQUISHY | STAFFED |
| SQUARING | SQUEEDGED | SQUILLS | SQUIT | STAFFER |
| SQUARINGS | SQUEEDGES | SQUINANCIES | SQUITCH | STAFFERS |
| SQUARISH | SQUEEDGING | SQUINANCY | SQUITCHES | STAFFING |
| SQUARROSE | SQUEEGEE | SQUINCH | SQUITS | STAFFROOM |
| SQUARSON | SQUEEGEED | SQUINCHES | SRADDHA | STAFFROOMS |
| SQUARSONS | SQUEEGEEING | SQUINIED | SRADDHAS | STAFFS |
| SQUASH | SQUEEGEES | SQUINIES | ST | STAG |
| SQUASHED | SQUEEZE | SQUINNIED | STAB | STAGE |
| SQUASHER | SQUEEZED | SQUINNIES | STABBED | STAGED |
| SQUASHERS | SQUEEZER | SQUINNY | STABBER | STAGER |
| SQUASHES | SQUEEZERS | SQUINNYING | STABBERS | STAGERIES |
| SQUASHIER | SQUEEZES | SQUINT | STABBING | STAGERS |
| SQUASHIEST | SQUEEZIER | SQUINTED | STABBINGS | STAGERY |
| SQUASHILY | SQUEEZIEST | SQUINTER | STABILE | STAGES |
| SQUASHING | SQUEEZING | SQUINTERS | STABILES | STAGEY |
| SQUASHY | SQUEEZINGS | SQUINTEST | STABILISE | STAGGARD |
| SQUAT | SQUEEZY | SQUINTING | STABILISED | STAGGARDS |
| SQUATNESS | SQUEG | SQUINTINGS | STABILISES | STAGGED |
| SQUATNESSES | SQUEGGED | SQUINTS | STABILISING | STAGGER |
| SQUATS | SQUEGGER | SQUINY | STABILITIES | STAGGERED |
| SQUATTED | SQUEGGERS | SQUINYING | STABILITY | STAGGERER |
| SQUATTER | SQUEGGING | SQUIRAGE | STABILIZE | STAGGERERS |
| SQUATTERED | SQUEGGINGS | SQUIRAGES | STABILIZED | STAGGERING |
| SQUATTERING | SQUEGS | SQUIRALTIES | STABILIZES | STAGGERINGS |
| SQUATTERS | SQUELCH | SQUIRALTY | STABILIZING | STAGGERS |
| SQUATTEST | SQUELCHED | SQUIRARCH | STABLE | STAGGING |
| SQUATTIER | SQUELCHER | SQUIRARCHS | STABLED | STAGHORN |
| SQUATTIEST | SQUELCHERS | SQUIRE | STABLER | STAGHORNS |
| SQUATTING | SQUELCHES | SQUIREAGE | STABLERS | STAGHOUND |
| SQUATTLE | SQUELCHIER | SQUIREAGES | STABLES | STAGHOUNDS |
| SQUATTLED | SQUELCHIEST | SQUIRED | STABLEST | STAGIER |
| SQUATTLES | SQUELCHING | SQUIREDOM | STABLING | STAGIEST |
| SQUATTLING | SQUELCHINGS | SQUIREDOMS | STABLINGS | STAGILY |
| SQUATTY | SQUELCHY | SQUIREEN | STABLISH | STAGINESS |
| SQUAW | SQUIB | SQUIREENS | STABLISHED | STAGINESSES |
| SQUAWK | SQUIBBED | SQUIRELY | STABLISHES | STAGING |
| SQUAWKED | SQUIBBING | SQUIRES | STABLISHING | STAGINGS |
| SQUAWKER | SQUIBBINGS | SQUIRESS | STABLY | STAGNANCIES |
| SQUAWKERS | SQUIBS | SQUIRESSES | STABS | STAGNANCY |
| SQUAWKIER | SQUID | SQUIRING | STACCATO | STAGNANT |
| SQUAWKIEST | SQUIDDED | SQUIRM | STACCATOS | STAGNATE |
| SQUAWKING | SQUIDDING | SQUIRMED | STACK | STAGNATED |

STAGNATES
STAGNATING
STAGS
STAGY
STAID
STAIDER
STAIDEST
STAIDLY
STAIDNESS
STAIDNESSES
STAIG
STAIGS
STAIN
STAINED
STAINER
STAINERS
STAINING
STAININGS
STAINLESS
STAINS
STAIR
STAIRCASE
STAIRCASES
STAIRED
STAIRFOOT
STAIRFOOTS
STAIRHEAD
STAIRHEADS
STAIRS
STAIRWAY
STAIRWAYS
STAIRWISE
STAITH
STAITHE
STAITHES
STAITHS
STAKE
STAKED
STAKES
STAKING
STALACTIC
STALAG
STALAGMA
STALAGMAS
STALAGS
STALE
STALED
STALELY
STALEMATE
STALEMATED
STALEMATES
STALEMATING
STALENESS
STALENESSES
STALER
STALES
STALEST
STALING
STALK
STALKED
STALKER
STALKERS
STALKIER
STALKIEST
STALKING
STALKINGS
STALKLESS
STALKO
STALKOES
STALKS

STALKY
STALL
STALLAGE
STALLAGES
STALLED
STALLING
STALLINGS
STALLION
STALLIONS
STALLMAN
STALLMEN
STALLS
STALWART
STALWARTS
STALWORTH
STALWORTHS
STAMEN
STAMENED
STAMENS
STAMINA
STAMINAL
STAMINAS
STAMINATE
STAMINEAL
STAMINODE
STAMINODES
STAMINODIES
STAMINODY
STAMINOID
STAMMEL
STAMMELS
STAMMER
STAMMERED
STAMMERER
STAMMERERS
STAMMERING
STAMMERINGS
STAMMERS
STAMNOI
STAMNOS
STAMP
STAMPED
STAMPEDE
STAMPEDED
STAMPEDES
STAMPEDING
STAMPEDO
STAMPEDOED
STAMPEDOING
STAMPEDOS
STAMPER
STAMPERS
STAMPING
STAMPINGS
STAMPS
STANCE
STANCES
STANCH
STANCHED
STANCHEL
STANCHELLED
STANCHELLING
STANCHELS
STANCHER
STANCHERED
STANCHERING
STANCHERS
STANCHES
STANCHEST
STANCHING

STANCHINGS
STANCHION
STANCHIONED
STANCHIONING
STANCHIONS
STANCHLY
STANCK
STAND
STANDARD
STANDARDS
STANDEN
STANDER
STANDERS
STANDGALE
STANDGALES
STANDING
STANDINGS
STANDISH
STANDISHES
STANDS
STANE
STANED
STANES
STANG
STANGED
STANGING
STANGS
STANHOPE
STANHOPES
STANIEL
STANIELS
STANING
STANK
STANKS
STANNARIES
STANNARY
STANNATE
STANNATES
STANNATOR
STANNATORS
STANNEL
STANNELS
STANNIC
STANNITE
STANNITES
STANNOUS
STANYEL
STANYELS
STANZA
STANZAIC
STANZAS
STANZE
STANZES
STANZO
STANZOES
STANZOS
STAP
STAPEDES
STAPEDIAL
STAPEDII
STAPEDIUS
STAPEDIUSES
STAPELIA
STAPELIAS
STAPES
STAPH
STAPHS
STAPHYLE
STAPHYLES
STAPLE

STAPLED
STAPLER
STAPLERS
STAPLES
STAPLING
STAPPED
STAPPING
STAPPLE
STAPPLES
STAPS
STAR
STARAGEN
STARAGENS
STARBOARD
STARBOARDED
STARBOARDING
STARBOARDS
STARCH
STARCHED
STARCHER
STARCHERS
STARCHES
STARCHIER
STARCHIEST
STARCHILY
STARCHING
STARCHY
STARDOM
STARDOMS
STARE
STARED
STARER
STARERS
STARES
STARETS
STARETSES
STARETZ
STARETZES
STARFISH
STARFISHES
STARING
STARINGLY
STARINGS
STARK
STARKED
STARKEN
STARKENED
STARKENING
STARKENS
STARKER
STARKERS
STARKEST
STARKING
STARKLY
STARKNESS
STARKNESSES
STARKS
STARLESS
STARLET
STARLETS
STARLIGHT
STARLIGHTS
STARLIKE
STARLING
STARLINGS
STARLIT
STARN
STARNED
STARNIE
STARNIES

STARNING
STARNS
STAROSTA
STAROSTAS
STAROSTIES
STAROSTY
STARR
STARRED
STARRIER
STARRIEST
STARRILY
STARRING
STARRINGS
STARRS
STARRY
STARS
STARSHINE
STARSHINES
STARSPOT
STARSPOTS
START
STARTED
STARTER
STARTERS
STARTFUL
STARTING
STARTINGS
STARTISH
STARTLE
STARTLED
STARTLER
STARTLERS
STARTLES
STARTLING
STARTLINGS
STARTLISH
STARTLY
STARTS
STARVE
STARVED
STARVES
STARVING
STARVINGS
STARWORT
STARWORTS
STASES
STASH
STASHED
STASHES
STASHIE
STASHIES
STASHING
STASIDION
STASIDIONS
STASIMA
STASIMON
STASIS
STATABLE
STATAL
STATANT
STATE
STATED
STATEDLY
STATEHOOD
STATEHOODS
STATELESS
STATELIER
STATELIEST
STATELILY
STATELY

| | | | | |
|---|---|---|---|---|
| STATEMENT | STAYING | STEARATES | STEENBOK | STEINBOCKS |
| STATEMENTS | STAYINGS | STEARD | STEENBOKS | STEINED |
| STATER | STAYLESS | STEARE | STEENBRAS | STEINING |
| STATEROOM | STAYNE | STEARED | STEENBRASES | STEININGS |
| STATEROOMS | STAYNED | STEARES | STEENED | STEINS |
| STATERS | STAYNES | STEARIC | STEENING | STELA |
| STATES | STAYNING | STEARIN | STEENINGS | STELAE |
| STATESIDE | STAYRE | STEARINE | STEENKIRK | STELAR |
| STATESMAN | STAYRES | STEARINES | STEENKIRKS | STELE |
| STATESMEN | STAYS | STEARING | STEENS | STELENE |
| STATEWIDE | STAYSAIL | STEARINS | STEEP | STELES |
| STATIC | STAYSAILS | STEARS | STEEPED | STELL |
| STATICAL | STEAD | STEARSMAN | STEEPEN | STELLAR |
| STATICS | STEADED | STEARSMEN | STEEPENED | STELLATE |
| STATING | STEADFAST | STEATITE | STEEPENING | STELLATED |
| STATION | STEADIED | STEATITES | STEEPENS | STELLED |
| STATIONAL | STEADIER | STEATITIC | STEEPER | STELLIFIED |
| STATIONED | STEADIES | STEATOMA | STEEPERS | STELLIFIES |
| STATIONER | STEADIEST | STEATOMAS | STEEPEST | STELLIFY |
| STATIONERS | STEADILY | STEATOSES | STEEPIER | STELLIFYING |
| STATIONING | STEADING | STEATOSIS | STEEPIEST | STELLIFYINGS |
| STATIONS | STEADINGS | STED | STEEPING | STELLING |
| STATISM | STEADS | STEDD | STEEPISH | STELLION |
| STATISMS | STEADY | STEDDE | STEEPLE | STELLIONS |
| STATIST | STEADYING | STEDDED | STEEPLED | STELLS |
| STATISTIC | STEAK | STEDDES | STEEPLES | STELLULAR |
| STATISTICS | STEAKS | STEDDIED | STEEPLY | STEM |
| STATISTS | STEAL | STEDDIES | STEEPNESS | STEMBOK |
| STATIVE | STEALE | STEDDING | STEEPNESSES | STEMBOKS |
| STATOCYST | STEALED | STEDDS | STEEPS | STEMBUCK |
| STATOCYSTS | STEALER | STEDDY | STEEPY | STEMBUCKS |
| STATOLITH | STEALERS | STEDDYING | STEER | STEME |
| STATOLITHS | STEALES | STEDE | STEERABLE | STEMED |
| STATOR | STEALING | STEDED | STEERAGE | STEMES |
| STATORS | STEALINGS | STEDES | STEERAGES | STEMING |
| STATUA | STEALS | STEDFAST | STEERED | STEMLESS |
| STATUARIES | STEALT | STEDING | STEERER | STEMLET |
| STATUARY | STEALTH | STEDS | STEERERS | STEMLETS |
| STATUAS | STEALTHIER | STEED | STEERIES | STEMMA |
| STATUE | STEALTHIEST | STEEDED | STEERING | STEMMATA |
| STATUED | STEALTHS | STEEDIED | STEERINGS | STEMME |
| STATUES | STEALTHY | STEEDIES | STEERLING | STEMMED |
| STATUETTE | STEAM | STEEDING | STEERLINGS | STEMMES |
| STATUETTES | STEAMBOAT | STEEDS | STEERS | STEMMING |
| STATURE | STEAMBOATS | STEEDY | STEERSMAN | STEMPEL |
| STATURED | STEAMED | STEEDYING | STEERSMEN | STEMPELS |
| STATURES | STEAMER | STEEK | STEERY | STEMPLE |
| STATUS | STEAMERS | STEEKING | STEEVE | STEMPLES |
| STATUTE | STEAMIE | STEEKIT | STEEVED | STEMS |
| STATUTES | STEAMIER | STEEKS | STEEVELY | STEMSON |
| STATUTORY | STEAMIES | STEEL | STEEVER | STEMSONS |
| STAUNCH | STEAMIEST | STEELBOW | STEEVES | STEN |
| STAUNCHED | STEAMILY | STEELBOWS | STEEVEST | STENCH |
| STAUNCHER | STEAMING | STEELD | STEEVING | STENCHED |
| STAUNCHES | STEAMINGS | STEELED | STEEVINGS | STENCHES |
| STAUNCHEST | STEAMS | STEELIER | STEGNOSES | STENCHIER |
| STAUNCHING | STEAMSHIP | STEELIEST | STEGNOSIS | STENCHIEST |
| STAUNCHLY | STEAMSHIPS | STEELING | STEGNOTIC | STENCHING |
| STAVE | STEAMY | STEELINGS | STEGODON | STENCHY |
| STAVED | STEAN | STEELS | STEGODONS | STENCIL |
| STAVES | STEANE | STEELWORK | STEGODONT | STENCILLED |
| STAVING | STEANED | STEELWORKS | STEGODONTS | STENCILLING |
| STAW | STEANES | STEELY | STEGOMYIA | STENCILLINGS |
| STAWED | STEANING | STEELYARD | STEGOMYIAS | STENCILS |
| STAWING | STEANINGS | STEELYARDS | STEGOSAUR | STEND |
| STAWS | STEANS | STEEM | STEGOSAURS | STENDED |
| STAY | STEAR | STEEMED | STEIL | STENDING |
| STAYED | STEARAGE | STEEMING | STEILS | STENDS |
| STAYER | STEARAGES | STEEMS | STEIN | STENGAH |
| STAYERS | STEARATE | STEEN | STEINBOCK | STENGAHS |

| | | | | |
|---|---|---|---|---|
| STENLOCK | STERILIZING | STEWPOTS | STIEVELY | STILTER |
| STENLOCKS | STERLET | STEWS | STIEVER | STILTERS |
| STENNED | STERLETS | STEWY | STIEVEST | STILTIER |
| STENNING | STERLING | STEY | STIFF | STILTIEST |
| STENOPAIC | STERLINGS | STEYER | STIFFED | STILTING |
| STENOSED | STERN | STEYEST | STIFFEN | STILTINGS |
| STENOSES | STERNAGE | STHENIC | STIFFENED | STILTISH |
| STENOSIS | STERNAGES | STIBBLE | STIFFENER | STILTS |
| STENOTIC | STERNAL | STIBBLER | STIFFENERS | STILTY |
| STENOTYPE | STERNEBRA | STIBBLERS | STIFFENING | STIME |
| STENOTYPES | STERNEBRAE | STIBBLES | STIFFENINGS | STIMED |
| STENOTYPIES | STERNED | STIBIAL | STIFFENS | STIMES |
| STENOTYPY | STERNER | STIBINE | STIFFER | STIMIE |
| STENS | STERNEST | STIBINES | STIFFEST | STIMIED |
| STENT | STERNING | STIBIUM | STIFFING | STIMIES |
| STENTED | STERNITE | STIBIUMS | STIFFISH | STIMING |
| STENTING | STERNITES | STIBNITE | STIFFLY | STIMULANT |
| STENTOR | STERNITIC | STIBNITES | STIFFNESS | STIMULANTS |
| STENTORS | STERNLY | STICCADO | STIFFNESSES | STIMULATE |
| STENTOUR | STERNMOST | STICCADOES | STIFFS | STIMULATED |
| STENTOURS | STERNNESS | STICCADOS | STIFLE | STIMULATES |
| STENTS | STERNNESSES | STICCATO | STIFLED | STIMULATING |
| STEP | STERNPORT | STICCATOES | STIFLER | STIMULI |
| STEPBAIRN | STERNPORTS | STICCATOS | STIFLERS | STIMULUS |
| STEPBAIRNS | STERNS | STICH | STIFLES | STIMY |
| STEPCHILD | STERNSON | STICHERON | STIFLING | STIMYING |
| STEPCHILDREN | STERNSONS | STICHERONS | STIFLINGS | STING |
| STEPDAME | STERNUM | STICHIC | STIGMA | STINGAREE |
| STEPDAMES | STERNUMS | STICHIDIA | STIGMAS | STINGAREES |
| STEPHANE | STERNWARD | STICHOI | STIGMATA | STINGED |
| STEPHANES | STERNWARDS | STICHOS | STIGMATIC | STINGER |
| STEPNEY | STERNWAY | STICHS | STIGMATICS | STINGERS |
| STEPNEYS | STERNWAYS | STICK | STIGME | STINGIER |
| STEPPE | STEROID | STICKED | STIGMES | STINGIEST |
| STEPPED | STEROIDS | STICKER | STILB | STINGILY |
| STEPPER | STEROL | STICKERS | STILBENE | STINGING |
| STEPPERS | STEROLS | STICKFUL | STILBENES | STINGINGS |
| STEPPES | STERVE | STICKFULS | STILBITE | STINGLESS |
| STEPPING | STERVED | STICKIED | STILBITES | STINGO |
| STEPS | STERVES | STICKIER | STILBS | STINGOS |
| STEPSON | STERVING | STICKIES | STILE | STINGS |
| STEPSONS | STET | STICKIEST | STILED | STINGY |
| STEPT | STETS | STICKILY | STILES | STINK |
| STEPWISE | STETTED | STICKING | STILET | STINKARD |
| STERADIAN | STETTING | STICKINGS | STILETS | STINKARDS |
| STERADIANS | STEVEDORE | STICKIT | STILETTO | STINKER |
| STERCORAL | STEVEDORED | STICKJAW | STILETTOED | STINKERS |
| STERCULIA | STEVEDORES | STICKJAWS | STILETTOING | STINKHORN |
| STERCULIAS | STEVEDORING | STICKLE | STILETTOS | STINKHORNS |
| STERE | STEVEN | STICKLED | STILING | STINKING |
| STEREO | STEVENS | STICKLER | STILL | STINKINGS |
| STEREOED | STEW | STICKLERS | STILLAGE | STINKS |
| STEREOING | STEWARD | STICKLES | STILLAGES | STINT |
| STEREOME | STEWARDRIES | STICKLING | STILLED | STINTED |
| STEREOMES | STEWARDRY | STICKS | STILLER | STINTEDLY |
| STEREOS | STEWARDS | STICKUP | STILLERS | STINTER |
| STERES | STEWARTRIES | STICKUPS | STILLEST | STINTERS |
| STERIC | STEWARTRY | STICKWORK | STILLIER | STINTIER |
| STERIGMA | STEWED | STICKWORKS | STILLIEST | STINTIEST |
| STERIGMATA | STEWER | STICKY | STILLING | STINTING |
| STERILE | STEWERS | STICKYING | STILLINGS | STINTINGS |
| STERILISE | STEWIER | STIDDIE | STILLION | STINTLESS |
| STERILISED | STEWIEST | STIDDIED | STILLIONS | STINTS |
| STERILISES | STEWING | STIDDIEING | STILLNESS | STINTY |
| STERILISING | STEWINGS | STIDDIES | STILLNESSES | STIPA |
| STERILITIES | STEWPAN | STIDDYING | STILLS | STIPAS |
| STERILITY | STEWPANS | STIE | STILLY | STIPE |
| STERILIZE | STEWPOND | STIED | STILT | STIPEL |
| STERILIZED | STEWPONDS | STIES | STILTED | STIPELS |
| STERILIZES | STEWPOT | STIEVE | STILTEDLY | STIPEND |

| | | | | |
|---|---|---|---|---|
| STIPENDS | STIVY | STOITED | STONESHOT | STOPE |
| STIPES | STOA | STOITER | STONESHOTS | STOPED |
| STIPITATE | STOAE | STOITERED | STONEWALL | STOPES |
| STIPITES | STOAI | STOITERING | STONEWALLED | STOPING |
| STIPPLE | STOAS | STOITERS | STONEWALLING | STOPINGS |
| STIPPLED | STOAT | STOITING | STONEWALLINGS | STOPLESS |
| STIPPLER | STOATS | STOITS | STONEWALLS | STOPPAGE |
| STIPPLERS | STOB | STOKE | STONEWARE | STOPPAGES |
| STIPPLES | STOBS | STOKED | STONEWARES | STOPPED |
| STIPPLING | STOCCADO | STOKEHOLD | STONEWORK | STOPPER |
| STIPPLINGS | STOCCADOS | STOKEHOLDS | STONEWORKS | STOPPERED |
| STIPULAR | STOCCATA | STOKER | STONEWORT | STOPPERING |
| STIPULARY | STOCCATAS | STOKERS | STONEWORTS | STOPPERS |
| STIPULATE | STOCK | STOKES | STONG | STOPPING |
| STIPULATED | STOCKADE | STOKING | STONIED | STOPPINGS |
| STIPULATES | STOCKADED | STOLA | STONIER | STOPPLE |
| STIPULATING | STOCKADES | STOLAS | STONIES | STOPPLED |
| STIPULE | STOCKADING | STOLE | STONIEST | STOPPLES |
| STIPULED | STOCKED | STOLED | STONILY | STOPPLING |
| STIPULES | STOCKFISH | STOLEN | STONINESS | STOPS |
| STIR | STOCKFISHES | STOLES | STONINESSES | STORABLE |
| STIRABOUT | STOCKIER | STOLID | STONING | STORAGE |
| STIRABOUTS | STOCKIEST | STOLIDER | STONINGS | STORAGES |
| STIRE | STOCKILY | STOLIDEST | STONK | STORAX |
| STIRED | STOCKINET | STOLIDITIES | STONKER | STORAXES |
| STIRES | STOCKINETS | STOLIDITY | STONKERED | STORE |
| STIRING | STOCKING | STOLIDLY | STONKERING | STORED |
| STIRK | STOCKINGS | STOLN | STONKERS | STOREMAN |
| STIRKS | STOCKISH | STOLON | STONKS | STOREMEN |
| STIRLESS | STOCKIST | STOLONS | STONN | STORER |
| STIRP | STOCKISTS | STOMA | STONNE | STOREROOM |
| STIRPES | STOCKLESS | STOMACH | STONNED | STOREROOMS |
| STIRPS | STOCKMAN | STOMACHAL | STONNES | STORERS |
| STIRRA | STOCKMEN | STOMACHED | STONNING | STORES |
| STIRRAH | STOCKPILE | STOMACHER | STONNS | STOREY |
| STIRRAHS | STOCKPILED | STOMACHERS | STONY | STOREYED |
| STIRRAS | STOCKPILES | STOMACHIC | STONYING | STOREYS |
| STIRRE | STOCKPILING | STOMACHICS | STOOD | STORGE |
| STIRRED | STOCKPILINGS | STOMACHING | STOODEN | STORGES |
| STIRRER | STOCKS | STOMACHS | STOOGE | STORIATED |
| STIRRERS | STOCKTAKE | STOMACHY | STOOGED | STORIED |
| STIRRES | STOCKTAKES | STOMATA | STOOGES | STORIES |
| STIRRING | STOCKWORK | STOMATAL | STOOGING | STORIETTE |
| STIRRINGS | STOCKWORKS | STOMATIC | STOOK | STORIETTES |
| STIRRUP | STOCKY | STOMODAEA | STOOKED | STORING |
| STIRRUPS | STOCKYARD | STOMODEA | STOOKER | STORK |
| STIRS | STOCKYARDS | STOMODEUM | STOOKERS | STORKS |
| STISHIE | STODGE | STOMODEUMS | STOOKING | STORM |
| STISHIES | STODGED | STOMP | STOOKS | STORMED |
| STITCH | STODGER | STOMPED | STOOL | STORMFUL |
| STITCHED | STODGERS | STOMPING | STOOLBALL | STORMIER |
| STITCHER | STODGES | STOMPS | STOOLBALLS | STORMIEST |
| STITCHERIES | STODGIER | STOND | STOOLED | STORMILY |
| STITCHERS | STODGIEST | STONDS | STOOLIE | STORMING |
| STITCHERY | STODGILY | STONE | STOOLIES | STORMINGS |
| STITCHES | STODGING | STONECHAT | STOOLING | STORMLESS |
| STITCHING | STODGY | STONECHATS | STOOLS | STORMS |
| STITCHINGS | STOEP | STONECROP | STOOP | STORMY |
| STITHIED | STOEPS | STONECROPS | STOOPE | STORNELLI |
| STITHIES | STOGEY | STONED | STOOPED | STORNELLO |
| STITHY | STOGEYS | STONEFISH | STOOPER | STORY |
| STITHYING | STOGIE | STONEFISHES | STOOPERS | STORYETTE |
| STIVE | STOGIES | STONEHAND | STOOPES | STORYETTES |
| STIVED | STOGY | STONEHANDS | STOOPING | STORYING |
| STIVER | STOIC | STONELESS | STOOPS | STORYINGS |
| STIVERS | STOICAL | STONEN | STOOR | STOT |
| STIVES | STOICALLY | STONER | STOORS | STOTINKA |
| STIVIER | STOICISM | STONERN | STOOSHIE | STOTINKI |
| STIVIEST | STOICISMS | STONERS | STOOSHIES | STOTIOUS |
| STIVING | STOIT | STONES | STOP | STOTS |

| | | | | |
|---|---|---|---|---|
| STOTTED | STOWNLINS | STRAK | STRATOSE | STREELING |
| STOTTER | STOWRE | STRAKE | STRATOUS | STREELS |
| STOTTERED | STOWRES | STRAKES | STRATUM | STREET |
| STOTTERING | STOWS | STRAMAÇON | STRATUS | STREETAGE |
| STOTTERS | STRABISM | STRAMAÇONS | STRATUSES | STREETAGES |
| STOTTING | STRABISMS | STRAMASH | STRAUCHT | STREETED |
| STOUN | STRACK | STRAMASHED | STRAUCHTED | STREETFUL |
| STOUND | STRAD | STRAMASHES | STRAUCHTER | STREETFULS |
| STOUNDED | STRADDLE | STRAMASHING | STRAUCHTEST | STREETIER |
| STOUNDING | STRADDLED | STRAMAZON | STRAUCHTING | STREETIEST |
| STOUNDS | STRADDLES | STRAMAZONS | STRAUCHTS | STREETS |
| STOUNING | STRADDLING | STRAMMEL | STRAUGHT | STREETWAY |
| STOUNS | STRADIOT | STRAMMELS | STRAUGHTED | STREETWAYS |
| STOUP | STRADIOTS | STRAMP | STRAUGHTER | STREETY |
| STOUPS | STRADS | STRAMPED | STRAUGHTEST | STREIGHT |
| STOUR | STRAE | STRAMPING | STRAUGHTING | STREIGNE |
| STOURIER | STRAES | STRAMPS | STRAUGHTS | STREIGNED |
| STOURIEST | STRAFE | STRAND | STRAUNGE | STREIGNES |
| STOURS | STRAFED | STRANDED | STRAVAIG | STREIGNING |
| STOURY | STRAFES | STRANDING | STRAVAIGED | STRELITZ |
| STOUSH | STRAFF | STRANDS | STRAVAIGING | STRELITZES |
| STOUSHED | STRAFFED | STRANGE | STRAVAIGS | STRELITZI |
| STOUSHES | STRAFFING | STRANGELY | STRAW | STRENE |
| STOUSHING | STRAFFS | STRANGER | STRAWED | STRENES |
| STOUT | STRAFING | STRANGERED | STRAWEN | STRENGTH |
| STOUTEN | STRAG | STRANGERING | STRAWIER | STRENGTHS |
| STOUTENED | STRAGGLE | STRANGERS | STRAWIEST | STRENUITIES |
| STOUTENING | STRAGGLED | STRANGEST | STRAWING | STRENUITY |
| STOUTENS | STRAGGLER | STRANGLE | STRAWLESS | STRENUOUS |
| STOUTER | STRAGGLERS | STRANGLED | STRAWN | STREP |
| STOUTEST | STRAGGLES | STRANGLER | STRAWS | STREPENT |
| STOUTH | STRAGGLIER | STRANGLERS | STRAWY | STREPS |
| STOUTHRIE | STRAGGLIEST | STRANGLES | STRAY | STRESS |
| STOUTHRIES | STRAGGLING | STRANGLING | STRAYED | STRESSED |
| STOUTHS | STRAGGLINGS | STRANGURIES | STRAYER | STRESSES |
| STOUTISH | STRAGGLY | STRANGURY | STRAYERS | STRESSFUL |
| STOUTLY | STRAGS | STRAP | STRAYING | STRESSING |
| STOUTNESS | STRAICHT | STRAPLESS | STRAYINGS | STRESSOR |
| STOUTNESSES | STRAICHTER | STRAPPADO | STRAYLING | STRESSORS |
| STOUTS | STRAICHTEST | STRAPPADOED | STRAYLINGS | STRETCH |
| STOVAINE | STRAIGHT | STRAPPADOING | STRAYS | STRETCHED |
| STOVAINES | STRAIGHTED | STRAPPADOS | STREAK | STRETCHER |
| STOVE | STRAIGHTER | STRAPPED | STREAKED | STRETCHERED |
| STOVED | STRAIGHTEST | STRAPPER | STREAKER | STRETCHERING |
| STOVEPIPE | STRAIGHTING | STRAPPERS | STREAKERS | STRETCHERS |
| STOVEPIPES | STRAIGHTS | STRAPPIER | STREAKIER | STRETCHES |
| STOVER | STRAIK | STRAPPIEST | STREAKIEST | STRETCHIER |
| STOVERS | STRAIKED | STRAPPING | STREAKILY | STRETCHIEST |
| STOVES | STRAIKING | STRAPPINGS | STREAKING | STRETCHING |
| STOVIES | STRAIKS | STRAPPY | STREAKINGS | STRETCHY |
| STOVING | STRAIN | STRAPS | STREAKS | STRETTA |
| STOVINGS | STRAINED | STRAPWORT | STREAKY | STRETTE |
| STOW | STRAINER | STRAPWORTS | STREAM | STRETTI |
| STOWAGE | STRAINERS | STRASS | STREAMED | STRETTO |
| STOWAGES | STRAINING | STRASSES | STREAMER | STREW |
| STOWAWAY | STRAININGS | STRATA | STREAMERS | STREWAGE |
| STOWAWAYS | STRAINS | STRATAGEM | STREAMIER | STREWAGES |
| STOWDOWN | STRAINT | STRATAGEMS | STREAMIEST | STREWED |
| STOWDOWNS | STRAINTS | STRATEGIC | STREAMING | STREWER |
| STOWED | STRAIT | STRATEGICS | STREAMINGS | STREWERS |
| STOWER | STRAITED | STRATEGIES | STREAMLET | STREWING |
| STOWERS | STRAITEN | STRATEGY | STREAMLETS | STREWINGS |
| STOWING | STRAITENED | STRATH | STREAMS | STREWMENT |
| STOWINGS | STRAITENING | STRATHS | STREAMY | STREWMENTS |
| STOWLINS | STRAITENS | STRATI | STREEK | STREWN |
| STOWN | STRAITER | STRATIFIED | STREEKED | STREWS |
| STOWND | STRAITEST | STRATIFIES | STREEKING | STREWTH |
| STOWNDED | STRAITING | STRATIFY | STREEKS | STRIA |
| STOWNDING | STRAITLY | STRATIFYING | STREEL | STRIAE |
| STOWNDS | STRAITS | STRATONIC | STREELED | STRIATA |

| | | | | |
|---|---|---|---|---|
| STRIATE | STRINGERS | STROLLED | STROYING | STUCCOER |
| STRIATED | STRINGIER | STROLLER | STROYS | STUCCOERS |
| STRIATES | STRINGIEST | STROLLERS | STRUCK | STUCCOING |
| STRIATING | STRINGILY | STROLLING | STRUCKEN | STUCCOS |
| STRIATION | STRINGING | STROLLINGS | STRUCTURE | STUCK |
| STRIATIONS | STRINGINGS | STROLLS | STRUCTURED | STUCKS |
| STRIATUM | STRINGS | STROMA | STRUCTURES | STUD |
| STRIATUMS | STRINGY | STROMATA | STRUCTURING | STUDDED |
| STRIATURE | STRINKLE | STROMATIC | STRUDEL | STUDDEN |
| STRIATURES | STRINKLED | STROMB | STRUDELS | STUDDING |
| STRICH | STRINKLES | STROMBS | STRUGGLE | STUDDINGS |
| STRICHES | STRINKLING | STROMBUS | STRUGGLED | STUDDLE |
| STRICKEN | STRINKLINGS | STROMBUSES | STRUGGLER | STUDDLES |
| STRICKLE | STRIP | STROND | STRUGGLERS | STUDENT |
| STRICKLED | STRIPE | STRONDS | STRUGGLES | STUDENTRIES |
| STRICKLES | STRIPED | STRONG | STRUGGLING | STUDENTRY |
| STRICKLING | STRIPES | STRONGARM | STRUGGLINGS | STUDENTS |
| STRICT | STRIPEY | STRONGARMED | STRUM | STUDIED |
| STRICTER | STRIPIER | STRONGARMING | STRUMA | STUDIEDLY |
| STRICTEST | STRIPIEST | STRONGARMS | STRUMAE | STUDIER |
| STRICTISH | STRIPING | STRONGER | STRUMATIC | STUDIERS |
| STRICTLY | STRIPINGS | STRONGEST | STRUMITIS | STUDIES |
| STRICTURE | STRIPLING | STRONGISH | STRUMITISES | STUDIO |
| STRICTURES | STRIPLINGS | STRONGLY | STRUMMED | STUDIOS |
| STRID | STRIPPED | STRONGMAN | STRUMMEL | STUDIOUS |
| STRIDDEN | STRIPPER | STRONGMEN | STRUMMELS | STUDS |
| STRIDDLE | STRIPPERS | STRONGYLE | STRUMMING | STUDWORK |
| STRIDDLED | STRIPPING | STRONGYLES | STRUMOSE | STUDWORKS |
| STRIDDLES | STRIPPINGS | STRONTIA | STRUMOUS | STUDY |
| STRIDDLING | STRIPS | STRONTIAN | STRUMPET | STUDYING |
| STRIDE | STRIPY | STRONTIANS | STRUMPETED | STUFF |
| STRIDENCE | STRIVE | STRONTIAS | STRUMPETING | STUFFED |
| STRIDENCES | STRIVED | STRONTIUM | STRUMPETS | STUFFER |
| STRIDENCIES | STRIVEN | STRONTIUMS | STRUMS | STUFFERS |
| STRIDENCY | STRIVER | STROOK | STRUNG | STUFFIER |
| STRIDENT | STRIVERS | STROOKE | STRUNT | STUFFIEST |
| STRIDES | STRIVES | STROOKEN | STRUNTED | STUFFILY |
| STRIDING | STRIVING | STROOKES | STRUNTING | STUFFING |
| STRIDLING | STRIVINGS | STROP | STRUNTS | STUFFINGS |
| STRIDOR | STROAM | STROPHE | STRUT | STUFFS |
| STRIDORS | STROAMED | STROPHES | STRUTS | STUFFY |
| STRIDS | STROAMING | STROPHIC | STRUTTED | STUGGIER |
| STRIFE | STROAMS | STROPPED | STRUTTER | STUGGIEST |
| STRIFEFUL | STROBE | STROPPIER | STRUTTERS | STUGGY |
| STRIFES | STROBES | STROPPIEST | STRUTTING | STULL |
| STRIFT | STROBIC | STROPPING | STRUTTINGS | STULLS |
| STRIFTS | STROBILA | STROPPY | STRYCHNIA | STULM |
| STRIG | STROBILAE | STROPS | STRYCHNIAS | STULMS |
| STRIGA | STROBILE | STROSSERS | STRYCHNIC | STULTIFIED |
| STRIGAE | STROBILES | STROUD | STRYFULL | STULTIFIES |
| STRIGATE | STROBILI | STROUDING | STUB | STULTIFY |
| STRIGGED | STROBILUS | STROUDINGS | STUBBED | STULTIFYING |
| STRIGGING | STRODDLE | STROUDS | STUBBIER | STUM |
| STRIGIL | STRODDLED | STROUP | STUBBIES | STUMBLE |
| STRIGILS | STRODDLES | STROUPS | STUBBIEST | STUMBLED |
| STRIGINE | STRODDLING | STROUT | STUBBING | STUMBLER |
| STRIGOSE | STRODE | STROUTED | STUBBLE | STUMBLERS |
| STRIGS | STRODLE | STROUTING | STUBBLED | STUMBLES |
| STRIKE | STRODLED | STROUTS | STUBBLES | STUMBLIER |
| STRIKEOUT | STRODLES | STROVE | STUBBLIER | STUMBLIEST |
| STRIKEOUTS | STRODLING | STROW | STUBBLIEST | STUMBLING |
| STRIKER | STROKE | STROWED | STUBBLY | STUMBLY |
| STRIKERS | STROKED | STROWER | STUBBORN | STUMER |
| STRIKES | STROKEN | STROWERS | STUBBORNED | STUMERS |
| STRIKING | STROKER | STROWING | STUBBORNING | STUMM |
| STRIKINGS | STROKERS | STROWINGS | STUBBORNS | STUMMED |
| STRING | STROKES | STROWN | STUBBY | STUMMEL |
| STRINGED | STROKING | STROWS | STUBS | STUMMELS |
| STRINGENT | STROKINGS | STROY | STUCCO | STUMMING |
| STRINGER | STROLL | STROYED | STUCCOED | STUMP |

STUMPAGE
STUMPAGES
STUMPED
STUMPER
STUMPERS
STUMPIER
STUMPIES
STUMPIEST
STUMPILY
STUMPING
STUMPS
STUMPY
STUMS
STUN
STUNG
STUNK
STUNKARD
STUNNED
STUNNER
STUNNERS
STUNNING
STUNNINGS
STUNS
STUNSAIL
STUNSAILS
STUNT
STUNTED
STUNTING
STUNTMAN
STUNTMEN
STUNTS
STUPA
STUPAS
STUPE
STUPED
STUPEFIED
STUPEFIER
STUPEFIERS
STUPEFIES
STUPEFY
STUPEFYING
STUPENT
STUPES
STUPID
STUPIDER
STUPIDEST
STUPIDITIES
STUPIDITY
STUPIDLY
STUPIDS
STUPING
STUPOR
STUPOROUS
STUPORS
STUPRATE
STUPRATED
STUPRATES
STUPRATING
STURDIED
STURDIER
STURDIES
STURDIEST
STURDILY
STURDY
STURE
STURGEON
STURGEONS
STURMER
STURMERS
STURNINE

STURNOID
STURT
STURTED
STURTING
STURTS
STUSHIE
STUSHIES
STUTTER
STUTTERED
STUTTERER
STUTTERERS
STUTTERING
STUTTERINGS
STUTTERS
STY
STYE
STYED
STYES
STYING
STYLAR
STYLATE
STYLE
STYLED
STYLELESS
STYLES
STYLET
STYLETS
STYLI
STYLIFORM
STYLING
STYLISE
STYLISED
STYLISES
STYLISH
STYLISHLY
STYLISING
STYLIST
STYLISTIC
STYLISTICS
STYLISTS
STYLITE
STYLITES
STYLIZE
STYLIZED
STYLIZES
STYLIZING
STYLO
STYLOBATE
STYLOBATES
STYLOID
STYLOIDS
STYLOS
STYLUS
STYLUSES
STYME
STYMED
STYMES
STYMIE
STYMIED
STYMIEING
STYMIES
STYMING
STYMYING
STYPSIS
STYPSISES
STYPTIC
STYPTICAL
STYPTICS
STYRAX
STYRAXES

STYRE
STYRED
STYRENE
STYRENES
STYRES
STYRING
SUABILITIES
SUABILITY
SUABLE
SUASIBLE
SUASION
SUASIONS
SUASIVE
SUASIVELY
SUASORY
SUAVE
SUAVELY
SUAVER
SUAVEST
SUAVITIES
SUAVITY
SUB
SUBACID
SUBACRID
SUBACT
SUBACTED
SUBACTING
SUBACTION
SUBACTIONS
SUBACTS
SUBACUTE
SUBADAR
SUBADARS
SUBADULT
SUBADULTS
SUBAERIAL
SUBAGENCIES
SUBAGENCY
SUBAGENT
SUBAGENTS
SUBAH
SUBAHDAR
SUBAHDARIES
SUBAHDARS
SUBAHDARY
SUBAHS
SUBAHSHIP
SUBAHSHIPS
SUBALPINE
SUBALTERN
SUBALTERNS
SUBAQUA
SUBARCTIC
SUBARID
SUBASTRAL
SUBATOM
SUBATOMIC
SUBATOMICS
SUBATOMS
SUBBASAL
SUBBASALS
SUBBED
SUBBING
SUBBINGS
SUBBRANCH
SUBBRANCHES
SUBBREED
SUBBREEDS
SUBCANTOR
SUBCANTORS

SUBCAUDAL
SUBCLASS
SUBCLASSES
SUBCLAUSE
SUBCLAUSES
SUBCOSTA
SUBCOSTAE
SUBCOSTAL
SUBCOSTALS
SUBDEACON
SUBDEACONS
SUBDEAN
SUBDEANS
SUBDEW
SUBDEWED
SUBDEWING
SUBDEWS
SUBDIVIDE
SUBDIVIDED
SUBDIVIDES
SUBDIVIDING
SUBDOLOUS
SUBDUABLE
SUBDUAL
SUBDUALS
SUBDUCE
SUBDUCED
SUBDUCES
SUBDUCING
SUBDUCT
SUBDUCTED
SUBDUCTING
SUBDUCTS
SUBDUE
SUBDUED
SUBDUEDLY
SUBDUER
SUBDUERS
SUBDUES
SUBDUING
SUBDUPLE
SUBEDAR
SUBEDARS
SUBEDIT
SUBEDITED
SUBEDITING
SUBEDITOR
SUBEDITORS
SUBEDITS
SUBENTIRE
SUBEQUAL
SUBER
SUBERATE
SUBERATES
SUBERECT
SUBEREOUS
SUBERIC
SUBERIN
SUBERINS
SUBERISE
SUBERISED
SUBERISES
SUBERISING
SUBERIZE
SUBERIZED
SUBERIZES
SUBERIZING
SUBEROSE
SUBEROUS
SUBERS

SUBFAMILIES
SUBFAMILY
SUBFEU
SUBFEUED
SUBFEUING
SUBFEUS
SUBFLOOR
SUBFLOORS
SUBFUSC
SUBFUSCS
SUBFUSK
SUBFUSKS
SUBGENERA
SUBGENUS
SUBGENUSES
SUBGRADE
SUBGRADES
SUBGROUP
SUBGROUPS
SUBHUMAN
SUBIMAGINES
SUBIMAGO
SUBIMAGOS
SUBINCISE
SUBINCISED
SUBINCISES
SUBINCISING
SUBITO
SUBJACENT
SUBJECT
SUBJECTED
SUBJECTING
SUBJECTS
SUBJOIN
SUBJOINED
SUBJOINING
SUBJOINS
SUBJUGATE
SUBJUGATED
SUBJUGATES
SUBJUGATING
SUBLATE
SUBLATED
SUBLATES
SUBLATING
SUBLATION
SUBLATIONS
SUBLEASE
SUBLEASED
SUBLEASES
SUBLEASING
SUBLESSEE
SUBLESSEES
SUBLESSOR
SUBLESSORS
SUBLET
SUBLETHAL
SUBLETS
SUBLETTER
SUBLETTERS
SUBLETTING
SUBLETTINGS
SUBLIMATE
SUBLIMATED
SUBLIMATES
SUBLIMATING
SUBLIME
SUBLIMED
SUBLIMELY
SUBLIMER

| | | | | |
|---|---|---|---|---|
| SUBLIMES | SUBOXIDE | SUBSTAGE | SUBTLETY | SUCCEEDERS |
| SUBLIMEST | SUBOXIDES | SUBSTAGES | SUBTLIST | SUCCEEDING |
| SUBLIMING | SUBPHYLA | SUBSTANCE | SUBTLISTS | SUCCEEDS |
| SUBLIMINGS | SUBPHYLUM | SUBSTANCES | SUBTLY | SUCCENTOR |
| SUBLIMISE | SUBPLOT | SUBSTRACT | SUBTONIC | SUCCENTORS |
| SUBLIMISED | SUBPLOTS | SUBSTRACTED | SUBTONICS | SUCCÈS |
| SUBLIMISES | SUBPOENA | SUBSTRACTING | SUBTOPIA | SUCCESS |
| SUBLIMISING | SUBPOENAED | SUBSTRACTS | SUBTOPIAN | SUCCESSES |
| SUBLIMITIES | SUBPOENAING | SUBSTRATA | SUBTOPIAS | SUCCESSOR |
| SUBLIMITY | SUBPOENAS | SUBSTRATE | SUBTOTAL | SUCCESSORS |
| SUBLIMIZE | SUBPRIOR | SUBSTRATES | SUBTOTALLED | SUCCI |
| SUBLIMIZED | SUBPRIORS | SUBSTRUCT | SUBTOTALLING | SUCCINATE |
| SUBLIMIZES | SUBREGION | SUBSTRUCTED | SUBTOTALS | SUCCINATES |
| SUBLIMIZING | SUBREGIONS | SUBSTRUCTING | SUBTRACT | SUCCINCT |
| SUBLINEAR | SUBROGATE | SUBSTRUCTS | SUBTRACTED | SUCCINCTER |
| SUBLUNAR | SUBROGATED | SUBSTYLAR | SUBTRACTING | SUCCINCTEST |
| SUBLUNARIES | SUBROGATES | SUBSTYLE | SUBTRACTS | SUCCINIC |
| SUBLUNARS | SUBROGATING | SUBSTYLES | SUBTRIBE | SUCCINITE |
| SUBLUNARY | SUBS | SUBSULTUS | SUBTRIBES | SUCCINITES |
| SUBLUNATE | SUBSACRAL | SUBSULTUSES | SUBTRIST | SUCCINUM |
| SUBMAN | SUBSCRIBE | SUBSUME | SUBTROPIC | SUCCINUMS |
| SUBMARINE | SUBSCRIBED | SUBSUMED | SUBTROPICS | SUCCOR |
| SUBMARINED | SUBSCRIBES | SUBSUMES | SUBTRUDE | SUCCORED |
| SUBMARINES | SUBSCRIBING | SUBSUMING | SUBTRUDED | SUCCORIES |
| SUBMARINING | SUBSCRIBINGS | SUBSYSTEM | SUBTRUDES | SUCCORING |
| SUBMEN | SUBSCRIPT | SUBSYSTEMS | SUBTRUDING | SUCCORS |
| SUBMENTAL | SUBSCRIPTS | SUBTACK | SUBTYPE | SUCCORY |
| SUBMENTUM | SUBSEA | SUBTACKS | SUBTYPES | SUCCOSE |
| SUBMENTUMS | SUBSECIVE | SUBTEEN | SUBUCULA | SUCCOTASH |
| SUBMERGE | SUBSELLIA | SUBTEENS | SUBUCULAS | SUCCOTASHES |
| SUBMERGED | SUBSERE | SUBTENANT | SUBULATE | SUCCOUR |
| SUBMERGES | SUBSERES | SUBTENANTS | SUBUNGUAL | SUCCOURED |
| SUBMERGING | SUBSERIES | SUBTEND | SUBUNIT | SUCCOURER |
| SUBMERSE | SUBSERVE | SUBTENDED | SUBUNITS | SUCCOURERS |
| SUBMERSED | SUBSERVED | SUBTENDING | SUBURB | SUCCOURING |
| SUBMERSES | SUBSERVES | SUBTENDS | SUBURBAN | SUCCOURS |
| SUBMERSING | SUBSERVING | SUBTENSE | SUBURBANS | SUCCOUS |
| SUBMICRON | SUBSET | SUBTENSES | SUBURBIA | SUCCUBA |
| SUBMICRONS | SUBSETS | SUBTEXT | SUBURBIAS | SUCCUBAE |
| SUBMISS | SUBSHRUB | SUBTEXTS | SUBURBS | SUCCUBAS |
| SUBMISSLY | SUBSHRUBS | SUBTIL | SUBURSINE | SUCCUBI |
| SUBMIT | SUBSIDE | SUBTILE | SUBVASSAL | SUCCUBINE |
| SUBMITS | SUBSIDED | SUBTILELY | SUBVASSALS | SUCCUBOUS |
| SUBMITTED | SUBSIDES | SUBTILER | SUBVERSAL | SUCCUBUS |
| SUBMITTER | SUBSIDIES | SUBTILEST | SUBVERSALS | SUCCUBUSES |
| SUBMITTERS | SUBSIDING | SUBTILETY | SUBVERSE | SUCCULENT |
| SUBMITTING | SUBSIDISE | SUBTILISE | SUBVERSED | SUCCULENTS |
| SUBMITTINGS | SUBSIDISED | SUBTILISED | SUBVERSES | SUCCUMB |
| SUBMUCOSA | SUBSIDISES | SUBTILISES | SUBVERSING | SUCCUMBED |
| SUBMUCOSAE | SUBSIDISING | SUBTILISING | SUBVERST | SUCCUMBING |
| SUBMUCOUS | SUBSIDIZE | SUBTILIST | SUBVERT | SUCCUMBS |
| SUBNEURAL | SUBSIDIZED | SUBTILISTS | SUBVERTED | SUCCURSAL |
| SUBNIVEAL | SUBSIDIZES | SUBTILITIES | SUBVERTER | SUCCURSALS |
| SUBNIVEAN | SUBSIDIZING | SUBTILITY | SUBVERTERS | SUCCUS |
| SUBNORMAL | SUBSIDY | SUBTILIZE | SUBVERTING | SUCCUSS |
| SUBNORMALS | SUBSIST | SUBTILIZED | SUBVERTS | SUCCUSSED |
| SUBOCTAVE | SUBSISTED | SUBTILIZES | SUBVIRAL | SUCCUSSES |
| SUBOCTAVES | SUBSISTING | SUBTILIZING | SUBWARDEN | SUCCUSSING |
| SUBOCULAR | SUBSISTS | SUBTILLY | SUBWARDENS | SUCH |
| SUBOFFICE | SUBSIZAR | SUBTILTIES | SUBWAY | SUCHLIKE |
| SUBOFFICES | SUBSIZARS | SUBTILTY | SUBWAYS | SUCHNESS |
| SUBORDER | SUBSOIL | SUBTITLE | SUBZERO | SUCHNESSES |
| SUBORDERS | SUBSOILED | SUBTITLED | SUBZONAL | SUCHWISE |
| SUBORN | SUBSOILER | SUBTITLES | SUBZONE | SUCK |
| SUBORNED | SUBSOILERS | SUBTITLING | SUBZONES | SUCKED |
| SUBORNER | SUBSOILING | SUBTLE | SUCCADE | SUCKEN |
| SUBORNERS | SUBSOILINGS | SUBTLER | SUCCADES | SUCKENER |
| SUBORNING | SUBSOILS | SUBTLEST | SUCCEED | SUCKENERS |
| SUBORNS | SUBSOLAR | SUBTLETIES | SUCCEEDED | SUCKENS |
| SUBOVATE | SUBSONIC | | SUCCEEDER | SUCKER |

SUCKERED
SUCKERING
SUCKERS
SUCKET
SUCKETS
SUCKING
SUCKINGS
SUCKLE
SUCKLED
SUCKLER
SUCKLERS
SUCKLES
SUCKLING
SUCKLINGS
SUCKS
SUCRASE
SUCRASES
SUCRE
SUCRES
SUCRIER
SUCRIERS
SUCROSE
SUCROSES
SUCTION
SUCTIONS
SUCTORIAL
SUCTORIAN
SUCTORIANS
SUCURUJÚ
SUCURUJÚS
SUD
SUDAMEN
SUDAMINA
SUDAMINAL
SUDANIC
SUDARIES
SUDARIUM
SUDARIUMS
SUDARY
SUDATE
SUDATED
SUDATES
SUDATING
SUDATION
SUDATIONS
SUDATORIES
SUDATORY
SUDD
SUDDEN
SUDDENLY
SUDDENTIES
SUDDENTY
SUDDER
SUDDERS
SUDDS
SUDOR
SUDORAL
SUDORIFIC
SUDORIFICS
SUDOROUS
SUDORS
SUDS
SUDSER
SUDSERS
SUDSIER
SUDSIEST
SUDSY
SUE
SUEABLE
SUED

SUEDE
SUÈDE
SUEDED
SUÈDED
SUEDES
SUÈDES
SUEDETTE
SUEDETTES
SUEDING
SUÈDING
SUER
SUERS
SUES
SUET
SUETIER
SUETIEST
SUETS
SUETTY
SUETY
SUFFER
SUFFERED
SUFFERER
SUFFERERS
SUFFERING
SUFFERINGS
SUFFERS
SUFFETE
SUFFETES
SUFFICE
SUFFICED
SUFFICER
SUFFICERS
SUFFICES
SUFFICING
SUFFIX
SUFFIXAL
SUFFIXED
SUFFIXES
SUFFIXING
SUFFLATE
SUFFLATED
SUFFLATES
SUFFLATING
SUFFOCATE
SUFFOCATED
SUFFOCATES
SUFFOCATING
SUFFOCATINGS
SUFFRAGAN
SUFFRAGANS
SUFFRAGE
SUFFRAGES
SUFFUSE
SUFFUSED
SUFFUSES
SUFFUSING
SUFFUSION
SUFFUSIONS
SUGAR
SUGARED
SUGARIER
SUGARIEST
SUGARING
SUGARINGS
SUGARLESS
SUGARS
SUGARY
SUGGEST
SUGGESTED
SUGGESTER

SUGGESTERS
SUGGESTING
SUGGESTS
SUI
SUICIDAL
SUICIDE
SUICIDES
SUIDIAN
SUILLINE
SUING
SUINGS
SUINT
SUINTS
SUIT
SUITABLE
SUITABLY
SUITE
SUITED
SUITES
SUITING
SUITINGS
SUITOR
SUITORED
SUITORING
SUITORS
SUITRESS
SUITRESSES
SUITS
SUIVEZ
SUJEE
SUJEES
SUK
SUKH
SUKHS
SUKIYAKI
SUKIYAKIS
SUKS
SULCAL
SULCALISE
SULCALISED
SULCALISES
SULCALISING
SULCALIZE
SULCALIZED
SULCALIZES
SULCALIZING
SULCATE
SULCATED
SULCATION
SULCATIONS
SULCI
SULCUS
SULFA
SULFATE
SULFATED
SULFATES
SULFATING
SULFUR
SULFURED
SULFURING
SULFURS
SULK
SULKED
SULKIER
SULKIES
SULKIEST
SULKILY
SULKINESS
SULKINESSES
SULKING

SULKS
SULKY
SULLAGE
SULLAGES
SULLEN
SULLENER
SULLENEST
SULLENLY
SULLENS
SULLIED
SULLIES
SULLY
SULLYING
SULPHA
SULPHATE
SULPHATED
SULPHATES
SULPHATIC
SULPHATING
SULPHIDE
SULPHIDES
SULPHITE
SULPHITES
SULPHONE
SULPHONES
SULPHONIC
SULPHUR
SULPHURED
SULPHURET
SULPHURETS
SULPHURIC
SULPHURING
SULPHURS
SULPHURY
SULTAN
SULTANA
SULTANAS
SULTANATE
SULTANATES
SULTANESS
SULTANESSES
SULTANIC
SULTANS
SULTRIER
SULTRIEST
SULTRILY
SULTRY
SUM
SUMAC
SUMACH
SUMACHS
SUMACS
SUMATRA
SUMATRAS
SUMLESS
SUMMA
SUMMAE
SUMMAND
SUMMANDS
SUMMAR
SUMMARIES
SUMMARILY
SUMMARISE
SUMMARISED
SUMMARISES
SUMMARISING
SUMMARIST
SUMMARISTS
SUMMARIZE
SUMMARIZED

SUMMARIZES
SUMMARIZING
SUMMARY
SUMMAT
SUMMATE
SUMMATED
SUMMATES
SUMMATING
SUMMATION
SUMMATIONS
SUMMATIVE
SUMMATS
SUMMED
SUMMER
SUMMERED
SUMMERIER
SUMMERIEST
SUMMERING
SUMMERINGS
SUMMERLY
SUMMERS
SUMMERSET
SUMMERSETS
SUMMERSETTED
SUMMERSETTING
SUMMERY
SUMMING
SUMMINGS
SUMMIST
SUMMISTS
SUMMIT
SUMMITEER
SUMMITEERS
SUMMITRIES
SUMMITRY
SUMMITS
SUMMON
SUMMONED
SUMMONER
SUMMONERS
SUMMONING
SUMMONS
SUMMONSED
SUMMONSES
SUMMONSING
SUMO
SUMOS
SUMOTORI
SUMOTORIS
SUMP
SUMPH
SUMPHISH
SUMPHS
SUMPIT
SUMPITAN
SUMPITANS
SUMPITS
SUMPS
SUMPSIMUS
SUMPSIMUSES
SUMPTER
SUMPTERS
SUMPTUARY
SUMPTUOUS
SUMS
SUN
SUNBATH
SUNBATHE
SUNBATHED
SUNBATHER

| | | | | |
|---|---|---|---|---|
| SUNBATHERS | SUNN | SUPERFINE | SUPPING | SURAS |
| SUNBATHES | SUNNED | SUPERFLUX | SUPPLANT | SURAT |
| SUNBATHING | SUNNIER | SUPERFLUXES | SUPPLANTED | SURATS |
| SUNBATHINGS | SUNNIEST | SUPERFUSE | SUPPLANTING | SURBAHAR |
| SUNBATHS | SUNNILY | SUPERFUSED | SUPPLANTS | SURBAHARS |
| SUNBEAM | SUNNINESS | SUPERFUSES | SUPPLE | SURBASE |
| SUNBEAMED | SUNNINESSES | SUPERFUSING | SUPPLED | SURBASED |
| SUNBEAMS | SUNNING | SUPERGLUE | SUPPLER | SURBASES |
| SUNBEAMY | SUNNS | SUPERGLUES | SUPPLES | SURBATE |
| SUNBED | SUNNY | SUPERHEAT | SUPPLEST | SURBATED |
| SUNBEDS | SUNPROOF | SUPERHEATED | SUPPLIAL | SURBATES |
| SUNBELT | SUNRAY | SUPERHEATING | SUPPLIALS | SURBATING |
| SUNBELTS | SUNRAYS | SUPERHEATS | SUPPLIANT | SURBED |
| SUNBLOCK | SUNRISE | SUPERHET | SUPPLIANTS | SURBEDDED |
| SUNBLOCKS | SUNRISES | SUPERHIVE | SUPPLICAT | SURBEDDING |
| SUNBOW | SUNRISING | SUPERHIVES | SUPPLICATS | SURBEDS |
| SUNBOWS | SUNRISINGS | SUPERING | SUPPLIED | SURBET |
| SUNBRIGHT | SUNS | SUPERIOR | SUPPLIER | SURCEASE |
| SUNBURN | SUNSCREEN | SUPERIORS | SUPPLIERS | SURCEASED |
| SUNBURNED | SUNSCREENS | SUPERMAN | SUPPLIES | SURCEASES |
| SUNBURNING | SUNSET | SUPERMART | SUPPLING | SURCEASING |
| SUNBURNS | SUNSETS | SUPERMARTS | SUPPLY | SURCHARGE |
| SUNBURNT | SUNSHINE | SUPERMEN | SUPPLYING | SURCHARGED |
| SUNBURST | SUNSHINES | SUPERNAL | SUPPORT | SURCHARGES |
| SUNBURSTS | SUNSHINY | SUPERNOVA | SUPPORTED | SURCHARGING |
| SUNDAE | SUNSPOT | SUPERNOVAE | SUPPORTER | SURCINGLE |
| SUNDAES | SUNSPOTS | SUPERNOVAS | SUPPORTERS | SURCINGLED |
| SUNDARI | SUNSTONE | SUPERPLUS | SUPPORTING | SURCINGLES |
| SUNDARIS | SUNSTONES | SUPERPLUSES | SUPPORTINGS | SURCINGLING |
| SUNDER | SUNSTROKE | SUPERPOSE | SUPPORTS | SURCOAT |
| SUNDERED | SUNSTROKES | SUPERPOSED | SUPPOSAL | SURCOATS |
| SUNDERER | SUNSTRUCK | SUPERPOSES | SUPPOSALS | SURCULI |
| SUNDERERS | SUNSUIT | SUPERPOSING | SUPPOSE | SURCULOSE |
| SUNDERING | SUNSUITS | SUPERS | SUPPOSED | SURCULUS |
| SUNDERINGS | SUNTAN | SUPERSALT | SUPPOSER | SURCULUSES |
| SUNDERS | SUNTANNED | SUPERSALTS | SUPPOSERS | SURD |
| SUNDIAL | SUNTANS | SUPERSEDE | SUPPOSES | SURDITIES |
| SUNDIALS | SUNTRAP | SUPERSEDED | SUPPOSING | SURDITY |
| SUNDOWN | SUNTRAPS | SUPERSEDES | SUPPOSINGS | SURDS |
| SUNDOWNS | SUNWARD | SUPERSEDING | SUPPRESS | SURE |
| SUNDRA | SUNWARDS | SUPERSTAR | SUPPRESSED | SURED |
| SUNDRAS | SUNWISE | SUPERSTARS | SUPPRESSES | SURELY |
| SUNDRI | SUP | SUPERTAX | SUPPRESSING | SURENESS |
| SUNDRIES | SUPAWN | SUPERTAXES | SUPPURATE | SURENESSES |
| SUNDRIS | SUPAWNS | SUPERVENE | SUPPURATED | SURER |
| SUNDRY | SUPER | SUPERVENED | SUPPURATES | SURES |
| SUNFAST | SUPERABLE | SUPERVENES | SUPPURATING | SUREST |
| SUNFLOWER | SUPERABLY | SUPERVENING | SUPREMACIES | SURETIED |
| SUNFLOWERS | SUPERADD | SUPERVISE | SUPREMACY | SURETIES |
| SUNG | SUPERADDED | SUPERVISED | SUPRÊME | SURETY |
| SUNGAR | SUPERADDING | SUPERVISES | SUPREME | SURETYING |
| SUNGARS | SUPERADDS | SUPERVISING | SUPREMELY | SURF |
| SUNGLASS | SUPERATE | SUPINATE | SUPREMER | SURFACE |
| SUNGLASSES | SUPERATED | SUPINATED | SUPREMES | SURFACED |
| SUNGLOW | SUPERATES | SUPINATES | SUPRÊMES | SURFACER |
| SUNGLOWS | SUPERATING | SUPINATING | SUPREMEST | SURFACERS |
| SUNHAT | SUPERB | SUPINATOR | SUPREMITIES | SURFACES |
| SUNHATS | SUPERBER | SUPINATORS | SUPREMITY | SURFACING |
| SUNK | SUPERBEST | SUPINE | SUPREMO | SURFACINGS |
| SUNKEN | SUPERBITIES | SUPINELY | SUPREMOS | SURFBOARD |
| SUNKET | SUPERBITY | SUPINES | SUPS | SURFBOARDS |
| SUNKETS | SUPERBLY | SUPPAWN | SUQ | SURFED |
| SUNKIE | SUPERCOLD | SUPPAWNS | SUQS | SURFEIT |
| SUNKIES | SUPERCOOL | SUPPEAGO | SUR | SURFEITED |
| SUNKS | SUPERCOOLED | SUPPEAGOES | SURA | SURFEITER |
| SUNLESS | SUPERCOOLING | SUPPED | SURAH | SURFEITERS |
| SUNLIGHT | SUPERCOOLS | SUPPER | SURAHS | SURFEITING |
| SUNLIGHTS | SUPERED | SUPPERED | SURAL | SURFEITINGS |
| SUNLIKE | SUPERETTE | SUPPERING | SURANCE | SURFEITS |
| SUNLIT | SUPERETTES | SUPPERS | SURANCES | SURFER |

SURFERS
SURFICIAL
SURFIER
SURFIEST
SURFING
SURFINGS
SURFMAN
SURFMEN
SURFS
SURFY
SURGE
SURGED
SURGEFUL
SURGELESS
SURGENT
SURGEON
SURGEONCIES
SURGEONCY
SURGEONS
SURGERIES
SURGERY
SURGES
SURGICAL
SURGIER
SURGIEST
SURGING
SURGINGS
SURGY
SURICATE
SURICATES
SURING
SURLIER
SURLIEST
SURLILY
SURLINESS
SURLINESSES
SURLOIN
SURLOINS
SURLY
SURMASTER
SURMASTERS
SURMISAL
SURMISALS
SURMISE
SURMISED
SURMISER
SURMISERS
SURMISES
SURMISING
SURMISINGS
SURMOUNT
SURMOUNTED
SURMOUNTING
SURMOUNTINGS
SURMOUNTS
SURMULLET
SURMULLETS
SURNAME
SURNAMED
SURNAMES
SURNAMING
SURPASS
SURPASSED
SURPASSES
SURPASSING
SURPLICE
SURPLICED
SURPLICES
SURPLUS
SURPLUSES

SURPRISAL
SURPRISALS
SURPRISE
SURPRISED
SURPRISER
SURPRISERS
SURPRISES
SURPRISING
SURPRISINGS
SURQUEDIES
SURQUEDRIES
SURQUEDRY
SURQUEDY
SURRA
SURRAS
SURREAL
SURREBUT
SURREBUTS
SURREBUTTED
SURREBUTTING
SURREINED
SURREJOIN
SURREJOINED
SURREJOINING
SURREJOINS
SURRENDER
SURRENDERED
SURRENDERING
SURRENDERS
SURRENDRIES
SURRENDRY
SURREY
SURREYS
SURROGACIES
SURROGACY
SURROGATE
SURROGATES
SURROUND
SURROUNDED
SURROUNDING
SURROUNDINGS
SURROUNDS
SURROYAL
SURROYALS
SURTAX
SURTAXED
SURTAXES
SURTAXING
SURTITLE
SURTITLES
SURTOUT
SURTOUTS
SURUCUCU
SURUCUCUS
SURVEILLE
SURVEILLED
SURVEILLES
SURVEILLING
SURVEW
SURVEWE
SURVEWED
SURVEWES
SURVEWING
SURVEWS
SURVEY
SURVEYAL
SURVEYALS
SURVEYED
SURVEYING
SURVEYINGS

SURVEYOR
SURVEYORS
SURVEYS
SURVIEW
SURVIEWED
SURVIEWING
SURVIEWS
SURVIVAL
SURVIVALS
SURVIVE
SURVIVED
SURVIVES
SURVIVING
SURVIVOR
SURVIVORS
SUS
SUSCEPTOR
SUSCEPTORS
SUSCITATE
SUSCITATED
SUSCITATES
SUSCITATING
SUSES
SUSHI
SUSHIS
SUSLIK
SUSLIKS
SUSPECT
SUSPECTED
SUSPECTING
SUSPECTS
SUSPENCE
SUSPEND
SUSPENDED
SUSPENDER
SUSPENDERS
SUSPENDING
SUSPENDS
SUSPENS
SUSPENSE
SUSPENSES
SUSPENSOR
SUSPENSORS
SUSPICION
SUSPICIONED
SUSPICIONING
SUSPICIONS
SUSPIRE
SUSPIRED
SUSPIRES
SUSPIRING
SUSS
SUSSARARA
SUSSARARAS
SUSSED
SUSSES
SUSSING
SUSTAIN
SUSTAINED
SUSTAINER
SUSTAINERS
SUSTAINING
SUSTAININGS
SUSTAINS
SUSTINENT
SUSURRANT
SUSURRATE
SUSURRATED
SUSURRATES
SUSURRATING

SUSURRUS
SUSURRUSES
SUTILE
SUTLER
SUTLERIES
SUTLERS
SUTLERY
SUTOR
SUTORIAL
SUTORIAN
SUTORS
SUTRA
SUTRAS
SUTTEE
SUTTEEISM
SUTTEEISMS
SUTTEES
SUTTLE
SUTTLED
SUTTLES
SUTTLETIE
SUTTLETIES
SUTTLING
SUTTLY
SUTURAL
SUTURALLY
SUTURE
SUTURED
SUTURES
SUTURING
SUVERSED
SUZERAIN
SUZERAINS
SVASTIKA
SVASTIKAS
SVELTE
SVELTER
SVELTEST
SWAB
SWABBED
SWABBER
SWABBERS
SWABBING
SWABS
SWACK
SWAD
SWADDIES
SWADDLE
SWADDLED
SWADDLER
SWADDLERS
SWADDLES
SWADDLING
SWADDY
SWADS
SWAG
SWAGE
SWAGED
SWAGES
SWAGGED
SWAGGER
SWAGGERED
SWAGGERER
SWAGGERERS
SWAGGERING
SWAGGERINGS
SWAGGERS
SWAGGIE
SWAGGIES
SWAGGING

SWAGING
SWAGMAN
SWAGMEN
SWAGS
SWAGSHOP
SWAGSHOPS
SWAGSMAN
SWAGSMEN
SWAIN
SWAINING
SWAININGS
SWAINISH
SWAINS
SWALE
SWALED
SWALES
SWALIER
SWALIEST
SWALING
SWALINGS
SWALLET
SWALLETS
SWALLOW
SWALLOWED
SWALLOWER
SWALLOWERS
SWALLOWING
SWALLOWS
SWALY
SWAM
SWAMI
SWAMIS
SWAMP
SWAMPED
SWAMPER
SWAMPERS
SWAMPIER
SWAMPIEST
SWAMPING
SWAMPLAND
SWAMPLANDS
SWAMPS
SWAMPY
SWAN
SWANG
SWANHERD
SWANHERDS
SWANK
SWANKED
SWANKER
SWANKERS
SWANKEST
SWANKEY
SWANKEYS
SWANKIER
SWANKIES
SWANKIEST
SWANKING
SWANKPOT
SWANKPOTS
SWANKS
SWANKY
SWANLIKE
SWANNERIES
SWANNERY
SWANNIER
SWANNIEST
SWANNY
SWANS
SWANSDOWN

SWANSDOWNS
SWAP
SWAPPED
SWAPPER
SWAPPERS
SWAPPING
SWAPPINGS
SWAPS
SWAPT
SWARAJ
SWARAJES
SWARAJISM
SWARAJISMS
SWARAJIST
SWARAJISTS
SWARD
SWARDED
SWARDIER
SWARDIEST
SWARDING
SWARDS
SWARDY
SWARE
SWARF
SWARFED
SWARFING
SWARFS
SWARM
SWARMED
SWARMER
SWARMERS
SWARMING
SWARMINGS
SWARMS
SWART
SWARTH
SWARTHIER
SWARTHIEST
SWARTHS
SWARTHY
SWARTIER
SWARTIEST
SWARTNESS
SWARTNESSES
SWARTY
SWARVE
SWARVED
SWARVES
SWARVING
SWASH
SWASHED
SWASHER
SWASHERS
SWASHES
SWASHIER
SWASHIEST
SWASHING
SWASHINGS
SWASHWORK
SWASHWORKS
SWASHY
SWASTIKA
SWASTIKAS
SWAT
SWATCH
SWATCHES
SWATH
SWATHE
SWATHED
SWATHES

SWATHIER
SWATHIEST
SWATHING
SWATHS
SWATHY
SWATS
SWATTED
SWATTER
SWATTERED
SWATTERING
SWATTERS
SWATTING
SWATTINGS
SWAY
SWAYBACK
SWAYBACKS
SWAYED
SWAYER
SWAYERS
SWAYING
SWAYINGS
SWAYL
SWAYLED
SWAYLING
SWAYLINGS
SWAYLS
SWAYS
SWAZZLE
SWAZZLES
SWEAL
SWEALED
SWEALING
SWEALINGS
SWEALS
SWEAR
SWEARD
SWEARDS
SWEARER
SWEARERS
SWEARING
SWEARINGS
SWEARS
SWEAT
SWEATED
SWEATER
SWEATERS
SWEATIER
SWEATIEST
SWEATING
SWEATINGS
SWEATS
SWEATY
SWEDE
SWEDES
SWEE
SWEED
SWEEING
SWEEL
SWEELED
SWEELING
SWEELS
SWEENEY
SWEENEYS
SWEENIES
SWEENY
SWEEP
SWEEPBACK
SWEEPBACKS
SWEEPER
SWEEPERS

SWEEPIER
SWEEPIEST
SWEEPING
SWEEPINGS
SWEEPS
SWEEPY
SWEER
SWEERED
SWEERT
SWEES
SWEET
SWEETED
SWEETEN
SWEETENED
SWEETENER
SWEETENERS
SWEETENING
SWEETENINGS
SWEETENS
SWEETER
SWEETEST
SWEETFISH
SWEETFISHES
SWEETIE
SWEETIES
SWEETING
SWEETINGS
SWEETISH
SWEETLY
SWEETMEAL
SWEETMEAT
SWEETMEATS
SWEETNESS
SWEETNESSES
SWEETPEA
SWEETPEAS
SWEETS
SWEETWOOD
SWEETWOODS
SWEETY
SWEIR
SWEIRNESS
SWEIRNESSES
SWEIRT
SWELCHIE
SWELCHIES
SWELL
SWELLDOM
SWELLDOMS
SWELLED
SWELLER
SWELLERS
SWELLEST
SWELLING
SWELLINGS
SWELLISH
SWELLS
SWELT
SWELTED
SWELTER
SWELTERED
SWELTERING
SWELTERINGS
SWELTERS
SWELTING
SWELTRIER
SWELTRIEST
SWELTRY
SWELTS
SWEPT

SWEPTBACK
SWEPTWING
SWERF
SWERFED
SWERFING
SWERFS
SWERVE
SWERVED
SWERVER
SWERVERS
SWERVES
SWERVING
SWERVINGS
SWEVEN
SWEVENS
SWIDDEN
SWIDDENS
SWIES
SWIFT
SWIFTED
SWIFTER
SWIFTERS
SWIFTEST
SWIFTING
SWIFTLET
SWIFTLETS
SWIFTLY
SWIFTNESS
SWIFTNESSES
SWIFTS
SWIG
SWIGGED
SWIGGER
SWIGGERS
SWIGGING
SWIGS
SWILL
SWILLED
SWILLER
SWILLERS
SWILLING
SWILLINGS
SWILLS
SWIM
SWIMMABLE
SWIMMER
SWIMMERET
SWIMMERETS
SWIMMERS
SWIMMIER
SWIMMIEST
SWIMMING
SWIMMINGS
SWIMMY
SWIMS
SWIMSUIT
SWIMSUITS
SWIMWEAR
SWIMWEARS
SWINDGE
SWINDGED
SWINDGES
SWINDGING
SWINDLE
SWINDLED
SWINDLER
SWINDLERS
SWINDLES
SWINDLING
SWINDLINGS

SWINE
SWINEHERD
SWINEHERDS
SWINEHOOD
SWINEHOODS
SWINERIES
SWINERY
SWING
SWINGBOAT
SWINGBOATS
SWINGE
SWINGED
SWINGEING
SWINGER
SWINGERS
SWINGES
SWINGING
SWINGINGS
SWINGISM
SWINGISMS
SWINGLE
SWINGLED
SWINGLES
SWINGLING
SWINGLINGS
SWINGS
SWINGTREE
SWINGTREES
SWINISH
SWINISHLY
SWINK
SWINKED
SWINKING
SWINKS
SWIPE
SWIPED
SWIPER
SWIPERS
SWIPES
SWIPEY
SWIPIER
SWIPIEST
SWIPING
SWIPPLE
SWIPPLES
SWIRE
SWIRES
SWIRL
SWIRLED
SWIRLIER
SWIRLIEST
SWIRLING
SWIRLS
SWIRLY
SWISH
SWISHED
SWISHER
SWISHERS
SWISHES
SWISHEST
SWISHIER
SWISHIEST
SWISHING
SWISHINGS
SWISHY
SWISSING
SWISSINGS
SWITCH
SWITCHED
SWITCHEL

| | | | | |
|---|---|---|---|---|
| SWITCHELS | SWORDSMAN | SYKE | SYMAR | SYNANDRIA |
| SWITCHES | SWORDSMEN | SYKER | SYMARS | SYNANGIA |
| SWITCHING | SWORE | SYKES | SYMBION | SYNANGIUM |
| SWITCHINGS | SWORN | SYLLABARIES | SYMBIONS | SYNANGIUMS |
| SWITCHMAN | SWOT | SYLLABARY | SYMBIONT | SYNANTHIC |
| SWITCHMEN | SWOTS | SYLLABI | SYMBIONTS | SYNANTHIES |
| SWITCHY | SWOTTED | SYLLABIC | SYMBIOSES | SYNANTHY |
| SWITH | SWOTTER | SYLLABICS | SYMBIOSIS | SYNAPHEA |
| SWITHER | SWOTTERS | SYLLABIFIED | SYMBIOTIC . | SYNAPHEAS |
| SWITHERED | SWOTTING | SYLLABIFIES | SYMBOL | SYNAPHEIA |
| SWITHERING | SWOTTINGS | SYLLABIFY | SYMBOLE | SYNAPHEIAS |
| SWITHERS | SWOUN | SYLLABIFYING | SYMBOLES | SYNAPSE |
| SWITS | SWOUND | SYLLABISE | SYMBOLIC | SYNAPSES |
| SWITSES | SWOUNDED | SYLLABISED | SYMBOLICS | SYNAPSIS |
| SWIVEL | SWOUNDING | SYLLABISES | SYMBOLISE | SYNAPTASE |
| SWIVELLED | SWOUNDS | SYLLABISING | SYMBOLISED | SYNAPTASES |
| SWIVELLING | SWOUNE | SYLLABISM | SYMBOLISES | SYNAPTE |
| SWIVELS | SWOUNED | SYLLABISMS | SYMBOLISING | SYNAPTES |
| SWIVET | SWOUNES | SYLLABIZE | SYMBOLISM | SYNAPTIC |
| SWIVETS | SWOUNING | SYLLABIZED | SYMBOLISMS | SYNARCHIES |
| SWIZ | SWOUNS | SYLLABIZES | SYMBOLIST | SYNARCHY |
| SWIZZES | SWOWND | SYLLABIZING | SYMBOLISTS | SYNASTRIES |
| SWIZZLE | SWOWNDS | SYLLABLE | SYMBOLIZE | SYNASTRY |
| SWIZZLED | SWOWNE | SYLLABLED | SYMBOLIZED | SYNAXES |
| SWIZZLES | SWOWNES | SYLLABLES | SYMBOLIZES | SYNAXIS |
| SWIZZLING | SWOZZLE | SYLLABLING | SYMBOLIZING | SYNC |
| SWOB | SWOZZLES | SYLLABUB | SYMBOLLED | SYNCARP |
| SWOBBED | SWUM | SYLLABUBS | SYMBOLLING | SYNCARPIES |
| SWOBBER | SWUNG | SYLLABUS | SYMBOLOGIES | SYNCARPS |
| SWOBBERS | SWY | SYLLABUSES | SYMBOLOGY | SYNCARPY |
| SWOBBING | SYBARITE | SYLLEPSES | SYMBOLS | SYNCED |
| SWOBS | SYBARITES | SYLLEPSIS | SYMITAR | SYNCH |
| SWOLLEN | SYBARITIC | SYLLEPTIC | SYMITARE | SYNCHED |
| SWOLN | SYBBE | SYLLOGISE | SYMITARES | SYNCHING |
| SWONE | SYBBES | SYLLOGISED | SYMITARS | SYNCHRONIES |
| SWONES | SYBIL | SYLLOGISES | SYMMETRAL | SYNCHRONY |
| SWOON | SYBILS | SYLLOGISING | SYMMETRIC | SYNCHS |
| SWOONED | SYBO | SYLLOGISM | SYMMETRIES | SYNCHYSES |
| SWOONING | SYBOE | SYLLOGISMS | SYMMETRY | SYNCHYSIS |
| SWOONINGS | SYBOES | SYLLOGIZE | SYMPATHIES | SYNCING |
| SWOONS | SYBOTIC | SYLLOGIZED | SYMPATHIN | SYNCLINAL |
| SWOOP | SYBOTISM | SYLLOGIZES | SYMPATHINS | SYNCLINALS |
| SWOOPED | SYBOTISMS | SYLLOGIZING | SYMPATHY | SYNCLINE |
| SWOOPING | SYBOW | SYLPH | SYMPHILE | SYNCLINES |
| SWOOPS | SYBOWS | SYLPHID | SYMPHILES | SYNCOPAL |
| SWOOSH | SYCAMINE | SYLPHIDE | SYMPHILIES | SYNCOPATE |
| SWOOSHED | SYCAMINES | SYLPHIDES | SYMPHILY | SYNCOPATED |
| SWOOSHES | SYCAMORE | SYLPHIDS | SYMPHONIC | SYNCOPATES |
| SWOOSHING | SYCAMORES | SYLPHINE | SYMPHONIES | SYNCOPATING |
| SWOP | SYCE | SYLPHISH | SYMPHONY | SYNCOPE |
| SWOPPED | SYCEE | SYLPHS | SYMPHYSES | SYNCOPES |
| SWOPPER | SYCEES | SYLVA | SYMPHYSIS | SYNCOPIC |
| SWOPPERS | SYCES | SYLVAE | SYMPHYTIC | SYNCOPTIC |
| SWOPPING | SYCOMORE | SYLVAN | SYMPLOCE | SYNCRETIC |
| SWOPPINGS | SYCOMORES | SYLVANER | SYMPLOCES | SYNCS |
| SWOPS | SYCONIUM | SYLVANERS | SYMPODIA | SYNCYTIA |
| SWOPT | SYCONIUMS | SYLVANITE | SYMPODIAL | SYNCYTIAL |
| SWORD | SYCOPHANT | SYLVANITES | SYMPODIUM | SYNCYTIUM |
| SWORDED | SYCOPHANTS | SYLVANS | SYMPOSIA | SYNCYTIUMS |
| SWORDER | SYCOSES | SYLVAS | SYMPOSIAC | SYND |
| SWORDERS | SYCOSIS | SYLVATIC | SYMPOSIAL | SYNDACTYL |
| SWORDFISH | SYE | SYLVIA | SYMPOSIUM | SYNDED |
| SWORDFISHES | SYED | SYLVIAS | SYMPTOM | SYNDESES |
| SWORDING | SYEING | SYLVIINE | SYMPTOMS | SYNDESIS |
| SWORDLESS | SYEN | SYLVINE | SYMPTOSES | SYNDET |
| SWORDMAN | SYENITE | SYLVINES | SYMPTOSIS | SYNDETIC |
| SWORDMEN | SYENITES | SYLVINITE | SYMPTOTIC | SYNDETS |
| SWORDPLAY | SYENITIC | SYLVINITES | SYNAGOGAL | SYNDIC |
| SWORDPLAYS | SYENS | SYLVITE | SYNAGOGUE | SYNDICAL |
| SWORDS | SYES | SYLVITES | SYNAGOGUES | SYNDICATE |

| | | | | |
|---|---|---|---|---|
| SYNDICATED | SYNESES | SYNONYMS | SYNTONINS | SYRINX |
| SYNDICATES | SYNESIS | SYNONYMY | SYNTONISE | SYRINXES |
| SYNDICATING | SYNFUEL | SYNOPSES | SYNTONISED | SYRLYE |
| SYNDICS | SYNFUELS | SYNOPSIS | SYNTONISES | SYRPHID |
| SYNDING | SYNGAMIC | SYNOPSISE | SYNTONISING | SYRPHIDS |
| SYNDINGS | SYNGAMIES | SYNOPSISED | SYNTONIZE | SYRTES |
| SYNDROME | SYNGAMOUS | SYNOPSISES | SYNTONIZED | SYRTIS |
| SYNDROMES | SYNGAMY | SYNOPSISING | SYNTONIZES | SYRUP |
| SYNDROMIC | SYNGENEIC | SYNOPSIZE | SYNTONIZING | SYRUPED |
| SYNDS | SYNGRAPH | SYNOPSIZED | SYNTONOUS | SYRUPING |
| SYNE | SYNGRAPHS | SYNOPSIZES | SYNTONY | SYRUPS |
| SYNECHIA | SYNING | SYNOPSIZING | SYPE | SYRUPY |
| SYNECHIAS | SYNIZESES | SYNOPTIC | SYPED | SYSSITIA |
| SYNECTIC | SYNIZESIS | SYNOPTIST | SYPES | SYSSITIAS |
| SYNECTICS | SYNOD | SYNOPTISTS | SYPHILIS | SYSTALTIC |
| SYNED | SYNODAL | SYNOVIA | SYPHILISE | SYSTEM |
| SYNEDRIA | SYNODALS | SYNOVIAL | SYPHILISED | SYSTEMED |
| SYNEDRIAL | SYNODIC | SYNOVIAS | SYPHILISES | SYSTEMIC |
| SYNEDRION | SYNODICAL | SYNOVITIC | SYPHILISING | SYSTEMISE |
| SYNEDRIUM | SYNODS | SYNOVITIS | SYPHILIZE | SYSTEMISED |
| SYNERESES | SYNODSMAN | SYNOVITISES | SYPHILIZED | SYSTEMISES |
| SYNERESIS | SYNODSMEN | SYNROC | SYPHILIZES | SYSTEMISING |
| SYNERGIC | SYNOECETE | SYNROCS | SYPHILIZING | SYSTEMIZE |
| SYNERGID | SYNOECETES | SYNTACTIC | SYPHILOID | SYSTEMIZED |
| SYNERGIDS | SYNOECISE | SYNTAGMA | SYPHILOMA | SYSTEMIZES |
| SYNERGIES | SYNOECISED | SYNTAGMATA | SYPHILOMAS | SYSTEMIZING |
| SYNERGISE | SYNOECISES | SYNTAN | SYPHON | SYSTEMS |
| SYNERGISED | SYNOECISING | SYNTANS | SYPHONED | SYSTOLE |
| SYNERGISES | SYNOECISM | SYNTAX | SYPHONING | SYSTOLES |
| SYNERGISING | SYNOECISMS | SYNTAXES | SYPHONS | SYSTOLIC |
| SYNERGISM | SYNOECIZE | SYNTECTIC | SYPING | SYSTYLE |
| SYNERGISMS | SYNOECIZED | SYNTEXIS | SYREN | SYSTYLES |
| SYNERGIST | SYNOECIZES | SYNTEXISES | SYRENS | SYTHE |
| SYNERGISTS | SYNOECIZING | SYNTHESES | SYRINGA | SYTHES |
| SYNERGIZE | SYNOEKETE | SYNTHESIS | SYRINGAS | SYVER |
| SYNERGIZED | SYNOEKETES | SYNTHETIC | SYRINGE | SYVERS |
| SYNERGIZES | SYNOICOUS | SYNTHETICS | SYRINGEAL | SYZYGIAL |
| SYNERGIZING | SYNONYM | SYNTONIC | SYRINGED | SYZYGIES |
| SYNERGY | SYNONYMIC | SYNTONIES | SYRINGES | SYZYGY |
| SYNES | SYNONYMIES | SYNTONIN | SYRINGING | |

# T

TA
TAAL
TAALS
TAB
TABANID
TABANIDS
TABARD
TABARDS
TABARET
TABARETS
TABASHEER
TABASHEERS
TABASHIR
TABASHIRS
TABBED
TABBIED
TABBIES
TABBINET
TABBINETS
TABBING
TABBOULEH
TABBOULEHS
TABBY
TABBYHOOD
TABBYHOODS
TABBYING
TABEFIED
TABEFIES
TABEFY
TABEFYING
TABELLION
TABELLIONS
TABERDAR
TABERDARS
TABES
TABESCENT
TABETIC
TABID
TABINET
TABINETS
TABLA
TABLAS
TABLATURE
TABLATURES
TABLE
TABLEAU
TABLEAUX
TABLED
TABLEFUL
TABLEFULS
TABLELAND
TABLELANDS
TABLES
TABLET
TABLETED
TABLETING
TABLETS
TABLEWISE
TABLING
TABLINGS
TABLOID
TABLOIDS
TABOGGAN

TABOGGANED
TABOGGANING
TABOGGANS
TABOO
TABOOED
TABOOING
TABOOS
TABOR
TABORED
TABORER
TABORERS
TABORET
TABORETS
TABORIN
TABORING
TABORINS
TABORS
TABOUR
TABOURED
TABOURET
TABOURETS
TABOURIN
TABOURING
TABOURINS
TABOURS
TABRERE
TABRERES
TABRET
TABRETS
TABS
TABU
TABUED
TABUING
TABULA
TABULAE
TABULAR
TABULARLY
TABULATE
TABULATED
TABULATES
TABULATING
TABULATOR
TABULATORS
TABUN
TABUNS
TABUS
TACAHOUT
TACAHOUTS
TACAMAHAC
TACAMAHACS
TACE
TACES
TACET
TACH
TACHE
TACHES
TACHISM
TACHISME
TACHISMES
TACHISMS
TACHIST
TACHISTE
TACHISTES

TACHISTS
TACHOGRAM
TACHOGRAMS
TACHYLITE
TACHYLITES
TACHYLYTE
TACHYLYTES
TACHYON
TACHYONS
TACIT
TACITLY
TACITNESS
TACITNESSES
TACITURN
TACK
TACKED
TACKER
TACKERS
TACKET
TACKETS
TACKETY
TACKIER
TACKIES
TACKIEST
TACKINESS
TACKINESSES
TACKING
TACKINGS
TACKLE
TACKLED
TACKLER
TACKLERS
TACKLES
TACKLING
TACKLINGS
TACKS
TACKSMAN
TACKSMEN
TACKY
TACO
TACONITE
TACONITES
TACOS
TACT
TACTFUL
TACTFULLY
TACTIC
TACTICAL
TACTICIAN
TACTICIANS
TACTICITIES
TACTICITY
TACTICS
TACTILE
TACTILIST
TACTILISTS
TACTILITIES
TACTILITY
TACTION
TACTIONS
TACTISM
TACTISMS
TACTLESS

TACTS
TACTUAL
TACTUALLY
TAD
TADPOLE
TADPOLES
TADS
TADVANCE
TAE
TAED
TAEDIUM
TAEDIUMS
TAEING
TAEL
TAELS
TAENIA
TAENIAE
TAENIAS
TAENIASES
TAENIASIS
TAENIATE
TAENIOID
TAES
TAFFEREL
TAFFERELS
TAFFETA
TAFFETAS
TAFFETASES
TAFFETIES
TAFFETY
TAFFIES
TAFFRAIL
TAFFRAILS
TAFFY
TAFIA
TAFIAS
TAG
TAGETES
TAGGED
TAGGER
TAGGERS
TAGGING
TAGHAIRM
TAGHAIRMS
TAGLIONI
TAGLIONIS
TAGMEME
TAGMEMES
TAGMEMIC
TAGMEMICS
TAGRAG
TAGRAGS
TAGS
TAGUAN
TAGUANS
TAHA
TAHAS
TAHINA
TAHINAS
TAHINI
TAHINIS
TAHR
TAHRS

TAHSIL
TAHSILDAR
TAHSILDARS
TAHSILS
TAI
TAIGA
TAIGAS
TAIGLE
TAIGLED
TAIGLES
TAIGLING
TAIL
TAILARD
TAILARDS
TAILBACK
TAILBACKS
TAILED
TAILING
TAILINGS
TAILLESS
TAILLEUR
TAILLEURS
TAILLIE
TAILLIES
TAILOR
TAILORED
TAILORESS
TAILORESSES
TAILORING
TAILORINGS
TAILORS
TAILPIECE
TAILPIECES
TAILPLANE
TAILPLANES
TAILRACE
TAILRACES
TAILS
TAILSKID
TAILSKIDS
TAILYE
TAILYES
TAILZIE
TAILZIES
TAINT
TAINTED
TAINTING
TAINTLESS
TAINTS
TAINTURE
TAINTURES
TAIPAN
TAIPANS
TAIRA
TAIRAS
TAIS
TAISCH
TAISCHES
TAISH
TAISHES
TAIT
TAITS
TAIVER

TAIVERED
TAIVERING
TAIVERS
TAIVERT
TAJ
TAJES
TAK
TAKA
TAKABLE
TAKAHE
TAKAHEA
TAKAHEAS
TAKAHES
TAKAMAKA
TAKAMAKAS
TAKAS
TAKE
TAKEABLE
TAKEN
TAKEOVER
TAKEOVERS
TAKER
TAKERS
TAKES
TAKIER
TAKIEST
TAKIN
TAKING
TAKINGLY
TAKINGS
TAKINS
TAKS
TAKY
TALA
TALAK
TALAKS
TALANT
TALANTS
TALAPOIN
TALAPOINS
TALAQ
TALAQS
TALAR
TALARIA
TALARS
TALAS
TALAUNT
TALAUNTS
TALAYOT
TALAYOTS
TALBOT
TALBOTS
TALBOTYPE
TALBOTYPES
TALC
TALCKIER
TALCKIEST
TALCKY
TALCOSE
TALCOUS
TALCS
TALCUM
TALCUMS
TALE
TALEFUL
TALEGALLA
TALEGALLAS
TALENT
TALENTED
TALENTS

TALES
TALESMAN
TALESMEN
TALI
TALION
TALIONIC
TALIONS
TALIPAT
TALIPATS
TALIPED
TALIPEDS
TALIPES
TALIPOT
TALIPOTS
TALISMAN
TALISMANS
TALK
TALKABLE
TALKATHON
TALKATHONS
TALKATIVE
TALKED
TALKER
TALKERS
TALKFEST
TALKFESTS
TALKIE
TALKIES
TALKING
TALKINGS
TALKS
TALL
TALLAGE
TALLAGED
TALLAGES
TALLAGING
TALLAT
TALLATS
TALLBOY
TALLBOYS
TALLENT
TALLENTS
TALLER
TALLEST
TALLET
TALLETS
TALLIABLE
TALLIATE
TALLIATED
TALLIATES
TALLIATING
TALLIED
TALLIER
TALLIERS
TALLIES
TALLITH
TALLITHS
TALLNESS
TALLNESSES
TALLOT
TALLOTS
TALLOW
TALLOWED
TALLOWING
TALLOWISH
TALLOWS
TALLOWY
TALLY
TALLYING
TALLYMAN

TALLYMEN
TALLYSHOP
TALLYSHOPS
TALMA
TALMAS
TALON
TALONED
TALONS
TALPA
TALPAE
TALPAS
TALUK
TALUKDAR
TALUKDARS
TALUKS
TALUS
TALUSES
TALWEG
TALWEGS
TAM
TAMABLE
TAMAL
TAMALE
TAMALES
TAMALS
TAMANDUA
TAMANDUAS
TAMANOIR
TAMANOIRS
TAMANU
TAMANUS
TAMARA
TAMARACK
TAMARACKS
TAMARAS
TAMARI
TAMARILLO
TAMARILLOS
TAMARIN
TAMARIND
TAMARINDS
TAMARINS
TAMARIS
TAMARISK
TAMARISKS
TAMASHA
TAMASHAS
TAMBER
TAMBERS
TAMBOUR
TAMBOURA
TAMBOURAS
TAMBOURED
TAMBOURIN
TAMBOURING
TAMBOURINS
TAMBOURS
TAMBURA
TAMBURAS
TAMBURIN
TAMBURINS
TAME
TAMEABLE
TAMED
TAMELESS
TAMELY
TAMENESS
TAMENESSES
TAMER
TAMERS

TAMES
TAMEST
TAMIN
TAMINE
TAMINES
TAMING
TAMINGS
TAMINS
TAMIS
TAMISE
TAMISES
TAMMIES
TAMMY
TAMP
TAMPED
TAMPER
TAMPERED
TAMPERER
TAMPERERS
TAMPERING
TAMPERINGS
TAMPERS
TAMPING
TAMPINGS
TAMPION
TAMPIONS
TAMPON
TAMPONADE
TAMPONADES
TAMPONAGE
TAMPONAGES
TAMPONED
TAMPONING
TAMPONS
TAMPS
TAMS
TAN
TANA
TANADAR
TANADARS
TANAGER
TANAGERS
TANAGRA
TANAGRAS
TANAGRINE
TANAISTE
TANAISTES
TANAS
TANDEM
TANDEMS
TANDOORI
TANDOORIS
TANE
TANG
TANGA
TANGAS
TANGED
TANGELO
TANGELOS
TANGENCIES
TANGENCY
TANGENT
TANGENTS
TANGERINE
TANGERINES
TANGHIN
TANGHININ
TANGHININS
TANGHINS
TANGIBLE

TANGIBLES
TANGIBLY
TANGIE
TANGIER
TANGIES
TANGIEST
TANGING
TANGLE
TANGLED
TANGLER
TANGLERS
TANGLES
TANGLIER
TANGLIEST
TANGLING
TANGLINGS
TANGLY
TANGO
TANGOED
TANGOING
TANGOIST
TANGOISTS
TANGOS
TANGRAM
TANGRAMS
TANGS
TANGUN
TANGUNS
TANGY
TANIST
TANISTRIES
TANISTRY
TANISTS
TANK
TANKA
TANKAGE
TANKAGES
TANKARD
TANKARDS
TANKAS
TANKED
TANKER
TANKERS
TANKFUL
TANKFULS
TANKIA
TANKIAS
TANKING
TANKINGS
TANKS
TANLING
TANLINGS
TANNA
TANNABLE
TANNAGE
TANNAGES
TANNAH
TANNAHS
TANNAS
TANNATE
TANNATES
TANNED
TANNER
TANNERIES
TANNERS
TANNERY
TANNEST
TANNIC
TANNIN
TANNING

| | | | | |
|---|---|---|---|---|
| TANNINGS | TAPERNESS | TARANTISM | TAROTS | TARTARS |
| TANNINS | TAPERNESSES | TARANTISMS | TARP | TARTER |
| TANREC | TAPERS | TARANTULA | TARPAN | TARTEST |
| TANRECS | TAPERWISE | TARANTULAS | TARPANS | TARTIER |
| TANS | TAPES | TARAS | TARPAULIN | TARTIEST |
| TANSIES | TAPESTRIED | TARAXACUM | TARPAULINS | TARTINE |
| TANSY | TAPESTRIES | TARAXACUMS | TARPON | TARTINES |
| TANTALATE | TAPESTRY | TARBOGGIN | TARPONS | TARTINESS |
| TANTALATES | TAPESTRYING | TARBOGGINED | TARPS | TARTINESSES |
| TANTALIC | TAPET | TARBOGGINING | TARRAGON | TARTISH |
| TANTALISE | TAPETA | TARBOGGINS | TARRAGONS | TARTLET |
| TANTALISED | TAPETAL | TARBOOSH | TARRAS | TARTLETS |
| TANTALISES | TAPETI | TARBOOSHES | TARRASES | TARTLY |
| TANTALISING | TAPETIS | TARBOUSH | TARRE | TARTNESS |
| TANTALISINGS | TAPETS | TARBOUSHES | TARRED | TARTNESSES |
| TANTALISM | TAPETUM | TARBUSH | TARRES | TARTRATE |
| TANTALISMS | TAPEWORM | TARBUSHES | TARRIANCE | TARTRATES |
| TANTALITE | TAPEWORMS | TARCEL | TARRIANCES | TARTS |
| TANTALITES | TAPING | TARCELS | TARRIED | TARTY |
| TANTALIZE | TAPIOCA | TARDIED | TARRIER | TARWEED |
| TANTALIZED | TAPIOCAS | TARDIER | TARRIERS | TARWEEDS |
| TANTALIZES | TAPIR | TARDIES | TARRIES | TARWHINE |
| TANTALIZING | TAPIROID | TARDIEST | TARRIEST | TARWHINES |
| TANTALIZINGS | TAPIRS | TARDILY | TARRINESS | TASAR |
| TANTALUM | TAPIS | TARDINESS | TARRINESSES | TASARS |
| TANTALUMS | TAPISES | TARDINESSES | TARRING | TASH |
| TANTALUS | TAPIST | TARDIVE | TARRINGS | TASHED |
| TANTALUSES | TAPISTS | TARDY | TARROCK | TASHES |
| TANTARA | TAPLASH | TARDYING | TARROCKS | TASHING |
| TANTARARA | TAPLASHES | TARE | TARROW | TASIMETER |
| TANTARARAS | TAPPA | TARED | TARROWED | TASIMETERS |
| TANTARAS | TAPPAS | TARES | TARROWING | TASK |
| TANTI | TAPPED | TARGE | TARROWS | TASKED |
| TANTIVIES | TAPPER | TARGED | TARRY | TASKER |
| TANTIVY | TAPPERS | TARGES | TARRYING | TASKERS |
| TANTO | TAPPET | TARGET | TARS | TASKING |
| TANTONIES | TAPPETS | TARGETED | TARSAL | TASKINGS |
| TANTONY | TAPPICE | TARGETEER | TARSALGIA | TASKS |
| TANTRA | TAPPICED | TARGETEERS | TARSALGIAS | TASLET |
| TANTRAS | TAPPICES | TARGETING | TARSALS | TASLETS |
| TANTRIC | TAPPICING | TARGETS | TARSEL | TASS |
| TANTRUM | TAPPING | TARGING | TARSELS | TASSE |
| TANTRUMS | TAPPINGS | TARIFF | TARSI | TASSEL |
| TANYARD | TAPPIT | TARIFFED | TARSIA | TASSELL |
| TANYARDS | TAPROOM | TARIFFING | TARSIAS | TASSELLED |
| TAOISEACH | TAPROOMS | TARIFFS | TARSIER | TASSELLING |
| TAOISEACHS | TAPROOT | TARING | TARSIERS | TASSELLINGS |
| TAP | TAPROOTS | TARLATAN | TARSIOID | TASSELLS |
| TAPA | TAPS | TARLATANS | TARSUS | TASSELLY |
| TAPACOLO | TAPSMAN | TARMAC | TART | TASSELS |
| TAPACOLOS | TAPSMEN | TARMACKED | TARTAN | TASSES |
| TAPACULO | TAPSTER | TARMACKING | TARTANA | TASSET |
| TAPACULOS | TAPSTERS | TARMACS | TARTANAS | TASSETS |
| TAPADERA | TAPSTRY | TARN | TARTANE | TASSIE |
| TAPADERAS | TAPU | TARNAL | TARTANED | TASSIES |
| TAPADERO | TAPUS | TARNATION | TARTANES | TASSWAGE |
| TAPADEROS | TAR | TARNISH | TARTANS | TASTABLE |
| TAPAS | TARA | TARNISHED | TARTAR | TASTE |
| TAPE | TARAKIHI | TARNISHER | TARTARE | TASTED |
| TAPED | TARAKIHIS | TARNISHERS | TARTARES | TASTEFUL |
| TAPELESS | TARAND | TARNISHES | TARTARIC | TASTELESS |
| TAPELINE | TARANDS | TARNISHING | TARTARISE | TASTER |
| TAPELINES | TARANTARA | TARNS | TARTARISED | TASTERS |
| TAPEN | TARANTARAED | TARO | TARTARISES | TASTES |
| TAPER | TARANTARAING | TAROC | TARTARISING | TASTEVIN |
| TAPERED | TARANTARAS | TAROCS | TARTARIZE | TASTEVINS |
| TAPERER | TARANTAS | TAROK | TARTARIZED | TASTIER |
| TAPERERS | TARANTASES | TAROKS | TARTARIZES | TASTIEST |
| TAPERING | TARANTASS | TAROS | TARTARIZING | TASTILY |
| TAPERINGS | TARANTASSES | TAROT | TARTARLY | TASTING |

TASTINGS
TASTY
TAT
TATAMI
TATAMIS
TATE
TATER
TATERS
TATES
TATH
TATHED
TATHING
TATHS
TATIE
TATIES
TATLER
TATLERS
TATOU
TATOUS
TATS
TATT
TATTED
TATTER
TATTERED
TATTERING
TATTERS
TATTERY
TATTIE
TATTIER
TATTIES
TATTIEST
TATTILY
TATTINESS
TATTINESSES
TATTING
TATTINGS
TATTLE
TATTLED
TATTLER
TATTLERS
TATTLES
TATTLING
TATTLINGS
TATTOO
TATTOOED
TATTOOER
TATTOOERS
TATTOOING
TATTOOIST
TATTOOISTS
TATTOOS
TATTOW
TATTOWED
TATTOWING
TATTOWS
TATTS
TATTY
TATU
TATUED
TATUING
TATUS
TAU
TAUBE
TAUBES
TAUGHT
TAULD
TAUNT
TAUNTED
TAUNTER
TAUNTERS

TAUNTING
TAUNTINGS
TAUNTS
TAUPE
TAUPES
TAUPIE
TAUPIES
TAUREAN
TAURIC
TAURIFORM
TAURINE
TAUS
TAUT
TAUTED
TAUTEN
TAUTENED
TAUTENING
TAUTENS
TAUTER
TAUTEST
TAUTING
TAUTIT
TAUTLY
TAUTNESS
TAUTNESSES
TAUTOG
TAUTOGS
TAUTOLOGIES
TAUTOLOGY
TAUTOMER
TAUTOMERS
TAUTONYM
TAUTONYMS
TAUTS
TAVER
TAVERED
TAVERING
TAVERN
TAVERNA
TAVERNAS
TAVERNER
TAVERNERS
TAVERNS
TAVERS
TAVERT
TAW
TAWDRIER
TAWDRIES
TAWDRIEST
TAWDRILY
TAWDRY
TAWED
TAWER
TAWERIES
TAWERS
TAWERY
TAWIE
TAWING
TAWINGS
TAWNEY
TAWNEYS
TAWNIER
TAWNIES
TAWNIEST
TAWNINESS
TAWNINESSES
TAWNY
TAWPIE
TAWPIES
TAWS

TAWSE
TAWSES
TAWT
TAWTED
TAWTIE
TAWTIER
TAWTIEST
TAWTING
TAWTS
TAX
TAXA
TAXABLE
TAXABLY
TAXAMETER
TAXAMETERS
TAXATION
TAXATIONS
TAXATIVE
TAXED
TAXER
TAXERS
TAXES
TAXI
TAXIARCH
TAXIARCHS
TAXICAB
TAXICABS
TAXIDERMIES
TAXIDERMY
TAXIED
TAXIES
TAXIING
TAXIMAN
TAXIMEN
TAXIMETER
TAXIMETERS
TAXING
TAXINGS
TAXIS
TAXIWAY
TAXIWAYS
TAXMAN
TAXMEN
TAXON
TAXONOMER
TAXONOMERS
TAXONOMIC
TAXONOMIES
TAXONOMY
TAXOR
TAXORS
TAXYING
TAYBERRIES
TAYBERRY
TAYRA
TAYRAS
TAZZA
TAZZAS
TAZZE
TCHICK
TCHICKED
TCHICKING
TCHICKS
TE
TEA
TEABERRIES
TEABERRY
TEACH
TEACHABLE
TEACHER

TEACHERS
TEACHES
TEACHIE
TEACHING
TEACHINGS
TEACHLESS
TEACUP
TEACUPFUL
TEACUPFULS
TEACUPS
TEAD
TEADE
TEADES
TEADS
TEAED
TEAGLE
TEAGLED
TEAGLES
TEAGLING
TEAING
TEAK
TEAKS
TEAL
TEALS
TEAM
TEAMED
TEAMER
TEAMERS
TEAMING
TEAMINGS
TEAMS
TEAMSTER
TEAMSTERS
TEAMWISE
TEAMWORK
TEAMWORKS
TEAPOT
TEAPOTS
TEAPOY
TEAPOYS
TEAR
TEARAWAY
TEARAWAYS
TEARER
TEARERS
TEARFUL
TEARFULLY
TEARIER
TEARIEST
TEARING
TEARLESS
TEARS
TEARY
TEAS
TEASE
TEASED
TEASEL
TEASELED
TEASELER
TEASELERS
TEASELING
TEASELINGS
TEASELLED
TEASELLER
TEASELLERS
TEASELLING
TEASELLINGS
TEASELS
TEASER
TEASERS

TEASES
TEASING
TEASINGLY
TEASINGS
TEASPOON
TEASPOONS
TEAT
TEATED
TEATIME
TEATIMES
TEATS
TEAZE
TEAZED
TEAZEL
TEAZELED
TEAZELING
TEAZELLED
TEAZELLING
TEAZELS
TEAZES
TEAZING
TEAZLE
TEAZLED
TEAZLES
TEAZLING
TEBBAD
TEBBADS
TECH
TECHIER
TECHIEST
TECHNIC
TECHNICAL
TECHNICS
TECHNIQUE
TECHNIQUES
TECHS
TECHY
TECKEL
TECKELS
TECTIFORM
TECTONIC
TECTONICS
TECTORIAL
TECTRICES
TECTRIX
TED
TEDDED
TEDDER
TEDDERS
TEDDIES
TEDDING
TEDDY
TEDESCA
TEDESCHE
TEDESCHI
TEDESCO
TEDIER
TEDIEST
TEDIOSITIES
TEDIOSITY
TEDIOUS
TEDIOUSLY
TEDISOME
TEDIUM
TEDIUMS
TEDS
TEDY
TEE
TEED
TEEHEE

TEEHEED
TEEHEEING
TEEHEES
TEEING
TEEL
TEELS
TEEM
TEEMED
TEEMER
TEEMERS
TEEMFUL
TEEMING
TEEMLESS
TEEMS
TEEN
TEENAGE
TEENAGED
TEENAGER
TEENAGERS
TEEND
TEENDED
TEENDING
TEENDS
TEENE
TEENED
TEENES
TEENIER
TEENIEST
TEENING
TEENS
TEENSIER
TEENSIEST
TEENSY
TEENTIER
TEENTIEST
TEENTSIER
TEENTSIEST
TEENTSY
TEENTY
TEENY
TEEPEE
TEEPEES
TEER
TEERED
TEERING
TEERS
TEES
TEETER
TEETERED
TEETERING
TEETERS
TEETH
TEETHE
TEETHED
TEETHES
TEETHING
TEETHINGS
TEETOTAL
TEETOTALS
TEETOTUM
TEETOTUMS
TEF
TEFF
TEFFS
TEFS
TEG
TEGG
TEGGS
TEGMEN
TEGMENTAL

TEGMENTUM
TEGMENTUMS
TEGMINA
TEGS
TEGUEXIN
TEGUEXINS
TEGULA
TEGULAE
TEGULAR
TEGULARLY
TEGULATED
TEGUMENT
TEGUMENTS
TEHEE
TEHEED
TEHEEING
TEHEES
TEHR
TEHRS
TEIL
TEILS
TEIND
TEINDED
TEINDING
TEINDS
TEKNONYMIES
TEKNONYMY
TEKTITE
TEKTITES
TEL
TELA
TELAE
TELAMON
TELAMONES
TELARY
TELD
TELECAST
TELECASTED
TELECASTING
TELECASTS
TELECHIR
TELECHIRS
TELECINE
TELECINES
TELECOM
TELECOMS
TELEDU
TELEDUS
TELEFILM
TELEFILMS
TELEGA
TELEGAS
TELEGENIC
TELEGONIES
TELEGONY
TELEGRAM
TELEGRAMS
TELEGRAPH
TELEGRAPHED
TELEGRAPHING
TELEGRAPHS
TELEMARK
TELEMARKED
TELEMARKING
TELEMARKS
TELEMETER
TELEMETERED
TELEMETERING
TELEMETERS
TELEMETRIES

TELEMETRY
TELEOLOGIES
TELEOLOGY
TELEONOMIES
TELEONOMY
TELEOSAUR
TELEOSAURS
TELEOST
TELEOSTS
TELEPATH
TELEPATHED
TELEPATHIES
TELEPATHING
TELEPATHS
TELEPATHY
TELEPHEME
TELEPHEMES
TELEPHONE
TELEPHONED
TELEPHONES
TELEPHONIES
TELEPHONING
TELEPHONY
TELEPHOTO
TELERGIC
TELERGIES
TELERGY
TELESALE
TELESALES
TELESCOPE
TELESCOPED
TELESCOPES
TELESCOPIES
TELESCOPING
TELESCOPY
TELESEME
TELESEMES
TELESES
TELESIS
TELESM
TELESMS
TELESTIC
TELESTICH
TELESTICHS
TELETEX
TELETEXES
TELETEXT
TELETEXTS
TELETHON
TELETHONS
TELETRON
TELETRONS
TELEVIEW
TELEVIEWED
TELEVIEWING
TELEVIEWS
TELEVISE
TELEVISED
TELEVISES
TELEVISING
TELEVISOR
TELEVISORS
TELEX
TELEXED
TELEXES
TELEXING
TELIC
TELL
TELLABLE
TELLAR

TELLARED
TELLARING
TELLARS
TELLER
TELLERED
TELLERING
TELLERS
TELLIES
TELLING
TELLINGLY
TELLINGS
TELLS
TELLTALE
TELLTALES
TELLURAL
TELLURATE
TELLURATES
TELLURIAN
TELLURIANS
TELLURIC
TELLURIDE
TELLURIDES
TELLURION
TELLURIONS
TELLURISE
TELLURISED
TELLURISES
TELLURISING
TELLURITE
TELLURITES
TELLURIUM
TELLURIUMS
TELLURIZE
TELLURIZED
TELLURIZES
TELLURIZING
TELLUROUS
TELLY
TELOPHASE
TELOPHASES
TELOS
TELOSES
TELPHER
TELPHERS
TELS
TELSON
TELSONS
TELT
TEMBLOR
TEMBLORES
TEME
TEMED
TEMENOS
TEMENOSES
TEMERITIES
TEMERITY
TEMEROUS
TEMES
TEMP
TEMPED
TEMPER
TEMPERA
TEMPERAS
TEMPERATE
TEMPERATED
TEMPERATES
TEMPERATING
TEMPERED
TEMPERER
TEMPERERS

TEMPERING
TEMPERINGS
TEMPERS
TEMPEST
TEMPESTED
TEMPESTING
TEMPESTS
TEMPI
TEMPING
TEMPLAR
TEMPLATE
TEMPLATES
TEMPLE
TEMPLED
TEMPLES
TEMPLET
TEMPLETS
TEMPO
TEMPORAL
TEMPORALS
TEMPORARIES
TEMPORARY
TEMPORE
TEMPORISE
TEMPORISED
TEMPORISES
TEMPORISING
TEMPORISINGS
TEMPORIZE
TEMPORIZED
TEMPORIZES
TEMPORIZING
TEMPORIZINGS
TEMPOS
TEMPS
TEMPT
TEMPTABLE
TEMPTED
TEMPTER
TEMPTERS
TEMPTING
TEMPTINGS
TEMPTRESS
TEMPTRESSES
TEMPTS
TEMPURA
TEMPURAS
TEMS
TEMSE
TEMSED
TEMSES
TEMSING
TEMULENCE
TEMULENCES
TEMULENCIES
TEMULENCY
TEMULENT
TEN
TENABLE
TENACE
TENACES
TENACIOUS
TENACITIES
TENACITY
TENACULUM
TENACULUMS
TENAIL
TENAILLE
TENAILLES
TENAILLON

TENAILLONS
TENAILS
TENANCIES
TENANCY
TENANT
TENANTED
TENANTING
TENANTRIES
TENANTRY
TENANTS
TENCH
TENCHES
TEND
TENDANCE
TENDANCES
TENDED
TENDENCE
TENDENCES
TENDENCIES
TENDENCY
TENDENZ
TENDENZEN
TENDER
TENDERED
TENDERER
TENDERERS
TENDEREST
TENDERING
TENDERINGS
TENDERISE
TENDERISED
TENDERISES
TENDERISING
TENDERIZE
TENDERIZED
TENDERIZES
TENDERIZING
TENDERLY
TENDERS
TENDING
TENDINOUS
TENDON
TENDONS
TENDRE
TENDRES
TENDRIL
TENDRILS
TENDRON
TENDRONS
TENDS
TENE
TENEBRAE
TENEBRIO
TENEBRIOS
TENEBRISM
TENEBRISMS
TENEBRIST
TENEBRISTS
TENEBRITIES
TENEBRITY
TENEBROSE
TENEBROUS
TENEMENT
TENEMENTS
TENENDUM
TENENDUMS
TENES
TENESMUS
TENESMUSES
TENET

TENETS
TENFOLD
TENIA
TENIAE
TENIAS
TENIOID
TENNÉ
TENNER
TENNERS
TENNÉS
TENNIS
TENNISES
TENON
TENONED
TENONER
TENONERS
TENONING
TENONS
TENOR
TENORIST
TENORISTS
TENORITE
TENORITES
TENOROON
TENOROONS
TENORS
TENOTOMIES
TENOTOMY
TENOUR
TENOURS
TENPENCE
TENPENCES
TENPENNY
TENPINS
TENREC
TENRECS
TENS
TENSE
TENSED
TENSELY
TENSENESS
TENSENESSES
TENSER
TENSES
TENSEST
TENSIBLE
TENSILE
TENSILITIES
TENSILITY
TENSING
TENSION
TENSIONS
TENSITIES
TENSITY
TENSIVE
TENSON
TENSONS
TENSOR
TENSORS
TENT
TENTACLE
TENTACLED
TENTACLES
TENTACULA
TENTAGE
TENTAGES
TENTATION
TENTATIONS
TENTATIVE
TENTATIVES

TENTED
TENTER
TENTERED
TENTERING
TENTERS
TENTFUL
TENTFULS
TENTH
TENTHLY
TENTHS
TENTIE
TENTIER
TENTIEST
TENTIGO
TENTIGOS
TENTING
TENTINGS
TENTORIA
TENTORIAL
TENTORIUM
TENTORIUMS
TENTS
TENTWISE
TENTY
TENUE
TENUES
TENUIOUS
TENUIS
TENUITIES
TENUITY
TENUOUS
TENUOUSLY
TENURABLE
TENURE
TENURES
TENURIAL
TENUTO
TENZON
TENZONS
TEOCALLI
TEOCALLIS
TEOSINTE
TEOSINTES
TEPAL
TEPALS
TEPEE
TEPEES
TEPEFIED
TEPEFIES
TEPEFY
TEPEFYING
TEPHIGRAM
TEPHIGRAMS
TEPHRA
TEPHRAS
TEPHRITE
TEPHRITES
TEPHRITIC
TEPHROITE
TEPHROITES
TEPID
TEPIDARIA
TEPIDER
TEPIDEST
TEPIDITIES
TEPIDITY
TEPIDLY
TEPIDNESS
TEPIDNESSES
TEQUILA

TEQUILAS
TEQUILLA
TEQUILLAS
TERAI
TERAIS
TERAKIHI
TERAKIHIS
TERAPH
TERAPHIM
TERAPHIMS
TERAS
TERATA
TERATISM
TERATISMS
TERATOGEN
TERATOGENS
TERATOID
TERATOMA
TERATOMATA
TERBIC
TERBIUM
TERBIUMS
TERCE
TERCEL
TERCELET
TERCELETS
TERCELS
TERCES
TERCET
TERCETS
TERCIO
TERCIOS
TEREBENE
TEREBENES
TEREBINTH
TEREBINTHS
TEREBRA
TEREBRAE
TEREBRANT
TEREBRANTS
TEREBRAS
TEREBRATE
TEREBRATED
TEREBRATES
TEREBRATING
TEREDINES
TEREDO
TEREDOS
TEREFA
TEREFAH
TEREK
TEREKS
TERETE
TERF
TERFE
TERFES
TERFS
TERGAL
TERGITE
TERGITES
TERGUM
TERGUMS
TERIYAKI
TERIYAKIS
TERM
TERMAGANT
TERMAGANTS
TERMED
TERMER
TERMERS

TERMINAL
TERMINALS
TERMINATE
TERMINATED
TERMINATES
TERMINATING
TERMINER
TERMINERS
TERMING
TERMINI
TERMINISM
TERMINISMS
TERMINIST
TERMINISTS
TERMINUS
TERMINUSES
TERMITARIES
TERMITARY
TERMITE
TERMITES
TERMLESS
TERMLIES
TERMLY
TERMOR
TERMORS
TERMS
TERN
TERNAL
TERNARIES
TERNARY
TERNATE
TERNATELY
TERNE
TERNED
TERNES
TERNING
TERNION
TERNIONS
TERNS
TERPENE
TERPENES
TERPENOID
TERPENOIDS
TERPINEOL
TERPINEOLS
TERRA
TERRACE
TERRACED
TERRACES
TERRACING
TERRACINGS
TERRAE
TERRAIN
TERRAINS
TERRAMARA
TERRAMARE
TERRANE
TERRANES
TERRAPIN
TERRAPINS
TERRARIA
TERRARIUM
TERRARIUMS
TERRAS
TERRASES
TERRAZZO
TERRAZZOS
TERREEN
TERREENS
TERRELLA

TERRELLAS
TERRENE
TERRENELY
TERRENES
TERRET
TERRETS
TERRIBLE
TERRIBLES
TERRIBLY
TERRICOLE
TERRICOLES
TERRIER
TERRIERS
TERRIES
TERRIFIC
TERRIFIED
TERRIFIES
TERRIFY
TERRIFYING
TERRINE
TERRINES
TERRIT
TERRITORIES
TERRITORY
TERRITS
TERROR
TERRORISE
TERRORISED
TERRORISES
TERRORISING
TERRORISM
TERRORISMS
TERRORIST
TERRORISTS
TERRORIZE
TERRORIZED
TERRORIZES
TERRORIZING
TERRORS
TERRY
TERSE
TERSELY
TERSENESS
TERSENESSES
TERSER
TERSEST
TERSION
TERSIONS
TERTIA
TERTIAL
TERTIALS
TERTIAN
TERTIANS
TERTIARIES
TERTIARY
TERTIAS
TERTIUS
TERTIUSES
TERTS
TERVALENT
TERZETTA
TERZETTAS
TERZETTI
TERZETTO
TERZETTOS
TES
TESLA
TESLAS
TESSELLA
TESSELLAE

TESSELLAR
TESSERA
TESSERACT
TESSERACTS
TESSERAE
TESSERAL
TESSITURA
TESSITURAS
TEST
TESTA
TESTABLE
TESTACIES
TESTACY
TESTAMENT
TESTAMENTS
TESTAMUR
TESTAMURS
TESTAS
TESTATE
TESTATION
TESTATIONS
TESTATOR
TESTATORS
TESTATRICES
TESTATRIX
TESTATRIXES
TESTATUM
TESTATUMS
TESTE
TESTED
TESTEE
TESTEES
TESTER
TESTERN
TESTERNED
TESTERNING
TESTERNS
TESTERS
TESTES
TESTICLE
TESTICLES
TESTIER
TESTIEST
TESTIFIED
TESTIFIER
TESTIFIERS
TESTIFIES
TESTIFY
TESTIFYING
TESTILY
TESTIMONIED
TESTIMONIES
TESTIMONY
TESTIMONYING
TESTINESS
TESTINESSES
TESTING
TESTINGS
TESTIS
TESTON
TESTONS
TESTOON
TESTOONS
TESTRIL
TESTRILL
TESTRILLS
TESTRILS
TESTS
TESTUDINES
TESTUDO

TESTUDOS
TESTY
TETANAL
TETANIC
TETANIES
TETANISE
TETANISED
TETANISES
TETANISING
TETANIZE
TETANIZED
TETANIZES
TETANIZING
TETANOID
TETANUS
TETANUSES
TETANY
TETCHIER
TETCHIEST
TETCHILY
TETCHY
TÊTE
TÊTES
TETHER
TETHERED
TETHERING
TETHERS
TETRA
TETRACID
TETRACT
TETRACTS
TETRAD
TETRADIC
TETRADITE
TETRADITES
TETRADS
TETRAGON
TETRAGONS
TETRAGRAM
TETRAGRAMS
TETRALOGIES
TETRALOGY
TETRAPLA
TETRAPLAS
TETRAPOD
TETRAPODIES
TETRAPODS
TETRAPODY
TETRARCH
TETRARCHIES
TETRARCHS
TETRARCHY
TETRAS
TETRAXON
TETRAXONS
TETRODE
TETRODES
TETRONAL
TETRONALS
TETROXIDE
TETROXIDES
TETRYL
TETRYLS
TETTER
TETTERED
TETTERING
TETTEROUS
TETTERS
TETTIX
TETTIXES

TEUCH
TEUCHAT
TEUCHATS
TEUCHER
TEUCHEST
TEUCHTER
TEUCHTERS
TEUGH
TEUGHER
TEUGHEST
TEW
TEWART
TEWARTS
TEWED
TEWEL
TEWELS
TEWHIT
TEWHITS
TEWING
TEWIT
TEWITS
TEWS
TEXAS
TEXASES
TEXT
TEXTBOOK
TEXTBOOKS
TEXTILE
TEXTILES
TEXTORIAL
TEXTS
TEXTUAL
TEXTUALLY
TEXTUARIES
TEXTUARY
TEXTURAL
TEXTURE
TEXTURED
TEXTURES
TEXTURING
TEXTURISE
TEXTURISED
TEXTURISES
TEXTURISING
TEXTURIZE
TEXTURIZED
TEXTURIZES
TEXTURIZING
THACK
THACKS
THAE
THAGI
THAGIS
THAIM
THAIRM
THAIRMS
THALAMI
THALAMIC
THALAMUS
THALASSIC
THALER
THALERS
THALIAN
THALLI
THALLIC
THALLINE
THALLIUM
THALLIUMS
THALLOID
THALLOUS

THALLUS
THALLUSES
THALWEG
THALWEGS
THAN
THANA
THANADAR
THANADARS
THANAGE
THANAGES
THANAH
THANAHS
THANAS
THANATISM
THANATISMS
THANATIST
THANATISTS
THANATOID
THANE
THANEDOM
THANEDOMS
THANEHOOD
THANEHOODS
THANES
THANESHIP
THANESHIPS
THANK
THANKED
THANKEE
THANKER
THANKERS
THANKFUL
THANKING
THANKINGS
THANKLESS
THANKS
THANNA
THANNAH
THANNAHS
THANNAS
THAR
THARS
THAT
THATAWAY
THATCH
THATCHED
THATCHER
THATCHERS
THATCHES
THATCHING
THATCHINGS
THATCHT
THATNESS
THATNESSES
THAUMATIN
THAUMATINS
THAW
THAWED
THAWER
THAWERS
THAWIER
THAWIEST
THAWING
THAWINGS
THAWLESS
THAWS
THAWY
THE
THEACEOUS
THEANDRIC

THEARCHIC
THEARCHIES
THEARCHY
THEATER
THEATERS
THEATRAL
THEATRE
THEATRES
THEATRIC
THEATRICS
THEAVE
THEAVES
THEBAINE
THEBAINES
THECA
THECAE
THECAL
THECATE
THECODONT
THECODONTS
THEE
THEED
THEEING
THEEK
THEEKED
THEEKING
THEEKS
THEES
THEFT
THEFTBOOT
THEFTBOOTS
THEFTBOTE
THEFTBOTES
THEFTS
THEFTUOUS
THEGITHER
THEGN
THEGNS
THEIC
THEICS
THEINE
THEINES
THEIR
THEIRS
THEISM
THEISMS
THEIST
THEISTIC
THEISTS
THELEMENT
THELEMENTS
THELF
THELVES
THELYTOKIES
THELYTOKY
THEM
THEMA
THEMATA
THEMATIC
THEME
THEMED
THEMES
THEMING
THEMSELVES
THEN
THENABOUT
THENABOUTS
THENAR
THENARS
THENCE

THENS
THEOCRACIES
THEOCRACY
THEOCRASIES
THEOCRASY
THEOCRAT
THEOCRATS
THEODICIES
THEODICY
THEOGONIC
THEOGONIES
THEOGONY
THEOLOGER
THEOLOGERS
THEOLOGIC
THEOLOGIES
THEOLOGUE
THEOLOGUES
THEOLOGY
THEOMACHIES
THEOMACHY
THEOMANCIES
THEOMANCY
THEOMANIA
THEOMANIAS
THEONOMIES
THEONOMY
THEOPATHIES
THEOPATHY
THEOPHAGIES
THEOPHAGY
THEOPHANIES
THEOPHANY
THEORBIST
THEORBISTS
THEORBO
THEORBOS
THEOREM
THEOREMS
THEORETIC
THEORETICS
THEORIC
THEORICS
THEORIES
THEORIQUE
THEORIQUES
THEORISE
THEORISED
THEORISER
THEORISERS
THEORISES
THEORISING
THEORIST
THEORISTS
THEORIZE
THEORIZED
THEORIZER
THEORIZERS
THEORIZES
THEORIZING
THEORY
THEOSOPH
THEOSOPHIES
THEOSOPHS
THEOSOPHY
THEOTOKOI
THEOTOKOS
THEOW
THEOWS
THERALITE

THERALITES
THERAPIES
THERAPIST
THERAPISTS
THERAPSID
THERAPSIDS
THERAPY
THERBLIG
THERBLIGS
THERE
THEREAT
THEREAWAY
THEREBY
THEREFOR
THEREFORE
THEREFROM
THEREIN
THEREINTO
THERENESS
THERENESSES
THEREOF
THEREON
THEREOUT
THERES
THERETO
THEREUNTO
THEREUPON
THEREWITH
THERIAC
THERIACA
THERIACAL
THERIACAS
THERIACS
THERM
THERMAE
THERMAL
THERMALLY
THERMALS
THERMIC
THERMICAL
THERMION
THERMIONS
THERMITE
THERMITES
THERMOS
THERMOSES
THERMOTIC
THERMOTICS
THERMS
THEROID
THEROLOGIES
THEROLOGY
THEROPOD
THEROPODS
THESAURUS
THESAURUSES
THESE
THESES
THESIS
THESPIAN
THESPIANS
THETA
THETAS
THETCH
THETCHED
THETCHES
THETCHING
THETE
THETES
THETHER

THETIC
THETICAL
THEURGIC
THEURGIES
THEURGIST
THEURGISTS
THEURGY
THEW
THEWED
THEWES
THEWIER
THEWIEST
THEWLESS
THEWS
THEWY
THEY
THIAMIN
THIAMINE
THIAMINES
THIAMINS
THIASUS
THIASUSES
THIAZIDE
THIAZIDES
THIBET
THIBETS
THIBLE
THIBLES
THICK
THICKED
THICKEN
THICKENED
THICKENER
THICKENERS
THICKENING
THICKENINGS
THICKENS
THICKER
THICKEST
THICKET
THICKETED
THICKETS
THICKETY
THICKHEAD
THICKHEADS
THICKING
THICKISH
THICKLY
THICKNESS
THICKNESSES
THICKO
THICKOES
THICKOS
THICKS
THICKSET
THICKSETS
THICKSKIN
THICKSKINS
THICKY
THIEF
THIEVE
THIEVED
THIEVERIES
THIEVERY
THIEVES
THIEVING
THIEVINGS
THIEVISH
THIG
THIGGER

THIGGERS
THIGGING
THIGGINGS
THIGGIT
THIGH
THIGHS
THIGS
THILK
THILL
THILLER
THILLERS
THILLS
THIMBLE
THIMBLED
THIMBLES
THIMBLING
THIN
THINE
THING
THINGAMIES
THINGAMY
THINGHOOD
THINGHOODS
THINGIER
THINGIES
THINGIEST
THINGNESS
THINGNESSES
THINGS
THINGUMMIES
THINGUMMY
THINGY
THINK
THINKABLE
THINKER
THINKERS
THINKING
THINKINGS
THINKS
THINLY
THINNED
THINNER
THINNERS
THINNESS
THINNESSES
THINNEST
THINNING
THINNINGS
THINNISH
THINS
THIOL
THIOLS
THIOUREA
THIOUREAS
THIR
THIRAM
THIRAMS
THIRD
THIRDED
THIRDING
THIRDINGS
THIRDLY
THIRDS
THIRDSMAN
THIRDSMEN
THIRL
THIRLAGE
THIRLAGES
THIRLED
THIRLING

THIRLS
THIRST
THIRSTED
THIRSTER
THIRSTERS
THIRSTFUL
THIRSTIER
THIRSTIEST
THIRSTILY
THIRSTING
THIRSTS
THIRSTY
THIRTEEN
THIRTEENS
THIRTIES
THIRTIETH
THIRTIETHS
THIRTY
THIRTYISH
THIS
THISNESS
THISNESSES
THISTLE
THISTLES
THISTLIER
THISTLIEST
THISTLY
THITHER
THIVEL
THIVELS
THLIPSES
THLIPSIS
THO
THOFT
THOFTS
THOLE
THOLED
THOLES
THOLI
THOLING
THOLOBATE
THOLOBATES
THOLOI
THOLOS
THOLUS
THON
THONDER
THONG
THONGED
THONGS
THORACES
THORACIC
THORAX
THORAXES
THORITE
THORITES
THORIUM
THORIUMS
THORN
THORNBACK
THORNBACKS
THORNED
THORNIER
THORNIEST
THORNING
THORNLESS
THORNS
THORNSET
THORNTREE
THORNTREES

THORNY
THORON
THORONS
THOROUGH
THOROUGHER
THOROUGHEST
THOROUGHS
THORP
THORPE
THORPES
THORPS
THOSE
THOTHER
THOU
THOUGH
THOUGHT
THOUGHTED
THOUGHTEN
THOUGHTS
THOUING
THOUS
THOUSAND
THOUSANDS
THOWEL
THOWELS
THOWL
THOWLESS
THOWLS
THRAE
THRALDOM
THRALDOMS
THRALL
THRALLDOM
THRALLDOMS
THRALLED
THRALLING
THRALLS
THRANG
THRANGED
THRANGING
THRANGS
THRAPPLE
THRAPPLED
THRAPPLES
THRAPPLING
THRASH
THRASHED
THRASHER
THRASHERS
THRASHES
THRASHING
THRASHINGS
THRASONIC
THRAVE
THRAVES
THRAW
THRAWARD
THRAWART
THRAWING
THRAWN
THRAWS
THREAD
THREADED
THREADEN
THREADER
THREADERS
THREADIER
THREADIEST
THREADING
THREADS

THREADY
THREAP
THREAPING
THREAPIT
THREAPS
THREAT
THREATED
THREATEN
THREATENED
THREATENING
THREATENINGS
THREATENS
THREATFUL
THREATING
THREATS
THREAVE
THREAVES
THREE
THREEFOLD
THREENESS
THREENESSES
THREEP
THREEPING
THREEPIT
THREEPS
THREES
THREESOME
THREESOMES
THRENE
THRENES
THRENETIC
THRENODE
THRENODES
THRENODIC
THRENODIES
THRENODY
THRENOS
THRENOSES
THREONINE
THREONINES
THRESH
THRESHED
THRESHEL
THRESHELS
THRESHER
THRESHERS
THRESHES
THRESHING
THRESHINGS
THRESHOLD
THRESHOLDS
THRETTIES
THRETTY
THREW
THRICE
THRID
THRIDACE
THRIDACES
THRIDDED
THRIDDING
THRIDS
THRIFT
THRIFTIER
THRIFTIEST
THRIFTILY
THRIFTS
THRIFTY /
THRILL
THRILLANT
THRILLED

THRILLER
THRILLERS
THRILLIER
THRILLIEST
THRILLING
THRILLS
THRILLY
THRIMSA
THRIMSAS
THRIP
THRIPS
THRIPSES
THRISSEL
THRISSELS
THRIST
THRISTED
THRISTING
THRISTLE
THRISTLES
THRISTS
THRISTY
THRIVE
THRIVED
THRIVEN
THRIVER
THRIVERS
THRIVES
THRIVING
THRIVINGS
THRO
THROAT
THROATED
THROATIER
THROATIEST
THROATILY
THROATS
THROATY
THROB
THROBBED
THROBBING
THROBBINGS
THROBLESS
THROBS
THROE
THROED
THROEING
THROES
THROMBI
THROMBIN
THROMBINS
THROMBOSE
THROMBOSED
THROMBOSES
THROMBOSING
THROMBUS
THRONE
THRONED
THRONES
THRONG
THRONGED
THRONGFUL
THRONGING
THRONGINGS
THRONGS
THRONING
THROPPLE
THROPPLED
THROPPLES
THROPPLING
THROSTLE

THROSTLES
THROTTLE
THROTTLED
THROTTLER
THROTTLERS
THROTTLES
THROTTLING
THROTTLINGS
THROUGH
THROUGHLY
THROVE
THROW
THROWE
THROWER
THROWERS
THROWES
THROWING
THROWINGS
THROWN
THROWS
THROWSTER
THROWSTERS
THRU
THRUM
THRUMMED
THRUMMER
THRUMMERS
THRUMMIER
THRUMMIEST
THRUMMING
THRUMMINGS
THRUMMY
THRUMS
THRUSH
THRUSHES
THRUST
THRUSTED
THRUSTER
THRUSTERS
THRUSTING
THRUSTINGS
THRUSTS
THRUTCH
THRUTCHED
THRUTCHES
THRUTCHING
THRUWAY
THRUWAYS
THRYMSA
THRYMSAS
THUD
THUDDED
THUDDING
THUDS
THUG
THUGGEE
THUGGEES
THUGGERIES
THUGGERY
THUGGISM
THUGGISMS
THUGS
THUJA
THUJAS
THULIA
THULIAS
THULITE
THULITES
THULIUM
THULIUMS

| | | | | |
|---|---|---|---|---|
| THUMB | THYMIDINES | TICKLERS | TIERS | TILE |
| THUMBED | THYMIER | TICKLES | TIES | TILED |
| THUMBIER | THYMIEST | TICKLIER | TIETAC | TILEFISH |
| THUMBIEST | THYMINE | TICKLIEST | TIETACK | TILEFISHES |
| THUMBING | THYMINES | TICKLING | TIETACKS | TILER |
| THUMBKINS | THYMOCYTE | TICKLINGS | TIETACS | TILERIES |
| THUMBLESS | THYMOCYTES | TICKLISH | TIFF | TILERS |
| THUMBLING | THYMOL | TICKLY | TIFFANIES | TILERY |
| THUMBLINGS | THYMOLS | TICKS | TIFFANY | TILES |
| THUMBNAIL | THYMUS | TICKY | TIFFED | TILING |
| THUMBNAILS | THYMUSES | TICS | TIFFIN | TILINGS |
| THUMBPOT | THYMY | TID | TIFFING | TILL |
| THUMBPOTS | THYRATRON | TIDAL | TIFFINGS | TILLABLE |
| THUMBS | THYRATRONS | TIDBIT | TIFFINS | TILLAGE |
| THUMBY | THYREOID | TIDBITS | TIFFS | TILLAGES |
| THUMP | THYRISTOR | TIDDIER | TIFT | TILLED |
| THUMPED | THYRISTORS | TIDDIES | TIFTED | TILLER |
| THUMPER | THYROID | TIDDIEST | TIFTING | TILLERED |
| THUMPERS | THYROIDS | TIDDLE | TIFTS | TILLERING |
| THUMPING | THYROXIN | TIDDLED | TIG | TILLERS |
| THUMPS | THYROXINE | TIDDLER | TIGE | TILLIER |
| THUNDER | THYROXINES | TIDDLERS | TIGER | TILLIEST |
| THUNDERED | THYROXINS | TIDDLES | TIGERISH | TILLING |
| THUNDERER | THYRSE | TIDDLEY | TIGERISM | TILLINGS |
| THUNDERERS | THYRSES | TIDDLEYS | TIGERISMS | TILLITE |
| THUNDERING | THYRSI | TIDDLIER | TIGERLY | TILLITES |
| THUNDERINGS | THYRSOID | TIDDLIES | TIGERS | TILLS |
| THUNDERS | THYRSUS | TIDDLIEST | TIGERY | TILLY |
| THUNDERY | THYSELF | TIDDLING | TIGES | TILS |
| THUNDROUS | TI | TIDDLY | TIGGED | TILT |
| THURIBLE | TIAR | TIDDY | TIGGING | TILTABLE |
| THURIBLES | TIARA | TIDE | TIGHT | TILTED |
| THURIFER | TIARAED | TIDED | TIGHTEN | TILTER |
| THURIFERS | TIARAS | TIDELESS | TIGHTENED | TILTERS |
| THURIFIED | TIARS | TIDEMARK | TIGHTENER | TILTH |
| THURIFIES | TIBIA | TIDEMARKS | TIGHTENERS | TILTHS |
| THURIFY | TIBIAE | TIDEMILL | TIGHTENING | TILTING |
| THURIFYING | TIBIAL | TIDEMILLS | TIGHTENS | TILTINGS |
| THUS | TIBIAS | TIDES | TIGHTER | TILTS |
| THUSES | TIC | TIDIED | TIGHTEST | TIMARIOT |
| THUSNESS | TICAL | TIDIER | TIGHTISH | TIMARIOTS |
| THUSNESSES | TICALS | TIDIES | TIGHTLY | TIMBAL |
| THUSWISE | TICCA | TIDIEST | TIGHTNESS | TIMBALE |
| THWACK | TICE | TIDILY | TIGHTNESSES | TIMBALES |
| THWACKED | TICED | TIDINESS | TIGHTS | TIMBALS |
| THWACKER | TICES | TIDINESSES | TIGHTWAD | TIMBER |
| THWACKERS | TICH | TIDING | TIGHTWADS | TIMBERED |
| THWACKING | TICHES | TIDINGS | TIGLON | TIMBERING |
| THWACKINGS | TICHIER | TIDIVATE | TIGLONS | TIMBERINGS |
| THWACKS | TICHIEST | TIDIVATED | TIGON | TIMBERS |
| THWAITE | TICHY | TIDIVATES | TIGONS | TIMBÓ |
| THWAITES | TICING | TIDIVATING | TIGRESS | TIMBÓS |
| THWART | TICK | TIDS | TIGRESSES | TIMBRE |
| THWARTED | TICKED | TIDY | TIGRINE | TIMBREL |
| THWARTER | TICKEN | TIDYING | TIGRISH | TIMBRELS |
| THWARTERS | TICKENS | TIE | TIGROID | TIMBRES |
| THWARTING | TICKER | TIED | TIGS | TIME |
| THWARTINGS | TICKERS | TIELESS | TIKA | TIMED |
| THWARTLY | TICKET | TIER | TIKAS | TIMELESS |
| THWARTS | TICKETED | TIERCE | TIKE | TIMELIER |
| THY | TICKETING | TIERCÉ | TIKES | TIMELIEST |
| THYINE | TICKETS | TIERCEL | TIKI | TIMELY |
| THYLACINE | TICKEY | TIERCELET | TIKIS | TIMENOGUY |
| THYLACINES | TICKEYS | TIERCELETS | TIL | TIMENOGUYS |
| THYLOSE | TICKIES | TIERCELS | TILAPIA | TIMEOUS |
| THYLOSES | TICKING | TIERCERON | TILAPIAS | TIMEOUSLY |
| THYLOSIS | TICKINGS | TIERCERONS | TILBURIES | TIMEPIECE |
| THYME | TICKLE | TIERCES | TILBURY | TIMEPIECES |
| THYMES | TICKLED | TIERED | TILDE | TIMER |
| THYMIDINE | TICKLER | TIERING | TILDES | TIMERS |

TIMES
TIMESCALE
TIMESCALES
TIMETABLE
TIMETABLED
TIMETABLES
TIMETABLING
TIMID
TIMIDER
TIMIDEST
TIMIDITIES
TIMIDITY
TIMIDLY
TIMIDNESS
TIMIDNESSES
TIMING
TIMINGS
TIMIST
TIMISTS
TIMOCRACIES
TIMOCRACY
TIMON
TIMONEER
TIMONEERS
TIMONS
TIMOROUS
TIMORSOME
TIMOTHIES
TIMOTHY
TIMOUS
TIMOUSLY
TIMPANI
TIMPANIST
TIMPANISTS
TIMPANO
TIMPS
TIN
TINAJA
TINAJAS
TINAMOU
TINAMOUS
TINCAL
TINCALS
TINCHEL
TINCHELS
TINCT
TINCTED
TINCTING
TINCTS
TINCTURE
TINCTURED
TINCTURES
TINCTURING
TIND
TINDAL
TINDALS
TINDED
TINDER
TINDERS
TINDERY
TINDING
TINDS
TINE
TINEA
TINEAS
TINED
TINEID
TINEIDS
TINES
TINFOIL

TINFOILS
TINFUL
TINFULS
TING
TINGE
TINGED
TINGES
TINGING
TINGLE
TINGLED
TINGLER
TINGLERS
TINGLES
TINGLIER
TINGLIEST
TINGLING
TINGLINGS
TINGLISH
TINGLY
TINGS
TINGUAITE
TINGUAITES
TINHORN
TINHORNS
TINIER
TINIEST
TININESS
TININESSES
TINING
TINK
TINKED
TINKER
TINKERED
TINKERING
TINKERINGS
TINKERS
TINKING
TINKLE
TINKLED
TINKLER
TINKLERS
TINKLES
TINKLIER
TINKLIEST
TINKLING
TINKLINGS
TINKLY
TINKS
TINMAN
TINMEN
TINNED
TINNER
TINNERS
TINNIE
TINNIER
TINNIES
TINNIEST
TINNING
TINNINGS
TINNITUS
TINNITUSES
TINNY
TINPOT
TINPOTS
TINS
TINSEL
TINSELLED
TINSELLING
TINSELLY
TINSELRIES

TINSELRY
TINSELS
TINSEY
TINSEYS
TINSMITH
TINSMITHS
TINSNIPS
TINSTONE
TINSTONES
TINT
TINTED
TINTER
TINTERS
TINTIER
TINTIEST
TINTINESS
TINTINESSES
TINTING
TINTINGS
TINTLESS
TINTS
TINTY
TINTYPE
TINTYPES
TINWARE
TINWARES
TINY
TIP
TIPI
TIPIS
TIPPED
TIPPER
TIPPERS
TIPPET
TIPPETS
TIPPIER
TIPPIEST
TIPPING
TIPPINGS
TIPPLE
TIPPLED
TIPPLER
TIPPLERS
TIPPLES
TIPPLING
TIPPY
TIPS
TIPSIER
TIPSIEST
TIPSIFIED
TIPSIFIES
TIPSIFY
TIPSIFYING
TIPSILY
TIPSINESS
TIPSINESSES
TIPSTAFF
TIPSTAFFS
TIPSTAVES
TIPSTER
TIPSTERS
TIPSY
TIPT
TIPTOE
TIPTOED
TIPTOEING
TIPTOES
TIPTOP
TIPTOPS
TIPULA

TIPULAS
TIRADE
TIRADES
TIRASSE
TIRASSES
TIRE
TIRED
TIREDER
TIREDEST
TIREDNESS
TIREDNESSES
TIRELESS
TIRELING
TIRELINGS
TIRES
TIRESOME
TIRING
TIRINGS
TIRL
TIRLED
TIRLING
TIRLS
TIRO
TIROES
TIROS
TIRR
TIRRED
TIRRING
TIRRIT
TIRRITS
TIRRIVEE
TIRRIVEES
TIRRIVIE
TIRRIVIES
TIRRS
TIS
TISANE
TISANES
TISICK
TISICKS
TISSUE
TISSUED
TISSUES
TISSUING
TISWAS
TISWASES
TIT
TITAN
TITANATE
TITANATES
TITANIC
TITANITE
TITANITES
TITANIUM
TITANIUMS
TITANOUS
TITANS
TITBIT
TITBITS
TITCH
TITCHES
TITE
TITELY
TITER
TITERS
TITFER
TITFERS
TITHABLE
TITHE
TITHED

TITHER
TITHERS
TITHES
TITHING
TITHINGS
TITI
TITIAN
TITIANS
TITILLATE
TITILLATED
TITILLATES
TITILLATING
TITIS
TITIVATE
TITIVATED
TITIVATES
TITIVATING
TITLARK
TITLARKS
TITLE
TITLED
TITLELESS
TITLER
TITLERS
TITLES
TITLING
TITLINGS
TITMICE
TITMOSE
TITMOUSE
TITOKI
TITOKIS
TITRATE
TITRATED
TITRATES
TITRATING
TITRATION
TITRATIONS
TITRE
TITRES
TITS
TITTED
TITTER
TITTERED
TITTERER
TITTERERS
TITTERING
TITTERINGS
TITTERS
TITTIES
TITTING
TITTIVATE
TITTIVATED
TITTIVATES
TITTIVATING
TITTLE
TITTLEBAT
TITTLEBATS
TITTLED
TITTLES
TITTLING
TITTUP
TITTUPED
TITTUPING
TITTUPS
TITTUPY
TITTY
TITUBANCIES
TITUBANCY
TITUBANT

TITUBATE
TITUBATED
TITUBATES
TITUBATING
TITULAR
TITULARIES
TITULARLY
TITULARS
TITULARY
TITULE
TITULED
TITULES
TITULING
TITUP
TITUPED
TITUPING
TITUPS
TITUPY
TIZWAS
TIZWASES
TIZZ
TIZZES
TIZZIES
TIZZY
TMESES
TMESIS
TO
TOAD
TOADFISH
TOADFISHES
TOADFLAX
TOADFLAXES
TOADGRASS
TOADGRASSES
TOADIED
TOADIES
TOADRUSH
TOADRUSHES
TOADS
TOADSTOOL
TOADSTOOLS
TOADY
TOADYING
TOADYISH
TOADYISM
TOADYISMS
TOAST
TOASTED
TOASTER
TOASTERS
TOASTIE
TOASTIES
TOASTING
TOASTINGS
TOASTS
TOASTY
TOAZE
TOAZED
TOAZES
TOAZING
TOBACCO
TOBACCOES
TOBACCOS
TOBIES
TOBOGGAN
TOBOGGANED
TOBOGGANING
TOBOGGANINGS
TOBOGGANS
TOBOGGIN

TOBOGGINED
TOBOGGINING
TOBOGGINS
TOBY
TOCCATA
TOCCATAS
TOCCATINA
TOCCATINAS
TOCHER
TOCHERED
TOCHERING
TOCHERS
TOCO
TOCOLOGIES
TOCOLOGY
TOCOS
TOCSIN
TOCSINS
TOD
TODAY
TODAYS
TODDE
TODDED
TODDES
TODDIES
TODDING
TODDLE
TODDLED
TODDLER
TODDLERS
TODDLES
TODDLING
TODDY
TODIES
TODS
TODY
TOE
TOECAP
TOECAPS
TOECLIP
TOECLIPS
TOED
TOEING
TOENAIL
TOENAILS
TOES
TOFF
TOFFEE
TOFFEES
TOFFIER
TOFFIES
TOFFIEST
TOFFISH
TOFFS
TOFFY
TOFORE
TOFT
TOFTS
TOFU
TOFUS
TOG
TOGA
TOGAED
TOGAS
TOGATE
TOGATED
TOGE
TOGED
TOGES
TOGETHER

TOGGED
TOGGERIES
TOGGERY
TOGGING
TOGGLE
TOGGLED
TOGGLES
TOGGLING
TOGS
TOGUE
TOGUES
TOHEROA
TOHEROAS
TOHO
TOHOS
TOIL
TOILE
TOILED
TOILER
TOILERS
TOILES
TOILET
TOILETED
TOILETING
TOILETRIES
TOILETRY
TOILETS
TOILETTE
TOILETTES
TOILFUL
TOILINET
TOILINETS
TOILING
TOILINGS
TOILLESS
TOILS
TOILSOME
TOISE
TOISEACH
TOISEACHS
TOISECH
TOISECHS
TOISES
TOISON
TOISONS
TOKAMAK
TOKAMAKS
TOKE
TOKED
TOKEN
TOKENED
TOKENING
TOKENISM
TOKENISMS
TOKENS
TOKES
TOKING
TOKO
TOKOLOGIES
TOKOLOGY
TOKOLOSHE
TOKOLOSHES
TOKOS
TOLA
TOLAS
TOLBOOTH
TOLBOOTHS
TOLD
TOLE
TOLED

TOLERABLE
TOLERABLY
TOLERANCE
TOLERANCES
TOLERANT
TOLERATE
TOLERATED
TOLERATES
TOLERATING
TOLERATOR
TOLERATORS
TOLES
TOLING
TOLINGS
TOLL
TOLLABLE
TOLLAGE
TOLLAGES
TOLLBOOTH
TOLLBOOTHS
TOLLDISH
TOLLDISHES
TOLLED
TOLLER
TOLLERS
TOLLGATE
TOLLGATES
TOLLING
TOLLINGS
TOLLMAN
TOLLMEN
TOLLS
TOLSEL
TOLSELS
TOLSEY
TOLSEYS
TOLT
TOLTER
TOLTERED
TOLTERING
TOLTERS
TOLTS
TOLU
TOLUATE
TOLUATES
TOLUENE
TOLUENES
TOLUIC
TOLUIDINE
TOLUIDINES
TOLUOL
TOLUOLS
TOLUS
TOLZEY
TOLZEYS
TOM
TOMAHAWK
TOMAHAWKED
TOMAHAWKING
TOMAHAWKS
TOMALLEY
TOMALLEYS
TOMAN
TOMANS
TOMATO
TOMATOES
TOMB
TOMBAC
TOMBACS
TOMBAK

TOMBAKS
TOMBED
TOMBIC
TOMBING
TOMBLESS
TOMBOC
TOMBOCS
TOMBOLA
TOMBOLAS
TOMBOLO
TOMBOLOS
TOMBOY
TOMBOYISH
TOMBOYS
TOMBS
TOMBSTONE
TOMBSTONES
TOME
TOMENTOSE
TOMENTOUS
TOMENTUM
TOMENTUMS
TOMES
TOMFOOL
TOMFOOLED
TOMFOOLING
TOMFOOLS
TOMIAL
TOMIUM
TOMIUMS
TOMMIED
TOMMIES
TOMMY
TOMMYING
TOMOGRAM
TOMOGRAMS
TOMOGRAPH
TOMOGRAPHS
TOMORROW
TOMORROWS
TOMPION
TOMPIONS
TOMPON
TOMPONS
TOMS
TOMTIT
TOMTITS
TON
TONAL
TONALITE
TONALITES
TONALITIES
TONALITY
TONANT
TONDI
TONDINI
TONDINO
TONDINOS
TONDO
TONDOS
TONE
TONED
TONELESS
TONEME
TONEMES
TONEMIC
TONES
TONETIC
TONEY
TONG

TONGA
TONGAS
TONGS
TONGUE
TONGUED
TONGUELET
TONGUELETS
TONGUES
TONGUING
TONGUINGS
TONIC
TONICITIES
TONICITY
TONICS
TONIER
TONIES
TONIEST
TONIGHT
TONIGHTS
TONING
TONISH
TONISHLY
TONITE
TONITES
TONK
TONKED
TONKER
TONKERS
TONKING
TONKS
TONLET
TONLETS
TONNAG
TONNAGE
TONNAGES
TONNAGS
TONNE
TONNEAU
TONNEAUS
TONNELL
TONNELLS
TONNES
TONNISH
TONNISHLY
TONOMETER
TONOMETERS
TONOMETRIES
TONOMETRY
TONS
TONSIL
TONSILLAR
TONSILS
TONSOR
TONSORIAL
TONSORS
TONSURE
TONSURED
TONSURES
TONTINE
TONTINER
TONTINERS
TONTINES
TONUS
TONUSES
TONY
TOO
TOOART
TOOARTS
TOOK
TOOL

TOOLBAG
TOOLBAGS
TOOLBOX
TOOLBOXES
TOOLED
TOOLER
TOOLERS
TOOLHOUSE
TOOLHOUSES
TOOLING
TOOLINGS
TOOLKIT
TOOLKITS
TOOLMAKER
TOOLMAKERS
TOOLMAN
TOOLMEN
TOOLROOM
TOOLROOMS
TOOLS
TOOM
TOOMED
TOOMER
TOOMEST
TOOMING
TOOMS
TOON
TOONS
TOORIE
TOORIES
TOOT
TOOTED
TOOTER
TOOTERS
TOOTH
TOOTHACHE
TOOTHACHES
TOOTHCOMB
TOOTHCOMBS
TOOTHED
TOOTHFUL
TOOTHFULS
TOOTHIER
TOOTHIEST
TOOTHING
TOOTHLESS
TOOTHPICK
TOOTHPICKS
TOOTHS
TOOTHSOME
TOOTHWASH
TOOTHWASHES
TOOTHWORT
TOOTHWORTS
TOOTHY
TOOTING
TOOTLE
TOOTLED
TOOTLES
TOOTLING
TOOTS
TOOTSIE
TOOTSIES
TOOTSY
TOP
TOPARCH
TOPARCHIES
TOPARCHS
TOPARCHY
TOPAZ

TOPAZES
TOPAZINE
TOPCOAT
TOPCOATS
TOPE
TOPECTOMIES
TOPECTOMY
TOPED
TOPEE
TOPEES
TOPEK
TOPEKS
TOPER
TOPERS
TOPES
TOPFULL
TOPHI
TOPHUS
TOPI
TOPIARIAN
TOPIARIES
TOPIARIST
TOPIARISTS
TOPIARY
TOPIC
TOPICAL
TOPICALLY
TOPICS
TOPING
TOPIS
TOPKNOT
TOPKNOTS
TOPLESS
TOPLOFTY
TOPMAKER
TOPMAKERS
TOPMAKING
TOPMAKINGS
TOPMAN
TOPMAST
TOPMASTS
TOPMEN
TOPMINNOW
TOPMINNOWS
TOPMOST
TOPOI
TOPOLOGIC
TOPOLOGIES
TOPOLOGY
TOPONYM
TOPONYMAL
TOPONYMIC
TOPONYMICS
TOPONYMIES
TOPONYMS
TOPONYMY
TOPOS
TOPPED
TOPPER
TOPPERS
TOPPING
TOPPINGLY
TOPPINGS
TOPPLE
TOPPLED
TOPPLES
TOPPLING
TOPS
TOPSAIL
TOPSAILS

TOPSIDE
TOPSIDES
TOPSMAN
TOPSMEN
TOPSPIN
TOPSPINS
TOQUE
TOQUES
TOR
TORAN
TORANA
TORANAS
TORANS
TORBANITE
TORBANITES
TORC
TORCH
TORCHED
TORCHER
TORCHÈRE
TORCHÈRES
TORCHERS
TORCHES
TORCHING
TORCHON
TORCHONS
TORCS
TORCULAR
TORCULARS
TORDION
TORDIONS
TORE
TOREADOR
TOREADORS
TORERO
TOREROS
TORES
TOREUTIC
TOREUTICS
TORGOCH
TORGOCHS
TORI
TORIC
TORII
TORIIS
TORMENT
TORMENTED
TORMENTIL
TORMENTILS
TORMENTING
TORMENTINGS
TORMENTOR
TORMENTORS
TORMENTS
TORMENTUM
TORMENTUMS
TORMINA
TORMINAL
TORMINOUS
TORN
TORNADE
TORNADES
TORNADIC
TORNADO
TORNADOES
TOROID
TOROIDAL
TOROIDS
TORPEDO
TORPEDOED

TORPEDOER
TORPEDOERS
TORPEDOES
TORPEDOING
TORPEDOS
TORPEFIED
TORPEFIES
TORPEFY
TORPEFYING
TORPID
TORPIDITIES
TORPIDITY
TORPIDLY
TORPIDS
TORPITUDE
TORPITUDES
TORPOR
TORPORS
TORQUATE
TORQUATED
TORQUE
TORQUED
TORQUES
TORR
TORREFIED
TORREFIES
TORREFY
TORREFYING
TORRENT
TORRENTS
TORRET
TORRETS
TORRID
TORRIDER
TORRIDEST
TORRIDITIES
TORRIDITY
TORRS
TORS
TORSADE
TORSADES
TORSE
TORSEL
TORSELS
TORSES
TORSION
TORSIONAL
TORSIONS
TORSIVE
TORSK
TORSKS
TORSO
TORSOS
TORT
TORTE
TORTEN
TORTES
TORTILE
TORTILITIES
TORTILITY
TORTILLA
TORTILLAS
TORTIOUS
TORTIVE
TORTOISE
TORTOISES
TORTRICES
TORTRICID
TORTRICIDS
TORTRIX

| | | | | |
|---|---|---|---|---|
| TORTS | TOTALS | TOUGHNESS | TOWAGE | TOWSE |
| TORTUOUS | TOTARA | TOUGHNESSES | TOWAGES | TOWSED |
| TORTURE | TOTARAS | TOUGHS | TOWARD | TOWSER |
| TORTURED | TOTE | TOUK | TOWARDLY | TOWSERS |
| TORTURER | TOTED | TOUKS | TOWARDS | TOWSES |
| TORTURERS | TOTEM | TOUN | TOWBAR | TOWSIER |
| TORTURES | TOTEMIC | TOUNS | TOWBARS | TOWSIEST |
| TORTURING | TOTEMISM | TOUPEE | TOWED | TOWSING |
| TORTURINGS | TOTEMISMS | TOUPEES | TOWEL | TOWSY |
| TORTUROUS | TOTEMIST | TOUPET | TOWELLED | TOWT |
| TORUFFLED | TOTEMISTS | TOUPETS | TOWELLING | TOWTED |
| TORULA | TOTEMS | TOUR | TOWELLINGS | TOWTING |
| TORULAS | TOTES | TOURACO | TOWELS | TOWTS |
| TORULIN | TOTHER | TOURACOS | TOWER | TOWY |
| TORULINS | TOTIENT | TOURED | TOWERED | TOWZE |
| TORULOSE | TOTIENTS | TOURER | TOWERIER | TOWZED |
| TORULOSES | TOTING | TOURERS | TOWERIEST | TOWZES |
| TORULOSIS | TOTITIVE | TOURING | TOWERING | TOWZING |
| TORULUS | TOTITIVES | TOURINGS | TOWERLESS | TOXAEMIA |
| TORULUSES | TOTS | TOURISM | TOWERS | TOXAEMIAS |
| TORUS | TOTTED | TOURISMS | TOWERY | TOXAEMIC |
| TOSE | TOTTER | TOURIST | TOWHEE | TOXAPHENE |
| TOSED | TOTTERED | TOURISTIC | TOWHEES | TOXAPHENES |
| TOSES | TOTTERER | TOURISTS | TOWIER | TOXIC |
| TOSH | TOTTERERS | TOURISTY | TOWIEST | TOXICAL |
| TOSHACH | TOTTERING | TOURNEDOS | TOWING | TOXICALLY |
| TOSHACHS | TOTTERINGS | TOURNEY | TOWINGS | TOXICANT |
| TOSHED | TOTTERS | TOURNEYED | TOWLINE | TOXICANTS |
| TOSHER | TOTTERY | TOURNEYER | TOWLINES | TOXICITIES |
| TOSHERS | TOTTIE | TOURNEYERS | TOWMON | TOXICITY |
| TOSHES | TOTTIER | TOURNEYING | TOWMOND | TOXIN |
| TOSHIER | TOTTIES | TOURNEYS | TOWMONDS | TOXINS |
| TOSHIEST | TOTTIEST | TOURNURE | TOWMONS | TOXOCARA |
| TOSHING | TOTTING | TOURNURES | TOWMONT | TOXOCARAS |
| TOSHY | TOTTINGS | TOURS | TOWMONTS | TOXOID |
| TOSING | TOTTY | TOUSE | TOWN | TOXOIDS |
| TOSS | TOUCAN | TOUSED | TOWNEE | TOXOPHILIES |
| TOSSED | TOUCANET | TOUSER | TOWNEES | TOXOPHILY |
| TOSSEN | TOUCANETS | TOUSERS | TOWNHOUSE | TOY |
| TOSSER | TOUCANS | TOUSES | TOWNHOUSES | TOYED |
| TOSSERS | TOUCH | TOUSIER | TOWNIE | TOYER |
| TOSSES | TOUCHABLE | TOUSIEST | TOWNIER | TOYERS |
| TOSSIER | TOUCHÉ | TOUSING | TOWNIES | TOYING |
| TOSSIEST | TOUCHED | TOUSINGS | TOWNIEST | TOYINGS |
| TOSSILY | TOUCHER | TOUSLE | TOWNISH | TOYISH |
| TOSSING | TOUCHERS | TOUSLED | TOWNLAND | TOYISHLY |
| TOSSINGS | TOUCHES | TOUSLES | TOWNLANDS | TOYLESOME |
| TOSSPOT | TOUCHIER | TOUSLING | TOWNLING | TOYLSOM |
| TOSSPOTS | TOUCHIEST | TOUSTIE | TOWNLINGS | TOYMAN |
| TOSSY | TOUCHILY | TOUSY | TOWNLY | TOYMEN |
| TOST | TOUCHING | TOUT | TOWNS | TOYS |
| TOT | TOUCHINGS | TOUTED | TOWNSCAPE | TOYSHOP |
| TOTAL | TOUCHLESS | TOUTER | TOWNSCAPED | TOYSHOPS |
| TOTALISE | TOUCHWOOD | TOUTERS | TOWNSCAPES | TOYSOME |
| TOTALISED | TOUCHWOODS | TOUTIE | TOWNSCAPING | TOYWOMAN |
| TOTALISER | TOUCHY | TOUTIER | TOWNSCAPINGS | TOYWOMEN |
| TOTALISERS | TOUGH | TOUTIEST | TOWNSFOLK | TOZE |
| TOTALISES | TOUGHEN | TOUTING | TOWNSFOLKS | TOZED |
| TOTALISING | TOUGHENED | TOUTS | TOWNSHIP | TOZES |
| TOTALITIES | TOUGHENER | TOUZE | TOWNSHIPS | TOZIE |
| TOTALITY | TOUGHENERS | TOUZED | TOWNSKIP | TOZIES |
| TOTALIZE | TOUGHENING | TOUZES | TOWNSKIPS | TOZING |
| TOTALIZED | TOUGHENINGS | TOUZING | TOWNSMAN | TRABEATE |
| TOTALIZER | TOUGHENS | TOUZLE | TOWNSMEN | TRABEATED |
| TOTALIZERS | TOUGHER | TOUZLED | TOWNY | TRABECULA |
| TOTALIZES | TOUGHEST | TOUZLES | TOWPATH | TRABECULAE |
| TOTALIZING | TOUGHIE | TOUZLING | TOWPATHS | TRACE |
| TOTALLED | TOUGHIES | TOVARISH | TOWROPE | TRACEABLE |
| TOTALLING | TOUGHISH | TOVARISHES | TOWROPES | TRACEABLY |
| TOTALLY | TOUGHLY | TOW | TOWS | TRACED |

TRACELESS
TRACER
TRACERIED
TRACERIES
TRACERS
TRACERY
TRACES
TRACHEA
TRACHEAE
TRACHEAL
TRACHEARIES
TRACHEARY
TRACHEATE
TRACHEID
TRACHEIDE
TRACHEIDES
TRACHEIDS
TRACHITIS
TRACHITISES
TRACHOMA
TRACHOMAS
TRACHYTE
TRACHYTES
TRACHYTIC
TRACING
TRACINGS
TRACK
TRACKAGE
TRACKAGES
TRACKED
TRACKER
TRACKERS
TRACKING
TRACKINGS
TRACKLESS
TRACKMAN
TRACKMEN
TRACKROAD
TRACKROADS
TRACKS
TRACKWAY
TRACKWAYS
TRACT
TRACTABLE
TRACTATE
TRACTATES
TRACTATOR
TRACTATORS
TRACTED
TRACTILE
TRACTING
TRACTION
TRACTIONS
TRACTIVE
TRACTOR
TRACTORS
TRACTRIX
TRACTRIXES
TRACTS
TRACTUS
TRACTUSES
TRAD
TRADABLE
TRADE
TRADEABLE
TRADED
TRADEFUL
TRADELESS
TRADEMARK
TRADEMARKS

TRADENAME
TRADENAMES
TRADER
TRADERS
TRADES
TRADESMAN
TRADESMEN
TRADING
TRADINGS
TRADITION
TRADITIONS
TRADITIVE
TRADITOR
TRADITORS
TRADS
TRADUCE
TRADUCED
TRADUCER
TRADUCERS
TRADUCES
TRADUCING
TRADUCINGS
TRAFFIC
TRAFFICKED
TRAFFICKING
TRAFFICKINGS
TRAFFICS
TRAGEDIAN
TRAGEDIANS
TRAGEDIES
TRAGEDY
TRAGELAPH
TRAGELAPHS
TRAGI
TRAGIC
TRAGICAL
TRAGOPAN
TRAGOPANS
TRAGULE
TRAGULES
TRAGULINE
TRAGUS
TRAHISON
TRAHISONS
TRAIK
TRAIKED
TRAIKING
TRAIKIT
TRAIKS
TRAIL
TRAILED
TRAILER
TRAILERED
TRAILERING
TRAILERS
TRAILING
TRAILS
TRAIN
TRAINABLE
TRAINED
TRAINEE
TRAINEES
TRAINER
TRAINERS
TRAINING
TRAININGS
TRAINS
TRAIPSE
TRAIPSED
TRAIPSES

TRAIPSING
TRAIPSINGS
TRAIT
TRAITOR
TRAITORLY
TRAITORS
TRAITRESS
TRAITRESSES
TRAITS
TRAJECT
TRAJECTED
TRAJECTING
TRAJECTS
TRAM
TRAMMEL
TRAMMELLED
TRAMMELLING
TRAMMELS
TRAMP
TRAMPED
TRAMPER
TRAMPERS
TRAMPET
TRAMPETS
TRAMPETTE
TRAMPETTES
TRAMPING
TRAMPLE
TRAMPLED
TRAMPLER
TRAMPLERS
TRAMPLES
TRAMPLING
TRAMPLINGS
TRAMPOLIN
TRAMPOLINS
TRAMPS
TRAMS
TRAMWAY
TRAMWAYS
TRANCE
TRANCED
TRANCEDLY
TRANCES
TRANCHE
TRANCHES
TRANCHET
TRANCHETS
TRANCING
TRANECT
TRANECTS
TRANGAM
TRANGAMS
TRANGLE
TRANGLES
TRANKUM
TRANKUMS
TRANNIE
TRANNIES
TRANNY
TRANQUIL
TRANQUILLER
TRANQUILLEST
TRANSACT
TRANSACTED
TRANSACTING
TRANSACTS
TRANSAXLE
TRANSAXLES
TRANSCEND

TRANSCENDED
TRANSCENDING
TRANSCENDS
TRANSE
TRANSECT
TRANSECTED
TRANSECTING
TRANSECTS
TRANSENNA
TRANSENNAS
TRANSEPT
TRANSEPTS
TRANSES
TRANSFARD
TRANSFECT
TRANSFECTED
TRANSFECTING
TRANSFECTS
TRANSFER
TRANSFERRED
TRANSFERRING
TRANSFERS
TRANSFIX
TRANSFIXED
TRANSFIXES
TRANSFIXING
TRANSFORM
TRANSFORMED
TRANSFORMING
TRANSFORMINGS
TRANSFORMS
TRANSFUSE
TRANSFUSED
TRANSFUSES
TRANSFUSING
TRANSHIP
TRANSHIPPED
TRANSHIPPING
TRANSHIPPINGS
TRANSHIPS
TRANSHUME
TRANSHUMED
TRANSHUMES
TRANSHUMING
TRANSIENT
TRANSIENTS
TRANSIRE
TRANSIRES
TRANSIT
TRANSITED
TRANSITING
TRANSITS
TRANSLATE
TRANSLATED
TRANSLATES
TRANSLATING
TRANSMEW
TRANSMEWED
TRANSMEWING
TRANSMEWS
TRANSMIT
TRANSMITS
TRANSMITTED
TRANSMITTING
TRANSMOVE
TRANSMOVED
TRANSMOVES
TRANSMOVING
TRANSMUTE
TRANSMUTED

TRANSMUTES
TRANSMUTING
TRANSOM
TRANSOMS
TRANSONIC
TRANSONICS
TRANSPIRE
TRANSPIRED
TRANSPIRES
TRANSPIRING
TRANSPORT
TRANSPORTED
TRANSPORTING
TRANSPORTINGS
TRANSPORTS
TRANSPOSE
TRANSPOSED
TRANSPOSES
TRANSPOSING
TRANSPOSINGS
TRANSSHIP
TRANSSHIPPED
TRANSSHIPPING
TRANSSHIPPINGS
TRANSSHIPS
TRANSUDE
TRANSUDED
TRANSUDES
TRANSUDING
TRANSUME
TRANSUMED
TRANSUMES
TRANSUMING
TRANSUMPT
TRANSUMPTS
TRANSVEST
TRANSVESTED
TRANSVESTING
TRANSVESTS
TRANT
TRANTED
TRANTER
TRANTERS
TRANTING
TRANTS
TRAP
TRAPAN
TRAPANNED
TRAPANNING
TRAPANS
TRAPE
TRAPED
TRAPES
TRAPESED
TRAPESES
TRAPESING
TRAPESINGS
TRAPEZE
TRAPEZED
TRAPEZES
TRAPEZIA
TRAPEZIAL
TRAPEZING
TRAPEZIUM
TRAPEZIUMS
TRAPEZIUS
TRAPEZIUSES
TRAPEZOID
TRAPEZOIDS
TRAPING

TRAPPEAN
TRAPPED
TRAPPER
TRAPPERS
TRAPPIER
TRAPPIEST
TRAPPING
TRAPPINGS
TRAPPY
TRAPS
TRAPUNTO
TRAPUNTOS
TRASH
TRASHED
TRASHERIES
TRASHERY
TRASHES
TRASHIER
TRASHIEST
TRASHILY
TRASHING
TRASHTRIE
TRASHTRIES
TRASHY
TRASS
TRASSES
TRATTORIA
TRATTORIAS
TRATTORIE
TRAUCHLE
TRAUCHLED
TRAUCHLES
TRAUCHLING
TRAUMA
TRAUMAS
TRAUMATA
TRAUMATIC
TRAVAIL
TRAVAILED
TRAVAILING
TRAVAILS
TRAVE
TRAVEL
TRAVELLED
TRAVELLER
TRAVELLERS
TRAVELLING
TRAVELLINGS
TRAVELS
TRAVERSAL
TRAVERSALS
TRAVERSE
TRAVERSED
TRAVERSER
TRAVERSERS
TRAVERSES
TRAVERSING
TRAVERSINGS
TRAVERTIN
TRAVERTINS
TRAVES
TRAVESTIED
TRAVESTIES
TRAVESTY
TRAVESTYING
TRAVIS
TRAVISES
TRAVOIS
TRAWL
TRAWLED

TRAWLER
TRAWLERS
TRAWLING
TRAWLINGS
TRAWLS
TRAY
TRAYBIT
TRAYBITS
TRAYFUL
TRAYFULS
TRAYNE
TRAYNED
TRAYNES
TRAYNING
TRAYS
TREACHER
TREACHERIES
TREACHERS
TREACHERY
TREACHOUR
TREACHOURS
TREACLE
TREACLED
TREACLES
TREACLIER
TREACLIEST
TREACLING
TREACLY
TREAD
TREADER
TREADERS
TREADING
TREADINGS
TREADLE
TREADLED
TREADLER
TREADLERS
TREADLES
TREADLING
TREADLINGS
TREADMILL
TREADMILLS
TREADS
TREAGUE
TREAGUES
TREASON
TREASONS
TREASURE
TREASURED
TREASURER
TREASURERS
TREASURES
TREASURIES
TREASURING
TREASURY
TREAT
TREATABLE
TREATED
TREATER
TREATERS
TREATIES
TREATING
TREATINGS
TREATISE
TREATISES
TREATMENT
TREATMENTS
TREATS
TREATY
TREBLE

TREBLED
TREBLES
TREBLING
TREBLY
TREBUCHET
TREBUCHETS
TRECENTO
TRECENTOS
TRECK
TRECKED
TRECKING
TRECKS
TREDDLE
TREDDLED
TREDDLES
TREDDLING
TREDILLE
TREDILLES
TREDRILLE
TREDRILLES
TREE
TREED
TREEING
TREELESS
TREEN
TREENAIL
TREENAILS
TREENS
TREES
TREESHIP
TREESHIPS
TREETOP
TREETOPS
TREF
TREFA
TREFOIL
TREFOILED
TREFOILS
TREGETOUR
TREGETOURS
TREHALA
TREHALAS
TREILLAGE
TREILLAGES
TREILLE
TREILLES
TREK
TREKKED
TREKKER
TREKKERS
TREKKING
TREKS
TRELLIS
TRELLISED
TRELLISES
TRELLISING
TREMA
TREMAS
TREMATIC
TREMATODE
TREMATODES
TREMATOID
TREMATOIDS
TREMBLANT
TREMBLE
TREMBLED
TREMBLER
TREMBLERS
TREMBLES
TREMBLIER

TREMBLIEST
TREMBLING
TREMBLINGS
TREMBLY
TRÉMIE
TREMIE
TREMIES
TRÉMIES
TREMOLANT
TREMOLANTS
TREMOLITE
TREMOLITES
TREMOLO
TREMOLOS
TREMOR
TREMORS
TREMULANT
TREMULANTS
TREMULATE
TREMULATED
TREMULATES
TREMULATING
TREMULOUS
TRENAIL
TRENAILS
TRENCH
TRENCHAND
TRENCHANT
TRENCHARD
TRENCHARDS
TRENCHED
TRENCHER
TRENCHERS
TRENCHES
TRENCHING
TREND
TRENDED
TRENDIER
TRENDIES
TRENDIEST
TRENDING
TRENDS
TRENDY
TRENISE
TRENISES
TRENTAL
TRENTALS
TREPAN
TREPANG
TREPANGS
TREPANNED
TREPANNER
TREPANNERS
TREPANNING
TREPANNINGS
TREPANS
TREPHINE
TREPHINED
TREPHINES
TREPHINING
TREPID
TREPIDANT
TREPIDER
TREPIDEST
TREPONEMA
TREPONEMAS
TREPONEMATA
TRESPASS
TRESPASSED
TRESPASSES

TRESPASSING
TRESS
TRESSED
TRESSEL
TRESSELS
TRESSES
TRESSIER
TRESSIEST
TRESSING
TRESSURE
TRESSURED
TRESSURES
TRESSY
TRESTLE
TRESTLES
TRET
TRETS
TREVALLIES
TREVALLY
TREVIS
TREVISES
TREVISS
TREVISSES
TREW
TREWS
TREWSMAN
TREWSMEN
TREY
TREYBIT
TREYBITS
TREYS
TREZ
TREZES
TRIABLE
TRIACID
TRIACT
TRIACTINE
TRIAD
TRIADIC
TRIADIST
TRIADISTS
TRIADS
TRIAGE
TRIAGES
TRIAL
TRIALISM
TRIALISMS
TRIALIST
TRIALISTS
TRIALITIES
TRIALITY
TRIALLIST
TRIALLISTS
TRIALOGUE
TRIALOGUES
TRIALS
TRIANGLE
TRIANGLED
TRIANGLES
TRIAPSAL
TRIARCH
TRIARCHIES
TRIARCHS
TRIARCHY
TRIATHLON
TRIATHLONS
TRIATIC
TRIATICS
TRIATOMIC
TRIAXIAL

TRIAXIALS
TRIAXON
TRIAXONS
TRIBADE
TRIBADES
TRIBADIC
TRIBADIES
TRIBADISM
TRIBADISMS
TRIBADY
TRIBAL
TRIBALISM
TRIBALISMS
TRIBALIST
TRIBALISTS
TRIBALLY
TRIBASIC
TRIBBLE
TRIBBLES
TRIBE
TRIBELESS
TRIBES
TRIBESMAN
TRIBESMEN
TRIBLET
TRIBLETS
TRIBOLOGIES
TRIBOLOGY
TRIBRACH
TRIBRACHS
TRIBUNAL
TRIBUNALS
TRIBUNATE
TRIBUNATES
TRIBUNE
TRIBUNES
TRIBUTARIES
TRIBUTARY
TRIBUTE
TRIBUTER
TRIBUTERS
TRIBUTES
TRICAR
TRICARS
TRICE
TRICED
TRICEPS
TRICEPSES
TRICERION
TRICERIONS
TRICES
TRICHINA
TRICHINAE
TRICHINAS
TRICHITE
TRICHITES
TRICHITIC
TRICHOID
TRICHOME
TRICHOMES
TRICHORD
TRICHORDS
TRICHOSES
TRICHOSIS
TRICHROIC
TRICHROME
TRICING
TRICK
TRICKED
TRICKER

TRICKERIES
TRICKERS
TRICKERY
TRICKIER
TRICKIEST
TRICKILY
TRICKING
TRICKINGS
TRICKISH
TRICKLE
TRICKLED
TRICKLES
TRICKLESS
TRICKLET
TRICKLETS
TRICKLIER
TRICKLIEST
TRICKLING
TRICKLINGS
TRICKLY
TRICKS
TRICKSIER
TRICKSIEST
TRICKSOME
TRICKSTER
TRICKSTERS
TRICKSY
TRICKY
TRICLINIA
TRICLINIC
TRICOLOR
TRICOLORS
TRICOLOUR
TRICOLOURS
TRICORN
TRICORNE
TRICORNES
TRICORNS
TRICOT
TRICOTS
TRICROTIC
TRICUSPID
TRICYCLE
TRICYCLED
TRICYCLER
TRICYCLERS
TRICYCLES
TRICYCLIC
TRICYCLING
TRICYCLINGS
TRIDACNA
TRIDACNAS
TRIDACTYL
TRIDARN
TRIDARNS
TRIDE
TRIDENT
TRIDENTAL
TRIDENTED
TRIDENTS
TRIDUAN
TRIDUUM
TRIDUUMS
TRIDYMITE
TRIDYMITES
TRIE
TRIED
TRIENNIAL
TRIER

TRIERARCH
TRIERARCHS
TRIERS
TRIES
TRIETERIC
TRIETHYL
TRIFACIAL
TRIFECTA
TRIFECTAS
TRIFFID
TRIFFIDS
TRIFFIDY
TRIFID
TRIFLE
TRIFLED
TRIFLER
TRIFLERS
TRIFLES
TRIFLING
TRIFOCAL
TRIFOCALS
TRIFOLIES
TRIFOLIUM
TRIFOLIUMS
TRIFOLY
TRIFORIA
TRIFORIUM
TRIFORM
TRIFORMED
TRIG
TRIGAMIES
TRIGAMIST
TRIGAMISTS
TRIGAMOUS
TRIGAMY
TRIGGED
TRIGGER
TRIGGERED
TRIGGERING
TRIGGERS
TRIGGEST
TRIGGING
TRIGLOT
TRIGLOTS
TRIGLY
TRIGLYPH
TRIGLYPHS
TRIGNESS
TRIGNESSES
TRIGON
TRIGONAL
TRIGONIC
TRIGONOUS
TRIGONS
TRIGRAM
TRIGRAMS
TRIGRAPH
TRIGRAPHS
TRIGS
TRIGYNIAN
TRIGYNOUS
TRIHEDRAL
TRIHEDRALS
TRIHEDRON
TRIHEDRONS
TRIHYBRID
TRIHYBRIDS
TRIHYDRIC
TRIKE
TRIKED

TRIKES
TRIKING
TRILBIES
TRILBY
TRILBYS
TRILD
TRILEMMA
TRILEMMAS
TRILINEAR
TRILITH
TRILITHIC
TRILITHON
TRILITHONS
TRILITHS
TRILL
TRILLED
TRILLING
TRILLINGS
TRILLION
TRILLIONS
TRILLIUM
TRILLIUMS
TRILLO
TRILLOES
TRILLS
TRILOBATE
TRILOBE
TRILOBED
TRILOBES
TRILOBITE
TRILOBITES
TRILOGIES
TRILOGY
TRIM
TRIMARAN
TRIMARANS
TRIMER
TRIMERIC
TRIMEROUS
TRIMERS
TRIMESTER
TRIMESTERS
TRIMETER
TRIMETERS
TRIMETHYL
TRIMETRIC
TRIMLY
TRIMMED
TRIMMER
TRIMMERS
TRIMMEST
TRIMMING
TRIMMINGS
TRIMNESS
TRIMNESSES
TRIMS
TRIMTAB
TRIMTABS
TRIN
TRINAL
TRINARY
TRINDLE
TRINDLED
TRINDLES
TRINDLING
TRINE
TRINED
TRINES
TRINGLE
TRINGLES

TRINING
TRINITIES
TRINITRIN
TRINITRINS
TRINITY
TRINKET
TRINKETED '
TRINKETER
TRINKETERS
TRINKETING
TRINKETINGS
TRINKETRIES
TRINKETRY
TRINKETS
TRINKUM
TRINKUMS
TRINOMIAL
TRINOMIALS
TRINS
TRIO
TRIODE
TRIODES
TRIOLET
TRIOLETS
TRIONES
TRIONYM
TRIONYMAL
TRIONYMS
TRIOR
TRIORS
TRIOS
TRIOXIDE
TRIOXIDES
TRIP
TRIPE
TRIPEDAL
TRIPEMAN
TRIPEMEN
TRIPERIES
TRIPERY
TRIPES
TRIPEWIFE
TRIPEWIVES
TRIPHONE
TRIPHONES
TRIPITAKA
TRIPITAKAS
TRIPLANE
TRIPLANES
TRIPLE
TRIPLED
TRIPLES
TRIPLET
TRIPLETS
TRIPLEX
TRIPLEXES
TRIPLIED
TRIPLIES
TRIPLING
TRIPLINGS
TRIPLOID
TRIPLOIDIES
TRIPLOIDY
TRIPLY
TRIPLYING
TRIPOD
TRIPODAL
TRIPODIES
TRIPODS
TRIPODY

| | | | | |
|---|---|---|---|---|
| TRIPOLI | TRITE | TROAT | TROLLOPEE | TROTLINES |
| TRIPOLIS | TRITELY | TROATED | TROLLOPEES | TROTS |
| TRIPOS | TRITENESS | TROATING | TROLLOPING | TROTTED |
| TRIPOSES | TRITENESSES | TROATS | TROLLOPS | TROTTER |
| TRIPPANT | TRITER | TROCAR | TROLLOPY | TROTTERS |
| TRIPPED | TRITES | TROCARS | TROLLS | TROTTING |
| TRIPPER | TRITEST | TROCHAIC | TROLLY | TROTTINGS |
| TRIPPERS | TRITHEISM | TROCHAICS | TROMBONE | TROTTOIR |
| TRIPPERY | TRITHEISMS | TROCHAL | TROMBONES | TROTTOIRS |
| TRIPPET | TRITHEIST | TROCHE | TROMINO | TROTYL |
| TRIPPETS | TRITHEISTS | TROCHEE | TROMINOES | TROTYLS |
| TRIPPING | TRITIATE | TROCHEES | TROMINOS | TROUBLE |
| TRIPPINGS | TRITIATED | TROCHES | TROMMEL | TROUBLED |
| TRIPPLE | TRITIATES | TROCHI | TROMMELS | TROUBLER |
| TRIPPLED | TRITIATING | TROCHILIC | TROMP | TROUBLERS |
| TRIPPLER | TRITICAL | TROCHILUS | TROMPE | TROUBLES |
| TRIPPLERS | TRITICALE | TROCHILUSES | TROMPES | TROUBLING |
| TRIPPLES | TRITICALES | TROCHISK | TROMPS | TROUBLINGS |
| TRIPPLING | TRITICISM | TROCHISKS | TRON | TROUBLOUS |
| TRIPS | TRITICISMS | TROCHITE | TRONA | TROUGH |
| TRIPSES | TRITIDE | TROCHITES | TRONAS | TROUGHS |
| TRIPSIS | TRITIDES | TROCHLEA | TRONC | TROULE |
| TRIPTANE | TRITIUM | TROCHLEAR | TRONCS | TROULED |
| TRIPTANES | TRITIUMS | TROCHLEAS | TRONE | TROULES |
| TRIPTOTE | TRITON | TROCHOID | TRONES | TROULING |
| TRIPTOTES | TRITONE | TROCHOIDS | TRONS | TROUNCE |
| TRIPTYCH | TRITONES | TROCHUS | TROOLIE | TROUNCED |
| TRIPTYCHS | TRITONIA | TROCHUSES | TROOLIES | TROUNCER |
| TRIPTYQUE | TRITONIAS | TROCK | TROOP | TROUNCERS |
| TRIPTYQUES | TRITONS | TROCKED | TROOPED | TROUNCES |
| TRIPUDIA | TRITURATE | TROCKING | TROOPER | TROUNCING |
| TRIPUDIUM | TRITURATED | TROCKS | TROOPERS | TROUNCINGS |
| TRIPUDIUMS | TRITURATES | TROD | TROOPIAL | TROUPE |
| TRIQUETRA | TRITURATING | TRODDEN | TROOPIALS | TROUPED |
| TRIQUETRAS | TRIUMPH | TRODE | TROOPING | TROUPER |
| TRIRADIAL | TRIUMPHAL | TRODES | TROOPS | TROUPERS |
| TRIREME | TRIUMPHALS | TRODS | TROPARIA | TROUPES |
| TRIREMES | TRIUMPHED | TROELIE | TROPARION | TROUPIAL |
| TRISAGION | TRIUMPHER | TROELIES | TROPE | TROUPIALS |
| TRISAGIONS | TRIUMPHERS | TROELY | TROPED | TROUPING |
| TRISECT | TRIUMPHING | TROG | TROPES | TROUSE |
| TRISECTED | TRIUMPHINGS | TROGGED | TROPHESIES | TROUSERED |
| TRISECTING | TRIUMPHS | TROGGING | TROPHESY | TROUSERS |
| TRISECTOR | TRIUMVIR | TROGGS | TROPHI | TROUSES |
| TRISECTORS | TRIUMVIRI | TROGON | TROPHIC | TROUSSEAU |
| TRISECTS | TRIUMVIRIES | TROGONS | TROPHIED | TROUSSEAUS |
| TRISEME | TRIUMVIRS | TROGS | TROPHIES | TROUSSEAUX |
| TRISEMES | TRIUMVIRY | TROIKA | TROPHY | TROUT |
| TRISEMIC | TRIUNE | TROIKAS | TROPHYING | TROUTER |
| TRISHAW | TRIUNES | TROILISM | TROPIC | TROUTERS |
| TRISHAWS | TRIUNITIES | TROILISMS | TROPICAL | TROUTFUL |
| TRISKELE | TRIUNITY | TROILIST | TROPICS | TROUTIER |
| TRISKELES | TRIVALENT | TROILISTS | TROPING | TROUTIEST |
| TRISKELIA | TRIVALVE | TROILITE | TROPISM | TROUTING |
| TRISMUS | TRIVALVED | TROILITES | TROPISMS | TROUTINGS |
| TRISMUSES | TRIVALVES | TROKE | TROPIST | TROUTLESS |
| TRISOME | TRIVET | TROKED | TROPISTIC | TROUTLET |
| TRISOMES | TRIVETS | TROKES | TROPISTS | TROUTLETS |
| TRISOMIC | TRIVIA | TROKING | TROPOLOGIES | TROUTLING |
| TRISOMIES | TRIVIAL | TROLL | TROPOLOGY | TROUTLINGS |
| TRISOMY | TRIVIALLY | TROLLED | TROPPO | TROUTS |
| TRIST | TRIVIUM | TROLLER | TROSSERS | TROUTY |
| TRISTE | TRIVIUMS | TROLLERS | TROT | TROUVÈRE |
| TRISTFUL | TRIZONAL | TROLLEY | TROTH | TROUVÈRES |
| TRISTICH | TRIZONE | TROLLEYS | TROTHED | TROUVEUR |
| TRISTICHS | TRIZONES | TROLLIES | TROTHFUL | TROUVEURS |
| TRISUL | TROAD | TROLLING | TROTHING | TROVER |
| TRISULA | TROADE | TROLLINGS | TROTHLESS | TROVERS |
| TRISULAS | TROADES | TROLLOP | TROTHS | TROW |
| TRISULS | TROADS | TROLLOPED | TROTLINE | TROWED |

TROWEL
TROWELLED
TROWELLER
TROWELLERS
TROWELLING
TROWELS
TROWING
TROWS
TROWSERS
TROY
TROYS
TRUANCIES
TRUANCY
TRUANT
TRUANTED
TRUANTING
TRUANTRIES
TRUANTRY
TRUANTS
TRUCAGE
TRUCAGES
TRUCE
TRUCELESS
TRUCES
TRUCHMAN
TRUCHMANS
TRUCHMEN
TRUCIAL
TRUCK
TRUCKAGE
TRUCKAGES
TRUCKED
TRUCKER
TRUCKERS
TRUCKING
TRUCKINGS
TRUCKLE
TRUCKLED
TRUCKLER
TRUCKLERS
TRUCKLES
TRUCKLING
TRUCKLINGS
TRUCKMAN
TRUCKMEN
TRUCKS
TRUCULENT
TRUDGE
TRUDGED
TRUDGEN
TRUDGENS
TRUDGEON
TRUDGEONS
TRUDGER
TRUDGERS
TRUDGES
TRUDGING
TRUDGINGS
TRUE
TRUED
TRUEING
TRUEMAN
TRUEMEN
TRUENESS
TRUENESSES
TRUEPENNIES
TRUEPENNY
TRUER
TRUES
TRUEST

TRUFFLE
TRUFFLED
TRUFFLES
TRUG
TRUGS
TRUING
TRUISM
TRUISMS
TRUISTIC
TRULL
TRULLS
TRULY
TRUMEAU
TRUMEAUX
TRUMP
TRUMPED
TRUMPERIES
TRUMPERY
TRUMPET
TRUMPETED
TRUMPETER
TRUMPETERS
TRUMPETING
TRUMPETINGS
TRUMPETS
TRUMPING
TRUMPINGS
TRUMPS
TRUNCAL
TRUNCATE
TRUNCATED
TRUNCATES
TRUNCATING
TRUNCHEON
TRUNCHEONED
TRUNCHEONING
TRUNCHEONS
TRUNDLE
TRUNDLED
TRUNDLES
TRUNDLING
TRUNK
TRUNKED
TRUNKFISH
TRUNKFISHES
TRUNKFUL
TRUNKFULS
TRUNKING
TRUNKINGS
TRUNKS
TRUNNION
TRUNNIONS
TRUQUAGE
TRUQUAGES
TRUQUEUR
TRUQUEURS
TRUSS
TRUSSED
TRUSSER
TRUSSERS
TRUSSES
TRUSSING
TRUSSINGS
TRUST
TRUSTED
TRUSTEE
TRUSTEES
TRUSTER
TRUSTERS
TRUSTFUL

TRUSTIER
TRUSTIES
TRUSTIEST
TRUSTILY
TRUSTING
TRUSTLESS
TRUSTS
TRUSTY
TRUTH
TRUTHFUL
TRUTHIER
TRUTHIEST
TRUTHLESS
TRUTHLIKE
TRUTHS
TRUTHY
TRY
TRYE
TRYER
TRYERS
TRYING
TRYINGLY
TRYINGS
TRYP
TRYPS
TRYPSIN
TRYPSINS
TRYPTIC
TRYSAIL
TRYSAILS
TRYST
TRYSTED
TRYSTER
TRYSTERS
TRYSTING
TRYSTS
TSADDIK
TSADDIKIM
TSADDIKS
TSADDIQ
TSADDIQIM
TSADDIQS
TSAMBA
TSAMBAS
TSAR
TSARDOM
TSARDOMS
TSAREVICH
TSAREVICHES
TSAREVNA
TSAREVNAS
TSARINA
TSARINAS
TSARISM
TSARISMS
TSARIST
TSARISTS
TSARITSA
TSARITSAS
TSARS
TSESSEBE
TSESSEBES
TSETSE
TSETSES
TSIGANE
TSIGANES
TSOTSI
TSOTSIS
TSUBA
TSUBAS

TSUNAMI
TSUNAMIS
TUAN
TUANS
TUART
TUARTS
TUATARA
TUATARAS
TUATH
TUATHS
TUB
TUBA
TUBAE
TUBAGE
TUBAGES
TUBAL
TUBAR
TUBAS
TUBATE
TUBBED
TUBBER
TUBBERS
TUBBIER
TUBBIEST
TUBBINESS
TUBBINESSES
TUBBING
TUBBINGS
TUBBISH
TUBBY
TUBE
TUBECTOMIES
TUBECTOMY
TUBED
TUBEFUL
TUBEFULS
TUBELESS
TUBER
TUBERCLE
TUBERCLED
TUBERCLES
TUBERCULA
TUBERCULE
TUBERCULES
TUBEROSE
TUBEROSES
TUBEROUS
TUBERS
TUBES
TUBFAST
TUBFASTS
TUBFISH
TUBFISHES
TUBFUL
TUBFULS
TUBICOLAR
TUBICOLE
TUBICOLES
TUBIFORM
TUBING
TUBINGS
TUBS
TUBULAR
TUBULATE
TUBULATED
TUBULATES
TUBULATING
TUBULE
TUBULES
TUBULOUS

TUCHUN
TUCHUNS
TUCK
TUCKAHOE
TUCKAHOES
TUCKED
TUCKER
TUCKERBAG
TUCKERBAGS
TUCKERBOX
TUCKERBOXES
TUCKERED
TUCKERING
TUCKERS
TUCKET
TUCKETS
TUCKING
TUCKS
TUCOTUCO
TUCOTUCOS
TUCUTUCO
TUCUTUCOS
TUFA
TUFACEOUS
TUFAS
TUFF
TUFFE
TUFFES
TUFFET
TUFFETS
TUFFS
TUFT
TUFTED
TUFTER
TUFTERS
TUFTIER
TUFTIEST
TUFTING
TUFTINGS
TUFTS
TUFTY
TUG
TUGGED
TUGGER
TUGGERS
TUGGING
TUGGINGLY
TUGGINGS
TUGRIK
TUGRIKS
TUGS
TUI
TUILLE
TUILLES
TUILLETTE
TUILLETTES
TUILYIE
TUILYIED
TUILYIEING
TUILYIES
TUILZIE
TUILZIED
TUILZIEING
TUILZIES
TUIS
TUISM
TUISMS
TUITION
TUITIONAL
TUITIONS

| | | | | |
|---|---|---|---|---|
| TULAREMIA | TUNABLY | TUPS | TURFS | TURNSPITS |
| TULAREMIAS | TUNAS | TUPTOWING | TURFY | TURNSTILE |
| TULAREMIC | TUNBELLIES | TUQUE | TURGENT | TURNSTILES |
| TULBAN | TUNBELLY | TUQUES | TURGENTLY | TURNSTONE |
| TULBANS | TUND | TURACIN | TURGID | TURNSTONES |
| TULCHAN | TUNDED | TURACINS | TURGIDITIES | TURNTABLE |
| TULCHANS | TUNDING | TURACO | TURGIDITY | TURNTABLES |
| TULE | TUNDRA | TURACOS | TURGIDLY | TURPETH |
| TULES | TUNDRAS | TURBAN | TURGOR | TURPETHS |
| TULIP | TUNDS | TURBAND | TURGORS | TURPITUDE |
| TULIPANT | TUNDUN | TURBANDS | TURION | TURPITUDES |
| TULIPANTS | TUNDUNS | TURBANED | TURIONS | TURPS |
| TULIPS | TUNE | TURBANS | TURKEY | TURQUOISE |
| TULLE | TUNEABLE | TURBANT | TURKEYS | TURQUOISES |
| TULLES | TUNED | TURBANTS | TURKIES | TURRET |
| TULWAR | TUNEFUL | TURBARIES | TURKIESES | TURRETED |
| TULWARS | TUNEFULLY | TURBARY | TURKIS | TURRETS |
| TUM | TUNELESS | TURBID | TURKISES | TURRIBANT |
| TUMBLE | TUNER | TURBIDITE | TURLOUGH | TURRIBANTS |
| TUMBLED | TUNERS | TURBIDITES | TURLOUGHS | TURTLE |
| TUMBLER | TUNES | TURBIDITIES | TURM | TURTLED |
| TUMBLERS | TUNESMITH | TURBIDITY | TURME | TURTLER |
| TUMBLES | TUNESMITHS | TURBIDLY | TURMERIC | TURTLERS |
| TUMBLING | TUNGSTATE | TURBINAL | TURMERICS | TURTLES |
| TUMBLINGS | TUNGSTATES | TURBINALS | TURMES | TURTLING |
| TUMBREL | TUNGSTEN | TURBINATE | TURMOIL | TURTLINGS |
| TUMBRELS | TUNGSTENS | TURBINATES | TURMOILED | TURVES |
| TUMBRIL | TUNIC | TURBINE | TURMOILING | TUSCHE |
| TUMBRILS | TUNICATE | TURBINED | TURMOILS | TUSCHES |
| TUMEFIED | TUNICATED | TURBINES | TURMS | TUSH |
| TUMEFIES | TUNICATES | TURBIT | TURN | TUSHED |
| TUMEFY | TUNICIN | TURBITH | TURNABOUT | TUSHERIES |
| TUMEFYING | TUNICINS | TURBITHS | TURNABOUTS | TUSHERY |
| TUMESCE | TUNICKED | TURBITS | TURNAGAIN | TUSHES |
| TUMESCED | TUNICLE | TURBO | TURNAGAINS | TUSHING |
| TUMESCENT | TUNICLES | TURBOCAR | TURNBACK | TUSK |
| TUMESCES | TUNICS | TURBOCARS | TURNBACKS | TUSKAR |
| TUMESCING | TUNIER | TURBOFAN | TURNCOAT | TUSKARS |
| TUMID | TUNIEST | TURBOFANS | TURNCOATS | TUSKED |
| TUMIDITIES | TUNING | TURBOND | TURNCOCK | TUSKER |
| TUMIDITY | TUNINGS | TURBONDS | TURNCOCKS | TUSKERS |
| TUMIDLY | TUNNAGE | TURBOPROP | TURNDUN | TUSKIER |
| TUMIDNESS | TUNNAGES | TURBOPROPS | TURNDUNS | TUSKIEST |
| TUMIDNESSES | TUNNED | TURBOS | TURNED | TUSKING |
| TUMMIES | TUNNEL | TURBOT | TURNER | TUSKLESS |
| TUMMY | TUNNELLED | TURBOTS | TURNERIES | TUSKS |
| TUMOR | TUNNELLER | TURBULENT | TURNERS | TUSKY |
| TUMOROUS | TUNNELLERS | TURCOPOLE | TURNERY | TUSSAH |
| TUMORS | TUNNELLING | TURCOPOLES | TURNING | TUSSAHS |
| TUMOUR | TUNNELLINGS | TURD | TURNINGS | TUSSAL |
| TUMOURS | TUNNELS | TURDINE | TURNIP | TUSSEH |
| TUMP | TUNNIES | TURDION | TURNIPED | TUSSEHS |
| TUMPED | TUNNING | TURDIONS | TURNIPING | TUSSER |
| TUMPHIES | TUNNINGS | TURDOID | TURNIPS | TUSSERS |
| TUMPHY | TUNNY | TURDS | TURNKEY | TUSSIS |
| TUMPING | TUNS | TUREEN | TURNKEYS | TUSSISES |
| TUMPS | TUNY | TUREENS | TURNOFF | TUSSIVE |
| TUMPY | TUP | TURF | TURNOFFS | TUSSLE |
| TUMS | TUPEK | TURFED | TURNOVER | TUSSLED |
| TUMULAR | TUPEKS | TURFEN | TURNOVERS | TUSSLES |
| TUMULARY | TUPELO | TURFIER | TURNPIKE | TUSSLING |
| TUMULI | TUPELOS | TURFIEST | TURNPIKES | TUSSOCK |
| TUMULT | TUPIK | TURFINESS | TURNROUND | TUSSOCKS |
| TUMULTED | TUPIKS | TURFINESSES | TURNROUNDS | TUSSOCKY |
| TUMULTING | TUPPED | TURFING | TURNS | TUSSORE |
| TUMULTS | TUPPENCE | TURFINGS | TURNSKIN | TUSSORES |
| TUMULUS | TUPPENCES | TURFITE | TURNSKINS | TUT |
| TUN | TUPPENNIES | TURFITES | TURNSOLE | TUTANIA |
| TUNA | TUPPENNY | TURFMAN | TURNSOLES | TUTANIAS |
| TUNABLE | TUPPING | TURFMEN | TURNSPIT | TUTEE |

TUTEES
TUTELAGE
TUTELAGES
TUTELAR
TUTELARIES
TUTELARS
TUTELARY
TUTENAG
TUTENAGS
TUTIORISM
TUTIORISMS
TUTIORIST
TUTIORISTS
TUTMAN
TUTMEN
TUTOR
TUTORAGE
TUTORAGES
TUTORED
TUTORESS
TUTORESSES
TUTORIAL
TUTORIALS
TUTORING
TUTORINGS
TUTORISE
TUTORISED
TUTORISES
TUTORISING
TUTORISM
TUTORISMS
TUTORIZE
TUTORIZED
TUTORIZES
TUTORIZING
TUTORS
TUTORSHIP
TUTORSHIPS
TUTRESS
TUTRESSES
TUTRICES
TUTRIX
TUTRIXES
TUTS
TUTSAN
TUTSANS
TUTTED
TUTTI
TUTTIES
TUTTING
TUTTIS
TUTTY
TUTU
TUTUS
TUTWORK
TUTWORKER
TUTWORKERS
TUTWORKS
TUXEDO
TUXEDOES
TUXEDOS
TUYÈRE
TUYÈRES
TUZZ
TUZZES
TWA
TWADDLE
TWADDLED
TWADDLER
TWADDLERS

TWADDLES
TWADDLIER
TWADDLIEST
TWADDLING
TWADDLINGS
TWADDLY
TWAE
TWAES
TWAFALD
TWAIN
TWAINS
TWAITE
TWAITES
TWAL
TWALHOURS
TWALPENNIES
TWALPENNY
TWALS
TWANG
TWANGED
TWANGIER
TWANGIEST
TWANGING
TWANGINGS
TWANGLE
TWANGLED
TWANGLES
TWANGLING
TWANGLINGS
TWANGS
TWANGY
TWANK
TWANKAY
TWANKAYS
TWANKS
TWAS
TWASOME
TWASOMES
TWAT
TWATS
TWATTLE
TWATTLED
TWATTLER
TWATTLERS
TWATTLES
TWATTLING
TWATTLINGS
TWAY
TWAYS
TWEAK
TWEAKED
TWEAKING
TWEAKS
TWEE
TWEED
TWEEDIER
TWEEDIEST
TWEEDLE
TWEEDLED
TWEEDLES
TWEEDLING
TWEEDS
TWEEDY
TWEEL
TWEELED
TWEELING
TWEELS
TWEELY
TWEENESS
TWEENESSES

TWEENIES
TWEENY
TWEER
TWEERED
TWEERING
TWEERS
TWEEST
TWEET
TWEETED
TWEETER
TWEETERS
TWEETING
TWEETS
TWEEZE
TWEEZED
TWEEZERS
TWEEZES
TWEEZING
TWELFTH
TWELFTHLY
TWELFTHS
TWELVE
TWELVEMO
TWELVEMOS
TWELVES
TWENTIES
TWENTIETH
TWENTIETHS
TWENTY
TWENTYISH
TWERP
TWERPS
TWIBILL
TWIBILLS
TWICE
TWICER
TWICERS
TWICHILD
TWICHILDREN
TWIDDLE
TWIDDLED
TWIDDLER
TWIDDLERS
TWIDDLES
TWIDDLIER
TWIDDLIEST
TWIDDLING
TWIDDLINGS
TWIDDLY
TWIER
TWIERS
TWIFOLD
TWIFORKED
TWIFORMED
TWIG
TWIGGED
TWIGGEN
TWIGGER
TWIGGERS
TWIGGIER
TWIGGIEST
TWIGGING
TWIGGY
TWIGHT
TWIGHTED
TWIGHTING
TWIGHTS
TWIGS
TWIGSOME
TWILIGHT

TWILIGHTED
TWILIGHTING
TWILIGHTS
TWILIT
TWILL
TWILLED
TWILLIES
TWILLING
TWILLS
TWILLY
TWILT
TWILTED
TWILTING
TWILTS
TWIN
TWINE
TWINED
TWINER
TWINERS
TWINES
TWINGE
TWINGED
TWINGES
TWINGING
TWINIER
TWINIEST
TWINING
TWININGLY
TWININGS
TWINK
TWINKED
TWINKING
TWINKLE
TWINKLED
TWINKLER
TWINKLERS
TWINKLES
TWINKLING
TWINKLINGS
TWINKS
TWINLING
TWINLINGS
TWINNED
TWINNING
TWINNINGS
TWINS
TWINSHIP
TWINSHIPS
TWINTER
TWINTERS
TWINY
TWIRE
TWIRED
TWIRES
TWIRING
TWIRL
TWIRLED
TWIRLER
TWIRLERS
TWIRLIER
TWIRLIEST
TWIRLING
TWIRLS
TWIRLY
TWIRP
TWIRPS
TWISCAR
TWISCARS
TWIST
TWISTABLE

TWISTED
TWISTER
TWISTERS
TWISTIER
TWISTIEST
TWISTING
TWISTINGS
TWISTS
TWISTY
TWIT
TWITCH
TWITCHED
TWITCHER
TWITCHERS
TWITCHES
TWITCHIER
TWITCHIEST
TWITCHING
TWITCHINGS
TWITCHY
TWITE
TWITES
TWITS
TWITTED
TWITTEN
TWITTENS
TWITTER
TWITTERED
TWITTERER
TWITTERERS
TWITTERING
TWITTERINGS
TWITTERS
TWITTERY
TWITTING
TWITTINGS
TWIZZLE
TWIZZLED
TWIZZLES
TWIZZLING
TWO
TWOER
TWOERS
TWOFOLD
TWONESS
TWONESSES
TWOPENCE
TWOPENCES
TWOPENNIES
TWOPENNY
TWOS
TWOSEATER
TWOSEATERS
TWOSOME
TWOSOMES
TWOSTROKE
TWYER
TWYERE
TWYERES
TWYERS
TWYFOLD
TWYFORKED
TWYFORMED
TYCHISM
TYCHISMS
TYCOON
TYCOONATE
TYCOONATES
TYCOONERIES
TYCOONERY

TYCOONS
TYDE
TYE
TYED
TYEING
TYES
TYG
TYGS
TYING
TYKE
TYKES
TYKISH
TYLECTOMIES
TYLECTOMY
TYLER
TYLERS
TYLOPOD
TYLOPODS
TYLOSES
TYLOSIS
TYLOTE
TYLOTES
TYMBAL
TYMBALS
TYMP
TYMPAN
TYMPANA
TYMPANAL
TYMPANI
TYMPANIC
TYMPANICS

TYMPANIES
TYMPANIST
TYMPANISTS
TYMPANO
TYMPANS
TYMPANUM
TYMPANY
TYMPS
TYND
TYNDE
TYNE
TYNED
TYNES
TYNING
TYPAL
TYPE
TYPECAST
TYPECASTING
TYPECASTS
TYPED
TYPES
TYPEWRITE
TYPEWRITES
TYPEWRITING
TYPEWRITINGS
TYPEWRITTEN
TYPEWROTE
TYPHLITIC
TYPHLITIS
TYPHLITISES
TYPHOID

TYPHOIDAL
TYPHOIDS
TYPHON
TYPHONIAN
TYPHONIC
TYPHONS
TYPHOON
TYPHOONS
TYPHOUS
TYPHUS
TYPHUSES
TYPIC
TYPICAL
TYPICALLY
TYPIFIED
TYPIFIER
TYPIFIERS
TYPIFIES
TYPIFY
TYPIFYING
TYPING
TYPINGS
TYPIST
TYPISTS
TYPO
TYPOLOGIES
TYPOLOGY
TYPOMANIA
TYPOMANIAS
TYPOS
TYPTO

TYPTOED
TYPTOING
TYPTOS
TYRAMINE
TYRAMINES
TYRAN
TYRANED
TYRANING
TYRANNE
TYRANNED
TYRANNES
TYRANNESS
TYRANNESSES
TYRANNIC
TYRANNIES
TYRANNING
TYRANNIS
TYRANNISE
TYRANNISED
TYRANNISES
TYRANNISING
TYRANNIZE
TYRANNIZED
TYRANNIZES
TYRANNIZING
TYRANNOUS
TYRANNY
TYRANS
TYRANT
TYRANTED
TYRANTING

TYRANTS
TYRE
TYRED
TYRELESS
TYRES
TYRO
TYROES
TYRONES
TYROSINE
TYROSINES
TYSTIE
TYSTIES
TYTE
TYTHE
TYTHED
TYTHES
TYTHING
TZADDIK
TZADDIKIM
TZADDIKS
TZADDIQ
TZADDIQIM
TZADDIQS
TZAR
TZARS
TZIGANIES
TZIGANY
TZIMMES

# U

UAKARI
UAKARIS
UBEROUS
UBERTIES
UBERTY
UBIETIES
UBIETY
UBIQUE
UBIQUITIES
UBIQUITY
UDAL
UDALLER
UDALLERS
UDALS
UDDER
UDDERED
UDDERFUL
UDDERLESS
UDDERS
UDO
UDOMETER
UDOMETERS
UDOMETRIC
UDOS
UDS
UEY
UEYS
UFO
UFOLOGIES
UFOLOGIST
UFOLOGISTS
UFOLOGY
UFOS
UG
UGGED
UGGING
UGH
UGHS
UGLI
UGLIED
UGLIER
UGLIES
UGLIEST
UGLIFIED
UGLIFIES
UGLIFY
UGLIFYING
UGLILY
UGLINESS
UGLINESSES
UGLIS
UGLY
UGLYING
UGS
UGSOME
UHLAN
UHLANS
UHURU
UHURUS
UINTAHITE
UINTAHITES
UINTAITE
UINTAITES

UITLANDER
UITLANDERS
UKASE
UKASES
UKELELE
UKELELES
UKULELE
UKULELES
ULCER
ULCERATE
ULCERATED
ULCERATES
ULCERATING
ULCERED
ULCERING
ULCEROUS
ULCERS
ULE
ULEMA
ULEMAS
ULES
ULEX
ULEXES
ULICHON
ULICHONS
ULICON
ULICONS
ULIGINOUS
ULIKON
ULIKONS
ULITIS
ULITISES
ULLAGE
ULLAGED
ULLAGES
ULLAGING
ULLING
ULLINGS
ULMACEOUS
ULMIN
ULMINS
ULNA
ULNAE
ULNAR
ULNARE
ULNARIA
ULOSES
ULOSIS
ULOTRICHIES
ULOTRICHY
ULSTER
ULSTERED
ULSTERS
ULTERIOR
ULTIMA
ULTIMACIES
ULTIMACY
ULTIMAS
ULTIMATA
ULTIMATE
ULTIMATES
ULTIMATUM
ULTIMO

ULTION
ULTIONS
ULTRA
ULTRAISM
ULTRAISMS
ULTRAIST
ULTRAISTS
ULTRARED
ULTRAS
ULULANT
ULULATE
ULULATED
ULULATES
ULULATING
ULULATION
ULULATIONS
ULYIE
ULYIES
ULZIE
ULZIES
UM
UMBEL
UMBELLAR
UMBELLATE
UMBELLULE
UMBELLULES
UMBELS
UMBER
UMBERED
UMBERING
UMBERS
UMBERY
UMBILICAL
UMBILICI
UMBILICUS
UMBILICUSES
UMBLES
UMBO
UMBONAL
UMBONATE
UMBONES
UMBOS
UMBRA
UMBRAE
UMBRAGE
UMBRAGED
UMBRAGES
UMBRAGING
UMBRAL
UMBRAS
UMBRATED
UMBRATIC
UMBRATILE
UMBRE
UMBREL
UMBRELLA
UMBRELLAS
UMBRELLO
UMBRELLOES
UMBRELLOS
UMBRELS
UMBRERE
UMBRERES

UMBRES
UMBRETTE
UMBRETTES
UMBRIERE
UMBRIERES
UMBRIL
UMBRILS
UMBROSE
UMBROUS
UMIAK
UMIAKS
UMLAUT
UMLAUTED
UMLAUTING
UMLAUTS
UMPH
UMPIRAGE
UMPIRAGES
UMPIRE
UMPIRED
UMPIRES
UMPIRING
UMPTEEN
UMPTEENTH
UMPTIETH
UMPTY
UMQUHILE
UMWHILE
UN
UNABASHED
UNABATED
UNABLE
UNACCUSED
UNACHING
UNACTABLE
UNACTED
UNACTIVE
UNADAPTED
UNADMIRED
UNADOPTED
UNADORED
UNADORNED
UNADVISED
UNAFRAID
UNAIDABLE
UNAIDED
UNAIMED
UNAIRED
UNAKING
UNALIGNED
UNALIKE
UNALIST
UNALISTS
UNALIVE
UNALLAYED
UNALLIED
UNALLOYED
UNALTERED
UNAMAZED
UNAMENDED
UNAMERCED
UNAMIABLE
UNAMUSED

UNAMUSING
UNANCHOR
UNANCHORED
UNANCHORING
UNANCHORS
UNANELED
UNANIMITIES
UNANIMITY
UNANIMOUS
UNANXIOUS
UNAPPAREL
UNAPPARELLED
UNAPPARELLING
UNAPPARELS
UNAPPLIED
UNAPT
UNAPTLY
UNAPTNESS
UNAPTNESSES
UNARGUED
UNARISEN
UNARM
UNARMED
UNARMING
UNARMS
UNARTFUL
UNASHAMED
UNASKED
UNASSAYED
UNASSUMED
UNASSURED
UNATONED
UNATTIRED
UNAU
UNAUS
UNAVENGED
UNAVOIDED
UNAVOWED
UNAWARE
UNAWARES
UNAWED
UNBACKED
UNBAFFLED
UNBAG
UNBAGGED
UNBAGGING
UNBAGS
UNBAITED
UNBAKED
UNBALANCE
UNBALANCED
UNBALANCES
UNBALANCING
UNBANDED
UNBANKED
UNBAPTISE
UNBAPTISED
UNBAPTISES
UNBAPTISING
UNBAPTIZE
UNBAPTIZED
UNBAPTIZES
UNBAPTIZING

| | | | | |
|---|---|---|---|---|
| UNBAR | UNBIAS | UNBOSOMING | UNCAGED | UNCHEWED |
| UNBARBED | UNBIASED | UNBOSOMS | UNCAGES | UNCHILD |
| UNBARE | UNBIASES | UNBOUGHT | UNCAGING | UNCHILDED |
| UNBARED | UNBIASING | UNBOUND | UNCALLED | UNCHILDING |
| UNBARES | UNBIASSED | UNBOUNDED | UNCANDID | UNCHILDS |
| UNBARING | UNBIASSES | UNBOWED | UNCANDOUR | UNCHOSEN |
| UNBARK | UNBIASSING | UNBOX | UNCANDOURS | UNCHRISOM |
| UNBARKED | UNBID | UNBOXED | UNCANNIER | UNCHURCH |
| UNBARKING | UNBIDDEN | UNBOXES | UNCANNIEST | UNCHURCHED |
| UNBARKS | UNBIND | UNBOXING | UNCANNILY | UNCHURCHES |
| UNBARRED | UNBINDING | UNBRACE | UNCANNY | UNCHURCHING |
| UNBARRING | UNBINDINGS | UNBRACED | UNCANONIC | UNCI |
| UNBARS | UNBINDS | UNBRACES | UNCAP | UNCIAL |
| UNBASHFUL | UNBISHOP | UNBRACING | UNCAPABLE | UNCIALS |
| UNBATED | UNBISHOPED | UNBRAIDED | UNCAPE | UNCIFORM |
| UNBATHED | UNBISHOPING | UNBRASTE | UNCAPED | UNCINATE |
| UNBE | UNBISHOPS | UNBRED | UNCAPES | UNCINATED |
| UNBEAR | UNBITT | UNBREECH | UNCAPING | UNCINI |
| UNBEARDED | UNBITTED | UNBREECHED | UNCAPPED | UNCINUS |
| UNBEARING | UNBITTING | UNBREECHES | UNCAPPING | UNCIPHER |
| UNBEARS | UNBITTS | UNBREECHING | UNCAPS | UNCIPHERED |
| UNBEATEN | UNBLAMED | UNBRIDGED | UNCAREFUL | UNCIPHERING |
| UNBED | UNBLENDED | UNBRIDLE | UNCARING | UNCIPHERS |
| UNBEDDED | UNBLENT | UNBRIDLED | UNCART | UNCIVIL |
| UNBEDDING | UNBLESS | UNBRIDLES | UNCARTED | UNCIVILLY |
| UNBEDS | UNBLESSED | UNBRIDLING | UNCARTING | UNCLAD |
| UNBEEN | UNBLESSES | UNBRIZZED | UNCARTS | UNCLAIMED |
| UNBEGET | UNBLESSING | UNBROKE | UNCASE | UNCLASP |
| UNBEGETS | UNBLEST | UNBROKEN | UNCASED | UNCLASPED |
| UNBEGETTING | UNBLIND | UNBRUISED | UNCASES | UNCLASPING |
| UNBEGGED | UNBLINDED | UNBRUSED | UNCASHED | UNCLASPS |
| UNBEGOT | UNBLINDING | UNBRUSHED | UNCASING | UNCLASSED |
| UNBEGOTTEN | UNBLINDS | UNBUCKLE | UNCATE | UNCLASSY |
| UNBEGUILE | UNBLOCK | UNBUCKLED | UNCAUGHT | UNCLE |
| UNBEGUILED | UNBLOCKED | UNBUCKLES | UNCAUSED | UNCLEAN |
| UNBEGUILES | UNBLOCKING | UNBUCKLING | UNCE | UNCLEANED |
| UNBEGUILING | UNBLOCKS | UNBUDDED | UNCEASING | UNCLEANER |
| UNBEGUN | UNBLOODED | UNBUILD | UNCERTAIN | UNCLEANEST |
| UNBEING | UNBLOODY | UNBUILDING | UNCES | UNCLEANLY |
| UNBEINGS | UNBLOTTED | UNBUILDS | UNCESSANT | UNCLEAR |
| UNBEKNOWN | UNBLOWED | UNBUILT | UNCHAIN | UNCLEARED |
| UNBELIEF | UNBLOWN | UNBUNDLE | UNCHAINED | UNCLEARER |
| UNBELIEFS | UNBLUNTED | UNBUNDLED | UNCHAINING | UNCLEAREST |
| UNBELIEVE | UNBODIED | UNBUNDLES | UNCHAINS | UNCLEARLY |
| UNBELIEVED | UNBODING | UNBUNDLING | UNCHANCIER | UNCLED |
| UNBELIEVES | UNBOLT | UNBUNDLINGS | UNCHANCIEST | UNCLENCH |
| UNBELIEVING | UNBOLTED | UNBURDEN | UNCHANCY | UNCLENCHED |
| UNBELOVED | UNBOLTING | UNBURDENED | UNCHANGED | UNCLENCHES |
| UNBELT | UNBOLTS | UNBURDENING | UNCHARGE | UNCLENCHING |
| UNBELTED | UNBONE | UNBURDENS | UNCHARGED | UNCLES |
| UNBELTING | UNBONED | UNBURIED | UNCHARGES | UNCLESHIP |
| UNBELTS | UNBONES | UNBURIES | UNCHARGING | UNCLESHIPS |
| UNBEND | UNBONING | UNBURNED | UNCHARITIES | UNCLEW |
| UNBENDED | UNBONNET | UNBURNT | UNCHARITY | UNCLEWED |
| UNBENDING | UNBONNETED | UNBURROW | UNCHARM | UNCLEWING |
| UNBENDINGS | UNBONNETING | UNBURROWED | UNCHARMED | UNCLEWS |
| UNBENDS | UNBONNETS | UNBURROWING | UNCHARMING | UNCLING |
| UNBENIGN | UNBOOKED | UNBURROWS | UNCHARMS | UNCLIPPED |
| UNBENT | UNBOOKISH | UNBURTHEN | UNCHARNEL | UNCLIPT |
| UNBEREFT | UNBOOT | UNBURTHENED | UNCHARNELLED | UNCLOAK |
| UNBERUFEN | UNBOOTED | UNBURTHENING | UNCHARNELLING | UNCLOAKED |
| UNBESEEM | UNBOOTING | UNBURTHENS | UNCHARNELS | UNCLOAKING |
| UNBESEEMED | UNBOOTS | UNBURY | UNCHARTED | UNCLOAKS |
| UNBESEEMING | UNBORE | UNBURYING | UNCHARY | UNCLOG |
| UNBESEEMS | UNBORN | UNBUSY | UNCHASTE | UNCLOGGED |
| UNBESPEAK | UNBORNE | UNBUTTON | UNCHECK | UNCLOGGING |
| UNBESPEAKING | UNBOSOM | UNBUTTONED | UNCHECKED | UNCLOGS |
| UNBESPEAKS | UNBOSOMED | UNBUTTONING | UNCHECKING | UNCLOSE |
| UNBESPOKE | UNBOSOMER | UNBUTTONS | UNCHECKS | UNCLOSED |
| UNBESPOKEN | UNBOSOMERS | UNCAGE | UNCHEERED | UNCLOSES |

| | | | | |
|---|---|---|---|---|
| UNCLOSING | UNCOUPLES | UNDASHED | UNDERBUSHED | UNDERGIRDED |
| UNCLOTHE | UNCOUPLING | UNDATE | UNDERBUSHES | UNDERGIRDING |
| UNCLOTHED | UNCOURTLY | UNDATED | UNDERBUSHING | UNDERGIRDS |
| UNCLOTHES | UNCOUTH | UNDAUNTED | UNDERBUY | UNDERGIRT |
| UNCLOTHING | UNCOUTHER | UNDAWNING | UNDERBUYING | UNDERGO |
| UNCLOUD | UNCOUTHEST | UNDAZZLE | UNDERBUYS | UNDERGOES |
| UNCLOUDED | UNCOUTHLY | UNDAZZLED | UNDERCARD | UNDERGOING |
| UNCLOUDING | UNCOVER | UNDAZZLES | UNDERCARDS | UNDERGONE |
| UNCLOUDS | UNCOVERED | UNDAZZLING | UNDERCART | UNDERGOWN |
| UNCLOUDY | UNCOVERING | UNDE | UNDERCARTS | UNDERGOWNS |
| UNCLOVEN | UNCOVERS | UNDÉ | UNDERCAST | UNDERGRAD |
| UNCLUTCH | UNCOWL | UNDEAD | UNDERCASTS | UNDERGRADS |
| UNCLUTCHED | UNCOWLED | UNDEAF | UNDERCLAD | UNDERHAND |
| UNCLUTCHES | UNCOWLING | UNDEAFED | UNDERCLAY | UNDERHANDS |
| UNCLUTCHING | UNCOWLS | UNDEAFING | UNDERCLAYS | UNDERHUNG |
| UNCO | UNCOYNED | UNDEAFS | UNDERCLUB | UNDERKEEP |
| UNCOCK | UNCRATE | UNDEALT | UNDERCLUBBED | UNDERKEEPING |
| UNCOCKED | UNCRATED | UNDEAR | UNDERCLUBBING | UNDERKEEPS |
| UNCOCKING | UNCRATES | UNDEBASED | UNDERCLUBS | UNDERKEPT |
| UNCOCKS | UNCRATING | UNDECAYED | UNDERCOAT | UNDERKING |
| UNCOIL | UNCREATE | UNDECEIVE | UNDERCOATS | UNDERKINGS |
| UNCOILED | UNCREATED | UNDECEIVED | UNDERCOOK | UNDERLAID |
| UNCOILING | UNCREATES | UNDECEIVES | UNDERCOOKS | UNDERLAIN |
| UNCOILS | UNCREATING | UNDECEIVING | UNDERCOOL | UNDERLAP |
| UNCOINED | UNCROPPED | UNDECENT | UNDERCOOLED | UNDERLAPPED |
| UNCOLT | UNCROSS | UNDECIDED | UNDERCOOLING | UNDERLAPPING |
| UNCOLTED | UNCROSSED | UNDECIMAL | UNDERCOOLS | UNDERLAPS |
| UNCOLTING | UNCROSSES | UNDECK | UNDERCUT | UNDERLAY |
| UNCOLTS | UNCROSSING | UNDECKED | UNDERCUTS | UNDERLAYING |
| UNCOMBED | UNCROWDED | UNDECKING | UNDERCUTTING | UNDERLAYS |
| UNCOMBINE | UNCROWN | UNDECKS | UNDERDECK | UNDERLET |
| UNCOMBINED | UNCROWNED | UNDEE | UNDERDECKS | UNDERLETS |
| UNCOMBINES | UNCROWNING | UNDÉE | UNDERDID | UNDERLETTING |
| UNCOMBINING | UNCROWNS | UNDEEDED | UNDERDO | UNDERLETTINGS |
| UNCOMELY | UNCRUDDED | UNDEFACED | UNDERDOER | UNDERLIE |
| UNCOMMON | UNCRUMPLE | UNDEFIDE | UNDERDOERS | UNDERLIES |
| UNCOMMONER | UNCRUMPLED | UNDEFIED | UNDERDOES | UNDERLINE |
| UNCOMMONEST | UNCRUMPLES | UNDEFILED | UNDERDOG | UNDERLINED |
| UNCONCERN | UNCRUMPLING | UNDEFINED | UNDERDOGS | UNDERLINES |
| UNCONCERNS | UNCTION | UNDEIFIED | UNDERDOING | UNDERLING |
| UNCONFINE | UNCTIONS | UNDEIFIES | UNDERDONE | UNDERLINGS |
| UNCONFINED | UNCTUOUS | UNDEIFY | UNDERDRAW | UNDERLINING |
| UNCONFINES | UNCULLED | UNDEIFYING | UNDERDRAWING | UNDERLIP |
| UNCONFINING | UNCURABLE | UNDELAYED | UNDERDRAWINGS | UNDERLIPS |
| UNCONFORM | UNCURBED | UNDELIGHT | UNDERDRAWN | UNDERLYING |
| UNCONGEAL | UNCURDLED | UNDELIGHTS | UNDERDRAWS | UNDERMAN |
| UNCONGEALED | UNCURED | UNDELUDED | UNDERDREW | UNDERMANNED |
| UNCONGEALING | UNCURIOUS | UNDER | UNDERFED | UNDERMANNING |
| UNCONGEALS | UNCURL | UNDERACT | UNDERFEED | UNDERMANS |
| UNCOOKED | UNCURLED | UNDERACTED | UNDERFEEDING | UNDERMEN |
| UNCOOL | UNCURLING | UNDERACTING | UNDERFEEDS | UNDERMINE |
| UNCOPE | UNCURLS | UNDERACTS | UNDERFELT | UNDERMINED |
| UNCOPED | UNCURRENT | UNDERARM | UNDERFELTS | UNDERMINES |
| UNCOPES | UNCURSE | UNDERBEAR | UNDERFIRE | UNDERMINING |
| UNCOPING | UNCURSED | UNDERBEARING | UNDERFIRED | UNDERMININGS |
| UNCORD | UNCURSES | UNDERBEARINGS | UNDERFIRES | UNDERMOST |
| UNCORDED | UNCURSING | UNDERBEARS | UNDERFIRING | UNDERN |
| UNCORDIAL | UNCURTAIN | UNDERBID | UNDERFLOW | UNDERNOTE |
| UNCORDING | UNCURTAINED | UNDERBIDDING | UNDERFLOWS | UNDERNOTED |
| UNCORDS | UNCURTAINING | UNDERBIDS | UNDERFONG | UNDERNOTES |
| UNCORK | UNCURTAINS | UNDERBIT | UNDERFONGED | UNDERNOTING |
| UNCORKED | UNCUS | UNDERBITE | UNDERFONGING | UNDERNS |
| UNCORKING | UNCUT | UNDERBITES | UNDERFONGS | UNDERPAID |
| UNCORKS | UNDAM | UNDERBITING | UNDERFOOT | UNDERPASS |
| UNCORRUPT | UNDAMAGED | UNDERBITTEN | UNDERFOOTED | UNDERPASSES |
| UNCOS | UNDAMMED | UNDERBORE | UNDERFOOTING | UNDERPAY |
| UNCOSTLY | UNDAMMING | UNDERBORNE | UNDERFOOTS | UNDERPAYING |
| UNCOUNTED | UNDAMNED | UNDERBOUGHT | UNDERFUR | UNDERPAYS |
| UNCOUPLE | UNDAMPED | UNDERBRED | UNDERFURS | UNDERPEEP |
| UNCOUPLED | UNDAMS | UNDERBUSH | UNDERGIRD | UNDERPEEPED |

| | | | | |
|---|---|---|---|---|
| UNDERPEEPING | UNDERTONE | UNDRAINED | UNENDOWED | UNFEUED |
| UNDERPEEPS | UNDERTONES | UNDRAPED | UNENGAGED | UNFIGURED |
| UNDERPIN | UNDERTOOK | UNDRAW | UNENTERED | UNFILDE |
| UNDERPINNED | UNDERTOW | UNDRAWING | UNENVIED | UNFILED |
| UNDERPINNING | UNDERTOWS | UNDRAWN | UNENVIOUS | UNFILIAL |
| UNDERPINNINGS | UNDERUSE | UNDRAWS | UNENVYING | UNFILLED |
| UNDERPINS | UNDERUSED | UNDREADED | UNEQUABLE | UNFILMED |
| UNDERPLAY | UNDERUSES | UNDREAMED | UNEQUAL | UNFINE |
| UNDERPLAYED | UNDERUSING | UNDREAMT | UNEQUALLY | UNFIRED |
| UNDERPLAYING | UNDERVEST | UNDRESS | UNEQUALS | UNFIRM |
| UNDERPLAYS | UNDERVESTS | UNDRESSED | UNERRING | UNFISHED |
| UNDERPLOT | UNDERWAY | UNDRESSES | UNESPIED | UNFIT |
| UNDERPLOTS | UNDERWEAR | UNDRESSING | UNESSAYED | UNFITLY |
| UNDERPROP | UNDERWEARS | UNDRESSINGS | UNESSENCE | UNFITNESS |
| UNDERPROPPED | UNDERWENT | UNDREST | UNESSENCED | UNFITNESSES |
| UNDERPROPPING | UNDERWING | UNDREW | UNESSENCES | UNFITS |
| UNDERPROPS | UNDERWINGS | UNDRIED | UNESSENCING | UNFITTED |
| UNDERRAN | UNDERWIT | UNDRILLED | UNETH | UNFITTER |
| UNDERRATE | UNDERWITS | UNDRIVEN | UNETHICAL | UNFITTEST |
| UNDERRATED | UNDERWOOD | UNDROSSY | UNEVEN | UNFITTING |
| UNDERRATES | UNDERWOODS | UNDROWNED | UNEVENER | UNFIX |
| UNDERRATING | UNDERWORK | UNDRUNK | UNEVENEST | UNFIXED |
| UNDERRUN | UNDERWORKED | UNDUBBED | UNEVENLY | UNFIXES |
| UNDERRUNNING | UNDERWORKING | UNDUE | UNEXALTED | UNFIXING |
| UNDERRUNNINGS | UNDERWORKS | UNDUG | UNEXCITED | UNFIXITIES |
| UNDERRUNS | UNDERWROUGHT | UNDULANCIES | UNEXPIRED | UNFIXITY |
| UNDERSAID | UNDESERT | UNDULANCY | UNEXPOSED | UNFLAWED |
| UNDERSAY | UNDESERTS | UNDULANT | UNEXTINCT | UNFLEDGED |
| UNDERSAYE | UNDESERVE | UNDULATE | UNEXTREME | UNFLESH |
| UNDERSAYES | UNDESERVED | UNDULATED | UNEYED | UNFLESHED |
| UNDERSAYING | UNDESERVES | UNDULATES | UNFABLED | UNFLESHES |
| UNDERSAYS | UNDESERVING | UNDULATING | UNFACT | UNFLESHING |
| UNDERSEA | UNDESIRED | UNDULLED | UNFACTS | UNFLESHLY |
| UNDERSEAL | UNDEVOUT | UNDULOSE | UNFADABLE | UNFLOORED |
| UNDERSEALED | UNDID | UNDULOUS | UNFADED | UNFLUSH |
| UNDERSEALING | UNDIES | UNDULY | UNFADING | UNFLUSHED |
| UNDERSEALINGS | UNDIGHT | UNDUTEOUS | UNFAILING | UNFLUSHES |
| UNDERSEALS | UNDIGHTING | UNDUTIFUL | UNFAIR | UNFLUSHING |
| UNDERSELF | UNDIGHTS | UNDYED | UNFAIRED | UNFOCUSED |
| UNDERSELL | UNDIGNIFIED | UNDYING | UNFAIRER | UNFOLD |
| UNDERSELLING | UNDIGNIFIES | UNDYINGLY | UNFAIREST | UNFOLDED |
| UNDERSELLS | UNDIGNIFY | UNEARED | UNFAIRING | UNFOLDER |
| UNDERSELVES | UNDIGNIFYING | UNEARNED | UNFAIRLY | UNFOLDERS |
| UNDERSET | UNDILUTED | UNEARTH | UNFAIRS | UNFOLDING |
| UNDERSETS | UNDIMMED | UNEARTHED | UNFAITH | UNFOLDINGS |
| UNDERSETTING | UNDINE | UNEARTHING | UNFAITHS | UNFOLDS |
| UNDERSHOT | UNDINES | UNEARTHLIER | UNFALLEN | UNFOOL |
| UNDERSIDE | UNDINISM | UNEARTHLIEST | UNFAMED | UNFOOLED |
| UNDERSIDES | UNDINISMS | UNEARTHLY | UNFANNED | UNFOOLING |
| UNDERSIGN | UNDINTED | UNEARTHS | UNFASTEN | UNFOOLS |
| UNDERSIGNED | UNDIPPED | UNEASE | UNFASTENED | UNFOOTED |
| UNDERSIGNING | UNDIVIDED | UNEASES | UNFASTENING | UNFORBID |
| UNDERSIGNS | UNDIVINE | UNEASIER | UNFASTENS | UNFORCED |
| UNDERSKIES | UNDO | UNEASIEST | UNFAULTY | UNFORGED |
| UNDERSKY | UNDOCK | UNEASILY | UNFAZED | UNFORGOT |
| UNDERSOIL | UNDOCKED | UNEASY | UNFEARED | UNFORM |
| UNDERSOILS | UNDOCKING | UNEATABLE | UNFEARFUL | UNFORMAL |
| UNDERSOLD | UNDOCKS | UNEATEN | UNFEARING | UNFORMED |
| UNDERSONG | UNDOER | UNEATH | UNFED | UNFORMING |
| UNDERSONGS | UNDOERS | UNEATHES | UNFEED | UNFORMS |
| UNDERTAKE | UNDOES | UNEDGE | UNFEELING | UNFORTUNE |
| UNDERTAKEN | UNDOING | UNEDGED | UNFEIGNED | UNFORTUNES |
| UNDERTAKES | UNDOINGS | UNEDGES | UNFELLED | UNFOUGHT |
| UNDERTAKING | UNDONE | UNEDGING | UNFELT | UNFOUND |
| UNDERTAKINGS | UNDOOMED | UNEDITED | UNFENCED | UNFOUNDED |
| UNDERTANE | UNDOUBLE | UNEFFACED | UNFETTER | UNFRAMED |
| UNDERTIME | UNDOUBLED | UNELATED | UNFETTERED | UNFRANKED |
| UNDERTIMES | UNDOUBLES | UNELECTED | UNFETTERING | UNFRAUGHT |
| UNDERTINT | UNDOUBLING | UNEMPTIED | UNFETTERS | UNFRAUGHTED |
| UNDERTINTS | UNDOUBTED | UNENDING | UNFEUDAL | UNFRAUGHTING |

UNFRAUGHTS
UNFREE
UNFREEMAN
UNFREEMEN
UNFREEZE
UNFREEZES
UNFREEZING
UNFRETTED
UNFRIEND
UNFRIENDS
UNFROCK
UNFROCKED
UNFROCKING
UNFROCKS
UNFROZE
UNFROZEN
UNFUELLED
UNFUMED
UNFUNDED
UNFUNNY
UNFURL
UNFURLED
UNFURLING
UNFURLS
UNFURNISH
UNFURNISHED
UNFURNISHES
UNFURNISHING
UNFURRED
UNGAIN
UNGAINFUL
UNGAINLIER
UNGAINLIEST
UNGAINLY
UNGALLANT
UNGALLED
UNGARBLED
UNGAUGED
UNGAZED
UNGEAR
UNGEARED
UNGEARING
UNGEARS
UNGENIAL
UNGENTEEL
UNGENTLE
UNGENTLY
UNGENUINE
UNGERMANE
UNGET
UNGETS
UNGETTING
UNGHOSTLY
UNGIFTED
UNGILD
UNGILDED
UNGILDING
UNGILDS
UNGILT
UNGIRD
UNGIRDED
UNGIRDING
UNGIRDS
UNGIRT
UNGIRTH
UNGIRTHED
UNGIRTHING
UNGIRTHS
UNGIVING
UNGLAD
UNGLAZED
UNGLOSSED
UNGLOVE
UNGLOVED
UNGLOVES
UNGLOVING
UNGLUE
UNGLUED
UNGLUES
UNGLUING
UNGOD
UNGODDED
UNGODDING
UNGODLIER
UNGODLIEST
UNGODLIKE
UNGODLILY
UNGODLY
UNGODS
UNGORD
UNGORED
UNGORGED
UNGOT
UNGOTTEN
UNGOWN
UNGOWNED
UNGOWNING
UNGOWNS
UNGRACED
UNGRADED
UNGRASSED
UNGRAVELY
UNGRAZED
UNGROOMED
UNGROUND
UNGROWN
UNGRUDGED
UNGUAL
UNGUARD
UNGUARDED
UNGUARDING
UNGUARDS
UNGUENT
UNGUENTS
UNGUES
UNGUESSED
UNGUIDED
UNGUIFORM
UNGUILTY
UNGUIS
UNGULA
UNGULAE
UNGULATE
UNGULATES
UNGULED
UNGUM
UNGUMMED
UNGUMMING
UNGUMS
UNGYVE
UNGYVED
UNGYVES
UNGYVING
UNHABLE
UNHACKED
UNHAILED
UNHAIR
UNHAIRED
UNHAIRING
UNHAIRS
UNHALLOW
UNHALLOWED
UNHALLOWING
UNHALLOWS
UNHALSED
UNHAND
UNHANDED
UNHANDILY
UNHANDING
UNHANDLED
UNHANDS
UNHANDY
UNHANG
UNHANGED
UNHANGING
UNHANGS
UNHAPPIED
UNHAPPIER
UNHAPPIES
UNHAPPIEST
UNHAPPILY
UNHAPPY
UNHAPPYING
UNHARBOUR
UNHARBOURED
UNHARBOURING
UNHARBOURS
UNHARDY
UNHARMED
UNHARMFUL
UNHARMING
UNHARNESS
UNHARNESSED
UNHARNESSES
UNHARNESSING
UNHASP
UNHASPED
UNHASPING
UNHASPS
UNHASTING
UNHASTY
UNHAT
UNHATCHED
UNHATS
UNHATTED
UNHATTING
UNHATTINGS
UNHAUNTED
UNHEAD
UNHEADED
UNHEADING
UNHEADS
UNHEAL
UNHEALED
UNHEALING
UNHEALS
UNHEALTH
UNHEALTHIER
UNHEALTHIEST
UNHEALTHS
UNHEALTHY
UNHEARD
UNHEARSE
UNHEARSED
UNHEARSES
UNHEARSING
UNHEART
UNHEARTED
UNHEARTING
UNHEARTS
UNHEATED
UNHEDGED
UNHEEDED
UNHEEDFUL
UNHEEDILY
UNHEEDING
UNHEEDY
UNHELE
UNHELED
UNHELES
UNHELING
UNHELM
UNHELMED
UNHELMING
UNHELMS
UNHELPED
UNHELPFUL
UNHEPPEN
UNHEROIC
UNHERST
UNHEWN
UNHIDDEN
UNHINGE
UNHINGED
UNHINGES
UNHINGING
UNHIP
UNHIRED
UNHITCH
UNHITCHED
UNHITCHES
UNHITCHING
UNHIVE
UNHIVED
UNHIVES
UNHIVING
UNHOARD
UNHOARDED
UNHOARDING
UNHOARDS
UNHOLIER
UNHOLIEST
UNHOLILY
UNHOLPEN
UNHOLY
UNHOMELY
UNHONEST
UNHOOD
UNHOODED
UNHOODING
UNHOODS
UNHOOK
UNHOOKED
UNHOOKING
UNHOOKS
UNHOOP
UNHOOPED
UNHOOPING
UNHOOPS
UNHOPED
UNHOPEFUL
UNHORSE
UNHORSED
UNHORSES
UNHORSING
UNHOUSE
UNHOUSED
UNHOUSES
UNHOUSING
UNHUMAN
UNHUMBLED
UNHUNG
UNHUNTED
UNHURRIED
UNHURT
UNHURTFUL
UNHUSK
UNHUSKED
UNHUSKING
UNHUSKS
UNI
UNIAXIAL
UNICITIES
UNICITY
UNICOLOR
UNICOLOUR
UNICORN
UNICORNS
UNICYCLE
UNICYCLES
UNIDEAL
UNIFIABLE
UNIFIC
UNIFIED
UNIFIER
UNIFIERS
UNIFIES
UNIFILAR
UNIFORM
UNIFORMED
UNIFORMING
UNIFORMLY
UNIFORMS
UNIFY
UNIFYING
UNIFYINGS
UNILLUMED
UNILOBAR
UNILOBED
UNIMBUED
UNIMPEDED
UNIMPOSED
UNINCITED
UNINDEXED
UNINJURED
UNINSURED
UNINURED
UNINVITED
UNION
UNIONISE
UNIONISED
UNIONISES
UNIONISING
UNIONISM
UNIONISMS
UNIONIST
UNIONISTS
UNIONIZE
UNIONIZED
UNIONIZES
UNIONIZING
UNIONS
UNIPAROUS
UNIPED
UNIPEDS
UNIPLANAR
UNIPOD
UNIPODS
UNIPOLAR
UNIQUE

| | | | | |
|---|---|---|---|---|
| UNIQUELY | UNKENNELS | UNLEADING | UNLOOSED | UNMEEK |
| UNIQUER | UNKENT | UNLEADS | UNLOOSEN | UNMEET |
| UNIQUES | UNKEPT | UNLEAL | UNLOOSENED | UNMEETLY |
| UNIQUEST | UNKET | UNLEARN | UNLOOSENING | UNMELTED |
| UNIRONED | UNKID | UNLEARNED | UNLOOSENS | UNMERITED |
| UNIS | UNKIND | UNLEARNING | UNLOOSES | UNMET |
| UNISERIAL | UNKINDER | UNLEARNS | UNLOOSING | UNMETED |
| UNISEX | UNKINDEST | UNLEARNT | UNLOPPED | UNMEW |
| UNISEXUAL | UNKINDLED | UNLEASED | UNLORD | UNMEWED |
| UNISON | UNKINDLIER | UNLEASH | UNLORDED | UNMEWING |
| UNISONAL | UNKINDLIEST | UNLEASHED | UNLORDING | UNMEWS |
| UNISONANT | UNKINDLY | UNLEASHES | UNLORDLY | UNMILKED |
| UNISONOUS | UNKING | UNLEASHING | UNLORDS | UNMILLED |
| UNISONS | UNKINGED | UNLED | UNLOSABLE | UNMINDED |
| UNIT | UNKINGING | UNLESS | UNLOST | UNMINDFUL |
| UNITAL | UNKINGLIER | UNLET | UNLOVABLE | UNMINGLED |
| UNITARIAN | UNKINGLIEST | UNLICH | UNLOVE | UNMIRY |
| UNITARIANS | UNKINGLY | UNLICKED | UNLOVED | UNMISSED |
| UNITARY | UNKINGS | UNLID | UNLOVELY | UNMIXED |
| UNITE | UNKISS | UNLIDDED | UNLOVES | UNMIXEDLY |
| UNITED | UNKISSED | UNLIDDING | UNLOVING | UNMOANED |
| UNITEDLY | UNKISSES | UNLIDS | UNLUCKIER | UNMODISH |
| UNITER | UNKISSING | UNLIGHTED | UNLUCKIEST | UNMONEYED |
| UNITERS | UNKNELLED | UNLIKABLE | UNLUCKILY | UNMONIED |
| UNITES | UNKNIGHT | UNLIKE | UNLUCKY | UNMOOR |
| UNITIES | UNKNIGHTED | UNLIKELIER | UNMADE | UNMOORED |
| UNITING | UNKNIGHTING | UNLIKELIEST | UNMAILED | UNMOORING |
| UNITINGS | UNKNIGHTS | UNLIKELY | UNMAIMED | UNMOORS |
| UNITION | UNKNIT | UNLIKES | UNMAKABLE | UNMORAL |
| UNITIONS | UNKNITS | UNLIMBER | UNMAKE | UNMOTIVED |
| UNITISE | UNKNITTED | UNLIMBERED | UNMAKES | UNMOULD |
| UNITISED | UNKNITTING | UNLIMBERING | UNMAKING | UNMOULDED |
| UNITISES | UNKNOT | UNLIMBERS | UNMAKINGS | UNMOULDING |
| UNITISING | UNKNOTS | UNLIME | UNMAN | UNMOULDS |
| UNITIVE | UNKNOTTED | UNLIMED | UNMANACLE | UNMOUNT |
| UNITIVELY | UNKNOTTING | UNLIMES | UNMANACLED | UNMOUNTED |
| UNITIZE | UNKNOWING | UNLIMING | UNMANACLES | UNMOUNTING |
| UNITIZED | UNKNOWN | UNLIMITED | UNMANACLING | UNMOUNTS |
| UNITIZES | UNKNOWNS | UNLINE | UNMANAGED | UNMOURNED |
| UNITIZING | UNLACE | UNLINEAL | UNMANLIER | UNMOVABLE |
| UNITS | UNLACED | UNLINED | UNMANLIEST | UNMOVABLY |
| UNITY | UNLACES | UNLINES | UNMANLIKE | UNMOVED |
| UNIVALENT | UNLACING | UNLINING | UNMANLY | UNMOVEDLY |
| UNIVALENTS | UNLADE | UNLINK | UNMANNED | UNMOVING |
| UNIVALVE | UNLADED | UNLINKED | UNMANNING | UNMOWN |
| UNIVALVES | UNLADEN | UNLINKING | UNMANS | UNMUFFLE |
| UNIVERSAL | UNLADES | UNLINKS | UNMANTLE | UNMUFFLED |
| UNIVERSALS | UNLADING | UNLISTED | UNMANTLED | UNMUFFLES |
| UNIVERSE | UNLADINGS | UNLIT | UNMANTLES | UNMUFFLING |
| UNIVERSES | UNLAID | UNLIVABLE | UNMANTLING | UNMUSICAL |
| UNIVOCAL | UNLASH | UNLIVE | UNMANURED | UNMUZZLE |
| UNIVOCALS | UNLASHED | UNLIVED | UNMARD | UNMUZZLED |
| UNJADED | UNLASHES | UNLIVELY | UNMARKED | UNMUZZLES |
| UNJEALOUS | UNLASHING | UNLIVES | UNMARRED | UNMUZZLING |
| UNJOINT | UNLAST | UNLIVING | UNMARRIED | UNMUZZLINGS |
| UNJOINTED | UNLASTE | UNLOAD | UNMARRIES | UNNAIL |
| UNJOINTING | UNLATCH | UNLOADED | UNMARRY | UNNAILED |
| UNJOINTS | UNLATCHED | UNLOADER | UNMARRYING | UNNAILING |
| UNJOYFUL | UNLATCHES | UNLOADERS | UNMASK | UNNAILS |
| UNJOYOUS | UNLATCHING | UNLOADING | UNMASKED | UNNAMABLE |
| UNJUST | UNLAW | UNLOADINGS | UNMASKER | UNNAMED |
| UNJUSTER | UNLAWED | UNLOADS | UNMASKERS | UNNANELD |
| UNJUSTEST | UNLAWFUL | UNLOCATED | UNMASKING | UNNATIVE |
| UNJUSTLY | UNLAWING | UNLOCK | UNMASKINGS | UNNATURAL |
| UNKED | UNLAWS | UNLOCKED | UNMASKS | UNNEATH |
| UNKEMPT | UNLAY | UNLOCKING | UNMATCHED | UNNEEDED |
| UNKENNED | UNLAYING | UNLOCKS | UNMATED | UNNEEDFUL |
| UNKENNEL | UNLAYS | UNLOGICAL | UNMATURED | UNNERVE |
| UNKENNELLED | UNLEAD | UNLOOKED | UNMEANING | UNNERVED |
| UNKENNELLING | UNLEADED | UNLOOSE | UNMEANT | UNNERVES |

| | | | | |
|---|---|---|---|---|
| UNNERVING | UNPEGS | UNPLUMBS | UNPROVIDE | UNREALLY |
| UNNEST | UNPEN | UNPLUME | UNPROVIDED | UNREAPED |
| UNNESTED | UNPENNED | UNPLUMED | UNPROVIDES | UNREASON |
| UNNESTING | UNPENNIED | UNPLUMES | UNPROVIDING | UNREASONS |
| UNNESTS | UNPENNING | UNPLUMING | UNPROVOKE | UNREAVE |
| UNNETHES | UNPENS | UNPOETIC | UNPROVOKED | UNREAVED |
| UNNETTED | UNPENT | UNPOINTED | UNPROVOKES | UNREAVES |
| UNNOBLE | UNPEOPLE | UNPOISED | UNPROVOKING | UNREAVING |
| UNNOBLED | UNPEOPLED | UNPOISON | UNPRUNED | UNREBATED |
| UNNOBLES | UNPEOPLES | UNPOISONED | UNPULLED | UNREBUKED |
| UNNOBLING | UNPEOPLING | UNPOISONING | UNPURGED | UNRECKED |
| UNNOTED | UNPERCH | UNPOISONS | UNPURSE | UNRED |
| UNNOTICED | UNPERCHED | UNPOLICED | UNPURSED | UNREDREST |
| UNOBEYED | UNPERCHES | UNPOLISH | UNPURSES | UNREDUCED |
| UNOBVIOUS | UNPERCHING | UNPOLISHED | UNPURSING | UNREEL |
| UNOFFERED | UNPERFECT | UNPOLISHES | UNPURSUED | UNREELED |
| UNOFTEN | UNPERPLEX | UNPOLISHING | UNQUALIFIED | UNREELING |
| UNOILED | UNPERPLEXED | UNPOLITE | UNQUALIFIES | UNREELS |
| UNOPENED | UNPERPLEXES | UNPOLITIC | UNQUALIFY | UNREEVE |
| UNOPPOSED | UNPERPLEXING | UNPOLLED | UNQUALIFYING | UNREEVED |
| UNORDER | UNPERSON | UNPOPE | UNQUEEN | UNREEVES |
| UNORDERED | UNPERSONED | UNPOPED | UNQUEENED | UNREEVING |
| UNORDERING | UNPERSONING | UNPOPES | UNQUEENING | UNREFINED |
| UNORDERLY | UNPERSONS | UNPOPING | UNQUEENLIER | UNREFUTED |
| UNORDERS | UNPERVERT | UNPOPULAR | UNQUEENLIEST | UNREIN |
| UNOWED | UNPERVERTED | UNPOSED | UNQUEENLY | UNREINED |
| UNOWNED | UNPERVERTING | UNPOSTED | UNQUEENS | UNREINING |
| UNPACK | UNPERVERTS | UNPOTABLE | UNQUELLED | UNREINS |
| UNPACKED | UNPICK | UNPRAISE | UNQUIET | UNRELATED |
| UNPACKER | UNPICKED | UNPRAISED | UNQUIETED | UNRELAXED |
| UNPACKERS | UNPICKING | UNPRAISES | UNQUIETING | UNREMOVED |
| UNPACKING | UNPICKS | UNPRAISING | UNQUIETLY | UNRENEWED |
| UNPACKINGS | UNPIERCED | UNPRAY | UNQUIETS | UNRENT |
| UNPACKS | UNPILOTED | UNPRAYED | UNQUOTE | UNREPAID |
| UNPAGED | UNPIN | UNPRAYING | UNQUOTED | UNREPAIR |
| UNPAID | UNPINKED | UNPRAYS | UNQUOTES | UNREPAIRS |
| UNPAINED | UNPINKT | UNPREACH | UNQUOTING | UNRESERVE |
| UNPAINFUL | UNPINNED | UNPREACHED | UNRACED | UNRESERVES |
| UNPAINT | UNPINNING | UNPREACHES | UNRACKED | UNREST |
| UNPAINTED | UNPINS | UNPREACHING | UNRAISED | UNRESTFUL |
| UNPAINTING | UNPITIED | UNPRECISE | UNRAKE | UNRESTING |
| UNPAINTS | UNPITIFUL | UNPREDICT | UNRAKED | UNRESTS |
| UNPAIRED | UNPITYING | UNPREDICTED | UNRAKES | UNREVISED |
| UNPALSIED | UNPLACE | UNPREDICTING | UNRAKING | UNREVOKED |
| UNPANEL | UNPLACED | UNPREDICTS | UNRATED | UNRHYMED |
| UNPANELLED | UNPLACES | UNPREPARE | UNRAVEL | UNRIBBED |
| UNPANELLING | UNPLACING | UNPREPARED | UNRAVELLED | UNRID |
| UNPANELS | UNPLAGUED | UNPREPARES | UNRAVELLING | UNRIDABLE |
| UNPANGED | UNPLAINED | UNPREPARING | UNRAVELLINGS | UNRIDDEN |
| UNPANNEL | UNPLAIT | UNPRESSED | UNRAVELS | UNRIDDLE |
| UNPANNELLED | UNPLAITED | UNPRETTY | UNRAZORED | UNRIDDLED |
| UNPANNELLING | UNPLAITING | UNPRICED | UNREACHED | UNRIDDLER |
| UNPANNELS | UNPLAITS | UNPRIEST | UNREAD | UNRIDDLERS |
| UNPAPER | UNPLANKED | UNPRIESTED | UNREADIER | UNRIDDLES |
| UNPAPERED | UNPLANNED | UNPRIESTING | UNREADIEST | UNRIDDLING |
| UNPAPERING | UNPLANTED | UNPRIESTS | UNREADILY | UNRIFLED |
| UNPAPERS | UNPLEASED | UNPRIMED | UNREADY | UNRIG |
| UNPARED | UNPLEATED | UNPRINTED | UNREAL | UNRIGGED |
| UNPARTIAL | UNPLEDGED | UNPRISON | UNREALISE | UNRIGGING |
| UNPATHED | UNPLIABLE | UNPRISONED | UNREALISED | UNRIGHT |
| UNPAVED | UNPLIABLY | UNPRISONING | UNREALISES | UNRIGHTS |
| UNPAY | UNPLIANT | UNPRISONS | UNREALISING | UNRIGS |
| UNPAYABLE | UNPLUCKED | UNPRIZED | UNREALISM | UNRIMED |
| UNPAYING | UNPLUG | UNPROP | UNREALISMS | UNRINGED |
| UNPAYS | UNPLUGGED | UNPROPER | UNREALITIES | UNRINGED |
| UNPEELED | UNPLUGGING | UNPROPPED | UNREALITY | UNRIP |
| UNPEERED | UNPLUGS | UNPROPPING | UNREALIZE | UNRIPE |
| UNPEG | UNPLUMB | UNPROPS | UNREALIZED | UNRIPENED |
| UNPEGGED | UNPLUMBED | UNPROVED | UNREALIZES | UNRIPER |
| UNPEGGING | UNPLUMBING | UNPROVEN | UNREALIZING | UNRIPEST |
| | | | | UNRIPPED |

| | | | | |
|---|---|---|---|---|
| UNRIPPING | UNSAFETY | UNSEEMLIER | UNSHED | UNSLUICED |
| UNRIPPINGS | UNSAID | UNSEEMLIEST | UNSHELL | UNSLUICES |
| UNRIPS | UNSAILED | UNSEEMLY | UNSHELLED | UNSLUICING |
| UNRISEN | UNSAINED | UNSEEN | UNSHELLING | UNSLUNG |
| UNRIVEN | UNSAINT | UNSEENS | UNSHELLS | UNSMART |
| UNRIVET | UNSAINTED | UNSEIZED | UNSHENT | UNSMILING |
| UNRIVETED | UNSAINTING | UNSELDOM | UNSHEWN | UNSMITTEN |
| UNRIVETING | UNSAINTLIER | UNSELF | UNSHIP | UNSMOOTH |
| UNRIVETS | UNSAINTLIEST | UNSELFED | UNSHIPPED | UNSMOOTHED |
| UNROBE | UNSAINTLY | UNSELFING | UNSHIPPING | UNSMOOTHING |
| UNROBED | UNSAINTS | UNSELFISH | UNSHIPS | UNSMOOTHS |
| UNROBES | UNSALABLE | UNSELFS | UNSHOCKED | UNSMOTE |
| UNROBING | UNSALTED | UNSELVES | UNSHOD | UNSNAP |
| UNROLL | UNSALUTED | UNSENSE | UNSHOE | UNSNAPPED |
| UNROLLED | UNSAPPED | UNSENSED | UNSHOED | UNSNAPPING |
| UNROLLING | UNSASHED | UNSENSES | UNSHOEING | UNSNAPS |
| UNROLLS | UNSATABLE | UNSENSING | UNSHOES | UNSNARL |
| UNROOF | UNSATED | UNSENT | UNSHOOT | UNSNARLED |
| UNROOFED | UNSATIATE | UNSERIOUS | UNSHOOTED | UNSNARLING |
| UNROOFING | UNSATING | UNSET | UNSHOOTING | UNSNARLS |
| UNROOFS | UNSAVED | UNSETS | UNSHOOTS | UNSNECK |
| UNROOST | UNSAVOURY | UNSETTING | UNSHORN | UNSNECKED |
| UNROOSTED | UNSAY | UNSETTLE | UNSHOT | UNSNECKING |
| UNROOSTING | UNSAYABLE | UNSETTLED | UNSHOUT | UNSNECKS |
| UNROOSTS | UNSAYING | UNSETTLES | UNSHOUTED | UNSNUFFED |
| UNROOT | UNSAYS | UNSETTLING | UNSHOUTING | UNSOAPED |
| UNROOTED | UNSCALE | UNSETTLINGS | UNSHOUTS | UNSOCIAL |
| UNROOTING | UNSCALED | UNSEVERED | UNSHOWN | UNSOCKET |
| UNROOTS | UNSCALES | UNSEW | UNSHRIVED | UNSOCKETED |
| UNROPE | UNSCALING | UNSEWED | UNSHRIVEN | UNSOCKETING |
| UNROPED | UNSCANNED | UNSEWING | UNSHROUD | UNSOCKETS |
| UNROPES | UNSCARRED | UNSEWN | UNSHROUDED | UNSOD |
| UNROPING | UNSCARY | UNSEWS | UNSHROUDING | UNSODDEN |
| UNROSINED | UNSCATHED | UNSEX | UNSHROUDS | UNSOFT |
| UNROTTED | UNSCENTED | UNSEXED | UNSHRUBD | UNSOILED |
| UNROTTEN | UNSCOURED | UNSEXES | UNSHUNNED | UNSOLACED |
| UNROUGED | UNSCREW | UNSEXING | UNSHUT | UNSOLD |
| UNROUGH | UNSCREWED | UNSEXIST | UNSHUTS | UNSOLDER |
| UNROUND | UNSCREWING | UNSEXUAL | UNSHUTTER | UNSOLDERED |
| UNROUNDED | UNSCREWS | UNSHACKLE | UNSHUTTERED | UNSOLDERING |
| UNROUNDING | UNSCYTHED | UNSHACKLED | UNSHUTTERING | UNSOLDERS |
| UNROUNDS | UNSEAL | UNSHACKLES | UNSHUTTERS | UNSOLEMN |
| UNROUSED | UNSEALED | UNSHACKLING | UNSHUTTING | UNSOLID |
| UNROVE | UNSEALING | UNSHADED | UNSICKER | UNSOLIDLY |
| UNROYAL | UNSEALS | UNSHADOW | UNSICKLED | UNSOLVED |
| UNROYALLY | UNSEAM | UNSHADOWED | UNSIFTED | UNSONSY |
| UNRUBBED | UNSEAMED | UNSHADOWING | UNSIGHING | UNSOOTE |
| UNRUDE | UNSEAMING | UNSHADOWS | UNSIGHT | UNSORTED |
| UNRUFFE | UNSEAMS | UNSHAKED | UNSIGHTED | UNSOUGHT |
| UNRUFFLE | UNSEASON | UNSHAKEN | UNSIGHTLIER | UNSOUL |
| UNRUFFLED | UNSEASONED | UNSHALE | UNSIGHTLIEST | UNSOULED |
| UNRUFFLES | UNSEASONING | UNSHALED | UNSIGHTLY | UNSOULING |
| UNRUFFLING | UNSEASONS | UNSHALES | UNSIGNED | UNSOULS |
| UNRULE | UNSEAT | UNSHALING | UNSINEW | UNSOUND |
| UNRULED | UNSEATED | UNSHAMED | UNSINEWED | UNSOUNDED |
| UNRULES | UNSEATING | UNSHAPE | UNSINEWING | UNSOUNDER |
| UNRULIER | UNSEATS | UNSHAPED | UNSINEWS | UNSOUNDEST |
| UNRULIEST | UNSECRET | UNSHAPELIER | UNSISTING | UNSOUNDLY |
| UNRULY | UNSECULAR | UNSHAPELIEST | UNSIZABLE | UNSOURCED |
| UNRUMPLED | UNSECURED | UNSHAPELY | UNSIZED | UNSOURED |
| UNS | UNSEDUCED | UNSHAPEN | UNSKILFUL | UNSOWN |
| UNSADDLE | UNSEEABLE | UNSHAPES | UNSKILLED | UNSPAR |
| UNSADDLED | UNSEEDED | UNSHAPING | UNSKIMMED | UNSPARED |
| UNSADDLES | UNSEEING | UNSHARED | UNSKINNED | UNSPARING |
| UNSADDLING | UNSEEL | UNSHAVED | UNSLAIN | UNSPARRED |
| UNSAFE | UNSEELED | UNSHAVEN | UNSLAKED | UNSPARRING |
| UNSAFELY | UNSEELING | UNSHEATHE | UNSLING | UNSPARS |
| UNSAFER | UNSEELS | UNSHEATHED | UNSLINGING | UNSPEAK |
| UNSAFEST | UNSEEMING | UNSHEATHES | UNSLINGS | UNSPEAKING |
| UNSAFETIES | UNSEEMINGS | UNSHEATHING | UNSLUICE | UNSPEAKS |

| | | | | |
|---|---|---|---|---|
| UNSPED | UNSTOCKS | UNSWORN | UNTHINKING | UNTRIMMING |
| UNSPELL | UNSTOP | UNTACK | UNTHINKS | UNTRIMS |
| UNSPELLED | UNSTOPPED | UNTACKED | UNTHOUGHT | UNTROD |
| UNSPELLING | UNSTOPPER | UNTACKING | UNTHREAD | UNTRODDEN |
| UNSPELLS | UNSTOPPERED | UNTACKLE | UNTHREADED | UNTRUE |
| UNSPENT | UNSTOPPERING | UNTACKLED | UNTHREADING | UNTRUER |
| UNSPHERE | UNSTOPPERS | UNTACKLES | UNTHREADS | UNTRUEST |
| UNSPHERED | UNSTOPPING | UNTACKLING | UNTHRIFT | UNTRUISM |
| UNSPHERES | UNSTOPS | UNTACKS | UNTHRIFTS | UNTRUISMS |
| UNSPHERING | UNSTOW | UNTAILED | UNTHRIFTY | UNTRULY |
| UNSPIDE | UNSTOWED | UNTAINTED | UNTHRONE | UNTRUSS |
| UNSPIED | UNSTOWING | UNTAKEN | UNTHRONED | UNTRUSSED |
| UNSPILLED | UNSTOWS | UNTAMABLE | UNTHRONES | UNTRUSSER |
| UNSPILT | UNSTRAP | UNTAMABLY | UNTHRONING | UNTRUSSERS |
| UNSPOILED | UNSTRAPPED | UNTAME | UNTIDIED | UNTRUSSES |
| UNSPOILT | UNSTRAPPING | UNTAMED | UNTIDIER | UNTRUSSING |
| UNSPOKE | UNSTRAPS | UNTAMES | UNTIDIES | UNTRUSSINGS |
| UNSPOKEN | UNSTRING | UNTAMING | UNTIDIEST | UNTRUST |
| UNSPOTTED | UNSTRINGED | UNTANGLE | UNTIDILY | UNTRUSTS |
| UNSPRUNG | UNSTRINGING | UNTANGLED | UNTIDY | UNTRUSTY |
| UNSPUN | UNSTRINGS | UNTANGLES | UNTIDYING | UNTRUTH |
| UNSQUARED | UNSTRIP | UNTANGLING | UNTIE | UNTRUTHS |
| UNSTABLE | UNSTRIPED | UNTANNED | UNTIED | UNTUCK |
| UNSTABLER | UNSTRIPPED | UNTAPPED | UNTIES | UNTUCKED |
| UNSTABLEST | UNSTRIPPING | UNTARRED | UNTIL | UNTUCKING |
| UNSTACK | UNSTRIPS | UNTASTED | UNTILE | UNTUCKS |
| UNSTACKED | UNSTRUCK | UNTAUGHT | UNTILED | UNTUMBLED |
| UNSTACKING | UNSTRUNG | UNTAX | UNTILES | UNTUNABLE |
| UNSTACKS | UNSTUCK | UNTAXED | UNTILING | UNTUNABLY |
| UNSTAID | UNSTUDIED | UNTAXES | UNTILLED | UNTUNE |
| UNSTAINED | UNSTUFFED | UNTAXING | UNTIMELIER | UNTUNED |
| UNSTAMPED | UNSTUFFY | UNTEACH | UNTIMELIEST | UNTUNEFUL |
| UNSTARCH | UNSTUFT | UNTEACHES | UNTIMELY | UNTUNES |
| UNSTARCHED | UNSUBDUED | UNTEACHING | UNTIMEOUS | UNTUNING |
| UNSTARCHES | UNSUBJECT | UNTEAM | UNTIN | UNTURBID |
| UNSTARCHING | UNSUBTLE | UNTEAMED | UNTINGED | UNTURF |
| UNSTATE | UNSUCCESS | UNTEAMING | UNTINNED | UNTURFED |
| UNSTATED | UNSUCCESSES | UNTEAMS | UNTINNING | UNTURFING |
| UNSTATES | UNSUCKED | UNTEMPER | UNTINS | UNTURFS |
| UNSTATING | UNSUIT | UNTEMPERED | UNTIRABLE | UNTURN |
| UNSTAYED | UNSUITED | UNTEMPERING | UNTIRED | UNTURNED |
| UNSTAYING | UNSUITING | UNTEMPERS | UNTIRING | UNTURNING |
| UNSTEADIED | UNSUITS | UNTEMPTED | UNTITLED | UNTURNS |
| UNSTEADIER | UNSULLIED | UNTENABLE | UNTO | UNTUTORED |
| UNSTEADIES | UNSUMMED | UNTENANT | UNTOILING | UNTWINE |
| UNSTEADIEST | UNSUNG | UNTENANTED | UNTOLD | UNTWINED |
| UNSTEADY | UNSUNNED | UNTENANTING | UNTOMB | UNTWINES |
| UNSTEADYING | UNSUNNY | UNTENANTS | UNTOMBED | UNTWINING |
| UNSTEEL | UNSUPPLE | UNTENDED | UNTOMBING | UNTWIST |
| UNSTEELED | UNSURE | UNTENDER | UNTOMBS | UNTWISTED |
| UNSTEELING | UNSURED | UNTENT | UNTONED | UNTWISTING |
| UNSTEELS | UNSURER | UNTENTED | UNTORN | UNTWISTINGS |
| UNSTEP | UNSUREST | UNTENTING | UNTOUCHED | UNTWISTS |
| UNSTEPPED | UNSUSPECT | UNTENTS | UNTOWARD | UNTYING |
| UNSTEPPING | UNSWADDLE | UNTENTY | UNTRACE | UNTYINGS |
| UNSTEPS | UNSWADDLED | UNTESTED | UNTRACED | UNTYPABLE |
| UNSTERILE | UNSWADDLES | UNTETHER | UNTRACES | UNTYPICAL |
| UNSTICK | UNSWADDLING | UNTETHERED | UNTRACING | UNURGED |
| UNSTICKING | UNSWATHE | UNTETHERING | UNTRACKED | UNUSABLE |
| UNSTICKS | UNSWATHED | UNTETHERS | UNTRADED | UNUSABLY |
| UNSTIFLED | UNSWATHES | UNTHANKED | UNTRAINED | UNUSED |
| UNSTILLED | UNSWATHING | UNTHATCH | UNTREAD | UNUSEFUL |
| UNSTINTED | UNSWAYED | UNTHATCHED | UNTREADING | UNUSHERED |
| UNSTITCH | UNSWEAR | UNTHATCHES | UNTREADS | UNUSUAL |
| UNSTITCHED | UNSWEARING | UNTHATCHING | UNTREATED | UNUSUALLY |
| UNSTITCHES | UNSWEARINGS | UNTHAW | UNTRESSED | UNUTTERED |
| UNSTITCHING | UNSWEARS | UNTHAWED | UNTRIDE | UNVAIL |
| UNSTOCK | UNSWEET | UNTHAWING | UNTRIED | UNVAILE |
| UNSTOCKED | UNSWEPT | UNTHAWS | UNTRIM | UNVAILED |
| UNSTOCKING | UNSWORE | UNTHINK | UNTRIMMED | UNVAILES |

UNVAILING
UNVAILS
UNVALUED
UNVARIED
UNVARYING
UNVEIL
UNVEILED
UNVEILER
UNVEILERS
UNVEILING
UNVEILINGS
UNVEILS
UNVENTED
UNVERSED
UNVEXED
UNVIABLE
UNVIEWED
UNVIRTUE
UNVIRTUES
UNVISITED
UNVISOR
UNVISORED
UNVISORING
UNVISORS
UNVITAL
UNVIZARD
UNVIZARDED
UNVIZARDING
UNVIZARDS
UNVOCAL
UNVOICE
UNVOICED
UNVOICES
UNVOICING
UNVOICINGS
UNVULGAR
UNWAGED
UNWAKED
UNWAKENED
UNWALLED
UNWANTED
UNWARDED
UNWARE
UNWARELY
UNWARES
UNWARIE
UNWARIER
UNWARIEST
UNWARILY
UNWARLIKE
UNWARMED
UNWARNED
UNWARPED
UNWARY
UNWASHED
UNWASHEN
UNWASTED
UNWASTING
UNWATCHED
UNWATER
UNWATERED
UNWATERING
UNWATERS
UNWATERY
UNWAYED
UNWEAL
UNWEALS
UNWEANED
UNWEAPON
UNWEAPONED

UNWEAPONING
UNWEAPONS
UNWEARIED
UNWEARY
UNWEAVE
UNWEAVES
UNWEAVING
UNWEBBED
UNWED
UNWEDDED
UNWEEDED
UNWEENED
UNWEETING
UNWEIGHED
UNWELCOME
UNWELDY
UNWELL
UNWEPT
UNWET
UNWETTED
UNWHIPPED
UNWHIPT
UNWIELDIER
UNWIELDIEST
UNWIELDY
UNWIFELIER
UNWIFELIEST
UNWIFELY
UNWIGGED
UNWILFUL
UNWILL
UNWILLED
UNWILLING
UNWILLS
UNWIND
UNWINDING
UNWINDINGS
UNWINDS
UNWINGED
UNWINKING
UNWIPED
UNWIRE
UNWIRED
UNWIRES
UNWIRING
UNWISDOM
UNWISDOMS
UNWISE
UNWISELY
UNWISER
UNWISEST
UNWISH
UNWISHED
UNWISHES
UNWISHFUL
UNWISHING
UNWIST
UNWIT
UNWITCH
UNWITCHED
UNWITCHES
UNWITCHING
UNWITS
UNWITTED
UNWITTILY
UNWITTING
UNWITTY
UNWIVE
UNWIVED
UNWIVES

UNWIVING
UNWOMAN
UNWOMANED
UNWOMANING
UNWOMANLIER
UNWOMANLIEST
UNWOMANLY
UNWOMANS
UNWON
UNWONT
UNWONTED
UNWOODED
UNWOOED
UNWORDED
UNWORK
UNWORKED
UNWORKING
UNWORKS
UNWORLDLIER
UNWORLDLIEST
UNWORLDLY
UNWORMED
UNWORN
UNWORRIED
UNWORTH
UNWORTHIER
UNWORTHIEST
UNWORTHS
UNWORTHY
UNWOUND
UNWOUNDED
UNWOVE
UNWOVEN
UNWRAP
UNWRAPPED
UNWRAPPING
UNWRAPS
UNWREAKED
UNWREATHE
UNWREATHED
UNWREATHES
UNWREATHING
UNWRINKLE
UNWRINKLED
UNWRINKLES
UNWRINKLING
UNWRITE
UNWRITES
UNWRITING
UNWRITTEN
UNWROTE
UNWROUGHT
UNWRUNG
UNYEANED
UNYOKE
UNYOKED
UNYOKES
UNYOKING
UNZEALOUS
UNZIP
UNZIPPED
UNZIPPING
UNZIPS
UNZONED
UP
UPADAISY
UPAITHRIC
UPAS
UPASES
UPBEAR

UPBEARING
UPBEARS
UPBEAT
UPBIND
UPBINDING
UPBINDS
UPBLEW
UPBLOW
UPBLOWING
UPBLOWN
UPBLOWS
UPBOIL
UPBOILED
UPBOILING
UPBOILS
UPBORE
UPBORNE
UPBOUND
UPBOUNDEN
UPBRAID
UPBRAIDED
UPBRAIDER
UPBRAIDERS
UPBRAIDING
UPBRAIDINGS
UPBRAIDS
UPBRAST
UPBRAY
UPBRAYED
UPBRAYING
UPBRAYS
UPBREAK
UPBREAKING
UPBREAKS
UPBRING
UPBRINGING
UPBRINGINGS
UPBRINGS
UPBROKE
UPBROKEN
UPBROUGHT
UPBUILD
UPBUILDING
UPBUILDINGS
UPBUILDS
UPBUILT
UPBURNING
UPBURST
UPBURSTING
UPBURSTS
UPBY
UPBYE
UPCAST
UPCASTING
UPCASTS
UPCATCH
UPCATCHES
UPCATCHING
UPCAUGHT
UPCHEARD
UPCHEER
UPCHEERED
UPCHEERING
UPCHEERS
UPCLIMB
UPCLIMBED
UPCLIMBING
UPCLIMBS
UPCLOSE
UPCLOSED

UPCLOSES
UPCLOSING
UPCOAST
UPCOIL
UPCOILED
UPCOILING
UPCOILS
UPCOME
UPCOMES
UPCURL
UPCURLED
UPCURLING
UPCURLS
UPCURVED
UPDATE
UPDATED
UPDATES
UPDATING
UPDRAG
UPDRAGGED
UPDRAGGING
UPDRAGS
UPDRAW
UPDRAWING
UPDRAWN
UPDRAWS
UPDREW
UPFILL
UPFILLED
UPFILLING
UPFILLINGS
UPFILLS
UPFLOW
UPFLOWED
UPFLOWING
UPFLOWS
UPFLUNG
UPFOLLOW
UPFOLLOWED
UPFOLLOWING
UPFOLLOWS
UPFRONT
UPFURL
UPFURLED
UPFURLING
UPFURLS
UPGANG
UPGANGS
UPGATHER
UPGATHERED
UPGATHERING
UPGATHERS
UPGAZE
UPGAZED
UPGAZES
UPGAZING
UPGO
UPGOES
UPGOING
UPGOINGS
UPGONE
UPGRADE
UPGRADED
UPGRADES
UPGRADING
UPGREW
UPGROW
UPGROWING
UPGROWINGS
UPGROWN

UPGROWS
UPGROWTH
UPGROWTHS
UPGUSH
UPGUSHED
UPGUSHES
UPGUSHING
UPHAND
UPHANG
UPHANGING
UPHANGS
UPHAUD
UPHAUDING
UPHAUDS
UPHEAP
UPHEAPED
UPHEAPING
UPHEAPINGS
UPHEAPS
UPHEAVAL
UPHEAVALS
UPHEAVE
UPHEAVED
UPHEAVES
UPHEAVING
UPHELD
UPHILD
UPHILL
UPHILLS
UPHOARD
UPHOARDED
UPHOARDING
UPHOARDS
UPHOIST
UPHOISTED
UPHOISTING
UPHOISTS
UPHOLD
UPHOLDER
UPHOLDERS
UPHOLDING
UPHOLDINGS
UPHOLDS
UPHOLSTER
UPHOLSTERED
UPHOLSTERING
UPHOLSTERS
UPHOORD
UPHOORDED
UPHOORDING
UPHOORDS
UPHROE
UPHROES
UPHUDDEN
UPHUNG
UPHURL
UPHURLED
UPHURLING
UPHURLS
UPJET
UPJETS
UPJETTED
UPJETTING
UPKEEP
UPKEEPS
UPKNIT
UPKNITS
UPKNITTED
UPKNITTING
UPLAID

UPLAND
UPLANDER
UPLANDERS
UPLANDISH
UPLANDS
UPLAY
UPLAYING
UPLAYS
UPLEAD
UPLEADING
UPLEADS
UPLEAN
UPLEANED
UPLEANING
UPLEANS
UPLEANT
UPLEAP
UPLEAPED
UPLEAPING
UPLEAPS
UPLEAPT
UPLED
UPLIFT
UPLIFTED
UPLIFTER
UPLIFTERS
UPLIFTING
UPLIFTINGS
UPLIFTS
UPLIGHTED
UPLIGHTER
UPLIGHTERS
UPLOCK
UPLOCKED
UPLOCKING
UPLOCKS
UPLOOK
UPLOOKED
UPLOOKING
UPLOOKS
UPLYING
UPMAKE
UPMAKER
UPMAKERS
UPMAKES
UPMAKING
UPMAKINGS
UPMOST
UPON
UPPED
UPPER
UPPERCUT
UPPERCUTS
UPPERMOST
UPPERS
UPPILED
UPPING
UPPINGS
UPPISH
UPPISHLY
UPPITY
UPRAISE
UPRAISED
UPRAISES
UPRAISING
UPRAN
UPRATE
UPRATED
UPRATES
UPRATING

UPREAR
UPREARED
UPREARING
UPREARS
UPREST
UPRESTS
UPRIGHT
UPRIGHTED
UPRIGHTING
UPRIGHTLY
UPRIGHTS
UPRISAL
UPRISALS
UPRISE
UPRISEN
UPRISES
UPRISING
UPRISINGS
UPRIST
UPRISTS
UPRIVER
UPROAR
UPROARED
UPROARING
UPROARS
UPROLL
UPROLLED
UPROLLING
UPROLLS
UPROOT
UPROOTAL
UPROOTALS
UPROOTED
UPROOTER
UPROOTERS
UPROOTING
UPROOTINGS
UPROOTS
UPROSE
UPROUSE
UPROUSED
UPROUSES
UPROUSING
UPRUN
UPRUNNING
UPRUNS
UPRUSH
UPRUSHED
UPRUSHES
UPRUSHING
UPRYST
UPS
UPSEE
UPSEES
UPSEND
UPSENDING
UPSENDS
UPSENT
UPSET
UPSETS
UPSETTER
UPSETTERS
UPSETTING
UPSETTINGS
UPSEY
UPSEYS
UPSHOOT
UPSHOOTING
UPSHOOTS
UPSHOT

UPSHOTS
UPSIDE
UPSIDES
UPSIES
UPSILON
UPSILONS
UPSITTING
UPSITTINGS
UPSPAKE
UPSPEAK
UPSPEAKING
UPSPEAKS
UPSPEAR
UPSPEARED
UPSPEARING
UPSPEARS
UPSPOKE
UPSPOKEN
UPSPRANG
UPSPRING
UPSPRINGING
UPSPRINGS
UPSPRUNG
UPSTAGE
UPSTAGED
UPSTAGES
UPSTAGING
UPSTAIR
UPSTAIRS
UPSTAND
UPSTANDING
UPSTANDS
UPSTARE
UPSTARED
UPSTARES
UPSTARING
UPSTART
UPSTARTED
UPSTARTING
UPSTARTS
UPSTATE
UPSTAY
UPSTAYED
UPSTAYING
UPSTAYS
UPSTOOD
UPSTREAM
UPSTREAMED
UPSTREAMING
UPSTREAMS
UPSTROKE
UPSTROKES
UPSURGE
UPSURGED
UPSURGES
UPSURGING
UPSWARM
UPSWARMED
UPSWARMING
UPSWARMS
UPSWAY
UPSWAYED
UPSWAYING
UPSWAYS
UPSWEEP
UPSWEEPS
UPSWELL
UPSWELLED
UPSWELLING
UPSWELLS

UPSWEPT
UPSWING
UPSWINGS
UPSWOLLEN
UPSY
UPTAK
UPTAKE
UPTAKEN
UPTAKES
UPTAKING
UPTAKS
UPTEAR
UPTEARING
UPTEARS
UPTHREW
UPTHROW
UPTHROWING
UPTHROWN
UPTHROWS
UPTHRUST
UPTHRUSTING
UPTHRUSTS
UPTHUNDER
UPTHUNDERED
UPTHUNDERING
UPTHUNDERS
UPTIE
UPTIED
UPTIES
UPTIGHT
UPTIGHTER
UPTIGHTEST
UPTILT
UPTILTED
UPTILTING
UPTILTS
UPTOOK
UPTORE
UPTORN
UPTOWN
UPTOWNS
UPTRAIN
UPTRAINED
UPTRAINING
UPTRAINS
UPTREND
UPTRENDS
UPTRILLED
UPTURN
UPTURNED
UPTURNING
UPTURNINGS
UPTURNS
UPTYING
UPVALUE
UPVALUED
UPVALUES
UPVALUING
UPWAFT
UPWAFTED
UPWAFTING
UPWAFTS
UPWARD
UPWARDLY
UPWARDS
UPWELL
UPWELLED
UPWELLING
UPWELLINGS
UPWELLS

UPWENT
UPWHIRL
UPWHIRLED
UPWHIRLING
UPWHIRLS
UPWIND
UPWINDING
UPWINDS
UPWOUND
UPWROUGHT
UR
URACHUS
URACHUSES
URACIL
URACILS
URAEMIA
URAEMIAS
URAEMIC
URAEUS
URAEUSES
URALI
URALIS
URALITE
URALITES
URALITIC
URALITISE
URALITISED
URALITISES
URALITISING
URALITIZE
URALITIZED
URALITIZES
URALITIZING
URANIAN
URANIC
URANIDE
URANIDES
URANIN
URANINITE
URANINITES
URANINS
URANISCUS
URANISCUSES
URANISM
URANISMS
URANITE
URANITES
URANITIC
URANIUM
URANIUMS
URANOLOGIES
URANOLOGY
URANOUS
URANYL
URANYLS
URAO
URAOS
URARI
URARIS
URATE
URATES
URBAN
URBANE
URBANELY
URBANER
URBANEST
URBANISE
URBANISED
URBANISES
URBANISING

URBANITE
URBANITES
URBANITIES
URBANITY
URBANIZE
URBANIZED
URBANIZES
URBANIZING
URCEOLATE
URCEOLI
URCEOLUS
URCEOLUSES
URCHIN
URCHINS
URD
URDÉ
URDEE
URDÉE
URDS
URDY
URE
UREA
UREAL
UREAS
UREDIA
UREDINE
UREDINES
UREDINIA
UREDINIAL
UREDINIUM
UREDINOUS
UREDIUM
UREDO
UREDOSORI
UREIDE
UREIDES
UREMIA
UREMIAS
UREMIC
URENA
URENAS
URENT
URES
URESES
URESIS
URETER
URETERAL
URETERIC
URETERS
URETHAN
URETHANE
URETHANES
URETHANS
URETHRA
URETHRAE
URETHRAL
URETHRAS
URETIC
URGE
URGED
URGENCE
URGENCES
URGENCIES
URGENCY
URGENT
URGENTLY
URGER
URGERS
URGES
URGING

URGINGS
URIAL
URIALS
URIC
URICASE
URICASES
URIDINE
URIDINES
URINAL
URINALS
URINANT
URINARIES
URINARY
URINATE
URINATED
URINATES
URINATING
URINATION
URINATIONS
URINATIVE
URINATOR
URINATORS
URINE
URINED
URINES
URINING
URINOLOGIES
URINOLOGY
URINOUS
URITE
URITES
URMAN
URMANS
URN
URNAL
URNED
URNFIELD
URNFIELDS
URNFUL
URNFULS
URNING
URNINGS
URNS
UROCHORD
UROCHORDS
UROCHROME
UROCHROMES
URODELAN
URODELANS
URODELE
URODELES
URODELOUS
UROGRAPHIES
UROGRAPHY
UROKINASE
UROKINASES
UROLAGNIA
UROLAGNIAS
UROLITH
UROLITHS
UROLOGIC
UROLOGIES
UROLOGIST
UROLOGISTS
UROLOGY
UROMERE
UROMERES
UROPOD
UROPODS
UROPYGIAL

UROPYGIUM
UROPYGIUMS
UROSCOPIES
UROSCOPY
UROSES
UROSIS
UROSOME
UROSOMES
UROSTEGE
UROSTEGES
UROSTYLE
UROSTYLES
URSINE
URSON
URSONS
URTICA
URTICANT
URTICARIA
URTICARIAS
URTICAS
URTICATE
URTICATED
URTICATES
URTICATING
URUBU
URUBUS
URUS
URUSES
URVA
URVAS
US
USABLE
USAGE
USAGER
USAGERS
USAGES
USANCE
USANCES
USE
USED
USEFUL
USEFULLY
USELESS
USELESSLY
USER
USERS
USES
USHER
USHERED
USHERESS
USHERESSES
USHERETTE
USHERETTES
USHERING
USHERINGS
USHERS
USHERSHIP
USHERSHIPS
USING
USNEA
USNEAS
USTION
USTIONS
USUAL
USUALLY
USUALNESS
USUALNESSES
USUALS
USUCAPION
USUCAPIONS

USUCAPT
USUCAPTED
USUCAPTING
USUCAPTS
USUFRUCT
USUFRUCTED
USUFRUCTING
USUFRUCTS
USURE
USURED
USURER
USURERS
USURES
USURESS
USURESSES
USURIES
USURING
USURIOUS
USUROUS
USURP
USURPED
USURPEDLY
USURPER
USURPERS
USURPING
USURPINGS
USURPS
USURY
USWARD
USWARDS
UT
UTAS
UTASES
UTE
UTENSIL
UTENSILS
UTERI
UTERINE
UTERITIS
UTERITISES
UTEROTOMIES
UTEROTOMY
UTERUS
UTES
UTILE
UTILISE
UTILISED
UTILISER
UTILISERS
UTILISES
UTILISING
UTILITIES
UTILITY
UTILIZE
UTILIZED
UTILIZER
UTILIZERS
UTILIZES
UTILIZING
UTIS
UTISES
UTMOST
UTMOSTS
UTOPIA
UTOPIAN
UTOPIANS
UTOPIAS
UTOPIAST
UTOPIASTS
UTOPISM

UTOPISMS
UTOPIST
UTOPISTS
UTRICLE
UTRICLES
UTRICULAR
UTRICULI
UTRICULUS
UTS
UTTER

UTTERABLE
UTTERANCE
UTTERANCES
UTTERED
UTTERER
UTTERERS
UTTEREST
UTTERING
UTTERINGS
UTTERLESS

UTTERLY
UTTERMOST
UTTERMOSTS
UTTERNESS
UTTERNESSES
UTTERS
UTU
UTUS
UVA
UVAROVITE

UVAROVITES
UVAS
UVEA
UVEAL
UVEAS
UVEITIS
UVEITISES
UVULA
UVULAE
UVULAR

UVULARLY
UVULAS
UVULITIS
UVULITISES
UXORIAL
UXORICIDE
UXORICIDES
UXORIOUS

# V

VAC
VACANCE
VACANCES
VACANCIES
VACANCY
VACANT
VACANTLY
VACATE
VACATED
VACATES
VACATING
VACATION
VACATIONED
VACATIONING
VACATIONS
VACATUR
VACATURS
VACCINAL
VACCINATE
VACCINATED
VACCINATES
VACCINATING
VACCINE
VACCINES
VACCINIA
VACCINIAL
VACCINIAS
VACCINIUM
VACCINIUMS
VACHERIN
VACHERINS
VACILLANT
VACILLATE
VACILLATED
VACILLATES
VACILLATING
VACKED
VACKING
VACS
VACUA
VACUATE
VACUATED
VACUATES
VACUATING
VACUATION
VACUATIONS
VACUIST
VACUISTS
VACUITIES
VACUITY
VACUOLAR
VACUOLATE
VACUOLE
VACUOLES
VACUOUS
VACUOUSLY
VACUUM
VACUUMED
VACUUMING
VACUUMS
VADE
VADED
VADES

VADING
VAE
VAES
VAGABOND
VAGABONDED
VAGABONDING
VAGABONDS
VAGAL
VAGARIES
VAGARIOUS
VAGARISH
VAGARY
VAGI
VAGILE
VAGILITIES
VAGILITY
VAGINA
VAGINAE
VAGINAL
VAGINALLY
VAGINANT
VAGINAS
VAGINATE
VAGINATED
VAGINITIS
VAGINITISES
VAGINULA
VAGINULAE
VAGINULE
VAGINULES
VAGITUS
VAGITUSES
VAGRANCIES
VAGRANCY
VAGRANT
VAGRANTS
VAGROM
VAGUE
VAGUED
VAGUELY
VAGUENESS
VAGUENESSES
VAGUER
VAGUES
VAGUEST
VAGUING
VAGUS
VAHINE
VAHINES
VAIL
VAILED
VAILING
VAILS
VAIN
VAINER
VAINESSE
VAINESSES
VAINEST
VAINGLORIED
VAINGLORIES
VAINGLORY
VAINGLORYING
VAINLY

VAINNESS
VAINNESSES
VAIR
VAIRÉ
VAIRIER
VAIRIEST
VAIRS
VAIRY
VAIVODE
VAIVODES
VAKASS
VAKASSES
VAKEEL
VAKEELS
VAKIL
VAKILS
VALANCE
VALANCED
VALANCES
VALE
VALENCE
VALENCES
VALENCIES
VALENCY
VALENTINE
VALENTINES
VALERIAN
VALERIANS
VALES
VALET
VALETA
VALETAS
VALETE
VALETED
VALETES
VALETING
VALETINGS
VALETS
VALGOUS
VALGUS
VALGUSES
VALI
VALIANCE
VALIANCES
VALIANCIES
VALIANCY
VALIANT
VALIANTLY
VALIANTS
VALID
VALIDATE
VALIDATED
VALIDATES
VALIDATING
VALIDER
VALIDEST
VALIDITIES
VALIDITY
VALIDLY
VALIDNESS
VALIDNESSES
VALINE
VALINES

VALIS
VALISE
VALISES
VALLAR
VALLARY
VALLECULA
VALLECULAE
VALLEY
VALLEYS
VALLONIA
VALLONIAS
VALLUM
VALLUMS
VALONEA
VALONEAS
VALONIA
VALONIAS
VALOR
VALORISE
VALORISED
VALORISES
VALORISING
VALORIZE
VALORIZED
VALORIZES
VALORIZING
VALOROUS
VALORS
VALOUR
VALOURS
VALSE
VALSED
VALSES
VALSING
VALUABLE
VALUABLES
VALUABLY
VALUATE
VALUATED
VALUATES
VALUATING
VALUATION
VALUATIONS
VALUATOR
VALUATORS
VALUE
VALUED
VALUELESS
VALUER
VALUERS
VALUES
VALUING
VALUTA
VALUTAS
VALVAL
VALVAR
VALVASSOR
VALVASSORS
VALVATE
VALVE
VALVED
VALVELESS
VALVELET

VALVELETS
VALVES
VALVING
VALVULA
VALVULAE
VALVULAR
VALVULE
VALVULES
VAMBRACE
VAMBRACED
VAMBRACES
VAMOOSE
VAMOOSED
VAMOOSES
VAMOOSING
VAMOSE
VAMOSED
VAMOSES
VAMOSING
VAMP
VAMPED
VAMPER
VAMPERS
VAMPING
VAMPINGS
VAMPIRE
VAMPIRED
VAMPIRES
VAMPIRIC
VAMPIRING
VAMPIRISE
VAMPIRISED
VAMPIRISES
VAMPIRISING
VAMPIRISM
VAMPIRISMS
VAMPIRIZE
VAMPIRIZED
VAMPIRIZES
VAMPIRIZING
VAMPISH
VAMPLATE
VAMPLATES
VAMPS
VAN
VANADATE
VANADATES
VANADIC
VANADIUM
VANADIUMS
VANADOUS
VANDAL
VANDALISE
VANDALISED
VANDALISES
VANDALISING
VANDALISM
VANDALISMS
VANDALIZE
VANDALIZED
VANDALIZES
VANDALIZING
VANDALS

VANDYKE
VANDYKED
VANDYKES
VANDYKING
VANE
VANED
VANELESS
VANES
VANESSA
VANESSAS
VANG
VANGS
VANGUARD
VANGUARDS
VANILLA
VANILLAS
VANILLIN
VANILLINS
VANISH
VANISHED
VANISHER
VANISHERS
VANISHES
VANISHING
VANISHINGS
VANITAS
VANITASES
VANITIES
VANITORIES
VANITORY
VANITY
VANNED
VANNER
VANNERS
VANNING
VANNINGS
VANQUISH
VANQUISHED
VANQUISHES
VANQUISHING
VANS
VANT
VANTAGE
VANTAGED
VANTAGES
VANTAGING
VANTBRACE
VANTBRACES
VANTS
VANWARD
VAPID
VAPIDER
VAPIDEST
VAPIDITIES
VAPIDITY
VAPIDLY
VAPIDNESS
VAPIDNESSES
VAPOR
VAPORABLE
VAPORED
VAPORETTI
VAPORETTO
VAPORETTOS
VAPORIFIC
VAPORING
VAPORISE
VAPORISED
VAPORISER
VAPORISERS

VAPORISES
VAPORISING
VAPORIZE
VAPORIZED
VAPORIZER
VAPORIZERS
VAPORIZES
VAPORIZING
VAPOROUS
VAPORS
VAPOUR
VAPOURED
VAPOURER
VAPOURERS
VAPOURING
VAPOURINGS
VAPOURISH
VAPOURS
VAPOURY
VAPULATE
VAPULATED
VAPULATES
VAPULATING
VAQUERO
VAQUEROS
VARA
VARACTOR
VARACTORS
VARAN
VARANS
VARAS
VARDIES
VARDY
VARE
VAREC
VARECH
VARECHS
VARECS
VARES
VAREUSE
VAREUSES
VARGUEÑO
VARGUEÑOS
VARIABLE
VARIABLES
VARIABLY
VARIANCE
VARIANCES
VARIANT
VARIANTS
VARIATE
VARIATED
VARIATES
VARIATING
VARIATION
VARIATIONS
VARIATIVE
VARICELLA
VARICELLAS
VARICES
VARICOSE
VARIED
VARIEDLY
VARIEGATE
VARIEGATED
VARIEGATES
VARIEGATING
VARIER
VARIERS
VARIES

VARIETAL
VARIETIES
VARIETY
VARIFORM
VARIOLA
VARIOLAR
VARIOLAS
VARIOLATE
VARIOLATED
VARIOLATES
VARIOLATING
VARIOLE
VARIOLES
VARIOLITE
VARIOLITES
VARIOLOID
VARIOLOUS
VARIORUM
VARIORUMS
VARIOUS
VARIOUSLY
VARISCITE
VARISCITES
VARISTOR
VARISTORS
VARIX
VARLET
VARLETESS
VARLETESSES
VARLETRIES
VARLETRY
VARLETS
VARLETTO
VARLETTOS
VARMENT
VARMENTS
VARMINT
VARMINTS
VARNA
VARNAS
VARNISH
VARNISHED
VARNISHER
VARNISHERS
VARNISHES
VARNISHING
VARNISHINGS
VARROA
VARROAS
VARSAL
VARSITIES
VARSITY
VARTABED
VARTABEDS
VARUS
VARUSES
VARVE
VARVED
VARVEL
VARVELLED
VARVELS
VARVES
VARY
VARYING
VARYINGS
VAS
VASA
VASAL
VASCULA
VASCULAR

VASCULUM
VASCULUMS
VASE
VASECTOMIES
VASECTOMY
VASES
VASIFORM
VASOMOTOR
VASSAIL
VASSAILS
VASSAL
VASSALAGE
VASSALAGES
VASSALESS
VASSALESSES
VASSALLED
VASSALLING
VASSALRIES
VASSALRY
VASSALS
VAST
VASTER
VASTEST
VASTIDITIES
VASTIDITY
VASTIER
VASTIEST
VASTITIES
VASTITUDE
VASTITUDES
VASTITY
VASTLY
VASTNESS
VASTNESSES
VASTS
VASTY
VAT
VATFUL
VATFULS
VATIC
VATICIDE
VATICIDES
VATICINAL
VATMAN
VATMEN
VATS
VATTED
VATTING
VAU
VAUDOO
VAUDOOS
VAUDOUX
VAULT
VAULTAGE
VAULTAGES
VAULTED
VAULTER
VAULTERS
VAULTING
VAULTINGS
VAULTS
VAULTY
VAUNCE
VAUNCED
VAUNCES
VAUNCING
VAUNT
VAUNTAGE
VAUNTAGES
VAUNTED

VAUNTER
VAUNTERIES
VAUNTERY
VAUNTFUL
VAUNTING
VAUNTINGS
VAUNTS
VAURIEN
VAURIENS
VAUS
VAUT
VAUTE
VAUTED
VAUTES
VAUTING
VAUTS
VAVASORIES
VAVASORY
VAVASOUR
VAVASOURS
VAWARD
VAWARDS
VAWTE
VAWTED
VAWTES
VAWTING
VEAL
VEALE
VEALES
VEALIER
VEALIEST
VEALS
VEALY
VECTOR
VECTORED
VECTORIAL
VECTORING
VECTORINGS
VECTORS
VEDALIA
VEDALIAS
VEDETTE
VEDETTES
VEDUTA
VEDUTE
VEDUTISTA
VEDUTISTI
VEE
VEENA
VEENAS
VEER
VEERED
VEERIES
VEERING
VEERINGLY
VEERINGS
VEERS
VEERY
VEES
VEG
VEGA
VEGAN
VEGANIC
VEGANISM
VEGANISMS
VEGANS
VEGAS
VEGETABLE
VEGETABLES

| | | | | |
|---|---|---|---|---|
| VEGETABLY | VELATE | VENATOR | VENGEMENTS | VENTRINGS |
| VEGETAL | VELATED | VENATORS | VENGER | VENTROUS |
| VEGETALS | VELATURA | VEND | VENGERS | VENTS |
| VEGETANT | VELATURAS | VENDACE | VENGES | VENTURE |
| VEGETATE | VELD | VENDACES | VENGING | VENTURED |
| VEGETATED | VELDS | VENDAGE | VENIAL | VENTURER |
| VEGETATES | VELDSKOEN | VENDAGES | VENIALITIES | VENTURERS |
| VEGETATING | VELDSKOENS | VENDANGE | VENIALITY | VENTURES |
| VEGETATINGS | VELDT | VENDANGES | VENIALLY | VENTURI |
| VEGETE | VELDTS | VENDED | VENIN | VENTURING |
| VEGETIVE | VELE | VENDEE | VENINS | VENTURINGS |
| VEGETIVES | VELES | VENDEES | VENIRE | VENTURIS |
| VEGGIE | VELETA | VENDER | VENIREMAN | VENTUROUS |
| VEGGIES | VELETAS | VENDERS | VENIREMEN | VENUE |
| VEGIE | VELIGER | VENDETTA | VENIRES | VENUES |
| VEGIES | VELIGERS | VENDETTAS | VENISON | VENULE |
| VEHEMENCE | VELL | VENDEUSE | VENISONS | VENULES |
| VEHEMENCES | VELLEITIES | VENDEUSES | VENITE | VENUS |
| VEHEMENCIES | VELLEITY | VENDIBLE | VENITES | VENUSES |
| VEHEMENCY | VELLENAGE | VENDIBLES | VENNEL | VENVILLE |
| VEHEMENT | VELLENAGES | VENDIBLY | VENNELS | VENVILLES |
| VEHICLE | VELLET | VENDING | VENOM | VERACIOUS |
| VEHICLES | VELLETS | VENDIS | VENOMED | VERACITIES |
| VEHICULAR | VELLICATE | VENDISES | VENOMING | VERACITY |
| VEHM | VELLICATED | VENDISS | VENOMOUS | VERANDA |
| VEHME | VELLICATES | VENDISSES | VENOMS | VERANDAH |
| VEHMIC | VELLICATING | VENDITION | VENOSE | VERANDAHS |
| VEHMIQUE | VELLON | VENDITIONS | VENOSITIES | VERANDAS |
| VEIL | VELLONS | VENDOR | VENOSITY | VERATRIN |
| VEILED | VELLS | VENDORS | VENOUS | VERATRINE |
| VEILIER | VELLUM | VENDS | VENT | VERATRINES |
| VEILIEST | VELLUMS | VENDUE | VENTAGE | VERATRINS |
| VEILING | VELOCE | VENDUES | VENTAGES | VERATRUM |
| VEILINGS | VELOCITIES | VENEER | VENTAIL | VERATRUMS |
| VEILLESS | VELOCITY | VENEERED | VENTAILE | VERB |
| VEILLEUSE | VELODROME | VENEERER | VENTAILES | VERBAL |
| VEILLEUSES | VELODROMES | VENEERERS | VENTAILS | VERBALISE |
| VEILS | VELOUR | VENEERING | VENTANA | VERBALISED |
| VEILY | VELOURS | VENEERINGS | VENTANAS | VERBALISES |
| VEIN | VELOUTÉ | VENEERS | VENTAYLE | VERBALISING |
| VEINED | VELOUTÉS | VENEFIC | VENTAYLES | VERBALISM |
| VEINIER | VELOUTINE | VENEFICAL | VENTED | VERBALISMS |
| VEINIEST | VELOUTINES | VENERABLE | VENTER | VERBALIST |
| VEINING | VELSKOEN | VENERABLY | VENTERS | VERBALISTS |
| VEININGS | VELSKOENS | VENERATE | VENTIDUCT | VERBALITIES |
| VEINLET | VELUM | VENERATED | VENTIDUCTS | VERBALITY |
| VEINLETS | VELURE | VENERATES | VENTIFACT | VERBALIZE |
| VEINOUS | VELURED | VENERATING | VENTIFACTS | VERBALIZED |
| VEINS | VELURES | VENERATOR | VENTIGE | VERBALIZES |
| VEINSTONE | VELURING | VENERATORS | VENTIGES | VERBALIZING |
| VEINSTONES | VELVERET | VENEREAL | VENTIL | VERBALLED |
| VEINSTUFF | VELVERETS | VENEREAN | VENTILATE | VERBALLING |
| VEINSTUFFS | VELVET | VENEREANS | VENTILATED | VERBALLY |
| VEINY | VELVETED | VENEREOUS | VENTILATES | VERBALS |
| VELA | VELVETEEN | VENERER | VENTILATING | VERBARIAN |
| VELAMEN | VELVETEENS | VENERERS | VENTILS | VERBARIANS |
| VELAMINA | VELVETING | VENERIES | VENTING | VERBATIM |
| VELAR | VELVETINGS | VENERY | VENTINGS | VERBENA |
| VELARIA | VELVETS | VENEWE | VENTOSE | VERBENAS |
| VELARIC | VELVETY | VENEWES | VENTOSITIES | VERBERATE |
| VELARISE | VENA | VENEY | VENTOSITY | VERBERATED |
| VELARISED | VENAE | VENEYS | VENTRAL | VERBERATES |
| VELARISES | VENAL | VENGE | VENTRALLY | VERBERATING |
| VELARISING | VENALITIES | VENGEABLE | VENTRALS | VERBIAGE |
| VELARIUM | VENALITY | VENGEABLY | VENTRE | VERBIAGES |
| VELARIZE | VENALLY | VENGEANCE | VENTRED | VERBICIDE |
| VELARIZED | VENATIC | VENGEANCES | VENTRES | VERBICIDES |
| VELARIZES | VENATICAL | VENGED | VENTRICLE | VERBLESS |
| VELARIZING | VENATION | VENGEFUL | VENTRICLES | VERBOSE |
| VELARS | VENATIONS | VENGEMENT | VENTRING | VERBOSELY |

VERBOSER
VERBOSEST
VERBOSITIES
VERBOSITY
VERBS
VERDANCIES
VERDANCY
VERDANT
VERDANTLY
VERDELHO
VERDELHOS
VERDERER
VERDERERS
VERDEROR
VERDERORS
VERDET
VERDETS
VERDICT
VERDICTS
VERDIGRIS
VERDIGRISED
VERDIGRISES
VERDIGRISING
VERDIT
VERDITER
VERDITERS
VERDITS
VERDOY
VERDURE
VERDURED
VERDURES
VERDUROUS
VERECUND
VERGE
VERGED
VERGENCIES
VERGENCY
VERGER
VERGERS
VERGES
VERGING
VERGLAS
VERGLASES
VERIDICAL
VERIER
VERIEST
VERIFIED
VERIFIER
VERIFIERS
VERIFIES
VERIFY
VERIFYING
VERILY
VERISM
VERISMO
VERISMOS
VERISMS
VERIST
VERISTIC
VERISTS
VERITABLE
VERITABLY
VERITIES
VERITY
VERJUICE
VERJUICED
VERJUICES
VERKRAMP
VERLIG
VERLIGTE

VERLIGTES
VERMEIL
VERMEILED
VERMEILING
VERMEILLE
VERMEILLED
VERMEILLES
VERMEILLING
VERMEILS
VERMELL
VERMELLS
VERMES
VERMIAN
VERMICIDE
VERMICIDES
VERMICULE
VERMICULES
VERMIFORM
VERMIFUGE
VERMIFUGES
VERMIL
VERMILIES
VERMILION
VERMILIONED
VERMILIONING
VERMILIONS
VERMILLED
VERMILLING
VERMILS
VERMILY
VERMIN
VERMINATE
VERMINATED
VERMINATES
VERMINATING
VERMINED
VERMINOUS
VERMINS
VERMINY
VERMIS
VERMISES
VERMOUTH
VERMOUTHS
VERNAL
VERNALISE
VERNALISED
VERNALISES
VERNALISING
VERNALITIES
VERNALITY
VERNALIZE
VERNALIZED
VERNALIZES
VERNALIZING
VERNALLY
VERNANT
VERNATION
VERNATIONS
VERNICLE
VERNICLES
VERNIER
VERNIERS
VERONAL
VERONALS
VERONICA
VERONICAS
VÉRONIQUE
VERQUERE
VERQUERES
VERQUIRE

VERQUIRES
VERREL
VERRELS
VERREY
VERRUCA
VERRUCAE
VERRUCAS
VERRUCOSE
VERRUCOUS
VERRUGA
VERRUGAS
VERRY
VERS
VERSAL
VERSALS
VERSANT
VERSANTS
VERSATILE
VERSE
VERSED
VERSELET
VERSELETS
VERSER
VERSERS
VERSES
VERSET
VERSETS
VERSICLE
VERSICLES
VERSIFIED
VERSIFIER
VERSIFIERS
VERSIFIES
VERSIFORM
VERSIFY
VERSIFYING
VERSIN
VERSINE
VERSINES
VERSING
VERSINGS
VERSINS
VERSION
VERSIONAL
VERSIONER
VERSIONERS
VERSIONS
VERSO
VERSOS
VERST
VERSTS
VERSUS
VERSUTE
VERT
VERTEBRA
VERTEBRAE
VERTEBRAL
VERTED
VERTEX
VERTICAL
VERTICALS
VERTICES
VERTICIL
VERTICILS
VERTICITIES
VERTICITY
VERTIGINES
VERTIGO
VERTIGOES
VERTIGOS

VERTING
VERTIPORT
VERTIPORTS
VERTS
VERTU
VERTUE
VERTUES
VERTUOUS
VERTUS
VERVAIN
VERVAINS
VERVE
VERVEL
VERVELLED
VERVELS
VERVEN
VERVENS
VERVES
VERVET
VERVETS
VERY
VESICA
VESICAE
VESICAL
VESICANT
VESICANTS
VESICATE
VESICATED
VESICATES
VESICATING
VESICLE
VESICLES
VESICULA
VESICULAE
VESICULAR
VESPA
VESPAS
VESPER
VESPERAL
VESPERS
VESPIARIES
VESPIARY
VESPINE
VESPOID
VESSAIL
VESSAILS
VESSEL
VESSELS
VEST
VESTA
VESTAL
VESTALS
VESTAS
VESTED
VESTIARIES
VESTIARY
VESTIBULE
VESTIBULED
VESTIBULES
VESTIBULING
VESTIGE
VESTIGES
VESTIGIA
VESTIGIAL
VESTIGIUM
VESTIMENT
VESTIMENTS
VESTING
VESTINGS
VESTITURE

VESTITURES
VESTMENT
VESTMENTS
VESTRAL
VESTRIES
VESTRY
VESTRYMAN
VESTRYMEN
VESTS
VESTURAL
VESTURE
VESTURED
VESTURER
VESTURERS
VESTURES
VESTURING
VESUVIAN
VESUVIANS
VET
VETCH
VETCHES
VETCHIER
VETCHIEST
VETCHLING
VETCHLINGS
VETCHY
VETERAN
VETERANS
VETIVER
VETIVERS
VETKOEK
VETKOEKS
VETO
VETOED
VETOES
VETOING
VETS
VETTED
VETTING
VETTURA
VETTURAS
VETTURINI
VETTURINO
VEX
VEXATION
VEXATIONS
VEXATIOUS
VEXATORY
VEXED
VEXEDLY
VEXEDNESS
VEXEDNESSES
VEXER
VEXERS
VEXES
VEXILLA
VEXILLARIES
VEXILLARY
VEXILLUM
VEXING
VEXINGLY
VEXINGS
VEZIR
VEZIRS
VIA
VIABILITIES
VIABILITY
VIABLE
VIADUCT
VIADUCTS

VIAE
VIAL
VIALFUL
VIALFULS
VIALLED
VIALS
VIAMETER
VIAMETERS
VIAND
VIANDS
VIAS
VIATICA
VIATICALS
VIATICUM
VIATICUMS
VIATOR
VIATORIAL
VIATORS
VIBE
VIBES
VIBEX
VIBICES
VIBIST
VIBISTS
VIBRACULA
VIBRAHARP
VIBRAHARPS
VIBRANCIES
VIBRANCY
VIBRANT
VIBRATE
VIBRATED
VIBRATES
VIBRATILE
VIBRATING
VIBRATION
VIBRATIONS
VIBRATIVE
VIBRATO
VIBRATOR
VIBRATORS
VIBRATORY
VIBRATOS
VIBRIO
VIBRIOS
VIBRIOSES
VIBRIOSIS
VIBRISSA
VIBRISSAE
VIBRONIC
VIBS
VIBURNUM
VIBURNUMS
VICAR
VICARAGE
VICARAGES
VICARATE
VICARATES
VICARESS
VICARESSES
VICARIAL
VICARIATE
VICARIATES
VICARIES
VICARIOUS
VICARS
VICARSHIP
VICARSHIPS
VICARY
VICE

VICED
VICENARY
VICENNIAL
VICEREINE
VICEREINES
VICEROY
VICEROYS
VICES
VICESIMAL
VICIATE
VICIATED
VICIATES
VICIATING
VICINAGE
VICINAGES
VICINAL
VICING
VICINITIES
VICINITY
VICIOSITIES
VICIOSITY
VICIOUS
VICIOUSLY
VICOMTE
VICOMTES
VICTIM
VICTIMISE
VICTIMISED
VICTIMISES
VICTIMISING
VICTIMIZE
VICTIMIZED
VICTIMIZES
VICTIMIZING
VICTIMS
VICTOR
VICTORESS
VICTORESSES
VICTORIA
VICTORIAS
VICTORIES
VICTORINE
VICTORINES
VICTORS
VICTORY
VICTRESS
VICTRESSES
VICTRIX
VICTRIXES
VICTUAL
VICTUALLED
VICTUALLING
VICTUALS
VICUÑA
VICUÑAS
VIDAME
VIDAMES
VIDE
VIDELICET
VIDENDA
VIDENDUM
VIDEO
VIDEODISC
VIDEODISCS
VIDEOED
VIDEOFIT
VIDEOFITS
VIDEOGRAM
VIDEOGRAMS
VIDEOING

VIDEOS
VIDEOTAPE
VIDEOTAPES
VIDEOTEX
VIDEOTEXES
VIDEOTEXT
VIDEOTEXTS
VIDETTE
VIDETTES
VIDIMUS
VIDIMUSES
VIDUAGE
VIDUAGES
VIDUAL
VIDUITIES
VIDUITY
VIDUOUS
VIE
VIED
VIELLE
VIELLES
VIER
VIERS
VIES
VIEW
VIEWABLE
VIEWDATA
VIEWDATAS
VIEWED
VIEWER
VIEWERS
VIEWIER
VIEWIEST
VIEWINESS
VIEWINESSES
VIEWING
VIEWINGS
VIEWLESS
VIEWLY
VIEWPHONE
VIEWPHONES
VIEWPOINT
VIEWPOINTS
VIEWS
VIEWY
VIFDA
VIFDAS
VIGESIMAL
VIGIA
VIGIAS
VIGIL
VIGILANCE
VIGILANCES
VIGILANT
VIGILANTE
VIGILANTES
VIGILS
VIGNERON
VIGNERONS
VIGNETTE
VIGNETTED
VIGNETTER
VIGNETTERS
VIGNETTES
VIGNETTING
VIGOR
VIGORISH
VIGORISHES
VIGORO
VIGOROS

VIGOROUS
VIGORS
VIGOUR
VIGOURS
VIHARA
VIHARAS
VIHUELA
VIHUELAS
VIKING
VIKINGISM
VIKINGISMS
VIKINGS
VILAYET
VILAYETS
VILD
VILDE
VILDLY
VILDNESS
VILDNESSES
VILE
VILELY
VILENESS
VILENESSES
VILER
VILEST
VILIACO
VILIACOES
VILIACOS
VILIAGO
VILIAGOES
VILIAGOS
VILIFIED
VILIFIER
VILIFIERS
VILIFIES
VILIFY
VILIFYING
VILIPEND
VILIPENDED
VILIPENDING
VILIPENDS
VILL
VILLA
VILLADOM
VILLADOMS
VILLAGE
VILLAGER
VILLAGERIES
VILLAGERS
VILLAGERY
VILLAGES
VILLAGIO
VILLAGIOES
VILLAGIOS
VILLAGREE
VILLAGREES
VILLAIN
VILLAINIES
VILLAINS
VILLAINY
VILLAN
VILLANAGE
VILLANAGES
VILLANIES
VILLANOUS
VILLANS
VILLANY
VILLAR
VILLAS
VILLATIC

VILLEIN
VILLEINS
VILLENAGE
VILLENAGES
VILLI
VILLIAGO
VILLIAGOES
VILLIAGOS
VILLIFORM
VILLOSE
VILLOSITIES
VILLOSITY
VILLOUS
VILLS
VILLUS
VIM
VIMANA
VIMANAS
VIMINEOUS
VIMS
VIN
VINA
VINACEOUS
VINAL
VINAS
VINASSE
VINASSES
VINCA
VINCAS
VINCIBLE
VINCULA
VINCULUM
VINDALOO
VINDALOOS
VINDEMIAL
VINDICATE
VINDICATED
VINDICATES
VINDICATING
VINE
VINED
VINEGAR
VINEGARED
VINEGARING
VINEGARS
VINEGARY
VINER
VINERIES
VINERS
VINERY
VINES
VINEW
VINEWED
VINEWING
VINEWS
VINEYARD
VINEYARDS
VINIER
VINIEST
VINING
VINO
VINOLENT
VINOLOGIES
VINOLOGY
VINOS
VINOSITIES
VINOSITY
VINOUS
VINS
VINT

VINTAGE
VINTAGED
VINTAGER
VINTAGERS
VINTAGES
VINTAGING
VINTAGINGS
VINTED
VINTING
VINTNER
VINTNERS
VINTRIES
VINTRY
VINTS
VINY
VINYL
VINYLS
VIOL
VIOLA
VIOLABLE
VIOLABLY
VIOLAS
VIOLATE
VIOLATED
VIOLATES
VIOLATING
VIOLATION
VIOLATIONS
VIOLATIVE
VIOLATOR
VIOLATORS
VIOLD
VIOLENCE
VIOLENCES
VIOLENT
VIOLENTED
VIOLENTING
VIOLENTLY
VIOLENTS
VIOLER
VIOLERS
VIOLET
VIOLETS
VIOLIN
VIOLINIST
VIOLINISTS
VIOLINS
VIOLIST
VIOLISTS
VIOLONE
VIOLONES
VIOLS
VIPER
VIPERINE
VIPERISH
VIPEROUS
VIPERS
VIRAEMIA
VIRAEMIAS
VIRAEMIC
VIRAGO
VIRAGOES
VIRAGOISH
VIRAGOS
VIRAL
VIRANDA
VIRANDAS
VIRANDO
VIRANDOS
VIRELAY

VIRELAYS
VIREMENT
VIREMENTS
VIRENT
VIREO
VIREOS
VIRES
VIRESCENT
VIRETOT
VIRETOTS
VIRGA
VIRGAS
VIRGATE
VIRGATES
VIRGE
VIRGER
VIRGERS
VIRGES
VIRGIN
VIRGINAL
VIRGINALLED
VIRGINALLING
VIRGINALS
VIRGINED
VIRGINING
VIRGINITIES
VIRGINITY
VIRGINIUM
VIRGINIUMS
VIRGINLY
VIRGINS
VIRGULATE
VIRGULE
VIRGULES
VIRICIDAL
VIRICIDE
VIRICIDES
VIRID
VIRIDIAN
VIRIDIANS
VIRIDITE
VIRIDITES
VIRIDITIES
VIRIDITY
VIRILE
VIRILISED
VIRILISM
VIRILISMS
VIRILITIES
VIRILITY
VIRILIZED
VIRION
VIRIONS
VIRL
VIRLS
VIROGENE
VIROGENES
VIROID
VIROIDS
VIROLOGIES
VIROLOGY
VIROSE
VIROSES
VIROSIS
VIROUS
VIRTU
VIRTUAL
VIRTUALLY
VIRTUE
VIRTUES

VIRTUOSA
VIRTUOSE
VIRTUOSI
VIRTUOSIC
VIRTUOSO
VIRTUOSOS
VIRTUOUS
VIRTUS
VIRUCIDAL
VIRUCIDE
VIRUCIDES
VIRULENCE
VIRULENCES
VIRULENCIES
VIRULENCY
VIRULENT
VIRUS
VIRUSES
VIS
VISA
VISAED
VISAGE
VISAGED
VISAGES
VISAGIST
VISAGISTE
VISAGISTES
VISAGISTS
VISAING
VISAS
VISCACHA
VISCACHAS
VISCERA
VISCERAL
VISCERATE
VISCERATED
VISCERATES
VISCERATING
VISCID
VISCIDITIES
VISCIDITY
VISCIN
VISCINS
VISCOSE
VISCOSES
VISCOSITIES
VISCOSITY
VISCOUNT
VISCOUNTIES
VISCOUNTS
VISCOUNTY
VISCOUS
VISCUM
VISCUMS
VISCUS
VISE
VISÉ
VISED
VISÉED
VISÉING
VISES
VISÉS
VISIBLE
VISIBLES
VISIBLY
VISIE
VISIED
VISIEING
VISIER
VISIERS

VISIES
VISILE
VISILES
VISING
VISION
VISIONAL
VISIONARIES
VISIONARY
VISIONED
VISIONER
VISIONERS
VISIONING
VISIONINGS
VISIONIST
VISIONISTS
VISIONS
VISIT
VISITABLE
VISITANT
VISITANTS
VISITATOR
VISITATORS
VISITE
VISITED
VISITEE
VISITEES
VISITER
VISITERS
VISITES
VISITING
VISITINGS
VISITOR
VISITORS
VISITRESS
VISITRESSES
VISITS
VISIVE
VISNE
VISNES
VISNOMIE
VISNOMIES
VISNOMY
VISON
VISONS
VISOR
VISORED
VISORING
VISORS
VISTA
VISTAED
VISTAING
VISTAL
VISTALESS
VISTAS
VISTO
VISTOS
VISUAL
VISUALISE
VISUALISED
VISUALISES
VISUALISING
VISUALIST
VISUALISTS
VISUALITIES
VISUALITY
VISUALIZE
VISUALIZED
VISUALIZES
VISUALIZING
VISUALLY

VISUALS
VITA
VITAE
VITAL
VITALISE
VITALISED
VITALISER
VITALISERS
VITALISES
VITALISING
VITALISM
VITALISMS
VITALIST
VITALISTS
VITALITIES
VITALITY
VITALIZE
VITALIZED
VITALIZER
VITALIZERS
VITALIZES
VITALIZING
VITALLY
VITALS
VITAMIN
VITAMINE
VITAMINES
VITAMINS
VITASCOPE
VITASCOPES
VITATIVE
VITE
VITELLARY
VITELLI
VITELLIN
VITELLINE
VITELLINES
VITELLINS
VITELLUS
VITEX
VITEXES
VITIABLE
VITIATE
VITIATED
VITIATES
VITIATING
VITIATION
VITIATIONS
VITIATOR
VITIATORS
VITICETA
VITICETUM
VITICETUMS
VITICIDE
VITICIDES
VITILIGO
VITILIGOS
VITIOSITIES
VITIOSITY
VITRAGE
VITRAGES
VITRAIL
VITRAIN
VITRAINS
VITRAUX
VITREOUS
VITREUM
VITREUMS
VITRIC
VITRICS

VITRIFIED
VITRIFIES
VITRIFORM
VITRIFY
VITRIFYING
VITRINE
VITRINES
VITRIOL
VITRIOLIC
VITRIOLS
VITTA
VITTAE
VITTATE
VITTLE
VITTLES
VITULAR
VITULINE
VIVA
VIVACE
VIVACIOUS
VIVACITIES
VIVACITY
VIVAED
VIVAING
VIVAMENTE
VIVANDIER
VIVANDIERS
VIVARIA
VIVARIES
VIVARIUM
VIVARIUMS
VIVARY
VIVAS
VIVAT
VIVDA
VIVDAS
VIVE
VIVELY
VIVENCIES
VIVENCY
VIVER
VIVERRINE
VIVERS
VIVES
VIVIANITE
VIVIANITES
VIVID
VIVIDER
VIVIDEST
VIVIDITIES
VIVIDITY
VIVIDLY
VIVIDNESS
VIVIDNESSES
VIVIFIC
VIVIFIED
VIVIFIER
VIVIFIERS
VIVIFIES
VIVIFY
VIVIFYING
VIVIPARIES
VIVIPARY
VIVISECT
VIVISECTED
VIVISECTING
VIVISECTS
VIVO
VIVRES
VIXEN

VIXENISH
VIXENLY
VIXENS
VIZAMENT
VIZAMENTS
VIZARD
VIZARDED
VIZARDING
VIZARDS
VIZCACHA
VIZCACHAS
VIZIER
VIZIERATE
VIZIERATES
VIZIERIAL
VIZIERS
VIZIES
VIZIR
VIZIRATE
VIZIRATES
VIZIRIAL
VIZIRS
VIZIRSHIP
VIZIRSHIPS
VIZOR
VIZORED
VIZORING
VIZORS
VIZSLA
VIZSLAS
VIZY
VIZZIE
VIZZIED
VIZZIEING
VIZZIES
VLEI
VLEIS
VLIES
VLY
VOAR
VOARS
VOCABLE
VOCABLES
VOCABULAR
VOCAL
VOCALIC
VOCALION
VOCALIONS
VOCALISE
VOCALISED
VOCALISER
VOCALISERS
VOCALISES
VOCALISING
VOCALISM
VOCALISMS
VOCALIST
VOCALISTS
VOCALITIES
VOCALITY
VOCALIZE
VOCALIZED
VOCALIZER
VOCALIZERS
VOCALIZES
VOCALIZING
VOCALLY
VOCALNESS
VOCALNESSES
VOCALS

VOCATION
VOCATIONS
VOCATIVE
VOCATIVES
VOCES
VOCODER
VOCODERS
VOCULAR
VOCULE
VOCULES
VODKA
VODKAS
VOE
VOES
VOGIE
VOGIER
VOGIEST
VOGUE
VOGUED
VOGUES
VOGUEY
VOGUIER
VOGUIEST
VOGUING
VOGUISH
VOICE
VOICED
VOICEFUL
VOICELESS
VOICER
VOICERS
VOICES
VOICING
VOICINGS
VOID
VOIDABLE
VOIDANCE
VOIDANCES
VOIDED
VOIDEE
VOIDEES
VOIDER
VOIDERS
VOIDING
VOIDINGS
VOIDNESS
VOIDNESSES
VOIDS
VOILÀ
VOILE
VOILES
VOISINAGE
VOISINAGES
VOITURE
VOITURES
VOITURIER
VOITURIERS
VOIVODE
VOIVODES
VOL
VOLA
VOLABLE
VOLAE
VOLAGE
VOLAGEOUS
VOLANT
VOLANTE
VOLANTES
VOLAR
VOLARIES

VOLARY
VOLATIC
VOLATILE
VOLATILES
VOLCANIAN
VOLCANIC
VOLCANISE
VOLCANISED
VOLCANISES
VOLCANISING
VOLCANISM
VOLCANISMS
VOLCANIST
VOLCANISTS
VOLCANIZE
VOLCANIZED
VOLCANIZES
VOLCANIZING
VOLCANO
VOLCANOES
VOLE
VOLED
VOLENS
VOLERIES
VOLERY
VOLES
VOLET
VOLETS
VOLING
VOLITANT
VOLITATE
VOLITATED
VOLITATES
VOLITATING
VOLITIENT
VOLITION
VOLITIONS
VOLITIVE
VOLITIVES
VOLKSRAAD
VOLKSRAADS
VOLLEY
VOLLEYED
VOLLEYING
VOLLEYS
VOLOST
VOLOSTS
VOLPINO
VOLPINOS
VOLPLANE
VOLPLANED
VOLPLANES
VOLPLANING
VOLS
VOLT
VOLTA
VOLTAGE
VOLTAGES
VOLTAIC
VOLTAISM
VOLTAISMS
VOLTE
VOLTES
VOLTIGEUR
VOLTIGEURS
VOLTINISM
VOLTINISMS
VOLTMETER
VOLTMETERS
VOLTS

VOLUBIL
VOLUBLE
VOLUBLY
VOLUCRINE
VOLUME
VOLUMED
VOLUMES
VOLUMETER
VOLUMETERS
VOLUMINAL
VOLUMING
VOLUMIST
VOLUMISTS
VOLUNTARIES
VOLUNTARY
VOLUNTEER
VOLUNTEERED
VOLUNTEERING
VOLUNTEERS
VÖLUSPA
VÖLUSPAS
VOLUTE
VOLUTED
VOLUTES
VOLUTIN
VOLUTINS
VOLUTION
VOLUTIONS
VOLUTOID
VOLVA
VOLVAS
VOLVATE
VOLVE
VOLVED
VOLVES
VOLVING
VOLVULUS
VOLVULUSES
VOMER
VOMERINE
VOMERS
VOMICA
VOMICAS
VOMIT
VOMITED
VOMITING
VOMITINGS
VOMITIVE
VOMITIVES
VOMITO
VOMITORIA
VOMITORIES
VOMITORY
VOMITOS
VOMITS
VOODOO
VOODOOED
VOODOOING
VOODOOISM
VOODOOISMS
VOODOOIST
VOODOOISTS
VOODOOS
VOR
VORACIOUS
VORACITIES
VORACITY
VORAGO
VORAGOES
VORANT

| | | | | |
|---|---|---|---|---|
| VORPAL | VOUCHSAFED | VOX | VULCANISMS | VULNERATES |
| VORRED | VOUCHSAFES | VOYAGE | VULCANIST | VULNERATING |
| VORRING | VOUCHSAFING | VOYAGED | VULCANISTS | VULNING |
| VORS | VOUDOU | VOYAGER | VULCANITE | VULNS |
| VORTEX | VOUDOUED | VOYAGERS | VULCANITES | VULPICIDE |
| VORTEXES | VOUDOUING | VOYAGES | VULCANIZE | VULPICIDES |
| VORTICAL | VOUDOUS | VOYAGEUR | VULCANIZED | VULPINE |
| VORTICES | VOUGE | VOYAGEURS | VULCANIZES | VULPINISM |
| VORTICISM | VOUGES | VOYAGING | VULCANIZING | VULPINISMS |
| VORTICISMS | VOULGE | VOYEUR | VULCANS | VULPINITE |
| VORTICIST | VOULGES | VOYEURISM | VULGAR | VULPINITES |
| VORTICISTS | VOULU | VOYEURISMS | VULGARER | VULSELLA |
| VORTICITIES | VOUSSOIR | VOYEURS | VULGAREST | VULSELLAE |
| VORTICITY | VOUSSOIRED | VRAIC | VULGARIAN | VULSELLUM |
| VORTICOSE | VOUSSOIRING | VRAICKER | VULGARIANS | VULTURE |
| VOTARESS | VOUSSOIRS | VRAICKERS | VULGARISE | VULTURES |
| VOTARESSES | VOUTSAFE | VRAICKING | VULGARISED | VULTURINE |
| VOTARIES | VOUTSAFED | VRAICKINGS | VULGARISES | VULTURISH |
| VOTARIST | VOUTSAFES | VRAICS | VULGARISING | VULTURISM |
| VOTARISTS | VOUTSAFING | VRIL | VULGARISM | VULTURISMS |
| VOTARY | VOW | VRILS | VULGARISMS | VULTURN |
| VOTE | VOWED | VROOM | VULGARITIES | VULTURNS |
| VOTED | VOWEL | VROOMED | VULGARITY | VULTUROUS |
| VOTEEN | VOWELISE | VROOMING | VULGARIZE | VULVA |
| VOTEENS | VOWELISED | VROOMS | VULGARIZED | VULVAL |
| VOTELESS | VOWELISES | VROUW | VULGARIZES | VULVAR |
| VOTER | VOWELISING | VROUWS | VULGARIZING | VULVAS |
| VOTERS | VOWELIZE | VUG | VULGARLY | VULVATE |
| VOTES | VOWELIZED | VUGGIER | VULGARS | VULVIFORM |
| VOTING | VOWELIZES | VUGGIEST | VULGATE | VULVITIS |
| VOTIVE | VOWELIZING | VUGGY | VULGATES | VULVITISES |
| VOUCH | VOWELLED | VUGS | VULGO | VUM |
| VOUCHED | VOWELLESS | VULCAN | VULGUS | VUMMED |
| VOUCHEE | VOWELLING | VULCANIAN | VULGUSES | VUMMING |
| VOUCHEES | VOWELLY | VULCANIC | VULN | VUMS |
| VOUCHER | VOWELS | VULCANISE | VULNED | VYING |
| VOUCHERS | VOWESS | VULCANISED | VULNERARIES | VYINGLY |
| VOUCHES | VOWESSES | VULCANISES | VULNERARY | |
| VOUCHING | VOWING | VULCANISING | VULNERATE | |
| VOUCHSAFE | VOWS | VULCANISM | VULNERATED | |

# W

WABAIN
WABAINS
WABBLE
WABBLED
WABBLER
WABBLERS
WABBLES
WABBLIER
WABBLIEST
WABBLING
WABBLY
WABOOM
WABOOMS
WABSTER
WABSTERS
WACKE
WACKES
WACKIER
WACKIEST
WACKINESS
WACKINESSES
WACKY
WAD
WADD
WADDED
WADDIE
WADDIED
WADDIES
WADDING
WADDINGS
WADDLE
WADDLED
WADDLES
WADDLING
WADDS
WADDY
WADDYING
WADE
WADED
WADER
WADERS
WADES
WADI
WADIES
WADING
WADINGS
WADIS
WADMAAL
WADMAALS
WADMAL
WADMALS
WADMOL
WADMOLL
WADMOLLS
WADMOLS
WADS
WADSET
WADSETS
WADSETT
WADSETTED
WADSETTER
WADSETTERS
WADSETTING

WADSETTS
WADY
WAE
WAEFUL
WAENESS
WAENESSES
WAES
WAESOME
WAESUCKS
WAFER
WAFERED
WAFERING
WAFERS
WAFERY
WAFF
WAFFED
WAFFING
WAFFLE
WAFFLED
WAFFLES
WAFFLING
WAFFS
WAFT
WAFTAGE
WAFTAGES
WAFTED
WAFTER
WAFTERS
WAFTING
WAFTINGS
WAFTS
WAFTURE
WAFTURES
WAG
WAGE
WAGED
WAGELESS
WAGENBOOM
WAGENBOOMS
WAGER
WAGERED
WAGERER
WAGERERS
WAGERING
WAGERS
WAGES
WAGGED
WAGGERIES
WAGGERY
WAGGING
WAGGISH
WAGGISHLY
WAGGLE
WAGGLED
WAGGLES
WAGGLIER
WAGGLIEST
WAGGLING
WAGGLY
WAGGON
WAGGONED
WAGGONER
WAGGONERS

WAGGONING
WAGGONS
WAGHALTER
WAGHALTERS
WAGING
WAGMOIRE
WAGMOIRES
WAGON
WAGONAGE
WAGONAGES
WAGONED
WAGONER
WAGONERS
WAGONETTE
WAGONETTES
WAGONFUL
WAGONFULS
WAGONING
WAGONS
WAGS
WAGTAIL
WAGTAILS
WAHINE
WAHINES
WAHOO
WAHOOS
WAID
WAIDE
WAIF
WAIFED
WAIFING
WAIFS
WAIFT
WAIFTS
WAIL
WAILED
WAILER
WAILERS
WAILFUL
WAILING
WAILINGLY
WAILINGS
WAILS
WAIN
WAINAGE
WAINAGES
WAINED
WAINING
WAINS
WAINSCOT
WAINSCOTED
WAINSCOTING
WAINSCOTINGS
WAINSCOTS
WAINSCOTTED
WAINSCOTTING
WAINSCOTTINGS
WAIST
WAISTBAND
WAISTBANDS
WAISTBELT
WAISTBELTS
WAISTBOAT

WAISTBOATS
WAISTCOAT
WAISTCOATS
WAISTED
WAISTER
WAISTERS
WAISTLINE
WAISTLINES
WAISTS
WAIT
WAITE
WAITED
WAITER
WAITERAGE
WAITERAGES
WAITERING
WAITERINGS
WAITERS
WAITES
WAITING
WAITINGLY
WAITINGS
WAITRESS
WAITRESSES
WAITS
WAIVE
WAIVED
WAIVER
WAIVERS
WAIVES
WAIVING
WAIVODE
WAIVODES
WAIWODE
WAIWODES
WAKE
WAKED
WAKEFUL
WAKEFULLY
WAKELESS
WAKEMAN
WAKEMEN
WAKEN
WAKENED
WAKENER
WAKENERS
WAKENING
WAKENINGS
WAKENS
WAKER
WAKERIFE
WAKERS
WAKES
WAKIKI
WAKIKIS
WAKING
WAKINGS
WALD
WALDFLUTE
WALDFLUTES
WALDGRAVE
WALDGRAVES
WALDHORN

WALDHORNS
WALDS
WALE
WALED
WALER
WALERS
WALES
WALI
WALIER
WALIES
WALIEST
WALING
WALIS
WALISE
WALISES
WALK
WALKABLE
WALKABOUT
WALKABOUTS
WALKED
WALKER
WALKERS
WALKING
WALKINGS
WALKS
WALKWAY
WALKWAYS
WALL
WALLA
WALLABA
WALLABAS
WALLABIES
WALLABY
WALLAH
WALLAHS
WALLAROO
WALLAROOS
WALLAS
WALLED
WALLER
WALLERS
WALLET
WALLETS
WALLFISH
WALLFISHES
WALLIER
WALLIES
WALLIEST
WALLING
WALLINGS
WALLOP
WALLOPED
WALLOPER
WALLOPERS
WALLOPING
WALLOPINGS
WALLOPS
WALLOW
WALLOWED
WALLOWER
WALLOWERS
WALLOWING
WALLOWINGS

| | | | | |
|---|---|---|---|---|
| WALLOWS | WANED | WANWORDY | WAREHOUSING | WARPING |
| WALLPAPER | WANES | WANWORTH | WAREHOUSINGS | WARPINGS |
| WALLPAPERS | WANEY | WANWORTHS | WARELESS | WARPLANE |
| WALLS | WANG | WANY | WARES | WARPLANES |
| WALLSEND | WANGAN | WANZE | WARFARE | WARPS |
| WALLSENDS | WANGANS | WANZED | WARFARED | WARRAGAL |
| WALLWORT | WANGLE | WANZES | WARFARER | WARRAGALS |
| WALLWORTS | WANGLED | WANZING | WARFARERS | WARRAGLE |
| WALLY | WANGLER | WAP | WARFARES | WARRAGLES |
| WALLYDRAG | WANGLERS | WAPENSHAW | WARFARIN | WARRAGUL |
| WALLYDRAGS | WANGLES | WAPENSHAWS | WARFARING | WARRAGULS |
| WALNUT | WANGLING | WAPENTAKE | WARFARINGS | WARRAN |
| WALNUTS | WANGLINGS | WAPENTAKES | WARFARINS | WARRAND |
| WALRUS | WANGS | WAPINSHAW | WARHABLE | WARRANDED |
| WALRUSES | WANGUN | WAPINSHAWS | WARHEAD | WARRANDING |
| WALTIER | WANGUNS | WAPITI | WARHEADS | WARRANDS |
| WALTIEST | WANHOPE | WAPITIS | WARIER | WARRANED |
| WALTY | WANHOPES | WAPPED | WARIEST | WARRANING |
| WALTZ | WANIER | WAPPEND | WARILY | WARRANS |
| WALTZED | WANIEST | WAPPER | WARIMENT | WARRANT |
| WALTZER | WANIGAN | WAPPERED | WARIMENTS | WARRANTED |
| WALTZERS | WANIGANS | WAPPERING | WARINESS | WARRANTEE |
| WALTZES | WANING | WAPPERS | WARINESSES | WARRANTEES |
| WALTZING | WANINGS | WAPPING | WARING | WARRANTER |
| WALTZINGS | WANK | WAPS | WARISON | WARRANTERS |
| WALY | WANKED | WAR | WARISONS | WARRANTIES |
| WAMBLE | WANKER | WARATAH | WARK | WARRANTING |
| WAMBLED | WANKERS | WARATAHS | WARKS | WARRANTINGS |
| WAMBLES | WANKING | WARBIER | WARLIKE | WARRANTOR |
| WAMBLIER | WANKLE | WARBIEST | WARLING | WARRANTORS |
| WAMBLIEST | WANKS | WARBLE | WARLINGS | WARRANTS |
| WAMBLING | WANLE | WARBLED | WARLOCK | WARRANTY |
| WAMBLINGS | WANLY | WARBLER | WARLOCKRIES | WARRAY |
| WAMBLY | WANNED | WARBLERS | WARLOCKRY | WARRAYED |
| WAME | WANNEL | WARBLES | WARLOCKS | WARRAYING |
| WAMED | WANNER | WARBLING | WARLORD | WARRAYS |
| WAMEFUL | WANNESS | WARBLINGS | WARLORDS | WARRE |
| WAMEFULS | WANNESSES | WARBY | WARM | WARRED |
| WAMES | WANNEST | WARD | WARMAN | WARREN |
| WAMMUS | WANNING | WARDED | WARMBLOOD | WARRENER |
| WAMMUSES | WANNISH | WARDEN | WARMBLOODS | WARRENERS |
| WAMPEE | WANS | WARDENED | WARMED | WARRENS |
| WAMPEES | WANT | WARDENING | WARMEN | WARREY |
| WAMPISH | WANTAGE | WARDENRIES | WARMER | WARREYED |
| WAMPISHED | WANTAGES | WARDENRY | WARMERS | WARREYING |
| WAMPISHES | WANTED | WARDENS | WARMEST | WARREYS |
| WAMPISHING | WANTER | WARDER | WARMING | WARRIGAL |
| WAMPUM | WANTERS | WARDERED | WARMINGS | WARRIGALS |
| WAMPUMS | WANTHILL | WARDERING | WARMLY | WARRING |
| WAMPUS | WANTHILLS | WARDERS | WARMNESS | WARRIOR |
| WAMPUSES | WANTIES | WARDING | WARMNESSES | WARRIORS |
| WAMUS | WANTING | WARDINGS | WARMONGER | WARRISON |
| WAMUSES | WANTINGS | WARDOG | WARMONGERS | WARRISONS |
| WAN | WANTON | WARDOGS | WARMS | WARS |
| WANCHANCY | WANTONED | WARDRESS | WARMTH | WARSHIP |
| WAND | WANTONER | WARDRESSES | WARMTHS | WARSHIPS |
| WANDER | WANTONEST | WARDROBE | WARN | WARSLE |
| WANDERED | WANTONING | WARDROBER | WARNED | WARSLED |
| WANDERER | WANTONISE | WARDROBERS | WARNER | WARSLES |
| WANDERERS | WANTONISED | WARDROBES | WARNERS | WARSLING |
| WANDERING | WANTONISES | WARDROP | WARNING | WARST |
| WANDERINGS | WANTONISING | WARDROPS | WARNINGLY | WART |
| WANDEROO | WANTONIZE | WARDS | WARNINGS | WARTED |
| WANDEROOS | WANTONIZED | WARDSHIP | WARNS | WARTIER |
| WANDERS | WANTONIZES | WARDSHIPS | WARP | WARTIEST |
| WANDLE | WANTONIZING | WARE | WARPATH | WARTIME |
| WANDOO | WANTONLY | WARED | WARPATHS | WARTIMES |
| WANDOOS | WANTONS | WAREHOUSE | WARPED | WARTLESS |
| WANDS | WANTS | WAREHOUSED | WARPER | WARTS |
| WANE | WANTY | WAREHOUSES | WARPERS | WARTWEED |

WARTWEEDS
WARTWORT
WARTWORTS
WARTY
WARWOLF
WARWOLVES
WARY
WAS
WASE
WASES
WASH
WASHABLE
WASHED
WASHEN
WASHER
WASHERED
WASHERIES
WASHERING
WASHERMAN
WASHERMEN
WASHERS
WASHERY
WASHES
WASHIER
WASHIEST
WASHINESS
WASHINESSES
WASHING
WASHINGS
WASHLAND
WASHLANDS
WASHROOM
WASHROOMS
WASHY
WASP
WASPIE
WASPIER
WASPIES
WASPIEST
WASPISH
WASPISHLY
WASPS
WASPY
WASSAIL
WASSAILED
WASSAILER
WASSAILERS
WASSAILING
WASSAILINGS
WASSAILRIES
WASSAILRY
WASSAILS
WASSERMAN
WASSERMEN
WAST
WASTAGE
WASTAGES
WASTE
WASTED
WASTEFUL
WASTEL
WASTELAND
WASTELANDS
WASTELS
WASTENESS
WASTENESSES
WASTER
WASTERED
WASTERFUL
WASTERIES

WASTERIFE
WASTERIFES
WASTERING
WASTERS
WASTERY
WASTES
WASTFULL
WASTING
WASTINGS
WASTNESS
WASTNESSES
WASTREL
WASTRELS
WASTRIES
WASTRY
WASTS
WAT
WATCH
WATCHABLE
WATCHCASE
WATCHCASES
WATCHED
WATCHER
WATCHERS
WATCHES
WATCHET
WATCHETS
WATCHFUL
WATCHING
WATCHMAN
WATCHMEN
WATCHWORD
WATCHWORDS
WATE
WATER
WATERAGE
WATERAGES
WATERED
WATERER
WATERERS
WATERFALL
WATERFALLS
WATERIER
WATERIEST
WATERING
WATERINGS
WATERISH
WATERLESS
WATERLILIES
WATERLILY
WATERLOG
WATERLOGGED
WATERLOGGING
WATERLOGS
WATERMAN
WATERMARK
WATERMARKED
WATERMARKING
WATERMARKS
WATERMEN
WATERS
WATERSHED
WATERSHEDS
WATERSIDE
WATERSIDES
WATERWAY
WATERWAYS
WATERWORK
WATERWORKS
WATERY

WATS
WATT
WATTAGE
WATTAGES
WATTER
WATTEST
WATTLE
WATTLED
WATTLES
WATTLING
WATTLINGS
WATTMETER
WATTMETERS
WATTS
WAUCHT
WAUCHTED
WAUCHTING
WAUCHTS
WAUFF
WAUFFED
WAUFFING
WAUFFS
WAUGH
WAUGHED
WAUGHING
WAUGHS
WAUGHT
WAUGHTED
WAUGHTING
WAUGHTS
WAUK
WAUKED
WAUKING
WAUKRIFE
WAUKS
WAUL
WAULED
WAULING
WAULINGS
WAULK
WAULKED
WAULKING
WAULKS
WAULS
WAUR
WAURED
WAURING
WAURS
WAURST
WAVE
WAVEBAND
WAVEBANDS
WAVED
WAVEFORM
WAVEFORMS
WAVEFRONT
WAVEFRONTS
WAVEGUIDE
WAVEGUIDES
WAVELESS
WAVELET
WAVELETS
WAVELIKE
WAVELLITE
WAVELLITES
WAVEMETER
WAVEMETERS
WAVER
WAVERED
WAVERER

WAVERERS
WAVERING
WAVERINGS
WAVEROUS
WAVERS
WAVERY
WAVES
WAVESHAPE
WAVESHAPES
WAVESON
WAVESONS
WAVEY
WAVEYS
WAVIER
WAVIES
WAVIEST
WAVINESS
WAVINESSES
WAVING
WAVINGS
WAVY
WAW
WAWE
WAWES
WAWL
WAWLED
WAWLING
WAWLINGS
WAWLS
WAWS
WAX
WAXBERRIES
WAXBERRY
WAXBILL
WAXBILLS
WAXED
WAXEN
WAXER
WAXERS
WAXES
WAXIER
WAXIEST
WAXINESS
WAXINESSES
WAXING
WAXINGS
WAXWING
WAXWINGS
WAXWORK
WAXWORKER
WAXWORKERS
WAXWORKS
WAXY
WAY
WAYBREAD
WAYBREADS
WAYED
WAYFARE
WAYFARED
WAYFARER
WAYFARERS
WAYFARES
WAYFARING
WAYFARINGS
WAYGONE
WAYGOOSE
WAYGOOSES
WAYING
WAYLAID
WAYLAY

WAYLAYER
WAYLAYERS
WAYLAYING
WAYLAYS
WAYLESS
WAYMARK
WAYMARKED
WAYMARKING
WAYMARKS
WAYMENT
WAYMENTED
WAYMENTING
WAYMENTS
WAYS
WAYSIDE
WAYSIDES
WAYWARD
WAYWARDLY
WAYWISER
WAYWISERS
WAYWORN
WAYZGOOSE
WAYZGOOSES
WAZIR
WAZIRS
WE
WEAK
WEAKEN
WEAKENED
WEAKENER
WEAKENERS
WEAKENING
WEAKENS
WEAKER
WEAKEST
WEAKFISH
WEAKFISHES
WEAKLIER
WEAKLIEST
WEAKLING
WEAKLINGS
WEAKLY
WEAKNESS
WEAKNESSES
WEAL
WEALD
WEALDS
WEALS
WEALSMAN
WEALSMEN
WEALTH
WEALTHIER
WEALTHIEST
WEALTHILY
WEALTHS
WEALTHY
WEAMB
WEAMBS
WEAN
WEANED
WEANEL
WEANELS
WEANER
WEANERS
WEANING
WEANLING
WEANLINGS
WEANS
WEAPON
WEAPONED

| | | | | |
|---|---|---|---|---|
| WEAPONRIES | WEBWORM | WEEPHOLE | WEIRDNESS | WELLING |
| WEAPONRY | WEBWORMS | WEEPHOLES | WEIRDNESSES | WELLINGS |
| WEAPONS | WECHT | WEEPIE | WEIRDO | WELLS |
| WEAR | WECHTS | WEEPIER | WEIRDOS | WELLY |
| WEARABLE | WED | WEEPIES | WEIRDS | WELSH |
| WEARED | WEDDED | WEEPIEST | WEIRED | WELSHED |
| WEARER | WEDDING | WEEPING | WEIRING | WELSHER |
| WEARERS | WEDDINGS | WEEPINGLY | WEIRS | WELSHERS |
| WEARIED | WEDELN | WEEPINGS | WEISE | WELSHES |
| WEARIER | WEDELNED | WEEPS | WEISED | WELSHING |
| WEARIES | WEDELNING | WEEPY | WEISES | WELT |
| WEARIEST | WEDELNS | WEER | WEISING | WELTED |
| WEARIFUL | WEDGE | WEES | WEIZE | WELTER |
| WEARILESS | WEDGED | WEEST | WEIZED | WELTERED |
| WEARILY | WEDGES | WEET | WEIZES | WELTERING |
| WEARINESS | WEDGEWISE | WEETE | WEIZING | WELTERS |
| WEARINESSES | WEDGIE | WEETEN | WEKA | WELTING |
| WEARING | WEDGIES | WEETING | WEKAS | WELTS |
| WEARINGS | WEDGING | WEETINGLY | WELAWAY | WEM |
| WEARISH | WEDGINGS | WEETLESS | WELCH | WEMB |
| WEARISOME | WEDLOCK | WEEVER | WELCHED | WEMBS |
| WEARS | WEDLOCKS | WEEVERS | WELCHER | WEMS |
| WEARY | WEDS | WEEVIL | WELCHERS | WEN |
| WEARYING | WEE | WEEVILED | WELCHES | WENCH |
| WEASAND | WEED | WEEVILLED | WELCHING | WENCHED |
| WEASANDS | WEEDED | WEEVILLY | WELCOME | WENCHER |
| WEASEL | WEEDER | WEEVILS | WELCOMED | WENCHERS |
| WEASELED | WEEDERIES | WEEVILY | WELCOMER | WENCHES |
| WEASELER | WEEDERS | WEFT | WELCOMERS | WENCHING |
| WEASELERS | WEEDERY | WEFTAGE | WELCOMES | WEND |
| WEASELING | WEEDICIDE | WEFTAGES | WELCOMING | WENDED |
| WEASELLED | WEEDICIDES | WEFTE | WELD | WENDIGO |
| WEASELLER | WEEDIER | WEFTED | WELDABLE | WENDIGOS |
| WEASELLERS | WEEDIEST | WEFTES | WELDED | WENDING |
| WEASELLING | WEEDINESS | WEFTING | WELDER | WENDS |
| WEASELLY | WEEDINESSES | WEFTS | WELDERS | WENNIER |
| WEASELS | WEEDING | WEID | WELDING | WENNIEST |
| WEATHER | WEEDINGS | WEIDS | WELDINGS | WENNISH |
| WEATHERED | WEEDLESS | WEIGELA | WELDLESS | WENNY |
| WEATHERING | WEEDS | WEIGELAS | WELDMENT | WENS |
| WEATHERINGS | WEEDY | WEIGH | WELDMENTS | WENT |
| WEATHERLY | WEEING | WEIGHABLE | WELDMESH | WENTS |
| WEATHERS | WEEK | WEIGHAGE | WELDMESH® | WEPT |
| WEAVE | WEEKDAY | WEIGHAGES | WELDMESHES | WERE |
| WEAVED | WEEKDAYS | WEIGHED | WELDMESHES® | WEREGILD |
| WEAVER | WEEKE | WEIGHER | WELDOR | WEREGILDS |
| WEAVERS | WEEKEND | WEIGHERS | WELDORS | WEREWOLF |
| WEAVES | WEEKENDED | WEIGHING | WELDS | WEREWOLVES |
| WEAVING | WEEKENDING | WEIGHINGS | WELFARE | WERGILD |
| WEAVINGS | WEEKENDS | WEIGHS | WELFARES | WERGILDS |
| WEAZAND | WEEKES | WEIGHT | WELFARISM | WERNERITE |
| WEAZANDS | WEEKLIES | WEIGHTED | WELFARISMS | WERNERITES |
| WEAZEN | WEEKLY | WEIGHTIER | WELFARIST | WERSH |
| WEAZENED | WEEKNIGHT | WEIGHTIEST | WELFARISTS | WERSHER |
| WEAZENING | WEEKNIGHTS | WEIGHTILY | WELK | WERSHEST |
| WEAZENS | WEEKS | WEIGHTING | WELKE | WERT |
| WEB | WEEL | WEIGHTINGS | WELKED | WERWOLF |
| WEBBED | WEELS | WEIGHTS | WELKES | WERWOLVES |
| WEBBIER | WEEM | WEIGHTY | WELKIN | WESAND |
| WEBBIEST | WEEMS | WEIL | WELKING | WESANDS |
| WEBBING | WEEN | WEILS | WELKINS | WEST |
| WEBBINGS | WEENED | WEIR | WELKS | WESTBOUND |
| WEBBY | WEENIER | WEIRD | WELKT | WESTED |
| WEBER | WEENIEST | WEIRDED | WELL | WESTER |
| WEBERS | WEENING | WEIRDER | WELLADAY | WESTERED |
| WEBS | WEENS | WEIRDEST | WELLANEAR | WESTERING |
| WEBSTER | WEENY | WEIRDIE | WELLAWAY | WESTERINGS |
| WEBSTERS | WEEP | WEIRDIES | WELLED | WESTERLIES |
| WEBWHEEL | WEEPER | WEIRDING | WELLIE | WESTERLY |
| WEBWHEELS | WEEPERS | WEIRDLY | WELLIES | WESTERN |

WESTERNER
WESTERNERS
WESTERNS
WESTERS
WESTING
WESTINGS
WESTLIN
WESTMOST
WESTS
WESTWARD
WESTWARDS
WET
WETBACK
WETBACKS
WETHER
WETHERS
WETLAND
WETLANDS
WETLY
WETNESS
WETNESSES
WETS
WETTED
WETTER
WETTEST
WETTING
WETTISH
WEX
WEXE
WEXED
WEXES
WEXING
WEY
WEYARD
WEYS
WEYWARD
WEZAND
WEZANDS
WHACK
WHACKED
WHACKER
WHACKERS
WHACKIER
WHACKIEST
WHACKING
WHACKINGS
WHACKO
WHACKOES
WHACKOS
WHACKS
WHACKY
WHAISLE
WHAISLED
WHAISLES
WHAISLING
WHAIZLE
WHAIZLED
WHAIZLES
WHAIZLING
WHALE
WHALEBONE
WHALEBONES
WHALED
WHALER
WHALERIES
WHALERS
WHALERY
WHALES
WHALING
WHALINGS

WHALLY
WHAM
WHAMMED
WHAMMING
WHAMPLE
WHAMPLES
WHAMS
WHANG
WHANGAM
WHANGAMS
WHANGED
WHANGEE
WHANGEES
WHANGING
WHANGS
WHAP
WHAPPED
WHAPPING
WHAPS
WHARE
WHARES
WHARF
WHARFAGE
WHARFAGES
WHARFED
WHARFING
WHARFINGS
WHARFS
WHARVE
WHARVES
WHAT
WHATEN
WHATEVER
WHATNA
WHATNESS
WHATNESSES
WHATNOT
WHATNOTS
WHATS
WHATSIS
WHATSISES
WHATSIT
WHATSITS
WHATSO
WHATTEN
WHAUP
WHAUPS
WHAUR
WHAURS
WHEAL
WHEALS
WHEAR
WHEARE
WHEAT
WHEATEAR
WHEATEARS
WHEATEN
WHEATS
WHEE
WHEECH
WHEECHED
WHEECHING
WHEECHS
WHEEDLE
WHEEDLED
WHEEDLER
WHEEDLERS
WHEEDLES
WHEEDLING
WHEEDLINGS

WHEEL
WHEELBASE
WHEELBASES
WHEELED
WHEELER
WHEELERS
WHEELIE
WHEELIER
WHEELIES
WHEELIEST
WHEELING
WHEELINGS
WHEELMAN
WHEELMEN
WHEELS
WHEELWORK
WHEELWORKS
WHEELY
WHEEN
WHEENGE
WHEENGED
WHEENGES
WHEENGING
WHEENS
WHEEPLE
WHEEPLED
WHEEPLES
WHEEPLING
WHEESHT
WHEESHTED
WHEESHTING
WHEESHTS
WHEEZE
WHEEZED
WHEEZES
WHEEZIER
WHEEZIEST
WHEEZILY
WHEEZING
WHEEZINGS
WHEEZLE
WHEEZLED
WHEEZLES
WHEEZLING
WHEEZY
WHEFT
WHEFTS
WHELK
WHELKED
WHELKIER
WHELKIEST
WHELKS
WHELKY
WHELM
WHELMED
WHELMING
WHELMS
WHELP
WHELPED
WHELPING
WHELPS
WHEMMLE
WHEMMLED
WHEMMLES
WHEMMLING
WHEN
WHENAS
WHENCE
WHENCES
WHENCEVER

WHENEVER
WHENS
WHERE
WHEREAS
WHEREAT
WHEREBY
WHEREFOR
WHEREFORE
WHEREFORES
WHEREFROM
WHEREIN
WHEREINTO
WHERENESS
WHERENESSES
WHEREOF
WHEREON
WHEREOUT
WHERES
WHERESO
WHERETO
WHEREUNTO
WHEREUPON
WHEREVER
WHEREWITH
WHEREWITHS
WHERRET
WHERRETED
WHERRETING
WHERRETS
WHERRIES
WHERRY
WHERRYMAN
WHERRYMEN
WHET
WHETHER
WHETS
WHETSTONE
WHETSTONES
WHETTED
WHETTER
WHETTERS
WHETTING
WHEUGH
WHEUGHED
WHEUGHING
WHEUGHS
WHEW
WHEWED
WHEWING
WHEWS
WHEY
WHEYEY
WHEYIER
WHEYIEST
WHEYISH
WHEYS
WHICH
WHICHEVER
WHICKER
WHICKERED
WHICKERING
WHICKERS
WHID
WHIDAH
WHIDAHS
WHIDDED
WHIDDER
WHIDDERED
WHIDDERING
WHIDDERS

WHIDDING
WHIDS
WHIFF
WHIFFED
WHIFFER
WHIFFERS
WHIFFET
WHIFFETS
WHIFFIER
WHIFFIEST
WHIFFING
WHIFFINGS
WHIFFLE
WHIFFLED
WHIFFLER
WHIFFLERIES
WHIFFLERS
WHIFFLERY
WHIFFLES
WHIFFLING
WHIFFLINGS
WHIFFS
WHIFFY
WHIFT
WHIFTS
WHIG
WHIGGED
WHIGGING
WHIGS
WHILE
WHILED
WHILES
WHILING
WHILK
WHILLIED
WHILLIES
WHILLY
WHILLYING
WHILLYWHA
WHILLYWHAED
WHILLYWHAING
WHILLYWHAS
WHILOM
WHILST
WHIM
WHIMBREL
WHIMBRELS
WHIMMED
WHIMMIER
WHIMMIEST
WHIMMING
WHIMMY
WHIMPER
WHIMPERED
WHIMPERER
WHIMPERERS
WHIMPERING
WHIMPERINGS
WHIMPERS
WHIMPLE
WHIMPLED
WHIMPLES
WHIMPLING
WHIMS
WHIMSEY
WHIMSEYS
WHIMSICAL
WHIMSIER
WHIMSIES
WHIMSIEST

WHIMSILY
WHIMSY
WHIN
WHINCHAT
WHINCHATS
WHINE
WHINED
WHINER
WHINERS
WHINES
WHINGE
WHINGED
WHINGEING
WHINGEINGS
WHINGER
WHINGERS
WHINGES
WHINIARD
WHINIARDS
WHINIER
WHINIEST
WHININESS
WHININESSES
WHINING
WHININGLY
WHININGS
WHINNIED
WHINNIER
WHINNIES
WHINNIEST
WHINNY
WHINNYING
WHINS
WHINSTONE
WHINSTONES
WHINY
WHINYARD
WHINYARDS
WHIP
WHIPBIRD
WHIPBIRDS
WHIPCAT
WHIPCATS
WHIPCORD
WHIPCORDS
WHIPCORDY
WHIPJACK
WHIPJACKS
WHIPLASH
WHIPLASHED
WHIPLASHES
WHIPLASHING
WHIPLIKE
WHIPPED
WHIPPER
WHIPPERS
WHIPPET
WHIPPETS
WHIPPIER
WHIPPIEST
WHIPPING
WHIPPINGS
WHIPPY
WHIPS
WHIPSTAFF
WHIPSTAFFS
WHIPSTALL
WHIPSTALLED
WHIPSTALLING
WHIPSTALLS

WHIPSTER
WHIPSTERS
WHIPT
WHIPWORM
WHIPWORMS
WHIR
WHIRL
WHIRLED
WHIRLER
WHIRLERS
WHIRLIGIG
WHIRLIGIGS
WHIRLING
WHIRLINGS
WHIRLPOOL
WHIRLPOOLS
WHIRLS
WHIRLWIND
WHIRLWINDS
WHIRR
WHIRRED
WHIRRET
WHIRRETED
WHIRRETING
WHIRRETS
WHIRRIED
WHIRRIES
WHIRRING
WHIRRINGS
WHIRRS
WHIRRY
WHIRRYING
WHIRS
WHIRTLE
WHIRTLES
WHISH
WHISHED
WHISHES
WHISHING
WHISHT
WHISHTED
WHISHTING
WHISHTS
WHISK
WHISKED
WHISKER
WHISKERED
WHISKERS
WHISKERY
WHISKET
WHISKETS
WHISKEY
WHISKEYS
WHISKIES
WHISKING
WHISKS
WHISKY
WHISPER
WHISPERED
WHISPERER
WHISPERERS
WHISPERING
WHISPERINGS
WHISPERS
WHISPERY
WHISS
WHISSED
WHISSES
WHISSING
WHIST

WHISTED
WHISTING
WHISTLE
WHISTLED
WHISTLER
WHISTLERS
WHISTLES
WHISTLING
WHISTLINGS
WHISTS
WHIT
WHITE
WHITEBAIT
WHITEBAITS
WHITEBASS
WHITEBASSES
WHITEBEAM
WHITEBEAMS
WHITECAP
WHITECAPS
WHITED
WHITEFISH
WHITEFISHES
WHITEHEAD
WHITEHEADS
WHITELY
WHITEN
WHITENED
WHITENER
WHITENERS
WHITENESS
WHITENESSES
WHITENING
WHITENINGS
WHITENS
WHITER
WHITES
WHITEST
WHITEWALL
WHITEWALLS
WHITEWARE
WHITEWARES
WHITEWASH
WHITEWASHED
WHITEWASHES
WHITEWASHING
WHITEWING
WHITEWINGS
WHITEWOOD
WHITEWOODS
WHITEY
WHITEYS
WHITHER
WHITHERED
WHITHERING
WHITHERS
WHITIER
WHITIES
WHITIEST
WHITING
WHITINGS
WHITISH
WHITLING
WHITLINGS
WHITLOW
WHITLOWS
WHITRET
WHITRETS
WHITS
WHITSTER

WHITSTERS
WHITTAW
WHITTAWER
WHITTAWERS
WHITTAWS
WHITTER
WHITTERED
WHITTERING
WHITTERS
WHITTLE
WHITTLED
WHITTLER
WHITTLERS
WHITTLES
WHITTLING
WHITTLINGS
WHITTRET
WHITTRETS
WHITY
WHIZ
WHIZZ
WHIZZED
WHIZZER
WHIZZERS
WHIZZES
WHIZZING
WHIZZINGS
WHO
WHOA
WHODUNNIT
WHODUNNITS
WHOEVER
WHOLE
WHOLEFOOD
WHOLEFOODS
WHOLEMEAL
WHOLEMEALS
WHOLENESS
WHOLENESSES
WHOLES
WHOLESALE
WHOLESALES
WHOLESOME
WHOLESOMER
WHOLESOMEST
WHOLISM
WHOLISMS
WHOLISTIC
WHOLLY
WHOM
WHOMBLE
WHOMBLED
WHOMBLES
WHOMBLING
WHOMEVER
WHOMMLE
WHOMMLED
WHOMMLES
WHOMMLING
WHOOBUB
WHOOBUBS
WHOOP
WHOOPED
WHOOPEE
WHOOPEES
WHOOPER
WHOOPERS
WHOOPING
WHOOPINGS
WHOOPS

WHOOSH
WHOOSHED
WHOOSHES
WHOOSHING
WHOOT
WHOOTED
WHOOTING
WHOOTS
WHOP
WHOPPED
WHOPPER
WHOPPERS
WHOPPING
WHOPPINGS
WHOPS
WHORE
WHORED
WHOREDOM
WHOREDOMS
WHORES
WHORESON
WHORESONS
WHORING
WHORISH
WHORISHLY
WHORL
WHORLED
WHORLS
WHORT
WHORTS
WHOSE
WHOSEVER
WHOSO
WHOSOEVER
WHOT
WHOW
WHUMMLE
WHUMMLED
WHUMMLES
WHUMMLING
WHUNSTANE
WHUNSTANES
WHY
WHYDAH
WHYDAHS
WHYEVER
WICK
WICKED
WICKEDER
WICKEDEST
WICKEDLY
WICKEN
WICKENS
WICKER
WICKERED
WICKERS
WICKET
WICKETS
WICKIES
WICKING
WICKS
WICKY
WIDDIES
WIDDLE
WIDDLED
WIDDLES
WIDDLING
WIDDY
WIDE
WIDELY

WIDEN
WIDENED
WIDENER
WIDENERS
WIDENESS
WIDENESSES
WIDENING
WIDENS
WIDER
WIDES
WIDEST
WIDGEON
WIDGEONS
WIDGET
WIDGETS
WIDISH
WIDOW
WIDOWED
WIDOWER
WIDOWERS
WIDOWHOOD
WIDOWHOODS
WIDOWING
WIDOWS
WIDTH
WIDTHS
WIDTHWAYS
WIDTHWISE
WIEL
WIELD
WIELDABLE
WIELDED
WIELDER
WIELDERS
WIELDIER
WIELDIEST
WIELDING
WIELDLESS
WIELDS
WIELDY
WIELS
WIFE
WIFEHOOD
WIFEHOODS
WIFELESS
WIFELIER
WIFELIEST
WIFELY
WIG
WIGAN
WIGANS
WIGEON
WIGEONS
WIGGED
WIGGERIES
WIGGERY
WIGGING
WIGGINGS
WIGGLE
WIGGLED
WIGGLER
WIGGLERS
WIGGLES
WIGGLIER
WIGGLIEST
WIGGLING
WIGGLY
WIGHT
WIGHTED
WIGHTING

WIGHTLY
WIGHTS
WIGLESS
WIGS
WIGWAG
WIGWAGGED
WIGWAGGING
WIGWAGS
WIGWAM
WIGWAMS
WILD
WILDCAT
WILDCATS
WILDCATTED
WILDCATTING
WILDED
WILDER
WILDERED
WILDERING
WILDERS
WILDEST
WILDFIRE
WILDFIRES
WILDGRAVE
WILDGRAVES
WILDING
WILDINGS
WILDISH
WILDLIFE
WILDLIFES
WILDLY
WILDNESS
WILDNESSES
WILDOAT
WILDOATS
WILDS
WILE
WILED
WILEFUL
WILES
WILFUL
WILFULLY
WILI
WILIER
WILIEST
WILILY
WILINESS
WILINESSES
WILING
WILIS
WILL
WILLABLE
WILLED
WILLEMITE
WILLEMITES
WILLER
WILLERS
WILLEST
WILLET
WILLETS
WILLEY
WILLEYED
WILLEYING
WILLEYS
WILLIE
WILLIED
WILLIES
WILLING
WILLINGLY
WILLIWAW

WILLIWAWS
WILLOW
WILLOWED
WILLOWING
WILLOWISH
WILLOWS
WILLOWY
WILLS
WILLY
WILLYARD
WILLYART
WILLYING
WILT
WILTED
WILTING
WILTS
WILY
WIMBLE
WIMBLED
WIMBLES
WIMBLING
WIMBREL
WIMBRELS
WIMP
WIMPIER
WIMPIEST
WIMPISH
WIMPLE
WIMPLED
WIMPLES
WIMPLING
WIMPS
WIMPY
WIN
WINCE
WINCED
WINCER
WINCERS
WINCES
WINCEY
WINCEYS
WINCH
WINCHED
WINCHES
WINCHING
WINCHMAN
WINCHMEN
WINCING
WINCINGS
WINCOPIPE
WINCOPIPES
WIND
WINDAC
WINDACS
WINDAGE
WINDAGES
WINDAS
WINDASES
WINDBLOW
WINDBLOWS
WINDBURN
WINDBURNS
WINDED
WINDER
WINDERS
WINDFALL
WINDFALLS
WINDIER
WINDIEST
WINDIGO

WINDIGOS
WINDILY
WINDINESS
WINDINESSES
WINDING
WINDINGLY
WINDINGS
WINDLASS
WINDLASSED
WINDLASSES
WINDLASSING
WINDLE
WINDLES
WINDLESS
WINDMILL
WINDMILLED
WINDMILLING
WINDMILLS
WINDOCK
WINDOCKS
WINDORE
WINDORES
WINDOW
WINDOWED
WINDOWING
WINDOWINGS
WINDOWS
WINDPIPE
WINDPIPES
WINDRING
WINDROSE
WINDROSES
WINDROW
WINDROWED
WINDROWING
WINDROWS
WINDS
WINDSES
WINDSHIP
WINDSHIPS
WINDSTORM
WINDSTORMS
WINDSURF
WINDSURFED
WINDSURFING
WINDSURFINGS
WINDSURFS
WINDSWEPT
WINDTHROW
WINDTHROWS
WINDWARD
WINDWARDS
WINDY
WINE
WINED
WINERIES
WINERY
WINES
WINEY
WING
WINGBEAT
WINGBEATS
WINGDING
WINGDINGS
WINGE
WINGED
WINGEDLY
WINGEING
WINGER
WINGERS

WINGES
WINGIER
WINGIEST
WINGING
WINGLESS
WINGLET
WINGLETS
WINGS
WINGSPAN
WINGSPANS
WINGY
WINIER
WINIEST
WINING
WINK
WINKED
WINKER
WINKERS
WINKING
WINKINGLY
WINKINGS
WINKLE
WINKLER
WINKLERS
WINKLES
WINKS
WINN
WINNA
WINNABLE
WINNER
WINNERS
WINNING
WINNINGLY
WINNINGS
WINNLE
WINNLES
WINNOCK
WINNOCKS
WINNOW
WINNOWED
WINNOWER
WINNOWERS
WINNOWING
WINNOWINGS
WINNOWS
WINNS
WINO
WINOS
WINS
WINSEY
WINSEYS
WINSOME
WINSOMELY
WINSOMER
WINSOMEST
WINTER
WINTERED
WINTERIER
WINTERIEST
WINTERING
WINTERISE
WINTERISED
WINTERISES
WINTERISING
WINTERIZE
WINTERIZED
WINTERIZES
WINTERIZING
WINTERLY
WINTERS

WINTERY
WINTLE
WINTLED
WINTLES
WINTLING
WINTRIER
WINTRIEST
WINTRY
WINY
WINZE
WINZES
WIPE
WIPED
WIPEOUT
WIPEOUTS
WIPER
WIPERS
WIPES
WIPING
WIPINGS
WIRE
WIRED
WIREDRAW
WIREDRAWING
WIREDRAWINGS
WIREDRAWN
WIREDRAWS
WIREDREW
WIRELESS
WIRELESSED
WIRELESSES
WIRELESSING
WIREPHOTO
WIREPHOTOS
WIRER
WIRERS
WIRES
WIRETAP
WIRETAPPED
WIRETAPPING
WIRETAPS
WIREWORK
WIREWORKS
WIREWOVE
WIRIER
WIRIEST
WIRILY
WIRINESS
WIRINESSES
WIRING
WIRINGS
WIRRICOW
WIRRICOWS
WIRY
WIS
WISARD
WISARDS
WISDOM
WISDOMS
WISE
WISEACRE
WISEACRES
WISECRACK
WISECRACKED
WISECRACKING
WISECRACKS
WISED
WISELING
WISELINGS
WISELY

WISENESS
WISENESSES
WISENT
WISENTS
WISER
WISES
WISEST
WISH
WISHBONE
WISHBONES
WISHED
WISHER
WISHERS
WISHES
WISHFUL
WISHFULLY
WISHING
WISHINGS
WISING
WISKET
WISKETS
WISP
WISPED
WISPIER
WISPIEST
WISPING
WISPS
WISPY
WISSED
WISSES
WISSING
WIST
WISTARIA
WISTARIAS
WISTED
WISTERIA
WISTERIAS
WISTFUL
WISTFULLY
WISTING
WISTITI
WISTITIS
WISTLY
WISTS
WIT
WITAN
WITCH
WITCHED
WITCHEN
WITCHENS
WITCHERIES
WITCHERY
WITCHES
WITCHETTIES
WITCHETTY
WITCHING
WITCHINGS
WITCHKNOT
WITCHKNOTS
WITE
WITED
WITELESS
WITES
WITGAT
WITGATS
WITH
WITHAL
WITHDRAW
WITHDRAWING
WITHDRAWN

WITHDRAWS
WITHDREW
WITHE
WITHED
WITHER
WITHERED
WITHERING
WITHERINGS
WITHERITE
WITHERITES
WITHERS
WITHES
WITHHAULT
WITHHELD
WITHHOLD
WITHHOLDEN
WITHHOLDING
WITHHOLDS
WITHIER
WITHIES
WITHIEST
WITHIN
WITHING
WITHOUT
WITHOUTEN
WITHS
WITHSTAND
WITHSTANDING
WITHSTANDS
WITHSTOOD
WITHWIND
WITHWINDS
WITHY
WITHYWIND
WITHYWINDS
WITING
WITLESS
WITLESSLY
WITLING
WITLINGS
WITLOOF
WITLOOFS
WITNESS
WITNESSED
WITNESSER
WITNESSERS
WITNESSES
WITNESSING
WITS
WITTED
WITTER
WITTERED
WITTERING
WITTERS
WITTICISM
WITTICISMS
WITTIER
WITTIEST
WITTILY
WITTINESS
WITTINESSES
WITTING
WITTINGLY
WITTINGS
WITTOL
WITTOLLY
WITTOLS
WITTY
WITWALL
WITWALLS

WITWANTON
WITWANTONED
WITWANTONING
WITWANTONS
WIVE
WIVED
WIVEHOOD
WIVEHOODS
WIVERN
WIVERNS
WIVES
WIVING
WIZARD
WIZARDLY
WIZARDRIES
WIZARDRY
WIZARDS
WIZEN
WIZENED
WIZENING
WIZENS
WIZIER
WIZIERS
WO
WOAD
WOADED
WOADS
WOBBEGONG
WOBBEGONGS
WOBBLE
WOBBLED
WOBBLER
WOBBLERS
WOBBLES
WOBBLIER
WOBBLIES
WOBBLIEST
WOBBLING
WOBBLINGS
WOBBLY
WOBEGONE
WOCK
WOCKS
WODGE
WODGES
WOE
WOEBEGONE
WOEFUL
WOEFULLER
WOEFULLEST
WOEFULLY
WOEFULNESS
WOEFULNESSES
WOES
WOESOME
WOFUL
WOFULLY
WOFULNESS
WOFULNESSES
WOG
WOGGLE
WOGGLES
WOGS
WOIWODE
WOIWODES
WOK
WOKE
WOKEN
WOKS
WOLD

WOLDS
WOLF
WOLFED
WOLFER
WOLFERS
WOLFING
WOLFINGS
WOLFISH
WOLFISHLY
WOLFKIN
WOLFKINS
WOLFLING
WOLFLINGS
WOLFRAM
WOLFRAMS
WOLFS
WOLFSBANE
WOLFSBANES
WOLLIES
WOLLY
WOLVE
WOLVED
WOLVER
WOLVERENE
WOLVERENES
WOLVERINE
WOLVERINES
WOLVERS
WOLVES
WOLVING
WOLVINGS
WOLVISH
WOLVISHLY
WOMAN
WOMANED
WOMANHOOD
WOMANHOODS
WOMANING
WOMANISE
WOMANISED
WOMANISER
WOMANISERS
WOMANISES
WOMANISH
WOMANISING
WOMANIZE
WOMANIZED
WOMANIZER
WOMANIZERS
WOMANIZES
WOMANIZING
WOMANKIND
WOMANKINDS
WOMANLIER
WOMANLIEST
WOMANLY
WOMANS
WOMB
WOMBAT
WOMBATS
WOMBED
WOMBING
WOMBS
WOMBY
WOMEN
WOMENFOLK
WOMENFOLKS
WOMENKIND
WOMENKINDS
WOMERA

| | | | | |
|---|---|---|---|---|
| WOMERAS | WOODMICE | WOOLSEYS | WORKER | WORRISOME |
| WON | WOODMOUSE | WOOLWARD | WORKERIST | WORRIT |
| WONDER | WOODNESS | WOOLWORK | WORKERISTS | WORRITED |
| WONDERED | WOODNESSES | WOOLWORKS | WORKERS | WORRITING |
| WONDERER | WOODRUFF | WOOMERA | WORKFOLK | WORRITS |
| WONDERERS | WOODRUFFS | WOOMERANG | WORKFOLKS | WORRY |
| WONDERFUL | WOODS | WOOMERANGS | WORKFORCE | WORRYCOW |
| WONDERING | WOODSHED | WOOMERAS | WORKFORCES | WORRYCOWS |
| WONDERINGS | WOODSHEDDED | WOON | WORKFUL | WORRYGUTS |
| WONDEROUS | WOODSHEDDING | WOONED | WORKHORSE | WORRYING |
| WONDERS | WOODSHEDS | WOONING | WORKHORSES | WORRYINGS |
| WONDRED | WOODSIER | WOONS | WORKHOUSE | WORRYWART |
| WONDROUS | WOODSIEST | WOORALI | WORKHOUSES | WORRYWARTS |
| WONED | WOODSMAN | WOORALIS | WORKING | WORSE |
| WONGA | WOODSMEN | WOORARA | WORKINGS | WORSED |
| WONGAS | WOODSY | WOORARAS | WORKLESS | WORSEN |
| WONING | WOODWALE | WOOS | WORKLOAD | WORSENED |
| WONINGS | WOODWALES | WOOSEL | WORKLOADS | WORSENESS |
| WONKIER | WOODWARD | WOOSELL | WORKMAN | WORSENESSES |
| WONKIEST | WOODWARDS | WOOSELLS | WORKMANLY | WORSENING |
| WONKY | WOODWIND | WOOSELS | WORKMEN | WORSENS |
| WONNED | WOODWINDS | WOOSH | WORKPIECE | WORSER |
| WONNING | WOODWORK | WOOSHED | WORKPIECES | WORSES |
| WONS | WOODWORKS | WOOSHES | WORKPLACE | WORSHIP |
| WONT | WOODWORM | WOOSHING | WORKPLACES | WORSHIPPED |
| WONTED | WOODWORMS | WOOT | WORKROOM | WORSHIPPING |
| WONTING | WOODWOSE | WOOTZ | WORKROOMS | WORSHIPS |
| WONTLESS | WOODWOSES | WOOTZES | WORKS | WORSING |
| WONTS | WOODY | WOOZIER | WORKSHOP | WORST |
| WOO | WOODYARD | WOOZIEST | WORKSHOPS | WORSTED |
| WOOBUT | WOODYARDS | WOOZILY | WORKSOME | WORSTEDS |
| WOOBUTS | WOOED | WOOZINESS | WORKTOP | WORSTING |
| WOOD | WOOER | WOOZINESSES | WORKTOPS | WORSTS |
| WOODBIND | WOOERS | WOOZY | WORKWEAR | WORT |
| WOODBINDS | WOOF | WOP | WORKWEARS | WORTH |
| WOODBINE | WOOFED | WOPPED | WORLD | WORTHED |
| WOODBINES | WOOFER | WOPPING | WORLDED | WORTHFUL |
| WOODBLOCK | WOOFERS | WOPS | WORLDLIER | WORTHIED |
| WOODBLOCKS | WOOFIER | WORCESTER | WORLDLIEST | WORTHIER |
| WOODCHIP | WOOFIEST | WORCESTERS | WORLDLING | WORTHIES |
| WOODCHIPS | WOOFS | WORD | WORLDLINGS | WORTHIEST |
| WOODCHUCK | WOOFY | WORDAGE | WORLDLY | WORTHILY |
| WOODCHUCKS | WOOING | WORDAGES | WORLDS | WORTHING |
| WOODCOCK | WOOINGLY | WORDBOOK | WORLDWIDE | WORTHLESS |
| WOODCOCKS | WOOINGS | WORDBOOKS | WORM | WORTHS |
| WOODCRAFT | WOOL | WORDBOUND | WORMED | WORTHY |
| WOODCRAFTS | WOOLD | WORDED | WORMER | WORTHYING |
| WOODCUT | WOOLDED | WORDIER | WORMERIES | WORTLE |
| WOODCUTS | WOOLDER | WORDIEST | WORMERS | WORTLES |
| WOODED | WOOLDERS | WORDILY | WORMERY | WORTS |
| WOODEN | WOOLDING | WORDINESS | WORMIER | WOS |
| WOODENER | WOOLDINGS | WORDINESSES | WORMIEST | WOSBIRD |
| WOODENEST | WOOLDS | WORDING | WORMING | WOSBIRDS |
| WOODENLY | WOOLFAT | WORDINGS | WORMS | WOST |
| WOODHOUSE | WOOLFATS | WORDISH | WORMWOOD | WOT |
| WOODHOUSES | WOOLFELL | WORDLESS | WORMWOODS | WOTCHER |
| WOODIE | WOOLFELLS | WORDS | WORMY | WOTS |
| WOODIER | WOOLLED | WORDSMITH | WORN | WOTTED |
| WOODIES | WOOLLEN | WORDSMITHS | WORRAL | WOTTEST |
| WOODIEST | WOOLLENS | WORDY | WORRALS | WOTTETH |
| WOODINESS | WOOLLIER | WORE | WORREL | WOTTING |
| WOODINESSES | WOOLLIES | WORK | WORRELS | WOUBIT |
| WOODING | WOOLLIEST | WORKABLE | WORRICOW | WOUBITS |
| WOODLAND | WOOLLY | WORKADAY | WORRICOWS | WOULD |
| WOODLANDS | WOOLMAN | WORKADAYS | WORRIED | WOULDS |
| WOODLESS | WOOLMEN | WORKBOAT | WORRIER | WOULDST |
| WOODLICE | WOOLS | WORKBOATS | WORRIERS | WOUND |
| WOODLOUSE | WOOLSACK | WORKBOOK | WORRIES | WOUNDABLE |
| WOODMAN | WOOLSACKS | WORKBOOKS | WORRIMENT | WOUNDED |
| WOODMEN | WOOLSEY | WORKED | WORRIMENTS | WOUNDER |

# WYVERNS

| | | | | |
|---|---|---|---|---|
| WOUNDERS | WRASTED | WRENCH | WRINKLIEST | WRY |
| WOUNDILY | WRASTING | WRENCHED | WRINKLING | WRYBILL |
| WOUNDING | WRASTS | WRENCHES | WRINKLY | WRYBILLS |
| WOUNDINGS | WRATE | WRENCHING | WRIST | WRYER |
| WOUNDLESS | WRATH | WRENCHINGS | WRISTBAND | WRYEST |
| WOUNDS | WRATHED | WRENS | WRISTBANDS | WRYING |
| WOUNDWORT | WRATHFUL | WREST | WRISTIER | WRYLY |
| WOUNDWORTS | WRATHIER | WRESTED | WRISTIEST | WRYNECK |
| WOUNDY | WRATHIEST | WRESTER | WRISTLET | WRYNECKS |
| WOURALI | WRATHILY | WRESTERS | WRISTLETS | WRYNESS |
| WOURALIS | WRATHING | WRESTING | WRISTS | WRYNESSES |
| WOVE | WRATHLESS | WRESTLE | WRISTY | WRYTHEN |
| WOVEN | WRATHS | WRESTLED | WRIT | WUD |
| WOW | WRATHY | WRESTLER | WRITABLE | WUDDED |
| WOWED | WRAWL | WRESTLERS | WRITATIVE | WUDDING |
| WOWEE | WRAWLED | WRESTLES | WRITE | WUDS |
| WOWF | WRAWLING | WRESTLING | WRITER | WULFENITE |
| WOWFER | WRAWLS | WRESTLINGS | WRITERESS | WULFENITES |
| WOWFEST | WRAXLE | WRESTS | WRITERESSES | WULL |
| WOWING | WRAXLED | WRETCH | WRITERLY | WULLED |
| WOWS | WRAXLES | WRETCHED | WRITERS | WULLING |
| WOWSER | WRAXLING | WRETCHES | WRITES | WULLS |
| WOWSERS | WRAXLINGS | WRETHE | WRITHE | WUNNER |
| WOX | WREAK | WRETHED | WRITHED | WUNNERS |
| WOXEN | WREAKE | WRETHES | WRITHEN | WURLEY |
| WRACK | WREAKED | WRETHING | WRITHES | WURLEYS |
| WRACKED | WREAKER | WRICK | WRITHING | WURLIES |
| WRACKFUL | WREAKERS | WRICKED | WRITHINGS | WURST |
| WRACKING | WREAKES | WRICKING | WRITHLED | WURSTS |
| WRACKS | WREAKFUL | WRICKS | WRITING | WURTZITE |
| WRAITH | WREAKING | WRIED | WRITINGS | WURTZITES |
| WRAITHS | WREAKLESS | WRIER | WRITS | WUSHU |
| WRANGLE | WREAKS | WRIES | WRITTEN | WUSHUS |
| WRANGLED | WREATH | WRIEST | WRIZLED | WUTHER |
| WRANGLER | WREATHE | WRIGGLE | WROATH | WUTHERED |
| WRANGLERS | WREATHED | WRIGGLED | WROATHS | WUTHERING |
| WRANGLES | WREATHEN | WRIGGLER | WROKE | WUTHERS |
| WRANGLING | WREATHER | WRIGGLERS | WROKEN | WUZZLE |
| WRANGLINGS | WREATHERS | WRIGGLES | WRONG | WUZZLED |
| WRAP | WREATHES | WRIGGLIER | WRONGED | WUZZLES |
| WRAPOVER | WREATHIER | WRIGGLIEST | WRONGER | WUZZLING |
| WRAPOVERS | WREATHIEST | WRIGGLING | WRONGERS | WYANDOTTE |
| WRAPPAGE | WREATHING | WRIGGLINGS | WRONGEST | WYANDOTTES |
| WRAPPAGES | WREATHS | WRIGGLY | WRONGFUL | WYE |
| WRAPPED | WREATHY | WRIGHT | WRONGING | WYES |
| WRAPPER | WRECK | WRIGHTS | WRONGLY | WYN |
| WRAPPERED | WRECKAGE | WRING | WRONGNESS | WYND |
| WRAPPERING | WRECKAGES | WRINGED | WRONGNESSES | WYNDS |
| WRAPPERS | WRECKED | WRINGER | WRONGOUS | WYNN |
| WRAPPING | WRECKER | WRINGERS | WRONGS | WYNNS |
| WRAPPINGS | WRECKERS | WRINGING | WROOT | WYNS |
| WRAPROUND | WRECKFISH | WRINGINGS | WROOTED | WYSIWYG |
| WRAPROUNDS | WRECKFISHES | WRINGS | WROOTING | WYTE |
| WRAPS | WRECKFUL | WRINKLE | WROOTS | WYTED |
| WRAPT | WRECKING | WRINKLED | WROTE | WYTES |
| WRASSE | WRECKINGS | WRINKLES | WROTH | WYTING |
| WRASSES | WRECKS | WRINKLIER | WROUGHT | WYVERN |
| WRAST | WREN | WRINKLIES | WRUNG | WYVERNS |

# X

XANTHATE
XANTHATES
XANTHEIN
XANTHEINS
XANTHENE
XANTHENES
XANTHIC
XANTHIN
XANTHINE
XANTHINES
XANTHINS
XANTHOMA
XANTHOMAS
XANTHOUS
XEBEC
XEBECS
XENIA
XENIAL
XENIAS
XENIUM
XENOCRYST
XENOCRYSTS
XENOGAMIES
XENOGAMY
XENOGRAFT
XENOGRAFTS
XENOLITH

XENOLITHS
XENOMANIA
XENOMANIAS
XENOMENIA
XENOMENIAS
XENON
XENONS
XENOPHILE
XENOPHILES
XENOPHOBE
XENOPHOBES
XENOPHOBIES
XENOPHOBY
XENOPHYA
XENOPHYAS
XENOTIME
XENOTIMES
XENURINE
XERAFIN
XERAFINS
XERANSES
XERANSIS
XERANTIC
XERAPHIM
XERAPHIMS
XERARCH
XERASIA

XERASIAS
XERIC
XEROCHASIES
XEROCHASY
XERODERMA
XERODERMAS
XEROMA
XEROMAS
XEROMORPH
XEROMORPHS
XEROPHAGIES
XEROPHAGY
XEROPHILIES
XEROPHILY
XEROPHYTE
XEROPHYTES
XEROSES
XEROSIS
XEROSTOMA
XEROSTOMAS
XEROTES
XEROTIC
XI
XIPHOID
XIPHOIDAL
XIS
XOANON

XOANONS
XYLEM
XYLEMS
XYLENE
XYLENES
XYLENOL
XYLENOLS
XYLIC
XYLITOL
XYLITOLS
XYLOCARP
XYLOCARPS
XYLOGEN
XYLOGENS
XYLOGRAPH
XYLOGRAPHS
XYLOID
XYLOIDIN
XYLOIDINE
XYLOIDINES
XYLOIDINS
XYLOL
XYLOLOGIES
XYLOLOGY
XYLOLS
XYLOMA
XYLOMAS

XYLOMETER
XYLOMETERS
XYLONIC
XYLONITE
XYLONITES
XYLOPHAGE
XYLOPHAGES
XYLOPHONE
XYLOPHONES
XYLORIMBA
XYLORIMBAS
XYLOSE
XYLOSES
XYLYL
XYLYLS
XYST
XYSTER
XYSTERS
XYSTI
XYSTOI
XYSTOS
XYSTOSES
XYSTS
XYSTUS
XYSTUSES

YABBER
YABBERED
YABBERING
YABBERS
YABBIE
YABBIES
YABBY
YACCA
YACCAS
YACHT
YACHTED
YACHTER
YACHTERS
YACHTING
YACHTINGS
YACHTS
YACHTSMAN
YACHTSMEN
YACK
YACKED
YACKER
YACKERS
YACKING
YAFF
YAFFED
YAFFING
YAFFLE
YAFFLES
YAFFS
YAGER
YAGERS
YAGGER
YAGGERS
YAH
YAHOO
YAHOOS
YAK
YAKHDAN
YAKHDANS
YAKKA
YAKKAS
YAKKED
YAKKER
YAKKERS
YAKKING
YAKS
YAKUZA
YALD
YALE
YALES
YAM
YAMEN
YAMENS
YAMMER
YAMMERED
YAMMERING
YAMMERINGS
YAMS
YAMULKA
YAMULKAS
YANG

YANGS
YANK
YANKED
YANKER
YANKERS
YANKIE
YANKIES
YANKS
YAOURT
YAOURTS
YAP
YAPOCK
YAPOCKS
YAPOK
YAPOKS
YAPON
YAPP
YAPPED
YAPPER
YAPPERS
YAPPING
YAPS
YAPSTER
YAPSTERS
YARD
YARDAGE
YARDAGES
YARDANG
YARDANGS
YARDED
YARDING
YARDLAND
YARDLANDS
YARDMAN
YARDMEN
YARDS
YARDSTICK
YARDSTICKS
YARDWAND
YARDWANDS
YARE
YARELY
YARER
YAREST
YARFA
YARFAS
YARMULKA
YARMULKAS
YARMULKE
YARMULKES
YARN
YARNED
YARNING
YARNS
YARPHA
YARPHAS
YARR
YARROW
YARROWS
YARRS

YARTA
YARTAS
YARTO
YARTOS
YASHMAK
YASHMAKS
YATAGAN
YATAGANS
YATAGHAN
YATAGHANS
YATE
YATES
YATTER
YATTERED
YATTERING
YATTERINGS
YATTERS
YAUD
YAUDS
YAULD
YAUP
YAUPON
YAUPONS
YAW
YAWED
YAWEY
YAWING
YAWL
YAWLED
YAWLING
YAWLS
YAWN
YAWNED
YAWNIER
YAWNIEST
YAWNING
YAWNINGLY
YAWNINGS
YAWNY
YAWP
YAWPED
YAWPER
YAWPERS
YAWPING
YAWPS
YAWS
YAWY
YBET
YBLENT
YBORE
YBOUND
YBOUNDEN
YBRENT
YCLAD
YCLED
YCLEPE
YCLEPED
YCLEPT
YCOND
YDRAD
YDRED
YE

YEA
YEAD
YEADING
YEADS
YEAH
YEALDON
YEALDONS
YEALM
YEALMED
YEALMING
YEALMS
YEAN
YEANED
YEANING
YEANLING
YEANLINGS
YEANS
YEAR
YEARD
YEARDS
YEARLING
YEARLINGS
YEARLONG
YEARLY
YEARN
YEARNED
YEARNING
YEARNINGS
YEARNS
YEAS
YEAST
YEASTED
YEASTIER
YEASTIEST
YEASTING
YEASTS
YEASTY
YEDE
YEDES
YEDING
YEED
YEEDING
YEEDS
YEGG
YEGGMAN
YEGGMEN
YEGGS
YELD
YELDRING
YELDRINGS
YELDROCK
YELDROCKS
YELK
YELKS
YELL
YELLED
YELLING
YELLINGS
YELLOCH

YELLOCHED
YELLOCHING
YELLOCHS
YELLOW
YELLOWED
YELLOWER
YELLOWEST
YELLOWING
YELLOWISH
YELLOWS
YELLOWY
YELLS
YELM
YELMED
YELMING
YELMS
YELP
YELPED
YELPER
YELPERS
YELPING
YELPINGS
YELPS
YELT
YELTS
YEN
YENNED
YENNING
YENS
YENTA
YENTAS
YEOMAN
YEOMANLY
YEOMANRIES
YEOMANRY
YEOMEN
YEP
YEPS
YERBA
YERBAS
YERD
YERDED
YERDING
YERDS
YERK
YERKED
YERKING
YERKS
YERSINIA
YERSINIAE
YERSINIAS
YES
YESES
YESHIVA
YESHIVAH
YESHIVAHS
YESHIVAS
YESHIVOTH
YESK
YESKED
YESKING
YESKS
YESSES

| | | | | |
|---|---|---|---|---|
| YEST | YIRKED | YOICKSED | YOUNGLING | YTTRIC |
| YESTER | YIRKING | YOICKSES | YOUNGLINGS | YTTRIOUS |
| YESTERDAY | YIRKS | YOICKSING | YOUNGLY | YTTRIUM |
| YESTERDAYS | YITE | YOJAN | YOUNGNESS | YTTRIUMS |
| YESTEREVE | YITES | YOJANA | YOUNGNESSES | YU |
| YESTEREVES | YLEM | YOJANAS | YOUNGS | YUAN |
| YESTERN | YLEMS | YOJANS | YOUNGSTER | YUCA |
| YESTREEN | YLIKE | YOK | YOUNGSTERS | YUCAS |
| YESTS | YLKE | YOKE | YOUNGTH | YUCCA |
| YESTY | YMOLT | YOKED | YOUNGTHLY | YUCCAS |
| YET | YMOLTEN | YOKEL | YOUNGTHS | YUCK |
| YETI | YMPE | YOKELISH | YOUNKER | YUCKED |
| YETIS | YMPES | YOKELS | YOUNKERS | YUCKER |
| YETT | YMPING | YOKES | YOUR | YUCKERS |
| YETTS | YMPT | YOKING | YOURN | YUCKIER |
| YEUK | YNAMBU | YOKINGS | YOURS | YUCKIEST |
| YEUKED | YNAMBUS | YOKKED | YOURSELF | YUCKING |
| YEUKING | YO | YOKKING | YOURSELVES | YUCKS |
| YEUKS | YOB | YOKS | YOURT | YUCKY |
| YEVE | YOBBISH | YOKUL | YOURTS | YUFT |
| YEVEN | YOBBISHLY | YOLD | YOUTH | YUFTS |
| YEVES | YOBBO | YOLDRING | YOUTHFUL | YUG |
| YEVING | YOBBOES | YOLDRINGS | YOUTHHEAD | YUGA |
| YEW | YOBBOS | YOLK | YOUTHHEADS | YUGAS |
| YEWEN | YOBS | YOLKED | YOUTHHOOD | YUGS |
| YEWS | YOCK | YOLKIER | YOUTHHOODS | YUK |
| YEX | YOCKED | YOLKIEST | YOUTHIER | YUKE |
| YEXED | YOCKING | YOLKS | YOUTHIEST | YUKED |
| YEXES | YOCKS | YOLKY | YOUTHLY | YUKES |
| YEXING | YOD | YOMP | YOUTHS | YUKIER |
| YFERE | YODE | YOMPED | YOUTHSOME | YUKIEST |
| YGLAUNST | YODEL | YOMPING | YOUTHY | YUKING |
| YGO | YODELLED | YOMPS | YOW | YUKKIER |
| YGOE | YODELLER | YON | YOWE | YUKKIEST |
| YIBBLES | YODELLERS | YOND | YOWES | YUKKY |
| YICKER | YODELLING | YONDER | YOWIE | YUKS |
| YICKERED | YODELS | YONDERLY | YOWIES | YUKY |
| YICKERING | YODLE | YONGTHLY | YOWL | YULAN |
| YICKERS | YODLED | YONI | YOWLED | YULANS |
| YIELD | YODLER | YONIS | YOWLEY | YULE |
| YIELDABLE | YODLERS | YONKER | YOWLEYS | YULES |
| YIELDED | YODLES | YONKERS | YOWLING | YULETIDE |
| YIELDER | YODLING | YONKS | YOWLINGS | YULETIDES |
| YIELDERS | YOGA | YONT | YOWLS | YUMMIER |
| YIELDING | YOGAS | YOOP | YOWS | YUMMIEST |
| YIELDINGS | YOGH | YOOPS | YPIGHT | YUMMY |
| YIELDS | YOGHOURT | YOPPER | YPLAST | YUMP |
| YIKKER | YOGHOURTS | YOPPERS | YPLIGHT | YUMPIE |
| YIKKERED | YOGHS | YORE | YPSILOID | YUMPIES |
| YIKKERING | YOGHURT | YORES | YPSILON | YUMPS |
| YIKKERS | YOGHURTS | YORK | YPSILONS | YUNX |
| YILL | YOGI | YORKED | YRAPT | YUNXES |
| YILLS | YOGIC | YORKER | YRAVISHED | YUP |
| YIN | YOGIN | YORKERS | YRENT | YUPON |
| YINCE | YOGINI | YORKIE | YRIVD | YUPONS |
| YINS | YOGINIS | YORKIES | YSAME | YUPPIE |
| YIP | YOGINS | YORKING | YSHEND | YUPPIES |
| YIPPED | YOGIS | YORKS | YSHENDING | YUPPY |
| YIPPEE | YOGISM | YOS | YSHENDS | YUPS |
| YIPPIES | YOGISMS | YOU | YSHENT | YURT |
| YIPPING | YOGURT | YOUK | YSLAKED | YURTS |
| YIPPY | YOGURTS | YOUKED | YTOST | YUS |
| YIPS | YOHIMBINE | YOUKING | YTTERBIA | YWIS |
| YIRD | YOHIMBINES | YOUKS | YTTERBIAS | YWRAKE |
| YIRDED | YOICK | YOUNG | YTTERBIUM | YWROKE |
| YIRDING | YOICKED | YOUNGER | YTTERBIUMS | YWROKEN |
| YIRDS | YOICKING | YOUNGEST | YTTRIA | |
| YIRK | YOICKS | YOUNGISH | YTTRIAS | |

# Z

| | | | | |
|---|---|---|---|---|
| ZABAIONE | ZANYISMS | ZEBRASS | ZERIBAS | ZILLIONTH |
| ZABAIONES | ZANZE | ZEBRASSES | ZERO | ZILLIONTHS |
| ZABETA | ZANZES | ZEBRINE | ZEROED | ZIMB |
| ZABETAS | ZAP | ZEBRINNIES | ZEROING | ZIMBI |
| ZABRA | ZAPATA | ZEBRINNY | ZEROS | ZIMBIS |
| ZABRAS | ZAPATEADO | ZEBROID | ZEROTH | ZIMBS |
| ZABTIEH | ZAPATEADOS | ZEBRULA | ZERUMBET | ZIMMER |
| ZABTIEHS | ZAPOTILLA | ZEBRULAS | ZERUMBETS | ZIMMERS |
| ZACK | ZAPOTILLAS | ZEBRULE | ZEST | ZIMOCCA |
| ZACKS | ZAPPED | ZEBRULES | ZESTFUL | ZIMOCCAS |
| ZADDIK | ZAPPIER | ZEBU | ZESTFULLY | ZINC |
| ZADDIKIM | ZAPPIEST | ZEBUB | ZESTIER | ZINCED |
| ZADDIKS | ZAPPING | ZEBUBS | ZESTIEST | ZINCIER |
| ZAFFER | ZAPPY | ZEBUS | ZESTS | ZINCIEST |
| ZAFFERS | ZAPS | ZECCHINE | ZESTY | ZINCIFIED |
| ZAFFRE | ZAPTIAH | ZECCHINES | ZETA | ZINCIFIES |
| ZAFFRES | ZAPTIAHS | ZECCHINI | ZETAS | ZINCIFY |
| ZAG | ZAPTIEH | ZECCHINO | ZETETIC | ZINCIFYING |
| ZAGGED | ZAPTIEHS | ZECCHINOS | ZETETICS | ZINCING |
| ZAGGING | ZARAPE | ZED | ZEUGMA | ZINCITE |
| ZAGS | ZARAPES | ZEDOARIES | ZEUGMAS | ZINCITES |
| ZAIRE | ZARATITE | ZEDOARY | ZEUGMATIC | ZINCKED |
| ZAKUSKA | ZARATITES | ZEDS | ZEUXITE | ZINCKIER |
| ZAKUSKI | ZAREBA | ZEE | ZEUXITES | ZINCKIEST |
| ZAMAN | ZAREBAS | ZEES | ZEZE | ZINCKIFIED |
| ZAMANG | ZAREEBA | ZEIN | ZEZES | ZINCKIFIES |
| ZAMANGS | ZAREEBAS | ZEINS | ZHO | ZINCKIFY |
| ZAMANS | ZARF | ZEITGEIST | ZHOMO | ZINCKIFYING |
| ZAMARRA | ZARFS | ZEITGEISTS | ZHOMOS | ZINCKING |
| ZAMARRAS | ZARIBA | ZEK | ZHOS | ZINCKY |
| ZAMARRO | ZARIBAS | ZEKS | ZIBELINE | ZINCO |
| ZAMARROS | ZARNEC | ZEL | ZIBELINES | ZINCODE |
| ZAMBO | ZARNECS | ZELANT | ZIBELLINE | ZINCODES |
| ZAMBOMBA | ZARNICH | ZELANTS | ZIBELLINES | ZINCOID |
| ZAMBOMBAS | ZARNICHS | ZELOSO | ZIBET | ZINCOS |
| ZAMBOORAK | ZARZUELA | ZELOTYPIA | ZIBETS | ZINCOUS |
| ZAMBOORAKS | ZARZUELAS | ZELOTYPIAS | ZIFF | ZINCS |
| ZAMBOS | ZASTRUGA | ZELS | ZIFFIUS | ZINCY |
| ZAMIA | ZASTRUGI | ZEMINDAR | ZIFFIUSES | ZINEB |
| ZAMIAS | ZATI | ZEMINDARI | ZIFFS | ZINEBS |
| ZAMINDAR | ZATIS | ZEMINDARIES | ZIG | ZINFANDEL |
| ZAMINDARI | ZAX | ZEMINDARIS | ZIGAN | ZINFANDELS |
| ZAMINDARIS | ZAXES | ZEMINDARS | ZIGANKA | ZING |
| ZAMINDARS | ZEA | ZEMINDARY | ZIGANKAS | ZINGED |
| ZAMOUSE | ZEAL | ZEMSTVO | ZIGANS | ZINGEL |
| ZAMOUSES | ZEALANT | ZEMSTVOS | ZIGGED | ZINGELS |
| ZAMPOGNA | ZEALANTS | ZENANA | ZIGGING | ZINGIBER |
| ZAMPOGNAS | ZEALFUL | ZENANAS | ZIGGURAT | ZINGIBERS |
| ZANDER | ZEALLESS | ZENDIK | ZIGGURATS | ZINGIER |
| ZANDERS | ZEALOT | ZENDIKS | ZIGS | ZINGIEST |
| ZANELLA | ZEALOTISM | ZENITH | ZIGZAG | ZINGING |
| ZANELLAS | ZEALOTISMS | ZENITHAL | ZIGZAGGED | ZINGS |
| ZANIED | ZEALOTRIES | ZENITHS | ZIGZAGGING | ZINGY |
| ZANIER | ZEALOTRY | ZEOLITE | ZIGZAGGY | ZINKE |
| ZANIES | ZEALOTS | ZEOLITES | ZIGZAGS | ZINKED |
| ZANIEST | ZEALOUS | ZEOLITIC | ZIKKURAT | ZINKENITE |
| ZANJA | ZEALOUSLY | ZEPHYR | ZIKKURATS | ZINKENITES |
| ZANJAS | ZEALS | ZEPHYRS | ZILA | ZINKES |
| ZANJERO | ZEAS | ZEPPELIN | ZILAS | ZINKIER |
| ZANJEROS | ZEBEC | ZEPPELINS | ZILCH | ZINKIEST |
| ZANTE | ZEBECK | ZERDA | ZILCHES | ZINKIFIED |
| ZANTES | ZEBECKS | ZERDAS | ZILLAH | ZINKIFIES |
| ZANY | ZEBECS | ZEREBA | ZILLAHS | ZINKIFY |
| ZANYING | ZEBRA | ZEREBAS | ZILLION | ZINKIFYING |
| ZANYISM | ZEBRAS | ZERIBA | ZILLIONS | ZINKING |

ZINKY
ZINNIA
ZINNIAS
ZIP
ZIPPED
ZIPPER
ZIPPERED
ZIPPERS
ZIPPIER
ZIPPIEST
ZIPPING
ZIPPY
ZIPS
ZIPTOP
ZIRCALLOY
ZIRCALLOYS
ZIRCON
ZIRCONIA
ZIRCONIAS
ZIRCONIC
ZIRCONIUM
ZIRCONIUMS
ZIRCONS
ZIT
ZITHER
ZITHERN
ZITHERNS
ZITHERS
ZITS
ZIZ
ZIZEL
ZIZELS
ZIZZ
ZIZZED
ZIZZES
ZIZZING
ZLOTY
ZLOTYS
ZO
ZOA
ZOARIUM
ZOARIUMS
ZOBO
ZOBOS
ZOBU
ZOBUS
ZOCCO
ZOCCOLO
ZOCCOLOS
ZOCCOS
ZODIAC
ZODIACAL
ZODIACS
ZOEA
ZOEAE
ZOEAL
ZOEAS
ZOECHROME
ZOECHROMES
ZOEFORM
ZOETIC
ZOETROPE
ZOETROPES
ZOETROPIC
ZOIATRIA
ZOIATRIAS
ZOIATRICS
ZOIC
ZOISITE
ZOISITES
ZOISM
ZOISMS
ZOIST
ZOISTS
ZOMBI
ZOMBIE
ZOMBIES
ZOMBIISM
ZOMBIISMS
ZOMBIS
ZOMBORUK
ZOMBORUKS
ZONA
ZONAE
ZONAL
ZONARY
ZONATE
ZONATED
ZONATION
ZONATIONS
ZONDA
ZONDAS
ZONE
ZONED
ZONELESS
ZONES
ZONING
ZONINGS
ZONKED
ZONOID
ZONULA
ZONULAR
ZONULAS
ZONULE
ZONULET
ZONULETS
ZOO
ZOOBIOTIC
ZOOBLAST
ZOOBLASTS
ZOOCHORE
ZOOCHORES
ZOOCHORIES
ZOOCHORY
ZOOCYTIA
ZOOCYTIUM
ZOOEA
ZOOEAE
ZOOEAL
ZOOEAS
ZOOECIA
ZOOECIUM
ZOOGAMETE
ZOOGAMETES
ZOOGAMIES
ZOOGAMOUS
ZOOGAMY
ZOOGENIC
ZOOGENIES
ZOOGENOUS
ZOOGENY
ZOOGLOEA
ZOOGLOEAS
ZOOGLOEIC
ZOOGONIES
ZOOGONOUS
ZOOGONY
ZOOGRAFT
ZOOGRAFTS
ZOOGRAPHIES
ZOOGRAPHY
ZOOID
ZOOIDAL
ZOOIDS·
ZOOKS
ZOOLATER
ZOOLATERS
ZOOLATRIA
ZOOLATRIAS
ZOOLATRIES
ZOOLATRY
ZOOLITE
ZOOLITES
ZOOLITH
ZOOLITHIC
ZOOLITHS
ZOOLITIC
ZOOLOGIES
ZOOLOGIST
ZOOLOGISTS
ZOOLOGY
ZOOM
ZOOMANCIES
ZOOMANCY
ZOOMANTIC
ZOOMED
ZOOMETRIC
ZOOMETRIES
ZOOMETRY
ZOOMING
ZOOMORPH
ZOOMORPHIES
ZOOMORPHS
ZOOMORPHY
ZOOMS
ZOON
ZOONAL
ZOONIC
ZOONITE
ZOONITES
ZOONITIC
ZOONOMIA
ZOONOMIAS
ZOONOMIC
ZOONOMIES
ZOONOMIST
ZOONOMISTS
ZOONOMY
ZOONOSES
ZOONOSIS
ZOONOTIC
ZOONS
ZOOPATHIES
ZOOPATHY
ZOOPERAL
ZOOPERIES
ZOOPERIST
ZOOPERISTS
ZOOPERY
ZOOPHAGAN
ZOOPHAGANS
ZOOPHILE
ZOOPHILES
ZOOPHILIA
ZOOPHILIAS
ZOOPHILIES
ZOOPHILY
ZOOPHOBIA
ZOOPHOBIAS
ZOOPHORIC
ZOOPHORUS
ZOOPHORUSES
ZOOPHYTE
ZOOPHYTES
ZOOPHYTIC
ZOOPLASTIES
ZOOPLASTY
ZOOS
ZOOSCOPIC
ZOOSCOPIES
ZOOSCOPY
ZOOSPERM
ZOOSPERMS
ZOOSPORE
ZOOSPORES
ZOOSPORIC
ZOOTAXIES
ZOOTAXY
ZOOTECHNIES
ZOOTECHNY
ZOOTHECIA
ZOOTHEISM
ZOOTHEISMS
ZOOTHOME
ZOOTHOMES
ZOOTOMIC
ZOOTOMIES
ZOOTOMIST
ZOOTOMISTS
ZOOTOMY
ZOOTOXIN
ZOOTOXINS
ZOOTROPE
ZOOTROPES
ZOOTROPHIES
ZOOTROPHY
ZOOTYPE
ZOOTYPES
ZOOTYPIC
ZOOZOO
ZOOZOOS
ZOPILOTE
ZOPILOTES
ZOPPO
ZORGITE
ZORGITES
ZORIL
ZORILLE
ZORILLES
ZORILLO
ZORILLOS
ZORILS
ZORINO
ZORINOS
ZORRO
ZORROS
ZOS
ZOSTER
ZOSTERS
ZOUNDS
ZOWIE
ZUCCHETTO
ZUCCHETTOS
ZUCCHINI
ZUCCHINIS
ZUCHETTA
ZUCHETTAS
ZUCHETTO
ZUCHETTOS
ZUFFOLI
ZUFFOLO
ZUFOLI
ZUFOLO
ZUGZWANG
ZUGZWANGS
ZULU
ZULUS
ZUMBOORUK
ZUMBOORUKS
ZUPA
ZUPAN
ZUPANS
ZUPAS
ZURF
ZURFS
ZUZ
ZUZES
ZYGAENID
ZYGAENINE
ZYGAENOID
ZYGAL
ZYGANTRA
ZYGANTRUM
ZYGANTRUMS
ZYGODONT
ZYGOMA
ZYGOMAS
ZYGOMATIC
ZYGON
ZYGONS
ZYGOPHYTE
ZYGOPHYTES
ZYGOSE
ZYGOSES
ZYGOSIS
ZYGOSPERM
ZYGOSPERMS
ZYGOSPORE
ZYGOSPORES
ZYGOTE
ZYGOTES
ZYGOTIC
ZYLONITE
ZYLONITES
ZYMASE
ZYMASES
ZYME
ZYMES
ZYMIC
ZYMITE
ZYMITES
ZYMOGEN
ZYMOGENIC
ZYMOGENS
ZYMOID
ZYMOLOGIC
ZYMOLOGIES
ZYMOLOGY
ZYMOLYSES
ZYMOLYSIS
ZYMOLYTIC
ZYMOME
ZYMOMES
ZYMOMETER
ZYMOMETERS
ZYMOSES
ZYMOSIS
ZYMOTIC
ZYMOTICS
ZYMURGIES
ZYMURGY
ZYTHUM
ZYTHUMS